Also by G. Scott Thomas

History
Counting the Votes
A New World to Be Won
Advice From the Presidents
The United States of Suburbia
The Pursuit of the White House

Demographics
The Rating Guide to Life in America's Fifty States
Where to Make Money
The Rating Guide to Life in America's Small Cities

Sports
The Best (and Worst) of Baseball's Modern Era
Leveling the Field

MICROPOLITAN AMERICA

MICROPOLITAN AMERICA

A STATISTICAL GUIDE
TO SMALL CITIES
ACROSS THE NATION

G. SCOTT THOMAS

n NIAWANDA BOOKS

Micropolitan America: A Statistical Guide to Small Cities Across the Nation

Copyright © 2017 by G. Scott Thomas

Niawanda Books
949 Delaware Road
Buffalo, NY 14223

Printed in the United States of America

First Edition
10 9 8 7 6 5 4 3 2 1

CONTENTS

MICROPOLITAN AMERICA

1

INSIDE MICROPOLITAN AMERICA

★ ★ ★ ★ ★

MICROPOLITAN AMERICA

The United States is dominated by belts of urban development that sprawl along the nation's various coasts.

These "megaregions," as they have been dubbed by demographers, are starkly visible from the air — the Atlantic seaboard from Boston to Virginia Beach, the Great Lakes chain from Buffalo to Milwaukee, most of the peninsula of Florida, the Gulf of Mexico shoreline from New Orleans to Houston, the extensive Pacific coast of California. They're supplemented by densely populated clusters that dot the nation's interior, emanating from cities such as Atlanta, Dallas, Denver, Minneapolis-St. Paul, and Phoenix.

Travel writers may wax poetically about America's wide, open spaces, but this airborne view tells the true story. Megaregions (and the metropolitan areas that are their building blocks) are massive forces that dictate the rhythms of the country's economic, cultural, and political life. "We are a much more big-urban nation than a lot of people think," admits William Frey, a demographer with the Brookings Institution.

The federal government accepted this reality decades ago, when it originated the concept of the metropolitan area. Each metro is a discrete package of a major city or cities and adjacent suburbs. The U.S. Office of Management and Budget (OMB), which bears the responsibility for delineating metropolitan areas, currently recognizes 382 in all.

A metro area isn't the same as a megaregion. Several of the former, as noted above, must be linked to create one of the latter. But every metro — from the biggest (the New York City area with 20.18 million residents) to the smallest (Carson City, Nevada, with 54,521) — wields unusual clout in its state, its section of the country, and (if it belongs to one) its megaregion.

This power is grounded in sheer numbers. More than 275 million persons live in the nation's 382 metros. That means 17 of every 20 Americans — 85.7 percent — reside in major cities or their suburbs. Only 46 million persons live beyond the boundaries of metropolitan America, scattered throughout the small cities and rural areas that comprise the rest of the country.

The extent of this metropolitan dominance is driven home by the following list. It shows the nation's 23 biggest metros, each designated by a lengthy (and excessively specific) name assigned by OMB. The righthand column tabulates the cumulative share of U.S. residents through a given row. The New York City area, for example, accounts for 6.3 percent of the nation's population all by itself. Add the Los Angeles metro, and the share rises to 10.4 percent. Mix in the Chicago area, and the sum climbs to 13.4 percent.

A quarter of all Americans, as shown by the list, live in the nine biggest metropolitan areas, which include the national capitals of business and media (New York City), government (Washington), entertainment (Los Angeles), and energy (Houston), as well as the dominant centers of the Midwest (Chicago) and the South (Atlanta). Toss in the subsequent 14 metros, and the share of U.S. population soars above 40 percent:

Metro area	2015 population	Cumulative share of U.S. population
New York-Newark-Jersey City, NY-NJ-PA	20,182,305	6.3%
Los Angeles-Long Beach-Anaheim, CA	13,340,068	10.4%
Chicago-Naperville-Elgin, IL-IN-WI	9,551,031	13.4%
Dallas-Fort Worth-Arlington, TX	7,102,796	15.6%
Houston-The Woodlands-Sugar Land, TX	6,656,947	17.7%
Washington-Arlington-Alexandria, DC-VA-MD-WV	6,097,684	19.6%
Philadelphia-Camden-Wilmington, PA-NJ-DE-MD	6,069,875	21.5%
Miami-Fort Lauderdale-West Palm Beach, FL	6,012,331	23.3%
Atlanta-Sandy Springs-Roswell, GA	5,710,795	25.1%
Boston-Cambridge-Newton, MA-NH	4,774,321	26.6%
San Francisco-Oakland-Hayward, CA	4,656,132	28.0%
Phoenix-Mesa-Scottsdale, AZ	4,574,531	29.5%
Riverside-San Bernardino-Ontario, CA	4,489,159	30.9%
Detroit-Warren-Dearborn, MI	4,302,043	32.2%
Seattle-Tacoma-Bellevue, WA	3,733,580	33.4%
Minneapolis-St. Paul-Bloomington, MN-WI	3,524,583	34.5%
San Diego-Carlsbad, CA	3,299,521	35.5%
Tampa-St. Petersburg-Clearwater, FL	2,975,225	36.4%
Denver-Aurora-Lakewood, CO	2,814,330	37.3%
St. Louis, MO-IL	2,811,588	38.2%
Baltimore-Columbia-Towson, MD	2,797,407	39.0%
Charlotte-Concord-Gastonia, NC-SC	2,426,363	39.8%
Portland-Vancouver-Hillsboro, OR-WA	2,389,228	40.5%

These behemoths are the engines of American life, the giant markets that propel the nation's economy and the rest of U.S. society. "In a world of rising urbanization, the degree of economic vigor that the economy of the United States derives from its cities is unmatched by any other region of the globe," concedes a recent report by the management-consulting firm of McKinsey & Company.

Yet it would be a mistake to assume that America's story is being written solely by its megaregions and metropolitan areas, no matter how robust and powerful they might be.

If you cross the nation on a nighttime flight, you will certainly be dazzled by the extensive networks of lights glowing from urban hubs. But you'll also see vast expanses of darkness, relieved occasionally by small communities or isolated farms. These places also have tales to tell.

America's 382 metropolitan areas occupy 979,411 square miles of urban and suburban land. That's an impressive sum, roughly the size of Alaska and Texas combined. But the rest of the country — the darkest zones outside your airplane window — would cover the remaining 48 states in their entirety, encompassing more than 2.8 million square miles.

Coastal elites may spurn this enormous territory as "flyover country," but savvy marketers, developers, and politicians know better. They're aware that opportunities abound in the small cities outside of metropolitan America. This book provides the data to support their expectations.

Metro Areas on a Smaller Scale

The Bureau of the Budget, as OMB was known at the time, published its first list of metropolitan areas in 1949, just as a heady period of unprecedented national growth was dawning. The postwar economy was expanding rapidly, and so was the population. Millions of urban dwellers were swarming to new homes in the surrounding countryside, challenging the traditional model of a city-based economy. Demographers came to believe that they needed a more inclusive concept to acknowledge this new pattern of development and the accompanying emergence of suburbia.

Hence the metropolitan area. OMB would tinker with its definition in the decades to come, but the basic idea would not change. Each metro would be "an area containing a significant population nucleus and adjacent communities that have a high degree of integration with that nucleus," as U.S. Census Bureau geographer Michael Ratcliffe has written.

OMB's current standards require a central city or urbanized area with a population of 50,000 or more. A metropolitan area includes this urban core, the rest of the county in which it is located, and any adjacent counties that have "a high degree of social and economic integration" with the central city. The resulting metro can be as extensive as the 25-county New York City area, which spans 190 miles from the Hudson River city of

Poughkeepsie to the tip of Long Island, or as compact as the 149 metros from Albany, Oregon, to Yuma, Arizona, that consist of a single county apiece.

We have now reached the point where I briefly pop into our story. It occurred to me in the late 1980s that OMB's standards could be adjusted to fit smaller circumstances. A city with 25,000 or even 15,000 residents might not be metropolitan, but no one could deny that it exerts influence beyond its geographic limits. Suburban-style developments can be found on its periphery, and residents of outlying communities commute to jobs within its core. The pattern is the same for Washington, D.C. (central city population: 672,228), and Washington Court House, Ohio (14,019). Only the scale is different.

I advanced this argument in a 1989 piece for the late, lamented *American Demographics*, a magazine of surprising liveliness published by Dow Jones. My article proposed the creation of micropolitan areas, based on the following criteria:

■ The central city was required to have at least 15,000 residents, but fewer than 50,000. (My threshold proved to be a bit too high for Washington Court House, but I had to draw the line somewhere.)

■ The county that included the central city had to have a total population of at least 40,000.

■ Most micros consisted of a single county. If a qualifying city had at least 40 percent of its population in each of two counties, the micro area extended to both counties.

These rules yielded a list of 219 micropolitan areas, which became the focus of *The Rating Guide to Life in America's Small Cities*, a 1990 book in which I analyzed these alternatives to metropolitan life. My 50-part formula crowned San Luis Obispo-Atascadero, California, as the nation's most desirable micropolitan area, followed by Corvallis, Oregon, and Fredericksburg, Virginia, as runners-up.

I don't recall how I initially landed on "micropolitan" as the adjective for my concept, though I do know it wasn't a difficult or especially imaginative choice. What name could be more logical for the smaller version of a metropolitan area? Two decades would pass before I learned that my creation had been predated by a pair of agricultural economists, Luther Tweeten and George Brinkman, in a 1976 academic tome, *Micropolitan Development*. But there was an essential difference in our uses of the term. They considered it to be a broad synonym for all things nonmetropolitan, not a designation for a particular type of community that is midway between the big city and the farm.

I moved on to other projects in the 1990s, though the topic would resurface late in the decade, when the aforementioned Michael Ratcliffe got in touch. He was calling on behalf of the Metropolitan Area Standards Review Project, a comprehensive study by the federal government of the metro classification system.

Our conversation was brief. Ratcliffe asked what had inspired me to come up with the micropolitan area. He was especially curious if I held any legal claim to the name. Had I trademarked it? The thought had never crossed my mind. I asked why he was interested, and he replied that the project's team was thinking about elevating the micro to official status.

The formal announcement came in December 2000, with the first group of micropolitan areas being delineated three years later. The standards adopted by the government are broader than mine, encompassing every city or urban cluster that has a minimum of 10,000 residents (not my 15,000) and a maximum of 49,999. Most micros consist of a single county, though additional counties can be added if at least 25 percent of their workers commute to the central city. (OMB saw no need to adopt my additional population threshold of 40,000 for an entire micropolitan area, taking both its central city and surrounding territory into account. The smallest micro under the current rules has just 12,937 residents.)

It's important to remember that micros are not densely populated from end to end. "The extent of a metropolitan or micropolitan statistical area reflects the field of influence surrounding an urban core," writes Ratcliffe, "but it does not imply that the entire area is urban in a structural sense." Yes, you will find a city at the center of each micro profiled in this book, but you will also see an outlying suburban ring and most likely a rural fringe.

OMB's current roster contains 551 micropolitan areas. Here's how they stack up against their metropolitan cousins and the sparsely settled counties that constitute the rest of the nation:

Type	Areas	Population	Share of U.S. population
Metropolitan areas	382	275,315,786	85.7%
Micropolitan areas	551	27,710,171	8.6%
Rest of nation	—	18,392,863	5.7%

There are two ways to react to these statistics. The typical observer is likely to remark upon the insignificance of micropolitan areas. Their collective population, after all, is only one-tenth the total for America's metros, which is yet another sign of metropolitan dominance.

The alternate response, one of greater subtlety and sophistication, is to acknowledge the importance of any group that has nearly 28 million members. Micros may play a secondary role — a distinction reinforced by their inferior prefix — but they still wield substantial clout. Simply consider the fact that micropolitan America's private-sector employees earned a total of $321 billion in 2015. A sum of such enormity is difficult to ignore.

Where to Find America's Micros

Micropolitan areas exist in almost all of these United States. The exceptions are Delaware, the District of Columbia, New Jersey, and Rhode Island. (D.C. is considered a state for statistical purposes.) All 30 counties in these four jurisdictions are classified as metropolitan, leaving no room for anything else.

Texas offers the widest array of micropolitan areas, 44 in all, accounting for 8 percent of the national total of 551. It's followed by Ohio with 32 micros, Indiana and North Carolina with 24 apiece, and Georgia with 23. (Sixteen micros straddle state lines. I have awarded each of those bifurcated areas to the state in which its primary city is located. New Hampshire, for example, is given credit for Claremont-Lebanon, NH-VT, the most populous micropolitan area of them all.)

A second way to analyze the relative distribution of micros is to add their state-by-state populations. Ohio's total of nearly 1.9 million micropolitan residents propels it past Texas. Here are the eight states above 1 million:

State	Micros	Micropolitan population
Ohio	32	1,892,315
Texas	44	1,655,607
North Carolina	24	1,566,216
Michigan	19	1,115,760
Pennsylvania	17	1,111,275
Indiana	24	1,009,987
New York	14	1,006,046
Mississippi	19	1,000,353

Six of the eight states on this chart are Southern or Midwestern, offering a strong hint as to which two sections of the country have the deepest concentrations of micropolitan areas.

Why does that matter? It's important because this book is organized along sectional lines. Chapters 4 through 7 offer single-page statistical profiles of all 551 micros, arranged alphabetically by region. This is how the states are grouped:

East: Connecticut, Delaware, District of Columbia, Maine, Maryland, Massachusetts, New Hampshire, New Jersey, New York, Pennsylvania, Rhode Island, Vermont, and West Virginia.

South: Alabama, Arkansas, Florida, Georgia, Kentucky, Louisiana, Mississippi, North Carolina, Oklahoma, South Carolina, Tennessee, Texas, and Virginia.

Midwest: Illinois, Indiana, Iowa, Kansas, Michigan, Minnesota, Missouri, Nebraska, North Dakota, Ohio, South Dakota, and Wisconsin.

West: Alaska, Arizona, California, Colorado, Hawaii, Idaho, Montana, Nevada, New Mexico, Oregon, Utah, Washington, and Wyoming.

A heavy imbalance exists between the four sections. Nearly three-quarters of all micros — 408 of 551 — are located in the South or Midwest. And 70 percent of the nation's micropolitan population is concentrated in those two sections:

Section	Chapter	Micros	Micropolitan population
East	4	51	3,627,240
South	5	214	10,482,361
Midwest	6	194	8,958,265
West	7	92	4,642,305

The South, as I define it, is the most populous section of the country. The total population of its 13 states (metropolitan + micropolitan + everything else) is more than 111 million, which gives it a substantial head start in the micropolitan derby. None of the other three regions is bigger than 76 million.

But this disparity doesn't mean as much as you might imagine. If we examine the percentage of micropolitan residents, rather than the raw count, the two leading sections remain on top. The highest density exists in the Midwest, where 13.2 percent of all residents live in micropolitan areas. It's followed by the South at 9.4 percent. Well off the pace are the West (where 6.1 percent live in micros) and the East (only 5.5 percent).

The Strengths of Micropolitan America

Big is better. That seems to be the American credo. Millions of our fellow citizens perceive an inextricable link between size and quality. They aspire to hold big jobs, earn big salaries, own big homes, and drive big cars.

And, of course, most of them live in big cities or adjacent suburbs. We've already established that two of every five Americans reside in the 23 largest metropolitan areas, and more than 85 percent of the nation's 321 million people are concentrated in its 382 metros.

But that doesn't mean they like it.

Polls consistently find that Americans would prefer to live in communities that are smaller than the ones they actually call home. The most comprehensive report on this subject was produced in 2009 by the Pew Research Center. It surveyed 2,260 adults, a massive sample with a tiny margin of error of 2.3 percentage points.

Pew posed dozens of questions about the qualities that make a place livable. I'm going to focus on three that seem especially relevant.

The first query dealt with the pace of life. Nearly three-quarters of the survey participants indicated a desire to live in a community with a minimal level of stress:

Type of community	Preference
Slower pace of life	71%
Faster pace of life	22%
Not sure	7%

Pew then asked about the ebb and flow of a typical day. Did the respondents prefer to keep to themselves, or did they enjoy interacting with neighbors and other community residents? The resulting numbers were virtually identical to those in the previous chart, with roughly three-quarters opting for a place where people know each other well:

Type of community	Preference
People know each other well	73%
People don't know each other's business	22%
Not sure	5%

These results lead to an indisputable conclusion: Tranquility and friendliness are important selling points for most Americans, which is why they are fascinated by smaller communities. This connection was reinforced when Pew asked a direct question: If you could live anywhere in the United States, which type of community would you prefer? Small towns emerged on top:

Type of community	Preference
Small town	30%
Suburban area	25%
City	23%
Rural area	21%
Not sure	1%

We can consider "small town" to be synonymous in this instance with "micropolitan area." Pew drew a clear distinction between small communities and rural areas, allowing us to say with a fair degree of certitude that nearly one-third of all Americans are attracted to micropolitan living.

There are several good reasons for their interest, several factors to be emphasized by officials and marketers seeking to attract new employers and residents to a micro. Tranquility and friendliness are naturally on the list, but so are the following five qualities.

1. Micropolitan areas are more stable than metropolitan areas.

A variety of yardsticks can be used to measure stability. I'm going to suggest two — the percentage of residents who have lived in the same housing unit for more than one year (residential stability) and the percentage of households that are occupied by married couples (family stability).

Here are the collective stats for all 551 micros: 85.2 percent of people stay in their homes for more than a year and 49.8 percent of households feature married couples. The respective figures for all 382 metros are 84.9 percent and 47.9 percent. The differences may be slight, but they tilt toward micropolitan areas in both cases.

2. Smaller cities are cheaper places to live.

Casual research — say, a quick Google search — will confirm that big cities are where the money is.

That's evident in the latest figures for per capita income, defined as the average amount of money received by each resident (including children) in a given year, encompassing such diverse sources as salaries, interest payments, dividends, rental income, and government checks. The per capita income for U.S. metropolitan areas is $29,988, which is 29.1 percent higher than the corresponding level of $23,225 for micropolitan areas. That's a huge difference.

We're all aware that this gap in wages can be offset by fluctuations in the cost of living. Expenses tend to be lower in small cities, making it possible to thrive on a smaller salary.

But how much smaller? It's impossible to obtain precise cost-of-living data for micros, but the U.S. Bureau of Economic Analysis offers something almost as good. It calculates an index with a bureaucratically intimidating name — regional price parities — for the metropolitan and nonmetropolitan portions of each state. The resulting numbers reflect the respective costs of goods and services.

Regional price parities indicate that the nonmetropolitan part of every state is less expensive than the metropolitan side. The gap is wider than 10 percent in these eight states:

State	Cost of living in nonmetropolitan portion (compared to metropolitan portion)
New York	-19.6%
Hawaii	-18.2%
Maryland	-18.0%
Illinois	-17.8%
Virginia	-15.9%
California	-14.7%
Minnesota	-13.1%
Arizona	-11.6%

What does this mean? A salary of $60,300 will go just as far in the nonmetropolitan portion of New York as $75,000 does in New York City or another of the state's metros, based on the reduction of 19.6 percent in the cost of living. That's a crucial distinction for anybody who is pondering a move from a major urban area to a smaller city.

3. The goal of home ownership is more easily attained in micropolitan areas.

This point is directly linked to the one immediately above. Homes are less expensive in micros, so they are easier to purchase. Simple as that.

Take a look at two comparisons selected at random. Each involves a major metropolitan area and a micro roughly two hours away by car.

The median value of an owner-occupied home in the Chicago area was $214,400 as of 2015, according to the U.S. Census Bureau. The corresponding figure for Freeport, Illinois, was $98,900, a reduction of 54 percent. The second comparison involves bigger dollar figures, yet the price disparity is much the same. The median home value was $617,000 in the San Francisco metro, but 50 percent lower at $308,400 in the Ukiah, California, micro.

It comes as no surprise, then, that the rate of home ownership is substantially higher in the nation's micropolitan areas (where 69.4 percent of households are occupied by their owners) than in their metropolitan counterparts (62.6 percent).

4. It's easier to commute or run errands in a micro.

Gridlock is nonexistent in the typical micropolitan area. Traffic usually flows easily, thanks to relatively light population densities and generally compact development patterns.

Short commutes are common in micros, as you can see in this comparison of travel times from home to work:

Type	Less than 15 minutes	15 to 44 minutes	45 minutes or more
Micropolitan areas	42.1%	46.0%	11.9%
Metropolitan areas	24.8%	58.4%	16.8%

The most striking divergence occurs in the first column of statistics. More than two-fifths of micropolitan commuters are on the road for less than 15 minutes, a distinction that only one-quarter of metropolitan workers can claim.

5. Entrepreneurial spirit seems to be stronger in micropolitan areas.

This is an unexpected factor, one that isn't easily explained. It emerges from the Census Bureau's latest count of fulltime workers who are self-employed. The rate for the nation's 551 micros is 1.1 percentage points larger than the corresponding figure for the 382 metros, which is a significant difference:

Type	Fulltime civilian workers	Self-employed	Share
Micropolitan areas	8,065,267	734,791	9.1%
Metropolitan areas	87,162,886	6,981,026	8.0%

We might speculate that self-employment is more common in micros because opportunities are fewer. But that doesn't account for the unusually high self-employment rates in several prosperous micros, such as 27.8 percent in Vineyard Haven, Massachusetts, or 20.4 percent in Fredericksburg, Texas, or 17.0 percent in Key West, Florida. The reasons may not be thoroughly understood, but it's clear that enterpreneurship is alive and well at the micropolitan level.

And the Weaknesses, Too

There is a flip side, of course. Micropolitan areas are blessed with several advantages, as we have just discussed, but they are also saddled with deficiencies. We focused on five of the former, so it seems only fair to examine five of the latter.

1. Residents of micropolitan areas tend to be older.

This isn't a case of age discrimination. It's a simple matter of demographic progress. If an area has an excess of senior citizens and a paucity of children, its prospects for future growth are usually quite dim.

That's why these numbers don't bode well for the nation's micros:

Type	Children per senior	Share of children (ages 0-17)	Share of seniors (ages 65+)
Micropolitan areas	1.39	22.7%	16.3%
Metropolitan areas	1.73	23.4%	13.6%

The respective shares of children aren't much different, but the variation in the righthand column is significant. The distribution of senior citizens is 2.7 percentage points larger in micros, which is why the micropolitan ratio of children per senior is so much smaller.

This imbalance is especially stark in the 46 micros with ratios lower than 1.00 — in other words, with more seniors than children. Twenty-two of these areas actually lost population between 2010 and 2015.

2. Micros are considerably less diverse.

Small cities are supposedly characterized by endless rows of white picket fences and infinite quantities of white residents. Yes, it's a stereotype, yet it does contain a kernel of racial truth.

The nation, as a whole, is rapidly diversifying, but most micropolitan areas are well behind the curve, as shown by the following chart:

Type	Whites	Blacks	Hispanics	Asians	Native Americans	Others
Micros	77.9%	7.9%	9.1%	1.3%	1.7%	2.1%
Metros	59.5%	13.0%	18.7%	6.0%	0.4%	2.5%

Asians are almost five times as numerous in an average metropolitan area than in a typical micro. Hispanics are roughly twice as common in the former, and blacks are nearly so. Native Americans are the only minority group to post a bigger share on the micropolitan side.

I have reduced this battery of racial percentages to a single head-to-head comparison, using a statistical tool known as the Gini-Simpson racial diversity index. A relatively simple calculation determines the likelihood that two randomly selected persons would come from different racial groups. The odds for the 382 micros are considerably better than half (59.0 percent), but the Gini-Simpson index for the 551 micros is just 37.8 percent.

So what? Demographic, sociological, and psychological studies consistently demonstrate that diverse groups grow and prosper more extensively than homogenous groups do. "Diversity enhances creativity," writes Katherine Phillips, a Columbia Business School professor. "It encourages the search for novel information and perspectives, leading to better decision making and problem solving."

The danger is that many micropolitan areas are missing out on these benefits.

3. There is a sizable education gap between urban hubs and small cities.

A number of prominent universities are located in micropolitan areas, including Dartmouth College (Claremont-Lebanon, NH-VT), Ohio University (Athens, OH), Oklahoma State University (Stillwater, OK), the University of Mississippi (Oxford, MS), and Washington State University (Pullman, WA), among several others.

The highly educated faculties at these schools greatly enhance the levels of brainpower in their communities. Take Pullman as an example. A quarter of its working-age adults (24.9 percent) hold advanced degrees, such as master's, doctoral, and professional degrees, which is more than twice the metropolitan rate of 12.2 percent.

But that's an exception to the rule. Educational attainment is typically much more impressive in metros than in micros, as the next chart makes clear:

Type	Adults (ages 25-64)	Bachelor's degrees	Advanced degrees
Micropolitan areas	14,052,410	20.6%	6.9%
Metropolitan areas	143,367,283	33.3%	12.2%

Roughly 2.9 million working-age residents of micropolitan areas hold bachelor's degrees. If micros had matched the metropolitan rate of 33.3 percent, that total would have been nearly 4.7 million. The resulting shortfall of 1.8 million college-educated adults puts micropolitan areas at a disadvantage.

4. Poverty is a bigger problem in micros.

It's a snap to calculate the poverty rate. The Census Bureau releases new guidelines every year, establishing a series of thresholds that vary according to the composition of a household. Everybody who falls below the relevant limit — such as $24,339 for a family of two adults and two children — is officially classified as poor.

Poverty, as we all know, is a serious issue in major cities. Two-fifths (40.3 percent) of the residents of Detroit (just the city itself, not the entire Detroit metro) are considered to be poor. The same is true for 36.2 percent in Cleveland, 34.8 percent in Syracuse, and 33.4 percent in Hartford.

But micropolitan areas aren't immune. Twenty-eight micros have poverty rates in excess of 30 percent, topped by Raymondville, Texas, at 39.0 percent, and Middlesborough, Kentucky, at 38.0 percent. Another 151 areas are stuck between 20 percent and 30 percent. (The rate for the entire country is 15.5 percent.)

The overall numbers favor metropolitan areas, largely thanks to the stability and relative affluence of suburbia. The collective poverty rate for metros is 15.0 percent, nearly three points better than the micropolitan average of 17.9 percent.

5. Top-level jobs are much harder to find in micropolitan areas.

American workers hold more than 145 million jobs, which the Census Bureau divides among 17 occupational subcategories. At the top of the resulting salary pyramid is the group of computer, engineering, and science jobs, with median annual earnings of $71,170 as of 2015. The runners-up are management, business, and financial jobs at $61,703 and health care practitioner and technical jobs at $53,488.

There's a substantial drop-off after that. Fourth on the list are protective service jobs (such as police officers and firefighters), with median earnings of $41,532. Salaries continue to dwindle until we reach the bottom four groups, which are all below $20,000. Food preparation and serving jobs rank 17th at $13,351.

So it makes sense to narrow our search for top-level positions to the three elite subcategories. Here are their relative concentrations:

Type	Management, business, and financial jobs	Computer, engineering, and science jobs	Health care practitioner and technical jobs
Micropolitan areas	11.4%	3.1%	5.6%
Metropolitan areas	15.2%	5.8%	5.8%

The health care column is a wash, but the other two are slanted heavily in favor of metropolitan areas. More than one-quarter of all metropolitan workers (26.8 percent) are employed in the top three occupational groups, compared to just one-fifth (20.1 percent) in the nation's micros.

To Rate or Not to Rate?

You won't find overall quality-of-life rankings in this book. My goal is simply to offer a comprehensive statistical snapshot of America's 551 micropolitan areas, something that has been unavailable up to now.

Not that I have any objection to rankings. I previously mentioned that I developed a 50-part formula in 1990 for *The Rating Guide to Life in America's Small Cities*, which ranked my original 219 micropolitan areas. These were the 11 most desirable micros back then:

1. San Luis Obispo-Atascadero, California
2. Corvallis, Oregon
3. Fredericksburg, Virginia
4. (tie) Fairbanks, Alaska
4. (tie) Wenatchee, Washington
6. Hattiesburg, Mississippi
7. (tie) Ames, Iowa
7. (tie) Port Angeles, Washington
9. Mankato, Minnesota
10. (tie) Aberdeen, Washington
10. (tie) Brunswick, Georgia

There is an ancient quality to this list, even though it is fewer than 30 years old. Nine of these 11 highly rated communities are no longer classified as micropolitan areas. San Luis Obispo, Corvallis, and six others have been elevated by OMB to full-fledged metropolitan status, while Fredericksburg has been absorbed into the rapidly expanding Washington, D.C., metro.

The irony is inescapable. Newcomers flocked to these micros during the 1990s and early years of the 21st century, attracted by the very small-town charm that would be muted by their arrival. The population of the San Luis Obispo area soared from 155,000 in 1980 to 281,000 in 2015. Traffic became so congested in Fredericksburg that one-fifth of local workers now spend at least three-quarters of an hour driving to work.

Port Angeles and Aberdeen are the only places on my original list that remain micropolitan areas today. Both have experienced growth in recent decades — 42 percent in the Port Angeles area and 7 percent in the Aberdeen micro since 1980 — but their populations remain small enough to qualify for this book. You'll find both of their profiles in Chapter 7.

You will also discover my inability to completely deny the desire to rank. Each micro's page contains a series of 10 ratings, which were designed to answer the following questions:

Children: Where are children more likely to have stable family lives, extended educational opportunities, and financial safety nets?

Diversity/Equality: Which areas embrace racial and geographic diversity, as well as economic equality?

Education: Where do substantial percentages of adults hold high school diplomas and college degrees?

Employment: Which micros are blessed with low unemployment, strong entrepreneurial spirit, and substantial numbers of good-paying jobs?

Growth Potential: Where do a variety of demographic factors suggest the possibility of future growth?

Housing: Which places have low vacancy percentages, high rates of home ownership, and diverse mixes of affordable and sizable houses?

Income: Which micros enjoy the highest income levels and lowest poverty rates?

Seniors: Where are senior citizens most likely to be self-sufficient and active in their families and communities?

Stability: Where do most residents have strong local roots, especially married couples and young adults of child-rearing age?

Transportation: Which areas offer their workers the shortest commutes and an array of transportation options?

Each of these ratings is based on five sets of current statistics. The best scores for children, for instance, have been awarded to micropolitan areas with high percentages of children who live with two parents, attend school, and speak English well, and low percentages who live in poverty and lack health insurance. Explanations of all statistical categories can be found in Chapter 2, while the ratings themselves are discussed in Chapter 3.

Micros are ranked in every case from first place all the way to 551st. If you are so inclined, it is possible to search out the best area for children (Pella, Iowa), as well as the worst (Arcadia, Florida). But I believe it's more useful to examine broader ranges, looking collectively at communities that have similar qualities. That's why I converted all of the ratings in this book to a five-star scale. The principle is the same as for movie or restaurant reviews. The more stars, the better the performance.

A Digression About Growth Potential

Nine of the 10 ratings are self-explanatory. Most of us agree on the qualities that distinguish a city with an impressive educational system, a place with a solid employment base, or an area with a strong housing stock. Those ratings are straightforward.

But growth potential is a different animal. It's an attempt to analyze existing conditions to predict the future, even though the results don't always align with expectations.

The highest scores for growth potential have been awarded to micropolitan areas with large proportions of children and young adults, proven abilities to attract newcomers from other states, and strong construction sectors. Logic dictates that outstanding performances in these statistical categories should foreshadow a growth spurt.

But I didn't stop there. I have also generated projections for all 551 micropolitan areas to forecast their populations in 2020 and 2030, totally independent of their growth potential ratings. Here, without getting too technical, are the steps I followed:

■ I used U.S. Census Bureau data to analyze population trends in all 3,142 U.S. counties and independent cities between 2000 and 2015, focusing on five different spans (three, six, nine, 12, and 15 years) that all ended in 2015. I determined the percentage of each state's population that was held by each of its counties and independent cities at the beginning and end of each period. (I'll use county as a blanket term from this point forward, encompassing independent cities as well.)

■ I calculated the annual rate of change in each county's percentage of state population during each period. Then I consolidated the five rates for each county, yielding an average annual rate.

■ I multiplied each county's share of its state's 2015 population by its average annual rate to determine its projected shares in future years. Multiplying by the annual rate to the power of five, for example, generated the raw share for 2020.

■ I added the raw shares for all counties within a state for each year. This total typically was more than 100 percent, so each county's raw share was then multiplied by the reciprocal of the statewide sum of all raw shares. The sum of the resulting adjusted shares for all counties in each state was 100 percent.

■ The University of Virginia's Weldon Cooper Center for Public Service has generated projections on a statewide basis through 2040. I took the projected population for a given state and multiplied it by the adjusted share for each county, yielding my county-by-county projections for any given year.

■ My final step was to add the projections at the county level to produce projections for micropolitan areas.

Many projection formulas are much, much more complicated than this one, yet all are bound by a thread of uncertainty. Some of my projections will prove to be uncannily accurate, while others will miss the mark. The only problem is that we won't be able to identify the winners and losers until 2030.

Which brings us back to growth potential.

My ratings and projections are generally in alignment. Heber, Utah, is projected to expand by 77.4 percent between 2015 and 2030, a truly meteoric rise. Also boasting impressive rates for the 15-year period are Dickinson, North Dakota, at 61.8 percent, Andrews, Texas, at 54.8 percent, and Bozeman, Montana, at 39.8 percent. It should come as no surprise that all of these micros earned five stars for growth potential.

I decided to test this linkage by adding the populations and projections for all micropolitan areas. The ratings, as you can see, match up pretty well:

Growth potential rating	2015 population	2030 projection	Change
5 stars	5,130,742	5,749,598	12.1%
4 stars	5,606,398	5,812,616	3.7%
3 stars	5,548,522	5,525,376	-0.4%
2 stars	5,677,564	5,534,043	-2.5%
1 star	5,746,945	5,394,226	-6.1%

The collective population of all five-star micros is expected to grow 12.1 percent between 2015 and 2030, and 21 of those areas are projected to grow 20 percent or more. But there are exceptions: 25 of the 110 five-star areas are actually projected to decline between 2015 and 2030. That's counterintuitive, I know, but it appears likely that these places will fail to capitalize on their demographic strengths.

The biggest disparities exist in four areas that marry five-star ratings for growth potential with projected population declines that are bewilderingly large, actually greater than 10 percent. Mountain Home, Idaho, is the worst of the bunch. It seems to be well-situated for future growth, but my computer expects its micropolitan population to slip from 25,876 in 2015 to 22,888 in 2030, a drop of 11.5 percent.

Putting Everything Together

The top 20 percent of the entries in any field — precisely 110 of the 551 micropolitan areas — are awarded five stars, the highest possible score on this book's scale.

A five-star rating is an indisputable sign of quality. Is Mayfield, Kentucky, a great place to raise children? Is Williston, North Dakota, a well-educated community? Does Norfolk, Nebraska, have a strong income base? The answer to all three questions is yes. Never mind that each of these communities is 110th in its respective field. It still outranks 80 percent of all other micros, and it still earns five stars, truly an outstanding accomplishment.

Yet the natural American impulse is to spin immediately to the highest point on any list. Five stars are all well and good, but these questions are foremost: Which micropolitan areas are the champions? Who holds first place in each of the 10 ratings? Here are the answers:

Children: Pella, Iowa.
Diversity/Equality: Kapaa, Hawaii.

Education: Laramie, Wyoming.
Employment: Summit Park, Utah.
Growth Potential: Rexburg, Idaho.
Housing: Hutchinson, Minnesota.
Income: Los Alamos, New Mexico.
Seniors: Heber, Utah.
Stability: Vernal, Utah.
Transportation: Ketchikan, Alaska.

You can find each field's full roster of five-star micropolitan areas in Chapter 3. The complete set of ratings for any given area can be seen on its profile page in Chapters 4 through 7.

If you peruse these various lists and profiles, you are likely to be struck by the wide distribution of quality across the nation. Seventy-two percent of all micros — a total of 398 — earned a five-star rating in one field or another. Only 153 areas were completely shut out, though most came close to breaking through. All but 22 members of this latter group received four stars in at least one instance.

The ultimate achievers — the dazzling standouts of micropolitan America — are the six areas that amassed five stars in eight fields apiece, giving them the highest possible score in all but two of the 10 ratings. A step behind are the 11 micros that earned top honors in seven fields. All of these high-flying micropolitan areas are included in their following chart, with an X signifying each five-star performance. The column for each rating is headed by a three-letter abbreviation:

Micro	5-star ratings	Chi	Div	Edu	Emp	Gro	Hou	Inc	Sen	Sta	Tra
Durango, CO	8	X	X	X	X	X		X	X		X
Edwards, CO	8		X	X	X	X		X	X	X	X
Helena, MT	8	X	X	X	X		X	X	X		X
Los Alamos, NM	8	X	X	X	X		X	X	X		X
McPherson, KS	8	X		X	X		X	X	X	X	X
Vineyard Haven, MA	8	X		X	X		X	X	X	X	X
Bozeman, MT	7	X		X	X	X		X	X		X
Breckenridge, CO	7		X	X	X	X		X	X		X

Micro	5-star ratings	Chi	Div	Edu	Emp	Gro	Hou	Inc	Sen	Sta	Tra
Dickinson, ND	7	X		X	X	X	X	X		X	
Jackson, WY-ID	7		X	X	X	X		X	X		X
Juneau, AK	7		X	X	X	X		X	X		X
Kearney, NE	7	X		X	X		X	X	X		X
Mitchell, SD	7	X		X	X	X	X	X			X
New Ulm, MN	7	X		X	X		X	X		X	X
Pierre, SD	7	X		X	X		X	X		X	X
Steamboat Springs, CO	7	X		X	X	X		X	X		X
Traverse City, MI	7	X		X	X		X	X	X	X	

These are indeed high-quality communities, though each has its flaws. Eleven of the 17 listed micros received a one-star rating in at least one field. (Breckenridge, McPherson, and New Ulm actually drew a pair of single stars.) Five of the remaining six top-rated micros have two-star scores somewhere on their records. The sole exception is Pierre, which boasts a sterling blend of five stars (seven times) and four stars (three times).

The spirit of equal time requires me to report that nearly 83 percent of the nation's micropolitan areas — 455 in all — received a lone star in one field or another, confirming that almost every community has serious deficiencies. The worst performances were turned in by three micros that registered eight one-star ratings apiece, followed by eight areas with seven sets of single stars. Here's the breakdown for these tailenders, with each X indicating a one-star rating:

Micro	1-star ratings	Chi	Div	Edu	Emp	Gro	Hou	Inc	Sen	Sta	Tra
Brownsville, TN	8			X	X	X	X	X	X	X	X
Helena-West Helena, AR	8	X		X	X	X	X	X	X		
Valley, AL	8	X		X	X	X		X	X	X	X
Atmore, AL	7	X		X	X		X	X	X		X
Bastrop, LA	7	X		X	X		X	X	X		X

Micro	1-star ratings	Chi	Div	Edu	Emp	Gro	Hou	Inc	Sen	Sta	Tra
Bennettsville, SC	7	X		X	X	X		X	X		X
Deming, NM	7	X		X	X		X	X	X	X	
Laurinburg, NC	7	X			X		X	X	X	X	X
Lumberton, NC	7	X		X	X		X	X	X		X
Palatka, FL	7	X		X	X		X	X		X	X
Roanoke Rapids, NC	7	X		X	X	X		X	X	X	

Yet there is cause for optimism even on this unfortunate list. Every single one of these low-scoring micros earned at least one mark as high as three stars. All but Bastrop and Brownsville reached four stars. And four achieved five-star ratings: Lumberton and Palatka for diversity/equality, Lumberton also for growth potential, and Deming and Helena-West Helena for transportation.

The temptation, of course, is to take the final step. Wouldn't it be a simple matter to combine the separate ratings for all 10 fields into a series of overall quality-of-life scores? Well, yes, it would. But I have decided to opt out. I'm more interested in highlighting the strengths and weaknesses of different areas, allowing you to make the final judgments.

Yet I am willing to say this. I have tinkered with several statistical tests, and my results suggest that three fields correlate especially well with the overall conditions in a community. Those golden indicators are education, employment, and income, a threesome that makes perfect sense. An excellent education improves a person's chances of landing a challenging job and a sizable paycheck. If a micropolitan area is fortunate enough to have a solid core of highly educated, steadily employed, and well-paid citizens, it is bound to prosper.

So I close with this final list. It shows the 51 micros that earned a trio of five-star ratings for education, employment, and income. They're arranged alphabetically by section of the country:

East (10 micros): Barre, VT; Claremont-Lebanon, NH-VT; Concord, NH; Easton, MD; Greenfield Town, MA; Hudson, NY; Keene, NH; Laconia, NH; Torrington, CT; and Vineyard Haven, MA.

South (2 micros): Key West, FL; and Pinehurst-Southern Pines, NC.

Midwest (23 micros): Aberdeen, SD; Alexandria, MN; Boone, IA; Dickinson, ND; Effingham, IL; Faribault-Northfield, MN; Fergus Falls, MN; Hastings, NE; Kearney, NE; Marshall, MN; McPherson, KS; Minot, ND; Mitchell, SD; New Ulm, MN; Owatonna, MN; Pella, IA; Pierre, SD; Port Clinton, OH; Red Wing, MN; Spirit Lake, IA; Traverse City, MI; Williston, ND; and Winona, MN.

West (16 micros): Bozeman, MT; Breckenridge, CO; Durango, CO; Edwards, CO; Glenwood Springs, CO; Heber, UT; Helena, MT; Jackson, WY-ID; Juneau, AK; Kalispell, MT; Los Alamos, NM; Oak Harbor, WA; Sheridan, WY; Steamboat Springs, CO; Summit Park, UT; and Truckee-Grass Valley, CA.

If I were to crown micropolitan America's quality-of-life champion, the winner would undoubtedly come from this list. But I'll leave it to you to make the ultimate statistical decision. You'll find all the numbers you need within the covers of this book.

2

CATEGORIES: THE TOP 25

★★★★★

MICROPOLITAN
AMERICA

The latter portion of this book — Chapters 4 through 7 — is devoted to single-page statistical profiles of the 551 micropolitan areas across the United States.

Each profile contains 75 statistics for a given micro, as well as 10 ratings on a five-star scale. A parenthetical rank accompanies each stat and rating, indicating an area's relative position among its peers.

Jamming all of this information onto a single sheet of paper was no simple matter. It was often necessary to use a linguistic shorthand, resulting in such entries as "living with two parents" and "racial diversity index" and "interest/dividends." The general idea comes across in each instance, though the process of abbreviation has obscured the necessary precision.

That's where this chapter comes in. It allocates one page to each of the 75 statistics, which are presented in the same sequence as in the profiles. (Forget about the five-star ratings for the moment. They're discussed in Chapter 3.) You'll find a detailed description of a given stat, telling you what it measures and what year it applies to. You'll also see the order in which the rankings run (biggest to smallest or vice versa) and the way the results are allocated.

The latter feature is known as a category's "splits," which allow you to quickly compare a given micro with all the others. The splits include the extreme statistics (top and bottom), as well as the figures at five intervening points. The number at the 80th percentile, for example, is superior to the corresponding numbers for 80 percent of the nation's micros, but inferior to the other 20 percent. The 50th percentile is the category's midpoint, better known as its median.

No value judgments have been imposed on the first 25 statistics, which are grouped under the headings of Population, Race, Age, Private Sector, and Household Income Ladder. These lists were designed to show each area's relative size, nothing more. They all run in the same order — biggest to smallest — so their 80th percentiles are always larger than 80 percent of the results for all micros.

But the story is different for the remaining 50 stats, which double as factors that determine each area's ratings in 10 fields from Children and Diversity/Equality to Stability and Transportation. Each of these categories is ordered from superior (top) to inferior (bottom) performances, with first place denoting the very best micro and 551st place the very worst.

Fifteen of the final 50 lists, for obvious reasons, put the smallest number at the top. Nobody could dispute that the lowest poverty rate is most desirable, or that the lowest vacancy rate or shortest commuting time is better. The splits are reversed in these instances. The number at the 80th percentile is smaller than 80 percent of the others.

Each page in this chapter is dominated by its final feature, a list of the top 25 micropolitan areas (or more in the case of ties) within a given category. That's why this chapter is called The Top 25. The micros on each list are displayed with their 2015 populations (except for the few initial lists that give populations for other years).

The raw data for this book came entirely from official sources, primarily the U.S. Census Bureau's 2015 American Community Survey, the same bureau's Population Estimates Program, and the U.S. Bureau of Labor Statistics's Quarterly Census of Employment and Wages. All figures were the latest available at presstime in February 2016.

But most of these stats were processed further before being set in print. The federal government typically — not always, but usually — contents itself with reporting raw numbers. I took the additional step of calculating percentages, rates, and ratios. And I ran the Census Bureau's population figures through a formula of my own creation to produce projections for 2020 and 2030.

It's important to keep in mind that most official stats are generated from surveys, which are extensively and comprehensively conducted, yet still carry the small margin of error that all polls do. My percentages, rates, and ratios are based on the precise numbers reported by the American Community Survey and other federal sources. You should be aware of the possibility of wiggle room in some instances, particularly in those rare cases where an area is credited with the always eyebrowing-raising figure of 100 percent.

Population: 2010 Census

Description: Residents counted by the U.S. Census Bureau (April 2010).
Order: Ranked from highest population (top) to lowest population (bottom).
Splits: 218,466 at the top, 67,077 at the 80th percentile, 47,759 at the 60th percentile, 43,041 at the median (50th percentile), 38,827 at the 40th percentile, 29,180 at the 20th percentile, and 13,477 at the bottom.

The Top 25

Rank	Micropolitan area	2010 census
1	Claremont-Lebanon, NH-VT	218,466
2	Torrington, CT	189,927
3	Hilo, HI	185,079
4	Ottawa-Peru, IL	154,908
5	Pottsville, PA	148,289
6	Concord, NH	146,445
7	Traverse City, MI	143,372
8	Tupelo, MS	136,268
9	Jamestown-Dunkirk-Fredonia, NY	134,905
10	Eureka-Arcata-Fortuna, CA	134,623
11	Lumberton, NC	134,168
12	London, KY	126,369
13	Augusta-Waterville, ME	122,151
14	Dunn, NC	114,678
15	Wooster, OH	114,520
16	Ogdensburg-Massena, NY	111,944
17	Holland, MI	111,408
18	Salem, OH	107,841
19	Roseburg, OR	107,667
20	Meridian, MS	107,449
20	Show Low, AZ	107,449
22	Bluefield, WV-VA	107,342
23	Danville, VA	106,561
24	Cookeville, TN	106,042
25	Whitewater-Elkhorn, WI	102,228

Population: 2015 Estimate

Description: Residents estimated by the U.S. Census Bureau (July 2015).
Order: Ranked from highest population (top) to lowest population (bottom).
Splits: 216,923 at the top, 67,215 at the 80th percentile, 48,494 at the 60th percentile, 43,664 at the median (50th percentile), 38,521 at the 40th percentile, 29,126 at the 20th percentile, and 12,937 at the bottom.

The Top 25

Rank	Micropolitan area	2015 estimate
1	Claremont-Lebanon, NH-VT	216,923
2	Hilo, HI	196,428
3	Torrington, CT	183,603
4	Ottawa-Peru, IL	150,564
5	Traverse City, MI	148,334
6	Concord, NH	147,994
7	Pottsville, PA	144,590
8	Tupelo, MS	139,817
9	Eureka-Arcata-Fortuna, CA	135,727
10	Lumberton, NC	134,197
11	Jamestown-Dunkirk-Fredonia, NY	130,779
12	Dunn, NC	128,140
13	London, KY	127,953
14	Augusta-Waterville, ME	119,980
15	Wooster, OH	116,063
16	Holland, MI	114,625
17	Ogdensburg-Massena, NY	111,007
18	Show Low, AZ	108,277
19	Cookeville, TN	108,191
20	Roseburg, OR	107,685
21	Twin Falls, ID	105,189
22	Salem, OH	104,806
23	Richmond-Berea, KY	104,766
24	Meridian, MS	104,499
25	Danville, VA	104,276

Population: 2010-2015 Change

Description: Percentage change in the area's population (2010 to 2015).
Order: Ranked from highest percentage (top) to lowest percentage (bottom).
Splits: 57.6% at the top, 2.4% at the 80th percentile, 0.5% at the 60th percentile, -0.2% at the median (50th percentile), -1.0% at the 40th percentile, -2.3% at the 20th percentile, and -10.3% at the bottom.

The Top 25

Rank	Micropolitan area	Population	2010-2015 change
1	Williston, ND	35,294	57.6%
2	Dickinson, ND	32,154	32.9%
3	Heber, UT	29,161	23.9%
4	Andrews, TX	18,105	22.4%
5	Vernal, UT	37,928	16.4%
6	Minot, ND	79,814	14.8%
7	Bozeman, MT	100,739	12.5%
8	Oxford, MS	53,154	12.3%
9	Dunn, NC	128,140	11.7%
10	Hobbs, NM	71,180	10.0%
11	Summit Park, UT	39,633	9.1%
12	Stephenville, TX	41,122	8.5%
13	Weatherford, OK	29,744	8.3%
14	Breckenridge, CO	30,257	8.1%
15	Junction City, KS	37,030	7.8%
16	Pullman, WA	48,177	7.6%
17	Elk City, OK	23,768	7.5%
18	Woodward, OK	21,559	7.4%
19	Gallup, NM	76,708	7.3%
20	Jackson, WY-ID	33,689	7.1%
21	Carlsbad-Artesia, NM	57,578	7.0%
22	Kapaa, HI	71,735	6.9%
22	Pecos, TX	14,732	6.9%
22	Pinehurst-Southern Pines, NC	94,352	6.9%
25	Gillette, WY	49,220	6.7%
25	Sevierville, TN	95,946	6.7%

Population: 2020 Projection

Description: Residents projected by the author's formula (July 2020).
Order: Ranked from highest population (top) to lowest population (bottom).
Splits: 216,497 at the top, 67,397 at the 80th percentile, 49,157 at the 60th percentile, 43,652 at the median (50th percentile), 38,853 at the 40th percentile, 28,884 at the 20th percentile, and 12,438 at the bottom.

The Top 25

Rank	Micropolitan area	2020 projection
1	Claremont-Lebanon, NH-VT	216,497
2	Hilo, HI	210,431
3	Torrington, CT	179,467
4	Traverse City, MI	153,682
5	Concord, NH	149,282
6	Ottawa-Peru, IL	147,385
7	Tupelo, MS	142,587
8	Pottsville, PA	141,496
9	Dunn, NC	140,046
10	Eureka-Arcata-Fortuna, CA	137,593
11	Lumberton, NC	133,510
12	London, KY	128,773
13	Jamestown-Dunkirk-Fredonia, NY	127,829
14	Augusta-Waterville, ME	118,610
15	Holland, MI	117,972
16	Wooster, OH	117,092
17	Bozeman, MT	112,664
18	Cookeville, TN	110,834
19	Twin Falls, ID	110,624
20	Ogdensburg-Massena, NY	110,393
21	Richmond-Berea, KY	109,139
22	Show Low, AZ	108,367
23	Roseburg, OR	108,166
24	Whitewater-Elkhorn, WI	103,686
25	Tullahoma-Manchester, TN	103,400

Population: 2030 Projection

Description: Residents projected by the author's formula (July 2030).
Order: Ranked from highest population (top) to lowest population (bottom).
Splits: 242,308 at the top, 68,706 at the 80th percentile, 49,658 at the 60th percentile, 43,880 at the median (50th percentile), 38,641 at the 40th percentile, 28,137 at the 20th percentile, and 11,327 at the bottom.

The Top 25

Rank	Micropolitan area	2030 projection
1	Hilo, HI	242,308
2	Claremont-Lebanon, NH-VT	215,496
3	Torrington, CT	171,309
4	Dunn, NC	166,598
5	Traverse City, MI	164,583
6	Concord, NH	151,833
7	Tupelo, MS	147,292
8	Eureka-Arcata-Fortuna, CA	141,790
9	Ottawa-Peru, IL	140,870
10	Bozeman, MT	140,788
11	Pottsville, PA	135,299
12	Lumberton, NC	131,572
13	London, KY	130,104
14	Holland, MI	124,532
15	Twin Falls, ID	122,259
16	Jamestown-Dunkirk-Fredonia, NY	122,181
17	Wooster, OH	118,724
18	Richmond-Berea, KY	118,241
19	Sevierville, TN	116,782
20	Kalispell, MT	116,045
21	Cookeville, TN	116,002
22	Augusta-Waterville, ME	115,710
23	Moses Lake, WA	110,341
24	Pinehurst-Southern Pines, NC	110,218
25	Roseburg, OR	109,321

Race: Whites

Description: Percentage of residents who are whites and not also classified as Hispanics or Latinos (2015). An area's racial percentages may not add to 100 because not all races are listed in its profile.

Order: Ranked from highest percentage (top) to lowest percentage (bottom).

Splits: 97.6% at the top, 92.9% at the 80th percentile, 88.0% at the 60th percentile, 84.2% at the median (50th percentile), 79.6% at the 40th percentile, 60.7% at the 20th percentile, and 0.9% at the bottom.

The Top 25

Rank	Micropolitan area	Population	Whites
1	St. Marys, PA	30,872	97.6%
2	Warren, PA	40,396	97.2%
3	Spirit Lake, IA	17,111	96.7%
4	Alexandria, MN	37,075	96.6%
5	Effingham, IL	34,371	96.5%
5	Greenville, OH	52,076	96.5%
5	Lewistown, PA	46,500	96.5%
5	Wapakoneta, OH	45,876	96.5%
9	Ashland, OH	53,213	96.2%
9	Celina, OH	40,968	96.2%
9	Coshocton, OH	36,569	96.2%
9	Elkins, WV	29,126	96.2%
9	Jackson, OH	32,596	96.2%
9	Sayre, PA	61,281	96.2%
15	Alpena, MI	28,803	96.1%
15	Bedford, IN	45,495	96.1%
15	Iron Mountain, MI-WI	30,252	96.1%
15	London, KY	127,953	96.1%
15	Merrill, WI	27,980	96.1%
15	Oil City, PA	53,119	96.1%
21	Bucyrus, OH	42,306	96.0%
21	Connersville, IN	23,434	96.0%
23	Rutland, VT	59,736	95.9%
24	Logan, WV	34,707	95.8%
25	Carroll, IA	20,498	95.7%

Race: Blacks

Description: Percentage of residents who are blacks and not also classi-fied as Hispanics or Latinos (2015). An area's racial percentages may not add to 100 because not all races are listed in its profile.

Order: Ranked from highest percentage (top) to lowest percentage (bottom).

Splits: 75.8% at the top, 11.0% at the 80th percentile, 3.2% at the 60th percentile, 2.2% at the median (50th percentile), 1.5% at the 40th percentile, 0.6% at the 20th percentile, and 0.0% at the bottom.

The Top 25

Rank	Micropolitan area	Population	Blacks
1	Clarksdale, MS	24,620	75.8%
2	Indianola, MS	27,005	72.7%
3	Greenville, MS	48,130	71.1%
4	Selma, AL	41,131	69.2%
5	Cleveland, MS	33,322	64.0%
6	Greenwood, MS	41,242	62.6%
7	Orangeburg, SC	89,208	61.6%
8	Helena-West Helena, AR	19,513	61.5%
9	West Point, MS	20,048	58.2%
10	Vicksburg, MS	56,635	53.7%
11	Roanoke Rapids, NC	72,882	53.3%
12	Forrest City, AR	26,589	51.7%
13	Bennettsville, SC	27,494	50.7%
14	McComb, MS	52,530	49.8%
15	Natchez, MS-LA	51,396	49.7%
16	Henderson, NC	44,568	49.3%
17	Brownsville, TN	18,023	49.0%
18	Americus, GA	35,947	47.7%
19	Bastrop, LA	26,395	47.3%
20	Eufaula, AL-GA	28,791	46.9%
21	Milledgeville, GA	54,010	46.6%
22	Columbus, MS	59,710	43.8%
23	Grenada, MS	21,578	43.5%
24	Cordele, GA	22,881	43.2%
25	Meridian, MS	104,499	42.9%

Race: Hispanics

Description: Percentage of residents who are Hispanics or Latinos (2015). An area's racial percentages may not add to 100 because not all races are listed in its profile.

Order: Ranked from highest percentage (top) to lowest percentage (bottom).

Splits: 98.7% at the top, 14.0% at the 80th percentile, 6.1% at the 60th percentile, 4.4% at the median (50th percentile), 3.2% at the 40th percentile, 2.0% at the 20th percentile, and 0.1% at the bottom.

The Top 25

Rank	Micropolitan area	Population	Hispanics
1	Rio Grande City, TX	63,795	98.7%
2	Eagle Pass, TX	57,706	95.2%
3	Zapata, TX	14,374	93.6%
4	Raymondville, TX	21,903	87.5%
5	Nogales, AZ	46,461	82.8%
6	Del Rio, TX	48,988	80.4%
7	Alice, TX	41,382	79.5%
8	Las Vegas, NM	27,967	76.9%
9	Pecos, TX	14,732	74.6%
10	Española, NM	39,465	71.5%
11	Kingsville, TX	32,264	71.2%
12	Uvalde, TX	27,245	70.2%
13	Hereford, TX	18,952	69.8%
14	Deming, NM	24,518	64.1%
15	Othello, WA	19,254	61.5%
16	Liberal, KS	23,152	58.3%
17	Plainview, TX	34,360	57.9%
18	Beeville, TX	32,874	57.3%
19	Taos, NM	32,907	56.2%
20	Lamesa, TX	13,520	54.7%
21	Hobbs, NM	71,180	54.5%
22	Roswell, NM	65,764	54.2%
23	Andrews, TX	18,105	53.2%
24	Dodge City, KS	34,536	52.8%
25	Dumas, TX	22,255	52.6%

Race: Asians

Description: Percentage of residents who are Asians, Native Hawaiians, or Pacific Islanders and not also classified as Hispanics or Latinos (2015). An area's racial percentages may not add to 100 because not all races are listed in its profile.

Order: Ranked from highest percentage (top) to lowest percentage (bottom).

Splits: 42.7% at the top, 1.4% at the 80th percentile, 0.8% at the 60th percentile, 0.7% at the median (50th percentile), 0.6% at the 40th percentile, 0.4% at the 20th percentile, and 0.0% at the bottom.

The Top 25

Rank	Micropolitan area	Population	Asians
1	Kapaa, HI	71,735	42.7%
2	Hilo, HI	196,428	32.5%
3	Dumas, TX	22,255	8.5%
3	Storm Lake, IA	20,493	8.5%
5	Fairfield, IA	17,555	7.9%
6	Huron, SD	18,372	7.8%
6	Pullman, WA	48,177	7.8%
8	Ketchikan, AK	13,709	7.4%
9	Juneau, AK	32,756	7.3%
10	Los Alamos, NM	17,785	6.8%
11	Worthington, MN	21,770	5.8%
12	Oak Harbor, WA	80,593	5.1%
13	Stillwater, OK	80,850	4.2%
14	Junction City, KS	37,030	3.8%
15	Garden City, KS	41,074	3.7%
16	Port Lavaca, TX	21,895	3.5%
17	Fort Leonard Wood, MO	53,221	3.4%
17	Mountain Home, ID	25,876	3.4%
17	Rolla, MO	44,794	3.4%
20	Athens, OH	65,886	3.3%
20	Marshall, MN	25,673	3.3%
22	Laramie, WY	37,956	3.1%
23	Fallon, NV	24,200	3.0%
23	Starkville, MS	49,800	3.0%
25	Brookings, SD	33,897	2.9%
25	Eureka-Arcata-Fortuna, CA	135,727	2.9%
25	Liberal, KS	23,152	2.9%
25	Marshalltown, IA	40,746	2.9%

Race: Native Americans

Description: Percentage of residents who are Native Americans or Native Alaskans and not also classified as Hispanics or Latinos (2015). An area's racial percentages may not add to 100 because not all races are listed in its profile.

Order: Ranked from highest percentage (top) to lowest percentage (bottom).

Splits: 72.3% at the top, 1.0% at the 80th percentile, 0.4% at the 60th percentile, 0.3% at the median (50th percentile), 0.2% at the 40th percentile, 0.1% at the 20th percentile, and 0.0% at the bottom.

The Top 25

Rank	Micropolitan area	Population	Native Americans
1	Gallup, NM	76,708	72.3%
2	Show Low, AZ	108,277	43.1%
3	Grants, NM	27,329	38.5%
4	Lumberton, NC	134,197	37.6%
5	Tahlequah, OK	48,447	32.1%
6	Bemidji, MN	45,672	20.0%
7	Riverton, WY	40,315	18.9%
8	Muskogee, OK	69,699	16.1%
9	Payson, AZ	53,159	15.1%
10	Sault Ste. Marie, MI	38,033	14.8%
11	Durant, OK	44,884	14.4%
11	Shawano, WI	45,877	14.4%
13	Española, NM	39,465	14.0%
14	Miami, OK	31,981	13.7%
15	Ketchikan, AK	13,709	13.6%
16	Shawnee, OK	71,875	13.1%
17	Safford, AZ	37,666	12.9%
18	Juneau, AK	32,756	11.8%
19	Laurinburg, NC	35,509	10.4%
20	Bartlesville, OK	52,021	9.7%
21	Pierre, SD	21,935	9.2%
22	McAlester, OK	44,610	9.0%
23	Cullowhee, NC	41,265	8.4%
24	Ardmore, OK	48,689	8.0%
25	Ada, OK	38,194	7.3%

Age: 0-17 Years Old

Description: Percentage of residents who are in the range from 0 through 17 years old (2015).
Order: Ranked from highest percentage (top) to lowest percentage (bottom).
Splits: 35.2% at the top, 25.2% at the 80th percentile, 23.7% at the 60th percentile, 22.9% at the median (50th percentile), 22.1% at the 40th percentile, 20.4% at the 20th percentile, and 13.4% at the bottom.

The Top 25

Rank	Micropolitan area	Population	0-17 years old
1	Othello, WA	19,254	35.2%
2	Vernal, UT	37,928	33.8%
3	Zapata, TX	14,374	33.7%
4	Rio Grande City, TX	63,795	33.3%
5	Heber, UT	29,161	33.1%
6	Eagle Pass, TX	57,706	32.3%
7	Blackfoot, ID	44,990	32.0%
8	Hereford, TX	18,952	31.8%
9	Dumas, TX	22,255	31.7%
10	Liberal, KS	23,152	31.6%
11	Decatur, IN	34,980	31.3%
12	Garden City, KS	41,074	31.2%
13	Junction City, KS	37,030	30.8%
14	Dodge City, KS	34,536	30.7%
15	Burley, ID	43,967	30.6%
16	Andrews, TX	18,105	30.5%
16	Gallup, NM	76,708	30.5%
18	Moses Lake, WA	93,259	30.3%
19	Hobbs, NM	71,180	29.8%
20	Evanston, WY	20,822	29.6%
21	Cedar City, UT	48,368	29.4%
22	Mount Pleasant, TX	32,623	29.3%
23	Del Rio, TX	48,988	29.2%
24	Washington, IN	32,906	29.1%
25	Nogales, AZ	46,461	28.8%

Age: 18-24 Years Old

Description: Percentage of residents who are in the range from 18 through 24 years old (2015).

Order: Ranked from highest percentage (top) to lowest percentage (bottom).

Splits: 37.0% at the top, 11.2% at the 80th percentile, 9.3% at the 60th percentile, 9.0% at the median (50th percentile), 8.5% at the 40th percentile, 7.9% at the 20th percentile, and 5.5% at the bottom.

The Top 25

Rank	Micropolitan area	Population	18-24 years old
1	Pullman, WA	48,177	37.0%
2	Vermillion, SD	13,964	32.8%
3	Starkville, MS	49,800	32.1%
4	Boone, NC	52,906	31.4%
5	Mount Pleasant, MI	70,698	30.5%
6	Athens, OH	65,886	30.2%
7	Laramie, WY	37,956	29.5%
8	Maryville, MO	22,810	29.1%
9	Brookings, SD	33,897	28.1%
10	Stillwater, OK	80,850	27.2%
11	Statesboro, GA	72,651	26.7%
12	Macomb, IL	31,333	26.3%
13	Oxford, MS	53,154	26.0%
14	Ruston, LA	47,774	25.9%
15	Moscow, ID	38,778	25.7%
15	Rexburg, ID	51,092	25.7%
17	Kirksville, MO	29,814	25.5%
18	Fort Leonard Wood, MO	53,221	23.4%
19	Ellensburg, WA	43,269	22.6%
20	Arkadelphia, AR	22,633	22.5%
21	Stephenville, TX	41,122	22.0%
22	Murray, KY	38,343	21.7%
23	Troy, AL	33,046	21.4%
24	Winona, MN	50,885	21.0%
25	Warrensburg, MO	53,951	20.8%

Age: 25-39 Years Old

Description: Percentage of residents who are in the range from 25 through 39 years old (2015).
Order: Ranked from highest percentage (top) to lowest percentage (bottom).
Splits: 27.9% at the top, 18.9% at the 80th percentile, 17.9% at the 60th percentile, 17.4% at the median (50th percentile), 17.0% at the 40th percentile, 16.2% at the 20th percentile, and 12.2% at the bottom.

The Top 25

Rank	Micropolitan area	Population	25-39 years old
1	Susanville, CA	31,345	27.9%
2	Junction City, KS	37,030	27.5%
3	Breckenridge, CO	30,257	27.3%
4	Jackson, WY-ID	33,689	27.2%
5	Edwards, CO	53,605	26.5%
6	Fort Polk South, LA	50,803	24.3%
7	Williston, ND	35,294	24.2%
8	Fort Leonard Wood, MO	53,221	24.0%
8	Palestine, TX	57,580	24.0%
10	Lamesa, TX	13,520	23.8%
11	Beeville, TX	32,874	23.7%
12	Vernal, UT	37,928	23.6%
13	Gillette, WY	49,220	23.4%
14	Bozeman, MT	100,739	23.2%
15	Pecos, TX	14,732	22.9%
16	Rock Springs, WY	44,626	22.8%
17	Elk City, OK	23,768	22.4%
18	Guymon, OK	21,489	22.3%
19	Juneau, AK	32,756	22.2%
20	Dickinson, ND	32,154	22.0%
20	Heber, UT	29,161	22.0%
22	Dunn, NC	128,140	21.9%
22	Raymondville, TX	21,903	21.9%
24	Bennettsville, SC	27,494	21.8%
24	Cañon City, CO	46,692	21.8%

Age: 40-54 Years Old

Description: Percentage of residents who are in the range from 40 through 54 years old (2015).

Order: Ranked from highest percentage (top) to lowest percentage (bottom).

Splits: 24.8% at the top, 21.0% at the 80th percentile, 20.1% at the 60th percentile, 19.7% at the median (50th percentile), 19.3% at the 40th percentile, 18.2% at the 20th percentile, and 12.0% at the bottom.

The Top 25

Rank	Micropolitan area	Population	40-54 years old
1	Oxford, NC	58,674	24.8%
2	Summit Park, UT	39,633	24.3%
3	Torrington, CT	183,603	24.0%
4	Vineyard Haven, MA	17,299	23.5%
5	Jefferson, GA	63,360	23.1%
5	Merrill, WI	27,980	23.1%
7	Concord, NH	147,994	22.9%
7	DuBois, PA	80,994	22.9%
7	Key West, FL	77,482	22.9%
10	Beaver Dam, WI	88,502	22.8%
10	Los Alamos, NM	17,785	22.8%
10	Steamboat Springs, CO	24,130	22.8%
13	Edwards, CO	53,605	22.7%
14	Palestine, TX	57,580	22.6%
14	St. Marys, PA	30,872	22.6%
16	Auburn, NY	78,288	22.5%
17	Beeville, TX	32,874	22.4%
17	Chillicothe, OH	77,170	22.4%
19	Augusta-Waterville, ME	119,980	22.3%
19	New Castle, IN	48,985	22.3%
21	Barre, VT	58,612	22.2%
21	Batavia, NY	58,937	22.2%
21	Greenfield Town, MA	70,601	22.2%
21	Kill Devil Hills, NC	39,733	22.2%
25	Albemarle, NC	60,714	22.1%
25	Breckenridge, CO	30,257	22.1%
25	Hailey, ID	27,955	22.1%
25	Ionia, MI	64,223	22.1%
25	Jasper, IN	55,055	22.1%
25	Malone, NY	50,660	22.1%

Age: 55-64 Years Old

Description: Percentage of residents who are in the range from 55 through 64 years old (2015).

Order: Ranked from highest percentage (top) to lowest percentage (bottom).

Splits: 19.3% at the top, 14.6% at the 80th percentile, 13.8% at the 60th percentile, 13.4% at the median (50th percentile), 13.1% at the 40th percentile, 12.0% at the 20th percentile, and 6.2% at the bottom.

The Top 25

Rank	Micropolitan area	Population	55-64 years old
1	Newport, OR	47,038	19.3%
2	Brookings, OR	22,483	18.9%
3	Truckee-Grass Valley, CA	98,877	18.6%
4	Sandpoint, ID	41,859	18.4%
5	Fairfield, IA	17,555	18.3%
6	Ruidoso, NM	19,420	17.9%
7	Gardnerville Ranchos, NV	47,710	17.5%
7	Greenfield Town, MA	70,601	17.5%
7	Sonora, CA	53,709	17.5%
10	Key West, FL	77,482	17.4%
10	Taos, NM	32,907	17.4%
12	Vineyard Haven, MA	17,299	17.3%
13	Berlin, NH-VT	37,375	17.2%
13	Pahrump, NV	42,477	17.2%
15	Clearlake, CA	64,591	17.1%
16	Kill Devil Hills, NC	39,733	17.0%
16	Port Clinton, OH	40,877	17.0%
18	Astoria, OR	37,831	16.9%
18	Coos Bay, OR	63,121	16.9%
18	Port Angeles, WA	73,486	16.9%
21	Laconia, NH	60,641	16.8%
21	Spirit Lake, IA	17,111	16.8%
23	Escanaba, MI	36,377	16.7%
23	Grand Rapids, MN	45,435	16.7%
25	Logan, WV	34,707	16.6%
25	Prineville, OR	21,630	16.6%

Age: 65+ Years Old

Description: Percentage of residents who are 65 years old or older (2015).
Order: Ranked from highest percentage (top) to lowest percentage (bottom).
Splits: 30.5% at the top, 18.2% at the 80th percentile, 16.8% at the 60th percentile, 16.3% at the median (50th percentile), 15.6% at the 40th percentile, 14.0% at the 20th percentile, and 6.6% at the bottom.

The Top 25

Rank	Micropolitan area	Population	65+ years old
1	Brookings, OR	22,483	30.5%
2	Mountain Home, AR	41,053	29.6%
3	Crossville, TN	58,229	28.4%
4	Fredericksburg, TX	25,963	27.9%
5	Brevard, NC	33,211	27.6%
6	Pahrump, NV	42,477	26.6%
7	Port Angeles, WA	73,486	26.2%
8	Kerrville, TX	50,955	26.1%
9	Easton, MD	37,512	25.7%
10	Payson, AZ	53,159	25.6%
11	Ruidoso, NM	19,420	25.3%
12	Newport, OR	47,038	24.0%
13	Pinehurst-Southern Pines, NC	94,352	23.6%
13	Spirit Lake, IA	17,111	23.6%
15	Gardnerville Ranchos, NV	47,710	23.5%
15	Silver City, NM	28,609	23.5%
17	Prineville, OR	21,630	23.4%
18	Coos Bay, OR	63,121	23.3%
19	Georgetown, SC	61,298	23.2%
20	Roseburg, OR	107,685	22.9%
21	Sonora, CA	53,709	22.7%
22	Truckee-Grass Valley, CA	98,877	22.3%
23	Fergus Falls, MN	57,716	22.0%
24	Branson, MO	85,535	21.8%
25	Fairmont, MN	20,022	21.5%

Private Sector: Businesses

Description: Annual average total of private-sector business establishments (2015).

Order: Ranked from highest total (top) to lowest total (bottom).

Splits: 6,875 at the top, 1,652 at the 80th percentile, 1,139 at the 60th percentile, 1,008 at the median (50th percentile), 871 at the 40th percentile, 679 at the 20th percentile, and 175 at the bottom.

The Top 25

Rank	Micropolitan area	Population	Businesses
1	Claremont-Lebanon, NH-VT	216,923	6,875
2	Bozeman, MT	100,739	5,872
3	Torrington, CT	183,603	5,585
4	Hilo, HI	196,428	4,768
5	Traverse City, MI	148,334	4,450
6	Eureka-Arcata-Fortuna, CA	135,727	4,340
7	Concord, NH	147,994	4,329
8	Key West, FL	77,482	4,295
9	Glenwood Springs, CO	75,882	4,249
10	Kalispell, MT	96,165	4,239
11	Ukiah, CA	87,649	3,917
12	Ottawa-Peru, IL	150,564	3,574
13	Augusta-Waterville, ME	119,980	3,480
14	Truckee-Grass Valley, CA	98,877	3,330
15	Edwards, CO	53,605	3,317
16	Twin Falls, ID	105,189	3,260
17	Tupelo, MS	139,817	3,153
18	Moses Lake, WA	93,259	3,126
19	Sturgis, MI	61,018	3,062
20	Jamestown-Dunkirk-Fredonia, NY	130,779	3,037
21	Pottsville, PA	144,590	2,921
22	Helena, MT	78,063	2,882
23	Paducah, KY-IL	97,312	2,876
24	Roseburg, OR	107,685	2,854
25	Danville, VA	104,276	2,815

Private Sector: Employees

Description: Annual average total of private-sector employees (2015).
Order: Ranked from highest total (top) to lowest total (bottom).
Splits: 81,681 at the top, 21,213 at the 80th percentile, 14,517 at the 60th percentile, 13,104 at the median (50th percentile), 11,383 at the 40th percentile, 8,246 at the 20th percentile, and 651 at the bottom.

The Top 25

Rank	Micropolitan area	Population	Employees
1	Claremont-Lebanon, NH-VT	216,923	81,681
2	Tupelo, MS	139,817	62,787
3	Concord, NH	147,994	59,565
4	Hilo, HI	196,428	54,545
5	Traverse City, MI	148,334	53,595
6	Torrington, CT	183,603	53,198
7	Ottawa-Peru, IL	150,564	47,391
8	Bozeman, MT	100,739	44,127
9	Augusta-Waterville, ME	119,980	43,228
10	Pottsville, PA	144,590	42,404
11	Findlay, OH	75,573	41,294
12	Jamestown-Dunkirk-Fredonia, NY	130,779	41,183
13	Paducah, KY-IL	97,312	40,966
14	Twin Falls, ID	105,189	40,843
15	Wooster, OH	116,063	39,408
16	Sevierville, TN	95,946	39,163
17	London, KY	127,953	38,340
18	Kalispell, MT	96,165	35,806
19	Key West, FL	77,482	35,102
20	Glenwood Springs, CO	75,882	34,340
21	LaGrange, GA	69,763	34,338
22	Eureka-Arcata-Fortuna, CA	135,727	34,291
23	Warsaw, IN	78,620	33,989
24	Williston, ND	35,294	33,793
25	Whitewater-Elkhorn, WI	102,804	33,711

Private Sector: Total Wages

Description: Annual total wages for private-sector employees (2015).
Order: Ranked from highest dollar figure (top) to lowest dollar figure (bottom).
Splits: $3,977,638,194 at the top, $839,208,768 at the 80th percentile, $539,117,449 at the 60th percentile, $468,939,754 at the median (50th percentile), $405,010,269 at the 40th percentile, $293,586,034 at the 20th percentile, and $21,937,071 at the bottom.

The Top 25

Rank	Micropolitan area	Population	Total wages
1	Claremont-Lebanon, NH-VT	216,923	$3,977,638,194
2	Concord, NH	147,994	$2,844,977,072
3	Williston, ND	35,294	$2,695,544,781
4	Torrington, CT	183,603	$2,307,099,360
5	Tupelo, MS	139,817	$2,255,280,185
6	Traverse City, MI	148,334	$2,123,864,614
7	Hilo, HI	196,428	$2,034,834,831
8	Ottawa-Peru, IL	150,564	$1,986,809,202
9	Warsaw, IN	78,620	$1,944,324,105
10	Findlay, OH	75,573	$1,927,507,671
11	Paducah, KY-IL	97,312	$1,752,111,923
12	Bozeman, MT	100,739	$1,704,252,996
13	Glenwood Springs, CO	75,882	$1,643,781,457
14	Wooster, OH	116,063	$1,637,332,777
15	Augusta-Waterville, ME	119,980	$1,624,408,486
16	Pottsville, PA	144,590	$1,604,911,407
17	Corning, NY	97,631	$1,586,041,211
18	Minot, ND	79,814	$1,519,042,797
19	Holland, MI	114,625	$1,479,708,183
20	Hobbs, NM	71,180	$1,456,669,357
21	LaGrange, GA	69,763	$1,440,396,391
22	Jamestown-Dunkirk-Fredonia, NY	130,779	$1,421,825,263
23	Carlsbad-Artesia, NM	57,578	$1,360,922,877
24	Tullahoma-Manchester, TN	102,048	$1,360,434,780
25	Gillette, WY	49,220	$1,359,051,684

Private Sector: Average Weekly Wages

Description: Average weekly wages for private-sector employees (2015).
Order: Ranked from highest dollar figure (top) to lowest dollar figure (bottom).
Splits: $1,575 at the top, $785 at the 80th percentile, $717 at the 60th percentile, $693 at the median (50th percentile), $672 at the 40th percentile, $627 at the 20th percentile, and $396 at the bottom.

The Top 25

Rank	Micropolitan area	Population	Average weekly wages
1	Los Alamos, NM	17,785	$1,575
2	Williston, ND	35,294	$1,534
3	Dickinson, ND	32,154	$1,245
4	Port Lavaca, TX	21,895	$1,229
5	Borger, TX	21,734	$1,219
6	Andrews, TX	18,105	$1,189
7	Rock Springs, WY	44,626	$1,176
8	Gillette, WY	49,220	$1,142
9	Warsaw, IN	78,620	$1,100
10	Elko, NV	53,951	$1,087
10	Winnemucca, NV	17,019	$1,087
12	Bay City, TX	36,770	$1,071
13	Carlsbad-Artesia, NM	57,578	$1,063
14	Corning, NY	97,631	$1,047
15	Snyder, TX	17,615	$1,046
16	Morgan City, LA	52,810	$1,018
17	Bartlesville, OK	52,021	$1,013
18	Hobbs, NM	71,180	$1,010
19	Levelland, TX	23,433	$976
20	Ozark, AL	49,565	$966
21	Pahrump, NV	42,477	$964
22	Marshall, TX	66,746	$962
23	Pampa, TX	23,210	$956
24	Claremont-Lebanon, NH-VT	216,923	$936
24	El Dorado, AR	40,144	$936

Household Income Ladder: 95th Percentile

Description: Household income that outranks 95 percent of incomes for other households in the same area (2015). The Census Bureau does not report incomes greater than $250,000. The designation of ">$250,000" is used for areas above that threshold.

Order: Ranked from highest dollar figure (top) to lowest dollar figure (bottom).

Splits: >$250,000 at the top, $157,696 at the 80th percentile, $145,582 at the 60th percentile, $141,253 at the median (50th percentile), $136,785 at the 40th percentile, $129,028 at the 20th percentile, and $95,527 at the bottom. (These splits serve the same function as those on other pages. Each percentile above is a specific point in the 95th percentile rankings.)

The Top 25

Rank	Micropolitan area	Population	95th percentile
1	Easton, MD	37,512	>$250,000
1	Edwards, CO	53,605	>$250,000
1	Jackson, WY-ID	33,689	>$250,000
1	Los Alamos, NM	17,785	>$250,000
1	Summit Park, UT	39,633	>$250,000
1	Williston, ND	35,294	>$250,000
7	Key West, FL	77,482	$234,261
8	Steamboat Springs, CO	24,130	$226,863
9	Juneau, AK	32,756	$225,829
10	Torrington, CT	183,603	$222,504
11	Vineyard Haven, MA	17,299	$219,163
12	Breckenridge, CO	30,257	$213,654
13	Andrews, TX	18,105	$211,960
14	Glenwood Springs, CO	75,882	$204,673
15	Hailey, ID	27,955	$203,983
16	Ketchikan, AK	13,709	$201,938
17	Elk City, OK	23,768	$201,552
18	Dickinson, ND	32,154	$200,146
19	Concord, NH	147,994	$198,240
20	Spirit Lake, IA	17,111	$197,892
21	Oxford, MS	53,154	$197,596
22	Elko, NV	53,951	$197,587
23	Fredericksburg, TX	25,963	$196,615
24	Kapaa, HI	71,735	$196,588
25	Hudson, NY	61,509	$196,394

Household Income Ladder: 80th Percentile

Description: Household income that outranks 80 percent of incomes for other households in the same area (2015).

Order: Ranked from highest dollar figure (top) to lowest dollar figure (bottom).

Splits: $178,719 at the top, $93,464 at the 80th percentile, $86,536 at the 60th percentile, $83,819 at the median (50th percentile), $81,649 at the 40th percentile, $75,895 at the 20th percentile, and $51,480 at the bottom. (These splits serve the same function as those on other pages. Each percentile above is a specific point in the 80th percentile rankings.)

The Top 25

Rank	Micropolitan area	Population	80th percentile
1	Summit Park, UT	39,633	$178,719
2	Los Alamos, NM	17,785	$176,866
3	Williston, ND	35,294	$153,948
4	Juneau, AK	32,756	$140,078
5	Edwards, CO	53,605	$138,742
6	Torrington, CT	183,603	$132,608
7	Gillette, WY	49,220	$127,547
8	Breckenridge, CO	30,257	$126,093
9	Jackson, WY-ID	33,689	$125,194
10	Andrews, TX	18,105	$124,366
11	Dickinson, ND	32,154	$121,575
12	Vineyard Haven, MA	17,299	$121,565
13	Easton, MD	37,512	$120,359
14	Concord, NH	147,994	$119,469
15	Elko, NV	53,951	$119,436
16	Heber, UT	29,161	$117,639
17	Ketchikan, AK	13,709	$117,281
18	Rock Springs, WY	44,626	$117,033
19	Kapaa, HI	71,735	$115,478
20	Steamboat Springs, CO	24,130	$114,838
21	Glenwood Springs, CO	75,882	$114,374
22	Key West, FL	77,482	$112,806
23	Durango, CO	54,688	$110,423
24	Truckee-Grass Valley, CA	98,877	$110,191
25	Laconia, NH	60,641	$109,832

Household Income Ladder: 60th Percentile

Description: Household income that outranks 60 percent of incomes for other households in the same area (2015).

Order: Ranked from highest dollar figure (top) to lowest dollar figure (bottom).

Splits: $121,215 at the top, $61,911 at the 80th percentile, $56,385 at the 60th percentile, $54,186 at the median (50th percentile), $51,783 at the 40th percentile, $47,169 at the 20th percentile, and $30,192 at the bottom. (These splits serve the same function as those on other pages. Each percentile above is a specific point in the 60th percentile rankings.)

The Top 25

Rank	Micropolitan area	Population	60th percentile
1	Los Alamos, NM	17,785	$121,215
2	Summit Park, UT	39,633	$112,935
3	Williston, ND	35,294	$106,784
4	Juneau, AK	32,756	$99,873
5	Gillette, WY	49,220	$93,072
6	Edwards, CO	53,605	$89,460
7	Torrington, CT	183,603	$88,082
8	Andrews, TX	18,105	$87,173
9	Dickinson, ND	32,154	$87,043
10	Elko, NV	53,951	$83,927
11	Rock Springs, WY	44,626	$83,854
12	Breckenridge, CO	30,257	$83,492
13	Jackson, WY-ID	33,689	$82,746
14	Heber, UT	29,161	$82,263
15	Vineyard Haven, MA	17,299	$81,548
16	Concord, NH	147,994	$80,885
17	Ketchikan, AK	13,709	$80,804
18	Kapaa, HI	71,735	$79,396
19	Vernal, UT	37,928	$77,473
20	Steamboat Springs, CO	24,130	$77,384
21	Glenwood Springs, CO	75,882	$76,425
22	Winnemucca, NV	17,019	$75,125
23	Laconia, NH	60,641	$74,933
24	Minot, ND	79,814	$74,649
25	Easton, MD	37,512	$73,664

Household Income Ladder: 40th Percentile

Description: Household income that outranks 40 percent of incomes for other households in the same area (2015).

Order: Ranked from highest dollar figure (top) to lowest dollar figure (bottom).

Splits: $84,845 at the top, $40,566 at the 80th percentile, $36,313 at the 60th percentile, $34,329 at the median (50th percentile), $32,834 at the 40th percentile, $28,978 at the 20th percentile, and $17,075 at the bottom. (These splits serve the same function as those on other pages. Each percentile above is a specific point in the 40th percentile rankings.)

The Top 25

Rank	Micropolitan area	Population	40th percentile
1	Los Alamos, NM	17,785	$84,845
2	Summit Park, UT	39,633	$74,304
3	Juneau, AK	32,756	$72,702
4	Williston, ND	35,294	$71,278
5	Gillette, WY	49,220	$66,565
6	Edwards, CO	53,605	$59,202
7	Elko, NV	53,951	$58,121
8	Torrington, CT	183,603	$58,104
9	Dickinson, ND	32,154	$57,772
10	Jackson, WY-ID	33,689	$56,143
11	Rock Springs, WY	44,626	$55,887
12	Heber, UT	29,161	$55,306
13	Vernal, UT	37,928	$54,106
14	Andrews, TX	18,105	$53,559
15	Breckenridge, CO	30,257	$52,663
16	Concord, NH	147,994	$52,473
17	Kapaa, HI	71,735	$52,065
18	Winnemucca, NV	17,019	$52,045
19	Ketchikan, AK	13,709	$51,075
20	Laconia, NH	60,641	$49,819
21	Glenwood Springs, CO	75,882	$49,585
22	Durango, CO	54,688	$49,345
23	Steamboat Springs, CO	24,130	$49,297
24	Vineyard Haven, MA	17,299	$48,847
25	Minot, ND	79,814	$48,776

Household Income Ladder: 20th Percentile

Description: Household income that outranks 20 percent of incomes for other households in the same area (2015).

Order: Ranked from highest dollar figure (top) to lowest dollar figure (bottom).

Splits: $43,919 at the top, $22,663 at the 80th percentile, $20,253 at the 60th percentile, $18,818 at the median (50th percentile), $17,706 at the 40th percentile, $15,403 at the 20th percentile, and $9,065 at the bottom. (These splits serve the same function as those on other pages. Each percentile above is a specific point in the 20th percentile rankings.)

The Top 25

Rank	Micropolitan area	Population	20th percentile
1	Summit Park, UT	39,633	$43,919
2	Juneau, AK	32,756	$43,058
3	Los Alamos, NM	17,785	$41,682
4	Edwards, CO	53,605	$38,057
5	Gillette, WY	49,220	$37,581
6	Williston, ND	35,294	$36,450
7	Elko, NV	53,951	$33,102
8	Breckenridge, CO	30,257	$31,896
9	Heber, UT	29,161	$31,863
10	Torrington, CT	183,603	$31,809
11	Jackson, WY-ID	33,689	$31,703
12	Rock Springs, WY	44,626	$30,837
13	Vernal, UT	37,928	$30,603
14	Dickinson, ND	32,154	$30,560
15	Ketchikan, AK	13,709	$29,797
16	McPherson, KS	28,941	$29,487
17	Minot, ND	79,814	$28,915
18	Andrews, TX	18,105	$28,903
19	Concord, NH	147,994	$28,712
20	Glenwood Springs, CO	75,882	$28,383
21	Kapaa, HI	71,735	$28,322
22	Watertown-Fort Atkinson, WI	84,559	$27,653
23	Dumas, TX	22,255	$27,015
24	Steamboat Springs, CO	24,130	$26,929
25	Vineyard Haven, MA	17,299	$26,833

Children: Living With Two Parents

Description: Percentage of children (0 to 17 years old) who live in a family setting with two parents (2015).

Order: Ranked from highest percentage (top) to lowest percentage (bottom).

Splits: 89.1% at the top, 71.5% at the 80th percentile, 66.9% at the 60th percentile, 64.8% at the median (50th percentile), 62.6% at the 40th percentile, 58.4% at the 20th percentile, and 26.8% at the bottom.

The Top 25

Rank	Micropolitan area	Population	Living with two parents
1	Rexburg, ID	51,092	89.1%
2	Los Alamos, NM	17,785	84.3%
3	Cedar City, UT	48,368	84.1%
4	Moscow, ID	38,778	82.4%
5	Heber, UT	29,161	82.2%
6	Summit Park, UT	39,633	81.9%
7	Washington, IN	32,906	81.1%
8	Celina, OH	40,968	80.9%
9	Decatur, IN	34,980	80.8%
9	Winona, MN	50,885	80.8%
11	Edwards, CO	53,605	80.4%
12	Bozeman, MT	100,739	79.8%
13	Vernal, UT	37,928	79.7%
14	Dickinson, ND	32,154	79.6%
15	Steamboat Springs, CO	24,130	79.0%
16	Pella, IA	33,294	78.8%
17	Wahpeton, ND-MN	22,798	78.4%
18	Laramie, WY	37,956	78.3%
19	Vermillion, SD	13,964	78.2%
20	Pierre, SD	21,935	78.0%
21	Torrington, CT	183,603	77.7%
21	Wooster, OH	116,063	77.7%
23	Wapakoneta, OH	45,876	77.6%
24	Alexandria, MN	37,075	77.5%
24	Evanston, WY	20,822	77.5%

Children: Older Teens in School

Description: Percentage of older teens (16 to 19 years old) who are enrolled in school (2015).

Order: Ranked from highest percentage (top) to lowest percentage (bottom).

Splits: 100.0% at the top, 87.6% at the 80th percentile, 84.5% at the 60th percentile, 83.0% at the median (50th percentile), 81.8% at the 40th percentile, 78.3% at the 20th percentile, and 53.2% at the bottom.

The Top 25

Rank	Micropolitan area	Population	Older teens in school
1	Zapata, TX	14,374	100.0%
2	Oxford, MS	53,154	99.1%
3	Pullman, WA	48,177	98.6%
4	Athens, OH	65,886	98.0%
5	Brookings, SD	33,897	97.9%
6	Boone, NC	52,906	97.7%
6	Starkville, MS	49,800	97.7%
8	Macomb, IL	31,333	97.5%
9	Laramie, WY	37,956	97.3%
10	Vermillion, SD	13,964	96.4%
11	Atchison, KS	16,398	96.3%
12	Maryville, MO	22,810	95.8%
12	Vincennes, IN	37,927	95.8%
14	Menomonie, WI	44,497	95.0%
15	Los Alamos, NM	17,785	94.7%
16	Jamestown, ND	21,103	94.6%
16	Murray, KY	38,343	94.6%
18	Martin, TN	33,960	94.2%
19	Americus, GA	35,947	94.1%
19	Faribault-Northfield, MN	65,400	94.1%
19	Kearney, NE	55,448	94.1%
22	Marquette, MI	67,215	94.0%
23	Bozeman, MT	100,739	93.8%
24	Charleston-Mattoon, IL	63,419	93.7%
25	Boone, IA	26,643	93.6%
25	Sheridan, WY	30,009	93.6%

Children: Speak English Very Well

Description: Percentage of school-age children (5 to 17 years old) who speak only English or are classified as speaking English "very well" as a second language (2015).

Order: Ranked from highest percentage (top) to lowest percentage (bottom).

Splits: 100.0% at the top, 99.5% at the 80th percentile, 99.0% at the 60th percentile, 98.7% at the median (50th percentile), 98.1% at the 40th percentile, 96.4% at the 20th percentile, and 63.4% at the bottom.

The Top 25

Rank	Micropolitan area	Population	Speak English very well
1	Bradford, PA	42,412	100.0%
1	Brevard, NC	33,211	100.0%
1	Fitzgerald, GA	17,403	100.0%
1	Greensburg, IN	26,521	100.0%
1	Grenada, MS	21,578	100.0%
1	Harrison, AR	45,135	100.0%
1	London, KY	127,953	100.0%
1	McPherson, KS	28,941	100.0%
1	Natchez, MS-LA	51,396	100.0%
1	North Platte, NE	36,908	100.0%
1	Pierre, SD	21,935	100.0%
1	Sandpoint, ID	41,859	100.0%
1	Selma, AL	41,131	100.0%
1	Spirit Lake, IA	17,111	100.0%
1	Sterling, CO	22,036	100.0%
1	Valley, AL	34,123	100.0%
1	Vineyard Haven, MA	17,299	100.0%
1	Wahpeton, ND-MN	22,798	100.0%
19	(19 micros tied)	—	99.9%

Children: Poverty Rate for Children

Description: Percentage of children (0 to 17 years old) who live in households that are below the federal poverty level (2015).

Order: Ranked from lowest percentage (top) to highest percentage (bottom).

Splits: 4.9% at the top, 17.5% at the 80th percentile, 22.0% at the 60th percentile, 24.1% at the median (50th percentile), 26.2% at the 40th percentile, 31.8% at the 20th percentile, and 53.8% at the bottom.

The Top 25

Rank	Micropolitan area	Population	Poverty rate for children
1	Dickinson, ND	32,154	4.9%
2	Spirit Lake, IA	17,111	6.1%
3	Torrington, CT	183,603	7.6%
4	Los Alamos, NM	17,785	7.7%
5	New Ulm, MN	25,313	8.1%
6	Aberdeen, SD	42,784	8.4%
6	Gillette, WY	49,220	8.4%
8	Steamboat Springs, CO	24,130	9.0%
9	Watertown, SD	27,939	9.1%
10	Brookings, SD	33,897	9.3%
11	McPherson, KS	28,941	9.4%
11	Vernal, UT	37,928	9.4%
13	Summit Park, UT	39,633	9.6%
14	Celina, OH	40,968	10.0%
15	Durango, CO	54,688	10.2%
16	Minot, ND	79,814	10.3%
17	Alexandria, MN	37,075	10.4%
18	Sheridan, WY	30,009	10.5%
19	Jackson, WY-ID	33,689	10.6%
20	Bozeman, MT	100,739	10.7%
21	Juneau, AK	32,756	11.0%
22	Newton, IA	36,827	11.1%
23	Carroll, IA	20,498	11.3%
23	Snyder, TX	17,615	11.3%
25	Columbus, NE	32,847	11.5%

Children: No Health Insurance

Description: Percentage of children (0 to 17 years old) who have no health insurance coverage (2015). Children in institutions are not included in this category.

Order: Ranked from lowest percentage (top) to highest percentage (bottom).

Splits: 0.8% at the top, 3.9% at the 80th percentile, 5.5% at the 60th percentile, 6.4% at the median (50th percentile), 7.2% at the 40th percentile, 10.7% at the 20th percentile, and 34.9% at the bottom.

The Top 25

Rank	Micropolitan area	Population	No health insurance
1	Oskaloosa, IA	22,324	0.8%
2	Carroll, IA	20,498	1.0%
3	Alexander City, AL	40,844	1.1%
4	Bennington, VT	36,317	1.3%
5	Freeport, IL	45,749	1.4%
5	Ruston, LA	47,774	1.4%
7	Beatrice, NE	21,900	1.6%
8	Greenfield Town, MA	70,601	1.7%
9	Clinton, IA	47,768	1.8%
9	Yankton, SD	22,702	1.8%
11	Jacksonville, IL	39,920	1.9%
11	Pella, IA	33,294	1.9%
13	Mason City, IA	50,586	2.0%
13	Newberry, SC	38,012	2.0%
15	Arkadelphia, AR	22,633	2.2%
15	Lincoln, IL	29,494	2.2%
15	Selma, AL	41,131	2.2%
15	Steamboat Springs, CO	24,130	2.2%
15	Talladega-Sylacauga, AL	91,586	2.2%
20	Barre, VT	58,612	2.3%
20	Canton, IL	35,699	2.3%
20	Fort Polk South, LA	50,803	2.3%
20	Huron, SD	18,372	2.3%
20	Jennings, LA	31,439	2.3%
20	Plattsburgh, NY	81,251	2.3%
20	Troy, AL	33,046	2.3%
20	Vineyard Haven, MA	17,299	2.3%

Diversity/Equality: Racial Diversity Index

Description: Statistical likelihood that two randomly selected persons would belong to different racial groups (2015). These are the groups: whites, blacks, Hispanics, Asians, Native Americans, or others.

Order: Ranked from highest percentage (top) to lowest percentage (bottom).

Splits: 72.9% at the top, 50.4% at the 80th percentile, 33.8% at the 60th percentile, 27.6% at the median (50th percentile), 21.5% at the 40th percentile, 13.3% at the 20th percentile, and 2.6% at the bottom.

The Top 25

Rank	Micropolitan area	Population	Racial diversity index
1	Hilo, HI	196,428	72.9%
2	Lumberton, NC	134,197	72.3%
3	Kapaa, HI	71,735	69.1%
4	Grants, NM	27,329	66.7%
5	Laurinburg, NC	35,509	64.0%
6	Tahlequah, OK	48,447	63.7%
7	Muskogee, OK	69,699	62.1%
8	Show Low, AZ	108,277	62.0%
9	Bay City, TX	36,770	61.7%
10	Clewiston, FL	39,119	61.5%
11	El Campo, TX	41,486	61.4%
11	Safford, AZ	37,666	61.4%
13	Wilson, NC	81,714	61.0%
14	Alamogordo, NM	64,362	60.3%
15	Junction City, KS	37,030	60.1%
16	Mount Pleasant, TX	32,623	59.8%
17	Dumas, TX	22,255	59.3%
18	Arcadia, FL	35,458	58.6%
18	Clovis, NM	50,398	58.6%
18	Moultrie, GA	45,844	58.6%
21	Sanford, NC	59,660	58.5%
22	Wauchula, FL	27,502	58.4%
23	Kinston, NC	58,106	58.3%
24	Bennettsville, SC	27,494	58.2%
24	Henderson, NC	44,568	58.2%

Diversity/Equality: Geographic Diversity Index

Description: Statistical likelihood that two randomly selected persons would have been born in different sections (2015). These are the sections: state of residence, other state in Northeast, other state in South, other state in Midwest, other state in West, U.S. territories, abroad of American parents, foreign-born naturalized citizen, or foreign-born non-citizen.

Order: Ranked from highest percentage (top) to lowest percentage (bottom).

Splits: 82.3% at the top, 61.5% at the 80th percentile, 49.5% at the 60th percentile, 45.4% at the median (50th percentile), 41.8% at the 40th percentile, 34.7% at the 20th percentile, and 13.9% at the bottom.

The Top 25

Rank	Micropolitan area	Population	Geographic diversity index
1	Key West, FL	77,482	82.3%
2	Jackson, WY-ID	33,689	81.8%
3	Breckenridge, CO	30,257	81.6%
4	Edwards, CO	53,605	80.7%
4	Fort Leonard Wood, MO	53,221	80.7%
6	Los Alamos, NM	17,785	80.6%
7	Junction City, KS	37,030	80.0%
8	Mountain Home, ID	25,876	79.1%
9	Steamboat Springs, CO	24,130	78.2%
10	Glenwood Springs, CO	75,882	78.1%
11	Pahrump, NV	42,477	78.0%
12	Alamogordo, NM	64,362	77.5%
12	Oak Harbor, WA	80,593	77.5%
14	Guymon, OK	21,489	77.0%
15	Durango, CO	54,688	76.9%
16	Summit Park, UT	39,633	75.3%
17	Hailey, ID	27,955	74.8%
18	Juneau, AK	32,756	74.7%
19	St. Marys, GA	52,102	74.4%
20	Laramie, WY	37,956	74.3%
21	Ruidoso, NM	19,420	73.0%
22	Cañon City, CO	46,692	72.8%
22	Fallon, NV	24,200	72.8%
24	Hood River, OR	23,137	72.7%
24	Ketchikan, AK	13,709	72.7%
24	Liberal, KS	23,152	72.7%

Diversity/Equality: Top 20% Share of Income

Description: Share of area's aggregate household income that goes to the households whose incomes are in the top 20 percent locally (2015). The Census Bureau calculates this percentage to two decimal places, so it is shown in that form on this page. (But only one decimal place is shown in the area profiles.)

Order: Ranked from lowest percentage (top) to highest percentage (bottom).

Splits: 41.64% at the top, 45.78% at the 80th percentile, 47.03% at the 60th percentile, 47.74% at the median (50th percentile), 48.65% at the 40th percentile, 50.22% at the 20th percentile, and 57.09% at the bottom.

The Top 25

Rank	Micropolitan area	Population	Top 20% share of income
1	Gillette, WY	49,220	41.64%
2	Winnemucca, NV	17,019	41.81%
3	Fort Leonard Wood, MO	53,221	42.21%
4	Rock Springs, WY	44,626	42.24%
5	Urbana, OH	38,987	42.83%
6	Los Alamos, NM	17,785	43.01%
7	Elko, NV	53,951	43.18%
8	Huntington, IN	36,630	43.25%
9	Beaver Dam, WI	88,502	43.29%
9	Wapakoneta, OH	45,876	43.29%
11	Watertown-Fort Atkinson, WI	84,559	43.40%
12	Columbus, NE	32,847	43.52%
13	Ionia, MI	64,223	43.60%
14	Pella, IA	33,294	43.65%
15	Juneau, AK	32,756	43.68%
16	Dumas, TX	22,255	43.71%
17	Hutchinson, MN	35,932	43.75%
18	Marshalltown, IA	40,746	43.77%
19	Greensburg, IN	26,521	43.78%
20	Blackfoot, ID	44,990	43.79%
21	Madison, IN	32,416	43.82%
21	Price, UT	20,479	43.82%
23	Batavia, NY	58,937	43.85%
24	Defiance, OH	38,352	43.91%
25	Crawfordsville, IN	38,227	43.93%

Diversity/Equality: Gender Gap in Earnings

Description: Disparity between the median annual earnings for male and female workers (2015). The gap is the absolute value of the decline from the higher figure to the lower figure, regardless of whether males or females have the higher median.

Order: Ranked from lowest percentage (top) to highest percentage (bottom).

Splits: 0.1% at the top, 26.6% at the 80th percentile, 31.8% at the 60th percentile, 33.7% at the median (50th percentile), 35.7% at the 40th percentile, 40.0% at the 20th percentile, and 63.3% at the bottom.

The Top 25

Rank	Micropolitan area	Population	Gender gap in earnings
1	Arcadia, FL	35,458	0.1%
2	Española, NM	39,465	1.8%
3	Boone, NC	52,906	1.9%
4	Henderson, NC	44,568	2.2%
5	Houghton, MI	38,548	2.6%
6	Susanville, CA	31,345	7.8%
7	Raymondville, TX	21,903	8.5%
8	Wauchula, FL	27,502	10.0%
9	Gallup, NM	76,708	10.1%
10	Clearlake, CA	64,591	10.5%
11	Kapaa, HI	71,735	11.3%
12	Tahlequah, OK	48,447	11.7%
13	Moultrie, GA	45,844	11.8%
14	Barre, VT	58,612	12.7%
15	Clewiston, FL	39,119	14.9%
16	Rolla, MO	44,794	15.2%
17	Toccoa, GA	25,586	15.9%
18	Douglas, GA	43,108	16.3%
19	Cañon City, CO	46,692	16.4%
19	Grants, NM	27,329	16.4%
21	Indianola, MS	27,005	16.5%
22	Bennettsville, SC	27,494	16.7%
22	North Wilkesboro, NC	68,502	16.7%
24	Mountain Home, AR	41,053	17.2%
25	Alexander City, AL	40,844	17.3%
25	Crescent City, CA	27,254	17.3%
25	Sanford, NC	59,660	17.3%

Diversity/Equality: White-Collar Gender Gap

Description: Disparity between the numbers of male and female workers in management, business, and financial occupations (2015). The gap is the absolute value of the decline from the higher figure to the lower figure, regardless of whether males or females have the higher number.

Order: Ranked from lowest percentage (top) to highest percentage (bottom).

Splits: 0.2% at the top, 11.8% at the 80th percentile, 21.2% at the 60th percentile, 25.3% at the median (50th percentile), 29.6% at the 40th percentile, 39.5% at the 20th percentile, and 67.3% at the bottom.

The Top 25

Rank	Micropolitan area	Population	White-collar gender gap
1	Ozark, AL	49,565	0.2%
2	Helena, MT	78,063	0.3%
2	Martinsville, VA	65,526	0.3%
4	Frankfort, KY	72,354	0.6%
5	Huntsville, TX	85,101	0.7%
6	Barre, VT	58,612	1.0%
7	Brenham, TX	34,765	1.1%
7	Rolla, MO	44,794	1.1%
9	Fairfield, IA	17,555	1.2%
10	Pahrump, NV	42,477	1.4%
11	Raymondville, TX	21,903	1.8%
12	Auburn, IN	42,589	2.2%
12	DuBois, PA	80,994	2.2%
12	Hope, AR	30,642	2.2%
15	Payson, AZ	53,159	2.3%
15	Seneca, SC	75,713	2.3%
17	North Vernon, IN	27,897	2.5%
18	Wilmington, OH	41,917	2.6%
19	Shelton, WA	61,023	3.0%
20	Marquette, MI	67,215	3.3%
20	Newton, IA	36,827	3.3%
20	Starkville, MS	49,800	3.3%
23	Centralia, WA	75,882	3.5%
23	Sandpoint, ID	41,859	3.5%
25	Albemarle, NC	60,714	3.6%

Education: Eighth Grade or Less

Description: Percentage of working-age adults (25 to 64 years old) who left school prior to ninth grade (2015).

Order: Ranked from lowest percentage (top) to highest percentage (bottom).

Splits: 0.4% at the top, 1.8% at the 80th percentile, 2.9% at the 60th percentile, 3.4% at the median (50th percentile), 4.0% at the 40th percentile, 6.3% at the 20th percentile, and 27.3% at the bottom.

The Top 25

Rank	Micropolitan area	Population	Eighth grade or less
1	Alexandria, MN	37,075	0.4%
2	Grand Rapids, MN	45,435	0.5%
2	Kalispell, MT	96,165	0.5%
2	Laramie, WY	37,956	0.5%
2	Spirit Lake, IA	17,111	0.5%
2	Vineyard Haven, MA	17,299	0.5%
7	Bozeman, MT	100,739	0.6%
7	Fairfield, IA	17,555	0.6%
9	Spearfish, SD	24,827	0.7%
10	Atchison, KS	16,398	0.8%
10	Fairmont, MN	20,022	0.8%
10	Newton, IA	36,827	0.8%
10	Sheridan, WY	30,009	0.8%
10	St. Marys, PA	30,872	0.8%
10	Van Wert, OH	28,562	0.8%
16	Brainerd, MN	92,134	0.9%
16	Macomb, IL	31,333	0.9%
16	Marquette, MI	67,215	0.9%
16	Moscow, ID	38,778	0.9%
20	Bemidji, MN	45,672	1.0%
20	Ottawa, KS	25,609	1.0%
20	Pullman, WA	48,177	1.0%
20	Riverton, WY	40,315	1.0%
20	Tiffin, OH	55,610	1.0%
20	Wapakoneta, OH	45,876	1.0%

Education: High School Diplomas

Description: Percentage of working-age adults (25 to 64 years old) who hold high school diplomas (2015).

Order: Ranked from highest percentage (top) to lowest percentage (bottom).

Splits: 97.6% at the top, 92.5% at the 80th percentile, 89.4% at the 60th percentile, 87.8% at the median (50th percentile), 86.4% at the 40th percentile, 82.3% at the 20th percentile, and 52.2% at the bottom.

The Top 25

Rank	Micropolitan area	Population	High school diplomas
1	Laramie, WY	37,956	97.6%
2	Bozeman, MT	100,739	97.5%
2	Vermillion, SD	13,964	97.5%
4	Spirit Lake, IA	17,111	97.2%
5	Los Alamos, NM	17,785	97.1%
6	Steamboat Springs, CO	24,130	96.8%
7	Spearfish, SD	24,827	96.7%
8	Moscow, ID	38,778	96.6%
9	Fairfield, IA	17,555	96.4%
10	Alexandria, MN	37,075	96.3%
11	Carroll, IA	20,498	96.1%
12	Marquette, MI	67,215	96.0%
12	Pullman, WA	48,177	96.0%
14	Brookings, SD	33,897	95.9%
15	Atchison, KS	16,398	95.8%
16	Wapakoneta, OH	45,876	95.7%
17	Sheridan, WY	30,009	95.6%
18	Celina, OH	40,968	95.5%
18	New Ulm, MN	25,313	95.5%
18	Newton, IA	36,827	95.5%
21	Aberdeen, SD	42,784	95.3%
21	Kalispell, MT	96,165	95.3%
23	Hays, KS	29,029	95.2%
23	Helena, MT	78,063	95.2%
23	Mason City, IA	50,586	95.2%
23	Minot, ND	79,814	95.2%

Education: Attended College

Description: Percentage of working-age adults (25 to 64 years old) who attended college at some point, regardless of whether they hold degrees (2015).

Order: Ranked from highest percentage (top) to lowest percentage (bottom).

Splits: 87.5% at the top, 61.1% at the 80th percentile, 55.1% at the 60th percentile, 52.4% at the median (50th percentile), 50.2% at the 40th percentile, 44.7% at the 20th percentile, and 26.3% at the bottom.

The Top 25

Rank	Micropolitan area	Population	Attended college
1	Los Alamos, NM	17,785	87.5%
2	Laramie, WY	37,956	82.5%
3	Pullman, WA	48,177	81.4%
4	Moscow, ID	38,778	79.4%
5	Bozeman, MT	100,739	78.7%
5	Summit Park, UT	39,633	78.7%
7	Steamboat Springs, CO	24,130	76.4%
8	Breckenridge, CO	30,257	75.7%
9	Jackson, WY-ID	33,689	75.3%
10	Durango, CO	54,688	75.2%
11	Truckee-Grass Valley, CA	98,877	74.2%
12	Juneau, AK	32,756	73.9%
13	Rexburg, ID	51,092	73.1%
14	Oxford, MS	53,154	72.8%
14	Vermillion, SD	13,964	72.8%
16	Brookings, SD	33,897	72.7%
17	Helena, MT	78,063	72.4%
17	Mitchell, SD	23,243	72.4%
19	Heber, UT	29,161	72.2%
20	Alexandria, MN	37,075	71.8%
21	Boone, NC	52,906	71.7%
21	Spirit Lake, IA	17,111	71.7%
23	Oak Harbor, WA	80,593	71.5%
24	Hays, KS	29,029	71.4%
25	Edwards, CO	53,605	71.1%

Education: Bachelor's Degrees

Description: Percentage of working-age adults (25 to 64 years old) who hold bachelor's degrees (2015).

Order: Ranked from highest percentage (top) to lowest percentage (bottom).

Splits: 65.0% at the top, 24.9% at the 80th percentile, 20.1% at the 60th percentile, 18.3% at the median (50th percentile), 17.0% at the 40th percentile, 14.6% at the 20th percentile, and 7.2% at the bottom.

The Top 25

Rank	Micropolitan area	Population	Bachelor's degrees
1	Los Alamos, NM	17,785	65.0%
2	Pullman, WA	48,177	52.7%
3	Summit Park, UT	39,633	51.3%
4	Laramie, WY	37,956	50.9%
5	Jackson, WY-ID	33,689	50.0%
6	Steamboat Springs, CO	24,130	49.7%
7	Bozeman, MT	100,739	48.8%
8	Vermillion, SD	13,964	48.6%
9	Moscow, ID	38,778	47.9%
10	Breckenridge, CO	30,257	46.1%
11	Edwards, CO	53,605	45.9%
12	Starkville, MS	49,800	44.8%
13	Brookings, SD	33,897	43.1%
14	Durango, CO	54,688	42.6%
15	Barre, VT	58,612	41.1%
16	Oxford, MS	53,154	40.9%
17	Boone, NC	52,906	39.1%
17	Stillwater, OK	80,850	39.1%
19	Helena, MT	78,063	38.1%
20	Vineyard Haven, MA	17,299	38.0%
21	Juneau, AK	32,756	37.4%
22	Greenfield Town, MA	70,601	36.2%
23	Macomb, IL	31,333	36.1%
24	Glenwood Springs, CO	75,882	35.8%
24	Ruston, LA	47,774	35.8%

Education: Advanced Degrees

Description: Percentage of working-age adults (25 to 64 years old) who hold master's, doctoral, and/or professional degrees (2015).

Order: Ranked from highest percentage (top) to lowest percentage (bottom).

Splits: 39.8% at the top, 8.4% at the 80th percentile, 6.5% at the 60th percentile, 5.9% at the median (50th percentile), 5.5% at the 40th percentile, 4.6% at the 20th percentile, and 1.7% at the bottom.

The Top 25

Rank	Micropolitan area	Population	Advanced degrees
1	Los Alamos, NM	17,785	39.8%
2	Pullman, WA	48,177	24.9%
3	Vermillion, SD	13,964	22.4%
4	Laramie, WY	37,956	21.5%
5	Starkville, MS	49,800	20.8%
6	Summit Park, UT	39,633	19.0%
7	Moscow, ID	38,778	17.6%
8	Boone, NC	52,906	16.8%
9	Barre, VT	58,612	16.6%
9	Oxford, MS	53,154	16.6%
11	Macomb, IL	31,333	16.2%
12	Greenfield Town, MA	70,601	16.0%
12	Stillwater, OK	80,850	16.0%
14	Bozeman, MT	100,739	15.3%
15	Athens, OH	65,886	14.8%
16	Claremont-Lebanon, NH-VT	216,923	14.6%
17	Steamboat Springs, CO	24,130	14.2%
18	Durango, CO	54,688	14.1%
19	Ruston, LA	47,774	14.0%
19	Torrington, CT	183,603	14.0%
21	Kirksville, MO	29,814	13.9%
22	Hudson, NY	61,509	13.7%
23	Fairfield, IA	17,555	13.6%
23	Oneonta, NY	60,636	13.6%
25	Easton, MD	37,512	13.5%

Employment: Average Jobless Rate

Description: Average unemployment rate for the civilian labor force (2011-2015).

Order: Ranked from lowest percentage (top) to highest percentage (bottom).

Splits: 1.7% at the top, 5.7% at the 80th percentile, 7.2% at the 60th percentile, 7.8% at the median (50th percentile), 8.4% at the 40th percentile, 10.5% at the 20th percentile, and 21.7% at the bottom.

The Top 25

Rank	Micropolitan area	Population	Average jobless rate
1	Williston, ND	35,294	1.7%
2	Aberdeen, SD	42,784	2.4%
3	Jamestown, ND	21,103	2.5%
4	Minot, ND	79,814	2.6%
5	Wahpeton, ND-MN	22,798	2.7%
6	Dickinson, ND	32,154	2.8%
6	Pierre, SD	21,935	2.8%
8	Elk City, OK	23,768	2.9%
8	Huron, SD	18,372	2.9%
8	Watertown, SD	27,939	2.9%
11	Mitchell, SD	23,243	3.0%
12	Brookings, SD	33,897	3.1%
12	McPherson, KS	28,941	3.1%
14	New Ulm, MN	25,313	3.2%
14	Summit Park, UT	39,633	3.2%
16	Carroll, IA	20,498	3.3%
16	Norfolk, NE	48,184	3.3%
16	Snyder, TX	17,615	3.3%
19	Sheridan, WY	30,009	3.4%
20	Fairmont, MN	20,022	3.5%
20	Guymon, OK	21,489	3.5%
20	Kearney, NE	55,448	3.5%
20	Los Alamos, NM	17,785	3.5%
24	Yankton, SD	22,702	3.6%
25	Jasper, IN	55,055	3.7%
25	Storm Lake, IA	20,493	3.7%
25	Weatherford, OK	29,744	3.7%

Employment: Self-Employed Workers

Description: Percentage of full-time, year-round workers who are self-employed by their own businesses, whether incorporated or unincorporated (2015).

Order: Ranked from highest percentage (top) to lowest percentage (bottom).

Splits: 27.8% at the top, 11.2% at the 80th percentile, 9.4% at the 60th percentile, 8.8% at the median (50th percentile), 8.1% at the 40th percentile, 6.9% at the 20th percentile, and 4.0% at the bottom.

The Top 25

Rank	Micropolitan area	Population	Self-employed workers
1	Vineyard Haven, MA	17,299	27.8%
2	Fredericksburg, TX	25,963	20.4%
3	Bennington, VT	36,317	17.7%
4	Kill Devil Hills, NC	39,733	17.4%
4	Truckee-Grass Valley, CA	98,877	17.4%
6	Hailey, ID	27,955	17.2%
7	Key West, FL	77,482	17.0%
7	Spirit Lake, IA	17,111	17.0%
9	Fairmont, MN	20,022	16.8%
10	Carroll, IA	20,498	16.6%
10	Summit Park, UT	39,633	16.6%
10	Williston, ND	35,294	16.6%
13	Wahpeton, ND-MN	22,798	16.4%
14	Beatrice, NE	21,900	15.6%
15	Bozeman, MT	100,739	15.3%
15	Heber, UT	29,161	15.3%
17	Boone, NC	52,906	15.1%
17	Ukiah, CA	87,649	15.1%
17	Yankton, SD	22,702	15.1%
20	Sandpoint, ID	41,859	15.0%
21	Montrose, CO	40,946	14.7%
22	Easton, MD	37,512	14.6%
22	Ellensburg, WA	43,269	14.6%
22	Fairfield, IA	17,555	14.6%
22	Fergus Falls, MN	57,716	14.6%
22	Morehead City, NC	68,879	14.6%
22	New Ulm, MN	25,313	14.6%
22	Worthington, MN	21,770	14.6%

Employment: Management/Financial Jobs

Description: Percentage of workers who are employed in management, business, and financial occupations (2015). The focus has been placed on this and the two adjacent occupational groups because they are the three groups with the highest median earnings on a national basis.

Order: Ranked from highest percentage (top) to lowest percentage (bottom).

Splits: 23.3% at the top, 12.6% at the 80th percentile, 11.3% at the 60th percentile, 10.9% at the median (50th percentile), 10.5% at the 40th percentile, 9.5% at the 20th percentile, and 5.5% at the bottom.

The Top 25

Rank	Micropolitan area	Population	Management/financial jobs
1	Los Alamos, NM	17,785	23.3%
2	Summit Park, UT	39,633	22.4%
3	Vineyard Haven, MA	17,299	21.8%
4	Pierre, SD	21,935	21.3%
5	Juneau, AK	32,756	20.4%
6	Helena, MT	78,063	19.5%
6	Jackson, WY-ID	33,689	19.5%
8	Edwards, CO	53,605	18.3%
9	McPherson, KS	28,941	18.1%
10	Barre, VT	58,612	17.3%
11	Spirit Lake, IA	17,111	16.7%
12	Kill Devil Hills, NC	39,733	16.6%
13	Easton, MD	37,512	16.4%
14	Wahpeton, ND-MN	22,798	16.1%
15	Marshall, MN	25,673	16.0%
16	Ruidoso, NM	19,420	15.9%
17	Española, NM	39,465	15.8%
17	Torrington, CT	183,603	15.8%
19	Durango, CO	54,688	15.7%
19	Glenwood Springs, CO	75,882	15.7%
19	Key West, FL	77,482	15.7%
22	Fairmont, MN	20,022	15.6%
22	Findlay, OH	75,573	15.6%
24	Truckee-Grass Valley, CA	98,877	15.5%
25	Concord, NH	147,994	15.4%
25	Hudson, NY	61,509	15.4%

Employment: Computer/Engineering Jobs

Description: Percentage of workers who are employed in computer, engineering, and science occupations (2015). The focus has been placed on this and the two adjacent occupational groups because they are the three groups with the highest median earnings on a national basis.

Order: Ranked from highest percentage (top) to lowest percentage (bottom).

Splits: 30.9% at the top, 3.7% at the 80th percentile, 2.9% at the 60th percentile, 2.7% at the median (50th percentile), 2.5% at the 40th percentile, 1.9% at the 20th percentile, and 0.4% at the bottom.

The Top 25

Rank	Micropolitan area	Population	Computer/engineering jobs
1	Los Alamos, NM	17,785	30.9%
2	Pullman, WA	48,177	9.4%
3	Helena, MT	78,063	7.9%
4	Bartlesville, OK	52,021	7.7%
5	Bozeman, MT	100,739	7.6%
5	Juneau, AK	32,756	7.6%
5	Moscow, ID	38,778	7.6%
8	Vicksburg, MS	56,635	7.3%
9	Houghton, MI	38,548	7.2%
10	Brookings, SD	33,897	7.0%
11	Laramie, WY	37,956	6.3%
11	Truckee-Grass Valley, CA	98,877	6.3%
13	Rolla, MO	44,794	6.1%
14	Pierre, SD	21,935	5.9%
14	Starkville, MS	49,800	5.9%
14	Summit Park, UT	39,633	5.9%
14	Winnemucca, NV	17,019	5.9%
18	Claremont-Lebanon, NH-VT	216,923	5.8%
19	Corning, NY	97,631	5.7%
19	Hood River, OR	23,137	5.7%
19	Sheridan, WY	30,009	5.7%
22	Concord, NH	147,994	5.5%
22	Durango, CO	54,688	5.5%
24	Barre, VT	58,612	5.4%
24	Oxford, NC	58,674	5.4%

Employment: Health Care Jobs

Description: Percentage of workers who are employed in health care practitioner and technical occupations (2015). The focus has been placed on this and the two adjacent occupational groups because they are the three groups with the highest median earnings on a national basis.

Order: Ranked from highest percentage (top) to lowest percentage (bottom).

Splits: 10.5% at the top, 6.7% at the 80th percentile, 5.8% at the 60th percentile, 5.4% at the median (50th percentile), 5.1% at the 40th percentile, 4.4% at the 20th percentile, and 0.7% at the bottom.

The Top 25

Rank	Micropolitan area	Population	Health care jobs
1	Portsmouth, OH	76,825	10.5%
2	Pinehurst-Southern Pines, NC	94,352	9.5%
3	Lake City, FL	68,348	9.4%
4	Sunbury, PA	93,246	9.0%
5	Bluefield, WV-VA	104,063	8.8%
6	Brookings, OR	22,483	8.7%
6	Fairmont, WV	56,925	8.7%
8	Brookhaven, MS	34,649	8.5%
8	Corinth, MS	37,388	8.5%
8	Douglas, GA	43,108	8.5%
11	Martin, TN	33,960	8.4%
11	Somerset, KY	63,782	8.4%
13	Alpena, MI	28,803	8.3%
13	Meridian, MS	104,499	8.3%
15	Iron Mountain, MI-WI	30,252	8.2%
16	Jackson, OH	32,596	8.1%
16	Marquette, MI	67,215	8.1%
16	Thomasville, GA	45,063	8.1%
19	Brownwood, TX	37,896	8.0%
19	Butte-Silver Bow, MT	34,622	8.0%
19	Crossville, TN	58,229	8.0%
19	Cullman, AL	82,005	8.0%
19	Mountain Home, AR	41,053	8.0%
19	Poplar Bluff, MO	42,951	8.0%
19	Yankton, SD	22,702	8.0%

Growth Potential: Children Per Senior

Description: Ratio of children (0 to 17 years old) to every senior citizen (65 years old or older) in the area (2015).
Order: Ranked from highest ratio (top) to lowest ratio (bottom).
Splits: 4.24 at the top, 1.76 at the 80th percentile, 1.49 at the 60th percentile, 1.41 at the median (50th percentile), 1.33 at the 40th percentile, 1.16 at the 20th percentile, and 0.51 at the bottom.

The Top 25

Rank	Micropolitan area	Population	Children per senior
1	Gillette, WY	49,220	4.24
2	Junction City, KS	37,030	4.13
3	Liberal, KS	23,152	3.70
3	Vernal, UT	37,928	3.70
5	Heber, UT	29,161	3.63
6	Othello, WA	19,254	3.49
7	Dumas, TX	22,255	3.32
8	Garden City, KS	41,074	3.24
9	Fort Leonard Wood, MO	53,221	3.21
10	Rexburg, ID	51,092	3.19
11	Edwards, CO	53,605	3.14
12	Elko, NV	53,951	3.05
13	Rio Grande City, TX	63,795	3.02
14	Andrews, TX	18,105	3.01
14	Dodge City, KS	34,536	3.01
16	Gallup, NM	76,708	2.99
17	Zapata, TX	14,374	2.97
18	Rock Springs, WY	44,626	2.94
19	Eagle Pass, TX	57,706	2.91
20	Evanston, WY	20,822	2.90
21	Summit Park, UT	39,633	2.88
22	Winnemucca, NV	17,019	2.83
23	Hobbs, NM	71,180	2.79
24	Hereford, TX	18,952	2.76
25	Guymon, OK	21,489	2.75

Growth Potential: Median Age

Description: Median age of all residents (2015).
Order: Ranked from lowest age (top) to highest age (bottom).
Splits: 24.1 at the top, 35.7 at the 80th percentile, 38.8 at the 60th percentile, 39.6 at the median (50th percentile), 40.5 at the 40th percentile, 42.6 at the 20th percentile, and 54.6 at the bottom.

The Top 25

Rank	Micropolitan area	Population	Median age
1	Rexburg, ID	51,092	24.1
2	Pullman, WA	48,177	24.2
3	Starkville, MS	49,800	25.0
4	Vermillion, SD	13,964	25.2
5	Junction City, KS	37,030	26.2
6	Mount Pleasant, MI	70,698	26.3
6	Statesboro, GA	72,651	26.3
8	Brookings, SD	33,897	26.4
9	Laramie, WY	37,956	26.6
10	Fort Leonard Wood, MO	53,221	26.8
11	Stillwater, OK	80,850	27.2
12	Ruston, LA	47,774	27.4
13	Athens, OH	65,886	28.0
13	Kingsville, TX	32,264	28.0
15	Cedar City, UT	48,368	28.1
16	Maryville, MO	22,810	28.3
17	Moscow, ID	38,778	28.5
17	Oxford, MS	53,154	28.5
19	Othello, WA	19,254	28.9
20	Rio Grande City, TX	63,795	29.1
21	Zapata, TX	14,374	29.2
22	Liberal, KS	23,152	29.4
22	Portales, NM	19,120	29.4
24	Boone, NC	52,906	29.5
25	Vernal, UT	37,928	29.7
25	Warrensburg, MO	53,951	29.7

Growth Potential: Moved From Different State

Description: Percentage of residents 1 year old or older who moved from a different state or nation within the past year (2015).

Order: Ranked from highest percentage (top) to lowest percentage (bottom).

Splits: 30.9% at the top, 3.5% at the 80th percentile, 2.4% at the 60th percentile, 2.1% at the median (50th percentile), 1.9% at the 40th percentile, 1.4% at the 20th percentile, and 0.4% at the bottom.

The Top 25

Rank	Micropolitan area	Population	Moved from different state
1	Fort Leonard Wood, MO	53,221	30.9%
2	Junction City, KS	37,030	14.5%
3	Rexburg, ID	51,092	13.3%
4	Fort Polk South, LA	50,803	10.8%
5	Laramie, WY	37,956	10.2%
6	Vermillion, SD	13,964	9.6%
7	Williston, ND	35,294	9.5%
8	Mountain Home, ID	25,876	9.1%
9	Moscow, ID	38,778	8.8%
10	Minot, ND	79,814	8.5%
11	Oxford, MS	53,154	8.4%
12	Clovis, NM	50,398	7.8%
13	Pullman, WA	48,177	7.7%
14	Alamogordo, NM	64,362	7.6%
14	Ozark, AL	49,565	7.6%
16	Brookings, OR	22,483	7.4%
16	Dickinson, ND	32,154	7.4%
16	St. Marys, GA	52,102	7.4%
19	Brookings, SD	33,897	7.3%
20	Jackson, WY-ID	33,689	7.2%
20	Rock Springs, WY	44,626	7.2%
22	Durango, CO	54,688	7.1%
23	Fallon, NV	24,200	7.0%
23	Gillette, WY	49,220	7.0%
25	Key West, FL	77,482	6.9%
25	Oak Harbor, WA	80,593	6.9%
25	Starkville, MS	49,800	6.9%

Growth Potential: Homes Built Since 2000

Description: Percentage of housing units that were built in 2000 or later (2015). Each house, duplex, condominium, apartment, or trailer is a separate housing unit.

Order: Ranked from highest percentage (top) to lowest percentage (bottom).

Splits: 41.7% at the top, 18.9% at the 80th percentile, 14.5% at the 60th percentile, 13.0% at the median (50th percentile), 11.6% at the 40th percentile, 8.9% at the 20th percentile, and 2.8% at the bottom.

The Top 25

Rank	Micropolitan area	Population	Homes built since 2000
1	Heber, UT	29,161	41.7%
2	Jefferson, GA	63,360	40.3%
3	Fernley, NV	52,585	39.9%
4	Fort Leonard Wood, MO	53,221	39.4%
5	Oxford, MS	53,154	36.7%
6	Pahrump, NV	42,477	36.0%
7	Gillette, WY	49,220	35.8%
8	Junction City, KS	37,030	34.3%
9	Bozeman, MT	100,739	33.7%
10	Vernal, UT	37,928	33.1%
11	Statesboro, GA	72,651	32.7%
12	Rexburg, ID	51,092	32.1%
13	Dunn, NC	128,140	29.6%
14	Eagle Pass, TX	57,706	29.1%
15	Branson, MO	85,535	28.7%
16	Cedar City, UT	48,368	28.3%
17	Jackson, WY-ID	33,689	28.2%
17	Williston, ND	35,294	28.2%
19	Sevierville, TN	95,946	28.0%
20	Picayune, MS	55,191	27.8%
20	Summit Park, UT	39,633	27.8%
22	Fredericksburg, TX	25,963	27.7%
23	Crossville, TN	58,229	27.5%
24	Oxford, NC	58,674	27.4%
25	St. Marys, GA	52,102	27.3%

Growth Potential: Construction Jobs

Description: Percentage of workers who are employed in the construction sector (2015).

Order: Ranked from highest percentage (top) to lowest percentage (bottom).

Splits: 15.2% at the top, 7.6% at the 80th percentile, 6.7% at the 60th percentile, 6.4% at the median (50th percentile), 6.0% at the 40th percentile, 5.3% at the 20th percentile, and 1.1% at the bottom.

The Top 25

Rank	Micropolitan area	Population	Construction jobs
1	Vineyard Haven, MA	17,299	15.2%
2	Glenwood Springs, CO	75,882	13.9%
3	Borger, TX	21,734	12.3%
4	Port Lavaca, TX	21,895	12.1%
5	Breckenridge, CO	30,257	11.9%
5	Rio Grande City, TX	63,795	11.9%
7	Brevard, NC	33,211	11.6%
8	Montrose, CO	40,946	11.3%
9	Edwards, CO	53,605	11.2%
9	Washington, IN	32,906	11.2%
11	Fredericksburg, TX	25,963	10.7%
12	Hailey, ID	27,955	10.6%
13	DeRidder, LA	36,462	10.3%
13	Sheridan, WY	30,009	10.3%
15	Albemarle, NC	60,714	10.2%
16	Athens, TX	79,545	10.1%
17	Bay City, TX	36,770	10.0%
17	Jackson, WY-ID	33,689	10.0%
17	Picayune, MS	55,191	10.0%
17	Ruidoso, NM	19,420	10.0%
21	Mineral Wells, TX	27,895	9.9%
21	Spearfish, SD	24,827	9.9%
21	Steamboat Springs, CO	24,130	9.9%
24	Williston, ND	35,294	9.8%
25	Dunn, NC	128,140	9.7%
25	Kill Devil Hills, NC	39,733	9.7%
25	Laconia, NH	60,641	9.7%
25	Wauchula, FL	27,502	9.7%

Housing: Home Vacancy Rate

Description: Percentage of housing units that are vacant, have not been sold or rented, and are not for seasonal use (2015).

Order: Ranked from lowest percentage (top) to highest percentage (bottom).

Splits: 3.0% at the top, 6.2% at the 80th percentile, 7.9% at the 60th percentile, 8.8% at the median (50th percentile), 9.6% at the 40th percentile, 11.6% at the 20th percentile, and 23.4% at the bottom.

The Top 25

Rank	Micropolitan area	Population	Home vacancy rate
1	Malvern, AR	33,426	3.0%
2	Watertown, SD	27,939	3.3%
3	Mayfield, KY	37,421	3.5%
4	Mitchell, SD	23,243	3.6%
5	Bennington, VT	36,317	3.7%
6	Vineyard Haven, MA	17,299	3.8%
7	Brainerd, MN	92,134	3.9%
8	Helena, MT	78,063	4.1%
9	Grand Rapids, MN	45,435	4.2%
9	Middlesborough, KY	27,337	4.2%
9	Truckee-Grass Valley, CA	98,877	4.2%
9	Watertown-Fort Atkinson, WI	84,559	4.2%
13	Lewisburg, PA	44,954	4.3%
14	Concord, NH	147,994	4.4%
14	Laconia, NH	60,641	4.4%
14	Los Alamos, NM	17,785	4.4%
17	Celina, OH	40,968	4.5%
17	Hutchinson, MN	35,932	4.5%
17	Kearney, NE	55,448	4.5%
20	Camden, AR	29,587	4.6%
20	Columbus, NE	32,847	4.6%
22	Barre, VT	58,612	4.7%
22	Edwards, CO	53,605	4.7%
22	Elko, NV	53,951	4.7%
22	Juneau, AK	32,756	4.7%
22	Kendallville, IN	47,733	4.7%

Housing: Home Ownership Rate

Description: Percentage of all occupied housing units that are occupied by their owners (2015).

Order: Ranked from highest percentage (top) to lowest percentage (bottom).

Splits: 82.0% at the top, 74.2% at the 80th percentile, 71.2% at the 60th percentile, 69.9% at the median (50th percentile), 68.4% at the 40th percentile, 64.8% at the 20th percentile, and 42.8% at the bottom.

The Top 25

Rank	Micropolitan area	Population	Home ownership rate
1	Iron Mountain, MI-WI	30,252	82.0%
2	Holland, MI	114,625	80.9%
3	Vineyard Haven, MA	17,299	79.9%
4	Central City, KY	31,183	79.5%
4	Grand Rapids, MN	45,435	79.5%
4	Port Clinton, OH	40,877	79.5%
7	Traverse City, MI	148,334	79.3%
8	Effingham, IL	34,371	79.1%
9	Ruidoso, NM	19,420	79.0%
10	Crossville, TN	58,229	78.6%
10	Escanaba, MI	36,377	78.6%
10	Somerset, PA	75,522	78.6%
13	Fergus Falls, MN	57,716	78.5%
13	Ionia, MI	64,223	78.5%
15	Cadillac, MI	47,906	78.4%
15	Decatur, IN	34,980	78.4%
17	St. Marys, PA	30,872	78.1%
18	Point Pleasant, WV-OH	57,179	78.0%
19	New Ulm, MN	25,313	77.7%
20	Española, NM	39,465	77.6%
21	Angola, IN	34,372	77.5%
22	Raymondville, TX	21,903	77.4%
23	Hillsdale, MI	45,941	77.3%
24	DuBois, PA	80,994	77.2%
24	Jasper, IN	55,055	77.2%

Housing: Housing Diversity Index

Description: Statistical likelihood that two randomly selected housing units would have been built in different periods (2015). These are the periods: 1939 or earlier, 1940-1949, 1950-1959, 1960-1969, 1970-1979, 1980-1989, 1990-1999, or 2000 or later.

Order: Ranked from highest percentage (top) to lowest percentage (bottom).

Splits: 87.1% at the top, 85.7% at the 80th percentile, 85.1% at the 60th percentile, 84.7% at the median (50th percentile), 84.2% at the 40th percentile, 82.5% at the 20th percentile, and 72.2% at the bottom.

The Top 25

Rank	Micropolitan area	Population	Housing diversity index
1	Albemarle, NC	60,714	87.1%
2	Danville, VA	104,276	86.9%
3	El Campo, TX	41,486	86.8%
3	Eureka-Arcata-Fortuna, CA	135,727	86.8%
3	Paducah, KY-IL	97,312	86.8%
6	Ardmore, OK	48,689	86.7%
6	Greenwood, SC	94,770	86.7%
6	Mount Vernon, IL	38,353	86.7%
6	Roanoke Rapids, NC	72,882	86.7%
6	Thomaston, GA	26,368	86.7%
6	Valley, AL	34,123	86.7%
12	Bogalusa, LA	46,371	86.6%
12	Centralia, IL	38,339	86.6%
12	Elkins, WV	29,126	86.6%
12	Mexico, MO	26,096	86.6%
12	Miami, OK	31,981	86.6%
12	Sault Ste. Marie, MI	38,033	86.6%
12	Wisconsin Rapids-Marshfield, WI	73,435	86.6%
19	Brownwood, TX	37,896	86.5%
19	Coos Bay, OR	63,121	86.5%
19	Forest City, NC	66,390	86.5%
19	Jennings, LA	31,439	86.5%
19	Magnolia, AR	24,114	86.5%
19	Seymour, IN	44,069	86.5%
19	Union City, TN-KY	36,877	86.5%

Housing: 4 or More Bedrooms

Description: Percentage of housing units that have four or more bedrooms (2015).

Order: Ranked from highest percentage (top) to lowest percentage (bottom).

Splits: 44.2% at the top, 20.7% at the 80th percentile, 17.7% at the 60th percentile, 16.4% at the median (50th percentile), 15.4% at the 40th percentile, 13.3% at the 20th percentile, and 6.8% at the bottom.

The Top 25

Rank	Micropolitan area	Population	4 or more bedrooms
1	Heber, UT	29,161	44.2%
2	Kill Devil Hills, NC	39,733	36.4%
3	Summit Park, UT	39,633	36.0%
4	Blackfoot, ID	44,990	34.9%
5	Carroll, IA	20,498	31.9%
6	Vineyard Haven, MA	17,299	31.3%
7	Mitchell, SD	23,243	29.8%
8	Hays, KS	29,029	29.4%
9	Garden City, KS	41,074	29.3%
9	Wahpeton, ND-MN	22,798	29.3%
11	Marshall, MN	25,673	29.2%
12	Cedar City, UT	48,368	29.1%
13	Faribault-Northfield, MN	65,400	29.0%
14	Vernal, UT	37,928	28.9%
15	Jefferson, GA	63,360	28.8%
15	McPherson, KS	28,941	28.8%
17	Alexandria, MN	37,075	28.6%
18	Dickinson, ND	32,154	28.4%
19	Rexburg, ID	51,092	28.3%
19	Watertown, SD	27,939	28.3%
21	Kearney, NE	55,448	28.0%
21	New Ulm, MN	25,313	28.0%
23	Gillette, WY	49,220	27.9%
24	Willmar, MN	42,542	27.7%
25	Edwards, CO	53,605	27.5%
25	Red Wing, MN	46,435	27.5%

Housing: Affordability/Income Ratio

Description: Ratio of the median value of owner-occupied housing units per $1,000 of median household income (2015). The lower the ratio, the more affordable the local housing. (Here's how it works: Pecos, TX, has a median home value of $44,600 and a median household income of $43,540, yielding a ratio of $1,024 in home value per $1,000 of income.)
Order: Ranked from lowest ratio (top) to highest ratio (bottom).
Splits: $1,024 at the top, $2,178 at the 80th percentile, $2,430 at the 60th percentile, $2,556 at the median (50th percentile), $2,708 at the 40th percentile, $3,251 at the 20th percentile, and $10,289 at the bottom.

The Top 25

Rank	Micropolitan area	Population	Affordability/income ratio
1	Pecos, TX	14,732	$1,024
2	Borger, TX	21,734	$1,489
3	Big Spring, TX	38,521	$1,509
4	Lamesa, TX	13,520	$1,511
5	Sweetwater, TX	15,107	$1,542
6	Snyder, TX	17,615	$1,568
7	Andrews, TX	18,105	$1,585
8	Levelland, TX	23,433	$1,611
9	Centralia, IL	38,339	$1,624
10	Alice, TX	41,382	$1,631
11	Vernon, TX	13,027	$1,662
12	Plainview, TX	34,360	$1,692
13	Parsons, KS	20,803	$1,694
14	Zapata, TX	14,374	$1,716
15	Coffeyville, KS	33,314	$1,718
16	Beeville, TX	32,874	$1,723
17	Pampa, TX	23,210	$1,728
18	Bradford, PA	42,412	$1,733
19	Canton, IL	35,699	$1,769
20	Great Bend, KS	27,103	$1,845
20	Guymon, OK	21,489	$1,845
22	Liberal, KS	23,152	$1,848
23	Taylorville, IL	33,642	$1,849
24	Lexington, NE	25,859	$1,851
25	Oil City, PA	53,119	$1,861

Income: Poverty Rate

Description: Percentage of all residents who live in households that are below the federal poverty level (2015).

Order: Ranked from lowest percentage (top) to highest percentage (bottom).

Splits: 6.1% at the top, 12.8% at the 80th percentile, 15.9% at the 60th percentile, 17.2% at the median (50th percentile), 18.8% at the 40th percentile, 22.7% at the 20th percentile, and 39.0% at the bottom.

The Top 25

Rank	Micropolitan area	Population	Poverty rate
1	Los Alamos, NM	17,785	6.1%
2	Juneau, AK	32,756	6.6%
2	Spirit Lake, IA	17,111	6.6%
4	Dickinson, ND	32,154	6.7%
5	Torrington, CT	183,603	7.0%
6	Gillette, WY	49,220	7.2%
6	McPherson, KS	28,941	7.2%
8	New Ulm, MN	25,313	7.8%
8	Summit Park, UT	39,633	7.8%
10	Minot, ND	79,814	7.9%
11	Hutchinson, MN	35,932	8.1%
12	Sheridan, WY	30,009	8.3%
13	Celina, OH	40,968	8.4%
14	Columbus, NE	32,847	8.5%
14	Jackson, WY-ID	33,689	8.5%
16	St. Marys, PA	30,872	8.8%
17	Wapakoneta, OH	45,876	8.9%
18	Concord, NH	147,994	9.1%
19	Beaver Dam, WI	88,502	9.2%
19	Edwards, CO	53,605	9.2%
21	Vernal, UT	37,928	9.3%
22	Pierre, SD	21,935	9.5%
23	Alexandria, MN	37,075	9.6%
23	Kill Devil Hills, NC	39,733	9.6%
23	Newton, IA	36,827	9.6%
23	Oak Harbor, WA	80,593	9.6%

Income: Median Household Income

Description: Median annual income for all households (2015). Household income is the total amount received from all sources (wages, interest, dividends, welfare, Social Security, etc.) by all persons in a housing unit.
Order: Ranked from highest dollar figure (top) to lowest dollar figure (bottom).
Splits: $101,934 at the top, $50,559 at the 80th percentile, $45,579 at the 60th percentile, $43,523 at the median (50th percentile), $41,630 at the 40th percentile, $37,106 at the 20th percentile, and $22,443 at the bottom.

The Top 25

Rank	Micropolitan area	Population	Median household income
1	Los Alamos, NM	17,785	$101,934
2	Summit Park, UT	39,633	$91,773
3	Williston, ND	35,294	$88,013
4	Juneau, AK	32,756	$85,746
5	Gillette, WY	49,220	$80,060
6	Edwards, CO	53,605	$72,214
7	Dickinson, ND	32,154	$72,099
8	Torrington, CT	183,603	$72,061
9	Elko, NV	53,951	$71,462
10	Andrews, TX	18,105	$70,423
11	Rock Springs, WY	44,626	$69,022
12	Jackson, WY-ID	33,689	$68,318
13	Breckenridge, CO	30,257	$67,983
14	Vernal, UT	37,928	$66,815
15	Heber, UT	29,161	$66,486
16	Concord, NH	147,994	$65,983
17	Winnemucca, NV	17,019	$65,212
18	Kapaa, HI	71,735	$65,101
19	Steamboat Springs, CO	24,130	$64,963
20	Ketchikan, AK	13,709	$64,222
20	Vineyard Haven, MA	17,299	$64,222
22	Laconia, NH	60,641	$62,159
23	Minot, ND	79,814	$61,213
24	Durango, CO	54,688	$60,278
25	Glenwood Springs, CO	75,882	$59,875

Income: Interest/Dividends

Description: Percentage of households that earned interest, dividends, or net rental income during the past year (2015).

Order: Ranked from highest percentage (top) to lowest percentage (bottom).

Splits: 50.6% at the top, 24.7% at the 80th percentile, 20.9% at the 60th percentile, 19.1% at the median (50th percentile), 17.5% at the 40th percentile, 14.1% at the 20th percentile, and 4.8% at the bottom.

The Top 25

Rank	Micropolitan area	Population	Interest/dividends
1	Juneau, AK	32,756	50.6%
2	Ketchikan, AK	13,709	47.8%
3	Los Alamos, NM	17,785	46.4%
4	Fredericksburg, TX	25,963	39.2%
5	Fairfield, IA	17,555	33.1%
6	Riverton, WY	40,315	33.0%
7	Easton, MD	37,512	32.7%
8	Bennington, VT	36,317	32.5%
9	Logan, WV	34,707	32.2%
10	Kapaa, HI	71,735	31.4%
10	Spirit Lake, IA	17,111	31.4%
12	Torrington, CT	183,603	31.3%
13	Gardnerville Ranchos, NV	47,710	31.2%
14	Breckenridge, CO	30,257	31.0%
15	Jackson, WY-ID	33,689	30.8%
15	Truckee-Grass Valley, CA	98,877	30.8%
17	Barre, VT	58,612	30.7%
18	Effingham, IL	34,371	30.6%
19	Kalispell, MT	96,165	30.5%
19	Oak Harbor, WA	80,593	30.5%
21	Bozeman, MT	100,739	30.4%
22	Sonora, CA	53,709	30.3%
23	Durango, CO	54,688	30.1%
23	Port Angeles, WA	73,486	30.1%
25	New Ulm, MN	25,313	30.0%

Income: Public Assistance

Description: Percentage of households that received cash public assistance and/or food stamps during the past year (2015).
Order: Ranked from lowest percentage (top) to highest percentage (bottom).
Splits: 2.4% at the top, 11.4% at the 80th percentile, 14.3% at the 60th percentile, 15.4% at the median (50th percentile), 16.9% at the 40th percentile, 20.4% at the 20th percentile, and 43.9% at the bottom.

The Top 25

Rank	Micropolitan area	Population	Public assistance
1	Los Alamos, NM	17,785	2.4%
2	Gillette, WY	49,220	3.0%
3	Vineyard Haven, MA	17,299	3.1%
4	Breckenridge, CO	30,257	3.2%
5	Summit Park, UT	39,633	3.6%
6	Jackson, WY-ID	33,689	3.7%
6	Steamboat Springs, CO	24,130	3.7%
8	Edwards, CO	53,605	3.8%
9	Rock Springs, WY	44,626	4.4%
10	Laramie, WY	37,956	4.6%
11	Sheridan, WY	30,009	5.0%
12	Bozeman, MT	100,739	5.7%
12	Minot, ND	79,814	5.7%
14	Heber, UT	29,161	5.8%
15	Durango, CO	54,688	6.3%
16	Columbus, NE	32,847	6.5%
16	Jasper, IN	55,055	6.5%
18	Elko, NV	53,951	6.6%
18	Glenwood Springs, CO	75,882	6.6%
20	McPherson, KS	28,941	6.7%
21	Fredericksburg, TX	25,963	7.0%
21	Red Wing, MN	46,435	7.0%
23	Hays, KS	29,029	7.1%
24	Brookings, SD	33,897	7.2%
24	Dickinson, ND	32,154	7.2%
24	Hutchinson, MN	35,932	7.2%

Income: Median Fulltime Earnings

Description: Median annual earnings for full-time, year-round workers (2015). Earnings are not the same as income. Earnings are confined to wages or salaries from employment, while income encompasses all sources of money.

Order: Ranked from highest dollar figure (top) to lowest dollar figure (bottom).

Splits: $87,975 at the top, $40,658 at the 80th percentile, $38,006 at the 60th percentile, $37,122 at the median (50th percentile), $36,054 at the 40th percentile, $33,453 at the 20th percentile, and $26,560 at the bottom.

The Top 25

Rank	Micropolitan area	Population	Median fulltime earnings
1	Los Alamos, NM	17,785	$87,975
2	Williston, ND	35,294	$56,718
3	Summit Park, UT	39,633	$56,116
4	Juneau, AK	32,756	$54,253
5	Gillette, WY	49,220	$54,198
6	Torrington, CT	183,603	$53,992
7	Rock Springs, WY	44,626	$53,503
8	Winnemucca, NV	17,019	$53,244
9	Elko, NV	53,951	$52,344
10	Vineyard Haven, MA	17,299	$51,538
11	Andrews, TX	18,105	$51,469
12	Susanville, CA	31,345	$50,150
13	Vernal, UT	37,928	$50,087
14	Concord, NH	147,994	$49,688
15	Heber, UT	29,161	$49,436
16	Dickinson, ND	32,154	$49,423
17	Oak Harbor, WA	80,593	$49,109
18	Truckee-Grass Valley, CA	98,877	$49,043
19	Ketchikan, AK	13,709	$48,190
20	Easton, MD	37,512	$47,162
21	Greenfield Town, MA	70,601	$46,974
22	Hudson, NY	61,509	$46,790
23	Sonora, CA	53,709	$46,782
24	Carlsbad-Artesia, NM	57,578	$46,380
25	Faribault-Northfield, MN	65,400	$46,282

Seniors: Seniors Living Alone

Description: Percentage of senior citizens (65 years old or older) who live alone (2015). Seniors in group quarters are not considered to be living alone.

Order: Ranked from lowest percentage (top) to highest percentage (bottom).

Splits: 16.5% at the top, 24.8% at the 80th percentile, 26.7% at the 60th percentile, 27.6% at the median (50th percentile), 28.4% at the 40th percentile, 30.3% at the 20th percentile, and 40.3% at the bottom.

The Top 25

Rank	Micropolitan area	Population	Seniors living alone
1	Breckenridge, CO	30,257	16.5%
2	Kapaa, HI	71,735	17.2%
3	Kingsville, TX	32,264	17.7%
4	Summit Park, UT	39,633	17.9%
5	Rio Grande City, TX	63,795	18.1%
6	Raymondville, TX	21,903	18.2%
7	Edwards, CO	53,605	18.6%
8	Heber, UT	29,161	18.8%
9	Gardnerville Ranchos, NV	47,710	18.9%
10	Wauchula, FL	27,502	19.1%
11	Fernley, NV	52,585	19.6%
12	St. Marys, GA	52,102	19.9%
12	Winnemucca, NV	17,019	19.9%
14	Hilo, HI	196,428	20.0%
14	Show Low, AZ	108,277	20.0%
16	Zapata, TX	14,374	20.2%
17	Del Rio, TX	48,988	20.3%
18	Dumas, TX	22,255	20.4%
18	Plainview, TX	34,360	20.4%
20	Crossville, TN	58,229	21.0%
21	Brevard, NC	33,211	21.1%
21	Nogales, AZ	46,461	21.1%
23	Cedar City, UT	48,368	21.2%
23	Malvern, AR	33,426	21.2%
23	Shelbyville, TN	47,183	21.2%

Seniors: Poverty Rate for Seniors

Description: Percentage of senior citizens (65 years old or older) who live in households that are below the federal poverty level (2015).

Order: Ranked from lowest percentage (top) to highest percentage (bottom).

Splits: 2.2% at the top, 7.1% at the 80th percentile, 8.4% at the 60th percentile, 9.3% at the median (50th percentile), 10.0% at the 40th percentile, 12.6% at the 20th percentile, and 34.1% at the bottom.

The Top 25

Rank	Micropolitan area	Population	Poverty rate for seniors
1	Juneau, AK	32,756	2.2%
2	Vermillion, SD	13,964	2.7%
3	Jackson, WY-ID	33,689	3.3%
4	Ketchikan, AK	13,709	3.5%
5	Los Alamos, NM	17,785	3.6%
5	Urbana, OH	38,987	3.6%
7	Angola, IN	34,372	3.8%
8	Bozeman, MT	100,739	4.0%
8	Dodge City, KS	34,536	4.0%
8	Oak Harbor, WA	80,593	4.0%
11	Brookings, SD	33,897	4.3%
12	Hood River, OR	23,137	4.6%
13	Findlay, OH	75,573	4.7%
13	Heber, UT	29,161	4.7%
15	Durango, CO	54,688	4.8%
16	Port Clinton, OH	40,877	4.9%
17	Brevard, NC	33,211	5.0%
17	Gardnerville Ranchos, NV	47,710	5.0%
17	Gillette, WY	49,220	5.0%
17	Pontiac, IL	36,671	5.0%
17	Spirit Lake, IA	17,111	5.0%
22	Concord, NH	147,994	5.1%
22	Decatur, IN	34,980	5.1%
22	Sterling, IL	57,079	5.1%
25	Greenville, OH	52,076	5.2%

Seniors: Median Income for Seniors

Description: Median annual income for households headed by persons who are 65 years old or older (2015).

Order: Ranked from highest dollar figure (top) to lowest dollar figure (bottom).

Splits: $89,293 at the top, $37,454 at the 80th percentile, $34,491 at the 60th percentile, $33,342 at the median (50th percentile), $32,032 at the 40th percentile, $29,435 at the 20th percentile, and $17,382 at the bottom.

The Top 25

Rank	Micropolitan area	Population	Median income for seniors
1	Los Alamos, NM	17,785	$89,293
2	Juneau, AK	32,756	$69,148
3	Summit Park, UT	39,633	$68,495
4	Breckenridge, CO	30,257	$68,015
5	Jackson, WY-ID	33,689	$65,134
6	Edwards, CO	53,605	$64,500
7	Durango, CO	54,688	$52,276
8	Easton, MD	37,512	$52,154
9	Gardnerville Ranchos, NV	47,710	$51,872
10	Vermillion, SD	13,964	$50,903
11	Williston, ND	35,294	$50,898
12	Kapaa, HI	71,735	$50,357
13	Oak Harbor, WA	80,593	$49,984
14	Elko, NV	53,951	$49,667
15	Key West, FL	77,482	$49,479
16	Glenwood Springs, CO	75,882	$49,370
17	Steamboat Springs, CO	24,130	$48,184
18	Vineyard Haven, MA	17,299	$47,563
19	Laramie, WY	37,956	$47,112
20	Gillette, WY	49,220	$46,849
21	Helena, MT	78,063	$46,104
22	Truckee-Grass Valley, CA	98,877	$46,011
23	Brevard, NC	33,211	$45,992
24	Bozeman, MT	100,739	$45,618
25	Hood River, OR	23,137	$45,403

Seniors: Seniors Who Work

Description: Percentage of senior citizens (65 years old or older) who were employed at some point during the past year (2015).

Order: Ranked from highest percentage (top) to lowest percentage (bottom).

Splits: 40.5% at the top, 23.1% at the 80th percentile, 19.6% at the 60th percentile, 18.3% at the median (50th percentile), 17.2% at the 40th percentile, 15.4% at the 20th percentile, and 7.5% at the bottom.

The Top 25

Rank	Micropolitan area	Population	Seniors who work
1	Edwards, CO	53,605	40.5%
2	Breckenridge, CO	30,257	39.3%
3	Summit Park, UT	39,633	35.7%
4	Vineyard Haven, MA	17,299	35.6%
5	Liberal, KS	23,152	35.3%
6	Glenwood Springs, CO	75,882	34.6%
7	Juneau, AK	32,756	34.4%
8	Jackson, WY-ID	33,689	34.1%
9	Guymon, OK	21,489	33.5%
10	Junction City, KS	37,030	33.3%
11	Hailey, ID	27,955	32.6%
12	Brookings, SD	33,897	32.5%
13	Vermillion, SD	13,964	32.2%
14	Ketchikan, AK	13,709	31.8%
15	Garden City, KS	41,074	31.7%
16	Gillette, WY	49,220	31.2%
17	Columbus, NE	32,847	31.1%
17	Pierre, SD	21,935	31.1%
19	Kearney, NE	55,448	30.9%
19	Scottsbluff, NE	38,309	30.9%
21	Winnemucca, NV	17,019	30.5%
22	Dodge City, KS	34,536	30.4%
22	Fairfield, IA	17,555	30.4%
24	Lexington, NE	25,859	30.3%
25	Craig, CO	12,937	30.1%

Seniors: Home Ownership by Seniors

Description: Percentage of senior citizens (65 years old or older) who own the housing units they occupy (2015).

Order: Ranked from highest percentage (top) to lowest percentage (bottom).

Splits: 93.4% at the top, 85.9% at the 80th percentile, 83.0% at the 60th percentile, 82.0% at the median (50th percentile), 81.1% at the 40th percentile, 78.3% at the 20th percentile, and 66.7% at the bottom.

The Top 25

Rank	Micropolitan area	Population	Home ownership by seniors
1	Vernal, UT	37,928	93.4%
2	Brevard, NC	33,211	92.7%
3	DeRidder, LA	36,462	92.4%
4	Arcadia, FL	35,458	92.3%
5	Heber, UT	29,161	92.0%
6	Ruidoso, NM	19,420	91.7%
7	Starkville, MS	49,800	90.9%
8	Grants, NM	27,329	90.8%
9	Seneca, SC	75,713	90.7%
10	Bardstown, KY	45,126	90.6%
11	Picayune, MS	55,191	90.5%
11	Point Pleasant, WV-OH	57,179	90.5%
13	Andrews, TX	18,105	90.4%
14	Boone, NC	52,906	90.2%
14	Okeechobee, FL	39,469	90.2%
16	Georgetown, SC	61,298	90.1%
17	Borger, TX	21,734	89.9%
17	Craig, CO	12,937	89.9%
19	Iron Mountain, MI-WI	30,252	89.5%
20	Española, NM	39,465	89.4%
21	Paris, TN	32,147	89.3%
22	Fort Leonard Wood, MO	53,221	89.2%
23	Cadillac, MI	47,906	89.1%
24	Guymon, OK	21,489	89.0%
24	Pecos, TX	14,732	89.0%

Stability: 25-39 Age Group

Description: Percentage of residents who are in the range from 25 through 39 years old (2015). This is the same as the list on page 53. It is repeated here because it is a category of the Stability rating.

Order: Ranked from highest percentage (top) to lowest percentage (bottom).

Splits: 27.9% at the top, 18.9% at the 80th percentile, 17.9% at the 60th percentile, 17.4% at the median (50th percentile), 17.0% at the 40th percentile, 16.2% at the 20th percentile, and 12.2% at the bottom.

The Top 25

Rank	Micropolitan area	Population	25-39 age group
1	Susanville, CA	31,345	27.9%
2	Junction City, KS	37,030	27.5%
3	Breckenridge, CO	30,257	27.3%
4	Jackson, WY-ID	33,689	27.2%
5	Edwards, CO	53,605	26.5%
6	Fort Polk South, LA	50,803	24.3%
7	Williston, ND	35,294	24.2%
8	Fort Leonard Wood, MO	53,221	24.0%
8	Palestine, TX	57,580	24.0%
10	Lamesa, TX	13,520	23.8%
11	Beeville, TX	32,874	23.7%
12	Vernal, UT	37,928	23.6%
13	Gillette, WY	49,220	23.4%
14	Bozeman, MT	100,739	23.2%
15	Pecos, TX	14,732	22.9%
16	Rock Springs, WY	44,626	22.8%
17	Elk City, OK	23,768	22.4%
18	Guymon, OK	21,489	22.3%
19	Juneau, AK	32,756	22.2%
20	Dickinson, ND	32,154	22.0%
20	Heber, UT	29,161	22.0%
22	Dunn, NC	128,140	21.9%
22	Raymondville, TX	21,903	21.9%
24	Bennettsville, SC	27,494	21.8%
24	Cañon City, CO	46,692	21.8%

Stability: Born in State of Residence

Description: Percentage of residents who were born in the state where they currently live (2015).

Order: Ranked from highest percentage (top) to lowest percentage (bottom).

Splits: 92.7% at the top, 80.1% at the 80th percentile, 75.0% at the 60th percentile, 72.1% at the median (50th percentile), 68.8% at the 40th percentile, 57.4% at the 20th percentile, and 17.6% at the bottom.

The Top 25

Rank	Micropolitan area	Population	Born in state of residence
1	Opelousas, LA	83,848	92.7%
2	Lewistown, PA	46,500	90.8%
3	St. Marys, PA	30,872	90.5%
4	Coshocton, OH	36,569	88.6%
5	Batavia, NY	58,937	88.4%
6	Alma, MI	41,540	88.3%
7	Ionia, MI	64,223	88.0%
7	Selma, AL	41,131	88.0%
9	Greenwood, MS	41,242	87.9%
10	Oil City, PA	53,119	87.5%
10	Owosso, MI	68,619	87.5%
12	Indianola, MS	27,005	87.3%
12	Wapakoneta, OH	45,876	87.3%
14	Alpena, MI	28,803	87.2%
14	Sunbury, PA	93,246	87.2%
16	Tiffin, OH	55,610	87.0%
17	Greenville, MS	48,130	86.9%
18	Decatur, IN	34,980	86.7%
18	Jennings, LA	31,439	86.7%
18	West Point, MS	20,048	86.7%
21	Cadillac, MI	47,906	86.6%
22	Shawano, WI	45,877	86.4%
23	Alice, TX	41,382	86.2%
23	Gloversville, NY	53,992	86.2%
23	Lock Haven, PA	39,441	86.2%

Stability: Same House as 1 Year Ago

Description: Percentage of residents 1 year old or older who have lived in the same housing unit for at least a year (2015).

Order: Ranked from highest percentage (top) to lowest percentage (bottom).

Splits: 94.6% at the top, 88.4% at the 80th percentile, 86.5% at the 60th percentile, 85.7% at the median (50th percentile), 84.4% at the 40th percentile, 82.0% at the 20th percentile, and 56.9% at the bottom.

The Top 25

Rank	Micropolitan area	Population	Same house as 1 year ago
1	Bastrop, LA	26,395	94.6%
2	Washington, NC	47,651	94.3%
3	Atmore, AL	37,789	93.9%
3	Española, NM	39,465	93.9%
5	North Wilkesboro, NC	68,502	93.3%
6	Manitowoc, WI	79,806	93.1%
7	Vineyard Haven, MA	17,299	92.8%
8	Vicksburg, MS	56,635	92.7%
9	Scottsboro, AL	52,419	92.5%
9	St. Marys, PA	30,872	92.5%
11	Brookhaven, MS	34,649	92.4%
11	Mount Airy, NC	72,743	92.4%
13	El Campo, TX	41,486	92.2%
13	Hood River, OR	23,137	92.2%
15	Somerset, PA	75,522	92.1%
16	Mayfield, KY	37,421	91.9%
17	Las Vegas, NM	27,967	91.8%
18	Cornelia, GA	43,996	91.7%
19	Brownwood, TX	37,896	91.6%
19	Gallup, NM	76,708	91.6%
19	Marion, NC	44,989	91.6%
22	Jefferson, GA	63,360	91.5%
22	Rio Grande City, TX	63,795	91.5%
24	Sayre, PA	61,281	91.4%
25	Hudson, NY	61,509	91.3%

Stability: Live and Work in County

Description: Percentage of workers who are employed in the county where they live (2015).

Order: Ranked from highest percentage (top) to lowest percentage (bottom).

Splits: 99.1% at the top, 86.3% at the 80th percentile, 79.8% at the 60th percentile, 75.9% at the median (50th percentile), 73.0% at the 40th percentile, 65.8% at the 20th percentile, and 37.2% at the bottom.

The Top 25

Rank	Micropolitan area	Population	Live and work in county
1	Juneau, AK	32,756	99.1%
1	Kapaa, HI	71,735	99.1%
3	Ketchikan, AK	13,709	98.8%
4	Hilo, HI	196,428	98.2%
5	Eureka-Arcata-Fortuna, CA	135,727	98.0%
6	Gillette, WY	49,220	97.2%
7	Rock Springs, WY	44,626	96.3%
8	Carlsbad-Artesia, NM	57,578	96.2%
8	Steamboat Springs, CO	24,130	96.2%
10	Marquette, MI	67,215	95.9%
11	Silver City, NM	28,609	95.7%
12	Williston, ND	35,294	95.6%
13	Kalispell, MT	96,165	95.5%
14	Coos Bay, OR	63,121	95.2%
15	Jamestown, ND	21,103	94.6%
15	Vineyard Haven, MA	17,299	94.6%
17	North Platte, NE	36,908	94.4%
18	Bozeman, MT	100,739	94.1%
19	Key West, FL	77,482	94.0%
20	Newport, OR	47,038	93.9%
21	Riverton, WY	40,315	93.8%
22	Astoria, OR	37,831	93.7%
22	Hobbs, NM	71,180	93.7%
24	Fort Leonard Wood, MO	53,221	93.6%
24	Laramie, WY	37,956	93.6%

Stability: Married-Couple Households

Description: Percentage of households that include both members of a married couple (2015).

Order: Ranked from highest percentage (top) to lowest percentage (bottom).

Splits: 71.0% at the top, 54.0% at the 80th percentile, 51.6% at the 60th percentile, 50.5% at the median (50th percentile), 49.4% at the 40th percentile, 46.1% at the 20th percentile, and 29.8% at the bottom.

The Top 25

Rank	Micropolitan area	Population	Married-couple households
1	Rexburg, ID	51,092	71.0%
2	Heber, UT	29,161	64.7%
3	Summit Park, UT	39,633	63.8%
4	Dumas, TX	22,255	63.0%
5	Andrews, TX	18,105	62.7%
6	Blackfoot, ID	44,990	62.6%
7	Burley, ID	43,967	61.5%
8	Vernal, UT	37,928	60.5%
9	Holland, MI	114,625	60.3%
10	Jefferson, GA	63,360	59.9%
11	Washington, IN	32,906	59.8%
12	Los Alamos, NM	17,785	59.6%
13	Jasper, IN	55,055	59.0%
14	Cedar City, UT	48,368	58.7%
15	Mountain Home, ID	25,876	58.6%
16	Decatur, IN	34,980	58.5%
16	Ottawa, KS	25,609	58.5%
18	Warsaw, IN	78,620	58.3%
19	Othello, WA	19,254	58.1%
19	Selinsgrove, PA	40,444	58.1%
21	Celina, OH	40,968	57.9%
21	Pella, IA	33,294	57.9%
23	Elko, NV	53,951	57.7%
24	Toccoa, GA	25,586	57.6%
24	Wooster, OH	116,063	57.6%

Transportation: Bicycle or Walk to Work

Description: Percentage of workers (not employed at home) who commute to their jobs by bicycle or on foot (2015).

Order: Ranked from highest percentage (top) to lowest percentage (bottom).

Splits: 19.6% at the top, 4.6% at the 80th percentile, 3.3% at the 60th percentile, 2.9% at the median (50th percentile), 2.4% at the 40th percentile, 1.7% at the 20th percentile, and 0.3% at the bottom.

The Top 25

Rank	Micropolitan area	Population	Bicycle or walk to work
1	Pullman, WA	48,177	19.6%
2	Athens, OH	65,886	17.6%
3	Vermillion, SD	13,964	17.4%
4	Moscow, ID	38,778	15.9%
5	Laramie, WY	37,956	15.5%
6	Ellensburg, WA	43,269	12.3%
7	Key West, FL	77,482	11.8%
8	Rexburg, ID	51,092	11.4%
9	Jackson, WY-ID	33,689	11.2%
10	Houghton, MI	38,548	11.1%
10	Ketchikan, AK	13,709	11.1%
12	La Grande, OR	25,790	10.9%
13	Bozeman, MT	100,739	10.5%
13	Breckenridge, CO	30,257	10.5%
15	Oneonta, NY	60,636	10.1%
16	Brookings, SD	33,897	9.6%
17	Eureka-Arcata-Fortuna, CA	135,727	9.2%
17	Steamboat Springs, CO	24,130	9.2%
19	Durango, CO	54,688	9.1%
19	Spearfish, SD	24,827	9.1%
21	Astoria, OR	37,831	8.9%
21	Mount Pleasant, MI	70,698	8.9%
23	Hood River, OR	23,137	8.8%
23	Macomb, IL	31,333	8.8%
25	Glenwood Springs, CO	75,882	8.4%
25	Maryville, MO	22,810	8.4%

Transportation: Carpool to Work

Description: Percentage of workers (not employed at home) who commute to their jobs in a carpool (2015).

Order: Ranked from highest percentage (top) to lowest percentage (bottom).

Splits: 24.2% at the top, 12.9% at the 80th percentile, 11.1% at the 60th percentile, 10.6% at the median (50th percentile), 10.1% at the 40th percentile, 8.9% at the 20th percentile, and 5.8% at the bottom.

The Top 25

Rank	Micropolitan area	Population	Carpool to work
1	Liberal, KS	23,152	24.2%
2	Rio Grande City, TX	63,795	21.5%
3	Moultrie, GA	45,844	20.6%
4	Guymon, OK	21,489	20.1%
5	Zapata, TX	14,374	19.6%
6	Gainesville, TX	39,229	19.0%
7	Dumas, TX	22,255	18.9%
7	Helena-West Helena, AR	19,513	18.9%
7	Marion, NC	44,989	18.9%
10	Andrews, TX	18,105	18.7%
11	Grants, NM	27,329	18.6%
12	Arcadia, FL	35,458	18.5%
13	Ketchikan, AK	13,709	18.4%
14	Storm Lake, IA	20,493	18.3%
15	Levelland, TX	23,433	18.1%
16	Craig, CO	12,937	18.0%
17	Wauchula, FL	27,502	17.9%
18	Worthington, MN	21,770	17.7%
19	Decatur, IN	34,980	17.5%
19	Lexington, NE	25,859	17.5%
21	Alamogordo, NM	64,362	17.3%
21	Fort Morgan, CO	28,360	17.3%
23	Eagle Pass, TX	57,706	17.2%
24	Kinston, NC	58,106	16.9%
24	Washington, IN	32,906	16.9%

Transportation: Public Transit to Work

Description: Percentage of workers (not employed at home) who commute to their jobs by bus, streetcar, subway, railroad, or ferryboat (2015).
Order: Ranked from highest percentage (top) to lowest percentage (bottom).
Splits: 14.5% at the top, 0.8% at the 80th percentile, 0.4% at the 60th percentile, 0.4% at the median (50th percentile), 0.3% at the 40th percentile, 0.1% at the 20th percentile, and 0.0% at the bottom.

The Top 25

Rank	Micropolitan area	Population	Public transit to work
1	Winnemucca, NV	17,019	14.5%
2	Elko, NV	53,951	12.2%
3	Clewiston, FL	39,119	8.2%
4	Edwards, CO	53,605	7.6%
5	Glenwood Springs, CO	75,882	6.8%
6	Arcadia, FL	35,458	6.3%
6	Jackson, WY-ID	33,689	6.3%
8	Breckenridge, CO	30,257	6.0%
9	Pullman, WA	48,177	5.4%
10	Juneau, AK	32,756	4.5%
11	Vineyard Haven, MA	17,299	4.3%
12	Los Alamos, NM	17,785	4.2%
13	Blackfoot, ID	44,990	3.0%
13	Ketchikan, AK	13,709	3.0%
13	Oak Harbor, WA	80,593	3.0%
16	Evanston, WY	20,822	2.8%
16	Laramie, WY	37,956	2.8%
18	Boone, NC	52,906	2.7%
18	Steamboat Springs, CO	24,130	2.7%
20	Moses Lake, WA	93,259	2.6%
20	Wauchula, FL	27,502	2.6%
22	Gillette, WY	49,220	2.5%
22	Hudson, NY	61,509	2.5%
22	Port Angeles, WA	73,486	2.5%
25	Rock Springs, WY	44,626	2.4%

Transportation: Commute <15 Minutes

Description: Percentage of workers (not employed at home) who commute from home to their jobs in less than 15 minutes (2015).

Order: Ranked from highest percentage (top) to lowest percentage (bottom).

Splits: 74.8% at the top, 52.9% at the 80th percentile, 46.8% at the 60th percentile, 43.2% at the median (50th percentile), 40.0% at the 40th percentile, 34.9% at the 20th percentile, and 19.1% at the bottom.

The Top 25

Rank	Micropolitan area	Population	Commute <15 minutes
1	Vernon, TX	13,027	74.8%
2	Hays, KS	29,029	74.4%
3	Laramie, WY	37,956	72.4%
4	Pierre, SD	21,935	71.7%
5	Vermillion, SD	13,964	71.0%
6	Pecos, TX	14,732	70.1%
7	Liberal, KS	23,152	69.8%
8	Yankton, SD	22,702	68.2%
9	Jamestown, ND	21,103	67.4%
10	Mitchell, SD	23,243	66.8%
11	Snyder, TX	17,615	66.6%
12	Storm Lake, IA	20,493	66.4%
13	Dodge City, KS	34,536	66.3%
14	Huron, SD	18,372	66.1%
15	Brookings, SD	33,897	65.9%
16	Lamesa, TX	13,520	65.6%
17	Watertown, SD	27,939	65.4%
18	Price, UT	20,479	64.9%
19	Plainview, TX	34,360	64.8%
19	Sterling, CO	22,036	64.8%
21	Brookings, OR	22,483	64.5%
22	Hereford, TX	18,952	64.3%
23	Kearney, NE	55,448	64.2%
24	Carroll, IA	20,498	64.0%
24	Sweetwater, TX	15,107	64.0%

Transportation: Commute >45 Minutes

Description: Percentage of workers (not employed at home) who commute from home to their jobs in 45 minutes or more (2015).

Order: Ranked from lowest percentage (top) to highest percentage (bottom).

Splits: 1.2% at the top, 7.6% at the 80th percentile, 9.8% at the 60th percentile, 11.1% at the median (50th percentile), 12.4% at the 40th percentile, 15.5% at the 20th percentile, and 31.1% at the bottom.

The Top 25

Rank	Micropolitan area	Population	Commute >45 minutes
1	Ketchikan, AK	13,709	1.2%
2	Pierre, SD	21,935	2.2%
3	Clovis, NM	50,398	2.5%
3	Juneau, AK	32,756	2.5%
5	Vineyard Haven, MA	17,299	2.7%
6	Aberdeen, SD	42,784	2.8%
7	Crescent City, CA	27,254	2.9%
8	Hays, KS	29,029	3.1%
9	Junction City, KS	37,030	3.2%
10	Brookings, OR	22,483	3.3%
11	Huron, SD	18,372	3.5%
12	Fort Leonard Wood, MO	53,221	3.7%
13	Columbus, NE	32,847	4.0%
13	Mountain Home, AR	41,053	4.0%
13	Storm Lake, IA	20,493	4.0%
16	Watertown, SD	27,939	4.1%
17	Jamestown, ND	21,103	4.2%
17	North Platte, NE	36,908	4.2%
19	Marshall, MN	25,673	4.3%
19	Salina, KS	61,666	4.3%
21	Houghton, MI	38,548	4.5%
21	McPherson, KS	28,941	4.5%
21	Portales, NM	19,120	4.5%
24	Hastings, NE	31,587	4.6%
24	Hereford, TX	18,952	4.6%

3

RATINGS: FIVE-STAR MICROS

★★★★★

MICROPOLITAN
AMERICA

This book does not rank the nation's micropolitan areas according to the quality of life they afford. There is no overall champion, no list of prime destinations, no roster of places to avoid.

My chief aim was a simple one. I set out to collect a broad array of data for 551 important markets that are frequently (and unfairly) overlooked. Hence the 75 sets of statistics that were described in the previous chapter.

But that's not to say that I completely resisted the urge to rate. Each area's profile page offers 10 exclusive grades on a five-star scale. These are independent ratings, not components of a broad formula. They are designed to stand alone, to illuminate different aspects of life in a given micro.

These are the 10 fields in alphabetical order:

- Children
- Diversity/Equality
- Education
- Employment
- Growth Potential
- Housing
- Income
- Seniors
- Stability
- Transportation

These 10 ratings offer a quick synopsis of any micropolitan area's strengths and weaknesses. You'll need to do a considerable amount of study, of course, if you're thinking about relocating to a specific micro or starting a business there. But the five-star ratings in this book are a decent place to start.

Take a look, for instance, at one of the first areas profiled in Chapter 4 — Auburn, New York. Auburn earns five stars for Income and four stars for Children, Education, and Employment, clearly stamping it as a good place to make a living and raise kids. But its two-star rating for Seniors and lone star for Growth Potential should give pause to older residents and entrepreneurs. You can draw similar conclusions about every area profiled in this book.

So how were the ratings determined? Let me walk you through the four-step procedure:

1. Statistics were gathered for the five components of each rating. The factors for Children, as noted in Chapter 2, are the percentages who live

with two parents, attend high school and college, speak English well, live below the poverty level, and go without health insurance.

2. Each stat for each area was measured against the correponding averages for all micros in the same categories. Superior performances received positive scores (known as z-scores), while inferior showings drew negative z-scores. Auburn's share of children who live with two parents is 62.1 percent, slightly worse than the micropolitan average of 64.0 percent (receiving a z-score of minus-0.203). But Auburn fares much better in the other four categories, especially with its poverty rate for children of 17.7 percent, a clear improvement upon the micropolitan benchmark of 25.0 percent (earning a z-score of plus-0.810).

3. The five z-scores in each field were averaged for each micro, yielding top-to-bottom national rankings. Auburn emerged with an average score of plus-0.370 for Children, good for 159th place in that field.

4. The standings were divided into five equal groups, with stars awarded accordingly. The highest quintile (first through 110th place) earned the highest rating of five stars. The scale descends step by step to four stars (111th through 220th), three stars (221st to 330th), two stars (331st to 440th), and one star (441st to 551st). Auburn's rank of 159th earns a four-star rating for Children.

The remainder of this chapter is precisely 10 pages long, one page for each field. You'll find a summary of the qualities worthy of a five-star rating, a rundown of the five relevant categories, and a list of all five-star micros (ranked in order from first place to 110th). This final feature is the largest on each page. Consider it a fitting celebration of America's outstanding micropolitan areas.

Children

Recipients of five-star ratings: Micropolitan areas where children are more likely to have stable family lives, extended educational opportunities, and a financial safety net.

Categories: (1) Living with two parents. (2) Older teens in school. (3) Speak English very well. (4) Poverty rate for children. (5) No health insurance. See pages 66-70 for details on each category.

Five-Star Micros

1. Pella, IA
2. Sheridan, WY
3. Los Alamos, NM
4. Alexandria, MN
5. Steamboat Springs, CO
6. Wapakoneta, OH
7. Vermillion, SD
8. Brookings, SD
9. Kearney, NE
10. Laramie, WY
11. Pierre, SD
12. Moscow, ID
13. Celina, OH
14. Bozeman, MT
15. Torrington, CT
16. Wahpeton, ND-MN
17. Stevens Point, WI
18. Pullman, WA
19. Carroll, IA
20. Macomb, IL
21. New Ulm, MN
22. Boone, IA
23. Newton, IA
24. Marquette, MI
25. Sidney, OH
26. Watertown, SD
27. Boone, NC
28. Rexburg, ID
29. Rochelle, IL
30. Menomonie, WI
31. Winona, MN
32. Aberdeen, SD
33. Owatonna, MN
34. Iron Mountain, MI-WI
35. Watertown-Fort Atkinson, WI
36. Beatrice, NE
37. McPherson, KS
38. Hastings, NE
39. Barre, VT
40. Oskaloosa, IA
41. Spencer, IA
42. Concord, NH
43. Ellensburg, WA
44. Spirit Lake, IA
45. Martin, TN
46. North Platte, NE
47. Richmond-Berea, KY
48. Hays, KS
49. Warrensburg, MO
50. Effingham, IL
51. Dixon, IL
52. Fergus Falls, MN
53. Price, UT
54. Keene, NH
55. Houghton, MI
56. Mason City, IA
57. Holland, MI
58. St. Marys, PA
59. Manitowoc, WI
60. Beaver Dam, WI
61. Van Wert, OH
62. Findlay, OH
63. Huntingdon, PA
64. Hutchinson, KS
65. Greenfield Town, MA
66. Faribault-Northfield, MN
67. Oneonta, NY
68. Plattsburgh, NY
69. Ottawa, KS
70. Pittsburg, KS
71. Merrill, WI
72. Yankton, SD
73. Clinton, IA
74. Ionia, MI
75. Wisconsin Rapids-Marshfield, WI
76. Vineyard Haven, MA
77. Hutchinson, MN
78. Whitewater-Elkhorn, WI
79. Jacksonville, IL
80. Claremont-Lebanon, NH-VT
81. Laconia, NH
82. Fairmont, MN
83. Greenville, OH
84. Jamestown, ND
85. Willmar, MN
86. Cortland, NY
87. Quincy, IL-MO
88. Mitchell, SD
89. Vincennes, IN
90. Marietta, OH
91. Rock Springs, WY
92. Gillette, WY
93. Charleston-Mattoon, IL
94. Summit Park, UT
95. Vernal, UT
96. Helena, MT
97. Durango, CO
98. Red Wing, MN
99. Traverse City, MI
100. Minot, ND
101. Platteville, WI
102. Searcy, AR
103. Dickinson, ND
104. Somerset, PA
105. Adrian, MI
106. Muscatine, IA
107. Rutland, VT
108. Oxford, MS
109. Escanaba, MI
110. Mayfield, KY

Diversity/Equality

Recipients of five-star ratings: Micropolitan areas with diverse mixtures of racial groups and geographic origins, and with relatively small financial disparities between the affluent and everybody else and between men and women.

Categories: (1) Racial diversity index. (2) Geographic diversity index. (3) Top 20% share of income. (4) Gender gap in earnings. (5) White-collar gender gap. See pages 71-75 for details on each category.

Five-Star Micros

1. Kapaa, HI
2. Liberal, KS
3. Fort Leonard Wood, MO
4. Ketchikan, AK
5. Juneau, AK
6. Arcadia, FL
7. Susanville, CA
8. Junction City, KS
9. Grants, NM
10. Alamogordo, NM
11. Cañon City, CO
12. Breckenridge, CO
13. Sanford, NC
14. Guymon, OK
15. Clewiston, FL
16. Hilo, HI
17. Shelton, WA
18. Payson, AZ
19. Edwards, CO
20. Miami, OK
21. Barre, VT
22. Mountain Home, ID
23. Clearlake, CA
24. Pahrump, NV
25. Tahlequah, OK
26. Helena, MT
27. Fallon, NV
28. Durango, CO
29. Oak Harbor, WA
30. Oxford, NC
31. Fort Morgan, CO
32. Hope, AR
33. Palatka, FL
34. Brevard, NC
35. Fort Polk South, LA
36. Henderson, NC
37. Silver City, NM

38. Martinsville, VA
39. Frankfort, KY
40. Taos, NM
41. Ada, OK
42. St. Marys, GA
43. Kill Devil Hills, NC
44. Riverton, WY
45. Ozark, AL
46. Gardnerville Ranchos, NV
47. Mount Pleasant, TX
48. Dodge City, KS
49. Lake City, FL
50. Newberry, SC
51. Fernley, NV
52. Durant, OK
53. Bonham, TX
54. Safford, AZ
55. Montrose, CO
56. Cambridge, MD
57. Rolla, MO
58. Warrensburg, MO
59. Hermiston-Pendleton, OR
60. Rockingham, NC
61. Eufaula, AL-GA
62. Huntsville, TX
63. Okeechobee, FL
64. Crescent City, CA
65. Aberdeen, WA
66. Moultrie, GA
67. Americus, GA
68. Clovis, NM
69. Port Angeles, WA
70. Elizabeth City, NC
71. Dunn, NC
72. Newport, OR
73. Winnemucca, NV

74. Bartlesville, OK
75. Marshalltown, IA
76. Los Alamos, NM
77. Altus, OK
78. Toccoa, GA
79. Crossville, TN
80. Plainview, TX
81. Klamath Falls, OR
82. Muskogee, OK
83. Roswell, NM
84. Centralia, WA
85. Lumberton, NC
86. Key West, FL
87. Concord, NH
88. Mountain Home, AR
89. Jackson, WY-ID
90. Ukiah, CA
91. Albemarle, NC
92. Gillette, WY
93. Garden City, KS
94. Sault Ste. Marie, MI
95. Moscow, ID
96. Marion, NC
97. Cullowhee, NC
98. Washington, NC
99. Gallup, NM
100. Wilson, NC
101. Brenham, TX
102. Madison, IN
103. Hood River, OR
104. Malone, NY
105. Worthington, MN
106. Emporia, KS
107. Eureka-Arcata-Fortuna, CA
108. Orangeburg, SC
109. Berlin, NH-VT
110. Fredericksburg, TX

Education

Recipients of five-star ratings: Micropolitan areas where substantial percentages of adults have picked up high school diplomas and college degrees.
Categories: (1) Eighth grade or less. (2) High school diplomas. (3) Attended college. (4) Bachelor's degrees. (5) Advanced degrees. See pages 76–80 for details on each category.

Five-Star Micros

1. Laramie, WY
2. Bozeman, MT
3. Moscow, ID
4. Los Alamos, NM
5. Pullman, WA
6. Vermillion, SD
7. Steamboat Springs, CO
8. Durango, CO
9. Summit Park, UT
10. Barre, VT
11. Oxford, MS
12. Brookings, SD
13. Juneau, AK
14. Helena, MT
15. Greenfield Town, MA
16. Jackson, WY-ID
17. Breckenridge, CO
18. Boone, NC
19. Macomb, IL
20. Stillwater, OK
21. Vineyard Haven, MA
22. Fairfield, IA
23. Starkville, MS
24. Concord, NH
25. Torrington, CT
26. Claremont-Lebanon, NH-VT
27. Hays, KS
28. Truckee-Grass Valley, CA
29. Houghton, MI
30. Spirit Lake, IA
31. Athens, OH
32. Kearney, NE
33. Sheridan, WY
34. Keene, NH
35. Heber, UT
36. Spearfish, SD
37. Oak Harbor, WA
38. Mitchell, SD
39. Edwards, CO
40. Marquette, MI
41. Alexandria, MN
42. Ruston, LA
43. Stevens Point, WI
44. Pinehurst-Southern Pines, NC
45. Traverse City, MI
46. Pierre, SD
47. Mount Pleasant, MI
48. Winona, MN
49. Rexburg, ID
50. Hudson, NY
51. Oneonta, NY
52. Bennington, VT
53. Ellensburg, WA
54. Pittsburg, KS
55. Aberdeen, SD
56. Rutland, VT
57. Cedar City, UT
58. Menomonie, WI
59. Kirksville, MO
60. Kalispell, MT
61. Gardnerville Ranchos, NV
62. Laconia, NH
63. Warrensburg, MO
64. Findlay, OH
65. Easton, MD
66. Minot, ND
67. Statesboro, GA
68. Key West, FL
69. Glenwood Springs, CO
70. Murray, KY
71. Bemidji, MN
72. Rolla, MO
73. Kapaa, HI
74. Pella, IA
75. Cullowhee, NC
76. McPherson, KS
77. Hilo, HI
78. Faribault-Northfield, MN
79. Dickinson, ND
80. Owatonna, MN
81. Cortland, NY
82. Fergus Falls, MN
83. Boone, IA
84. Augusta-Waterville, ME
85. New Ulm, MN
86. Astoria, OR
87. Morehead City, NC
88. Red Wing, MN
89. Marshall, MN
90. Grand Rapids, MN
91. Fort Leonard Wood, MO
92. Eureka-Arcata-Fortuna, CA
93. Effingham, IL
94. Brevard, NC
95. Bartlesville, OK
96. Mason City, IA
97. Brainerd, MN
98. Ada, OK
99. Silver City, NM
100. Port Clinton, OH
101. Hastings, NE
102. La Grande, OR
103. Yankton, SD
104. Whitewater-Elkhorn, WI
105. Maryville, MO
106. Charleston-Mattoon, IL
107. Arkadelphia, AR
108. Taos, NM
109. Butte-Silver Bow, MT
110. Williston, ND

Employment

Recipients of five-star ratings: Micropolitan areas where unemployment is low, entrepreneurial spirit is high, and a substantial number of good-paying jobs are available.

Categories: (1) Average jobless rate. (2) Self-employed workers. (3) Management/financial jobs. (4) Computer/engineering jobs. (5) Health care jobs. See pages 81-85 for details on each category.

Five-Star Micros

1. Summit Park, UT
2. Sheridan, WY
3. Helena, MT
4. Yankton, SD
5. Truckee-Grass Valley, CA
6. Spirit Lake, IA
7. Bozeman, MT
8. Durango, CO
9. Wahpeton, ND-MN
10. Claremont-Lebanon, NH-VT
11. Heber, UT
12. Beatrice, NE
13. Barre, VT
14. Vineyard Haven, MA
15. Fairmont, MN
16. Aberdeen, SD
17. Fredericksburg, TX
18. Juneau, AK
19. Laconia, NH
20. Concord, NH
21. Williston, ND
22. Pierre, SD
23. Hood River, OR
24. Easton, MD
25. Fergus Falls, MN
26. Torrington, CT
27. Los Alamos, NM
28. Carroll, IA
29. Red Wing, MN
30. Bennington, VT
31. Kalispell, MT
32. Mitchell, SD
33. McPherson, KS
34. Marshall, MN
35. Edwards, CO
36. Alexandria, MN
37. Key West, FL
38. Fairfield, IA
39. Bartlesville, OK
40. Pinehurst-Southern Pines, NC
41. Butte-Silver Bow, MT
42. Steamboat Springs, CO
43. New Ulm, MN
44. Morehead City, NC
45. Hailey, ID
46. Norfolk, NE
47. Greenfield Town, MA
48. Traverse City, MI
49. Jackson, WY-ID
50. Breckenridge, CO
51. Pella, IA
52. Brookings, SD
53. Willmar, MN
54. Brownwood, TX
55. Hudson, NY
56. Jamestown, ND
57. Keene, NH
58. Laramie, WY
59. Spearfish, SD
60. Mason City, IA
61. Minot, ND
62. Oneonta, NY
63. Boone, IA
64. Brainerd, MN
65. Lewisburg, PA
66. Fairmont, WV
67. Spencer, IA
68. Hastings, NE
69. Kearney, NE
70. Glenwood Springs, CO
71. Salina, KS
72. Hutchinson, MN
73. Faribault-Northfield, MN
74. Kill Devil Hills, NC
75. Hays, KS
76. Oak Harbor, WA
77. Ruidoso, NM
78. Platteville, WI
79. Winona, MN
80. Clarksburg, WV
81. Moscow, ID
82. Rutland, VT
83. Dickinson, ND
84. Silver City, NM
85. Pullman, WA
86. Wisconsin Rapids-Marshfield, WI
87. Brookings, OR
88. Augusta-Waterville, ME
89. Owatonna, MN
90. Wooster, OH
91. Huron, SD
92. Menomonie, WI
93. Houghton, MI
94. Effingham, IL
95. Austin, MN
96. Riverton, WY
97. Oxford, NC
98. Kerrville, TX
99. Mountain Home, AR
100. Berlin, NH-VT
101. Fort Dodge, IA
102. Paducah, KY-IL
103. Meadville, PA
104. Scottsbluff, NE
105. Alpena, MI
106. Sayre, PA
107. Port Clinton, OH
108. Sandpoint, ID
109. Rexburg, ID
110. Douglas, GA

Growth Potential

Recipients of five-star ratings: Micropolitan areas where a solid core of young people, an influx of newcomers, and a strong construction sector suggest the possibility of future growth. (This is a rating of *potential*. A few areas with five-star ratings are actually projected to lose population by 2030.) **Categories:** (1) Children per senior. (2) Median age. (3) Moved from different state. (4) Homes built since 2000. (5) Construction jobs. See pages 86-90 for details on each category.

Five-Star Micros

1. Rexburg, ID
2. Williston, ND
3. Junction City, KS
4. Fort Leonard Wood, MO
5. Gillette, WY
6. Rio Grande City, TX
7. Dunn, NC
8. Cedar City, UT
9. Heber, UT
10. Jackson, WY-ID
11. Bozeman, MT
12. Edwards, CO
13. Fort Polk South, LA
14. St. Marys, GA
15. Vernal, UT
16. Oxford, MS
17. Rock Springs, WY
18. Glenwood Springs, CO
19. Mountain Home, ID
20. Minot, ND
21. Clewiston, FL
22. Eagle Pass, TX
23. Laramie, WY
24. Stillwater, OK
25. Zapata, TX
26. Clovis, NM
27. Warrensburg, MO
28. Starkville, MS
29. Brookings, SD
30. Breckenridge, CO
31. Summit Park, UT
32. Statesboro, GA
33. Dickinson, ND
34. Steamboat Springs, CO
35. Evanston, WY
36. Elko, NV
37. Alamogordo, NM
38. Vermillion, SD
39. Liberal, KS
40. Safford, AZ
41. Picayune, MS
42. Hobbs, NM
43. Durango, CO
44. Moscow, ID
45. DeRidder, LA
46. Jesup, GA
47. Wauchula, FL
48. Blackfoot, ID
49. Fernley, NV
50. Calhoun, GA
51. Show Low, AZ
52. Washington, IN
53. Nacogdoches, TX
54. Hailey, ID
55. Portales, NM
56. Jefferson, GA
57. Montrose, CO
58. Uvalde, TX
59. Andrews, TX
60. Ruston, LA
61. Kalispell, MT
62. Gallup, NM
63. Spearfish, SD
64. Del Rio, TX
65. Shelbyville, TN
66. Maryville, MO
67. Garden City, KS
68. Ellensburg, WA
69. Port Lavaca, TX
70. Cullowhee, NC
71. Bemidji, MN
72. Mount Pleasant, TX
73. Pullman, WA
74. Ketchikan, AK
75. Hereford, TX
76. Boone, NC
77. Sheridan, WY
78. Moses Lake, WA
79. Borger, TX
80. Kingsville, TX
81. Weatherford, OK
82. Durant, OK
83. Searcy, AR
84. Altus, OK
85. Ozark, AL
86. Twin Falls, ID
87. Elk City, OK
88. Cedartown, GA
89. Lumberton, NC
90. Dumas, TX
91. Fallon, NV
92. Mitchell, SD
93. Guymon, OK
94. Juneau, AK
95. Craig, CO
96. Stephenville, TX
97. Columbus, MS
98. Dodge City, KS
99. Enterprise, AL
100. Decatur, IN
101. Rolla, MO
102. Winnemucca, NV
103. Nogales, AZ
104. Emporia, KS
105. Sevierville, TN
106. Vidalia, GA
107. Murray, KY
108. Opelousas, LA
109. Mount Pleasant, MI
110. Faribault-Northfield, MN

Housing

Recipients of five-star ratings: Micropolitan areas where vacant houses are rare, home ownership is common, and there is a diverse mix of affordable and sizable houses.

Categories: (1) Home vacancy rate. (2) Home ownership rate. (3) Housing diversity index. (4) 4 or more bedrooms. (5) Affordability/income ratio. See pages 91-95 for details on each category.

Five-Star Micros

1. Hutchinson, MN
2. Holland, MI
3. Owatonna, MN
4. Columbus, NE
5. McPherson, KS
6. Blackfoot, ID
7. Willmar, MN
8. Fergus Falls, MN
9. Iron Mountain, MI-WI
10. Alexandria, MN
11. Celina, OH
12. Wahpeton, ND-MN
13. Red Wing, MN
14. Carroll, IA
15. Watertown, SD
16. Faribault-Northfield, MN
17. Port Clinton, OH
18. New Ulm, MN
19. Adrian, MI
20. Decatur, IN
21. Los Alamos, NM
22. Burley, ID
23. Pella, IA
24. Worthington, MN
25. Effingham, IL
26. Mitchell, SD
27. Wisconsin Rapids-Marshfield, WI
28. Garden City, KS
29. Grand Rapids, MN
30. Yankton, SD
31. Warsaw, IN
32. Aberdeen, SD
33. Rochelle, IL
34. Plymouth, IN
35. Hillsdale, MI
36. Sturgis, MI
37. Wooster, OH

38. Norfolk, NE
39. Shawano, WI
40. Mayfield, KY
41. Ionia, MI
42. Spirit Lake, IA
43. Cadillac, MI
44. Kearney, NE
45. Brainerd, MN
46. Selinsgrove, PA
47. Angola, IN
48. Wapakoneta, OH
49. Somerset, PA
50. Marshall, MN
51. Owosso, MI
52. Vineyard Haven, MA
53. Alpena, MI
54. Merrill, WI
55. Washington, IN
56. Lewisburg, PA
57. Jasper, IN
58. Alma, MI
59. St. Marys, PA
60. Hays, KS
61. Coldwater, MI
62. Big Rapids, MI
63. Sterling, IL
64. Pierre, SD
65. Hastings, NE
66. Torrington, CT
67. Jamestown, ND
68. Van Wert, OH
69. Traverse City, MI
70. Ludington, MI
71. Helena, MT
72. Kendallville, IN
73. Salina, KS
74. Mount Vernon, IL

75. Platteville, WI
76. Huntingdon, PA
77. Marinette, WI-MI
78. Albert Lea, MN
79. Storm Lake, IA
80. Sidney, OH
81. Dickinson, ND
82. Lexington, NE
83. Ashland, OH
84. Fairmont, MN
85. Bennington, VT
86. Warren, PA
87. Meadville, PA
88. Malvern, AR
89. Fremont, NE
90. Price, UT
91. Manitowoc, WI
92. Bartlesville, OK
93. Defiance, OH
94. Othello, WA
95. Clinton, IA
96. Spencer, IA
97. Austin, MN
98. Whitewater-Elkhorn, WI
99. Findlay, OH
100. Marietta, OH
101. Menomonie, WI
102. Dodge City, KS
103. Auburn, IN
104. Watertown-Fort Atkinson, WI
105. Plattsburgh, NY
106. Elkins, WV
107. Laconia, NH
108. Stevens Point, WI
109. DeRidder, LA
110. Lawrenceburg, TN

Income

Recipients of five-star ratings: Micropolitan areas where income levels are strong and poverty is relatively rare.
Categories: (1) Poverty rate. (2) Median household income. (3) Interest/dividends. (4) Public assistance. (5) Median fulltime earnings. See pages 96-100 for details on each category.

Five-Star Micros

1. Los Alamos, NM
2. Juneau, AK
3. Summit Park, UT
4. Torrington, CT
5. Dickinson, ND
6. Jackson, WY-ID
7. Williston, ND
8. Vineyard Haven, MA
9. Vernal, UT
10. Gillette, WY
11. Edwards, CO
12. Concord, NH
13. Rock Springs, WY
14. Breckenridge, CO
15. Heber, UT
16. Ketchikan, AK
17. Oak Harbor, WA
18. Truckee-Grass Valley, CA
19. Elko, NV
20. Steamboat Springs, CO
21. Gardnerville Ranchos, NV
22. Durango, CO
23. Easton, MD
24. McPherson, KS
25. Spirit Lake, IA
26. Sheridan, WY
27. Red Wing, MN
28. Barre, VT
29. Hudson, NY
30. Minot, ND
31. Kapaa, HI
32. Hutchinson, MN
33. Faribault-Northfield, MN
34. Glenwood Springs, CO
35. Fredericksburg, TX
36. Andrews, TX

37. Bozeman, MT
38. Winnemucca, NV
39. New Ulm, MN
40. Laconia, NH
41. Owatonna, MN
42. Keene, NH
43. Sonora, CA
44. Helena, MT
45. Alexandria, MN
46. Wahpeton, ND-MN
47. Columbus, NE
48. Port Clinton, OH
49. Rochelle, IL
50. Greenfield Town, MA
51. Claremont-Lebanon, NH-VT
52. Key West, FL
53. Pierre, SD
54. Riverton, WY
55. Fergus Falls, MN
56. Watertown-Fort Atkinson, WI
57. Wapakoneta, OH
58. Snyder, TX
59. Pella, IA
60. Boone, IA
61. Beaver Dam, WI
62. Aberdeen, SD
63. Celina, OH
64. Evanston, WY
65. Carroll, IA
66. Jasper, IN
67. Manitowoc, WI
68. Pontiac, IL
69. Effingham, IL
70. Kill Devil Hills, NC
71. Sidney, OH
72. Newton, IA
73. Jamestown, ND

74. Fairmont, MN
75. Kearney, NE
76. Whitewater-Elkhorn, WI
77. Dixon, IL
78. Beatrice, NE
79. Kalispell, MT
80. Muscatine, IA
81. Carlsbad-Artesia, NM
82. Warsaw, IN
83. Spencer, IA
84. Pinehurst-Southern Pines, NC
85. Woodward, OK
86. Sayre, PA
87. Findlay, OH
88. Lewisburg, PA
89. St. Marys, PA
90. Susanville, CA
91. Marshall, MN
92. Holland, MI
93. Traverse City, MI
94. Winona, MN
95. Fremont, NE
96. Merrill, WI
97. Hastings, NE
98. Stevens Point, WI
99. Wisconsin Rapids-Marshfield, WI
100. Gainesville, TX
101. Auburn, NY
102. Ottawa-Peru, IL
103. Albert Lea, MN
104. Baraboo, WI
105. Willmar, MN
106. Wooster, OH
107. Hailey, ID
108. Mitchell, SD
109. Selinsgrove, PA
110. Norfolk, NE

Seniors

Recipients of five-star ratings: Micropolitan areas where senior citizens are most likely to be self-sufficient and active in their families and communities.

Categories: (1) Seniors living alone. (2) Poverty rate for seniors. (3) Median income for seniors. (4) Seniors who work. (5) Home ownership by seniors. See pages 101–105 for details on each category.

Five-Star Micros

1. Heber, UT
2. Summit Park, UT
3. Edwards, CO
4. Breckenridge, CO
5. Jackson, WY-ID
6. Elko, NV
7. Durango, CO
8. Vineyard Haven, MA
9. Juneau, AK
10. Brevard, NC
11. Winnemucca, NV
12. Los Alamos, NM
13. Gardnerville Ranchos, NV
14. Vermillion, SD
15. Weatherford, OK
16. Kill Devil Hills, NC
17. Oak Harbor, WA
18. Kapaa, HI
19. Guymon, OK
20. Spirit Lake, IA
21. Cedar City, UT
22. Glenwood Springs, CO
23. Gillette, WY
24. Williston, ND
25. Vernal, UT
26. Rexburg, ID
27. Port Lavaca, TX
28. Warrensburg, MO
29. Angola, IN
30. Hailey, ID
31. Easton, MD
32. Blackfoot, ID
33. Boone, NC
34. Laconia, NH
35. Gainesville, TX
36. Bozeman, MT
37. Fernley, NV

38. Muscatine, IA
39. Bardstown, KY
40. Port Clinton, OH
41. Truckee-Grass Valley, CA
42. Dumas, TX
43. Shelton, WA
44. Morehead City, NC
45. Hilo, HI
46. Traverse City, MI
47. Sevierville, TN
48. Urbana, OH
49. Steamboat Springs, CO
50. McPherson, KS
51. Claremont-Lebanon, NH-VT
52. Laramie, WY
53. Shelbyville, TN
54. Hudson, NY
55. Ruidoso, NM
56. Torrington, CT
57. Georgetown, SC
58. Key West, FL
59. Fort Leonard Wood, MO
60. Sterling, CO
61. Kearney, NE
62. Snyder, TX
63. Ketchikan, AK
64. Evanston, WY
65. Warsaw, IN
66. Holland, MI
67. Brookings, SD
68. Helena, MT
69. Pinehurst-Southern Pines, NC
70. Fredericksburg, TX
71. Lincoln, IL
72. Crossville, TN

73. Rock Springs, WY
74. Greensburg, IN
75. Sulphur Springs, TX
76. Andrews, TX
77. Toccoa, GA
78. Ellensburg, WA
79. Seneca, SC
80. Brenham, TX
81. Owosso, MI
82. Athens, TX
83. Cadillac, MI
84. Kerrville, TX
85. Barre, VT
86. Boone, IA
87. St. Marys, GA
88. Newton, IA
89. Willmar, MN
90. Worthington, MN
91. Branson, MO
92. Ashland, OH
93. Pontiac, IL
94. Cullowhee, NC
95. Concord, NH
96. Malvern, AR
97. Craig, CO
98. Riverton, WY
99. Sonora, CA
100. Sanford, NC
101. Freeport, IL
102. Wooster, OH
103. Frankfort, IN
104. Defiance, OH
105. Brainerd, MN
106. Bedford, IN
107. Elizabeth City, NC
108. Sidney, OH
109. Starkville, MS
110. Dodge City, KS

Stability

Recipients of five-star ratings: Micropolitan areas where most residents have strong local roots, especially married couples and young adults of child-rearing age.

Categories: (1) 25-39 age group. (2) Born in state of residence. (3) Same house as 1 year ago. (4) Live and work in county. (5) Married-couple households. See pages 106-110 for details on each category.

Five-Star Micros

1. Vernal, UT
2. Snyder, TX
3. Effingham, IL
4. Andrews, TX
5. Dumas, TX
6. Palestine, TX
7. Brownwood, TX
8. Zapata, TX
9. Lamesa, TX
10. Elk City, OK
11. Hereford, TX
12. Jasper, IN
13. Del Rio, TX
14. Woodward, OK
15. Somerset, PA
16. Willmar, MN
17. Logan, WV
18. Hobbs, NM
19. Elkins, WV
20. Carroll, IA
21. Douglas, GA
22. Dickinson, ND
23. Manitowoc, WI
24. Washington, IN
25. St. Marys, PA
26. Decatur, IN
27. Dodge City, KS
28. Pecos, TX
29. Seymour, IN
30. Mount Pleasant, TX
31. Kapaa, HI
32. Marshall, MN
33. Muscatine, IA
34. Blackfoot, ID
35. Rio Grande City, TX
36. Columbus, NE
37. New Philadelphia-Dover, OH

38. Quincy, IL-MO
39. North Wilkesboro, NC
40. Sidney, OH
41. Gillette, WY
42. Alexandria, MN
43. Garden City, KS
44. Warsaw, IN
45. Edwards, CO
46. Alice, TX
47. Celina, OH
48. North Platte, NE
49. Sault Ste. Marie, MI
50. Raymondville, TX
51. Cedar City, UT
52. Cullman, AL
53. Coshocton, OH
54. Gallup, NM
55. New Ulm, MN
56. Price, UT
57. Carlsbad-Artesia, NM
58. Baraboo, WI
59. Fort Polk South, LA
60. Beeville, TX
61. Cornelia, GA
62. Selinsgrove, PA
63. Bardstown, KY
64. DuBois, PA
65. El Campo, TX
66. El Dorado, AR
67. Rock Springs, WY
68. Othello, WA
69. Central City, KY
70. Huntingdon, PA
71. Safford, AZ
72. Laurel, MS
73. Chillicothe, OH
74. Somerset, KY

75. Vineyard Haven, MA
76. Scottsboro, AL
77. Pampa, TX
78. Batesville, AR
79. Vicksburg, MS
80. Grand Rapids, MN
81. Port Lavaca, TX
82. Wisconsin Rapids-Marshfield, WI
83. Heber, UT
84. Hutchinson, MN
85. Bay City, TX
86. Alpena, MI
87. Jamestown, ND
88. Warren, PA
89. Susanville, CA
90. Pierre, SD
91. Madisonville, KY
92. Williston, ND
93. Big Spring, TX
94. Ardmore, OK
95. Watertown, SD
96. Clarksburg, WV
97. Wooster, OH
98. Eagle Pass, TX
99. Poplar Bluff, MO
100. Brookhaven, MS
101. Mount Vernon, IL
102. Findlay, OH
103. Traverse City, MI
104. Sayre, PA
105. Cadillac, MI
106. McPherson, KS
107. Moses Lake, WA
108. Marshalltown, IA
109. Uvalde, TX
110. Borger, TX

Transportation

Recipients of five-star ratings: Micropolitan areas where most workers have short commutes, and where several modes of transportation are readily available.

Categories: (1) Bicycle or walk to work. (2) Carpool to work. (3) Public transit to work. (4) Commute <15 minutes. (5) Commute >45 minutes. See pages 111-115 for details on each category.

Five-Star Micros

1. Ketchikan, AK
2. Pullman, WA
3. Juneau, AK
4. Laramie, WY
5. Storm Lake, IA
6. Breckenridge, CO
7. Jackson, WY-ID
8. Houghton, MI
9. Steamboat Springs, CO
10. Spearfish, SD
11. Liberal, KS
12. Brookings, SD
13. Rexburg, ID
14. La Grande, OR
15. Huron, SD
16. Crescent City, CA
17. Vermillion, SD
18. Marshall, MN
19. Vineyard Haven, MA
20. Kingsville, TX
21. Pierre, SD
22. Eureka-Arcata-Fortuna, CA
23. Key West, FL
24. Cedar City, UT
25. Macomb, IL
26. Brookings, OR
27. Moscow, ID
28. Newport, OR
29. Lexington, NE
30. Garden City, KS
31. Astoria, OR
32. Vernon, TX
33. Worthington, MN
34. The Dalles, OR
35. Hood River, OR
36. Los Alamos, NM
37. Maryville, MO
38. Sterling, CO
39. Craig, CO
40. Stillwater, OK
41. Dodge City, KS
42. Fort Morgan, CO
43. Evanston, WY
44. Sault Ste. Marie, MI
45. Zapata, TX
46. Portales, NM
47. Emporia, KS
48. Yankton, SD
49. Bozeman, MT
50. Kearney, NE
51. Winona, MN
52. Price, UT
53. Rio Grande City, TX
54. Durango, CO
55. New Ulm, MN
56. Mount Pleasant, MI
57. Guymon, OK
58. Dumas, TX
59. Boone, NC
60. Columbus, NE
61. Hereford, TX
62. Jamestown, ND
63. Ukiah, CA
64. Elko, NV
65. Marshalltown, IA
66. Port Angeles, WA
67. Rock Springs, WY
68. Moses Lake, WA
69. Riverton, WY
70. Austin, MN
71. Oneonta, NY
72. Mitchell, SD
73. Hays, KS
74. Altus, OK
75. Arcadia, FL
76. Marshall, MO
77. Del Rio, TX
78. Spencer, IA
79. Kirksville, MO
80. Alamogordo, NM
81. Charleston-Mattoon, IL
82. Lamesa, TX
83. Levelland, TX
84. Coos Bay, OR
85. Aberdeen, SD
86. Glenwood Springs, CO
87. Othello, WA
88. Sheridan, WY
89. McPherson, KS
90. Bemidji, MN
91. Ellensburg, WA
92. Helena, MT
93. Fairfield, IA
94. Deming, NM
95. Helena-West Helena, AR
96. Marquette, MI
97. Sweetwater, TX
98. Watertown, SD
99. Cortland, NY
100. Snyder, TX
101. Edwards, CO
102. Starkville, MS
103. Ruidoso, NM
104. Carroll, IA
105. Scottsbluff, NE
106. Moultrie, GA
107. Fredericksburg, TX
108. Big Spring, TX
109. Ontario, OR-ID
110. Show Low, AZ

4

EAST

★★★★★

MICROPOLITAN
AMERICA

Amsterdam, NY
(Montgomery County, NY)

POPULATION

2010 census	50,219 (210)
2015 estimate	49,642 (213)
2010-2015 change	-1.1% (335)
2020 projection	49,646 (216)
2030 projection	49,658 (221)

RACE

Whites	83.6% (285)
Blacks	1.5% (329)
Hispanics	12.3% (124)
Asians	0.7% (241)
Native Americans	0.1% (402)

AGE

0-17 years old	22.8% (277)
18-24 years old	8.3% (362)
25-39 years old	17.5% (258)
40-54 years old	20.0% (233)
55-64 years old	14.0% (182)
65+ years old	17.4% (165)

PRIVATE SECTOR

Businesses	1,139 (220)
Employees	15,759 (197)
Total wages	$579,846,946 (197)
Average weekly wages	$708 (237)

HOUSEHOLD INCOME LADDER

95th percentile	$145,820 (217)
80th percentile	$86,172 (229)
60th percentile	$55,216 (243)
40th percentile	$34,329 (276)
20th percentile	$17,706 (331)

CHILDREN ★ **(456)**

Living with two parents	59.1% (425)
Older teens in school	77.3% (466)
Speak English very well	96.7% (428)
Poverty rate for children	32.4% (455)
No health insurance	8.4% (371)

DIVERSITY/EQUALITY ★★★ **(235)**

Racial diversity index	28.5% (265)
Geographic diversity index	32.0% (463)
Top 20% share of income	48.3% (312)
Gender gap in earnings	25.2% (90)
White-collar gender gap	16.1% (167)

EDUCATION ★★★ **(288)**

Eighth grade or less	3.5% (284)
High school diplomas	86.5% (327)
Attended college	53.0% (262)
Bachelor's degrees	17.3% (309)
Advanced degrees	6.1% (250)

EMPLOYMENT ★★★ **(312)**

Average jobless rate	8.9% (351)
Self-employed workers	7.0% (428)
Management/financial jobs	12.4% (126)
Computer/engineering jobs	2.6% (288)
Health care jobs	5.6% (240)

GROWTH POTENTIAL ★★ **(420)**

Children per senior	1.32 (334)
Median age	41.0 (357)
Moved from different state	1.4% (425)
Homes built since 2000	5.5% (534)
Construction jobs	7.5% (122)

HOUSING ★ **(522)**

Home vacancy rate	13.7% (512)
Home ownership rate	67.1% (382)
Housing diversity index	73.4% (550)
4 or more bedrooms	18.0% (202)
Affordability/income ratio	$2,322 (175)

INCOME ★★★ **(286)**

Poverty rate	20.6% (392)
Median household income	$43,764 (270)
Interest/dividends	21.3% (206)
Public assistance	20.2% (435)
Median fulltime earnings	$40,384 (127)

SENIORS ★ **(508)**

Seniors living alone	32.1% (514)
Poverty rate for seniors	12.0% (413)
Median income for seniors	$29,350 (424)
Seniors who work	17.1% (339)
Home ownership by seniors	76.7% (497)

STABILITY ★ **(462)**

25-39 age group	17.5% (258)
Born in state of residence	82.1% (81)
Same house as 1 year ago	86.5% (219)
Live and work in county	56.5% (514)
Married-couple households	43.7% (485)

TRANSPORTATION ★★ **(339)**

Bicycle or walk to work	4.1% (147)
Carpool to work	10.7% (260)
Public transit to work	1.4% (46)
Commute <15 minutes	36.6% (407)
Commute >45 minutes	17.0% (482)

See pages 37-130 for explanations of statistics, stars, and ranks.

Auburn, NY
(Cayuga County, NY)

POPULATION

2010 census	80,026 (68)
2015 estimate	78,288 (73)
2010-2015 change	-2.2% (427)
2020 projection	76,952 (79)
2030 projection	74,329 (92)

RACE

Whites	90.7% (167)
Blacks	4.1% (185)
Hispanics	2.7% (361)
Asians	0.4% (413)
Native Americans	0.3% (231)

AGE

0-17 years old	20.7% (420)
18-24 years old	9.1% (251)
25-39 years old	16.9% (338)
40-54 years old	22.5% (16)
55-64 years old	14.4% (136)
65+ years old	16.5% (247)

PRIVATE SECTOR

Businesses	1,672 (107)
Employees	20,426 (122)
Total wages	$802,808,189 (118)
Average weekly wages	$756 (152)

HOUSEHOLD INCOME LADDER

95th percentile	$155,176 (118)
80th percentile	$97,263 (74)
60th percentile	$62,634 (99)
40th percentile	$41,718 (83)
20th percentile	$22,686 (109)

CHILDREN ★★★★ (159)

Living with two parents	62.1% (349)
Older teens in school	84.5% (220)
Speak English very well	98.9% (226)
Poverty rate for children	17.7% (116)
No health insurance	4.8% (173)

DIVERSITY/EQUALITY ★★★ (293)

Racial diversity index	17.5% (381)
Geographic diversity index	26.8% (508)
Top 20% share of income	45.4% (82)
Gender gap in earnings	30.8% (190)
White-collar gender gap	17.8% (185)

EDUCATION ★★★★ (143)

Eighth grade or less	2.1% (136)
High school diplomas	89.0% (231)
Attended college	56.4% (198)
Bachelor's degrees	22.7% (139)
Advanced degrees	9.0% (87)

EMPLOYMENT ★★★★ (191)

Average jobless rate	7.3% (228)
Self-employed workers	9.1% (243)
Management/financial jobs	12.6% (111)
Computer/engineering jobs	3.2% (158)
Health care jobs	5.0% (339)

GROWTH POTENTIAL ★ (492)

Children per senior	1.25 (385)
Median age	42.5 (432)
Moved from different state	1.3% (452)
Homes built since 2000	7.4% (491)
Construction jobs	6.2% (295)

HOUSING ★★★ (271)

Home vacancy rate	6.7% (141)
Home ownership rate	71.1% (222)
Housing diversity index	78.0% (534)
4 or more bedrooms	21.7% (90)
Affordability/income ratio	$2,181 (115)

INCOME ★★★★★ (101)

Poverty rate	12.0% (85)
Median household income	$52,082 (87)
Interest/dividends	20.9% (221)
Public assistance	13.7% (197)
Median fulltime earnings	$43,301 (42)

SENIORS ★★ (362)

Seniors living alone	30.8% (462)
Poverty rate for seniors	7.2% (114)
Median income for seniors	$36,131 (150)
Seniors who work	20.6% (173)
Home ownership by seniors	76.3% (505)

STABILITY ★★ (359)

25-39 age group	16.9% (338)
Born in state of residence	85.3% (41)
Same house as 1 year ago	87.5% (165)
Live and work in county	62.7% (467)
Married-couple households	45.8% (447)

TRANSPORTATION ★★★ (328)

Bicycle or walk to work	4.1% (147)
Carpool to work	8.9% (439)
Public transit to work	1.0% (69)
Commute <15 minutes	39.7% (334)
Commute >45 minutes	12.8% (346)

See pages 37-130 for explanations of statistics, stars, and ranks.

Augusta-Waterville, ME
(Kennebec County, ME)

POPULATION	
2010 census	122,151 (13)
2015 estimate	119,980 (14)
2010-2015 change	-1.8% (389)
2020 projection	118,610 (14)
2030 projection	115,710 (22)

RACE	
Whites	95.1% (42)
Blacks	0.8% (404)
Hispanics	1.4% (488)
Asians	0.8% (201)
Native Americans	0.6% (150)

AGE	
0-17 years old	20.0% (458)
18-24 years old	8.6% (317)
25-39 years old	16.6% (388)
40-54 years old	22.3% (19)
55-64 years old	15.5% (59)
65+ years old	17.0% (197)

PRIVATE SECTOR	
Businesses	3,480 (13)
Employees	43,228 (9)
Total wages	$1,624,408,486 (15)
Average weekly wages	$723 (211)

HOUSEHOLD INCOME LADDER	
95th percentile	$149,924 (164)
80th percentile	$91,569 (133)
60th percentile	$58,853 (164)
40th percentile	$36,683 (213)
20th percentile	$20,579 (203)

CHILDREN	★★★★ (160)
Living with two parents	64.0% (297)
Older teens in school	83.5% (255)
Speak English very well	98.9% (226)
Poverty rate for children	19.2% (149)
No health insurance	4.5% (150)

DIVERSITY/EQUALITY	★★★★ (126)
Racial diversity index	9.5% (505)
Geographic diversity index	44.6% (286)
Top 20% share of income	46.8% (188)
Gender gap in earnings	21.7% (56)
White-collar gender gap	7.7% (60)

EDUCATION	★★★★★ (84)
Eighth grade or less	2.1% (136)
High school diplomas	93.5% (75)
Attended college	58.8% (149)
Bachelor's degrees	25.3% (105)
Advanced degrees	9.6% (71)

EMPLOYMENT	★★★★★ (88)
Average jobless rate	7.7% (260)
Self-employed workers	9.0% (254)
Management/financial jobs	14.0% (49)
Computer/engineering jobs	4.3% (63)
Health care jobs	6.0% (181)

GROWTH POTENTIAL	★★ (394)
Children per senior	1.18 (427)
Median age	44.0 (477)
Moved from different state	2.2% (248)
Homes built since 2000	12.3% (303)
Construction jobs	7.1% (173)

HOUSING	★★★★ (188)
Home vacancy rate	6.2% (109)
Home ownership rate	70.3% (256)
Housing diversity index	85.3% (170)
4 or more bedrooms	15.9% (303)
Affordability/income ratio	$3,210 (433)

INCOME	★★★★ (218)
Poverty rate	13.8% (149)
Median household income	$46,917 (195)
Interest/dividends	22.2% (174)
Public assistance	20.9% (452)
Median fulltime earnings	$40,457 (121)

SENIORS	★★ (331)
Seniors living alone	29.8% (422)
Poverty rate for seniors	8.6% (234)
Median income for seniors	$33,481 (260)
Seniors who work	20.6% (173)
Home ownership by seniors	79.7% (385)

STABILITY	★★ (339)
25-39 age group	16.6% (388)
Born in state of residence	72.7% (265)
Same house as 1 year ago	84.9% (306)
Live and work in county	79.7% (222)
Married-couple households	47.2% (413)

TRANSPORTATION	★★ (384)
Bicycle or walk to work	4.3% (130)
Carpool to work	10.3% (299)
Public transit to work	0.2% (363)
Commute <15 minutes	32.7% (480)
Commute >45 minutes	12.8% (346)

See pages 37-130 for explanations of statistics, stars, and ranks.

Barre, VT
(Washington County, VT)

POPULATION			Attended college	67.0% (37)
2010 census	59,534 (155)		Bachelor's degrees	41.1% (15)
2015 estimate	58,612 (155)		Advanced degrees	16.6% (9)
2010-2015 change	-1.5% (373)		**EMPLOYMENT**	**★★★★★ (13)**
2020 projection	57,947 (159)		Average jobless rate	4.8% (58)
2030 projection	56,519 (171)		Self-employed workers	11.7% (86)
			Management/financial jobs	17.3% (10)
RACE			Computer/engineering jobs	5.4% (24)
Whites	94.4% (66)		Health care jobs	5.1% (319)
Blacks	0.9% (388)			
Hispanics	1.9% (442)		**GROWTH POTENTIAL**	**★★ (405)**
Asians	0.8% (201)		Children per senior	1.21 (411)
Native Americans	0.3% (231)		Median age	43.2 (456)
			Moved from different state	3.3% (129)
AGE			Homes built since 2000	10.7% (370)
0-17 years old	19.8% (468)		Construction jobs	6.1% (310)
18-24 years old	9.2% (234)			
25-39 years old	16.7% (375)		**HOUSING**	**★★★★ (171)**
40-54 years old	22.2% (21)		Home vacancy rate	4.7% (22)
55-64 years old	15.8% (51)		Home ownership rate	73.6% (132)
65+ years old	16.3% (268)		Housing diversity index	82.2% (450)
			4 or more bedrooms	20.1% (122)
PRIVATE SECTOR			Affordability/income ratio	$3,593 (468)
Businesses	2,364 (41)			
Employees	25,764 (70)		**INCOME**	**★★★★★ (28)**
Total wages	$1,181,200,500 (43)		Poverty rate	10.1% (34)
Average weekly wages	$882 (41)		Median household income	$58,788 (30)
			Interest/dividends	30.7% (17)
HOUSEHOLD INCOME LADDER			Public assistance	11.7% (120)
95th percentile	$173,744 (48)		Median fulltime earnings	$44,523 (35)
80th percentile	$105,058 (37)			
60th percentile	$72,316 (29)		**SENIORS**	**★★★★★ (85)**
40th percentile	$47,421 (28)		Seniors living alone	30.3% (440)
20th percentile	$24,745 (51)		Poverty rate for seniors	5.7% (42)
			Median income for seniors	$40,821 (53)
CHILDREN	**★★★★★ (39)**		Seniors who work	28.5% (29)
Living with two parents	67.3% (209)		Home ownership by seniors	80.5% (356)
Older teens in school	87.4% (116)			
Speak English very well	99.7% (57)		**STABILITY**	**★★ (348)**
Poverty rate for children	12.4% (39)		25-39 age group	16.7% (375)
No health insurance	2.3% (20)		Born in state of residence	55.0% (464)
			Same house as 1 year ago	88.8% (93)
DIVERSITY/EQUALITY	**★★★★★ (21)**		Live and work in county	80.8% (206)
Racial diversity index	10.8% (482)		Married-couple households	48.4% (366)
Geographic diversity index	61.4% (112)			
Top 20% share of income	45.5% (89)		**TRANSPORTATION**	**★★★★ (174)**
Gender gap in earnings	12.7% (14)		Bicycle or walk to work	7.0% (41)
White-collar gender gap	1.0% (6)		Carpool to work	11.2% (211)
			Public transit to work	1.5% (42)
EDUCATION	**★★★★★ (10)**		Commute <15 minutes	37.8% (381)
Eighth grade or less	1.1% (26)		Commute >45 minutes	14.3% (402)
High school diplomas	95.1% (27)			

See pages 37-130 for explanations of statistics, stars, and ranks.

Batavia, NY
(Genesee County, NY)

POPULATION		Attended college	58.5% (157)
2010 census	60,079 (151)	Bachelor's degrees	21.3% (182)
2015 estimate	58,937 (152)	Advanced degrees	8.4% (106)
2010-2015 change	-1.9% (399)	**EMPLOYMENT**	★★★★ (220)
2020 projection	58,264 (157)	Average jobless rate	6.7% (169)
2030 projection	56,944 (167)	Self-employed workers	7.7% (362)
RACE		Management/financial jobs	11.0% (252)
Whites	90.9% (164)	Computer/engineering jobs	3.4% (131)
Blacks	2.5% (253)	Health care jobs	5.8% (209)
Hispanics	3.0% (343)	**GROWTH POTENTIAL**	★ (516)
Asians	0.7% (241)	Children per senior	1.24 (390)
Native Americans	1.0% (103)	Median age	42.7 (442)
AGE		Moved from different state	1.2% (474)
0-17 years old	21.0% (411)	Homes built since 2000	4.5% (544)
18-24 years old	9.2% (234)	Construction jobs	6.5% (253)
25-39 years old	16.6% (388)	**HOUSING**	★★★★ (201)
40-54 years old	22.2% (21)	Home vacancy rate	4.8% (27)
55-64 years old	14.0% (182)	Home ownership rate	73.0% (151)
65+ years old	16.9% (207)	Housing diversity index	77.9% (535)
PRIVATE SECTOR		4 or more bedrooms	20.9% (103)
Businesses	1,371 (160)	Affordability/income ratio	$2,103 (83)
Employees	17,624 (158)	**INCOME**	★★★★ (112)
Total wages	$638,987,984 (170)	Poverty rate	13.2% (123)
Average weekly wages	$697 (261)	Median household income	$50,880 (104)
HOUSEHOLD INCOME LADDER		Interest/dividends	22.0% (185)
95th percentile	$144,543 (236)	Public assistance	12.0% (132)
80th percentile	$93,381 (112)	Median fulltime earnings	$40,976 (98)
60th percentile	$63,433 (92)	**SENIORS**	★★★★ (219)
40th percentile	$40,916 (102)	Seniors living alone	25.8% (160)
20th percentile	$22,234 (127)	Poverty rate for seniors	6.8% (77)
CHILDREN	★★★★ (113)	Median income for seniors	$34,103 (231)
Living with two parents	67.2% (214)	Seniors who work	20.0% (195)
Older teens in school	84.9% (201)	Home ownership by seniors	78.3% (441)
Speak English very well	99.6% (77)	**STABILITY**	★★★★ (165)
Poverty rate for children	20.5% (180)	25-39 age group	16.6% (388)
No health insurance	3.9% (111)	Born in state of residence	88.4% (5)
DIVERSITY/EQUALITY	★★ (378)	Same house as 1 year ago	89.3% (71)
Racial diversity index	17.2% (384)	Live and work in county	61.9% (476)
Geographic diversity index	21.6% (547)	Married-couple households	51.6% (218)
Top 20% share of income	43.9% (23)	**TRANSPORTATION**	★★ (366)
Gender gap in earnings	36.5% (354)	Bicycle or walk to work	4.3% (130)
White-collar gender gap	25.3% (274)	Carpool to work	8.8% (448)
EDUCATION	★★★★ (118)	Public transit to work	0.4% (219)
Eighth grade or less	1.4% (60)	Commute <15 minutes	39.4% (339)
High school diplomas	93.1% (91)	Commute >45 minutes	13.1% (359)

See pages 37-130 for explanations of statistics, stars, and ranks.

Bennington, VT
(Bennington County, VT)

POPULATION

2010 census	37,125 (352)
2015 estimate	36,317 (369)
2010-2015 change	-2.2% (427)
2020 projection	35,732 (375)
2030 projection	34,516 (379)

RACE

Whites	95.0% (46)
Blacks	0.5% (466)
Hispanics	1.7% (464)
Asians	0.5% (355)
Native Americans	0.2% (300)

AGE

0-17 years old	19.5% (486)
18-24 years old	9.2% (234)
25-39 years old	14.5% (531)
40-54 years old	20.4% (169)
55-64 years old	15.7% (52)
65+ years old	20.7% (40)

PRIVATE SECTOR

Businesses	1,441 (149)
Employees	14,709 (218)
Total wages	$593,690,471 (190)
Average weekly wages	$776 (121)

HOUSEHOLD INCOME LADDER

95th percentile	$181,281 (39)
80th percentile	$94,247 (96)
60th percentile	$61,100 (127)
40th percentile	$39,589 (139)
20th percentile	$22,855 (102)

CHILDREN ★★★★ (122)

Living with two parents	61.5% (367)
Older teens in school	87.5% (112)
Speak English very well	98.9% (226)
Poverty rate for children	23.6% (260)
No health insurance	1.3% (4)

DIVERSITY/EQUALITY ★★★★ (205)

Racial diversity index	9.7% (500)
Geographic diversity index	61.9% (104)
Top 20% share of income	49.7% (412)
Gender gap in earnings	28.4% (144)
White-collar gender gap	13.0% (126)

EDUCATION ★★★★★ (52)

Eighth grade or less	1.5% (72)
High school diplomas	92.3% (117)
Attended college	60.5% (120)
Bachelor's degrees	32.5% (39)
Advanced degrees	10.8% (44)

EMPLOYMENT ★★★★★ (30)

Average jobless rate	5.7% (109)
Self-employed workers	17.7% (3)
Management/financial jobs	13.8% (54)
Computer/engineering jobs	3.6% (112)
Health care jobs	5.5% (250)

GROWTH POTENTIAL ★★ (393)

Children per senior	0.94 (517)
Median age	46.1 (514)
Moved from different state	4.1% (76)
Homes built since 2000	9.4% (414)
Construction jobs	7.9% (93)

HOUSING ★★★★★ (85)

Home vacancy rate	3.7% (5)
Home ownership rate	71.9% (192)
Housing diversity index	84.8% (248)
4 or more bedrooms	24.1% (48)
Affordability/income ratio	$4,262 (506)

INCOME ★★★★ (114)

Poverty rate	13.5% (137)
Median household income	$49,573 (137)
Interest/dividends	32.5% (8)
Public assistance	18.4% (381)
Median fulltime earnings	$38,274 (210)

SENIORS ★★★★ (118)

Seniors living alone	30.1% (433)
Poverty rate for seniors	7.0% (93)
Median income for seniors	$38,643 (79)
Seniors who work	26.6% (40)
Home ownership by seniors	81.6% (299)

STABILITY ★ (489)

25-39 age group	14.5% (531)
Born in state of residence	46.9% (497)
Same house as 1 year ago	86.8% (206)
Live and work in county	83.1% (161)
Married-couple households	49.1% (345)

TRANSPORTATION ★★★★ (130)

Bicycle or walk to work	6.9% (43)
Carpool to work	10.0% (337)
Public transit to work	0.4% (219)
Commute <15 minutes	48.8% (178)
Commute >45 minutes	9.1% (180)

See pages 37-130 for explanations of statistics, stars, and ranks.

Berlin, NH-VT
(Coos County, NH, and Essex County, VT)

POPULATION		
2010 census	39,361 (320)	
2015 estimate	37,375 (353)	
2010-2015 change	-5.0% (532)	
2020 projection	35,965 (369)	
2030 projection	33,284 (398)	

RACE		
Whites	94.7% (55)	
Blacks	1.5% (329)	
Hispanics	1.5% (480)	
Asians	0.4% (413)	
Native Americans	0.6% (150)	

AGE		
0-17 years old	17.8% (530)	
18-24 years old	6.6% (535)	
25-39 years old	15.2% (498)	
40-54 years old	21.7% (42)	
55-64 years old	17.2% (13)	
65+ years old	21.4% (26)	

PRIVATE SECTOR		
Businesses	1,005 (277)	
Employees	651 (551)	
Total wages	$21,937,071 (551)	
Average weekly wages	$648 (397)	

HOUSEHOLD INCOME LADDER		
95th percentile	$130,163 (432)	
80th percentile	$79,008 (381)	
60th percentile	$51,837 (326)	
40th percentile	$32,547 (337)	
20th percentile	$17,757 (329)	

CHILDREN	★★★★ (202)	
Living with two parents	58.6% (437)	
Older teens in school	81.3% (357)	
Speak English very well	99.7% (57)	
Poverty rate for children	20.9% (191)	
No health insurance	3.3% (72)	

DIVERSITY/EQUALITY	★★★★★ (109)	
Racial diversity index	10.3% (492)	
Geographic diversity index	56.3% (143)	
Top 20% share of income	47.1% (224)	
Gender gap in earnings	26.4% (109)	
White-collar gender gap	6.8% (53)	

EDUCATION	★★★ (225)	
Eighth grade or less	1.9% (114)	
High school diplomas	90.5% (186)	

Attended college	52.1% (281)	
Bachelor's degrees	19.0% (248)	
Advanced degrees	5.7% (292)	

EMPLOYMENT	★★★★★ (100)	
Average jobless rate	7.3% (228)	
Self-employed workers	11.3% (104)	
Management/financial jobs	12.2% (139)	
Computer/engineering jobs	2.1% (399)	
Health care jobs	7.0% (69)	

GROWTH POTENTIAL	★ (499)	
Children per senior	0.83 (533)	
Median age	48.2 (536)	
Moved from different state	2.6% (187)	
Homes built since 2000	11.7% (324)	
Construction jobs	7.4% (134)	

HOUSING	★★★ (237)	
Home vacancy rate	6.7% (141)	
Home ownership rate	71.6% (201)	
Housing diversity index	83.8% (369)	
4 or more bedrooms	15.2% (344)	
Affordability/income ratio	$2,992 (403)	

INCOME	★★★ (247)	
Poverty rate	14.2% (160)	
Median household income	$41,214 (347)	
Interest/dividends	21.7% (190)	
Public assistance	17.2% (344)	
Median fulltime earnings	$37,962 (223)	

SENIORS	★★ (430)	
Seniors living alone	30.6% (454)	
Poverty rate for seniors	8.6% (234)	
Median income for seniors	$30,897 (377)	
Seniors who work	19.5% (226)	
Home ownership by seniors	77.5% (471)	

STABILITY	★ (456)	
25-39 age group	15.2% (498)	
Born in state of residence	58.9% (427)	
Same house as 1 year ago	88.0% (133)	
Live and work in county	74.9% (291)	
Married-couple households	48.5% (361)	

TRANSPORTATION	★★★ (307)	
Bicycle or walk to work	3.7% (173)	
Carpool to work	10.8% (249)	
Public transit to work	0.2% (363)	
Commute <15 minutes	43.8% (264)	
Commute >45 minutes	12.6% (336)	

See pages 37-130 for explanations of statistics, stars, and ranks.

Bluefield, WV-VA
(Mercer County, WV, and Tazewell County, VA)

POPULATION	
2010 census	107,342 (22)
2015 estimate	104,063 (26)
2010-2015 change	-3.1% (487)
2020 projection	101,277 (31)
2030 projection	95,420 (38)

RACE	
Whites	91.9% (141)
Blacks	4.6% (173)
Hispanics	0.9% (535)
Asians	0.5% (355)
Native Americans	0.2% (300)

AGE	
0-17 years old	20.3% (445)
18-24 years old	8.6% (317)
25-39 years old	17.8% (227)
40-54 years old	19.2% (336)
55-64 years old	15.4% (66)
65+ years old	18.7% (97)

PRIVATE SECTOR	
Businesses	2,394 (39)
Employees	27,154 (58)
Total wages	$891,647,631 (94)
Average weekly wages	$631 (435)

HOUSEHOLD INCOME LADDER	
95th percentile	$130,381 (426)
80th percentile	$76,332 (435)
60th percentile	$46,155 (455)
40th percentile	$28,278 (456)
20th percentile	$15,569 (429)

CHILDREN	★★★ (273)
Living with two parents	63.3% (316)
Older teens in school	82.1% (313)
Speak English very well	98.9% (226)
Poverty rate for children	29.5% (391)
No health insurance	4.8% (173)

DIVERSITY/EQUALITY	★★ (412)
Racial diversity index	15.3% (405)
Geographic diversity index	45.4% (274)
Top 20% share of income	50.7% (458)
Gender gap in earnings	32.9% (255)
White-collar gender gap	22.7% (245)

EDUCATION	★★ (336)
Eighth grade or less	4.4% (346)
High school diplomas	85.9% (345)
Attended college	48.8% (362)
Bachelor's degrees	18.2% (277)
Advanced degrees	6.1% (250)

EMPLOYMENT	★★★ (232)
Average jobless rate	6.4% (147)
Self-employed workers	5.6% (523)
Management/financial jobs	9.3% (453)
Computer/engineering jobs	1.8% (457)
Health care jobs	8.8% (5)

GROWTH POTENTIAL	★ (514)
Children per senior	1.08 (471)
Median age	42.6 (437)
Moved from different state	2.8% (171)
Homes built since 2000	9.4% (414)
Construction jobs	4.5% (504)

HOUSING	★★★★ (166)
Home vacancy rate	10.9% (400)
Home ownership rate	73.4% (142)
Housing diversity index	86.4% (26)
4 or more bedrooms	15.9% (303)
Affordability/income ratio	$2,389 (209)

INCOME	★★ (432)
Poverty rate	20.2% (380)
Median household income	$36,754 (448)
Interest/dividends	15.1% (405)
Public assistance	20.6% (445)
Median fulltime earnings	$35,081 (380)

SENIORS	★★ (373)
Seniors living alone	28.6% (336)
Poverty rate for seniors	10.9% (370)
Median income for seniors	$29,284 (428)
Seniors who work	14.6% (472)
Home ownership by seniors	86.1% (93)

STABILITY	★★★★ (191)
25-39 age group	17.8% (227)
Born in state of residence	70.8% (295)
Same house as 1 year ago	87.9% (140)
Live and work in county	74.3% (306)
Married-couple households	50.1% (291)

TRANSPORTATION	★★ (398)
Bicycle or walk to work	2.3% (348)
Carpool to work	9.8% (358)
Public transit to work	0.3% (291)
Commute <15 minutes	38.6% (360)
Commute >45 minutes	12.3% (325)

See pages 37-130 for explanations of statistics, stars, and ranks.

Bradford, PA
(McKean County, PA)

POPULATION			
2010 census	43,450 (274)	Attended college	46.1% (418)
2015 estimate	42,412 (287)	Bachelor's degrees	18.3% (274)
2010-2015 change	-2.4% (443)	Advanced degrees	6.8% (191)

POPULATION
2010 census — 43,450 (274)
2015 estimate — 42,412 (287)
2010-2015 change — -2.4% (443)
2020 projection — 41,144 (299)
2030 projection — 38,636 (332)

RACE
Whites — 93.8% (80)
Blacks — 2.3% (267)
Hispanics — 2.0% (428)
Asians — 0.5% (355)
Native Americans — 0.2% (300)

AGE
0-17 years old — 20.4% (437)
18-24 years old — 9.1% (251)
25-39 years old — 17.2% (290)
40-54 years old — 21.3% (73)
55-64 years old — 14.2% (161)
65+ years old — 17.7% (142)

PRIVATE SECTOR
Businesses — 1,108 (240)
Employees — 13,259 (270)
Total wages — $531,117,585 (225)
Average weekly wages — $770 (128)

HOUSEHOLD INCOME LADDER
95th percentile — $132,846 (389)
80th percentile — $79,721 (375)
60th percentile — $53,315 (292)
40th percentile — $35,395 (254)
20th percentile — $18,370 (299)

CHILDREN ★★★★ (215)
Living with two parents — 55.5% (475)
Older teens in school — 86.1% (164)
Speak English very well — 100.0% (1)
Poverty rate for children — 24.8% (293)
No health insurance — 4.1% (126)

DIVERSITY/EQUALITY ★★ (331)
Racial diversity index — 11.9% (468)
Geographic diversity index — 45.6% (270)
Top 20% share of income — 48.5% (323)
Gender gap in earnings — 32.9% (255)
White-collar gender gap — 16.1% (167)

EDUCATION ★★★ (226)
Eighth grade or less — 1.2% (42)
High school diplomas — 91.7% (135)
Attended college — 46.1% (418)
Bachelor's degrees — 18.3% (274)
Advanced degrees — 6.8% (191)

EMPLOYMENT ★★★★ (162)
Average jobless rate — 9.1% (370)
Self-employed workers — 7.9% (345)
Management/financial jobs — 12.3% (133)
Computer/engineering jobs — 3.4% (131)
Health care jobs — 6.9% (79)

GROWTH POTENTIAL ★ (524)
Children per senior — 1.15 (442)
Median age — 42.4 (429)
Moved from different state — 1.9% (310)
Homes built since 2000 — 4.7% (542)
Construction jobs — 5.7% (373)

HOUSING ★★★★ (205)
Home vacancy rate — 5.1% (39)
Home ownership rate — 73.7% (129)
Housing diversity index — 78.7% (531)
4 or more bedrooms — 17.1% (239)
Affordability/income ratio — $1,733 (18)

INCOME ★★★ (238)
Poverty rate — 17.2% (270)
Median household income — $43,965 (263)
Interest/dividends — 22.2% (174)
Public assistance — 17.2% (344)
Median fulltime earnings — $39,586 (154)

SENIORS ★★ (374)
Seniors living alone — 29.4% (394)
Poverty rate for seniors — 6.7% (73)
Median income for seniors — $31,115 (366)
Seniors who work — 16.9% (348)
Home ownership by seniors — 79.5% (394)

STABILITY ★★★ (315)
25-39 age group — 17.2% (290)
Born in state of residence — 71.7% (284)
Same house as 1 year ago — 87.1% (192)
Live and work in county — 78.9% (234)
Married-couple households — 44.6% (471)

TRANSPORTATION ★★★ (227)
Bicycle or walk to work — 4.3% (130)
Carpool to work — 9.7% (369)
Public transit to work — 0.5% (178)
Commute <15 minutes — 45.7% (237)
Commute >45 minutes — 9.4% (197)

See pages 37-130 for explanations of statistics, stars, and ranks.

Cambridge, MD
(Dorchester County, MD)

POPULATION			
2010 census	32,618 (407)		
2015 estimate	32,384 (416)		
2010-2015 change	-0.7% (303)		
2020 projection	32,620 (413)		
2030 projection	33,124 (400)		

RACE
Whites	64.8% (417)
Blacks	27.7% (62)
Hispanics	4.3% (279)
Asians	1.0% (158)
Native Americans	0.0% (523)

AGE
0-17 years old	21.3% (383)
18-24 years old	7.7% (454)
25-39 years old	17.7% (236)
40-54 years old	19.6% (289)
55-64 years old	14.6% (107)
65+ years old	19.1% (76)

PRIVATE SECTOR
Businesses	692 (432)
Employees	8,790 (422)
Total wages	$314,669,144 (417)
Average weekly wages	$688 (290)

HOUSEHOLD INCOME LADDER
95th percentile	$152,847 (135)
80th percentile	$94,414 (93)
60th percentile	$61,657 (119)
40th percentile	$37,113 (204)
20th percentile	$20,068 (225)

CHILDREN ★★★ (322)
Living with two parents	53.6% (482)
Older teens in school	81.3% (357)
Speak English very well	99.1% (179)
Poverty rate for children	28.5% (377)
No health insurance	3.3% (72)

DIVERSITY/EQUALITY ★★★★★ (56)
Racial diversity index	50.1% (113)
Geographic diversity index	42.1% (326)
Top 20% share of income	49.8% (417)
Gender gap in earnings	19.6% (39)
White-collar gender gap	3.9% (27)

EDUCATION ★★★ (228)
Eighth grade or less	2.6% (185)
High school diplomas	87.6% (284)
Attended college	49.4% (348)
Bachelor's degrees	20.4% (213)
Advanced degrees	7.9% (126)

EMPLOYMENT ★★★ (254)
Average jobless rate	10.4% (437)
Self-employed workers	9.3% (224)
Management/financial jobs	11.1% (240)
Computer/engineering jobs	3.3% (145)
Health care jobs	6.2% (156)

GROWTH POTENTIAL ★★★ (288)
Children per senior	1.11 (457)
Median age	43.8 (472)
Moved from different state	1.5% (406)
Homes built since 2000	20.3% (87)
Construction jobs	7.5% (122)

HOUSING ★ (488)
Home vacancy rate	13.4% (504)
Home ownership rate	65.6% (421)
Housing diversity index	85.7% (108)
4 or more bedrooms	16.1% (286)
Affordability/income ratio	$3,986 (496)

INCOME ★★★ (275)
Poverty rate	16.5% (246)
Median household income	$47,093 (191)
Interest/dividends	18.3% (299)
Public assistance	23.7% (506)
Median fulltime earnings	$41,704 (69)

SENIORS ★★★★ (158)
Seniors living alone	25.6% (149)
Poverty rate for seniors	8.5% (223)
Median income for seniors	$35,855 (159)
Seniors who work	24.5% (79)
Home ownership by seniors	78.4% (435)

STABILITY ★★ (391)
25-39 age group	17.7% (236)
Born in state of residence	75.0% (221)
Same house as 1 year ago	89.1% (77)
Live and work in county	62.8% (466)
Married-couple households	44.5% (474)

TRANSPORTATION ★★ (361)
Bicycle or walk to work	2.5% (322)
Carpool to work	13.0% (101)
Public transit to work	0.5% (178)
Commute <15 minutes	33.2% (473)
Commute >45 minutes	14.2% (395)

See pages 37-130 for explanations of statistics, stars, and ranks.

Claremont-Lebanon, NH-VT
(Grafton and Sullivan Counties, NH, Orange and Windsor Counties, VT)

POPULATION

2010 census	218,466 (1)
2015 estimate	216,923 (1)
2010-2015 change	-0.7% (303)
2020 projection	216,497 (1)
2030 projection	215,496 (2)

RACE

Whites	93.8% (80)
Blacks	0.6% (438)
Hispanics	1.7% (464)
Asians	1.8% (60)
Native Americans	0.4% (203)

AGE

0-17 years old	18.7% (507)
18-24 years old	9.8% (176)
25-39 years old	16.5% (403)
40-54 years old	20.7% (132)
55-64 years old	16.2% (38)
65+ years old	18.1% (117)

PRIVATE SECTOR

Businesses	6,875 (1)
Employees	81,681 (1)
Total wages	$3,977,638,194 (1)
Average weekly wages	$936 (24)

HOUSEHOLD INCOME LADDER

95th percentile	$191,407 (30)
80th percentile	$104,552 (39)
60th percentile	$67,844 (46)
40th percentile	$44,054 (55)
20th percentile	$24,234 (61)

CHILDREN ★★★★★ (80)

Living with two parents	65.3% (263)
Older teens in school	87.3% (124)
Speak English very well	99.0% (200)
Poverty rate for children	15.1% (65)
No health insurance	4.6% (159)

DIVERSITY/EQUALITY ★★★★ (117)

Racial diversity index	11.9% (468)
Geographic diversity index	65.2% (72)
Top 20% share of income	49.1% (374)
Gender gap in earnings	24.1% (76)
White-collar gender gap	13.2% (130)

EDUCATION ★★★★★ (26)

Eighth grade or less	1.4% (60)
High school diplomas	93.2% (88)

Attended college	61.6% (102)
Bachelor's degrees	34.8% (29)
Advanced degrees	14.6% (16)

EMPLOYMENT ★★★★★ (10)

Average jobless rate	5.1% (69)
Self-employed workers	11.2% (108)
Management/financial jobs	13.7% (59)
Computer/engineering jobs	5.8% (18)
Health care jobs	7.5% (44)

GROWTH POTENTIAL ★★★ (277)

Children per senior	1.03 (492)
Median age	44.4 (491)
Moved from different state	5.0% (51)
Homes built since 2000	12.7% (290)
Construction jobs	7.4% (134)

HOUSING ★★★ (226)

Home vacancy rate	6.2% (109)
Home ownership rate	71.5% (204)
Housing diversity index	84.0% (344)
4 or more bedrooms	17.7% (220)
Affordability/income ratio	$3,644 (476)

INCOME ★★★★★ (51)

Poverty rate	11.2% (61)
Median household income	$54,744 (56)
Interest/dividends	27.2% (47)
Public assistance	11.1% (96)
Median fulltime earnings	$43,474 (40)

SENIORS ★★★★★ (51)

Seniors living alone	25.7% (154)
Poverty rate for seniors	6.8% (77)
Median income for seniors	$40,049 (59)
Seniors who work	27.1% (36)
Home ownership by seniors	81.8% (286)

STABILITY ★ (523)

25-39 age group	16.5% (403)
Born in state of residence	41.9% (516)
Same house as 1 year ago	86.3% (232)
Live and work in county	65.2% (448)
Married-couple households	50.0% (296)

TRANSPORTATION ★★★ (224)

Bicycle or walk to work	6.5% (51)
Carpool to work	10.7% (260)
Public transit to work	1.1% (58)
Commute <15 minutes	34.4% (452)
Commute >45 minutes	12.5% (334)

See pages 37-130 for explanations of statistics, stars, and ranks.

Clarksburg, WV
(Doddridge, Harrison, and Taylor Counties, WV)

POPULATION

2010 census	94,196 (37)
2015 estimate	93,802 (41)
2010-2015 change	-0.4% (286)
2020 projection	93,360 (43)
2030 projection	91,906 (44)

RACE

Whites	95.0% (46)
Blacks	1.6% (320)
Hispanics	1.3% (503)
Asians	0.7% (241)
Native Americans	0.2% (300)

AGE

0-17 years old	21.2% (397)
18-24 years old	7.7% (454)
25-39 years old	18.1% (186)
40-54 years old	21.0% (107)
55-64 years old	14.6% (107)
65+ years old	17.4% (165)

PRIVATE SECTOR

Businesses	2,282 (46)
Employees	30,493 (40)
Total wages	$1,293,696,772 (31)
Average weekly wages	$816 (69)

HOUSEHOLD INCOME LADDER

95th percentile	$147,000 (198)
80th percentile	$87,652 (189)
60th percentile	$54,795 (256)
40th percentile	$33,879 (292)
20th percentile	$18,025 (319)

CHILDREN ★★★★ (166)

Living with two parents	68.4% (181)
Older teens in school	79.9% (401)
Speak English very well	99.3% (142)
Poverty rate for children	23.6% (260)
No health insurance	3.0% (59)

DIVERSITY/EQUALITY ★★ (332)

Racial diversity index	9.7% (500)
Geographic diversity index	36.8% (407)
Top 20% share of income	48.3% (308)
Gender gap in earnings	32.9% (255)
White-collar gender gap	6.7% (51)

EDUCATION ★★★★ (218)

Eighth grade or less	2.6% (185)
High school diplomas	88.6% (251)

Attended college	50.2% (325)
Bachelor's degrees	21.5% (174)
Advanced degrees	7.1% (176)

EMPLOYMENT ★★★★★ (80)

Average jobless rate	7.7% (260)
Self-employed workers	8.0% (333)
Management/financial jobs	11.5% (202)
Computer/engineering jobs	5.1% (28)
Health care jobs	7.6% (39)

GROWTH POTENTIAL ★★ (384)

Children per senior	1.22 (401)
Median age	42.2 (412)
Moved from different state	1.8% (338)
Homes built since 2000	9.9% (389)
Construction jobs	7.4% (134)

HOUSING ★★★★ (146)

Home vacancy rate	10.7% (390)
Home ownership rate	75.4% (69)
Housing diversity index	85.1% (212)
4 or more bedrooms	17.0% (247)
Affordability/income ratio	$2,177 (110)

INCOME ★★★ (242)

Poverty rate	16.3% (234)
Median household income	$43,728 (271)
Interest/dividends	17.4% (334)
Public assistance	15.2% (266)
Median fulltime earnings	$40,436 (123)

SENIORS ★★ (348)

Seniors living alone	29.6% (413)
Poverty rate for seniors	8.7% (241)
Median income for seniors	$31,676 (338)
Seniors who work	14.3% (493)
Home ownership by seniors	85.2% (132)

STABILITY ★★★★★ (96)

25-39 age group	18.1% (186)
Born in state of residence	78.7% (139)
Same house as 1 year ago	90.0% (44)
Live and work in county	70.4% (363)
Married-couple households	50.4% (278)

TRANSPORTATION ★ (488)

Bicycle or walk to work	2.3% (348)
Carpool to work	8.2% (480)
Public transit to work	0.5% (178)
Commute <15 minutes	31.0% (511)
Commute >45 minutes	13.5% (374)

See pages 37-130 for explanations of statistics, stars, and ranks.

Concord, NH
(Merrimack County, NH)

POPULATION		
2010 census	146,445 (6)	
2015 estimate	147,994 (6)	
2010-2015 change	1.1% (181)	
2020 projection	149,282 (5)	
2030 projection	151,833 (6)	

RACE	
Whites	93.6% (87)
Blacks	1.1% (367)
Hispanics	1.8% (455)
Asians	1.6% (77)
Native Americans	0.1% (402)

AGE	
0-17 years old	20.4% (437)
18-24 years old	9.6% (189)
25-39 years old	16.7% (375)
40-54 years old	22.9% (7)
55-64 years old	15.1% (74)
65+ years old	15.4% (344)

PRIVATE SECTOR	
Businesses	4,329 (7)
Employees	59,565 (3)
Total wages	$2,844,977,072 (2)
Average weekly wages	$919 (29)

HOUSEHOLD INCOME LADDER	
95th percentile	$198,240 (19)
80th percentile	$119,469 (14)
60th percentile	$80,885 (16)
40th percentile	$52,473 (16)
20th percentile	$28,712 (19)

CHILDREN	★★★★★ (42)
Living with two parents	70.5% (131)
Older teens in school	86.7% (141)
Speak English very well	99.0% (200)
Poverty rate for children	12.3% (33)
No health insurance	2.8% (50)

DIVERSITY/EQUALITY	★★★★★ (87)
Racial diversity index	12.3% (459)
Geographic diversity index	61.4% (112)
Top 20% share of income	45.5% (91)
Gender gap in earnings	27.1% (120)
White-collar gender gap	16.4% (173)

EDUCATION	★★★★★ (24)
Eighth grade or less	1.3% (52)
High school diplomas	94.0% (57)
Attended college	67.0% (37)
Bachelor's degrees	35.2% (27)
Advanced degrees	12.9% (28)

EMPLOYMENT	★★★★★ (20)
Average jobless rate	5.2% (76)
Self-employed workers	9.8% (186)
Management/financial jobs	15.4% (25)
Computer/engineering jobs	5.5% (22)
Health care jobs	6.5% (121)

GROWTH POTENTIAL	★★★ (279)
Children per senior	1.33 (325)
Median age	42.6 (437)
Moved from different state	2.6% (187)
Homes built since 2000	13.9% (240)
Construction jobs	7.3% (151)

HOUSING	★★★★ (144)
Home vacancy rate	4.4% (14)
Home ownership rate	72.1% (181)
Housing diversity index	83.8% (369)
4 or more bedrooms	18.6% (174)
Affordability/income ratio	$3,413 (454)

INCOME	★★★★★ (12)
Poverty rate	9.1% (18)
Median household income	$65,983 (16)
Interest/dividends	25.9% (71)
Public assistance	10.1% (66)
Median fulltime earnings	$49,688 (14)

SENIORS	★★★★★ (95)
Seniors living alone	25.8% (160)
Poverty rate for seniors	5.1% (22)
Median income for seniors	$42,812 (41)
Seniors who work	23.5% (95)
Home ownership by seniors	76.4% (502)

STABILITY	★★ (423)
25-39 age group	16.7% (375)
Born in state of residence	53.6% (470)
Same house as 1 year ago	87.6% (157)
Live and work in county	66.0% (435)
Married-couple households	53.1% (148)

TRANSPORTATION	★ (523)
Bicycle or walk to work	3.0% (249)
Carpool to work	8.2% (480)
Public transit to work	0.4% (219)
Commute <15 minutes	27.6% (538)
Commute >45 minutes	16.1% (459)

See pages 37-130 for explanations of statistics, stars, and ranks.

Corning, NY
(Steuben County, NY)

POPULATION

2010 census	98,990 (31)
2015 estimate	97,631 (33)
2010-2015 change	-1.4% (364)
2020 projection	96,851 (36)
2030 projection	95,326 (39)

RACE

Whites	93.9% (78)
Blacks	1.5% (329)
Hispanics	1.5% (480)
Asians	1.5% (85)
Native Americans	0.2% (300)

AGE

0-17 years old	22.5% (300)
18-24 years old	8.2% (379)
25-39 years old	16.6% (388)
40-54 years old	21.2% (85)
55-64 years old	14.5% (122)
65+ years old	17.0% (197)

PRIVATE SECTOR

Businesses	1,946 (67)
Employees	29,131 (48)
Total wages	$1,586,041,211 (17)
Average weekly wages	$1,047 (14)

HOUSEHOLD INCOME LADDER

95th percentile	$148,624 (176)
80th percentile	$89,339 (165)
60th percentile	$58,149 (177)
40th percentile	$37,461 (193)
20th percentile	$19,966 (231)

CHILDREN   ★★ (343)

Living with two parents	65.4% (260)
Older teens in school	78.2% (442)
Speak English very well	97.6% (375)
Poverty rate for children	24.6% (289)
No health insurance	8.1% (364)

DIVERSITY/EQUALITY   ★★ (338)

Racial diversity index	11.7% (471)
Geographic diversity index	35.8% (425)
Top 20% share of income	48.0% (299)
Gender gap in earnings	30.8% (190)
White-collar gender gap	14.0% (141)

EDUCATION   ★★★★ (123)

Eighth grade or less	2.1% (136)
High school diplomas	91.7% (135)
Attended college	55.1% (221)
Bachelor's degrees	22.2% (153)
Advanced degrees	10.3% (51)

EMPLOYMENT   ★★★★ (141)

Average jobless rate	8.2% (310)
Self-employed workers	7.7% (362)
Management/financial jobs	11.9% (165)
Computer/engineering jobs	5.7% (19)
Health care jobs	5.4% (273)

GROWTH POTENTIAL   ★★ (438)

Children per senior	1.32 (334)
Median age	42.0 (398)
Moved from different state	1.4% (425)
Homes built since 2000	7.9% (470)
Construction jobs	6.9% (198)

HOUSING   ★★★★ (172)

Home vacancy rate	6.5% (130)
Home ownership rate	70.0% (272)
Housing diversity index	81.0% (495)
4 or more bedrooms	20.1% (122)
Affordability/income ratio	$1,925 (34)

INCOME   ★★★★ (163)

Poverty rate	16.3% (234)
Median household income	$47,280 (185)
Interest/dividends	22.3% (172)
Public assistance	14.8% (249)
Median fulltime earnings	$41,631 (74)

SENIORS   ★★★ (290)

Seniors living alone	28.4% (325)
Poverty rate for seniors	7.4% (128)
Median income for seniors	$35,022 (186)
Seniors who work	16.6% (367)
Home ownership by seniors	81.3% (316)

STABILITY   ★★★ (262)

25-39 age group	16.6% (388)
Born in state of residence	79.4% (122)
Same house as 1 year ago	87.5% (165)
Live and work in county	74.8% (294)
Married-couple households	47.0% (417)

TRANSPORTATION   ★★★ (234)

Bicycle or walk to work	4.5% (117)
Carpool to work	11.1% (221)
Public transit to work	0.7% (119)
Commute <15 minutes	41.0% (317)
Commute >45 minutes	11.3% (285)

See pages 37-130 for explanations of statistics, stars, and ranks.

Cortland, NY
(Cortland County, NY)

POPULATION		Attended college	58.9% (145)
2010 census	49,336 (216)	Bachelor's degrees	24.8% (114)
2015 estimate	48,494 (221)	Advanced degrees	10.1% (56)
2010-2015 change	-1.7% (384)	**EMPLOYMENT**	**★★★★ (167)**
2020 projection	48,032 (229)	Average jobless rate	6.1% (121)
2030 projection	47,117 (245)	Self-employed workers	8.4% (297)
RACE		Management/financial jobs	10.7% (287)
Whites	92.9% (110)	Computer/engineering jobs	4.5% (58)
Blacks	1.5% (329)	Health care jobs	5.3% (286)
Hispanics	2.5% (384)	**GROWTH POTENTIAL**	**★ (443)**
Asians	0.9% (178)	Children per senior	1.36 (304)
Native Americans	0.1% (402)	Median age	36.1 (118)
AGE		Moved from different state	0.8% (524)
0-17 years old	20.1% (457)	Homes built since 2000	4.9% (540)
18-24 years old	17.8% (38)	Construction jobs	5.9% (345)
25-39 years old	16.0% (449)	**HOUSING**	**★★★ (326)**
40-54 years old	19.1% (354)	Home vacancy rate	7.1% (165)
55-64 years old	12.4% (408)	Home ownership rate	65.7% (419)
65+ years old	14.7% (389)	Housing diversity index	74.5% (549)
PRIVATE SECTOR		4 or more bedrooms	23.6% (53)
Businesses	1,049 (258)	Affordability/income ratio	$2,185 (118)
Employees	14,304 (226)	**INCOME**	**★★★★ (161)**
Total wages	$600,638,856 (186)	Poverty rate	14.7% (182)
Average weekly wages	$808 (78)	Median household income	$49,514 (138)
HOUSEHOLD INCOME LADDER		Interest/dividends	22.1% (181)
95th percentile	$158,219 (108)	Public assistance	15.0% (254)
80th percentile	$93,966 (102)	Median fulltime earnings	$39,533 (156)
60th percentile	$60,795 (136)	**SENIORS**	**★★ (414)**
40th percentile	$40,675 (109)	Seniors living alone	31.6% (503)
20th percentile	$21,254 (176)	Poverty rate for seniors	10.0% (321)
CHILDREN	**★★★★★ (86)**	Median income for seniors	$34,985 (190)
Living with two parents	64.0% (297)	Seniors who work	24.5% (79)
Older teens in school	88.8% (86)	Home ownership by seniors	74.3% (532)
Speak English very well	99.6% (77)	**STABILITY**	**★★ (341)**
Poverty rate for children	15.3% (68)	25-39 age group	16.0% (449)
No health insurance	6.1% (258)	Born in state of residence	85.8% (33)
DIVERSITY/EQUALITY	**★★ (363)**	Same house as 1 year ago	87.0% (198)
Racial diversity index	13.6% (437)	Live and work in county	70.9% (356)
Geographic diversity index	25.9% (516)	Married-couple households	45.2% (461)
Top 20% share of income	46.8% (196)	**TRANSPORTATION**	**★★★★★ (99)**
Gender gap in earnings	25.6% (97)	Bicycle or walk to work	7.4% (38)
White-collar gender gap	26.4% (291)	Carpool to work	12.5% (121)
EDUCATION	**★★★★★ (81)**	Public transit to work	0.9% (83)
Eighth grade or less	1.2% (42)	Commute <15 minutes	42.6% (284)
High school diplomas	92.2% (120)	Commute >45 minutes	10.8% (266)

See pages 37-130 for explanations of statistics, stars, and ranks.

DuBois, PA
(Clearfield County, PA)

POPULATION		
2010 census	81,642 (63)	
2015 estimate	80,994 (65)	
2010-2015 change	-0.8% (314)	
2020 projection	79,877 (70)	
2030 projection	77,586 (83)	

RACE	
Whites	93.4% (94)
Blacks	2.2% (276)
Hispanics	2.8% (355)
Asians	0.5% (355)
Native Americans	0.1% (402)

AGE	
0-17 years old	19.0% (501)
18-24 years old	8.1% (396)
25-39 years old	17.2% (290)
40-54 years old	22.9% (7)
55-64 years old	14.3% (148)
65+ years old	18.5% (104)

PRIVATE SECTOR	
Businesses	1,961 (64)
Employees	25,304 (74)
Total wages	$898,341,500 (92)
Average weekly wages	$683 (305)

HOUSEHOLD INCOME LADDER	
95th percentile	$127,691 (461)
80th percentile	$77,359 (413)
60th percentile	$52,083 (314)
40th percentile	$33,487 (311)
20th percentile	$18,066 (317)

CHILDREN	★★★★ (154)
Living with two parents	68.7% (174)
Older teens in school	83.5% (255)
Speak English very well	98.7% (265)
Poverty rate for children	22.9% (246)
No health insurance	4.2% (134)

DIVERSITY/EQUALITY	★★★ (276)
Racial diversity index	12.6% (453)
Geographic diversity index	26.5% (511)
Top 20% share of income	45.8% (111)
Gender gap in earnings	35.0% (314)
White-collar gender gap	2.2% (12)

EDUCATION	★★ (388)
Eighth grade or less	2.5% (180)
High school diplomas	89.8% (207)
Attended college	40.2% (511)
Bachelor's degrees	14.5% (443)
Advanced degrees	4.0% (478)

EMPLOYMENT	★★★ (294)
Average jobless rate	7.8% (270)
Self-employed workers	8.0% (333)
Management/financial jobs	9.7% (416)
Computer/engineering jobs	2.8% (246)
Health care jobs	6.3% (144)

GROWTH POTENTIAL	★ (507)
Children per senior	1.03 (492)
Median age	43.9 (475)
Moved from different state	1.8% (338)
Homes built since 2000	7.4% (491)
Construction jobs	6.7% (219)

HOUSING	★★★★ (132)
Home vacancy rate	8.5% (253)
Home ownership rate	77.2% (24)
Housing diversity index	83.1% (414)
4 or more bedrooms	16.5% (267)
Affordability/income ratio	$2,066 (71)

INCOME	★★★ (266)
Poverty rate	15.0% (190)
Median household income	$42,257 (311)
Interest/dividends	20.8% (224)
Public assistance	17.3% (351)
Median fulltime earnings	$36,584 (311)

SENIORS	★★ (376)
Seniors living alone	29.1% (371)
Poverty rate for seniors	8.8% (250)
Median income for seniors	$28,890 (439)
Seniors who work	14.7% (467)
Home ownership by seniors	84.5% (165)

STABILITY	★★★★★ (64)
25-39 age group	17.2% (290)
Born in state of residence	85.5% (38)
Same house as 1 year ago	88.9% (86)
Live and work in county	72.1% (337)
Married-couple households	52.8% (164)

TRANSPORTATION	★★ (428)
Bicycle or walk to work	3.0% (249)
Carpool to work	10.7% (260)
Public transit to work	0.2% (363)
Commute <15 minutes	38.4% (366)
Commute >45 minutes	16.4% (466)

See pages 37-130 for explanations of statistics, stars, and ranks.

Easton, MD
(Talbot County, MD)

POPULATION			Attended college	61.0% (113)
2010 census	37,782 (345)		Bachelor's degrees	31.4% (44)
2015 estimate	37,512 (350)		Advanced degrees	13.5% (25)
2010-2015 change	-0.7% (303)			
2020 projection	37,780 (344)		**EMPLOYMENT**	★★★★★ **(24)**
2030 projection	38,375 (333)		Average jobless rate	6.7% (169)
			Self-employed workers	14.6% (22)
RACE			Management/financial jobs	16.4% (13)
Whites	78.2% (336)		Computer/engineering jobs	3.5% (122)
Blacks	11.7% (104)		Health care jobs	5.6% (240)
Hispanics	6.0% (222)			
Asians	1.5% (85)		**GROWTH POTENTIAL**	★★ **(406)**
Native Americans	0.1% (402)		Children per senior	0.73 (543)
			Median age	49.0 (540)
AGE			Moved from different state	3.2% (136)
0-17 years old	18.8% (504)		Homes built since 2000	18.1% (131)
18-24 years old	6.7% (531)		Construction jobs	7.8% (98)
25-39 years old	13.9% (543)			
40-54 years old	19.7% (273)		**HOUSING**	★★★ **(295)**
55-64 years old	15.2% (72)		Home vacancy rate	8.1% (227)
65+ years old	25.7% (9)		Home ownership rate	68.6% (321)
			Housing diversity index	85.8% (97)
PRIVATE SECTOR			4 or more bedrooms	24.2% (47)
Businesses	1,505 (134)		Affordability/income ratio	$5,487 (535)
Employees	16,908 (173)			
Total wages	$657,058,549 (163)		**INCOME**	★★★★★ **(23)**
Average weekly wages	$747 (162)		Poverty rate	11.2% (61)
			Median household income	$58,228 (32)
HOUSEHOLD INCOME LADDER			Interest/dividends	32.7% (7)
95th percentile	>$250,000 (1)		Public assistance	12.5% (148)
80th percentile	$120,359 (13)		Median fulltime earnings	$47,162 (20)
60th percentile	$73,664 (25)			
40th percentile	$44,996 (46)		**SENIORS**	★★★★★ **(31)**
20th percentile	$23,930 (70)		Seniors living alone	25.3% (127)
			Poverty rate for seniors	6.9% (84)
CHILDREN	★★★★ **(151)**		Median income for seniors	$52,154 (8)
Living with two parents	59.0% (429)		Seniors who work	22.6% (116)
Older teens in school	86.9% (138)		Home ownership by seniors	82.9% (225)
Speak English very well	97.9% (352)			
Poverty rate for children	16.1% (83)		**STABILITY**	★ **(488)**
No health insurance	4.1% (126)		25-39 age group	13.9% (543)
			Born in state of residence	56.9% (444)
DIVERSITY/EQUALITY	★★★ **(252)**		Same house as 1 year ago	88.0% (133)
Racial diversity index	37.0% (206)		Live and work in county	71.3% (352)
Geographic diversity index	62.8% (93)		Married-couple households	50.7% (264)
Top 20% share of income	54.0% (535)			
Gender gap in earnings	26.0% (105)		**TRANSPORTATION**	★★ **(406)**
White-collar gender gap	26.4% (291)		Bicycle or walk to work	2.6% (308)
			Carpool to work	11.3% (201)
EDUCATION	★★★★★ **(65)**		Public transit to work	0.8% (96)
Eighth grade or less	4.8% (374)		Commute <15 minutes	37.4% (390)
High school diplomas	88.5% (253)		Commute >45 minutes	17.6% (495)

See pages 37-130 for explanations of statistics, stars, and ranks.

Elkins, WV
(Randolph County, WV)

POPULATION

2010 census	29,405 (439)
2015 estimate	29,126 (441)
2010-2015 change	-0.9% (323)
2020 projection	28,884 (441)
2030 projection	28,228 (439)

RACE

Whites	96.2% (9)
Blacks	1.9% (295)
Hispanics	0.8% (542)
Asians	0.2% (509)
Native Americans	0.2% (300)

AGE

0-17 years old	19.3% (492)
18-24 years old	8.6% (317)
25-39 years old	17.7% (236)
40-54 years old	20.8% (122)
55-64 years old	14.4% (136)
65+ years old	19.2% (72)

PRIVATE SECTOR

Businesses	741 (409)
Employees	9,420 (396)
Total wages	$293,557,491 (442)
Average weekly wages	$599 (489)

HOUSEHOLD INCOME LADDER

95th percentile	$132,252 (397)
80th percentile	$75,895 (441)
60th percentile	$47,875 (428)
40th percentile	$30,145 (415)
20th percentile	$16,664 (376)

CHILDREN   ★★★ (237)

Living with two parents	62.6% (330)
Older teens in school	79.1% (424)
Speak English very well	99.8% (38)
Poverty rate for children	21.5% (206)
No health insurance	5.2% (197)

DIVERSITY/EQUALITY   ★ (515)

Racial diversity index	7.4% (537)
Geographic diversity index	38.8% (373)
Top 20% share of income	49.1% (366)
Gender gap in earnings	36.9% (360)
White-collar gender gap	33.0% (375)

EDUCATION   ★★ (360)

Eighth grade or less	5.2% (398)
High school diplomas	86.1% (339)

Attended college	39.7% (520)
Bachelor's degrees	19.2% (241)
Advanced degrees	8.4% (106)

EMPLOYMENT   ★★★ (257)

Average jobless rate	6.7% (169)
Self-employed workers	5.5% (530)
Management/financial jobs	8.8% (488)
Computer/engineering jobs	3.5% (122)
Health care jobs	7.6% (39)

GROWTH POTENTIAL   ★ (513)

Children per senior	1.00 (503)
Median age	43.2 (456)
Moved from different state	0.8% (524)
Homes built since 2000	9.3% (420)
Construction jobs	6.6% (241)

HOUSING   ★★★★★ (106)

Home vacancy rate	9.3% (305)
Home ownership rate	72.9% (159)
Housing diversity index	86.6% (12)
4 or more bedrooms	18.4% (183)
Affordability/income ratio	$2,565 (280)

INCOME   ★★ (375)

Poverty rate	17.0% (262)
Median household income	$39,457 (396)
Interest/dividends	14.6% (424)
Public assistance	15.2% (266)
Median fulltime earnings	$33,387 (443)

SENIORS   ★★★ (243)

Seniors living alone	26.2% (186)
Poverty rate for seniors	8.5% (223)
Median income for seniors	$30,382 (396)
Seniors who work	16.4% (383)
Home ownership by seniors	85.1% (137)

STABILITY   ★★★★★ (19)

25-39 age group	17.7% (236)
Born in state of residence	77.3% (174)
Same house as 1 year ago	90.5% (34)
Live and work in county	85.5% (129)
Married-couple households	52.0% (194)

TRANSPORTATION   ★★★★ (167)

Bicycle or walk to work	3.8% (161)
Carpool to work	13.6% (80)
Public transit to work	0.0% (511)
Commute <15 minutes	47.3% (204)
Commute >45 minutes	10.4% (248)

See pages 37-130 for explanations of statistics, stars, and ranks.

Fairmont, WV
(Marion County, WV)

POPULATION				
2010 census	56,418 (165)		Attended college	52.6% (270)
2015 estimate	56,925 (166)		Bachelor's degrees	24.6% (118)
2010-2015 change	0.9% (186)		Advanced degrees	7.5% (142)
2020 projection	56,775 (165)			
2030 projection	56,126 (173)		**EMPLOYMENT**	**★★★★★ (66)**
			Average jobless rate	4.9% (63)
RACE			Self-employed workers	5.6% (523)
Whites	93.1% (107)		Management/financial jobs	11.3% (218)
Blacks	3.6% (206)		Computer/engineering jobs	4.6% (48)
Hispanics	1.2% (513)		Health care jobs	8.7% (6)
Asians	0.5% (355)			
Native Americans	0.1% (402)		**GROWTH POTENTIAL**	**★ (471)**
			Children per senior	1.14 (446)
AGE			Median age	41.1 (362)
0-17 years old	20.2% (452)		Moved from different state	1.7% (355)
18-24 years old	11.2% (110)		Homes built since 2000	8.7% (445)
25-39 years old	17.0% (317)		Construction jobs	6.0% (326)
40-54 years old	19.8% (261)			
55-64 years old	14.2% (161)		**HOUSING**	**★★★★ (206)**
65+ years old	17.7% (142)		Home vacancy rate	10.8% (397)
			Home ownership rate	76.6% (38)
PRIVATE SECTOR			Housing diversity index	84.5% (287)
Businesses	1,263 (186)		4 or more bedrooms	14.4% (381)
Employees	15,161 (207)		Affordability/income ratio	$2,312 (172)
Total wages	$636,920,718 (172)			
Average weekly wages	$808 (78)		**INCOME**	**★★★ (248)**
			Poverty rate	16.2% (232)
HOUSEHOLD INCOME LADDER			Median household income	$43,165 (286)
95th percentile	$149,044 (171)		Interest/dividends	17.5% (329)
80th percentile	$89,021 (169)		Public assistance	14.2% (215)
60th percentile	$55,587 (235)		Median fulltime earnings	$39,377 (162)
40th percentile	$34,223 (279)			
20th percentile	$18,743 (280)		**SENIORS**	**★★★ (271)**
			Seniors living alone	29.5% (405)
CHILDREN	**★★★★ (179)**		Poverty rate for seniors	7.6% (145)
Living with two parents	62.8% (323)		Median income for seniors	$29,919 (410)
Older teens in school	84.5% (220)		Seniors who work	15.4% (441)
Speak English very well	99.5% (96)		Home ownership by seniors	87.9% (42)
Poverty rate for children	24.9% (297)			
No health insurance	4.0% (118)		**STABILITY**	**★★★ (255)**
			25-39 age group	17.0% (317)
DIVERSITY/EQUALITY	**★★★ (319)**		Born in state of residence	80.4% (104)
Racial diversity index	13.2% (442)		Same house as 1 year ago	89.4% (64)
Geographic diversity index	34.4% (444)		Live and work in county	61.7% (478)
Top 20% share of income	46.9% (210)		Married-couple households	49.5% (323)
Gender gap in earnings	38.2% (399)			
White-collar gender gap	4.4% (30)		**TRANSPORTATION**	**★ (447)**
			Bicycle or walk to work	2.9% (265)
EDUCATION	**★★★★ (148)**		Carpool to work	8.3% (471)
Eighth grade or less	1.6% (84)		Public transit to work	0.8% (96)
High school diplomas	91.5% (145)		Commute <15 minutes	27.5% (540)
			Commute >45 minutes	10.8% (266)

See pages 37-130 for explanations of statistics, stars, and ranks.

Gloversville, NY
(Fulton County, NY)

POPULATION		
2010 census	55,531 (168)
2015 estimate	53,992 (178)
2010-2015 change	-2.8% (467)
2020 projection	53,198 (188)
2030 projection	51,653 (207)

RACE		
Whites	93.3% (98)
Blacks	1.6% (320)
Hispanics	2.7% (361)
Asians	0.7% (241)
Native Americans	0.1% (402)

AGE		
0-17 years old	21.0% (411)
18-24 years old	8.0% (407)
25-39 years old	17.5% (258)
40-54 years old	22.0% (31)
55-64 years old	14.2% (161)
65+ years old	17.3% (172)

PRIVATE SECTOR		
Businesses	1,114 (234)
Employees	13,469 (258)
Total wages	$474,504,073 (267)
Average weekly wages	$677 (319)

HOUSEHOLD INCOME LADDER		
95th percentile	$141,985 (266)
80th percentile	$88,460 (177)
60th percentile	$56,822 (214)
40th percentile	$37,286 (199)
20th percentile	$20,317 (217)

CHILDREN	★★★ (296)
Living with two parents	59.9% (399)
Older teens in school	81.7% (337)
Speak English very well	98.9% (226)
Poverty rate for children	24.3% (280)
No health insurance	6.5% (282)

DIVERSITY/EQUALITY	★★★ (285)
Racial diversity index	12.8% (447)
Geographic diversity index	25.3% (526)
Top 20% share of income	46.2% (138)
Gender gap in earnings	27.3% (124)
White-collar gender gap	12.0% (113)

EDUCATION	★★★ (284)
Eighth grade or less	3.2% (250)
High school diplomas	87.1% (301)
Attended college	50.5% (314)
Bachelor's degrees	15.8% (391)
Advanced degrees	7.1% (176)

EMPLOYMENT	★ (445)
Average jobless rate	9.3% (387)
Self-employed workers	6.1% (495)
Management/financial jobs	9.6% (427)
Computer/engineering jobs	2.8% (246)
Health care jobs	5.5% (250)

GROWTH POTENTIAL	★ (504)
Children per senior	1.21 (411)
Median age	42.8 (447)
Moved from different state	1.1% (487)
Homes built since 2000	7.3% (496)
Construction jobs	6.4% (270)

HOUSING	★★ (340)
Home vacancy rate	8.8% (273)
Home ownership rate	70.4% (251)
Housing diversity index	80.2% (510)
4 or more bedrooms	17.8% (215)
Affordability/income ratio	$2,304 (167)

INCOME	★★★ (252)
Poverty rate	17.1% (267)
Median household income	$46,969 (193)
Interest/dividends	19.9% (247)
Public assistance	16.8% (324)
Median fulltime earnings	$37,474 (249)

SENIORS	★★ (382)
Seniors living alone	31.5% (498)
Poverty rate for seniors	8.5% (223)
Median income for seniors	$34,170 (226)
Seniors who work	17.6% (306)
Home ownership by seniors	80.9% (339)

STABILITY	★★ (342)
25-39 age group	17.5% (258)
Born in state of residence	86.2% (23)
Same house as 1 year ago	86.5% (219)
Live and work in county	60.5% (488)
Married-couple households	46.5% (432)

TRANSPORTATION	★★ (439)
Bicycle or walk to work	2.2% (358)
Carpool to work	10.7% (260)
Public transit to work	0.6% (141)
Commute <15 minutes	37.7% (384)
Commute >45 minutes	17.1% (483)

See pages 37-130 for explanations of statistics, stars, and ranks.

Greenfield Town, MA
(Franklin County, MA)

POPULATION	
2010 census	71,372 (93)
2015 estimate	70,601 (101)
2010-2015 change	-1.1% (335)
2020 projection	70,152 (104)
2030 projection	69,384 (108)

RACE	
Whites	91.6% (151)
Blacks	1.1% (367)
Hispanics	3.6% (314)
Asians	1.6% (77)
Native Americans	0.2% (300)

AGE	
0-17 years old	18.6% (509)
18-24 years old	7.9% (424)
25-39 years old	16.4% (411)
40-54 years old	22.2% (21)
55-64 years old	17.5% (7)
65+ years old	17.4% (165)

PRIVATE SECTOR	
Businesses	2,112 (55)
Employees	21,213 (111)
Total wages	$841,252,023 (110)
Average weekly wages	$763 (135)

HOUSEHOLD INCOME LADDER	
95th percentile	$165,814 (68)
80th percentile	$100,820 (52)
60th percentile	$67,497 (51)
40th percentile	$44,047 (57)
20th percentile	$22,754 (106)

CHILDREN	★★★★★ (65)
Living with two parents	67.7% (202)
Older teens in school	84.5% (220)
Speak English very well	98.7% (265)
Poverty rate for children	15.3% (68)
No health insurance	1.7% (8)

DIVERSITY/EQUALITY	★★★★ (164)
Racial diversity index	15.9% (398)
Geographic diversity index	50.4% (209)
Top 20% share of income	47.1% (229)
Gender gap in earnings	30.9% (198)
White-collar gender gap	9.6% (86)

EDUCATION	★★★★★ (15)
Eighth grade or less	1.2% (42)
High school diplomas	94.1% (54)

Attended college	68.4% (31)
Bachelor's degrees	36.2% (22)
Advanced degrees	16.0% (12)

EMPLOYMENT	★★★★★ (47)
Average jobless rate	6.7% (169)
Self-employed workers	10.1% (158)
Management/financial jobs	14.5% (38)
Computer/engineering jobs	4.7% (40)
Health care jobs	6.3% (144)

GROWTH POTENTIAL	★ (521)
Children per senior	1.07 (477)
Median age	45.1 (500)
Moved from different state	2.5% (203)
Homes built since 2000	7.0% (505)
Construction jobs	5.9% (345)

HOUSING	★★ (397)
Home vacancy rate	5.7% (74)
Home ownership rate	69.0% (303)
Housing diversity index	80.3% (505)
4 or more bedrooms	19.1% (157)
Affordability/income ratio	$3,998 (497)

INCOME	★★★★★ (50)
Poverty rate	11.7% (77)
Median household income	$55,221 (52)
Interest/dividends	27.4% (45)
Public assistance	15.0% (254)
Median fulltime earnings	$46,974 (21)

SENIORS	★★★★ (176)
Seniors living alone	30.7% (460)
Poverty rate for seniors	7.3% (119)
Median income for seniors	$37,941 (91)
Seniors who work	28.0% (33)
Home ownership by seniors	78.3% (441)

STABILITY	★ (497)
25-39 age group	16.4% (411)
Born in state of residence	68.2% (342)
Same house as 1 year ago	87.3% (181)
Live and work in county	60.5% (488)
Married-couple households	44.8% (467)

TRANSPORTATION	★★★ (278)
Bicycle or walk to work	5.7% (64)
Carpool to work	9.1% (419)
Public transit to work	1.7% (36)
Commute <15 minutes	33.9% (463)
Commute >45 minutes	13.4% (371)

See pages 37-130 for explanations of statistics, stars, and ranks.

Hudson, NY
(Columbia County, NY)

POPULATION		Attended college	61.1% (108)
2010 census	63,096 (131)	Bachelor's degrees	29.0% (62)
2015 estimate	61,509 (137)	Advanced degrees	13.7% (22)
2010-2015 change	-2.5% (451)		
2020 projection	60,605 (145)	**EMPLOYMENT**	**★★★★★ (55)**
2030 projection	58,813 (157)	Average jobless rate	6.7% (169)
		Self-employed workers	11.6% (90)
RACE		Management/financial jobs	15.4% (25)
Whites	87.5% (232)	Computer/engineering jobs	2.8% (246)
Blacks	4.1% (185)	Health care jobs	6.1% (168)
Hispanics	4.3% (279)		
Asians	1.8% (60)	**GROWTH POTENTIAL**	**★ (494)**
Native Americans	0.1% (402)	Children per senior	0.94 (517)
		Median age	46.6 (522)
AGE		Moved from different state	1.3% (452)
0-17 years old	19.0% (501)	Homes built since 2000	9.9% (389)
18-24 years old	7.7% (454)	Construction jobs	8.0% (89)
25-39 years old	14.9% (515)		
40-54 years old	22.0% (31)	**HOUSING**	**★★★ (260)**
55-64 years old	16.2% (38)	Home vacancy rate	7.5% (186)
65+ years old	20.1% (54)	Home ownership rate	71.9% (192)
		Housing diversity index	82.4% (444)
PRIVATE SECTOR		4 or more bedrooms	21.6% (92)
Businesses	1,874 (77)	Affordability/income ratio	$3,758 (485)
Employees	16,930 (171)		
Total wages	$638,351,943 (171)	**INCOME**	**★★★★★ (29)**
Average weekly wages	$725 (207)	Poverty rate	11.7% (77)
		Median household income	$59,105 (27)
HOUSEHOLD INCOME LADDER		Interest/dividends	28.3% (33)
95th percentile	$196,394 (25)	Public assistance	10.9% (91)
80th percentile	$109,274 (26)	Median fulltime earnings	$46,790 (22)
60th percentile	$72,106 (31)		
40th percentile	$46,630 (34)	**SENIORS**	**★★★★★ (54)**
20th percentile	$25,932 (37)	Seniors living alone	26.2% (186)
		Poverty rate for seniors	7.4% (128)
CHILDREN	**★★★★ (164)**	Median income for seniors	$43,512 (39)
Living with two parents	61.8% (361)	Seniors who work	23.3% (103)
Older teens in school	79.8% (405)	Home ownership by seniors	84.0% (179)
Speak English very well	99.1% (179)		
Poverty rate for children	16.8% (91)	**STABILITY**	**★★ (433)**
No health insurance	2.7% (43)	25-39 age group	14.9% (515)
		Born in state of residence	71.3% (287)
DIVERSITY/EQUALITY	**★★★★ (154)**	Same house as 1 year ago	91.3% (25)
Racial diversity index	23.0% (314)	Live and work in county	60.5% (488)
Geographic diversity index	46.9% (256)	Married-couple households	48.4% (366)
Top 20% share of income	49.4% (396)		
Gender gap in earnings	19.9% (42)	**TRANSPORTATION**	**★★★ (295)**
White-collar gender gap	14.9% (151)	Bicycle or walk to work	4.5% (117)
		Carpool to work	9.6% (378)
EDUCATION	**★★★★★ (50)**	Public transit to work	2.5% (22)
Eighth grade or less	2.4% (169)	Commute <15 minutes	32.3% (489)
High school diplomas	90.8% (167)	Commute >45 minutes	15.4% (436)

See pages 37-130 for explanations of statistics, stars, and ranks.

Huntingdon, PA
(Huntingdon County, PA)

POPULATION

2010 census	45,913 (250)
2015 estimate	45,668 (251)
2010-2015 change	-0.5% (292)
2020 projection	45,309 (257)
2030 projection	44,533 (267)

RACE

Whites	91.2% (159)
Blacks	5.1% (160)
Hispanics	1.8% (455)
Asians	0.5% (355)
Native Americans	0.0% (523)

AGE

0-17 years old	19.1% (498)
18-24 years old	9.7% (183)
25-39 years old	18.0% (201)
40-54 years old	21.1% (97)
55-64 years old	14.0% (182)
65+ years old	18.0% (122)

PRIVATE SECTOR

Businesses	817 (364)
Employees	9,328 (402)
Total wages	$307,603,585 (427)
Average weekly wages	$634 (425)

HOUSEHOLD INCOME LADDER

95th percentile	$126,758 (470)
80th percentile	$81,250 (345)
60th percentile	$54,499 (265)
40th percentile	$35,636 (248)
20th percentile	$19,357 (252)

CHILDREN ★★★★★ (63)

Living with two parents	72.7% (89)
Older teens in school	87.9% (103)
Speak English very well	99.3% (142)
Poverty rate for children	19.9% (163)
No health insurance	4.6% (159)

DIVERSITY/EQUALITY ★★★ (263)

Racial diversity index	16.5% (390)
Geographic diversity index	26.2% (515)
Top 20% share of income	44.1% (30)
Gender gap in earnings	32.4% (239)
White-collar gender gap	16.4% (173)

EDUCATION ★★ (348)

Eighth grade or less	1.6% (84)
High school diplomas	91.8% (132)

Attended college	40.0% (515)
Bachelor's degrees	14.4% (448)
Advanced degrees	4.9% (396)

EMPLOYMENT ★★★ (272)

Average jobless rate	8.1% (298)
Self-employed workers	9.0% (254)
Management/financial jobs	10.1% (365)
Computer/engineering jobs	3.0% (193)
Health care jobs	5.9% (193)

GROWTH POTENTIAL ★★★ (278)

Children per senior	1.06 (483)
Median age	42.5 (432)
Moved from different state	1.9% (310)
Homes built since 2000	10.5% (377)
Construction jobs	9.6% (29)

HOUSING ★★★★★ (76)

Home vacancy rate	6.0% (95)
Home ownership rate	76.2% (49)
Housing diversity index	84.2% (325)
4 or more bedrooms	18.6% (174)
Affordability/income ratio	$2,680 (321)

INCOME ★★★★ (215)

Poverty rate	13.7% (145)
Median household income	$44,396 (252)
Interest/dividends	20.9% (221)
Public assistance	15.8% (286)
Median fulltime earnings	$38,563 (204)

SENIORS ★★ (360)

Seniors living alone	27.8% (283)
Poverty rate for seniors	9.2% (270)
Median income for seniors	$31,024 (370)
Seniors who work	16.0% (410)
Home ownership by seniors	82.0% (274)

STABILITY ★★★★★ (70)

25-39 age group	18.0% (201)
Born in state of residence	85.6% (36)
Same house as 1 year ago	88.1% (126)
Live and work in county	63.2% (462)
Married-couple households	55.1% (69)

TRANSPORTATION ★★ (430)

Bicycle or walk to work	6.3% (53)
Carpool to work	11.5% (184)
Public transit to work	0.3% (291)
Commute <15 minutes	32.9% (477)
Commute >45 minutes	22.3% (537)

See pages 37-130 for explanations of statistics, stars, and ranks.

Indiana, PA
(Indiana County, PA)

POPULATION

2010 census	88,880 (48)
2015 estimate	86,966 (53)
2010-2015 change	-2.2% (427)
2020 projection	85,331 (59)
2030 projection	82,032 (69)

RACE

Whites	93.9% (78)
Blacks	2.3% (267)
Hispanics	1.3% (503)
Asians	1.1% (139)
Native Americans	0.2% (300)

AGE

0-17 years old	18.4% (522)
18-24 years old	17.6% (39)
25-39 years old	15.1% (507)
40-54 years old	18.6% (412)
55-64 years old	13.8% (203)
65+ years old	16.6% (237)

PRIVATE SECTOR

Businesses	1,900 (74)
Employees	26,027 (66)
Total wages	$1,074,146,095 (58)
Average weekly wages	$794 (101)

HOUSEHOLD INCOME LADDER

95th percentile	$150,181 (160)
80th percentile	$86,126 (230)
60th percentile	$54,946 (250)
40th percentile	$34,703 (272)
20th percentile	$18,218 (305)

CHILDREN ★★★ (325)

Living with two parents	75.5% (44)
Older teens in school	87.1% (133)
Speak English very well	93.8% (497)
Poverty rate for children	20.5% (180)
No health insurance	14.8% (523)

DIVERSITY/EQUALITY ★ (545)

Racial diversity index	11.7% (471)
Geographic diversity index	27.7% (505)
Top 20% share of income	48.7% (331)
Gender gap in earnings	45.4% (504)
White-collar gender gap	37.9% (421)

EDUCATION ★★★★ (145)

Eighth grade or less	3.0% (231)
High school diplomas	91.4% (151)

Attended college	50.3% (321)
Bachelor's degrees	24.9% (111)
Advanced degrees	9.7% (68)

EMPLOYMENT ★★★★ (205)

Average jobless rate	7.8% (270)
Self-employed workers	9.4% (216)
Management/financial jobs	10.4% (332)
Computer/engineering jobs	3.0% (193)
Health care jobs	6.3% (144)

GROWTH POTENTIAL ★★ (339)

Children per senior	1.11 (457)
Median age	38.9 (228)
Moved from different state	2.3% (234)
Homes built since 2000	10.4% (381)
Construction jobs	6.8% (204)

HOUSING ★★★★ (157)

Home vacancy rate	8.5% (253)
Home ownership rate	70.8% (239)
Housing diversity index	84.9% (235)
4 or more bedrooms	18.1% (197)
Affordability/income ratio	$2,368 (198)

INCOME ★★★★ (151)

Poverty rate	17.3% (280)
Median household income	$45,195 (231)
Interest/dividends	25.4% (85)
Public assistance	12.0% (132)
Median fulltime earnings	$39,823 (146)

SENIORS ★★★ (269)

Seniors living alone	27.0% (239)
Poverty rate for seniors	7.6% (145)
Median income for seniors	$32,329 (310)
Seniors who work	16.5% (376)
Home ownership by seniors	82.4% (257)

STABILITY ★★ (381)

25-39 age group	15.1% (507)
Born in state of residence	84.7% (47)
Same house as 1 year ago	81.3% (470)
Live and work in county	76.3% (266)
Married-couple households	50.6% (267)

TRANSPORTATION ★★★ (272)

Bicycle or walk to work	6.2% (55)
Carpool to work	8.8% (448)
Public transit to work	0.6% (141)
Commute <15 minutes	39.7% (334)
Commute >45 minutes	11.7% (300)

See pages 37-130 for explanations of statistics, stars, and ranks.

Jamestown-Dunkirk-Fredonia, NY
(Chautauqua County, NY)

POPULATION	
2010 census	134,905 (9)
2015 estimate	130,779 (11)
2010-2015 change	-3.1% (487)
2020 projection	127,829 (13)
2030 projection	122,181 (16)

RACE	
Whites	88.2% (219)
Blacks	2.3% (267)
Hispanics	6.8% (203)
Asians	0.7% (241)
Native Americans	0.5% (174)

AGE	
0-17 years old	21.0% (411)
18-24 years old	10.9% (119)
25-39 years old	16.3% (418)
40-54 years old	19.9% (250)
55-64 years old	14.4% (136)
65+ years old	17.6% (151)

PRIVATE SECTOR	
Businesses	3,037 (20)
Employees	41,183 (12)
Total wages	$1,421,825,263 (22)
Average weekly wages	$664 (344)

HOUSEHOLD INCOME LADDER	
95th percentile	$134,064 (374)
80th percentile	$81,649 (331)
60th percentile	$52,704 (307)
40th percentile	$33,753 (297)
20th percentile	$17,523 (341)

CHILDREN	★★★ (324)
Living with two parents	61.4% (370)
Older teens in school	86.2% (158)
Speak English very well	96.8% (421)
Poverty rate for children	29.9% (400)
No health insurance	6.9% (307)

DIVERSITY/EQUALITY	★★★★ (204)
Racial diversity index	21.7% (328)
Geographic diversity index	39.8% (357)
Top 20% share of income	47.1% (231)
Gender gap in earnings	32.9% (255)
White-collar gender gap	7.5% (58)

EDUCATION	★★★★ (159)
Eighth grade or less	3.4% (269)
High school diplomas	89.8% (207)
Attended college	56.0% (204)
Bachelor's degrees	21.4% (180)
Advanced degrees	9.3% (76)

EMPLOYMENT	★★★ (290)
Average jobless rate	7.8% (270)
Self-employed workers	9.6% (200)
Management/financial jobs	10.7% (287)
Computer/engineering jobs	2.5% (307)
Health care jobs	5.2% (307)

GROWTH POTENTIAL	★ (509)
Children per senior	1.19 (423)
Median age	41.7 (390)
Moved from different state	2.0% (288)
Homes built since 2000	6.0% (531)
Construction jobs	5.5% (404)

HOUSING	★★ (373)
Home vacancy rate	7.9% (213)
Home ownership rate	69.6% (284)
Housing diversity index	76.5% (542)
4 or more bedrooms	18.4% (183)
Affordability/income ratio	$1,965 (46)

INCOME	★★★ (274)
Poverty rate	18.9% (334)
Median household income	$42,993 (288)
Interest/dividends	22.1% (181)
Public assistance	19.0% (399)
Median fulltime earnings	$38,680 (194)

SENIORS	★★ (341)
Seniors living alone	28.3% (318)
Poverty rate for seniors	7.9% (170)
Median income for seniors	$33,003 (282)
Seniors who work	16.9% (348)
Home ownership by seniors	80.0% (375)

STABILITY	★★★ (251)
25-39 age group	16.3% (418)
Born in state of residence	76.6% (188)
Same house as 1 year ago	85.4% (285)
Live and work in county	88.3% (86)
Married-couple households	45.6% (451)

TRANSPORTATION	★★★★ (160)
Bicycle or walk to work	5.0% (91)
Carpool to work	10.0% (337)
Public transit to work	0.3% (291)
Commute <15 minutes	49.3% (166)
Commute >45 minutes	7.8% (122)

See pages 37-130 for explanations of statistics, stars, and ranks.

Keene, NH
(Cheshire County, NH)

POPULATION

2010 census	77,117 (77)
2015 estimate	75,909 (81)
2010-2015 change	-1.6% (381)
2020 projection	74,980 (89)
2030 projection	73,126 (95)

RACE

Whites	94.7% (55)
Blacks	0.7% (423)
Hispanics	1.6% (472)
Asians	1.2% (125)
Native Americans	0.2% (300)

AGE

0-17 years old	18.8% (504)
18-24 years old	12.8% (74)
25-39 years old	16.4% (411)
40-54 years old	20.4% (169)
55-64 years old	15.0% (87)
65+ years old	16.6% (237)

PRIVATE SECTOR

Businesses	1,998 (60)
Employees	27,098 (59)
Total wages	$1,175,575,379 (45)
Average weekly wages	$834 (59)

HOUSEHOLD INCOME LADDER

95th percentile	$177,197 (42)
80th percentile	$104,259 (42)
60th percentile	$69,416 (41)
40th percentile	$45,917 (38)
20th percentile	$24,493 (55)

CHILDREN ★★★★★ (54)

Living with two parents	65.6% (256)
Older teens in school	91.2% (51)
Speak English very well	99.5% (96)
Poverty rate for children	16.9% (94)
No health insurance	4.0% (118)

DIVERSITY/EQUALITY ★★★★ (194)

Racial diversity index	10.2% (493)
Geographic diversity index	62.5% (95)
Top 20% share of income	48.0% (296)
Gender gap in earnings	31.6% (218)
White-collar gender gap	15.7% (159)

EDUCATION ★★★★★ (34)

Eighth grade or less	1.2% (42)
High school diplomas	94.3% (47)
Attended college	61.7% (100)
Bachelor's degrees	32.9% (36)
Advanced degrees	12.0% (37)

EMPLOYMENT ★★★★★ (57)

Average jobless rate	6.1% (121)
Self-employed workers	9.2% (231)
Management/financial jobs	13.9% (50)
Computer/engineering jobs	4.9% (33)
Health care jobs	6.0% (181)

GROWTH POTENTIAL ★★★★ (184)

Children per senior	1.13 (452)
Median age	42.0 (398)
Moved from different state	5.5% (39)
Homes built since 2000	11.3% (344)
Construction jobs	8.2% (78)

HOUSING ★★★★ (212)

Home vacancy rate	4.9% (31)
Home ownership rate	70.9% (232)
Housing diversity index	83.1% (414)
4 or more bedrooms	17.1% (239)
Affordability/income ratio	$3,267 (444)

INCOME ★★★★★ (42)

Poverty rate	11.8% (82)
Median household income	$57,782 (34)
Interest/dividends	26.5% (62)
Public assistance	10.6% (84)
Median fulltime earnings	$44,575 (34)

SENIORS ★★★★ (146)

Seniors living alone	26.9% (230)
Poverty rate for seniors	8.7% (241)
Median income for seniors	$39,059 (71)
Seniors who work	25.6% (57)
Home ownership by seniors	78.2% (445)

STABILITY ★ (516)

25-39 age group	16.4% (411)
Born in state of residence	43.7% (509)
Same house as 1 year ago	82.8% (406)
Live and work in county	77.3% (250)
Married-couple households	48.9% (351)

TRANSPORTATION ★★ (344)

Bicycle or walk to work	4.2% (142)
Carpool to work	8.9% (439)
Public transit to work	0.4% (219)
Commute <15 minutes	38.6% (360)
Commute >45 minutes	11.3% (285)

See pages 37-130 for explanations of statistics, stars, and ranks.

Laconia, NH
(Belknap County, NH)

POPULATION	
2010 census	60,088 (150)
2015 estimate	60,641 (145)
2010-2015 change	0.9% (186)
2020 projection	60,967 (141)
2030 projection	61,600 (143)

RACE	
Whites	95.1% (42)
Blacks	0.5% (466)
Hispanics	1.6% (472)
Asians	1.1% (139)
Native Americans	0.2% (300)

AGE	
0-17 years old	19.8% (468)
18-24 years old	7.3% (503)
25-39 years old	15.6% (474)
40-54 years old	21.6% (50)
55-64 years old	16.8% (21)
65+ years old	18.9% (85)

PRIVATE SECTOR	
Businesses	1,876 (76)
Employees	21,458 (105)
Total wages	$863,979,216 (103)
Average weekly wages	$774 (123)

HOUSEHOLD INCOME LADDER	
95th percentile	$184,046 (36)
80th percentile	$109,832 (25)
60th percentile	$74,933 (23)
40th percentile	$49,819 (20)
20th percentile	$25,673 (42)

CHILDREN	★★★★★ (81)
Living with two parents	67.2% (214)
Older teens in school	85.3% (193)
Speak English very well	99.6% (77)
Poverty rate for children	18.2% (128)
No health insurance	3.5% (82)

DIVERSITY/EQUALITY	★★★★ (111)
Racial diversity index	9.5% (505)
Geographic diversity index	59.9% (123)
Top 20% share of income	46.8% (198)
Gender gap in earnings	22.6% (63)
White-collar gender gap	18.1% (189)

EDUCATION	★★★★★ (62)
Eighth grade or less	1.4% (60)
High school diplomas	92.5% (110)
Attended college	61.8% (96)
Bachelor's degrees	29.7% (55)
Advanced degrees	9.6% (71)

EMPLOYMENT	★★★★★ (19)
Average jobless rate	5.3% (82)
Self-employed workers	11.5% (99)
Management/financial jobs	14.9% (32)
Computer/engineering jobs	3.8% (96)
Health care jobs	7.5% (44)

GROWTH POTENTIAL	★★★ (241)
Children per senior	1.05 (485)
Median age	46.1 (514)
Moved from different state	2.3% (234)
Homes built since 2000	16.6% (164)
Construction jobs	9.7% (25)

HOUSING	★★★★★ (107)
Home vacancy rate	4.4% (14)
Home ownership rate	74.9% (83)
Housing diversity index	85.4% (156)
4 or more bedrooms	16.3% (279)
Affordability/income ratio	$3,533 (462)

INCOME	★★★★★ (40)
Poverty rate	10.5% (44)
Median household income	$62,159 (22)
Interest/dividends	24.2% (126)
Public assistance	10.7% (88)
Median fulltime earnings	$43,423 (41)

SENIORS	★★★★★ (34)
Seniors living alone	21.7% (32)
Poverty rate for seniors	7.4% (128)
Median income for seniors	$41,081 (52)
Seniors who work	23.4% (98)
Home ownership by seniors	82.5% (251)

STABILITY	★ (459)
25-39 age group	15.6% (474)
Born in state of residence	53.1% (475)
Same house as 1 year ago	90.0% (44)
Live and work in county	61.0% (483)
Married-couple households	53.4% (134)

TRANSPORTATION	★ (532)
Bicycle or walk to work	1.5% (457)
Carpool to work	8.9% (439)
Public transit to work	0.0% (511)
Commute <15 minutes	32.0% (499)
Commute >45 minutes	17.2% (486)

See pages 37-130 for explanations of statistics, stars, and ranks.

Lewisburg, PA
(Union County, PA)

POPULATION
2010 census	44,947 (263)
2015 estimate	44,954 (262)
2010-2015 change	0.0% (255)
2020 projection	45,193 (258)
2030 projection	45,592 (258)

RACE
Whites	84.6% (270)
Blacks	6.5% (142)
Hispanics	5.6% (233)
Asians	1.3% (112)
Native Americans	0.3% (231)

AGE
0-17 years old	18.5% (517)
18-24 years old	13.7% (63)
25-39 years old	19.4% (78)
40-54 years old	20.7% (132)
55-64 years old	11.9% (447)
65+ years old	15.8% (305)

PRIVATE SECTOR
Businesses	906 (308)
Employees	14,009 (233)
Total wages	$542,987,063 (218)
Average weekly wages	$745 (165)

HOUSEHOLD INCOME LADDER
95th percentile	$173,870 (46)
80th percentile	$94,061 (99)
60th percentile	$60,708 (138)
40th percentile	$41,394 (92)
20th percentile	$23,292 (87)

CHILDREN ★★★★ (220)
Living with two parents	73.0% (80)
Older teens in school	89.6% (72)
Speak English very well	97.1% (408)
Poverty rate for children	17.8% (120)
No health insurance	14.4% (518)

DIVERSITY/EQUALITY ★★ (419)
Racial diversity index	27.6% (275)
Geographic diversity index	50.7% (202)
Top 20% share of income	49.6% (407)
Gender gap in earnings	36.1% (343)
White-collar gender gap	41.0% (456)

EDUCATION ★★★ (317)
Eighth grade or less	4.9% (380)
High school diplomas	85.2% (368)
Attended college	45.0% (439)
Bachelor's degrees	21.0% (188)
Advanced degrees	7.8% (129)

EMPLOYMENT ★★★★★ (65)
Average jobless rate	6.1% (121)
Self-employed workers	13.8% (35)
Management/financial jobs	9.9% (392)
Computer/engineering jobs	4.4% (60)
Health care jobs	6.2% (156)

GROWTH POTENTIAL ★★★★ (150)
Children per senior	1.18 (427)
Median age	38.6 (207)
Moved from different state	5.7% (33)
Homes built since 2000	10.2% (386)
Construction jobs	7.9% (93)

HOUSING ★★★★★ (56)
Home vacancy rate	4.3% (13)
Home ownership rate	71.5% (204)
Housing diversity index	85.5% (143)
4 or more bedrooms	21.8% (85)
Affordability/income ratio	$3,217 (436)

INCOME ★★★★★ (88)
Poverty rate	12.8% (109)
Median household income	$49,803 (130)
Interest/dividends	25.9% (71)
Public assistance	11.8% (122)
Median fulltime earnings	$40,970 (99)

SENIORS ★★★ (297)
Seniors living alone	23.6% (73)
Poverty rate for seniors	6.7% (73)
Median income for seniors	$31,891 (324)
Seniors who work	16.4% (383)
Home ownership by seniors	76.2% (509)

STABILITY ★★★ (266)
25-39 age group	19.4% (78)
Born in state of residence	68.5% (336)
Same house as 1 year ago	83.8% (347)
Live and work in county	60.7% (486)
Married-couple households	54.4% (93)

TRANSPORTATION ★★★ (305)
Bicycle or walk to work	6.0% (59)
Carpool to work	9.9% (348)
Public transit to work	0.1% (441)
Commute <15 minutes	36.0% (418)
Commute >45 minutes	11.4% (292)

See pages 37-130 for explanations of statistics, stars, and ranks.

Lewistown, PA
(Mifflin County, PA)

POPULATION		
2010 census	46,682 (239)	
2015 estimate	46,500 (239)	
2010-2015 change	-0.4% (286)	
2020 projection	46,185 (244)	
2030 projection	45,461 (259)	

RACE		
Whites	96.5% (5)	
Blacks	0.7% (423)	
Hispanics	1.3% (503)	
Asians	0.5% (355)	
Native Americans	0.0% (523)	

AGE		
0-17 years old	22.7% (284)	
18-24 years old	7.3% (503)	
25-39 years old	15.6% (474)	
40-54 years old	20.9% (112)	
55-64 years old	13.8% (203)	
65+ years old	19.7% (59)	

PRIVATE SECTOR		
Businesses	960 (290)	
Employees	13,706 (248)	
Total wages	$503,050,453 (242)	
Average weekly wages	$706 (240)	

HOUSEHOLD INCOME LADDER		
95th percentile	$121,993 (502)	
80th percentile	$75,701 (445)	
60th percentile	$50,140 (378)	
40th percentile	$32,956 (325)	
20th percentile	$19,032 (263)	

CHILDREN	★ (537)	
Living with two parents	70.5% (131)	
Older teens in school	74.3% (507)	
Speak English very well	88.0% (533)	
Poverty rate for children	25.8% (320)	
No health insurance	18.7% (542)	

DIVERSITY/EQUALITY	★ (467)	
Racial diversity index	6.8% (543)	
Geographic diversity index	17.4% (550)	
Top 20% share of income	44.5% (41)	
Gender gap in earnings	33.8% (280)	
White-collar gender gap	28.1% (310)	

EDUCATION	★ (493)	
Eighth grade or less	6.0% (424)	
High school diplomas	85.1% (374)	
Attended college	36.8% (536)	
Bachelor's degrees	12.6% (504)	
Advanced degrees	3.1% (524)	

EMPLOYMENT	★★★ (302)	
Average jobless rate	6.4% (147)	
Self-employed workers	8.5% (290)	
Management/financial jobs	8.3% (513)	
Computer/engineering jobs	2.8% (246)	
Health care jobs	6.2% (156)	

GROWTH POTENTIAL	★ (502)	
Children per senior	1.15 (442)	
Median age	43.5 (464)	
Moved from different state	0.7% (540)	
Homes built since 2000	7.3% (496)	
Construction jobs	7.2% (162)	

HOUSING	★★★★ (189)	
Home vacancy rate	6.7% (141)	
Home ownership rate	70.4% (251)	
Housing diversity index	84.2% (325)	
4 or more bedrooms	14.7% (370)	
Affordability/income ratio	$2,369 (200)	

INCOME	★★★ (314)	
Poverty rate	15.8% (217)	
Median household income	$41,288 (344)	
Interest/dividends	20.9% (221)	
Public assistance	19.3% (409)	
Median fulltime earnings	$35,225 (374)	

SENIORS	★★ (403)	
Seniors living alone	26.9% (230)	
Poverty rate for seniors	8.5% (223)	
Median income for seniors	$30,357 (398)	
Seniors who work	16.3% (391)	
Home ownership by seniors	77.8% (461)	

STABILITY	★★★★ (120)	
25-39 age group	15.6% (474)	
Born in state of residence	90.8% (2)	
Same house as 1 year ago	88.4% (109)	
Live and work in county	73.0% (329)	
Married-couple households	51.2% (242)	

TRANSPORTATION	★★★ (280)	
Bicycle or walk to work	4.3% (130)	
Carpool to work	13.0% (101)	
Public transit to work	0.2% (363)	
Commute <15 minutes	39.2% (343)	
Commute >45 minutes	14.2% (395)	

See pages 37-130 for explanations of statistics, stars, and ranks.

Lock Haven, PA
(Clinton County, PA)

POPULATION		Attended college	46.2% (414)
2010 census	39,238 (321)	Bachelor's degrees	18.3% (274)
2015 estimate	39,441 (319)	Advanced degrees	6.0% (264)
2010-2015 change	0.5% (219)		
2020 projection	39,532 (319)	**EMPLOYMENT**	**★★ (391)**
2030 projection	39,643 (323)	Average jobless rate	6.1% (121)
		Self-employed workers	7.6% (376)
RACE		Management/financial jobs	9.4% (444)
Whites	95.4% (31)	Computer/engineering jobs	2.6% (288)
Blacks	1.4% (340)	Health care jobs	4.6% (401)
Hispanics	1.3% (503)		
Asians	0.6% (291)	**GROWTH POTENTIAL**	**★★ (355)**
Native Americans	0.1% (402)	Children per senior	1.22 (401)
		Median age	38.1 (187)
AGE		Moved from different state	1.4% (425)
0-17 years old	20.6% (423)	Homes built since 2000	7.9% (470)
18-24 years old	16.2% (51)	Construction jobs	7.3% (151)
25-39 years old	15.2% (498)		
40-54 years old	18.6% (412)	**HOUSING**	**★★★★ (122)**
55-64 years old	12.6% (385)	Home vacancy rate	5.8% (79)
65+ years old	16.9% (207)	Home ownership rate	71.3% (215)
		Housing diversity index	84.4% (299)
PRIVATE SECTOR		4 or more bedrooms	17.7% (220)
Businesses	792 (378)	Affordability/income ratio	$2,604 (290)
Employees	10,541 (359)		
Total wages	$400,599,540 (336)	**INCOME**	**★★★ (263)**
Average weekly wages	$731 (194)	Poverty rate	16.4% (241)
		Median household income	$45,078 (235)
HOUSEHOLD INCOME LADDER		Interest/dividends	18.3% (299)
95th percentile	$131,141 (415)	Public assistance	16.4% (309)
80th percentile	$85,765 (236)	Median fulltime earnings	$37,647 (240)
60th percentile	$56,621 (219)		
40th percentile	$35,626 (249)	**SENIORS**	**★★ (336)**
20th percentile	$19,109 (261)	Seniors living alone	28.3% (318)
		Poverty rate for seniors	8.3% (202)
CHILDREN	**★★ (366)**	Median income for seniors	$31,291 (361)
Living with two parents	66.4% (235)	Seniors who work	17.0% (341)
Older teens in school	87.5% (112)	Home ownership by seniors	81.6% (299)
Speak English very well	93.9% (495)		
Poverty rate for children	25.3% (307)	**STABILITY**	**★★★ (297)**
No health insurance	11.6% (462)	25-39 age group	15.2% (498)
		Born in state of residence	86.2% (23)
DIVERSITY/EQUALITY	**★★ (372)**	Same house as 1 year ago	86.1% (245)
Racial diversity index	8.9% (518)	Live and work in county	66.9% (419)
Geographic diversity index	25.3% (526)	Married-couple households	51.4% (231)
Top 20% share of income	45.3% (79)		
Gender gap in earnings	42.0% (471)	**TRANSPORTATION**	**★★★ (311)**
White-collar gender gap	4.4% (30)	Bicycle or walk to work	4.4% (123)
		Carpool to work	10.7% (260)
EDUCATION	**★★★ (266)**	Public transit to work	0.3% (291)
Eighth grade or less	2.5% (180)	Commute <15 minutes	40.8% (320)
High school diplomas	90.1% (200)	Commute >45 minutes	12.9% (353)

See pages 37-130 for explanations of statistics, stars, and ranks.

Logan, WV
(Logan County, WV)

POPULATION

2010 census	36,743 (362)
2015 estimate	34,707 (385)
2010-2015 change	-5.5% (538)
2020 projection	33,073 (406)
2030 projection	29,842 (424)

RACE

Whites	95.8% (24)
Blacks	2.1% (283)
Hispanics	0.9% (535)
Asians	0.4% (413)
Native Americans	0.2% (300)

AGE

0-17 years old	20.8% (417)
18-24 years old	7.3% (503)
25-39 years old	18.1% (186)
40-54 years old	20.9% (112)
55-64 years old	16.6% (25)
65+ years old	16.3% (268)

PRIVATE SECTOR

Businesses	780 (382)
Employees	8,157 (443)
Total wages	$336,565,356 (396)
Average weekly wages	$793 (103)

HOUSEHOLD INCOME LADDER

95th percentile	$130,340 (428)
80th percentile	$82,425 (312)
60th percentile	$49,900 (386)
40th percentile	$27,333 (473)
20th percentile	$15,463 (436)

CHILDREN ★★★★ (176)

Living with two parents	72.7% (89)
Older teens in school	77.9% (452)
Speak English very well	99.1% (179)
Poverty rate for children	23.8% (268)
No health insurance	3.9% (111)

DIVERSITY/EQUALITY ★ (508)

Racial diversity index	8.2% (527)
Geographic diversity index	26.5% (511)
Top 20% share of income	47.9% (286)
Gender gap in earnings	47.8% (518)
White-collar gender gap	8.1% (65)

EDUCATION ★ (510)

Eighth grade or less	5.8% (413)
High school diplomas	82.5% (431)
Attended college	38.8% (526)
Bachelor's degrees	8.2% (548)
Advanced degrees	2.6% (544)

EMPLOYMENT ★ (448)

Average jobless rate	10.9% (454)
Self-employed workers	5.8% (508)
Management/financial jobs	8.4% (510)
Computer/engineering jobs	3.0% (193)
Health care jobs	6.9% (79)

GROWTH POTENTIAL ★ (532)

Children per senior	1.28 (357)
Median age	42.6 (437)
Moved from different state	1.2% (474)
Homes built since 2000	11.9% (318)
Construction jobs	3.7% (542)

HOUSING ★★★★ (164)

Home vacancy rate	12.3% (469)
Home ownership rate	75.9% (58)
Housing diversity index	86.3% (36)
4 or more bedrooms	15.7% (315)
Affordability/income ratio	$2,233 (135)

INCOME ★★★ (246)

Poverty rate	19.7% (362)
Median household income	$36,763 (447)
Interest/dividends	32.2% (9)
Public assistance	22.3% (482)
Median fulltime earnings	$40,686 (109)

SENIORS ★★★ (327)

Seniors living alone	27.2% (254)
Poverty rate for seniors	8.2% (196)
Median income for seniors	$31,954 (321)
Seniors who work	10.6% (548)
Home ownership by seniors	85.9% (105)

STABILITY ★★★★★ (17)

25-39 age group	18.1% (186)
Born in state of residence	85.3% (41)
Same house as 1 year ago	89.2% (72)
Live and work in county	79.3% (229)
Married-couple households	52.3% (180)

TRANSPORTATION ★ (481)

Bicycle or walk to work	3.8% (161)
Carpool to work	9.4% (394)
Public transit to work	0.0% (511)
Commute <15 minutes	34.0% (460)
Commute >45 minutes	17.7% (497)

See pages 37-130 for explanations of statistics, stars, and ranks.

Malone, NY
(Franklin County, NY)

POPULATION

2010 census	51,599 (198)
2015 estimate	50,660 (209)
2010-2015 change	-1.8% (389)
2020 projection	50,050 (211)
2030 projection	48,881 (225)

RACE

Whites	81.9% (302)
Blacks	5.4% (153)
Hispanics	3.3% (324)
Asians	0.4% (413)
Native Americans	7.2% (26)

AGE

0-17 years old	20.3% (445)
18-24 years old	10.0% (163)
25-39 years old	19.9% (63)
40-54 years old	22.1% (25)
55-64 years old	13.2% (297)
65+ years old	14.5% (412)

PRIVATE SECTOR

Businesses	1,008 (273)
Employees	10,438 (361)
Total wages	$350,707,341 (382)
Average weekly wages	$646 (401)

HOUSEHOLD INCOME LADDER

95th percentile	$142,480 (260)
80th percentile	$90,355 (152)
60th percentile	$58,679 (169)
40th percentile	$36,199 (225)
20th percentile	$17,289 (349)

CHILDREN ★★ (405)

Living with two parents	59.1% (425)
Older teens in school	83.0% (276)
Speak English very well	98.7% (265)
Poverty rate for children	29.9% (400)
No health insurance	11.2% (452)

DIVERSITY/EQUALITY ★★★★★ (104)

Racial diversity index	32.0% (237)
Geographic diversity index	36.5% (416)
Top 20% share of income	46.8% (188)
Gender gap in earnings	17.8% (31)
White-collar gender gap	19.4% (200)

EDUCATION ★★★ (267)

Eighth grade or less	3.8% (307)
High school diplomas	86.5% (327)
Attended college	50.5% (314)
Bachelor's degrees	17.0% (328)
Advanced degrees	8.0% (123)

EMPLOYMENT ★★★ (235)

Average jobless rate	8.8% (344)
Self-employed workers	10.5% (139)
Management/financial jobs	10.1% (365)
Computer/engineering jobs	2.6% (288)
Health care jobs	6.3% (144)

GROWTH POTENTIAL ★★ (397)

Children per senior	1.40 (279)
Median age	39.8 (285)
Moved from different state	1.7% (355)
Homes built since 2000	9.7% (399)
Construction jobs	5.9% (345)

HOUSING ★★★★ (118)

Home vacancy rate	5.8% (79)
Home ownership rate	72.7% (162)
Housing diversity index	81.4% (479)
4 or more bedrooms	20.6% (114)
Affordability/income ratio	$2,120 (89)

INCOME ★★★ (261)

Poverty rate	20.3% (384)
Median household income	$47,923 (179)
Interest/dividends	18.2% (305)
Public assistance	17.7% (361)
Median fulltime earnings	$40,666 (110)

SENIORS ★★★ (275)

Seniors living alone	28.2% (311)
Poverty rate for seniors	10.7% (357)
Median income for seniors	$35,384 (177)
Seniors who work	17.0% (341)
Home ownership by seniors	84.6% (159)

STABILITY ★★★★ (173)

25-39 age group	19.9% (63)
Born in state of residence	79.2% (125)
Same house as 1 year ago	82.4% (422)
Live and work in county	81.2% (200)
Married-couple households	46.0% (443)

TRANSPORTATION ★★★★ (193)

Bicycle or walk to work	4.8% (98)
Carpool to work	10.9% (239)
Public transit to work	0.7% (119)
Commute <15 minutes	45.7% (237)
Commute >45 minutes	11.3% (285)

See pages 37-130 for explanations of statistics, stars, and ranks.

Meadville, PA
(Crawford County, PA)

POPULATION	
2010 census	88,765 (49)
2015 estimate	86,484 (54)
2010-2015 change	-2.6% (455)
2020 projection	84,467 (60)
2030 projection	80,463 (75)

RACE	
Whites	95.2% (38)
Blacks	1.8% (309)
Hispanics	1.2% (513)
Asians	0.5% (355)
Native Americans	0.1% (402)

AGE	
0-17 years old	21.6% (366)
18-24 years old	9.7% (183)
25-39 years old	15.6% (474)
40-54 years old	20.5% (151)
55-64 years old	14.7% (97)
65+ years old	17.9% (132)

PRIVATE SECTOR	
Businesses	2,038 (58)
Employees	27,073 (60)
Total wages	$976,273,256 (72)
Average weekly wages	$693 (274)

HOUSEHOLD INCOME LADDER	
95th percentile	$135,910 (344)
80th percentile	$82,475 (307)
60th percentile	$54,298 (274)
40th percentile	$35,684 (245)
20th percentile	$19,793 (237)

CHILDREN	★★ (412)
Living with two parents	69.1% (164)
Older teens in school	76.5% (482)
Speak English very well	95.3% (471)
Poverty rate for children	22.1% (224)
No health insurance	11.7% (466)

DIVERSITY/EQUALITY	★ (444)
Racial diversity index	9.3% (509)
Geographic diversity index	31.2% (474)
Top 20% share of income	46.5% (162)
Gender gap in earnings	38.4% (406)
White-collar gender gap	21.5% (226)

EDUCATION	★★★ (245)
Eighth grade or less	3.8% (307)
High school diplomas	89.4% (220)

Attended college	46.6% (405)
Bachelor's degrees	21.5% (174)
Advanced degrees	7.4% (149)

EMPLOYMENT	★★★★★ (103)
Average jobless rate	7.2% (218)
Self-employed workers	11.5% (99)
Management/financial jobs	10.7% (287)
Computer/engineering jobs	3.1% (180)
Health care jobs	6.9% (79)

GROWTH POTENTIAL	★ (490)
Children per senior	1.21 (411)
Median age	42.4 (429)
Moved from different state	1.5% (406)
Homes built since 2000	8.1% (465)
Construction jobs	6.0% (326)

HOUSING	★★★★★ (87)
Home vacancy rate	6.8% (151)
Home ownership rate	73.5% (137)
Housing diversity index	84.1% (337)
4 or more bedrooms	19.5% (141)
Affordability/income ratio	$2,351 (191)

INCOME	★★★★ (209)
Poverty rate	14.7% (182)
Median household income	$44,579 (247)
Interest/dividends	23.7% (137)
Public assistance	16.2% (301)
Median fulltime earnings	$37,868 (228)

SENIORS	★★★ (312)
Seniors living alone	26.9% (230)
Poverty rate for seniors	8.0% (177)
Median income for seniors	$32,482 (303)
Seniors who work	18.3% (272)
Home ownership by seniors	79.0% (417)

STABILITY	★★★★ (151)
25-39 age group	15.6% (474)
Born in state of residence	82.5% (75)
Same house as 1 year ago	87.8% (149)
Live and work in county	76.2% (269)
Married-couple households	52.1% (190)

TRANSPORTATION	★★★★ (207)
Bicycle or walk to work	5.7% (64)
Carpool to work	12.3% (130)
Public transit to work	0.3% (291)
Commute <15 minutes	40.1% (328)
Commute >45 minutes	12.2% (321)

See pages 37-130 for explanations of statistics, stars, and ranks.

New Castle, PA
(Lawrence County, PA)

POPULATION

2010 census	91,108 (42)
2015 estimate	88,082 (50)
2010-2015 change	-3.3% (495)
2020 projection	85,344 (58)
2030 projection	80,005 (79)

RACE

Whites	92.3% (124)
Blacks	3.7% (202)
Hispanics	1.2% (513)
Asians	0.4% (413)
Native Americans	0.1% (402)

AGE

0-17 years old	20.5% (433)
18-24 years old	8.3% (362)
25-39 years old	16.1% (442)
40-54 years old	20.2% (202)
55-64 years old	15.3% (68)
65+ years old	19.6% (61)

PRIVATE SECTOR

Businesses	1,948 (66)
Employees	25,207 (75)
Total wages	$955,260,282 (79)
Average weekly wages	$729 (196)

HOUSEHOLD INCOME LADDER

95th percentile	$147,188 (195)
80th percentile	$86,013 (231)
60th percentile	$54,974 (249)
40th percentile	$35,023 (260)
20th percentile	$18,464 (291)

CHILDREN ★★★ (224)

Living with two parents	59.9% (399)
Older teens in school	84.5% (220)
Speak English very well	98.4% (300)
Poverty rate for children	24.3% (280)
No health insurance	4.0% (118)

DIVERSITY/EQUALITY ★ (506)

Racial diversity index	14.6% (422)
Geographic diversity index	30.5% (478)
Top 20% share of income	48.4% (316)
Gender gap in earnings	41.2% (459)
White-collar gender gap	25.4% (277)

EDUCATION ★★★★ (173)

Eighth grade or less	1.7% (97)
High school diplomas	92.4% (115)
Attended college	50.2% (325)
Bachelor's degrees	22.4% (145)
Advanced degrees	6.8% (191)

EMPLOYMENT ★★★★ (206)

Average jobless rate	7.0% (196)
Self-employed workers	7.9% (345)
Management/financial jobs	9.7% (416)
Computer/engineering jobs	3.0% (193)
Health care jobs	7.1% (63)

GROWTH POTENTIAL ★ (525)

Children per senior	1.04 (487)
Median age	44.4 (491)
Moved from different state	1.4% (425)
Homes built since 2000	7.5% (487)
Construction jobs	6.4% (270)

HOUSING ★★★★ (191)

Home vacancy rate	9.4% (309)
Home ownership rate	73.9% (122)
Housing diversity index	83.6% (385)
4 or more bedrooms	16.3% (279)
Affordability/income ratio	$2,183 (117)

INCOME ★★★★ (210)

Poverty rate	15.2% (199)
Median household income	$44,571 (248)
Interest/dividends	23.9% (130)
Public assistance	18.9% (397)
Median fulltime earnings	$40,430 (124)

SENIORS ★★ (363)

Seniors living alone	28.5% (332)
Poverty rate for seniors	7.3% (119)
Median income for seniors	$30,787 (379)
Seniors who work	17.7% (302)
Home ownership by seniors	79.4% (400)

STABILITY ★★★ (227)

25-39 age group	16.1% (442)
Born in state of residence	82.9% (68)
Same house as 1 year ago	90.9% (31)
Live and work in county	63.7% (456)
Married-couple households	49.5% (323)

TRANSPORTATION ★★ (412)

Bicycle or walk to work	2.5% (322)
Carpool to work	8.5% (462)
Public transit to work	1.2% (54)
Commute <15 minutes	36.1% (415)
Commute >45 minutes	13.7% (379)

See pages 37-130 for explanations of statistics, stars, and ranks.

Ogdensburg-Massena, NY
(St. Lawrence County, NY)

POPULATION			Attended college	55.1% (221)
2010 census	111,944 (16)		Bachelor's degrees	23.4% (127)
2015 estimate	111,007 (17)		Advanced degrees	11.6% (41)
2010-2015 change	-0.8% (314)		**EMPLOYMENT**	★★★ (297)
2020 projection	110,393 (20)		Average jobless rate	10.0% (420)
2030 projection	109,163 (26)		Self-employed workers	9.9% (171)
			Management/financial jobs	10.5% (318)
RACE			Computer/engineering jobs	2.5% (307)
Whites	92.2% (128)		Health care jobs	6.1% (168)
Blacks	2.1% (283)			
Hispanics	2.2% (406)		**GROWTH POTENTIAL**	★★★ (300)
Asians	1.1% (139)		Children per senior	1.39 (286)
Native Americans	0.8% (125)		Median age	37.8 (174)
			Moved from different state	2.2% (248)
AGE			Homes built since 2000	8.6% (449)
0-17 years old	20.7% (420)		Construction jobs	6.7% (219)
18-24 years old	14.9% (57)			
25-39 years old	16.8% (359)		**HOUSING**	★★★★ (128)
40-54 years old	19.7% (273)		Home vacancy rate	6.6% (136)
55-64 years old	12.9% (343)		Home ownership rate	71.4% (209)
65+ years old	14.9% (374)		Housing diversity index	82.6% (433)
			4 or more bedrooms	19.1% (157)
PRIVATE SECTOR			Affordability/income ratio	$1,960 (44)
Businesses	1,952 (65)			
Employees	24,905 (77)		**INCOME**	★★★ (255)
Total wages	$935,821,845 (84)		Poverty rate	19.4% (353)
Average weekly wages	$723 (211)		Median household income	$44,705 (242)
			Interest/dividends	19.8% (254)
HOUSEHOLD INCOME LADDER			Public assistance	17.7% (361)
95th percentile	$144,945 (229)		Median fulltime earnings	$41,061 (93)
80th percentile	$84,579 (261)			
60th percentile	$54,773 (257)		**SENIORS**	★★ (365)
40th percentile	$34,870 (266)		Seniors living alone	28.6% (336)
20th percentile	$18,216 (306)		Poverty rate for seniors	9.1% (263)
			Median income for seniors	$35,018 (187)
CHILDREN	★★★ (276)		Seniors who work	13.6% (515)
Living with two parents	63.9% (301)		Home ownership by seniors	82.0% (274)
Older teens in school	88.1% (100)			
Speak English very well	97.8% (361)		**STABILITY**	★★★★ (217)
Poverty rate for children	27.5% (356)		25-39 age group	16.8% (359)
No health insurance	8.8% (385)		Born in state of residence	80.2% (109)
			Same house as 1 year ago	83.4% (375)
DIVERSITY/EQUALITY	★★ (368)		Live and work in county	89.6% (72)
Racial diversity index	14.9% (417)		Married-couple households	46.3% (437)
Geographic diversity index	35.0% (436)			
Top 20% share of income	48.9% (349)		**TRANSPORTATION**	★★★★ (157)
Gender gap in earnings	32.7% (245)		Bicycle or walk to work	7.8% (32)
White-collar gender gap	14.2% (142)		Carpool to work	9.9% (348)
			Public transit to work	0.5% (178)
EDUCATION	★★★★ (117)		Commute <15 minutes	44.3% (257)
Eighth grade or less	3.1% (238)		Commute >45 minutes	11.2% (278)
High school diplomas	90.3% (192)			

See pages 37-130 for explanations of statistics, stars, and ranks.

Oil City, PA
(Venango County, PA)

POPULATION	
2010 census	54,984 (174)
2015 estimate	53,119 (189)
2010-2015 change	-3.4% (501)
2020 projection	51,382 (205)
2030 projection	48,011 (231)

RACE	
Whites	96.1% (15)
Blacks	0.8% (404)
Hispanics	1.0% (530)
Asians	0.4% (413)
Native Americans	0.1% (402)

AGE	
0-17 years old	20.6% (423)
18-24 years old	7.5% (483)
25-39 years old	15.6% (474)
40-54 years old	20.7% (132)
55-64 years old	16.3% (35)
65+ years old	19.3% (68)

PRIVATE SECTOR	
Businesses	1,190 (208)
Employees	15,650 (198)
Total wages	$556,877,930 (212)
Average weekly wages	$684 (302)

HOUSEHOLD INCOME LADDER	
95th percentile	$130,778 (421)
80th percentile	$80,497 (363)
60th percentile	$53,776 (283)
40th percentile	$35,329 (255)
20th percentile	$20,302 (218)

CHILDREN	★★★ (282)
Living with two parents	63.5% (310)
Older teens in school	77.3% (466)
Speak English very well	99.3% (142)
Poverty rate for children	25.9% (321)
No health insurance	4.3% (140)

DIVERSITY/EQUALITY	★ (533)
Racial diversity index	7.6% (531)
Geographic diversity index	23.1% (541)
Top 20% share of income	46.2% (139)
Gender gap in earnings	38.2% (399)
White-collar gender gap	41.3% (459)

EDUCATION	★★★ (311)
Eighth grade or less	2.7% (195)
High school diplomas	91.9% (128)
Attended college	43.6% (459)
Bachelor's degrees	17.2% (315)
Advanced degrees	5.0% (378)

EMPLOYMENT	★★★ (260)
Average jobless rate	8.1% (298)
Self-employed workers	8.3% (302)
Management/financial jobs	10.1% (365)
Computer/engineering jobs	2.9% (219)
Health care jobs	6.5% (121)

GROWTH POTENTIAL	★ (540)
Children per senior	1.06 (483)
Median age	45.4 (504)
Moved from different state	1.4% (425)
Homes built since 2000	7.5% (487)
Construction jobs	6.0% (326)

HOUSING	★★★★ (204)
Home vacancy rate	8.1% (227)
Home ownership rate	76.3% (47)
Housing diversity index	80.8% (497)
4 or more bedrooms	16.1% (286)
Affordability/income ratio	$1,861 (25)

INCOME	★★★★ (217)
Poverty rate	15.4% (211)
Median household income	$43,644 (272)
Interest/dividends	25.2% (87)
Public assistance	16.0% (295)
Median fulltime earnings	$36,827 (301)

SENIORS	★★★ (309)
Seniors living alone	27.7% (278)
Poverty rate for seniors	8.3% (202)
Median income for seniors	$31,918 (322)
Seniors who work	15.6% (432)
Home ownership by seniors	83.1% (217)

STABILITY	★★★★ (128)
25-39 age group	15.6% (474)
Born in state of residence	87.5% (10)
Same house as 1 year ago	87.2% (190)
Live and work in county	76.3% (266)
Married-couple households	51.9% (199)

TRANSPORTATION	★★★ (270)
Bicycle or walk to work	3.6% (180)
Carpool to work	11.8% (152)
Public transit to work	0.6% (141)
Commute <15 minutes	36.1% (415)
Commute >45 minutes	10.1% (228)

See pages 37-130 for explanations of statistics, stars, and ranks.

Olean, NY
(Cattaraugus County, NY)

POPULATION		Attended college	50.6% (311)
2010 census	80,317 (67)	Bachelor's degrees	18.7% (262)
2015 estimate	77,922 (75)	Advanced degrees	7.6% (139)
2010-2015 change	-3.0% (481)	**EMPLOYMENT**	★★ (353)
2020 projection	76,003 (85)	Average jobless rate	8.2% (310)
2030 projection	72,335 (96)	Self-employed workers	9.0% (254)
RACE		Management/financial jobs	10.3% (339)
Whites	91.2% (159)	Computer/engineering jobs	2.4% (336)
Blacks	1.5% (329)	Health care jobs	5.1% (319)
Hispanics	1.9% (442)	**GROWTH POTENTIAL**	★★ (382)
Asians	0.8% (201)	Children per senior	1.38 (291)
Native Americans	2.8% (56)	Median age	41.4 (376)
AGE		Moved from different state	1.6% (383)
0-17 years old	22.9% (270)	Homes built since 2000	7.3% (496)
18-24 years old	9.5% (197)	Construction jobs	7.5% (122)
25-39 years old	15.9% (453)	**HOUSING**	★★★ (242)
40-54 years old	20.5% (151)	Home vacancy rate	7.6% (193)
55-64 years old	14.6% (107)	Home ownership rate	71.3% (215)
65+ years old	16.6% (237)	Housing diversity index	80.3% (505)
PRIVATE SECTOR		4 or more bedrooms	18.9% (164)
Businesses	1,634 (116)	Affordability/income ratio	$1,986 (53)
Employees	19,898 (128)	**INCOME**	★★★ (293)
Total wages	$751,421,886 (134)	Poverty rate	18.3% (309)
Average weekly wages	$726 (203)	Median household income	$42,601 (297)
HOUSEHOLD INCOME LADDER		Interest/dividends	20.8% (224)
95th percentile	$133,561 (381)	Public assistance	18.1% (376)
80th percentile	$81,918 (327)	Median fulltime earnings	$36,989 (288)
60th percentile	$52,727 (305)	**SENIORS**	★★ (400)
40th percentile	$33,802 (295)	Seniors living alone	29.5% (405)
20th percentile	$18,931 (269)	Poverty rate for seniors	9.9% (315)
CHILDREN	★★ (393)	Median income for seniors	$30,966 (375)
Living with two parents	64.1% (293)	Seniors who work	16.7% (360)
Older teens in school	81.8% (329)	Home ownership by seniors	81.8% (286)
Speak English very well	96.0% (453)	**STABILITY**	★★★ (313)
Poverty rate for children	27.7% (362)	25-39 age group	15.9% (453)
No health insurance	9.9% (420)	Born in state of residence	81.1% (98)
DIVERSITY/EQUALITY	★★★ (303)	Same house as 1 year ago	88.6% (101)
Racial diversity index	16.6% (387)	Live and work in county	69.2% (382)
Geographic diversity index	33.3% (452)	Married-couple households	46.9% (419)
Top 20% share of income	46.1% (126)	**TRANSPORTATION**	★★★ (273)
Gender gap in earnings	30.6% (187)	Bicycle or walk to work	6.3% (53)
White-collar gender gap	21.6% (229)	Carpool to work	8.8% (448)
EDUCATION	★★★ (233)	Public transit to work	0.5% (178)
Eighth grade or less	3.4% (269)	Commute <15 minutes	43.2% (276)
High school diplomas	89.9% (206)	Commute >45 minutes	13.2% (363)

See pages 37-130 for explanations of statistics, stars, and ranks.

Oneonta, NY
(Otsego County, NY)

POPULATION	
2010 census	62,259 (135)
2015 estimate	60,636 (146)
2010-2015 change	-2.6% (455)
2020 projection	59,636 (150)
2030 projection	57,658 (162)

RACE	
Whites	91.9% (141)
Blacks	1.8% (309)
Hispanics	3.4% (322)
Asians	1.2% (125)
Native Americans	0.1% (402)

AGE	
0-17 years old	17.2% (535)
18-24 years old	17.5% (42)
25-39 years old	13.6% (547)
40-54 years old	19.3% (323)
55-64 years old	14.4% (136)
65+ years old	18.0% (122)

PRIVATE SECTOR	
Businesses	1,454 (146)
Employees	19,293 (134)
Total wages	$754,938,941 (133)
Average weekly wages	$753 (155)

HOUSEHOLD INCOME LADDER	
95th percentile	$156,397 (117)
80th percentile	$91,186 (137)
60th percentile	$59,674 (157)
40th percentile	$38,120 (177)
20th percentile	$21,215 (180)

CHILDREN	★★★★★ (67)
Living with two parents	67.0% (217)
Older teens in school	89.8% (68)
Speak English very well	99.2% (163)
Poverty rate for children	19.5% (152)
No health insurance	3.7% (98)

DIVERSITY/EQUALITY	★★★ (265)
Racial diversity index	15.4% (404)
Geographic diversity index	37.0% (403)
Top 20% share of income	47.6% (260)
Gender gap in earnings	30.9% (198)
White-collar gender gap	10.1% (90)

EDUCATION	★★★★★ (51)
Eighth grade or less	1.9% (114)
High school diplomas	91.6% (141)
Attended college	58.9% (145)
Bachelor's degrees	29.0% (62)
Advanced degrees	13.6% (23)

EMPLOYMENT	★★★★★ (62)
Average jobless rate	7.1% (208)
Self-employed workers	11.3% (104)
Management/financial jobs	12.7% (103)
Computer/engineering jobs	3.2% (158)
Health care jobs	7.3% (55)

GROWTH POTENTIAL	★ (464)
Children per senior	0.95 (516)
Median age	41.6 (387)
Moved from different state	1.9% (310)
Homes built since 2000	9.7% (399)
Construction jobs	6.5% (253)

HOUSING	★★ (341)
Home vacancy rate	9.0% (287)
Home ownership rate	73.4% (142)
Housing diversity index	76.7% (540)
4 or more bedrooms	23.5% (56)
Affordability/income ratio	$2,939 (390)

INCOME	★★★★ (152)
Poverty rate	16.5% (246)
Median household income	$48,588 (158)
Interest/dividends	24.5% (115)
Public assistance	11.6% (116)
Median fulltime earnings	$37,432 (253)

SENIORS	★★★★ (116)
Seniors living alone	27.3% (260)
Poverty rate for seniors	7.4% (128)
Median income for seniors	$37,958 (90)
Seniors who work	22.0% (130)
Home ownership by seniors	83.2% (210)

STABILITY	★ (466)
25-39 age group	13.6% (547)
Born in state of residence	78.7% (139)
Same house as 1 year ago	82.9% (403)
Live and work in county	78.2% (241)
Married-couple households	48.5% (361)

TRANSPORTATION	★★★★★ (71)
Bicycle or walk to work	10.1% (15)
Carpool to work	10.1% (322)
Public transit to work	2.0% (32)
Commute <15 minutes	38.4% (366)
Commute >45 minutes	10.5% (254)

See pages 37-130 for explanations of statistics, stars, and ranks.

Plattsburgh, NY
(Clinton County, NY)

POPULATION	
2010 census	82,128 (62)
2015 estimate	81,251 (64)
2010-2015 change	-1.1% (335)
2020 projection	80,968 (69)
2030 projection	80,439 (76)

RACE	
Whites	90.3% (173)
Blacks	4.0% (189)
Hispanics	2.7% (361)
Asians	1.4% (99)
Native Americans	0.3% (231)

AGE	
0-17 years old	18.5% (517)
18-24 years old	14.0% (62)
25-39 years old	18.4% (151)
40-54 years old	21.2% (85)
55-64 years old	13.3% (282)
65+ years old	14.7% (389)

PRIVATE SECTOR	
Businesses	1,904 (73)
Employees	25,333 (73)
Total wages	$953,306,462 (80)
Average weekly wages	$724 (210)

HOUSEHOLD INCOME LADDER	
95th percentile	$154,434 (121)
80th percentile	$94,933 (91)
60th percentile	$61,770 (114)
40th percentile	$38,663 (164)
20th percentile	$20,253 (221)

CHILDREN	★★★★★ (68)
Living with two parents	61.0% (380)
Older teens in school	92.8% (33)
Speak English very well	99.6% (77)
Poverty rate for children	22.1% (224)
No health insurance	2.3% (20)

DIVERSITY/EQUALITY	★★★ (324)
Racial diversity index	18.2% (372)
Geographic diversity index	37.9% (392)
Top 20% share of income	47.0% (213)
Gender gap in earnings	26.7% (112)
White-collar gender gap	31.5% (359)

EDUCATION	★★★★ (166)
Eighth grade or less	3.8% (307)
High school diplomas	87.8% (274)
Attended college	53.4% (257)
Bachelor's degrees	23.2% (132)
Advanced degrees	10.2% (53)

EMPLOYMENT	★★★ (283)
Average jobless rate	6.9% (185)
Self-employed workers	7.3% (401)
Management/financial jobs	10.0% (381)
Computer/engineering jobs	3.0% (193)
Health care jobs	6.1% (168)

GROWTH POTENTIAL	★★ (407)
Children per senior	1.26 (378)
Median age	39.4 (262)
Moved from different state	2.0% (288)
Homes built since 2000	12.1% (310)
Construction jobs	5.2% (442)

HOUSING	★★★★★ (105)
Home vacancy rate	5.7% (74)
Home ownership rate	68.1% (339)
Housing diversity index	85.8% (97)
4 or more bedrooms	17.9% (209)
Affordability/income ratio	$2,487 (244)

INCOME	★★★ (232)
Poverty rate	16.5% (246)
Median household income	$49,930 (128)
Interest/dividends	18.3% (299)
Public assistance	19.3% (409)
Median fulltime earnings	$41,674 (72)

SENIORS	★★ (427)
Seniors living alone	32.3% (519)
Poverty rate for seniors	7.1% (101)
Median income for seniors	$35,421 (174)
Seniors who work	16.5% (376)
Home ownership by seniors	78.0% (454)

STABILITY	★★★★ (158)
25-39 age group	18.4% (151)
Born in state of residence	78.1% (153)
Same house as 1 year ago	82.6% (416)
Live and work in county	90.4% (59)
Married-couple households	46.4% (435)

TRANSPORTATION	★★★★ (132)
Bicycle or walk to work	5.2% (85)
Carpool to work	12.9% (106)
Public transit to work	0.6% (141)
Commute <15 minutes	42.6% (284)
Commute >45 minutes	9.0% (175)

See pages 37-130 for explanations of statistics, stars, and ranks.

Point Pleasant, WV-OH
(Mason County, WV, and Gallia County, OH)

POPULATION

2010 census	58,258 (161)
2015 estimate	57,179 (164)
2010-2015 change	-1.9% (399)
2020 projection	56,373 (169)
2030 projection	54,525 (189)

RACE

Whites	95.2% (38)
Blacks	1.7% (315)
Hispanics	1.1% (525)
Asians	0.4% (413)
Native Americans	0.1% (402)

AGE

0-17 years old	22.4% (306)
18-24 years old	7.9% (424)
25-39 years old	17.2% (290)
40-54 years old	20.4% (169)
55-64 years old	14.5% (122)
65+ years old	17.6% (151)

PRIVATE SECTOR

Businesses	933 (300)
Employees	13,380 (262)
Total wages	$505,500,142 (241)
Average weekly wages	$727 (200)

HOUSEHOLD INCOME LADDER

95th percentile	$135,038 (359)
80th percentile	$78,157 (399)
60th percentile	$47,169 (441)
40th percentile	$29,690 (430)
20th percentile	$16,395 (390)

CHILDREN ★★★ (316)

Living with two parents	63.1% (320)
Older teens in school	79.4% (415)
Speak English very well	98.9% (226)
Poverty rate for children	27.9% (366)
No health insurance	5.7% (233)

DIVERSITY/EQUALITY ★ (463)

Racial diversity index	9.3% (509)
Geographic diversity index	51.7% (191)
Top 20% share of income	49.1% (377)
Gender gap in earnings	38.6% (409)
White-collar gender gap	32.0% (364)

EDUCATION ★★ (406)

Eighth grade or less	3.4% (269)
High school diplomas	85.9% (345)
Attended college	43.2% (469)
Bachelor's degrees	14.2% (454)
Advanced degrees	4.8% (405)

EMPLOYMENT ★★ (343)

Average jobless rate	8.7% (340)
Self-employed workers	5.8% (508)
Management/financial jobs	9.1% (463)
Computer/engineering jobs	2.4% (336)
Health care jobs	7.8% (28)

GROWTH POTENTIAL ★★ (386)

Children per senior	1.28 (357)
Median age	42.0 (398)
Moved from different state	2.3% (234)
Homes built since 2000	13.1% (274)
Construction jobs	5.9% (345)

HOUSING ★★★★ (156)

Home vacancy rate	11.6% (441)
Home ownership rate	78.0% (18)
Housing diversity index	86.0% (71)
4 or more bedrooms	15.0% (356)
Affordability/income ratio	$2,380 (203)

INCOME ★★ (415)

Poverty rate	20.1% (373)
Median household income	$36,850 (445)
Interest/dividends	14.7% (418)
Public assistance	22.3% (482)
Median fulltime earnings	$38,934 (181)

SENIORS ★★ (356)

Seniors living alone	29.4% (394)
Poverty rate for seniors	10.6% (350)
Median income for seniors	$28,860 (441)
Seniors who work	11.8% (542)
Home ownership by seniors	90.5% (11)

STABILITY ★★ (340)

25-39 age group	17.2% (290)
Born in state of residence	66.1% (373)
Same house as 1 year ago	88.6% (101)
Live and work in county	62.3% (473)
Married-couple households	51.6% (218)

TRANSPORTATION ★ (543)

Bicycle or walk to work	3.0% (249)
Carpool to work	8.9% (439)
Public transit to work	0.1% (441)
Commute <15 minutes	27.4% (541)
Commute >45 minutes	21.4% (530)

See pages 37-130 for explanations of statistics, stars, and ranks.

Pottsville, PA
(Schuylkill County, PA)

POPULATION

2010 census	148,289 (5)
2015 estimate	144,590 (7)
2010-2015 change	-2.5% (451)
2020 projection	141,496 (8)
2030 projection	135,299 (11)

RACE

Whites	92.2% (128)
Blacks	2.6% (247)
Hispanics	3.4% (322)
Asians	0.5% (355)
Native Americans	0.1% (402)

AGE

0-17 years old	19.7% (473)
18-24 years old	7.4% (489)
25-39 years old	17.6% (248)
40-54 years old	22.0% (31)
55-64 years old	14.4% (136)
65+ years old	18.9% (85)

PRIVATE SECTOR

Businesses	2,921 (21)
Employees	42,404 (10)
Total wages	$1,604,911,407 (16)
Average weekly wages	$728 (198)

HOUSEHOLD INCOME LADDER

95th percentile	$136,289 (339)
80th percentile	$86,814 (213)
60th percentile	$56,949 (208)
40th percentile	$35,805 (237)
20th percentile	$20,102 (224)

CHILDREN ★★★★ (156)

Living with two parents	65.1% (268)
Older teens in school	85.5% (183)
Speak English very well	99.0% (200)
Poverty rate for children	19.6% (155)
No health insurance	5.9% (244)

DIVERSITY/EQUALITY ★★ (416)

Racial diversity index	14.8% (418)
Geographic diversity index	25.4% (521)
Top 20% share of income	45.7% (105)
Gender gap in earnings	32.9% (255)
White-collar gender gap	29.6% (331)

EDUCATION ★★★ (280)

Eighth grade or less	2.1% (136)
High school diplomas	90.3% (192)
Attended college	45.2% (435)
Bachelor's degrees	17.2% (315)
Advanced degrees	6.0% (264)

EMPLOYMENT ★★★ (320)

Average jobless rate	8.8% (344)
Self-employed workers	6.9% (435)
Management/financial jobs	9.7% (416)
Computer/engineering jobs	2.7% (270)
Health care jobs	7.0% (69)

GROWTH POTENTIAL ★ (543)

Children per senior	1.04 (487)
Median age	43.8 (472)
Moved from different state	0.9% (515)
Homes built since 2000	5.9% (532)
Construction jobs	6.1% (310)

HOUSING ★★ (367)

Home vacancy rate	11.6% (441)
Home ownership rate	74.9% (83)
Housing diversity index	72.2% (551)
4 or more bedrooms	20.7% (110)
Affordability/income ratio	$2,042 (67)

INCOME ★★★★ (164)

Poverty rate	13.1% (119)
Median household income	$45,535 (223)
Interest/dividends	22.0% (185)
Public assistance	15.0% (254)
Median fulltime earnings	$40,365 (128)

SENIORS ★★ (398)

Seniors living alone	29.4% (394)
Poverty rate for seniors	8.1% (187)
Median income for seniors	$30,307 (401)
Seniors who work	16.1% (400)
Home ownership by seniors	81.1% (325)

STABILITY ★★★★ (116)

25-39 age group	17.6% (248)
Born in state of residence	86.1% (26)
Same house as 1 year ago	90.4% (36)
Live and work in county	67.2% (415)
Married-couple households	48.4% (366)

TRANSPORTATION ★ (461)

Bicycle or walk to work	3.7% (173)
Carpool to work	10.1% (322)
Public transit to work	0.6% (141)
Commute <15 minutes	31.0% (511)
Commute >45 minutes	18.0% (499)

See pages 37-130 for explanations of statistics, stars, and ranks.

Rutland, VT
(Rutland County, VT)

POPULATION	
2010 census	61,642 (140)
2015 estimate	59,736 (148)
2010-2015 change	-3.1% (487)
2020 projection	57,943 (160)
2030 projection	54,400 (190)

RACE	
Whites	95.9% (23)
Blacks	0.6% (438)
Hispanics	1.3% (503)
Asians	0.7% (241)
Native Americans	0.2% (300)

AGE	
0-17 years old	18.5% (517)
18-24 years old	9.9% (168)
25-39 years old	14.8% (520)
40-54 years old	21.7% (42)
55-64 years old	16.5% (27)
65+ years old	18.6% (101)

PRIVATE SECTOR	
Businesses	2,213 (48)
Employees	23,241 (87)
Total wages	$927,187,508 (85)
Average weekly wages	$767 (131)

HOUSEHOLD INCOME LADDER	
95th percentile	$156,458 (116)
80th percentile	$91,040 (140)
60th percentile	$60,801 (135)
40th percentile	$39,181 (150)
20th percentile	$20,693 (198)

CHILDREN	★★★★★ (107)
Living with two parents	66.7% (226)
Older teens in school	83.8% (245)
Speak English very well	99.3% (142)
Poverty rate for children	17.4% (109)
No health insurance	3.8% (108)

DIVERSITY/EQUALITY	★★★★ (157)
Racial diversity index	8.0% (528)
Geographic diversity index	56.2% (144)
Top 20% share of income	47.4% (248)
Gender gap in earnings	25.4% (94)
White-collar gender gap	14.9% (151)

EDUCATION	★★★★★ (56)
Eighth grade or less	1.5% (72)
High school diplomas	93.1% (91)
Attended college	59.8% (129)
Bachelor's degrees	30.6% (49)
Advanced degrees	10.7% (46)

EMPLOYMENT	★★★★★ (82)
Average jobless rate	6.6% (161)
Self-employed workers	11.6% (90)
Management/financial jobs	11.9% (165)
Computer/engineering jobs	3.7% (103)
Health care jobs	6.1% (168)

GROWTH POTENTIAL	★ (449)
Children per senior	1.00 (503)
Median age	45.5 (508)
Moved from different state	3.1% (147)
Homes built since 2000	7.2% (500)
Construction jobs	7.8% (98)

HOUSING	★★★ (278)
Home vacancy rate	6.2% (109)
Home ownership rate	70.1% (267)
Housing diversity index	82.2% (450)
4 or more bedrooms	19.7% (132)
Affordability/income ratio	$3,615 (473)

INCOME	★★★★ (122)
Poverty rate	12.5% (101)
Median household income	$49,372 (141)
Interest/dividends	27.0% (51)
Public assistance	17.4% (352)
Median fulltime earnings	$40,728 (108)

SENIORS	★★★★ (209)
Seniors living alone	28.9% (358)
Poverty rate for seniors	8.0% (177)
Median income for seniors	$34,126 (228)
Seniors who work	25.2% (69)
Home ownership by seniors	79.2% (406)

STABILITY	★★ (372)
25-39 age group	14.8% (520)
Born in state of residence	59.3% (423)
Same house as 1 year ago	89.0% (79)
Live and work in county	86.5% (108)
Married-couple households	47.9% (387)

TRANSPORTATION	★★★★ (213)
Bicycle or walk to work	5.8% (63)
Carpool to work	8.4% (466)
Public transit to work	0.9% (83)
Commute <15 minutes	41.9% (300)
Commute >45 minutes	9.0% (175)

See pages 37-130 for explanations of statistics, stars, and ranks.

St. Marys, PA
(Elk County, PA)

POPULATION	
2010 census	31,946 (417)
2015 estimate	30,872 (429)
2010-2015 change	-3.4% (501)
2020 projection	29,540 (435)
2030 projection	27,026 (456)

RACE	
Whites	97.6% (1)
Blacks	0.5% (466)
Hispanics	0.7% (544)
Asians	0.4% (413)
Native Americans	0.2% (300)

AGE	
0-17 years old	20.0% (458)
18-24 years old	6.8% (527)
25-39 years old	15.0% (511)
40-54 years old	22.6% (14)
55-64 years old	15.5% (59)
65+ years old	20.1% (54)

PRIVATE SECTOR	
Businesses	870 (333)
Employees	13,634 (250)
Total wages	$546,273,544 (215)
Average weekly wages	$771 (127)

HOUSEHOLD INCOME LADDER	
95th percentile	$135,141 (357)
80th percentile	$82,513 (304)
60th percentile	$57,150 (202)
40th percentile	$38,046 (182)
20th percentile	$21,846 (145)

CHILDREN	★★★★★ (58)
Living with two parents	70.8% (125)
Older teens in school	81.9% (325)
Speak English very well	99.2% (163)
Poverty rate for children	12.6% (44)
No health insurance	2.5% (34)

DIVERSITY/EQUALITY	★ (518)
Racial diversity index	4.7% (550)
Geographic diversity index	17.9% (549)
Top 20% share of income	44.3% (34)
Gender gap in earnings	44.3% (492)
White-collar gender gap	25.3% (274)

EDUCATION	★★★★ (194)
Eighth grade or less	0.8% (10)
High school diplomas	95.0% (31)
Attended college	47.3% (392)
Bachelor's degrees	19.2% (241)
Advanced degrees	5.8% (283)

EMPLOYMENT	★★★ (230)
Average jobless rate	5.2% (76)
Self-employed workers	7.9% (345)
Management/financial jobs	8.3% (513)
Computer/engineering jobs	4.6% (48)
Health care jobs	5.5% (250)

GROWTH POTENTIAL	★ (551)
Children per senior	0.99 (506)
Median age	46.4 (518)
Moved from different state	0.5% (549)
Homes built since 2000	6.3% (518)
Construction jobs	4.5% (504)

HOUSING	★★★★★ (59)
Home vacancy rate	5.3% (50)
Home ownership rate	78.1% (17)
Housing diversity index	83.4% (396)
4 or more bedrooms	16.0% (293)
Affordability/income ratio	$1,943 (38)

INCOME	★★★★★ (89)
Poverty rate	8.8% (16)
Median household income	$46,671 (200)
Interest/dividends	23.6% (139)
Public assistance	10.4% (76)
Median fulltime earnings	$39,998 (141)

SENIORS	★★ (416)
Seniors living alone	31.1% (476)
Poverty rate for seniors	5.6% (40)
Median income for seniors	$30,293 (402)
Seniors who work	14.0% (503)
Home ownership by seniors	80.9% (339)

STABILITY	★★★★★ (25)
25-39 age group	15.0% (511)
Born in state of residence	90.5% (3)
Same house as 1 year ago	92.5% (9)
Live and work in county	85.9% (119)
Married-couple households	50.4% (278)

TRANSPORTATION	★★★★ (170)
Bicycle or walk to work	3.0% (249)
Carpool to work	10.8% (249)
Public transit to work	0.8% (96)
Commute <15 minutes	47.2% (211)
Commute >45 minutes	7.2% (91)

See pages 37-130 for explanations of statistics, stars, and ranks.

Sayre, PA
(Bradford County, PA)

POPULATION

2010 census	62,622 (134)
2015 estimate	61,281 (139)
2010-2015 change	-2.1% (418)
2020 projection	60,046 (148)
2030 projection	57,530 (164)

RACE

Whites	96.2% (9)
Blacks	0.5% (466)
Hispanics	1.4% (488)
Asians	0.6% (291)
Native Americans	0.1% (402)

AGE

0-17 years old	22.2% (320)
18-24 years old	7.4% (489)
25-39 years old	15.5% (484)
40-54 years old	21.3% (73)
55-64 years old	14.7% (97)
65+ years old	18.9% (85)

PRIVATE SECTOR

Businesses	1,512 (132)
Employees	21,267 (110)
Total wages	$937,213,039 (83)
Average weekly wages	$847 (53)

HOUSEHOLD INCOME LADDER

95th percentile	$149,975 (163)
80th percentile	$91,998 (128)
60th percentile	$60,965 (130)
40th percentile	$38,747 (160)
20th percentile	$21,229 (178)

CHILDREN ★★★★ (211)

Living with two parents	66.6% (228)
Older teens in school	84.2% (232)
Speak English very well	98.9% (226)
Poverty rate for children	20.3% (173)
No health insurance	8.5% (379)

DIVERSITY/EQUALITY ★★ (439)

Racial diversity index	7.4% (537)
Geographic diversity index	44.6% (286)
Top 20% share of income	47.4% (250)
Gender gap in earnings	38.7% (411)
White-collar gender gap	27.6% (304)

EDUCATION ★★★ (282)

Eighth grade or less	2.1% (136)
High school diplomas	90.2% (196)
Attended college	43.3% (468)
Bachelor's degrees	18.8% (259)
Advanced degrees	5.9% (272)

EMPLOYMENT ★★★★★ (106)

Average jobless rate	5.6% (106)
Self-employed workers	9.9% (171)
Management/financial jobs	10.4% (332)
Computer/engineering jobs	2.9% (219)
Health care jobs	7.2% (58)

GROWTH POTENTIAL ★ (458)

Children per senior	1.18 (427)
Median age	44.1 (481)
Moved from different state	1.7% (355)
Homes built since 2000	9.2% (427)
Construction jobs	7.2% (162)

HOUSING ★★★★ (131)

Home vacancy rate	5.8% (79)
Home ownership rate	74.6% (91)
Housing diversity index	81.3% (484)
4 or more bedrooms	21.8% (85)
Affordability/income ratio	$2,774 (352)

INCOME ★★★★★ (86)

Poverty rate	13.6% (142)
Median household income	$48,987 (149)
Interest/dividends	29.5% (28)
Public assistance	11.8% (122)
Median fulltime earnings	$39,455 (158)

SENIORS ★★★ (274)

Seniors living alone	24.9% (113)
Poverty rate for seniors	8.4% (214)
Median income for seniors	$34,008 (234)
Seniors who work	15.1% (455)
Home ownership by seniors	80.7% (350)

STABILITY ★★★★★ (104)

25-39 age group	15.5% (484)
Born in state of residence	71.8% (278)
Same house as 1 year ago	91.4% (24)
Live and work in county	79.1% (232)
Married-couple households	53.5% (131)

TRANSPORTATION ★★★ (286)

Bicycle or walk to work	5.9% (60)
Carpool to work	9.5% (388)
Public transit to work	0.3% (291)
Commute <15 minutes	39.1% (348)
Commute >45 minutes	12.0% (311)

See pages 37-130 for explanations of statistics, stars, and ranks.

Selinsgrove, PA
(Snyder County, PA)

POPULATION

2010 census	39,702 (317)
2015 estimate	40,444 (308)
2010-2015 change	1.9% (136)
2020 projection	41,196 (298)
2030 projection	42,676 (290)

RACE

Whites	95.5% (29)
Blacks	1.0% (381)
Hispanics	2.1% (416)
Asians	0.7% (241)
Native Americans	0.1% (402)

AGE

0-17 years old	21.7% (359)
18-24 years old	12.2% (83)
25-39 years old	16.9% (338)
40-54 years old	19.5% (301)
55-64 years old	13.3% (282)
65+ years old	16.4% (255)

PRIVATE SECTOR

Businesses	879 (325)
Employees	13,523 (256)
Total wages	$420,599,890 (314)
Average weekly wages	$598 (491)

HOUSEHOLD INCOME LADDER

95th percentile	$145,949 (213)
80th percentile	$87,440 (192)
60th percentile	$59,753 (156)
40th percentile	$40,448 (114)
20th percentile	$23,185 (90)

CHILDREN ★★ (420)

Living with two parents	73.9% (68)
Older teens in school	80.9% (370)
Speak English very well	94.1% (493)
Poverty rate for children	17.2% (104)
No health insurance	18.8% (543)

DIVERSITY/EQUALITY ★ (549)

Racial diversity index	8.7% (521)
Geographic diversity index	28.8% (495)
Top 20% share of income	47.0% (222)
Gender gap in earnings	38.7% (411)
White-collar gender gap	63.0% (546)

EDUCATION ★★ (401)

Eighth grade or less	5.1% (390)
High school diplomas	85.4% (363)
Attended college	40.1% (514)
Bachelor's degrees	17.6% (301)
Advanced degrees	6.3% (234)

EMPLOYMENT ★★★★ (190)

Average jobless rate	5.0% (66)
Self-employed workers	9.7% (196)
Management/financial jobs	9.0% (475)
Computer/engineering jobs	2.5% (307)
Health care jobs	6.4% (132)

GROWTH POTENTIAL ★★★ (232)

Children per senior	1.33 (325)
Median age	39.3 (256)
Moved from different state	2.3% (234)
Homes built since 2000	11.7% (324)
Construction jobs	7.9% (93)

HOUSING ★★★★★ (46)

Home vacancy rate	5.7% (74)
Home ownership rate	74.6% (91)
Housing diversity index	85.7% (108)
4 or more bedrooms	20.7% (110)
Affordability/income ratio	$2,899 (377)

INCOME ★★★★★ (109)

Poverty rate	10.8% (54)
Median household income	$49,917 (129)
Interest/dividends	25.9% (71)
Public assistance	11.9% (127)
Median fulltime earnings	$36,450 (315)

SENIORS ★★★ (272)

Seniors living alone	24.2% (89)
Poverty rate for seniors	8.8% (250)
Median income for seniors	$31,639 (344)
Seniors who work	15.9% (418)
Home ownership by seniors	81.1% (325)

STABILITY ★★★★★ (62)

25-39 age group	16.9% (338)
Born in state of residence	84.0% (55)
Same house as 1 year ago	89.0% (79)
Live and work in county	62.9% (465)
Married-couple households	58.1% (19)

TRANSPORTATION ★★ (372)

Bicycle or walk to work	4.6% (110)
Carpool to work	9.6% (378)
Public transit to work	0.4% (219)
Commute <15 minutes	35.8% (426)
Commute >45 minutes	13.6% (377)

See pages 37-130 for explanations of statistics, stars, and ranks.

Seneca Falls, NY
(Seneca County, NY)

POPULATION

2010 census	35,251 (381)
2015 estimate	34,833 (383)
2010-2015 change	-1.2% (345)
2020 projection	34,692 (387)
2030 projection	34,372 (384)

RACE

Whites	89.7% (189)
Blacks	4.2% (181)
Hispanics	3.1% (333)
Asians	0.8% (201)
Native Americans	0.3% (231)

AGE

0-17 years old	20.4% (437)
18-24 years old	8.7% (299)
25-39 years old	18.2% (167)
40-54 years old	21.5% (57)
55-64 years old	14.5% (122)
65+ years old	16.7% (225)

PRIVATE SECTOR

Businesses	687 (435)
Employees	8,655 (429)
Total wages	$353,509,542 (381)
Average weekly wages	$785 (110)

HOUSEHOLD INCOME LADDER

95th percentile	$149,236 (170)
80th percentile	$92,848 (116)
60th percentile	$61,290 (124)
40th percentile	$40,166 (126)
20th percentile	$21,207 (181)

CHILDREN   ★★★ (228)

Living with two parents	70.0% (143)
Older teens in school	81.6% (341)
Speak English very well	98.5% (287)
Poverty rate for children	15.9% (75)
No health insurance	10.7% (441)

DIVERSITY/EQUALITY   ★★★ (236)

Racial diversity index	19.2% (358)
Geographic diversity index	33.3% (452)
Top 20% share of income	46.4% (153)
Gender gap in earnings	21.9% (58)
White-collar gender gap	25.4% (277)

EDUCATION   ★★★★ (195)

Eighth grade or less	3.2% (250)
High school diplomas	87.1% (301)
Attended college	54.0% (243)
Bachelor's degrees	21.2% (185)
Advanced degrees	8.6% (99)

EMPLOYMENT   ★★★★ (188)

Average jobless rate	5.5% (98)
Self-employed workers	8.0% (333)
Management/financial jobs	12.7% (103)
Computer/engineering jobs	2.8% (246)
Health care jobs	5.0% (339)

GROWTH POTENTIAL   ★★ (426)

Children per senior	1.22 (401)
Median age	42.3 (427)
Moved from different state	1.6% (383)
Homes built since 2000	9.1% (430)
Construction jobs	7.1% (173)

HOUSING   ★★★★ (167)

Home vacancy rate	7.0% (162)
Home ownership rate	72.3% (175)
Housing diversity index	81.1% (492)
4 or more bedrooms	19.6% (135)
Affordability/income ratio	$1,968 (47)

INCOME   ★★★★ (125)

Poverty rate	12.7% (105)
Median household income	$49,292 (145)
Interest/dividends	21.0% (214)
Public assistance	12.6% (150)
Median fulltime earnings	$41,681 (71)

SENIORS   ★★★ (231)

Seniors living alone	29.0% (366)
Poverty rate for seniors	7.1% (101)
Median income for seniors	$36,141 (149)
Seniors who work	18.5% (268)
Home ownership by seniors	82.2% (264)

STABILITY   ★★ (389)

25-39 age group	18.2% (167)
Born in state of residence	81.2% (97)
Same house as 1 year ago	86.6% (213)
Live and work in county	55.3% (519)
Married-couple households	47.3% (409)

TRANSPORTATION   ★★ (349)

Bicycle or walk to work	3.8% (161)
Carpool to work	10.5% (280)
Public transit to work	0.5% (178)
Commute <15 minutes	37.3% (394)
Commute >45 minutes	13.5% (374)

See pages 37-130 for explanations of statistics, stars, and ranks.

Somerset, PA
(Somerset County, PA)

POPULATION	
2010 census	77,742 (73)
2015 estimate	75,522 (87)
2010-2015 change	-2.9% (477)
2020 projection	73,275 (93)
2030 projection	68,879 (110)

RACE	
Whites	95.0% (46)
Blacks	2.6% (247)
Hispanics	1.3% (503)
Asians	0.3% (473)
Native Americans	0.1% (402)

AGE	
0-17 years old	18.6% (509)
18-24 years old	7.4% (489)
25-39 years old	17.2% (290)
40-54 years old	21.4% (67)
55-64 years old	15.5% (59)
65+ years old	19.9% (57)

PRIVATE SECTOR	
Businesses	1,745 (94)
Employees	19,684 (129)
Total wages	$682,922,791 (154)
Average weekly wages	$667 (341)

HOUSEHOLD INCOME LADDER	
95th percentile	$135,263 (356)
80th percentile	$83,267 (285)
60th percentile	$54,578 (260)
40th percentile	$35,405 (253)
20th percentile	$20,536 (205)

CHILDREN	★★★★★ (104)
Living with two parents	74.8% (54)
Older teens in school	85.7% (176)
Speak English very well	97.5% (388)
Poverty rate for children	19.6% (155)
No health insurance	5.5% (218)

DIVERSITY/EQUALITY	★ (512)
Racial diversity index	9.7% (500)
Geographic diversity index	25.7% (518)
Top 20% share of income	46.7% (181)
Gender gap in earnings	35.4% (326)
White-collar gender gap	36.2% (398)

EDUCATION	★★ (349)
Eighth grade or less	3.1% (238)
High school diplomas	89.6% (214)
Attended college	42.0% (490)
Bachelor's degrees	16.9% (334)
Advanced degrees	5.5% (318)

EMPLOYMENT	★★★★ (136)
Average jobless rate	6.9% (185)
Self-employed workers	9.9% (171)
Management/financial jobs	9.8% (408)
Computer/engineering jobs	2.4% (336)
Health care jobs	7.7% (35)

GROWTH POTENTIAL	★ (530)
Children per senior	0.93 (519)
Median age	45.3 (502)
Moved from different state	0.8% (524)
Homes built since 2000	8.1% (465)
Construction jobs	7.1% (173)

HOUSING	★★★★★ (49)
Home vacancy rate	5.8% (79)
Home ownership rate	78.6% (10)
Housing diversity index	83.5% (391)
4 or more bedrooms	18.4% (183)
Affordability/income ratio	$2,216 (128)

INCOME	★★★★ (187)
Poverty rate	12.7% (105)
Median household income	$44,587 (246)
Interest/dividends	22.2% (174)
Public assistance	13.6% (195)
Median fulltime earnings	$37,128 (275)

SENIORS	★★ (434)
Seniors living alone	27.7% (278)
Poverty rate for seniors	9.8% (308)
Median income for seniors	$28,615 (445)
Seniors who work	14.5% (478)
Home ownership by seniors	80.8% (346)

STABILITY	★★★★★ (15)
25-39 age group	17.2% (290)
Born in state of residence	85.8% (33)
Same house as 1 year ago	92.1% (15)
Live and work in county	67.9% (407)
Married-couple households	56.7% (34)

TRANSPORTATION	★★ (429)
Bicycle or walk to work	2.4% (331)
Carpool to work	10.1% (322)
Public transit to work	0.1% (441)
Commute <15 minutes	34.1% (457)
Commute >45 minutes	11.9% (308)

See pages 37-130 for explanations of statistics, stars, and ranks.

Sunbury, PA
(Northumberland County, PA)

POPULATION

2010 census	94,528 (36)
2015 estimate	93,246 (43)
2010-2015 change	-1.4% (364)
2020 projection	91,984 (45)
2030 projection	89,393 (50)

RACE

Whites	93.3% (98)
Blacks	2.5% (253)
Hispanics	2.9% (350)
Asians	0.3% (473)
Native Americans	0.2% (300)

AGE

0-17 years old	19.6% (478)
18-24 years old	7.9% (424)
25-39 years old	17.6% (248)
40-54 years old	21.0% (107)
55-64 years old	14.6% (107)
65+ years old	19.3% (68)

PRIVATE SECTOR

Businesses	1,715 (98)
Employees	23,285 (86)
Total wages	$842,804,640 (109)
Average weekly wages	$696 (262)

HOUSEHOLD INCOME LADDER

95th percentile	$131,524 (409)
80th percentile	$82,200 (321)
60th percentile	$52,807 (302)
40th percentile	$33,672 (302)
20th percentile	$19,167 (257)

CHILDREN ★★★ (268)

Living with two parents	68.5% (180)
Older teens in school	79.6% (412)
Speak English very well	97.6% (375)
Poverty rate for children	21.3% (200)
No health insurance	7.5% (344)

DIVERSITY/EQUALITY ★ (486)

Racial diversity index	12.8% (447)
Geographic diversity index	23.6% (537)
Top 20% share of income	46.9% (207)
Gender gap in earnings	33.9% (284)
White-collar gender gap	30.5% (344)

EDUCATION ★★ (361)

Eighth grade or less	2.8% (205)
High school diplomas	88.6% (251)
Attended college	40.3% (510)
Bachelor's degrees	17.0% (328)
Advanced degrees	5.8% (283)

EMPLOYMENT ★★★★ (213)

Average jobless rate	7.2% (218)
Self-employed workers	6.6% (461)
Management/financial jobs	8.3% (513)
Computer/engineering jobs	2.5% (307)
Health care jobs	9.0% (4)

GROWTH POTENTIAL ★ (544)

Children per senior	1.02 (497)
Median age	43.8 (472)
Moved from different state	1.0% (504)
Homes built since 2000	5.5% (534)
Construction jobs	6.0% (326)

HOUSING ★ (456)

Home vacancy rate	10.6% (385)
Home ownership rate	71.2% (218)
Housing diversity index	75.8% (544)
4 or more bedrooms	18.8% (168)
Affordability/income ratio	$2,460 (236)

INCOME ★★★★ (216)

Poverty rate	13.8% (149)
Median household income	$42,406 (305)
Interest/dividends	20.0% (245)
Public assistance	13.2% (181)
Median fulltime earnings	$38,098 (218)

SENIORS ★ (500)

Seniors living alone	30.6% (454)
Poverty rate for seniors	8.9% (254)
Median income for seniors	$28,936 (437)
Seniors who work	17.7% (302)
Home ownership by seniors	73.3% (540)

STABILITY ★★★ (299)

25-39 age group	17.6% (248)
Born in state of residence	87.2% (14)
Same house as 1 year ago	89.4% (64)
Live and work in county	51.8% (535)
Married-couple households	48.0% (378)

TRANSPORTATION ★★ (436)

Bicycle or walk to work	3.1% (232)
Carpool to work	9.1% (419)
Public transit to work	0.3% (291)
Commute <15 minutes	32.3% (489)
Commute >45 minutes	12.0% (311)

See pages 37-130 for explanations of statistics, stars, and ranks.

Torrington, CT
(Litchfield County, CT)

POPULATION		
2010 census	189,927 (2)	
2015 estimate	183,603 (3)	
2010-2015 change	-3.3% (495)	
2020 projection	179,467 (3)	
2030 projection	171,309 (3)	

RACE	
Whites	90.2% (175)
Blacks	1.4% (340)
Hispanics	5.2% (247)
Asians	1.8% (60)
Native Americans	0.1% (402)

AGE	
0-17 years old	20.0% (458)
18-24 years old	7.4% (489)
25-39 years old	14.6% (527)
40-54 years old	24.0% (3)
55-64 years old	16.3% (35)
65+ years old	17.7% (142)

PRIVATE SECTOR	
Businesses	5,585 (3)
Employees	53,198 (6)
Total wages	$2,307,099,360 (4)
Average weekly wages	$834 (59)

HOUSEHOLD INCOME LADDER	
95th percentile	$222,504 (10)
80th percentile	$132,608 (6)
60th percentile	$88,082 (7)
40th percentile	$58,104 (8)
20th percentile	$31,809 (10)

CHILDREN	★★★★★ (15)
Living with two parents	77.7% (21)
Older teens in school	86.5% (149)
Speak English very well	98.8% (251)
Poverty rate for children	7.6% (3)
No health insurance	3.4% (79)

DIVERSITY/EQUALITY	★★★ (221)
Racial diversity index	18.3% (368)
Geographic diversity index	52.9% (175)
Top 20% share of income	48.6% (324)
Gender gap in earnings	32.0% (227)
White-collar gender gap	14.2% (142)

EDUCATION	★★★★★ (25)
Eighth grade or less	1.9% (114)
High school diplomas	93.5% (75)
Attended college	65.2% (57)
Bachelor's degrees	35.2% (27)
Advanced degrees	14.0% (19)

EMPLOYMENT	★★★★★ (26)
Average jobless rate	7.1% (208)
Self-employed workers	12.1% (71)
Management/financial jobs	15.8% (17)
Computer/engineering jobs	4.9% (33)
Health care jobs	6.2% (156)

GROWTH POTENTIAL	★ (482)
Children per senior	1.13 (452)
Median age	46.0 (513)
Moved from different state	1.4% (425)
Homes built since 2000	8.2% (462)
Construction jobs	7.8% (98)

HOUSING	★★★★★ (66)
Home vacancy rate	6.5% (130)
Home ownership rate	77.0% (27)
Housing diversity index	85.0% (226)
4 or more bedrooms	22.4% (76)
Affordability/income ratio	$3,533 (462)

INCOME	★★★★★ (4)
Poverty rate	7.0% (5)
Median household income	$72,061 (8)
Interest/dividends	31.3% (12)
Public assistance	8.8% (42)
Median fulltime earnings	$53,992 (6)

SENIORS	★★★★★ (56)
Seniors living alone	27.0% (239)
Poverty rate for seniors	6.4% (57)
Median income for seniors	$44,721 (29)
Seniors who work	25.8% (55)
Home ownership by seniors	80.4% (362)

STABILITY	★★ (434)
25-39 age group	14.6% (527)
Born in state of residence	65.6% (381)
Same house as 1 year ago	91.1% (29)
Live and work in county	55.4% (518)
Married-couple households	53.7% (123)

TRANSPORTATION	★ (515)
Bicycle or walk to work	2.9% (265)
Carpool to work	7.4% (518)
Public transit to work	1.5% (42)
Commute <15 minutes	30.3% (521)
Commute >45 minutes	19.1% (510)

See pages 37-130 for explanations of statistics, stars, and ranks.

Vineyard Haven, MA
(Dukes County, MA)

POPULATION	
2010 census	16,535 (541)
2015 estimate	17,299 (538)
2010-2015 change	4.6% (47)
2020 projection	18,204 (532)
2030 projection	20,191 (519)

RACE	
Whites	92.1% (133)
Blacks	3.1% (222)
Hispanics	0.8% (542)
Asians	0.8% (201)
Native Americans	0.8% (125)

AGE	
0-17 years old	18.6% (509)
18-24 years old	6.5% (541)
25-39 years old	15.1% (507)
40-54 years old	23.5% (4)
55-64 years old	17.3% (12)
65+ years old	19.0% (80)

PRIVATE SECTOR	
Businesses	1,132 (225)
Employees	7,181 (467)
Total wages	$332,642,287 (397)
Average weekly wages	$891 (38)

HOUSEHOLD INCOME LADDER	
95th percentile	$219,163 (11)
80th percentile	$121,565 (12)
60th percentile	$81,548 (15)
40th percentile	$48,847 (24)
20th percentile	$26,833 (25)

CHILDREN	★★★★★ (76)
Living with two parents	62.8% (323)
Older teens in school	88.0% (101)
Speak English very well	100.0% (1)
Poverty rate for children	19.9% (163)
No health insurance	2.3% (20)

DIVERSITY/EQUALITY	★★ (404)
Racial diversity index	15.0% (415)
Geographic diversity index	62.4% (98)
Top 20% share of income	54.7% (544)
Gender gap in earnings	18.3% (34)
White-collar gender gap	39.6% (442)

EDUCATION	★★★★★ (21)
Eighth grade or less	0.5% (2)
High school diplomas	93.4% (82)
Attended college	69.9% (27)
Bachelor's degrees	38.0% (20)
Advanced degrees	12.5% (32)

EMPLOYMENT	★★★★★ (14)
Average jobless rate	5.2% (76)
Self-employed workers	27.8% (1)
Management/financial jobs	21.8% (3)
Computer/engineering jobs	3.8% (96)
Health care jobs	4.1% (462)

GROWTH POTENTIAL	★★★★ (165)
Children per senior	0.98 (509)
Median age	45.9 (511)
Moved from different state	4.2% (70)
Homes built since 2000	13.5% (256)
Construction jobs	15.2% (1)

HOUSING	★★★★★ (52)
Home vacancy rate	3.8% (6)
Home ownership rate	79.9% (3)
Housing diversity index	83.4% (396)
4 or more bedrooms	31.3% (6)
Affordability/income ratio	$10,289 (551)

INCOME	★★★★★ (8)
Poverty rate	11.7% (77)
Median household income	$64,222 (20)
Interest/dividends	25.8% (77)
Public assistance	3.1% (3)
Median fulltime earnings	$51,538 (10)

SENIORS	★★★★★ (8)
Seniors living alone	22.6% (52)
Poverty rate for seniors	10.0% (321)
Median income for seniors	$47,563 (18)
Seniors who work	35.6% (4)
Home ownership by seniors	87.7% (48)

STABILITY	★★★★★ (75)
25-39 age group	15.1% (507)
Born in state of residence	57.0% (443)
Same house as 1 year ago	92.8% (7)
Live and work in county	94.6% (15)
Married-couple households	53.4% (134)

TRANSPORTATION	★★★★★ (19)
Bicycle or walk to work	6.8% (46)
Carpool to work	6.8% (534)
Public transit to work	4.3% (11)
Commute <15 minutes	49.6% (162)
Commute >45 minutes	2.7% (5)

See pages 37-130 for explanations of statistics, stars, and ranks.

Warren, PA
(Warren County, PA)

POPULATION	
2010 census	41,815 (292)
2015 estimate	40,396 (310)
2010-2015 change	-3.4% (501)
2020 projection	39,145 (325)
2030 projection	36,701 (349)

RACE	
Whites	97.2% (2)
Blacks	0.5% (466)
Hispanics	0.9% (535)
Asians	0.5% (355)
Native Americans	0.1% (402)

AGE	
0-17 years old	20.0% (458)
18-24 years old	7.2% (510)
25-39 years old	15.5% (484)
40-54 years old	21.1% (97)
55-64 years old	16.0% (46)
65+ years old	20.2% (50)

PRIVATE SECTOR	
Businesses	1,049 (258)
Employees	12,977 (283)
Total wages	$480,548,188 (260)
Average weekly wages	$712 (229)

HOUSEHOLD INCOME LADDER	
95th percentile	$136,323 (338)
80th percentile	$82,701 (299)
60th percentile	$53,548 (287)
40th percentile	$34,727 (271)
20th percentile	$20,730 (196)

CHILDREN	★★★★ (197)
Living with two parents	72.3% (101)
Older teens in school	79.0% (428)
Speak English very well	98.3% (312)
Poverty rate for children	19.9% (163)
No health insurance	6.5% (282)

DIVERSITY/EQUALITY	★ (461)
Racial diversity index	5.5% (549)
Geographic diversity index	35.7% (428)
Top 20% share of income	47.1% (231)
Gender gap in earnings	34.5% (301)
White-collar gender gap	29.5% (330)

EDUCATION	★★★★ (196)
Eighth grade or less	1.6% (84)
High school diplomas	93.2% (88)
Attended college	47.5% (390)
Bachelor's degrees	20.1% (220)
Advanced degrees	6.8% (191)

EMPLOYMENT	★★★★ (151)
Average jobless rate	6.6% (161)
Self-employed workers	8.3% (302)
Management/financial jobs	11.8% (173)
Computer/engineering jobs	3.1% (180)
Health care jobs	6.3% (144)

GROWTH POTENTIAL	★ (550)
Children per senior	0.99 (506)
Median age	46.2 (517)
Moved from different state	1.4% (425)
Homes built since 2000	5.2% (539)
Construction jobs	4.2% (524)

HOUSING	★★★★★ (86)
Home vacancy rate	5.6% (69)
Home ownership rate	76.6% (38)
Housing diversity index	82.8% (426)
4 or more bedrooms	16.4% (272)
Affordability/income ratio	$2,038 (66)

INCOME	★★★★ (167)
Poverty rate	12.2% (91)
Median household income	$44,020 (259)
Interest/dividends	23.9% (130)
Public assistance	13.8% (202)
Median fulltime earnings	$37,387 (254)

SENIORS	★★★ (330)
Seniors living alone	28.7% (344)
Poverty rate for seniors	6.8% (77)
Median income for seniors	$31,694 (336)
Seniors who work	15.5% (436)
Home ownership by seniors	82.1% (268)

STABILITY	★★★★★ (88)
25-39 age group	15.5% (484)
Born in state of residence	79.3% (123)
Same house as 1 year ago	90.3% (39)
Live and work in county	80.4% (213)
Married-couple households	52.2% (188)

TRANSPORTATION	★★★ (242)
Bicycle or walk to work	5.1% (90)
Carpool to work	9.3% (401)
Public transit to work	0.4% (219)
Commute <15 minutes	42.5% (287)
Commute >45 minutes	9.3% (188)

See pages 37-130 for explanations of statistics, stars, and ranks.

5

SOUTH

★★★★★

MICROPOLITAN
AMERICA

Ada, OK
(Pontotoc County, OK)

POPULATION				
2010 census	37,492 (348)		Attended college	57.1% (185)
2015 estimate	38,194 (338)		Bachelor's degrees	28.2% (72)
2010-2015 change	1.9% (136)		Advanced degrees	10.1% (56)
2020 projection	38,918 (330)			
2030 projection	40,366 (312)			

POPULATION
2010 census — 37,492 (348)
2015 estimate — 38,194 (338)
2010-2015 change — 1.9% (136)
2020 projection — 38,918 (330)
2030 projection — 40,366 (312)

RACE
Whites — 67.6% (402)
Blacks — 2.3% (267)
Hispanics — 4.7% (260)
Asians — 0.9% (178)
Native Americans — 7.3% (25)

AGE
0-17 years old — 23.8% (206)
18-24 years old — 12.2% (83)
25-39 years old — 19.2% (88)
40-54 years old — 17.9% (454)
55-64 years old — 11.5% (478)
65+ years old — 15.5% (333)

PRIVATE SECTOR
Businesses — 955 (292)
Employees — 11,447 (327)
Total wages — $379,070,606 (355)
Average weekly wages — $637 (420)

HOUSEHOLD INCOME LADDER
95th percentile — $131,973 (402)
80th percentile — $83,176 (289)
60th percentile — $53,911 (280)
40th percentile — $33,488 (310)
20th percentile — $18,633 (284)

CHILDREN ★★ (396)
Living with two parents — 59.9% (399)
Older teens in school — 80.9% (370)
Speak English very well — 99.8% (38)
Poverty rate for children — 24.4% (284)
No health insurance — 13.4% (503)

DIVERSITY/EQUALITY ★★★★★ (41)
Racial diversity index — 50.5% (109)
Geographic diversity index — 47.5% (250)
Top 20% share of income — 45.8% (112)
Gender gap in earnings — 21.4% (53)
White-collar gender gap — 21.5% (226)

EDUCATION ★★★★★ (98)
Eighth grade or less — 2.5% (180)
High school diplomas — 89.5% (215)
Attended college — 57.1% (185)
Bachelor's degrees — 28.2% (72)
Advanced degrees — 10.1% (56)

EMPLOYMENT ★★★★ (184)
Average jobless rate — 6.2% (131)
Self-employed workers — 8.3% (302)
Management/financial jobs — 11.2% (229)
Computer/engineering jobs — 2.6% (288)
Health care jobs — 6.3% (144)

GROWTH POTENTIAL ★★★★ (212)
Children per senior — 1.54 (197)
Median age — 35.3 (100)
Moved from different state — 2.4% (218)
Homes built since 2000 — 14.3% (227)
Construction jobs — 5.6% (392)

HOUSING ★★ (368)
Home vacancy rate — 11.4% (432)
Home ownership rate — 64.1% (453)
Housing diversity index — 86.2% (43)
4 or more bedrooms — 14.0% (401)
Affordability/income ratio — $2,492 (247)

INCOME ★★ (365)
Poverty rate — 18.5% (317)
Median household income — $43,261 (283)
Interest/dividends — 15.1% (405)
Public assistance — 16.2% (301)
Median fulltime earnings — $33,930 (425)

SENIORS ★★★★ (151)
Seniors living alone — 26.6% (209)
Poverty rate for seniors — 8.7% (241)
Median income for seniors — $37,405 (109)
Seniors who work — 22.2% (126)
Home ownership by seniors — 81.5% (305)

STABILITY ★★★★ (202)
25-39 age group — 19.2% (88)
Born in state of residence — 70.8% (295)
Same house as 1 year ago — 81.7% (454)
Live and work in county — 91.3% (51)
Married-couple households — 45.8% (447)

TRANSPORTATION ★★★ (274)
Bicycle or walk to work — 2.7% (292)
Carpool to work — 7.3% (523)
Public transit to work — 0.5% (178)
Commute <15 minutes — 48.8% (178)
Commute >45 minutes — 6.3% (65)

See pages 37-130 for explanations of statistics, stars, and ranks.

Albemarle, NC
(Stanly County, NC)

POPULATION

2010 census	60,585 (147)
2015 estimate	60,714 (144)
2010-2015 change	0.2% (241)
2020 projection	60,172 (147)
2030 projection	58,829 (156)

RACE

Whites	81.6% (310)
Blacks	10.3% (113)
Hispanics	3.9% (302)
Asians	1.9% (58)
Native Americans	0.3% (231)

AGE

0-17 years old	22.0% (335)
18-24 years old	9.3% (217)
25-39 years old	16.2% (434)
40-54 years old	22.1% (25)
55-64 years old	13.4% (274)
65+ years old	17.1% (186)

PRIVATE SECTOR

Businesses	1,289 (179)
Employees	15,403 (202)
Total wages	$484,825,321 (255)
Average weekly wages	$605 (479)

HOUSEHOLD INCOME LADDER

95th percentile	$130,948 (418)
80th percentile	$80,898 (352)
60th percentile	$51,671 (336)
40th percentile	$32,442 (341)
20th percentile	$18,171 (309)

CHILDREN   ★★★ (311)

Living with two parents	61.8% (361)
Older teens in school	78.1% (446)
Speak English very well	98.9% (226)
Poverty rate for children	25.1% (302)
No health insurance	5.4% (209)

DIVERSITY/EQUALITY   ★★★★★ (91)

Racial diversity index	32.1% (236)
Geographic diversity index	38.4% (383)
Top 20% share of income	45.8% (110)
Gender gap in earnings	30.8% (190)
White-collar gender gap	3.6% (25)

EDUCATION   ★★★ (316)

Eighth grade or less	3.4% (269)
High school diplomas	85.6% (357)
Attended college	52.4% (276)
Bachelor's degrees	17.8% (290)
Advanced degrees	5.2% (352)

EMPLOYMENT   ★★ (380)

Average jobless rate	12.2% (497)
Self-employed workers	9.0% (254)
Management/financial jobs	10.0% (381)
Computer/engineering jobs	2.8% (246)
Health care jobs	6.4% (132)

GROWTH POTENTIAL   ★★★★ (202)

Children per senior	1.28 (357)
Median age	41.8 (394)
Moved from different state	1.0% (504)
Homes built since 2000	13.3% (263)
Construction jobs	10.2% (15)

HOUSING   ★★★ (256)

Home vacancy rate	9.3% (305)
Home ownership rate	71.0% (229)
Housing diversity index	87.1% (1)
4 or more bedrooms	12.5% (478)
Affordability/income ratio	$3,134 (424)

INCOME   ★★ (333)

Poverty rate	17.7% (290)
Median household income	$40,910 (356)
Interest/dividends	17.2% (339)
Public assistance	16.3% (305)
Median fulltime earnings	$36,047 (332)

SENIORS   ★★★★ (189)

Seniors living alone	26.0% (172)
Poverty rate for seniors	7.8% (163)
Median income for seniors	$30,994 (374)
Seniors who work	17.0% (341)
Home ownership by seniors	85.9% (105)

STABILITY   ★★★ (314)

25-39 age group	16.2% (434)
Born in state of residence	77.7% (163)
Same house as 1 year ago	86.0% (250)
Live and work in county	65.8% (440)
Married-couple households	51.9% (199)

TRANSPORTATION   ★ (507)

Bicycle or walk to work	2.4% (331)
Carpool to work	11.2% (211)
Public transit to work	0.2% (363)
Commute <15 minutes	34.5% (448)
Commute >45 minutes	20.4% (520)

See pages 37-130 for explanations of statistics, stars, and ranks.

Albertville, AL
(Marshall County, AL)

POPULATION	
2010 census	93,019 (39)
2015 estimate	94,725 (39)
2010-2015 change	1.8% (142)
2020 projection	96,757 (37)
2030 projection	100,447 (31)

RACE	
Whites	82.7% (293)
Blacks	1.9% (295)
Hispanics	12.7% (121)
Asians	0.5% (355)
Native Americans	0.4% (203)

AGE	
0-17 years old	24.6% (144)
18-24 years old	8.5% (330)
25-39 years old	18.2% (167)
40-54 years old	20.3% (186)
55-64 years old	12.3% (414)
65+ years old	16.0% (291)

PRIVATE SECTOR	
Businesses	1,861 (81)
Employees	28,850 (50)
Total wages	$945,221,822 (81)
Average weekly wages	$630 (438)

HOUSEHOLD INCOME LADDER	
95th percentile	$150,733 (154)
80th percentile	$82,942 (294)
60th percentile	$49,161 (398)
40th percentile	$30,217 (411)
20th percentile	$17,196 (351)

CHILDREN	★★ (423)
Living with two parents	63.5% (310)
Older teens in school	80.0% (397)
Speak English very well	93.9% (495)
Poverty rate for children	32.9% (462)
No health insurance	5.5% (218)

DIVERSITY/EQUALITY	★★★★ (179)
Racial diversity index	29.9% (253)
Geographic diversity index	48.9% (230)
Top 20% share of income	51.3% (478)
Gender gap in earnings	24.2% (79)
White-collar gender gap	9.6% (86)

EDUCATION	★ (470)
Eighth grade or less	8.7% (502)
High school diplomas	78.4% (504)
Attended college	48.1% (381)
Bachelor's degrees	17.0% (328)
Advanced degrees	5.4% (334)

EMPLOYMENT	★★★ (241)
Average jobless rate	8.4% (323)
Self-employed workers	9.2% (231)
Management/financial jobs	11.1% (240)
Computer/engineering jobs	3.2% (158)
Health care jobs	5.6% (240)

GROWTH POTENTIAL	★★★★ (193)
Children per senior	1.54 (197)
Median age	38.8 (217)
Moved from different state	1.7% (355)
Homes built since 2000	13.5% (256)
Construction jobs	7.9% (93)

HOUSING	★★★ (291)
Home vacancy rate	11.2% (423)
Home ownership rate	71.8% (196)
Housing diversity index	84.7% (260)
4 or more bedrooms	17.1% (239)
Affordability/income ratio	$2,963 (396)

INCOME	★★ (410)
Poverty rate	20.2% (380)
Median household income	$38,983 (405)
Interest/dividends	15.0% (410)
Public assistance	17.6% (359)
Median fulltime earnings	$33,935 (424)

SENIORS	★★★ (325)
Seniors living alone	27.8% (283)
Poverty rate for seniors	9.5% (291)
Median income for seniors	$30,084 (406)
Seniors who work	15.4% (441)
Home ownership by seniors	85.1% (137)

STABILITY	★★★★ (142)
25-39 age group	18.2% (167)
Born in state of residence	69.8% (312)
Same house as 1 year ago	86.0% (250)
Live and work in county	73.8% (317)
Married-couple households	53.8% (116)

TRANSPORTATION	★★ (417)
Bicycle or walk to work	1.1% (501)
Carpool to work	13.3% (88)
Public transit to work	0.2% (363)
Commute <15 minutes	38.0% (375)
Commute >45 minutes	16.6% (473)

See pages 37-130 for explanations of statistics, stars, and ranks.

Alexander City, AL
(Tallapoosa County, AL)

POPULATION

2010 census	41,616 (294)
2015 estimate	40,844 (305)
2010-2015 change	-1.9% (399)
2020 projection	39,997 (315)
2030 projection	38,157 (340)

RACE

Whites	69.0% (397)
Blacks	27.4% (63)
Hispanics	2.5% (384)
Asians	0.0% (546)
Native Americans	0.3% (231)

AGE

0-17 years old	21.5% (373)
18-24 years old	8.3% (362)
25-39 years old	16.1% (442)
40-54 years old	20.4% (169)
55-64 years old	14.8% (91)
65+ years old	18.9% (85)

PRIVATE SECTOR

Businesses	733 (412)
Employees	11,360 (332)
Total wages	$356,556,497 (376)
Average weekly wages	$604 (484)

HOUSEHOLD INCOME LADDER

95th percentile	$135,583 (352)
80th percentile	$78,957 (383)
60th percentile	$49,943 (385)
40th percentile	$30,142 (416)
20th percentile	$15,673 (421)

CHILDREN ★ **(444)**

Living with two parents	50.8% (502)
Older teens in school	73.4% (514)
Speak English very well	99.9% (19)
Poverty rate for children	40.2% (516)
No health insurance	1.1% (3)

DIVERSITY/EQUALITY ★★★★ **(114)**

Racial diversity index	44.8% (153)
Geographic diversity index	30.4% (481)
Top 20% share of income	48.3% (310)
Gender gap in earnings	17.3% (25)
White-collar gender gap	20.7% (216)

EDUCATION ★★ **(410)**

Eighth grade or less	4.1% (332)
High school diplomas	79.7% (484)
Attended college	46.9% (399)
Bachelor's degrees	17.1% (322)
Advanced degrees	5.7% (292)

EMPLOYMENT ★★★ **(310)**

Average jobless rate	9.0% (358)
Self-employed workers	8.2% (314)
Management/financial jobs	10.1% (365)
Computer/engineering jobs	2.7% (270)
Health care jobs	6.4% (132)

GROWTH POTENTIAL ★★★ **(298)**

Children per senior	1.14 (446)
Median age	42.8 (447)
Moved from different state	1.3% (452)
Homes built since 2000	17.2% (150)
Construction jobs	7.8% (98)

HOUSING ★★★ **(247)**

Home vacancy rate	10.4% (371)
Home ownership rate	71.4% (209)
Housing diversity index	85.6% (127)
4 or more bedrooms	15.1% (347)
Affordability/income ratio	$2,637 (304)

INCOME ★ **(442)**

Poverty rate	22.5% (437)
Median household income	$39,206 (400)
Interest/dividends	14.6% (424)
Public assistance	18.6% (389)
Median fulltime earnings	$33,770 (430)

SENIORS ★★★ **(229)**

Seniors living alone	25.4% (132)
Poverty rate for seniors	11.0% (374)
Median income for seniors	$35,253 (180)
Seniors who work	16.5% (376)
Home ownership by seniors	84.2% (175)

STABILITY ★★★ **(253)**

25-39 age group	16.1% (442)
Born in state of residence	82.8% (71)
Same house as 1 year ago	88.6% (101)
Live and work in county	66.6% (425)
Married-couple households	49.6% (317)

TRANSPORTATION ★ **(476)**

Bicycle or walk to work	0.5% (547)
Carpool to work	12.9% (106)
Public transit to work	0.3% (291)
Commute <15 minutes	28.3% (534)
Commute >45 minutes	15.4% (436)

See pages 37-130 for explanations of statistics, stars, and ranks.

Alice, TX
(Jim Wells County, TX)

POPULATION		
2010 census	40,838 (303)	
2015 estimate	41,382 (295)	
2010-2015 change	1.3% (167)	
2020 projection	41,212 (297)	
2030 projection	40,910 (303)	

RACE

Whites	19.0% (542)	
Blacks	0.5% (466)	
Hispanics	79.5% (7)	
Asians	0.5% (355)	
Native Americans	0.1% (402)	

AGE

0-17 years old	28.3% (28)	
18-24 years old	9.8% (176)	
25-39 years old	18.0% (201)	
40-54 years old	18.7% (399)	
55-64 years old	11.4% (482)	
65+ years old	13.8% (448)	

PRIVATE SECTOR

Businesses	934 (299)	
Employees	16,495 (181)	
Total wages	$747,685,631 (136)	
Average weekly wages	$872 (46)	

HOUSEHOLD INCOME LADDER

95th percentile	$165,864 (67)	
80th percentile	$98,646 (66)	
60th percentile	$57,611 (192)	
40th percentile	$32,049 (359)	
20th percentile	$16,531 (384)	

CHILDREN ★ (509)

Living with two parents	60.1% (395)	
Older teens in school	72.1% (520)	
Speak English very well	96.6% (430)	
Poverty rate for children	31.6% (437)	
No health insurance	12.1% (473)	

DIVERSITY/EQUALITY ★ (551)

Racial diversity index	33.2% (227)	
Geographic diversity index	25.3% (526)	
Top 20% share of income	52.9% (519)	
Gender gap in earnings	52.9% (536)	
White-collar gender gap	34.1% (385)	

EDUCATION ★ (520)

Eighth grade or less	7.8% (488)	
High school diplomas	75.9% (520)	
Attended college	40.2% (511)	
Bachelor's degrees	12.0% (516)	
Advanced degrees	3.8% (496)	

EMPLOYMENT ★★★★ (180)

Average jobless rate	6.6% (161)	
Self-employed workers	8.6% (285)	
Management/financial jobs	11.4% (210)	
Computer/engineering jobs	2.8% (246)	
Health care jobs	6.1% (168)	

GROWTH POTENTIAL ★★★★ (169)

Children per senior	2.05 (54)	
Median age	34.6 (84)	
Moved from different state	1.1% (487)	
Homes built since 2000	14.4% (222)	
Construction jobs	5.5% (404)	

HOUSING ★★★ (232)

Home vacancy rate	10.4% (371)	
Home ownership rate	68.3% (332)	
Housing diversity index	85.3% (170)	
4 or more bedrooms	14.0% (401)	
Affordability/income ratio	$1,631 (10)	

INCOME ★★ (421)

Poverty rate	22.3% (432)	
Median household income	$42,986 (289)	
Interest/dividends	8.3% (540)	
Public assistance	17.2% (344)	
Median fulltime earnings	$37,750 (232)	

SENIORS ★★ (364)

Seniors living alone	22.2% (41)	
Poverty rate for seniors	16.9% (516)	
Median income for seniors	$24,292 (512)	
Seniors who work	20.4% (183)	
Home ownership by seniors	83.2% (210)	

STABILITY ★★★★★ (46)

25-39 age group	18.0% (201)	
Born in state of residence	86.2% (23)	
Same house as 1 year ago	88.4% (109)	
Live and work in county	73.9% (313)	
Married-couple households	51.7% (212)	

TRANSPORTATION ★ (528)

Bicycle or walk to work	1.3% (485)	
Carpool to work	11.7% (170)	
Public transit to work	0.0% (511)	
Commute <15 minutes	28.9% (531)	
Commute >45 minutes	18.8% (508)	

See pages 37-130 for explanations of statistics, stars, and ranks.

Altus, OK
(Jackson County, OK)

POPULATION	
2010 census	26,446 (466)
2015 estimate	25,574 (480)
2010-2015 change	-3.3% (495)
2020 projection	24,624 (486)
2030 projection	22,813 (495)

RACE	
Whites	64.2% (420)
Blacks	7.4% (131)
Hispanics	22.4% (67)
Asians	1.6% (77)
Native Americans	1.1% (96)

AGE	
0-17 years old	25.8% (75)
18-24 years old	10.7% (124)
25-39 years old	19.8% (64)
40-54 years old	18.6% (412)
55-64 years old	11.5% (478)
65+ years old	13.6% (454)

PRIVATE SECTOR	
Businesses	573 (487)
Employees	5,845 (513)
Total wages	$180,091,707 (519)
Average weekly wages	$593 (497)

HOUSEHOLD INCOME LADDER	
95th percentile	$145,135 (226)
80th percentile	$81,651 (330)
60th percentile	$51,690 (335)
40th percentile	$32,429 (342)
20th percentile	$17,417 (345)

CHILDREN	★★ (367)
Living with two parents	66.5% (231)
Older teens in school	74.0% (510)
Speak English very well	95.3% (471)
Poverty rate for children	21.2% (198)
No health insurance	6.4% (276)

DIVERSITY/EQUALITY	★★★★★ (77)
Racial diversity index	53.1% (80)
Geographic diversity index	70.3% (42)
Top 20% share of income	48.3% (310)
Gender gap in earnings	39.0% (421)
White-collar gender gap	24.6% (265)

EDUCATION	★★ (368)
Eighth grade or less	9.9% (511)
High school diplomas	84.0% (400)
Attended college	56.9% (188)
Bachelor's degrees	19.8% (224)
Advanced degrees	6.5% (220)

EMPLOYMENT	★ (442)
Average jobless rate	7.6% (250)
Self-employed workers	8.2% (314)
Management/financial jobs	9.3% (453)
Computer/engineering jobs	2.0% (420)
Health care jobs	4.6% (401)

GROWTH POTENTIAL	★★★★★ (84)
Children per senior	1.90 (71)
Median age	34.1 (78)
Moved from different state	6.0% (30)
Homes built since 2000	8.9% (439)
Construction jobs	6.8% (204)

HOUSING	★ (501)
Home vacancy rate	14.5% (529)
Home ownership rate	58.7% (517)
Housing diversity index	85.7% (108)
4 or more bedrooms	12.8% (462)
Affordability/income ratio	$2,173 (109)

INCOME	★★ (332)
Poverty rate	17.0% (262)
Median household income	$41,560 (335)
Interest/dividends	21.8% (188)
Public assistance	17.4% (352)
Median fulltime earnings	$32,320 (479)

SENIORS	★★ (438)
Seniors living alone	27.9% (290)
Poverty rate for seniors	12.8% (442)
Median income for seniors	$28,146 (453)
Seniors who work	17.5% (310)
Home ownership by seniors	81.5% (305)

STABILITY	★★ (411)
25-39 age group	19.8% (64)
Born in state of residence	48.4% (490)
Same house as 1 year ago	78.7% (512)
Live and work in county	90.3% (61)
Married-couple households	47.8% (390)

TRANSPORTATION	★★★★★ (74)
Bicycle or walk to work	2.6% (308)
Carpool to work	13.0% (101)
Public transit to work	0.2% (363)
Commute <15 minutes	63.1% (30)
Commute >45 minutes	6.0% (53)

See pages 37-130 for explanations of statistics, stars, and ranks.

Americus, GA
(Schley and Sumter Counties, GA)

POPULATION
2010 census	37,829 (344)
2015 estimate	35,947 (372)
2010-2015 change	-5.0% (532)
2020 projection	34,668 (388)
2030 projection	32,307 (404)

RACE
Whites	44.5% (504)
Blacks	47.7% (18)
Hispanics	5.1% (249)
Asians	1.2% (125)
Native Americans	0.2% (300)

AGE
0-17 years old	25.2% (108)
18-24 years old	12.3% (80)
25-39 years old	17.5% (258)
40-54 years old	18.8% (386)
55-64 years old	11.7% (463)
65+ years old	14.5% (412)

PRIVATE SECTOR
Businesses	702 (427)
Employees	8,978 (413)
Total wages	$319,859,068 (409)
Average weekly wages	$685 (300)

HOUSEHOLD INCOME LADDER
95th percentile	$125,589 (483)
80th percentile	$71,730 (495)
60th percentile	$43,393 (496)
40th percentile	$24,704 (513)
20th percentile	$12,103 (517)

CHILDREN ★ (450)
Living with two parents	42.8% (534)
Older teens in school	94.1% (19)
Speak English very well	98.7% (265)
Poverty rate for children	49.6% (543)
No health insurance	6.3% (271)

DIVERSITY/EQUALITY ★★★★★ (67)
Racial diversity index	57.2% (30)
Geographic diversity index	34.1% (447)
Top 20% share of income	50.7% (458)
Gender gap in earnings	17.5% (29)
White-collar gender gap	7.3% (57)

EDUCATION ★★ (397)
Eighth grade or less	6.1% (429)
High school diplomas	78.7% (500)
Attended college	46.4% (409)
Bachelor's degrees	17.8% (290)
Advanced degrees	8.5% (103)

EMPLOYMENT ★★ (412)
Average jobless rate	14.1% (528)
Self-employed workers	6.8% (446)
Management/financial jobs	13.0% (86)
Computer/engineering jobs	1.9% (441)
Health care jobs	6.6% (114)

GROWTH POTENTIAL ★★★ (304)
Children per senior	1.74 (113)
Median age	35.1 (94)
Moved from different state	1.1% (487)
Homes built since 2000	13.3% (263)
Construction jobs	4.2% (524)

HOUSING ★★ (424)
Home vacancy rate	11.8% (454)
Home ownership rate	59.2% (512)
Housing diversity index	84.9% (235)
4 or more bedrooms	17.9% (209)
Affordability/income ratio	$2,539 (263)

INCOME ★ (524)
Poverty rate	31.7% (533)
Median household income	$33,798 (500)
Interest/dividends	14.2% (435)
Public assistance	27.2% (525)
Median fulltime earnings	$32,857 (458)

SENIORS ★ (533)
Seniors living alone	31.3% (486)
Poverty rate for seniors	16.6% (512)
Median income for seniors	$27,969 (461)
Seniors who work	17.0% (341)
Home ownership by seniors	76.0% (511)

STABILITY ★ (494)
25-39 age group	17.5% (258)
Born in state of residence	80.4% (104)
Same house as 1 year ago	81.8% (452)
Live and work in county	68.9% (390)
Married-couple households	40.7% (519)

TRANSPORTATION ★★★ (251)
Bicycle or walk to work	3.3% (211)
Carpool to work	14.3% (57)
Public transit to work	0.1% (441)
Commute <15 minutes	39.1% (348)
Commute >45 minutes	12.3% (325)

See pages 37-130 for explanations of statistics, stars, and ranks.

Andrews, TX
(Andrews County, TX)

POPULATION

2010 census	14,786 (544)
2015 estimate	18,105 (532)
2010-2015 change	22.4% (4)
2020 projection	20,948 (519)
2030 projection	28,035 (444)

RACE

Whites	43.1% (506)
Blacks	1.3% (351)
Hispanics	53.2% (23)
Asians	0.4% (413)
Native Americans	0.2% (300)

AGE

0-17 years old	30.5% (16)
18-24 years old	10.1% (157)
25-39 years old	20.4% (52)
40-54 years old	19.0% (364)
55-64 years old	9.9% (524)
65+ years old	10.1% (528)

PRIVATE SECTOR

Businesses	453 (526)
Employees	6,117 (505)
Total wages	$378,098,992 (356)
Average weekly wages	$1,189 (6)

HOUSEHOLD INCOME LADDER

95th percentile	$211,960 (13)
80th percentile	$124,366 (10)
60th percentile	$87,173 (8)
40th percentile	$53,559 (14)
20th percentile	$28,903 (18)

CHILDREN ★ (506)

Living with two parents	74.3% (64)
Older teens in school	67.7% (544)
Speak English very well	92.8% (510)
Poverty rate for children	17.0% (97)
No health insurance	17.4% (536)

DIVERSITY/EQUALITY ★ (453)

Racial diversity index	53.1% (80)
Geographic diversity index	55.6% (149)
Top 20% share of income	47.6% (261)
Gender gap in earnings	57.7% (549)
White-collar gender gap	50.7% (514)

EDUCATION ★ (527)

Eighth grade or less	10.6% (518)
High school diplomas	76.8% (516)
Attended college	42.4% (483)
Bachelor's degrees	12.2% (512)
Advanced degrees	2.5% (546)

EMPLOYMENT ★★ (368)

Average jobless rate	3.9% (31)
Self-employed workers	7.9% (345)
Management/financial jobs	9.6% (427)
Computer/engineering jobs	2.5% (307)
Health care jobs	3.8% (494)

GROWTH POTENTIAL ★★★★★ (59)

Children per senior	3.01 (14)
Median age	31.3 (40)
Moved from different state	0.8% (524)
Homes built since 2000	9.5% (408)
Construction jobs	8.0% (89)

HOUSING ★★★★ (119)

Home vacancy rate	7.8% (205)
Home ownership rate	74.7% (89)
Housing diversity index	82.2% (450)
4 or more bedrooms	17.8% (215)
Affordability/income ratio	$1,585 (7)

INCOME ★★★★★ (36)

Poverty rate	12.3% (94)
Median household income	$70,423 (10)
Interest/dividends	14.0% (442)
Public assistance	9.7% (57)
Median fulltime earnings	$51,469 (11)

SENIORS ★★★★★ (76)

Seniors living alone	21.7% (32)
Poverty rate for seniors	14.2% (475)
Median income for seniors	$30,625 (388)
Seniors who work	23.1% (107)
Home ownership by seniors	90.4% (13)

STABILITY ★★★★★ (4)

25-39 age group	20.4% (52)
Born in state of residence	64.7% (389)
Same house as 1 year ago	86.2% (237)
Live and work in county	80.0% (219)
Married-couple households	62.7% (5)

TRANSPORTATION ★★★★ (134)

Bicycle or walk to work	0.3% (550)
Carpool to work	18.7% (10)
Public transit to work	0.0% (511)
Commute <15 minutes	58.0% (65)
Commute >45 minutes	13.4% (371)

See pages 37-130 for explanations of statistics, stars, and ranks.

Arcadia, FL
(DeSoto County, FL)

POPULATION

2010 census	34,862 (386)
2015 estimate	35,458 (379)
2010-2015 change	1.7% (150)
2020 projection	36,152 (367)
2030 projection	37,681 (342)

RACE

Whites	55.2% (471)
Blacks	12.9% (99)
Hispanics	30.5% (48)
Asians	0.4% (413)
Native Americans	0.1% (402)

AGE

0-17 years old	21.2% (397)
18-24 years old	10.3% (146)
25-39 years old	18.4% (151)
40-54 years old	19.2% (336)
55-64 years old	12.1% (430)
65+ years old	18.8% (94)

PRIVATE SECTOR

Businesses	580 (483)
Employees	6,266 (498)
Total wages	$203,593,357 (506)
Average weekly wages	$625 (443)

HOUSEHOLD INCOME LADDER

95th percentile	$117,203 (531)
80th percentile	$63,891 (537)
60th percentile	$42,278 (505)
40th percentile	$26,912 (487)
20th percentile	$16,298 (396)

CHILDREN ★ **(551)**

Living with two parents	51.5% (496)
Older teens in school	61.1% (547)
Speak English very well	86.3% (541)
Poverty rate for children	42.4% (527)
No health insurance	11.5% (459)

DIVERSITY/EQUALITY ★★★★★ **(6)**

Racial diversity index	58.6% (18)
Geographic diversity index	72.3% (29)
Top 20% share of income	48.7% (334)
Gender gap in earnings	0.1% (1)
White-collar gender gap	17.1% (182)

EDUCATION ★ **(551)**

Eighth grade or less	19.8% (543)
High school diplomas	67.1% (542)
Attended college	26.3% (551)
Bachelor's degrees	7.2% (551)
Advanced degrees	1.9% (550)

EMPLOYMENT ★ **(548)**

Average jobless rate	9.4% (394)
Self-employed workers	7.2% (410)
Management/financial jobs	6.9% (547)
Computer/engineering jobs	0.8% (543)
Health care jobs	2.7% (542)

GROWTH POTENTIAL ★★★★ **(113)**

Children per senior	1.13 (452)
Median age	40.1 (309)
Moved from different state	2.7% (179)
Homes built since 2000	22.7% (55)
Construction jobs	9.1% (40)

HOUSING ★ **(475)**

Home vacancy rate	9.1% (296)
Home ownership rate	70.4% (251)
Housing diversity index	81.3% (484)
4 or more bedrooms	7.4% (549)
Affordability/income ratio	$2,286 (158)

INCOME ★ **(510)**

Poverty rate	30.6% (526)
Median household income	$35,165 (485)
Interest/dividends	17.0% (344)
Public assistance	22.4% (489)
Median fulltime earnings	$28,254 (549)

SENIORS ★★★★ **(144)**

Seniors living alone	23.3% (63)
Poverty rate for seniors	12.3% (427)
Median income for seniors	$33,342 (265)
Seniors who work	12.8% (530)
Home ownership by seniors	92.3% (4)

STABILITY ★ **(482)**

25-39 age group	18.4% (151)
Born in state of residence	46.9% (497)
Same house as 1 year ago	82.6% (416)
Live and work in county	76.2% (269)
Married-couple households	48.1% (376)

TRANSPORTATION ★★★★★ **(75)**

Bicycle or walk to work	2.9% (265)
Carpool to work	18.5% (12)
Public transit to work	6.3% (6)
Commute <15 minutes	32.7% (480)
Commute >45 minutes	15.8% (446)

See pages 37-130 for explanations of statistics, stars, and ranks.

Ardmore, OK
(Carter County, OK)

POPULATION	
2010 census	47,557 (227)
2015 estimate	48,689 (220)
2010-2015 change	2.4% (111)
2020 projection	49,458 (217)
2030 projection	50,991 (210)

RACE	
Whites	71.4% (381)
Blacks	6.9% (135)
Hispanics	6.4% (210)
Asians	1.0% (158)
Native Americans	8.0% (24)

AGE	
0-17 years old	25.4% (96)
18-24 years old	8.3% (362)
25-39 years old	18.0% (201)
40-54 years old	20.0% (233)
55-64 years old	12.7% (375)
65+ years old	15.6% (328)

PRIVATE SECTOR	
Businesses	1,643 (114)
Employees	20,833 (117)
Total wages	$858,513,805 (104)
Average weekly wages	$792 (105)

HOUSEHOLD INCOME LADDER	
95th percentile	$145,599 (220)
80th percentile	$84,667 (258)
60th percentile	$55,188 (244)
40th percentile	$34,026 (289)
20th percentile	$19,430 (250)

CHILDREN	★★★ (286)
Living with two parents	63.6% (306)
Older teens in school	82.3% (304)
Speak English very well	99.0% (200)
Poverty rate for children	20.8% (187)
No health insurance	9.9% (420)

DIVERSITY/EQUALITY	★★★★ (158)
Racial diversity index	47.1% (135)
Geographic diversity index	47.4% (252)
Top 20% share of income	48.8% (348)
Gender gap in earnings	38.8% (415)
White-collar gender gap	10.7% (96)

EDUCATION	★★★ (301)
Eighth grade or less	3.4% (269)
High school diplomas	87.8% (274)
Attended college	48.9% (357)
Bachelor's degrees	18.9% (254)
Advanced degrees	5.6% (304)

EMPLOYMENT	★★★★ (149)
Average jobless rate	6.1% (121)
Self-employed workers	8.5% (290)
Management/financial jobs	11.9% (165)
Computer/engineering jobs	2.9% (219)
Health care jobs	6.1% (168)

GROWTH POTENTIAL	★★★ (227)
Children per senior	1.63 (158)
Median age	38.6 (207)
Moved from different state	2.4% (218)
Homes built since 2000	13.6% (251)
Construction jobs	6.2% (295)

HOUSING	★★★ (284)
Home vacancy rate	13.0% (490)
Home ownership rate	69.9% (275)
Housing diversity index	86.7% (6)
4 or more bedrooms	13.8% (409)
Affordability/income ratio	$2,178 (111)

INCOME	★★★ (267)
Poverty rate	15.3% (204)
Median household income	$44,531 (249)
Interest/dividends	16.8% (349)
Public assistance	14.0% (207)
Median fulltime earnings	$35,930 (337)

SENIORS	★ (458)
Seniors living alone	31.4% (495)
Poverty rate for seniors	12.8% (442)
Median income for seniors	$29,064 (431)
Seniors who work	19.9% (201)
Home ownership by seniors	81.7% (294)

STABILITY	★★★★★ (94)
25-39 age group	18.0% (201)
Born in state of residence	70.7% (299)
Same house as 1 year ago	86.4% (225)
Live and work in county	90.2% (62)
Married-couple households	49.1% (345)

TRANSPORTATION	★★★ (235)
Bicycle or walk to work	1.7% (428)
Carpool to work	11.3% (201)
Public transit to work	0.6% (141)
Commute <15 minutes	46.8% (219)
Commute >45 minutes	8.5% (152)

See pages 37-130 for explanations of statistics, stars, and ranks.

Arkadelphia, AR
(Clark County, AR)

POPULATION		
2010 census	22,995 (494)	
2015 estimate	22,633 (503)	
2010-2015 change	-1.6% (381)	
2020 projection	22,067 (512)	
2030 projection	20,784 (513)	

RACE		
Whites	69.6% (395)	
Blacks	23.9% (69)	
Hispanics	4.3% (279)	
Asians	0.8% (201)	
Native Americans	0.1% (402)	

AGE		
0-17 years old	19.6% (478)	
18-24 years old	22.5% (20)	
25-39 years old	13.7% (545)	
40-54 years old	17.6% (470)	
55-64 years old	11.2% (489)	
65+ years old	15.5% (333)	

PRIVATE SECTOR		
Businesses	568 (491)	
Employees	6,906 (477)	
Total wages	$223,413,397 (490)	
Average weekly wages	$622 (448)	

HOUSEHOLD INCOME LADDER		
95th percentile	$129,631 (435)	
80th percentile	$75,262 (454)	
60th percentile	$43,389 (497)	
40th percentile	$27,123 (481)	
20th percentile	$13,685 (484)	

CHILDREN	★★★★ (135)	
Living with two parents	61.1% (378)	
Older teens in school	93.3% (30)	
Speak English very well	99.6% (77)	
Poverty rate for children	32.6% (457)	
No health insurance	2.2% (15)	

DIVERSITY/EQUALITY	★★ (361)	
Racial diversity index	45.6% (144)	
Geographic diversity index	48.3% (239)	
Top 20% share of income	51.5% (487)	
Gender gap in earnings	37.0% (364)	
White-collar gender gap	33.6% (379)	

EDUCATION	★★★★★ (107)	
Eighth grade or less	3.0% (231)	
High school diplomas	90.2% (196)	

Attended college	58.5% (157)	
Bachelor's degrees	26.6% (92)	
Advanced degrees	10.1% (56)	

EMPLOYMENT	★★★ (309)	
Average jobless rate	8.4% (323)	
Self-employed workers	7.8% (355)	
Management/financial jobs	10.5% (318)	
Computer/engineering jobs	2.2% (381)	
Health care jobs	6.5% (121)	

GROWTH POTENTIAL	★★ (340)	
Children per senior	1.27 (370)	
Median age	34.0 (77)	
Moved from different state	3.4% (118)	
Homes built since 2000	11.5% (333)	
Construction jobs	3.4% (545)	

HOUSING	★★★ (251)	
Home vacancy rate	5.0% (33)	
Home ownership rate	63.5% (469)	
Housing diversity index	85.0% (226)	
4 or more bedrooms	13.1% (448)	
Affordability/income ratio	$2,489 (246)	

INCOME	★★ (408)	
Poverty rate	23.7% (462)	
Median household income	$35,031 (486)	
Interest/dividends	15.7% (388)	
Public assistance	14.4% (225)	
Median fulltime earnings	$35,688 (351)	

SENIORS	★ (517)	
Seniors living alone	40.3% (551)	
Poverty rate for seniors	11.5% (388)	
Median income for seniors	$26,472 (486)	
Seniors who work	19.4% (230)	
Home ownership by seniors	79.6% (388)	

STABILITY	★ (540)	
25-39 age group	13.7% (545)	
Born in state of residence	69.6% (317)	
Same house as 1 year ago	81.4% (465)	
Live and work in county	71.5% (349)	
Married-couple households	44.1% (479)	

TRANSPORTATION	★★★ (288)	
Bicycle or walk to work	4.6% (110)	
Carpool to work	11.2% (211)	
Public transit to work	0.4% (219)	
Commute <15 minutes	47.3% (204)	
Commute >45 minutes	16.8% (479)	

See pages 37-130 for explanations of statistics, stars, and ranks.

Athens, TN
(McMinn County, TN)

POPULATION	
2010 census	52,266 (194)
2015 estimate	52,639 (192)
2010-2015 change	0.7% (202)
2020 projection	52,736 (191)
2030 projection	52,755 (195)

RACE	
Whites	90.0% (184)
Blacks	4.0% (189)
Hispanics	3.3% (324)
Asians	0.5% (355)
Native Americans	0.2% (300)

AGE	
0-17 years old	21.7% (359)
18-24 years old	8.7% (299)
25-39 years old	16.3% (418)
40-54 years old	21.0% (107)
55-64 years old	13.9% (192)
65+ years old	18.3% (108)

PRIVATE SECTOR	
Businesses	826 (358)
Employees	15,290 (204)
Total wages	$623,110,166 (176)
Average weekly wages	$784 (114)

HOUSEHOLD INCOME LADDER	
95th percentile	$127,504 (462)
80th percentile	$74,467 (465)
60th percentile	$48,435 (411)
40th percentile	$28,704 (444)
20th percentile	$15,067 (451)

CHILDREN	★★★★ (138)
Living with two parents	70.9% (122)
Older teens in school	86.7% (141)
Speak English very well	99.3% (142)
Poverty rate for children	28.3% (375)
No health insurance	4.2% (134)

DIVERSITY/EQUALITY	★★ (341)
Racial diversity index	18.7% (364)
Geographic diversity index	48.5% (237)
Top 20% share of income	48.8% (342)
Gender gap in earnings	40.0% (438)
White-collar gender gap	15.6% (157)

EDUCATION	★★ (356)
Eighth grade or less	3.4% (269)
High school diplomas	87.8% (274)
Attended college	43.9% (453)
Bachelor's degrees	17.2% (315)
Advanced degrees	5.5% (318)

EMPLOYMENT	★ (459)
Average jobless rate	9.3% (387)
Self-employed workers	5.6% (523)
Management/financial jobs	9.0% (475)
Computer/engineering jobs	3.4% (131)
Health care jobs	5.3% (286)

GROWTH POTENTIAL	★★ (362)
Children per senior	1.19 (423)
Median age	42.7 (442)
Moved from different state	1.6% (383)
Homes built since 2000	13.3% (263)
Construction jobs	7.3% (151)

HOUSING	★★★ (265)
Home vacancy rate	12.3% (469)
Home ownership rate	73.8% (126)
Housing diversity index	85.6% (127)
4 or more bedrooms	16.6% (264)
Affordability/income ratio	$2,938 (388)

INCOME	★★ (405)
Poverty rate	19.9% (366)
Median household income	$38,535 (417)
Interest/dividends	15.2% (401)
Public assistance	18.4% (381)
Median fulltime earnings	$34,920 (386)

SENIORS	★ (457)
Seniors living alone	27.1% (247)
Poverty rate for seniors	12.3% (427)
Median income for seniors	$28,725 (443)
Seniors who work	14.5% (478)
Home ownership by seniors	80.9% (339)

STABILITY	★★★ (326)
25-39 age group	16.3% (418)
Born in state of residence	69.9% (310)
Same house as 1 year ago	85.9% (257)
Live and work in county	68.4% (400)
Married-couple households	53.2% (143)

TRANSPORTATION	★ (473)
Bicycle or walk to work	0.8% (531)
Carpool to work	10.1% (322)
Public transit to work	0.1% (441)
Commute <15 minutes	35.4% (433)
Commute >45 minutes	13.2% (363)

See pages 37-130 for explanations of statistics, stars, and ranks.

Athens, TX
(Henderson County, TX)

POPULATION		
2010 census		78,532 (70)
2015 estimate		79,545 (70)
2010-2015 change		1.3% (167)
2020 projection		79,805 (72)
2030 projection		80,236 (77)

RACE		
Whites		79.5% (332)
Blacks		6.5% (142)
Hispanics		11.7% (128)
Asians		0.7% (241)
Native Americans		0.6% (150)

AGE		
0-17 years old		22.2% (320)
18-24 years old		8.2% (379)
25-39 years old		15.2% (498)
40-54 years old		19.7% (273)
55-64 years old		14.3% (148)
65+ years old		20.4% (45)

PRIVATE SECTOR		
Businesses		1,329 (170)
Employees		12,793 (286)
Total wages		$422,341,736 (312)
Average weekly wages		$635 (422)

HOUSEHOLD INCOME LADDER		
95th percentile		$147,143 (196)
80th percentile		$82,166 (323)
60th percentile		$51,783 (331)
40th percentile		$33,095 (322)
20th percentile		$18,796 (277)

CHILDREN	★ (461)
Living with two parents	66.0% (246)
Older teens in school	76.0% (490)
Speak English very well	96.8% (421)
Poverty rate for children	30.0% (404)
No health insurance	12.1% (473)

DIVERSITY/EQUALITY	★★★ (224)
Racial diversity index	35.0% (212)
Geographic diversity index	46.8% (257)
Top 20% share of income	50.2% (438)
Gender gap in earnings	27.8% (133)
White-collar gender gap	20.6% (215)

EDUCATION	★ (449)
Eighth grade or less	6.9% (467)
High school diplomas	82.6% (428)
Attended college	48.3% (374)
Bachelor's degrees	15.8% (391)
Advanced degrees	4.1% (472)

EMPLOYMENT	★★★ (229)
Average jobless rate	7.8% (270)
Self-employed workers	11.3% (104)
Management/financial jobs	10.5% (318)
Computer/engineering jobs	2.1% (399)
Health care jobs	5.7% (222)

GROWTH POTENTIAL	★★★★ (162)
Children per senior	1.09 (469)
Median age	43.4 (462)
Moved from different state	2.1% (269)
Homes built since 2000	18.6% (117)
Construction jobs	10.1% (16)

HOUSING	★★ (377)
Home vacancy rate	11.0% (405)
Home ownership rate	74.3% (105)
Housing diversity index	81.8% (466)
4 or more bedrooms	12.3% (482)
Affordability/income ratio	$2,199 (124)

INCOME	★★ (348)
Poverty rate	18.8% (329)
Median household income	$41,607 (334)
Interest/dividends	16.9% (345)
Public assistance	15.2% (266)
Median fulltime earnings	$34,341 (409)

SENIORS	★★★★★ (82)
Seniors living alone	22.8% (54)
Poverty rate for seniors	8.3% (202)
Median income for seniors	$35,668 (163)
Seniors who work	16.7% (360)
Home ownership by seniors	87.7% (48)

STABILITY	★★ (419)
25-39 age group	15.2% (498)
Born in state of residence	71.8% (278)
Same house as 1 year ago	86.3% (232)
Live and work in county	58.7% (497)
Married-couple households	55.2% (65)

TRANSPORTATION	★ (480)
Bicycle or walk to work	1.3% (485)
Carpool to work	15.2% (45)
Public transit to work	0.1% (441)
Commute <15 minutes	32.2% (496)
Commute >45 minutes	22.6% (538)

See pages 37-130 for explanations of statistics, stars, and ranks.

Atmore, AL
(Escambia County, AL)

POPULATION	
2010 census	38,319 (339)
2015 estimate	37,789 (348)
2010-2015 change	-1.4% (364)
2020 projection	37,161 (359)
2030 projection	35,758 (366)

RACE	
Whites	60.7% (441)
Blacks	33.4% (44)
Hispanics	1.2% (513)
Asians	0.1% (529)
Native Americans	3.2% (47)

AGE	
0-17 years old	22.3% (312)
18-24 years old	9.2% (234)
25-39 years old	18.1% (186)
40-54 years old	21.5% (57)
55-64 years old	12.8% (356)
65+ years old	16.1% (286)

PRIVATE SECTOR	
Businesses	750 (400)
Employees	8,690 (428)
Total wages	$324,133,067 (405)
Average weekly wages	$717 (221)

HOUSEHOLD INCOME LADDER	
95th percentile	$120,573 (512)
80th percentile	$68,728 (518)
60th percentile	$41,782 (509)
40th percentile	$24,384 (516)
20th percentile	$12,997 (503)

CHILDREN	★ (507)
Living with two parents	50.5% (505)
Older teens in school	73.0% (515)
Speak English very well	99.8% (38)
Poverty rate for children	31.8% (441)
No health insurance	11.6% (462)

DIVERSITY/EQUALITY	★★★ (274)
Racial diversity index	51.9% (98)
Geographic diversity index	43.7% (299)
Top 20% share of income	49.6% (405)
Gender gap in earnings	35.7% (331)
White-collar gender gap	31.9% (363)

EDUCATION	★ (492)
Eighth grade or less	5.4% (405)
High school diplomas	81.4% (458)
Attended college	40.4% (507)
Bachelor's degrees	12.3% (510)
Advanced degrees	3.7% (498)

EMPLOYMENT	★ (538)
Average jobless rate	15.6% (543)
Self-employed workers	6.6% (461)
Management/financial jobs	9.6% (427)
Computer/engineering jobs	1.5% (499)
Health care jobs	5.4% (273)

GROWTH POTENTIAL	★★ (391)
Children per senior	1.38 (291)
Median age	40.3 (319)
Moved from different state	1.3% (452)
Homes built since 2000	11.4% (338)
Construction jobs	6.1% (310)

HOUSING	★ (489)
Home vacancy rate	16.5% (541)
Home ownership rate	71.6% (201)
Housing diversity index	84.3% (314)
4 or more bedrooms	13.7% (415)
Affordability/income ratio	$2,901 (379)

INCOME	★ (497)
Poverty rate	24.2% (469)
Median household income	$32,330 (516)
Interest/dividends	12.1% (489)
Public assistance	22.1% (478)
Median fulltime earnings	$32,454 (469)

SENIORS	★ (515)
Seniors living alone	31.7% (504)
Poverty rate for seniors	14.4% (477)
Median income for seniors	$25,242 (501)
Seniors who work	11.1% (547)
Home ownership by seniors	85.2% (132)

STABILITY	★★★★ (134)
25-39 age group	18.1% (186)
Born in state of residence	72.1% (273)
Same house as 1 year ago	93.9% (3)
Live and work in county	74.8% (294)
Married-couple households	44.1% (479)

TRANSPORTATION	★ (527)
Bicycle or walk to work	1.2% (492)
Carpool to work	6.0% (547)
Public transit to work	0.4% (219)
Commute <15 minutes	43.5% (270)
Commute >45 minutes	16.8% (479)

See pages 37-130 for explanations of statistics, stars, and ranks.

Bainbridge, GA
(Decatur County, GA)

POPULATION		Attended college	46.2% (414)
2010 census	27,842 (457)	Bachelor's degrees	15.0% (422)
2015 estimate	27,174 (463)	Advanced degrees	6.5% (220)
2010-2015 change	-2.4% (443)		
2020 projection	26,309 (465)	**EMPLOYMENT**	**★★★★ (179)**
2030 projection	24,586 (476)	Average jobless rate	6.5% (157)
		Self-employed workers	11.1% (115)
RACE		Management/financial jobs	12.2% (139)
Whites	51.5% (481)	Computer/engineering jobs	2.5% (307)
Blacks	41.5% (26)	Health care jobs	4.6% (401)
Hispanics	5.5% (237)		
Asians	0.3% (473)	**GROWTH POTENTIAL**	**★★★★ (175)**
Native Americans	0.3% (231)	Children per senior	1.65 (148)
		Median age	37.4 (160)
AGE		Moved from different state	2.3% (234)
0-17 years old	24.9% (131)	Homes built since 2000	14.2% (231)
18-24 years old	9.4% (203)	Construction jobs	6.8% (204)
25-39 years old	18.4% (151)		
40-54 years old	19.6% (289)	**HOUSING**	**★ (474)**
55-64 years old	12.6% (385)	Home vacancy rate	8.4% (245)
65+ years old	15.1% (363)	Home ownership rate	59.4% (511)
		Housing diversity index	85.3% (170)
PRIVATE SECTOR		4 or more bedrooms	13.8% (409)
Businesses	642 (453)	Affordability/income ratio	$3,657 (478)
Employees	5,896 (511)		
Total wages	$188,956,288 (514)	**INCOME**	**★ (520)**
Average weekly wages	$616 (454)	Poverty rate	28.4% (513)
		Median household income	$31,284 (528)
HOUSEHOLD INCOME LADDER		Interest/dividends	9.4% (535)
95th percentile	$137,705 (314)	Public assistance	21.0% (455)
80th percentile	$67,276 (522)	Median fulltime earnings	$31,966 (495)
60th percentile	$41,009 (516)		
40th percentile	$23,282 (531)	**SENIORS**	**★ (542)**
20th percentile	$10,767 (539)	Seniors living alone	33.1% (530)
		Poverty rate for seniors	16.5% (508)
CHILDREN	**★ (519)**	Median income for seniors	$26,178 (489)
Living with two parents	40.5% (539)	Seniors who work	17.5% (310)
Older teens in school	77.2% (469)	Home ownership by seniors	72.6% (542)
Speak English very well	97.8% (361)		
Poverty rate for children	39.8% (513)	**STABILITY**	**★★ (337)**
No health insurance	6.1% (258)	25-39 age group	18.4% (151)
		Born in state of residence	73.0% (259)
DIVERSITY/EQUALITY	**★ (450)**	Same house as 1 year ago	89.4% (64)
Racial diversity index	55.9% (41)	Live and work in county	71.8% (346)
Geographic diversity index	43.2% (308)	Married-couple households	41.0% (516)
Top 20% share of income	54.6% (542)		
Gender gap in earnings	23.3% (68)	**TRANSPORTATION**	**★★ (415)**
White-collar gender gap	55.8% (531)	Bicycle or walk to work	0.8% (531)
		Carpool to work	11.4% (190)
EDUCATION	**★★ (422)**	Public transit to work	1.2% (54)
Eighth grade or less	6.0% (424)	Commute <15 minutes	33.1% (476)
High school diplomas	81.9% (449)	Commute >45 minutes	14.3% (402)

See pages 37-130 for explanations of statistics, stars, and ranks.

Bardstown, KY
(Nelson County, KY)

POPULATION

2010 census	43,437 (275)
2015 estimate	45,126 (258)
2010-2015 change	3.9% (64)
2020 projection	46,883 (238)
2030 projection	50,454 (213)

RACE

Whites	90.7% (167)
Blacks	5.2% (155)
Hispanics	2.1% (416)
Asians	0.3% (473)
Native Americans	0.2% (300)

AGE

0-17 years old	25.2% (108)
18-24 years old	8.6% (317)
25-39 years old	18.6% (135)
40-54 years old	21.7% (42)
55-64 years old	13.1% (318)
65+ years old	12.8% (478)

PRIVATE SECTOR

Businesses	1,140 (219)
Employees	13,068 (277)
Total wages	$502,009,205 (243)
Average weekly wages	$739 (180)

HOUSEHOLD INCOME LADDER

95th percentile	$144,046 (241)
80th percentile	$89,540 (160)
60th percentile	$60,623 (139)
40th percentile	$39,458 (143)
20th percentile	$21,275 (174)

CHILDREN ★★★★ (187)

Living with two parents	66.7% (226)
Older teens in school	80.8% (376)
Speak English very well	99.2% (163)
Poverty rate for children	24.7% (290)
No health insurance	3.6% (93)

DIVERSITY/EQUALITY ★★ (366)

Racial diversity index	17.4% (382)
Geographic diversity index	30.5% (478)
Top 20% share of income	48.9% (353)
Gender gap in earnings	33.7% (276)
White-collar gender gap	9.8% (88)

EDUCATION ★★★ (298)

Eighth grade or less	1.8% (102)
High school diplomas	89.7% (211)
Attended college	46.5% (406)
Bachelor's degrees	15.9% (382)
Advanced degrees	5.5% (318)

EMPLOYMENT ★★★ (308)

Average jobless rate	9.8% (415)
Self-employed workers	8.0% (333)
Management/financial jobs	12.1% (149)
Computer/engineering jobs	2.3% (354)
Health care jobs	6.0% (181)

GROWTH POTENTIAL ★★★★ (111)

Children per senior	1.96 (65)
Median age	37.9 (179)
Moved from different state	1.1% (487)
Homes built since 2000	24.2% (41)
Construction jobs	6.5% (253)

HOUSING ★★★★ (158)

Home vacancy rate	6.7% (141)
Home ownership rate	76.1% (55)
Housing diversity index	82.6% (433)
4 or more bedrooms	17.4% (226)
Affordability/income ratio	$2,710 (332)

INCOME ★★★ (237)

Poverty rate	16.0% (227)
Median household income	$49,298 (144)
Interest/dividends	19.7% (259)
Public assistance	17.1% (338)
Median fulltime earnings	$37,707 (237)

SENIORS ★★★★★ (39)

Seniors living alone	22.3% (45)
Poverty rate for seniors	10.7% (357)
Median income for seniors	$36,097 (152)
Seniors who work	21.9% (132)
Home ownership by seniors	90.6% (10)

STABILITY ★★★★★ (63)

25-39 age group	18.6% (135)
Born in state of residence	82.8% (71)
Same house as 1 year ago	87.4% (173)
Live and work in county	63.5% (459)
Married-couple households	55.9% (50)

TRANSPORTATION ★ (541)

Bicycle or walk to work	1.1% (501)
Carpool to work	10.3% (299)
Public transit to work	0.0% (511)
Commute <15 minutes	32.0% (499)
Commute >45 minutes	21.1% (524)

See pages 37-130 for explanations of statistics, stars, and ranks.

Bartlesville, OK
(Washington County, OK)

POPULATION	
2010 census	50,976 (204)
2015 estimate	52,021 (199)
2010-2015 change	2.0% (128)
2020 projection	52,740 (190)
2030 projection	54,168 (191)

RACE	
Whites	74.2% (363)
Blacks	2.6% (247)
Hispanics	5.5% (237)
Asians	1.7% (69)
Native Americans	9.7% (20)

AGE	
0-17 years old	23.7% (218)
18-24 years old	8.3% (362)
25-39 years old	17.5% (258)
40-54 years old	18.8% (386)
55-64 years old	13.5% (258)
65+ years old	18.2% (111)

PRIVATE SECTOR	
Businesses	1,279 (184)
Employees	18,748 (144)
Total wages	$987,632,041 (71)
Average weekly wages	$1,013 (17)

HOUSEHOLD INCOME LADDER	
95th percentile	$188,662 (32)
80th percentile	$100,295 (57)
60th percentile	$62,063 (107)
40th percentile	$37,971 (183)
20th percentile	$21,800 (147)

CHILDREN	★★★ (235)
Living with two parents	67.6% (204)
Older teens in school	83.4% (258)
Speak English very well	99.0% (200)
Poverty rate for children	22.0% (221)
No health insurance	8.9% (390)

DIVERSITY/EQUALITY	★★★★★ (74)
Racial diversity index	43.2% (167)
Geographic diversity index	60.2% (122)
Top 20% share of income	50.0% (430)
Gender gap in earnings	30.1% (171)
White-collar gender gap	8.2% (66)

EDUCATION	★★★★★ (95)
Eighth grade or less	1.6% (84)
High school diplomas	90.9% (162)
Attended college	58.8% (149)
Bachelor's degrees	28.3% (70)
Advanced degrees	8.1% (120)

EMPLOYMENT	★★★★★ (39)
Average jobless rate	5.3% (82)
Self-employed workers	7.7% (362)
Management/financial jobs	14.2% (44)
Computer/engineering jobs	7.7% (4)
Health care jobs	5.5% (250)

GROWTH POTENTIAL	★★★ (256)
Children per senior	1.30 (347)
Median age	40.5 (329)
Moved from different state	3.6% (104)
Homes built since 2000	11.2% (351)
Construction jobs	7.0% (185)

HOUSING	★★★★★ (92)
Home vacancy rate	10.2% (358)
Home ownership rate	72.3% (175)
Housing diversity index	86.1% (51)
4 or more bedrooms	20.5% (117)
Affordability/income ratio	$2,225 (131)

INCOME	★★★★ (119)
Poverty rate	14.4% (172)
Median household income	$50,023 (126)
Interest/dividends	23.6% (139)
Public assistance	11.4% (107)
Median fulltime earnings	$39,783 (147)

SENIORS	★★★ (256)
Seniors living alone	30.3% (440)
Poverty rate for seniors	7.5% (140)
Median income for seniors	$36,744 (124)
Seniors who work	17.0% (341)
Home ownership by seniors	84.1% (178)

STABILITY	★★ (352)
25-39 age group	17.5% (258)
Born in state of residence	59.5% (421)
Same house as 1 year ago	82.0% (439)
Live and work in county	82.0% (181)
Married-couple households	51.9% (199)

TRANSPORTATION	★★★★ (171)
Bicycle or walk to work	2.7% (292)
Carpool to work	11.8% (152)
Public transit to work	0.4% (219)
Commute <15 minutes	50.1% (149)
Commute >45 minutes	8.2% (138)

See pages 37-130 for explanations of statistics, stars, and ranks.

Bastrop, LA
(Morehouse Parish, LA)

POPULATION

2010 census	27,979 (456)
2015 estimate	26,395 (469)
2010-2015 change	-5.7% (539)
2020 projection	24,861 (481)
2030 projection	21,986 (501)

RACE

Whites	49.8% (487)
Blacks	47.3% (19)
Hispanics	1.2% (513)
Asians	0.3% (473)
Native Americans	0.1% (402)

AGE

0-17 years old	24.6% (144)
18-24 years old	8.6% (317)
25-39 years old	17.6% (248)
40-54 years old	18.9% (376)
55-64 years old	13.8% (203)
65+ years old	16.4% (255)

PRIVATE SECTOR

Businesses	461 (525)
Employees	5,546 (519)
Total wages	$165,542,018 (528)
Average weekly wages	$574 (517)

HOUSEHOLD INCOME LADDER

95th percentile	$114,257 (539)
80th percentile	$62,599 (544)
60th percentile	$35,892 (545)
40th percentile	$22,093 (538)
20th percentile	$11,424 (535)

CHILDREN   ★ (526)

Living with two parents	45.9% (527)
Older teens in school	71.7% (523)
Speak English very well	99.0% (200)
Poverty rate for children	42.0% (525)
No health insurance	6.0% (248)

DIVERSITY/EQUALITY   ★★ (399)

Racial diversity index	52.8% (85)
Geographic diversity index	25.7% (518)
Top 20% share of income	55.6% (547)
Gender gap in earnings	24.5% (81)
White-collar gender gap	21.7% (232)

EDUCATION   ★ (506)

Eighth grade or less	5.8% (413)
High school diplomas	81.7% (452)
Attended college	36.1% (538)
Bachelor's degrees	12.8% (501)
Advanced degrees	3.1% (524)

EMPLOYMENT   ★ (443)

Average jobless rate	8.0% (291)
Self-employed workers	5.1% (540)
Management/financial jobs	7.9% (530)
Computer/engineering jobs	1.7% (470)
Health care jobs	7.4% (49)

GROWTH POTENTIAL   ★★ (366)

Children per senior	1.50 (216)
Median age	39.3 (256)
Moved from different state	0.8% (524)
Homes built since 2000	10.8% (364)
Construction jobs	6.3% (284)

HOUSING   ★ (454)

Home vacancy rate	9.7% (334)
Home ownership rate	65.6% (421)
Housing diversity index	84.8% (248)
4 or more bedrooms	9.7% (536)
Affordability/income ratio	$2,878 (373)

INCOME   ★ (533)

Poverty rate	28.5% (514)
Median household income	$28,003 (542)
Interest/dividends	9.9% (532)
Public assistance	22.1% (478)
Median fulltime earnings	$28,931 (545)

SENIORS   ★ (539)

Seniors living alone	32.2% (517)
Poverty rate for seniors	19.7% (537)
Median income for seniors	$23,669 (516)
Seniors who work	15.7% (427)
Home ownership by seniors	81.9% (280)

STABILITY   ★★★ (241)

25-39 age group	17.6% (248)
Born in state of residence	85.6% (36)
Same house as 1 year ago	94.6% (1)
Live and work in county	58.5% (500)
Married-couple households	42.0% (506)

TRANSPORTATION   ★ (504)

Bicycle or walk to work	0.8% (531)
Carpool to work	9.5% (388)
Public transit to work	0.1% (441)
Commute <15 minutes	38.5% (364)
Commute >45 minutes	15.5% (441)

See pages 37-130 for explanations of statistics, stars, and ranks.

Batesville, AR
(Independence County, AR)

POPULATION	
2010 census	36,647 (366)
2015 estimate	37,052 (356)
2010-2015 change	1.1% (181)
2020 projection	37,285 (354)
2030 projection	37,423 (345)

RACE	
Whites	89.3% (198)
Blacks	2.0% (290)
Hispanics	6.0% (222)
Asians	0.9% (178)
Native Americans	0.3% (231)

AGE	
0-17 years old	24.0% (184)
18-24 years old	8.5% (330)
25-39 years old	19.1% (95)
40-54 years old	19.2% (336)
55-64 years old	12.8% (356)
65+ years old	16.4% (255)

PRIVATE SECTOR	
Businesses	841 (352)
Employees	12,711 (292)
Total wages	$452,383,736 (290)
Average weekly wages	$684 (302)

HOUSEHOLD INCOME LADDER	
95th percentile	$129,603 (436)
80th percentile	$73,733 (476)
60th percentile	$45,009 (478)
40th percentile	$30,453 (404)
20th percentile	$15,779 (415)

CHILDREN	★★ (352)
Living with two parents	59.3% (422)
Older teens in school	83.8% (245)
Speak English very well	96.1% (446)
Poverty rate for children	32.0% (445)
No health insurance	4.3% (140)

DIVERSITY/EQUALITY	★★★★ (151)
Racial diversity index	19.8% (350)
Geographic diversity index	49.2% (224)
Top 20% share of income	49.7% (413)
Gender gap in earnings	24.7% (85)
White-collar gender gap	4.6% (39)

EDUCATION	★★ (347)
Eighth grade or less	3.9% (316)
High school diplomas	86.7% (319)
Attended college	48.3% (374)
Bachelor's degrees	16.8% (339)
Advanced degrees	5.6% (304)

EMPLOYMENT	★★★ (259)
Average jobless rate	6.9% (185)
Self-employed workers	9.2% (231)
Management/financial jobs	9.7% (416)
Computer/engineering jobs	1.6% (486)
Health care jobs	6.8% (91)

GROWTH POTENTIAL	★★★★ (126)
Children per senior	1.46 (237)
Median age	38.7 (211)
Moved from different state	2.3% (234)
Homes built since 2000	17.8% (136)
Construction jobs	8.6% (61)

HOUSING	★★★ (313)
Home vacancy rate	9.5% (317)
Home ownership rate	71.4% (209)
Housing diversity index	83.8% (369)
4 or more bedrooms	13.6% (424)
Affordability/income ratio	$2,647 (310)

INCOME	★★ (429)
Poverty rate	21.8% (424)
Median household income	$36,265 (461)
Interest/dividends	16.2% (369)
Public assistance	14.9% (253)
Median fulltime earnings	$31,575 (516)

SENIORS	★ (475)
Seniors living alone	27.2% (254)
Poverty rate for seniors	14.0% (470)
Median income for seniors	$30,391 (395)
Seniors who work	13.8% (513)
Home ownership by seniors	79.6% (388)

STABILITY	★★★★★ (78)
25-39 age group	19.1% (95)
Born in state of residence	69.6% (317)
Same house as 1 year ago	85.0% (299)
Live and work in county	85.6% (125)
Married-couple households	51.6% (218)

TRANSPORTATION	★★★★ (212)
Bicycle or walk to work	2.1% (374)
Carpool to work	13.8% (76)
Public transit to work	0.1% (441)
Commute <15 minutes	41.5% (308)
Commute >45 minutes	7.9% (126)

See pages 37-130 for explanations of statistics, stars, and ranks.

Bay City, TX
(Matagorda County, TX)

POPULATION

2010 census	36,702 (363)
2015 estimate	36,770 (361)
2010-2015 change	0.2% (241)
2020 projection	36,272 (365)
2030 projection	35,246 (371)

RACE

Whites	46.2% (499)
Blacks	9.9% (115)
Hispanics	39.9% (36)
Asians	2.3% (36)
Native Americans	0.4% (203)

AGE

0-17 years old	25.8% (75)
18-24 years old	9.0% (265)
25-39 years old	18.9% (111)
40-54 years old	17.5% (483)
55-64 years old	13.7% (225)
65+ years old	15.1% (363)

PRIVATE SECTOR

Businesses	752 (398)
Employees	8,725 (426)
Total wages	$486,114,704 (253)
Average weekly wages	$1,071 (12)

HOUSEHOLD INCOME LADDER

95th percentile	$147,296 (194)
80th percentile	$93,464 (111)
60th percentile	$52,627 (308)
40th percentile	$30,864 (389)
20th percentile	$15,339 (442)

CHILDREN ★ (528)

Living with two parents	59.5% (415)
Older teens in school	75.8% (494)
Speak English very well	90.0% (528)
Poverty rate for children	35.2% (479)
No health insurance	9.3% (401)

DIVERSITY/EQUALITY ★★★★ (214)

Racial diversity index	61.7% (9)
Geographic diversity index	41.8% (331)
Top 20% share of income	49.1% (369)
Gender gap in earnings	52.3% (534)
White-collar gender gap	4.4% (30)

EDUCATION ★ (524)

Eighth grade or less	11.5% (525)
High school diplomas	79.1% (496)
Attended college	42.4% (483)
Bachelor's degrees	14.6% (435)
Advanced degrees	2.4% (547)

EMPLOYMENT ★ (477)

Average jobless rate	6.4% (147)
Self-employed workers	9.5% (207)
Management/financial jobs	7.0% (546)
Computer/engineering jobs	3.4% (131)
Health care jobs	2.8% (540)

GROWTH POTENTIAL ★★★★ (131)

Children per senior	1.71 (127)
Median age	37.2 (154)
Moved from different state	0.7% (540)
Homes built since 2000	11.0% (358)
Construction jobs	10.0% (17)

HOUSING ★ (463)

Home vacancy rate	14.3% (524)
Home ownership rate	67.8% (349)
Housing diversity index	85.4% (156)
4 or more bedrooms	10.2% (529)
Affordability/income ratio	$2,297 (164)

INCOME ★★ (383)

Poverty rate	21.7% (421)
Median household income	$40,797 (361)
Interest/dividends	14.9% (413)
Public assistance	17.9% (368)
Median fulltime earnings	$37,476 (248)

SENIORS ★ (492)

Seniors living alone	30.5% (451)
Poverty rate for seniors	18.4% (528)
Median income for seniors	$26,974 (478)
Seniors who work	16.3% (391)
Home ownership by seniors	86.3% (87)

STABILITY ★★★★★ (85)

25-39 age group	18.9% (111)
Born in state of residence	75.5% (215)
Same house as 1 year ago	89.4% (64)
Live and work in county	73.0% (329)
Married-couple households	49.7% (311)

TRANSPORTATION ★★★ (293)

Bicycle or walk to work	2.6% (308)
Carpool to work	14.0% (66)
Public transit to work	0.7% (119)
Commute <15 minutes	39.2% (343)
Commute >45 minutes	15.4% (436)

See pages 37-130 for explanations of statistics, stars, and ranks.

Beeville, TX
(Bee County, TX)

POPULATION		Attended college	40.2% (511)
2010 census	31,861 (418)	Bachelor's degrees	8.7% (545)
2015 estimate	32,874 (408)	Advanced degrees	3.1% (524)
2010-2015 change	3.2% (74)		
2020 projection	32,969 (408)	**EMPLOYMENT**	★ (517)
2030 projection	33,065 (401)	Average jobless rate	7.0% (196)
		Self-employed workers	6.8% (446)
RACE		Management/financial jobs	7.4% (540)
Whites	33.1% (527)	Computer/engineering jobs	1.7% (470)
Blacks	8.6% (121)	Health care jobs	4.0% (476)
Hispanics	57.3% (18)		
Asians	0.2% (509)	**GROWTH POTENTIAL**	★★★ (226)
Native Americans	0.5% (174)	Children per senior	1.89 (72)
		Median age	35.3 (100)
AGE		Moved from different state	1.4% (425)
0-17 years old	21.1% (407)	Homes built since 2000	9.5% (408)
18-24 years old	11.2% (110)	Construction jobs	6.1% (310)
25-39 years old	23.7% (11)		
40-54 years old	22.4% (17)	**HOUSING**	★ (477)
55-64 years old	10.4% (506)	Home vacancy rate	14.4% (527)
65+ years old	11.2% (507)	Home ownership rate	61.8% (483)
		Housing diversity index	84.4% (299)
PRIVATE SECTOR		4 or more bedrooms	13.4% (433)
Businesses	559 (496)	Affordability/income ratio	$1,723 (16)
Employees	5,976 (510)		
Total wages	$236,292,227 (477)	**INCOME**	★★ (393)
Average weekly wages	$760 (145)	Poverty rate	21.2% (407)
		Median household income	$42,302 (308)
HOUSEHOLD INCOME LADDER		Interest/dividends	14.1% (439)
95th percentile	$163,150 (80)	Public assistance	16.5% (313)
80th percentile	$77,055 (421)	Median fulltime earnings	$34,389 (406)
60th percentile	$50,960 (360)		
40th percentile	$33,996 (290)	**SENIORS**	★★★★ (199)
20th percentile	$17,084 (360)	Seniors living alone	22.4% (49)
		Poverty rate for seniors	12.8% (442)
CHILDREN	★ (493)	Median income for seniors	$34,102 (232)
Living with two parents	52.4% (491)	Seniors who work	19.0% (243)
Older teens in school	76.4% (483)	Home ownership by seniors	82.1% (268)
Speak English very well	98.8% (251)		
Poverty rate for children	35.6% (483)	**STABILITY**	★★★★★ (60)
No health insurance	9.7% (412)	25-39 age group	23.7% (11)
		Born in state of residence	82.2% (79)
DIVERSITY/EQUALITY	★★ (411)	Same house as 1 year ago	79.9% (499)
Racial diversity index	55.5% (45)	Live and work in county	77.5% (247)
Geographic diversity index	31.8% (465)	Married-couple households	47.3% (409)
Top 20% share of income	51.4% (484)		
Gender gap in earnings	48.2% (520)	**TRANSPORTATION**	★★★ (243)
White-collar gender gap	15.2% (154)	Bicycle or walk to work	3.0% (249)
		Carpool to work	13.4% (87)
EDUCATION	★ (529)	Public transit to work	0.0% (511)
Eighth grade or less	7.9% (489)	Commute <15 minutes	53.2% (107)
High school diplomas	74.2% (531)	Commute >45 minutes	16.0% (453)

See pages 37-130 for explanations of statistics, stars, and ranks.

Bennettsville, SC
(Marlboro County, SC)

POPULATION

2010 census	28,933 (444)
2015 estimate	27,494 (458)
2010-2015 change	-5.0% (532)
2020 projection	26,269 (467)
2030 projection	23,914 (480)

RACE

Whites	39.8% (513)
Blacks	50.7% (13)
Hispanics	3.1% (333)
Asians	0.3% (473)
Native Americans	3.7% (44)

AGE

0-17 years old	20.6% (423)
18-24 years old	8.4% (349)
25-39 years old	21.8% (24)
40-54 years old	21.1% (97)
55-64 years old	13.1% (318)
65+ years old	15.0% (371)

PRIVATE SECTOR

Businesses	334 (544)
Employees	4,974 (529)
Total wages	$197,949,107 (509)
Average weekly wages	$765 (132)

HOUSEHOLD INCOME LADDER

95th percentile	$111,031 (543)
80th percentile	$63,266 (543)
60th percentile	$38,597 (535)
40th percentile	$23,559 (528)
20th percentile	$12,052 (520)

CHILDREN ★ (473)

Living with two parents	40.6% (538)
Older teens in school	82.7% (289)
Speak English very well	99.3% (142)
Poverty rate for children	43.9% (530)
No health insurance	2.8% (50)

DIVERSITY/EQUALITY ★★★★ (156)

Racial diversity index	58.2% (24)
Geographic diversity index	45.5% (271)
Top 20% share of income	49.9% (420)
Gender gap in earnings	16.7% (22)
White-collar gender gap	47.6% (496)

EDUCATION ★ (525)

Eighth grade or less	5.9% (420)
High school diplomas	76.9% (515)
Attended college	35.1% (540)
Bachelor's degrees	8.3% (547)
Advanced degrees	3.0% (532)

EMPLOYMENT ★ (546)

Average jobless rate	15.5% (539)
Self-employed workers	4.5% (547)
Management/financial jobs	7.9% (530)
Computer/engineering jobs	1.7% (470)
Health care jobs	6.0% (181)

GROWTH POTENTIAL ★ (446)

Children per senior	1.38 (291)
Median age	39.4 (262)
Moved from different state	2.4% (218)
Homes built since 2000	10.6% (374)
Construction jobs	4.2% (524)

HOUSING ★★ (360)

Home vacancy rate	12.2% (468)
Home ownership rate	65.6% (421)
Housing diversity index	85.2% (190)
4 or more bedrooms	13.8% (409)
Affordability/income ratio	$1,957 (40)

INCOME ★ (535)

Poverty rate	29.0% (517)
Median household income	$30,767 (533)
Interest/dividends	6.6% (550)
Public assistance	25.0% (515)
Median fulltime earnings	$32,172 (487)

SENIORS ★ (525)

Seniors living alone	29.6% (413)
Poverty rate for seniors	18.5% (529)
Median income for seniors	$26,161 (491)
Seniors who work	13.5% (518)
Home ownership by seniors	82.2% (264)

STABILITY ★★★ (317)

25-39 age group	21.8% (24)
Born in state of residence	71.1% (289)
Same house as 1 year ago	89.7% (54)
Live and work in county	54.6% (523)
Married-couple households	41.2% (513)

TRANSPORTATION ★ (467)

Bicycle or walk to work	1.5% (457)
Carpool to work	11.7% (170)
Public transit to work	0.4% (219)
Commute <15 minutes	30.2% (522)
Commute >45 minutes	15.8% (446)

See pages 37-130 for explanations of statistics, stars, and ranks.

Big Spring, TX
(Glasscock and Howard Counties, TX)

POPULATION	
2010 census	36,238 (373)
2015 estimate	38,521 (331)
2010-2015 change	6.3% (29)
2020 projection	40,141 (313)
2030 projection	43,477 (281)

RACE	
Whites	52.0% (479)
Blacks	5.1% (160)
Hispanics	39.7% (38)
Asians	1.3% (112)
Native Americans	0.6% (150)

AGE	
0-17 years old	22.5% (300)
18-24 years old	10.4% (144)
25-39 years old	21.5% (32)
40-54 years old	21.2% (85)
55-64 years old	11.7% (463)
65+ years old	12.7% (480)

PRIVATE SECTOR	
Businesses	896 (315)
Employees	9,745 (383)
Total wages	$435,935,335 (301)
Average weekly wages	$860 (49)

HOUSEHOLD INCOME LADDER	
95th percentile	$171,584 (52)
80th percentile	$93,768 (106)
60th percentile	$61,904 (112)
40th percentile	$39,089 (155)
20th percentile	$20,472 (206)

CHILDREN	★★★ (312)
Living with two parents	64.7% (278)
Older teens in school	86.2% (158)
Speak English very well	97.8% (361)
Poverty rate for children	21.2% (198)
No health insurance	12.5% (485)

DIVERSITY/EQUALITY	★★★ (226)
Racial diversity index	56.9% (31)
Geographic diversity index	49.6% (216)
Top 20% share of income	50.0% (427)
Gender gap in earnings	31.9% (223)
White-collar gender gap	38.1% (423)

EDUCATION	★ (491)
Eighth grade or less	7.5% (478)
High school diplomas	79.4% (492)
Attended college	47.4% (391)
Bachelor's degrees	13.6% (474)
Advanced degrees	3.6% (505)

EMPLOYMENT	★★★ (289)
Average jobless rate	6.3% (140)
Self-employed workers	6.9% (435)
Management/financial jobs	11.5% (202)
Computer/engineering jobs	1.0% (536)
Health care jobs	6.6% (114)

GROWTH POTENTIAL	★★★★ (154)
Children per senior	1.77 (104)
Median age	37.0 (143)
Moved from different state	3.6% (104)
Homes built since 2000	6.4% (516)
Construction jobs	7.8% (98)

HOUSING	★★ (412)
Home vacancy rate	12.3% (469)
Home ownership rate	67.2% (379)
Housing diversity index	83.0% (417)
4 or more bedrooms	11.7% (505)
Affordability/income ratio	$1,509 (3)

INCOME	★★★★ (178)
Poverty rate	15.2% (199)
Median household income	$50,091 (123)
Interest/dividends	19.8% (254)
Public assistance	12.7% (155)
Median fulltime earnings	$38,138 (214)

SENIORS	★★ (368)
Seniors living alone	30.0% (427)
Poverty rate for seniors	11.8% (401)
Median income for seniors	$33,734 (249)
Seniors who work	19.0% (243)
Home ownership by seniors	82.5% (251)

STABILITY	★★★★★ (93)
25-39 age group	21.5% (32)
Born in state of residence	69.7% (315)
Same house as 1 year ago	81.2% (474)
Live and work in county	85.6% (125)
Married-couple households	48.9% (351)

TRANSPORTATION	★★★★★ (108)
Bicycle or walk to work	1.8% (409)
Carpool to work	15.7% (36)
Public transit to work	0.2% (363)
Commute <15 minutes	58.1% (62)
Commute >45 minutes	10.9% (268)

See pages 37-130 for explanations of statistics, stars, and ranks.

Big Stone Gap, VA
(Dickenson and Wise Counties and City of Norton, VA)

POPULATION

2010 census	61,313 (141)
2015 estimate	58,772 (153)
2010-2015 change	-4.1% (522)
2020 projection	56,462 (167)
2030 projection	51,879 (205)

RACE

Whites	93.2% (103)
Blacks	4.0% (189)
Hispanics	1.2% (513)
Asians	0.7% (241)
Native Americans	0.1% (402)

AGE

0-17 years old	20.3% (445)
18-24 years old	9.9% (168)
25-39 years old	19.1% (95)
40-54 years old	20.4% (169)
55-64 years old	14.4% (136)
65+ years old	16.0% (291)

PRIVATE SECTOR

Businesses	1,481 (138)
Employees	14,395 (223)
Total wages	$513,203,781 (235)
Average weekly wages	$686 (297)

HOUSEHOLD INCOME LADDER

95th percentile	$124,997 (487)
80th percentile	$73,395 (480)
60th percentile	$45,565 (468)
40th percentile	$27,286 (476)
20th percentile	$14,314 (472)

CHILDREN ★★★★ (203)

Living with two parents	67.6% (204)
Older teens in school	86.6% (144)
Speak English very well	99.3% (142)
Poverty rate for children	32.2% (449)
No health insurance	5.1% (188)

DIVERSITY/EQUALITY ★ (452)

Racial diversity index	13.0% (443)
Geographic diversity index	40.4% (344)
Top 20% share of income	50.8% (463)
Gender gap in earnings	37.6% (379)
White-collar gender gap	13.3% (131)

EDUCATION ★ (465)

Eighth grade or less	6.2% (433)
High school diplomas	80.3% (475)
Attended college	46.4% (409)
Bachelor's degrees	14.3% (451)
Advanced degrees	4.7% (419)

EMPLOYMENT ★★ (422)

Average jobless rate	10.4% (437)
Self-employed workers	4.4% (549)
Management/financial jobs	8.6% (498)
Computer/engineering jobs	3.2% (158)
Health care jobs	7.6% (39)

GROWTH POTENTIAL ★ (442)

Children per senior	1.27 (370)
Median age	40.5 (329)
Moved from different state	1.8% (338)
Homes built since 2000	11.3% (344)
Construction jobs	5.3% (425)

HOUSING ★★★★ (182)

Home vacancy rate	7.0% (162)
Home ownership rate	70.3% (256)
Housing diversity index	85.7% (108)
4 or more bedrooms	12.6% (472)
Affordability/income ratio	$2,377 (202)

INCOME ★ (450)

Poverty rate	22.3% (432)
Median household income	$35,556 (477)
Interest/dividends	15.4% (396)
Public assistance	21.8% (474)
Median fulltime earnings	$36,895 (295)

SENIORS ★ (468)

Seniors living alone	29.5% (405)
Poverty rate for seniors	11.0% (374)
Median income for seniors	$28,342 (449)
Seniors who work	12.3% (538)
Home ownership by seniors	82.8% (232)

STABILITY ★★★★ (145)

25-39 age group	19.1% (95)
Born in state of residence	75.4% (217)
Same house as 1 year ago	88.3% (115)
Live and work in county	68.1% (404)
Married-couple households	49.3% (333)

TRANSPORTATION ★★ (422)

Bicycle or walk to work	2.1% (374)
Carpool to work	11.4% (190)
Public transit to work	0.6% (141)
Commute <15 minutes	36.0% (418)
Commute >45 minutes	16.0% (453)

See pages 37-130 for explanations of statistics, stars, and ranks.

Blytheville, AR
(Mississippi County, AR)

POPULATION	
2010 census	46,480 (242)
2015 estimate	43,738 (275)
2010-2015 change	-5.9% (540)
2020 projection	40,906 (303)
2030 projection	35,459 (368)

RACE	
Whites	59.6% (448)
Blacks	34.5% (41)
Hispanics	3.8% (308)
Asians	0.3% (473)
Native Americans	0.1% (402)

AGE	
0-17 years old	27.1% (43)
18-24 years old	9.4% (203)
25-39 years old	18.2% (167)
40-54 years old	20.1% (221)
55-64 years old	12.1% (430)
65+ years old	13.0% (474)

PRIVATE SECTOR	
Businesses	1,114 (234)
Employees	15,183 (206)
Total wages	$645,896,288 (167)
Average weekly wages	$818 (67)

HOUSEHOLD INCOME LADDER	
95th percentile	$131,179 (413)
80th percentile	$75,280 (453)
60th percentile	$43,946 (492)
40th percentile	$27,110 (482)
20th percentile	$13,281 (495)

CHILDREN	★ (449)
Living with two parents	48.9% (515)
Older teens in school	81.3% (357)
Speak English very well	98.2% (320)
Poverty rate for children	40.9% (522)
No health insurance	3.5% (82)

DIVERSITY/EQUALITY	★★ (396)
Racial diversity index	52.4% (92)
Geographic diversity index	49.5% (217)
Top 20% share of income	50.6% (451)
Gender gap in earnings	44.4% (493)
White-collar gender gap	38.6% (428)

EDUCATION	★★ (435)
Eighth grade or less	4.9% (380)
High school diplomas	83.7% (406)
Attended college	45.9% (422)
Bachelor's degrees	13.1% (491)
Advanced degrees	4.8% (405)

EMPLOYMENT	★ (532)
Average jobless rate	12.0% (492)
Self-employed workers	7.3% (401)
Management/financial jobs	8.3% (513)
Computer/engineering jobs	2.2% (381)
Health care jobs	4.1% (462)

GROWTH POTENTIAL	★★★★ (205)
Children per senior	2.07 (51)
Median age	35.6 (105)
Moved from different state	3.3% (129)
Homes built since 2000	9.5% (408)
Construction jobs	4.6% (494)

HOUSING	★ (518)
Home vacancy rate	14.7% (531)
Home ownership rate	57.6% (528)
Housing diversity index	85.3% (170)
4 or more bedrooms	12.7% (466)
Affordability/income ratio	$2,300 (166)

INCOME	★ (503)
Poverty rate	26.8% (500)
Median household income	$34,612 (491)
Interest/dividends	10.5% (522)
Public assistance	23.8% (507)
Median fulltime earnings	$33,908 (426)

SENIORS	★ (521)
Seniors living alone	31.2% (479)
Poverty rate for seniors	15.9% (500)
Median income for seniors	$24,775 (505)
Seniors who work	20.3% (185)
Home ownership by seniors	77.0% (490)

STABILITY	★★★ (312)
25-39 age group	18.2% (167)
Born in state of residence	68.5% (336)
Same house as 1 year ago	82.0% (439)
Live and work in county	91.6% (48)
Married-couple households	43.7% (485)

TRANSPORTATION	★★★★ (135)
Bicycle or walk to work	1.7% (428)
Carpool to work	14.7% (51)
Public transit to work	0.1% (441)
Commute <15 minutes	50.8% (137)
Commute >45 minutes	7.4% (99)

See pages 37-130 for explanations of statistics, stars, and ranks.

Bogalusa, LA
(Washington Parish, LA)

POPULATION

2010 census	47,168 (231)
2015 estimate	46,371 (242)
2010-2015 change	-1.7% (384)
2020 projection	46,445 (243)
2030 projection	46,449 (252)

RACE

Whites	65.9% (411)
Blacks	30.1% (54)
Hispanics	2.0% (428)
Asians	0.2% (509)
Native Americans	0.2% (300)

AGE

0-17 years old	24.4% (155)
18-24 years old	8.3% (362)
25-39 years old	17.9% (214)
40-54 years old	19.9% (250)
55-64 years old	13.9% (192)
65+ years old	15.7% (318)

PRIVATE SECTOR

Businesses	657 (448)
Employees	7,685 (450)
Total wages	$263,038,082 (463)
Average weekly wages	$658 (370)

HOUSEHOLD INCOME LADDER

95th percentile	$129,013 (442)
80th percentile	$72,528 (489)
60th percentile	$39,805 (531)
40th percentile	$23,080 (535)
20th percentile	$11,788 (528)

CHILDREN ★★★ (315)

Living with two parents	57.2% (457)
Older teens in school	86.2% (158)
Speak English very well	97.4% (395)
Poverty rate for children	32.3% (450)
No health insurance	3.7% (98)

DIVERSITY/EQUALITY ★ (516)

Racial diversity index	47.4% (133)
Geographic diversity index	35.9% (423)
Top 20% share of income	52.5% (514)
Gender gap in earnings	41.8% (468)
White-collar gender gap	38.7% (429)

EDUCATION ★ (515)

Eighth grade or less	6.6% (452)
High school diplomas	79.1% (496)
Attended college	37.5% (532)
Bachelor's degrees	12.2% (512)
Advanced degrees	3.1% (524)

EMPLOYMENT ★ (516)

Average jobless rate	15.0% (535)
Self-employed workers	6.2% (488)
Management/financial jobs	9.1% (463)
Computer/engineering jobs	1.3% (519)
Health care jobs	7.3% (55)

GROWTH POTENTIAL ★★★★ (179)

Children per senior	1.56 (189)
Median age	39.2 (248)
Moved from different state	1.8% (338)
Homes built since 2000	17.9% (135)
Construction jobs	7.0% (185)

HOUSING ★★★ (258)

Home vacancy rate	12.7% (483)
Home ownership rate	72.4% (170)
Housing diversity index	86.6% (12)
4 or more bedrooms	15.0% (356)
Affordability/income ratio	$2,592 (288)

INCOME ★ (527)

Poverty rate	26.4% (493)
Median household income	$30,705 (534)
Interest/dividends	10.1% (530)
Public assistance	29.1% (535)
Median fulltime earnings	$34,331 (411)

SENIORS ★ (514)

Seniors living alone	28.7% (344)
Poverty rate for seniors	16.5% (508)
Median income for seniors	$24,329 (511)
Seniors who work	14.5% (478)
Home ownership by seniors	81.9% (280)

STABILITY ★★★ (300)

25-39 age group	17.9% (214)
Born in state of residence	78.7% (139)
Same house as 1 year ago	88.0% (133)
Live and work in county	67.0% (417)
Married-couple households	45.3% (459)

TRANSPORTATION ★ (521)

Bicycle or walk to work	1.6% (443)
Carpool to work	13.6% (80)
Public transit to work	0.1% (441)
Commute <15 minutes	33.4% (471)
Commute >45 minutes	28.5% (549)

See pages 37-130 for explanations of statistics, stars, and ranks.

Bonham, TX
(Fannin County, TX)

POPULATION

2010 census	33,915 (395)
2015 estimate	33,693 (396)
2010-2015 change	-0.7% (303)
2020 projection	33,535 (397)
2030 projection	33,241 (399)

RACE

Whites	79.7% (328)
Blacks	6.8% (136)
Hispanics	10.3% (147)
Asians	0.6% (291)
Native Americans	0.3% (231)

AGE

0-17 years old	21.3% (383)
18-24 years old	8.9% (282)
25-39 years old	18.2% (167)
40-54 years old	20.1% (221)
55-64 years old	13.0% (334)
65+ years old	18.5% (104)

PRIVATE SECTOR

Businesses	451 (529)
Employees	4,531 (535)
Total wages	$154,305,407 (531)
Average weekly wages	$655 (381)

HOUSEHOLD INCOME LADDER

95th percentile	$134,693 (364)
80th percentile	$86,264 (227)
60th percentile	$55,611 (234)
40th percentile	$34,741 (270)
20th percentile	$17,973 (321)

CHILDREN ★★ (368)

Living with two parents	64.8% (276)
Older teens in school	78.9% (430)
Speak English very well	97.9% (352)
Poverty rate for children	22.5% (235)
No health insurance	11.2% (452)

DIVERSITY/EQUALITY ★★★★★ (53)

Racial diversity index	34.9% (213)
Geographic diversity index	46.8% (257)
Top 20% share of income	45.7% (107)
Gender gap in earnings	21.6% (54)
White-collar gender gap	13.6% (136)

EDUCATION ★★ (395)

Eighth grade or less	5.1% (390)
High school diplomas	83.9% (403)

Attended college	48.6% (367)
Bachelor's degrees	15.8% (391)
Advanced degrees	5.1% (364)

EMPLOYMENT ★★★★ (131)

Average jobless rate	6.7% (169)
Self-employed workers	8.2% (314)
Management/financial jobs	12.9% (92)
Computer/engineering jobs	2.9% (219)
Health care jobs	6.3% (144)

GROWTH POTENTIAL ★★★★ (186)

Children per senior	1.15 (442)
Median age	41.3 (371)
Moved from different state	2.1% (269)
Homes built since 2000	23.2% (48)
Construction jobs	7.4% (134)

HOUSING ★★★★ (160)

Home vacancy rate	10.4% (371)
Home ownership rate	74.5% (98)
Housing diversity index	85.2% (190)
4 or more bedrooms	16.1% (286)
Affordability/income ratio	$2,147 (100)

INCOME ★★★ (295)

Poverty rate	17.2% (270)
Median household income	$44,071 (258)
Interest/dividends	14.7% (418)
Public assistance	14.5% (234)
Median fulltime earnings	$37,069 (280)

SENIORS ★★★★ (127)

Seniors living alone	22.8% (54)
Poverty rate for seniors	9.8% (308)
Median income for seniors	$33,170 (272)
Seniors who work	19.1% (238)
Home ownership by seniors	84.9% (145)

STABILITY ★ (451)

25-39 age group	18.2% (167)
Born in state of residence	71.8% (278)
Same house as 1 year ago	81.0% (478)
Live and work in county	54.1% (526)
Married-couple households	53.8% (116)

TRANSPORTATION ★ (540)

Bicycle or walk to work	1.9% (401)
Carpool to work	11.0% (229)
Public transit to work	0.1% (441)
Commute <15 minutes	32.1% (497)
Commute >45 minutes	24.4% (545)

See pages 37-130 for explanations of statistics, stars, and ranks.

Boone, NC
(Watauga County, NC)

POPULATION	
2010 census	51,079 (203)
2015 estimate	52,906 (190)
2010-2015 change	3.6% (68)
2020 projection	54,614 (180)
2030 projection	57,958 (160)

RACE	
Whites	92.1% (133)
Blacks	1.1% (367)
Hispanics	3.5% (318)
Asians	0.9% (178)
Native Americans	0.3% (231)

AGE	
0-17 years old	13.4% (551)
18-24 years old	31.4% (4)
25-39 years old	14.8% (520)
40-54 years old	15.0% (534)
55-64 years old	11.6% (471)
65+ years old	13.7% (453)

PRIVATE SECTOR	
Businesses	1,633 (117)
Employees	17,075 (168)
Total wages	$523,585,550 (227)
Average weekly wages	$590 (504)

HOUSEHOLD INCOME LADDER	
95th percentile	$154,488 (120)
80th percentile	$85,251 (247)
60th percentile	$50,086 (382)
40th percentile	$27,876 (465)
20th percentile	$10,905 (538)

CHILDREN	★★★★★ (27)
Living with two parents	72.8% (83)
Older teens in school	97.7% (6)
Speak English very well	99.1% (179)
Poverty rate for children	21.8% (216)
No health insurance	4.5% (150)

DIVERSITY/EQUALITY	★★★ (241)
Racial diversity index	15.0% (415)
Geographic diversity index	61.5% (109)
Top 20% share of income	54.4% (538)
Gender gap in earnings	1.9% (3)
White-collar gender gap	28.1% (310)

EDUCATION	★★★★★ (18)
Eighth grade or less	2.7% (195)
High school diplomas	90.9% (162)
Attended college	71.7% (21)
Bachelor's degrees	39.1% (17)
Advanced degrees	16.8% (8)

EMPLOYMENT	★★★★ (118)
Average jobless rate	9.5% (400)
Self-employed workers	15.1% (17)
Management/financial jobs	13.1% (78)
Computer/engineering jobs	3.1% (180)
Health care jobs	4.2% (454)

GROWTH POTENTIAL	★★★★★ (76)
Children per senior	0.98 (509)
Median age	29.5 (24)
Moved from different state	3.5% (109)
Homes built since 2000	21.8% (72)
Construction jobs	7.0% (185)

HOUSING	★ (540)
Home vacancy rate	8.6% (260)
Home ownership rate	57.9% (524)
Housing diversity index	82.9% (422)
4 or more bedrooms	18.0% (202)
Affordability/income ratio	$6,153 (545)

INCOME	★★★ (308)
Poverty rate	31.4% (531)
Median household income	$37,656 (436)
Interest/dividends	26.8% (56)
Public assistance	9.9% (59)
Median fulltime earnings	$37,443 (252)

SENIORS	★★★★★ (33)
Seniors living alone	24.7% (105)
Poverty rate for seniors	8.3% (202)
Median income for seniors	$38,517 (82)
Seniors who work	21.8% (135)
Home ownership by seniors	90.2% (14)

STABILITY	★ (547)
25-39 age group	14.8% (520)
Born in state of residence	57.7% (438)
Same house as 1 year ago	72.1% (538)
Live and work in county	87.8% (92)
Married-couple households	43.2% (491)

TRANSPORTATION	★★★★★ (59)
Bicycle or walk to work	6.6% (49)
Carpool to work	10.7% (260)
Public transit to work	2.7% (18)
Commute <15 minutes	38.3% (370)
Commute >45 minutes	6.4% (67)

See pages 37-130 for explanations of statistics, stars, and ranks.

Borger, TX
(Hutchinson County, TX)

POPULATION	
2010 census	22,150 (507)
2015 estimate	21,734 (513)
2010-2015 change	-1.9% (399)
2020 projection	21,037 (518)
2030 projection	19,734 (522)

RACE	
Whites	71.8% (379)
Blacks	2.6% (247)
Hispanics	22.0% (68)
Asians	0.6% (291)
Native Americans	1.0% (103)

AGE	
0-17 years old	26.3% (57)
18-24 years old	8.4% (349)
25-39 years old	18.6% (135)
40-54 years old	18.7% (399)
55-64 years old	13.3% (282)
65+ years old	14.7% (389)

PRIVATE SECTOR	
Businesses	473 (519)
Employees	7,582 (454)
Total wages	$480,436,433 (261)
Average weekly wages	$1,219 (5)

HOUSEHOLD INCOME LADDER	
95th percentile	$157,661 (112)
80th percentile	$95,065 (88)
60th percentile	$60,462 (141)
40th percentile	$38,053 (181)
20th percentile	$20,021 (229)

CHILDREN	★★ (418)
Living with two parents	56.8% (464)
Older teens in school	79.0% (428)
Speak English very well	97.3% (399)
Poverty rate for children	21.7% (211)
No health insurance	10.8% (445)

DIVERSITY/EQUALITY	★★ (385)
Racial diversity index	43.5% (164)
Geographic diversity index	51.3% (195)
Top 20% share of income	46.4% (156)
Gender gap in earnings	51.1% (530)
White-collar gender gap	42.6% (468)

EDUCATION	★★ (351)
Eighth grade or less	4.1% (332)
High school diplomas	86.1% (339)
Attended college	55.2% (216)
Bachelor's degrees	15.7% (399)
Advanced degrees	3.9% (489)

EMPLOYMENT	★★ (387)
Average jobless rate	5.3% (82)
Self-employed workers	5.8% (508)
Management/financial jobs	8.0% (528)
Computer/engineering jobs	3.4% (131)
Health care jobs	5.5% (250)

GROWTH POTENTIAL	★★★★★ (79)
Children per senior	1.80 (96)
Median age	37.3 (157)
Moved from different state	3.7% (96)
Homes built since 2000	6.1% (525)
Construction jobs	12.3% (3)

HOUSING	★★ (337)
Home vacancy rate	17.4% (545)
Home ownership rate	76.8% (34)
Housing diversity index	84.4% (299)
4 or more bedrooms	12.9% (458)
Affordability/income ratio	$1,489 (2)

INCOME	★★★★ (166)
Poverty rate	16.1% (228)
Median household income	$49,353 (142)
Interest/dividends	18.2% (305)
Public assistance	14.4% (225)
Median fulltime earnings	$43,277 (44)

SENIORS	★★★ (270)
Seniors living alone	28.6% (336)
Poverty rate for seniors	12.1% (416)
Median income for seniors	$32,034 (317)
Seniors who work	15.7% (427)
Home ownership by seniors	89.9% (17)

STABILITY	★★★★★ (110)
25-39 age group	18.6% (135)
Born in state of residence	68.1% (344)
Same house as 1 year ago	87.4% (173)
Live and work in county	84.7% (139)
Married-couple households	48.9% (351)

TRANSPORTATION	★★★ (322)
Bicycle or walk to work	0.9% (521)
Carpool to work	11.1% (221)
Public transit to work	0.2% (363)
Commute <15 minutes	54.0% (95)
Commute >45 minutes	13.5% (374)

See pages 37-130 for explanations of statistics, stars, and ranks.

Brenham, TX
(Washington County, TX)

POPULATION

2010 census	33,718 (397)
2015 estimate	34,765 (384)
2010-2015 change	3.1% (78)
2020 projection	35,796 (373)
2030 projection	37,920 (341)

RACE

Whites	65.1% (415)
Blacks	17.1% (86)
Hispanics	14.8% (104)
Asians	1.8% (60)
Native Americans	0.4% (203)

AGE

0-17 years old	21.8% (351)
18-24 years old	11.5% (100)
25-39 years old	14.1% (538)
40-54 years old	19.5% (301)
55-64 years old	13.6% (247)
65+ years old	19.6% (61)

PRIVATE SECTOR

Businesses	876 (327)
Employees	12,137 (305)
Total wages	$458,211,299 (286)
Average weekly wages	$726 (203)

HOUSEHOLD INCOME LADDER

95th percentile	$162,621 (81)
80th percentile	$89,123 (168)
60th percentile	$63,088 (98)
40th percentile	$40,355 (119)
20th percentile	$22,202 (130)

CHILDREN ★★ (419)

Living with two parents	62.5% (334)
Older teens in school	80.7% (379)
Speak English very well	95.5% (468)
Poverty rate for children	20.0% (167)
No health insurance	13.2% (500)

DIVERSITY/EQUALITY ★★★★★ (101)

Racial diversity index	52.5% (90)
Geographic diversity index	43.9% (296)
Top 20% share of income	48.1% (304)
Gender gap in earnings	40.3% (444)
White-collar gender gap	1.1% (7)

EDUCATION ★★★ (274)

Eighth grade or less	3.9% (316)
High school diplomas	85.4% (363)
Attended college	53.7% (251)
Bachelor's degrees	21.6% (172)
Advanced degrees	5.3% (347)

EMPLOYMENT ★★★★ (169)

Average jobless rate	5.1% (69)
Self-employed workers	9.9% (171)
Management/financial jobs	12.9% (92)
Computer/engineering jobs	2.3% (354)
Health care jobs	4.5% (419)

GROWTH POTENTIAL ★★★ (273)

Children per senior	1.11 (457)
Median age	42.0 (398)
Moved from different state	0.7% (540)
Homes built since 2000	21.2% (76)
Construction jobs	7.5% (122)

HOUSING ★★★★ (154)

Home vacancy rate	5.5% (60)
Home ownership rate	73.8% (126)
Housing diversity index	84.8% (248)
4 or more bedrooms	14.3% (387)
Affordability/income ratio	$2,980 (399)

INCOME ★★★★ (129)

Poverty rate	13.5% (137)
Median household income	$51,269 (95)
Interest/dividends	23.6% (139)
Public assistance	11.0% (94)
Median fulltime earnings	$36,837 (298)

SENIORS ★★★★★ (80)

Seniors living alone	21.4% (27)
Poverty rate for seniors	12.2% (422)
Median income for seniors	$38,484 (84)
Seniors who work	19.4% (230)
Home ownership by seniors	86.1% (93)

STABILITY ★★★★ (180)

25-39 age group	14.1% (538)
Born in state of residence	74.1% (242)
Same house as 1 year ago	89.8% (52)
Live and work in county	82.7% (167)
Married-couple households	52.6% (167)

TRANSPORTATION ★★★ (296)

Bicycle or walk to work	2.0% (386)
Carpool to work	11.1% (221)
Public transit to work	0.3% (291)
Commute <15 minutes	47.3% (204)
Commute >45 minutes	11.4% (292)

See pages 37-130 for explanations of statistics, stars, and ranks.

Brevard, NC
(Transylvania County, NC)

POPULATION

2010 census	33,090 (402)
2015 estimate	33,211 (404)
2010-2015 change	0.4% (228)
2020 projection	33,512 (398)
2030 projection	33,958 (393)

RACE

Whites	89.2% (199)
Blacks	3.8% (198)
Hispanics	3.1% (333)
Asians	0.5% (355)
Native Americans	0.5% (174)

AGE

0-17 years old	16.8% (540)
18-24 years old	8.7% (299)
25-39 years old	13.7% (545)
40-54 years old	17.6% (470)
55-64 years old	15.6% (56)
65+ years old	27.6% (5)

PRIVATE SECTOR

Businesses	844 (349)
Employees	7,046 (475)
Total wages	$219,309,950 (496)
Average weekly wages	$599 (489)

HOUSEHOLD INCOME LADDER

95th percentile	$131,218 (412)
80th percentile	$79,987 (370)
60th percentile	$54,440 (269)
40th percentile	$37,307 (198)
20th percentile	$20,936 (189)

CHILDREN ★★★ (236)

Living with two parents	66.3% (241)
Older teens in school	81.4% (350)
Speak English very well	100.0% (1)
Poverty rate for children	21.7% (211)
No health insurance	8.4% (371)

DIVERSITY/EQUALITY ★★★★★ (34)

Racial diversity index	20.1% (347)
Geographic diversity index	66.9% (64)
Top 20% share of income	45.5% (91)
Gender gap in earnings	23.2% (67)
White-collar gender gap	10.3% (91)

EDUCATION ★★★★★ (94)

Eighth grade or less	2.9% (217)
High school diplomas	88.1% (263)

Attended college	59.8% (129)
Bachelor's degrees	27.6% (79)
Advanced degrees	10.9% (42)

EMPLOYMENT ★★★ (248)

Average jobless rate	6.9% (185)
Self-employed workers	12.0% (75)
Management/financial jobs	10.3% (339)
Computer/engineering jobs	1.7% (470)
Health care jobs	5.1% (319)

GROWTH POTENTIAL ★★★ (319)

Children per senior	0.61 (549)
Median age	50.1 (544)
Moved from different state	2.8% (171)
Homes built since 2000	15.8% (184)
Construction jobs	11.6% (7)

HOUSING ★★★ (306)

Home vacancy rate	8.7% (268)
Home ownership rate	76.7% (36)
Housing diversity index	84.2% (325)
4 or more bedrooms	15.8% (307)
Affordability/income ratio	$4,256 (505)

INCOME ★★★★ (132)

Poverty rate	12.6% (103)
Median household income	$45,114 (234)
Interest/dividends	29.9% (26)
Public assistance	12.4% (143)
Median fulltime earnings	$35,240 (371)

SENIORS ★★★★★ (10)

Seniors living alone	21.1% (21)
Poverty rate for seniors	5.0% (17)
Median income for seniors	$45,992 (23)
Seniors who work	17.9% (292)
Home ownership by seniors	92.7% (2)

STABILITY ★ (470)

25-39 age group	13.7% (545)
Born in state of residence	51.1% (483)
Same house as 1 year ago	86.9% (202)
Live and work in county	71.3% (352)
Married-couple households	56.4% (39)

TRANSPORTATION ★★ (419)

Bicycle or walk to work	2.4% (331)
Carpool to work	11.0% (229)
Public transit to work	0.4% (219)
Commute <15 minutes	35.8% (426)
Commute >45 minutes	14.9% (420)

See pages 37-130 for explanations of statistics, stars, and ranks.

Brookhaven, MS
(Lincoln County, MS)

POPULATION	
2010 census	34,869 (385)
2015 estimate	34,649 (386)
2010-2015 change	-0.6% (298)
2020 projection	34,497 (389)
2030 projection	33,956 (394)

RACE	
Whites	67.2% (403)
Blacks	30.8% (51)
Hispanics	1.1% (525)
Asians	0.6% (291)
Native Americans	0.0% (523)

AGE	
0-17 years old	25.2% (108)
18-24 years old	9.3% (217)
25-39 years old	18.0% (201)
40-54 years old	19.3% (323)
55-64 years old	13.1% (318)
65+ years old	15.1% (363)

PRIVATE SECTOR	
Businesses	746 (405)
Employees	9,872 (380)
Total wages	$346,480,013 (386)
Average weekly wages	$675 (320)

HOUSEHOLD INCOME LADDER	
95th percentile	$129,341 (438)
80th percentile	$76,023 (439)
60th percentile	$45,946 (461)
40th percentile	$28,215 (460)
20th percentile	$15,511 (431)

CHILDREN	★★ (413)
Living with two parents	59.1% (425)
Older teens in school	81.8% (329)
Speak English very well	97.7% (370)
Poverty rate for children	40.7% (520)
No health insurance	4.8% (173)

DIVERSITY/EQUALITY	★ (466)
Racial diversity index	45.3% (146)
Geographic diversity index	31.6% (469)
Top 20% share of income	49.0% (358)
Gender gap in earnings	36.0% (339)
White-collar gender gap	47.9% (499)

EDUCATION	★★★ (259)
Eighth grade or less	3.2% (250)
High school diplomas	87.1% (301)
Attended college	53.5% (255)
Bachelor's degrees	17.0% (328)
Advanced degrees	6.6% (211)

EMPLOYMENT	★★★★ (187)
Average jobless rate	7.5% (242)
Self-employed workers	9.1% (243)
Management/financial jobs	9.9% (392)
Computer/engineering jobs	1.0% (536)
Health care jobs	8.5% (8)

GROWTH POTENTIAL	★★★★ (143)
Children per senior	1.67 (144)
Median age	37.7 (172)
Moved from different state	0.7% (540)
Homes built since 2000	20.2% (89)
Construction jobs	7.5% (122)

HOUSING	★★★ (274)
Home vacancy rate	9.5% (317)
Home ownership rate	74.6% (91)
Housing diversity index	83.9% (360)
4 or more bedrooms	11.6% (510)
Affordability/income ratio	$2,339 (186)

INCOME	★ (456)
Poverty rate	26.6% (496)
Median household income	$36,473 (458)
Interest/dividends	11.4% (502)
Public assistance	13.5% (188)
Median fulltime earnings	$35,287 (369)

SENIORS	★ (477)
Seniors living alone	27.0% (239)
Poverty rate for seniors	16.9% (516)
Median income for seniors	$24,055 (513)
Seniors who work	13.1% (523)
Home ownership by seniors	86.6% (78)

STABILITY	★★★★★ (100)
25-39 age group	18.0% (201)
Born in state of residence	81.7% (89)
Same house as 1 year ago	92.4% (11)
Live and work in county	66.1% (434)
Married-couple households	48.4% (366)

TRANSPORTATION	★ (546)
Bicycle or walk to work	1.0% (512)
Carpool to work	6.5% (539)
Public transit to work	0.0% (511)
Commute <15 minutes	34.5% (448)
Commute >45 minutes	19.8% (515)

See pages 37-130 for explanations of statistics, stars, and ranks.

Brownsville, TN
(Haywood County, TN)

POPULATION
2010 census	18,787 (530)
2015 estimate	18,023 (533)
2010-2015 change	-4.1% (522)
2020 projection	17,269 (537)
2030 projection	15,793 (541)

RACE
Whites	45.2% (502)
Blacks	49.0% (17)
Hispanics	4.2% (287)
Asians	0.0% (546)
Native Americans	0.1% (402)

AGE
0-17 years old	23.9% (194)
18-24 years old	8.5% (330)
25-39 years old	17.6% (248)
40-54 years old	19.8% (261)
55-64 years old	14.5% (122)
65+ years old	15.7% (318)

PRIVATE SECTOR
Businesses	305 (546)
Employees	3,692 (543)
Total wages	$137,464,351 (540)
Average weekly wages	$716 (223)

HOUSEHOLD INCOME LADDER
95th percentile	$118,833 (525)
80th percentile	$67,326 (520)
60th percentile	$41,775 (510)
40th percentile	$26,103 (497)
20th percentile	$11,911 (526)

CHILDREN ★★ (333)
Living with two parents	57.4% (456)
Older teens in school	86.2% (158)
Speak English very well	98.2% (320)
Poverty rate for children	32.3% (450)
No health insurance	6.0% (248)

DIVERSITY/EQUALITY ★★★ (262)
Racial diversity index	55.4% (47)
Geographic diversity index	29.0% (492)
Top 20% share of income	51.6% (494)
Gender gap in earnings	27.5% (126)
White-collar gender gap	19.6% (202)

EDUCATION ★ (444)
Eighth grade or less	3.3% (259)
High school diplomas	82.3% (437)
Attended college	38.3% (529)
Bachelor's degrees	13.2% (489)
Advanced degrees	6.1% (250)

EMPLOYMENT ★ (491)
Average jobless rate	10.5% (441)
Self-employed workers	6.2% (488)
Management/financial jobs	10.0% (381)
Computer/engineering jobs	1.9% (441)
Health care jobs	5.4% (273)

GROWTH POTENTIAL ★ (480)
Children per senior	1.53 (206)
Median age	39.9 (292)
Moved from different state	1.9% (310)
Homes built since 2000	9.4% (414)
Construction jobs	3.7% (542)

HOUSING ★ (493)
Home vacancy rate	11.1% (409)
Home ownership rate	62.1% (479)
Housing diversity index	84.3% (314)
4 or more bedrooms	12.2% (487)
Affordability/income ratio	$2,899 (377)

INCOME ★ (519)
Poverty rate	22.8% (442)
Median household income	$34,182 (495)
Interest/dividends	11.4% (502)
Public assistance	29.4% (536)
Median fulltime earnings	$31,701 (508)

SENIORS ★ (541)
Seniors living alone	36.4% (547)
Poverty rate for seniors	16.5% (508)
Median income for seniors	n.a.
Seniors who work	18.3% (272)
Home ownership by seniors	78.9% (422)

STABILITY ★ (445)
25-39 age group	17.6% (248)
Born in state of residence	83.8% (59)
Same house as 1 year ago	88.5% (108)
Live and work in county	53.2% (531)
Married-couple households	42.8% (497)

TRANSPORTATION ★ (537)
Bicycle or walk to work	0.5% (547)
Carpool to work	7.8% (504)
Public transit to work	0.0% (511)
Commute <15 minutes	36.1% (415)
Commute >45 minutes	15.9% (451)

See pages 37-130 for explanations of statistics, stars, and ranks.

Brownwood, TX
(Brown County, TX)

POPULATION
2010 census	38,106 (341)
2015 estimate	37,896 (345)
2010-2015 change	-0.6% (298)
2020 projection	37,403 (350)
2030 projection	36,372 (355)

RACE
Whites	73.5% (367)
Blacks	4.2% (181)
Hispanics	20.7% (75)
Asians	0.5% (355)
Native Americans	0.2% (300)

AGE
0-17 years old	23.0% (259)
18-24 years old	9.4% (203)
25-39 years old	16.5% (403)
40-54 years old	19.1% (354)
55-64 years old	13.2% (297)
65+ years old	18.7% (97)

PRIVATE SECTOR
Businesses	854 (339)
Employees	12,780 (288)
Total wages	$439,536,276 (299)
Average weekly wages	$661 (360)

HOUSEHOLD INCOME LADDER
95th percentile	$135,657 (351)
80th percentile	$81,016 (351)
60th percentile	$51,120 (357)
40th percentile	$32,010 (362)
20th percentile	$18,199 (307)

CHILDREN ★★★ (291)
Living with two parents	65.8% (253)
Older teens in school	82.1% (313)
Speak English very well	98.7% (265)
Poverty rate for children	30.2% (408)
No health insurance	6.3% (271)

DIVERSITY/EQUALITY ★★★ (245)
Racial diversity index	41.5% (177)
Geographic diversity index	38.2% (388)
Top 20% share of income	50.2% (438)
Gender gap in earnings	31.1% (208)
White-collar gender gap	16.0% (166)

EDUCATION ★★ (380)
Eighth grade or less	5.0% (385)
High school diplomas	86.6% (322)
Attended college	48.8% (362)
Bachelor's degrees	17.3% (309)
Advanced degrees	4.3% (456)

EMPLOYMENT ★★★★★ (54)
Average jobless rate	4.3% (38)
Self-employed workers	10.1% (158)
Management/financial jobs	13.3% (70)
Computer/engineering jobs	1.6% (486)
Health care jobs	8.0% (19)

GROWTH POTENTIAL ★ (468)
Children per senior	1.23 (393)
Median age	41.0 (357)
Moved from different state	0.5% (549)
Homes built since 2000	12.3% (303)
Construction jobs	5.7% (373)

HOUSING ★★ (410)
Home vacancy rate	15.2% (535)
Home ownership rate	70.7% (244)
Housing diversity index	86.5% (19)
4 or more bedrooms	9.6% (539)
Affordability/income ratio	$2,154 (102)

INCOME ★★ (373)
Poverty rate	18.3% (309)
Median household income	$41,962 (323)
Interest/dividends	14.1% (439)
Public assistance	15.1% (262)
Median fulltime earnings	$33,624 (435)

SENIORS ★★★★ (196)
Seniors living alone	25.4% (132)
Poverty rate for seniors	8.0% (177)
Median income for seniors	$31,579 (349)
Seniors who work	17.2% (330)
Home ownership by seniors	84.0% (179)

STABILITY ★★★★★ (7)
25-39 age group	16.5% (403)
Born in state of residence	78.0% (156)
Same house as 1 year ago	91.6% (19)
Live and work in county	90.8% (56)
Married-couple households	53.8% (116)

TRANSPORTATION ★★★ (226)
Bicycle or walk to work	0.8% (531)
Carpool to work	9.6% (378)
Public transit to work	0.4% (219)
Commute <15 minutes	52.2% (118)
Commute >45 minutes	5.0% (33)

See pages 37-130 for explanations of statistics, stars, and ranks.

Calhoun, GA
(Gordon County, GA)

POPULATION	
2010 census	55,186 (171)
2015 estimate	56,574 (168)
2010-2015 change	2.5% (107)
2020 projection	58,427 (155)
2030 projection	62,139 (139)

RACE	
Whites	78.5% (334)
Blacks	4.2% (181)
Hispanics	14.8% (104)
Asians	1.1% (139)
Native Americans	0.3% (231)

AGE	
0-17 years old	25.8% (75)
18-24 years old	9.0% (265)
25-39 years old	19.4% (78)
40-54 years old	21.2% (85)
55-64 years old	11.9% (447)
65+ years old	12.8% (478)

PRIVATE SECTOR	
Businesses	1,008 (273)
Employees	18,768 (143)
Total wages	$694,647,083 (151)
Average weekly wages	$712 (229)

HOUSEHOLD INCOME LADDER	
95th percentile	$142,907 (254)
80th percentile	$78,577 (390)
60th percentile	$50,137 (379)
40th percentile	$33,140 (320)
20th percentile	$18,758 (279)

CHILDREN	★★★ (310)
Living with two parents	72.5% (97)
Older teens in school	84.8% (207)
Speak English very well	95.0% (477)
Poverty rate for children	30.0% (404)
No health insurance	7.8% (357)

DIVERSITY/EQUALITY	★★★ (225)
Racial diversity index	36.0% (209)
Geographic diversity index	52.9% (175)
Top 20% share of income	48.0% (292)
Gender gap in earnings	28.7% (147)
White-collar gender gap	39.2% (436)

EDUCATION	★ (501)
Eighth grade or less	8.7% (502)
High school diplomas	77.8% (510)
Attended college	43.0% (471)
Bachelor's degrees	14.1% (457)
Advanced degrees	5.6% (304)

EMPLOYMENT	★ (492)
Average jobless rate	8.3% (314)
Self-employed workers	5.7% (515)
Management/financial jobs	10.2% (357)
Computer/engineering jobs	2.0% (420)
Health care jobs	4.4% (433)

GROWTH POTENTIAL	★★★★★ (50)
Children per senior	2.02 (60)
Median age	37.0 (143)
Moved from different state	2.0% (288)
Homes built since 2000	23.2% (48)
Construction jobs	9.1% (40)

HOUSING	★★ (437)
Home vacancy rate	11.0% (405)
Home ownership rate	65.4% (425)
Housing diversity index	82.7% (429)
4 or more bedrooms	16.4% (272)
Affordability/income ratio	$2,716 (335)

INCOME	★★ (416)
Poverty rate	20.4% (388)
Median household income	$41,612 (333)
Interest/dividends	13.2% (463)
Public assistance	18.0% (371)
Median fulltime earnings	$34,066 (419)

SENIORS	★★★ (277)
Seniors living alone	23.5% (69)
Poverty rate for seniors	11.0% (374)
Median income for seniors	$32,196 (315)
Seniors who work	17.3% (324)
Home ownership by seniors	80.8% (346)

STABILITY	★★★★ (129)
25-39 age group	19.4% (78)
Born in state of residence	66.5% (368)
Same house as 1 year ago	85.3% (290)
Live and work in county	69.5% (379)
Married-couple households	55.6% (56)

TRANSPORTATION	★★ (335)
Bicycle or walk to work	1.1% (501)
Carpool to work	14.1% (61)
Public transit to work	0.6% (141)
Commute <15 minutes	30.5% (517)
Commute >45 minutes	10.7% (262)

See pages 37-130 for explanations of statistics, stars, and ranks.

Camden, AR
(Calhoun and Ouachita Counties, AR)

POPULATION

2010 census	31,488 (425)
2015 estimate	29,587 (437)
2010-2015 change	-6.0% (545)
2020 projection	27,707 (450)
2030 projection	24,080 (477)

RACE

Whites	58.7% (452)
Blacks	37.0% (35)
Hispanics	2.2% (406)
Asians	0.2% (509)
Native Americans	0.2% (300)

AGE

0-17 years old	22.3% (312)
18-24 years old	8.2% (379)
25-39 years old	16.3% (418)
40-54 years old	20.1% (221)
55-64 years old	15.2% (72)
65+ years old	18.0% (122)

PRIVATE SECTOR

Businesses	706 (425)
Employees	7,685 (450)
Total wages	$293,586,034 (441)
Average weekly wages	$735 (187)

HOUSEHOLD INCOME LADDER

95th percentile	$126,918 (469)
80th percentile	$70,032 (504)
60th percentile	$42,254 (506)
40th percentile	$25,237 (509)
20th percentile	$13,326 (493)

CHILDREN   ★★ **(378)**

Living with two parents	51.3% (498)
Older teens in school	84.2% (232)
Speak English very well	99.5% (96)
Poverty rate for children	36.4% (490)
No health insurance	4.8% (173)

DIVERSITY/EQUALITY   ★★★ **(222)**

Racial diversity index	51.8% (99)
Geographic diversity index	35.9% (423)
Top 20% share of income	49.7% (408)
Gender gap in earnings	38.9% (418)
White-collar gender gap	8.8% (77)

EDUCATION   ★★ **(344)**

Eighth grade or less	2.0% (126)
High school diplomas	89.2% (227)

Attended college	43.6% (459)
Bachelor's degrees	16.0% (372)
Advanced degrees	4.8% (405)

EMPLOYMENT   ★ **(458)**

Average jobless rate	8.1% (298)
Self-employed workers	6.6% (461)
Management/financial jobs	8.6% (498)
Computer/engineering jobs	3.4% (131)
Health care jobs	4.5% (419)

GROWTH POTENTIAL   ★ **(491)**

Children per senior	1.24 (390)
Median age	43.1 (453)
Moved from different state	1.0% (504)
Homes built since 2000	7.7% (475)
Construction jobs	6.6% (241)

HOUSING   ★★★★ **(155)**

Home vacancy rate	4.6% (20)
Home ownership rate	69.1% (298)
Housing diversity index	85.2% (190)
4 or more bedrooms	11.3% (515)
Affordability/income ratio	$2,081 (74)

INCOME   ★ **(474)**

Poverty rate	23.0% (444)
Median household income	$32,194 (517)
Interest/dividends	13.9% (444)
Public assistance	18.2% (378)
Median fulltime earnings	$32,367 (474)

SENIORS   ★ **(469)**

Seniors living alone	31.7% (504)
Poverty rate for seniors	14.4% (477)
Median income for seniors	$26,436 (487)
Seniors who work	18.6% (265)
Home ownership by seniors	84.5% (165)

STABILITY   ★★ **(366)**

25-39 age group	16.3% (418)
Born in state of residence	79.1% (130)
Same house as 1 year ago	89.7% (54)
Live and work in county	65.9% (436)
Married-couple households	45.5% (453)

TRANSPORTATION   ★★ **(375)**

Bicycle or walk to work	2.8% (279)
Carpool to work	10.0% (337)
Public transit to work	0.8% (96)
Commute <15 minutes	36.9% (401)
Commute >45 minutes	13.1% (359)

See pages 37-130 for explanations of statistics, stars, and ranks.

Campbellsville, KY
(Taylor County, KY)

POPULATION	
2010 census	24,512 (485)
2015 estimate	25,420 (481)
2010-2015 change	3.7% (66)
2020 projection	26,115 (470)
2030 projection	27,481 (449)

RACE	
Whites	90.4% (172)
Blacks	4.0% (189)
Hispanics	2.1% (416)
Asians	0.9% (178)
Native Americans	0.1% (402)

AGE	
0-17 years old	22.3% (312)
18-24 years old	12.1% (85)
25-39 years old	16.6% (388)
40-54 years old	19.0% (364)
55-64 years old	12.9% (343)
65+ years old	17.1% (186)

PRIVATE SECTOR	
Businesses	704 (426)
Employees	9,384 (397)
Total wages	$295,050,056 (439)
Average weekly wages	$605 (479)

HOUSEHOLD INCOME LADDER	
95th percentile	$115,366 (535)
80th percentile	$67,543 (519)
60th percentile	$41,943 (508)
40th percentile	$25,896 (501)
20th percentile	$14,370 (470)

CHILDREN	★ (466)
Living with two parents	49.7% (510)
Older teens in school	76.7% (476)
Speak English very well	99.5% (96)
Poverty rate for children	36.5% (492)
No health insurance	5.8% (236)

DIVERSITY/EQUALITY	★ (448)
Racial diversity index	18.0% (377)
Geographic diversity index	35.4% (431)
Top 20% share of income	47.2% (238)
Gender gap in earnings	37.9% (389)
White-collar gender gap	31.8% (361)

EDUCATION	★★★ (268)
Eighth grade or less	2.8% (205)
High school diplomas	88.8% (240)
Attended college	46.1% (418)
Bachelor's degrees	16.6% (348)
Advanced degrees	7.6% (139)

EMPLOYMENT	★ (463)
Average jobless rate	9.6% (402)
Self-employed workers	8.3% (302)
Management/financial jobs	8.6% (498)
Computer/engineering jobs	0.7% (548)
Health care jobs	6.4% (132)

GROWTH POTENTIAL	★★★ (289)
Children per senior	1.31 (344)
Median age	39.2 (248)
Moved from different state	2.5% (203)
Homes built since 2000	15.3% (195)
Construction jobs	5.7% (373)

HOUSING	★★ (363)
Home vacancy rate	9.7% (334)
Home ownership rate	65.4% (425)
Housing diversity index	85.2% (190)
4 or more bedrooms	14.2% (392)
Affordability/income ratio	$2,810 (360)

INCOME	★ (487)
Poverty rate	23.7% (462)
Median household income	$33,340 (503)
Interest/dividends	15.9% (380)
Public assistance	20.8% (450)
Median fulltime earnings	$30,632 (534)

SENIORS	★ (529)
Seniors living alone	31.3% (486)
Poverty rate for seniors	16.9% (516)
Median income for seniors	$25,704 (496)
Seniors who work	17.2% (330)
Home ownership by seniors	79.0% (417)

STABILITY	★★ (394)
25-39 age group	16.6% (388)
Born in state of residence	79.6% (120)
Same house as 1 year ago	82.0% (439)
Live and work in county	80.3% (214)
Married-couple households	45.7% (449)

TRANSPORTATION	★★★★ (148)
Bicycle or walk to work	4.3% (130)
Carpool to work	11.0% (229)
Public transit to work	0.1% (441)
Commute <15 minutes	53.5% (103)
Commute >45 minutes	8.2% (138)

See pages 37-130 for explanations of statistics, stars, and ranks.

Cedartown, GA
(Polk County, GA)

POPULATION

2010 census	41,475 (296)
2015 estimate	41,524 (293)
2010-2015 change	0.1% (250)
2020 projection	41,559 (295)
2030 projection	41,497 (299)

RACE

Whites	71.9% (377)
Blacks	13.3% (95)
Hispanics	12.7% (121)
Asians	0.9% (178)
Native Americans	0.0% (523)

AGE

0-17 years old	26.2% (63)
18-24 years old	8.7% (299)
25-39 years old	17.7% (236)
40-54 years old	20.9% (112)
55-64 years old	12.0% (438)
65+ years old	14.5% (412)

PRIVATE SECTOR

Businesses	622 (461)
Employees	9,582 (387)
Total wages	$330,215,356 (398)
Average weekly wages	$663 (352)

HOUSEHOLD INCOME LADDER

95th percentile	$125,047 (486)
80th percentile	$78,630 (389)
60th percentile	$49,678 (389)
40th percentile	$30,849 (392)
20th percentile	$17,126 (355)

CHILDREN ★★ (383)

Living with two parents	65.3% (263)
Older teens in school	82.6% (293)
Speak English very well	94.9% (479)
Poverty rate for children	31.6% (437)
No health insurance	7.3% (333)

DIVERSITY/EQUALITY ★★★★ (175)

Racial diversity index	44.9% (150)
Geographic diversity index	42.6% (313)
Top 20% share of income	50.2% (435)
Gender gap in earnings	21.6% (54)
White-collar gender gap	26.4% (291)

EDUCATION ★ (497)

Eighth grade or less	8.1% (491)
High school diplomas	77.8% (510)
Attended college	40.0% (515)
Bachelor's degrees	13.6% (474)
Advanced degrees	6.8% (191)

EMPLOYMENT ★ (519)

Average jobless rate	10.2% (427)
Self-employed workers	6.6% (461)
Management/financial jobs	8.3% (513)
Computer/engineering jobs	0.9% (542)
Health care jobs	5.6% (240)

GROWTH POTENTIAL ★★★★★ (88)

Children per senior	1.81 (93)
Median age	37.2 (154)
Moved from different state	0.9% (515)
Homes built since 2000	18.5% (119)
Construction jobs	9.5% (31)

HOUSING ★★ (392)

Home vacancy rate	13.0% (490)
Home ownership rate	67.2% (379)
Housing diversity index	86.1% (51)
4 or more bedrooms	13.8% (409)
Affordability/income ratio	$2,710 (332)

INCOME ★ (479)

Poverty rate	21.5% (416)
Median household income	$37,853 (429)
Interest/dividends	10.1% (530)
Public assistance	21.7% (472)
Median fulltime earnings	$33,240 (446)

SENIORS ★★ (355)

Seniors living alone	26.9% (230)
Poverty rate for seniors	11.1% (378)
Median income for seniors	$33,040 (280)
Seniors who work	15.0% (459)
Home ownership by seniors	82.6% (242)

STABILITY ★★ (333)

25-39 age group	17.7% (236)
Born in state of residence	74.7% (227)
Same house as 1 year ago	86.3% (232)
Live and work in county	58.7% (497)
Married-couple households	51.6% (218)

TRANSPORTATION ★ (529)

Bicycle or walk to work	1.5% (457)
Carpool to work	8.9% (439)
Public transit to work	0.4% (219)
Commute <15 minutes	35.7% (429)
Commute >45 minutes	19.1% (510)

See pages 37-130 for explanations of statistics, stars, and ranks.

Central City, KY
(Muhlenberg County, KY)

POPULATION
2010 census	31,499 (424)
2015 estimate	31,183 (427)
2010-2015 change	-1.0% (326)
2020 projection	30,682 (428)
2030 projection	29,615 (427)

RACE
Whites	92.4% (121)
Blacks	5.2% (155)
Hispanics	0.5% (545)
Asians	0.5% (355)
Native Americans	0.3% (231)

AGE
0-17 years old	21.2% (397)
18-24 years old	9.2% (234)
25-39 years old	17.4% (269)
40-54 years old	21.3% (73)
55-64 years old	13.4% (274)
65+ years old	17.5% (158)

PRIVATE SECTOR
Businesses	566 (493)
Employees	6,802 (480)
Total wages	$277,458,383 (449)
Average weekly wages	$784 (114)

HOUSEHOLD INCOME LADDER
95th percentile	$133,826 (378)
80th percentile	$77,354 (414)
60th percentile	$49,105 (399)
40th percentile	$30,005 (424)
20th percentile	$16,176 (402)

CHILDREN ★★★ (240)
Living with two parents	66.3% (241)
Older teens in school	84.6% (214)
Speak English very well	99.6% (77)
Poverty rate for children	29.7% (395)
No health insurance	6.5% (282)

DIVERSITY/EQUALITY ★★ (337)
Racial diversity index	14.3% (427)
Geographic diversity index	30.5% (478)
Top 20% share of income	46.5% (159)
Gender gap in earnings	33.7% (276)
White-collar gender gap	13.4% (133)

EDUCATION ★ (474)
Eighth grade or less	6.8% (463)
High school diplomas	81.5% (455)

Attended college	41.4% (498)
Bachelor's degrees	12.3% (510)
Advanced degrees	6.4% (229)

EMPLOYMENT ★ (521)
Average jobless rate	10.3% (432)
Self-employed workers	5.6% (523)
Management/financial jobs	6.5% (549)
Computer/engineering jobs	1.5% (499)
Health care jobs	6.7% (104)

GROWTH POTENTIAL ★ (447)
Children per senior	1.22 (401)
Median age	41.5 (380)
Moved from different state	1.4% (425)
Homes built since 2000	10.9% (361)
Construction jobs	6.1% (310)

HOUSING ★★★★ (219)
Home vacancy rate	14.0% (518)
Home ownership rate	79.5% (4)
Housing diversity index	85.2% (190)
4 or more bedrooms	13.6% (424)
Affordability/income ratio	$1,997 (56)

INCOME ★★ (414)
Poverty rate	19.9% (366)
Median household income	$38,961 (407)
Interest/dividends	12.1% (489)
Public assistance	18.8% (394)
Median fulltime earnings	$36,802 (303)

SENIORS ★★★ (315)
Seniors living alone	23.4% (65)
Poverty rate for seniors	11.9% (408)
Median income for seniors	$26,608 (482)
Seniors who work	13.6% (515)
Home ownership by seniors	86.4% (82)

STABILITY ★★★★★ (69)
25-39 age group	17.4% (269)
Born in state of residence	82.7% (73)
Same house as 1 year ago	87.4% (173)
Live and work in county	67.9% (407)
Married-couple households	56.4% (39)

TRANSPORTATION ★ (456)
Bicycle or walk to work	0.9% (521)
Carpool to work	9.2% (408)
Public transit to work	0.2% (363)
Commute <15 minutes	37.9% (378)
Commute >45 minutes	11.7% (300)

See pages 37-130 for explanations of statistics, stars, and ranks.

Clarksdale, MS
(Coahoma County, MS)

POPULATION

2010 census	26,151 (471)
2015 estimate	24,620 (486)
2010-2015 change	-5.9% (540)
2020 projection	22,876 (498)
2030 projection	19,613 (523)

RACE

Whites	22.6% (538)
Blacks	75.8% (1)
Hispanics	0.3% (549)
Asians	0.6% (291)
Native Americans	0.1% (402)

AGE

0-17 years old	28.4% (27)
18-24 years old	11.0% (115)
25-39 years old	18.4% (151)
40-54 years old	17.3% (487)
55-64 years old	12.0% (438)
65+ years old	12.9% (477)

PRIVATE SECTOR

Businesses	608 (467)
Employees	6,248 (501)
Total wages	$205,513,107 (505)
Average weekly wages	$633 (429)

HOUSEHOLD INCOME LADDER

95th percentile	$110,924 (545)
80th percentile	$61,871 (547)
60th percentile	$37,191 (540)
40th percentile	$20,586 (546)
20th percentile	$9,853 (546)

CHILDREN ★ (498)

Living with two parents	28.3% (549)
Older teens in school	82.7% (289)
Speak English very well	99.6% (77)
Poverty rate for children	44.8% (532)
No health insurance	5.4% (209)

DIVERSITY/EQUALITY ★ (446)

Racial diversity index	37.4% (200)
Geographic diversity index	25.8% (517)
Top 20% share of income	51.8% (496)
Gender gap in earnings	19.2% (37)
White-collar gender gap	43.3% (471)

EDUCATION ★★ (411)

Eighth grade or less	6.0% (424)
High school diplomas	80.9% (468)
Attended college	52.4% (276)
Bachelor's degrees	17.3% (309)
Advanced degrees	4.7% (419)

EMPLOYMENT ★ (512)

Average jobless rate	20.3% (550)
Self-employed workers	7.7% (362)
Management/financial jobs	10.7% (287)
Computer/engineering jobs	1.3% (519)
Health care jobs	6.2% (156)

GROWTH POTENTIAL ★★★ (237)

Children per senior	2.21 (40)
Median age	33.5 (64)
Moved from different state	2.1% (269)
Homes built since 2000	6.3% (518)
Construction jobs	4.4% (509)

HOUSING ★ (457)

Home vacancy rate	11.1% (409)
Home ownership rate	52.2% (543)
Housing diversity index	86.0% (71)
4 or more bedrooms	15.4% (329)
Affordability/income ratio	$2,146 (99)

INCOME ★ (547)

Poverty rate	34.1% (539)
Median household income	$28,851 (540)
Interest/dividends	8.1% (542)
Public assistance	39.4% (550)
Median fulltime earnings	$30,363 (539)

SENIORS ★ (547)

Seniors living alone	33.0% (529)
Poverty rate for seniors	19.2% (535)
Median income for seniors	$26,178 (489)
Seniors who work	19.8% (206)
Home ownership by seniors	70.5% (549)

STABILITY ★★★ (316)

25-39 age group	18.4% (151)
Born in state of residence	85.7% (35)
Same house as 1 year ago	87.4% (173)
Live and work in county	78.4% (237)
Married-couple households	29.8% (551)

TRANSPORTATION ★★★★ (131)

Bicycle or walk to work	2.8% (279)
Carpool to work	15.3% (42)
Public transit to work	1.0% (69)
Commute <15 minutes	52.2% (118)
Commute >45 minutes	14.6% (414)

See pages 37-130 for explanations of statistics, stars, and ranks.

Cleveland, MS
(Bolivar County, MS)

POPULATION	
2010 census	34,145 (394)
2015 estimate	33,322 (401)
2010-2015 change	-2.4% (443)
2020 projection	31,569 (423)
2030 projection	28,137 (441)

RACE	
Whites	32.6% (529)
Blacks	64.0% (5)
Hispanics	2.1% (416)
Asians	0.7% (241)
Native Americans	0.2% (300)

AGE	
0-17 years old	25.3% (97)
18-24 years old	11.7% (94)
25-39 years old	19.5% (74)
40-54 years old	17.6% (470)
55-64 years old	12.4% (408)
65+ years old	13.5% (459)

PRIVATE SECTOR	
Businesses	770 (387)
Employees	9,338 (400)
Total wages	$318,798,947 (411)
Average weekly wages	$657 (373)

HOUSEHOLD INCOME LADDER	
95th percentile	$122,902 (494)
80th percentile	$65,446 (531)
60th percentile	$35,743 (547)
40th percentile	$20,916 (545)
20th percentile	$11,052 (537)

CHILDREN	★ (525)
Living with two parents	31.4% (546)
Older teens in school	84.1% (237)
Speak English very well	99.8% (38)
Poverty rate for children	53.3% (550)
No health insurance	9.1% (397)

DIVERSITY/EQUALITY	★★★ (295)
Racial diversity index	48.4% (127)
Geographic diversity index	26.4% (513)
Top 20% share of income	52.5% (513)
Gender gap in earnings	30.3% (175)
White-collar gender gap	6.0% (46)

EDUCATION	★★ (412)
Eighth grade or less	8.7% (502)
High school diplomas	76.6% (517)
Attended college	51.9% (284)
Bachelor's degrees	22.0% (159)
Advanced degrees	7.2% (164)

EMPLOYMENT	★★ (341)
Average jobless rate	15.3% (537)
Self-employed workers	10.9% (120)
Management/financial jobs	12.0% (156)
Computer/engineering jobs	4.7% (40)
Health care jobs	4.7% (385)

GROWTH POTENTIAL	★★★ (266)
Children per senior	1.87 (77)
Median age	34.7 (86)
Moved from different state	1.7% (355)
Homes built since 2000	10.6% (374)
Construction jobs	4.6% (494)

HOUSING	★ (496)
Home vacancy rate	10.5% (381)
Home ownership rate	55.9% (532)
Housing diversity index	84.7% (260)
4 or more bedrooms	16.3% (279)
Affordability/income ratio	$3,085 (413)

INCOME	★ (544)
Poverty rate	37.1% (547)
Median household income	$27,585 (543)
Interest/dividends	10.9% (512)
Public assistance	32.4% (542)
Median fulltime earnings	$31,600 (512)

SENIORS	★ (549)
Seniors living alone	35.0% (542)
Poverty rate for seniors	18.1% (526)
Median income for seniors	$22,621 (524)
Seniors who work	12.8% (530)
Home ownership by seniors	75.1% (524)

STABILITY	★★★ (247)
25-39 age group	19.5% (74)
Born in state of residence	85.4% (39)
Same house as 1 year ago	86.2% (237)
Live and work in county	82.5% (172)
Married-couple households	31.5% (549)

TRANSPORTATION	★★★★ (126)
Bicycle or walk to work	3.1% (232)
Carpool to work	12.8% (112)
Public transit to work	0.2% (363)
Commute <15 minutes	52.9% (110)
Commute >45 minutes	7.5% (105)

See pages 37-130 for explanations of statistics, stars, and ranks.

Clewiston, FL
(Hendry County, FL)

POPULATION	
2010 census	39,140 (324)
2015 estimate	39,119 (324)
2010-2015 change	-0.1% (266)
2020 projection	39,928 (316)
2030 projection	41,634 (297)

RACE	
Whites	34.1% (523)
Blacks	11.7% (104)
Hispanics	50.5% (26)
Asians	1.1% (139)
Native Americans	1.4% (84)

AGE	
0-17 years old	27.9% (34)
18-24 years old	9.8% (176)
25-39 years old	20.9% (44)
40-54 years old	18.8% (386)
55-64 years old	10.3% (510)
65+ years old	12.3% (491)

PRIVATE SECTOR	
Businesses	786 (381)
Employees	9,237 (405)
Total wages	$338,162,342 (393)
Average weekly wages	$704 (246)

HOUSEHOLD INCOME LADDER	
95th percentile	$147,684 (190)
80th percentile	$76,863 (427)
60th percentile	$48,261 (416)
40th percentile	$27,312 (475)
20th percentile	$16,541 (382)

CHILDREN	★ (547)
Living with two parents	56.6% (468)
Older teens in school	76.1% (488)
Speak English very well	87.4% (536)
Poverty rate for children	32.1% (447)
No health insurance	19.9% (547)

DIVERSITY/EQUALITY	★★★★★ (15)
Racial diversity index	61.5% (10)
Geographic diversity index	70.3% (42)
Top 20% share of income	51.6% (493)
Gender gap in earnings	14.9% (15)
White-collar gender gap	10.8% (98)

EDUCATION	★ (546)
Eighth grade or less	22.3% (547)
High school diplomas	63.1% (548)
Attended college	30.8% (546)
Bachelor's degrees	9.9% (542)
Advanced degrees	3.4% (514)

EMPLOYMENT	★ (537)
Average jobless rate	11.9% (488)
Self-employed workers	9.8% (186)
Management/financial jobs	9.6% (427)
Computer/engineering jobs	1.2% (530)
Health care jobs	2.5% (547)

GROWTH POTENTIAL	★★★★★ (21)
Children per senior	2.27 (38)
Median age	33.8 (70)
Moved from different state	5.2% (47)
Homes built since 2000	22.6% (59)
Construction jobs	8.9% (51)

HOUSING	★ (469)
Home vacancy rate	12.4% (475)
Home ownership rate	68.8% (313)
Housing diversity index	80.2% (510)
4 or more bedrooms	15.3% (333)
Affordability/income ratio	$1,969 (48)

INCOME	★ (522)
Poverty rate	26.4% (493)
Median household income	$36,771 (446)
Interest/dividends	11.3% (505)
Public assistance	27.8% (532)
Median fulltime earnings	$30,822 (530)

SENIORS	★★★ (299)
Seniors living alone	26.0% (172)
Poverty rate for seniors	14.0% (470)
Median income for seniors	n.a.
Seniors who work	16.6% (367)
Home ownership by seniors	85.4% (129)

STABILITY	★★ (401)
25-39 age group	20.9% (44)
Born in state of residence	49.1% (489)
Same house as 1 year ago	82.1% (434)
Live and work in county	75.5% (282)
Married-couple households	48.0% (378)

TRANSPORTATION	★★★★ (189)
Bicycle or walk to work	2.9% (265)
Carpool to work	14.9% (49)
Public transit to work	8.2% (3)
Commute <15 minutes	34.7% (444)
Commute >45 minutes	21.3% (528)

See pages 37-130 for explanations of statistics, stars, and ranks.

Columbus, MS
(Lowndes County, MS)

POPULATION	
2010 census	59,779 (153)
2015 estimate	59,710 (149)
2010-2015 change	-0.1% (266)
2020 projection	59,127 (152)
2030 projection	57,575 (163)

RACE	
Whites	52.7% (478)
Blacks	43.8% (22)
Hispanics	1.9% (442)
Asians	0.7% (241)
Native Americans	0.2% (300)

AGE	
0-17 years old	24.1% (180)
18-24 years old	10.7% (124)
25-39 years old	19.5% (74)
40-54 years old	19.2% (336)
55-64 years old	12.5% (396)
65+ years old	13.9% (444)

PRIVATE SECTOR	
Businesses	1,491 (137)
Employees	20,435 (121)
Total wages	$803,728,404 (117)
Average weekly wages	$756 (152)

HOUSEHOLD INCOME LADDER	
95th percentile	$134,596 (367)
80th percentile	$81,466 (339)
60th percentile	$50,994 (359)
40th percentile	$30,041 (422)
20th percentile	$14,706 (461)

CHILDREN	★★ (410)
Living with two parents	51.8% (493)
Older teens in school	82.5% (296)
Speak English very well	99.4% (124)
Poverty rate for children	32.9% (462)
No health insurance	7.4% (341)

DIVERSITY/EQUALITY	★★★ (302)
Racial diversity index	53.0% (83)
Geographic diversity index	48.1% (241)
Top 20% share of income	48.7% (338)
Gender gap in earnings	42.7% (479)
White-collar gender gap	34.9% (389)

EDUCATION	★★★★ (190)
Eighth grade or less	3.6% (292)
High school diplomas	86.0% (343)
Attended college	57.2% (183)
Bachelor's degrees	22.7% (139)
Advanced degrees	7.9% (126)

EMPLOYMENT	★ (475)
Average jobless rate	12.6% (509)
Self-employed workers	7.8% (355)
Management/financial jobs	11.8% (173)
Computer/engineering jobs	2.0% (420)
Health care jobs	4.8% (369)

GROWTH POTENTIAL	★★★★★ (97)
Children per senior	1.73 (120)
Median age	36.3 (127)
Moved from different state	3.7% (96)
Homes built since 2000	16.0% (178)
Construction jobs	7.4% (134)

HOUSING	★ (494)
Home vacancy rate	11.8% (454)
Home ownership rate	61.5% (485)
Housing diversity index	83.9% (360)
4 or more bedrooms	14.5% (377)
Affordability/income ratio	$2,875 (372)

INCOME	★ (445)
Poverty rate	23.5% (457)
Median household income	$40,239 (376)
Interest/dividends	15.8% (385)
Public assistance	22.2% (481)
Median fulltime earnings	$36,024 (334)

SENIORS	★★★ (316)
Seniors living alone	27.5% (264)
Poverty rate for seniors	14.4% (477)
Median income for seniors	$31,177 (364)
Seniors who work	19.5% (226)
Home ownership by seniors	86.0% (102)

STABILITY	★★★★ (215)
25-39 age group	19.5% (74)
Born in state of residence	69.7% (315)
Same house as 1 year ago	84.5% (325)
Live and work in county	84.4% (142)
Married-couple households	44.7% (468)

TRANSPORTATION	★★ (373)
Bicycle or walk to work	1.1% (501)
Carpool to work	10.1% (322)
Public transit to work	0.1% (441)
Commute <15 minutes	39.4% (339)
Commute >45 minutes	8.2% (138)

See pages 37-130 for explanations of statistics, stars, and ranks.

Cookeville, TN
(Jackson, Overton, and Putnam Counties, TN)

POPULATION

2010 census	106,042 (24)
2015 estimate	108,191 (19)
2010-2015 change	2.0% (128)
2020 projection	110,834 (18)
2030 projection	116,002 (21)

RACE

Whites	91.5% (152)
Blacks	1.9% (295)
Hispanics	4.4% (270)
Asians	0.9% (178)
Native Americans	0.1% (402)

AGE

0-17 years old	21.3% (383)
18-24 years old	12.9% (73)
25-39 years old	17.1% (308)
40-54 years old	19.2% (336)
55-64 years old	12.8% (356)
65+ years old	16.7% (225)

PRIVATE SECTOR

Businesses	2,124 (52)
Employees	30,679 (39)
Total wages	$1,057,835,633 (61)
Average weekly wages	$663 (352)

HOUSEHOLD INCOME LADDER

95th percentile	$129,028 (441)
80th percentile	$72,309 (491)
60th percentile	$45,246 (473)
40th percentile	$26,865 (490)
20th percentile	$13,977 (476)

CHILDREN ★★★★ (193)

Living with two parents	68.4% (181)
Older teens in school	88.2% (97)
Speak English very well	99.1% (179)
Poverty rate for children	32.7% (459)
No health insurance	5.5% (218)

DIVERSITY/EQUALITY ★★ (407)

Racial diversity index	16.0% (397)
Geographic diversity index	52.8% (178)
Top 20% share of income	53.2% (526)
Gender gap in earnings	29.0% (153)
White-collar gender gap	22.2% (239)

EDUCATION ★★★ (312)

Eighth grade or less	4.5% (354)
High school diplomas	87.1% (301)
Attended college	45.1% (438)
Bachelor's degrees	20.9% (192)
Advanced degrees	6.8% (191)

EMPLOYMENT ★★★★ (172)

Average jobless rate	8.9% (351)
Self-employed workers	8.6% (285)
Management/financial jobs	11.2% (229)
Computer/engineering jobs	3.0% (193)
Health care jobs	7.3% (55)

GROWTH POTENTIAL ★★★★ (149)

Children per senior	1.27 (370)
Median age	38.8 (217)
Moved from different state	1.8% (338)
Homes built since 2000	20.5% (85)
Construction jobs	8.1% (86)

HOUSING ★★ (408)

Home vacancy rate	8.6% (260)
Home ownership rate	67.1% (382)
Housing diversity index	84.0% (344)
4 or more bedrooms	15.3% (333)
Affordability/income ratio	$3,725 (481)

INCOME ★ (443)

Poverty rate	24.6% (473)
Median household income	$34,841 (487)
Interest/dividends	15.7% (388)
Public assistance	14.6% (240)
Median fulltime earnings	$33,471 (439)

SENIORS ★★ (406)

Seniors living alone	26.0% (172)
Poverty rate for seniors	12.5% (436)
Median income for seniors	$28,849 (442)
Seniors who work	14.5% (478)
Home ownership by seniors	83.2% (210)

STABILITY ★★★ (294)

25-39 age group	17.1% (308)
Born in state of residence	66.5% (368)
Same house as 1 year ago	87.4% (173)
Live and work in county	74.9% (291)
Married-couple households	49.2% (340)

TRANSPORTATION ★ (539)

Bicycle or walk to work	0.9% (521)
Carpool to work	7.3% (523)
Public transit to work	0.1% (441)
Commute <15 minutes	27.2% (543)
Commute >45 minutes	13.0% (356)

See pages 37-130 for explanations of statistics, stars, and ranks.

Cordele, GA
(Crisp County, GA)

POPULATION
2010 census	23,439 (491)
2015 estimate	22,881 (499)
2010-2015 change	-2.4% (443)
2020 projection	22,301 (505)
2030 projection	21,139 (511)

RACE
Whites	51.0% (483)
Blacks	43.2% (24)
Hispanics	3.3% (324)
Asians	1.3% (112)
Native Americans	0.1% (402)

AGE
0-17 years old	25.1% (116)
18-24 years old	9.0% (265)
25-39 years old	17.5% (258)
40-54 years old	19.7% (273)
55-64 years old	13.9% (192)
65+ years old	14.9% (374)

PRIVATE SECTOR
Businesses	547 (499)
Employees	6,846 (479)
Total wages	$219,346,037 (495)
Average weekly wages	$616 (454)

HOUSEHOLD INCOME LADDER
95th percentile	$134,918 (361)
80th percentile	$74,372 (467)
60th percentile	$41,733 (512)
40th percentile	$23,661 (526)
20th percentile	$11,453 (534)

CHILDREN ★ (533)
Living with two parents	49.4% (511)
Older teens in school	70.6% (529)
Speak English very well	99.7% (57)
Poverty rate for children	46.9% (538)
No health insurance	8.2% (366)

DIVERSITY/EQUALITY ★ (535)
Racial diversity index	55.2% (50)
Geographic diversity index	27.8% (504)
Top 20% share of income	55.3% (545)
Gender gap in earnings	26.8% (114)
White-collar gender gap	58.3% (539)

EDUCATION ★★ (402)
Eighth grade or less	4.1% (332)
High school diplomas	83.0% (420)
Attended college	45.4% (433)
Bachelor's degrees	15.3% (412)
Advanced degrees	5.8% (283)

EMPLOYMENT ★★ (337)
Average jobless rate	15.5% (539)
Self-employed workers	11.8% (81)
Management/financial jobs	11.5% (202)
Computer/engineering jobs	2.0% (420)
Health care jobs	6.9% (79)

GROWTH POTENTIAL ★★★ (272)
Children per senior	1.69 (137)
Median age	38.4 (202)
Moved from different state	0.8% (524)
Homes built since 2000	12.8% (286)
Construction jobs	6.5% (253)

HOUSING ★ (484)
Home vacancy rate	12.0% (460)
Home ownership rate	59.0% (513)
Housing diversity index	85.8% (97)
4 or more bedrooms	15.0% (356)
Affordability/income ratio	$3,106 (418)

INCOME ★ (532)
Poverty rate	32.8% (535)
Median household income	$31,615 (525)
Interest/dividends	15.1% (405)
Public assistance	30.1% (538)
Median fulltime earnings	$33,837 (427)

SENIORS ★ (518)
Seniors living alone	28.3% (318)
Poverty rate for seniors	14.9% (491)
Median income for seniors	n.a.
Seniors who work	16.5% (376)
Home ownership by seniors	74.8% (528)

STABILITY ★★★ (229)
25-39 age group	17.5% (258)
Born in state of residence	84.5% (48)
Same house as 1 year ago	84.7% (314)
Live and work in county	78.0% (245)
Married-couple households	45.9% (445)

TRANSPORTATION ★★ (348)
Bicycle or walk to work	0.4% (549)
Carpool to work	10.4% (289)
Public transit to work	0.0% (511)
Commute <15 minutes	46.3% (227)
Commute >45 minutes	8.8% (165)

See pages 37-130 for explanations of statistics, stars, and ranks.

Corinth, MS
(Alcorn County, MS)

POPULATION	
2010 census	37,057 (357)
2015 estimate	37,388 (352)
2010-2015 change	0.9% (186)
2020 projection	37,738 (346)
2030 projection	38,176 (338)

RACE	
Whites	83.2% (289)
Blacks	11.4% (108)
Hispanics	3.0% (343)
Asians	0.3% (473)
Native Americans	0.1% (402)

AGE	
0-17 years old	24.0% (184)
18-24 years old	8.3% (362)
25-39 years old	17.9% (214)
40-54 years old	20.7% (132)
55-64 years old	12.5% (396)
65+ years old	16.6% (237)

PRIVATE SECTOR	
Businesses	758 (394)
Employees	10,827 (347)
Total wages	$360,425,269 (369)
Average weekly wages	$640 (415)

HOUSEHOLD INCOME LADDER	
95th percentile	$127,250 (468)
80th percentile	$69,831 (506)
60th percentile	$44,403 (485)
40th percentile	$28,248 (459)
20th percentile	$15,487 (433)

CHILDREN	★★★ (259)
Living with two parents	64.1% (293)
Older teens in school	85.5% (183)
Speak English very well	99.3% (142)
Poverty rate for children	30.6% (416)
No health insurance	6.5% (282)

DIVERSITY/EQUALITY	★★★★ (212)
Racial diversity index	29.4% (259)
Geographic diversity index	50.6% (203)
Top 20% share of income	48.8% (345)
Gender gap in earnings	24.1% (76)
White-collar gender gap	32.0% (364)

EDUCATION	★★ (394)
Eighth grade or less	5.3% (402)
High school diplomas	84.3% (393)
Attended college	48.3% (374)
Bachelor's degrees	16.4% (354)
Advanced degrees	5.0% (378)

EMPLOYMENT	★★★★ (153)
Average jobless rate	9.0% (358)
Self-employed workers	10.9% (120)
Management/financial jobs	8.2% (522)
Computer/engineering jobs	2.8% (246)
Health care jobs	8.5% (8)

GROWTH POTENTIAL	★★★ (268)
Children per senior	1.44 (253)
Median age	39.9 (292)
Moved from different state	3.0% (157)
Homes built since 2000	11.7% (324)
Construction jobs	6.5% (253)

HOUSING	★★★ (269)
Home vacancy rate	10.0% (347)
Home ownership rate	68.7% (317)
Housing diversity index	85.6% (127)
4 or more bedrooms	13.9% (406)
Affordability/income ratio	$2,345 (188)

INCOME	★★ (438)
Poverty rate	21.2% (407)
Median household income	$36,163 (463)
Interest/dividends	13.0% (472)
Public assistance	17.4% (352)
Median fulltime earnings	$34,807 (395)

SENIORS	★ (467)
Seniors living alone	30.3% (440)
Poverty rate for seniors	10.5% (345)
Median income for seniors	$29,084 (430)
Seniors who work	14.2% (496)
Home ownership by seniors	81.5% (305)

STABILITY	★★★ (329)
25-39 age group	17.9% (214)
Born in state of residence	66.8% (366)
Same house as 1 year ago	85.3% (290)
Live and work in county	74.1% (308)
Married-couple households	48.5% (361)

TRANSPORTATION	★★ (433)
Bicycle or walk to work	0.8% (531)
Carpool to work	8.6% (457)
Public transit to work	0.2% (363)
Commute <15 minutes	45.1% (245)
Commute >45 minutes	12.0% (311)

See pages 37-130 for explanations of statistics, stars, and ranks.

Cornelia, GA
(Habersham County, GA)

POPULATION		
2010 census	43,041 (276)	
2015 estimate	43,996 (272)	
2010-2015 change	2.2% (118)	
2020 projection	45,149 (260)	
2030 projection	47,395 (241)	

RACE
Whites	78.0% (339)
Blacks	3.8% (198)
Hispanics	13.5% (115)
Asians	2.4% (33)
Native Americans	0.2% (300)

AGE
0-17 years old	23.1% (256)
18-24 years old	9.3% (217)
25-39 years old	18.9% (111)
40-54 years old	19.3% (323)
55-64 years old	12.2% (424)
65+ years old	17.1% (186)

PRIVATE SECTOR
Businesses	838 (353)
Employees	11,628 (322)
Total wages	$370,050,153 (364)
Average weekly wages	$612 (464)

HOUSEHOLD INCOME LADDER
95th percentile	$135,689 (348)
80th percentile	$80,898 (352)
60th percentile	$51,146 (355)
40th percentile	$33,151 (318)
20th percentile	$18,883 (273)

CHILDREN ★★ (379)
Living with two parents	72.5% (97)
Older teens in school	81.9% (325)
Speak English very well	93.5% (500)
Poverty rate for children	26.2% (328)
No health insurance	10.7% (441)

DIVERSITY/EQUALITY ★★★★ (131)
Racial diversity index	37.1% (204)
Geographic diversity index	54.1% (163)
Top 20% share of income	46.1% (129)
Gender gap in earnings	28.8% (149)
White-collar gender gap	35.3% (395)

EDUCATION ★★ (426)
Eighth grade or less	8.1% (491)
High school diplomas	79.6% (486)
Attended college	46.7% (403)
Bachelor's degrees	18.2% (277)
Advanced degrees	7.7% (133)

EMPLOYMENT ★★ (385)
Average jobless rate	7.7% (260)
Self-employed workers	9.4% (216)
Management/financial jobs	8.9% (483)
Computer/engineering jobs	3.0% (193)
Health care jobs	4.6% (401)

GROWTH POTENTIAL ★★★★ (180)
Children per senior	1.35 (313)
Median age	38.8 (217)
Moved from different state	1.7% (355)
Homes built since 2000	22.6% (59)
Construction jobs	6.4% (270)

HOUSING ★★★ (316)
Home vacancy rate	9.2% (302)
Home ownership rate	74.9% (83)
Housing diversity index	82.6% (433)
4 or more bedrooms	15.5% (324)
Affordability/income ratio	$3,215 (435)

INCOME ★★ (352)
Poverty rate	17.8% (292)
Median household income	$40,907 (357)
Interest/dividends	16.4% (363)
Public assistance	15.8% (286)
Median fulltime earnings	$34,057 (420)

SENIORS ★★★★ (124)
Seniors living alone	22.8% (54)
Poverty rate for seniors	8.3% (202)
Median income for seniors	$33,077 (278)
Seniors who work	14.3% (493)
Home ownership by seniors	87.8% (46)

STABILITY ★★★★★ (61)
25-39 age group	18.9% (111)
Born in state of residence	65.5% (382)
Same house as 1 year ago	91.7% (18)
Live and work in county	62.4% (471)
Married-couple households	57.3% (27)

TRANSPORTATION ★ (498)
Bicycle or walk to work	2.0% (386)
Carpool to work	9.1% (419)
Public transit to work	0.5% (178)
Commute <15 minutes	34.6% (445)
Commute >45 minutes	16.6% (473)

See pages 37-130 for explanations of statistics, stars, and ranks.

Corsicana, TX
(Navarro County, TX)

POPULATION

2010 census	47,735 (222)
2015 estimate	48,323 (224)
2010-2015 change	1.2% (173)
2020 projection	48,413 (228)
2030 projection	48,613 (227)

RACE

Whites	58.4% (454)
Blacks	13.3% (95)
Hispanics	25.2% (60)
Asians	1.6% (77)
Native Americans	0.2% (300)

AGE

0-17 years old	26.3% (57)
18-24 years old	8.6% (317)
25-39 years old	16.9% (338)
40-54 years old	20.1% (221)
55-64 years old	12.3% (414)
65+ years old	15.7% (318)

PRIVATE SECTOR

Businesses	884 (323)
Employees	13,341 (265)
Total wages	$479,816,198 (262)
Average weekly wages	$692 (277)

HOUSEHOLD INCOME LADDER

95th percentile	$143,650 (248)
80th percentile	$85,804 (234)
60th percentile	$52,757 (304)
40th percentile	$33,226 (315)
20th percentile	$18,241 (304)

CHILDREN ★ (529)

Living with two parents	58.4% (441)
Older teens in school	78.1% (446)
Speak English very well	90.7% (524)
Poverty rate for children	31.5% (435)
No health insurance	12.9% (494)

DIVERSITY/EQUALITY ★★★ (237)

Racial diversity index	57.7% (28)
Geographic diversity index	46.5% (260)
Top 20% share of income	49.0% (358)
Gender gap in earnings	31.2% (210)
White-collar gender gap	43.9% (474)

EDUCATION ★ (500)

Eighth grade or less	10.7% (519)
High school diplomas	77.2% (514)
Attended college	48.9% (357)
Bachelor's degrees	15.8% (391)
Advanced degrees	4.9% (396)

EMPLOYMENT ★ (522)

Average jobless rate	10.9% (454)
Self-employed workers	7.2% (410)
Management/financial jobs	10.2% (357)
Computer/engineering jobs	1.6% (486)
Health care jobs	3.8% (494)

GROWTH POTENTIAL ★★★★ (167)

Children per senior	1.67 (144)
Median age	38.2 (189)
Moved from different state	1.5% (406)
Homes built since 2000	19.1% (105)
Construction jobs	6.5% (253)

HOUSING ★★★ (259)

Home vacancy rate	9.4% (309)
Home ownership rate	66.5% (405)
Housing diversity index	85.6% (127)
4 or more bedrooms	13.4% (433)
Affordability/income ratio	$1,959 (42)

INCOME ★★ (434)

Poverty rate	20.7% (395)
Median household income	$41,505 (336)
Interest/dividends	14.9% (413)
Public assistance	20.8% (450)
Median fulltime earnings	$33,111 (450)

SENIORS ★★ (381)

Seniors living alone	26.1% (179)
Poverty rate for seniors	13.8% (467)
Median income for seniors	$31,772 (333)
Seniors who work	23.1% (107)
Home ownership by seniors	76.5% (500)

STABILITY ★★★ (286)

25-39 age group	16.9% (338)
Born in state of residence	72.1% (273)
Same house as 1 year ago	84.3% (333)
Live and work in county	76.2% (269)
Married-couple households	51.0% (248)

TRANSPORTATION ★ (442)

Bicycle or walk to work	1.7% (428)
Carpool to work	12.4% (128)
Public transit to work	0.1% (441)
Commute <15 minutes	35.4% (433)
Commute >45 minutes	16.3% (464)

See pages 37-130 for explanations of statistics, stars, and ranks.

Crossville, TN
(Cumberland County, TN)

POPULATION

2010 census	56,053 (166)
2015 estimate	58,229 (157)
2010-2015 change	3.9% (64)
2020 projection	60,642 (144)
2030 projection	65,552 (124)

RACE

Whites	94.9% (51)
Blacks	0.6% (438)
Hispanics	2.7% (361)
Asians	0.4% (413)
Native Americans	0.3% (231)

AGE

0-17 years old	18.2% (523)
18-24 years old	6.6% (535)
25-39 years old	14.2% (537)
40-54 years old	18.1% (446)
55-64 years old	14.6% (107)
65+ years old	28.4% (3)

PRIVATE SECTOR

Businesses	1,046 (260)
Employees	14,936 (211)
Total wages	$485,711,892 (254)
Average weekly wages	$625 (443)

HOUSEHOLD INCOME LADDER

95th percentile	$127,816 (458)
80th percentile	$73,848 (475)
60th percentile	$46,060 (458)
40th percentile	$32,095 (358)
20th percentile	$18,266 (302)

CHILDREN ★★ (350)

Living with two parents	56.9% (461)
Older teens in school	74.7% (504)
Speak English very well	99.7% (57)
Poverty rate for children	24.1% (276)
No health insurance	5.0% (181)

DIVERSITY/EQUALITY ★★★★★ (79)

Racial diversity index	9.9% (496)
Geographic diversity index	66.5% (66)
Top 20% share of income	47.3% (243)
Gender gap in earnings	22.6% (63)
White-collar gender gap	14.8% (149)

EDUCATION ★★ (414)

Eighth grade or less	5.0% (385)
High school diplomas	84.4% (389)
Attended college	43.4% (464)
Bachelor's degrees	16.2% (360)
Advanced degrees	5.5% (318)

EMPLOYMENT ★★★ (268)

Average jobless rate	9.0% (358)
Self-employed workers	9.5% (207)
Management/financial jobs	9.1% (463)
Computer/engineering jobs	1.4% (510)
Health care jobs	8.0% (19)

GROWTH POTENTIAL ★★ (379)

Children per senior	0.64 (548)
Median age	49.7 (543)
Moved from different state	2.4% (218)
Homes built since 2000	27.5% (23)
Construction jobs	7.0% (185)

HOUSING ★★ (418)

Home vacancy rate	7.9% (213)
Home ownership rate	78.6% (10)
Housing diversity index	80.0% (514)
4 or more bedrooms	12.0% (496)
Affordability/income ratio	$3,616 (474)

INCOME ★★★ (328)

Poverty rate	16.5% (246)
Median household income	$38,576 (415)
Interest/dividends	24.3% (122)
Public assistance	18.1% (376)
Median fulltime earnings	$32,325 (478)

SENIORS ★★★★★ (72)

Seniors living alone	21.0% (20)
Poverty rate for seniors	7.1% (101)
Median income for seniors	$36,796 (122)
Seniors who work	12.5% (535)
Home ownership by seniors	88.2% (37)

STABILITY ★★ (430)

25-39 age group	14.2% (537)
Born in state of residence	51.5% (480)
Same house as 1 year ago	85.5% (280)
Live and work in county	83.7% (148)
Married-couple households	54.1% (105)

TRANSPORTATION ★★ (435)

Bicycle or walk to work	1.2% (492)
Carpool to work	10.4% (289)
Public transit to work	0.2% (363)
Commute <15 minutes	32.7% (480)
Commute >45 minutes	10.3% (237)

See pages 37-130 for explanations of statistics, stars, and ranks.

Cullman, AL
(Cullman County, AL)

POPULATION	
2010 census	80,406 (66)
2015 estimate	82,005 (62)
2010-2015 change	2.0% (128)
2020 projection	82,884 (64)
2030 projection	84,250 (64)

RACE	
Whites	92.2% (128)
Blacks	1.1% (367)
Hispanics	4.3% (279)
Asians	0.6% (291)
Native Americans	0.4% (203)

AGE	
0-17 years old	22.6% (291)
18-24 years old	8.5% (330)
25-39 years old	18.0% (201)
40-54 years old	20.3% (186)
55-64 years old	13.2% (297)
65+ years old	17.3% (172)

PRIVATE SECTOR	
Businesses	1,699 (100)
Employees	23,425 (85)
Total wages	$866,305,178 (101)
Average weekly wages	$711 (231)

HOUSEHOLD INCOME LADDER	
95th percentile	$134,358 (371)
80th percentile	$77,324 (416)
60th percentile	$47,628 (431)
40th percentile	$31,314 (379)
20th percentile	$16,793 (371)

CHILDREN	★★★★ (191)
Living with two parents	69.0% (166)
Older teens in school	86.6% (144)
Speak English very well	97.6% (375)
Poverty rate for children	25.0% (298)
No health insurance	6.5% (282)

DIVERSITY/EQUALITY	★★ (391)
Racial diversity index	14.8% (418)
Geographic diversity index	38.4% (383)
Top 20% share of income	48.8% (341)
Gender gap in earnings	29.1% (155)
White-collar gender gap	27.5% (302)

EDUCATION	★★ (366)
Eighth grade or less	4.2% (337)
High school diplomas	85.0% (375)
Attended college	51.5% (291)
Bachelor's degrees	14.9% (424)
Advanced degrees	5.4% (334)

EMPLOYMENT	★★★★ (132)
Average jobless rate	7.3% (228)
Self-employed workers	9.2% (231)
Management/financial jobs	10.1% (365)
Computer/engineering jobs	2.6% (288)
Health care jobs	8.0% (19)

GROWTH POTENTIAL	★★★★ (203)
Children per senior	1.30 (347)
Median age	40.5 (329)
Moved from different state	1.4% (425)
Homes built since 2000	17.4% (145)
Construction jobs	8.3% (67)

HOUSING	★★★ (264)
Home vacancy rate	10.6% (385)
Home ownership rate	75.3% (72)
Housing diversity index	84.5% (287)
4 or more bedrooms	15.1% (347)
Affordability/income ratio	$2,956 (395)

INCOME	★★ (366)
Poverty rate	18.5% (317)
Median household income	$38,971 (406)
Interest/dividends	12.7% (477)
Public assistance	14.4% (225)
Median fulltime earnings	$36,571 (313)

SENIORS	★★ (440)
Seniors living alone	26.5% (201)
Poverty rate for seniors	13.3% (455)
Median income for seniors	$27,975 (460)
Seniors who work	14.0% (503)
Home ownership by seniors	83.4% (202)

STABILITY	★★★★★ (52)
25-39 age group	18.0% (201)
Born in state of residence	77.5% (168)
Same house as 1 year ago	89.8% (52)
Live and work in county	69.0% (388)
Married-couple households	54.9% (75)

TRANSPORTATION	★ (542)
Bicycle or walk to work	1.6% (443)
Carpool to work	10.2% (312)
Public transit to work	0.1% (441)
Commute <15 minutes	32.6% (484)
Commute >45 minutes	23.1% (540)

See pages 37-130 for explanations of statistics, stars, and ranks.

Cullowhee, NC
(Jackson County, NC)

POPULATION	
2010 census	40,271 (309)
2015 estimate	41,265 (296)
2010-2015 change	2.5% (107)
2020 projection	42,405 (290)
2030 projection	44,600 (266)

RACE	
Whites	81.0% (317)
Blacks	2.2% (276)
Hispanics	5.3% (244)
Asians	0.9% (178)
Native Americans	8.4% (23)

AGE	
0-17 years old	17.4% (533)
18-24 years old	18.9% (31)
25-39 years old	17.3% (280)
40-54 years old	16.5% (516)
55-64 years old	13.1% (318)
65+ years old	16.8% (215)

PRIVATE SECTOR	
Businesses	984 (285)
Employees	8,827 (418)
Total wages	$267,502,209 (457)
Average weekly wages	$583 (511)

HOUSEHOLD INCOME LADDER	
95th percentile	$128,763 (445)
80th percentile	$77,737 (405)
60th percentile	$49,407 (395)
40th percentile	$29,380 (437)
20th percentile	$15,554 (430)

CHILDREN	★★★ (314)
Living with two parents	60.4% (391)
Older teens in school	91.7% (44)
Speak English very well	97.5% (388)
Poverty rate for children	31.2% (427)
No health insurance	9.3% (401)

DIVERSITY/EQUALITY	★★★★★ (97)
Racial diversity index	33.3% (225)
Geographic diversity index	60.7% (120)
Top 20% share of income	49.5% (402)
Gender gap in earnings	28.3% (140)
White-collar gender gap	12.4% (121)

EDUCATION	★★★★★ (75)
Eighth grade or less	2.7% (195)
High school diplomas	90.6% (178)
Attended college	62.8% (85)
Bachelor's degrees	28.8% (65)
Advanced degrees	9.7% (68)

EMPLOYMENT	★★★★ (210)
Average jobless rate	6.2% (131)
Self-employed workers	9.4% (216)
Management/financial jobs	10.7% (287)
Computer/engineering jobs	2.8% (246)
Health care jobs	5.5% (250)

GROWTH POTENTIAL	★★★★★ (70)
Children per senior	1.03 (492)
Median age	36.8 (138)
Moved from different state	2.9% (165)
Homes built since 2000	27.0% (27)
Construction jobs	8.7% (58)

HOUSING	★ (511)
Home vacancy rate	8.3% (241)
Home ownership rate	67.6% (362)
Housing diversity index	81.6% (475)
4 or more bedrooms	14.1% (398)
Affordability/income ratio	$4,522 (516)

INCOME	★★ (357)
Poverty rate	22.0% (427)
Median household income	$38,015 (427)
Interest/dividends	21.7% (190)
Public assistance	13.0% (169)
Median fulltime earnings	$31,811 (505)

SENIORS	★★★★★ (94)
Seniors living alone	23.7% (76)
Poverty rate for seniors	9.4% (282)
Median income for seniors	$37,490 (104)
Seniors who work	17.1% (339)
Home ownership by seniors	87.5% (56)

STABILITY	★ (481)
25-39 age group	17.3% (280)
Born in state of residence	58.3% (436)
Same house as 1 year ago	83.4% (375)
Live and work in county	74.8% (294)
Married-couple households	46.3% (437)

TRANSPORTATION	★★★★ (155)
Bicycle or walk to work	4.7% (106)
Carpool to work	12.6% (116)
Public transit to work	0.6% (141)
Commute <15 minutes	40.0% (329)
Commute >45 minutes	8.2% (138)

See pages 37-130 for explanations of statistics, stars, and ranks.

Danville, KY
(Boyle and Lincoln Counties, KY)

POPULATION

2010 census	53,174 (184)
2015 estimate	54,272 (176)
2010-2015 change	2.1% (125)
2020 projection	54,932 (177)
2030 projection	56,167 (172)

RACE

Whites	90.0% (184)
Blacks	5.0% (164)
Hispanics	2.4% (389)
Asians	0.6% (291)
Native Americans	0.1% (402)

AGE

0-17 years old	22.1% (330)
18-24 years old	10.2% (151)
25-39 years old	17.0% (317)
40-54 years old	20.7% (132)
55-64 years old	13.1% (318)
65+ years old	17.0% (197)

PRIVATE SECTOR

Businesses	1,175 (210)
Employees	14,618 (220)
Total wages	$545,752,686 (216)
Average weekly wages	$718 (219)

HOUSEHOLD INCOME LADDER

95th percentile	$127,804 (459)
80th percentile	$80,646 (357)
60th percentile	$47,617 (432)
40th percentile	$30,311 (408)
20th percentile	$15,714 (419)

CHILDREN ★★★★ (189)

Living with two parents	64.4% (283)
Older teens in school	85.5% (183)
Speak English very well	99.5% (96)
Poverty rate for children	26.8% (346)
No health insurance	5.0% (181)

DIVERSITY/EQUALITY ★ (503)

Racial diversity index	18.7% (364)
Geographic diversity index	40.1% (350)
Top 20% share of income	49.3% (388)
Gender gap in earnings	32.1% (230)
White-collar gender gap	47.9% (499)

EDUCATION ★★ (343)

Eighth grade or less	5.0% (385)
High school diplomas	86.2% (333)
Attended college	46.2% (414)
Bachelor's degrees	17.2% (315)
Advanced degrees	7.5% (142)

EMPLOYMENT ★★★ (246)

Average jobless rate	8.6% (335)
Self-employed workers	8.4% (297)
Management/financial jobs	11.3% (218)
Computer/engineering jobs	2.2% (381)
Health care jobs	6.7% (104)

GROWTH POTENTIAL ★★★ (293)

Children per senior	1.30 (347)
Median age	40.7 (341)
Moved from different state	2.0% (288)
Homes built since 2000	16.4% (172)
Construction jobs	6.3% (284)

HOUSING ★★★ (227)

Home vacancy rate	9.0% (287)
Home ownership rate	69.3% (294)
Housing diversity index	85.7% (108)
4 or more bedrooms	16.4% (272)
Affordability/income ratio	$2,846 (365)

INCOME ★★ (420)

Poverty rate	20.3% (384)
Median household income	$38,436 (419)
Interest/dividends	16.1% (372)
Public assistance	21.6% (470)
Median fulltime earnings	$36,116 (327)

SENIORS ★★ (353)

Seniors living alone	28.9% (358)
Poverty rate for seniors	11.9% (408)
Median income for seniors	$30,648 (386)
Seniors who work	18.2% (280)
Home ownership by seniors	84.7% (155)

STABILITY ★ (450)

25-39 age group	17.0% (317)
Born in state of residence	76.3% (198)
Same house as 1 year ago	83.4% (375)
Live and work in county	57.1% (511)
Married-couple households	51.0% (248)

TRANSPORTATION ★★ (424)

Bicycle or walk to work	3.2% (225)
Carpool to work	11.4% (190)
Public transit to work	0.1% (441)
Commute <15 minutes	34.0% (460)
Commute >45 minutes	15.3% (435)

See pages 37-130 for explanations of statistics, stars, and ranks.

Danville, VA
(Pittsylvania County and City of Danville, VA)

POPULATION			
2010 census	106,561 (23)	Attended college	53.7% (251)
2015 estimate	104,276 (25)	Bachelor's degrees	17.3% (309)
2010-2015 change	-2.1% (418)	Advanced degrees	5.9% (272)
2020 projection	101,320 (30)	**EMPLOYMENT**	**★★ (398)**
2030 projection	95,250 (40)	Average jobless rate	9.6% (402)

RACE

Whites	62.5% (432)	Self-employed workers	7.0% (428)
Blacks	32.3% (47)	Management/financial jobs	9.5% (440)
Hispanics	2.8% (355)	Computer/engineering jobs	2.2% (381)
Asians	0.7% (241)	Health care jobs	6.6% (114)
Native Americans	0.1% (402)		

POPULATION
2010 census — 106,561 (23)
2015 estimate — 104,276 (25)
2010-2015 change — -2.1% (418)
2020 projection — 101,320 (30)
2030 projection — 95,250 (40)

RACE
Whites — 62.5% (432)
Blacks — 32.3% (47)
Hispanics — 2.8% (355)
Asians — 0.7% (241)
Native Americans — 0.1% (402)

AGE
0-17 years old — 20.9% (416)
18-24 years old — 8.1% (396)
25-39 years old — 15.9% (453)
40-54 years old — 20.8% (122)
55-64 years old — 15.1% (74)
65+ years old — 19.2% (72)

PRIVATE SECTOR
Businesses — 2,815 (25)
Employees — 32,105 (29)
Total wages — $1,074,834,726 (57)
Average weekly wages — $644 (405)

HOUSEHOLD INCOME LADDER
95th percentile — $129,494 (437)
80th percentile — $74,749 (460)
60th percentile — $46,636 (450)
40th percentile — $30,202 (412)
20th percentile — $15,938 (411)

CHILDREN ★★ (365)
Living with two parents — 52.7% (489)
Older teens in school — 84.6% (214)
Speak English very well — 99.0% (200)
Poverty rate for children — 29.8% (398)
No health insurance — 7.3% (333)

DIVERSITY/EQUALITY ★★★★ (168)
Racial diversity index — 50.4% (110)
Geographic diversity index — 40.4% (344)
Top 20% share of income — 48.3% (315)
Gender gap in earnings — 30.5% (183)
White-collar gender gap — 24.1% (259)

EDUCATION ★★★ (309)
Eighth grade or less — 4.1% (332)
High school diplomas — 85.6% (357)
Attended college — 53.7% (251)
Bachelor's degrees — 17.3% (309)
Advanced degrees — 5.9% (272)

EMPLOYMENT ★★ (398)
Average jobless rate — 9.6% (402)
Self-employed workers — 7.0% (428)
Management/financial jobs — 9.5% (440)
Computer/engineering jobs — 2.2% (381)
Health care jobs — 6.6% (114)

GROWTH POTENTIAL ★ (467)
Children per senior — 1.08 (471)
Median age — 44.2 (484)
Moved from different state — 2.0% (288)
Homes built since 2000 — 11.0% (358)
Construction jobs — 6.5% (253)

HOUSING ★★ (358)
Home vacancy rate — 13.9% (514)
Home ownership rate — 67.3% (377)
Housing diversity index — 86.9% (2)
4 or more bedrooms — 15.1% (347)
Affordability/income ratio — $2,666 (318)

INCOME ★★ (397)
Poverty rate — 19.1% (341)
Median household income — $38,228 (423)
Interest/dividends — 16.6% (357)
Public assistance — 20.6% (445)
Median fulltime earnings — $36,126 (326)

SENIORS ★★ (418)
Seniors living alone — 30.3% (440)
Poverty rate for seniors — 11.1% (378)
Median income for seniors — $30,097 (405)
Seniors who work — 18.8% (253)
Home ownership by seniors — 81.5% (305)

STABILITY ★ (521)
25-39 age group — 15.9% (453)
Born in state of residence — 75.9% (207)
Same house as 1 year ago — 87.0% (198)
Live and work in county — 52.3% (534)
Married-couple households — 44.0% (482)

TRANSPORTATION ★★ (421)
Bicycle or walk to work — 1.4% (472)
Carpool to work — 10.6% (271)
Public transit to work — 1.0% (69)
Commute <15 minutes — 31.3% (508)
Commute >45 minutes — 12.6% (336)

See pages 37-130 for explanations of statistics, stars, and ranks.

Dayton, TN
(Rhea County, TN)

POPULATION

2010 census	31,809 (420)
2015 estimate	32,526 (414)
2010-2015 change	2.3% (114)
2020 projection	33,204 (405)
2030 projection	34,488 (380)

RACE

Whites	91.3% (155)
Blacks	2.5% (253)
Hispanics	4.4% (270)
Asians	0.1% (529)
Native Americans	0.1% (402)

AGE

0-17 years old	23.0% (259)
18-24 years old	9.4% (203)
25-39 years old	16.8% (359)
40-54 years old	20.5% (151)
55-64 years old	13.2% (297)
65+ years old	17.1% (186)

PRIVATE SECTOR

Businesses	449 (531)
Employees	7,859 (449)
Total wages	$272,942,950 (453)
Average weekly wages	$668 (338)

HOUSEHOLD INCOME LADDER

95th percentile	$134,816 (362)
80th percentile	$76,265 (437)
60th percentile	$46,596 (453)
40th percentile	$27,496 (468)
20th percentile	$14,922 (453)

CHILDREN ★★ (382)

Living with two parents	64.0% (297)
Older teens in school	75.2% (501)
Speak English very well	98.4% (300)
Poverty rate for children	37.3% (499)
No health insurance	3.2% (69)

DIVERSITY/EQUALITY ★★ (425)

Racial diversity index	16.4% (391)
Geographic diversity index	50.1% (212)
Top 20% share of income	49.9% (421)
Gender gap in earnings	37.5% (375)
White-collar gender gap	27.1% (298)

EDUCATION ★ (516)

Eighth grade or less	7.7% (484)
High school diplomas	77.4% (512)
Attended college	37.5% (532)
Bachelor's degrees	12.4% (509)
Advanced degrees	4.8% (405)

EMPLOYMENT ★ (497)

Average jobless rate	11.1% (460)
Self-employed workers	6.0% (502)
Management/financial jobs	10.2% (357)
Computer/engineering jobs	3.9% (86)
Health care jobs	3.7% (503)

GROWTH POTENTIAL ★★★★ (187)

Children per senior	1.34 (321)
Median age	40.5 (329)
Moved from different state	3.8% (89)
Homes built since 2000	18.8% (112)
Construction jobs	6.3% (284)

HOUSING ★★★ (303)

Home vacancy rate	7.4% (180)
Home ownership rate	68.3% (332)
Housing diversity index	84.0% (344)
4 or more bedrooms	14.6% (373)
Affordability/income ratio	$2,944 (393)

INCOME ★ (466)

Poverty rate	24.5% (472)
Median household income	$36,146 (464)
Interest/dividends	17.7% (321)
Public assistance	23.0% (496)
Median fulltime earnings	$35,247 (370)

SENIORS ★★ (361)

Seniors living alone	27.0% (239)
Poverty rate for seniors	11.7% (397)
Median income for seniors	$30,733 (381)
Seniors who work	18.6% (265)
Home ownership by seniors	81.5% (305)

STABILITY ★ (461)

25-39 age group	16.8% (359)
Born in state of residence	68.7% (333)
Same house as 1 year ago	80.3% (494)
Live and work in county	75.8% (278)
Married-couple households	49.1% (345)

TRANSPORTATION ★★★ (265)

Bicycle or walk to work	2.8% (279)
Carpool to work	15.0% (48)
Public transit to work	0.0% (511)
Commute <15 minutes	41.6% (307)
Commute >45 minutes	14.1% (392)

See pages 37-130 for explanations of statistics, stars, and ranks.

Del Rio, TX
(Val Verde County, TX)

POPULATION

2010 census	48,879 (218)
2015 estimate	48,988 (217)
2010-2015 change	0.2% (241)
2020 projection	49,157 (221)
2030 projection	49,457 (222)

RACE

Whites	16.9% (544)
Blacks	0.9% (388)
Hispanics	80.4% (6)
Asians	0.6% (291)
Native Americans	0.1% (402)

AGE

0-17 years old	29.2% (23)
18-24 years old	11.0% (115)
25-39 years old	20.1% (57)
40-54 years old	16.8% (507)
55-64 years old	9.5% (538)
65+ years old	13.4% (463)

PRIVATE SECTOR

Businesses	798 (374)
Employees	12,132 (307)
Total wages	$357,706,669 (372)
Average weekly wages	$567 (522)

HOUSEHOLD INCOME LADDER

95th percentile	$141,615 (271)
80th percentile	$87,143 (201)
60th percentile	$53,192 (294)
40th percentile	$34,514 (274)
20th percentile	$17,533 (340)

CHILDREN ★ (523)

Living with two parents	62.6% (330)
Older teens in school	77.4% (463)
Speak English very well	91.1% (521)
Poverty rate for children	27.8% (363)
No health insurance	14.4% (518)

DIVERSITY/EQUALITY ★★★ (280)

Racial diversity index	32.5% (231)
Geographic diversity index	57.9% (134)
Top 20% share of income	48.3% (312)
Gender gap in earnings	41.0% (456)
White-collar gender gap	29.7% (333)

EDUCATION ★ (532)

Eighth grade or less	15.1% (535)
High school diplomas	72.1% (534)
Attended college	42.9% (473)
Bachelor's degrees	18.3% (274)
Advanced degrees	4.2% (466)

EMPLOYMENT ★ (534)

Average jobless rate	9.3% (387)
Self-employed workers	6.3% (484)
Management/financial jobs	8.0% (528)
Computer/engineering jobs	0.8% (543)
Health care jobs	4.6% (401)

GROWTH POTENTIAL ★★★★★ (64)

Children per senior	2.19 (41)
Median age	31.7 (45)
Moved from different state	3.2% (136)
Homes built since 2000	19.9% (92)
Construction jobs	5.2% (442)

HOUSING ★★★ (301)

Home vacancy rate	9.5% (317)
Home ownership rate	64.8% (438)
Housing diversity index	84.9% (235)
4 or more bedrooms	15.3% (333)
Affordability/income ratio	$2,191 (120)

INCOME ★ (459)

Poverty rate	20.6% (392)
Median household income	$42,174 (314)
Interest/dividends	10.3% (526)
Public assistance	22.0% (477)
Median fulltime earnings	$34,920 (386)

SENIORS ★ (494)

Seniors living alone	20.3% (17)
Poverty rate for seniors	22.3% (545)
Median income for seniors	$22,810 (522)
Seniors who work	18.0% (287)
Home ownership by seniors	77.2% (478)

STABILITY ★★★★★ (13)

25-39 age group	20.1% (57)
Born in state of residence	62.4% (409)
Same house as 1 year ago	84.8% (313)
Live and work in county	92.1% (44)
Married-couple households	56.4% (39)

TRANSPORTATION ★★★★★ (77)

Bicycle or walk to work	3.4% (199)
Carpool to work	14.1% (61)
Public transit to work	0.2% (363)
Commute <15 minutes	56.3% (78)
Commute >45 minutes	6.7% (77)

See pages 37-130 for explanations of statistics, stars, and ranks.

DeRidder, LA
(Beauregard Parish, LA)

POPULATION

2010 census	35,654 (378)
2015 estimate	36,462 (367)
2010-2015 change	2.3% (114)
2020 projection	37,367 (352)
2030 projection	39,122 (327)

RACE

Whites	79.6% (330)
Blacks	13.1% (98)
Hispanics	3.5% (318)
Asians	0.6% (291)
Native Americans	0.8% (125)

AGE

0-17 years old	25.3% (97)
18-24 years old	8.8% (292)
25-39 years old	19.0% (104)
40-54 years old	20.5% (151)
55-64 years old	12.5% (396)
65+ years old	13.8% (448)

PRIVATE SECTOR

Businesses	640 (454)
Employees	7,061 (474)
Total wages	$282,867,692 (446)
Average weekly wages	$770 (128)

HOUSEHOLD INCOME LADDER

95th percentile	$159,040 (104)
80th percentile	$92,782 (118)
60th percentile	$60,966 (129)
40th percentile	$36,313 (221)
20th percentile	$17,616 (337)

CHILDREN ★★ (428)

Living with two parents	60.8% (382)
Older teens in school	68.9% (534)
Speak English very well	99.7% (57)
Poverty rate for children	27.4% (354)
No health insurance	6.5% (282)

DIVERSITY/EQUALITY ★ (459)

Racial diversity index	34.7% (217)
Geographic diversity index	47.5% (250)
Top 20% share of income	47.7% (269)
Gender gap in earnings	55.7% (544)
White-collar gender gap	30.1% (339)

EDUCATION ★ (450)

Eighth grade or less	6.2% (433)
High school diplomas	84.8% (377)
Attended college	43.0% (471)
Bachelor's degrees	15.8% (391)
Advanced degrees	4.0% (478)

EMPLOYMENT ★★★ (307)

Average jobless rate	5.7% (109)
Self-employed workers	9.8% (186)
Management/financial jobs	10.0% (381)
Computer/engineering jobs	2.6% (288)
Health care jobs	4.3% (444)

GROWTH POTENTIAL ★★★★★ (45)

Children per senior	1.83 (88)
Median age	37.5 (162)
Moved from different state	2.8% (171)
Homes built since 2000	20.3% (87)
Construction jobs	10.3% (13)

HOUSING ★★★★★ (109)

Home vacancy rate	8.4% (245)
Home ownership rate	76.4% (43)
Housing diversity index	84.3% (314)
4 or more bedrooms	17.3% (232)
Affordability/income ratio	$2,265 (147)

INCOME ★★★ (285)

Poverty rate	20.2% (380)
Median household income	$45,969 (213)
Interest/dividends	13.6% (450)
Public assistance	15.0% (254)
Median fulltime earnings	$40,808 (106)

SENIORS ★★★★ (120)

Seniors living alone	23.8% (78)
Poverty rate for seniors	12.4% (434)
Median income for seniors	$34,272 (221)
Seniors who work	14.8% (465)
Home ownership by seniors	92.4% (3)

STABILITY ★★★ (271)

25-39 age group	19.0% (104)
Born in state of residence	70.3% (305)
Same house as 1 year ago	85.4% (285)
Live and work in county	54.0% (528)
Married-couple households	55.7% (53)

TRANSPORTATION ★ (526)

Bicycle or walk to work	2.1% (374)
Carpool to work	11.1% (221)
Public transit to work	0.4% (219)
Commute <15 minutes	30.5% (517)
Commute >45 minutes	21.5% (532)

See pages 37-130 for explanations of statistics, stars, and ranks.

Douglas, GA
(Coffee County, GA)

POPULATION

2010 census	42,356 (285)
2015 estimate	43,108 (278)
2010-2015 change	1.8% (142)
2020 projection	43,606 (277)
2030 projection	44,458 (269)

RACE

Whites	59.3% (449)
Blacks	28.2% (61)
Hispanics	10.9% (139)
Asians	0.6% (291)
Native Americans	0.1% (402)

AGE

0-17 years old	25.1% (116)
18-24 years old	11.4% (104)
25-39 years old	20.3% (54)
40-54 years old	20.2% (202)
55-64 years old	11.1% (492)
65+ years old	12.0% (495)

PRIVATE SECTOR

Businesses	891 (320)
Employees	13,351 (263)
Total wages	$426,410,782 (307)
Average weekly wages	$614 (461)

HOUSEHOLD INCOME LADDER

95th percentile	$143,677 (246)
80th percentile	$70,660 (501)
60th percentile	$41,083 (515)
40th percentile	$25,922 (500)
20th percentile	$12,993 (504)

CHILDREN ★ (496)

Living with two parents	51.3% (498)
Older teens in school	82.0% (319)
Speak English very well	96.1% (446)
Poverty rate for children	35.6% (483)
No health insurance	10.3% (428)

DIVERSITY/EQUALITY ★★ (406)

Racial diversity index	55.7% (42)
Geographic diversity index	36.6% (414)
Top 20% share of income	53.6% (530)
Gender gap in earnings	16.3% (18)
White-collar gender gap	58.2% (538)

EDUCATION ★ (479)

Eighth grade or less	4.4% (346)
High school diplomas	79.3% (494)
Attended college	40.0% (515)
Bachelor's degrees	14.0% (462)
Advanced degrees	4.9% (396)

EMPLOYMENT ★★★★★ (110)

Average jobless rate	8.3% (314)
Self-employed workers	9.9% (171)
Management/financial jobs	12.2% (139)
Computer/engineering jobs	1.3% (519)
Health care jobs	8.5% (8)

GROWTH POTENTIAL ★★★★ (168)

Children per senior	2.08 (49)
Median age	35.2 (98)
Moved from different state	1.5% (406)
Homes built since 2000	16.8% (159)
Construction jobs	4.7% (487)

HOUSING ★ (449)

Home vacancy rate	14.1% (520)
Home ownership rate	66.7% (399)
Housing diversity index	83.3% (402)
4 or more bedrooms	17.2% (236)
Affordability/income ratio	$2,455 (232)

INCOME ★ (501)

Poverty rate	25.5% (480)
Median household income	$33,965 (498)
Interest/dividends	10.9% (512)
Public assistance	20.0% (430)
Median fulltime earnings	$30,751 (532)

SENIORS ★ (523)

Seniors living alone	30.8% (462)
Poverty rate for seniors	21.1% (543)
Median income for seniors	$24,700 (506)
Seniors who work	18.7% (259)
Home ownership by seniors	82.7% (236)

STABILITY ★★★★★ (21)

25-39 age group	20.3% (54)
Born in state of residence	78.9% (136)
Same house as 1 year ago	90.3% (39)
Live and work in county	86.3% (111)
Married-couple households	44.4% (477)

TRANSPORTATION ★★ (360)

Bicycle or walk to work	2.0% (386)
Carpool to work	9.9% (348)
Public transit to work	0.6% (141)
Commute <15 minutes	36.7% (405)
Commute >45 minutes	9.7% (214)

See pages 37-130 for explanations of statistics, stars, and ranks.

Dublin, GA
(Johnson and Laurens Counties, GA)

POPULATION	
2010 census	58,414 (159)
2015 estimate	57,387 (163)
2010-2015 change	-1.8% (389)
2020 projection	56,551 (166)
2030 projection	54,761 (188)

RACE	
Whites	59.9% (447)
Blacks	35.8% (38)
Hispanics	2.1% (416)
Asians	1.2% (125)
Native Americans	0.1% (402)

AGE	
0-17 years old	24.0% (184)
18-24 years old	9.1% (251)
25-39 years old	18.7% (127)
40-54 years old	19.5% (301)
55-64 years old	12.9% (343)
65+ years old	15.8% (305)

PRIVATE SECTOR	
Businesses	1,151 (216)
Employees	14,349 (224)
Total wages	$475,742,111 (265)
Average weekly wages	$638 (417)

HOUSEHOLD INCOME LADDER	
95th percentile	$131,960 (403)
80th percentile	$74,832 (458)
60th percentile	$42,448 (503)
40th percentile	$23,945 (523)
20th percentile	$12,110 (515)

CHILDREN	★★ (438)
Living with two parents	55.9% (474)
Older teens in school	79.9% (401)
Speak English very well	99.5% (96)
Poverty rate for children	38.0% (501)
No health insurance	7.3% (333)

DIVERSITY/EQUALITY	★ (495)
Racial diversity index	51.2% (103)
Geographic diversity index	31.2% (474)
Top 20% share of income	53.4% (529)
Gender gap in earnings	33.2% (264)
White-collar gender gap	40.4% (449)

EDUCATION	★★ (427)
Eighth grade or less	4.7% (366)
High school diplomas	82.4% (433)
Attended college	40.4% (507)
Bachelor's degrees	14.6% (435)
Advanced degrees	7.1% (176)

EMPLOYMENT	★★★★ (114)
Average jobless rate	7.0% (196)
Self-employed workers	10.7% (129)
Management/financial jobs	10.8% (280)
Computer/engineering jobs	1.7% (470)
Health care jobs	7.8% (28)

GROWTH POTENTIAL	★★★ (276)
Children per senior	1.52 (208)
Median age	38.7 (211)
Moved from different state	1.1% (487)
Homes built since 2000	13.3% (263)
Construction jobs	6.7% (219)

HOUSING	★ (466)
Home vacancy rate	13.2% (497)
Home ownership rate	64.8% (438)
Housing diversity index	84.8% (248)
4 or more bedrooms	12.9% (458)
Affordability/income ratio	$2,467 (240)

INCOME	★ (494)
Poverty rate	26.8% (500)
Median household income	$32,594 (512)
Interest/dividends	11.8% (497)
Public assistance	21.2% (461)
Median fulltime earnings	$34,806 (396)

SENIORS	★ (503)
Seniors living alone	28.6% (336)
Poverty rate for seniors	15.4% (495)
Median income for seniors	$25,957 (495)
Seniors who work	15.9% (418)
Home ownership by seniors	80.3% (365)

STABILITY	★★★★ (152)
25-39 age group	18.7% (127)
Born in state of residence	82.4% (77)
Same house as 1 year ago	87.2% (190)
Live and work in county	75.0% (289)
Married-couple households	45.7% (449)

TRANSPORTATION	★★ (432)
Bicycle or walk to work	1.7% (428)
Carpool to work	11.8% (152)
Public transit to work	0.2% (363)
Commute <15 minutes	35.2% (437)
Commute >45 minutes	14.6% (414)

See pages 37-130 for explanations of statistics, stars, and ranks.

Dumas, TX
(Moore County, TX)

POPULATION

2010 census	21,904 (511)
2015 estimate	22,255 (506)
2010-2015 change	1.6% (157)
2020 projection	22,555 (501)
2030 projection	23,111 (491)

RACE

Whites	35.0% (522)
Blacks	2.5% (253)
Hispanics	52.6% (25)
Asians	8.5% (3)
Native Americans	0.4% (203)

AGE

0-17 years old	31.7% (9)
18-24 years old	10.4% (144)
25-39 years old	20.8% (47)
40-54 years old	17.6% (470)
55-64 years old	9.9% (524)
65+ years old	9.5% (539)

PRIVATE SECTOR

Businesses	487 (518)
Employees	8,941 (415)
Total wages	$393,027,381 (346)
Average weekly wages	$845 (54)

HOUSEHOLD INCOME LADDER

95th percentile	$148,198 (182)
80th percentile	$89,521 (161)
60th percentile	$57,224 (201)
40th percentile	$40,989 (99)
20th percentile	$27,015 (23)

CHILDREN ★ (515)

Living with two parents	64.4% (283)
Older teens in school	80.9% (370)
Speak English very well	89.9% (529)
Poverty rate for children	31.5% (435)
No health insurance	13.0% (496)

DIVERSITY/EQUALITY ★★★★ (120)

Racial diversity index	59.3% (17)
Geographic diversity index	65.2% (72)
Top 20% share of income	43.7% (16)
Gender gap in earnings	38.4% (406)
White-collar gender gap	62.7% (545)

EDUCATION ★ (543)

Eighth grade or less	24.0% (548)
High school diplomas	64.0% (547)
Attended college	38.8% (526)
Bachelor's degrees	11.8% (519)
Advanced degrees	2.3% (548)

EMPLOYMENT ★ (462)

Average jobless rate	4.1% (35)
Self-employed workers	7.5% (385)
Management/financial jobs	9.0% (475)
Computer/engineering jobs	1.4% (510)
Health care jobs	3.5% (512)

GROWTH POTENTIAL ★★★★★ (90)

Children per senior	3.32 (7)
Median age	31.1 (39)
Moved from different state	1.6% (383)
Homes built since 2000	11.8% (321)
Construction jobs	5.2% (442)

HOUSING ★★ (394)

Home vacancy rate	11.3% (426)
Home ownership rate	67.5% (368)
Housing diversity index	83.9% (360)
4 or more bedrooms	11.2% (518)
Affordability/income ratio	$1,867 (26)

INCOME ★★ (343)

Poverty rate	20.1% (373)
Median household income	$49,802 (131)
Interest/dividends	13.4% (458)
Public assistance	14.3% (220)
Median fulltime earnings	$33,712 (431)

SENIORS ★★★★★ (42)

Seniors living alone	20.4% (18)
Poverty rate for seniors	11.1% (378)
Median income for seniors	$36,578 (132)
Seniors who work	25.4% (63)
Home ownership by seniors	85.0% (142)

STABILITY ★★★★★ (5)

25-39 age group	20.8% (47)
Born in state of residence	53.4% (471)
Same house as 1 year ago	84.2% (341)
Live and work in county	90.9% (54)
Married-couple households	63.0% (4)

TRANSPORTATION ★★★★★ (58)

Bicycle or walk to work	1.7% (428)
Carpool to work	18.9% (7)
Public transit to work	0.4% (219)
Commute <15 minutes	52.6% (115)
Commute >45 minutes	7.0% (86)

See pages 37-130 for explanations of statistics, stars, and ranks.

Duncan, OK
(Stephens County, OK)

POPULATION

2010 census	45,048 (261)
2015 estimate	44,581 (267)
2010-2015 change	-1.0% (326)
2020 projection	44,478 (267)
2030 projection	44,233 (271)

RACE

Whites	81.4% (311)
Blacks	1.9% (295)
Hispanics	6.8% (203)
Asians	0.6% (291)
Native Americans	5.7% (30)

AGE

0-17 years old	23.9% (194)
18-24 years old	8.0% (407)
25-39 years old	17.9% (214)
40-54 years old	18.7% (399)
55-64 years old	13.8% (203)
65+ years old	17.7% (142)

PRIVATE SECTOR

Businesses	1,088 (249)
Employees	13,634 (250)
Total wages	$593,419,177 (191)
Average weekly wages	$837 (58)

HOUSEHOLD INCOME LADDER

95th percentile	$149,452 (168)
80th percentile	$87,237 (195)
60th percentile	$55,049 (247)
40th percentile	$34,324 (277)
20th percentile	$18,444 (293)

CHILDREN ★★★★ (140)

Living with two parents	70.6% (128)
Older teens in school	86.0% (166)
Speak English very well	99.1% (179)
Poverty rate for children	21.0% (193)
No health insurance	7.2% (330)

DIVERSITY/EQUALITY ★★ (413)

Racial diversity index	32.8% (228)
Geographic diversity index	54.0% (164)
Top 20% share of income	49.5% (397)
Gender gap in earnings	45.0% (500)
White-collar gender gap	34.7% (387)

EDUCATION ★★★ (330)

Eighth grade or less	2.9% (217)
High school diplomas	87.5% (286)
Attended college	49.6% (342)
Bachelor's degrees	18.0% (284)
Advanced degrees	4.2% (466)

EMPLOYMENT ★★★★ (176)

Average jobless rate	6.6% (161)
Self-employed workers	9.0% (254)
Management/financial jobs	11.6% (196)
Computer/engineering jobs	4.0% (76)
Health care jobs	4.9% (355)

GROWTH POTENTIAL ★★ (342)

Children per senior	1.35 (313)
Median age	40.1 (309)
Moved from different state	2.5% (203)
Homes built since 2000	9.8% (395)
Construction jobs	6.4% (270)

HOUSING ★★★ (309)

Home vacancy rate	11.7% (451)
Home ownership rate	70.3% (256)
Housing diversity index	86.0% (71)
4 or more bedrooms	11.9% (500)
Affordability/income ratio	$2,248 (141)

INCOME ★★★ (245)

Poverty rate	15.3% (204)
Median household income	$43,781 (269)
Interest/dividends	20.1% (241)
Public assistance	14.2% (215)
Median fulltime earnings	$36,297 (318)

SENIORS ★★★ (318)

Seniors living alone	27.8% (283)
Poverty rate for seniors	10.0% (321)
Median income for seniors	$31,080 (367)
Seniors who work	17.9% (292)
Home ownership by seniors	83.2% (210)

STABILITY ★★★ (256)

25-39 age group	17.9% (214)
Born in state of residence	65.2% (383)
Same house as 1 year ago	81.9% (450)
Live and work in county	81.8% (186)
Married-couple households	52.6% (167)

TRANSPORTATION ★★★ (266)

Bicycle or walk to work	2.2% (358)
Carpool to work	11.5% (184)
Public transit to work	0.6% (141)
Commute <15 minutes	45.1% (245)
Commute >45 minutes	10.9% (268)

See pages 37-130 for explanations of statistics, stars, and ranks.

Dunn, NC
(Harnett County, NC)

POPULATION			
2010 census	114,678 (14)	Attended college	58.6% (153)
2015 estimate	128,140 (12)	Bachelor's degrees	20.9% (192)
2010-2015 change	11.7% (9)	Advanced degrees	6.6% (211)
2020 projection	140,046 (9)	**EMPLOYMENT**	**★★★ (292)**
2030 projection	166,598 (4)	Average jobless rate	11.3% (466)

POPULATION

2010 census	114,678 (14)
2015 estimate	128,140 (12)
2010-2015 change	11.7% (9)
2020 projection	140,046 (9)
2030 projection	166,598 (4)

RACE

Whites	62.8% (429)
Blacks	20.4% (77)
Hispanics	11.7% (128)
Asians	1.1% (139)
Native Americans	1.0% (103)

AGE

0-17 years old	27.4% (39)
18-24 years old	9.8% (176)
25-39 years old	21.9% (22)
40-54 years old	19.7% (273)
55-64 years old	10.4% (506)
65+ years old	10.8% (515)

PRIVATE SECTOR

Businesses	1,652 (110)
Employees	18,053 (153)
Total wages	$557,988,687 (211)
Average weekly wages	$594 (495)

HOUSEHOLD INCOME LADDER

95th percentile	$142,417 (261)
80th percentile	$87,188 (198)
60th percentile	$56,900 (211)
40th percentile	$36,289 (223)
20th percentile	$20,321 (216)

CHILDREN ★★★★ (152)

Living with two parents	68.7% (174)
Older teens in school	85.9% (169)
Speak English very well	98.1% (331)
Poverty rate for children	24.0% (274)
No health insurance	4.4% (145)

DIVERSITY/EQUALITY ★★★★★ (71)

Racial diversity index	54.9% (56)
Geographic diversity index	64.8% (75)
Top 20% share of income	46.2% (139)
Gender gap in earnings	33.6% (271)
White-collar gender gap	37.8% (417)

EDUCATION ★★★★ (205)

Eighth grade or less	4.0% (325)
High school diplomas	87.9% (272)
Attended college	58.6% (153)
Bachelor's degrees	20.9% (192)
Advanced degrees	6.6% (211)

EMPLOYMENT ★★★ (292)

Average jobless rate	11.3% (466)
Self-employed workers	7.8% (355)
Management/financial jobs	12.5% (119)
Computer/engineering jobs	4.2% (66)
Health care jobs	5.2% (307)

GROWTH POTENTIAL ★★★★★ (7)

Children per senior	2.54 (29)
Median age	33.6 (66)
Moved from different state	5.0% (51)
Homes built since 2000	29.6% (13)
Construction jobs	9.7% (25)

HOUSING ★★ (422)

Home vacancy rate	10.1% (352)
Home ownership rate	65.9% (418)
Housing diversity index	81.4% (479)
4 or more bedrooms	19.3% (145)
Affordability/income ratio	$2,921 (386)

INCOME ★★★ (327)

Poverty rate	18.3% (309)
Median household income	$46,353 (205)
Interest/dividends	13.1% (467)
Public assistance	15.9% (290)
Median fulltime earnings	$36,968 (292)

SENIORS ★★ (371)

Seniors living alone	28.0% (296)
Poverty rate for seniors	12.1% (416)
Median income for seniors	$30,926 (376)
Seniors who work	18.2% (280)
Home ownership by seniors	82.7% (236)

STABILITY ★★ (438)

25-39 age group	21.9% (22)
Born in state of residence	55.7% (459)
Same house as 1 year ago	83.2% (388)
Live and work in county	37.2% (551)
Married-couple households	53.1% (148)

TRANSPORTATION ★ (547)

Bicycle or walk to work	1.1% (501)
Carpool to work	10.4% (289)
Public transit to work	0.1% (441)
Commute <15 minutes	20.1% (549)
Commute >45 minutes	21.2% (525)

See pages 37-130 for explanations of statistics, stars, and ranks.

Durant, OK
(Bryan County, OK)

POPULATION	
2010 census	42,416 (283)
2015 estimate	44,884 (263)
2010-2015 change	5.8% (34)
2020 projection	47,549 (235)
2030 projection	53,315 (193)

RACE	
Whites	72.6% (374)
Blacks	1.9% (295)
Hispanics	5.4% (240)
Asians	0.5% (355)
Native Americans	14.4% (11)

AGE	
0-17 years old	23.3% (246)
18-24 years old	10.7% (124)
25-39 years old	19.0% (104)
40-54 years old	18.3% (439)
55-64 years old	12.0% (438)
65+ years old	16.7% (225)

PRIVATE SECTOR	
Businesses	792 (378)
Employees	9,521 (390)
Total wages	$320,394,377 (408)
Average weekly wages	$647 (400)

HOUSEHOLD INCOME LADDER	
95th percentile	$133,927 (375)
80th percentile	$80,033 (368)
60th percentile	$48,197 (417)
40th percentile	$30,478 (402)
20th percentile	$16,262 (399)

CHILDREN	★★ (334)
Living with two parents	65.4% (260)
Older teens in school	84.5% (220)
Speak English very well	98.1% (331)
Poverty rate for children	23.1% (250)
No health insurance	12.6% (488)

DIVERSITY/EQUALITY	★★★★★ (52)
Racial diversity index	44.6% (156)
Geographic diversity index	62.6% (94)
Top 20% share of income	48.5% (321)
Gender gap in earnings	29.2% (156)
White-collar gender gap	10.7% (96)

EDUCATION	★★★ (234)
Eighth grade or less	3.6% (292)
High school diplomas	86.2% (333)
Attended college	52.8% (266)
Bachelor's degrees	22.3% (148)
Advanced degrees	7.2% (164)

EMPLOYMENT	★★★ (313)
Average jobless rate	8.1% (298)
Self-employed workers	9.2% (231)
Management/financial jobs	12.1% (149)
Computer/engineering jobs	1.8% (457)
Health care jobs	4.9% (355)

GROWTH POTENTIAL	★★★★★ (82)
Children per senior	1.39 (286)
Median age	37.1 (149)
Moved from different state	4.9% (57)
Homes built since 2000	23.7% (46)
Construction jobs	6.6% (241)

HOUSING	★ (441)
Home vacancy rate	10.7% (390)
Home ownership rate	64.6% (447)
Housing diversity index	84.0% (344)
4 or more bedrooms	11.7% (505)
Affordability/income ratio	$2,319 (174)

INCOME	★★ (387)
Poverty rate	18.3% (309)
Median household income	$38,847 (409)
Interest/dividends	13.8% (446)
Public assistance	15.7% (280)
Median fulltime earnings	$34,554 (402)

SENIORS	★★ (390)
Seniors living alone	29.1% (371)
Poverty rate for seniors	9.6% (295)
Median income for seniors	$31,329 (358)
Seniors who work	16.4% (383)
Home ownership by seniors	81.6% (299)

STABILITY	★ (444)
25-39 age group	19.0% (104)
Born in state of residence	51.7% (479)
Same house as 1 year ago	82.6% (416)
Live and work in county	76.2% (269)
Married-couple households	48.0% (378)

TRANSPORTATION	★★★ (263)
Bicycle or walk to work	2.3% (348)
Carpool to work	11.8% (152)
Public transit to work	0.5% (178)
Commute <15 minutes	43.5% (270)
Commute >45 minutes	10.1% (228)

See pages 37-130 for explanations of statistics, stars, and ranks.

Dyersburg, TN
(Dyer County, TN)

POPULATION

2010 census	38,335 (337)
2015 estimate	37,893 (346)
2010-2015 change	-1.2% (345)
2020 projection	37,375 (351)
2030 projection	36,240 (356)

RACE

Whites	80.3% (323)
Blacks	13.3% (95)
Hispanics	3.0% (343)
Asians	0.6% (291)
Native Americans	0.2% (300)

AGE

0-17 years old	24.4% (155)
18-24 years old	8.7% (299)
25-39 years old	16.5% (403)
40-54 years old	21.5% (57)
55-64 years old	13.2% (297)
65+ years old	15.8% (305)

PRIVATE SECTOR

Businesses	757 (396)
Employees	13,104 (276)
Total wages	$481,190,058 (259)
Average weekly wages	$706 (240)

HOUSEHOLD INCOME LADDER

95th percentile	$147,808 (186)
80th percentile	$81,404 (340)
60th percentile	$55,735 (232)
40th percentile	$33,216 (316)
20th percentile	$17,830 (326)

CHILDREN ★★★ (227)

Living with two parents	61.3% (373)
Older teens in school	83.0% (276)
Speak English very well	98.6% (278)
Poverty rate for children	25.1% (302)
No health insurance	3.6% (93)

DIVERSITY/EQUALITY ★ (473)

Racial diversity index	33.6% (222)
Geographic diversity index	45.5% (271)
Top 20% share of income	49.0% (355)
Gender gap in earnings	39.3% (425)
White-collar gender gap	49.1% (507)

EDUCATION ★★★ (224)

Eighth grade or less	3.4% (269)
High school diplomas	88.2% (260)
Attended college	48.5% (371)
Bachelor's degrees	21.4% (180)
Advanced degrees	8.4% (106)

EMPLOYMENT ★★★ (276)

Average jobless rate	6.6% (161)
Self-employed workers	6.1% (495)
Management/financial jobs	10.1% (365)
Computer/engineering jobs	2.5% (307)
Health care jobs	7.0% (69)

GROWTH POTENTIAL ★★★★ (207)

Children per senior	1.54 (197)
Median age	40.3 (319)
Moved from different state	3.3% (129)
Homes built since 2000	14.7% (210)
Construction jobs	6.6% (241)

HOUSING ★★★ (262)

Home vacancy rate	8.1% (227)
Home ownership rate	64.3% (451)
Housing diversity index	86.0% (71)
4 or more bedrooms	13.9% (406)
Affordability/income ratio	$2,326 (178)

INCOME ★★ (353)

Poverty rate	17.8% (292)
Median household income	$42,468 (300)
Interest/dividends	13.5% (456)
Public assistance	18.5% (385)
Median fulltime earnings	$37,918 (224)

SENIORS ★ (505)

Seniors living alone	28.1% (306)
Poverty rate for seniors	15.2% (493)
Median income for seniors	$28,511 (446)
Seniors who work	12.5% (535)
Home ownership by seniors	80.3% (365)

STABILITY ★★ (343)

25-39 age group	16.5% (403)
Born in state of residence	72.1% (273)
Same house as 1 year ago	83.0% (397)
Live and work in county	78.1% (243)
Married-couple households	50.4% (278)

TRANSPORTATION ★ (479)

Bicycle or walk to work	1.1% (501)
Carpool to work	6.7% (536)
Public transit to work	0.0% (511)
Commute <15 minutes	46.8% (219)
Commute >45 minutes	13.3% (368)

See pages 37-130 for explanations of statistics, stars, and ranks.

Eagle Pass, TX
(Maverick County, TX)

POPULATION	
2010 census	54,258 (177)
2015 estimate	57,706 (160)
2010-2015 change	6.4% (28)
2020 projection	60,761 (143)
2030 projection	67,292 (117)

RACE	
Whites	3.1% (550)
Blacks	0.1% (544)
Hispanics	95.2% (2)
Asians	0.5% (355)
Native Americans	0.9% (115)

AGE	
0-17 years old	32.3% (6)
18-24 years old	11.5% (100)
25-39 years old	17.6% (248)
40-54 years old	17.9% (454)
55-64 years old	9.6% (536)
65+ years old	11.1% (509)

PRIVATE SECTOR	
Businesses	825 (360)
Employees	11,512 (326)
Total wages	$291,778,525 (443)
Average weekly wages	$487 (548)

HOUSEHOLD INCOME LADDER	
95th percentile	$138,387 (306)
80th percentile	$77,395 (411)
60th percentile	$44,036 (491)
40th percentile	$25,575 (506)
20th percentile	$14,039 (474)

CHILDREN	★ (542)
Living with two parents	62.6% (330)
Older teens in school	83.0% (276)
Speak English very well	74.1% (549)
Poverty rate for children	34.9% (477)
No health insurance	21.4% (549)

DIVERSITY/EQUALITY	★ (538)
Racial diversity index	9.3% (509)
Geographic diversity index	62.0% (103)
Top 20% share of income	51.0% (471)
Gender gap in earnings	41.3% (462)
White-collar gender gap	57.0% (534)

EDUCATION	★ (541)
Eighth grade or less	18.0% (541)
High school diplomas	66.3% (544)
Attended college	41.5% (497)
Bachelor's degrees	11.9% (517)
Advanced degrees	2.9% (534)

EMPLOYMENT	★ (550)
Average jobless rate	13.1% (518)
Self-employed workers	7.9% (345)
Management/financial jobs	7.9% (530)
Computer/engineering jobs	0.6% (550)
Health care jobs	2.7% (542)

GROWTH POTENTIAL	★★★★★ (22)
Children per senior	2.91 (19)
Median age	29.9 (27)
Moved from different state	2.3% (234)
Homes built since 2000	29.1% (14)
Construction jobs	6.2% (295)

HOUSING	★★ (407)
Home vacancy rate	9.1% (296)
Home ownership rate	70.0% (272)
Housing diversity index	81.2% (491)
4 or more bedrooms	14.3% (387)
Affordability/income ratio	$2,628 (301)

INCOME	★ (538)
Poverty rate	26.7% (499)
Median household income	$33,747 (501)
Interest/dividends	7.8% (544)
Public assistance	33.1% (545)
Median fulltime earnings	$31,118 (525)

SENIORS	★ (530)
Seniors living alone	22.1% (39)
Poverty rate for seniors	34.1% (551)
Median income for seniors	$17,382 (529)
Seniors who work	15.5% (436)
Home ownership by seniors	78.0% (454)

STABILITY	★★★★★ (98)
25-39 age group	17.6% (248)
Born in state of residence	56.3% (454)
Same house as 1 year ago	88.1% (126)
Live and work in county	81.7% (191)
Married-couple households	57.1% (29)

TRANSPORTATION	★★★★ (153)
Bicycle or walk to work	2.5% (322)
Carpool to work	17.2% (23)
Public transit to work	0.5% (178)
Commute <15 minutes	48.8% (178)
Commute >45 minutes	15.6% (443)

See pages 37-130 for explanations of statistics, stars, and ranks.

El Campo, TX
(Wharton County, TX)

POPULATION

2010 census	41,280 (298)
2015 estimate	41,486 (294)
2010-2015 change	0.5% (219)
2020 projection	41,242 (296)
2030 projection	40,769 (308)

RACE

Whites	46.1% (500)
Blacks	14.2% (92)
Hispanics	39.2% (40)
Asians	0.1% (529)
Native Americans	0.0% (523)

AGE

0-17 years old	26.1% (66)
18-24 years old	9.2% (234)
25-39 years old	17.8% (227)
40-54 years old	18.6% (412)
55-64 years old	12.9% (343)
65+ years old	15.4% (344)

PRIVATE SECTOR

Businesses	1,070 (254)
Employees	12,785 (287)
Total wages	$469,767,087 (275)
Average weekly wages	$707 (238)

HOUSEHOLD INCOME LADDER

95th percentile	$150,088 (162)
80th percentile	$86,349 (226)
60th percentile	$55,127 (245)
40th percentile	$35,727 (241)
20th percentile	$17,409 (347)

CHILDREN ★ (451)

Living with two parents	58.8% (433)
Older teens in school	78.6% (437)
Speak English very well	96.2% (443)
Poverty rate for children	28.4% (376)
No health insurance	9.8% (417)

DIVERSITY/EQUALITY ★★★★ (207)

Racial diversity index	61.4% (11)
Geographic diversity index	30.1% (485)
Top 20% share of income	47.9% (289)
Gender gap in earnings	38.1% (396)
White-collar gender gap	20.0% (207)

EDUCATION ★ (495)

Eighth grade or less	9.8% (510)
High school diplomas	80.3% (475)

Attended college	45.8% (426)
Bachelor's degrees	14.8% (429)
Advanced degrees	4.5% (442)

EMPLOYMENT ★★★ (322)

Average jobless rate	6.6% (161)
Self-employed workers	9.5% (207)
Management/financial jobs	12.1% (149)
Computer/engineering jobs	1.5% (499)
Health care jobs	4.2% (454)

GROWTH POTENTIAL ★★★★ (173)

Children per senior	1.69 (137)
Median age	37.3 (157)
Moved from different state	0.6% (546)
Homes built since 2000	11.0% (358)
Construction jobs	8.8% (55)

HOUSING ★★ (331)

Home vacancy rate	12.1% (463)
Home ownership rate	67.7% (356)
Housing diversity index	86.8% (3)
4 or more bedrooms	11.6% (510)
Affordability/income ratio	$2,264 (146)

INCOME ★★★ (306)

Poverty rate	17.6% (287)
Median household income	$45,176 (233)
Interest/dividends	16.2% (369)
Public assistance	14.5% (234)
Median fulltime earnings	$35,090 (379)

SENIORS ★ (472)

Seniors living alone	32.8% (526)
Poverty rate for seniors	13.4% (457)
Median income for seniors	$28,871 (440)
Seniors who work	21.4% (148)
Home ownership by seniors	80.4% (362)

STABILITY ★★★★★ (65)

25-39 age group	17.8% (227)
Born in state of residence	83.2% (66)
Same house as 1 year ago	92.2% (13)
Live and work in county	73.7% (320)
Married-couple households	47.5% (399)

TRANSPORTATION ★★ (370)

Bicycle or walk to work	1.6% (443)
Carpool to work	12.2% (132)
Public transit to work	0.3% (291)
Commute <15 minutes	44.5% (254)
Commute >45 minutes	16.0% (453)

See pages 37-130 for explanations of statistics, stars, and ranks.

El Dorado, AR
(Union County, AR)

POPULATION
2010 census	41,639 (293)
2015 estimate	40,144 (312)
2010-2015 change	-3.6% (510)
2020 projection	38,138 (339)
2030 projection	34,117 (389)

RACE
Whites	61.5% (438)
Blacks	32.8% (45)
Hispanics	3.6% (314)
Asians	0.5% (355)
Native Americans	0.5% (174)

AGE
0-17 years old	23.8% (206)
18-24 years old	8.1% (396)
25-39 years old	18.6% (135)
40-54 years old	19.3% (323)
55-64 years old	13.8% (203)
65+ years old	16.4% (255)

PRIVATE SECTOR
Businesses	1,284 (181)
Employees	15,941 (195)
Total wages	$775,840,681 (123)
Average weekly wages	$936 (24)

HOUSEHOLD INCOME LADDER
95th percentile	$135,803 (345)
80th percentile	$81,468 (338)
60th percentile	$50,535 (369)
40th percentile	$30,732 (395)
20th percentile	$15,657 (424)

CHILDREN ★★ (348)
Living with two parents	56.9% (461)
Older teens in school	83.1% (271)
Speak English very well	98.4% (300)
Poverty rate for children	31.8% (441)
No health insurance	5.4% (209)

DIVERSITY/EQUALITY ★★★★ (189)
Racial diversity index	51.3% (102)
Geographic diversity index	43.4% (306)
Top 20% share of income	49.6% (404)
Gender gap in earnings	35.7% (331)
White-collar gender gap	15.7% (159)

EDUCATION ★★★ (325)
Eighth grade or less	3.4% (269)
High school diplomas	85.6% (357)
Attended college	50.6% (311)
Bachelor's degrees	18.8% (259)
Advanced degrees	5.1% (364)

EMPLOYMENT ★★★ (231)
Average jobless rate	9.7% (409)
Self-employed workers	6.8% (446)
Management/financial jobs	11.1% (240)
Computer/engineering jobs	3.2% (158)
Health care jobs	7.5% (44)

GROWTH POTENTIAL ★★★ (240)
Children per senior	1.46 (237)
Median age	39.7 (279)
Moved from different state	2.2% (248)
Homes built since 2000	11.3% (344)
Construction jobs	7.6% (110)

HOUSING ★★★ (244)
Home vacancy rate	11.1% (409)
Home ownership rate	70.9% (232)
Housing diversity index	86.1% (51)
4 or more bedrooms	12.2% (487)
Affordability/income ratio	$1,929 (36)

INCOME ★★ (368)
Poverty rate	20.4% (388)
Median household income	$38,678 (413)
Interest/dividends	16.6% (357)
Public assistance	17.0% (334)
Median fulltime earnings	$37,079 (279)

SENIORS ★★★ (300)
Seniors living alone	28.0% (296)
Poverty rate for seniors	10.4% (342)
Median income for seniors	$31,032 (369)
Seniors who work	17.9% (292)
Home ownership by seniors	84.5% (165)

STABILITY ★★★★★ (66)
25-39 age group	18.6% (135)
Born in state of residence	73.2% (258)
Same house as 1 year ago	86.8% (206)
Live and work in county	90.8% (56)
Married-couple households	47.8% (390)

TRANSPORTATION ★★ (362)
Bicycle or walk to work	1.7% (428)
Carpool to work	8.0% (493)
Public transit to work	0.1% (441)
Commute <15 minutes	42.9% (280)
Commute >45 minutes	6.7% (77)

See pages 37-130 for explanations of statistics, stars, and ranks.

Elizabeth City, NC
(Camden, Pasquotank, and Perquimans Counties, NC)

POPULATION

2010 census	64,094 (127)
2015 estimate	63,578 (131)
2010-2015 change	-0.8% (314)
2020 projection	64,012 (129)
2030 projection	64,736 (130)

RACE

Whites	62.5% (432)
Blacks	30.5% (53)
Hispanics	3.7% (311)
Asians	1.4% (99)
Native Americans	0.2% (300)

AGE

0-17 years old	22.0% (335)
18-24 years old	9.8% (176)
25-39 years old	18.2% (167)
40-54 years old	20.2% (202)
55-64 years old	13.1% (318)
65+ years old	16.7% (225)

PRIVATE SECTOR

Businesses	1,312 (173)
Employees	13,765 (244)
Total wages	$470,218,983 (274)
Average weekly wages	$657 (373)

HOUSEHOLD INCOME LADDER

95th percentile	$148,491 (178)
80th percentile	$89,798 (156)
60th percentile	$57,225 (200)
40th percentile	$36,739 (209)
20th percentile	$18,554 (287)

CHILDREN ★★★ (242)

Living with two parents	59.2% (424)
Older teens in school	89.1% (78)
Speak English very well	98.5% (287)
Poverty rate for children	27.6% (357)
No health insurance	6.1% (258)

DIVERSITY/EQUALITY ★★★★★ (70)

Racial diversity index	51.5% (100)
Geographic diversity index	64.0% (84)
Top 20% share of income	47.5% (258)
Gender gap in earnings	36.2% (346)
White-collar gender gap	21.8% (234)

EDUCATION ★★★ (229)

Eighth grade or less	3.7% (303)
High school diplomas	87.3% (296)
Attended college	58.6% (153)
Bachelor's degrees	19.8% (224)
Advanced degrees	6.0% (264)

EMPLOYMENT ★★★ (317)

Average jobless rate	10.5% (441)
Self-employed workers	6.9% (435)
Management/financial jobs	11.4% (210)
Computer/engineering jobs	3.8% (96)
Health care jobs	5.9% (193)

GROWTH POTENTIAL ★★★★ (127)

Children per senior	1.32 (334)
Median age	40.0 (303)
Moved from different state	3.2% (136)
Homes built since 2000	22.3% (66)
Construction jobs	7.6% (110)

HOUSING ★★ (352)

Home vacancy rate	12.1% (463)
Home ownership rate	69.5% (287)
Housing diversity index	85.7% (108)
4 or more bedrooms	18.0% (202)
Affordability/income ratio	$3,607 (471)

INCOME ★★★ (280)

Poverty rate	17.4% (283)
Median household income	$46,386 (204)
Interest/dividends	17.1% (343)
Public assistance	18.9% (397)
Median fulltime earnings	$38,985 (179)

SENIORS ★★★★★ (107)

Seniors living alone	24.2% (89)
Poverty rate for seniors	9.1% (263)
Median income for seniors	n.a.
Seniors who work	17.7% (302)
Home ownership by seniors	86.1% (93)

STABILITY ★★ (429)

25-39 age group	18.2% (167)
Born in state of residence	54.0% (468)
Same house as 1 year ago	88.3% (115)
Live and work in county	54.9% (522)
Married-couple households	52.9% (157)

TRANSPORTATION ★ (525)

Bicycle or walk to work	2.2% (358)
Carpool to work	11.8% (152)
Public transit to work	0.4% (219)
Commute <15 minutes	32.4% (487)
Commute >45 minutes	23.5% (541)

See pages 37-130 for explanations of statistics, stars, and ranks.

Elk City, OK
(Beckham County, OK)

POPULATION		Attended college	44.3% (450)
2010 census	22,119 (509)	Bachelor's degrees	18.1% (282)
2015 estimate	23,768 (491)	Advanced degrees	5.8% (283)
2010-2015 change	7.5% (17)		
2020 projection	25,204 (478)	**EMPLOYMENT**	★★★★ (202)
2030 projection	28,318 (438)	Average jobless rate	2.9% (8)
		Self-employed workers	10.4% (145)
RACE		Management/financial jobs	10.9% (263)
Whites	76.7% (347)	Computer/engineering jobs	2.1% (399)
Blacks	3.4% (214)	Health care jobs	4.0% (476)
Hispanics	13.5% (115)		
Asians	0.9% (178)	**GROWTH POTENTIAL**	★★★★★ (87)
Native Americans	1.0% (103)	Children per senior	2.03 (57)
		Median age	34.7 (86)
AGE		Moved from different state	3.2% (136)
0-17 years old	25.3% (97)	Homes built since 2000	17.3% (149)
18-24 years old	9.3% (217)	Construction jobs	6.5% (253)
25-39 years old	22.4% (17)		
40-54 years old	19.1% (354)	**HOUSING**	★ (509)
55-64 years old	11.6% (471)	Home vacancy rate	21.2% (550)
65+ years old	12.4% (487)	Home ownership rate	63.9% (456)
		Housing diversity index	85.8% (97)
PRIVATE SECTOR		4 or more bedrooms	12.8% (462)
Businesses	850 (345)	Affordability/income ratio	$2,518 (257)
Employees	9,810 (382)		
Total wages	$450,016,173 (293)	**INCOME**	★★★★ (134)
Average weekly wages	$882 (41)	Poverty rate	13.0% (114)
		Median household income	$48,601 (157)
HOUSEHOLD INCOME LADDER		Interest/dividends	18.0% (313)
95th percentile	$201,552 (17)	Public assistance	9.4% (51)
80th percentile	$101,693 (50)	Median fulltime earnings	$40,915 (102)
60th percentile	$66,173 (65)		
40th percentile	$36,781 (207)	**SENIORS**	★★★★ (213)
20th percentile	$22,832 (103)	Seniors living alone	21.3% (26)
		Poverty rate for seniors	9.6% (295)
CHILDREN	★★★ (330)	Median income for seniors	$28,681 (444)
Living with two parents	67.3% (209)	Seniors who work	22.5% (120)
Older teens in school	70.9% (527)	Home ownership by seniors	77.2% (478)
Speak English very well	98.8% (251)		
Poverty rate for children	12.3% (33)	**STABILITY**	★★★★★ (10)
No health insurance	10.3% (428)	25-39 age group	22.4% (17)
		Born in state of residence	62.5% (407)
DIVERSITY/EQUALITY	★★★ (308)	Same house as 1 year ago	87.6% (157)
Racial diversity index	39.0% (190)	Live and work in county	86.1% (113)
Geographic diversity index	56.9% (141)	Married-couple households	50.7% (264)
Top 20% share of income	52.2% (507)		
Gender gap in earnings	35.2% (318)	**TRANSPORTATION**	★★★ (221)
White-collar gender gap	25.7% (284)	Bicycle or walk to work	1.3% (485)
		Carpool to work	10.3% (299)
EDUCATION	★★ (405)	Public transit to work	0.1% (441)
Eighth grade or less	6.2% (433)	Commute <15 minutes	62.5% (34)
High school diplomas	84.6% (387)	Commute >45 minutes	10.5% (254)

See pages 37-130 for explanations of statistics, stars, and ranks.

Enterprise, AL
(Coffee County, AL)

POPULATION
2010 census	49,948 (211)
2015 estimate	51,211 (204)
2010-2015 change	2.5% (107)
2020 projection	52,672 (192)
2030 projection	55,447 (178)

RACE
Whites	71.5% (380)
Blacks	17.2% (85)
Hispanics	6.4% (210)
Asians	1.2% (125)
Native Americans	0.8% (125)

AGE
0-17 years old	23.8% (206)
18-24 years old	8.4% (349)
25-39 years old	19.5% (74)
40-54 years old	20.5% (151)
55-64 years old	12.3% (414)
65+ years old	15.4% (344)

PRIVATE SECTOR
Businesses	972 (286)
Employees	12,730 (289)
Total wages	$401,039,367 (335)
Average weekly wages	$606 (478)

HOUSEHOLD INCOME LADDER
95th percentile	$160,368 (92)
80th percentile	$98,707 (65)
60th percentile	$60,893 (133)
40th percentile	$35,651 (246)
20th percentile	$19,466 (246)

CHILDREN ★★★ (243)
Living with two parents	59.5% (415)
Older teens in school	87.1% (133)
Speak English very well	96.9% (419)
Poverty rate for children	26.4% (339)
No health insurance	3.7% (98)

DIVERSITY/EQUALITY ★★★★ (185)
Racial diversity index	45.4% (145)
Geographic diversity index	61.3% (114)
Top 20% share of income	47.7% (273)
Gender gap in earnings	41.3% (462)
White-collar gender gap	29.7% (333)

EDUCATION ★★★★ (152)
Eighth grade or less	3.6% (292)
High school diplomas	87.7% (280)
Attended college	58.7% (151)
Bachelor's degrees	25.2% (106)
Advanced degrees	8.6% (99)

EMPLOYMENT ★★★ (223)
Average jobless rate	7.1% (208)
Self-employed workers	7.3% (401)
Management/financial jobs	10.3% (339)
Computer/engineering jobs	2.8% (246)
Health care jobs	7.0% (69)

GROWTH POTENTIAL ★★★★★ (99)
Children per senior	1.54 (197)
Median age	38.8 (217)
Moved from different state	5.7% (33)
Homes built since 2000	23.9% (44)
Construction jobs	5.2% (442)

HOUSING ★★ (433)
Home vacancy rate	13.7% (512)
Home ownership rate	67.6% (362)
Housing diversity index	84.0% (344)
4 or more bedrooms	17.9% (209)
Affordability/income ratio	$3,047 (409)

INCOME ★★★ (250)
Poverty rate	17.1% (267)
Median household income	$46,729 (198)
Interest/dividends	17.5% (329)
Public assistance	13.8% (202)
Median fulltime earnings	$37,113 (277)

SENIORS ★★★★ (190)
Seniors living alone	27.6% (269)
Poverty rate for seniors	9.7% (301)
Median income for seniors	$35,437 (173)
Seniors who work	16.9% (348)
Home ownership by seniors	87.1% (69)

STABILITY ★★ (425)
25-39 age group	19.5% (74)
Born in state of residence	58.6% (431)
Same house as 1 year ago	84.3% (333)
Live and work in county	61.5% (480)
Married-couple households	49.9% (302)

TRANSPORTATION ★★ (420)
Bicycle or walk to work	1.1% (501)
Carpool to work	9.9% (348)
Public transit to work	0.1% (441)
Commute <15 minutes	34.5% (448)
Commute >45 minutes	8.6% (154)

See pages 37-130 for explanations of statistics, stars, and ranks.

Eufaula, AL-GA
(Barbour County, AL, and Quitman County, GA)

POPULATION	
2010 census	29,970 (435)
2015 estimate	28,791 (445)
2010-2015 change	-3.9% (517)
2020 projection	27,463 (454)
2030 projection	24,872 (472)

RACE	
Whites	46.5% (497)
Blacks	46.9% (20)
Hispanics	4.2% (287)
Asians	0.4% (413)
Native Americans	0.2% (300)

AGE	
0-17 years old	21.2% (397)
18-24 years old	8.7% (299)
25-39 years old	20.9% (44)
40-54 years old	19.2% (336)
55-64 years old	13.2% (297)
65+ years old	16.9% (207)

PRIVATE SECTOR	
Businesses	530 (505)
Employees	6,784 (481)
Total wages	$234,058,196 (479)
Average weekly wages	$663 (352)

HOUSEHOLD INCOME LADDER	
95th percentile	$118,251 (527)
80th percentile	$69,532 (510)
60th percentile	$40,985 (517)
40th percentile	$24,862 (512)
20th percentile	$12,769 (505)

CHILDREN	★ (517)
Living with two parents	42.9% (533)
Older teens in school	81.7% (337)
Speak English very well	97.0% (413)
Poverty rate for children	45.2% (535)
No health insurance	5.8% (236)

DIVERSITY/EQUALITY	★★★★★ (61)
Racial diversity index	56.2% (37)
Geographic diversity index	49.5% (217)
Top 20% share of income	49.3% (388)
Gender gap in earnings	27.9% (137)
White-collar gender gap	11.3% (100)

EDUCATION	★ (505)
Eighth grade or less	5.8% (413)
High school diplomas	76.5% (518)
Attended college	41.1% (501)
Bachelor's degrees	11.7% (521)
Advanced degrees	4.5% (442)

EMPLOYMENT	★ (536)
Average jobless rate	17.2% (546)
Self-employed workers	8.9% (266)
Management/financial jobs	9.3% (453)
Computer/engineering jobs	2.0% (420)
Health care jobs	4.5% (419)

GROWTH POTENTIAL	★★ (369)
Children per senior	1.26 (378)
Median age	39.6 (276)
Moved from different state	2.5% (203)
Homes built since 2000	11.4% (338)
Construction jobs	5.7% (373)

HOUSING	★ (465)
Home vacancy rate	14.3% (524)
Home ownership rate	64.7% (443)
Housing diversity index	84.7% (260)
4 or more bedrooms	16.4% (272)
Affordability/income ratio	$2,752 (347)

INCOME	★ (509)
Poverty rate	26.5% (495)
Median household income	$32,847 (507)
Interest/dividends	13.0% (472)
Public assistance	26.2% (519)
Median fulltime earnings	$32,796 (460)

SENIORS	★ (488)
Seniors living alone	28.0% (296)
Poverty rate for seniors	15.7% (498)
Median income for seniors	$27,079 (474)
Seniors who work	16.1% (400)
Home ownership by seniors	81.1% (325)

STABILITY	★★ (361)
25-39 age group	20.9% (44)
Born in state of residence	67.7% (352)
Same house as 1 year ago	85.0% (299)
Live and work in county	68.4% (400)
Married-couple households	42.8% (497)

TRANSPORTATION	★★ (402)
Bicycle or walk to work	1.9% (401)
Carpool to work	11.5% (184)
Public transit to work	0.4% (219)
Commute <15 minutes	38.8% (356)
Commute >45 minutes	15.2% (430)

See pages 37-130 for explanations of statistics, stars, and ranks.

Fitzgerald, GA
(Ben Hill County, GA)

POPULATION

2010 census	17,634 (533)
2015 estimate	17,403 (537)
2010-2015 change	-1.3% (355)
2020 projection	17,061 (540)
2030 projection	16,343 (538)

RACE

Whites	56.5% (467)
Blacks	35.7% (39)
Hispanics	6.2% (214)
Asians	0.0% (546)
Native Americans	0.0% (523)

AGE

0-17 years old	25.9% (72)
18-24 years old	9.1% (251)
25-39 years old	16.8% (359)
40-54 years old	20.2% (202)
55-64 years old	13.2% (297)
65+ years old	14.9% (374)

PRIVATE SECTOR

Businesses	337 (543)
Employees	4,380 (537)
Total wages	$132,710,993 (543)
Average weekly wages	$583 (511)

HOUSEHOLD INCOME LADDER

95th percentile	$107,834 (549)
80th percentile	$63,923 (536)
60th percentile	$38,798 (534)
40th percentile	$24,209 (518)
20th percentile	$9,697 (547)

CHILDREN ★ (543)

Living with two parents	47.2% (520)
Older teens in school	68.8% (535)
Speak English very well	100.0% (1)
Poverty rate for children	49.5% (542)
No health insurance	9.8% (417)

DIVERSITY/EQUALITY ★★★★ (171)

Racial diversity index	54.9% (56)
Geographic diversity index	40.2% (348)
Top 20% share of income	48.8% (344)
Gender gap in earnings	41.0% (456)
White-collar gender gap	8.4% (68)

EDUCATION ★ (480)

Eighth grade or less	3.4% (269)
High school diplomas	81.9% (449)
Attended college	41.0% (502)
Bachelor's degrees	11.3% (529)
Advanced degrees	3.5% (511)

EMPLOYMENT ★ (457)

Average jobless rate	9.7% (409)
Self-employed workers	7.5% (385)
Management/financial jobs	10.3% (339)
Computer/engineering jobs	2.0% (420)
Health care jobs	4.9% (355)

GROWTH POTENTIAL ★★★ (306)

Children per senior	1.74 (113)
Median age	38.6 (207)
Moved from different state	1.3% (452)
Homes built since 2000	13.5% (256)
Construction jobs	5.2% (442)

HOUSING ★ (525)

Home vacancy rate	16.8% (544)
Home ownership rate	63.9% (456)
Housing diversity index	84.7% (260)
4 or more bedrooms	12.7% (466)
Affordability/income ratio	$2,697 (329)

INCOME ★ (534)

Poverty rate	35.3% (542)
Median household income	$29,994 (536)
Interest/dividends	12.1% (489)
Public assistance	26.6% (523)
Median fulltime earnings	$34,181 (415)

SENIORS ★ (481)

Seniors living alone	24.6% (100)
Poverty rate for seniors	21.9% (544)
Median income for seniors	n.a.
Seniors who work	16.5% (376)
Home ownership by seniors	81.0% (335)

STABILITY ★★ (351)

25-39 age group	16.8% (359)
Born in state of residence	75.9% (207)
Same house as 1 year ago	88.9% (86)
Live and work in county	78.3% (239)
Married-couple households	41.2% (513)

TRANSPORTATION ★★★ (222)

Bicycle or walk to work	2.3% (348)
Carpool to work	11.5% (184)
Public transit to work	0.0% (511)
Commute <15 minutes	46.0% (233)
Commute >45 minutes	6.5% (71)

See pages 37-130 for explanations of statistics, stars, and ranks.

Forest City, NC
(Rutherford County, NC)

POPULATION			Attended college	52.1% (281)
2010 census	67,810 (108)		Bachelor's degrees	15.8% (391)
2015 estimate	66,390 (115)		Advanced degrees	5.4% (334)
2010-2015 change	-2.1% (418)		**EMPLOYMENT**	**★ (455)**
2020 projection	65,108 (123)		Average jobless rate	12.2% (497)
2030 projection	62,345 (136)		Self-employed workers	8.1% (323)
			Management/financial jobs	8.7% (493)
RACE			Computer/engineering jobs	2.3% (354)
Whites	83.9% (280)		Health care jobs	6.5% (121)
Blacks	10.0% (114)			
Hispanics	3.9% (302)		**GROWTH POTENTIAL**	**★★ (404)**
Asians	0.6% (291)		Children per senior	1.14 (446)
Native Americans	0.3% (231)		Median age	43.3 (460)
			Moved from different state	1.6% (383)
AGE			Homes built since 2000	13.0% (276)
0-17 years old	21.5% (373)		Construction jobs	7.1% (173)
18-24 years old	7.8% (447)			
25-39 years old	16.3% (418)		**HOUSING**	**★★★ (292)**
40-54 years old	20.9% (112)		Home vacancy rate	11.1% (409)
55-64 years old	14.7% (97)		Home ownership rate	71.4% (209)
65+ years old	18.9% (85)		Housing diversity index	86.5% (19)
			4 or more bedrooms	13.5% (431)
PRIVATE SECTOR			Affordability/income ratio	$2,992 (403)
Businesses	1,224 (199)			
Employees	14,815 (216)		**INCOME**	**★ (464)**
Total wages	$468,939,754 (276)		Poverty rate	19.9% (366)
Average weekly wages	$609 (473)		Median household income	$35,630 (475)
			Interest/dividends	15.2% (401)
HOUSEHOLD INCOME LADDER			Public assistance	23.2% (500)
95th percentile	$120,361 (513)		Median fulltime earnings	$34,222 (414)
80th percentile	$68,829 (515)			
60th percentile	$44,273 (488)		**SENIORS**	**★ (442)**
40th percentile	$28,978 (441)		Seniors living alone	28.7% (344)
20th percentile	$15,604 (426)		Poverty rate for seniors	8.5% (223)
			Median income for seniors	$27,423 (471)
CHILDREN	**★★ (356)**		Seniors who work	12.9% (526)
Living with two parents	58.8% (433)		Home ownership by seniors	82.3% (261)
Older teens in school	82.0% (319)			
Speak English very well	97.6% (375)		**STABILITY**	**★★★ (290)**
Poverty rate for children	29.6% (392)		25-39 age group	16.3% (418)
No health insurance	6.0% (248)		Born in state of residence	71.8% (278)
			Same house as 1 year ago	89.1% (77)
DIVERSITY/EQUALITY	**★★★★ (148)**		Live and work in county	69.2% (382)
Racial diversity index	28.4% (267)		Married-couple households	50.0% (296)
Geographic diversity index	46.2% (265)			
Top 20% share of income	48.1% (301)		**TRANSPORTATION**	**★★ (404)**
Gender gap in earnings	26.1% (106)		Bicycle or walk to work	1.0% (512)
White-collar gender gap	15.8% (162)		Carpool to work	14.5% (55)
			Public transit to work	0.2% (363)
EDUCATION	**★★ (371)**		Commute <15 minutes	30.4% (520)
Eighth grade or less	4.5% (354)		Commute >45 minutes	14.3% (402)
High school diplomas	83.4% (411)			

See pages 37-130 for explanations of statistics, stars, and ranks.

Forrest City, AR
(St. Francis County, AR)

POPULATION	
2010 census	28,258 (452)
2015 estimate	26,589 (467)
2010-2015 change	-5.9% (540)
2020 projection	24,981 (480)
2030 projection	21,848 (505)

RACE	
Whites	41.2% (511)
Blacks	51.7% (12)
Hispanics	4.4% (270)
Asians	0.3% (473)
Native Americans	0.3% (231)

AGE	
0-17 years old	23.0% (259)
18-24 years old	8.7% (299)
25-39 years old	21.2% (37)
40-54 years old	20.9% (112)
55-64 years old	12.9% (343)
65+ years old	13.3% (465)

PRIVATE SECTOR	
Businesses	715 (421)
Employees	5,873 (512)
Total wages	$174,651,070 (523)
Average weekly wages	$572 (518)

HOUSEHOLD INCOME LADDER	
95th percentile	$107,917 (548)
80th percentile	$63,750 (539)
60th percentile	$38,484 (536)
40th percentile	$23,966 (521)
20th percentile	$13,100 (501)

CHILDREN	★★ (439)
Living with two parents	41.5% (536)
Older teens in school	84.9% (201)
Speak English very well	98.6% (278)
Poverty rate for children	36.7% (494)
No health insurance	3.9% (111)

DIVERSITY/EQUALITY	★★★★ (118)
Racial diversity index	56.1% (39)
Geographic diversity index	50.9% (198)
Top 20% share of income	49.1% (374)
Gender gap in earnings	19.5% (38)
White-collar gender gap	44.9% (479)

EDUCATION	★ (490)
Eighth grade or less	4.9% (380)
High school diplomas	82.3% (437)
Attended college	40.6% (505)
Bachelor's degrees	10.2% (539)
Advanced degrees	3.8% (496)

EMPLOYMENT	★ (533)
Average jobless rate	11.7% (481)
Self-employed workers	7.9% (345)
Management/financial jobs	8.7% (493)
Computer/engineering jobs	1.2% (530)
Health care jobs	4.2% (454)

GROWTH POTENTIAL	★★★★ (157)
Children per senior	1.72 (122)
Median age	37.5 (162)
Moved from different state	4.1% (76)
Homes built since 2000	10.5% (377)
Construction jobs	6.6% (241)

HOUSING	★ (521)
Home vacancy rate	11.5% (436)
Home ownership rate	55.6% (534)
Housing diversity index	83.7% (378)
4 or more bedrooms	9.7% (536)
Affordability/income ratio	$1,894 (32)

INCOME	★ (531)
Poverty rate	24.8% (476)
Median household income	$32,105 (519)
Interest/dividends	7.5% (545)
Public assistance	27.1% (524)
Median fulltime earnings	$31,344 (520)

SENIORS	★ (534)
Seniors living alone	30.4% (447)
Poverty rate for seniors	13.1% (450)
Median income for seniors	$23,818 (514)
Seniors who work	16.8% (356)
Home ownership by seniors	73.5% (539)

STABILITY	★ (475)
25-39 age group	21.2% (37)
Born in state of residence	67.3% (356)
Same house as 1 year ago	81.5% (460)
Live and work in county	72.2% (336)
Married-couple households	37.1% (540)

TRANSPORTATION	★★★★ (214)
Bicycle or walk to work	3.6% (180)
Carpool to work	13.1% (98)
Public transit to work	0.1% (441)
Commute <15 minutes	48.5% (187)
Commute >45 minutes	12.9% (353)

See pages 37-130 for explanations of statistics, stars, and ranks.

Fort Payne, AL
(DeKalb County, AL)

POPULATION

2010 census	71,109 (94)
2015 estimate	71,130 (98)
2010-2015 change	0.0% (255)
2020 projection	71,556 (97)
2030 projection	72,045 (97)

RACE

Whites	80.9% (319)
Blacks	1.8% (309)
Hispanics	14.0% (111)
Asians	0.4% (413)
Native Americans	1.1% (96)

AGE

0-17 years old	25.2% (108)
18-24 years old	8.4% (349)
25-39 years old	17.3% (280)
40-54 years old	21.3% (73)
55-64 years old	12.9% (343)
65+ years old	14.9% (374)

PRIVATE SECTOR

Businesses	1,041 (261)
Employees	17,585 (160)
Total wages	$595,395,293 (187)
Average weekly wages	$651 (388)

HOUSEHOLD INCOME LADDER

95th percentile	$116,591 (534)
80th percentile	$71,947 (494)
60th percentile	$47,383 (437)
40th percentile	$29,665 (432)
20th percentile	$15,899 (412)

CHILDREN ★★★ (262)

Living with two parents	69.6% (151)
Older teens in school	85.5% (183)
Speak English very well	95.6% (466)
Poverty rate for children	25.2% (304)
No health insurance	7.4% (341)

DIVERSITY/EQUALITY ★★★ (254)

Racial diversity index	32.5% (231)
Geographic diversity index	49.5% (217)
Top 20% share of income	47.7% (268)
Gender gap in earnings	28.3% (140)
White-collar gender gap	40.4% (449)

EDUCATION ★ (528)

Eighth grade or less	11.2% (523)
High school diplomas	75.1% (524)
Attended college	40.4% (507)
Bachelor's degrees	11.5% (525)
Advanced degrees	4.7% (419)

EMPLOYMENT ★★ (352)

Average jobless rate	7.7% (260)
Self-employed workers	9.1% (243)
Management/financial jobs	9.6% (427)
Computer/engineering jobs	2.1% (399)
Health care jobs	5.5% (250)

GROWTH POTENTIAL ★★★★ (182)

Children per senior	1.69 (137)
Median age	39.3 (256)
Moved from different state	1.6% (383)
Homes built since 2000	15.4% (193)
Construction jobs	7.4% (134)

HOUSING ★★★ (289)

Home vacancy rate	11.1% (409)
Home ownership rate	73.2% (146)
Housing diversity index	84.2% (325)
4 or more bedrooms	15.1% (347)
Affordability/income ratio	$2,579 (283)

INCOME ★ (448)

Poverty rate	18.7% (326)
Median household income	$38,192 (424)
Interest/dividends	12.2% (488)
Public assistance	16.9% (327)
Median fulltime earnings	$31,204 (522)

SENIORS ★ (454)

Seniors living alone	25.4% (132)
Poverty rate for seniors	13.1% (450)
Median income for seniors	$27,551 (467)
Seniors who work	14.4% (485)
Home ownership by seniors	80.9% (339)

STABILITY ★★★★ (133)

25-39 age group	17.3% (280)
Born in state of residence	68.8% (331)
Same house as 1 year ago	88.0% (133)
Live and work in county	72.1% (337)
Married-couple households	55.4% (61)

TRANSPORTATION ★ (512)

Bicycle or walk to work	0.6% (541)
Carpool to work	10.6% (271)
Public transit to work	0.0% (511)
Commute <15 minutes	30.6% (515)
Commute >45 minutes	13.7% (379)

See pages 37-130 for explanations of statistics, stars, and ranks.

Fort Polk South, LA
(Vernon Parish, LA)

POPULATION

2010 census	52,334 (191)
2015 estimate	50,803 (208)
2010-2015 change	-2.9% (477)
2020 projection	49,401 (218)
2030 projection	46,556 (251)

RACE

Whites	70.5% (387)
Blacks	13.9% (93)
Hispanics	9.0% (166)
Asians	2.1% (45)
Native Americans	1.1% (96)

AGE

0-17 years old	27.0% (46)
18-24 years old	13.6% (64)
25-39 years old	24.3% (6)
40-54 years old	16.0% (523)
55-64 years old	9.0% (544)
65+ years old	10.2% (524)

PRIVATE SECTOR

Businesses	844 (349)
Employees	9,141 (409)
Total wages	$301,466,454 (433)
Average weekly wages	$634 (425)

HOUSEHOLD INCOME LADDER

95th percentile	$138,096 (309)
80th percentile	$85,381 (244)
60th percentile	$55,965 (227)
40th percentile	$37,384 (195)
20th percentile	$21,359 (170)

CHILDREN ★★★ (222)

Living with two parents	74.4% (63)
Older teens in school	63.4% (545)
Speak English very well	99.5% (96)
Poverty rate for children	18.9% (145)
No health insurance	2.3% (20)

DIVERSITY/EQUALITY ★★★★★ (35)

Racial diversity index	47.4% (133)
Geographic diversity index	70.9% (41)
Top 20% share of income	45.3% (71)
Gender gap in earnings	38.6% (409)
White-collar gender gap	15.6% (157)

EDUCATION ★★★★ (213)

Eighth grade or less	2.7% (195)
High school diplomas	89.8% (207)
Attended college	55.2% (216)
Bachelor's degrees	20.5% (207)
Advanced degrees	5.6% (304)

EMPLOYMENT ★★ (351)

Average jobless rate	7.5% (242)
Self-employed workers	5.6% (523)
Management/financial jobs	11.1% (240)
Computer/engineering jobs	3.3% (145)
Health care jobs	5.3% (286)

GROWTH POTENTIAL ★★★★★ (13)

Children per senior	2.66 (26)
Median age	30.0 (29)
Moved from different state	10.8% (4)
Homes built since 2000	18.4% (123)
Construction jobs	7.1% (173)

HOUSING ★ (528)

Home vacancy rate	12.1% (463)
Home ownership rate	53.5% (540)
Housing diversity index	82.1% (454)
4 or more bedrooms	15.8% (307)
Affordability/income ratio	$2,116 (87)

INCOME ★★★ (297)

Poverty rate	14.7% (182)
Median household income	$46,312 (207)
Interest/dividends	10.4% (524)
Public assistance	12.4% (143)
Median fulltime earnings	$35,463 (362)

SENIORS ★★★ (323)

Seniors living alone	26.1% (179)
Poverty rate for seniors	11.0% (374)
Median income for seniors	$32,379 (308)
Seniors who work	16.1% (400)
Home ownership by seniors	82.7% (236)

STABILITY ★★★★★ (59)

25-39 age group	24.3% (6)
Born in state of residence	46.3% (500)
Same house as 1 year ago	81.0% (478)
Live and work in county	85.8% (122)
Married-couple households	55.9% (50)

TRANSPORTATION ★★ (345)

Bicycle or walk to work	2.9% (265)
Carpool to work	9.5% (388)
Public transit to work	0.1% (441)
Commute <15 minutes	38.6% (360)
Commute >45 minutes	8.7% (158)

See pages 37-130 for explanations of statistics, stars, and ranks.

Frankfort, KY
(Anderson and Franklin Counties, KY)

POPULATION	
2010 census	70,706 (96)
2015 estimate	72,354 (93)
2010-2015 change	2.3% (114)
2020 projection	73,566 (92)
2030 projection	75,833 (88)

RACE	
Whites	85.9% (256)
Blacks	7.9% (128)
Hispanics	2.5% (384)
Asians	1.3% (112)
Native Americans	0.1% (402)

AGE	
0-17 years old	22.2% (320)
18-24 years old	8.9% (282)
25-39 years old	18.0% (201)
40-54 years old	22.0% (31)
55-64 years old	14.0% (182)
65+ years old	14.8% (384)

PRIVATE SECTOR	
Businesses	1,969 (63)
Employees	21,448 (106)
Total wages	$794,831,085 (119)
Average weekly wages	$713 (228)

HOUSEHOLD INCOME LADDER	
95th percentile	$148,533 (177)
80th percentile	$91,974 (129)
60th percentile	$62,120 (106)
40th percentile	$40,418 (116)
20th percentile	$23,868 (72)

CHILDREN	★★★ (246)
Living with two parents	61.3% (373)
Older teens in school	80.4% (386)
Speak English very well	97.5% (388)
Poverty rate for children	19.6% (155)
No health insurance	4.1% (126)

DIVERSITY/EQUALITY	★★★★★ (39)
Racial diversity index	25.5% (291)
Geographic diversity index	38.7% (375)
Top 20% share of income	44.6% (46)
Gender gap in earnings	18.8% (36)
White-collar gender gap	0.6% (4)

EDUCATION	★★★★ (158)
Eighth grade or less	3.9% (316)
High school diplomas	89.2% (227)
Attended college	54.9% (227)
Bachelor's degrees	25.0% (108)
Advanced degrees	9.1% (83)

EMPLOYMENT	★★★★ (212)
Average jobless rate	8.2% (310)
Self-employed workers	6.6% (461)
Management/financial jobs	15.1% (29)
Computer/engineering jobs	4.7% (40)
Health care jobs	3.6% (508)

GROWTH POTENTIAL	★★★ (236)
Children per senior	1.50 (216)
Median age	40.5 (329)
Moved from different state	2.1% (269)
Homes built since 2000	16.1% (176)
Construction jobs	6.7% (219)

HOUSING	★★★ (253)
Home vacancy rate	8.3% (241)
Home ownership rate	67.0% (386)
Housing diversity index	86.1% (51)
4 or more bedrooms	14.4% (381)
Affordability/income ratio	$2,745 (343)

INCOME	★★★★ (138)
Poverty rate	13.3% (130)
Median household income	$50,025 (125)
Interest/dividends	22.6% (166)
Public assistance	13.4% (185)
Median fulltime earnings	$39,293 (164)

SENIORS	★★★★ (137)
Seniors living alone	29.2% (381)
Poverty rate for seniors	6.4% (57)
Median income for seniors	$42,810 (42)
Seniors who work	17.9% (292)
Home ownership by seniors	83.5% (197)

STABILITY	★★ (422)
25-39 age group	18.0% (201)
Born in state of residence	77.4% (172)
Same house as 1 year ago	82.8% (406)
Live and work in county	66.2% (432)
Married-couple households	46.7% (427)

TRANSPORTATION	★★★ (306)
Bicycle or walk to work	1.6% (443)
Carpool to work	11.8% (152)
Public transit to work	1.0% (69)
Commute <15 minutes	38.9% (353)
Commute >45 minutes	11.2% (278)

See pages 37-130 for explanations of statistics, stars, and ranks.

Fredericksburg, TX
(Gillespie County, TX)

POPULATION
2010 census	24,837 (483)
2015 estimate	25,963 (472)
2010-2015 change	4.5% (51)
2020 projection	27,167 (457)
2030 projection	29,794 (425)

RACE
Whites	76.7% (347)
Blacks	0.3% (519)
Hispanics	21.4% (72)
Asians	0.2% (509)
Native Americans	0.0% (523)

AGE
0-17 years old	19.6% (478)
18-24 years old	6.6% (535)
25-39 years old	12.2% (550)
40-54 years old	17.9% (454)
55-64 years old	15.7% (52)
65+ years old	27.9% (4)

PRIVATE SECTOR
Businesses	992 (281)
Employees	8,943 (414)
Total wages	$308,734,056 (424)
Average weekly wages	$664 (344)

HOUSEHOLD INCOME LADDER
95th percentile	$196,615 (23)
80th percentile	$104,516 (40)
60th percentile	$66,500 (60)
40th percentile	$41,112 (98)
20th percentile	$22,325 (121)

CHILDREN ★★★★ (184)
Living with two parents	74.1% (67)
Older teens in school	87.3% (124)
Speak English very well	95.8% (459)
Poverty rate for children	18.8% (142)
No health insurance	9.9% (420)

DIVERSITY/EQUALITY ★★★★★ (110)
Racial diversity index	36.6% (207)
Geographic diversity index	51.9% (190)
Top 20% share of income	49.2% (379)
Gender gap in earnings	29.8% (167)
White-collar gender gap	8.6% (71)

EDUCATION ★★★★ (147)
Eighth grade or less	7.6% (482)
High school diplomas	85.8% (352)
Attended college	58.3% (163)
Bachelor's degrees	31.7% (42)
Advanced degrees	10.5% (48)

EMPLOYMENT ★★★★★ (17)
Average jobless rate	6.8% (179)
Self-employed workers	20.4% (2)
Management/financial jobs	13.7% (59)
Computer/engineering jobs	3.7% (103)
Health care jobs	6.8% (91)

GROWTH POTENTIAL ★★★★ (195)
Children per senior	0.70 (546)
Median age	50.6 (548)
Moved from different state	2.1% (269)
Homes built since 2000	27.7% (22)
Construction jobs	10.7% (11)

HOUSING ★ (453)
Home vacancy rate	10.0% (347)
Home ownership rate	76.5% (41)
Housing diversity index	83.2% (405)
4 or more bedrooms	12.0% (496)
Affordability/income ratio	$4,344 (509)

INCOME ★★★★★ (35)
Poverty rate	11.2% (61)
Median household income	$54,859 (54)
Interest/dividends	39.2% (4)
Public assistance	7.0% (21)
Median fulltime earnings	$37,470 (250)

SENIORS ★★★★★ (70)
Seniors living alone	25.4% (132)
Poverty rate for seniors	6.9% (84)
Median income for seniors	n.a.
Seniors who work	19.8% (206)
Home ownership by seniors	86.3% (87)

STABILITY ★★★ (325)
25-39 age group	12.2% (550)
Born in state of residence	68.1% (344)
Same house as 1 year ago	86.6% (213)
Live and work in county	83.1% (161)
Married-couple households	56.7% (34)

TRANSPORTATION ★★★★★ (107)
Bicycle or walk to work	2.7% (292)
Carpool to work	16.0% (32)
Public transit to work	0.4% (219)
Commute <15 minutes	47.3% (204)
Commute >45 minutes	8.8% (165)

See pages 37-130 for explanations of statistics, stars, and ranks.

Gaffney, SC
(Cherokee County, SC)

POPULATION

2010 census	55,342 (170)
2015 estimate	56,194 (169)
2010-2015 change	1.5% (160)
2020 projection	56,419 (168)
2030 projection	56,690 (169)

RACE

Whites	73.2% (372)
Blacks	20.1% (79)
Hispanics	4.0% (296)
Asians	0.6% (291)
Native Americans	0.2% (300)

AGE

0-17 years old	23.9% (194)
18-24 years old	10.0% (163)
25-39 years old	17.7% (236)
40-54 years old	20.9% (112)
55-64 years old	12.8% (356)
65+ years old	14.7% (389)

PRIVATE SECTOR

Businesses	854 (339)
Employees	16,534 (180)
Total wages	$577,074,069 (200)
Average weekly wages	$671 (333)

HOUSEHOLD INCOME LADDER

95th percentile	$133,345 (384)
80th percentile	$73,304 (481)
60th percentile	$45,584 (467)
40th percentile	$27,396 (472)
20th percentile	$14,361 (471)

CHILDREN ★★ **(388)**

Living with two parents	56.7% (465)
Older teens in school	79.4% (415)
Speak English very well	99.9% (19)
Poverty rate for children	34.8% (474)
No health insurance	5.9% (244)

DIVERSITY/EQUALITY ★★★ **(247)**

Racial diversity index	42.2% (172)
Geographic diversity index	44.8% (285)
Top 20% share of income	50.7% (456)
Gender gap in earnings	36.2% (346)
White-collar gender gap	13.3% (131)

EDUCATION ★★ **(439)**

Eighth grade or less	4.8% (374)
High school diplomas	81.4% (458)
Attended college	44.4% (447)
Bachelor's degrees	16.0% (372)
Advanced degrees	4.8% (405)

EMPLOYMENT ★ **(513)**

Average jobless rate	10.6% (446)
Self-employed workers	5.5% (530)
Management/financial jobs	10.6% (306)
Computer/engineering jobs	1.8% (457)
Health care jobs	4.5% (419)

GROWTH POTENTIAL ★★★ **(315)**

Children per senior	1.63 (158)
Median age	38.8 (217)
Moved from different state	1.8% (338)
Homes built since 2000	15.3% (195)
Construction jobs	4.6% (494)

HOUSING ★★ **(425)**

Home vacancy rate	12.9% (489)
Home ownership rate	67.9% (347)
Housing diversity index	85.1% (212)
4 or more bedrooms	11.7% (505)
Affordability/income ratio	$2,444 (224)

INCOME ★ **(470)**

Poverty rate	23.8% (468)
Median household income	$35,389 (482)
Interest/dividends	11.3% (505)
Public assistance	21.0% (455)
Median fulltime earnings	$36,970 (291)

SENIORS ★ **(489)**

Seniors living alone	29.4% (394)
Poverty rate for seniors	13.7% (465)
Median income for seniors	$27,395 (472)
Seniors who work	14.4% (485)
Home ownership by seniors	81.8% (286)

STABILITY ★★ **(370)**

25-39 age group	17.7% (236)
Born in state of residence	72.0% (277)
Same house as 1 year ago	88.0% (133)
Live and work in county	65.9% (436)
Married-couple households	46.5% (432)

TRANSPORTATION ★★ **(396)**

Bicycle or walk to work	1.5% (457)
Carpool to work	10.3% (299)
Public transit to work	0.1% (441)
Commute <15 minutes	36.8% (402)
Commute >45 minutes	9.7% (214)

See pages 37-130 for explanations of statistics, stars, and ranks.

Gainesville, TX
(Cooke County, TX)

POPULATION	
2010 census	38,437 (336)
2015 estimate	39,229 (321)
2010-2015 change	2.1% (125)
2020 projection	39,456 (320)
2030 projection	39,890 (319)

RACE	
Whites	77.1% (346)
Blacks	2.4% (263)
Hispanics	16.9% (90)
Asians	0.8% (201)
Native Americans	0.8% (125)

AGE	
0-17 years old	24.4% (155)
18-24 years old	8.8% (292)
25-39 years old	17.1% (308)
40-54 years old	18.5% (425)
55-64 years old	14.0% (182)
65+ years old	17.1% (186)

PRIVATE SECTOR	
Businesses	895 (316)
Employees	13,130 (275)
Total wages	$602,097,814 (184)
Average weekly wages	$882 (41)

HOUSEHOLD INCOME LADDER	
95th percentile	$168,917 (58)
80th percentile	$103,378 (46)
60th percentile	$66,083 (66)
40th percentile	$41,206 (96)
20th percentile	$22,118 (134)

CHILDREN	★★★ (295)
Living with two parents	71.7% (109)
Older teens in school	80.7% (379)
Speak English very well	97.9% (352)
Poverty rate for children	22.0% (221)
No health insurance	11.0% (448)

DIVERSITY/EQUALITY	★★★★ (203)
Racial diversity index	37.6% (198)
Geographic diversity index	52.5% (183)
Top 20% share of income	47.6% (264)
Gender gap in earnings	42.0% (471)
White-collar gender gap	16.6% (176)

EDUCATION	★★★ (293)
Eighth grade or less	4.2% (337)
High school diplomas	87.3% (296)
Attended college	54.4% (236)
Bachelor's degrees	19.8% (224)
Advanced degrees	4.5% (442)

EMPLOYMENT	★★★ (239)
Average jobless rate	7.0% (196)
Self-employed workers	8.1% (323)
Management/financial jobs	10.6% (306)
Computer/engineering jobs	4.0% (76)
Health care jobs	5.2% (307)

GROWTH POTENTIAL	★★★ (254)
Children per senior	1.43 (261)
Median age	39.6 (276)
Moved from different state	1.9% (310)
Homes built since 2000	19.8% (94)
Construction jobs	5.4% (413)

HOUSING	★★★★ (133)
Home vacancy rate	7.3% (176)
Home ownership rate	69.5% (287)
Housing diversity index	85.8% (97)
4 or more bedrooms	16.5% (267)
Affordability/income ratio	$2,341 (187)

INCOME	★★★★★ (100)
Poverty rate	13.9% (151)
Median household income	$52,406 (81)
Interest/dividends	26.3% (66)
Public assistance	13.8% (202)
Median fulltime earnings	$40,303 (131)

SENIORS	★★★★★ (35)
Seniors living alone	23.4% (65)
Poverty rate for seniors	5.4% (29)
Median income for seniors	$41,743 (47)
Seniors who work	21.4% (148)
Home ownership by seniors	83.8% (186)

STABILITY	★★★ (327)
25-39 age group	17.1% (308)
Born in state of residence	67.4% (354)
Same house as 1 year ago	84.1% (344)
Live and work in county	65.2% (448)
Married-couple households	55.6% (56)

TRANSPORTATION	★★★ (267)
Bicycle or walk to work	1.5% (457)
Carpool to work	19.0% (6)
Public transit to work	0.2% (363)
Commute <15 minutes	39.1% (348)
Commute >45 minutes	16.7% (477)

See pages 37-130 for explanations of statistics, stars, and ranks.

Georgetown, SC
(Georgetown County, SC)

POPULATION
2010 census	60,158 (149)
2015 estimate	61,298 (138)
2010-2015 change	1.9% (136)
2020 projection	61,697 (138)
2030 projection	62,308 (137)

RACE
Whites	62.7% (430)
Blacks	32.5% (46)
Hispanics	3.1% (333)
Asians	0.4% (413)
Native Americans	0.2% (300)

AGE
0-17 years old	20.3% (445)
18-24 years old	7.0% (521)
25-39 years old	14.0% (541)
40-54 years old	19.1% (354)
55-64 years old	16.4% (30)
65+ years old	23.2% (19)

PRIVATE SECTOR
Businesses	1,916 (70)
Employees	18,176 (149)
Total wages	$645,213,460 (169)
Average weekly wages	$683 (305)

HOUSEHOLD INCOME LADDER
95th percentile	$168,533 (61)
80th percentile	$90,682 (148)
60th percentile	$55,936 (228)
40th percentile	$33,655 (304)
20th percentile	$17,074 (362)

CHILDREN ★ (511)
Living with two parents	47.2% (520)
Older teens in school	83.3% (263)
Speak English very well	98.8% (251)
Poverty rate for children	36.0% (486)
No health insurance	14.3% (516)

DIVERSITY/EQUALITY ★★★ (328)
Racial diversity index	50.0% (114)
Geographic diversity index	57.9% (134)
Top 20% share of income	51.9% (500)
Gender gap in earnings	34.3% (296)
White-collar gender gap	41.1% (458)

EDUCATION ★★★★ (155)
Eighth grade or less	3.7% (303)
High school diplomas	88.0% (267)
Attended college	56.1% (202)
Bachelor's degrees	24.7% (116)
Advanced degrees	9.4% (75)

EMPLOYMENT ★★★★ (164)
Average jobless rate	11.2% (464)
Self-employed workers	11.5% (99)
Management/financial jobs	13.8% (54)
Computer/engineering jobs	2.7% (270)
Health care jobs	5.7% (222)

GROWTH POTENTIAL ★★ (351)
Children per senior	0.88 (528)
Median age	47.5 (532)
Moved from different state	2.6% (187)
Homes built since 2000	23.5% (47)
Construction jobs	6.8% (204)

HOUSING ★★★★ (200)
Home vacancy rate	7.7% (199)
Home ownership rate	76.8% (34)
Housing diversity index	81.9% (461)
4 or more bedrooms	22.2% (79)
Affordability/income ratio	$3,726 (483)

INCOME ★★★ (299)
Poverty rate	21.0% (400)
Median household income	$42,835 (293)
Interest/dividends	23.5% (142)
Public assistance	17.4% (352)
Median fulltime earnings	$35,886 (339)

SENIORS ★★★★★ (57)
Seniors living alone	23.4% (65)
Poverty rate for seniors	8.6% (234)
Median income for seniors	$39,302 (67)
Seniors who work	16.0% (410)
Home ownership by seniors	90.1% (16)

STABILITY ★ (487)
25-39 age group	14.0% (541)
Born in state of residence	61.1% (414)
Same house as 1 year ago	87.6% (157)
Live and work in county	70.8% (357)
Married-couple households	49.9% (302)

TRANSPORTATION ★ (514)
Bicycle or walk to work	1.8% (409)
Carpool to work	8.7% (453)
Public transit to work	0.6% (141)
Commute <15 minutes	34.6% (445)
Commute >45 minutes	17.4% (490)

See pages 37-130 for explanations of statistics, stars, and ranks.

Glasgow, KY
(Barren and Metcalfe Counties, KY)

POPULATION		
2010 census	52,272 (193)	
2015 estimate	53,479 (183)	
2010-2015 change	2.3% (114)	
2020 projection	54,576 (181)	
2030 projection	56,732 (168)	

RACE	
Whites	91.5% (152)
Blacks	3.5% (209)
Hispanics	2.6% (378)
Asians	0.5% (355)
Native Americans	0.3% (231)

AGE	
0-17 years old	23.5% (232)
18-24 years old	8.0% (407)
25-39 years old	17.3% (280)
40-54 years old	21.2% (85)
55-64 years old	13.2% (297)
65+ years old	16.8% (215)

PRIVATE SECTOR	
Businesses	1,136 (222)
Employees	15,456 (200)
Total wages	$533,274,614 (223)
Average weekly wages	$664 (344)

HOUSEHOLD INCOME LADDER	
95th percentile	$121,163 (506)
80th percentile	$74,775 (459)
60th percentile	$45,861 (464)
40th percentile	$28,796 (443)
20th percentile	$15,137 (448)

CHILDREN	★★ (363)
Living with two parents	71.3% (114)
Older teens in school	77.5% (460)
Speak English very well	98.5% (287)
Poverty rate for children	29.1% (387)
No health insurance	10.6% (440)

DIVERSITY/EQUALITY	★★ (362)
Racial diversity index	16.1% (396)
Geographic diversity index	38.7% (375)
Top 20% share of income	48.3% (308)
Gender gap in earnings	22.2% (59)
White-collar gender gap	39.3% (438)

EDUCATION	★★ (384)
Eighth grade or less	4.6% (361)
High school diplomas	85.8% (352)
Attended college	42.8% (476)
Bachelor's degrees	16.1% (366)
Advanced degrees	6.7% (205)

EMPLOYMENT	★★★ (280)
Average jobless rate	7.6% (250)
Self-employed workers	9.9% (171)
Management/financial jobs	10.5% (318)
Computer/engineering jobs	2.2% (381)
Health care jobs	5.5% (250)

GROWTH POTENTIAL	★★★ (287)
Children per senior	1.40 (279)
Median age	41.1 (362)
Moved from different state	1.5% (406)
Homes built since 2000	18.4% (123)
Construction jobs	6.1% (310)

HOUSING	★★★★ (181)
Home vacancy rate	7.9% (213)
Home ownership rate	69.3% (294)
Housing diversity index	85.7% (108)
4 or more bedrooms	16.4% (272)
Affordability/income ratio	$2,692 (325)

INCOME	★ (452)
Poverty rate	20.7% (395)
Median household income	$37,369 (439)
Interest/dividends	17.3% (336)
Public assistance	20.7% (448)
Median fulltime earnings	$31,639 (511)

SENIORS	★ (524)
Seniors living alone	29.5% (405)
Poverty rate for seniors	18.2% (527)
Median income for seniors	$23,378 (517)
Seniors who work	16.8% (356)
Home ownership by seniors	80.9% (339)

STABILITY	★★★★ (172)
25-39 age group	17.3% (280)
Born in state of residence	77.2% (175)
Same house as 1 year ago	86.0% (250)
Live and work in county	70.7% (360)
Married-couple households	53.7% (123)

TRANSPORTATION	★★ (383)
Bicycle or walk to work	1.6% (443)
Carpool to work	10.5% (280)
Public transit to work	0.3% (291)
Commute <15 minutes	37.5% (387)
Commute >45 minutes	10.5% (254)

See pages 37-130 for explanations of statistics, stars, and ranks.

Greeneville, TN
(Greene County, TN)

POPULATION

2010 census	68,831 (106)
2015 estimate	68,580 (107)
2010-2015 change	-0.4% (286)
2020 projection	68,664 (107)
2030 projection	68,592 (113)

RACE

Whites	93.4% (94)
Blacks	2.1% (283)
Hispanics	2.7% (361)
Asians	0.5% (355)
Native Americans	0.1% (402)

AGE

0-17 years old	20.3% (445)
18-24 years old	8.3% (362)
25-39 years old	16.6% (388)
40-54 years old	21.1% (97)
55-64 years old	14.6% (107)
65+ years old	19.1% (76)

PRIVATE SECTOR

Businesses	1,058 (255)
Employees	21,553 (103)
Total wages	$779,942,478 (121)
Average weekly wages	$696 (262)

HOUSEHOLD INCOME LADDER

95th percentile	$118,988 (524)
80th percentile	$69,552 (509)
60th percentile	$43,291 (498)
40th percentile	$29,034 (440)
20th percentile	$16,466 (387)

CHILDREN ★★ **(341)**

Living with two parents	65.2% (266)
Older teens in school	78.1% (446)
Speak English very well	98.3% (312)
Poverty rate for children	32.1% (447)
No health insurance	5.1% (188)

DIVERSITY/EQUALITY ★★★ **(299)**

Racial diversity index	12.6% (453)
Geographic diversity index	50.5% (206)
Top 20% share of income	49.3% (385)
Gender gap in earnings	30.3% (175)
White-collar gender gap	17.9% (187)

EDUCATION ★★ **(433)**

Eighth grade or less	4.8% (374)
High school diplomas	84.7% (380)
Attended college	40.0% (515)
Bachelor's degrees	16.0% (372)
Advanced degrees	5.2% (352)

EMPLOYMENT ★★ **(388)**

Average jobless rate	8.7% (340)
Self-employed workers	6.2% (488)
Management/financial jobs	10.0% (381)
Computer/engineering jobs	2.3% (354)
Health care jobs	6.5% (121)

GROWTH POTENTIAL ★★ **(346)**

Children per senior	1.07 (477)
Median age	43.7 (470)
Moved from different state	2.2% (248)
Homes built since 2000	17.4% (145)
Construction jobs	6.8% (204)

HOUSING ★★★ **(234)**

Home vacancy rate	8.9% (280)
Home ownership rate	71.5% (204)
Housing diversity index	85.9% (83)
4 or more bedrooms	15.1% (347)
Affordability/income ratio	$3,117 (422)

INCOME ★★ **(439)**

Poverty rate	20.5% (391)
Median household income	$35,196 (484)
Interest/dividends	18.0% (313)
Public assistance	19.4% (414)
Median fulltime earnings	$32,333 (477)

SENIORS ★★★ **(322)**

Seniors living alone	24.7% (105)
Poverty rate for seniors	11.5% (388)
Median income for seniors	$30,131 (404)
Seniors who work	16.5% (376)
Home ownership by seniors	82.6% (242)

STABILITY ★★★★ **(210)**

25-39 age group	16.6% (388)
Born in state of residence	68.2% (342)
Same house as 1 year ago	87.3% (181)
Live and work in county	80.6% (208)
Married-couple households	51.2% (242)

TRANSPORTATION ★ **(472)**

Bicycle or walk to work	1.4% (472)
Carpool to work	9.2% (408)
Public transit to work	0.2% (363)
Commute <15 minutes	31.4% (507)
Commute >45 minutes	11.3% (285)

See pages 37-130 for explanations of statistics, stars, and ranks.

Greenville, MS
(Washington County, MS)

POPULATION	
2010 census	51,137 (202)
2015 estimate	48,130 (227)
2010-2015 change	-5.9% (540)
2020 projection	44,428 (269)
2030 projection	37,598 (344)

RACE	
Whites	26.4% (536)
Blacks	71.1% (3)
Hispanics	1.3% (503)
Asians	0.7% (241)
Native Americans	0.1% (402)

AGE	
0-17 years old	26.9% (47)
18-24 years old	9.7% (183)
25-39 years old	18.1% (186)
40-54 years old	18.7% (399)
55-64 years old	13.4% (274)
65+ years old	13.2% (470)

PRIVATE SECTOR	
Businesses	1,216 (203)
Employees	13,405 (259)
Total wages	$418,513,281 (315)
Average weekly wages	$600 (487)

HOUSEHOLD INCOME LADDER	
95th percentile	$137,155 (324)
80th percentile	$64,316 (533)
60th percentile	$38,178 (539)
40th percentile	$21,165 (544)
20th percentile	$11,085 (536)

CHILDREN	★ (534)
Living with two parents	28.9% (548)
Older teens in school	82.0% (319)
Speak English very well	99.1% (179)
Poverty rate for children	52.5% (549)
No health insurance	10.3% (428)

DIVERSITY/EQUALITY	★ (514)
Racial diversity index	42.5% (170)
Geographic diversity index	23.8% (536)
Top 20% share of income	54.4% (540)
Gender gap in earnings	35.3% (321)
White-collar gender gap	20.3% (212)

EDUCATION	★★ (407)
Eighth grade or less	6.0% (424)
High school diplomas	80.1% (478)
Attended college	48.6% (367)
Bachelor's degrees	18.8% (259)
Advanced degrees	6.1% (250)

EMPLOYMENT	★★ (393)
Average jobless rate	21.7% (551)
Self-employed workers	9.6% (200)
Management/financial jobs	11.1% (240)
Computer/engineering jobs	3.3% (145)
Health care jobs	6.5% (121)

GROWTH POTENTIAL	★★ (341)
Children per senior	2.03 (57)
Median age	36.2 (122)
Moved from different state	1.6% (383)
Homes built since 2000	7.5% (487)
Construction jobs	4.1% (530)

HOUSING	★ (524)
Home vacancy rate	13.2% (497)
Home ownership rate	55.0% (535)
Housing diversity index	84.8% (248)
4 or more bedrooms	13.3% (437)
Affordability/income ratio	$2,536 (262)

INCOME	★ (545)
Poverty rate	36.0% (544)
Median household income	$29,144 (538)
Interest/dividends	8.9% (537)
Public assistance	32.9% (544)
Median fulltime earnings	$32,395 (471)

SENIORS	★ (535)
Seniors living alone	31.2% (479)
Poverty rate for seniors	18.6% (530)
Median income for seniors	$26,129 (492)
Seniors who work	19.7% (214)
Home ownership by seniors	75.7% (515)

STABILITY	★★★ (284)
25-39 age group	18.1% (186)
Born in state of residence	86.9% (17)
Same house as 1 year ago	84.9% (306)
Live and work in county	89.0% (82)
Married-couple households	32.2% (547)

TRANSPORTATION	★★★★ (195)
Bicycle or walk to work	1.4% (472)
Carpool to work	10.0% (337)
Public transit to work	0.5% (178)
Commute <15 minutes	53.1% (109)
Commute >45 minutes	6.0% (53)

See pages 37-130 for explanations of statistics, stars, and ranks.

Greenwood, MS
(Carroll and Leflore Counties, MS)

POPULATION

2010 census	42,914 (278)
2015 estimate	41,242 (297)
2010-2015 change	-3.9% (517)
2020 projection	39,312 (321)
2030 projection	35,483 (367)

RACE

Whites	34.0% (524)
Blacks	62.6% (6)
Hispanics	2.0% (428)
Asians	0.6% (291)
Native Americans	0.0% (523)

AGE

0-17 years old	25.2% (108)
18-24 years old	11.1% (113)
25-39 years old	18.2% (167)
40-54 years old	18.6% (412)
55-64 years old	12.5% (396)
65+ years old	14.3% (423)

PRIVATE SECTOR

Businesses	861 (338)
Employees	10,946 (344)
Total wages	$324,874,607 (404)
Average weekly wages	$571 (520)

HOUSEHOLD INCOME LADDER

95th percentile	$140,285 (284)
80th percentile	$62,485 (546)
60th percentile	$36,301 (543)
40th percentile	$20,422 (549)
20th percentile	$9,503 (548)

CHILDREN ★ (458)

Living with two parents	33.5% (545)
Older teens in school	91.9% (40)
Speak English very well	99.2% (163)
Poverty rate for children	52.1% (547)
No health insurance	4.7% (166)

DIVERSITY/EQUALITY ★ (543)

Racial diversity index	49.2% (119)
Geographic diversity index	22.2% (543)
Top 20% share of income	54.6% (542)
Gender gap in earnings	23.6% (73)
White-collar gender gap	64.5% (548)

EDUCATION ★★ (424)

Eighth grade or less	6.5% (449)
High school diplomas	82.0% (445)
Attended college	46.1% (418)
Bachelor's degrees	17.3% (309)
Advanced degrees	5.8% (283)

EMPLOYMENT ★★ (363)

Average jobless rate	15.1% (536)
Self-employed workers	8.4% (297)
Management/financial jobs	11.8% (173)
Computer/engineering jobs	2.0% (420)
Health care jobs	7.8% (28)

GROWTH POTENTIAL ★★★★ (217)

Children per senior	1.77 (104)
Median age	35.7 (109)
Moved from different state	1.6% (383)
Homes built since 2000	14.1% (237)
Construction jobs	5.5% (404)

HOUSING ★ (467)

Home vacancy rate	11.9% (458)
Home ownership rate	59.8% (505)
Housing diversity index	85.4% (156)
4 or more bedrooms	15.0% (356)
Affordability/income ratio	$2,754 (348)

INCOME ★ (536)

Poverty rate	36.5% (545)
Median household income	$26,836 (548)
Interest/dividends	6.9% (549)
Public assistance	21.8% (474)
Median fulltime earnings	$35,022 (383)

SENIORS ★ (545)

Seniors living alone	28.9% (358)
Poverty rate for seniors	22.8% (546)
Median income for seniors	$22,990 (520)
Seniors who work	14.0% (503)
Home ownership by seniors	76.0% (511)

STABILITY ★★★ (302)

25-39 age group	18.2% (167)
Born in state of residence	87.9% (9)
Same house as 1 year ago	91.2% (26)
Live and work in county	69.2% (382)
Married-couple households	36.4% (542)

TRANSPORTATION ★★ (401)

Bicycle or walk to work	1.7% (428)
Carpool to work	6.6% (537)
Public transit to work	0.1% (441)
Commute <15 minutes	48.0% (196)
Commute >45 minutes	9.2% (182)

See pages 37-130 for explanations of statistics, stars, and ranks.

Greenwood, SC
(Abbeville and Greenwood Counties, SC)

POPULATION	
2010 census	95,078 (35)
2015 estimate	94,770 (38)
2010-2015 change	-0.3% (279)
2020 projection	93,621 (42)
2030 projection	91,112 (48)

RACE	
Whites	62.7% (430)
Blacks	29.9% (56)
Hispanics	4.5% (265)
Asians	0.7% (241)
Native Americans	0.1% (402)

AGE	
0-17 years old	22.9% (270)
18-24 years old	10.3% (146)
25-39 years old	16.7% (375)
40-54 years old	20.1% (221)
55-64 years old	13.0% (334)
65+ years old	17.0% (197)

PRIVATE SECTOR	
Businesses	1,653 (109)
Employees	25,918 (67)
Total wages	$925,828,921 (87)
Average weekly wages	$687 (295)

HOUSEHOLD INCOME LADDER	
95th percentile	$130,577 (424)
80th percentile	$77,543 (406)
60th percentile	$46,915 (446)
40th percentile	$28,662 (445)
20th percentile	$15,472 (435)

CHILDREN	★★ (392)
Living with two parents	51.4% (497)
Older teens in school	86.4% (152)
Speak English very well	98.2% (320)
Poverty rate for children	35.5% (480)
No health insurance	6.0% (248)

DIVERSITY/EQUALITY	★★★★ (184)
Racial diversity index	51.5% (100)
Geographic diversity index	42.4% (316)
Top 20% share of income	49.9% (422)
Gender gap in earnings	30.9% (198)
White-collar gender gap	19.8% (203)

EDUCATION	★★★ (322)
Eighth grade or less	4.6% (361)
High school diplomas	83.3% (415)
Attended college	51.5% (291)
Bachelor's degrees	20.2% (216)
Advanced degrees	6.5% (220)

EMPLOYMENT	★★ (356)
Average jobless rate	12.4% (506)
Self-employed workers	6.5% (474)
Management/financial jobs	9.6% (427)
Computer/engineering jobs	3.7% (103)
Health care jobs	7.6% (39)

GROWTH POTENTIAL	★★ (345)
Children per senior	1.35 (313)
Median age	40.1 (309)
Moved from different state	1.9% (310)
Homes built since 2000	13.4% (260)
Construction jobs	5.9% (345)

HOUSING	★★★ (286)
Home vacancy rate	11.1% (409)
Home ownership rate	68.9% (308)
Housing diversity index	86.7% (6)
4 or more bedrooms	14.2% (392)
Affordability/income ratio	$2,717 (336)

INCOME	★★ (431)
Poverty rate	23.4% (456)
Median household income	$36,623 (452)
Interest/dividends	15.5% (393)
Public assistance	18.4% (381)
Median fulltime earnings	$35,781 (343)

SENIORS	★★ (408)
Seniors living alone	28.2% (311)
Poverty rate for seniors	11.9% (408)
Median income for seniors	$30,428 (392)
Seniors who work	15.1% (455)
Home ownership by seniors	83.7% (190)

STABILITY	★ (447)
25-39 age group	16.7% (375)
Born in state of residence	74.6% (228)
Same house as 1 year ago	85.3% (290)
Live and work in county	70.2% (369)
Married-couple households	44.5% (474)

TRANSPORTATION	★ (451)
Bicycle or walk to work	2.2% (358)
Carpool to work	9.3% (401)
Public transit to work	0.3% (291)
Commute <15 minutes	36.4% (411)
Commute >45 minutes	13.8% (382)

See pages 37-130 for explanations of statistics, stars, and ranks.

Grenada, MS
(Grenada County, MS)

POPULATION	
2010 census	21,906 (510)
2015 estimate	21,578 (515)
2010-2015 change	-1.5% (373)
2020 projection	21,049 (517)
2030 projection	19,895 (520)

RACE	
Whites	55.5% (470)
Blacks	43.5% (23)
Hispanics	0.1% (551)
Asians	0.5% (355)
Native Americans	0.0% (523)

AGE	
0-17 years old	24.0% (184)
18-24 years old	9.7% (183)
25-39 years old	15.5% (484)
40-54 years old	21.5% (57)
55-64 years old	13.2% (297)
65+ years old	16.1% (286)

PRIVATE SECTOR	
Businesses	514 (512)
Employees	8,553 (434)
Total wages	$259,196,935 (464)
Average weekly wages	$583 (511)

HOUSEHOLD INCOME LADDER	
95th percentile	$137,406 (317)
80th percentile	$73,105 (484)
60th percentile	$41,132 (514)
40th percentile	$24,147 (520)
20th percentile	$13,119 (500)

CHILDREN	★★ (391)
Living with two parents	48.9% (515)
Older teens in school	79.1% (424)
Speak English very well	100.0% (1)
Poverty rate for children	34.8% (474)
No health insurance	2.5% (34)

DIVERSITY/EQUALITY	★★★ (300)
Racial diversity index	50.3% (112)
Geographic diversity index	28.9% (493)
Top 20% share of income	53.2% (522)
Gender gap in earnings	31.9% (223)
White-collar gender gap	4.4% (30)

EDUCATION	★★ (417)
Eighth grade or less	6.9% (467)
High school diplomas	80.4% (473)
Attended college	50.9% (304)
Bachelor's degrees	16.1% (366)
Advanced degrees	6.3% (234)

EMPLOYMENT	★★ (406)
Average jobless rate	9.4% (394)
Self-employed workers	8.9% (266)
Management/financial jobs	10.9% (263)
Computer/engineering jobs	2.0% (420)
Health care jobs	4.7% (385)

GROWTH POTENTIAL	★★ (364)
Children per senior	1.49 (220)
Median age	40.4 (325)
Moved from different state	1.8% (338)
Homes built since 2000	12.9% (280)
Construction jobs	5.4% (413)

HOUSING	★★ (421)
Home vacancy rate	23.4% (551)
Home ownership rate	73.4% (142)
Housing diversity index	85.4% (156)
4 or more bedrooms	15.8% (307)
Affordability/income ratio	$2,914 (383)

INCOME	★ (477)
Poverty rate	22.3% (432)
Median household income	$31,779 (520)
Interest/dividends	11.4% (502)
Public assistance	17.1% (338)
Median fulltime earnings	$32,558 (468)

SENIORS	★ (520)
Seniors living alone	33.4% (533)
Poverty rate for seniors	15.9% (500)
Median income for seniors	n.a.
Seniors who work	16.1% (400)
Home ownership by seniors	81.8% (286)

STABILITY	★★★ (330)
25-39 age group	15.5% (484)
Born in state of residence	83.7% (60)
Same house as 1 year ago	87.8% (149)
Live and work in county	79.3% (229)
Married-couple households	42.9% (495)

TRANSPORTATION	★★★ (239)
Bicycle or walk to work	0.7% (537)
Carpool to work	11.0% (229)
Public transit to work	1.5% (42)
Commute <15 minutes	51.5% (128)
Commute >45 minutes	12.3% (325)

See pages 37-130 for explanations of statistics, stars, and ranks.

Guymon, OK
(Texas County, OK)

POPULATION	
2010 census	20,640 (523)
2015 estimate	21,489 (517)
2010-2015 change	4.1% (57)
2020 projection	22,089 (510)
2030 projection	23,327 (489)

RACE	
Whites	47.7% (493)
Blacks	2.2% (276)
Hispanics	45.2% (32)
Asians	2.2% (40)
Native Americans	0.2% (300)

AGE	
0-17 years old	27.6% (37)
18-24 years old	12.0% (87)
25-39 years old	22.3% (18)
40-54 years old	17.3% (487)
55-64 years old	10.8% (497)
65+ years old	10.1% (528)

PRIVATE SECTOR	
Businesses	527 (507)
Employees	8,208 (442)
Total wages	$325,184,860 (403)
Average weekly wages	$762 (139)

HOUSEHOLD INCOME LADDER	
95th percentile	$145,441 (223)
80th percentile	$85,631 (237)
60th percentile	$58,755 (168)
40th percentile	$37,233 (201)
20th percentile	$22,030 (139)

CHILDREN	★★ (437)
Living with two parents	66.6% (228)
Older teens in school	86.5% (149)
Speak English very well	81.5% (545)
Poverty rate for children	18.2% (128)
No health insurance	12.3% (479)

DIVERSITY/EQUALITY	★★★★★ (14)
Racial diversity index	56.7% (34)
Geographic diversity index	77.0% (14)
Top 20% share of income	45.1% (66)
Gender gap in earnings	32.2% (233)
White-collar gender gap	21.3% (222)

EDUCATION	★ (536)
Eighth grade or less	19.9% (544)
High school diplomas	68.3% (539)
Attended college	40.6% (505)
Bachelor's degrees	19.0% (248)
Advanced degrees	4.0% (478)

EMPLOYMENT	★★ (340)
Average jobless rate	3.5% (20)
Self-employed workers	9.0% (254)
Management/financial jobs	10.9% (263)
Computer/engineering jobs	2.3% (354)
Health care jobs	2.9% (537)

GROWTH POTENTIAL	★★★★★ (93)
Children per senior	2.75 (25)
Median age	31.5 (42)
Moved from different state	5.6% (36)
Homes built since 2000	5.5% (534)
Construction jobs	3.9% (538)

HOUSING	★★★ (319)
Home vacancy rate	10.1% (352)
Home ownership rate	62.1% (479)
Housing diversity index	85.5% (143)
4 or more bedrooms	14.3% (387)
Affordability/income ratio	$1,845 (20)

INCOME	★★★★ (219)
Poverty rate	13.0% (114)
Median household income	$50,242 (119)
Interest/dividends	15.3% (399)
Public assistance	9.5% (55)
Median fulltime earnings	$33,820 (428)

SENIORS	★★★★★ (19)
Seniors living alone	25.5% (142)
Poverty rate for seniors	9.3% (276)
Median income for seniors	$38,033 (89)
Seniors who work	33.5% (9)
Home ownership by seniors	89.0% (24)

STABILITY	★★★★ (213)
25-39 age group	22.3% (18)
Born in state of residence	36.3% (533)
Same house as 1 year ago	83.3% (382)
Live and work in county	81.8% (186)
Married-couple households	53.1% (148)

TRANSPORTATION	★★★★★ (57)
Bicycle or walk to work	2.6% (308)
Carpool to work	20.1% (4)
Public transit to work	0.0% (511)
Commute <15 minutes	60.0% (47)
Commute >45 minutes	10.6% (261)

See pages 37-130 for explanations of statistics, stars, and ranks.

Harrison, AR
(Boone and Newton Counties, AR)

POPULATION

2010 census	45,233 (257)
2015 estimate	45,135 (257)
2010-2015 change	-0.2% (273)
2020 projection	44,844 (264)
2030 projection	43,927 (274)

RACE

Whites	94.5% (61)
Blacks	0.3% (519)
Hispanics	2.0% (428)
Asians	0.5% (355)
Native Americans	0.8% (125)

AGE

0-17 years old	22.2% (320)
18-24 years old	7.5% (483)
25-39 years old	17.0% (317)
40-54 years old	19.5% (301)
55-64 years old	13.8% (203)
65+ years old	20.0% (56)

PRIVATE SECTOR

Businesses	1,029 (268)
Employees	11,296 (335)
Total wages	$386,347,669 (350)
Average weekly wages	$658 (370)

HOUSEHOLD INCOME LADDER

95th percentile	$129,868 (434)
80th percentile	$72,604 (488)
60th percentile	$45,951 (460)
40th percentile	$30,659 (397)
20th percentile	$17,649 (333)

CHILDREN ★★★★ (139)

Living with two parents	68.6% (177)
Older teens in school	83.2% (268)
Speak English very well	100.0% (1)
Poverty rate for children	25.4% (310)
No health insurance	3.1% (64)

DIVERSITY/EQUALITY ★★★ (286)

Racial diversity index	10.6% (485)
Geographic diversity index	62.2% (102)
Top 20% share of income	49.1% (369)
Gender gap in earnings	29.2% (156)
White-collar gender gap	30.0% (338)

EDUCATION ★★★ (285)

Eighth grade or less	3.1% (238)
High school diplomas	88.7% (245)
Attended college	53.2% (260)
Bachelor's degrees	15.9% (382)
Advanced degrees	5.2% (352)

EMPLOYMENT ★★★★ (125)

Average jobless rate	7.8% (270)
Self-employed workers	12.1% (71)
Management/financial jobs	12.0% (156)
Computer/engineering jobs	3.4% (131)
Health care jobs	5.2% (307)

GROWTH POTENTIAL ★★★ (285)

Children per senior	1.11 (457)
Median age	42.6 (437)
Moved from different state	3.2% (136)
Homes built since 2000	16.3% (175)
Construction jobs	6.8% (204)

HOUSING ★★★ (252)

Home vacancy rate	9.0% (287)
Home ownership rate	73.6% (132)
Housing diversity index	84.7% (260)
4 or more bedrooms	13.1% (448)
Affordability/income ratio	$2,732 (339)

INCOME ★★ (367)

Poverty rate	18.2% (304)
Median household income	$38,395 (420)
Interest/dividends	20.0% (245)
Public assistance	16.6% (316)
Median fulltime earnings	$32,381 (472)

SENIORS ★★★ (291)

Seniors living alone	26.3% (190)
Poverty rate for seniors	10.8% (365)
Median income for seniors	$30,816 (378)
Seniors who work	15.4% (441)
Home ownership by seniors	85.9% (105)

STABILITY ★★★ (310)

25-39 age group	17.0% (317)
Born in state of residence	56.8% (446)
Same house as 1 year ago	83.5% (366)
Live and work in county	78.2% (241)
Married-couple households	55.3% (62)

TRANSPORTATION ★★ (414)

Bicycle or walk to work	2.0% (386)
Carpool to work	10.3% (299)
Public transit to work	0.1% (441)
Commute <15 minutes	39.5% (338)
Commute >45 minutes	13.2% (363)

See pages 37-130 for explanations of statistics, stars, and ranks.

Helena-West Helena, AR
(Phillips County, AR)

POPULATION

2010 census	21,757 (512)
2015 estimate	19,513 (526)
2010-2015 change	-10.3% (551)
2020 projection	17,434 (535)
2030 projection	13,791 (547)

RACE

Whites	35.2% (521)
Blacks	61.5% (8)
Hispanics	1.6% (472)
Asians	0.1% (529)
Native Americans	0.1% (402)

AGE

0-17 years old	27.2% (41)
18-24 years old	9.5% (197)
25-39 years old	16.1% (442)
40-54 years old	17.9% (454)
55-64 years old	13.5% (258)
65+ years old	15.8% (305)

PRIVATE SECTOR

Businesses	773 (386)
Employees	4,348 (538)
Total wages	$134,222,380 (541)
Average weekly wages	$594 (495)

HOUSEHOLD INCOME LADDER

95th percentile	$134,757 (363)
80th percentile	$59,316 (549)
60th percentile	$35,021 (549)
40th percentile	$21,250 (542)
20th percentile	$12,037 (521)

CHILDREN ★ (531)

Living with two parents	26.8% (551)
Older teens in school	77.6% (458)
Speak English very well	99.6% (77)
Poverty rate for children	52.4% (548)
No health insurance	6.9% (307)

DIVERSITY/EQUALITY ★★ (417)

Racial diversity index	49.7% (115)
Geographic diversity index	38.5% (379)
Top 20% share of income	53.8% (533)
Gender gap in earnings	19.7% (40)
White-collar gender gap	50.6% (512)

EDUCATION ★ (476)

Eighth grade or less	4.6% (361)
High school diplomas	82.0% (445)
Attended college	46.5% (406)
Bachelor's degrees	9.9% (542)
Advanced degrees	3.4% (514)

EMPLOYMENT ★ (539)

Average jobless rate	18.1% (547)
Self-employed workers	7.2% (410)
Management/financial jobs	7.4% (540)
Computer/engineering jobs	0.8% (543)
Health care jobs	7.1% (63)

GROWTH POTENTIAL ★ (512)

Children per senior	1.72 (122)
Median age	37.8 (174)
Moved from different state	1.9% (310)
Homes built since 2000	6.6% (513)
Construction jobs	2.0% (550)

HOUSING ★ (542)

Home vacancy rate	14.9% (533)
Home ownership rate	51.3% (545)
Housing diversity index	83.8% (369)
4 or more bedrooms	12.6% (472)
Affordability/income ratio	$2,280 (155)

INCOME ★ (546)

Poverty rate	34.1% (539)
Median household income	$26,844 (547)
Interest/dividends	11.3% (505)
Public assistance	34.8% (547)
Median fulltime earnings	$28,967 (544)

SENIORS ★ (548)

Seniors living alone	34.6% (540)
Poverty rate for seniors	17.3% (521)
Median income for seniors	$24,444 (508)
Seniors who work	19.6% (221)
Home ownership by seniors	71.2% (546)

STABILITY ★ (513)

25-39 age group	16.1% (442)
Born in state of residence	76.8% (180)
Same house as 1 year ago	83.4% (375)
Live and work in county	78.9% (234)
Married-couple households	32.8% (546)

TRANSPORTATION ★★★★★ (95)

Bicycle or walk to work	2.2% (358)
Carpool to work	18.9% (7)
Public transit to work	0.1% (441)
Commute <15 minutes	52.1% (123)
Commute >45 minutes	11.0% (273)

See pages 37-130 for explanations of statistics, stars, and ranks.

Henderson, NC
(Vance County, NC)

POPULATION

2010 census	45,422 (255)
2015 estimate	44,568 (268)
2010-2015 change	-1.9% (399)
2020 projection	43,605 (278)
2030 projection	41,560 (298)

RACE

Whites	41.2% (511)
Blacks	49.3% (16)
Hispanics	7.1% (197)
Asians	0.5% (355)
Native Americans	0.3% (231)

AGE

0-17 years old	24.4% (155)
18-24 years old	9.4% (203)
25-39 years old	16.2% (434)
40-54 years old	20.2% (202)
55-64 years old	14.1% (174)
65+ years old	15.6% (328)

PRIVATE SECTOR

Businesses	807 (369)
Employees	12,333 (299)
Total wages	$401,306,084 (334)
Average weekly wages	$626 (442)

HOUSEHOLD INCOME LADDER

95th percentile	$119,735 (518)
80th percentile	$70,617 (502)
60th percentile	$42,321 (504)
40th percentile	$26,143 (495)
20th percentile	$14,166 (473)

CHILDREN ★ **(500)**

Living with two parents	38.5% (540)
Older teens in school	81.4% (350)
Speak English very well	98.1% (331)
Poverty rate for children	37.0% (495)
No health insurance	6.7% (296)

DIVERSITY/EQUALITY ★★★★★ **(36)**

Racial diversity index	58.2% (24)
Geographic diversity index	35.5% (430)
Top 20% share of income	50.1% (433)
Gender gap in earnings	2.2% (4)
White-collar gender gap	9.0% (82)

EDUCATION ★ **(504)**

Eighth grade or less	6.8% (463)
High school diplomas	79.4% (492)

Attended college	42.7% (479)
Bachelor's degrees	11.9% (517)
Advanced degrees	3.3% (520)

EMPLOYMENT ★ **(541)**

Average jobless rate	12.2% (497)
Self-employed workers	4.7% (544)
Management/financial jobs	8.8% (488)
Computer/engineering jobs	1.3% (519)
Health care jobs	5.3% (286)

GROWTH POTENTIAL ★★ **(409)**

Children per senior	1.56 (189)
Median age	40.0 (303)
Moved from different state	1.1% (487)
Homes built since 2000	11.7% (324)
Construction jobs	5.2% (442)

HOUSING ★★ **(384)**

Home vacancy rate	8.8% (273)
Home ownership rate	62.8% (477)
Housing diversity index	85.3% (170)
4 or more bedrooms	14.0% (401)
Affordability/income ratio	$2,939 (390)

INCOME ★ **(514)**

Poverty rate	25.1% (478)
Median household income	$33,316 (504)
Interest/dividends	12.1% (489)
Public assistance	26.2% (519)
Median fulltime earnings	$31,778 (506)

SENIORS ★ **(474)**

Seniors living alone	27.6% (269)
Poverty rate for seniors	14.8% (485)
Median income for seniors	$29,529 (422)
Seniors who work	16.4% (383)
Home ownership by seniors	79.3% (403)

STABILITY ★ **(485)**

25-39 age group	16.2% (434)
Born in state of residence	79.6% (120)
Same house as 1 year ago	90.4% (36)
Live and work in county	65.3% (446)
Married-couple households	36.9% (541)

TRANSPORTATION ★★ **(431)**

Bicycle or walk to work	2.2% (358)
Carpool to work	10.6% (271)
Public transit to work	0.1% (441)
Commute <15 minutes	33.7% (465)
Commute >45 minutes	12.3% (325)

See pages 37-130 for explanations of statistics, stars, and ranks.

Hereford, TX
(Deaf Smith County, TX)

POPULATION	
2010 census	19,372 (529)
2015 estimate	18,952 (530)
2010-2015 change	-2.2% (427)
2020 projection	18,627 (529)
2030 projection	17,975 (531)

RACE	
Whites	27.8% (534)
Blacks	0.8% (404)
Hispanics	69.8% (13)
Asians	0.3% (473)
Native Americans	0.6% (150)

AGE	
0-17 years old	31.8% (8)
18-24 years old	10.0% (163)
25-39 years old	19.6% (71)
40-54 years old	16.7% (508)
55-64 years old	10.3% (510)
65+ years old	11.5% (499)

PRIVATE SECTOR	
Businesses	466 (522)
Employees	6,241 (502)
Total wages	$255,514,895 (468)
Average weekly wages	$787 (108)

HOUSEHOLD INCOME LADDER	
95th percentile	$132,009 (400)
80th percentile	$88,697 (171)
60th percentile	$51,991 (319)
40th percentile	$35,925 (235)
20th percentile	$18,605 (285)

CHILDREN	★★ (414)
Living with two parents	61.9% (359)
Older teens in school	89.8% (68)
Speak English very well	90.8% (523)
Poverty rate for children	28.8% (384)
No health insurance	9.0% (393)

DIVERSITY/EQUALITY	★★★ (290)
Racial diversity index	43.5% (164)
Geographic diversity index	50.2% (210)
Top 20% share of income	46.7% (179)
Gender gap in earnings	32.6% (243)
White-collar gender gap	55.0% (527)

EDUCATION	★ (537)
Eighth grade or less	14.7% (530)
High school diplomas	74.3% (528)
Attended college	42.2% (489)
Bachelor's degrees	14.3% (451)
Advanced degrees	2.9% (534)

EMPLOYMENT	★★ (369)
Average jobless rate	5.4% (89)
Self-employed workers	11.1% (115)
Management/financial jobs	11.1% (240)
Computer/engineering jobs	2.1% (399)
Health care jobs	2.3% (548)

GROWTH POTENTIAL	★★★★★ (75)
Children per senior	2.76 (24)
Median age	31.5 (42)
Moved from different state	1.3% (452)
Homes built since 2000	7.2% (500)
Construction jobs	7.4% (134)

HOUSING	★★★ (245)
Home vacancy rate	10.3% (366)
Home ownership rate	68.0% (343)
Housing diversity index	84.4% (299)
4 or more bedrooms	17.1% (239)
Affordability/income ratio	$1,999 (57)

INCOME	★★ (394)
Poverty rate	20.8% (397)
Median household income	$43,373 (280)
Interest/dividends	10.8% (517)
Public assistance	16.0% (295)
Median fulltime earnings	$35,711 (349)

SENIORS	★★★ (236)
Seniors living alone	27.9% (290)
Poverty rate for seniors	12.4% (434)
Median income for seniors	$33,078 (277)
Seniors who work	26.4% (43)
Home ownership by seniors	81.0% (335)

STABILITY	★★★★★ (11)
25-39 age group	19.6% (71)
Born in state of residence	68.6% (334)
Same house as 1 year ago	88.9% (86)
Live and work in county	85.3% (132)
Married-couple households	53.8% (116)

TRANSPORTATION	★★★★★ (61)
Bicycle or walk to work	1.1% (501)
Carpool to work	14.2% (58)
Public transit to work	0.3% (291)
Commute <15 minutes	64.3% (22)
Commute >45 minutes	4.6% (24)

See pages 37-130 for explanations of statistics, stars, and ranks.

Hope, AR
(Hempstead and Nevada Counties, AR)

POPULATION	
2010 census	31,606 (422)
2015 estimate	30,642 (430)
2010-2015 change	-3.1% (487)
2020 projection	29,346 (436)
2030 projection	26,691 (459)

RACE	
Whites	58.1% (458)
Blacks	29.9% (56)
Hispanics	9.9% (153)
Asians	0.4% (413)
Native Americans	0.2% (300)

AGE	
0-17 years old	25.6% (85)
18-24 years old	7.5% (483)
25-39 years old	17.5% (258)
40-54 years old	19.3% (323)
55-64 years old	13.0% (334)
65+ years old	17.0% (197)

PRIVATE SECTOR	
Businesses	615 (464)
Employees	8,006 (447)
Total wages	$267,782,096 (456)
Average weekly wages	$643 (409)

HOUSEHOLD INCOME LADDER	
95th percentile	$117,854 (528)
80th percentile	$63,304 (542)
60th percentile	$40,544 (524)
40th percentile	$24,423 (515)
20th percentile	$13,788 (482)

CHILDREN	★ (478)
Living with two parents	59.8% (404)
Older teens in school	80.3% (388)
Speak English very well	95.8% (459)
Poverty rate for children	43.1% (528)
No health insurance	6.7% (296)

DIVERSITY/EQUALITY	★★★★★ (32)
Racial diversity index	56.3% (36)
Geographic diversity index	50.8% (200)
Top 20% share of income	50.0% (427)
Gender gap in earnings	21.7% (56)
White-collar gender gap	2.2% (12)

EDUCATION	★ (485)
Eighth grade or less	7.0% (472)
High school diplomas	81.7% (452)
Attended college	43.9% (453)
Bachelor's degrees	12.9% (497)
Advanced degrees	4.3% (456)

EMPLOYMENT	★ (502)
Average jobless rate	8.4% (323)
Self-employed workers	6.7% (457)
Management/financial jobs	7.4% (540)
Computer/engineering jobs	2.1% (399)
Health care jobs	5.0% (339)

GROWTH POTENTIAL	★★★ (264)
Children per senior	1.51 (210)
Median age	39.9 (292)
Moved from different state	1.9% (310)
Homes built since 2000	10.8% (364)
Construction jobs	7.4% (134)

HOUSING	★ (492)
Home vacancy rate	18.3% (547)
Home ownership rate	68.8% (313)
Housing diversity index	85.9% (83)
4 or more bedrooms	9.9% (533)
Affordability/income ratio	$2,283 (157)

INCOME	★ (500)
Poverty rate	27.3% (506)
Median household income	$31,718 (522)
Interest/dividends	13.2% (463)
Public assistance	16.5% (313)
Median fulltime earnings	$28,680 (547)

SENIORS	★ (527)
Seniors living alone	31.3% (486)
Poverty rate for seniors	17.9% (525)
Median income for seniors	$25,188 (502)
Seniors who work	20.0% (195)
Home ownership by seniors	78.3% (441)

STABILITY	★★ (350)
25-39 age group	17.5% (258)
Born in state of residence	67.3% (356)
Same house as 1 year ago	89.0% (79)
Live and work in county	68.6% (395)
Married-couple households	46.9% (419)

TRANSPORTATION	★★ (342)
Bicycle or walk to work	0.9% (521)
Carpool to work	12.6% (116)
Public transit to work	0.4% (219)
Commute <15 minutes	38.3% (370)
Commute >45 minutes	11.2% (278)

See pages 37-130 for explanations of statistics, stars, and ranks.

Huntsville, TX
(Trinity and Walker Counties, TX)

POPULATION	
2010 census	82,446 (61)
2015 estimate	85,101 (58)
2010-2015 change	3.2% (74)
2020 projection	87,393 (53)
2030 projection	92,196 (43)

RACE	
Whites	61.2% (440)
Blacks	20.5% (76)
Hispanics	16.2% (94)
Asians	1.0% (158)
Native Americans	0.3% (231)

AGE	
0-17 years old	16.5% (544)
18-24 years old	17.6% (39)
25-39 years old	19.7% (68)
40-54 years old	20.9% (112)
55-64 years old	11.7% (463)
65+ years old	13.5% (459)

PRIVATE SECTOR	
Businesses	1,141 (218)
Employees	13,012 (281)
Total wages	$417,219,378 (318)
Average weekly wages	$617 (452)

HOUSEHOLD INCOME LADDER	
95th percentile	$138,381 (307)
80th percentile	$81,064 (350)
60th percentile	$48,077 (424)
40th percentile	$29,299 (438)
20th percentile	$13,940 (478)

CHILDREN	★ (480)
Living with two parents	62.2% (344)
Older teens in school	88.8% (86)
Speak English very well	94.4% (490)
Poverty rate for children	29.7% (395)
No health insurance	18.1% (539)

DIVERSITY/EQUALITY	★★★★★ (62)
Racial diversity index	55.7% (42)
Geographic diversity index	43.8% (297)
Top 20% share of income	50.6% (454)
Gender gap in earnings	25.9% (103)
White-collar gender gap	0.7% (5)

EDUCATION	★ (459)
Eighth grade or less	6.7% (459)
High school diplomas	82.0% (445)
Attended college	45.2% (435)
Bachelor's degrees	16.4% (354)
Advanced degrees	4.2% (466)

EMPLOYMENT	★★★ (274)
Average jobless rate	5.4% (89)
Self-employed workers	10.1% (158)
Management/financial jobs	9.9% (392)
Computer/engineering jobs	2.5% (307)
Health care jobs	4.6% (401)

GROWTH POTENTIAL	★★★ (262)
Children per senior	1.23 (393)
Median age	36.7 (137)
Moved from different state	1.7% (355)
Homes built since 2000	22.7% (55)
Construction jobs	4.3% (514)

HOUSING	★ (543)
Home vacancy rate	13.3% (500)
Home ownership rate	60.5% (497)
Housing diversity index	81.4% (479)
4 or more bedrooms	12.0% (496)
Affordability/income ratio	$2,847 (366)

INCOME	★★ (413)
Poverty rate	23.7% (462)
Median household income	$36,738 (449)
Interest/dividends	10.9% (512)
Public assistance	10.0% (63)
Median fulltime earnings	$34,640 (400)

SENIORS	★★★ (242)
Seniors living alone	28.6% (336)
Poverty rate for seniors	10.8% (365)
Median income for seniors	$34,167 (227)
Seniors who work	17.9% (292)
Home ownership by seniors	86.8% (72)

STABILITY	★★ (384)
25-39 age group	19.7% (68)
Born in state of residence	74.1% (242)
Same house as 1 year ago	82.2% (432)
Live and work in county	71.6% (348)
Married-couple households	44.2% (478)

TRANSPORTATION	★ (466)
Bicycle or walk to work	4.6% (110)
Carpool to work	10.2% (312)
Public transit to work	0.2% (363)
Commute <15 minutes	27.3% (542)
Commute >45 minutes	16.9% (481)

See pages 37-130 for explanations of statistics, stars, and ranks.

Indianola, MS
(Sunflower County, MS)

POPULATION

2010 census	29,450 (438)
2015 estimate	27,005 (465)
2010-2015 change	-8.3% (549)
2020 projection	24,634 (485)
2030 projection	20,351 (518)

RACE

Whites	25.0% (537)
Blacks	72.7% (2)
Hispanics	1.5% (480)
Asians	0.4% (413)
Native Americans	0.0% (523)

AGE

0-17 years old	23.7% (218)
18-24 years old	11.6% (98)
25-39 years old	21.4% (33)
40-54 years old	20.4% (169)
55-64 years old	11.6% (471)
65+ years old	11.2% (507)

PRIVATE SECTOR

Businesses	499 (515)
Employees	5,041 (527)
Total wages	$143,835,350 (536)
Average weekly wages	$549 (532)

HOUSEHOLD INCOME LADDER

95th percentile	$118,789 (526)
80th percentile	$63,345 (541)
60th percentile	$36,359 (542)
40th percentile	$22,017 (539)
20th percentile	$11,538 (533)

CHILDREN ★ (527)

Living with two parents	30.3% (547)
Older teens in school	79.7% (407)
Speak English very well	98.9% (226)
Poverty rate for children	51.2% (544)
No health insurance	6.0% (248)

DIVERSITY/EQUALITY ★ (519)

Racial diversity index	40.9% (184)
Geographic diversity index	23.2% (540)
Top 20% share of income	53.2% (525)
Gender gap in earnings	16.5% (21)
White-collar gender gap	58.3% (539)

EDUCATION ★ (509)

Eighth grade or less	7.6% (482)
High school diplomas	73.9% (532)
Attended college	44.5% (444)
Bachelor's degrees	13.9% (466)
Advanced degrees	4.3% (456)

EMPLOYMENT ★ (499)

Average jobless rate	20.1% (549)
Self-employed workers	8.0% (333)
Management/financial jobs	11.1% (240)
Computer/engineering jobs	0.7% (548)
Health care jobs	6.8% (91)

GROWTH POTENTIAL ★★★ (247)

Children per senior	2.11 (47)
Median age	34.1 (78)
Moved from different state	1.5% (406)
Homes built since 2000	9.8% (395)
Construction jobs	4.3% (514)

HOUSING ★★ (416)

Home vacancy rate	11.1% (409)
Home ownership rate	57.6% (528)
Housing diversity index	84.7% (260)
4 or more bedrooms	19.0% (159)
Affordability/income ratio	$2,556 (276)

INCOME ★ (548)

Poverty rate	35.5% (543)
Median household income	$27,384 (545)
Interest/dividends	8.4% (539)
Public assistance	35.3% (549)
Median fulltime earnings	$30,412 (537)

SENIORS ★ (506)

Seniors living alone	26.9% (230)
Poverty rate for seniors	17.0% (519)
Median income for seniors	$24,875 (504)
Seniors who work	17.2% (330)
Home ownership by seniors	78.3% (441)

STABILITY ★★★ (274)

25-39 age group	21.4% (33)
Born in state of residence	87.3% (12)
Same house as 1 year ago	85.9% (257)
Live and work in county	68.2% (403)
Married-couple households	33.2% (545)

TRANSPORTATION ★★★★ (147)

Bicycle or walk to work	3.6% (180)
Carpool to work	11.2% (211)
Public transit to work	0.6% (141)
Commute <15 minutes	49.9% (154)
Commute >45 minutes	7.5% (105)

See pages 37-130 for explanations of statistics, stars, and ranks.

Jacksonville, TX
(Cherokee County, TX)

POPULATION

2010 census	50,845 (205)
2015 estimate	51,542 (201)
2010-2015 change	1.4% (165)
2020 projection	52,103 (198)
2030 projection	53,186 (194)

RACE

Whites	61.6% (437)
Blacks	14.4% (91)
Hispanics	21.9% (70)
Asians	0.5% (355)
Native Americans	0.1% (402)

AGE

0-17 years old	25.7% (81)
18-24 years old	9.5% (197)
25-39 years old	17.9% (214)
40-54 years old	18.7% (399)
55-64 years old	12.5% (396)
65+ years old	15.7% (318)

PRIVATE SECTOR

Businesses	743 (407)
Employees	10,345 (365)
Total wages	$340,482,570 (392)
Average weekly wages	$633 (429)

HOUSEHOLD INCOME LADDER

95th percentile	$159,085 (103)
80th percentile	$81,542 (336)
60th percentile	$48,480 (410)
40th percentile	$30,727 (396)
20th percentile	$17,087 (359)

CHILDREN ★ (486)

Living with two parents	59.3% (422)
Older teens in school	83.8% (245)
Speak English very well	92.5% (512)
Poverty rate for children	34.8% (474)
No health insurance	9.7% (412)

DIVERSITY/EQUALITY ★★★★ (129)

Racial diversity index	55.2% (50)
Geographic diversity index	42.8% (311)
Top 20% share of income	50.5% (449)
Gender gap in earnings	22.7% (65)
White-collar gender gap	24.1% (259)

EDUCATION ★ (508)

Eighth grade or less	9.5% (509)
High school diplomas	78.3% (505)
Attended college	43.5% (463)
Bachelor's degrees	15.4% (410)
Advanced degrees	3.6% (505)

EMPLOYMENT ★★ (334)

Average jobless rate	6.4% (147)
Self-employed workers	6.8% (446)
Management/financial jobs	10.1% (365)
Computer/engineering jobs	2.5% (307)
Health care jobs	5.7% (222)

GROWTH POTENTIAL ★★★★ (122)

Children per senior	1.63 (158)
Median age	37.6 (168)
Moved from different state	1.6% (383)
Homes built since 2000	15.8% (184)
Construction jobs	8.9% (51)

HOUSING ★★★★ (211)

Home vacancy rate	9.5% (317)
Home ownership rate	71.7% (199)
Housing diversity index	86.0% (71)
4 or more bedrooms	12.1% (492)
Affordability/income ratio	$2,134 (96)

INCOME ★ (446)

Poverty rate	22.1% (429)
Median household income	$39,595 (391)
Interest/dividends	14.9% (413)
Public assistance	17.9% (368)
Median fulltime earnings	$32,199 (484)

SENIORS ★★★★ (141)

Seniors living alone	23.5% (69)
Poverty rate for seniors	12.3% (427)
Median income for seniors	$32,541 (300)
Seniors who work	18.9% (247)
Home ownership by seniors	87.9% (42)

STABILITY ★★★ (221)

25-39 age group	17.9% (214)
Born in state of residence	74.8% (224)
Same house as 1 year ago	86.7% (210)
Live and work in county	66.7% (424)
Married-couple households	51.8% (206)

TRANSPORTATION ★★ (385)

Bicycle or walk to work	2.2% (358)
Carpool to work	13.3% (88)
Public transit to work	0.0% (511)
Commute <15 minutes	34.3% (453)
Commute >45 minutes	14.2% (395)

See pages 37-130 for explanations of statistics, stars, and ranks.

Jefferson, GA
(Jackson County, GA)

POPULATION

2010 census	60,485 (148)
2015 estimate	63,360 (133)
2010-2015 change	4.8% (42)
2020 projection	68,618 (108)
2030 projection	80,211 (78)

RACE

Whites	82.7% (293)
Blacks	7.1% (133)
Hispanics	6.7% (206)
Asians	1.9% (58)
Native Americans	0.1% (402)

AGE

0-17 years old	25.9% (72)
18-24 years old	7.9% (424)
25-39 years old	18.3% (159)
40-54 years old	23.1% (5)
55-64 years old	11.8% (456)
65+ years old	13.0% (474)

PRIVATE SECTOR

Businesses	1,347 (165)
Employees	19,140 (136)
Total wages	$735,191,311 (141)
Average weekly wages	$739 (180)

HOUSEHOLD INCOME LADDER

95th percentile	$162,412 (83)
80th percentile	$99,895 (61)
60th percentile	$65,310 (72)
40th percentile	$43,794 (63)
20th percentile	$22,216 (129)

CHILDREN ★★★★ (150)

Living with two parents	71.5% (111)
Older teens in school	81.5% (345)
Speak English very well	99.3% (142)
Poverty rate for children	15.6% (71)
No health insurance	7.9% (359)

DIVERSITY/EQUALITY ★★★★ (210)

Racial diversity index	30.6% (250)
Geographic diversity index	50.0% (214)
Top 20% share of income	46.0% (122)
Gender gap in earnings	30.8% (190)
White-collar gender gap	37.1% (408)

EDUCATION ★★★ (321)

Eighth grade or less	5.2% (398)
High school diplomas	84.4% (389)
Attended college	50.9% (304)
Bachelor's degrees	20.6% (204)
Advanced degrees	6.5% (220)

EMPLOYMENT ★★★★ (133)

Average jobless rate	7.9% (286)
Self-employed workers	9.6% (200)
Management/financial jobs	13.9% (50)
Computer/engineering jobs	3.0% (193)
Health care jobs	5.4% (273)

GROWTH POTENTIAL ★★★★★ (56)

Children per senior	2.00 (61)
Median age	38.3 (197)
Moved from different state	1.3% (452)
Homes built since 2000	40.3% (2)
Construction jobs	7.4% (134)

HOUSING ★★★★ (186)

Home vacancy rate	8.9% (280)
Home ownership rate	77.0% (27)
Housing diversity index	75.7% (545)
4 or more bedrooms	28.8% (15)
Affordability/income ratio	$2,917 (384)

INCOME ★★★★ (170)

Poverty rate	13.7% (145)
Median household income	$53,379 (69)
Interest/dividends	14.8% (417)
Public assistance	13.1% (177)
Median fulltime earnings	$39,952 (142)

SENIORS ★★★★ (114)

Seniors living alone	22.0% (35)
Poverty rate for seniors	10.5% (345)
Median income for seniors	$35,000 (189)
Seniors who work	15.0% (459)
Home ownership by seniors	87.9% (42)

STABILITY ★★★★ (163)

25-39 age group	18.3% (159)
Born in state of residence	68.9% (326)
Same house as 1 year ago	91.5% (22)
Live and work in county	38.0% (550)
Married-couple households	59.9% (10)

TRANSPORTATION ★ (551)

Bicycle or walk to work	0.6% (541)
Carpool to work	8.4% (466)
Public transit to work	0.2% (363)
Commute <15 minutes	19.1% (551)
Commute >45 minutes	20.7% (523)

See pages 37-130 for explanations of statistics, stars, and ranks.

Jennings, LA
(Jefferson Davis Parish, LA)

POPULATION
2010 census	31,594 (423)
2015 estimate	31,439 (424)
2010-2015 change	-0.5% (292)
2020 projection	31,340 (426)
2030 projection	31,039 (419)

RACE
Whites	78.2% (336)
Blacks	17.1% (86)
Hispanics	2.1% (416)
Asians	0.3% (473)
Native Americans	0.5% (174)

AGE
0-17 years old	25.8% (75)
18-24 years old	8.5% (330)
25-39 years old	17.7% (236)
40-54 years old	20.3% (186)
55-64 years old	12.6% (385)
65+ years old	15.1% (363)

PRIVATE SECTOR
Businesses	654 (449)
Employees	6,652 (485)
Total wages	$236,316,314 (476)
Average weekly wages	$683 (305)

HOUSEHOLD INCOME LADDER
95th percentile	$153,591 (125)
80th percentile	$92,353 (125)
60th percentile	$50,135 (380)
40th percentile	$28,557 (447)
20th percentile	$14,493 (465)

CHILDREN ★★★ (300)
Living with two parents	53.7% (481)
Older teens in school	79.4% (415)
Speak English very well	99.5% (96)
Poverty rate for children	26.3% (333)
No health insurance	2.3% (20)

DIVERSITY/EQUALITY ★ (522)
Racial diversity index	35.8% (211)
Geographic diversity index	24.1% (533)
Top 20% share of income	51.6% (492)
Gender gap in earnings	49.8% (526)
White-collar gender gap	11.6% (105)

EDUCATION ★ (456)
Eighth grade or less	4.7% (366)
High school diplomas	82.6% (428)
Attended college	41.7% (495)
Bachelor's degrees	15.2% (415)
Advanced degrees	4.0% (478)

EMPLOYMENT ★★★ (304)
Average jobless rate	9.2% (377)
Self-employed workers	10.3% (150)
Management/financial jobs	10.9% (263)
Computer/engineering jobs	1.9% (441)
Health care jobs	5.7% (222)

GROWTH POTENTIAL ★★★★ (148)
Children per senior	1.71 (127)
Median age	38.4 (202)
Moved from different state	1.2% (474)
Homes built since 2000	18.6% (117)
Construction jobs	7.5% (122)

HOUSING ★★★★ (183)
Home vacancy rate	10.1% (352)
Home ownership rate	74.0% (120)
Housing diversity index	86.5% (19)
4 or more bedrooms	12.7% (466)
Affordability/income ratio	$2,353 (194)

INCOME ★★ (354)
Poverty rate	21.1% (403)
Median household income	$39,063 (404)
Interest/dividends	16.9% (345)
Public assistance	18.5% (385)
Median fulltime earnings	$39,281 (166)

SENIORS ★ (501)
Seniors living alone	27.9% (290)
Poverty rate for seniors	16.7% (513)
Median income for seniors	$25,645 (497)
Seniors who work	16.6% (367)
Home ownership by seniors	80.7% (350)

STABILITY ★ (449)
25-39 age group	17.7% (236)
Born in state of residence	86.7% (18)
Same house as 1 year ago	83.7% (353)
Live and work in county	55.3% (519)
Married-couple households	45.9% (445)

TRANSPORTATION ★ (509)
Bicycle or walk to work	1.2% (492)
Carpool to work	12.6% (116)
Public transit to work	0.0% (511)
Commute <15 minutes	38.0% (375)
Commute >45 minutes	21.7% (533)

See pages 37-130 for explanations of statistics, stars, and ranks.

Jesup, GA
(Wayne County, GA)

POPULATION	
2010 census	30,099 (433)
2015 estimate	29,534 (438)
2010-2015 change	-1.9% (399)
2020 projection	29,117 (439)
2030 projection	28,198 (440)

RACE	
Whites	71.1% (382)
Blacks	20.4% (77)
Hispanics	6.1% (218)
Asians	0.1% (529)
Native Americans	0.2% (300)

AGE	
0-17 years old	24.6% (144)
18-24 years old	8.4% (349)
25-39 years old	20.0% (58)
40-54 years old	20.6% (145)
55-64 years old	12.3% (414)
65+ years old	14.1% (431)

PRIVATE SECTOR	
Businesses	574 (486)
Employees	5,595 (518)
Total wages	$205,782,088 (504)
Average weekly wages	$707 (238)

HOUSEHOLD INCOME LADDER	
95th percentile	$132,948 (387)
80th percentile	$80,143 (365)
60th percentile	$51,277 (351)
40th percentile	$30,322 (407)
20th percentile	$15,602 (427)

CHILDREN	★★ (381)
Living with two parents	65.8% (253)
Older teens in school	77.9% (452)
Speak English very well	98.7% (265)
Poverty rate for children	23.5% (255)
No health insurance	12.4% (482)

DIVERSITY/EQUALITY	★★★ (229)
Racial diversity index	44.9% (150)
Geographic diversity index	45.3% (277)
Top 20% share of income	47.5% (259)
Gender gap in earnings	39.3% (425)
White-collar gender gap	25.0% (271)

EDUCATION	★★ (421)
Eighth grade or less	5.5% (409)
High school diplomas	85.4% (363)
Attended college	42.9% (473)
Bachelor's degrees	14.1% (457)
Advanced degrees	5.9% (272)

EMPLOYMENT	★★ (418)
Average jobless rate	11.3% (466)
Self-employed workers	7.1% (421)
Management/financial jobs	8.5% (505)
Computer/engineering jobs	3.2% (158)
Health care jobs	6.8% (91)

GROWTH POTENTIAL	★★★★★ (46)
Children per senior	1.74 (113)
Median age	37.3 (157)
Moved from different state	3.5% (109)
Homes built since 2000	22.5% (64)
Construction jobs	9.4% (36)

HOUSING	★★ (390)
Home vacancy rate	13.3% (500)
Home ownership rate	68.4% (329)
Housing diversity index	84.5% (287)
4 or more bedrooms	14.9% (363)
Affordability/income ratio	$2,346 (189)

INCOME	★★ (401)
Poverty rate	20.3% (384)
Median household income	$38,955 (408)
Interest/dividends	12.7% (477)
Public assistance	19.6% (416)
Median fulltime earnings	$38,728 (192)

SENIORS	★★ (358)
Seniors living alone	24.1% (86)
Poverty rate for seniors	10.0% (321)
Median income for seniors	$26,887 (479)
Seniors who work	10.5% (549)
Home ownership by seniors	85.7% (118)

STABILITY	★★★★ (113)
25-39 age group	20.0% (58)
Born in state of residence	72.2% (272)
Same house as 1 year ago	83.5% (366)
Live and work in county	77.1% (256)
Married-couple households	51.6% (218)

TRANSPORTATION	★ (454)
Bicycle or walk to work	1.5% (457)
Carpool to work	9.2% (408)
Public transit to work	0.2% (363)
Commute <15 minutes	40.3% (324)
Commute >45 minutes	13.9% (387)

See pages 37-130 for explanations of statistics, stars, and ranks.

Kerrville, TX
(Kerr County, TX)

POPULATION

2010 census	49,625 (213)
2015 estimate	50,955 (206)
2010-2015 change	2.7% (96)
2020 projection	52,370 (197)
2030 projection	55,262 (181)

RACE

Whites	70.6% (386)
Blacks	1.6% (320)
Hispanics	25.3% (58)
Asians	0.9% (178)
Native Americans	0.3% (231)

AGE

0-17 years old	19.5% (486)
18-24 years old	8.5% (330)
25-39 years old	14.1% (538)
40-54 years old	17.2% (494)
55-64 years old	14.6% (107)
65+ years old	26.1% (8)

PRIVATE SECTOR

Businesses	1,391 (155)
Employees	14,508 (222)
Total wages	$548,233,757 (213)
Average weekly wages	$727 (200)

HOUSEHOLD INCOME LADDER

95th percentile	$162,226 (85)
80th percentile	$86,723 (215)
60th percentile	$54,562 (261)
40th percentile	$35,269 (257)
20th percentile	$19,112 (259)

CHILDREN ★★ (361)

Living with two parents	62.5% (334)
Older teens in school	82.1% (313)
Speak English very well	98.0% (341)
Poverty rate for children	23.5% (255)
No health insurance	11.6% (462)

DIVERSITY/EQUALITY ★★ (333)

Racial diversity index	43.7% (161)
Geographic diversity index	56.4% (142)
Top 20% share of income	51.1% (472)
Gender gap in earnings	28.8% (149)
White-collar gender gap	48.6% (505)

EDUCATION ★★★★ (184)

Eighth grade or less	4.8% (374)
High school diplomas	86.7% (319)
Attended college	58.0% (168)
Bachelor's degrees	25.4% (101)
Advanced degrees	7.6% (139)

EMPLOYMENT ★★★★★ (98)

Average jobless rate	8.0% (291)
Self-employed workers	13.5% (42)
Management/financial jobs	13.2% (73)
Computer/engineering jobs	2.9% (219)
Health care jobs	5.1% (319)

GROWTH POTENTIAL ★★★ (310)

Children per senior	0.75 (540)
Median age	47.9 (533)
Moved from different state	1.6% (383)
Homes built since 2000	21.3% (75)
Construction jobs	9.4% (36)

HOUSING ★★ (386)

Home vacancy rate	7.1% (165)
Home ownership rate	69.6% (284)
Housing diversity index	84.0% (344)
4 or more bedrooms	11.6% (510)
Affordability/income ratio	$3,611 (472)

INCOME ★★★★ (156)

Poverty rate	15.9% (219)
Median household income	$43,810 (268)
Interest/dividends	28.0% (37)
Public assistance	11.5% (112)
Median fulltime earnings	$36,289 (319)

SENIORS ★★★★★ (84)

Seniors living alone	26.4% (193)
Poverty rate for seniors	6.1% (51)
Median income for seniors	$39,947 (60)
Seniors who work	19.3% (232)
Home ownership by seniors	84.8% (150)

STABILITY ★ (476)

25-39 age group	14.1% (538)
Born in state of residence	64.2% (395)
Same house as 1 year ago	82.7% (411)
Live and work in county	85.6% (125)
Married-couple households	48.4% (366)

TRANSPORTATION ★★★★ (204)

Bicycle or walk to work	1.9% (401)
Carpool to work	13.5% (83)
Public transit to work	0.1% (441)
Commute <15 minutes	46.3% (227)
Commute >45 minutes	8.9% (171)

See pages 37-130 for explanations of statistics, stars, and ranks.

Key West, FL
(Monroe County, FL)

POPULATION	
2010 census	73,090 (89)
2015 estimate	77,482 (76)
2010-2015 change	6.0% (32)
2020 projection	78,988 (75)
2030 projection	82,267 (68)

RACE	
Whites	69.0% (397)
Blacks	6.1% (145)
Hispanics	22.0% (68)
Asians	1.0% (158)
Native Americans	0.4% (203)

AGE	
0-17 years old	15.2% (548)
18-24 years old	7.1% (515)
25-39 years old	17.9% (214)
40-54 years old	22.9% (7)
55-64 years old	17.4% (10)
65+ years old	19.6% (61)

PRIVATE SECTOR	
Businesses	4,295 (8)
Employees	35,102 (19)
Total wages	$1,270,600,261 (33)
Average weekly wages	$696 (262)

HOUSEHOLD INCOME LADDER	
95th percentile	$234,261 (7)
80th percentile	$112,806 (22)
60th percentile	$71,923 (32)
40th percentile	$45,877 (39)
20th percentile	$23,934 (69)

CHILDREN	★ (481)
Living with two parents	64.2% (291)
Older teens in school	80.0% (397)
Speak English very well	92.5% (512)
Poverty rate for children	19.5% (152)
No health insurance	16.0% (530)

DIVERSITY/EQUALITY	★★★★★ (86)
Racial diversity index	47.1% (135)
Geographic diversity index	82.3% (1)
Top 20% share of income	54.4% (539)
Gender gap in earnings	20.2% (44)
White-collar gender gap	30.6% (347)

EDUCATION	★★★★★ (68)
Eighth grade or less	3.3% (259)
High school diplomas	91.9% (128)
Attended college	62.5% (89)
Bachelor's degrees	30.0% (53)
Advanced degrees	10.4% (50)

EMPLOYMENT	★★★★★ (37)
Average jobless rate	6.0% (117)
Self-employed workers	17.0% (7)
Management/financial jobs	15.7% (19)
Computer/engineering jobs	3.5% (122)
Health care jobs	4.1% (462)

GROWTH POTENTIAL	★★ (336)
Children per senior	0.77 (539)
Median age	46.8 (524)
Moved from different state	6.9% (25)
Homes built since 2000	11.6% (330)
Construction jobs	6.8% (204)

HOUSING	★ (551)
Home vacancy rate	10.7% (390)
Home ownership rate	61.1% (489)
Housing diversity index	83.8% (369)
4 or more bedrooms	7.7% (548)
Affordability/income ratio	$6,745 (547)

INCOME	★★★★★ (52)
Poverty rate	13.4% (135)
Median household income	$57,290 (36)
Interest/dividends	29.8% (27)
Public assistance	7.4% (28)
Median fulltime earnings	$38,466 (206)

SENIORS	★★★★★ (58)
Seniors living alone	26.0% (172)
Poverty rate for seniors	10.2% (334)
Median income for seniors	$49,479 (15)
Seniors who work	24.0% (89)
Home ownership by seniors	81.6% (299)

STABILITY	★ (499)
25-39 age group	17.9% (214)
Born in state of residence	28.8% (546)
Same house as 1 year ago	81.4% (465)
Live and work in county	94.0% (19)
Married-couple households	46.1% (441)

TRANSPORTATION	★★★★★ (23)
Bicycle or walk to work	11.8% (7)
Carpool to work	10.3% (299)
Public transit to work	2.3% (26)
Commute <15 minutes	47.1% (213)
Commute >45 minutes	9.0% (175)

See pages 37-130 for explanations of statistics, stars, and ranks.

Kill Devil Hills, NC
(Dare and Tyrrell Counties, NC)

POPULATION

2010 census	38,327 (338)
2015 estimate	39,733 (315)
2010-2015 change	3.7% (66)
2020 projection	40,511 (310)
2030 projection	42,013 (295)

RACE

Whites	84.4% (273)
Blacks	5.2% (155)
Hispanics	7.1% (197)
Asians	0.8% (201)
Native Americans	0.2% (300)

AGE

0-17 years old	19.3% (492)
18-24 years old	6.7% (531)
25-39 years old	17.0% (317)
40-54 years old	22.2% (21)
55-64 years old	17.0% (16)
65+ years old	17.8% (137)

PRIVATE SECTOR

Businesses	1,921 (69)
Employees	16,788 (174)
Total wages	$475,237,669 (266)
Average weekly wages	$544 (537)

HOUSEHOLD INCOME LADDER

95th percentile	$171,500 (53)
80th percentile	$97,432 (73)
60th percentile	$61,650 (120)
40th percentile	$43,549 (64)
20th percentile	$26,316 (33)

CHILDREN ★★★ (233)

Living with two parents	63.9% (301)
Older teens in school	82.7% (289)
Speak English very well	97.6% (375)
Poverty rate for children	12.6% (44)
No health insurance	9.5% (410)

DIVERSITY/EQUALITY ★★★★★ (43)

Racial diversity index	27.9% (270)
Geographic diversity index	72.0% (31)
Top 20% share of income	47.0% (222)
Gender gap in earnings	20.5% (48)
White-collar gender gap	24.2% (262)

EDUCATION ★★★★ (124)

Eighth grade or less	3.6% (292)
High school diplomas	90.1% (200)
Attended college	65.2% (57)
Bachelor's degrees	26.0% (95)
Advanced degrees	7.1% (176)

EMPLOYMENT ★★★★★ (74)

Average jobless rate	7.0% (196)
Self-employed workers	17.4% (4)
Management/financial jobs	16.6% (12)
Computer/engineering jobs	1.6% (486)
Health care jobs	3.2% (525)

GROWTH POTENTIAL ★★★★ (151)

Children per senior	1.08 (471)
Median age	44.9 (496)
Moved from different state	3.7% (96)
Homes built since 2000	18.9% (110)
Construction jobs	9.7% (25)

HOUSING ★★ (415)

Home vacancy rate	7.9% (213)
Home ownership rate	68.6% (321)
Housing diversity index	78.9% (528)
4 or more bedrooms	36.4% (2)
Affordability/income ratio	$5,107 (527)

INCOME ★★★★★ (70)

Poverty rate	9.6% (23)
Median household income	$52,591 (79)
Interest/dividends	26.6% (60)
Public assistance	10.8% (89)
Median fulltime earnings	$38,761 (189)

SENIORS ★★★★★ (16)

Seniors living alone	24.9% (113)
Poverty rate for seniors	7.2% (114)
Median income for seniors	$45,319 (26)
Seniors who work	27.0% (37)
Home ownership by seniors	88.1% (39)

STABILITY ★★ (397)

25-39 age group	17.0% (317)
Born in state of residence	40.1% (520)
Same house as 1 year ago	85.7% (272)
Live and work in county	89.4% (78)
Married-couple households	51.1% (245)

TRANSPORTATION ★★★ (269)

Bicycle or walk to work	3.6% (180)
Carpool to work	10.1% (322)
Public transit to work	0.0% (511)
Commute <15 minutes	46.4% (226)
Commute >45 minutes	9.4% (197)

See pages 37-130 for explanations of statistics, stars, and ranks.

Kingsville, TX
(Kenedy and Kleberg Counties, TX)

POPULATION

2010 census	32,477 (410)
2015 estimate	32,264 (417)
2010-2015 change	-0.7% (303)
2020 projection	31,928 (418)
2030 projection	31,236 (418)

RACE

Whites	22.1% (539)
Blacks	3.9% (195)
Hispanics	71.2% (11)
Asians	2.0% (51)
Native Americans	0.1% (402)

AGE

0-17 years old	24.9% (131)
18-24 years old	19.5% (29)
25-39 years old	18.8% (121)
40-54 years old	14.8% (537)
55-64 years old	9.7% (532)
65+ years old	12.2% (492)

PRIVATE SECTOR

Businesses	589 (478)
Employees	8,521 (435)
Total wages	$296,619,484 (438)
Average weekly wages	$669 (336)

HOUSEHOLD INCOME LADDER

95th percentile	$150,177 (161)
80th percentile	$88,358 (179)
60th percentile	$50,007 (384)
40th percentile	$30,056 (421)
20th percentile	$14,375 (469)

CHILDREN ★ (485)

Living with two parents	55.3% (476)
Older teens in school	83.8% (245)
Speak English very well	94.1% (493)
Poverty rate for children	31.2% (427)
No health insurance	11.3% (455)

DIVERSITY/EQUALITY ★★★★ (208)

Racial diversity index	44.2% (159)
Geographic diversity index	36.8% (407)
Top 20% share of income	49.4% (394)
Gender gap in earnings	31.8% (221)
White-collar gender gap	14.3% (144)

EDUCATION ★★★ (326)

Eighth grade or less	10.1% (513)
High school diplomas	79.1% (496)
Attended college	57.0% (187)
Bachelor's degrees	27.6% (79)
Advanced degrees	8.1% (120)

EMPLOYMENT ★ (515)

Average jobless rate	11.6% (479)
Self-employed workers	7.2% (410)
Management/financial jobs	10.2% (357)
Computer/engineering jobs	2.8% (246)
Health care jobs	3.4% (513)

GROWTH POTENTIAL ★★★★★ (80)

Children per senior	2.04 (55)
Median age	28.0 (13)
Moved from different state	1.2% (474)
Homes built since 2000	14.9% (206)
Construction jobs	6.5% (253)

HOUSING ★★ (378)

Home vacancy rate	9.7% (334)
Home ownership rate	52.6% (542)
Housing diversity index	86.4% (26)
4 or more bedrooms	17.0% (247)
Affordability/income ratio	$2,116 (87)

INCOME ★ (482)

Poverty rate	26.1% (487)
Median household income	$38,191 (425)
Interest/dividends	10.4% (524)
Public assistance	19.3% (409)
Median fulltime earnings	$33,675 (432)

SENIORS ★★★★ (195)

Seniors living alone	17.7% (3)
Poverty rate for seniors	12.3% (427)
Median income for seniors	$34,117 (230)
Seniors who work	15.7% (427)
Home ownership by seniors	79.8% (382)

STABILITY ★★ (405)

25-39 age group	18.8% (121)
Born in state of residence	79.0% (132)
Same house as 1 year ago	81.6% (456)
Live and work in county	74.2% (307)
Married-couple households	42.9% (495)

TRANSPORTATION ★★★★★ (20)

Bicycle or walk to work	6.9% (43)
Carpool to work	16.8% (26)
Public transit to work	0.0% (511)
Commute <15 minutes	58.9% (54)
Commute >45 minutes	10.2% (235)

See pages 37-130 for explanations of statistics, stars, and ranks.

Kinston, NC
(Lenoir County, NC)

POPULATION

2010 census	59,495 (156)
2015 estimate	58,106 (158)
2010-2015 change	-2.3% (436)
2020 projection	56,151 (171)
2030 projection	52,213 (202)

RACE

Whites	50.5% (484)
Blacks	39.5% (31)
Hispanics	7.1% (197)
Asians	0.7% (241)
Native Americans	0.3% (231)

AGE

0-17 years old	23.0% (259)
18-24 years old	8.5% (330)
25-39 years old	16.1% (442)
40-54 years old	20.4% (169)
55-64 years old	14.4% (136)
65+ years old	17.5% (158)

PRIVATE SECTOR

Businesses	1,305 (174)
Employees	22,037 (97)
Total wages	$743,455,323 (139)
Average weekly wages	$649 (393)

HOUSEHOLD INCOME LADDER

95th percentile	$119,820 (517)
80th percentile	$70,366 (503)
60th percentile	$44,344 (486)
40th percentile	$27,318 (474)
20th percentile	$15,238 (444)

CHILDREN ★★ **(434)**

Living with two parents	49.3% (512)
Older teens in school	84.6% (214)
Speak English very well	96.8% (421)
Poverty rate for children	36.2% (489)
No health insurance	4.6% (159)

DIVERSITY/EQUALITY ★★★ **(287)**

Racial diversity index	58.3% (23)
Geographic diversity index	38.3% (385)
Top 20% share of income	51.2% (475)
Gender gap in earnings	20.3% (46)
White-collar gender gap	50.2% (511)

EDUCATION ★ **(472)**

Eighth grade or less	7.9% (489)
High school diplomas	81.4% (458)
Attended college	51.1% (300)
Bachelor's degrees	12.8% (501)
Advanced degrees	3.9% (489)

EMPLOYMENT ★ **(469)**

Average jobless rate	13.1% (518)
Self-employed workers	8.1% (323)
Management/financial jobs	10.2% (357)
Computer/engineering jobs	2.2% (381)
Health care jobs	5.8% (209)

GROWTH POTENTIAL ★★ **(410)**

Children per senior	1.32 (334)
Median age	42.1 (408)
Moved from different state	1.5% (406)
Homes built since 2000	8.2% (462)
Construction jobs	7.3% (151)

HOUSING ★★ **(414)**

Home vacancy rate	10.4% (371)
Home ownership rate	60.4% (499)
Housing diversity index	85.9% (83)
4 or more bedrooms	13.7% (415)
Affordability/income ratio	$2,664 (317)

INCOME ★ **(499)**

Poverty rate	23.2% (452)
Median household income	$34,717 (489)
Interest/dividends	14.2% (435)
Public assistance	27.2% (525)
Median fulltime earnings	$32,134 (489)

SENIORS ★ **(491)**

Seniors living alone	30.9% (469)
Poverty rate for seniors	13.2% (454)
Median income for seniors	$31,467 (351)
Seniors who work	18.1% (284)
Home ownership by seniors	77.2% (478)

STABILITY ★ **(477)**

25-39 age group	16.1% (442)
Born in state of residence	77.8% (159)
Same house as 1 year ago	83.4% (375)
Live and work in county	76.3% (266)
Married-couple households	41.6% (509)

TRANSPORTATION ★★★★ **(162)**

Bicycle or walk to work	2.6% (308)
Carpool to work	16.9% (24)
Public transit to work	0.8% (96)
Commute <15 minutes	34.1% (457)
Commute >45 minutes	10.7% (262)

See pages 37-130 for explanations of statistics, stars, and ranks.

LaGrange, GA
(Troup County, GA)

POPULATION

2010 census	67,044 (112)
2015 estimate	69,763 (103)
2010-2015 change	4.1% (57)
2020 projection	71,951 (96)
2030 projection	76,256 (87)

RACE

Whites	58.4% (454)
Blacks	34.3% (42)
Hispanics	3.6% (314)
Asians	1.8% (60)
Native Americans	0.1% (402)

AGE

0-17 years old	25.6% (85)
18-24 years old	10.5% (136)
25-39 years old	18.2% (167)
40-54 years old	20.2% (202)
55-64 years old	12.1% (430)
65+ years old	13.3% (465)

PRIVATE SECTOR

Businesses	1,511 (133)
Employees	34,338 (21)
Total wages	$1,440,396,391 (21)
Average weekly wages	$807 (81)

HOUSEHOLD INCOME LADDER

95th percentile	$150,710 (156)
80th percentile	$82,886 (295)
60th percentile	$52,767 (303)
40th percentile	$32,414 (344)
20th percentile	$15,661 (423)

CHILDREN ★ **(472)**

Living with two parents	49.8% (508)
Older teens in school	76.1% (488)
Speak English very well	98.9% (226)
Poverty rate for children	31.1% (423)
No health insurance	8.0% (362)

DIVERSITY/EQUALITY ★★★★ **(202)**

Racial diversity index	53.9% (69)
Geographic diversity index	50.6% (203)
Top 20% share of income	52.0% (503)
Gender gap in earnings	30.8% (190)
White-collar gender gap	22.6% (242)

EDUCATION ★★★ **(247)**

Eighth grade or less	3.9% (316)
High school diplomas	87.1% (301)
Attended college	51.1% (300)
Bachelor's degrees	19.4% (235)
Advanced degrees	7.8% (129)

EMPLOYMENT ★ **(466)**

Average jobless rate	11.9% (488)
Self-employed workers	6.6% (461)
Management/financial jobs	12.2% (139)
Computer/engineering jobs	2.5% (307)
Health care jobs	4.6% (401)

GROWTH POTENTIAL ★★★★ **(135)**

Children per senior	1.92 (69)
Median age	36.1 (118)
Moved from different state	3.8% (89)
Homes built since 2000	19.1% (105)
Construction jobs	4.3% (514)

HOUSING ★★ **(389)**

Home vacancy rate	9.8% (341)
Home ownership rate	57.9% (524)
Housing diversity index	85.9% (83)
4 or more bedrooms	17.2% (236)
Affordability/income ratio	$2,803 (359)

INCOME ★★ **(437)**

Poverty rate	21.4% (412)
Median household income	$41,489 (337)
Interest/dividends	12.0% (494)
Public assistance	19.8% (419)
Median fulltime earnings	$35,149 (378)

SENIORS ★ **(499)**

Seniors living alone	28.3% (318)
Poverty rate for seniors	13.8% (467)
Median income for seniors	$30,588 (389)
Seniors who work	15.7% (427)
Home ownership by seniors	76.3% (505)

STABILITY ★ **(441)**

25-39 age group	18.2% (167)
Born in state of residence	67.2% (358)
Same house as 1 year ago	81.6% (456)
Live and work in county	81.0% (204)
Married-couple households	43.4% (488)

TRANSPORTATION ★ **(490)**

Bicycle or walk to work	1.4% (472)
Carpool to work	8.6% (457)
Public transit to work	0.3% (291)
Commute <15 minutes	31.2% (510)
Commute >45 minutes	11.8% (306)

See pages 37-130 for explanations of statistics, stars, and ranks.

Lake City, FL
(Columbia County, FL)

POPULATION	
2010 census	67,531 (109)
2015 estimate	68,348 (109)
2010-2015 change	1.2% (173)
2020 projection	70,243 (103)
2030 projection	74,311 (93)

RACE	
Whites	73.4% (369)
Blacks	17.7% (84)
Hispanics	5.4% (240)
Asians	0.8% (201)
Native Americans	0.3% (231)

AGE	
0-17 years old	21.8% (351)
18-24 years old	9.4% (203)
25-39 years old	18.3% (159)
40-54 years old	19.8% (261)
55-64 years old	13.8% (203)
65+ years old	16.8% (215)

PRIVATE SECTOR	
Businesses	1,407 (153)
Employees	18,088 (151)
Total wages	$594,604,496 (188)
Average weekly wages	$632 (432)

HOUSEHOLD INCOME LADDER	
95th percentile	$136,175 (340)
80th percentile	$80,055 (367)
60th percentile	$51,814 (328)
40th percentile	$33,258 (314)
20th percentile	$18,346 (301)

CHILDREN	★ (477)
Living with two parents	57.7% (453)
Older teens in school	73.5% (513)
Speak English very well	98.8% (251)
Poverty rate for children	30.6% (416)
No health insurance	10.3% (428)

DIVERSITY/EQUALITY	★★★★★ (49)
Racial diversity index	42.6% (169)
Geographic diversity index	60.8% (119)
Top 20% share of income	48.0% (298)
Gender gap in earnings	26.9% (116)
White-collar gender gap	12.7% (123)

EDUCATION	★★ (333)
Eighth grade or less	3.3% (259)
High school diplomas	86.6% (322)

Attended college	51.3% (298)
Bachelor's degrees	14.9% (424)
Advanced degrees	5.6% (304)

EMPLOYMENT	★★ (374)
Average jobless rate	14.8% (534)
Self-employed workers	6.9% (435)
Management/financial jobs	9.6% (427)
Computer/engineering jobs	2.7% (270)
Health care jobs	9.4% (3)

GROWTH POTENTIAL	★★★★ (129)
Children per senior	1.30 (347)
Median age	40.4 (325)
Moved from different state	2.7% (179)
Homes built since 2000	25.2% (34)
Construction jobs	7.3% (151)

HOUSING	★ (455)
Home vacancy rate	12.5% (476)
Home ownership rate	71.4% (209)
Housing diversity index	81.4% (479)
4 or more bedrooms	14.5% (377)
Affordability/income ratio	$2,469 (241)

INCOME	★★ (402)
Poverty rate	19.9% (366)
Median household income	$41,926 (325)
Interest/dividends	15.1% (405)
Public assistance	20.5% (442)
Median fulltime earnings	$35,468 (361)

SENIORS	★★★★ (194)
Seniors living alone	25.1% (120)
Poverty rate for seniors	9.9% (315)
Median income for seniors	$36,380 (145)
Seniors who work	12.0% (540)
Home ownership by seniors	87.3% (62)

STABILITY	★ (503)
25-39 age group	18.3% (159)
Born in state of residence	59.4% (422)
Same house as 1 year ago	79.2% (507)
Live and work in county	74.6% (301)
Married-couple households	45.6% (451)

TRANSPORTATION	★ (474)
Bicycle or walk to work	1.3% (485)
Carpool to work	11.9% (145)
Public transit to work	0.1% (441)
Commute <15 minutes	32.5% (486)
Commute >45 minutes	16.1% (459)

See pages 37-130 for explanations of statistics, stars, and ranks.

Lamesa, TX
(Dawson County, TX)

POPULATION

2010 census	13,833 (547)
2015 estimate	13,520 (549)
2010-2015 change	-2.3% (436)
2020 projection	13,063 (549)
2030 projection	12,206 (549)

RACE

Whites	37.8% (517)
Blacks	5.6% (150)
Hispanics	54.7% (20)
Asians	0.8% (201)
Native Americans	0.3% (231)

AGE

0-17 years old	23.9% (194)
18-24 years old	10.7% (124)
25-39 years old	23.8% (10)
40-54 years old	17.2% (494)
55-64 years old	9.9% (524)
65+ years old	14.5% (412)

PRIVATE SECTOR

Businesses	466 (522)
Employees	3,031 (548)
Total wages	$109,497,549 (547)
Average weekly wages	$695 (268)

HOUSEHOLD INCOME LADDER

95th percentile	$170,438 (56)
80th percentile	$86,867 (211)
60th percentile	$51,522 (343)
40th percentile	$32,110 (357)
20th percentile	$16,668 (375)

CHILDREN   ★ (443)

Living with two parents	70.4% (135)
Older teens in school	84.7% (210)
Speak English very well	91.1% (521)
Poverty rate for children	17.2% (104)
No health insurance	17.7% (537)

DIVERSITY/EQUALITY   ★ (527)

Racial diversity index	55.5% (45)
Geographic diversity index	34.7% (441)
Top 20% share of income	51.8% (498)
Gender gap in earnings	50.7% (529)
White-collar gender gap	40.9% (453)

EDUCATION   ★ (533)

Eighth grade or less	10.3% (514)
High school diplomas	75.5% (521)
Attended college	37.5% (532)
Bachelor's degrees	11.7% (521)
Advanced degrees	3.2% (521)

EMPLOYMENT   ★★ (405)

Average jobless rate	9.5% (400)
Self-employed workers	10.2% (155)
Management/financial jobs	12.7% (103)
Computer/engineering jobs	0.4% (551)
Health care jobs	4.3% (444)

GROWTH POTENTIAL   ★★★ (258)

Children per senior	1.65 (148)
Median age	33.4 (63)
Moved from different state	3.3% (129)
Homes built since 2000	3.0% (550)
Construction jobs	5.7% (373)

HOUSING   ★ (451)

Home vacancy rate	14.1% (520)
Home ownership rate	72.0% (189)
Housing diversity index	82.3% (448)
4 or more bedrooms	10.3% (528)
Affordability/income ratio	$1,511 (4)

INCOME   ★★ (360)

Poverty rate	16.6% (252)
Median household income	$41,095 (350)
Interest/dividends	14.4% (429)
Public assistance	17.8% (366)
Median fulltime earnings	$35,697 (350)

SENIORS   ★★ (372)

Seniors living alone	30.6% (454)
Poverty rate for seniors	16.7% (513)
Median income for seniors	$27,065 (475)
Seniors who work	25.6% (57)
Home ownership by seniors	86.6% (78)

STABILITY   ★★★★★ (9)

25-39 age group	23.8% (10)
Born in state of residence	80.3% (107)
Same house as 1 year ago	79.6% (503)
Live and work in county	81.9% (184)
Married-couple households	53.2% (143)

TRANSPORTATION   ★★★★★ (82)

Bicycle or walk to work	1.2% (492)
Carpool to work	15.3% (42)
Public transit to work	0.3% (291)
Commute <15 minutes	65.6% (16)
Commute >45 minutes	10.3% (237)

See pages 37-130 for explanations of statistics, stars, and ranks.

Laurel, MS
(Jasper and Jones Counties, MS)

POPULATION	
2010 census	84,823 (56)
2015 estimate	84,784 (59)
2010-2015 change	0.0% (255)
2020 projection	84,455 (61)
2030 projection	83,274 (66)

RACE	
Whites	61.4% (439)
Blacks	33.6% (43)
Hispanics	3.5% (318)
Asians	0.4% (413)
Native Americans	0.2% (300)

AGE	
0-17 years old	25.1% (116)
18-24 years old	9.2% (234)
25-39 years old	18.6% (135)
40-54 years old	18.6% (412)
55-64 years old	13.0% (334)
65+ years old	15.5% (333)

PRIVATE SECTOR	
Businesses	1,476 (140)
Employees	24,071 (81)
Total wages	$975,306,254 (74)
Average weekly wages	$779 (120)

HOUSEHOLD INCOME LADDER	
95th percentile	$140,629 (282)
80th percentile	$74,306 (470)
60th percentile	$45,077 (477)
40th percentile	$27,461 (470)
20th percentile	$14,709 (460)

CHILDREN	★ (469)
Living with two parents	46.3% (525)
Older teens in school	80.3% (388)
Speak English very well	98.3% (312)
Poverty rate for children	35.5% (480)
No health insurance	6.2% (262)

DIVERSITY/EQUALITY	★★ (408)
Racial diversity index	50.9% (105)
Geographic diversity index	33.4% (451)
Top 20% share of income	52.3% (509)
Gender gap in earnings	29.8% (167)
White-collar gender gap	37.3% (411)

EDUCATION	★★ (377)
Eighth grade or less	6.5% (449)
High school diplomas	81.2% (463)

Attended college	52.4% (276)
Bachelor's degrees	17.3% (309)
Advanced degrees	7.2% (164)

EMPLOYMENT	★★★ (269)
Average jobless rate	7.5% (242)
Self-employed workers	7.3% (401)
Management/financial jobs	9.9% (392)
Computer/engineering jobs	2.3% (354)
Health care jobs	7.2% (58)

GROWTH POTENTIAL	★★★★ (191)
Children per senior	1.62 (164)
Median age	37.5 (162)
Moved from different state	1.5% (406)
Homes built since 2000	17.2% (150)
Construction jobs	6.4% (270)

HOUSING	★★★★ (153)
Home vacancy rate	10.7% (390)
Home ownership rate	75.3% (72)
Housing diversity index	85.7% (108)
4 or more bedrooms	16.0% (293)
Affordability/income ratio	$2,281 (156)

INCOME	★ (475)
Poverty rate	23.0% (444)
Median household income	$36,032 (466)
Interest/dividends	10.7% (520)
Public assistance	18.2% (378)
Median fulltime earnings	$32,623 (465)

SENIORS	★★ (349)
Seniors living alone	26.0% (172)
Poverty rate for seniors	14.6% (484)
Median income for seniors	$26,688 (480)
Seniors who work	16.1% (400)
Home ownership by seniors	88.4% (31)

STABILITY	★★★★★ (72)
25-39 age group	18.6% (135)
Born in state of residence	80.7% (103)
Same house as 1 year ago	91.0% (30)
Live and work in county	71.5% (349)
Married-couple households	48.4% (366)

TRANSPORTATION	★ (518)
Bicycle or walk to work	1.0% (512)
Carpool to work	7.6% (510)
Public transit to work	0.4% (219)
Commute <15 minutes	26.4% (544)
Commute >45 minutes	9.6% (210)

See pages 37-130 for explanations of statistics, stars, and ranks.

Laurinburg, NC
(Scotland County, NC)

POPULATION	
2010 census	36,157 (374)
2015 estimate	35,509 (377)
2010-2015 change	-1.8% (389)
2020 projection	34,385 (391)
2030 projection	32,101 (407)

RACE	
Whites	44.8% (503)
Blacks	38.3% (32)
Hispanics	2.7% (361)
Asians	0.8% (201)
Native Americans	10.4% (19)

AGE	
0-17 years old	23.7% (218)
18-24 years old	10.2% (151)
25-39 years old	17.2% (290)
40-54 years old	19.8% (261)
55-64 years old	13.8% (203)
65+ years old	15.2% (354)

PRIVATE SECTOR	
Businesses	596 (472)
Employees	9,525 (389)
Total wages	$328,695,871 (400)
Average weekly wages	$664 (344)

HOUSEHOLD INCOME LADDER	
95th percentile	$112,989 (541)
80th percentile	$63,838 (538)
60th percentile	$39,988 (528)
40th percentile	$23,269 (532)
20th percentile	$11,662 (530)

CHILDREN	★ (504)
Living with two parents	37.8% (542)
Older teens in school	86.4% (152)
Speak English very well	99.1% (179)
Poverty rate for children	46.9% (538)
No health insurance	6.8% (302)

DIVERSITY/EQUALITY	★★★★ (187)
Racial diversity index	64.0% (5)
Geographic diversity index	44.4% (291)
Top 20% share of income	49.5% (401)
Gender gap in earnings	20.5% (48)
White-collar gender gap	52.5% (520)

EDUCATION	★★ (416)
Eighth grade or less	4.7% (366)
High school diplomas	81.5% (455)
Attended college	46.5% (406)
Bachelor's degrees	15.7% (399)
Advanced degrees	5.6% (304)

EMPLOYMENT	★ (505)
Average jobless rate	15.5% (539)
Self-employed workers	7.9% (345)
Management/financial jobs	10.9% (263)
Computer/engineering jobs	1.9% (441)
Health care jobs	5.6% (240)

GROWTH POTENTIAL	★★★ (295)
Children per senior	1.56 (189)
Median age	39.1 (244)
Moved from different state	2.4% (218)
Homes built since 2000	10.8% (364)
Construction jobs	6.0% (326)

HOUSING	★ (452)
Home vacancy rate	12.6% (481)
Home ownership rate	63.1% (471)
Housing diversity index	85.1% (212)
4 or more bedrooms	14.3% (387)
Affordability/income ratio	$2,555 (274)

INCOME	★ (537)
Poverty rate	31.2% (528)
Median household income	$30,958 (531)
Interest/dividends	11.2% (508)
Public assistance	27.8% (532)
Median fulltime earnings	$31,841 (504)

SENIORS	★ (496)
Seniors living alone	28.0% (296)
Poverty rate for seniors	13.1% (450)
Median income for seniors	n.a.
Seniors who work	14.4% (485)
Home ownership by seniors	77.6% (466)

STABILITY	★ (492)
25-39 age group	17.2% (290)
Born in state of residence	72.9% (261)
Same house as 1 year ago	85.8% (264)
Live and work in county	67.8% (409)
Married-couple households	40.2% (530)

TRANSPORTATION	★ (477)
Bicycle or walk to work	1.7% (428)
Carpool to work	8.1% (489)
Public transit to work	0.3% (291)
Commute <15 minutes	35.9% (421)
Commute >45 minutes	12.8% (346)

See pages 37-130 for explanations of statistics, stars, and ranks.

Lawrenceburg, TN
(Lawrence County, TN)

POPULATION

2010 census	41,869 (291)
2015 estimate	42,564 (284)
2010-2015 change	1.7% (150)
2020 projection	42,970 (282)
2030 projection	43,654 (280)

RACE

Whites	94.2% (70)
Blacks	1.9% (295)
Hispanics	1.9% (442)
Asians	0.5% (355)
Native Americans	0.2% (300)

AGE

0-17 years old	25.0% (126)
18-24 years old	7.8% (447)
25-39 years old	17.2% (290)
40-54 years old	20.0% (233)
55-64 years old	12.8% (356)
65+ years old	17.2% (182)

PRIVATE SECTOR

Businesses	676 (444)
Employees	8,046 (446)
Total wages	$257,264,115 (467)
Average weekly wages	$615 (456)

HOUSEHOLD INCOME LADDER

95th percentile	$117,023 (532)
80th percentile	$73,939 (474)
60th percentile	$48,095 (423)
40th percentile	$30,528 (400)
20th percentile	$17,095 (358)

CHILDREN ★ (522)

Living with two parents	73.0% (80)
Older teens in school	72.5% (517)
Speak English very well	94.5% (486)
Poverty rate for children	31.0% (421)
No health insurance	18.5% (541)

DIVERSITY/EQUALITY ★★ (401)

Racial diversity index	11.2% (477)
Geographic diversity index	46.3% (264)
Top 20% share of income	46.7% (184)
Gender gap in earnings	35.3% (321)
White-collar gender gap	35.9% (397)

EDUCATION ★ (447)

Eighth grade or less	5.4% (405)
High school diplomas	85.2% (368)

Attended college	41.3% (500)
Bachelor's degrees	13.6% (474)
Advanced degrees	4.9% (396)

EMPLOYMENT ★★ (384)

Average jobless rate	10.8% (453)
Self-employed workers	10.2% (155)
Management/financial jobs	7.8% (537)
Computer/engineering jobs	2.0% (420)
Health care jobs	7.1% (63)

GROWTH POTENTIAL ★★★★ (138)

Children per senior	1.45 (244)
Median age	39.9 (292)
Moved from different state	1.8% (338)
Homes built since 2000	17.1% (153)
Construction jobs	9.2% (39)

HOUSING ★★★★★ (110)

Home vacancy rate	8.5% (253)
Home ownership rate	74.9% (83)
Housing diversity index	85.4% (156)
4 or more bedrooms	18.0% (202)
Affordability/income ratio	$2,607 (294)

INCOME ★ (453)

Poverty rate	20.3% (384)
Median household income	$37,814 (431)
Interest/dividends	13.6% (450)
Public assistance	19.8% (419)
Median fulltime earnings	$33,279 (444)

SENIORS ★ (451)

Seniors living alone	26.1% (179)
Poverty rate for seniors	12.9% (449)
Median income for seniors	$28,091 (455)
Seniors who work	13.2% (522)
Home ownership by seniors	82.4% (257)

STABILITY ★★★★ (176)

25-39 age group	17.2% (290)
Born in state of residence	71.0% (293)
Same house as 1 year ago	89.7% (54)
Live and work in county	65.8% (440)
Married-couple households	54.0% (108)

TRANSPORTATION ★ (536)

Bicycle or walk to work	0.6% (541)
Carpool to work	9.6% (378)
Public transit to work	0.3% (291)
Commute <15 minutes	32.3% (489)
Commute >45 minutes	18.7% (506)

See pages 37-130 for explanations of statistics, stars, and ranks.

Levelland, TX
(Hockley County, TX)

POPULATION

2010 census	22,935 (496)
2015 estimate	23,433 (493)
2010-2015 change	2.2% (118)
2020 projection	23,448 (491)
2030 projection	23,462 (487)

RACE

Whites	48.4% (490)
Blacks	3.3% (217)
Hispanics	45.9% (30)
Asians	0.4% (413)
Native Americans	0.4% (203)

AGE

0-17 years old	26.7% (52)
18-24 years old	12.5% (77)
25-39 years old	17.6% (248)
40-54 years old	18.4% (430)
55-64 years old	11.4% (482)
65+ years old	13.5% (459)

PRIVATE SECTOR

Businesses	604 (468)
Employees	8,288 (440)
Total wages	$420,728,612 (313)
Average weekly wages	$976 (19)

HOUSEHOLD INCOME LADDER

95th percentile	$163,240 (79)
80th percentile	$94,163 (97)
60th percentile	$61,708 (117)
40th percentile	$40,381 (118)
20th percentile	$21,456 (166)

CHILDREN ★★★ (329)

Living with two parents	64.1% (293)
Older teens in school	91.9% (40)
Speak English very well	96.5% (436)
Poverty rate for children	16.8% (91)
No health insurance	17.8% (538)

DIVERSITY/EQUALITY ★★ (370)

Racial diversity index	55.4% (47)
Geographic diversity index	35.3% (433)
Top 20% share of income	47.4% (252)
Gender gap in earnings	45.8% (508)
White-collar gender gap	37.9% (421)

EDUCATION ★★ (434)

Eighth grade or less	6.6% (452)
High school diplomas	80.8% (470)
Attended college	54.1% (241)
Bachelor's degrees	15.8% (391)
Advanced degrees	3.7% (498)

EMPLOYMENT ★★★ (330)

Average jobless rate	6.4% (147)
Self-employed workers	9.9% (171)
Management/financial jobs	10.7% (287)
Computer/engineering jobs	1.8% (457)
Health care jobs	4.4% (433)

GROWTH POTENTIAL ★★★★ (119)

Children per senior	1.98 (64)
Median age	32.8 (57)
Moved from different state	2.0% (288)
Homes built since 2000	9.1% (430)
Construction jobs	7.6% (110)

HOUSING ★★★ (302)

Home vacancy rate	10.9% (400)
Home ownership rate	68.0% (343)
Housing diversity index	85.2% (190)
4 or more bedrooms	11.3% (515)
Affordability/income ratio	$1,611 (8)

INCOME ★★★★ (204)

Poverty rate	14.6% (178)
Median household income	$50,665 (107)
Interest/dividends	16.6% (357)
Public assistance	14.0% (207)
Median fulltime earnings	$38,720 (193)

SENIORS ★★★★ (133)

Seniors living alone	26.6% (209)
Poverty rate for seniors	12.3% (427)
Median income for seniors	$37,464 (106)
Seniors who work	26.6% (40)
Home ownership by seniors	82.6% (242)

STABILITY ★★★ (298)

25-39 age group	17.6% (248)
Born in state of residence	79.9% (117)
Same house as 1 year ago	79.1% (509)
Live and work in county	69.8% (374)
Married-couple households	54.6% (84)

TRANSPORTATION ★★★★★ (83)

Bicycle or walk to work	2.4% (331)
Carpool to work	18.1% (15)
Public transit to work	0.1% (441)
Commute <15 minutes	49.0% (174)
Commute >45 minutes	8.9% (171)

See pages 37-130 for explanations of statistics, stars, and ranks.

Lewisburg, TN
(Marshall County, TN)

POPULATION	
2010 census	30,617 (430)
2015 estimate	31,552 (423)
2010-2015 change	3.1% (78)
2020 projection	32,643 (412)
2030 projection	34,812 (378)

RACE	
Whites	86.0% (255)
Blacks	7.0% (134)
Hispanics	4.9% (254)
Asians	0.5% (355)
Native Americans	0.0% (523)

AGE	
0-17 years old	23.9% (194)
18-24 years old	7.8% (447)
25-39 years old	19.1% (95)
40-54 years old	20.7% (132)
55-64 years old	13.9% (192)
65+ years old	14.5% (412)

PRIVATE SECTOR	
Businesses	468 (521)
Employees	6,693 (484)
Total wages	$248,988,044 (471)
Average weekly wages	$715 (225)

HOUSEHOLD INCOME LADDER	
95th percentile	$144,431 (237)
80th percentile	$84,433 (263)
60th percentile	$51,812 (329)
40th percentile	$33,973 (291)
20th percentile	$20,004 (230)

CHILDREN	★★★ (247)
Living with two parents	64.5% (281)
Older teens in school	82.4% (301)
Speak English very well	99.0% (200)
Poverty rate for children	25.3% (307)
No health insurance	6.0% (248)

DIVERSITY/EQUALITY	★★★★ (128)
Racial diversity index	25.3% (292)
Geographic diversity index	54.2% (161)
Top 20% share of income	47.6% (261)
Gender gap in earnings	27.8% (133)
White-collar gender gap	17.5% (183)

EDUCATION	★ (475)
Eighth grade or less	6.2% (433)
High school diplomas	84.2% (396)
Attended college	42.8% (476)
Bachelor's degrees	14.4% (448)
Advanced degrees	3.1% (524)

EMPLOYMENT	★★ (440)
Average jobless rate	8.4% (323)
Self-employed workers	5.5% (530)
Management/financial jobs	7.6% (539)
Computer/engineering jobs	4.1% (70)
Health care jobs	5.7% (222)

GROWTH POTENTIAL	★★★★ (156)
Children per senior	1.65 (148)
Median age	39.4 (262)
Moved from different state	1.5% (406)
Homes built since 2000	22.6% (59)
Construction jobs	6.4% (270)

HOUSING	★★★★ (129)
Home vacancy rate	6.9% (158)
Home ownership rate	72.8% (160)
Housing diversity index	84.9% (235)
4 or more bedrooms	16.8% (258)
Affordability/income ratio	$2,632 (302)

INCOME	★★★ (322)
Poverty rate	16.2% (232)
Median household income	$42,661 (296)
Interest/dividends	16.5% (360)
Public assistance	16.7% (319)
Median fulltime earnings	$35,462 (363)

SENIORS	★★★★ (134)
Seniors living alone	26.5% (201)
Poverty rate for seniors	5.8% (45)
Median income for seniors	$32,395 (306)
Seniors who work	18.2% (280)
Home ownership by seniors	86.2% (90)

STABILITY	★★★ (296)
25-39 age group	19.1% (95)
Born in state of residence	65.2% (383)
Same house as 1 year ago	88.6% (101)
Live and work in county	54.5% (524)
Married-couple households	52.4% (177)

TRANSPORTATION	★ (549)
Bicycle or walk to work	1.0% (512)
Carpool to work	9.1% (419)
Public transit to work	0.2% (363)
Commute <15 minutes	29.8% (526)
Commute >45 minutes	27.3% (547)

See pages 37-130 for explanations of statistics, stars, and ranks.

London, KY
(Knox, Laurel, and Whitley Counties, KY)

POPULATION

2010 census	126,369 (12)
2015 estimate	127,953 (13)
2010-2015 change	1.3% (167)
2020 projection	128,773 (12)
2030 projection	130,104 (13)

RACE

Whites	96.1% (15)
Blacks	0.9% (388)
Hispanics	1.2% (513)
Asians	0.4% (413)
Native Americans	0.3% (231)

AGE

0-17 years old	23.9% (194)
18-24 years old	9.4% (203)
25-39 years old	18.7% (127)
40-54 years old	20.2% (202)
55-64 years old	12.8% (356)
65+ years old	14.9% (374)

PRIVATE SECTOR

Businesses	2,671 (29)
Employees	38,340 (17)
Total wages	$1,296,654,982 (30)
Average weekly wages	$650 (389)

HOUSEHOLD INCOME LADDER

95th percentile	$117,252 (530)
80th percentile	$65,220 (532)
60th percentile	$40,199 (526)
40th percentile	$25,239 (508)
20th percentile	$13,206 (497)

CHILDREN   ★★★ (319)

Living with two parents	62.6% (330)
Older teens in school	81.8% (329)
Speak English very well	100.0% (1)
Poverty rate for children	38.2% (502)
No health insurance	3.8% (108)

DIVERSITY/EQUALITY   ★ (494)

Racial diversity index	7.6% (531)
Geographic diversity index	39.6% (361)
Top 20% share of income	50.2% (440)
Gender gap in earnings	27.9% (137)
White-collar gender gap	36.8% (404)

EDUCATION   ★ (494)

Eighth grade or less	8.1% (491)
High school diplomas	79.2% (495)
Attended college	39.5% (521)
Bachelor's degrees	14.1% (457)
Advanced degrees	6.2% (243)

EMPLOYMENT   ★ (528)

Average jobless rate	12.5% (508)
Self-employed workers	6.7% (457)
Management/financial jobs	9.1% (463)
Computer/engineering jobs	1.6% (486)
Health care jobs	5.0% (339)

GROWTH POTENTIAL   ★★★ (245)

Children per senior	1.61 (167)
Median age	38.3 (197)
Moved from different state	2.1% (269)
Homes built since 2000	17.5% (140)
Construction jobs	5.0% (467)

HOUSING   ★★ (400)

Home vacancy rate	9.6% (327)
Home ownership rate	66.9% (392)
Housing diversity index	83.4% (396)
4 or more bedrooms	13.3% (437)
Affordability/income ratio	$2,624 (300)

INCOME   ★ (525)

Poverty rate	26.3% (490)
Median household income	$32,428 (514)
Interest/dividends	11.0% (511)
Public assistance	27.7% (531)
Median fulltime earnings	$32,148 (488)

SENIORS   ★ (510)

Seniors living alone	27.6% (269)
Poverty rate for seniors	14.8% (485)
Median income for seniors	$25,970 (494)
Seniors who work	11.8% (542)
Home ownership by seniors	80.4% (362)

STABILITY   ★★★★ (214)

25-39 age group	18.7% (127)
Born in state of residence	76.4% (195)
Same house as 1 year ago	85.8% (264)
Live and work in county	68.8% (392)
Married-couple households	49.7% (311)

TRANSPORTATION   ★★★ (329)

Bicycle or walk to work	2.1% (374)
Carpool to work	10.7% (260)
Public transit to work	0.5% (178)
Commute <15 minutes	36.8% (402)
Commute >45 minutes	8.7% (158)

See pages 37-130 for explanations of statistics, stars, and ranks.

Lufkin, TX
(Angelina County, TX)

POPULATION	
2010 census	86,771 (54)
2015 estimate	88,255 (49)
2010-2015 change	1.7% (150)
2020 projection	89,387 (46)
2030 projection	91,563 (46)

RACE	
Whites	61.9% (436)
Blacks	14.9% (90)
Hispanics	20.9% (74)
Asians	1.0% (158)
Native Americans	0.1% (402)

AGE	
0-17 years old	26.3% (57)
18-24 years old	9.3% (217)
25-39 years old	18.5% (144)
40-54 years old	19.5% (301)
55-64 years old	11.8% (456)
65+ years old	14.6% (400)

PRIVATE SECTOR	
Businesses	1,786 (88)
Employees	29,548 (45)
Total wages	$1,164,446,840 (47)
Average weekly wages	$758 (148)

HOUSEHOLD INCOME LADDER	
95th percentile	$146,063 (212)
80th percentile	$84,301 (270)
60th percentile	$54,026 (279)
40th percentile	$35,698 (243)
20th percentile	$19,279 (254)

CHILDREN	★ (470)
Living with two parents	58.4% (441)
Older teens in school	79.2% (421)
Speak English very well	96.6% (430)
Poverty rate for children	30.0% (404)
No health insurance	11.6% (462)

DIVERSITY/EQUALITY	★★★★ (121)
Racial diversity index	55.1% (53)
Geographic diversity index	40.7% (341)
Top 20% share of income	50.0% (431)
Gender gap in earnings	30.8% (190)
White-collar gender gap	10.4% (93)

EDUCATION	★ (466)
Eighth grade or less	8.4% (497)
High school diplomas	80.3% (475)

Attended college	49.9% (335)
Bachelor's degrees	15.0% (422)
Advanced degrees	5.0% (378)

EMPLOYMENT	★★ (432)
Average jobless rate	9.1% (370)
Self-employed workers	8.3% (302)
Management/financial jobs	9.5% (440)
Computer/engineering jobs	1.8% (457)
Health care jobs	5.5% (250)

GROWTH POTENTIAL	★★★★ (152)
Children per senior	1.80 (96)
Median age	36.4 (128)
Moved from different state	1.6% (383)
Homes built since 2000	16.1% (176)
Construction jobs	6.7% (219)

HOUSING	★★ (342)
Home vacancy rate	10.1% (352)
Home ownership rate	66.0% (415)
Housing diversity index	85.0% (226)
4 or more bedrooms	11.6% (510)
Affordability/income ratio	$1,970 (49)

INCOME	★★ (396)
Poverty rate	19.4% (353)
Median household income	$44,223 (255)
Interest/dividends	14.7% (418)
Public assistance	19.9% (424)
Median fulltime earnings	$34,107 (418)

SENIORS	★★★★ (218)
Seniors living alone	24.7% (105)
Poverty rate for seniors	8.9% (254)
Median income for seniors	$35,157 (182)
Seniors who work	16.2% (398)
Home ownership by seniors	81.8% (286)

STABILITY	★★★★ (114)
25-39 age group	18.5% (144)
Born in state of residence	76.2% (201)
Same house as 1 year ago	81.4% (465)
Live and work in county	88.3% (86)
Married-couple households	51.1% (245)

TRANSPORTATION	★★★★ (172)
Bicycle or walk to work	1.6% (443)
Carpool to work	12.8% (112)
Public transit to work	0.1% (441)
Commute <15 minutes	47.9% (197)
Commute >45 minutes	5.6% (43)

See pages 37-130 for explanations of statistics, stars, and ranks.

Lumberton, NC
(Robeson County, NC)

POPULATION		Attended college	44.5% (444)
2010 census	134,168 (11)	Bachelor's degrees	13.0% (493)
2015 estimate	134,197 (10)	Advanced degrees	3.7% (498)
2010-2015 change	0.0% (255)		
2020 projection	133,510 (11)	**EMPLOYMENT**	**★ (530)**
2030 projection	131,572 (12)	Average jobless rate	12.1% (493)
		Self-employed workers	7.1% (421)
RACE		Management/financial jobs	8.3% (513)
Whites	26.6% (535)	Computer/engineering jobs	1.4% (510)
Blacks	24.0% (67)	Health care jobs	5.0% (339)
Hispanics	8.2% (177)		
Asians	0.8% (201)	**GROWTH POTENTIAL**	**★★★★★ (89)**
Native Americans	37.6% (4)	Children per senior	2.08 (49)
		Median age	35.2 (98)
AGE		Moved from different state	1.3% (452)
0-17 years old	26.1% (66)	Homes built since 2000	12.7% (290)
18-24 years old	11.0% (115)	Construction jobs	9.1% (40)
25-39 years old	18.9% (111)		
40-54 years old	19.2% (336)	**HOUSING**	**★ (444)**
55-64 years old	12.1% (430)	Home vacancy rate	11.0% (405)
65+ years old	12.6% (482)	Home ownership rate	63.1% (471)
		Housing diversity index	84.0% (344)
PRIVATE SECTOR		4 or more bedrooms	13.1% (448)
Businesses	1,913 (71)	Affordability/income ratio	$2,294 (162)
Employees	30,862 (37)		
Total wages	$926,700,213 (86)	**INCOME**	**★ (543)**
Average weekly wages	$577 (516)	Poverty rate	31.6% (532)
		Median household income	$30,608 (535)
HOUSEHOLD INCOME LADDER		Interest/dividends	7.3% (547)
95th percentile	$112,028 (542)	Public assistance	31.5% (539)
80th percentile	$65,758 (529)	Median fulltime earnings	$31,145 (524)
60th percentile	$39,184 (532)		
40th percentile	$23,365 (530)	**SENIORS**	**★ (538)**
20th percentile	$11,936 (523)	Seniors living alone	27.7% (278)
		Poverty rate for seniors	19.9% (538)
CHILDREN	**★ (516)**	Median income for seniors	$24,699 (507)
Living with two parents	43.1% (532)	Seniors who work	13.0% (525)
Older teens in school	80.9% (370)	Home ownership by seniors	78.6% (432)
Speak English very well	97.3% (399)		
Poverty rate for children	44.9% (533)	**STABILITY**	**★★★ (238)**
No health insurance	5.7% (233)	25-39 age group	18.9% (111)
		Born in state of residence	79.8% (119)
DIVERSITY/EQUALITY	**★★★★★ (85)**	Same house as 1 year ago	90.0% (44)
Racial diversity index	72.3% (2)	Live and work in county	71.9% (344)
Geographic diversity index	35.3% (433)	Married-couple households	40.6% (521)
Top 20% share of income	51.1% (474)		
Gender gap in earnings	20.6% (50)	**TRANSPORTATION**	**★ (475)**
White-collar gender gap	20.1% (209)	Bicycle or walk to work	1.2% (492)
		Carpool to work	10.7% (260)
EDUCATION	**★ (503)**	Public transit to work	0.1% (441)
Eighth grade or less	7.5% (478)	Commute <15 minutes	27.6% (538)
High school diplomas	78.0% (507)	Commute >45 minutes	11.6% (296)

See pages 37-130 for explanations of statistics, stars, and ranks.

Madisonville, KY
(Hopkins County, KY)

POPULATION	
2010 census	46,920 (235)
2015 estimate	46,222 (243)
2010-2015 change	-1.5% (373)
2020 projection	45,442 (255)
2030 projection	43,794 (277)

RACE	
Whites	89.0% (205)
Blacks	5.9% (147)
Hispanics	1.8% (455)
Asians	0.5% (355)
Native Americans	0.2% (300)

AGE	
0-17 years old	22.9% (270)
18-24 years old	7.7% (454)
25-39 years old	18.3% (159)
40-54 years old	20.2% (202)
55-64 years old	14.3% (148)
65+ years old	16.6% (237)

PRIVATE SECTOR	
Businesses	1,033 (265)
Employees	14,275 (228)
Total wages	$606,757,968 (183)
Average weekly wages	$817 (68)

HOUSEHOLD INCOME LADDER	
95th percentile	$128,308 (451)
80th percentile	$82,488 (306)
60th percentile	$53,740 (284)
40th percentile	$33,661 (303)
20th percentile	$17,648 (334)

CHILDREN	★★★ (287)
Living with two parents	64.1% (293)
Older teens in school	85.5% (183)
Speak English very well	99.7% (57)
Poverty rate for children	26.6% (341)
No health insurance	10.3% (428)

DIVERSITY/EQUALITY	★★ (365)
Racial diversity index	20.3% (343)
Geographic diversity index	38.5% (379)
Top 20% share of income	46.8% (194)
Gender gap in earnings	41.6% (465)
White-collar gender gap	19.9% (205)

EDUCATION	★★★ (279)
Eighth grade or less	3.5% (284)
High school diplomas	87.4% (291)
Attended college	49.5% (345)
Bachelor's degrees	16.8% (339)
Advanced degrees	7.4% (149)

EMPLOYMENT	★★★ (242)
Average jobless rate	6.7% (169)
Self-employed workers	5.8% (508)
Management/financial jobs	10.7% (287)
Computer/engineering jobs	2.0% (420)
Health care jobs	7.7% (35)

GROWTH POTENTIAL	★ (470)
Children per senior	1.38 (291)
Median age	40.8 (347)
Moved from different state	0.8% (524)
Homes built since 2000	9.9% (389)
Construction jobs	5.5% (404)

HOUSING	★★★★ (193)
Home vacancy rate	10.6% (385)
Home ownership rate	71.5% (204)
Housing diversity index	86.1% (51)
4 or more bedrooms	14.5% (377)
Affordability/income ratio	$2,114 (86)

INCOME	★★★ (318)
Poverty rate	17.2% (270)
Median household income	$42,346 (306)
Interest/dividends	13.8% (446)
Public assistance	17.0% (334)
Median fulltime earnings	$39,436 (160)

SENIORS	★★★ (232)
Seniors living alone	27.8% (283)
Poverty rate for seniors	7.6% (145)
Median income for seniors	$31,658 (340)
Seniors who work	14.4% (485)
Home ownership by seniors	87.5% (56)

STABILITY	★★★★★ (91)
25-39 age group	18.3% (159)
Born in state of residence	77.2% (175)
Same house as 1 year ago	86.1% (245)
Live and work in county	78.3% (239)
Married-couple households	51.6% (218)

TRANSPORTATION	★ (464)
Bicycle or walk to work	2.2% (358)
Carpool to work	6.6% (537)
Public transit to work	0.1% (441)
Commute <15 minutes	43.5% (270)
Commute >45 minutes	12.9% (353)

See pages 37-130 for explanations of statistics, stars, and ranks.

Magnolia, AR
(Columbia County, AR)

POPULATION	
2010 census	24,552 (484)
2015 estimate	24,114 (490)
2010-2015 change	-1.8% (389)
2020 projection	23,317 (493)
2030 projection	21,602 (510)

RACE	
Whites	59.2% (450)
Blacks	35.5% (40)
Hispanics	2.7% (361)
Asians	0.7% (241)
Native Americans	0.3% (231)

AGE	
0-17 years old	21.8% (351)
18-24 years old	16.4% (47)
25-39 years old	15.8% (460)
40-54 years old	17.8% (462)
55-64 years old	11.9% (447)
65+ years old	16.3% (268)

PRIVATE SECTOR	
Businesses	697 (430)
Employees	6,590 (489)
Total wages	$253,541,237 (469)
Average weekly wages	$740 (178)

HOUSEHOLD INCOME LADDER	
95th percentile	$136,672 (332)
80th percentile	$85,236 (249)
60th percentile	$48,833 (406)
40th percentile	$27,974 (464)
20th percentile	$13,138 (499)

CHILDREN	★★ (409)
Living with two parents	52.9% (485)
Older teens in school	76.3% (484)
Speak English very well	99.9% (19)
Poverty rate for children	36.1% (487)
No health insurance	2.9% (56)

DIVERSITY/EQUALITY	★★★★ (213)
Racial diversity index	52.2% (95)
Geographic diversity index	45.3% (277)
Top 20% share of income	48.8% (342)
Gender gap in earnings	48.8% (523)
White-collar gender gap	7.0% (56)

EDUCATION	★★★ (240)
Eighth grade or less	3.3% (259)
High school diplomas	87.5% (286)
Attended college	50.3% (321)
Bachelor's degrees	21.6% (172)
Advanced degrees	6.9% (186)

EMPLOYMENT	★ (524)
Average jobless rate	10.1% (423)
Self-employed workers	5.2% (538)
Management/financial jobs	9.9% (392)
Computer/engineering jobs	3.1% (180)
Health care jobs	3.2% (525)

GROWTH POTENTIAL	★★ (343)
Children per senior	1.34 (321)
Median age	36.0 (116)
Moved from different state	2.4% (218)
Homes built since 2000	14.3% (227)
Construction jobs	3.9% (538)

HOUSING	★★★ (267)
Home vacancy rate	11.8% (454)
Home ownership rate	68.2% (336)
Housing diversity index	86.5% (19)
4 or more bedrooms	14.4% (381)
Affordability/income ratio	$2,157 (104)

INCOME	★ (454)
Poverty rate	25.6% (481)
Median household income	$36,619 (453)
Interest/dividends	16.5% (360)
Public assistance	21.2% (461)
Median fulltime earnings	$37,010 (286)

SENIORS	★ (516)
Seniors living alone	29.3% (389)
Poverty rate for seniors	14.8% (485)
Median income for seniors	$27,463 (470)
Seniors who work	16.1% (400)
Home ownership by seniors	76.8% (495)

STABILITY	★★ (436)
25-39 age group	15.8% (460)
Born in state of residence	71.1% (289)
Same house as 1 year ago	81.7% (454)
Live and work in county	82.4% (174)
Married-couple households	47.4% (401)

TRANSPORTATION	★★★ (264)
Bicycle or walk to work	3.8% (161)
Carpool to work	7.0% (531)
Public transit to work	0.1% (441)
Commute <15 minutes	52.5% (116)
Commute >45 minutes	7.3% (95)

See pages 37-130 for explanations of statistics, stars, and ranks.

Malvern, AR
(Hot Spring County, AR)

POPULATION	
2010 census	32,923 (404)
2015 estimate	33,426 (399)
2010-2015 change	1.5% (160)
2020 projection	33,648 (395)
2030 projection	33,792 (396)

RACE	
Whites	83.0% (290)
Blacks	11.7% (104)
Hispanics	3.1% (333)
Asians	0.2% (509)
Native Americans	0.6% (150)

AGE	
0-17 years old	21.7% (359)
18-24 years old	8.3% (362)
25-39 years old	18.8% (121)
40-54 years old	20.1% (221)
55-64 years old	14.1% (174)
65+ years old	17.1% (186)

PRIVATE SECTOR	
Businesses	582 (482)
Employees	6,610 (486)
Total wages	$222,806,886 (491)
Average weekly wages	$648 (397)

HOUSEHOLD INCOME LADDER	
95th percentile	$124,500 (489)
80th percentile	$75,241 (455)
60th percentile	$49,224 (396)
40th percentile	$30,248 (409)
20th percentile	$16,374 (392)

CHILDREN	★★★ (304)
Living with two parents	60.2% (393)
Older teens in school	78.7% (435)
Speak English very well	99.8% (38)
Poverty rate for children	27.9% (366)
No health insurance	4.5% (150)

DIVERSITY/EQUALITY	★★★★ (188)
Racial diversity index	29.6% (257)
Geographic diversity index	43.4% (306)
Top 20% share of income	47.0% (221)
Gender gap in earnings	27.9% (137)
White-collar gender gap	22.7% (245)

EDUCATION	★★ (392)
Eighth grade or less	3.6% (292)
High school diplomas	87.5% (286)
Attended college	45.9% (422)
Bachelor's degrees	13.3% (487)
Advanced degrees	4.5% (442)

EMPLOYMENT	★ (461)
Average jobless rate	7.6% (250)
Self-employed workers	5.9% (506)
Management/financial jobs	9.1% (463)
Computer/engineering jobs	2.5% (307)
Health care jobs	5.0% (339)

GROWTH POTENTIAL	★★★ (282)
Children per senior	1.27 (370)
Median age	40.9 (350)
Moved from different state	1.0% (504)
Homes built since 2000	16.5% (167)
Construction jobs	7.4% (134)

HOUSING	★★★★★ (88)
Home vacancy rate	3.0% (1)
Home ownership rate	72.0% (189)
Housing diversity index	85.7% (108)
4 or more bedrooms	9.9% (533)
Affordability/income ratio	$2,083 (75)

INCOME	★★ (418)
Poverty rate	19.1% (341)
Median household income	$40,000 (381)
Interest/dividends	15.0% (410)
Public assistance	17.2% (344)
Median fulltime earnings	$31,586 (514)

SENIORS	★★★★★ (96)
Seniors living alone	21.2% (23)
Poverty rate for seniors	10.6% (350)
Median income for seniors	$33,317 (267)
Seniors who work	17.5% (310)
Home ownership by seniors	87.6% (52)

STABILITY	★★★ (275)
25-39 age group	18.8% (121)
Born in state of residence	73.9% (247)
Same house as 1 year ago	86.7% (210)
Live and work in county	54.1% (526)
Married-couple households	53.0% (152)

TRANSPORTATION	★ (463)
Bicycle or walk to work	1.1% (501)
Carpool to work	12.5% (121)
Public transit to work	0.6% (141)
Commute <15 minutes	29.5% (527)
Commute >45 minutes	16.6% (473)

See pages 37-130 for explanations of statistics, stars, and ranks.

Marion, NC
(McDowell County, NC)

POPULATION

2010 census	44,996 (262)
2015 estimate	44,989 (261)
2010-2015 change	0.0% (255)
2020 projection	44,605 (266)
2030 projection	43,672 (278)

RACE

Whites	87.9% (222)
Blacks	3.8% (198)
Hispanics	5.6% (233)
Asians	0.8% (201)
Native Americans	0.5% (174)

AGE

0-17 years old	21.1% (407)
18-24 years old	7.9% (424)
25-39 years old	16.9% (338)
40-54 years old	22.0% (31)
55-64 years old	14.2% (161)
65+ years old	17.9% (132)

PRIVATE SECTOR

Businesses	722 (419)
Employees	13,866 (237)
Total wages	$452,316,325 (291)
Average weekly wages	$627 (441)

HOUSEHOLD INCOME LADDER

95th percentile	$116,880 (533)
80th percentile	$69,072 (511)
60th percentile	$45,531 (470)
40th percentile	$28,483 (450)
20th percentile	$15,657 (424)

CHILDREN ★★ (337)

Living with two parents	65.5% (259)
Older teens in school	75.8% (494)
Speak English very well	99.6% (77)
Poverty rate for children	31.2% (427)
No health insurance	5.1% (188)

DIVERSITY/EQUALITY ★★★★★ (96)

Racial diversity index	22.3% (319)
Geographic diversity index	41.7% (333)
Top 20% share of income	46.6% (169)
Gender gap in earnings	22.2% (59)
White-collar gender gap	8.6% (71)

EDUCATION ★★ (415)

Eighth grade or less	4.5% (354)
High school diplomas	85.9% (345)
Attended college	48.5% (371)
Bachelor's degrees	13.5% (478)
Advanced degrees	3.5% (511)

EMPLOYMENT ★ (473)

Average jobless rate	11.1% (460)
Self-employed workers	6.1% (495)
Management/financial jobs	8.1% (524)
Computer/engineering jobs	2.3% (354)
Health care jobs	7.0% (69)

GROWTH POTENTIAL ★ (523)

Children per senior	1.18 (427)
Median age	43.1 (453)
Moved from different state	1.2% (474)
Homes built since 2000	12.4% (301)
Construction jobs	4.4% (509)

HOUSING ★★★ (246)

Home vacancy rate	8.1% (227)
Home ownership rate	70.2% (264)
Housing diversity index	85.9% (83)
4 or more bedrooms	12.3% (482)
Affordability/income ratio	$2,736 (340)

INCOME ★ (463)

Poverty rate	20.2% (380)
Median household income	$35,965 (469)
Interest/dividends	13.6% (450)
Public assistance	19.1% (406)
Median fulltime earnings	$32,078 (492)

SENIORS ★★ (389)

Seniors living alone	24.2% (89)
Poverty rate for seniors	12.0% (413)
Median income for seniors	$26,250 (488)
Seniors who work	14.5% (478)
Home ownership by seniors	83.0% (221)

STABILITY ★★★★ (124)

25-39 age group	16.9% (338)
Born in state of residence	75.4% (217)
Same house as 1 year ago	91.6% (19)
Live and work in county	72.7% (334)
Married-couple households	50.0% (296)

TRANSPORTATION ★★★ (297)

Bicycle or walk to work	0.7% (537)
Carpool to work	18.9% (7)
Public transit to work	0.0% (511)
Commute <15 minutes	31.0% (511)
Commute >45 minutes	12.4% (331)

See pages 37-130 for explanations of statistics, stars, and ranks.

Marshall, TX
(Harrison County, TX)

POPULATION	
2010 census	65,631 (118)
2015 estimate	66,746 (113)
2010-2015 change	1.7% (150)
2020 projection	67,397 (111)
2030 projection	68,664 (112)

RACE	
Whites	64.2% (420)
Blacks	21.6% (72)
Hispanics	12.1% (126)
Asians	0.5% (355)
Native Americans	0.3% (231)

AGE	
0-17 years old	25.3% (97)
18-24 years old	9.1% (251)
25-39 years old	18.5% (144)
40-54 years old	19.2% (336)
55-64 years old	13.1% (318)
65+ years old	14.9% (374)

PRIVATE SECTOR	
Businesses	1,304 (175)
Employees	21,547 (104)
Total wages	$1,077,342,319 (56)
Average weekly wages	$962 (22)

HOUSEHOLD INCOME LADDER	
95th percentile	$162,483 (82)
80th percentile	$93,247 (113)
60th percentile	$58,610 (170)
40th percentile	$35,759 (239)
20th percentile	$18,907 (271)

CHILDREN	★ (455)
Living with two parents	65.0% (270)
Older teens in school	82.3% (304)
Speak English very well	94.4% (490)
Poverty rate for children	25.4% (310)
No health insurance	14.6% (521)

DIVERSITY/EQUALITY	★★★★ (150)
Racial diversity index	52.6% (89)
Geographic diversity index	50.6% (203)
Top 20% share of income	50.2% (441)
Gender gap in earnings	40.5% (449)
White-collar gender gap	6.7% (51)

EDUCATION	★★ (337)
Eighth grade or less	4.8% (374)
High school diplomas	84.7% (380)
Attended college	51.8% (285)
Bachelor's degrees	20.0% (222)
Advanced degrees	5.2% (352)

EMPLOYMENT	★★★★ (159)
Average jobless rate	7.7% (260)
Self-employed workers	8.2% (314)
Management/financial jobs	12.7% (103)
Computer/engineering jobs	3.2% (158)
Health care jobs	6.1% (168)

GROWTH POTENTIAL	★★★★ (139)
Children per senior	1.71 (127)
Median age	37.5 (162)
Moved from different state	1.8% (338)
Homes built since 2000	18.1% (131)
Construction jobs	7.2% (162)

HOUSING	★★★★ (214)
Home vacancy rate	11.5% (436)
Home ownership rate	74.3% (105)
Housing diversity index	85.9% (83)
4 or more bedrooms	14.9% (363)
Affordability/income ratio	$2,451 (225)

INCOME	★★★ (226)
Poverty rate	17.2% (270)
Median household income	$45,974 (212)
Interest/dividends	17.8% (316)
Public assistance	13.5% (188)
Median fulltime earnings	$40,171 (135)

SENIORS	★★★ (249)
Seniors living alone	26.9% (230)
Poverty rate for seniors	12.3% (427)
Median income for seniors	$30,742 (380)
Seniors who work	18.7% (259)
Home ownership by seniors	87.4% (60)

STABILITY	★★★★ (184)
25-39 age group	18.5% (144)
Born in state of residence	68.0% (347)
Same house as 1 year ago	89.2% (72)
Live and work in county	56.7% (512)
Married-couple households	56.1% (46)

TRANSPORTATION	★ (500)
Bicycle or walk to work	0.9% (521)
Carpool to work	7.4% (518)
Public transit to work	0.1% (441)
Commute <15 minutes	35.7% (429)
Commute >45 minutes	10.5% (254)

See pages 37-130 for explanations of statistics, stars, and ranks.

Martin, TN
(Weakley County, TN)

POPULATION		Attended college	49.0% (355)
2010 census	35,021 (383)	Bachelor's degrees	22.0% (159)
2015 estimate	33,960 (394)	Advanced degrees	6.2% (243)
2010-2015 change	-3.0% (481)		
2020 projection	33,067 (407)	**EMPLOYMENT**	**★★★ (286)**
2030 projection	31,255 (417)	Average jobless rate	11.2% (464)
		Self-employed workers	8.4% (297)
RACE		Management/financial jobs	10.3% (339)
Whites	87.1% (239)	Computer/engineering jobs	1.6% (486)
Blacks	9.1% (118)	Health care jobs	8.4% (11)
Hispanics	2.2% (406)		
Asians	0.1% (529)	**GROWTH POTENTIAL**	**★★ (415)**
Native Americans	0.1% (402)	Children per senior	1.20 (417)
		Median age	36.9 (142)
AGE		Moved from different state	2.0% (288)
0-17 years old	19.6% (478)	Homes built since 2000	10.9% (361)
18-24 years old	17.5% (42)	Construction jobs	4.7% (487)
25-39 years old	16.3% (418)		
40-54 years old	17.7% (464)	**HOUSING**	**★★★ (314)**
55-64 years old	12.5% (396)	Home vacancy rate	10.0% (347)
65+ years old	16.4% (255)	Home ownership rate	67.8% (349)
		Housing diversity index	85.1% (212)
PRIVATE SECTOR		4 or more bedrooms	14.0% (401)
Businesses	495 (517)	Affordability/income ratio	$2,541 (267)
Employees	7,161 (469)		
Total wages	$225,449,875 (487)	**INCOME**	**★★ (403)**
Average weekly wages	$605 (479)	Poverty rate	19.1% (341)
		Median household income	$37,037 (443)
HOUSEHOLD INCOME LADDER		Interest/dividends	17.6% (325)
95th percentile	$127,867 (457)	Public assistance	20.2% (435)
80th percentile	$74,321 (469)	Median fulltime earnings	$34,843 (391)
60th percentile	$45,714 (465)		
40th percentile	$29,401 (434)	**SENIORS**	**★★★ (262)**
20th percentile	$14,853 (457)	Seniors living alone	27.5% (264)
		Poverty rate for seniors	11.2% (384)
CHILDREN	**★★★★★ (45)**	Median income for seniors	$30,346 (399)
Living with two parents	68.9% (168)	Seniors who work	17.5% (310)
Older teens in school	94.2% (18)	Home ownership by seniors	87.6% (52)
Speak English very well	99.5% (96)		
Poverty rate for children	22.6% (238)	**STABILITY**	**★ (464)**
No health insurance	3.5% (82)	25-39 age group	16.3% (418)
		Born in state of residence	73.3% (254)
DIVERSITY/EQUALITY	**★★★ (250)**	Same house as 1 year ago	82.7% (411)
Racial diversity index	23.2% (311)	Live and work in county	66.4% (428)
Geographic diversity index	43.8% (297)	Married-couple households	49.5% (323)
Top 20% share of income	48.2% (305)		
Gender gap in earnings	27.8% (133)	**TRANSPORTATION**	**★★ (393)**
White-collar gender gap	23.5% (256)	Bicycle or walk to work	4.0% (155)
		Carpool to work	6.5% (539)
EDUCATION	**★★★ (227)**	Public transit to work	0.2% (363)
Eighth grade or less	2.3% (161)	Commute <15 minutes	41.9% (300)
High school diplomas	89.4% (220)	Commute >45 minutes	10.4% (248)

See pages 37-130 for explanations of statistics, stars, and ranks.

Martinsville, VA
(Henry County and City of Martinsville, VA)

POPULATION
2010 census	67,972 (107)
2015 estimate	65,526 (120)
2010-2015 change	-3.6% (510)
2020 projection	62,714 (135)
2030 projection	57,176 (165)

RACE
Whites	65.9% (411)
Blacks	27.0% (64)
Hispanics	5.0% (252)
Asians	0.4% (413)
Native Americans	0.1% (402)

AGE
0-17 years old	20.6% (423)
18-24 years old	7.3% (503)
25-39 years old	15.6% (474)
40-54 years old	20.9% (112)
55-64 years old	14.5% (122)
65+ years old	21.0% (34)

PRIVATE SECTOR
Businesses	2,457 (36)
Employees	20,836 (116)
Total wages	$657,343,227 (162)
Average weekly wages	$607 (477)

HOUSEHOLD INCOME LADDER
95th percentile	$119,097 (523)
80th percentile	$68,977 (512)
60th percentile	$43,554 (495)
40th percentile	$26,900 (488)
20th percentile	$15,420 (440)

CHILDREN ★★ (422)
Living with two parents	56.5% (470)
Older teens in school	80.3% (388)
Speak English very well	97.1% (408)
Poverty rate for children	30.5% (413)
No health insurance	7.3% (333)

DIVERSITY/EQUALITY ★★★★★ (38)
Racial diversity index	49.0% (122)
Geographic diversity index	46.4% (261)
Top 20% share of income	49.5% (397)
Gender gap in earnings	20.1% (43)
White-collar gender gap	0.3% (2)

EDUCATION ★★ (383)
Eighth grade or less	3.5% (284)
High school diplomas	83.3% (415)
Attended college	51.0% (303)
Bachelor's degrees	13.9% (466)
Advanced degrees	5.2% (352)

EMPLOYMENT ★ (493)
Average jobless rate	10.3% (432)
Self-employed workers	6.6% (461)
Management/financial jobs	9.0% (475)
Computer/engineering jobs	1.8% (457)
Health care jobs	5.7% (222)

GROWTH POTENTIAL ★ (548)
Children per senior	0.98 (509)
Median age	45.3 (502)
Moved from different state	1.4% (425)
Homes built since 2000	7.2% (500)
Construction jobs	5.3% (425)

HOUSING ★★ (334)
Home vacancy rate	13.4% (504)
Home ownership rate	70.1% (267)
Housing diversity index	85.8% (97)
4 or more bedrooms	15.9% (303)
Affordability/income ratio	$2,746 (344)

INCOME ★ (447)
Poverty rate	19.4% (353)
Median household income	$34,382 (493)
Interest/dividends	17.7% (321)
Public assistance	21.0% (455)
Median fulltime earnings	$33,026 (452)

SENIORS ★★ (415)
Seniors living alone	29.8% (422)
Poverty rate for seniors	9.7% (301)
Median income for seniors	$27,533 (468)
Seniors who work	16.6% (367)
Home ownership by seniors	83.3% (206)

STABILITY ★ (527)
25-39 age group	15.6% (474)
Born in state of residence	70.4% (304)
Same house as 1 year ago	88.3% (115)
Live and work in county	51.1% (537)
Married-couple households	44.7% (468)

TRANSPORTATION ★ (486)
Bicycle or walk to work	0.6% (541)
Carpool to work	10.4% (289)
Public transit to work	0.4% (219)
Commute <15 minutes	29.2% (530)
Commute >45 minutes	12.7% (343)

See pages 37-130 for explanations of statistics, stars, and ranks.

Mayfield, KY
(Graves County, KY)

POPULATION

2010 census	37,121 (354)
2015 estimate	37,421 (351)
2010-2015 change	0.8% (194)
2020 projection	37,276 (355)
2030 projection	36,873 (348)

RACE

Whites	87.2% (236)
Blacks	5.0% (164)
Hispanics	5.9% (227)
Asians	0.3% (473)
Native Americans	0.1% (402)

AGE

0-17 years old	24.4% (155)
18-24 years old	7.9% (424)
25-39 years old	17.0% (317)
40-54 years old	20.5% (151)
55-64 years old	13.3% (282)
65+ years old	16.8% (215)

PRIVATE SECTOR

Businesses	812 (366)
Employees	8,785 (424)
Total wages	$302,998,521 (430)
Average weekly wages	$663 (352)

HOUSEHOLD INCOME LADDER

95th percentile	$130,273 (429)
80th percentile	$81,674 (329)
60th percentile	$49,591 (391)
40th percentile	$31,448 (376)
20th percentile	$16,312 (395)

CHILDREN ★★★★★ (110)

Living with two parents	68.2% (189)
Older teens in school	90.8% (57)
Speak English very well	98.9% (226)
Poverty rate for children	23.1% (250)
No health insurance	6.0% (248)

DIVERSITY/EQUALITY ★ (443)

Racial diversity index	23.3% (309)
Geographic diversity index	48.9% (230)
Top 20% share of income	47.6% (264)
Gender gap in earnings	33.9% (284)
White-collar gender gap	53.3% (525)

EDUCATION ★★★ (290)

Eighth grade or less	5.1% (390)
High school diplomas	85.8% (352)
Attended college	50.8% (306)
Bachelor's degrees	19.6% (229)
Advanced degrees	7.5% (142)

EMPLOYMENT ★★★★ (128)

Average jobless rate	7.2% (218)
Self-employed workers	10.4% (145)
Management/financial jobs	10.7% (287)
Computer/engineering jobs	2.2% (381)
Health care jobs	7.4% (49)

GROWTH POTENTIAL ★★ (348)

Children per senior	1.45 (244)
Median age	40.3 (319)
Moved from different state	1.9% (310)
Homes built since 2000	9.2% (427)
Construction jobs	6.7% (219)

HOUSING ★★★★★ (40)

Home vacancy rate	3.5% (3)
Home ownership rate	74.3% (105)
Housing diversity index	85.6% (127)
4 or more bedrooms	16.1% (286)
Affordability/income ratio	$2,350 (190)

INCOME ★★★ (326)

Poverty rate	17.3% (280)
Median household income	$39,530 (393)
Interest/dividends	16.2% (369)
Public assistance	15.7% (280)
Median fulltime earnings	$37,248 (265)

SENIORS ★★ (407)

Seniors living alone	27.1% (247)
Poverty rate for seniors	12.6% (439)
Median income for seniors	$26,603 (483)
Seniors who work	16.1% (400)
Home ownership by seniors	84.6% (159)

STABILITY ★★★★ (170)

25-39 age group	17.0% (317)
Born in state of residence	69.5% (321)
Same house as 1 year ago	91.9% (16)
Live and work in county	63.7% (456)
Married-couple households	53.7% (123)

TRANSPORTATION ★ (484)

Bicycle or walk to work	0.9% (521)
Carpool to work	7.4% (518)
Public transit to work	0.5% (178)
Commute <15 minutes	33.2% (473)
Commute >45 minutes	10.2% (235)

See pages 37-130 for explanations of statistics, stars, and ranks.

Maysville, KY
(Mason County, KY)

POPULATION	
2010 census	17,490 (534)
2015 estimate	17,099 (540)
2010-2015 change	-2.2% (427)
2020 projection	16,823 (541)
2030 projection	16,239 (539)

RACE	
Whites	89.6% (191)
Blacks	6.8% (136)
Hispanics	0.4% (547)
Asians	0.3% (473)
Native Americans	0.2% (300)

AGE	
0-17 years old	23.9% (194)
18-24 years old	8.5% (330)
25-39 years old	15.6% (474)
40-54 years old	21.7% (42)
55-64 years old	14.4% (136)
65+ years old	15.8% (305)

PRIVATE SECTOR	
Businesses	505 (514)
Employees	7,581 (455)
Total wages	$314,867,904 (416)
Average weekly wages	$799 (90)

HOUSEHOLD INCOME LADDER	
95th percentile	$139,410 (298)
80th percentile	$82,557 (302)
60th percentile	$48,369 (414)
40th percentile	$29,230 (439)
20th percentile	$16,540 (383)

CHILDREN	★★★ (270)
Living with two parents	66.5% (231)
Older teens in school	81.0% (366)
Speak English very well	99.8% (38)
Poverty rate for children	25.0% (298)
No health insurance	8.4% (371)

DIVERSITY/EQUALITY	★ (451)
Racial diversity index	19.2% (358)
Geographic diversity index	39.4% (367)
Top 20% share of income	55.7% (548)
Gender gap in earnings	29.0% (153)
White-collar gender gap	7.6% (59)

EDUCATION	★★★ (299)
Eighth grade or less	4.7% (366)
High school diplomas	87.0% (309)
Attended college	49.7% (340)
Bachelor's degrees	16.0% (372)
Advanced degrees	8.2% (114)

EMPLOYMENT	★★★★ (113)
Average jobless rate	6.2% (131)
Self-employed workers	6.6% (461)
Management/financial jobs	13.2% (73)
Computer/engineering jobs	2.0% (420)
Health care jobs	7.8% (28)

GROWTH POTENTIAL	★★★ (224)
Children per senior	1.51 (210)
Median age	41.1 (362)
Moved from different state	2.6% (187)
Homes built since 2000	15.3% (195)
Construction jobs	7.0% (185)

HOUSING	★★★ (261)
Home vacancy rate	10.3% (366)
Home ownership rate	67.0% (386)
Housing diversity index	86.1% (51)
4 or more bedrooms	16.5% (267)
Affordability/income ratio	$2,604 (290)

INCOME	★★ (390)
Poverty rate	18.2% (304)
Median household income	$38,824 (411)
Interest/dividends	14.4% (429)
Public assistance	18.8% (394)
Median fulltime earnings	$36,220 (324)

SENIORS	★★★ (245)
Seniors living alone	22.8% (54)
Poverty rate for seniors	10.7% (357)
Median income for seniors	$30,422 (393)
Seniors who work	19.1% (238)
Home ownership by seniors	80.8% (346)

STABILITY	★★★ (319)
25-39 age group	15.6% (474)
Born in state of residence	76.2% (201)
Same house as 1 year ago	85.8% (264)
Live and work in county	70.3% (366)
Married-couple households	52.0% (194)

TRANSPORTATION	★★ (394)
Bicycle or walk to work	2.1% (374)
Carpool to work	11.9% (145)
Public transit to work	0.6% (141)
Commute <15 minutes	40.5% (323)
Commute >45 minutes	17.3% (489)

See pages 37-130 for explanations of statistics, stars, and ranks.

McAlester, OK
(Pittsburg County, OK)

POPULATION	
2010 census	45,837 (252)
2015 estimate	44,610 (266)
2010-2015 change	-2.7% (459)
2020 projection	43,983 (274)
2030 projection	42,722 (289)

RACE	
Whites	70.4% (390)
Blacks	3.3% (217)
Hispanics	4.5% (265)
Asians	0.5% (355)
Native Americans	9.0% (22)

AGE	
0-17 years old	22.3% (312)
18-24 years old	8.0% (407)
25-39 years old	18.9% (111)
40-54 years old	19.7% (273)
55-64 years old	13.2% (297)
65+ years old	18.1% (117)

PRIVATE SECTOR	
Businesses	898 (314)
Employees	10,628 (355)
Total wages	$411,620,909 (325)
Average weekly wages	$745 (165)

HOUSEHOLD INCOME LADDER	
95th percentile	$141,680 (269)
80th percentile	$85,401 (242)
60th percentile	$52,997 (297)
40th percentile	$33,111 (321)
20th percentile	$17,038 (364)

CHILDREN	★★ (407)
Living with two parents	62.4% (338)
Older teens in school	80.6% (382)
Speak English very well	99.5% (96)
Poverty rate for children	25.6% (314)
No health insurance	14.1% (510)

DIVERSITY/EQUALITY	★★★ (238)
Racial diversity index	47.8% (131)
Geographic diversity index	53.4% (166)
Top 20% share of income	49.1% (372)
Gender gap in earnings	36.4% (352)
White-collar gender gap	33.6% (379)

EDUCATION	★★★ (296)
Eighth grade or less	2.5% (180)
High school diplomas	87.4% (291)
Attended college	51.5% (291)
Bachelor's degrees	17.1% (322)
Advanced degrees	5.1% (364)

EMPLOYMENT	★★★ (250)
Average jobless rate	6.2% (131)
Self-employed workers	7.6% (376)
Management/financial jobs	10.6% (306)
Computer/engineering jobs	3.5% (122)
Health care jobs	5.3% (286)

GROWTH POTENTIAL	★★★ (321)
Children per senior	1.23 (393)
Median age	40.7 (341)
Moved from different state	2.2% (248)
Homes built since 2000	15.9% (179)
Construction jobs	6.0% (326)

HOUSING	★★★ (228)
Home vacancy rate	11.1% (409)
Home ownership rate	72.4% (170)
Housing diversity index	86.2% (43)
4 or more bedrooms	13.0% (456)
Affordability/income ratio	$2,220 (129)

INCOME	★★★ (296)
Poverty rate	18.7% (326)
Median household income	$42,576 (298)
Interest/dividends	19.5% (264)
Public assistance	16.9% (327)
Median fulltime earnings	$37,193 (270)

SENIORS	★★ (420)
Seniors living alone	30.9% (469)
Poverty rate for seniors	11.8% (401)
Median income for seniors	$31,354 (356)
Seniors who work	17.2% (330)
Home ownership by seniors	83.4% (202)

STABILITY	★★★★ (204)
25-39 age group	18.9% (111)
Born in state of residence	65.7% (380)
Same house as 1 year ago	82.4% (422)
Live and work in county	87.6% (94)
Married-couple households	49.2% (340)

TRANSPORTATION	★★★ (245)
Bicycle or walk to work	1.2% (492)
Carpool to work	12.0% (141)
Public transit to work	0.4% (219)
Commute <15 minutes	44.3% (257)
Commute >45 minutes	7.6% (111)

See pages 37-130 for explanations of statistics, stars, and ranks.

McComb, MS
(Amite and Pike Counties, MS)

POPULATION

2010 census	53,535 (181)
2015 estimate	52,530 (194)
2010-2015 change	-1.9% (399)
2020 projection	51,667 (202)
2030 projection	49,672 (219)

RACE

Whites	47.9% (492)
Blacks	49.8% (14)
Hispanics	1.1% (525)
Asians	0.4% (413)
Native Americans	0.3% (231)

AGE

0-17 years old	25.5% (90)
18-24 years old	8.7% (299)
25-39 years old	16.7% (375)
40-54 years old	19.2% (336)
55-64 years old	13.6% (247)
65+ years old	16.4% (255)

PRIVATE SECTOR

Businesses	1,100 (244)
Employees	12,652 (293)
Total wages	$370,596,308 (362)
Average weekly wages	$563 (526)

HOUSEHOLD INCOME LADDER

95th percentile	$122,064 (500)
80th percentile	$68,787 (516)
60th percentile	$40,937 (519)
40th percentile	$24,255 (517)
20th percentile	$12,232 (513)

CHILDREN ★ (467)

Living with two parents	45.3% (529)
Older teens in school	80.8% (376)
Speak English very well	98.3% (312)
Poverty rate for children	39.8% (513)
No health insurance	3.7% (98)

DIVERSITY/EQUALITY ★★★ (291)

Racial diversity index	52.2% (95)
Geographic diversity index	40.8% (339)
Top 20% share of income	50.9% (467)
Gender gap in earnings	33.2% (264)
White-collar gender gap	28.1% (310)

EDUCATION ★ (446)

Eighth grade or less	5.9% (420)
High school diplomas	81.3% (462)
Attended college	46.3% (412)
Bachelor's degrees	14.5% (443)
Advanced degrees	5.2% (352)

EMPLOYMENT ★★ (428)

Average jobless rate	10.3% (432)
Self-employed workers	9.5% (207)
Management/financial jobs	9.1% (463)
Computer/engineering jobs	1.1% (532)
Health care jobs	6.3% (144)

GROWTH POTENTIAL ★★★ (229)

Children per senior	1.56 (189)
Median age	39.1 (244)
Moved from different state	2.0% (288)
Homes built since 2000	15.9% (179)
Construction jobs	6.3% (284)

HOUSING ★★★ (225)

Home vacancy rate	10.5% (381)
Home ownership rate	70.9% (232)
Housing diversity index	86.1% (51)
4 or more bedrooms	15.4% (329)
Affordability/income ratio	$2,546 (270)

INCOME ★ (515)

Poverty rate	27.4% (507)
Median household income	$31,425 (526)
Interest/dividends	10.5% (522)
Public assistance	21.5% (467)
Median fulltime earnings	$31,671 (509)

SENIORS ★ (536)

Seniors living alone	34.0% (539)
Poverty rate for seniors	17.8% (524)
Median income for seniors	$25,492 (498)
Seniors who work	16.9% (348)
Home ownership by seniors	80.9% (339)

STABILITY ★ (455)

25-39 age group	16.7% (375)
Born in state of residence	74.5% (231)
Same house as 1 year ago	88.3% (115)
Live and work in county	69.8% (374)
Married-couple households	40.9% (517)

TRANSPORTATION ★ (448)

Bicycle or walk to work	1.7% (428)
Carpool to work	10.9% (239)
Public transit to work	1.2% (54)
Commute <15 minutes	34.8% (442)
Commute >45 minutes	18.2% (504)

See pages 37-130 for explanations of statistics, stars, and ranks.

McMinnville, TN
(Warren County, TN)

POPULATION

2010 census	39,839 (316)
2015 estimate	40,435 (309)
2010-2015 change	1.5% (160)
2020 projection	40,754 (306)
2030 projection	41,269 (301)

RACE

Whites	86.5% (248)
Blacks	1.3% (351)
Hispanics	8.4% (175)
Asians	0.5% (355)
Native Americans	0.1% (402)

AGE

0-17 years old	23.9% (194)
18-24 years old	7.9% (424)
25-39 years old	18.5% (144)
40-54 years old	20.4% (169)
55-64 years old	12.9% (343)
65+ years old	16.4% (255)

PRIVATE SECTOR

Businesses	752 (398)
Employees	11,804 (314)
Total wages	$424,492,386 (310)
Average weekly wages	$692 (277)

HOUSEHOLD INCOME LADDER

95th percentile	$125,139 (485)
80th percentile	$71,407 (497)
60th percentile	$46,066 (457)
40th percentile	$28,540 (448)
20th percentile	$15,664 (422)

CHILDREN ★★ **(353)**

Living with two parents	61.8% (361)
Older teens in school	78.0% (451)
Speak English very well	98.9% (226)
Poverty rate for children	30.3% (409)
No health insurance	5.6% (225)

DIVERSITY/EQUALITY ★★ **(379)**

Racial diversity index	24.3% (301)
Geographic diversity index	44.6% (286)
Top 20% share of income	50.6% (453)
Gender gap in earnings	27.1% (120)
White-collar gender gap	33.5% (378)

EDUCATION ★ **(478)**

Eighth grade or less	6.6% (452)
High school diplomas	81.0% (467)
Attended college	39.1% (524)
Bachelor's degrees	14.7% (431)
Advanced degrees	6.0% (264)

EMPLOYMENT ★★ **(413)**

Average jobless rate	8.0% (291)
Self-employed workers	7.9% (345)
Management/financial jobs	8.3% (513)
Computer/engineering jobs	2.4% (336)
Health care jobs	5.7% (222)

GROWTH POTENTIAL ★★ **(335)**

Children per senior	1.46 (237)
Median age	39.7 (279)
Moved from different state	1.4% (425)
Homes built since 2000	13.0% (276)
Construction jobs	6.0% (326)

HOUSING ★★ **(347)**

Home vacancy rate	10.2% (358)
Home ownership rate	69.0% (303)
Housing diversity index	85.0% (226)
4 or more bedrooms	13.0% (456)
Affordability/income ratio	$2,762 (350)

INCOME ★ **(458)**

Poverty rate	21.2% (407)
Median household income	$35,376 (483)
Interest/dividends	16.7% (354)
Public assistance	21.1% (460)
Median fulltime earnings	$33,070 (451)

SENIORS ★★ **(436)**

Seniors living alone	32.2% (517)
Poverty rate for seniors	11.6% (392)
Median income for seniors	$27,781 (463)
Seniors who work	19.9% (201)
Home ownership by seniors	83.7% (190)

STABILITY ★★★★ **(181)**

25-39 age group	18.5% (144)
Born in state of residence	73.3% (254)
Same house as 1 year ago	87.9% (140)
Live and work in county	75.4% (284)
Married-couple households	47.4% (401)

TRANSPORTATION ★★ **(434)**

Bicycle or walk to work	1.4% (472)
Carpool to work	12.8% (112)
Public transit to work	0.0% (511)
Commute <15 minutes	34.6% (445)
Commute >45 minutes	15.0% (424)

See pages 37-130 for explanations of statistics, stars, and ranks.

Meridian, MS
(Clarke, Kemper, and Lauderdale Counties, MS)

POPULATION				
2010 census	107,449 (20)		Attended college	54.7% (230)
2015 estimate	104,499 (24)		Bachelor's degrees	18.0% (284)
2010-2015 change	-2.7% (459)		Advanced degrees	5.7% (292)
2020 projection	101,937 (29)			
2030 projection	96,352 (34)		**EMPLOYMENT**	**★★★ (298)**

			Average jobless rate	10.0% (420)
RACE			Self-employed workers	5.7% (515)
Whites	53.2% (477)		Management/financial jobs	10.8% (280)
Blacks	42.9% (25)		Computer/engineering jobs	2.1% (399)
Hispanics	1.9% (442)		Health care jobs	8.3% (13)
Asians	0.7% (241)			
Native Americans	0.5% (174)		**GROWTH POTENTIAL**	**★★★★ (163)**

			Children per senior	1.55 (196)
AGE			Median age	38.2 (189)
0-17 years old	23.7% (218)		Moved from different state	2.9% (165)
18-24 years old	10.0% (163)		Homes built since 2000	12.8% (286)
25-39 years old	17.9% (214)		Construction jobs	7.6% (110)
40-54 years old	20.0% (233)			
55-64 years old	13.0% (334)		**HOUSING**	**★★★ (282)**
65+ years old	15.3% (348)		Home vacancy rate	12.0% (460)

PRIVATE SECTOR			Home ownership rate	69.0% (303)
Businesses	2,182 (49)		Housing diversity index	85.9% (83)
Employees	31,647 (32)		4 or more bedrooms	15.0% (356)
Total wages	$1,128,233,153 (51)		Affordability/income ratio	$2,247 (140)
Average weekly wages	$686 (297)			
			INCOME	**★ (480)**

HOUSEHOLD INCOME LADDER			Poverty rate	23.3% (454)
95th percentile	$142,526 (259)		Median household income	$36,398 (459)
80th percentile	$77,896 (402)		Interest/dividends	11.8% (497)
60th percentile	$46,536 (454)		Public assistance	19.8% (419)
40th percentile	$28,017 (463)		Median fulltime earnings	$32,020 (494)
20th percentile	$15,403 (441)			
			SENIORS	**★ (493)**

CHILDREN	**★★ (358)**		Seniors living alone	31.2% (479)
Living with two parents	49.2% (514)		Poverty rate for seniors	15.7% (498)
Older teens in school	87.4% (116)		Median income for seniors	$27,930 (462)
Speak English very well	99.0% (200)		Seniors who work	17.2% (330)
Poverty rate for children	36.4% (490)		Home ownership by seniors	82.9% (225)
No health insurance	4.1% (126)			
			STABILITY	**★★★ (301)**

DIVERSITY/EQUALITY	**★★★ (258)**		25-39 age group	17.9% (214)
Racial diversity index	53.2% (79)		Born in state of residence	77.5% (168)
Geographic diversity index	37.9% (392)		Same house as 1 year ago	86.3% (232)
Top 20% share of income	51.5% (489)		Live and work in county	79.4% (224)
Gender gap in earnings	31.2% (210)		Married-couple households	42.2% (504)
White-collar gender gap	21.3% (222)			
			TRANSPORTATION	**★★ (358)**

EDUCATION	**★★★ (275)**		Bicycle or walk to work	2.4% (331)
Eighth grade or less	3.2% (250)		Carpool to work	11.8% (152)
High school diplomas	85.8% (352)		Public transit to work	0.3% (291)
			Commute <15 minutes	32.1% (497)
			Commute >45 minutes	10.4% (248)

See pages 37-130 for explanations of statistics, stars, and ranks.

Miami, OK
(Ottawa County, OK)

POPULATION		Attended college	48.7% (365)
2010 census	31,848 (419)	Bachelor's degrees	14.2% (454)
2015 estimate	31,981 (421)	Advanced degrees	4.4% (451)
2010-2015 change	0.4% (228)		
2020 projection	31,460 (425)	**EMPLOYMENT**	**★ (488)**
2030 projection	30,423 (422)	Average jobless rate	9.4% (394)
		Self-employed workers	5.9% (506)
RACE		Management/financial jobs	9.3% (453)
Whites	66.3% (408)	Computer/engineering jobs	1.5% (499)
Blacks	0.9% (388)	Health care jobs	5.9% (193)
Hispanics	5.1% (249)		
Asians	1.4% (99)	**GROWTH POTENTIAL**	**★★★ (249)**
Native Americans	13.7% (14)	Children per senior	1.40 (279)
		Median age	38.5 (206)
AGE		Moved from different state	3.8% (89)
0-17 years old	24.8% (135)	Homes built since 2000	11.6% (330)
18-24 years old	10.1% (157)	Construction jobs	5.9% (345)
25-39 years old	16.7% (375)		
40-54 years old	18.4% (430)	**HOUSING**	**★★★ (266)**
55-64 years old	12.3% (414)	Home vacancy rate	11.1% (409)
65+ years old	17.7% (142)	Home ownership rate	69.9% (275)
		Housing diversity index	86.6% (12)
PRIVATE SECTOR		4 or more bedrooms	12.4% (480)
Businesses	589 (478)	Affordability/income ratio	$2,273 (150)
Employees	6,610 (486)		
Total wages	$201,965,171 (507)	**INCOME**	**★ (492)**
Average weekly wages	$588 (508)	Poverty rate	22.9% (443)
		Median household income	$36,347 (460)
HOUSEHOLD INCOME LADDER		Interest/dividends	12.4% (483)
95th percentile	$114,817 (538)	Public assistance	20.3% (437)
80th percentile	$69,619 (508)	Median fulltime earnings	$29,786 (542)
60th percentile	$45,171 (474)		
40th percentile	$28,347 (452)	**SENIORS**	**★★ (369)**
20th percentile	$15,491 (432)	Seniors living alone	28.7% (344)
		Poverty rate for seniors	11.6% (392)
CHILDREN	**★★ (429)**	Median income for seniors	$29,338 (426)
Living with two parents	59.8% (404)	Seniors who work	19.6% (221)
Older teens in school	81.3% (357)	Home ownership by seniors	82.9% (225)
Speak English very well	97.7% (370)		
Poverty rate for children	35.5% (480)	**STABILITY**	**★★ (440)**
No health insurance	8.1% (364)	25-39 age group	16.7% (375)
		Born in state of residence	55.2% (461)
DIVERSITY/EQUALITY	**★★★★★ (20)**	Same house as 1 year ago	86.5% (219)
Racial diversity index	52.3% (93)	Live and work in county	72.0% (341)
Geographic diversity index	62.3% (100)	Married-couple households	50.0% (296)
Top 20% share of income	46.7% (184)		
Gender gap in earnings	25.2% (90)	**TRANSPORTATION**	**★★ (395)**
White-collar gender gap	11.0% (99)	Bicycle or walk to work	2.0% (386)
		Carpool to work	8.3% (471)
EDUCATION	**★★ (400)**	Public transit to work	0.2% (363)
Eighth grade or less	4.2% (337)	Commute <15 minutes	39.3% (341)
High school diplomas	84.7% (380)	Commute >45 minutes	8.7% (158)

See pages 37-130 for explanations of statistics, stars, and ranks.

Middlesborough, KY
(Bell County, KY)

POPULATION	
2010 census	28,691 (448)
2015 estimate	27,337 (459)
2010-2015 change	-4.7% (529)
2020 projection	26,128 (469)
2030 projection	23,796 (483)

RACE	
Whites	94.6% (59)
Blacks	3.2% (220)
Hispanics	0.5% (545)
Asians	0.3% (473)
Native Americans	0.0% (523)

AGE	
0-17 years old	21.6% (366)
18-24 years old	8.7% (299)
25-39 years old	18.0% (201)
40-54 years old	21.1% (97)
55-64 years old	13.8% (203)
65+ years old	16.8% (215)

PRIVATE SECTOR	
Businesses	538 (501)
Employees	6,720 (483)
Total wages	$215,075,775 (500)
Average weekly wages	$615 (456)

HOUSEHOLD INCOME LADDER	
95th percentile	$95,527 (551)
80th percentile	$51,480 (551)
60th percentile	$30,192 (551)
40th percentile	$17,075 (551)
20th percentile	$9,448 (549)

CHILDREN	★ (474)
Living with two parents	57.8% (452)
Older teens in school	81.2% (362)
Speak English very well	98.4% (300)
Poverty rate for children	51.6% (545)
No health insurance	6.5% (282)

DIVERSITY/EQUALITY	★ (520)
Racial diversity index	10.4% (490)
Geographic diversity index	36.8% (407)
Top 20% share of income	51.4% (481)
Gender gap in earnings	33.5% (270)
White-collar gender gap	28.6% (317)

EDUCATION	★ (539)
Eighth grade or less	10.5% (515)
High school diplomas	71.0% (536)

Attended college	33.9% (543)
Bachelor's degrees	10.2% (539)
Advanced degrees	5.0% (378)

EMPLOYMENT	★ (544)
Average jobless rate	11.6% (479)
Self-employed workers	5.5% (530)
Management/financial jobs	5.5% (551)
Computer/engineering jobs	1.3% (519)
Health care jobs	5.8% (209)

GROWTH POTENTIAL	★★ (381)
Children per senior	1.28 (357)
Median age	41.1 (362)
Moved from different state	2.0% (288)
Homes built since 2000	12.0% (315)
Construction jobs	6.2% (295)

HOUSING	★★★★ (179)
Home vacancy rate	4.2% (9)
Home ownership rate	66.2% (413)
Housing diversity index	86.1% (51)
4 or more bedrooms	12.3% (482)
Affordability/income ratio	$2,691 (324)

INCOME	★ (549)
Poverty rate	38.0% (550)
Median household income	$22,443 (551)
Interest/dividends	9.5% (534)
Public assistance	35.2% (548)
Median fulltime earnings	$30,606 (535)

SENIORS	★ (551)
Seniors living alone	33.8% (538)
Poverty rate for seniors	23.8% (547)
Median income for seniors	$20,495 (526)
Seniors who work	7.5% (551)
Home ownership by seniors	77.1% (486)

STABILITY	★★★★ (143)
25-39 age group	18.0% (201)
Born in state of residence	78.3% (149)
Same house as 1 year ago	91.2% (26)
Live and work in county	80.6% (208)
Married-couple households	42.1% (505)

TRANSPORTATION	★★★★ (137)
Bicycle or walk to work	3.9% (158)
Carpool to work	16.8% (26)
Public transit to work	0.2% (363)
Commute <15 minutes	45.9% (236)
Commute >45 minutes	13.9% (387)

See pages 37-130 for explanations of statistics, stars, and ranks.

Milledgeville, GA
(Baldwin and Hancock Counties, GA)

POPULATION

2010 census	55,149 (172)
2015 estimate	54,010 (177)
2010-2015 change	-2.1% (418)
2020 projection	51,911 (199)
2030 projection	47,856 (234)

RACE

Whites	48.7% (489)
Blacks	46.6% (21)
Hispanics	2.1% (416)
Asians	1.4% (99)
Native Americans	0.2% (300)

AGE

0-17 years old	19.1% (498)
18-24 years old	18.3% (33)
25-39 years old	16.7% (375)
40-54 years old	18.9% (376)
55-64 years old	12.9% (343)
65+ years old	14.2% (429)

PRIVATE SECTOR

Businesses	893 (317)
Employees	11,393 (330)
Total wages	$365,889,232 (367)
Average weekly wages	$618 (451)

HOUSEHOLD INCOME LADDER

95th percentile	$125,902 (481)
80th percentile	$74,738 (461)
60th percentile	$40,904 (520)
40th percentile	$23,147 (534)
20th percentile	$11,631 (531)

CHILDREN ★ (484)

Living with two parents	43.4% (531)
Older teens in school	84.0% (239)
Speak English very well	99.9% (19)
Poverty rate for children	43.3% (529)
No health insurance	7.0% (319)

DIVERSITY/EQUALITY ★★ (357)

Racial diversity index	54.5% (61)
Geographic diversity index	34.9% (437)
Top 20% share of income	53.4% (527)
Gender gap in earnings	32.3% (234)
White-collar gender gap	23.2% (252)

EDUCATION ★★ (369)

Eighth grade or less	2.8% (205)
High school diplomas	83.7% (406)
Attended college	42.7% (479)
Bachelor's degrees	15.7% (399)
Advanced degrees	7.2% (164)

EMPLOYMENT ★★ (342)

Average jobless rate	9.2% (377)
Self-employed workers	5.6% (523)
Management/financial jobs	8.7% (493)
Computer/engineering jobs	4.0% (76)
Health care jobs	7.1% (63)

GROWTH POTENTIAL ★★★ (253)

Children per senior	1.35 (313)
Median age	35.8 (112)
Moved from different state	1.3% (452)
Homes built since 2000	21.0% (79)
Construction jobs	4.5% (504)

HOUSING ★ (532)

Home vacancy rate	13.9% (514)
Home ownership rate	57.9% (524)
Housing diversity index	84.1% (337)
4 or more bedrooms	14.9% (363)
Affordability/income ratio	$3,098 (417)

INCOME ★ (506)

Poverty rate	31.2% (528)
Median household income	$30,791 (532)
Interest/dividends	12.6% (480)
Public assistance	17.8% (366)
Median fulltime earnings	$31,950 (496)

SENIORS ★★ (437)

Seniors living alone	27.8% (283)
Poverty rate for seniors	14.5% (481)
Median income for seniors	$34,403 (216)
Seniors who work	12.5% (535)
Home ownership by seniors	83.6% (195)

STABILITY ★ (533)

25-39 age group	16.7% (375)
Born in state of residence	80.1% (111)
Same house as 1 year ago	80.7% (489)
Live and work in county	69.8% (374)
Married-couple households	36.0% (544)

TRANSPORTATION ★★ (354)

Bicycle or walk to work	2.7% (292)
Carpool to work	10.3% (299)
Public transit to work	0.2% (363)
Commute <15 minutes	41.8% (303)
Commute >45 minutes	12.2% (321)

See pages 37-130 for explanations of statistics, stars, and ranks.

Mineral Wells, TX
(Palo Pinto County, TX)

POPULATION

2010 census	28,111 (454)
2015 estimate	27,895 (456)
2010-2015 change	-0.8% (314)
2020 projection	27,673 (451)
2030 projection	27,226 (455)

RACE

Whites	76.1% (352)
Blacks	2.4% (263)
Hispanics	19.4% (79)
Asians	0.4% (413)
Native Americans	0.6% (150)

AGE

0-17 years old	24.1% (180)
18-24 years old	8.5% (330)
25-39 years old	16.0% (449)
40-54 years old	19.9% (250)
55-64 years old	13.6% (247)
65+ years old	17.8% (137)

PRIVATE SECTOR

Businesses	633 (456)
Employees	6,605 (488)
Total wages	$276,727,042 (450)
Average weekly wages	$806 (83)

HOUSEHOLD INCOME LADDER

95th percentile	$147,799 (187)
80th percentile	$84,355 (268)
60th percentile	$50,736 (365)
40th percentile	$32,481 (339)
20th percentile	$16,928 (367)

CHILDREN ★ (540)

Living with two parents	60.8% (382)
Older teens in school	68.5% (538)
Speak English very well	93.1% (507)
Poverty rate for children	27.0% (348)
No health insurance	16.9% (535)

DIVERSITY/EQUALITY ★ (537)

Racial diversity index	38.2% (195)
Geographic diversity index	45.0% (280)
Top 20% share of income	52.0% (502)
Gender gap in earnings	44.2% (491)
White-collar gender gap	51.6% (515)

EDUCATION ★ (463)

Eighth grade or less	5.6% (410)
High school diplomas	83.1% (417)
Attended college	44.7% (441)
Bachelor's degrees	13.4% (482)
Advanced degrees	3.9% (489)

EMPLOYMENT ★★ (429)

Average jobless rate	8.3% (314)
Self-employed workers	9.1% (243)
Management/financial jobs	9.6% (427)
Computer/engineering jobs	2.2% (381)
Health care jobs	4.4% (433)

GROWTH POTENTIAL ★★★★ (140)

Children per senior	1.35 (313)
Median age	41.2 (368)
Moved from different state	1.4% (425)
Homes built since 2000	18.1% (131)
Construction jobs	9.9% (21)

HOUSING ★★★ (288)

Home vacancy rate	12.0% (460)
Home ownership rate	68.1% (339)
Housing diversity index	86.4% (26)
4 or more bedrooms	13.7% (415)
Affordability/income ratio	$2,095 (81)

INCOME ★★ (347)

Poverty rate	19.8% (364)
Median household income	$39,516 (394)
Interest/dividends	19.1% (273)
Public assistance	15.1% (262)
Median fulltime earnings	$34,422 (405)

SENIORS ★★★★ (117)

Seniors living alone	26.5% (201)
Poverty rate for seniors	11.4% (387)
Median income for seniors	$34,309 (220)
Seniors who work	23.5% (95)
Home ownership by seniors	87.2% (63)

STABILITY ★ (491)

25-39 age group	16.0% (449)
Born in state of residence	73.3% (254)
Same house as 1 year ago	81.8% (452)
Live and work in county	63.5% (459)
Married-couple households	49.6% (317)

TRANSPORTATION ★ (496)

Bicycle or walk to work	2.0% (386)
Carpool to work	7.9% (498)
Public transit to work	0.3% (291)
Commute <15 minutes	44.2% (259)
Commute >45 minutes	18.1% (502)

See pages 37-130 for explanations of statistics, stars, and ranks.

Morehead City, NC
(Carteret County, NC)

POPULATION		Attended college	64.8% (63)
2010 census	66,469 (114)	Bachelor's degrees	25.4% (101)
2015 estimate	68,879 (105)	Advanced degrees	8.9% (90)
2010-2015 change	3.6% (68)	**EMPLOYMENT**	★★★★★ **(44)**
2020 projection	70,423 (102)	Average jobless rate	10.2% (427)
2030 projection	73,301 (94)	Self-employed workers	14.6% (22)
		Management/financial jobs	14.4% (41)
RACE		Computer/engineering jobs	3.9% (86)
Whites	86.4% (250)	Health care jobs	6.5% (121)
Blacks	6.0% (146)		
Hispanics	4.1% (292)	**GROWTH POTENTIAL**	★★★ **(248)**
Asians	1.2% (125)	Children per senior	0.88 (528)
Native Americans	0.4% (203)	Median age	46.4 (518)
		Moved from different state	3.4% (118)
AGE		Homes built since 2000	20.8% (81)
0-17 years old	18.6% (509)	Construction jobs	8.3% (67)
18-24 years old	7.1% (515)		
25-39 years old	16.3% (418)	**HOUSING**	★★ **(387)**
40-54 years old	20.8% (122)	Home vacancy rate	8.4% (245)
55-64 years old	16.1% (42)	Home ownership rate	71.1% (222)
65+ years old	21.1% (29)	Housing diversity index	82.6% (433)
		4 or more bedrooms	17.6% (225)
PRIVATE SECTOR		Affordability/income ratio	$4,061 (500)
Businesses	2,055 (56)	**INCOME**	★★★★ **(146)**
Employees	18,125 (150)	Poverty rate	15.0% (190)
Total wages	$517,760,872 (231)	Median household income	$48,457 (163)
Average weekly wages	$549 (532)	Interest/dividends	24.7% (109)
		Public assistance	14.3% (220)
HOUSEHOLD INCOME LADDER		Median fulltime earnings	$39,370 (163)
95th percentile	$162,389 (84)	**SENIORS**	★★★★★ **(44)**
80th percentile	$92,319 (126)	Seniors living alone	25.9% (164)
60th percentile	$60,112 (148)	Poverty rate for seniors	6.7% (73)
40th percentile	$38,097 (178)	Median income for seniors	$43,423 (40)
20th percentile	$20,679 (199)	Seniors who work	20.2% (187)
		Home ownership by seniors	87.2% (63)
CHILDREN	★★★ **(326)**		
Living with two parents	61.8% (361)	**STABILITY**	★ **(478)**
Older teens in school	79.2% (421)	25-39 age group	16.3% (418)
Speak English very well	97.9% (352)	Born in state of residence	56.3% (454)
Poverty rate for children	24.5% (286)	Same house as 1 year ago	83.8% (347)
No health insurance	6.4% (276)	Live and work in county	74.8% (294)
		Married-couple households	49.3% (333)
DIVERSITY/EQUALITY	★★★★ **(198)**		
Racial diversity index	24.8% (296)	**TRANSPORTATION**	★★ **(376)**
Geographic diversity index	63.7% (87)	Bicycle or walk to work	1.8% (409)
Top 20% share of income	49.6% (403)	Carpool to work	11.4% (190)
Gender gap in earnings	31.1% (208)	Public transit to work	0.5% (178)
White-collar gender gap	22.6% (242)	Commute <15 minutes	36.0% (418)
		Commute >45 minutes	12.1% (316)
EDUCATION	★★★★★ **(87)**		
Eighth grade or less	2.4% (169)		
High school diplomas	90.9% (162)		

See pages 37-130 for explanations of statistics, stars, and ranks.

Morgan City, LA
(St. Mary Parish, LA)

POPULATION

2010 census	54,650 (176)
2015 estimate	52,810 (191)
2010-2015 change	-3.4% (501)
2020 projection	51,877 (200)
2030 projection	49,895 (215)

RACE

Whites	56.5% (467)
Blacks	31.1% (50)
Hispanics	6.2% (214)
Asians	1.6% (77)
Native Americans	1.2% (89)

AGE

0-17 years old	24.7% (141)
18-24 years old	9.2% (234)
25-39 years old	18.7% (127)
40-54 years old	20.5% (151)
55-64 years old	12.7% (375)
65+ years old	14.1% (431)

PRIVATE SECTOR

Businesses	1,368 (161)
Employees	20,923 (115)
Total wages	$1,107,814,833 (54)
Average weekly wages	$1,018 (16)

HOUSEHOLD INCOME LADDER

95th percentile	$152,158 (141)
80th percentile	$82,332 (316)
60th percentile	$50,800 (364)
40th percentile	$30,470 (403)
20th percentile	$15,430 (438)

CHILDREN ★ (453)

Living with two parents	50.6% (504)
Older teens in school	74.3% (507)
Speak English very well	98.2% (320)
Poverty rate for children	30.6% (416)
No health insurance	4.7% (166)

DIVERSITY/EQUALITY ★ (529)

Racial diversity index	57.9% (26)
Geographic diversity index	29.6% (490)
Top 20% share of income	50.7% (460)
Gender gap in earnings	54.4% (541)
White-collar gender gap	39.0% (433)

EDUCATION ★ (521)

Eighth grade or less	6.7% (459)
High school diplomas	78.6% (502)
Attended college	34.5% (542)
Bachelor's degrees	11.7% (521)
Advanced degrees	3.4% (514)

EMPLOYMENT ★ (485)

Average jobless rate	12.2% (497)
Self-employed workers	8.0% (333)
Management/financial jobs	11.7% (185)
Computer/engineering jobs	1.3% (519)
Health care jobs	4.9% (355)

GROWTH POTENTIAL ★★★★ (185)

Children per senior	1.76 (111)
Median age	37.7 (172)
Moved from different state	1.9% (310)
Homes built since 2000	12.9% (280)
Construction jobs	7.0% (185)

HOUSING ★★★ (280)

Home vacancy rate	9.6% (327)
Home ownership rate	67.0% (386)
Housing diversity index	86.0% (71)
4 or more bedrooms	12.8% (462)
Affordability/income ratio	$2,278 (153)

INCOME ★★ (411)

Poverty rate	22.4% (435)
Median household income	$40,781 (363)
Interest/dividends	12.8% (474)
Public assistance	22.3% (482)
Median fulltime earnings	$40,627 (113)

SENIORS ★ (502)

Seniors living alone	30.0% (427)
Poverty rate for seniors	15.5% (497)
Median income for seniors	$24,348 (510)
Seniors who work	17.6% (306)
Home ownership by seniors	81.9% (280)

STABILITY ★★★★ (162)

25-39 age group	18.7% (127)
Born in state of residence	83.5% (62)
Same house as 1 year ago	87.3% (181)
Live and work in county	82.1% (179)
Married-couple households	41.7% (508)

TRANSPORTATION ★★★★ (209)

Bicycle or walk to work	3.0% (249)
Carpool to work	11.2% (211)
Public transit to work	0.4% (219)
Commute <15 minutes	53.3% (106)
Commute >45 minutes	11.7% (300)

See pages 37-130 for explanations of statistics, stars, and ranks.

Moultrie, GA
(Colquitt County, GA)

POPULATION

2010 census	45,498 (254)
2015 estimate	45,844 (248)
2010-2015 change	0.8% (194)
2020 projection	45,910 (248)
2030 projection	45,891 (257)

RACE

Whites	57.3% (463)
Blacks	23.0% (70)
Hispanics	18.1% (88)
Asians	0.3% (473)
Native Americans	0.3% (231)

AGE

0-17 years old	27.1% (43)
18-24 years old	8.9% (282)
25-39 years old	19.1% (95)
40-54 years old	20.0% (233)
55-64 years old	11.3% (486)
65+ years old	13.6% (454)

PRIVATE SECTOR

Businesses	989 (284)
Employees	10,927 (345)
Total wages	$320,595,460 (406)
Average weekly wages	$564 (525)

HOUSEHOLD INCOME LADDER

95th percentile	$131,985 (401)
80th percentile	$69,703 (507)
60th percentile	$40,980 (518)
40th percentile	$25,632 (505)
20th percentile	$14,639 (464)

CHILDREN   ★ **(514)**

Living with two parents	56.7% (465)
Older teens in school	77.6% (458)
Speak English very well	96.4% (440)
Poverty rate for children	39.2% (510)
No health insurance	11.2% (452)

DIVERSITY/EQUALITY   ★★★★★ **(66)**

Racial diversity index	58.6% (18)
Geographic diversity index	44.6% (286)
Top 20% share of income	51.3% (479)
Gender gap in earnings	11.8% (13)
White-collar gender gap	24.7% (268)

EDUCATION   ★ **(526)**

Eighth grade or less	10.7% (519)
High school diplomas	74.6% (526)
Attended college	37.8% (530)
Bachelor's degrees	13.5% (478)
Advanced degrees	5.0% (378)

EMPLOYMENT   ★★ **(423)**

Average jobless rate	8.3% (314)
Self-employed workers	7.8% (355)
Management/financial jobs	9.8% (408)
Computer/engineering jobs	1.6% (486)
Health care jobs	5.5% (250)

GROWTH POTENTIAL   ★★★★ **(164)**

Children per senior	1.99 (63)
Median age	35.5 (104)
Moved from different state	2.2% (248)
Homes built since 2000	14.4% (222)
Construction jobs	5.3% (425)

HOUSING   ★★ **(369)**

Home vacancy rate	10.9% (400)
Home ownership rate	64.8% (438)
Housing diversity index	84.0% (344)
4 or more bedrooms	17.0% (247)
Affordability/income ratio	$2,456 (234)

INCOME   ★ **(518)**

Poverty rate	26.8% (500)
Median household income	$32,409 (515)
Interest/dividends	13.5% (456)
Public assistance	24.1% (509)
Median fulltime earnings	$29,914 (541)

SENIORS   ★★★ **(228)**

Seniors living alone	24.0% (84)
Poverty rate for seniors	10.3% (340)
Median income for seniors	$28,939 (436)
Seniors who work	21.7% (138)
Home ownership by seniors	81.2% (322)

STABILITY   ★★★★ **(200)**

25-39 age group	19.1% (95)
Born in state of residence	72.9% (261)
Same house as 1 year ago	83.4% (375)
Live and work in county	77.1% (256)
Married-couple households	49.6% (317)

TRANSPORTATION   ★★★★★ **(106)**

Bicycle or walk to work	3.0% (249)
Carpool to work	20.6% (3)
Public transit to work	1.4% (46)
Commute <15 minutes	37.3% (394)
Commute >45 minutes	12.3% (325)

See pages 37-130 for explanations of statistics, stars, and ranks.

Mountain Home, AR
(Baxter County, AR)

POPULATION			
2010 census	41,513 (295)	Attended college	56.4% (198)
2015 estimate	41,053 (301)	Bachelor's degrees	19.4% (235)
2010-2015 change	-1.1% (335)	Advanced degrees	4.8% (405)
2020 projection	40,785 (305)	**EMPLOYMENT**	**★★★★★ (99)**
2030 projection	39,895 (318)	Average jobless rate	7.6% (250)

POPULATION
2010 census — 41,513 (295)
2015 estimate — 41,053 (301)
2010-2015 change — -1.1% (335)
2020 projection — 40,785 (305)
2030 projection — 39,895 (318)

RACE
Whites — 95.3% (34)
Blacks — 0.3% (519)
Hispanics — 1.9% (442)
Asians — 0.5% (355)
Native Americans — 0.6% (150)

AGE
0-17 years old — 17.6% (532)
18-24 years old — 5.8% (548)
25-39 years old — 13.8% (544)
40-54 years old — 17.4% (485)
55-64 years old — 15.7% (52)
65+ years old — 29.6% (2)

PRIVATE SECTOR
Businesses — 1,170 (212)
Employees — 13,017 (279)
Total wages — $417,456,326 (317)
Average weekly wages — $617 (452)

HOUSEHOLD INCOME LADDER
95th percentile — $120,193 (515)
80th percentile — $68,832 (514)
60th percentile — $43,848 (493)
40th percentile — $28,493 (449)
20th percentile — $17,120 (356)

CHILDREN ★★★★ (207)
Living with two parents — 64.3% (288)
Older teens in school — 85.7% (176)
Speak English very well — 99.2% (163)
Poverty rate for children — 25.7% (315)
No health insurance — 6.2% (262)

DIVERSITY/EQUALITY ★★★★★ (88)
Racial diversity index — 9.1% (514)
Geographic diversity index — 71.3% (36)
Top 20% share of income — 50.0% (424)
Gender gap in earnings — 17.2% (24)
White-collar gender gap — 15.5% (156)

EDUCATION ★★★★ (217)
Eighth grade or less — 2.8% (205)
High school diplomas — 91.0% (160)
Attended college — 56.4% (198)
Bachelor's degrees — 19.4% (235)
Advanced degrees — 4.8% (405)

EMPLOYMENT ★★★★★ (99)
Average jobless rate — 7.6% (250)
Self-employed workers — 9.8% (186)
Management/financial jobs — 10.9% (263)
Computer/engineering jobs — 3.0% (193)
Health care jobs — 8.0% (19)

GROWTH POTENTIAL ★ (522)
Children per senior — 0.60 (550)
Median age — 51.5 (550)
Moved from different state — 2.6% (187)
Homes built since 2000 — 23.9% (44)
Construction jobs — 5.2% (442)

HOUSING ★★ (430)
Home vacancy rate — 7.4% (180)
Home ownership rate — 75.6% (66)
Housing diversity index — 81.0% (495)
4 or more bedrooms — 9.7% (536)
Affordability/income ratio — $3,402 (453)

INCOME ★★★ (303)
Poverty rate — 15.9% (219)
Median household income — $35,396 (481)
Interest/dividends — 25.2% (87)
Public assistance — 13.7% (197)
Median fulltime earnings — $31,037 (528)

SENIORS ★★★ (246)
Seniors living alone — 26.4% (193)
Poverty rate for seniors — 8.0% (177)
Median income for seniors — $31,689 (337)
Seniors who work — 13.6% (515)
Home ownership by seniors — 86.4% (82)

STABILITY ★ (524)
25-39 age group — 13.8% (544)
Born in state of residence — 37.3% (529)
Same house as 1 year ago — 83.5% (366)
Live and work in county — 84.8% (137)
Married-couple households — 52.9% (157)

TRANSPORTATION ★★★ (238)
Bicycle or walk to work — 1.5% (457)
Carpool to work — 9.3% (401)
Public transit to work — 0.4% (219)
Commute <15 minutes — 46.8% (219)
Commute >45 minutes — 4.0% (13)

See pages 37-130 for explanations of statistics, stars, and ranks.

Mount Airy, NC
(Surry County, NC)

POPULATION	
2010 census	73,673 (87)
2015 estimate	72,743 (91)
2010-2015 change	-1.3% (355)
2020 projection	71,086 (98)
2030 projection	67,591 (116)

RACE	
Whites	84.5% (272)
Blacks	3.6% (206)
Hispanics	10.0% (150)
Asians	0.6% (291)
Native Americans	0.3% (231)

AGE	
0-17 years old	22.4% (306)
18-24 years old	8.1% (396)
25-39 years old	16.2% (434)
40-54 years old	21.3% (73)
55-64 years old	13.7% (225)
65+ years old	18.3% (108)

PRIVATE SECTOR	
Businesses	1,717 (97)
Employees	23,757 (83)
Total wages	$760,352,748 (130)
Average weekly wages	$615 (456)

HOUSEHOLD INCOME LADDER	
95th percentile	$123,862 (491)
80th percentile	$75,544 (449)
60th percentile	$45,504 (471)
40th percentile	$29,595 (433)
20th percentile	$15,960 (410)

CHILDREN	★★ (421)
Living with two parents	69.4% (156)
Older teens in school	77.2% (469)
Speak English very well	93.8% (497)
Poverty rate for children	26.8% (346)
No health insurance	9.0% (393)

DIVERSITY/EQUALITY	★★★★ (165)
Racial diversity index	27.5% (277)
Geographic diversity index	47.4% (252)
Top 20% share of income	49.1% (366)
Gender gap in earnings	30.2% (172)
White-collar gender gap	6.9% (54)

EDUCATION	★★ (438)
Eighth grade or less	7.0% (472)
High school diplomas	80.4% (473)
Attended college	50.2% (325)
Bachelor's degrees	16.2% (360)
Advanced degrees	5.1% (364)

EMPLOYMENT	★★★ (278)
Average jobless rate	6.9% (185)
Self-employed workers	7.8% (355)
Management/financial jobs	10.7% (287)
Computer/engineering jobs	2.4% (336)
Health care jobs	6.0% (181)

GROWTH POTENTIAL	★★★ (290)
Children per senior	1.22 (401)
Median age	42.7 (442)
Moved from different state	0.9% (515)
Homes built since 2000	11.3% (344)
Construction jobs	9.5% (31)

HOUSING	★★★ (324)
Home vacancy rate	10.3% (366)
Home ownership rate	72.1% (181)
Housing diversity index	86.0% (71)
4 or more bedrooms	11.9% (500)
Affordability/income ratio	$3,194 (431)

INCOME	★★ (425)
Poverty rate	19.7% (362)
Median household income	$36,164 (462)
Interest/dividends	15.3% (399)
Public assistance	17.7% (361)
Median fulltime earnings	$33,656 (433)

SENIORS	★ (486)
Seniors living alone	29.5% (405)
Poverty rate for seniors	13.4% (457)
Median income for seniors	$26,483 (485)
Seniors who work	15.6% (432)
Home ownership by seniors	81.7% (294)

STABILITY	★★★★ (157)
25-39 age group	16.2% (434)
Born in state of residence	70.8% (295)
Same house as 1 year ago	92.4% (11)
Live and work in county	70.8% (357)
Married-couple households	52.0% (194)

TRANSPORTATION	★ (465)
Bicycle or walk to work	0.7% (537)
Carpool to work	10.5% (280)
Public transit to work	0.7% (119)
Commute <15 minutes	33.3% (472)
Commute >45 minutes	14.6% (414)

See pages 37-130 for explanations of statistics, stars, and ranks.

Mount Pleasant, TX
(Titus County, TX)

POPULATION	
2010 census	32,334 (412)
2015 estimate	32,623 (411)
2010-2015 change	0.9% (186)
2020 projection	33,356 (401)
2030 projection	34,930 (376)

RACE	
Whites	47.3% (496)
Blacks	9.6% (117)
Hispanics	41.1% (34)
Asians	0.8% (201)
Native Americans	0.3% (231)

AGE	
0-17 years old	29.3% (22)
18-24 years old	10.6% (131)
25-39 years old	18.0% (201)
40-54 years old	18.8% (386)
55-64 years old	10.6% (502)
65+ years old	12.7% (480)

PRIVATE SECTOR	
Businesses	630 (457)
Employees	12,611 (294)
Total wages	$462,578,999 (279)
Average weekly wages	$705 (244)

HOUSEHOLD INCOME LADDER	
95th percentile	$140,814 (280)
80th percentile	$84,579 (261)
60th percentile	$55,301 (240)
40th percentile	$35,234 (258)
20th percentile	$20,443 (207)

CHILDREN	★ (530)
Living with two parents	68.7% (174)
Older teens in school	77.3% (466)
Speak English very well	86.5% (540)
Poverty rate for children	31.6% (437)
No health insurance	13.9% (508)

DIVERSITY/EQUALITY	★★★★★ (47)
Racial diversity index	59.8% (16)
Geographic diversity index	54.8% (156)
Top 20% share of income	48.1% (302)
Gender gap in earnings	26.6% (111)
White-collar gender gap	21.2% (221)

EDUCATION	★ (534)
Eighth grade or less	15.2% (536)
High school diplomas	72.1% (534)
Attended college	43.7% (456)
Bachelor's degrees	14.6% (435)
Advanced degrees	4.5% (442)

EMPLOYMENT	★ (496)
Average jobless rate	7.5% (242)
Self-employed workers	7.7% (362)
Management/financial jobs	8.6% (498)
Computer/engineering jobs	1.3% (519)
Health care jobs	4.4% (433)

GROWTH POTENTIAL	★★★★★ (72)
Children per senior	2.30 (36)
Median age	33.8 (70)
Moved from different state	2.2% (248)
Homes built since 2000	19.1% (105)
Construction jobs	6.0% (326)

HOUSING	★★ (356)
Home vacancy rate	10.6% (385)
Home ownership rate	67.8% (349)
Housing diversity index	83.9% (360)
4 or more bedrooms	13.6% (424)
Affordability/income ratio	$2,207 (126)

INCOME	★★ (430)
Poverty rate	21.4% (412)
Median household income	$44,178 (256)
Interest/dividends	12.7% (477)
Public assistance	16.2% (301)
Median fulltime earnings	$30,584 (536)

SENIORS	★★★ (247)
Seniors living alone	22.9% (58)
Poverty rate for seniors	11.7% (397)
Median income for seniors	$33,952 (238)
Seniors who work	19.7% (214)
Home ownership by seniors	79.2% (406)

STABILITY	★★★★★ (30)
25-39 age group	18.0% (201)
Born in state of residence	64.9% (387)
Same house as 1 year ago	90.2% (41)
Live and work in county	80.3% (214)
Married-couple households	56.9% (32)

TRANSPORTATION	★★★ (244)
Bicycle or walk to work	1.2% (492)
Carpool to work	10.6% (271)
Public transit to work	0.4% (219)
Commute <15 minutes	46.1% (230)
Commute >45 minutes	5.9% (51)

See pages 37-130 for explanations of statistics, stars, and ranks.

Mount Sterling, KY
(Bath, Menifee, and Montgomery Counties, KY)

POPULATION

2010 census	44,396 (267)
2015 estimate	46,194 (244)
2010-2015 change	4.0% (61)
2020 projection	47,753 (230)
2030 projection	50,940 (211)

RACE

Whites	94.2% (70)
Blacks	2.2% (276)
Hispanics	2.2% (406)
Asians	0.1% (529)
Native Americans	0.2% (300)

AGE

0-17 years old	23.9% (194)
18-24 years old	8.0% (407)
25-39 years old	18.7% (127)
40-54 years old	21.7% (42)
55-64 years old	12.7% (375)
65+ years old	15.1% (363)

PRIVATE SECTOR

Businesses	883 (324)
Employees	11,577 (323)
Total wages	$414,150,690 (321)
Average weekly wages	$688 (290)

HOUSEHOLD INCOME LADDER

95th percentile	$128,528 (450)
80th percentile	$74,669 (462)
60th percentile	$45,083 (476)
40th percentile	$27,254 (477)
20th percentile	$13,666 (486)

CHILDREN ★★★ (327)

Living with two parents	62.0% (353)
Older teens in school	79.3% (419)
Speak English very well	99.8% (38)
Poverty rate for children	37.0% (495)
No health insurance	3.0% (59)

DIVERSITY/EQUALITY ★ (468)

Racial diversity index	11.2% (477)
Geographic diversity index	36.4% (418)
Top 20% share of income	51.0% (470)
Gender gap in earnings	27.5% (126)
White-collar gender gap	26.0% (289)

EDUCATION ★★ (429)

Eighth grade or less	6.8% (463)
High school diplomas	82.8% (425)
Attended college	44.8% (440)
Bachelor's degrees	16.8% (339)
Advanced degrees	6.1% (250)

EMPLOYMENT ★★ (409)

Average jobless rate	11.8% (486)
Self-employed workers	8.5% (290)
Management/financial jobs	10.7% (287)
Computer/engineering jobs	2.7% (270)
Health care jobs	5.5% (250)

GROWTH POTENTIAL ★★★★ (181)

Children per senior	1.59 (175)
Median age	39.6 (276)
Moved from different state	1.6% (383)
Homes built since 2000	19.0% (109)
Construction jobs	6.9% (198)

HOUSING ★★ (393)

Home vacancy rate	11.6% (441)
Home ownership rate	68.9% (308)
Housing diversity index	84.3% (314)
4 or more bedrooms	13.3% (437)
Affordability/income ratio	$2,584 (285)

INCOME ★ (483)

Poverty rate	26.6% (496)
Median household income	$35,987 (468)
Interest/dividends	13.8% (446)
Public assistance	23.5% (502)
Median fulltime earnings	$35,857 (340)

SENIORS ★ (478)

Seniors living alone	26.5% (201)
Poverty rate for seniors	16.0% (503)
Median income for seniors	$25,300 (500)
Seniors who work	15.3% (446)
Home ownership by seniors	82.3% (261)

STABILITY ★★ (413)

25-39 age group	18.7% (127)
Born in state of residence	78.7% (139)
Same house as 1 year ago	82.7% (411)
Live and work in county	55.7% (517)
Married-couple households	49.8% (307)

TRANSPORTATION ★ (449)

Bicycle or walk to work	1.3% (485)
Carpool to work	13.0% (101)
Public transit to work	0.4% (219)
Commute <15 minutes	33.6% (469)
Commute >45 minutes	17.4% (490)

See pages 37-130 for explanations of statistics, stars, and ranks.

Murray, KY
(Calloway County, KY)

POPULATION

2010 census	37,191 (351)
2015 estimate	38,343 (334)
2010-2015 change	3.1% (78)
2020 projection	39,186 (324)
2030 projection	40,791 (307)

RACE

Whites	89.6% (191)
Blacks	3.9% (195)
Hispanics	2.5% (384)
Asians	2.2% (40)
Native Americans	0.3% (231)

AGE

0-17 years old	17.9% (528)
18-24 years old	21.7% (22)
25-39 years old	16.3% (418)
40-54 years old	17.0% (502)
55-64 years old	11.4% (482)
65+ years old	15.6% (328)

PRIVATE SECTOR

Businesses	944 (296)
Employees	11,889 (312)
Total wages	$365,616,778 (368)
Average weekly wages	$591 (501)

HOUSEHOLD INCOME LADDER

95th percentile	$131,701 (407)
80th percentile	$78,529 (391)
60th percentile	$47,771 (430)
40th percentile	$28,254 (458)
20th percentile	$12,288 (512)

CHILDREN ★★★★ (128)

Living with two parents	69.4% (156)
Older teens in school	94.6% (16)
Speak English very well	98.0% (341)
Poverty rate for children	22.6% (238)
No health insurance	9.2% (399)

DIVERSITY/EQUALITY ★★ (433)

Racial diversity index	19.4% (355)
Geographic diversity index	60.4% (121)
Top 20% share of income	50.8% (464)
Gender gap in earnings	44.4% (493)
White-collar gender gap	25.4% (277)

EDUCATION ★★★★★ (70)

Eighth grade or less	3.6% (292)
High school diplomas	90.7% (173)
Attended college	59.7% (134)
Bachelor's degrees	29.7% (55)
Advanced degrees	12.0% (37)

EMPLOYMENT ★★ (349)

Average jobless rate	9.1% (370)
Self-employed workers	9.0% (254)
Management/financial jobs	10.5% (318)
Computer/engineering jobs	2.5% (307)
Health care jobs	5.4% (273)

GROWTH POTENTIAL ★★★★★ (107)

Children per senior	1.14 (446)
Median age	33.7 (68)
Moved from different state	4.8% (61)
Homes built since 2000	18.8% (112)
Construction jobs	6.5% (253)

HOUSING ★★ (375)

Home vacancy rate	7.8% (205)
Home ownership rate	63.1% (471)
Housing diversity index	84.9% (235)
4 or more bedrooms	15.0% (356)
Affordability/income ratio	$3,238 (438)

INCOME ★★ (340)

Poverty rate	23.1% (448)
Median household income	$37,034 (444)
Interest/dividends	18.2% (305)
Public assistance	12.6% (150)
Median fulltime earnings	$38,157 (213)

SENIORS ★★★ (282)

Seniors living alone	30.7% (460)
Poverty rate for seniors	9.9% (315)
Median income for seniors	$33,330 (266)
Seniors who work	18.3% (272)
Home ownership by seniors	86.7% (76)

STABILITY ★ (510)

25-39 age group	16.3% (418)
Born in state of residence	58.8% (430)
Same house as 1 year ago	80.2% (495)
Live and work in county	83.8% (147)
Married-couple households	45.0% (465)

TRANSPORTATION ★★★★ (156)

Bicycle or walk to work	6.8% (46)
Carpool to work	7.5% (515)
Public transit to work	0.3% (291)
Commute <15 minutes	55.2% (89)
Commute >45 minutes	9.2% (182)

See pages 37-130 for explanations of statistics, stars, and ranks.

Muskogee, OK
(Muskogee County, OK)

POPULATION

2010 census	70,990 (95)
2015 estimate	69,699 (104)
2010-2015 change	-1.8% (389)
2020 projection	68,749 (106)
2030 projection	66,831 (121)

RACE

Whites	57.4% (461)
Blacks	11.0% (111)
Hispanics	5.7% (231)
Asians	0.7% (241)
Native Americans	16.1% (8)

AGE

0-17 years old	24.6% (144)
18-24 years old	9.1% (251)
25-39 years old	18.9% (111)
40-54 years old	19.1% (354)
55-64 years old	12.8% (356)
65+ years old	15.5% (333)

PRIVATE SECTOR

Businesses	1,441 (149)
Employees	21,297 (108)
Total wages	$769,983,155 (127)
Average weekly wages	$695 (268)

HOUSEHOLD INCOME LADDER

95th percentile	$137,131 (326)
80th percentile	$76,915 (425)
60th percentile	$50,291 (376)
40th percentile	$30,790 (393)
20th percentile	$16,065 (405)

CHILDREN ★ (464)

Living with two parents	58.4% (441)
Older teens in school	80.8% (376)
Speak English very well	99.4% (124)
Poverty rate for children	32.0% (445)
No health insurance	14.1% (510)

DIVERSITY/EQUALITY ★★★★★ (82)

Racial diversity index	62.1% (7)
Geographic diversity index	48.2% (240)
Top 20% share of income	49.0% (357)
Gender gap in earnings	35.5% (327)
White-collar gender gap	11.8% (109)

EDUCATION ★★★ (323)

Eighth grade or less	2.9% (217)
High school diplomas	86.8% (314)
Attended college	50.4% (319)
Bachelor's degrees	17.9% (289)
Advanced degrees	4.6% (431)

EMPLOYMENT ★★★ (325)

Average jobless rate	8.2% (310)
Self-employed workers	7.4% (393)
Management/financial jobs	9.4% (444)
Computer/engineering jobs	2.6% (288)
Health care jobs	6.7% (104)

GROWTH POTENTIAL ★★★★ (177)

Children per senior	1.59 (175)
Median age	37.8 (174)
Moved from different state	2.7% (179)
Homes built since 2000	12.2% (306)
Construction jobs	7.3% (151)

HOUSING ★★ (362)

Home vacancy rate	13.1% (494)
Home ownership rate	67.0% (386)
Housing diversity index	86.4% (26)
4 or more bedrooms	13.2% (445)
Affordability/income ratio	$2,288 (159)

INCOME ★ (465)

Poverty rate	22.2% (430)
Median household income	$39,984 (382)
Interest/dividends	12.8% (474)
Public assistance	22.3% (482)
Median fulltime earnings	$34,910 (389)

SENIORS ★★ (395)

Seniors living alone	28.5% (332)
Poverty rate for seniors	10.0% (321)
Median income for seniors	$31,813 (328)
Seniors who work	15.8% (423)
Home ownership by seniors	81.4% (315)

STABILITY ★★★ (320)

25-39 age group	18.9% (111)
Born in state of residence	70.5% (301)
Same house as 1 year ago	81.0% (478)
Live and work in county	81.2% (200)
Married-couple households	46.7% (427)

TRANSPORTATION ★★★ (285)

Bicycle or walk to work	2.1% (374)
Carpool to work	11.8% (152)
Public transit to work	0.4% (219)
Commute <15 minutes	44.0% (260)
Commute >45 minutes	11.3% (285)

See pages 37-130 for explanations of statistics, stars, and ranks.

Nacogdoches, TX
(Nacogdoches County, TX)

POPULATION

2010 census	64,524 (124)
2015 estimate	65,664 (119)
2010-2015 change	1.8% (142)
2020 projection	66,445 (116)
2030 projection	67,995 (115)

RACE

Whites	60.4% (444)
Blacks	18.0% (83)
Hispanics	18.5% (85)
Asians	1.6% (77)
Native Americans	0.4% (203)

AGE

0-17 years old	23.5% (232)
18-24 years old	19.9% (27)
25-39 years old	16.9% (338)
40-54 years old	16.2% (521)
55-64 years old	11.1% (492)
65+ years old	12.4% (487)

PRIVATE SECTOR

Businesses	1,272 (185)
Employees	16,774 (177)
Total wages	$559,929,333 (207)
Average weekly wages	$642 (412)

HOUSEHOLD INCOME LADDER

95th percentile	$143,288 (252)
80th percentile	$82,875 (297)
60th percentile	$50,422 (370)
40th percentile	$30,003 (425)
20th percentile	$13,951 (477)

CHILDREN ★★ (425)

Living with two parents	62.3% (339)
Older teens in school	91.8% (43)
Speak English very well	94.5% (486)
Poverty rate for children	31.8% (441)
No health insurance	13.9% (508)

DIVERSITY/EQUALITY ★ (489)

Racial diversity index	56.8% (33)
Geographic diversity index	43.7% (299)
Top 20% share of income	52.1% (506)
Gender gap in earnings	38.7% (411)
White-collar gender gap	54.8% (526)

EDUCATION ★★★ (258)

Eighth grade or less	7.5% (478)
High school diplomas	82.1% (444)
Attended college	54.5% (233)
Bachelor's degrees	24.8% (114)
Advanced degrees	9.2% (81)

EMPLOYMENT ★★★ (251)

Average jobless rate	8.6% (335)
Self-employed workers	9.3% (224)
Management/financial jobs	10.6% (306)
Computer/engineering jobs	2.8% (246)
Health care jobs	6.1% (168)

GROWTH POTENTIAL ★★★★★ (53)

Children per senior	1.89 (72)
Median age	30.2 (30)
Moved from different state	1.3% (452)
Homes built since 2000	19.3% (102)
Construction jobs	8.3% (67)

HOUSING ★ (512)

Home vacancy rate	9.2% (302)
Home ownership rate	55.7% (533)
Housing diversity index	84.3% (314)
4 or more bedrooms	10.7% (522)
Affordability/income ratio	$2,792 (357)

INCOME ★★ (391)

Poverty rate	24.6% (473)
Median household income	$39,538 (392)
Interest/dividends	16.8% (349)
Public assistance	15.7% (280)
Median fulltime earnings	$36,238 (322)

SENIORS ★ (487)

Seniors living alone	32.9% (527)
Poverty rate for seniors	12.2% (422)
Median income for seniors	$31,590 (348)
Seniors who work	18.0% (287)
Home ownership by seniors	79.3% (403)

STABILITY ★ (473)

25-39 age group	16.9% (338)
Born in state of residence	74.1% (242)
Same house as 1 year ago	78.0% (518)
Live and work in county	82.6% (170)
Married-couple households	44.6% (471)

TRANSPORTATION ★★★★ (145)

Bicycle or walk to work	4.8% (98)
Carpool to work	12.1% (135)
Public transit to work	0.2% (363)
Commute <15 minutes	49.2% (170)
Commute >45 minutes	9.3% (188)

See pages 37-130 for explanations of statistics, stars, and ranks.

Natchez, MS-LA
(Adams County, MS, and Concordia Parish, LA)

POPULATION

2010 census	53,119 (186)
2015 estimate	51,396 (203)
2010-2015 change	-3.2% (494)
2020 projection	49,816 (213)
2030 projection	46,568 (250)

RACE

Whites	45.4% (501)
Blacks	49.7% (15)
Hispanics	4.1% (292)
Asians	0.2% (509)
Native Americans	0.1% (402)

AGE

0-17 years old	22.5% (300)
18-24 years old	8.5% (330)
25-39 years old	19.1% (95)
40-54 years old	19.5% (301)
55-64 years old	14.3% (148)
65+ years old	16.0% (291)

PRIVATE SECTOR

Businesses	1,199 (206)
Employees	13,309 (269)
Total wages	$432,384,257 (304)
Average weekly wages	$625 (443)

HOUSEHOLD INCOME LADDER

95th percentile	$126,319 (476)
80th percentile	$66,427 (528)
60th percentile	$38,240 (538)
40th percentile	$22,376 (536)
20th percentile	$12,014 (522)

CHILDREN   ★ (546)

Living with two parents	35.4% (543)
Older teens in school	81.8% (329)
Speak English very well	100.0% (1)
Poverty rate for children	48.3% (540)
No health insurance	20.2% (548)

DIVERSITY/EQUALITY   ★★★★ (190)

Racial diversity index	54.5% (61)
Geographic diversity index	48.4% (238)
Top 20% share of income	53.9% (534)
Gender gap in earnings	22.4% (62)
White-collar gender gap	21.3% (222)

EDUCATION   ★ (469)

Eighth grade or less	6.5% (449)
High school diplomas	81.2% (463)
Attended college	42.8% (476)
Bachelor's degrees	14.8% (429)
Advanced degrees	5.1% (364)

EMPLOYMENT   ★★ (437)

Average jobless rate	11.5% (474)
Self-employed workers	9.8% (186)
Management/financial jobs	9.4% (444)
Computer/engineering jobs	1.4% (510)
Health care jobs	6.1% (168)

GROWTH POTENTIAL   ★★ (368)

Children per senior	1.41 (269)
Median age	39.9 (292)
Moved from different state	2.4% (218)
Homes built since 2000	7.9% (470)
Construction jobs	6.3% (284)

HOUSING   ★ (498)

Home vacancy rate	10.6% (385)
Home ownership rate	63.0% (475)
Housing diversity index	82.6% (433)
4 or more bedrooms	13.7% (415)
Affordability/income ratio	$2,850 (368)

INCOME   ★ (513)

Poverty rate	30.3% (525)
Median household income	$29,088 (539)
Interest/dividends	10.3% (526)
Public assistance	16.3% (305)
Median fulltime earnings	$31,440 (518)

SENIORS   ★ (470)

Seniors living alone	28.1% (306)
Poverty rate for seniors	15.9% (500)
Median income for seniors	$27,020 (477)
Seniors who work	17.8% (299)
Home ownership by seniors	81.9% (280)

STABILITY   ★★ (375)

25-39 age group	19.1% (95)
Born in state of residence	67.9% (349)
Same house as 1 year ago	90.0% (44)
Live and work in county	75.1% (287)
Married-couple households	37.9% (537)

TRANSPORTATION   ★★★ (316)

Bicycle or walk to work	2.0% (386)
Carpool to work	7.0% (531)
Public transit to work	0.3% (291)
Commute <15 minutes	56.3% (78)
Commute >45 minutes	9.5% (203)

See pages 37-130 for explanations of statistics, stars, and ranks.

Natchitoches, LA
(Natchitoches Parish, LA)

POPULATION	
2010 census	39,566 (318)
2015 estimate	39,179 (323)
2010-2015 change	-1.0% (326)
2020 projection	38,950 (329)
2030 projection	38,366 (334)

RACE	
Whites	53.4% (475)
Blacks	40.5% (28)
Hispanics	2.1% (416)
Asians	0.6% (291)
Native Americans	1.0% (103)

AGE	
0-17 years old	24.0% (184)
18-24 years old	16.4% (47)
25-39 years old	16.6% (388)
40-54 years old	16.3% (520)
55-64 years old	11.9% (447)
65+ years old	14.7% (389)

PRIVATE SECTOR	
Businesses	830 (357)
Employees	9,097 (411)
Total wages	$288,882,843 (444)
Average weekly wages	$611 (467)

HOUSEHOLD INCOME LADDER	
95th percentile	$151,870 (142)
80th percentile	$77,480 (407)
60th percentile	$40,850 (522)
40th percentile	$22,180 (537)
20th percentile	$10,357 (543)

CHILDREN	★★ (404)
Living with two parents	48.5% (518)
Older teens in school	82.1% (313)
Speak English very well	99.5% (96)
Poverty rate for children	37.3% (499)
No health insurance	3.3% (72)

DIVERSITY/EQUALITY	★ (479)
Racial diversity index	55.0% (55)
Geographic diversity index	30.4% (481)
Top 20% share of income	57.1% (551)
Gender gap in earnings	45.4% (504)
White-collar gender gap	9.2% (84)

EDUCATION	★★★ (273)
Eighth grade or less	3.9% (316)
High school diplomas	85.6% (357)
Attended college	50.5% (314)
Bachelor's degrees	19.3% (239)
Advanced degrees	7.4% (149)

EMPLOYMENT	★ (501)
Average jobless rate	12.2% (497)
Self-employed workers	9.7% (196)
Management/financial jobs	8.2% (522)
Computer/engineering jobs	2.9% (219)
Health care jobs	4.2% (454)

GROWTH POTENTIAL	★★★★ (160)
Children per senior	1.62 (164)
Median age	33.8 (70)
Moved from different state	1.6% (383)
Homes built since 2000	18.4% (123)
Construction jobs	5.5% (404)

HOUSING	★ (541)
Home vacancy rate	16.7% (542)
Home ownership rate	58.0% (522)
Housing diversity index	84.8% (248)
4 or more bedrooms	15.1% (347)
Affordability/income ratio	$3,251 (441)

INCOME	★ (517)
Poverty rate	29.2% (518)
Median household income	$31,345 (527)
Interest/dividends	11.9% (495)
Public assistance	24.7% (512)
Median fulltime earnings	$34,341 (409)

SENIORS	★ (455)
Seniors living alone	27.5% (264)
Poverty rate for seniors	14.8% (485)
Median income for seniors	$31,035 (368)
Seniors who work	18.7% (259)
Home ownership by seniors	79.2% (406)

STABILITY	★★★ (295)
25-39 age group	16.6% (388)
Born in state of residence	82.7% (73)
Same house as 1 year ago	88.1% (126)
Live and work in county	81.8% (186)
Married-couple households	40.5% (526)

TRANSPORTATION	★★★ (236)
Bicycle or walk to work	2.7% (292)
Carpool to work	11.1% (221)
Public transit to work	0.7% (119)
Commute <15 minutes	48.3% (189)
Commute >45 minutes	11.3% (285)

See pages 37-130 for explanations of statistics, stars, and ranks.

Newberry, SC
(Newberry County, SC)

POPULATION

2010 census	37,508 (347)
2015 estimate	38,012 (340)
2010-2015 change	1.3% (167)
2020 projection	38,130 (340)
2030 projection	38,245 (336)

RACE

Whites	60.2% (445)
Blacks	30.0% (55)
Hispanics	7.3% (193)
Asians	0.7% (241)
Native Americans	0.2% (300)

AGE

0-17 years old	22.2% (320)
18-24 years old	10.3% (146)
25-39 years old	16.1% (442)
40-54 years old	20.0% (233)
55-64 years old	14.1% (174)
65+ years old	17.3% (172)

PRIVATE SECTOR

Businesses	689 (434)
Employees	11,747 (316)
Total wages	$414,751,023 (320)
Average weekly wages	$679 (315)

HOUSEHOLD INCOME LADDER

95th percentile	$139,583 (297)
80th percentile	$82,749 (298)
60th percentile	$51,852 (324)
40th percentile	$32,032 (361)
20th percentile	$19,384 (251)

CHILDREN ★★★★ (181)

Living with two parents	54.5% (479)
Older teens in school	88.9% (82)
Speak English very well	99.1% (179)
Poverty rate for children	27.1% (350)
No health insurance	2.0% (13)

DIVERSITY/EQUALITY ★★★★★ (50)

Racial diversity index	54.2% (67)
Geographic diversity index	39.7% (360)
Top 20% share of income	47.2% (240)
Gender gap in earnings	27.1% (120)
White-collar gender gap	5.0% (43)

EDUCATION ★ (464)

Eighth grade or less	8.1% (491)
High school diplomas	79.6% (486)
Attended college	46.0% (421)
Bachelor's degrees	16.1% (366)
Advanced degrees	6.1% (250)

EMPLOYMENT ★ (487)

Average jobless rate	10.2% (427)
Self-employed workers	6.5% (474)
Management/financial jobs	9.2% (459)
Computer/engineering jobs	2.8% (246)
Health care jobs	5.0% (339)

GROWTH POTENTIAL ★★ (337)

Children per senior	1.28 (357)
Median age	40.9 (350)
Moved from different state	1.5% (406)
Homes built since 2000	16.5% (167)
Construction jobs	6.0% (326)

HOUSING ★★★ (272)

Home vacancy rate	11.6% (441)
Home ownership rate	73.2% (146)
Housing diversity index	85.7% (108)
4 or more bedrooms	13.2% (445)
Affordability/income ratio	$2,512 (253)

INCOME ★★ (369)

Poverty rate	17.6% (287)
Median household income	$40,127 (378)
Interest/dividends	17.8% (316)
Public assistance	18.6% (389)
Median fulltime earnings	$34,362 (407)

SENIORS ★★★ (237)

Seniors living alone	27.6% (269)
Poverty rate for seniors	10.2% (334)
Median income for seniors	$32,407 (305)
Seniors who work	19.7% (214)
Home ownership by seniors	84.6% (159)

STABILITY ★★ (409)

25-39 age group	16.1% (442)
Born in state of residence	76.8% (180)
Same house as 1 year ago	88.2% (124)
Live and work in county	65.7% (443)
Married-couple households	46.4% (435)

TRANSPORTATION ★ (478)

Bicycle or walk to work	1.6% (443)
Carpool to work	9.4% (394)
Public transit to work	0.7% (119)
Commute <15 minutes	31.8% (503)
Commute >45 minutes	14.7% (418)

See pages 37-130 for explanations of statistics, stars, and ranks.

Newport, TN
(Cocke County, TN)

POPULATION	
2010 census	35,662 (377)
2015 estimate	35,162 (381)
2010-2015 change	-1.4% (364)
2020 projection	34,777 (385)
2030 projection	33,891 (395)

RACE	
Whites	93.7% (83)
Blacks	1.5% (329)
Hispanics	2.0% (428)
Asians	0.0% (546)
Native Americans	0.2% (300)

AGE	
0-17 years old	20.8% (417)
18-24 years old	7.7% (454)
25-39 years old	15.7% (465)
40-54 years old	21.6% (50)
55-64 years old	15.3% (68)
65+ years old	18.9% (85)

PRIVATE SECTOR	
Businesses	433 (533)
Employees	5,683 (517)
Total wages	$190,332,447 (512)
Average weekly wages	$644 (405)

HOUSEHOLD INCOME LADDER	
95th percentile	$110,910 (546)
80th percentile	$64,307 (534)
60th percentile	$39,928 (530)
40th percentile	$23,269 (532)
20th percentile	$11,893 (527)

CHILDREN	★ (505)
Living with two parents	46.3% (525)
Older teens in school	71.9% (522)
Speak English very well	99.4% (124)
Poverty rate for children	39.9% (515)
No health insurance	4.4% (145)

DIVERSITY/EQUALITY	★★ (389)
Racial diversity index	12.1% (462)
Geographic diversity index	51.0% (196)
Top 20% share of income	50.7% (462)
Gender gap in earnings	39.9% (435)
White-collar gender gap	9.1% (83)

EDUCATION	★ (496)
Eighth grade or less	5.4% (405)
High school diplomas	84.8% (377)
Attended college	35.4% (539)
Bachelor's degrees	11.1% (534)
Advanced degrees	3.6% (505)

EMPLOYMENT	★ (531)
Average jobless rate	11.1% (460)
Self-employed workers	6.7% (457)
Management/financial jobs	7.3% (543)
Computer/engineering jobs	1.3% (519)
Health care jobs	5.4% (273)

GROWTH POTENTIAL	★★ (423)
Children per senior	1.10 (464)
Median age	44.3 (487)
Moved from different state	2.6% (187)
Homes built since 2000	15.6% (189)
Construction jobs	5.8% (360)

HOUSING	★★ (401)
Home vacancy rate	9.0% (287)
Home ownership rate	68.8% (313)
Housing diversity index	84.9% (235)
4 or more bedrooms	10.4% (526)
Affordability/income ratio	$3,190 (430)

INCOME	★ (523)
Poverty rate	26.1% (487)
Median household income	$31,187 (529)
Interest/dividends	13.9% (444)
Public assistance	28.0% (534)
Median fulltime earnings	$30,926 (529)

SENIORS	★★ (409)
Seniors living alone	29.7% (416)
Poverty rate for seniors	16.4% (507)
Median income for seniors	$27,753 (464)
Seniors who work	20.7% (170)
Home ownership by seniors	86.8% (72)

STABILITY	★ (504)
25-39 age group	15.7% (465)
Born in state of residence	67.2% (358)
Same house as 1 year ago	86.9% (202)
Live and work in county	57.6% (508)
Married-couple households	47.7% (394)

TRANSPORTATION	★ (544)
Bicycle or walk to work	1.0% (512)
Carpool to work	10.5% (280)
Public transit to work	0.0% (511)
Commute <15 minutes	29.5% (527)
Commute >45 minutes	21.2% (525)

See pages 37-130 for explanations of statistics, stars, and ranks.

North Wilkesboro, NC
(Wilkes County, NC)

POPULATION	
2010 census	69,340 (104)
2015 estimate	68,502 (108)
2010-2015 change	-1.2% (345)
2020 projection	67,087 (114)
2030 projection	64,086 (132)

RACE	
Whites	88.3% (218)
Blacks	4.5% (176)
Hispanics	5.8% (230)
Asians	0.3% (473)
Native Americans	0.2% (300)

AGE	
0-17 years old	21.5% (373)
18-24 years old	7.8% (447)
25-39 years old	15.9% (453)
40-54 years old	21.2% (85)
55-64 years old	14.2% (161)
65+ years old	19.4% (65)

PRIVATE SECTOR	
Businesses	1,193 (207)
Employees	17,033 (169)
Total wages	$567,718,214 (204)
Average weekly wages	$641 (414)

HOUSEHOLD INCOME LADDER	
95th percentile	$121,623 (503)
80th percentile	$70,968 (500)
60th percentile	$43,004 (501)
40th percentile	$25,680 (504)
20th percentile	$14,408 (467)

CHILDREN	★★★ (293)
Living with two parents	68.3% (185)
Older teens in school	82.0% (319)
Speak English very well	97.7% (370)
Poverty rate for children	32.3% (450)
No health insurance	5.3% (206)

DIVERSITY/EQUALITY	★★★ (297)
Racial diversity index	21.5% (331)
Geographic diversity index	36.9% (405)
Top 20% share of income	50.4% (447)
Gender gap in earnings	16.7% (22)
White-collar gender gap	27.5% (302)

EDUCATION	★ (483)
Eighth grade or less	6.7% (459)
High school diplomas	78.5% (503)
Attended college	47.7% (388)
Bachelor's degrees	14.3% (451)
Advanced degrees	4.0% (478)

EMPLOYMENT	★ (489)
Average jobless rate	11.7% (481)
Self-employed workers	8.0% (333)
Management/financial jobs	10.4% (332)
Computer/engineering jobs	1.9% (441)
Health care jobs	4.9% (355)

GROWTH POTENTIAL	★★ (422)
Children per senior	1.11 (457)
Median age	43.7 (470)
Moved from different state	0.6% (546)
Homes built since 2000	12.6% (294)
Construction jobs	7.9% (93)

HOUSING	★★ (355)
Home vacancy rate	11.1% (409)
Home ownership rate	74.3% (105)
Housing diversity index	85.3% (170)
4 or more bedrooms	12.4% (480)
Affordability/income ratio	$3,455 (458)

INCOME	★ (469)
Poverty rate	23.3% (454)
Median household income	$33,232 (505)
Interest/dividends	17.7% (321)
Public assistance	20.4% (441)
Median fulltime earnings	$32,199 (484)

SENIORS	★ (449)
Seniors living alone	26.5% (201)
Poverty rate for seniors	15.2% (493)
Median income for seniors	$24,903 (503)
Seniors who work	14.3% (493)
Home ownership by seniors	86.5% (80)

STABILITY	★★★★★ (39)
25-39 age group	15.9% (453)
Born in state of residence	78.7% (139)
Same house as 1 year ago	93.3% (5)
Live and work in county	74.7% (299)
Married-couple households	54.2% (102)

TRANSPORTATION	★ (491)
Bicycle or walk to work	1.0% (512)
Carpool to work	11.9% (145)
Public transit to work	0.1% (441)
Commute <15 minutes	28.8% (532)
Commute >45 minutes	15.0% (424)

See pages 37-130 for explanations of statistics, stars, and ranks.

Okeechobee, FL
(Okeechobee County, FL)

POPULATION

2010 census	39,996 (315)
2015 estimate	39,469 (317)
2010-2015 change	-1.3% (355)
2020 projection	39,646 (317)
2030 projection	40,108 (315)

RACE

Whites	63.9% (424)
Blacks	8.6% (121)
Hispanics	25.0% (61)
Asians	1.0% (158)
Native Americans	0.7% (136)

AGE

0-17 years old	23.0% (259)
18-24 years old	9.0% (265)
25-39 years old	18.2% (167)
40-54 years old	20.3% (186)
55-64 years old	12.1% (430)
65+ years old	17.4% (165)

PRIVATE SECTOR

Businesses	900 (312)
Employees	8,850 (417)
Total wages	$301,266,172 (435)
Average weekly wages	$655 (381)

HOUSEHOLD INCOME LADDER

95th percentile	$125,815 (482)
80th percentile	$67,142 (524)
60th percentile	$42,998 (502)
40th percentile	$28,046 (462)
20th percentile	$15,434 (437)

CHILDREN ★ (544)

Living with two parents	54.0% (480)
Older teens in school	81.4% (350)
Speak English very well	87.2% (537)
Poverty rate for children	41.5% (524)
No health insurance	11.0% (448)

DIVERSITY/EQUALITY ★★★★★ (63)

Racial diversity index	52.2% (95)
Geographic diversity index	68.0% (57)
Top 20% share of income	49.8% (415)
Gender gap in earnings	23.4% (70)
White-collar gender gap	32.2% (367)

EDUCATION ★ (544)

Eighth grade or less	14.7% (530)
High school diplomas	71.0% (536)
Attended college	34.8% (541)
Bachelor's degrees	10.6% (536)
Advanced degrees	3.2% (521)

EMPLOYMENT ★ (529)

Average jobless rate	11.8% (486)
Self-employed workers	9.2% (231)
Management/financial jobs	10.1% (365)
Computer/engineering jobs	1.6% (486)
Health care jobs	2.6% (545)

GROWTH POTENTIAL ★★★★ (183)

Children per senior	1.32 (334)
Median age	39.9 (292)
Moved from different state	2.1% (269)
Homes built since 2000	16.7% (162)
Construction jobs	8.1% (86)

HOUSING ★ (505)

Home vacancy rate	10.1% (352)
Home ownership rate	70.7% (244)
Housing diversity index	79.9% (517)
4 or more bedrooms	9.8% (535)
Affordability/income ratio	$2,649 (311)

INCOME ★ (502)

Poverty rate	27.7% (510)
Median household income	$35,405 (480)
Interest/dividends	13.1% (467)
Public assistance	20.9% (452)
Median fulltime earnings	$30,407 (538)

SENIORS ★★★ (230)

Seniors living alone	23.2% (62)
Poverty rate for seniors	14.5% (481)
Median income for seniors	$31,773 (332)
Seniors who work	13.1% (523)
Home ownership by seniors	90.2% (14)

STABILITY ★★★ (250)

25-39 age group	18.2% (167)
Born in state of residence	52.2% (478)
Same house as 1 year ago	90.2% (41)
Live and work in county	79.0% (233)
Married-couple households	48.7% (356)

TRANSPORTATION ★★★ (232)

Bicycle or walk to work	3.1% (232)
Carpool to work	13.7% (77)
Public transit to work	0.8% (96)
Commute <15 minutes	42.0% (298)
Commute >45 minutes	14.0% (391)

See pages 37-130 for explanations of statistics, stars, and ranks.

Opelousas, LA
(St. Landry Parish, LA)

POPULATION

2010 census	83,384 (60)
2015 estimate	83,848 (61)
2010-2015 change	0.6% (209)
2020 projection	83,193 (63)
2030 projection	81,639 (71)

RACE

Whites	55.1% (472)
Blacks	40.8% (27)
Hispanics	1.9% (442)
Asians	0.4% (413)
Native Americans	0.1% (402)

AGE

0-17 years old	26.9% (47)
18-24 years old	8.8% (292)
25-39 years old	18.2% (167)
40-54 years old	19.0% (364)
55-64 years old	12.7% (375)
65+ years old	14.5% (412)

PRIVATE SECTOR

Businesses	1,699 (100)
Employees	18,785 (142)
Total wages	$659,117,269 (161)
Average weekly wages	$675 (320)

HOUSEHOLD INCOME LADDER

95th percentile	$136,947 (328)
80th percentile	$75,879 (442)
60th percentile	$44,732 (481)
40th percentile	$23,660 (527)
20th percentile	$12,075 (518)

CHILDREN ★ (501)

Living with two parents	48.1% (519)
Older teens in school	75.8% (494)
Speak English very well	99.1% (179)
Poverty rate for children	40.7% (520)
No health insurance	6.3% (271)

DIVERSITY/EQUALITY ★ (532)

Racial diversity index	52.9% (84)
Geographic diversity index	13.9% (551)
Top 20% share of income	53.2% (524)
Gender gap in earnings	46.0% (510)
White-collar gender gap	19.2% (197)

EDUCATION ★ (519)

Eighth grade or less	7.1% (475)
High school diplomas	79.6% (486)
Attended college	33.4% (544)
Bachelor's degrees	13.0% (493)
Advanced degrees	3.4% (514)

EMPLOYMENT ★★★ (262)

Average jobless rate	6.1% (121)
Self-employed workers	8.1% (323)
Management/financial jobs	8.8% (488)
Computer/engineering jobs	1.7% (470)
Health care jobs	7.4% (49)

GROWTH POTENTIAL ★★★★★ (108)

Children per senior	1.86 (82)
Median age	36.6 (134)
Moved from different state	1.3% (452)
Homes built since 2000	13.9% (240)
Construction jobs	9.1% (40)

HOUSING ★★ (339)

Home vacancy rate	9.5% (317)
Home ownership rate	69.7% (281)
Housing diversity index	84.8% (248)
4 or more bedrooms	12.2% (487)
Affordability/income ratio	$2,783 (354)

INCOME ★ (512)

Poverty rate	27.9% (512)
Median household income	$32,625 (511)
Interest/dividends	8.0% (543)
Public assistance	19.5% (415)
Median fulltime earnings	$32,304 (480)

SENIORS ★ (528)

Seniors living alone	30.6% (454)
Poverty rate for seniors	20.0% (540)
Median income for seniors	$22,740 (523)
Seniors who work	17.3% (324)
Home ownership by seniors	83.4% (202)

STABILITY ★★★ (230)

25-39 age group	18.2% (167)
Born in state of residence	92.7% (1)
Same house as 1 year ago	91.2% (26)
Live and work in county	57.4% (510)
Married-couple households	42.7% (499)

TRANSPORTATION ★ (485)

Bicycle or walk to work	1.7% (428)
Carpool to work	9.7% (369)
Public transit to work	0.2% (363)
Commute <15 minutes	35.9% (421)
Commute >45 minutes	15.9% (451)

See pages 37-130 for explanations of statistics, stars, and ranks.

Orangeburg, SC
(Orangeburg County, SC)

POPULATION	
2010 census	92,501 (41)
2015 estimate	89,208 (47)
2010-2015 change	-3.6% (510)
2020 projection	86,007 (56)
2030 projection	79,703 (80)

RACE	
Whites	33.6% (526)
Blacks	61.6% (7)
Hispanics	2.0% (428)
Asians	1.0% (158)
Native Americans	0.3% (231)

AGE	
0-17 years old	22.6% (291)
18-24 years old	11.7% (94)
25-39 years old	16.7% (375)
40-54 years old	18.8% (386)
55-64 years old	13.7% (225)
65+ years old	16.5% (247)

PRIVATE SECTOR	
Businesses	1,577 (123)
Employees	22,206 (93)
Total wages	$757,354,404 (132)
Average weekly wages	$656 (378)

HOUSEHOLD INCOME LADDER	
95th percentile	$123,254 (493)
80th percentile	$68,914 (513)
60th percentile	$43,069 (500)
40th percentile	$27,124 (480)
20th percentile	$12,395 (510)

CHILDREN	★ (459)
Living with two parents	40.9% (537)
Older teens in school	83.4% (258)
Speak English very well	99.2% (163)
Poverty rate for children	34.9% (477)
No health insurance	6.0% (248)

DIVERSITY/EQUALITY	★★★★★ (108)
Racial diversity index	50.7% (108)
Geographic diversity index	36.0% (421)
Top 20% share of income	49.8% (414)
Gender gap in earnings	24.3% (80)
White-collar gender gap	9.4% (85)

EDUCATION	★★★ (235)
Eighth grade or less	2.8% (205)
High school diplomas	86.1% (339)

Attended college	51.3% (298)
Bachelor's degrees	20.5% (207)
Advanced degrees	7.7% (133)

EMPLOYMENT	★ (498)
Average jobless rate	12.8% (514)
Self-employed workers	7.0% (428)
Management/financial jobs	9.3% (453)
Computer/engineering jobs	3.0% (193)
Health care jobs	5.2% (307)

GROWTH POTENTIAL	★★ (402)
Children per senior	1.38 (291)
Median age	38.7 (211)
Moved from different state	1.3% (452)
Homes built since 2000	12.1% (310)
Construction jobs	5.2% (442)

HOUSING	★★ (350)
Home vacancy rate	12.8% (488)
Home ownership rate	69.1% (298)
Housing diversity index	84.4% (299)
4 or more bedrooms	17.0% (247)
Affordability/income ratio	$2,560 (279)

INCOME	★ (498)
Poverty rate	23.5% (457)
Median household income	$34,218 (494)
Interest/dividends	10.9% (512)
Public assistance	22.6% (491)
Median fulltime earnings	$31,438 (519)

SENIORS	★★ (394)
Seniors living alone	27.2% (254)
Poverty rate for seniors	14.8% (485)
Median income for seniors	$31,201 (363)
Seniors who work	16.0% (410)
Home ownership by seniors	85.0% (142)

STABILITY	★★ (400)
25-39 age group	16.7% (375)
Born in state of residence	79.2% (125)
Same house as 1 year ago	89.4% (64)
Live and work in county	75.7% (280)
Married-couple households	38.7% (536)

TRANSPORTATION	★ (531)
Bicycle or walk to work	1.8% (409)
Carpool to work	10.2% (312)
Public transit to work	0.2% (363)
Commute <15 minutes	32.0% (499)
Commute >45 minutes	20.5% (522)

See pages 37-130 for explanations of statistics, stars, and ranks.

Oxford, MS
(Lafayette County, MS)

POPULATION	
2010 census	47,351 (230)
2015 estimate	53,154 (188)
2010-2015 change	12.3% (8)
2020 projection	58,328 (156)
2030 projection	69,748 (106)

RACE	
Whites	70.4% (390)
Blacks	24.0% (67)
Hispanics	2.3% (398)
Asians	2.0% (51)
Native Americans	0.1% (402)

AGE	
0-17 years old	18.2% (523)
18-24 years old	26.0% (13)
25-39 years old	19.5% (74)
40-54 years old	15.5% (529)
55-64 years old	9.9% (524)
65+ years old	10.9% (514)

PRIVATE SECTOR	
Businesses	1,128 (228)
Employees	14,888 (213)
Total wages	$497,865,294 (247)
Average weekly wages	$643 (409)

HOUSEHOLD INCOME LADDER	
95th percentile	$197,596 (21)
80th percentile	$91,538 (134)
60th percentile	$56,656 (218)
40th percentile	$32,143 (355)
20th percentile	$13,404 (491)

CHILDREN	★★★★★ (108)
Living with two parents	59.5% (415)
Older teens in school	99.1% (2)
Speak English very well	98.6% (278)
Poverty rate for children	25.5% (312)
No health insurance	6.0% (248)

DIVERSITY/EQUALITY	★★★ (243)
Racial diversity index	44.6% (156)
Geographic diversity index	58.0% (132)
Top 20% share of income	54.6% (541)
Gender gap in earnings	30.9% (198)
White-collar gender gap	14.8% (149)

EDUCATION	★★★★★ (11)
Eighth grade or less	2.1% (136)
High school diplomas	91.7% (135)
Attended college	72.8% (14)
Bachelor's degrees	40.9% (16)
Advanced degrees	16.6% (9)

EMPLOYMENT	★★★★ (160)
Average jobless rate	8.4% (323)
Self-employed workers	9.5% (207)
Management/financial jobs	11.6% (196)
Computer/engineering jobs	2.6% (288)
Health care jobs	6.9% (79)

GROWTH POTENTIAL	★★★★★ (16)
Children per senior	1.66 (147)
Median age	28.5 (17)
Moved from different state	8.4% (11)
Homes built since 2000	36.7% (5)
Construction jobs	5.6% (392)

HOUSING	★ (548)
Home vacancy rate	13.0% (490)
Home ownership rate	59.7% (507)
Housing diversity index	77.7% (536)
4 or more bedrooms	19.3% (145)
Affordability/income ratio	$3,566 (467)

INCOME	★★★ (284)
Poverty rate	25.8% (484)
Median household income	$44,643 (244)
Interest/dividends	18.0% (313)
Public assistance	8.4% (39)
Median fulltime earnings	$36,807 (302)

SENIORS	★★★★ (150)
Seniors living alone	26.9% (230)
Poverty rate for seniors	8.5% (223)
Median income for seniors	$36,861 (120)
Seniors who work	19.0% (243)
Home ownership by seniors	84.8% (150)

STABILITY	★ (530)
25-39 age group	19.5% (74)
Born in state of residence	59.3% (423)
Same house as 1 year ago	73.1% (535)
Live and work in county	83.4% (155)
Married-couple households	40.6% (521)

TRANSPORTATION	★★★★ (194)
Bicycle or walk to work	3.1% (232)
Carpool to work	9.7% (369)
Public transit to work	0.7% (119)
Commute <15 minutes	51.3% (129)
Commute >45 minutes	8.7% (158)

See pages 37-130 for explanations of statistics, stars, and ranks.

Oxford, NC
(Granville County, NC)

POPULATION	
2010 census	59,916 (152)
2015 estimate	58,674 (154)
2010-2015 change	-2.1% (418)
2020 projection	59,351 (151)
2030 projection	60,488 (150)

RACE	
Whites	58.6% (453)
Blacks	30.6% (52)
Hispanics	7.4% (190)
Asians	0.5% (355)
Native Americans	0.6% (150)

AGE	
0-17 years old	21.8% (351)
18-24 years old	9.3% (217)
25-39 years old	15.7% (465)
40-54 years old	24.8% (1)
55-64 years old	13.5% (258)
65+ years old	14.7% (389)

PRIVATE SECTOR	
Businesses	893 (317)
Employees	12,198 (302)
Total wages	$462,398,964 (281)
Average weekly wages	$729 (196)

HOUSEHOLD INCOME LADDER	
95th percentile	$153,359 (128)
80th percentile	$95,422 (85)
60th percentile	$62,163 (104)
40th percentile	$39,223 (149)
20th percentile	$22,551 (115)

CHILDREN	★★ (359)
Living with two parents	60.2% (393)
Older teens in school	78.1% (446)
Speak English very well	95.5% (468)
Poverty rate for children	21.1% (197)
No health insurance	6.2% (262)

DIVERSITY/EQUALITY	★★★★★ (30)
Racial diversity index	55.7% (42)
Geographic diversity index	52.0% (189)
Top 20% share of income	45.3% (71)
Gender gap in earnings	17.6% (30)
White-collar gender gap	35.0% (393)

EDUCATION	★★ (354)
Eighth grade or less	5.8% (413)
High school diplomas	84.7% (380)
Attended college	54.1% (241)
Bachelor's degrees	18.7% (262)
Advanced degrees	5.0% (378)

EMPLOYMENT	★★★★★ (97)
Average jobless rate	8.3% (314)
Self-employed workers	5.1% (540)
Management/financial jobs	13.1% (78)
Computer/engineering jobs	5.4% (24)
Health care jobs	7.5% (44)

GROWTH POTENTIAL	★★★★ (120)
Children per senior	1.48 (227)
Median age	41.4 (376)
Moved from different state	2.6% (187)
Homes built since 2000	27.4% (24)
Construction jobs	7.0% (185)

HOUSING	★★★ (254)
Home vacancy rate	9.5% (317)
Home ownership rate	72.5% (167)
Housing diversity index	82.9% (422)
4 or more bedrooms	19.0% (159)
Affordability/income ratio	$2,839 (363)

INCOME	★★★ (225)
Poverty rate	16.3% (234)
Median household income	$50,225 (120)
Interest/dividends	15.2% (401)
Public assistance	14.4% (225)
Median fulltime earnings	$40,510 (118)

SENIORS	★ (444)
Seniors living alone	21.7% (32)
Poverty rate for seniors	14.4% (477)
Median income for seniors	$30,367 (397)
Seniors who work	14.0% (503)
Home ownership by seniors	77.0% (490)

STABILITY	★ (522)
25-39 age group	15.7% (465)
Born in state of residence	67.2% (358)
Same house as 1 year ago	87.9% (140)
Live and work in county	43.7% (548)
Married-couple households	49.8% (307)

TRANSPORTATION	★ (550)
Bicycle or walk to work	0.7% (537)
Carpool to work	10.0% (337)
Public transit to work	0.0% (511)
Commute <15 minutes	19.8% (550)
Commute >45 minutes	20.4% (520)

See pages 37-130 for explanations of statistics, stars, and ranks.

Ozark, AL
(Dale County, AL)

POPULATION

2010 census	50,251 (209)
2015 estimate	49,565 (214)
2010-2015 change	-1.4% (364)
2020 projection	48,805 (223)
2030 projection	47,079 (246)

RACE

Whites	69.8% (394)
Blacks	19.4% (80)
Hispanics	6.0% (222)
Asians	1.2% (125)
Native Americans	0.5% (174)

AGE

0-17 years old	23.9% (194)
18-24 years old	9.4% (203)
25-39 years old	20.5% (50)
40-54 years old	19.0% (364)
55-64 years old	12.3% (414)
65+ years old	14.9% (374)

PRIVATE SECTOR

Businesses	762 (391)
Employees	11,383 (331)
Total wages	$571,883,558 (202)
Average weekly wages	$966 (20)

HOUSEHOLD INCOME LADDER

95th percentile	$143,347 (251)
80th percentile	$83,346 (284)
60th percentile	$55,807 (231)
40th percentile	$34,044 (286)
20th percentile	$16,240 (400)

CHILDREN ★★★★ (188)

Living with two parents	64.5% (281)
Older teens in school	82.5% (296)
Speak English very well	98.9% (226)
Poverty rate for children	26.2% (328)
No health insurance	2.7% (43)

DIVERSITY/EQUALITY ★★★★★ (45)

Racial diversity index	47.0% (138)
Geographic diversity index	62.5% (95)
Top 20% share of income	47.0% (216)
Gender gap in earnings	40.4% (445)
White-collar gender gap	0.2% (1)

EDUCATION ★★★ (272)

Eighth grade or less	3.4% (269)
High school diplomas	87.4% (291)
Attended college	56.8% (191)
Bachelor's degrees	16.9% (334)
Advanced degrees	4.9% (396)

EMPLOYMENT ★ (456)

Average jobless rate	10.9% (454)
Self-employed workers	5.5% (530)
Management/financial jobs	10.7% (287)
Computer/engineering jobs	2.0% (420)
Health care jobs	6.2% (156)

GROWTH POTENTIAL ★★★★★ (85)

Children per senior	1.60 (169)
Median age	36.8 (138)
Moved from different state	7.6% (14)
Homes built since 2000	17.5% (140)
Construction jobs	5.2% (442)

HOUSING ★ (479)

Home vacancy rate	14.1% (520)
Home ownership rate	62.0% (482)
Housing diversity index	84.0% (344)
4 or more bedrooms	16.0% (293)
Affordability/income ratio	$2,259 (143)

INCOME ★★★ (329)

Poverty rate	19.1% (341)
Median household income	$45,028 (236)
Interest/dividends	15.5% (393)
Public assistance	16.9% (327)
Median fulltime earnings	$37,187 (272)

SENIORS ★★★ (239)

Seniors living alone	27.3% (260)
Poverty rate for seniors	10.9% (370)
Median income for seniors	$36,875 (119)
Seniors who work	15.5% (436)
Home ownership by seniors	85.8% (115)

STABILITY ★ (486)

25-39 age group	20.5% (50)
Born in state of residence	56.5% (451)
Same house as 1 year ago	81.5% (460)
Live and work in county	57.8% (504)
Married-couple households	48.5% (361)

TRANSPORTATION ★ (455)

Bicycle or walk to work	1.8% (409)
Carpool to work	6.8% (534)
Public transit to work	0.1% (441)
Commute <15 minutes	35.7% (429)
Commute >45 minutes	7.7% (115)

See pages 37-130 for explanations of statistics, stars, and ranks.

Paducah, KY-IL

(Ballard, Livingston, and McCracken Counties, KY, Massac County, IL)

POPULATION	
2010 census	98,762 (33)
2015 estimate	97,312 (34)
2010-2015 change	-1.5% (373)
2020 projection	95,711 (39)
2030 projection	92,323 (42)

RACE	
Whites	86.6% (245)
Blacks	8.4% (124)
Hispanics	2.2% (406)
Asians	0.8% (201)
Native Americans	0.2% (300)

AGE	
0-17 years old	21.9% (344)
18-24 years old	7.5% (483)
25-39 years old	16.6% (388)
40-54 years old	21.2% (85)
55-64 years old	14.5% (122)
65+ years old	18.3% (108)

PRIVATE SECTOR	
Businesses	2,876 (23)
Employees	40,966 (13)
Total wages	$1,752,111,923 (11)
Average weekly wages	$822 (63)

HOUSEHOLD INCOME LADDER	
95th percentile	$153,254 (130)
80th percentile	$87,342 (193)
60th percentile	$53,880 (282)
40th percentile	$33,729 (299)
20th percentile	$18,110 (313)

CHILDREN	★★★★ (199)
Living with two parents	59.8% (404)
Older teens in school	85.0% (197)
Speak English very well	99.5% (96)
Poverty rate for children	25.5% (312)
No health insurance	3.7% (98)

DIVERSITY/EQUALITY	★ (510)
Racial diversity index	24.2% (303)
Geographic diversity index	55.7% (148)
Top 20% share of income	53.0% (521)
Gender gap in earnings	42.8% (481)
White-collar gender gap	32.5% (370)

EDUCATION	★★★★ (153)
Eighth grade or less	2.1% (136)
High school diplomas	89.3% (223)
Attended college	57.2% (183)
Bachelor's degrees	22.2% (153)
Advanced degrees	8.2% (114)

EMPLOYMENT	★★★★★ (102)
Average jobless rate	6.5% (157)
Self-employed workers	9.1% (243)
Management/financial jobs	11.0% (252)
Computer/engineering jobs	3.6% (112)
Health care jobs	7.2% (58)

GROWTH POTENTIAL	★★ (363)
Children per senior	1.20 (417)
Median age	43.0 (450)
Moved from different state	2.1% (269)
Homes built since 2000	13.4% (260)
Construction jobs	6.9% (198)

HOUSING	★★★★ (136)
Home vacancy rate	7.5% (186)
Home ownership rate	70.4% (251)
Housing diversity index	86.8% (3)
4 or more bedrooms	14.8% (368)
Affordability/income ratio	$2,529 (259)

INCOME	★★★ (260)
Poverty rate	16.8% (257)
Median household income	$43,222 (285)
Interest/dividends	18.3% (299)
Public assistance	16.8% (324)
Median fulltime earnings	$39,552 (155)

SENIORS	★★ (402)
Seniors living alone	30.1% (433)
Poverty rate for seniors	9.7% (301)
Median income for seniors	$33,097 (276)
Seniors who work	16.6% (367)
Home ownership by seniors	81.0% (335)

STABILITY	★★ (390)
25-39 age group	16.6% (388)
Born in state of residence	62.9% (405)
Same house as 1 year ago	89.0% (79)
Live and work in county	72.8% (332)
Married-couple households	47.5% (399)

TRANSPORTATION	★★ (413)
Bicycle or walk to work	1.4% (472)
Carpool to work	7.5% (515)
Public transit to work	0.5% (178)
Commute <15 minutes	37.8% (381)
Commute >45 minutes	7.8% (122)

See pages 37-130 for explanations of statistics, stars, and ranks.

Palatka, FL
(Putnam County, FL)

POPULATION

2010 census	74,364 (85)
2015 estimate	72,023 (94)
2010-2015 change	-3.1% (487)
2020 projection	70,699 (100)
2030 projection	68,256 (114)

RACE

Whites	71.9% (377)
Blacks	16.2% (88)
Hispanics	9.4% (159)
Asians	0.7% (241)
Native Americans	0.2% (300)

AGE

0-17 years old	22.0% (335)
18-24 years old	7.6% (468)
25-39 years old	15.6% (474)
40-54 years old	19.2% (336)
55-64 years old	15.0% (87)
65+ years old	20.6% (42)

PRIVATE SECTOR

Businesses	1,342 (166)
Employees	12,413 (298)
Total wages	$415,749,100 (319)
Average weekly wages	$644 (405)

HOUSEHOLD INCOME LADDER

95th percentile	$117,274 (529)
80th percentile	$66,954 (525)
60th percentile	$39,963 (529)
40th percentile	$23,951 (522)
20th percentile	$13,229 (496)

CHILDREN   ★ (538)

Living with two parents	46.4% (524)
Older teens in school	77.5% (460)
Speak English very well	97.8% (361)
Poverty rate for children	45.8% (537)
No health insurance	12.8% (493)

DIVERSITY/EQUALITY   ★★★★★ (33)

Racial diversity index	44.8% (153)
Geographic diversity index	62.5% (95)
Top 20% share of income	50.0% (425)
Gender gap in earnings	19.7% (40)
White-collar gender gap	7.8% (62)

EDUCATION   ★ (512)

Eighth grade or less	7.5% (478)
High school diplomas	79.5% (490)
Attended college	41.4% (498)
Bachelor's degrees	11.4% (526)
Advanced degrees	3.1% (524)

EMPLOYMENT   ★ (506)

Average jobless rate	12.6% (509)
Self-employed workers	9.1% (243)
Management/financial jobs	8.8% (488)
Computer/engineering jobs	1.7% (470)
Health care jobs	5.1% (319)

GROWTH POTENTIAL   ★★★ (328)

Children per senior	1.07 (477)
Median age	44.1 (481)
Moved from different state	2.5% (203)
Homes built since 2000	15.0% (204)
Construction jobs	7.6% (110)

HOUSING   ★ (480)

Home vacancy rate	14.0% (518)
Home ownership rate	73.6% (132)
Housing diversity index	83.2% (405)
4 or more bedrooms	10.1% (531)
Affordability/income ratio	$2,696 (328)

INCOME   ★ (511)

Poverty rate	28.7% (516)
Median household income	$31,715 (523)
Interest/dividends	14.4% (429)
Public assistance	23.5% (502)
Median fulltime earnings	$31,648 (510)

SENIORS   ★★★ (310)

Seniors living alone	27.0% (239)
Poverty rate for seniors	13.4% (457)
Median income for seniors	n.a.
Seniors who work	12.9% (526)
Home ownership by seniors	88.9% (26)

STABILITY   ★ (514)

25-39 age group	15.6% (474)
Born in state of residence	57.6% (439)
Same house as 1 year ago	88.1% (126)
Live and work in county	68.7% (394)
Married-couple households	43.6% (487)

TRANSPORTATION   ★ (502)

Bicycle or walk to work	1.9% (401)
Carpool to work	13.7% (77)
Public transit to work	0.7% (119)
Commute <15 minutes	30.2% (522)
Commute >45 minutes	23.6% (542)

See pages 37-130 for explanations of statistics, stars, and ranks.

Palestine, TX
(Anderson County, TX)

POPULATION	
2010 census	58,458 (158)
2015 estimate	57,580 (161)
2010-2015 change	-1.5% (373)
2020 projection	56,863 (164)
2030 projection	55,473 (177)

RACE	
Whites	60.2% (445)
Blacks	21.1% (74)
Hispanics	16.8% (92)
Asians	0.6% (291)
Native Americans	0.4% (203)

AGE	
0-17 years old	19.4% (489)
18-24 years old	8.7% (299)
25-39 years old	24.0% (8)
40-54 years old	22.6% (14)
55-64 years old	12.0% (438)
65+ years old	13.3% (465)

PRIVATE SECTOR	
Businesses	1,384 (158)
Employees	14,334 (225)
Total wages	$592,373,821 (193)
Average weekly wages	$795 (99)

HOUSEHOLD INCOME LADDER	
95th percentile	$152,465 (138)
80th percentile	$84,605 (260)
60th percentile	$52,066 (315)
40th percentile	$32,256 (353)
20th percentile	$18,037 (318)

CHILDREN	★ (476)
Living with two parents	59.8% (404)
Older teens in school	78.2% (442)
Speak English very well	94.5% (486)
Poverty rate for children	27.0% (348)
No health insurance	11.1% (450)

DIVERSITY/EQUALITY	★★★★ (155)
Racial diversity index	56.5% (35)
Geographic diversity index	41.8% (331)
Top 20% share of income	49.2% (381)
Gender gap in earnings	26.7% (112)
White-collar gender gap	29.7% (333)

EDUCATION	★ (507)
Eighth grade or less	6.3% (439)
High school diplomas	80.0% (479)
Attended college	42.3% (486)
Bachelor's degrees	10.1% (541)
Advanced degrees	2.9% (534)

EMPLOYMENT	★ (470)
Average jobless rate	4.3% (38)
Self-employed workers	6.1% (495)
Management/financial jobs	8.1% (524)
Computer/engineering jobs	1.5% (499)
Health care jobs	4.6% (401)

GROWTH POTENTIAL	★★★★ (197)
Children per senior	1.46 (237)
Median age	38.9 (228)
Moved from different state	1.2% (474)
Homes built since 2000	18.5% (119)
Construction jobs	7.2% (162)

HOUSING	★★★ (285)
Home vacancy rate	10.2% (358)
Home ownership rate	70.4% (251)
Housing diversity index	85.3% (170)
4 or more bedrooms	11.0% (521)
Affordability/income ratio	$2,008 (58)

INCOME	★★ (380)
Poverty rate	18.5% (317)
Median household income	$41,327 (341)
Interest/dividends	13.6% (450)
Public assistance	14.3% (220)
Median fulltime earnings	$32,906 (456)

SENIORS	★★★ (259)
Seniors living alone	26.9% (230)
Poverty rate for seniors	9.3% (276)
Median income for seniors	$32,210 (313)
Seniors who work	17.2% (330)
Home ownership by seniors	84.2% (175)

STABILITY	★★★★★ (6)
25-39 age group	24.0% (8)
Born in state of residence	75.5% (215)
Same house as 1 year ago	83.2% (388)
Live and work in county	81.5% (197)
Married-couple households	52.9% (157)

TRANSPORTATION	★★ (380)
Bicycle or walk to work	1.4% (472)
Carpool to work	10.9% (239)
Public transit to work	0.2% (363)
Commute <15 minutes	38.8% (356)
Commute >45 minutes	10.7% (262)

See pages 37-130 for explanations of statistics, stars, and ranks.

Pampa, TX
(Gray County, TX)

POPULATION

2010 census	22,535 (500)
2015 estimate	23,210 (496)
2010-2015 change	3.0% (86)
2020 projection	23,418 (492)
2030 projection	23,814 (482)

RACE

Whites	65.9% (411)
Blacks	4.4% (179)
Hispanics	26.4% (54)
Asians	0.6% (291)
Native Americans	0.8% (125)

AGE

0-17 years old	25.3% (97)
18-24 years old	7.9% (424)
25-39 years old	21.4% (33)
40-54 years old	18.5% (425)
55-64 years old	11.4% (482)
65+ years old	15.5% (333)

PRIVATE SECTOR

Businesses	593 (474)
Employees	7,140 (470)
Total wages	$355,075,572 (378)
Average weekly wages	$956 (23)

HOUSEHOLD INCOME LADDER

95th percentile	$141,993 (265)
80th percentile	$90,016 (155)
60th percentile	$54,816 (254)
40th percentile	$34,456 (275)
20th percentile	$20,804 (192)

CHILDREN ★ **(479)**

Living with two parents	68.0% (195)
Older teens in school	69.0% (533)
Speak English very well	95.9% (457)
Poverty rate for children	17.2% (104)
No health insurance	15.2% (525)

DIVERSITY/EQUALITY ★★ **(375)**

Racial diversity index	49.4% (117)
Geographic diversity index	54.3% (160)
Top 20% share of income	46.3% (143)
Gender gap in earnings	45.0% (500)
White-collar gender gap	60.8% (543)

EDUCATION ★ **(473)**

Eighth grade or less	7.3% (476)
High school diplomas	80.9% (468)

Attended college	49.2% (352)
Bachelor's degrees	13.7% (470)
Advanced degrees	3.9% (489)

EMPLOYMENT ★★ **(365)**

Average jobless rate	5.4% (89)
Self-employed workers	8.7% (281)
Management/financial jobs	8.9% (483)
Computer/engineering jobs	2.7% (270)
Health care jobs	4.4% (433)

GROWTH POTENTIAL ★★★ **(267)**

Children per senior	1.63 (158)
Median age	37.0 (143)
Moved from different state	1.7% (355)
Homes built since 2000	2.8% (551)
Construction jobs	8.2% (78)

HOUSING ★★ **(348)**

Home vacancy rate	15.6% (537)
Home ownership rate	73.5% (137)
Housing diversity index	84.7% (260)
4 or more bedrooms	13.3% (437)
Affordability/income ratio	$1,728 (17)

INCOME ★★★★ **(176)**

Poverty rate	13.3% (130)
Median household income	$43,288 (282)
Interest/dividends	21.0% (214)
Public assistance	10.3% (72)
Median fulltime earnings	$37,334 (259)

SENIORS ★★★★ **(217)**

Seniors living alone	30.2% (436)
Poverty rate for seniors	7.1% (101)
Median income for seniors	$33,019 (281)
Seniors who work	21.2% (153)
Home ownership by seniors	83.7% (190)

STABILITY ★★★★★ **(77)**

25-39 age group	21.4% (33)
Born in state of residence	65.9% (376)
Same house as 1 year ago	82.5% (420)
Live and work in county	80.9% (205)
Married-couple households	52.3% (180)

TRANSPORTATION ★★★ **(248)**

Bicycle or walk to work	1.4% (472)
Carpool to work	13.1% (98)
Public transit to work	0.0% (511)
Commute <15 minutes	59.3% (49)
Commute >45 minutes	15.4% (436)

See pages 37-130 for explanations of statistics, stars, and ranks.

Paragould, AR
(Greene County, AR)

POPULATION	
2010 census	42,090 (289)
2015 estimate	44,196 (270)
2010-2015 change	5.0% (41)
2020 projection	45,791 (249)
2030 projection	48,713 (226)

RACE	
Whites	94.5% (61)
Blacks	0.9% (388)
Hispanics	2.6% (378)
Asians	0.2% (509)
Native Americans	0.2% (300)

AGE	
0-17 years old	24.7% (141)
18-24 years old	9.1% (251)
25-39 years old	18.3% (159)
40-54 years old	21.1% (97)
55-64 years old	12.1% (430)
65+ years old	14.7% (389)

PRIVATE SECTOR	
Businesses	846 (347)
Employees	13,403 (261)
Total wages	$475,789,766 (264)
Average weekly wages	$683 (305)

HOUSEHOLD INCOME LADDER	
95th percentile	$133,330 (385)
80th percentile	$78,292 (398)
60th percentile	$51,923 (322)
40th percentile	$33,054 (323)
20th percentile	$17,078 (361)

CHILDREN	★★★★ (185)
Living with two parents	67.3% (209)
Older teens in school	79.6% (412)
Speak English very well	99.4% (124)
Poverty rate for children	22.8% (244)
No health insurance	4.1% (126)

DIVERSITY/EQUALITY	★★ (384)
Racial diversity index	10.6% (485)
Geographic diversity index	52.4% (185)
Top 20% share of income	46.6% (170)
Gender gap in earnings	34.1% (291)
White-collar gender gap	40.9% (453)

EDUCATION	★★★ (320)
Eighth grade or less	2.8% (205)
High school diplomas	88.9% (236)
Attended college	45.9% (422)
Bachelor's degrees	16.9% (334)
Advanced degrees	5.5% (318)

EMPLOYMENT	★★★ (267)
Average jobless rate	9.0% (358)
Self-employed workers	9.5% (207)
Management/financial jobs	10.9% (263)
Computer/engineering jobs	1.3% (519)
Health care jobs	7.0% (69)

GROWTH POTENTIAL	★★★★ (216)
Children per senior	1.67 (144)
Median age	38.3 (197)
Moved from different state	1.9% (310)
Homes built since 2000	21.9% (70)
Construction jobs	4.5% (504)

HOUSING	★★★ (329)
Home vacancy rate	6.7% (141)
Home ownership rate	64.7% (443)
Housing diversity index	83.7% (378)
4 or more bedrooms	13.7% (415)
Affordability/income ratio	$2,609 (295)

INCOME	★★ (337)
Poverty rate	17.8% (292)
Median household income	$41,286 (345)
Interest/dividends	18.4% (296)
Public assistance	16.6% (316)
Median fulltime earnings	$34,971 (385)

SENIORS	★★ (393)
Seniors living alone	26.7% (217)
Poverty rate for seniors	10.0% (321)
Median income for seniors	$31,446 (352)
Seniors who work	14.6% (472)
Home ownership by seniors	80.5% (356)

STABILITY	★★★ (323)
25-39 age group	18.3% (159)
Born in state of residence	65.9% (376)
Same house as 1 year ago	80.9% (484)
Live and work in county	73.7% (320)
Married-couple households	53.3% (140)

TRANSPORTATION	★★ (427)
Bicycle or walk to work	0.9% (521)
Carpool to work	8.5% (462)
Public transit to work	0.1% (441)
Commute <15 minutes	43.6% (269)
Commute >45 minutes	10.3% (237)

See pages 37-130 for explanations of statistics, stars, and ranks.

Paris, TN
(Henry County, TN)

POPULATION	
2010 census	32,330 (413)
2015 estimate	32,147 (419)
2010-2015 change	-0.6% (298)
2020 projection	31,918 (420)
2030 projection	31,344 (416)

RACE	
Whites	87.6% (230)
Blacks	8.6% (121)
Hispanics	2.1% (416)
Asians	0.2% (509)
Native Americans	0.3% (231)

AGE	
0-17 years old	21.1% (407)
18-24 years old	7.1% (515)
25-39 years old	15.7% (465)
40-54 years old	20.5% (151)
55-64 years old	14.6% (107)
65+ years old	21.0% (34)

PRIVATE SECTOR	
Businesses	684 (436)
Employees	8,788 (423)
Total wages	$302,489,030 (432)
Average weekly wages	$662 (358)

HOUSEHOLD INCOME LADDER	
95th percentile	$135,663 (350)
80th percentile	$72,210 (492)
60th percentile	$45,994 (459)
40th percentile	$30,787 (394)
20th percentile	$16,748 (372)

CHILDREN	★★ (342)
Living with two parents	62.1% (349)
Older teens in school	74.2% (509)
Speak English very well	99.3% (142)
Poverty rate for children	27.4% (354)
No health insurance	4.6% (159)

DIVERSITY/EQUALITY	★★ (434)
Racial diversity index	22.5% (317)
Geographic diversity index	61.9% (104)
Top 20% share of income	50.8% (465)
Gender gap in earnings	28.3% (140)
White-collar gender gap	55.9% (533)

EDUCATION	★★ (341)
Eighth grade or less	3.6% (292)
High school diplomas	87.8% (274)
Attended college	41.6% (496)
Bachelor's degrees	16.8% (339)
Advanced degrees	7.4% (149)

EMPLOYMENT	★★★ (234)
Average jobless rate	9.7% (409)
Self-employed workers	12.6% (55)
Management/financial jobs	9.6% (427)
Computer/engineering jobs	2.7% (270)
Health care jobs	5.9% (193)

GROWTH POTENTIAL	★ (462)
Children per senior	1.01 (500)
Median age	44.9 (496)
Moved from different state	1.6% (383)
Homes built since 2000	13.9% (240)
Construction jobs	6.7% (219)

HOUSING	★★★★ (185)
Home vacancy rate	10.2% (358)
Home ownership rate	74.1% (115)
Housing diversity index	85.3% (170)
4 or more bedrooms	15.6% (320)
Affordability/income ratio	$2,466 (239)

INCOME	★★ (417)
Poverty rate	18.5% (317)
Median household income	$38,234 (422)
Interest/dividends	18.6% (288)
Public assistance	20.5% (442)
Median fulltime earnings	$31,933 (500)

SENIORS	★★★★ (131)
Seniors living alone	25.2% (124)
Poverty rate for seniors	9.0% (260)
Median income for seniors	$32,964 (285)
Seniors who work	16.3% (391)
Home ownership by seniors	89.3% (21)

STABILITY	★★ (415)
25-39 age group	15.7% (465)
Born in state of residence	56.6% (448)
Same house as 1 year ago	87.4% (173)
Live and work in county	75.2% (286)
Married-couple households	51.3% (241)

TRANSPORTATION	★ (483)
Bicycle or walk to work	1.3% (485)
Carpool to work	6.2% (543)
Public transit to work	0.1% (441)
Commute <15 minutes	40.2% (327)
Commute >45 minutes	10.5% (254)

See pages 37-130 for explanations of statistics, stars, and ranks.

Paris, TX
(Lamar County, TX)

POPULATION

2010 census	49,793 (212)
2015 estimate	49,440 (215)
2010-2015 change	-0.7% (303)
2020 projection	48,770 (224)
2030 projection	47,417 (239)

RACE

Whites	75.1% (357)
Blacks	12.4% (101)
Hispanics	7.2% (194)
Asians	1.1% (139)
Native Americans	0.3% (231)

AGE

0-17 years old	23.7% (218)
18-24 years old	9.3% (217)
25-39 years old	16.8% (359)
40-54 years old	19.6% (289)
55-64 years old	12.7% (375)
65+ years old	18.0% (122)

PRIVATE SECTOR

Businesses	1,098 (245)
Employees	16,929 (172)
Total wages	$699,972,507 (149)
Average weekly wages	$795 (99)

HOUSEHOLD INCOME LADDER

95th percentile	$146,602 (204)
80th percentile	$82,883 (296)
60th percentile	$51,505 (344)
40th percentile	$31,944 (364)
20th percentile	$16,297 (397)

CHILDREN ★★ (416)

Living with two parents	58.0% (448)
Older teens in school	83.4% (258)
Speak English very well	97.6% (375)
Poverty rate for children	27.6% (357)
No health insurance	11.5% (459)

DIVERSITY/EQUALITY ★★★ (288)

Racial diversity index	41.4% (179)
Geographic diversity index	42.0% (327)
Top 20% share of income	50.3% (444)
Gender gap in earnings	34.2% (293)
White-collar gender gap	21.6% (229)

EDUCATION ★★ (338)

Eighth grade or less	4.5% (354)
High school diplomas	87.0% (309)
Attended college	53.2% (260)
Bachelor's degrees	16.0% (372)
Advanced degrees	5.0% (378)

EMPLOYMENT ★★★ (327)

Average jobless rate	7.4% (237)
Self-employed workers	8.1% (323)
Management/financial jobs	9.9% (392)
Computer/engineering jobs	1.9% (441)
Health care jobs	6.2% (156)

GROWTH POTENTIAL ★★★ (221)

Children per senior	1.32 (334)
Median age	40.3 (319)
Moved from different state	2.4% (218)
Homes built since 2000	14.3% (227)
Construction jobs	7.8% (98)

HOUSING ★★ (370)

Home vacancy rate	12.1% (463)
Home ownership rate	65.3% (429)
Housing diversity index	85.7% (108)
4 or more bedrooms	13.1% (448)
Affordability/income ratio	$2,108 (84)

INCOME ★★ (389)

Poverty rate	18.6% (322)
Median household income	$40,748 (364)
Interest/dividends	14.7% (418)
Public assistance	19.0% (399)
Median fulltime earnings	$35,729 (348)

SENIORS ★★ (391)

Seniors living alone	26.5% (201)
Poverty rate for seniors	11.3% (386)
Median income for seniors	$30,715 (383)
Seniors who work	17.6% (306)
Home ownership by seniors	79.5% (394)

STABILITY ★★★★ (192)

25-39 age group	16.8% (359)
Born in state of residence	75.2% (219)
Same house as 1 year ago	82.5% (420)
Live and work in county	86.9% (102)
Married-couple households	51.5% (226)

TRANSPORTATION ★★★ (275)

Bicycle or walk to work	2.1% (374)
Carpool to work	10.5% (280)
Public transit to work	0.0% (511)
Commute <15 minutes	48.4% (188)
Commute >45 minutes	8.7% (158)

See pages 37-130 for explanations of statistics, stars, and ranks.

Pecos, TX
(Reeves County, TX)

POPULATION

2010 census	13,783 (549)
2015 estimate	14,732 (545)
2010-2015 change	6.9% (22)
2020 projection	15,562 (544)
2030 projection	17,342 (534)

RACE

Whites	20.1% (541)
Blacks	3.5% (209)
Hispanics	74.6% (9)
Asians	0.8% (201)
Native Americans	0.3% (231)

AGE

0-17 years old	22.2% (320)
18-24 years old	10.7% (124)
25-39 years old	22.9% (15)
40-54 years old	20.3% (186)
55-64 years old	10.7% (500)
65+ years old	13.2% (470)

PRIVATE SECTOR

Businesses	246 (550)
Employees	2,674 (549)
Total wages	$102,811,576 (548)
Average weekly wages	$739 (180)

HOUSEHOLD INCOME LADDER

95th percentile	$150,969 (152)
80th percentile	$90,528 (150)
60th percentile	$56,366 (222)
40th percentile	$29,396 (435)
20th percentile	$14,650 (463)

CHILDREN   ★ (518)

Living with two parents	63.8% (304)
Older teens in school	70.1% (532)
Speak English very well	93.2% (505)
Poverty rate for children	24.5% (286)
No health insurance	13.1% (498)

DIVERSITY/EQUALITY   ★★ (342)

Racial diversity index	40.2% (187)
Geographic diversity index	54.2% (161)
Top 20% share of income	50.3% (443)
Gender gap in earnings	34.5% (301)
White-collar gender gap	41.5% (462)

EDUCATION   ★ (545)

Eighth grade or less	17.5% (539)
High school diplomas	64.8% (546)
Attended college	37.2% (535)
Bachelor's degrees	11.8% (519)
Advanced degrees	2.2% (549)

EMPLOYMENT   ★★ (436)

Average jobless rate	6.7% (169)
Self-employed workers	7.3% (401)
Management/financial jobs	9.5% (440)
Computer/engineering jobs	1.4% (510)
Health care jobs	5.1% (319)

GROWTH POTENTIAL   ★★★★ (174)

Children per senior	1.68 (141)
Median age	35.6 (105)
Moved from different state	5.2% (47)
Homes built since 2000	5.4% (538)
Construction jobs	6.1% (310)

HOUSING   ★★ (436)

Home vacancy rate	14.6% (530)
Home ownership rate	74.4% (103)
Housing diversity index	81.3% (484)
4 or more bedrooms	9.4% (542)
Affordability/income ratio	$1,024 (1)

INCOME   ★★ (331)

Poverty rate	16.8% (257)
Median household income	$43,540 (274)
Interest/dividends	8.3% (540)
Public assistance	16.4% (309)
Median fulltime earnings	$41,492 (78)

SENIORS   ★ (507)

Seniors living alone	31.1% (476)
Poverty rate for seniors	19.1% (533)
Median income for seniors	$20,224 (527)
Seniors who work	16.6% (367)
Home ownership by seniors	89.0% (24)

STABILITY   ★★★★★ (28)

25-39 age group	22.9% (15)
Born in state of residence	64.2% (395)
Same house as 1 year ago	80.9% (484)
Live and work in county	92.4% (41)
Married-couple households	50.5% (271)

TRANSPORTATION   ★★★★ (201)

Bicycle or walk to work	1.8% (409)
Carpool to work	8.0% (493)
Public transit to work	0.0% (511)
Commute <15 minutes	70.1% (6)
Commute >45 minutes	9.5% (203)

See pages 37-130 for explanations of statistics, stars, and ranks.

Picayune, MS
(Pearl River County, MS)

POPULATION	
2010 census	55,834 (167)
2015 estimate	55,191 (172)
2010-2015 change	-1.2% (345)
2020 projection	55,527 (174)
2030 projection	55,812 (175)

RACE	
Whites	81.8% (304)
Blacks	13.6% (94)
Hispanics	3.0% (343)
Asians	0.1% (529)
Native Americans	0.2% (300)

AGE	
0-17 years old	23.8% (206)
18-24 years old	9.6% (189)
25-39 years old	15.2% (498)
40-54 years old	21.2% (85)
55-64 years old	13.7% (225)
65+ years old	16.5% (247)

PRIVATE SECTOR	
Businesses	759 (393)
Employees	6,876 (478)
Total wages	$218,559,242 (498)
Average weekly wages	$611 (467)

HOUSEHOLD INCOME LADDER	
95th percentile	$131,552 (408)
80th percentile	$80,790 (355)
60th percentile	$51,313 (349)
40th percentile	$32,196 (354)
20th percentile	$15,973 (409)

CHILDREN	★★ (400)
Living with two parents	58.9% (431)
Older teens in school	83.0% (276)
Speak English very well	99.9% (19)
Poverty rate for children	32.3% (450)
No health insurance	10.9% (447)

DIVERSITY/EQUALITY	★★★★ (138)
Racial diversity index	31.1% (247)
Geographic diversity index	61.3% (114)
Top 20% share of income	45.6% (94)
Gender gap in earnings	45.1% (502)
White-collar gender gap	15.8% (162)

EDUCATION	★★ (423)
Eighth grade or less	5.8% (413)
High school diplomas	82.7% (427)
Attended college	52.7% (269)
Bachelor's degrees	14.1% (457)
Advanced degrees	4.0% (478)

EMPLOYMENT	★★★ (288)
Average jobless rate	12.1% (493)
Self-employed workers	6.8% (446)
Management/financial jobs	9.9% (392)
Computer/engineering jobs	4.1% (70)
Health care jobs	7.8% (28)

GROWTH POTENTIAL	★★★★★ (41)
Children per senior	1.45 (244)
Median age	40.7 (341)
Moved from different state	4.1% (76)
Homes built since 2000	27.8% (20)
Construction jobs	10.0% (17)

HOUSING	★★ (332)
Home vacancy rate	10.7% (390)
Home ownership rate	76.2% (49)
Housing diversity index	81.7% (470)
4 or more bedrooms	15.6% (320)
Affordability/income ratio	$2,785 (355)

INCOME	★★ (399)
Poverty rate	21.5% (416)
Median household income	$40,976 (354)
Interest/dividends	14.2% (435)
Public assistance	21.7% (472)
Median fulltime earnings	$39,293 (164)

SENIORS	★★★ (257)
Seniors living alone	26.7% (217)
Poverty rate for seniors	11.8% (401)
Median income for seniors	$30,252 (403)
Seniors who work	14.1% (500)
Home ownership by seniors	90.5% (11)

STABILITY	★ (542)
25-39 age group	15.2% (498)
Born in state of residence	43.6% (510)
Same house as 1 year ago	86.6% (213)
Live and work in county	46.8% (543)
Married-couple households	51.9% (199)

TRANSPORTATION	★ (548)
Bicycle or walk to work	1.0% (512)
Carpool to work	11.2% (211)
Public transit to work	0.1% (441)
Commute <15 minutes	23.0% (546)
Commute >45 minutes	31.1% (550)

See pages 37-130 for explanations of statistics, stars, and ranks.

Pinehurst-Southern Pines, NC
(Moore County, NC)

POPULATION	
2010 census	88,247 (51)
2015 estimate	94,352 (40)
2010-2015 change	6.9% (22)
2020 projection	99,504 (33)
2030 projection	110,218 (24)

RACE	
Whites	77.3% (344)
Blacks	12.3% (102)
Hispanics	6.2% (214)
Asians	1.1% (139)
Native Americans	0.7% (136)

AGE	
0-17 years old	21.3% (383)
18-24 years old	6.7% (531)
25-39 years old	16.1% (442)
40-54 years old	19.0% (364)
55-64 years old	13.3% (282)
65+ years old	23.6% (13)

PRIVATE SECTOR	
Businesses	2,435 (37)
Employees	28,778 (51)
Total wages	$1,060,739,961 (60)
Average weekly wages	$709 (234)

HOUSEHOLD INCOME LADDER	
95th percentile	$193,704 (28)
80th percentile	$100,724 (54)
60th percentile	$63,792 (87)
40th percentile	$39,854 (132)
20th percentile	$21,076 (183)

CHILDREN	★★★★ (180)
Living with two parents	66.4% (235)
Older teens in school	86.6% (144)
Speak English very well	97.4% (395)
Poverty rate for children	25.9% (321)
No health insurance	4.4% (145)

DIVERSITY/EQUALITY	★★★ (260)
Racial diversity index	38.3% (194)
Geographic diversity index	67.4% (59)
Top 20% share of income	50.6% (454)
Gender gap in earnings	37.6% (379)
White-collar gender gap	34.0% (382)

EDUCATION	★★★★★ (44)
Eighth grade or less	3.6% (292)
High school diplomas	90.2% (196)
Attended college	65.8% (46)
Bachelor's degrees	32.6% (38)
Advanced degrees	12.6% (29)

EMPLOYMENT	★★★★★ (40)
Average jobless rate	8.0% (291)
Self-employed workers	11.6% (90)
Management/financial jobs	13.0% (86)
Computer/engineering jobs	2.9% (219)
Health care jobs	9.5% (2)

GROWTH POTENTIAL	★★ (349)
Children per senior	0.90 (527)
Median age	45.1 (500)
Moved from different state	3.2% (136)
Homes built since 2000	22.9% (54)
Construction jobs	5.6% (392)

HOUSING	★★ (354)
Home vacancy rate	9.4% (309)
Home ownership rate	74.6% (91)
Housing diversity index	82.4% (444)
4 or more bedrooms	17.9% (209)
Affordability/income ratio	$3,904 (490)

INCOME	★★★★★ (84)
Poverty rate	15.2% (199)
Median household income	$50,998 (101)
Interest/dividends	26.1% (69)
Public assistance	9.4% (51)
Median fulltime earnings	$40,826 (105)

SENIORS	★★★★★ (69)
Seniors living alone	24.5% (99)
Poverty rate for seniors	7.0% (93)
Median income for seniors	$44,549 (31)
Seniors who work	16.3% (391)
Home ownership by seniors	84.5% (165)

STABILITY	★★ (332)
25-39 age group	16.1% (442)
Born in state of residence	52.4% (476)
Same house as 1 year ago	89.6% (57)
Live and work in county	73.9% (313)
Married-couple households	53.4% (134)

TRANSPORTATION	★ (534)
Bicycle or walk to work	2.4% (331)
Carpool to work	6.2% (543)
Public transit to work	0.1% (441)
Commute <15 minutes	32.7% (480)
Commute >45 minutes	15.2% (430)

See pages 37-130 for explanations of statistics, stars, and ranks.

Plainview, TX
(Hale County, TX)

POPULATION

2010 census	36,273 (372)
2015 estimate	34,360 (392)
2010-2015 change	-5.3% (536)
2020 projection	32,672 (411)
2030 projection	29,477 (429)

RACE

Whites	35.4% (520)
Blacks	4.6% (173)
Hispanics	57.9% (17)
Asians	0.4% (413)
Native Americans	0.1% (402)

AGE

0-17 years old	28.1% (30)
18-24 years old	11.8% (90)
25-39 years old	19.2% (88)
40-54 years old	18.2% (441)
55-64 years old	10.2% (516)
65+ years old	12.5% (484)

PRIVATE SECTOR

Businesses	824 (361)
Employees	9,506 (391)
Total wages	$318,037,336 (412)
Average weekly wages	$643 (409)

HOUSEHOLD INCOME LADDER

95th percentile	$132,682 (391)
80th percentile	$76,579 (431)
60th percentile	$51,634 (338)
40th percentile	$34,835 (267)
20th percentile	$17,888 (325)

CHILDREN ★ (494)

Living with two parents	60.8% (382)
Older teens in school	77.5% (460)
Speak English very well	96.6% (430)
Poverty rate for children	34.7% (472)
No health insurance	12.1% (473)

DIVERSITY/EQUALITY ★★★★★ (80)

Racial diversity index	53.7% (71)
Geographic diversity index	40.4% (344)
Top 20% share of income	46.1% (124)
Gender gap in earnings	37.7% (382)
White-collar gender gap	8.8% (77)

EDUCATION ★ (518)

Eighth grade or less	11.1% (522)
High school diplomas	75.4% (523)
Attended college	42.6% (482)
Bachelor's degrees	14.9% (424)
Advanced degrees	5.3% (347)

EMPLOYMENT ★ (482)

Average jobless rate	8.1% (298)
Self-employed workers	9.9% (171)
Management/financial jobs	9.4% (444)
Computer/engineering jobs	1.1% (532)
Health care jobs	3.7% (503)

GROWTH POTENTIAL ★★★★ (137)

Children per senior	2.25 (39)
Median age	32.5 (52)
Moved from different state	1.9% (310)
Homes built since 2000	3.3% (548)
Construction jobs	7.5% (122)

HOUSING ★ (497)

Home vacancy rate	13.0% (490)
Home ownership rate	61.0% (493)
Housing diversity index	83.9% (360)
4 or more bedrooms	10.7% (522)
Affordability/income ratio	$1,692 (12)

INCOME ★ (460)

Poverty rate	23.0% (444)
Median household income	$43,375 (279)
Interest/dividends	11.1% (509)
Public assistance	19.3% (409)
Median fulltime earnings	$32,741 (462)

SENIORS ★★★★ (193)

Seniors living alone	20.4% (18)
Poverty rate for seniors	12.2% (422)
Median income for seniors	$31,277 (362)
Seniors who work	23.6% (94)
Home ownership by seniors	77.4% (476)

STABILITY ★★★★ (175)

25-39 age group	19.2% (88)
Born in state of residence	76.5% (191)
Same house as 1 year ago	78.1% (516)
Live and work in county	82.4% (174)
Married-couple households	53.0% (152)

TRANSPORTATION ★★★★ (115)

Bicycle or walk to work	1.5% (457)
Carpool to work	11.5% (184)
Public transit to work	0.4% (219)
Commute <15 minutes	64.8% (19)
Commute >45 minutes	7.6% (111)

See pages 37-130 for explanations of statistics, stars, and ranks.

Ponca City, OK
(Kay County, OK)

POPULATION		Attended college	53.6% (254)
2010 census	46,562 (241)	Bachelor's degrees	18.1% (282)
2015 estimate	45,366 (256)	Advanced degrees	4.7% (419)
2010-2015 change	-2.6% (455)		
2020 projection	44,275 (272)	**EMPLOYMENT**	★★★ (295)
2030 projection	42,137 (294)	Average jobless rate	7.8% (270)
		Self-employed workers	8.3% (302)
RACE		Management/financial jobs	11.7% (185)
Whites	76.0% (354)	Computer/engineering jobs	2.6% (288)
Blacks	1.9% (295)	Health care jobs	5.1% (319)
Hispanics	7.2% (194)		
Asians	0.6% (291)	**GROWTH POTENTIAL**	★★ (360)
Native Americans	7.1% (27)	Children per senior	1.41 (269)
		Median age	38.8 (217)
AGE		Moved from different state	3.4% (118)
0-17 years old	25.1% (116)	Homes built since 2000	4.5% (544)
18-24 years old	9.0% (265)	Construction jobs	6.1% (310)
25-39 years old	17.0% (317)		
40-54 years old	18.1% (446)	**HOUSING**	★★★ (294)
55-64 years old	13.0% (334)	Home vacancy rate	12.5% (476)
65+ years old	17.8% (137)	Home ownership rate	68.9% (308)
		Housing diversity index	85.4% (156)
PRIVATE SECTOR		4 or more bedrooms	14.4% (381)
Businesses	1,129 (227)	Affordability/income ratio	$1,870 (27)
Employees	13,904 (236)		
Total wages	$577,764,995 (199)	**INCOME**	★★★ (309)
Average weekly wages	$799 (90)	Poverty rate	18.3% (309)
		Median household income	$42,134 (316)
HOUSEHOLD INCOME LADDER		Interest/dividends	20.6% (231)
95th percentile	$151,261 (148)	Public assistance	17.1% (338)
80th percentile	$82,509 (305)	Median fulltime earnings	$35,577 (358)
60th percentile	$51,758 (334)		
40th percentile	$32,890 (330)	**SENIORS**	★ (443)
20th percentile	$18,480 (289)	Seniors living alone	34.6% (540)
		Poverty rate for seniors	9.8% (308)
CHILDREN	★★ (339)	Median income for seniors	$29,717 (416)
Living with two parents	59.9% (399)	Seniors who work	20.4% (183)
Older teens in school	82.8% (286)	Home ownership by seniors	82.9% (225)
Speak English very well	98.8% (251)		
Poverty rate for children	25.9% (321)	**STABILITY**	★★ (408)
No health insurance	8.9% (390)	25-39 age group	17.0% (317)
		Born in state of residence	66.3% (371)
DIVERSITY/EQUALITY	★★★★ (180)	Same house as 1 year ago	81.4% (465)
Racial diversity index	40.7% (185)	Live and work in county	88.0% (91)
Geographic diversity index	52.8% (178)	Married-couple households	46.1% (441)
Top 20% share of income	48.6% (326)		
Gender gap in earnings	40.5% (449)	**TRANSPORTATION**	★★★★ (149)
White-collar gender gap	12.3% (119)	Bicycle or walk to work	3.4% (199)
		Carpool to work	10.7% (260)
EDUCATION	★★★ (291)	Public transit to work	0.3% (291)
Eighth grade or less	3.2% (250)	Commute <15 minutes	56.1% (84)
High school diplomas	87.4% (291)	Commute >45 minutes	8.0% (131)

See pages 37-130 for explanations of statistics, stars, and ranks.

Port Lavaca, TX
(Calhoun County, TX)

POPULATION			Attended college	49.9% (335)
2010 census	21,381 (515)		Bachelor's degrees	15.7% (399)
2015 estimate	21,895 (511)		Advanced degrees	5.0% (378)
2010-2015 change	2.4% (111)		**EMPLOYMENT**	**★★★ (275)**
2020 projection	22,138 (509)		Average jobless rate	7.2% (218)
2030 projection	22,618 (498)		Self-employed workers	8.6% (285)
			Management/financial jobs	10.3% (339)
RACE			Computer/engineering jobs	4.9% (33)
Whites	44.1% (505)		Health care jobs	4.0% (476)
Blacks	2.8% (232)			
Hispanics	47.8% (28)		**GROWTH POTENTIAL**	**★★★★★ (69)**
Asians	3.5% (16)		Children per senior	1.60 (169)
Native Americans	0.1% (402)		Median age	38.1 (187)
			Moved from different state	2.2% (248)
AGE			Homes built since 2000	15.2% (199)
0-17 years old	25.6% (85)		Construction jobs	12.1% (4)
18-24 years old	7.9% (424)			
25-39 years old	18.2% (167)		**HOUSING**	**★★ (359)**
40-54 years old	19.8% (261)		Home vacancy rate	11.6% (441)
55-64 years old	12.5% (396)		Home ownership rate	70.8% (239)
65+ years old	15.9% (297)		Housing diversity index	84.7% (260)
			4 or more bedrooms	10.0% (532)
PRIVATE SECTOR			Affordability/income ratio	$2,013 (60)
Businesses	520 (511)			
Employees	11,117 (340)		**INCOME**	**★★★★ (160)**
Total wages	$710,296,142 (148)		Poverty rate	19.3% (348)
Average weekly wages	$1,229 (4)		Median household income	$51,078 (99)
			Interest/dividends	21.0% (214)
HOUSEHOLD INCOME LADDER			Public assistance	12.6% (150)
95th percentile	$151,008 (151)		Median fulltime earnings	$41,554 (76)
80th percentile	$102,888 (48)			
60th percentile	$65,753 (70)		**SENIORS**	**★★★★★ (27)**
40th percentile	$40,596 (110)		Seniors living alone	22.1% (39)
20th percentile	$22,378 (119)		Poverty rate for seniors	7.6% (145)
			Median income for seniors	n.a.
CHILDREN	**★ (475)**		Seniors who work	21.4% (148)
Living with two parents	63.7% (305)		Home ownership by seniors	88.4% (31)
Older teens in school	87.7% (107)			
Speak English very well	93.3% (504)		**STABILITY**	**★★★★★ (81)**
Poverty rate for children	30.4% (411)		25-39 age group	18.2% (167)
No health insurance	15.9% (529)		Born in state of residence	78.0% (156)
			Same house as 1 year ago	87.1% (192)
DIVERSITY/EQUALITY	**★★★ (270)**		Live and work in county	75.3% (285)
Racial diversity index	57.5% (29)		Married-couple households	52.5% (171)
Geographic diversity index	38.2% (388)			
Top 20% share of income	44.6% (45)		**TRANSPORTATION**	**★★★ (260)**
Gender gap in earnings	48.1% (519)		Bicycle or walk to work	0.9% (521)
White-collar gender gap	38.2% (424)		Carpool to work	15.1% (46)
			Public transit to work	0.8% (96)
EDUCATION	**★ (452)**		Commute <15 minutes	38.8% (356)
Eighth grade or less	8.4% (497)		Commute >45 minutes	12.1% (316)
High school diplomas	81.4% (458)			

See pages 37-130 for explanations of statistics, stars, and ranks.

Raymondville, TX
(Willacy County, TX)

POPULATION	
2010 census	22,134 (508)
2015 estimate	21,903 (509)
2010-2015 change	-1.0% (326)
2020 projection	21,841 (514)
2030 projection	21,739 (507)

RACE

Whites	10.4% (547)
Blacks	1.6% (320)
Hispanics	87.5% (4)
Asians	0.1% (529)
Native Americans	0.0% (523)

AGE

0-17 years old	25.5% (90)
18-24 years old	13.0% (71)
25-39 years old	21.9% (22)
40-54 years old	17.6% (470)
55-64 years old	9.7% (532)
65+ years old	12.4% (487)

PRIVATE SECTOR

Businesses	256 (549)
Employees	2,418 (550)
Total wages	$76,389,479 (550)
Average weekly wages	$608 (476)

HOUSEHOLD INCOME LADDER

95th percentile	$120,761 (510)
80th percentile	$61,592 (548)
60th percentile	$35,785 (546)
40th percentile	$19,124 (550)
20th percentile	$9,065 (551)

CHILDREN ★ (549)

Living with two parents	54.8% (478)
Older teens in school	71.6% (525)
Speak English very well	92.5% (512)
Poverty rate for children	49.2% (541)
No health insurance	15.2% (525)

DIVERSITY/EQUALITY ★★★★ (147)

Racial diversity index	22.3% (319)
Geographic diversity index	41.9% (329)
Top 20% share of income	53.6% (532)
Gender gap in earnings	8.5% (7)
White-collar gender gap	1.8% (11)

EDUCATION ★ (550)

Eighth grade or less	17.9% (540)
High school diplomas	68.3% (539)
Attended college	29.7% (547)
Bachelor's degrees	8.2% (548)
Advanced degrees	1.7% (551)

EMPLOYMENT ★ (549)

Average jobless rate	11.5% (474)
Self-employed workers	6.9% (435)
Management/financial jobs	8.3% (513)
Computer/engineering jobs	0.8% (543)
Health care jobs	2.9% (537)

GROWTH POTENTIAL ★★★★ (128)

Children per senior	2.06 (53)
Median age	32.3 (51)
Moved from different state	2.0% (288)
Homes built since 2000	13.3% (263)
Construction jobs	5.7% (373)

HOUSING ★★★ (221)

Home vacancy rate	12.3% (469)
Home ownership rate	77.4% (22)
Housing diversity index	85.6% (127)
4 or more bedrooms	11.1% (519)
Affordability/income ratio	$1,876 (28)

INCOME ★ (550)

Poverty rate	39.0% (551)
Median household income	$26,495 (549)
Interest/dividends	4.8% (551)
Public assistance	32.5% (543)
Median fulltime earnings	$28,750 (546)

SENIORS ★★ (379)

Seniors living alone	18.2% (6)
Poverty rate for seniors	32.5% (549)
Median income for seniors	n.a.
Seniors who work	10.1% (550)
Home ownership by seniors	85.6% (120)

STABILITY ★★★★★ (50)

25-39 age group	21.9% (22)
Born in state of residence	75.0% (221)
Same house as 1 year ago	87.5% (165)
Live and work in county	60.9% (484)
Married-couple households	52.8% (164)

TRANSPORTATION ★ (489)

Bicycle or walk to work	3.1% (232)
Carpool to work	6.0% (547)
Public transit to work	0.0% (511)
Commute <15 minutes	37.2% (396)
Commute >45 minutes	12.1% (316)

See pages 37-130 for explanations of statistics, stars, and ranks.

Richmond-Berea, KY
(Madison and Rockcastle Counties, KY)

POPULATION

2010 census	99,972 (28)
2015 estimate	104,766 (23)
2010-2015 change	4.8% (42)
2020 projection	109,139 (21)
2030 projection	118,241 (18)

RACE

Whites	91.3% (155)
Blacks	3.7% (202)
Hispanics	2.0% (428)
Asians	0.8% (201)
Native Americans	0.5% (174)

AGE

0-17 years old	21.3% (383)
18-24 years old	16.0% (52)
25-39 years old	18.1% (186)
40-54 years old	19.9% (250)
55-64 years old	11.6% (471)
65+ years old	13.0% (474)

PRIVATE SECTOR

Businesses	2,125 (51)
Employees	29,562 (44)
Total wages	$1,032,312,873 (64)
Average weekly wages	$672 (330)

HOUSEHOLD INCOME LADDER

95th percentile	$144,811 (231)
80th percentile	$83,221 (288)
60th percentile	$51,781 (332)
40th percentile	$31,207 (385)
20th percentile	$15,262 (443)

CHILDREN ★★★★★ (47)

Living with two parents	68.9% (168)
Older teens in school	93.4% (28)
Speak English very well	99.6% (77)
Poverty rate for children	23.6% (260)
No health insurance	2.8% (50)

DIVERSITY/EQUALITY ★ (497)

Racial diversity index	16.4% (391)
Geographic diversity index	44.0% (295)
Top 20% share of income	49.1% (366)
Gender gap in earnings	40.4% (445)
White-collar gender gap	36.6% (402)

EDUCATION ★★★★ (136)

Eighth grade or less	4.2% (337)
High school diplomas	88.7% (245)
Attended college	56.5% (196)
Bachelor's degrees	26.4% (93)
Advanced degrees	10.0% (61)

EMPLOYMENT ★★★ (301)

Average jobless rate	9.0% (358)
Self-employed workers	6.1% (495)
Management/financial jobs	11.9% (165)
Computer/engineering jobs	3.8% (96)
Health care jobs	5.6% (240)

GROWTH POTENTIAL ★★★★ (118)

Children per senior	1.63 (158)
Median age	35.4 (103)
Moved from different state	2.6% (187)
Homes built since 2000	24.1% (42)
Construction jobs	5.3% (425)

HOUSING ★★ (423)

Home vacancy rate	8.0% (223)
Home ownership rate	62.1% (479)
Housing diversity index	83.1% (414)
4 or more bedrooms	16.7% (261)
Affordability/income ratio	$3,189 (429)

INCOME ★★ (377)

Poverty rate	21.7% (421)
Median household income	$40,828 (360)
Interest/dividends	14.6% (424)
Public assistance	19.0% (399)
Median fulltime earnings	$39,477 (157)

SENIORS ★ (446)

Seniors living alone	27.0% (239)
Poverty rate for seniors	12.8% (442)
Median income for seniors	$30,319 (400)
Seniors who work	14.7% (467)
Home ownership by seniors	81.1% (325)

STABILITY ★★ (428)

25-39 age group	18.1% (186)
Born in state of residence	73.4% (252)
Same house as 1 year ago	80.8% (486)
Live and work in county	69.1% (386)
Married-couple households	48.2% (373)

TRANSPORTATION ★★★ (320)

Bicycle or walk to work	6.2% (55)
Carpool to work	9.4% (394)
Public transit to work	0.5% (178)
Commute <15 minutes	37.6% (385)
Commute >45 minutes	14.1% (392)

See pages 37-130 for explanations of statistics, stars, and ranks.

Rio Grande City, TX
(Starr County, TX)

POPULATION
2010 census	60,968 (143)
2015 estimate	63,795 (127)
2010-2015 change	4.6% (47)
2020 projection	66,088 (117)
2030 projection	70,880 (102)

RACE
Whites	0.9% (551)
Blacks	0.0% (550)
Hispanics	98.7% (1)
Asians	0.1% (529)
Native Americans	0.0% (523)

AGE
0-17 years old	33.3% (4)
18-24 years old	11.5% (100)
25-39 years old	19.4% (78)
40-54 years old	16.4% (518)
55-64 years old	8.3% (548)
65+ years old	11.0% (511)

PRIVATE SECTOR
Businesses	533 (504)
Employees	9,143 (408)
Total wages	$188,126,579 (515)
Average weekly wages	$396 (551)

HOUSEHOLD INCOME LADDER
95th percentile	$119,241 (521)
80th percentile	$63,588 (540)
60th percentile	$34,539 (550)
40th percentile	$20,490 (548)
20th percentile	$11,917 (525)

CHILDREN ★ (548)
Living with two parents	57.1% (459)
Older teens in school	84.2% (232)
Speak English very well	69.2% (550)
Poverty rate for children	45.1% (534)
No health insurance	19.0% (544)

DIVERSITY/EQUALITY ★ (546)
Racial diversity index	2.6% (551)
Geographic diversity index	56.0% (145)
Top 20% share of income	54.1% (536)
Gender gap in earnings	37.8% (385)
White-collar gender gap	42.1% (465)

EDUCATION ★ (548)
Eighth grade or less	26.8% (550)
High school diplomas	52.2% (551)

Attended college	27.7% (549)
Bachelor's degrees	10.3% (538)
Advanced degrees	2.6% (544)

EMPLOYMENT ★ (551)
Average jobless rate	13.8% (525)
Self-employed workers	9.2% (231)
Management/financial jobs	6.0% (550)
Computer/engineering jobs	1.0% (536)
Health care jobs	2.6% (545)

GROWTH POTENTIAL ★★★★★ (6)
Children per senior	3.02 (13)
Median age	29.1 (20)
Moved from different state	1.9% (310)
Homes built since 2000	24.7% (37)
Construction jobs	11.9% (5)

HOUSING ★★★ (308)
Home vacancy rate	10.4% (371)
Home ownership rate	75.2% (76)
Housing diversity index	81.1% (492)
4 or more bedrooms	17.4% (226)
Affordability/income ratio	$2,487 (244)

INCOME ★ (551)
Poverty rate	36.6% (546)
Median household income	$26,172 (550)
Interest/dividends	7.1% (548)
Public assistance	43.9% (551)
Median fulltime earnings	$26,560 (551)

SENIORS ★ (509)
Seniors living alone	18.1% (5)
Poverty rate for seniors	33.2% (550)
Median income for seniors	$17,584 (528)
Seniors who work	15.3% (446)
Home ownership by seniors	77.6% (466)

STABILITY ★★★★★ (35)
25-39 age group	19.4% (78)
Born in state of residence	61.0% (416)
Same house as 1 year ago	91.5% (22)
Live and work in county	75.8% (278)
Married-couple households	54.2% (102)

TRANSPORTATION ★★★★★ (53)
Bicycle or walk to work	4.7% (106)
Carpool to work	21.5% (2)
Public transit to work	0.4% (219)
Commute <15 minutes	50.2% (146)
Commute >45 minutes	11.1% (275)

See pages 37-130 for explanations of statistics, stars, and ranks.

Roanoke Rapids, NC
(Halifax and Northampton Counties, NC)

POPULATION

2010 census	76,790 (80)
2015 estimate	72,882 (90)
2010-2015 change	-5.1% (535)
2020 projection	68,750 (105)
2030 projection	60,906 (147)

RACE

Whites	39.0% (516)
Blacks	53.3% (11)
Hispanics	2.4% (389)
Asians	0.6% (291)
Native Americans	2.4% (65)

AGE

0-17 years old	21.3% (383)
18-24 years old	8.7% (299)
25-39 years old	15.6% (474)
40-54 years old	20.3% (186)
55-64 years old	15.1% (74)
65+ years old	19.0% (80)

PRIVATE SECTOR

Businesses	1,262 (187)
Employees	15,792 (196)
Total wages	$499,703,590 (244)
Average weekly wages	$609 (473)

HOUSEHOLD INCOME LADDER

95th percentile	$120,281 (514)
80th percentile	$68,782 (517)
60th percentile	$40,184 (527)
40th percentile	$24,169 (519)
20th percentile	$12,074 (519)

CHILDREN ★ (492)

Living with two parents	34.7% (544)
Older teens in school	82.3% (304)
Speak English very well	99.4% (124)
Poverty rate for children	40.2% (516)
No health insurance	6.3% (271)

DIVERSITY/EQUALITY ★★★★ (162)

Racial diversity index	56.2% (37)
Geographic diversity index	36.7% (413)
Top 20% share of income	51.8% (496)
Gender gap in earnings	31.0% (204)
White-collar gender gap	4.2% (28)

EDUCATION ★ (454)

Eighth grade or less	3.8% (307)
High school diplomas	81.2% (463)
Attended college	44.4% (447)
Bachelor's degrees	12.9% (497)
Advanced degrees	4.1% (472)

EMPLOYMENT ★ (495)

Average jobless rate	14.6% (532)
Self-employed workers	7.3% (401)
Management/financial jobs	9.7% (416)
Computer/engineering jobs	2.2% (381)
Health care jobs	6.5% (121)

GROWTH POTENTIAL ★ (506)

Children per senior	1.12 (455)
Median age	43.6 (468)
Moved from different state	1.4% (425)
Homes built since 2000	12.5% (297)
Construction jobs	5.3% (425)

HOUSING ★★★ (320)

Home vacancy rate	11.0% (405)
Home ownership rate	64.7% (443)
Housing diversity index	86.7% (6)
4 or more bedrooms	15.3% (333)
Affordability/income ratio	$2,695 (327)

INCOME ★ (530)

Poverty rate	26.8% (500)
Median household income	$31,724 (521)
Interest/dividends	12.5% (482)
Public assistance	31.9% (540)
Median fulltime earnings	$32,853 (459)

SENIORS ★ (537)

Seniors living alone	30.8% (462)
Poverty rate for seniors	17.7% (523)
Median income for seniors	$25,993 (493)
Seniors who work	15.1% (455)
Home ownership by seniors	77.6% (466)

STABILITY ★ (531)

25-39 age group	15.6% (474)
Born in state of residence	78.4% (148)
Same house as 1 year ago	87.5% (165)
Live and work in county	57.8% (504)
Married-couple households	37.5% (538)

TRANSPORTATION ★★ (408)

Bicycle or walk to work	2.4% (331)
Carpool to work	11.3% (201)
Public transit to work	0.1% (441)
Commute <15 minutes	34.9% (441)
Commute >45 minutes	13.3% (368)

See pages 37-130 for explanations of statistics, stars, and ranks.

Rockingham, NC
(Richmond County, NC)

POPULATION

2010 census	46,639 (240)
2015 estimate	45,437 (253)
2010-2015 change	-2.6% (455)
2020 projection	43,858 (275)
2030 projection	40,701 (309)

RACE

Whites	57.9% (459)
Blacks	31.6% (49)
Hispanics	6.2% (214)
Asians	0.2% (509)
Native Americans	2.4% (65)

AGE

0-17 years old	23.8% (206)
18-24 years old	9.6% (189)
25-39 years old	16.7% (375)
40-54 years old	21.2% (85)
55-64 years old	13.2% (297)
65+ years old	15.5% (333)

PRIVATE SECTOR

Businesses	808 (368)
Employees	10,567 (358)
Total wages	$343,250,330 (387)
Average weekly wages	$625 (443)

HOUSEHOLD INCOME LADDER

95th percentile	$119,945 (516)
80th percentile	$66,775 (527)
60th percentile	$40,870 (521)
40th percentile	$25,019 (511)
20th percentile	$12,731 (507)

CHILDREN ★ (452)

Living with two parents	51.3% (498)
Older teens in school	84.4% (226)
Speak English very well	97.5% (388)
Poverty rate for children	39.0% (508)
No health insurance	6.8% (302)

DIVERSITY/EQUALITY ★★★★★ (60)

Racial diversity index	56.0% (40)
Geographic diversity index	40.2% (348)
Top 20% share of income	49.3% (391)
Gender gap in earnings	23.4% (70)
White-collar gender gap	8.5% (70)

EDUCATION ★ (442)

Eighth grade or less	5.2% (398)
High school diplomas	84.0% (400)
Attended college	47.8% (387)
Bachelor's degrees	13.4% (482)
Advanced degrees	3.6% (505)

EMPLOYMENT ★ (540)

Average jobless rate	13.8% (525)
Self-employed workers	6.2% (488)
Management/financial jobs	10.1% (365)
Computer/engineering jobs	1.5% (499)
Health care jobs	4.4% (433)

GROWTH POTENTIAL ★★★★ (201)

Children per senior	1.54 (197)
Median age	39.9 (292)
Moved from different state	1.3% (452)
Homes built since 2000	8.9% (439)
Construction jobs	9.6% (29)

HOUSING ★★ (371)

Home vacancy rate	10.2% (358)
Home ownership rate	62.7% (478)
Housing diversity index	86.2% (43)
4 or more bedrooms	12.6% (472)
Affordability/income ratio	$2,405 (215)

INCOME ★ (516)

Poverty rate	25.7% (482)
Median household income	$32,687 (510)
Interest/dividends	10.2% (529)
Public assistance	25.4% (516)
Median fulltime earnings	$32,982 (453)

SENIORS ★ (484)

Seniors living alone	28.9% (358)
Poverty rate for seniors	14.2% (475)
Median income for seniors	$26,659 (481)
Seniors who work	14.0% (503)
Home ownership by seniors	83.2% (210)

STABILITY ★ (467)

25-39 age group	16.7% (375)
Born in state of residence	76.4% (195)
Same house as 1 year ago	86.1% (245)
Live and work in county	72.0% (341)
Married-couple households	40.4% (527)

TRANSPORTATION ★★★★ (210)

Bicycle or walk to work	2.8% (279)
Carpool to work	13.9% (72)
Public transit to work	0.3% (291)
Commute <15 minutes	39.6% (336)
Commute >45 minutes	9.3% (188)

See pages 37-130 for explanations of statistics, stars, and ranks.

Russellville, AR
(Pope and Yell Counties, AR)

POPULATION

2010 census	83,939 (57)
2015 estimate	85,103 (57)
2010-2015 change	1.4% (165)
2020 projection	86,396 (55)
2030 projection	88,311 (56)

RACE

Whites	83.0% (290)
Blacks	2.7% (241)
Hispanics	10.7% (144)
Asians	0.9% (178)
Native Americans	0.5% (174)

AGE

0-17 years old	23.4% (240)
18-24 years old	12.7% (75)
25-39 years old	18.1% (186)
40-54 years old	19.3% (323)
55-64 years old	11.9% (447)
65+ years old	14.6% (400)

PRIVATE SECTOR

Businesses	2,115 (53)
Employees	27,870 (55)
Total wages	$1,004,194,186 (69)
Average weekly wages	$693 (274)

HOUSEHOLD INCOME LADDER

95th percentile	$136,785 (331)
80th percentile	$78,368 (396)
60th percentile	$48,813 (407)
40th percentile	$31,724 (370)
20th percentile	$17,175 (353)

CHILDREN ★★★★ (195)

Living with two parents	68.6% (177)
Older teens in school	88.7% (88)
Speak English very well	96.1% (446)
Poverty rate for children	26.6% (341)
No health insurance	5.4% (209)

DIVERSITY/EQUALITY ★★★★ (197)

Racial diversity index	29.8% (254)
Geographic diversity index	57.7% (137)
Top 20% share of income	47.7% (267)
Gender gap in earnings	38.9% (418)
White-collar gender gap	18.6% (194)

EDUCATION ★★ (379)

Eighth grade or less	6.1% (429)
High school diplomas	82.9% (423)
Attended college	48.1% (381)
Bachelor's degrees	19.6% (229)
Advanced degrees	6.4% (229)

EMPLOYMENT ★★ (336)

Average jobless rate	7.8% (270)
Self-employed workers	9.2% (231)
Management/financial jobs	10.0% (381)
Computer/engineering jobs	3.0% (193)
Health care jobs	4.8% (369)

GROWTH POTENTIAL ★★★★ (136)

Children per senior	1.60 (169)
Median age	36.5 (131)
Moved from different state	1.9% (310)
Homes built since 2000	19.7% (97)
Construction jobs	6.8% (204)

HOUSING ★★ (399)

Home vacancy rate	9.5% (317)
Home ownership rate	67.6% (362)
Housing diversity index	83.5% (391)
4 or more bedrooms	13.9% (406)
Affordability/income ratio	$2,879 (374)

INCOME ★★ (379)

Poverty rate	19.6% (360)
Median household income	$39,071 (403)
Interest/dividends	16.0% (375)
Public assistance	13.1% (177)
Median fulltime earnings	$32,290 (481)

SENIORS ★★ (412)

Seniors living alone	26.3% (190)
Poverty rate for seniors	10.3% (340)
Median income for seniors	$28,914 (438)
Seniors who work	16.4% (383)
Home ownership by seniors	79.2% (406)

STABILITY ★★★ (279)

25-39 age group	18.1% (186)
Born in state of residence	62.5% (407)
Same house as 1 year ago	83.6% (359)
Live and work in county	74.4% (304)
Married-couple households	53.5% (131)

TRANSPORTATION ★★★ (277)

Bicycle or walk to work	2.2% (358)
Carpool to work	11.0% (229)
Public transit to work	0.1% (441)
Commute <15 minutes	42.4% (291)
Commute >45 minutes	7.4% (99)

See pages 37-130 for explanations of statistics, stars, and ranks.

Ruston, LA
(Lincoln Parish, LA)

POPULATION	
2010 census	46,735 (237)
2015 estimate	47,774 (229)
2010-2015 change	2.2% (118)
2020 projection	49,171 (220)
2030 projection	51,924 (204)

RACE	
Whites	53.3% (476)
Blacks	40.4% (29)
Hispanics	2.7% (361)
Asians	1.8% (60)
Native Americans	0.1% (402)

AGE	
0-17 years old	20.3% (445)
18-24 years old	25.9% (14)
25-39 years old	17.9% (214)
40-54 years old	14.1% (545)
55-64 years old	9.8% (530)
65+ years old	11.9% (497)

PRIVATE SECTOR	
Businesses	1,090 (247)
Employees	14,160 (229)
Total wages	$495,212,411 (249)
Average weekly wages	$673 (327)

HOUSEHOLD INCOME LADDER	
95th percentile	$161,917 (87)
80th percentile	$83,654 (280)
60th percentile	$47,511 (436)
40th percentile	$25,086 (510)
20th percentile	$11,671 (529)

CHILDREN	★★★ (271)
Living with two parents	55.1% (477)
Older teens in school	85.6% (179)
Speak English very well	98.2% (320)
Poverty rate for children	31.9% (444)
No health insurance	1.4% (5)

DIVERSITY/EQUALITY	★★★ (246)
Racial diversity index	55.1% (53)
Geographic diversity index	45.9% (268)
Top 20% share of income	55.9% (549)
Gender gap in earnings	31.4% (213)
White-collar gender gap	8.9% (80)

EDUCATION	★★★★★ (42)
Eighth grade or less	2.9% (217)
High school diplomas	87.6% (284)
Attended college	60.3% (123)
Bachelor's degrees	35.8% (24)
Advanced degrees	14.0% (19)

EMPLOYMENT	★★ (402)
Average jobless rate	11.9% (488)
Self-employed workers	7.2% (410)
Management/financial jobs	12.7% (103)
Computer/engineering jobs	2.5% (307)
Health care jobs	5.3% (286)

GROWTH POTENTIAL	★★★★★ (60)
Children per senior	1.70 (133)
Median age	27.4 (12)
Moved from different state	3.0% (157)
Homes built since 2000	20.5% (85)
Construction jobs	5.7% (373)

HOUSING	★ (523)
Home vacancy rate	9.5% (317)
Home ownership rate	53.8% (539)
Housing diversity index	84.5% (287)
4 or more bedrooms	15.3% (333)
Affordability/income ratio	$3,768 (487)

INCOME	★ (485)
Poverty rate	32.1% (534)
Median household income	$33,467 (502)
Interest/dividends	16.3% (366)
Public assistance	20.0% (430)
Median fulltime earnings	$36,604 (309)

SENIORS	★★★ (294)
Seniors living alone	29.4% (394)
Poverty rate for seniors	11.5% (388)
Median income for seniors	$34,880 (194)
Seniors who work	19.6% (221)
Home ownership by seniors	83.9% (183)

STABILITY	★ (532)
25-39 age group	17.9% (214)
Born in state of residence	71.8% (278)
Same house as 1 year ago	76.1% (529)
Live and work in county	80.1% (216)
Married-couple households	37.3% (539)

TRANSPORTATION	★★★★ (173)
Bicycle or walk to work	4.4% (123)
Carpool to work	11.3% (201)
Public transit to work	0.1% (441)
Commute <15 minutes	50.8% (137)
Commute >45 minutes	9.8% (218)

See pages 37-130 for explanations of statistics, stars, and ranks.

St. Marys, GA
(Camden County, GA)

POPULATION

2010 census	50,513 (208)
2015 estimate	52,102 (197)
2010-2015 change	3.1% (78)
2020 projection	53,743 (185)
2030 projection	56,999 (166)

RACE

Whites	70.5% (387)
Blacks	18.7% (82)
Hispanics	5.9% (227)
Asians	1.5% (85)
Native Americans	0.4% (203)

AGE

0-17 years old	25.6% (85)
18-24 years old	13.1% (70)
25-39 years old	21.1% (39)
40-54 years old	19.0% (364)
55-64 years old	10.6% (502)
65+ years old	10.6% (519)

PRIVATE SECTOR

Businesses	869 (334)
Employees	11,644 (320)
Total wages	$498,336,413 (246)
Average weekly wages	$823 (61)

HOUSEHOLD INCOME LADDER

95th percentile	$151,419 (146)
80th percentile	$92,391 (123)
60th percentile	$64,641 (78)
40th percentile	$42,995 (68)
20th percentile	$23,908 (71)

CHILDREN ★★★ (290)

Living with two parents	68.1% (192)
Older teens in school	73.9% (511)
Speak English very well	98.0% (341)
Poverty rate for children	17.9% (123)
No health insurance	6.9% (307)

DIVERSITY/EQUALITY ★★★★★ (42)

Racial diversity index	46.3% (140)
Geographic diversity index	74.4% (19)
Top 20% share of income	44.0% (27)
Gender gap in earnings	45.9% (509)
White-collar gender gap	16.8% (178)

EDUCATION ★★★★ (121)

Eighth grade or less	1.8% (102)
High school diplomas	92.7% (106)
Attended college	62.5% (89)
Bachelor's degrees	21.2% (185)
Advanced degrees	7.5% (142)

EMPLOYMENT ★★★★ (204)

Average jobless rate	8.5% (332)
Self-employed workers	6.4% (479)
Management/financial jobs	13.6% (62)
Computer/engineering jobs	4.6% (48)
Health care jobs	4.9% (355)

GROWTH POTENTIAL ★★★★★ (14)

Children per senior	2.42 (32)
Median age	31.6 (44)
Moved from different state	7.4% (16)
Homes built since 2000	27.3% (25)
Construction jobs	6.2% (295)

HOUSING ★★ (417)

Home vacancy rate	8.2% (234)
Home ownership rate	61.1% (489)
Housing diversity index	79.0% (525)
4 or more bedrooms	25.1% (41)
Affordability/income ratio	$2,880 (375)

INCOME ★★★★ (182)

Poverty rate	12.8% (109)
Median household income	$52,473 (80)
Interest/dividends	14.5% (428)
Public assistance	12.3% (140)
Median fulltime earnings	$38,654 (195)

SENIORS ★★★★★ (87)

Seniors living alone	19.9% (12)
Poverty rate for seniors	11.8% (401)
Median income for seniors	$45,255 (27)
Seniors who work	12.8% (530)
Home ownership by seniors	84.9% (145)

STABILITY ★★ (407)

25-39 age group	21.1% (39)
Born in state of residence	34.4% (536)
Same house as 1 year ago	79.1% (509)
Live and work in county	73.9% (313)
Married-couple households	56.9% (32)

TRANSPORTATION ★ (470)

Bicycle or walk to work	3.0% (249)
Carpool to work	7.9% (498)
Public transit to work	0.2% (363)
Commute <15 minutes	34.1% (457)
Commute >45 minutes	13.3% (368)

See pages 37-130 for explanations of statistics, stars, and ranks.

Sanford, NC
(Lee County, NC)

POPULATION	
2010 census	57,866 (162)
2015 estimate	59,660 (151)
2010-2015 change	3.1% (78)
2020 projection	61,550 (140)
2030 projection	65,235 (126)

RACE
Whites	58.4% (454)
Blacks	19.1% (81)
Hispanics	19.2% (81)
Asians	1.2% (125)
Native Americans	0.6% (150)

AGE
0-17 years old	25.5% (90)
18-24 years old	8.7% (299)
25-39 years old	18.4% (151)
40-54 years old	20.5% (151)
55-64 years old	12.4% (408)
65+ years old	14.6% (400)

PRIVATE SECTOR
Businesses	1,362 (162)
Employees	21,963 (98)
Total wages	$839,208,768 (111)
Average weekly wages	$735 (187)

HOUSEHOLD INCOME LADDER
95th percentile	$146,653 (203)
80th percentile	$84,311 (269)
60th percentile	$56,828 (212)
40th percentile	$36,006 (233)
20th percentile	$18,818 (276)

CHILDREN ★★ (397)
Living with two parents	62.2% (344)
Older teens in school	82.3% (304)
Speak English very well	93.4% (501)
Poverty rate for children	26.3% (333)
No health insurance	7.3% (333)

DIVERSITY/EQUALITY ★★★★★ (13)
Racial diversity index	58.5% (21)
Geographic diversity index	59.8% (126)
Top 20% share of income	46.4% (151)
Gender gap in earnings	17.3% (25)
White-collar gender gap	20.8% (218)

EDUCATION ★★ (376)
Eighth grade or less	8.5% (501)
High school diplomas	81.7% (452)
Attended college	56.7% (193)
Bachelor's degrees	20.8% (194)
Advanced degrees	5.7% (292)

EMPLOYMENT ★★ (404)
Average jobless rate	10.3% (432)
Self-employed workers	7.1% (421)
Management/financial jobs	10.5% (318)
Computer/engineering jobs	3.7% (103)
Health care jobs	4.9% (355)

GROWTH POTENTIAL ★★★★ (123)
Children per senior	1.74 (113)
Median age	37.5 (162)
Moved from different state	2.3% (234)
Homes built since 2000	20.6% (84)
Construction jobs	6.7% (219)

HOUSING ★★ (376)
Home vacancy rate	9.6% (327)
Home ownership rate	66.7% (399)
Housing diversity index	84.5% (287)
4 or more bedrooms	14.6% (373)
Affordability/income ratio	$3,002 (405)

INCOME ★★ (334)
Poverty rate	18.1% (300)
Median household income	$45,608 (220)
Interest/dividends	15.9% (380)
Public assistance	16.9% (327)
Median fulltime earnings	$35,375 (365)

SENIORS ★★★★★ (100)
Seniors living alone	24.7% (105)
Poverty rate for seniors	10.4% (342)
Median income for seniors	$37,741 (98)
Seniors who work	20.0% (195)
Home ownership by seniors	86.4% (82)

STABILITY ★★ (380)
25-39 age group	18.4% (151)
Born in state of residence	61.1% (414)
Same house as 1 year ago	85.2% (294)
Live and work in county	70.1% (371)
Married-couple households	49.6% (317)

TRANSPORTATION ★ (492)
Bicycle or walk to work	1.5% (457)
Carpool to work	10.5% (280)
Public transit to work	0.3% (291)
Commute <15 minutes	33.6% (469)
Commute >45 minutes	16.6% (473)

See pages 37-130 for explanations of statistics, stars, and ranks.

Scottsboro, AL
(Jackson County, AL)

POPULATION	
2010 census	53,227 (183)
2015 estimate	52,419 (195)
2010-2015 change	-1.5% (373)
2020 projection	51,113 (207)
2030 projection	48,360 (228)

RACE	
Whites	89.4% (197)
Blacks	3.1% (222)
Hispanics	2.7% (361)
Asians	0.5% (355)
Native Americans	1.1% (96)

AGE	
0-17 years old	21.9% (344)
18-24 years old	7.7% (454)
25-39 years old	17.7% (236)
40-54 years old	20.3% (186)
55-64 years old	14.5% (122)
65+ years old	17.9% (132)

PRIVATE SECTOR	
Businesses	862 (337)
Employees	13,009 (282)
Total wages	$428,268,530 (306)
Average weekly wages	$633 (429)

HOUSEHOLD INCOME LADDER	
95th percentile	$126,625 (471)
80th percentile	$74,092 (472)
60th percentile	$46,613 (451)
40th percentile	$29,825 (429)
20th percentile	$15,725 (418)

CHILDREN	★★★★ (161)
Living with two parents	71.0% (118)
Older teens in school	85.0% (197)
Speak English very well	98.7% (265)
Poverty rate for children	25.9% (321)
No health insurance	5.3% (206)

DIVERSITY/EQUALITY	★★ (440)
Racial diversity index	19.8% (350)
Geographic diversity index	48.1% (241)
Top 20% share of income	47.7% (270)
Gender gap in earnings	31.9% (223)
White-collar gender gap	51.7% (516)

EDUCATION	★ (489)
Eighth grade or less	5.4% (405)
High school diplomas	79.9% (482)
Attended college	39.5% (521)
Bachelor's degrees	13.0% (493)
Advanced degrees	5.1% (364)

EMPLOYMENT	★ (460)
Average jobless rate	10.1% (423)
Self-employed workers	7.4% (393)
Management/financial jobs	8.1% (524)
Computer/engineering jobs	2.9% (219)
Health care jobs	5.7% (222)

GROWTH POTENTIAL	★★ (399)
Children per senior	1.23 (393)
Median age	42.2 (412)
Moved from different state	1.3% (452)
Homes built since 2000	11.9% (318)
Construction jobs	7.0% (185)

HOUSING	★★★ (255)
Home vacancy rate	10.4% (371)
Home ownership rate	73.5% (137)
Housing diversity index	84.0% (344)
4 or more bedrooms	16.2% (284)
Affordability/income ratio	$2,620 (299)

INCOME	★★ (388)
Poverty rate	18.0% (299)
Median household income	$37,745 (434)
Interest/dividends	13.8% (446)
Public assistance	15.0% (254)
Median fulltime earnings	$34,229 (412)

SENIORS	★ (471)
Seniors living alone	31.2% (479)
Poverty rate for seniors	12.5% (436)
Median income for seniors	$27,469 (469)
Seniors who work	16.0% (410)
Home ownership by seniors	83.1% (217)

STABILITY	★★★★★ (76)
25-39 age group	17.7% (236)
Born in state of residence	68.9% (326)
Same house as 1 year ago	92.5% (9)
Live and work in county	66.3% (430)
Married-couple households	55.3% (62)

TRANSPORTATION	★ (545)
Bicycle or walk to work	1.4% (472)
Carpool to work	7.6% (510)
Public transit to work	0.1% (441)
Commute <15 minutes	30.2% (522)
Commute >45 minutes	18.7% (506)

See pages 37-130 for explanations of statistics, stars, and ranks.

Searcy, AR
(White County, AR)

POPULATION

2010 census	77,076 (79)
2015 estimate	79,161 (71)
2010-2015 change	2.7% (96)
2020 projection	81,190 (68)
2030 projection	84,639 (62)

RACE

Whites	88.6% (213)
Blacks	4.5% (176)
Hispanics	4.1% (292)
Asians	0.6% (291)
Native Americans	0.2% (300)

AGE

0-17 years old	23.7% (218)
18-24 years old	12.5% (77)
25-39 years old	18.0% (201)
40-54 years old	19.7% (273)
55-64 years old	11.2% (489)
65+ years old	14.9% (374)

PRIVATE SECTOR

Businesses	1,752 (91)
Employees	20,980 (114)
Total wages	$745,092,369 (138)
Average weekly wages	$683 (305)

HOUSEHOLD INCOME LADDER

95th percentile	$152,664 (137)
80th percentile	$88,613 (173)
60th percentile	$54,352 (271)
40th percentile	$32,370 (346)
20th percentile	$16,734 (373)

CHILDREN ★★★★★ (102)

Living with two parents	70.0% (143)
Older teens in school	85.7% (176)
Speak English very well	98.6% (278)
Poverty rate for children	21.7% (211)
No health insurance	3.5% (82)

DIVERSITY/EQUALITY ★ (502)

Racial diversity index	21.1% (334)
Geographic diversity index	52.6% (182)
Top 20% share of income	50.2% (442)
Gender gap in earnings	43.2% (483)
White-collar gender gap	39.9% (446)

EDUCATION ★★★ (262)

Eighth grade or less	3.9% (316)
High school diplomas	86.0% (343)
Attended college	49.4% (348)
Bachelor's degrees	20.8% (194)
Advanced degrees	7.4% (149)

EMPLOYMENT ★★★ (228)

Average jobless rate	7.1% (208)
Self-employed workers	7.3% (401)
Management/financial jobs	10.9% (263)
Computer/engineering jobs	2.4% (336)
Health care jobs	6.9% (79)

GROWTH POTENTIAL ★★★★★ (83)

Children per senior	1.59 (175)
Median age	36.2 (122)
Moved from different state	2.5% (203)
Homes built since 2000	23.2% (48)
Construction jobs	7.6% (110)

HOUSING ★★ (382)

Home vacancy rate	8.8% (273)
Home ownership rate	68.6% (321)
Housing diversity index	82.7% (429)
4 or more bedrooms	13.1% (448)
Affordability/income ratio	$2,557 (277)

INCOME ★★★ (258)

Poverty rate	19.0% (338)
Median household income	$42,554 (299)
Interest/dividends	19.4% (269)
Public assistance	12.4% (143)
Median fulltime earnings	$37,270 (263)

SENIORS ★★★ (287)

Seniors living alone	25.8% (160)
Poverty rate for seniors	12.1% (416)
Median income for seniors	$33,138 (275)
Seniors who work	17.4% (318)
Home ownership by seniors	83.6% (195)

STABILITY ★★★ (293)

25-39 age group	18.0% (201)
Born in state of residence	66.5% (368)
Same house as 1 year ago	81.2% (474)
Live and work in county	74.0% (310)
Married-couple households	54.5% (88)

TRANSPORTATION ★★ (337)

Bicycle or walk to work	3.0% (249)
Carpool to work	13.6% (80)
Public transit to work	0.2% (363)
Commute <15 minutes	39.2% (343)
Commute >45 minutes	16.2% (463)

See pages 37-130 for explanations of statistics, stars, and ranks.

Selma, AL
(Dallas County, AL)

POPULATION

2010 census	43,820 (271)
2015 estimate	41,131 (298)
2010-2015 change	-6.1% (546)
2020 projection	38,774 (332)
2030 projection	34,279 (386)

RACE

Whites	28.6% (532)
Blacks	69.2% (4)
Hispanics	0.3% (549)
Asians	0.4% (413)
Native Americans	0.2% (300)

AGE

0-17 years old	25.5% (90)
18-24 years old	9.3% (217)
25-39 years old	16.9% (338)
40-54 years old	19.3% (323)
55-64 years old	13.7% (225)
65+ years old	15.2% (354)

PRIVATE SECTOR

Businesses	744 (406)
Employees	10,045 (374)
Total wages	$357,196,480 (374)
Average weekly wages	$684 (302)

HOUSEHOLD INCOME LADDER

95th percentile	$129,262 (439)
80th percentile	$67,258 (523)
60th percentile	$36,138 (544)
40th percentile	$20,517 (547)
20th percentile	$9,862 (545)

CHILDREN ★ (463)

Living with two parents	27.8% (550)
Older teens in school	86.0% (166)
Speak English very well	100.0% (1)
Poverty rate for children	53.8% (551)
No health insurance	2.2% (15)

DIVERSITY/EQUALITY ★ (492)

Racial diversity index	43.9% (160)
Geographic diversity index	22.1% (545)
Top 20% share of income	55.5% (546)
Gender gap in earnings	36.2% (346)
White-collar gender gap	8.9% (80)

EDUCATION ★ (457)

Eighth grade or less	4.9% (380)
High school diplomas	80.5% (472)
Attended college	45.4% (433)
Bachelor's degrees	12.7% (503)
Advanced degrees	5.0% (378)

EMPLOYMENT ★ (523)

Average jobless rate	16.4% (545)
Self-employed workers	7.0% (428)
Management/financial jobs	9.0% (475)
Computer/engineering jobs	2.2% (381)
Health care jobs	6.4% (132)

GROWTH POTENTIAL ★★★ (314)

Children per senior	1.68 (141)
Median age	38.7 (211)
Moved from different state	1.4% (425)
Homes built since 2000	10.2% (386)
Construction jobs	6.1% (310)

HOUSING ★★ (429)

Home vacancy rate	13.3% (500)
Home ownership rate	58.8% (514)
Housing diversity index	86.1% (51)
4 or more bedrooms	19.9% (129)
Affordability/income ratio	$2,985 (401)

INCOME ★ (541)

Poverty rate	35.0% (541)
Median household income	$27,306 (546)
Interest/dividends	10.8% (517)
Public assistance	32.2% (541)
Median fulltime earnings	$32,684 (464)

SENIORS ★ (544)

Seniors living alone	32.0% (512)
Poverty rate for seniors	18.7% (531)
Median income for seniors	n.a.
Seniors who work	14.0% (503)
Home ownership by seniors	76.9% (493)

STABILITY ★★ (364)

25-39 age group	16.9% (338)
Born in state of residence	88.0% (7)
Same house as 1 year ago	87.9% (140)
Live and work in county	80.6% (208)
Married-couple households	31.0% (550)

TRANSPORTATION ★★ (409)

Bicycle or walk to work	2.7% (292)
Carpool to work	11.7% (170)
Public transit to work	0.3% (291)
Commute <15 minutes	35.6% (432)
Commute >45 minutes	15.8% (446)

See pages 37-130 for explanations of statistics, stars, and ranks.

Seneca, SC
(Oconee County, SC)

POPULATION

2010 census	74,273 (86)
2015 estimate	75,713 (84)
2010-2015 change	1.9% (136)
2020 projection	77,038 (78)
2030 projection	79,508 (81)

RACE

Whites	85.3% (263)
Blacks	7.4% (131)
Hispanics	4.8% (256)
Asians	0.6% (291)
Native Americans	0.2% (300)

AGE

0-17 years old	20.4% (437)
18-24 years old	8.2% (379)
25-39 years old	16.7% (375)
40-54 years old	18.8% (386)
55-64 years old	15.1% (74)
65+ years old	20.8% (39)

PRIVATE SECTOR

Businesses	1,461 (145)
Employees	19,359 (133)
Total wages	$921,071,901 (89)
Average weekly wages	$915 (30)

HOUSEHOLD INCOME LADDER

95th percentile	$160,956 (91)
80th percentile	$81,763 (328)
60th percentile	$52,406 (311)
40th percentile	$31,905 (365)
20th percentile	$18,173 (308)

CHILDREN ★★★ (317)

Living with two parents	61.8% (361)
Older teens in school	85.6% (179)
Speak English very well	98.9% (226)
Poverty rate for children	28.5% (377)
No health insurance	9.0% (393)

DIVERSITY/EQUALITY ★★★★ (181)

Racial diversity index	26.4% (283)
Geographic diversity index	59.1% (128)
Top 20% share of income	51.7% (495)
Gender gap in earnings	32.1% (230)
White-collar gender gap	2.3% (15)

EDUCATION ★★★ (252)

Eighth grade or less	4.7% (366)
High school diplomas	84.9% (376)
Attended college	52.5% (272)
Bachelor's degrees	21.8% (167)
Advanced degrees	7.7% (133)

EMPLOYMENT ★★ (347)

Average jobless rate	10.4% (437)
Self-employed workers	7.4% (393)
Management/financial jobs	11.6% (196)
Computer/engineering jobs	3.8% (96)
Health care jobs	5.1% (319)

GROWTH POTENTIAL ★★★ (250)

Children per senior	0.98 (509)
Median age	44.3 (487)
Moved from different state	3.0% (157)
Homes built since 2000	23.1% (52)
Construction jobs	6.9% (198)

HOUSING ★★★ (325)

Home vacancy rate	10.9% (400)
Home ownership rate	74.1% (115)
Housing diversity index	83.4% (396)
4 or more bedrooms	18.4% (183)
Affordability/income ratio	$3,565 (466)

INCOME ★★★ (294)

Poverty rate	20.1% (373)
Median household income	$41,237 (346)
Interest/dividends	22.1% (181)
Public assistance	15.8% (286)
Median fulltime earnings	$36,093 (329)

SENIORS ★★★★★ (79)

Seniors living alone	23.9% (80)
Poverty rate for seniors	9.3% (276)
Median income for seniors	$36,569 (133)
Seniors who work	15.6% (432)
Home ownership by seniors	90.7% (9)

STABILITY ★★ (416)

25-39 age group	16.7% (375)
Born in state of residence	60.1% (418)
Same house as 1 year ago	84.6% (319)
Live and work in county	72.1% (337)
Married-couple households	52.1% (190)

TRANSPORTATION ★ (462)

Bicycle or walk to work	1.0% (512)
Carpool to work	10.3% (299)
Public transit to work	0.5% (178)
Commute <15 minutes	32.3% (489)
Commute >45 minutes	13.4% (371)

See pages 37-130 for explanations of statistics, stars, and ranks.

Sevierville, TN
(Sevier County, TN)

POPULATION		
2010 census	89,889 (45)	
2015 estimate	95,946 (37)	
2010-2015 change	6.7% (25)	
2020 projection	102,558 (26)	
2030 projection	116,782 (19)	

RACE		
Whites	91.0% (163)	
Blacks	0.7% (423)	
Hispanics	5.4% (240)	
Asians	1.2% (125)	
Native Americans	0.3% (231)	

AGE		
0-17 years old	21.5% (373)	
18-24 years old	8.3% (362)	
25-39 years old	17.3% (280)	
40-54 years old	21.5% (57)	
55-64 years old	14.1% (174)	
65+ years old	17.2% (182)	

PRIVATE SECTOR		
Businesses	2,555 (32)	
Employees	39,163 (16)	
Total wages	$1,064,950,390 (59)	
Average weekly wages	$523 (540)	

HOUSEHOLD INCOME LADDER		
95th percentile	$135,308 (354)	
80th percentile	$80,358 (364)	
60th percentile	$52,957 (299)	
40th percentile	$34,274 (278)	
20th percentile	$19,456 (247)	

CHILDREN	★★ (401)	
Living with two parents	61.3% (373)	
Older teens in school	77.9% (452)	
Speak English very well	97.0% (413)	
Poverty rate for children	21.5% (206)	
No health insurance	10.5% (437)	

DIVERSITY/EQUALITY	★★★★ (199)	
Racial diversity index	16.9% (386)	
Geographic diversity index	66.9% (64)	
Top 20% share of income	47.9% (286)	
Gender gap in earnings	28.7% (147)	
White-collar gender gap	32.2% (367)	

EDUCATION	★★ (374)	
Eighth grade or less	5.1% (390)	
High school diplomas	85.3% (367)	
Attended college	47.0% (397)	
Bachelor's degrees	16.9% (334)	
Advanced degrees	6.1% (250)	

EMPLOYMENT	★★ (362)	
Average jobless rate	7.4% (237)	
Self-employed workers	11.1% (115)	
Management/financial jobs	10.6% (306)	
Computer/engineering jobs	2.1% (399)	
Health care jobs	3.6% (508)	

GROWTH POTENTIAL	★★★★★ (105)	
Children per senior	1.25 (385)	
Median age	42.2 (412)	
Moved from different state	4.0% (79)	
Homes built since 2000	28.0% (19)	
Construction jobs	7.4% (134)	

HOUSING	★ (546)	
Home vacancy rate	11.3% (426)	
Home ownership rate	66.5% (405)	
Housing diversity index	78.8% (529)	
4 or more bedrooms	12.7% (466)	
Affordability/income ratio	$3,763 (486)	

INCOME	★★ (346)	
Poverty rate	15.3% (204)	
Median household income	$42,258 (310)	
Interest/dividends	17.6% (325)	
Public assistance	16.7% (319)	
Median fulltime earnings	$31,891 (502)	

SENIORS	★★★★★ (47)	
Seniors living alone	21.4% (27)	
Poverty rate for seniors	7.4% (128)	
Median income for seniors	$35,969 (154)	
Seniors who work	24.3% (83)	
Home ownership by seniors	82.8% (232)	

STABILITY	★★ (427)	
25-39 age group	17.3% (280)	
Born in state of residence	51.4% (481)	
Same house as 1 year ago	82.9% (403)	
Live and work in county	76.1% (274)	
Married-couple households	53.0% (152)	

TRANSPORTATION	★★ (359)	
Bicycle or walk to work	1.7% (428)	
Carpool to work	16.1% (31)	
Public transit to work	0.7% (119)	
Commute <15 minutes	22.1% (547)	
Commute >45 minutes	13.6% (377)	

See pages 37-130 for explanations of statistics, stars, and ranks.

Shawnee, OK
(Pottawatomie County, OK)

POPULATION	
2010 census	69,442 (103)
2015 estimate	71,875 (95)
2010-2015 change	3.5% (70)
2020 projection	73,574 (91)
2030 projection	77,033 (85)

RACE	
Whites	73.5% (367)
Blacks	2.8% (232)
Hispanics	4.7% (260)
Asians	0.6% (291)
Native Americans	13.1% (16)

AGE	
0-17 years old	24.5% (149)
18-24 years old	10.3% (146)
25-39 years old	18.2% (167)
40-54 years old	19.7% (273)
55-64 years old	12.2% (424)
65+ years old	15.2% (354)

PRIVATE SECTOR	
Businesses	1,280 (183)
Employees	16,618 (179)
Total wages	$570,177,986 (203)
Average weekly wages	$660 (364)

HOUSEHOLD INCOME LADDER	
95th percentile	$150,711 (155)
80th percentile	$85,333 (246)
60th percentile	$54,340 (272)
40th percentile	$34,946 (265)
20th percentile	$18,914 (270)

CHILDREN	★★ (355)
Living with two parents	63.5% (310)
Older teens in school	81.2% (362)
Speak English very well	98.4% (300)
Poverty rate for children	25.7% (315)
No health insurance	10.2% (426)

DIVERSITY/EQUALITY	★★★★ (152)
Racial diversity index	43.7% (161)
Geographic diversity index	48.7% (234)
Top 20% share of income	48.6% (328)
Gender gap in earnings	36.6% (356)
White-collar gender gap	12.3% (119)

EDUCATION	★★★ (251)
Eighth grade or less	2.6% (185)
High school diplomas	88.1% (263)
Attended college	53.8% (249)
Bachelor's degrees	18.9% (254)
Advanced degrees	5.3% (347)

EMPLOYMENT	★★★ (284)
Average jobless rate	6.8% (179)
Self-employed workers	7.7% (362)
Management/financial jobs	12.3% (133)
Computer/engineering jobs	2.7% (270)
Health care jobs	4.7% (385)

GROWTH POTENTIAL	★★★★ (189)
Children per senior	1.61 (167)
Median age	37.6 (168)
Moved from different state	1.8% (338)
Homes built since 2000	16.8% (159)
Construction jobs	6.4% (270)

HOUSING	★★★ (293)
Home vacancy rate	10.4% (371)
Home ownership rate	68.8% (313)
Housing diversity index	85.6% (127)
4 or more bedrooms	12.9% (458)
Affordability/income ratio	$2,298 (165)

INCOME	★★★ (319)
Poverty rate	18.2% (304)
Median household income	$44,688 (243)
Interest/dividends	18.2% (305)
Public assistance	18.0% (371)
Median fulltime earnings	$35,988 (336)

SENIORS	★★★★ (202)
Seniors living alone	27.1% (247)
Poverty rate for seniors	9.2% (270)
Median income for seniors	$34,659 (205)
Seniors who work	18.1% (284)
Home ownership by seniors	84.5% (165)

STABILITY	★★★ (309)
25-39 age group	18.2% (167)
Born in state of residence	70.0% (309)
Same house as 1 year ago	83.7% (353)
Live and work in county	68.1% (404)
Married-couple households	51.7% (212)

TRANSPORTATION	★ (497)
Bicycle or walk to work	2.3% (348)
Carpool to work	8.6% (457)
Public transit to work	0.2% (363)
Commute <15 minutes	36.6% (407)
Commute >45 minutes	16.0% (453)

See pages 37-130 for explanations of statistics, stars, and ranks.

Shelby, NC
(Cleveland County, NC)

POPULATION	
2010 census	98,078 (34)
2015 estimate	96,879 (35)
2010-2015 change	-1.2% (345)
2020 projection	94,630 (40)
2030 projection	89,908 (49)

RACE	
Whites	73.6% (366)
Blacks	20.6% (75)
Hispanics	3.1% (333)
Asians	0.9% (178)
Native Americans	0.3% (231)

AGE	
0-17 years old	22.5% (300)
18-24 years old	9.6% (189)
25-39 years old	16.2% (434)
40-54 years old	21.4% (67)
55-64 years old	13.6% (247)
65+ years old	16.7% (225)

PRIVATE SECTOR	
Businesses	1,912 (72)
Employees	26,759 (63)
Total wages	$966,255,425 (77)
Average weekly wages	$694 (272)

HOUSEHOLD INCOME LADDER	
95th percentile	$130,975 (417)
80th percentile	$76,963 (422)
60th percentile	$48,746 (408)
40th percentile	$30,169 (414)
20th percentile	$15,709 (420)

CHILDREN	★★★ (289)
Living with two parents	56.7% (465)
Older teens in school	86.2% (158)
Speak English very well	99.0% (200)
Poverty rate for children	30.5% (413)
No health insurance	5.0% (181)

DIVERSITY/EQUALITY	★★★ (251)
Racial diversity index	41.5% (177)
Geographic diversity index	39.4% (367)
Top 20% share of income	49.3% (383)
Gender gap in earnings	30.2% (172)
White-collar gender gap	25.3% (274)

EDUCATION	★★★ (306)
Eighth grade or less	3.6% (292)
High school diplomas	86.1% (339)
Attended college	51.4% (295)
Bachelor's degrees	17.2% (315)
Advanced degrees	6.3% (234)

EMPLOYMENT	★ (481)
Average jobless rate	12.6% (509)
Self-employed workers	6.1% (495)
Management/financial jobs	9.1% (463)
Computer/engineering jobs	2.5% (307)
Health care jobs	6.7% (104)

GROWTH POTENTIAL	★★ (418)
Children per senior	1.35 (313)
Median age	41.4 (376)
Moved from different state	1.6% (383)
Homes built since 2000	12.1% (310)
Construction jobs	5.7% (373)

HOUSING	★★ (409)
Home vacancy rate	11.6% (441)
Home ownership rate	68.2% (336)
Housing diversity index	85.2% (190)
4 or more bedrooms	11.3% (515)
Affordability/income ratio	$2,646 (309)

INCOME	★★ (422)
Poverty rate	20.1% (373)
Median household income	$39,453 (397)
Interest/dividends	14.6% (424)
Public assistance	19.8% (419)
Median fulltime earnings	$34,842 (392)

SENIORS	★ (463)
Seniors living alone	30.0% (427)
Poverty rate for seniors	11.8% (401)
Median income for seniors	$29,342 (425)
Seniors who work	15.9% (418)
Home ownership by seniors	81.8% (286)

STABILITY	★★★ (278)
25-39 age group	16.2% (434)
Born in state of residence	76.8% (180)
Same house as 1 year ago	90.8% (32)
Live and work in county	67.1% (416)
Married-couple households	47.8% (390)

TRANSPORTATION	★ (495)
Bicycle or walk to work	1.9% (401)
Carpool to work	9.4% (394)
Public transit to work	0.5% (178)
Commute <15 minutes	29.4% (529)
Commute >45 minutes	14.4% (407)

See pages 37-130 for explanations of statistics, stars, and ranks.

Shelbyville, TN
(Bedford County, TN)

POPULATION

2010 census	45,058 (259)
2015 estimate	47,183 (234)
2010-2015 change	4.7% (45)
2020 projection	49,658 (215)
2030 projection	54,794 (187)

RACE

Whites	78.1% (338)
Blacks	6.6% (139)
Hispanics	11.6% (130)
Asians	0.7% (241)
Native Americans	0.1% (402)

AGE

0-17 years old	26.2% (63)
18-24 years old	8.7% (299)
25-39 years old	18.9% (111)
40-54 years old	20.3% (186)
55-64 years old	11.6% (471)
65+ years old	14.4% (419)

PRIVATE SECTOR

Businesses	766 (389)
Employees	16,004 (193)
Total wages	$617,833,127 (180)
Average weekly wages	$742 (173)

HOUSEHOLD INCOME LADDER

95th percentile	$129,963 (433)
80th percentile	$77,421 (410)
60th percentile	$50,620 (367)
40th percentile	$32,908 (328)
20th percentile	$19,111 (260)

CHILDREN ★★ (331)

Living with two parents	64.3% (288)
Older teens in school	80.2% (392)
Speak English very well	95.2% (473)
Poverty rate for children	24.1% (276)
No health insurance	5.5% (218)

DIVERSITY/EQUALITY ★★★★ (125)

Racial diversity index	37.1% (204)
Geographic diversity index	54.6% (157)
Top 20% share of income	47.3% (245)
Gender gap in earnings	22.8% (66)
White-collar gender gap	37.4% (412)

EDUCATION ★ (499)

Eighth grade or less	6.3% (439)
High school diplomas	80.6% (471)
Attended college	39.2% (523)
Bachelor's degrees	13.8% (469)
Advanced degrees	3.7% (498)

EMPLOYMENT ★★★ (238)

Average jobless rate	7.7% (260)
Self-employed workers	12.3% (62)
Management/financial jobs	10.9% (263)
Computer/engineering jobs	2.2% (381)
Health care jobs	4.7% (385)

GROWTH POTENTIAL ★★★★★ (65)

Children per senior	1.82 (90)
Median age	36.6 (134)
Moved from different state	2.4% (218)
Homes built since 2000	21.5% (74)
Construction jobs	8.2% (78)

HOUSING ★★★ (222)

Home vacancy rate	8.4% (245)
Home ownership rate	68.2% (336)
Housing diversity index	85.0% (226)
4 or more bedrooms	17.9% (209)
Affordability/income ratio	$2,756 (349)

INCOME ★★ (398)

Poverty rate	17.1% (267)
Median household income	$41,984 (322)
Interest/dividends	17.2% (339)
Public assistance	20.3% (437)
Median fulltime earnings	$31,496 (517)

SENIORS ★★★★★ (53)

Seniors living alone	21.2% (23)
Poverty rate for seniors	9.1% (263)
Median income for seniors	$33,975 (235)
Seniors who work	20.8% (166)
Home ownership by seniors	87.9% (42)

STABILITY ★★★ (248)

25-39 age group	18.9% (111)
Born in state of residence	65.1% (385)
Same house as 1 year ago	85.2% (294)
Live and work in county	64.7% (450)
Married-couple households	54.3% (99)

TRANSPORTATION ★ (443)

Bicycle or walk to work	1.1% (501)
Carpool to work	14.1% (61)
Public transit to work	0.2% (363)
Commute <15 minutes	37.6% (385)
Commute >45 minutes	19.6% (513)

See pages 37-130 for explanations of statistics, stars, and ranks.

Snyder, TX
(Scurry County, TX)

POPULATION	
2010 census	16,921 (537)
2015 estimate	17,615 (535)
2010-2015 change	4.1% (57)
2020 projection	18,092 (534)
2030 projection	19,065 (526)

RACE	
Whites	55.1% (472)
Blacks	4.5% (176)
Hispanics	38.7% (41)
Asians	0.3% (473)
Native Americans	0.2% (300)

AGE	
0-17 years old	25.3% (97)
18-24 years old	9.9% (168)
25-39 years old	20.6% (49)
40-54 years old	18.6% (412)
55-64 years old	11.5% (478)
65+ years old	14.1% (431)

PRIVATE SECTOR	
Businesses	441 (532)
Employees	6,206 (503)
Total wages	$337,498,588 (394)
Average weekly wages	$1,046 (15)

HOUSEHOLD INCOME LADDER	
95th percentile	$179,500 (40)
80th percentile	$103,245 (47)
60th percentile	$69,689 (39)
40th percentile	$45,078 (45)
20th percentile	$26,455 (32)

CHILDREN	★★★ (230)
Living with two parents	72.9% (82)
Older teens in school	84.3% (229)
Speak English very well	96.1% (446)
Poverty rate for children	11.3% (23)
No health insurance	13.3% (502)

DIVERSITY/EQUALITY	★★★ (314)
Racial diversity index	54.4% (63)
Geographic diversity index	39.5% (363)
Top 20% share of income	46.3% (142)
Gender gap in earnings	53.4% (538)
White-collar gender gap	25.2% (273)

EDUCATION	★ (448)
Eighth grade or less	8.9% (505)
High school diplomas	82.4% (433)
Attended college	54.9% (227)
Bachelor's degrees	14.9% (424)
Advanced degrees	4.0% (478)

EMPLOYMENT	★ (450)
Average jobless rate	3.3% (16)
Self-employed workers	6.8% (446)
Management/financial jobs	9.4% (444)
Computer/engineering jobs	1.7% (470)
Health care jobs	3.3% (517)

GROWTH POTENTIAL	★★★★ (170)
Children per senior	1.79 (99)
Median age	36.0 (116)
Moved from different state	1.0% (504)
Homes built since 2000	6.2% (522)
Construction jobs	9.0% (47)

HOUSING	★★★ (276)
Home vacancy rate	11.9% (458)
Home ownership rate	75.8% (60)
Housing diversity index	83.8% (369)
4 or more bedrooms	10.7% (522)
Affordability/income ratio	$1,568 (6)

INCOME	★★★★★ (58)
Poverty rate	9.9% (28)
Median household income	$56,842 (41)
Interest/dividends	23.9% (130)
Public assistance	11.6% (116)
Median fulltime earnings	$42,765 (50)

SENIORS	★★★★★ (62)
Seniors living alone	25.1% (120)
Poverty rate for seniors	9.6% (295)
Median income for seniors	$37,500 (102)
Seniors who work	24.8% (74)
Home ownership by seniors	86.3% (87)

STABILITY	★★★★★ (2)
25-39 age group	20.6% (49)
Born in state of residence	77.2% (175)
Same house as 1 year ago	83.7% (353)
Live and work in county	90.4% (59)
Married-couple households	57.3% (27)

TRANSPORTATION	★★★★★ (100)
Bicycle or walk to work	1.4% (472)
Carpool to work	10.9% (239)
Public transit to work	0.9% (83)
Commute <15 minutes	66.6% (11)
Commute >45 minutes	7.5% (105)

See pages 37-130 for explanations of statistics, stars, and ranks.

Somerset, KY
(Pulaski County, KY)

POPULATION

2010 census	63,063 (132)
2015 estimate	63,782 (128)
2010-2015 change	1.1% (181)
2020 projection	64,868 (125)
2030 projection	66,890 (120)

RACE

Whites	94.5% (61)
Blacks	0.9% (388)
Hispanics	2.3% (398)
Asians	0.8% (201)
Native Americans	0.1% (402)

AGE

0-17 years old	22.6% (291)
18-24 years old	7.7% (454)
25-39 years old	17.2% (290)
40-54 years old	21.3% (73)
55-64 years old	13.8% (203)
65+ years old	17.3% (172)

PRIVATE SECTOR

Businesses	1,624 (118)
Employees	21,576 (102)
Total wages	$745,368,542 (137)
Average weekly wages	$664 (344)

HOUSEHOLD INCOME LADDER

95th percentile	$127,761 (460)
80th percentile	$72,420 (490)
60th percentile	$44,330 (487)
40th percentile	$26,105 (496)
20th percentile	$11,924 (524)

CHILDREN ★★★ (284)

Living with two parents	58.2% (445)
Older teens in school	85.4% (191)
Speak English very well	99.7% (57)
Poverty rate for children	35.6% (483)
No health insurance	3.3% (72)

DIVERSITY/EQUALITY ★ (457)

Racial diversity index	10.6% (485)
Geographic diversity index	40.5% (342)
Top 20% share of income	52.3% (511)
Gender gap in earnings	24.6% (83)
White-collar gender gap	25.6% (281)

EDUCATION ★★ (408)

Eighth grade or less	6.2% (433)
High school diplomas	85.9% (345)
Attended college	43.9% (453)
Bachelor's degrees	16.0% (372)
Advanced degrees	6.0% (264)

EMPLOYMENT ★★★★ (199)

Average jobless rate	9.1% (370)
Self-employed workers	9.0% (254)
Management/financial jobs	9.9% (392)
Computer/engineering jobs	1.8% (457)
Health care jobs	8.4% (11)

GROWTH POTENTIAL ★★★ (239)

Children per senior	1.31 (344)
Median age	42.0 (398)
Moved from different state	1.7% (355)
Homes built since 2000	19.9% (92)
Construction jobs	7.1% (173)

HOUSING ★★★ (281)

Home vacancy rate	7.6% (193)
Home ownership rate	69.0% (303)
Housing diversity index	84.0% (344)
4 or more bedrooms	16.1% (286)
Affordability/income ratio	$3,070 (412)

INCOME ★ (488)

Poverty rate	26.3% (490)
Median household income	$34,790 (488)
Interest/dividends	15.6% (390)
Public assistance	20.6% (445)
Median fulltime earnings	$31,946 (498)

SENIORS ★ (461)

Seniors living alone	26.5% (201)
Poverty rate for seniors	17.0% (519)
Median income for seniors	$27,326 (473)
Seniors who work	14.1% (500)
Home ownership by seniors	85.9% (105)

STABILITY ★★★★★ (74)

25-39 age group	17.2% (290)
Born in state of residence	75.7% (211)
Same house as 1 year ago	87.7% (154)
Live and work in county	89.7% (68)
Married-couple households	49.3% (333)

TRANSPORTATION ★★★ (321)

Bicycle or walk to work	1.8% (409)
Carpool to work	10.1% (322)
Public transit to work	0.3% (291)
Commute <15 minutes	42.1% (296)
Commute >45 minutes	8.1% (135)

See pages 37-130 for explanations of statistics, stars, and ranks.

Starkville, MS
(Oktibbeha County, MS)

POPULATION	
2010 census	47,671 (224)
2015 estimate	49,800 (212)
2010-2015 change	4.5% (51)
2020 projection	51,728 (201)
2030 projection	55,424 (179)

RACE	
Whites	57.4% (461)
Blacks	36.9% (36)
Hispanics	1.6% (472)
Asians	3.0% (23)
Native Americans	0.2% (300)

AGE	
0-17 years old	17.9% (528)
18-24 years old	32.1% (3)
25-39 years old	17.0% (317)
40-54 years old	14.2% (543)
55-64 years old	8.8% (545)
65+ years old	9.9% (532)

PRIVATE SECTOR	
Businesses	865 (335)
Employees	11,843 (313)
Total wages	$314,973,716 (415)
Average weekly wages	$511 (543)

HOUSEHOLD INCOME LADDER	
95th percentile	$164,035 (76)
80th percentile	$81,262 (342)
60th percentile	$42,001 (507)
40th percentile	$23,912 (524)
20th percentile	$10,458 (541)

CHILDREN	★★★★ (214)
Living with two parents	56.1% (472)
Older teens in school	97.7% (6)
Speak English very well	98.6% (278)
Poverty rate for children	31.6% (437)
No health insurance	7.1% (324)

DIVERSITY/EQUALITY	★★★ (289)
Racial diversity index	53.3% (75)
Geographic diversity index	49.0% (228)
Top 20% share of income	56.7% (550)
Gender gap in earnings	40.0% (438)
White-collar gender gap	3.3% (20)

EDUCATION	★★★★★ (23)
Eighth grade or less	2.9% (217)
High school diplomas	87.9% (272)
Attended college	69.4% (30)
Bachelor's degrees	44.8% (12)
Advanced degrees	20.8% (5)

EMPLOYMENT	★★ (381)
Average jobless rate	13.3% (521)
Self-employed workers	5.1% (540)
Management/financial jobs	10.9% (263)
Computer/engineering jobs	5.9% (14)
Health care jobs	5.8% (209)

GROWTH POTENTIAL	★★★★★ (28)
Children per senior	1.81 (93)
Median age	25.0 (3)
Moved from different state	6.9% (25)
Homes built since 2000	26.7% (30)
Construction jobs	4.3% (514)

HOUSING	★ (550)
Home vacancy rate	12.5% (476)
Home ownership rate	52.7% (541)
Housing diversity index	81.6% (475)
4 or more bedrooms	17.3% (232)
Affordability/income ratio	$4,374 (510)

INCOME	★ (473)
Poverty rate	33.7% (538)
Median household income	$32,485 (513)
Interest/dividends	15.9% (380)
Public assistance	15.3% (272)
Median fulltime earnings	$37,018 (285)

SENIORS	★★★★★ (109)
Seniors living alone	25.2% (124)
Poverty rate for seniors	11.2% (384)
Median income for seniors	$39,945 (61)
Seniors who work	13.7% (514)
Home ownership by seniors	90.9% (7)

STABILITY	★ (545)
25-39 age group	17.0% (317)
Born in state of residence	68.8% (331)
Same house as 1 year ago	73.6% (533)
Live and work in county	80.8% (206)
Married-couple households	36.1% (543)

TRANSPORTATION	★★★★★ (102)
Bicycle or walk to work	4.1% (147)
Carpool to work	12.1% (135)
Public transit to work	0.2% (363)
Commute <15 minutes	55.4% (87)
Commute >45 minutes	7.1% (88)

See pages 37-130 for explanations of statistics, stars, and ranks.

Statesboro, GA
(Bulloch County, GA)

POPULATION

2010 census	70,217 (99)
2015 estimate	72,651 (92)
2010-2015 change	3.5% (70)
2020 projection	75,594 (87)
2030 projection	81,597 (72)

RACE

Whites	64.0% (422)
Blacks	28.3% (60)
Hispanics	3.6% (314)
Asians	1.8% (60)
Native Americans	0.3% (231)

AGE

0-17 years old	20.4% (437)
18-24 years old	26.7% (11)
25-39 years old	17.6% (248)
40-54 years old	16.2% (521)
55-64 years old	9.3% (539)
65+ years old	9.9% (532)

PRIVATE SECTOR

Businesses	1,473 (141)
Employees	18,082 (152)
Total wages	$537,603,633 (222)
Average weekly wages	$572 (518)

HOUSEHOLD INCOME LADDER

95th percentile	$141,253 (276)
80th percentile	$79,670 (376)
60th percentile	$47,611 (433)
40th percentile	$27,109 (483)
20th percentile	$12,131 (514)

CHILDREN ★★★ (245)

Living with two parents	59.7% (408)
Older teens in school	91.9% (40)
Speak English very well	99.2% (163)
Poverty rate for children	32.4% (455)
No health insurance	6.8% (302)

DIVERSITY/EQUALITY ★★ (382)

Racial diversity index	50.8% (107)
Geographic diversity index	49.0% (228)
Top 20% share of income	52.0% (504)
Gender gap in earnings	35.3% (321)
White-collar gender gap	40.9% (453)

EDUCATION ★★★★★ (67)

Eighth grade or less	3.1% (238)
High school diplomas	88.5% (253)
Attended college	61.7% (100)
Bachelor's degrees	30.5% (50)
Advanced degrees	12.1% (36)

EMPLOYMENT ★★★ (243)

Average jobless rate	9.1% (370)
Self-employed workers	10.0% (168)
Management/financial jobs	11.2% (229)
Computer/engineering jobs	2.6% (288)
Health care jobs	5.9% (193)

GROWTH POTENTIAL ★★★★★ (32)

Children per senior	2.07 (51)
Median age	26.3 (6)
Moved from different state	1.7% (355)
Homes built since 2000	32.7% (11)
Construction jobs	6.0% (326)

HOUSING ★ (535)

Home vacancy rate	8.4% (245)
Home ownership rate	49.6% (547)
Housing diversity index	79.9% (517)
4 or more bedrooms	20.1% (122)
Affordability/income ratio	$3,600 (469)

INCOME ★ (496)

Poverty rate	32.9% (536)
Median household income	$36,032 (466)
Interest/dividends	10.6% (521)
Public assistance	16.6% (316)
Median fulltime earnings	$34,224 (413)

SENIORS ★★★★ (135)

Seniors living alone	24.4% (94)
Poverty rate for seniors	11.6% (392)
Median income for seniors	$38,584 (80)
Seniors who work	22.7% (114)
Home ownership by seniors	81.6% (299)

STABILITY ★ (528)

25-39 age group	17.6% (248)
Born in state of residence	69.5% (321)
Same house as 1 year ago	77.1% (522)
Live and work in county	76.6% (261)
Married-couple households	41.1% (515)

TRANSPORTATION ★★★ (254)

Bicycle or walk to work	3.1% (232)
Carpool to work	11.7% (170)
Public transit to work	1.0% (69)
Commute <15 minutes	47.2% (211)
Commute >45 minutes	14.8% (419)

See pages 37-130 for explanations of statistics, stars, and ranks.

Stephenville, TX
(Erath County, TX)

POPULATION	
2010 census	37,890 (343)
2015 estimate	41,122 (299)
2010-2015 change	8.5% (12)
2020 projection	43,652 (276)
2030 projection	49,106 (224)

RACE	
Whites	76.2% (351)
Blacks	1.4% (340)
Hispanics	19.9% (78)
Asians	0.7% (241)
Native Americans	0.6% (150)

AGE	
0-17 years old	21.3% (383)
18-24 years old	22.0% (21)
25-39 years old	16.6% (388)
40-54 years old	16.5% (516)
55-64 years old	10.3% (510)
65+ years old	13.4% (463)

PRIVATE SECTOR	
Businesses	1,008 (273)
Employees	12,180 (303)
Total wages	$398,453,171 (339)
Average weekly wages	$629 (439)

HOUSEHOLD INCOME LADDER	
95th percentile	$144,779 (232)
80th percentile	$82,433 (310)
60th percentile	$50,293 (375)
40th percentile	$31,372 (377)
20th percentile	$13,521 (490)

CHILDREN	★★ (408)
Living with two parents	69.3% (161)
Older teens in school	91.3% (49)
Speak English very well	93.4% (501)
Poverty rate for children	23.8% (268)
No health insurance	18.2% (540)

DIVERSITY/EQUALITY	★ (530)
Racial diversity index	37.9% (196)
Geographic diversity index	49.5% (217)
Top 20% share of income	52.8% (518)
Gender gap in earnings	45.2% (503)
White-collar gender gap	45.7% (484)

EDUCATION	★★★★ (211)
Eighth grade or less	7.4% (477)
High school diplomas	85.2% (368)
Attended college	58.4% (161)
Bachelor's degrees	27.6% (79)
Advanced degrees	7.9% (126)

EMPLOYMENT	★★★★ (155)
Average jobless rate	4.1% (35)
Self-employed workers	12.5% (56)
Management/financial jobs	12.6% (111)
Computer/engineering jobs	2.3% (354)
Health care jobs	3.2% (525)

GROWTH POTENTIAL	★★★★★ (96)
Children per senior	1.59 (175)
Median age	30.3 (31)
Moved from different state	1.7% (355)
Homes built since 2000	21.2% (76)
Construction jobs	6.1% (310)

HOUSING	★ (490)
Home vacancy rate	10.2% (358)
Home ownership rate	59.8% (505)
Housing diversity index	84.5% (287)
4 or more bedrooms	12.7% (466)
Affordability/income ratio	$2,938 (388)

INCOME	★★ (385)
Poverty rate	24.4% (471)
Median household income	$41,416 (339)
Interest/dividends	13.4% (458)
Public assistance	11.1% (96)
Median fulltime earnings	$34,532 (403)

SENIORS	★★ (351)
Seniors living alone	25.1% (120)
Poverty rate for seniors	17.4% (522)
Median income for seniors	$34,712 (202)
Seniors who work	24.9% (73)
Home ownership by seniors	77.5% (471)

STABILITY	★★ (396)
25-39 age group	16.6% (388)
Born in state of residence	69.9% (310)
Same house as 1 year ago	81.6% (456)
Live and work in county	83.2% (159)
Married-couple households	48.4% (366)

TRANSPORTATION	★★★★ (178)
Bicycle or walk to work	3.3% (211)
Carpool to work	11.7% (170)
Public transit to work	0.4% (219)
Commute <15 minutes	52.2% (118)
Commute >45 minutes	10.5% (254)

See pages 37-130 for explanations of statistics, stars, and ranks.

Stillwater, OK
(Payne County, OK)

POPULATION	
2010 census	77,350 (75)
2015 estimate	80,850 (66)
2010-2015 change	4.5% (51)
2020 projection	84,168 (62)
2030 projection	91,146 (47)

RACE	
Whites	77.8% (341)
Blacks	3.6% (206)
Hispanics	4.4% (270)
Asians	4.2% (13)
Native Americans	4.3% (40)

AGE	
0-17 years old	19.3% (492)
18-24 years old	27.2% (10)
25-39 years old	19.2% (88)
40-54 years old	14.2% (543)
55-64 years old	9.3% (539)
65+ years old	10.8% (515)

PRIVATE SECTOR	
Businesses	1,874 (77)
Employees	21,283 (109)
Total wages	$722,489,122 (145)
Average weekly wages	$653 (385)

HOUSEHOLD INCOME LADDER	
95th percentile	$159,801 (99)
80th percentile	$82,325 (317)
60th percentile	$47,570 (434)
40th percentile	$28,255 (457)
20th percentile	$13,365 (492)

CHILDREN	★★★★ (175)
Living with two parents	66.4% (235)
Older teens in school	90.3% (62)
Speak English very well	98.1% (331)
Poverty rate for children	24.7% (290)
No health insurance	7.5% (344)

DIVERSITY/EQUALITY	★★★ (304)
Racial diversity index	38.5% (192)
Geographic diversity index	61.6% (108)
Top 20% share of income	53.6% (530)
Gender gap in earnings	29.3% (160)
White-collar gender gap	31.1% (355)

EDUCATION	★★★★★ (20)
Eighth grade or less	2.3% (161)
High school diplomas	92.5% (110)
Attended college	66.7% (40)
Bachelor's degrees	39.1% (17)
Advanced degrees	16.0% (12)

EMPLOYMENT	★★★ (222)
Average jobless rate	6.3% (140)
Self-employed workers	7.4% (393)
Management/financial jobs	10.7% (287)
Computer/engineering jobs	4.9% (33)
Health care jobs	4.7% (385)

GROWTH POTENTIAL	★★★★★ (24)
Children per senior	1.79 (99)
Median age	27.2 (11)
Moved from different state	5.8% (32)
Homes built since 2000	25.7% (33)
Construction jobs	6.6% (241)

HOUSING	★ (519)
Home vacancy rate	9.8% (341)
Home ownership rate	50.2% (546)
Housing diversity index	84.4% (299)
4 or more bedrooms	16.3% (279)
Affordability/income ratio	$3,600 (469)

INCOME	★★ (363)
Poverty rate	25.9% (485)
Median household income	$37,667 (435)
Interest/dividends	19.9% (247)
Public assistance	11.1% (96)
Median fulltime earnings	$34,776 (397)

SENIORS	★★★★ (192)
Seniors living alone	29.3% (389)
Poverty rate for seniors	6.6% (68)
Median income for seniors	$39,440 (64)
Seniors who work	21.1% (156)
Home ownership by seniors	79.6% (388)

STABILITY	★ (525)
25-39 age group	19.2% (88)
Born in state of residence	58.6% (431)
Same house as 1 year ago	71.7% (540)
Live and work in county	86.7% (104)
Married-couple households	42.7% (499)

TRANSPORTATION	★★★★★ (40)
Bicycle or walk to work	6.6% (49)
Carpool to work	11.6% (178)
Public transit to work	1.4% (46)
Commute <15 minutes	55.5% (86)
Commute >45 minutes	7.6% (111)

See pages 37-130 for explanations of statistics, stars, and ranks.

Sulphur Springs, TX
(Hopkins County, TX)

POPULATION	
2010 census	35,161 (382)
2015 estimate	36,223 (370)
2010-2015 change	3.0% (86)
2020 projection	37,195 (357)
2030 projection	39,151 (326)

RACE	
Whites	74.4% (362)
Blacks	6.8% (136)
Hispanics	16.0% (98)
Asians	0.7% (241)
Native Americans	0.3% (231)

AGE	
0-17 years old	25.3% (97)
18-24 years old	8.2% (379)
25-39 years old	17.8% (227)
40-54 years old	19.1% (354)
55-64 years old	12.6% (385)
65+ years old	17.0% (197)

PRIVATE SECTOR	
Businesses	764 (390)
Employees	10,120 (372)
Total wages	$369,242,774 (365)
Average weekly wages	$702 (251)

HOUSEHOLD INCOME LADDER	
95th percentile	$145,582 (221)
80th percentile	$84,618 (259)
60th percentile	$55,699 (233)
40th percentile	$34,149 (283)
20th percentile	$18,960 (268)

CHILDREN	★ (512)
Living with two parents	66.9% (220)
Older teens in school	68.1% (540)
Speak English very well	98.5% (287)
Poverty rate for children	31.3% (431)
No health insurance	15.3% (527)

DIVERSITY/EQUALITY	★★ (387)
Racial diversity index	41.6% (176)
Geographic diversity index	44.1% (293)
Top 20% share of income	49.1% (364)
Gender gap in earnings	35.0% (314)
White-collar gender gap	45.0% (481)

EDUCATION	★ (461)
Eighth grade or less	8.1% (491)
High school diplomas	83.1% (417)
Attended college	45.8% (426)
Bachelor's degrees	15.6% (407)
Advanced degrees	4.9% (396)

EMPLOYMENT	★★★★ (134)
Average jobless rate	7.1% (208)
Self-employed workers	10.7% (129)
Management/financial jobs	12.0% (156)
Computer/engineering jobs	1.9% (441)
Health care jobs	6.5% (121)

GROWTH POTENTIAL	★★★★ (192)
Children per senior	1.49 (220)
Median age	39.2 (248)
Moved from different state	1.9% (310)
Homes built since 2000	17.2% (150)
Construction jobs	7.1% (173)

HOUSING	★★★★ (180)
Home vacancy rate	7.3% (176)
Home ownership rate	71.1% (222)
Housing diversity index	85.3% (170)
4 or more bedrooms	11.9% (500)
Affordability/income ratio	$2,090 (79)

INCOME	★★★ (315)
Poverty rate	19.9% (366)
Median household income	$44,396 (252)
Interest/dividends	18.4% (296)
Public assistance	14.4% (225)
Median fulltime earnings	$34,665 (399)

SENIORS	★★★★★ (75)
Seniors living alone	24.0% (84)
Poverty rate for seniors	10.4% (342)
Median income for seniors	$34,624 (207)
Seniors who work	24.8% (74)
Home ownership by seniors	85.5% (126)

STABILITY	★★★★ (166)
25-39 age group	17.8% (227)
Born in state of residence	73.9% (247)
Same house as 1 year ago	82.9% (403)
Live and work in county	72.8% (332)
Married-couple households	56.6% (37)

TRANSPORTATION	★★★ (323)
Bicycle or walk to work	2.9% (265)
Carpool to work	10.4% (289)
Public transit to work	0.1% (441)
Commute <15 minutes	43.8% (264)
Commute >45 minutes	11.0% (273)

See pages 37-130 for explanations of statistics, stars, and ranks.

Summerville, GA
(Chattooga County, GA)

POPULATION

2010 census	26,015 (472)
2015 estimate	24,922 (484)
2010-2015 change	-4.2% (525)
2020 projection	23,951 (488)
2030 projection	22,039 (500)

RACE

Whites	82.6% (295)
Blacks	10.7% (112)
Hispanics	4.6% (264)
Asians	0.6% (291)
Native Americans	0.1% (402)

AGE

0-17 years old	22.7% (284)
18-24 years old	8.6% (317)
25-39 years old	18.2% (167)
40-54 years old	21.5% (57)
55-64 years old	13.4% (274)
65+ years old	15.6% (328)

PRIVATE SECTOR

Businesses	294 (548)
Employees	4,931 (530)
Total wages	$154,302,874 (532)
Average weekly wages	$602 (486)

HOUSEHOLD INCOME LADDER

95th percentile	$111,000 (544)
80th percentile	$62,502 (545)
60th percentile	$40,517 (525)
40th percentile	$25,444 (507)
20th percentile	$13,574 (489)

CHILDREN ★ (447)

Living with two parents	58.1% (447)
Older teens in school	75.0% (503)
Speak English very well	96.1% (446)
Poverty rate for children	31.3% (431)
No health insurance	5.4% (209)

DIVERSITY/EQUALITY ★★★★ (124)

Racial diversity index	30.4% (251)
Geographic diversity index	39.8% (357)
Top 20% share of income	49.0% (362)
Gender gap in earnings	20.2% (44)
White-collar gender gap	10.4% (93)

EDUCATION ★ (535)

Eighth grade or less	7.7% (484)
High school diplomas	74.4% (527)
Attended college	33.4% (544)
Bachelor's degrees	8.6% (546)
Advanced degrees	3.0% (532)

EMPLOYMENT ★★ (394)

Average jobless rate	10.0% (420)
Self-employed workers	9.3% (224)
Management/financial jobs	9.6% (427)
Computer/engineering jobs	2.2% (381)
Health care jobs	5.7% (222)

GROWTH POTENTIAL ★★★ (312)

Children per senior	1.45 (244)
Median age	40.3 (319)
Moved from different state	1.5% (406)
Homes built since 2000	9.4% (414)
Construction jobs	7.6% (110)

HOUSING ★★ (404)

Home vacancy rate	12.6% (481)
Home ownership rate	66.3% (410)
Housing diversity index	86.1% (51)
4 or more bedrooms	9.2% (544)
Affordability/income ratio	$1,941 (37)

INCOME ★ (505)

Poverty rate	23.7% (462)
Median household income	$32,913 (506)
Interest/dividends	9.3% (536)
Public assistance	21.9% (476)
Median fulltime earnings	$31,209 (521)

SENIORS ★ (546)

Seniors living alone	29.1% (371)
Poverty rate for seniors	20.4% (542)
Median income for seniors	$22,885 (521)
Seniors who work	11.4% (546)
Home ownership by seniors	77.2% (478)

STABILITY ★★ (378)

25-39 age group	18.2% (167)
Born in state of residence	75.9% (207)
Same house as 1 year ago	87.5% (165)
Live and work in county	59.1% (494)
Married-couple households	46.8% (425)

TRANSPORTATION ★ (513)

Bicycle or walk to work	1.6% (443)
Carpool to work	9.0% (435)
Public transit to work	0.6% (141)
Commute <15 minutes	30.5% (517)
Commute >45 minutes	15.5% (441)

See pages 37-130 for explanations of statistics, stars, and ranks.

Sweetwater, TX
(Nolan County, TX)

POPULATION				
2010 census	15,216 (543)		Attended college	47.1% (396)
2015 estimate	15,107 (544)		Bachelor's degrees	12.1% (515)
2010-2015 change	-0.7% (303)		Advanced degrees	2.8% (540)
2020 projection	14,967 (545)		**EMPLOYMENT**	**★★ (425)**
2030 projection	14,668 (545)		Average jobless rate	7.7% (260)

RACE		Self-employed workers	8.1% (323)
Whites	58.2% (457)	Management/financial jobs	10.3% (339)
Blacks	4.2% (181)	Computer/engineering jobs	1.0% (536)
Hispanics	35.5% (44)	Health care jobs	5.2% (307)
Asians	0.4% (413)	**GROWTH POTENTIAL**	**★ (441)**
Native Americans	0.2% (300)	Children per senior	1.49 (220)
		Median age	37.9 (179)
AGE		Moved from different state	1.9% (310)
0-17 years old	25.0% (126)	Homes built since 2000	3.2% (549)
18-24 years old	10.2% (151)	Construction jobs	5.7% (373)
25-39 years old	16.9% (338)	**HOUSING**	**★ (445)**
40-54 years old	17.9% (454)	Home vacancy rate	14.1% (520)
55-64 years old	13.2% (297)	Home ownership rate	67.3% (377)
65+ years old	16.8% (215)	Housing diversity index	84.6% (277)
		4 or more bedrooms	9.6% (539)
PRIVATE SECTOR		Affordability/income ratio	$1,542 (5)
Businesses	355 (539)	**INCOME**	**★★ (423)**
Employees	4,531 (535)	Poverty rate	21.2% (407)
Total wages	$182,070,590 (517)	Median household income	$37,102 (442)
Average weekly wages	$773 (125)	Interest/dividends	16.5% (360)
		Public assistance	17.4% (352)
HOUSEHOLD INCOME LADDER		Median fulltime earnings	$33,235 (447)
95th percentile	$126,260 (477)	**SENIORS**	**★ (462)**
80th percentile	$78,471 (393)	Seniors living alone	30.6% (454)
60th percentile	$45,913 (463)	Poverty rate for seniors	13.7% (465)
40th percentile	$28,333 (453)	Median income for seniors	$27,690 (465)
20th percentile	$16,379 (391)	Seniors who work	20.5% (180)
		Home ownership by seniors	81.7% (294)
CHILDREN	**★★ (430)**	**STABILITY**	**★★★ (267)**
Living with two parents	60.7% (386)	25-39 age group	16.9% (338)
Older teens in school	79.7% (407)	Born in state of residence	82.4% (77)
Speak English very well	98.0% (341)	Same house as 1 year ago	81.2% (474)
Poverty rate for children	30.4% (411)	Live and work in county	87.0% (100)
No health insurance	10.2% (426)	Married-couple households	46.7% (427)
DIVERSITY/EQUALITY	**★★ (347)**	**TRANSPORTATION**	**★★★★★ (97)**
Racial diversity index	53.3% (75)	Bicycle or walk to work	3.0% (249)
Geographic diversity index	31.5% (472)	Carpool to work	11.7% (170)
Top 20% share of income	49.8% (415)	Public transit to work	0.2% (363)
Gender gap in earnings	33.4% (268)	Commute <15 minutes	64.0% (24)
White-collar gender gap	34.0% (382)	Commute >45 minutes	7.5% (105)
EDUCATION	**★ (482)**		
Eighth grade or less	6.3% (439)		
High school diplomas	82.9% (423)		

See pages 37-130 for explanations of statistics, stars, and ranks.

Tahlequah, OK
(Cherokee County, OK)

POPULATION

2010 census	46,987 (234)
2015 estimate	48,447 (222)
2010-2015 change	3.1% (78)
2020 projection	49,706 (214)
2030 projection	52,274 (200)

RACE

Whites	49.5% (488)
Blacks	1.2% (361)
Hispanics	6.6% (207)
Asians	0.6% (291)
Native Americans	32.1% (5)

AGE

0-17 years old	23.2% (251)
18-24 years old	14.9% (57)
25-39 years old	17.5% (258)
40-54 years old	17.7% (464)
55-64 years old	11.9% (447)
65+ years old	14.7% (389)

PRIVATE SECTOR

Businesses	678 (442)
Employees	7,306 (461)
Total wages	$189,188,409 (513)
Average weekly wages	$498 (545)

HOUSEHOLD INCOME LADDER

95th percentile	$132,659 (392)
80th percentile	$80,059 (366)
60th percentile	$49,457 (394)
40th percentile	$30,083 (417)
20th percentile	$15,480 (434)

CHILDREN ★ **(446)**

Living with two parents	59.0% (429)
Older teens in school	81.9% (325)
Speak English very well	99.0% (200)
Poverty rate for children	29.7% (395)
No health insurance	14.2% (513)

DIVERSITY/EQUALITY ★★★★★ **(25)**

Racial diversity index	63.7% (6)
Geographic diversity index	51.0% (196)
Top 20% share of income	49.1% (377)
Gender gap in earnings	11.7% (12)
White-collar gender gap	23.3% (254)

EDUCATION ★★★★ **(165)**

Eighth grade or less	3.3% (259)
High school diplomas	87.2% (299)
Attended college	55.7% (209)
Bachelor's degrees	24.4% (120)
Advanced degrees	8.8% (92)

EMPLOYMENT ★★★ **(271)**

Average jobless rate	7.9% (286)
Self-employed workers	8.2% (314)
Management/financial jobs	12.0% (156)
Computer/engineering jobs	1.6% (486)
Health care jobs	6.2% (156)

GROWTH POTENTIAL ★★★★ **(132)**

Children per senior	1.58 (182)
Median age	34.8 (88)
Moved from different state	1.9% (310)
Homes built since 2000	20.0% (91)
Construction jobs	6.3% (284)

HOUSING ★ **(517)**

Home vacancy rate	14.4% (527)
Home ownership rate	66.8% (396)
Housing diversity index	83.0% (417)
4 or more bedrooms	12.2% (487)
Affordability/income ratio	$2,794 (358)

INCOME ★ **(441)**

Poverty rate	22.6% (438)
Median household income	$38,694 (412)
Interest/dividends	14.0% (442)
Public assistance	16.9% (327)
Median fulltime earnings	$33,211 (448)

SENIORS ★★ **(334)**

Seniors living alone	24.9% (113)
Poverty rate for seniors	12.6% (439)
Median income for seniors	$32,949 (287)
Seniors who work	16.9% (348)
Home ownership by seniors	81.3% (316)

STABILITY ★★ **(383)**

25-39 age group	17.5% (258)
Born in state of residence	68.1% (344)
Same house as 1 year ago	85.1% (298)
Live and work in county	73.8% (317)
Married-couple households	47.6% (395)

TRANSPORTATION ★★★ **(324)**

Bicycle or walk to work	2.6% (308)
Carpool to work	12.2% (132)
Public transit to work	0.9% (83)
Commute <15 minutes	37.0% (399)
Commute >45 minutes	13.8% (382)

See pages 37-130 for explanations of statistics, stars, and ranks.

Talladega-Sylacauga, AL
(Coosa and Talladega Counties, AL)

POPULATION	
2010 census	93,830 (38)
2015 estimate	91,586 (46)
2010-2015 change	-2.4% (443)
2020 projection	89,275 (47)
2030 projection	84,444 (63)

RACE	
Whites	63.9% (424)
Blacks	31.8% (48)
Hispanics	2.2% (406)
Asians	0.4% (413)
Native Americans	0.2% (300)

AGE	
0-17 years old	21.9% (344)
18-24 years old	8.8% (292)
25-39 years old	17.4% (269)
40-54 years old	21.9% (38)
55-64 years old	14.2% (161)
65+ years old	15.9% (297)

PRIVATE SECTOR	
Businesses	1,292 (178)
Employees	25,543 (71)
Total wages	$1,161,949,774 (48)
Average weekly wages	$875 (45)

HOUSEHOLD INCOME LADDER	
95th percentile	$128,578 (448)
80th percentile	$73,679 (477)
60th percentile	$44,478 (483)
40th percentile	$26,986 (484)
20th percentile	$14,655 (462)

CHILDREN	★★ (351)
Living with two parents	52.8% (486)
Older teens in school	81.4% (350)
Speak English very well	99.9% (19)
Poverty rate for children	36.1% (487)
No health insurance	2.2% (15)

DIVERSITY/EQUALITY	★★★★ (119)
Racial diversity index	49.0% (122)
Geographic diversity index	31.9% (464)
Top 20% share of income	49.3% (382)
Gender gap in earnings	27.6% (130)
White-collar gender gap	4.9% (41)

EDUCATION	★ (471)
Eighth grade or less	5.9% (420)
High school diplomas	81.1% (466)
Attended college	44.6% (443)
Bachelor's degrees	12.9% (497)
Advanced degrees	4.6% (431)

EMPLOYMENT	★ (504)
Average jobless rate	14.1% (528)
Self-employed workers	7.1% (421)
Management/financial jobs	10.5% (318)
Computer/engineering jobs	2.3% (354)
Health care jobs	5.3% (286)

GROWTH POTENTIAL	★★★ (326)
Children per senior	1.38 (291)
Median age	41.6 (387)
Moved from different state	1.8% (338)
Homes built since 2000	15.7% (186)
Construction jobs	6.1% (310)

HOUSING	★★★ (238)
Home vacancy rate	10.5% (381)
Home ownership rate	72.1% (181)
Housing diversity index	85.7% (108)
4 or more bedrooms	15.0% (356)
Affordability/income ratio	$2,649 (311)

INCOME	★ (472)
Poverty rate	22.6% (438)
Median household income	$34,691 (490)
Interest/dividends	11.9% (495)
Public assistance	21.3% (465)
Median fulltime earnings	$35,479 (360)

SENIORS	★★ (433)
Seniors living alone	30.2% (436)
Poverty rate for seniors	12.1% (416)
Median income for seniors	$28,340 (450)
Seniors who work	16.6% (367)
Home ownership by seniors	84.6% (159)

STABILITY	★ (442)
25-39 age group	17.4% (269)
Born in state of residence	81.9% (87)
Same house as 1 year ago	85.7% (272)
Live and work in county	58.1% (502)
Married-couple households	45.2% (461)

TRANSPORTATION	★ (503)
Bicycle or walk to work	1.4% (472)
Carpool to work	10.8% (249)
Public transit to work	0.7% (119)
Commute <15 minutes	31.5% (506)
Commute >45 minutes	18.1% (502)

See pages 37-130 for explanations of statistics, stars, and ranks.

Thomaston, GA
(Upson County, GA)

POPULATION	
2010 census	27,153 (464)
2015 estimate	26,368 (470)
2010-2015 change	-2.9% (477)
2020 projection	25,409 (475)
2030 projection	23,532 (486)

RACE	
Whites	67.9% (401)
Blacks	28.4% (59)
Hispanics	2.4% (389)
Asians	0.2% (509)
Native Americans	0.2% (300)

AGE	
0-17 years old	22.9% (270)
18-24 years old	9.1% (251)
25-39 years old	15.8% (460)
40-54 years old	21.2% (85)
55-64 years old	13.7% (225)
65+ years old	17.2% (182)

PRIVATE SECTOR	
Businesses	452 (528)
Employees	5,335 (521)
Total wages	$181,658,503 (518)
Average weekly wages	$655 (381)

HOUSEHOLD INCOME LADDER	
95th percentile	$119,474 (520)
80th percentile	$71,154 (498)
60th percentile	$46,121 (456)
40th percentile	$27,418 (471)
20th percentile	$15,094 (450)

CHILDREN	★★ (432)
Living with two parents	58.3% (444)
Older teens in school	80.2% (392)
Speak English very well	98.5% (287)
Poverty rate for children	36.5% (492)
No health insurance	7.3% (333)

DIVERSITY/EQUALITY	★★★ (271)
Racial diversity index	45.8% (143)
Geographic diversity index	27.9% (503)
Top 20% share of income	49.2% (379)
Gender gap in earnings	32.9% (255)
White-collar gender gap	16.1% (167)

EDUCATION	★ (487)
Eighth grade or less	5.0% (385)
High school diplomas	79.8% (483)
Attended college	43.4% (464)
Bachelor's degrees	11.2% (531)
Advanced degrees	4.4% (451)

EMPLOYMENT	★ (476)
Average jobless rate	11.1% (460)
Self-employed workers	6.6% (461)
Management/financial jobs	9.2% (459)
Computer/engineering jobs	2.6% (288)
Health care jobs	5.7% (222)

GROWTH POTENTIAL	★★ (414)
Children per senior	1.33 (325)
Median age	41.5 (380)
Moved from different state	0.8% (524)
Homes built since 2000	11.4% (338)
Construction jobs	6.7% (219)

HOUSING	★★ (434)
Home vacancy rate	14.3% (524)
Home ownership rate	63.7% (462)
Housing diversity index	86.7% (6)
4 or more bedrooms	13.1% (448)
Affordability/income ratio	$2,393 (211)

INCOME	★ (491)
Poverty rate	23.7% (462)
Median household income	$35,774 (473)
Interest/dividends	12.4% (483)
Public assistance	21.2% (461)
Median fulltime earnings	$31,749 (507)

SENIORS	★ (466)
Seniors living alone	23.9% (80)
Poverty rate for seniors	12.6% (439)
Median income for seniors	$30,023 (408)
Seniors who work	14.2% (496)
Home ownership by seniors	75.7% (515)

STABILITY	★★ (406)
25-39 age group	15.8% (460)
Born in state of residence	84.5% (48)
Same house as 1 year ago	83.4% (375)
Live and work in county	65.7% (443)
Married-couple households	49.9% (302)

TRANSPORTATION	★★★ (309)
Bicycle or walk to work	0.6% (541)
Carpool to work	16.4% (28)
Public transit to work	0.5% (178)
Commute <15 minutes	43.4% (273)
Commute >45 minutes	17.6% (495)

See pages 37-130 for explanations of statistics, stars, and ranks.

Thomasville, GA
(Thomas County, GA)

POPULATION	
2010 census	44,720 (265)
2015 estimate	45,063 (259)
2010-2015 change	0.8% (194)
2020 projection	45,031 (261)
2030 projection	44,801 (265)

RACE	
Whites	57.8% (460)
Blacks	36.3% (37)
Hispanics	3.3% (324)
Asians	0.9% (178)
Native Americans	0.0% (523)

AGE	
0-17 years old	24.4% (155)
18-24 years old	8.1% (396)
25-39 years old	18.2% (167)
40-54 years old	19.8% (261)
55-64 years old	13.4% (274)
65+ years old	16.1% (286)

PRIVATE SECTOR	
Businesses	1,357 (163)
Employees	17,206 (166)
Total wages	$719,686,589 (146)
Average weekly wages	$804 (85)

HOUSEHOLD INCOME LADDER	
95th percentile	$139,375 (299)
80th percentile	$72,175 (493)
60th percentile	$46,602 (452)
40th percentile	$28,094 (461)
20th percentile	$14,006 (475)

CHILDREN	★★ (390)
Living with two parents	51.3% (498)
Older teens in school	83.9% (243)
Speak English very well	99.0% (200)
Poverty rate for children	28.5% (377)
No health insurance	8.4% (371)

DIVERSITY/EQUALITY	★★ (374)
Racial diversity index	53.3% (75)
Geographic diversity index	47.8% (247)
Top 20% share of income	51.9% (499)
Gender gap in earnings	30.4% (178)
White-collar gender gap	49.7% (509)

EDUCATION	★★★ (253)
Eighth grade or less	3.3% (259)
High school diplomas	83.4% (411)
Attended college	51.4% (295)
Bachelor's degrees	19.6% (229)
Advanced degrees	8.6% (99)

EMPLOYMENT	★★★★ (208)
Average jobless rate	10.5% (441)
Self-employed workers	7.6% (376)
Management/financial jobs	12.1% (149)
Computer/engineering jobs	2.1% (399)
Health care jobs	8.1% (16)

GROWTH POTENTIAL	★★★ (260)
Children per senior	1.51 (210)
Median age	39.4 (262)
Moved from different state	2.1% (269)
Homes built since 2000	19.4% (100)
Construction jobs	4.9% (473)

HOUSING	★ (499)
Home vacancy rate	11.8% (454)
Home ownership rate	59.9% (504)
Housing diversity index	85.6% (127)
4 or more bedrooms	14.3% (387)
Affordability/income ratio	$3,360 (450)

INCOME	★ (468)
Poverty rate	23.6% (461)
Median household income	$36,641 (450)
Interest/dividends	14.4% (429)
Public assistance	22.3% (482)
Median fulltime earnings	$35,183 (376)

SENIORS	★★ (345)
Seniors living alone	26.4% (193)
Poverty rate for seniors	10.8% (365)
Median income for seniors	n.a.
Seniors who work	18.9% (247)
Home ownership by seniors	78.9% (422)

STABILITY	★★ (349)
25-39 age group	18.2% (167)
Born in state of residence	69.6% (317)
Same house as 1 year ago	85.2% (294)
Live and work in county	79.5% (223)
Married-couple households	43.9% (483)

TRANSPORTATION	★★★ (294)
Bicycle or walk to work	1.8% (409)
Carpool to work	13.9% (72)
Public transit to work	0.2% (363)
Commute <15 minutes	41.2% (314)
Commute >45 minutes	12.6% (336)

See pages 37-130 for explanations of statistics, stars, and ranks.

Tifton, GA
(Tift County, GA)

POPULATION	
2010 census	40,118 (312)
2015 estimate	40,764 (306)
2010-2015 change	1.6% (157)
2020 projection	40,734 (307)
2030 projection	40,526 (311)

RACE	
Whites	56.6% (466)
Blacks	29.7% (58)
Hispanics	10.8% (143)
Asians	1.4% (99)
Native Americans	0.1% (402)

AGE	
0-17 years old	25.1% (116)
18-24 years old	12.3% (80)
25-39 years old	18.3% (159)
40-54 years old	19.6% (289)
55-64 years old	11.2% (489)
65+ years old	13.6% (454)

PRIVATE SECTOR	
Businesses	1,108 (240)
Employees	13,750 (245)
Total wages	$426,057,325 (308)
Average weekly wages	$596 (494)

HOUSEHOLD INCOME LADDER	
95th percentile	$153,080 (132)
80th percentile	$81,594 (335)
60th percentile	$48,048 (425)
40th percentile	$29,859 (427)
20th percentile	$13,315 (494)

CHILDREN	★ (483)
Living with two parents	48.6% (517)
Older teens in school	91.0% (55)
Speak English very well	99.2% (163)
Poverty rate for children	42.2% (526)
No health insurance	13.5% (505)

DIVERSITY/EQUALITY	★★★★ (177)
Racial diversity index	57.9% (26)
Geographic diversity index	37.3% (401)
Top 20% share of income	52.8% (517)
Gender gap in earnings	18.2% (33)
White-collar gender gap	23.3% (254)

EDUCATION	★★ (353)
Eighth grade or less	4.5% (354)
High school diplomas	82.4% (433)
Attended college	48.7% (365)
Bachelor's degrees	17.0% (328)
Advanced degrees	7.7% (133)

EMPLOYMENT	★★★★ (142)
Average jobless rate	5.8% (113)
Self-employed workers	8.8% (273)
Management/financial jobs	10.9% (263)
Computer/engineering jobs	1.9% (441)
Health care jobs	7.4% (49)

GROWTH POTENTIAL	★★★★ (145)
Children per senior	1.84 (86)
Median age	35.1 (94)
Moved from different state	1.5% (406)
Homes built since 2000	14.6% (213)
Construction jobs	6.8% (204)

HOUSING	★ (520)
Home vacancy rate	13.4% (504)
Home ownership rate	58.1% (520)
Housing diversity index	84.9% (235)
4 or more bedrooms	14.1% (398)
Affordability/income ratio	$2,985 (401)

INCOME	★ (490)
Poverty rate	29.2% (518)
Median household income	$37,653 (437)
Interest/dividends	13.6% (450)
Public assistance	20.1% (434)
Median fulltime earnings	$33,507 (438)

SENIORS	★★ (385)
Seniors living alone	23.7% (76)
Poverty rate for seniors	16.5% (508)
Median income for seniors	$33,401 (262)
Seniors who work	17.5% (310)
Home ownership by seniors	80.1% (369)

STABILITY	★★★★ (161)
25-39 age group	18.3% (159)
Born in state of residence	78.5% (146)
Same house as 1 year ago	88.9% (86)
Live and work in county	83.3% (157)
Married-couple households	42.3% (503)

TRANSPORTATION	★★★ (229)
Bicycle or walk to work	2.3% (348)
Carpool to work	14.1% (61)
Public transit to work	0.2% (363)
Commute <15 minutes	43.8% (264)
Commute >45 minutes	11.3% (285)

See pages 37-130 for explanations of statistics, stars, and ranks.

Toccoa, GA
(Stephens County, GA)

POPULATION

2010 census	26,175 (470)
2015 estimate	25,586 (479)
2010-2015 change	-2.3% (436)
2020 projection	25,087 (479)
2030 projection	24,029 (478)

RACE

Whites	83.0% (290)
Blacks	12.2% (103)
Hispanics	2.9% (350)
Asians	0.4% (413)
Native Americans	0.3% (231)

AGE

0-17 years old	22.4% (306)
18-24 years old	10.6% (131)
25-39 years old	15.2% (498)
40-54 years old	20.2% (202)
55-64 years old	13.8% (203)
65+ years old	17.7% (142)

PRIVATE SECTOR

Businesses	560 (495)
Employees	7,306 (461)
Total wages	$283,323,153 (445)
Average weekly wages	$746 (163)

HOUSEHOLD INCOME LADDER

95th percentile	$138,721 (304)
80th percentile	$82,007 (325)
60th percentile	$50,409 (372)
40th percentile	$31,298 (381)
20th percentile	$16,581 (379)

CHILDREN ★★★ (263)

Living with two parents	65.0% (270)
Older teens in school	83.0% (276)
Speak English very well	99.8% (38)
Poverty rate for children	25.3% (307)
No health insurance	8.5% (379)

DIVERSITY/EQUALITY ★★★★★ (78)

Racial diversity index	29.5% (258)
Geographic diversity index	45.5% (271)
Top 20% share of income	49.4% (395)
Gender gap in earnings	15.9% (17)
White-collar gender gap	8.6% (71)

EDUCATION ★★★ (328)

Eighth grade or less	3.1% (238)
High school diplomas	83.0% (420)
Attended college	45.9% (422)
Bachelor's degrees	17.2% (315)
Advanced degrees	8.4% (106)

EMPLOYMENT ★★ (403)

Average jobless rate	10.6% (446)
Self-employed workers	9.4% (216)
Management/financial jobs	7.9% (530)
Computer/engineering jobs	1.8% (457)
Health care jobs	7.0% (69)

GROWTH POTENTIAL ★★ (400)

Children per senior	1.26 (378)
Median age	41.2 (368)
Moved from different state	1.5% (406)
Homes built since 2000	15.7% (186)
Construction jobs	5.4% (413)

HOUSING ★ (459)

Home vacancy rate	19.3% (548)
Home ownership rate	72.0% (189)
Housing diversity index	85.5% (143)
4 or more bedrooms	12.5% (478)
Affordability/income ratio	$2,508 (251)

INCOME ★★ (428)

Poverty rate	18.9% (334)
Median household income	$40,315 (373)
Interest/dividends	14.4% (429)
Public assistance	19.2% (408)
Median fulltime earnings	$32,337 (476)

SENIORS ★★★★★ (77)

Seniors living alone	24.1% (86)
Poverty rate for seniors	7.3% (119)
Median income for seniors	$33,649 (254)
Seniors who work	24.7% (77)
Home ownership by seniors	82.9% (225)

STABILITY ★★★★ (219)

25-39 age group	15.2% (498)
Born in state of residence	71.7% (284)
Same house as 1 year ago	88.3% (115)
Live and work in county	67.4% (413)
Married-couple households	57.6% (24)

TRANSPORTATION ★★ (379)

Bicycle or walk to work	2.9% (265)
Carpool to work	9.8% (358)
Public transit to work	0.0% (511)
Commute <15 minutes	42.5% (287)
Commute >45 minutes	12.6% (336)

See pages 37-130 for explanations of statistics, stars, and ranks.

Troy, AL
(Pike County, AL)

POPULATION

2010 census	32,899 (405)
2015 estimate	33,046 (405)
2010-2015 change	0.4% (228)
2020 projection	33,413 (399)
2030 projection	33,984 (391)

RACE

Whites	57.1% (465)
Blacks	38.2% (33)
Hispanics	0.9% (535)
Asians	2.1% (45)
Native Americans	0.8% (125)

AGE

0-17 years old	19.7% (473)
18-24 years old	21.4% (23)
25-39 years old	17.5% (258)
40-54 years old	16.6% (511)
55-64 years old	11.1% (492)
65+ years old	13.8% (448)

PRIVATE SECTOR

Businesses	648 (452)
Employees	10,669 (354)
Total wages	$402,294,058 (333)
Average weekly wages	$725 (207)

HOUSEHOLD INCOME LADDER

95th percentile	$141,856 (267)
80th percentile	$74,483 (464)
60th percentile	$43,761 (494)
40th percentile	$25,857 (502)
20th percentile	$12,110 (515)

CHILDREN ★★★ (248)

Living with two parents	52.3% (492)
Older teens in school	91.0% (55)
Speak English very well	97.4% (395)
Poverty rate for children	30.3% (409)
No health insurance	2.3% (20)

DIVERSITY/EQUALITY ★★ (345)

Racial diversity index	52.7% (87)
Geographic diversity index	39.5% (363)
Top 20% share of income	52.7% (515)
Gender gap in earnings	33.3% (266)
White-collar gender gap	25.9% (287)

EDUCATION ★★★★ (214)

Eighth grade or less	2.8% (205)
High school diplomas	82.3% (437)
Attended college	48.9% (357)
Bachelor's degrees	24.9% (111)
Advanced degrees	9.8% (66)

EMPLOYMENT ★ (511)

Average jobless rate	10.2% (427)
Self-employed workers	5.7% (515)
Management/financial jobs	10.2% (357)
Computer/engineering jobs	2.4% (336)
Health care jobs	4.0% (476)

GROWTH POTENTIAL ★★★★ (133)

Children per senior	1.43 (261)
Median age	31.3 (40)
Moved from different state	2.7% (179)
Homes built since 2000	18.2% (128)
Construction jobs	5.4% (413)

HOUSING ★ (534)

Home vacancy rate	13.6% (507)
Home ownership rate	58.0% (522)
Housing diversity index	84.7% (260)
4 or more bedrooms	12.8% (462)
Affordability/income ratio	$3,214 (434)

INCOME ★ (493)

Poverty rate	26.1% (487)
Median household income	$32,825 (508)
Interest/dividends	13.6% (450)
Public assistance	19.3% (409)
Median fulltime earnings	$32,209 (483)

SENIORS ★ (450)

Seniors living alone	28.7% (344)
Poverty rate for seniors	13.6% (463)
Median income for seniors	$30,630 (387)
Seniors who work	18.3% (272)
Home ownership by seniors	80.3% (365)

STABILITY ★★★ (321)

25-39 age group	17.5% (258)
Born in state of residence	76.6% (188)
Same house as 1 year ago	85.4% (285)
Live and work in county	85.5% (129)
Married-couple households	40.9% (517)

TRANSPORTATION ★★ (382)

Bicycle or walk to work	2.3% (348)
Carpool to work	6.0% (547)
Public transit to work	0.7% (119)
Commute <15 minutes	45.6% (240)
Commute >45 minutes	9.2% (182)

See pages 37-130 for explanations of statistics, stars, and ranks.

Tullahoma-Manchester, TN
(Coffee, Franklin, and Moore Counties, TN)

POPULATION		
2010 census	100,210 (27)	
2015 estimate	102,048 (28)	
2010-2015 change	1.8% (142)	
2020 projection	103,400 (25)	
2030 projection	105,849 (28)	

RACE		
Whites	89.6% (191)	
Blacks	2.5% (253)	
Hispanics	3.2% (330)	
Asians	0.8% (201)	
Native Americans	0.3% (231)	

AGE		
0-17 years old	22.6% (291)	
18-24 years old	9.3% (217)	
25-39 years old	17.3% (280)	
40-54 years old	19.7% (273)	
55-64 years old	13.5% (258)	
65+ years old	17.5% (158)	

PRIVATE SECTOR		
Businesses	1,935 (68)	
Employees	33,219 (26)	
Total wages	$1,360,434,780 (24)	
Average weekly wages	$788 (107)	

HOUSEHOLD INCOME LADDER		
95th percentile	$141,003 (279)	
80th percentile	$81,259 (343)	
60th percentile	$51,843 (325)	
40th percentile	$34,168 (282)	
20th percentile	$17,818 (327)	

CHILDREN	★★★★ (196)	
Living with two parents	64.4% (283)	
Older teens in school	84.2% (232)	
Speak English very well	99.2% (163)	
Poverty rate for children	23.4% (254)	
No health insurance	5.6% (225)	

DIVERSITY/EQUALITY	★★★ (330)	
Racial diversity index	19.4% (355)	
Geographic diversity index	55.4% (151)	
Top 20% share of income	48.9% (351)	
Gender gap in earnings	34.0% (289)	
White-collar gender gap	29.2% (323)	

EDUCATION	★★★ (308)	
Eighth grade or less	4.2% (337)	
High school diplomas	86.8% (314)	
Attended college	48.2% (379)	
Bachelor's degrees	19.0% (248)	
Advanced degrees	6.7% (205)	

EMPLOYMENT	★★★ (227)	
Average jobless rate	8.9% (351)	
Self-employed workers	8.7% (281)	
Management/financial jobs	11.6% (196)	
Computer/engineering jobs	3.9% (86)	
Health care jobs	5.4% (273)	

GROWTH POTENTIAL	★★★ (305)	
Children per senior	1.29 (353)	
Median age	40.8 (347)	
Moved from different state	3.2% (136)	
Homes built since 2000	16.5% (167)	
Construction jobs	5.2% (442)	

HOUSING	★★★★ (152)	
Home vacancy rate	7.9% (213)	
Home ownership rate	71.2% (218)	
Housing diversity index	85.6% (127)	
4 or more bedrooms	17.2% (236)	
Affordability/income ratio	$2,702 (330)	

INCOME	★★★ (304)	
Poverty rate	17.5% (286)	
Median household income	$42,447 (302)	
Interest/dividends	20.6% (231)	
Public assistance	18.0% (371)	
Median fulltime earnings	$36,054 (331)	

SENIORS	★★★★ (181)	
Seniors living alone	25.3% (127)	
Poverty rate for seniors	10.1% (332)	
Median income for seniors	$35,567 (169)	
Seniors who work	16.3% (391)	
Home ownership by seniors	85.9% (105)	

STABILITY	★★ (418)	
25-39 age group	17.3% (280)	
Born in state of residence	63.7% (401)	
Same house as 1 year ago	84.5% (325)	
Live and work in county	64.6% (451)	
Married-couple households	52.6% (167)	

TRANSPORTATION	★ (444)	
Bicycle or walk to work	2.0% (386)	
Carpool to work	9.4% (394)	
Public transit to work	0.0% (511)	
Commute <15 minutes	35.2% (437)	
Commute >45 minutes	11.2% (278)	

See pages 37-130 for explanations of statistics, stars, and ranks.

Tupelo, MS
(Itawamba, Lee, and Pontotoc Counties, MS)

POPULATION	
2010 census	136,268 (8)
2015 estimate	139,817 (8)
2010-2015 change	2.6% (103)
2020 projection	142,587 (7)
2030 projection	147,292 (7)

RACE	
Whites	73.4% (369)
Blacks	21.4% (73)
Hispanics	3.1% (333)
Asians	0.5% (355)
Native Americans	0.1% (402)

AGE	
0-17 years old	25.5% (90)
18-24 years old	9.1% (251)
25-39 years old	19.0% (104)
40-54 years old	20.2% (202)
55-64 years old	11.8% (456)
65+ years old	14.4% (419)

PRIVATE SECTOR	
Businesses	3,153 (17)
Employees	62,787 (2)
Total wages	$2,255,280,185 (5)
Average weekly wages	$691 (282)

HOUSEHOLD INCOME LADDER	
95th percentile	$133,914 (376)
80th percentile	$81,211 (346)
60th percentile	$51,957 (320)
40th percentile	$32,292 (352)
20th percentile	$16,795 (370)

CHILDREN	★★★★ (212)
Living with two parents	60.4% (391)
Older teens in school	85.4% (191)
Speak English very well	99.6% (77)
Poverty rate for children	26.3% (333)
No health insurance	4.6% (159)

DIVERSITY/EQUALITY	★★★ (311)
Racial diversity index	41.4% (179)
Geographic diversity index	39.2% (371)
Top 20% share of income	48.7% (335)
Gender gap in earnings	29.3% (160)
White-collar gender gap	38.4% (427)

EDUCATION	★★★ (310)
Eighth grade or less	4.4% (346)
High school diplomas	83.6% (409)
Attended college	55.2% (216)
Bachelor's degrees	19.0% (248)
Advanced degrees	5.9% (272)

EMPLOYMENT	★★★ (319)
Average jobless rate	7.7% (260)
Self-employed workers	7.2% (410)
Management/financial jobs	10.1% (365)
Computer/engineering jobs	2.1% (399)
Health care jobs	6.6% (114)

GROWTH POTENTIAL	★★★ (223)
Children per senior	1.77 (104)
Median age	37.1 (149)
Moved from different state	1.7% (355)
Homes built since 2000	17.5% (140)
Construction jobs	4.9% (473)

HOUSING	★★★ (248)
Home vacancy rate	9.4% (309)
Home ownership rate	71.6% (201)
Housing diversity index	83.9% (360)
4 or more bedrooms	16.1% (286)
Affordability/income ratio	$2,484 (243)

INCOME	★★ (384)
Poverty rate	17.9% (297)
Median household income	$41,190 (348)
Interest/dividends	13.1% (467)
Public assistance	16.0% (295)
Median fulltime earnings	$33,966 (423)

SENIORS	★★ (429)
Seniors living alone	30.3% (440)
Poverty rate for seniors	10.5% (345)
Median income for seniors	$28,984 (434)
Seniors who work	16.8% (356)
Home ownership by seniors	82.7% (236)

STABILITY	★★★★ (203)
25-39 age group	19.0% (104)
Born in state of residence	76.7% (185)
Same house as 1 year ago	85.3% (290)
Live and work in county	69.6% (377)
Married-couple households	49.5% (323)

TRANSPORTATION	★ (450)
Bicycle or walk to work	0.9% (521)
Carpool to work	8.9% (439)
Public transit to work	0.2% (363)
Commute <15 minutes	32.3% (489)
Commute >45 minutes	8.1% (135)

See pages 37-130 for explanations of statistics, stars, and ranks.

Union City, TN-KY
(Obion County, TN, and Fulton County, KY)

POPULATION

2010 census	38,620 (333)
2015 estimate	36,877 (359)
2010-2015 change	-4.5% (528)
2020 projection	35,271 (379)
2030 projection	32,182 (406)

RACE

Whites	81.8% (304)
Blacks	12.8% (100)
Hispanics	3.2% (330)
Asians	0.3% (473)
Native Americans	0.2% (300)

AGE

0-17 years old	22.0% (335)
18-24 years old	8.6% (317)
25-39 years old	16.2% (434)
40-54 years old	20.8% (122)
55-64 years old	14.2% (161)
65+ years old	18.2% (111)

PRIVATE SECTOR

Businesses	792 (378)
Employees	9,591 (386)
Total wages	$326,588,886 (402)
Average weekly wages	$655 (381)

HOUSEHOLD INCOME LADDER

95th percentile	$135,090 (358)
80th percentile	$75,623 (448)
60th percentile	$47,519 (435)
40th percentile	$29,394 (436)
20th percentile	$14,753 (459)

CHILDREN ★★ (395)

Living with two parents	59.4% (419)
Older teens in school	78.7% (435)
Speak English very well	98.4% (300)
Poverty rate for children	31.1% (423)
No health insurance	7.0% (319)

DIVERSITY/EQUALITY ★★★ (264)

Racial diversity index	31.3% (242)
Geographic diversity index	53.3% (169)
Top 20% share of income	49.7% (409)
Gender gap in earnings	24.6% (83)
White-collar gender gap	39.7% (444)

EDUCATION ★★ (418)

Eighth grade or less	6.2% (433)
High school diplomas	84.7% (380)
Attended college	44.0% (452)
Bachelor's degrees	16.5% (350)
Advanced degrees	5.7% (292)

EMPLOYMENT ★★ (358)

Average jobless rate	11.3% (466)
Self-employed workers	9.6% (200)
Management/financial jobs	11.2% (229)
Computer/engineering jobs	2.0% (420)
Health care jobs	5.9% (193)

GROWTH POTENTIAL ★ (459)

Children per senior	1.21 (411)
Median age	42.2 (412)
Moved from different state	2.6% (187)
Homes built since 2000	10.7% (370)
Construction jobs	5.3% (425)

HOUSING ★★★ (304)

Home vacancy rate	11.5% (436)
Home ownership rate	66.9% (392)
Housing diversity index	86.5% (19)
4 or more bedrooms	13.3% (437)
Affordability/income ratio	$2,210 (127)

INCOME ★ (462)

Poverty rate	21.7% (421)
Median household income	$38,012 (428)
Interest/dividends	15.8% (385)
Public assistance	21.3% (465)
Median fulltime earnings	$32,377 (473)

SENIORS ★★ (338)

Seniors living alone	25.9% (164)
Poverty rate for seniors	12.8% (442)
Median income for seniors	$30,409 (394)
Seniors who work	18.5% (268)
Home ownership by seniors	82.5% (251)

STABILITY ★ (446)

25-39 age group	16.2% (434)
Born in state of residence	64.7% (389)
Same house as 1 year ago	86.2% (237)
Live and work in county	67.7% (410)
Married-couple households	49.6% (317)

TRANSPORTATION ★★ (407)

Bicycle or walk to work	1.7% (428)
Carpool to work	6.4% (541)
Public transit to work	0.3% (291)
Commute <15 minutes	44.0% (260)
Commute >45 minutes	8.3% (144)

See pages 37-130 for explanations of statistics, stars, and ranks.

Uvalde, TX
(Uvalde County, TX)

POPULATION

2010 census	26,405 (467)
2015 estimate	27,245 (462)
2010-2015 change	3.2% (74)
2020 projection	27,524 (452)
2030 projection	28,106 (443)

RACE

Whites	27.9% (533)
Blacks	0.2% (537)
Hispanics	70.2% (12)
Asians	1.0% (158)
Native Americans	0.5% (174)

AGE

0-17 years old	28.1% (30)
18-24 years old	10.6% (131)
25-39 years old	17.7% (236)
40-54 years old	16.9% (504)
55-64 years old	10.8% (497)
65+ years old	15.9% (297)

PRIVATE SECTOR

Businesses	678 (442)
Employees	7,177 (468)
Total wages	$208,492,227 (502)
Average weekly wages	$559 (528)

HOUSEHOLD INCOME LADDER

95th percentile	$127,425 (464)
80th percentile	$81,163 (347)
60th percentile	$51,545 (342)
40th percentile	$31,225 (383)
20th percentile	$15,984 (408)

CHILDREN ★★ (387)

Living with two parents	59.7% (408)
Older teens in school	85.9% (169)
Speak English very well	95.8% (459)
Poverty rate for children	29.1% (387)
No health insurance	9.4% (406)

DIVERSITY/EQUALITY ★★★★ (192)

Racial diversity index	42.9% (168)
Geographic diversity index	41.2% (337)
Top 20% share of income	47.4% (252)
Gender gap in earnings	32.8% (249)
White-collar gender gap	23.2% (252)

EDUCATION ★ (514)

Eighth grade or less	12.3% (528)
High school diplomas	75.0% (525)
Attended college	51.1% (300)
Bachelor's degrees	15.9% (382)
Advanced degrees	3.9% (489)

EMPLOYMENT ★★ (386)

Average jobless rate	8.1% (298)
Self-employed workers	8.9% (266)
Management/financial jobs	8.3% (513)
Computer/engineering jobs	2.1% (399)
Health care jobs	6.1% (168)

GROWTH POTENTIAL ★★★★★ (58)

Children per senior	1.77 (104)
Median age	34.1 (78)
Moved from different state	3.0% (157)
Homes built since 2000	17.6% (139)
Construction jobs	8.7% (58)

HOUSING ★★★ (235)

Home vacancy rate	13.2% (497)
Home ownership rate	73.6% (132)
Housing diversity index	85.5% (143)
4 or more bedrooms	15.5% (324)
Affordability/income ratio	$1,996 (55)

INCOME ★ (451)

Poverty rate	19.9% (366)
Median household income	$38,568 (416)
Interest/dividends	12.3% (486)
Public assistance	17.7% (361)
Median fulltime earnings	$31,937 (499)

SENIORS ★★ (335)

Seniors living alone	26.6% (209)
Poverty rate for seniors	14.1% (472)
Median income for seniors	$25,473 (499)
Seniors who work	19.1% (238)
Home ownership by seniors	87.4% (60)

STABILITY ★★★★★ (109)

25-39 age group	17.7% (236)
Born in state of residence	75.9% (207)
Same house as 1 year ago	85.8% (264)
Live and work in county	86.7% (104)
Married-couple households	49.3% (333)

TRANSPORTATION ★★★ (253)

Bicycle or walk to work	1.3% (485)
Carpool to work	11.7% (170)
Public transit to work	0.1% (441)
Commute <15 minutes	56.3% (78)
Commute >45 minutes	11.9% (308)

See pages 37-130 for explanations of statistics, stars, and ranks.

Valley, AL
(Chambers County, AL)

POPULATION		
2010 census	34,215 (391)	
2015 estimate	34,123 (393)	
2010-2015 change	-0.3% (279)	
2020 projection	33,334 (402)	
2030 projection	31,645 (413)	

RACE		
Whites	57.3% (463)	
Blacks	40.3% (30)	
Hispanics	0.4% (547)	
Asians	0.8% (201)	
Native Americans	0.2% (300)	

AGE		
0-17 years old	21.6% (366)	
18-24 years old	8.5% (330)	
25-39 years old	16.8% (359)	
40-54 years old	21.1% (97)	
55-64 years old	14.1% (174)	
65+ years old	18.0% (122)	

PRIVATE SECTOR		
Businesses	511 (513)	
Employees	6,191 (504)	
Total wages	$212,937,450 (501)	
Average weekly wages	$661 (360)	

HOUSEHOLD INCOME LADDER		
95th percentile	$120,663 (511)	
80th percentile	$71,126 (499)	
60th percentile	$43,263 (499)	
40th percentile	$27,240 (478)	
20th percentile	$14,919 (454)	

CHILDREN	★ (462)	
Living with two parents	45.6% (528)	
Older teens in school	76.7% (476)	
Speak English very well	100.0% (1)	
Poverty rate for children	37.2% (498)	
No health insurance	3.8% (108)	

DIVERSITY/EQUALITY	★★★★ (183)	
Racial diversity index	50.9% (105)	
Geographic diversity index	38.3% (385)	
Top 20% share of income	51.6% (490)	
Gender gap in earnings	27.5% (126)	
White-collar gender gap	11.3% (100)	

EDUCATION	★ (462)	
Eighth grade or less	3.8% (307)	
High school diplomas	82.6% (428)	

Attended college	43.4% (464)	
Bachelor's degrees	11.7% (521)	
Advanced degrees	3.9% (489)	

EMPLOYMENT	★ (486)	
Average jobless rate	8.9% (351)	
Self-employed workers	4.0% (551)	
Management/financial jobs	9.9% (392)	
Computer/engineering jobs	2.1% (399)	
Health care jobs	5.8% (209)	

GROWTH POTENTIAL	★ (448)	
Children per senior	1.20 (417)	
Median age	43.0 (450)	
Moved from different state	2.2% (248)	
Homes built since 2000	12.6% (294)	
Construction jobs	5.6% (392)	

HOUSING	★★ (351)	
Home vacancy rate	13.3% (500)	
Home ownership rate	67.6% (362)	
Housing diversity index	86.7% (6)	
4 or more bedrooms	13.2% (445)	
Affordability/income ratio	$2,364 (196)	

INCOME	★ (471)	
Poverty rate	21.6% (419)	
Median household income	$34,177 (496)	
Interest/dividends	10.3% (526)	
Public assistance	17.2% (344)	
Median fulltime earnings	$32,933 (454)	

SENIORS	★ (476)	
Seniors living alone	31.5% (498)	
Poverty rate for seniors	12.1% (416)	
Median income for seniors	$28,084 (456)	
Seniors who work	14.9% (464)	
Home ownership by seniors	83.3% (206)	

STABILITY	★ (538)	
25-39 age group	16.8% (359)	
Born in state of residence	76.2% (201)	
Same house as 1 year ago	86.7% (210)	
Live and work in county	39.9% (549)	
Married-couple households	40.6% (521)	

TRANSPORTATION	★ (516)	
Bicycle or walk to work	0.3% (550)	
Carpool to work	12.1% (135)	
Public transit to work	0.2% (363)	
Commute <15 minutes	20.6% (548)	
Commute >45 minutes	12.6% (336)	

See pages 37-130 for explanations of statistics, stars, and ranks.

Vernon, TX
(Wilbarger County, TX)

POPULATION		Attended college	52.8% (266)
2010 census	13,535 (550)	Bachelor's degrees	16.2% (360)
2015 estimate	13,027 (550)	Advanced degrees	2.9% (534)
2010-2015 change	-3.8% (516)		
2020 projection	12,438 (551)	**EMPLOYMENT**	**★★ (377)**
2030 projection	11,327 (551)	Average jobless rate	7.5% (242)
		Self-employed workers	5.1% (540)
RACE		Management/financial jobs	9.8% (408)
Whites	60.5% (442)	Computer/engineering jobs	2.5% (307)
Blacks	8.9% (120)	Health care jobs	6.6% (114)
Hispanics	28.0% (53)		
Asians	0.5% (355)	**GROWTH POTENTIAL**	**★★ (361)**
Native Americans	0.2% (300)	Children per senior	1.45 (244)
		Median age	37.6 (168)
AGE		Moved from different state	2.9% (165)
0-17 years old	24.0% (184)	Homes built since 2000	8.5% (453)
18-24 years old	10.1% (157)	Construction jobs	4.9% (473)
25-39 years old	17.5% (258)		
40-54 years old	18.7% (399)	**HOUSING**	**★ (446)**
55-64 years old	13.1% (318)	Home vacancy rate	13.6% (507)
65+ years old	16.6% (237)	Home ownership rate	65.4% (425)
		Housing diversity index	85.7% (108)
PRIVATE SECTOR		4 or more bedrooms	8.6% (546)
Businesses	302 (547)	Affordability/income ratio	$1,662 (11)
Employees	3,541 (545)		
Total wages	$132,783,323 (542)	**INCOME**	**★★ (409)**
Average weekly wages	$721 (215)	Poverty rate	17.8% (292)
		Median household income	$41,630 (331)
HOUSEHOLD INCOME LADDER		Interest/dividends	14.4% (429)
95th percentile	$122,733 (496)	Public assistance	17.6% (359)
80th percentile	$78,020 (400)	Median fulltime earnings	$31,050 (527)
60th percentile	$54,200 (275)		
40th percentile	$31,672 (371)	**SENIORS**	**★ (532)**
20th percentile	$15,795 (414)	Seniors living alone	39.0% (550)
		Poverty rate for seniors	16.2% (506)
CHILDREN	**★★ (427)**	Median income for seniors	$27,557 (466)
Living with two parents	49.8% (508)	Seniors who work	22.6% (116)
Older teens in school	82.6% (293)	Home ownership by seniors	78.1% (450)
Speak English very well	98.1% (331)		
Poverty rate for children	23.3% (252)	**STABILITY**	**★★★ (303)**
No health insurance	10.4% (434)	25-39 age group	17.5% (258)
		Born in state of residence	77.0% (179)
DIVERSITY/EQUALITY	**★★★★ (174)**	Same house as 1 year ago	80.4% (492)
Racial diversity index	54.7% (58)	Live and work in county	89.7% (68)
Geographic diversity index	39.3% (370)	Married-couple households	45.5% (453)
Top 20% share of income	45.4% (84)		
Gender gap in earnings	34.5% (301)	**TRANSPORTATION**	**★★★★★ (32)**
White-collar gender gap	37.0% (407)	Bicycle or walk to work	1.7% (428)
		Carpool to work	15.1% (46)
EDUCATION	**★★ (425)**	Public transit to work	0.0% (511)
Eighth grade or less	5.1% (390)	Commute <15 minutes	74.8% (1)
High school diplomas	81.5% (455)	Commute >45 minutes	4.8% (29)

See pages 37-130 for explanations of statistics, stars, and ranks.

Vicksburg, MS
(Claiborne and Warren Counties, MS)

POPULATION

2010 census	58,377 (160)
2015 estimate	56,635 (167)
2010-2015 change	-3.0% (481)
2020 projection	54,738 (179)
2030 projection	50,808 (212)

RACE

Whites	42.9% (507)
Blacks	53.7% (10)
Hispanics	1.9% (442)
Asians	0.8% (201)
Native Americans	0.1% (402)

AGE

0-17 years old	24.8% (135)
18-24 years old	10.5% (136)
25-39 years old	17.9% (214)
40-54 years old	18.9% (376)
55-64 years old	13.7% (225)
65+ years old	14.3% (423)

PRIVATE SECTOR

Businesses	1,180 (209)
Employees	17,836 (155)
Total wages	$690,710,819 (153)
Average weekly wages	$745 (165)

HOUSEHOLD INCOME LADDER

95th percentile	$148,254 (180)
80th percentile	$81,632 (332)
60th percentile	$49,483 (393)
40th percentile	$28,325 (454)
20th percentile	$13,668 (485)

CHILDREN ★ **(489)**

Living with two parents	46.9% (523)
Older teens in school	79.1% (424)
Speak English very well	99.6% (77)
Poverty rate for children	38.9% (507)
No health insurance	7.6% (349)

DIVERSITY/EQUALITY ★★★★ **(139)**

Racial diversity index	52.7% (87)
Geographic diversity index	32.2% (462)
Top 20% share of income	50.9% (468)
Gender gap in earnings	25.6% (97)
White-collar gender gap	6.0% (46)

EDUCATION ★★★★ **(157)**

Eighth grade or less	2.7% (195)
High school diplomas	87.4% (291)

Attended college	56.8% (191)
Bachelor's degrees	23.1% (133)
Advanced degrees	9.2% (81)

EMPLOYMENT ★★★★ **(189)**

Average jobless rate	9.2% (377)
Self-employed workers	5.2% (538)
Management/financial jobs	11.0% (252)
Computer/engineering jobs	7.3% (8)
Health care jobs	5.5% (250)

GROWTH POTENTIAL ★★★★ **(176)**

Children per senior	1.74 (113)
Median age	37.2 (154)
Moved from different state	1.1% (487)
Homes built since 2000	10.5% (377)
Construction jobs	8.3% (67)

HOUSING ★ **(450)**

Home vacancy rate	11.3% (426)
Home ownership rate	65.6% (421)
Housing diversity index	81.8% (466)
4 or more bedrooms	16.7% (261)
Affordability/income ratio	$2,439 (223)

INCOME ★ **(449)**

Poverty rate	25.7% (482)
Median household income	$38,044 (426)
Interest/dividends	11.5% (500)
Public assistance	14.7% (243)
Median fulltime earnings	$35,491 (359)

SENIORS ★★ **(386)**

Seniors living alone	28.2% (311)
Poverty rate for seniors	11.7% (397)
Median income for seniors	$33,768 (246)
Seniors who work	18.0% (287)
Home ownership by seniors	79.9% (377)

STABILITY ★★★★★ **(79)**

25-39 age group	17.9% (214)
Born in state of residence	81.5% (93)
Same house as 1 year ago	92.7% (8)
Live and work in county	85.2% (133)
Married-couple households	41.3% (511)

TRANSPORTATION ★★ **(340)**

Bicycle or walk to work	1.5% (457)
Carpool to work	8.6% (457)
Public transit to work	0.1% (441)
Commute <15 minutes	47.9% (197)
Commute >45 minutes	8.5% (152)

See pages 37-130 for explanations of statistics, stars, and ranks.

Vidalia, GA
(Montgomery and Toombs Counties, GA)

POPULATION		
2010 census	36,346 (368)	
2015 estimate	36,192 (371)	
2010-2015 change	-0.4% (286)	
2020 projection	35,890 (370)	
2030 projection	35,185 (373)	

RACE		
Whites	62.4% (435)	
Blacks	25.8% (65)	
Hispanics	10.1% (149)	
Asians	0.8% (201)	
Native Americans	0.1% (402)	

AGE		
0-17 years old	26.1% (66)	
18-24 years old	9.3% (217)	
25-39 years old	19.4% (78)	
40-54 years old	18.4% (430)	
55-64 years old	12.1% (430)	
65+ years old	14.6% (400)	

PRIVATE SECTOR		
Businesses	836 (354)	
Employees	11,640 (321)	
Total wages	$390,402,664 (348)	
Average weekly wages	$645 (402)	

HOUSEHOLD INCOME LADDER		
95th percentile	$136,595 (333)	
80th percentile	$74,349 (468)	
60th percentile	$44,827 (479)	
40th percentile	$26,038 (498)	
20th percentile	$13,660 (487)	

CHILDREN	★★ (424)	
Living with two parents	62.3% (339)	
Older teens in school	84.3% (229)	
Speak English very well	98.5% (287)	
Poverty rate for children	33.9% (469)	
No health insurance	12.5% (485)	

DIVERSITY/EQUALITY	★★★ (272)	
Racial diversity index	53.4% (74)	
Geographic diversity index	39.0% (372)	
Top 20% share of income	51.4% (481)	
Gender gap in earnings	28.9% (151)	
White-collar gender gap	28.8% (320)	

EDUCATION	★ (453)	
Eighth grade or less	5.7% (412)	
High school diplomas	82.3% (437)	

Attended college	42.3% (486)	
Bachelor's degrees	15.3% (412)	
Advanced degrees	5.0% (378)	

EMPLOYMENT	★★ (427)	
Average jobless rate	8.9% (351)	
Self-employed workers	9.8% (186)	
Management/financial jobs	7.7% (538)	
Computer/engineering jobs	2.2% (381)	
Health care jobs	5.5% (250)	

GROWTH POTENTIAL	★★★★★ (106)	
Children per senior	1.78 (102)	
Median age	35.9 (113)	
Moved from different state	1.1% (487)	
Homes built since 2000	15.9% (179)	
Construction jobs	8.8% (55)	

HOUSING	★★ (344)	
Home vacancy rate	9.5% (317)	
Home ownership rate	63.9% (456)	
Housing diversity index	84.3% (314)	
4 or more bedrooms	16.4% (272)	
Affordability/income ratio	$2,519 (258)	

INCOME	★ (504)	
Poverty rate	24.9% (477)	
Median household income	$34,140 (497)	
Interest/dividends	10.9% (512)	
Public assistance	23.5% (502)	
Median fulltime earnings	$31,867 (503)	

SENIORS	★ (550)	
Seniors living alone	33.3% (531)	
Poverty rate for seniors	19.9% (538)	
Median income for seniors	$22,364 (525)	
Seniors who work	16.9% (348)	
Home ownership by seniors	70.8% (547)	

STABILITY	★★★★ (122)	
25-39 age group	19.4% (78)	
Born in state of residence	77.1% (178)	
Same house as 1 year ago	89.5% (61)	
Live and work in county	66.4% (428)	
Married-couple households	48.5% (361)	

TRANSPORTATION	★★★ (302)	
Bicycle or walk to work	1.5% (457)	
Carpool to work	12.1% (135)	
Public transit to work	0.6% (141)	
Commute <15 minutes	38.3% (370)	
Commute >45 minutes	9.5% (203)	

See pages 37-130 for explanations of statistics, stars, and ranks.

Washington, NC
(Beaufort County, NC)

POPULATION	
2010 census	47,759 (221)
2015 estimate	47,651 (233)
2010-2015 change	-0.2% (273)
2020 projection	47,289 (236)
2030 projection	46,399 (253)

RACE	
Whites	66.0% (409)
Blacks	25.7% (66)
Hispanics	7.4% (190)
Asians	0.0% (546)
Native Americans	0.0% (523)

AGE	
0-17 years old	21.3% (383)
18-24 years old	8.0% (407)
25-39 years old	14.7% (523)
40-54 years old	19.6% (289)
55-64 years old	15.5% (59)
65+ years old	20.9% (38)

PRIVATE SECTOR	
Businesses	1,114 (234)
Employees	12,496 (297)
Total wages	$440,904,662 (298)
Average weekly wages	$679 (315)

HOUSEHOLD INCOME LADDER	
95th percentile	$131,719 (406)
80th percentile	$80,649 (356)
60th percentile	$50,172 (377)
40th percentile	$31,861 (367)
20th percentile	$16,347 (393)

CHILDREN	★★ (399)
Living with two parents	59.7% (408)
Older teens in school	78.4% (440)
Speak English very well	98.2% (320)
Poverty rate for children	25.9% (321)
No health insurance	9.3% (401)

DIVERSITY/EQUALITY	★★★★★ (98)
Racial diversity index	49.3% (118)
Geographic diversity index	43.5% (305)
Top 20% share of income	48.6% (324)
Gender gap in earnings	27.6% (130)
White-collar gender gap	15.0% (153)

EDUCATION	★★ (375)
Eighth grade or less	5.2% (398)
High school diplomas	84.4% (389)
Attended college	52.3% (280)
Bachelor's degrees	16.3% (357)
Advanced degrees	5.0% (378)

EMPLOYMENT	★★★★ (174)
Average jobless rate	11.5% (474)
Self-employed workers	10.8% (125)
Management/financial jobs	10.6% (306)
Computer/engineering jobs	3.0% (193)
Health care jobs	7.7% (35)

GROWTH POTENTIAL	★★ (439)
Children per senior	1.02 (497)
Median age	44.9 (496)
Moved from different state	1.3% (452)
Homes built since 2000	15.1% (202)
Construction jobs	7.1% (173)

HOUSING	★★ (406)
Home vacancy rate	15.3% (536)
Home ownership rate	70.8% (239)
Housing diversity index	85.2% (190)
4 or more bedrooms	16.2% (284)
Affordability/income ratio	$2,850 (368)

INCOME	★★ (362)
Poverty rate	18.4% (315)
Median household income	$40,391 (371)
Interest/dividends	19.7% (259)
Public assistance	20.7% (448)
Median fulltime earnings	$35,637 (354)

SENIORS	★★★ (311)
Seniors living alone	27.6% (269)
Poverty rate for seniors	10.7% (357)
Median income for seniors	$34,191 (224)
Seniors who work	16.5% (376)
Home ownership by seniors	83.2% (210)

STABILITY	★★★ (223)
25-39 age group	14.7% (523)
Born in state of residence	74.0% (245)
Same house as 1 year ago	94.3% (2)
Live and work in county	74.0% (310)
Married-couple households	48.0% (378)

TRANSPORTATION	★ (487)
Bicycle or walk to work	2.2% (358)
Carpool to work	7.9% (498)
Public transit to work	0.2% (363)
Commute <15 minutes	40.7% (321)
Commute >45 minutes	16.1% (459)

See pages 37-130 for explanations of statistics, stars, and ranks.

Wauchula, FL
(Hardee County, FL)

POPULATION

2010 census	27,731 (458)
2015 estimate	27,502 (457)
2010-2015 change	-0.8% (314)
2020 projection	27,516 (453)
2030 projection	27,623 (447)

RACE

Whites	47.4% (495)
Blacks	7.7% (130)
Hispanics	43.0% (33)
Asians	0.2% (509)
Native Americans	0.3% (231)

AGE

0-17 years old	26.6% (55)
18-24 years old	9.6% (189)
25-39 years old	20.0% (58)
40-54 years old	19.4% (315)
55-64 years old	10.4% (506)
65+ years old	14.1% (431)

PRIVATE SECTOR

Businesses	523 (509)
Employees	5,764 (515)
Total wages	$173,391,977 (525)
Average weekly wages	$578 (515)

HOUSEHOLD INCOME LADDER

95th percentile	$141,023 (278)
80th percentile	$76,443 (433)
60th percentile	$45,623 (466)
40th percentile	$28,836 (442)
20th percentile	$16,549 (381)

CHILDREN ★ (550)

Living with two parents	58.6% (437)
Older teens in school	70.6% (529)
Speak English very well	79.9% (547)
Poverty rate for children	39.7% (512)
No health insurance	15.1% (524)

DIVERSITY/EQUALITY ★★★★ (145)

Racial diversity index	58.4% (22)
Geographic diversity index	61.8% (107)
Top 20% share of income	51.6% (490)
Gender gap in earnings	10.0% (8)
White-collar gender gap	64.7% (549)

EDUCATION ★ (547)

Eighth grade or less	21.1% (545)
High school diplomas	67.7% (541)
Attended college	27.2% (550)
Bachelor's degrees	9.9% (542)
Advanced degrees	2.8% (540)

EMPLOYMENT ★ (542)

Average jobless rate	11.0% (459)
Self-employed workers	7.4% (393)
Management/financial jobs	9.9% (392)
Computer/engineering jobs	1.1% (532)
Health care jobs	2.8% (540)

GROWTH POTENTIAL ★★★★★ (47)

Children per senior	1.89 (72)
Median age	34.8 (88)
Moved from different state	2.2% (248)
Homes built since 2000	19.8% (94)
Construction jobs	9.7% (25)

HOUSING ★★ (391)

Home vacancy rate	12.7% (483)
Home ownership rate	69.6% (284)
Housing diversity index	84.5% (287)
4 or more bedrooms	12.6% (472)
Affordability/income ratio	$2,276 (151)

INCOME ★ (508)

Poverty rate	27.4% (507)
Median household income	$35,457 (479)
Interest/dividends	14.9% (413)
Public assistance	24.5% (511)
Median fulltime earnings	$29,079 (543)

SENIORS ★★★★ (165)

Seniors living alone	19.1% (10)
Poverty rate for seniors	14.1% (472)
Median income for seniors	$31,385 (355)
Seniors who work	15.5% (436)
Home ownership by seniors	86.5% (80)

STABILITY ★★★★ (115)

25-39 age group	20.0% (58)
Born in state of residence	58.9% (427)
Same house as 1 year ago	88.7% (95)
Live and work in county	72.7% (334)
Married-couple households	52.3% (180)

TRANSPORTATION ★★★★ (122)

Bicycle or walk to work	3.2% (225)
Carpool to work	17.9% (17)
Public transit to work	2.6% (20)
Commute <15 minutes	31.3% (508)
Commute >45 minutes	16.1% (459)

See pages 37-130 for explanations of statistics, stars, and ranks.

Waycross, GA
(Pierce and Ware Counties, GA)

POPULATION	
2010 census	55,070 (173)
2015 estimate	54,473 (175)
2010-2015 change	-1.1% (335)
2020 projection	54,204 (184)
2030 projection	53,576 (192)

RACE	
Whites	71.1% (382)
Blacks	22.0% (71)
Hispanics	4.2% (287)
Asians	0.9% (178)
Native Americans	0.4% (203)

AGE	
0-17 years old	24.3% (164)
18-24 years old	9.3% (217)
25-39 years old	18.6% (135)
40-54 years old	19.5% (301)
55-64 years old	12.8% (356)
65+ years old	15.5% (333)

PRIVATE SECTOR	
Businesses	1,248 (190)
Employees	15,010 (208)
Total wages	$499,224,976 (245)
Average weekly wages	$640 (415)

HOUSEHOLD INCOME LADDER	
95th percentile	$133,399 (383)
80th percentile	$75,307 (452)
60th percentile	$45,561 (469)
40th percentile	$27,484 (469)
20th percentile	$14,395 (468)

CHILDREN	★ (508)
Living with two parents	50.2% (506)
Older teens in school	77.9% (452)
Speak English very well	98.1% (331)
Poverty rate for children	40.4% (518)
No health insurance	8.8% (385)

DIVERSITY/EQUALITY	★★ (376)
Racial diversity index	44.4% (158)
Geographic diversity index	39.5% (363)
Top 20% share of income	50.5% (448)
Gender gap in earnings	37.8% (385)
White-collar gender gap	28.9% (321)

EDUCATION	★★ (440)
Eighth grade or less	4.7% (366)
High school diplomas	82.4% (433)
Attended college	42.3% (486)
Bachelor's degrees	13.3% (487)
Advanced degrees	6.1% (250)

EMPLOYMENT	★★★★ (117)
Average jobless rate	7.8% (270)
Self-employed workers	10.7% (129)
Management/financial jobs	11.8% (173)
Computer/engineering jobs	1.6% (486)
Health care jobs	7.6% (39)

GROWTH POTENTIAL	★★★★ (218)
Children per senior	1.57 (186)
Median age	38.2 (189)
Moved from different state	1.8% (338)
Homes built since 2000	15.4% (193)
Construction jobs	6.5% (253)

HOUSING	★★★ (311)
Home vacancy rate	11.6% (441)
Home ownership rate	67.7% (356)
Housing diversity index	85.8% (97)
4 or more bedrooms	14.4% (381)
Affordability/income ratio	$2,308 (168)

INCOME	★ (495)
Poverty rate	27.2% (505)
Median household income	$36,605 (455)
Interest/dividends	11.5% (500)
Public assistance	23.2% (500)
Median fulltime earnings	$34,913 (388)

SENIORS	★ (497)
Seniors living alone	28.3% (318)
Poverty rate for seniors	13.5% (461)
Median income for seniors	$28,940 (435)
Seniors who work	15.3% (446)
Home ownership by seniors	77.6% (466)

STABILITY	★★ (344)
25-39 age group	18.6% (135)
Born in state of residence	76.5% (191)
Same house as 1 year ago	82.8% (406)
Live and work in county	69.5% (379)
Married-couple households	47.6% (395)

TRANSPORTATION	★★★ (301)
Bicycle or walk to work	1.8% (409)
Carpool to work	11.1% (221)
Public transit to work	1.0% (69)
Commute <15 minutes	43.0% (278)
Commute >45 minutes	12.1% (316)

See pages 37-130 for explanations of statistics, stars, and ranks.

Weatherford, OK
(Custer County, OK)

POPULATION	
2010 census	27,469 (461)
2015 estimate	29,744 (436)
2010-2015 change	8.3% (13)
2020 projection	31,476 (424)
2030 projection	35,208 (372)

RACE	
Whites	70.7% (384)
Blacks	3.1% (222)
Hispanics	16.2% (94)
Asians	1.5% (85)
Native Americans	2.5% (60)

AGE	
0-17 years old	24.3% (164)
18-24 years old	17.1% (44)
25-39 years old	19.4% (78)
40-54 years old	15.8% (524)
55-64 years old	10.2% (516)
65+ years old	13.1% (473)

PRIVATE SECTOR	
Businesses	924 (303)
Employees	10,028 (375)
Total wages	$409,511,773 (326)
Average weekly wages	$785 (110)

HOUSEHOLD INCOME LADDER	
95th percentile	$151,232 (149)
80th percentile	$92,803 (117)
60th percentile	$56,658 (217)
40th percentile	$36,693 (212)
20th percentile	$18,862 (274)

CHILDREN	★★★★ (200)
Living with two parents	66.4% (235)
Older teens in school	91.2% (51)
Speak English very well	97.2% (403)
Poverty rate for children	16.8% (91)
No health insurance	12.1% (473)

DIVERSITY/EQUALITY	★★★ (307)
Racial diversity index	46.8% (139)
Geographic diversity index	54.9% (155)
Top 20% share of income	48.7% (336)
Gender gap in earnings	44.4% (493)
White-collar gender gap	34.9% (389)

EDUCATION	★★★ (243)
Eighth grade or less	6.3% (439)
High school diplomas	85.9% (345)

Attended college	52.0% (283)
Bachelor's degrees	26.8% (90)
Advanced degrees	7.2% (164)

EMPLOYMENT	★★★ (252)
Average jobless rate	3.7% (25)
Self-employed workers	9.8% (186)
Management/financial jobs	9.2% (459)
Computer/engineering jobs	2.5% (307)
Health care jobs	4.7% (385)

GROWTH POTENTIAL	★★★★★ (81)
Children per senior	1.85 (84)
Median age	30.7 (33)
Moved from different state	3.1% (147)
Homes built since 2000	14.8% (208)
Construction jobs	6.6% (241)

HOUSING	★ (458)
Home vacancy rate	12.5% (476)
Home ownership rate	59.7% (507)
Housing diversity index	85.9% (83)
4 or more bedrooms	14.8% (368)
Affordability/income ratio	$2,580 (284)

INCOME	★★★★ (205)
Poverty rate	16.7% (255)
Median household income	$46,125 (209)
Interest/dividends	19.3% (271)
Public assistance	8.3% (37)
Median fulltime earnings	$35,600 (356)

SENIORS	★★★★★ (15)
Seniors living alone	22.0% (35)
Poverty rate for seniors	8.4% (214)
Median income for seniors	$43,920 (36)
Seniors who work	25.6% (57)
Home ownership by seniors	88.4% (31)

STABILITY	★★★★ (178)
25-39 age group	19.4% (78)
Born in state of residence	65.1% (385)
Same house as 1 year ago	83.2% (388)
Live and work in county	83.6% (151)
Married-couple households	50.3% (284)

TRANSPORTATION	★★★★ (185)
Bicycle or walk to work	2.7% (292)
Carpool to work	11.0% (229)
Public transit to work	0.2% (363)
Commute <15 minutes	56.8% (74)
Commute >45 minutes	9.8% (218)

See pages 37-130 for explanations of statistics, stars, and ranks.

West Point, MS
(Clay County, MS)

POPULATION

2010 census	20,634 (524)
2015 estimate	20,048 (524)
2010-2015 change	-2.8% (467)
2020 projection	19,303 (527)
2030 projection	17,771 (532)

RACE

Whites	39.6% (514)
Blacks	58.2% (9)
Hispanics	1.2% (513)
Asians	0.6% (291)
Native Americans	0.1% (402)

AGE

0-17 years old	24.7% (141)
18-24 years old	9.2% (234)
25-39 years old	17.6% (248)
40-54 years old	19.0% (364)
55-64 years old	13.6% (247)
65+ years old	15.8% (305)

PRIVATE SECTOR

Businesses	341 (541)
Employees	4,340 (539)
Total wages	$147,410,405 (535)
Average weekly wages	$653 (385)

HOUSEHOLD INCOME LADDER

95th percentile	$135,533 (353)
80th percentile	$73,527 (479)
60th percentile	$41,219 (513)
40th percentile	$23,806 (525)
20th percentile	$12,346 (511)

CHILDREN ★ (460)

Living with two parents	41.6% (535)
Older teens in school	88.3% (94)
Speak English very well	99.5% (96)
Poverty rate for children	41.2% (523)
No health insurance	7.1% (324)

DIVERSITY/EQUALITY ★ (480)

Racial diversity index	50.4% (110)
Geographic diversity index	24.2% (532)
Top 20% share of income	51.4% (486)
Gender gap in earnings	39.1% (424)
White-collar gender gap	29.4% (328)

EDUCATION ★★ (370)

Eighth grade or less	2.4% (169)
High school diplomas	81.9% (449)
Attended college	48.6% (367)
Bachelor's degrees	16.8% (339)
Advanced degrees	5.2% (352)

EMPLOYMENT ★ (478)

Average jobless rate	16.2% (544)
Self-employed workers	9.0% (254)
Management/financial jobs	9.3% (453)
Computer/engineering jobs	2.4% (336)
Health care jobs	6.8% (91)

GROWTH POTENTIAL ★ (474)

Children per senior	1.57 (186)
Median age	38.8 (217)
Moved from different state	0.9% (515)
Homes built since 2000	7.7% (475)
Construction jobs	4.6% (494)

HOUSING ★★ (353)

Home vacancy rate	12.7% (483)
Home ownership rate	69.7% (281)
Housing diversity index	84.0% (344)
4 or more bedrooms	17.1% (239)
Affordability/income ratio	$2,555 (274)

INCOME ★ (521)

Poverty rate	26.6% (496)
Median household income	$31,669 (524)
Interest/dividends	11.7% (499)
Public assistance	26.5% (522)
Median fulltime earnings	$32,923 (455)

SENIORS ★★★ (302)

Seniors living alone	22.0% (35)
Poverty rate for seniors	16.1% (504)
Median income for seniors	$28,385 (447)
Seniors who work	18.2% (280)
Home ownership by seniors	84.4% (172)

STABILITY ★★ (354)

25-39 age group	17.6% (248)
Born in state of residence	86.7% (18)
Same house as 1 year ago	90.7% (33)
Live and work in county	55.3% (519)
Married-couple households	43.2% (491)

TRANSPORTATION ★ (458)

Bicycle or walk to work	1.7% (428)
Carpool to work	7.9% (498)
Public transit to work	0.1% (441)
Commute <15 minutes	36.3% (413)
Commute >45 minutes	10.3% (237)

See pages 37-130 for explanations of statistics, stars, and ranks.

Wilson, NC
(Wilson County, NC)

POPULATION

2010 census	81,234 (65)
2015 estimate	81,714 (63)
2010-2015 change	0.6% (209)
2020 projection	81,864 (66)
2030 projection	81,796 (70)

RACE

Whites	48.3% (491)
Blacks	38.2% (33)
Hispanics	9.9% (153)
Asians	1.0% (158)
Native Americans	0.3% (231)

AGE

0-17 years old	23.8% (206)
18-24 years old	9.0% (265)
25-39 years old	17.3% (280)
40-54 years old	20.4% (169)
55-64 years old	13.5% (258)
65+ years old	15.9% (297)

PRIVATE SECTOR

Businesses	1,807 (87)
Employees	31,988 (30)
Total wages	$1,302,615,839 (29)
Average weekly wages	$783 (116)

HOUSEHOLD INCOME LADDER

95th percentile	$139,793 (292)
80th percentile	$77,295 (417)
60th percentile	$48,987 (403)
40th percentile	$32,541 (338)
20th percentile	$16,172 (403)

CHILDREN ★ **(495)**

Living with two parents	53.6% (482)
Older teens in school	79.4% (415)
Speak English very well	96.0% (453)
Poverty rate for children	38.3% (503)
No health insurance	7.9% (359)

DIVERSITY/EQUALITY ★★★★★ **(100)**

Racial diversity index	61.0% (13)
Geographic diversity index	42.6% (313)
Top 20% share of income	49.3% (388)
Gender gap in earnings	24.1% (76)
White-collar gender gap	26.6% (294)

EDUCATION ★★ **(393)**

Eighth grade or less	6.4% (446)
High school diplomas	82.8% (425)
Attended college	50.2% (325)
Bachelor's degrees	18.4% (268)
Advanced degrees	5.4% (334)

EMPLOYMENT ★★ **(399)**

Average jobless rate	10.1% (423)
Self-employed workers	5.8% (508)
Management/financial jobs	10.0% (381)
Computer/engineering jobs	3.1% (180)
Health care jobs	6.4% (132)

GROWTH POTENTIAL ★★★ **(228)**

Children per senior	1.50 (216)
Median age	39.9 (292)
Moved from different state	1.7% (355)
Homes built since 2000	18.3% (126)
Construction jobs	6.4% (270)

HOUSING ★★ **(413)**

Home vacancy rate	9.4% (309)
Home ownership rate	60.0% (503)
Housing diversity index	85.9% (83)
4 or more bedrooms	13.8% (409)
Affordability/income ratio	$2,919 (385)

INCOME ★★ **(436)**

Poverty rate	23.1% (448)
Median household income	$39,847 (385)
Interest/dividends	15.1% (405)
Public assistance	19.9% (424)
Median fulltime earnings	$34,999 (384)

SENIORS ★ **(482)**

Seniors living alone	30.9% (469)
Poverty rate for seniors	11.9% (408)
Median income for seniors	$31,446 (352)
Seniors who work	19.5% (226)
Home ownership by seniors	75.7% (515)

STABILITY ★★ **(412)**

25-39 age group	17.3% (280)
Born in state of residence	74.8% (224)
Same house as 1 year ago	85.6% (277)
Live and work in county	75.6% (281)
Married-couple households	42.6% (502)

TRANSPORTATION ★★ **(391)**

Bicycle or walk to work	1.9% (401)
Carpool to work	8.8% (448)
Public transit to work	0.2% (363)
Commute <15 minutes	41.3% (313)
Commute >45 minutes	9.9% (225)

See pages 37-130 for explanations of statistics, stars, and ranks.

Woodward, OK
(Woodward County, OK)

POPULATION	
2010 census	20,081 (527)
2015 estimate	21,559 (516)
2010-2015 change	7.4% (18)
2020 projection	22,678 (499)
2030 projection	25,076 (471)

RACE	
Whites	81.4% (311)
Blacks	0.6% (438)
Hispanics	11.5% (135)
Asians	0.1% (529)
Native Americans	1.9% (72)

AGE	
0-17 years old	25.1% (116)
18-24 years old	9.1% (251)
25-39 years old	21.0% (42)
40-54 years old	19.3% (323)
55-64 years old	11.6% (471)
65+ years old	13.8% (448)

PRIVATE SECTOR	
Businesses	799 (372)
Employees	8,120 (444)
Total wages	$375,192,828 (359)
Average weekly wages	$889 (39)

HOUSEHOLD INCOME LADDER	
95th percentile	$167,922 (63)
80th percentile	$102,537 (49)
60th percentile	$68,908 (42)
40th percentile	$41,736 (82)
20th percentile	$21,868 (144)

CHILDREN	★★★ (249)
Living with two parents	75.7% (41)
Older teens in school	70.3% (531)
Speak English very well	99.7% (57)
Poverty rate for children	17.9% (123)
No health insurance	7.6% (349)

DIVERSITY/EQUALITY	★★★ (309)
Racial diversity index	32.2% (234)
Geographic diversity index	52.1% (188)
Top 20% share of income	47.0% (219)
Gender gap in earnings	47.3% (517)
White-collar gender gap	24.1% (259)

EDUCATION	★★ (345)
Eighth grade or less	4.4% (346)
High school diplomas	86.6% (322)
Attended college	47.2% (394)
Bachelor's degrees	18.6% (265)
Advanced degrees	5.8% (283)

EMPLOYMENT	★★★★ (200)
Average jobless rate	5.1% (69)
Self-employed workers	10.1% (158)
Management/financial jobs	11.8% (173)
Computer/engineering jobs	1.5% (499)
Health care jobs	5.1% (319)

GROWTH POTENTIAL	★★★★ (155)
Children per senior	1.82 (90)
Median age	36.1 (118)
Moved from different state	2.0% (288)
Homes built since 2000	11.2% (351)
Construction jobs	7.3% (151)

HOUSING	★★ (427)
Home vacancy rate	15.7% (538)
Home ownership rate	71.2% (218)
Housing diversity index	84.7% (260)
4 or more bedrooms	12.3% (482)
Affordability/income ratio	$2,087 (78)

INCOME	★★★★★ (85)
Poverty rate	13.0% (114)
Median household income	$55,300 (51)
Interest/dividends	20.8% (224)
Public assistance	11.1% (96)
Median fulltime earnings	$42,212 (60)

SENIORS	★★★★ (207)
Seniors living alone	29.9% (426)
Poverty rate for seniors	11.1% (378)
Median income for seniors	$32,985 (283)
Seniors who work	24.1% (86)
Home ownership by seniors	85.5% (126)

STABILITY	★★★★★ (14)
25-39 age group	21.0% (42)
Born in state of residence	67.2% (358)
Same house as 1 year ago	82.6% (416)
Live and work in county	90.7% (58)
Married-couple households	55.5% (59)

TRANSPORTATION	★★★ (281)
Bicycle or walk to work	0.6% (541)
Carpool to work	7.1% (528)
Public transit to work	0.9% (83)
Commute <15 minutes	58.4% (57)
Commute >45 minutes	8.4% (148)

See pages 37-130 for explanations of statistics, stars, and ranks.

Zapata, TX
(Zapata County, TX)

POPULATION

2010 census	14,018 (545)
2015 estimate	14,374 (546)
2010-2015 change	2.5% (107)
2020 projection	14,789 (546)
2030 projection	15,653 (542)

RACE

Whites	6.4% (549)
Blacks	0.0% (550)
Hispanics	93.6% (3)
Asians	0.0% (546)
Native Americans	0.0% (523)

AGE

0-17 years old	33.7% (3)
18-24 years old	10.6% (131)
25-39 years old	21.0% (42)
40-54 years old	14.4% (541)
55-64 years old	8.8% (545)
65+ years old	11.4% (501)

PRIVATE SECTOR

Businesses	175 (551)
Employees	3,217 (547)
Total wages	$151,435,672 (533)
Average weekly wages	$905 (34)

HOUSEHOLD INCOME LADDER

95th percentile	$140,179 (289)
80th percentile	$75,034 (456)
60th percentile	$40,810 (523)
40th percentile	$26,327 (491)
20th percentile	$10,426 (542)

CHILDREN ★ (521)

Living with two parents	56.6% (468)
Older teens in school	100.0% (1)
Speak English very well	63.4% (551)
Poverty rate for children	51.6% (545)
No health insurance	12.7% (489)

DIVERSITY/EQUALITY ★ (539)

Racial diversity index	12.0% (467)
Geographic diversity index	53.1% (173)
Top 20% share of income	54.2% (537)
Gender gap in earnings	43.3% (487)
White-collar gender gap	29.3% (324)

EDUCATION ★ (549)

Eighth grade or less	27.3% (551)
High school diplomas	55.4% (550)
Attended college	28.2% (548)
Bachelor's degrees	7.8% (550)
Advanced degrees	2.9% (534)

EMPLOYMENT ★ (543)

Average jobless rate	12.2% (497)
Self-employed workers	10.8% (125)
Management/financial jobs	8.1% (524)
Computer/engineering jobs	1.5% (499)
Health care jobs	0.7% (551)

GROWTH POTENTIAL ★★★★★ (25)

Children per senior	2.97 (17)
Median age	29.2 (21)
Moved from different state	0.4% (551)
Homes built since 2000	21.6% (73)
Construction jobs	8.9% (51)

HOUSING ★★ (364)

Home vacancy rate	12.1% (463)
Home ownership rate	75.2% (76)
Housing diversity index	81.6% (475)
4 or more bedrooms	12.2% (487)
Affordability/income ratio	$1,716 (14)

INCOME ★ (542)

Poverty rate	37.4% (548)
Median household income	$32,162 (518)
Interest/dividends	12.3% (486)
Public assistance	33.8% (546)
Median fulltime earnings	$28,601 (548)

SENIORS ★★★ (329)

Seniors living alone	20.2% (16)
Poverty rate for seniors	16.8% (515)
Median income for seniors	$29,132 (429)
Seniors who work	18.8% (253)
Home ownership by seniors	80.8% (346)

STABILITY ★★★★★ (8)

25-39 age group	21.0% (42)
Born in state of residence	64.5% (392)
Same house as 1 year ago	88.4% (109)
Live and work in county	83.3% (157)
Married-couple households	54.5% (88)

TRANSPORTATION ★★★★★ (45)

Bicycle or walk to work	3.5% (189)
Carpool to work	19.6% (5)
Public transit to work	0.3% (291)
Commute <15 minutes	61.0% (41)
Commute >45 minutes	12.1% (316)

See pages 37-130 for explanations of statistics, stars, and ranks.

6

MIDWEST

★★★★★

MICROPOLITAN
AMERICA

Aberdeen, SD
(Brown and Edmunds Counties, SD)

POPULATION
2010 census	40,602 (307)
2015 estimate	42,784 (282)
2010-2015 change	5.4% (39)
2020 projection	44,333 (271)
2030 projection	47,424 (238)

RACE
Whites	90.6% (169)
Blacks	1.4% (340)
Hispanics	2.2% (406)
Asians	1.7% (69)
Native Americans	3.1% (49)

AGE
0-17 years old	23.5% (232)
18-24 years old	9.9% (168)
25-39 years old	17.7% (236)
40-54 years old	19.4% (315)
55-64 years old	13.1% (318)
65+ years old	16.3% (268)

PRIVATE SECTOR
Businesses	1,517 (130)
Employees	18,898 (141)
Total wages	$734,887,331 (142)
Average weekly wages	$748 (160)

HOUSEHOLD INCOME LADDER
95th percentile	$165,556 (71)
80th percentile	$96,532 (77)
60th percentile	$66,354 (62)
40th percentile	$43,797 (62)
20th percentile	$23,672 (75)

CHILDREN ★★★★★ (32)
Living with two parents	72.7% (89)
Older teens in school	87.7% (107)
Speak English very well	98.8% (251)
Poverty rate for children	8.4% (6)
No health insurance	4.3% (140)

DIVERSITY/EQUALITY ★★★ (320)
Racial diversity index	17.7% (378)
Geographic diversity index	46.1% (266)
Top 20% share of income	46.5% (163)
Gender gap in earnings	32.8% (249)
White-collar gender gap	31.8% (361)

EDUCATION ★★★★★ (55)
Eighth grade or less	1.4% (60)
High school diplomas	95.3% (21)
Attended college	65.1% (60)
Bachelor's degrees	30.7% (48)
Advanced degrees	8.0% (123)

EMPLOYMENT ★★★★★ (16)
Average jobless rate	2.4% (2)
Self-employed workers	12.0% (75)
Management/financial jobs	14.7% (33)
Computer/engineering jobs	3.3% (145)
Health care jobs	6.7% (104)

GROWTH POTENTIAL ★★★ (235)
Children per senior	1.44 (253)
Median age	38.9 (228)
Moved from different state	3.7% (96)
Homes built since 2000	13.4% (260)
Construction jobs	5.8% (360)

HOUSING ★★★★★ (32)
Home vacancy rate	6.0% (95)
Home ownership rate	69.8% (279)
Housing diversity index	85.2% (190)
4 or more bedrooms	26.5% (33)
Affordability/income ratio	$2,657 (315)

INCOME ★★★★★ (62)
Poverty rate	10.1% (34)
Median household income	$53,289 (71)
Interest/dividends	25.4% (85)
Public assistance	8.1% (34)
Median fulltime earnings	$39,194 (171)

SENIORS ★★ (404)
Seniors living alone	29.5% (405)
Poverty rate for seniors	11.1% (378)
Median income for seniors	$36,473 (139)
Seniors who work	26.0% (47)
Home ownership by seniors	71.4% (545)

STABILITY ★★★★ (148)
25-39 age group	17.7% (236)
Born in state of residence	71.1% (289)
Same house as 1 year ago	82.0% (439)
Live and work in county	93.3% (31)
Married-couple households	50.4% (278)

TRANSPORTATION ★★★★★ (85)
Bicycle or walk to work	3.6% (180)
Carpool to work	9.3% (401)
Public transit to work	0.3% (291)
Commute <15 minutes	61.9% (36)
Commute >45 minutes	2.8% (6)

See pages 37-130 for explanations of statistics, stars, and ranks.

Adrian, MI
(Lenawee County, MI)

POPULATION

2010 census	99,892 (29)
2015 estimate	98,573 (32)
2010-2015 change	-1.3% (355)
2020 projection	97,896 (35)
2030 projection	96,218 (36)

RACE

Whites	87.3% (235)
Blacks	2.2% (276)
Hispanics	7.6% (189)
Asians	0.4% (413)
Native Americans	0.4% (203)

AGE

0-17 years old	22.1% (330)
18-24 years old	9.8% (176)
25-39 years old	16.9% (338)
40-54 years old	20.8% (122)
55-64 years old	14.2% (161)
65+ years old	16.2% (279)

PRIVATE SECTOR

Businesses	1,651 (112)
Employees	22,501 (92)
Total wages	$889,925,447 (95)
Average weekly wages	$761 (144)

HOUSEHOLD INCOME LADDER

95th percentile	$139,979 (290)
80th percentile	$88,331 (180)
60th percentile	$58,472 (173)
40th percentile	$38,409 (170)
20th percentile	$21,577 (158)

CHILDREN ★★★★★ (105)

Living with two parents	63.4% (315)
Older teens in school	88.5% (92)
Speak English very well	99.3% (142)
Poverty rate for children	21.3% (200)
No health insurance	3.5% (82)

DIVERSITY/EQUALITY ★★★★ (182)

Racial diversity index	23.1% (312)
Geographic diversity index	42.4% (316)
Top 20% share of income	44.8% (52)
Gender gap in earnings	33.1% (262)
White-collar gender gap	19.9% (205)

EDUCATION ★★★★ (177)

Eighth grade or less	2.2% (152)
High school diplomas	91.6% (141)
Attended college	57.4% (179)
Bachelor's degrees	20.2% (216)
Advanced degrees	5.9% (272)

EMPLOYMENT ★★★ (329)

Average jobless rate	8.6% (335)
Self-employed workers	7.6% (376)
Management/financial jobs	10.8% (280)
Computer/engineering jobs	3.3% (145)
Health care jobs	5.3% (286)

GROWTH POTENTIAL ★★ (419)

Children per senior	1.37 (301)
Median age	40.9 (350)
Moved from different state	2.1% (269)
Homes built since 2000	11.5% (333)
Construction jobs	5.2% (442)

HOUSING ★★★★★ (19)

Home vacancy rate	5.8% (79)
Home ownership rate	76.9% (31)
Housing diversity index	85.3% (170)
4 or more bedrooms	21.6% (92)
Affordability/income ratio	$2,392 (210)

INCOME ★★★★ (177)

Poverty rate	14.3% (168)
Median household income	$48,043 (175)
Interest/dividends	20.6% (231)
Public assistance	15.4% (274)
Median fulltime earnings	$40,227 (133)

SENIORS ★★★★ (132)

Seniors living alone	26.1% (179)
Poverty rate for seniors	7.3% (119)
Median income for seniors	$36,404 (142)
Seniors who work	15.0% (459)
Home ownership by seniors	87.6% (52)

STABILITY ★★ (410)

25-39 age group	16.9% (338)
Born in state of residence	74.4% (235)
Same house as 1 year ago	85.0% (299)
Live and work in county	61.3% (481)
Married-couple households	50.9% (253)

TRANSPORTATION ★ (517)

Bicycle or walk to work	3.4% (199)
Carpool to work	10.3% (299)
Public transit to work	0.3% (291)
Commute <15 minutes	32.3% (489)
Commute >45 minutes	21.4% (530)

See pages 37-130 for explanations of statistics, stars, and ranks.

Albert Lea, MN
(Freeborn County, MN)

POPULATION	
2010 census	31,255 (429)
2015 estimate	30,613 (431)
2010-2015 change	-2.1% (418)
2020 projection	29,890 (431)
2030 projection	28,500 (434)

RACE	
Whites	87.2% (236)
Blacks	1.1% (367)
Hispanics	9.3% (162)
Asians	1.2% (125)
Native Americans	0.2% (300)

AGE	
0-17 years old	21.9% (344)
18-24 years old	7.1% (515)
25-39 years old	15.7% (465)
40-54 years old	20.1% (221)
55-64 years old	14.1% (174)
65+ years old	21.1% (29)

PRIVATE SECTOR	
Businesses	725 (417)
Employees	10,571 (357)
Total wages	$407,460,856 (328)
Average weekly wages	$741 (176)

HOUSEHOLD INCOME LADDER	
95th percentile	$147,722 (189)
80th percentile	$88,120 (185)
60th percentile	$58,060 (180)
40th percentile	$38,499 (167)
20th percentile	$21,791 (148)

CHILDREN	★★★★ (126)
Living with two parents	62.0% (353)
Older teens in school	85.1% (196)
Speak English very well	99.0% (200)
Poverty rate for children	17.6% (112)
No health insurance	3.1% (64)

DIVERSITY/EQUALITY	★★ (380)
Racial diversity index	23.1% (312)
Geographic diversity index	39.5% (363)
Top 20% share of income	47.5% (254)
Gender gap in earnings	37.1% (366)
White-collar gender gap	28.3% (315)

EDUCATION	★★★★ (200)
Eighth grade or less	2.3% (161)
High school diplomas	91.8% (132)
Attended college	59.3% (142)
Bachelor's degrees	17.6% (301)
Advanced degrees	4.8% (405)

EMPLOYMENT	★★★★ (129)
Average jobless rate	4.9% (63)
Self-employed workers	11.6% (90)
Management/financial jobs	11.5% (202)
Computer/engineering jobs	1.9% (441)
Health care jobs	5.5% (250)

GROWTH POTENTIAL	★ (542)
Children per senior	1.03 (492)
Median age	44.6 (494)
Moved from different state	1.2% (474)
Homes built since 2000	6.3% (518)
Construction jobs	6.1% (310)

HOUSING	★★★★★ (78)
Home vacancy rate	7.2% (172)
Home ownership rate	76.4% (43)
Housing diversity index	82.9% (422)
4 or more bedrooms	20.4% (118)
Affordability/income ratio	$2,225 (131)

INCOME	★★★★★ (103)
Poverty rate	12.1% (88)
Median household income	$47,105 (190)
Interest/dividends	26.1% (69)
Public assistance	10.6% (84)
Median fulltime earnings	$38,544 (205)

SENIORS	★★★★ (156)
Seniors living alone	28.8% (355)
Poverty rate for seniors	7.4% (128)
Median income for seniors	$35,582 (168)
Seniors who work	20.8% (166)
Home ownership by seniors	84.6% (159)

STABILITY	★★★ (270)
25-39 age group	15.7% (465)
Born in state of residence	76.5% (191)
Same house as 1 year ago	88.2% (124)
Live and work in county	74.4% (304)
Married-couple households	49.3% (333)

TRANSPORTATION	★★★★ (188)
Bicycle or walk to work	2.8% (279)
Carpool to work	9.8% (358)
Public transit to work	0.9% (83)
Commute <15 minutes	50.7% (141)
Commute >45 minutes	8.0% (131)

See pages 37-130 for explanations of statistics, stars, and ranks.

Alexandria, MN
(Douglas County, MN)

POPULATION

2010 census	36,009 (376)
2015 estimate	37,075 (354)
2010-2015 change	3.0% (86)
2020 projection	38,051 (343)
2030 projection	40,086 (316)

RACE

Whites	96.6% (4)
Blacks	0.6% (438)
Hispanics	1.3% (503)
Asians	0.2% (509)
Native Americans	0.2% (300)

AGE

0-17 years old	21.3% (383)
18-24 years old	7.8% (447)
25-39 years old	16.7% (375)
40-54 years old	18.8% (386)
55-64 years old	14.4% (136)
65+ years old	21.1% (29)

PRIVATE SECTOR

Businesses	1,235 (193)
Employees	14,856 (215)
Total wages	$564,213,233 (205)
Average weekly wages	$730 (195)

HOUSEHOLD INCOME LADDER

95th percentile	$168,357 (62)
80th percentile	$99,313 (62)
60th percentile	$66,500 (60)
40th percentile	$43,848 (61)
20th percentile	$24,020 (65)

CHILDREN ★★★★★ (4)

Living with two parents	77.5% (24)
Older teens in school	92.6% (35)
Speak English very well	99.9% (19)
Poverty rate for children	10.4% (17)
No health insurance	3.5% (82)

DIVERSITY/EQUALITY ★ (521)

Racial diversity index	6.7% (547)
Geographic diversity index	35.4% (431)
Top 20% share of income	47.8% (282)
Gender gap in earnings	39.0% (421)
White-collar gender gap	35.1% (394)

EDUCATION ★★★★★ (41)

Eighth grade or less	0.4% (1)
High school diplomas	96.3% (10)

Attended college	71.8% (20)
Bachelor's degrees	26.8% (90)
Advanced degrees	7.3% (157)

EMPLOYMENT ★★★★★ (36)

Average jobless rate	4.5% (47)
Self-employed workers	13.6% (38)
Management/financial jobs	15.2% (27)
Computer/engineering jobs	3.0% (193)
Health care jobs	5.5% (250)

GROWTH POTENTIAL ★★★ (311)

Children per senior	1.01 (500)
Median age	44.1 (481)
Moved from different state	1.3% (452)
Homes built since 2000	23.0% (53)
Construction jobs	7.0% (185)

HOUSING ★★★★★ (10)

Home vacancy rate	4.8% (27)
Home ownership rate	76.3% (47)
Housing diversity index	84.8% (248)
4 or more bedrooms	28.6% (17)
Affordability/income ratio	$3,455 (458)

INCOME ★★★★★ (45)

Poverty rate	9.6% (23)
Median household income	$54,531 (59)
Interest/dividends	28.4% (30)
Public assistance	9.4% (51)
Median fulltime earnings	$41,411 (82)

SENIORS ★★★★ (147)

Seniors living alone	25.3% (127)
Poverty rate for seniors	8.5% (223)
Median income for seniors	$37,447 (107)
Seniors who work	23.3% (103)
Home ownership by seniors	79.0% (417)

STABILITY ★★★★★ (42)

25-39 age group	16.7% (375)
Born in state of residence	79.2% (125)
Same house as 1 year ago	85.0% (299)
Live and work in county	85.9% (119)
Married-couple households	56.4% (39)

TRANSPORTATION ★★★ (228)

Bicycle or walk to work	3.0% (249)
Carpool to work	7.8% (504)
Public transit to work	0.4% (219)
Commute <15 minutes	51.0% (131)
Commute >45 minutes	5.6% (43)

See pages 37-130 for explanations of statistics, stars, and ranks.

Alma, MI
(Gratiot County, MI)

POPULATION

2010 census	42,476 (282)
2015 estimate	41,540 (292)
2010-2015 change	-2.2% (427)
2020 projection	41,106 (300)
2030 projection	40,131 (314)

RACE

Whites	86.9% (243)
Blacks	5.6% (150)
Hispanics	5.6% (233)
Asians	0.4% (413)
Native Americans	0.3% (231)

AGE

0-17 years old	20.6% (423)
18-24 years old	11.8% (90)
25-39 years old	18.8% (121)
40-54 years old	20.5% (151)
55-64 years old	12.4% (408)
65+ years old	15.9% (297)

PRIVATE SECTOR

Businesses	672 (445)
Employees	10,447 (360)
Total wages	$397,650,303 (340)
Average weekly wages	$732 (193)

HOUSEHOLD INCOME LADDER

95th percentile	$133,433 (382)
80th percentile	$79,918 (372)
60th percentile	$51,653 (337)
40th percentile	$33,527 (309)
20th percentile	$18,003 (320)

CHILDREN ★★★★ (192)

Living with two parents	61.4% (370)
Older teens in school	88.7% (88)
Speak English very well	99.0% (200)
Poverty rate for children	27.1% (350)
No health insurance	5.1% (188)

DIVERSITY/EQUALITY ★★ (398)

Racial diversity index	23.8% (306)
Geographic diversity index	21.7% (546)
Top 20% share of income	47.2% (240)
Gender gap in earnings	32.6% (243)
White-collar gender gap	21.9% (237)

EDUCATION ★★★ (278)

Eighth grade or less	2.9% (217)
High school diplomas	90.6% (178)
Attended college	51.8% (285)
Bachelor's degrees	14.6% (435)
Advanced degrees	5.4% (334)

EMPLOYMENT ★★★ (293)

Average jobless rate	8.5% (332)
Self-employed workers	9.4% (216)
Management/financial jobs	10.8% (280)
Computer/engineering jobs	3.0% (193)
Health care jobs	5.1% (319)

GROWTH POTENTIAL ★ (500)

Children per senior	1.29 (353)
Median age	38.9 (228)
Moved from different state	1.3% (452)
Homes built since 2000	8.4% (455)
Construction jobs	4.5% (504)

HOUSING ★★★★★ (58)

Home vacancy rate	6.7% (141)
Home ownership rate	73.7% (129)
Housing diversity index	84.5% (287)
4 or more bedrooms	20.4% (118)
Affordability/income ratio	$2,121 (90)

INCOME ★★ (358)

Poverty rate	18.9% (334)
Median household income	$41,912 (326)
Interest/dividends	17.3% (336)
Public assistance	19.8% (419)
Median fulltime earnings	$36,591 (310)

SENIORS ★★★ (293)

Seniors living alone	26.4% (193)
Poverty rate for seniors	10.2% (334)
Median income for seniors	$32,823 (292)
Seniors who work	13.5% (518)
Home ownership by seniors	85.5% (126)

STABILITY ★★★★ (130)

25-39 age group	18.8% (121)
Born in state of residence	88.3% (6)
Same house as 1 year ago	84.0% (346)
Live and work in county	66.3% (430)
Married-couple households	51.6% (218)

TRANSPORTATION ★★ (353)

Bicycle or walk to work	4.1% (147)
Carpool to work	10.6% (271)
Public transit to work	0.1% (441)
Commute <15 minutes	41.7% (306)
Commute >45 minutes	14.9% (420)

See pages 37-130 for explanations of statistics, stars, and ranks.

Alpena, MI
(Alpena County, MI)

POPULATION	
2010 census	29,598 (436)
2015 estimate	28,803 (444)
2010-2015 change	-2.7% (459)
2020 projection	28,131 (448)
2030 projection	26,741 (458)

RACE	
Whites	96.1% (15)
Blacks	0.5% (466)
Hispanics	1.2% (513)
Asians	0.5% (355)
Native Americans	0.6% (150)

AGE	
0-17 years old	19.7% (473)
18-24 years old	7.4% (489)
25-39 years old	15.6% (474)
40-54 years old	20.2% (202)
55-64 years old	16.1% (42)
65+ years old	21.1% (29)

PRIVATE SECTOR	
Businesses	710 (423)
Employees	8,626 (430)
Total wages	$297,747,490 (437)
Average weekly wages	$664 (344)

HOUSEHOLD INCOME LADDER	
95th percentile	$120,849 (509)
80th percentile	$74,640 (463)
60th percentile	$46,739 (449)
40th percentile	$31,304 (380)
20th percentile	$16,971 (366)

CHILDREN	★★★★ (198)
Living with two parents	68.9% (168)
Older teens in school	83.4% (258)
Speak English very well	98.5% (287)
Poverty rate for children	25.0% (298)
No health insurance	5.8% (236)

DIVERSITY/EQUALITY	★★ (423)
Racial diversity index	7.6% (531)
Geographic diversity index	23.6% (537)
Top 20% share of income	46.8% (203)
Gender gap in earnings	28.6% (146)
White-collar gender gap	22.8% (248)

EDUCATION	★★★★ (151)
Eighth grade or less	1.6% (84)
High school diplomas	92.9% (98)
Attended college	62.8% (85)
Bachelor's degrees	17.7% (295)
Advanced degrees	6.1% (250)

EMPLOYMENT	★★★★★ (105)
Average jobless rate	9.3% (387)
Self-employed workers	11.3% (104)
Management/financial jobs	10.3% (339)
Computer/engineering jobs	2.9% (219)
Health care jobs	8.3% (13)

GROWTH POTENTIAL	★ (541)
Children per senior	0.93 (519)
Median age	47.1 (527)
Moved from different state	1.4% (425)
Homes built since 2000	6.9% (506)
Construction jobs	7.0% (185)

HOUSING	★★★★★ (53)
Home vacancy rate	6.0% (95)
Home ownership rate	76.2% (49)
Housing diversity index	85.9% (83)
4 or more bedrooms	16.3% (279)
Affordability/income ratio	$2,403 (214)

INCOME	★★ (335)
Poverty rate	17.2% (270)
Median household income	$38,829 (410)
Interest/dividends	23.7% (137)
Public assistance	21.5% (467)
Median fulltime earnings	$35,767 (345)

SENIORS	★★★★ (220)
Seniors living alone	26.4% (193)
Poverty rate for seniors	9.5% (291)
Median income for seniors	$32,723 (295)
Seniors who work	13.4% (520)
Home ownership by seniors	88.4% (31)

STABILITY	★★★★★ (86)
25-39 age group	15.6% (474)
Born in state of residence	87.2% (14)
Same house as 1 year ago	86.5% (219)
Live and work in county	89.9% (65)
Married-couple households	49.2% (340)

TRANSPORTATION	★★★★ (180)
Bicycle or walk to work	2.5% (322)
Carpool to work	10.1% (322)
Public transit to work	0.5% (178)
Commute <15 minutes	50.9% (135)
Commute >45 minutes	6.0% (53)

See pages 37-130 for explanations of statistics, stars, and ranks.

Angola, IN
(Steuben County, IN)

POPULATION	
2010 census	34,185 (393)
2015 estimate	34,372 (390)
2010-2015 change	0.5% (219)
2020 projection	34,366 (392)
2030 projection	34,236 (387)

RACE	
Whites	94.3% (69)
Blacks	0.3% (519)
Hispanics	3.2% (330)
Asians	0.5% (355)
Native Americans	0.0% (523)

AGE	
0-17 years old	21.5% (373)
18-24 years old	10.9% (119)
25-39 years old	15.6% (474)
40-54 years old	20.7% (132)
55-64 years old	14.7% (97)
65+ years old	16.6% (237)

PRIVATE SECTOR	
Businesses	889 (321)
Employees	14,155 (230)
Total wages	$472,698,756 (270)
Average weekly wages	$642 (412)

HOUSEHOLD INCOME LADDER	
95th percentile	$147,672 (191)
80th percentile	$86,983 (205)
60th percentile	$57,933 (183)
40th percentile	$40,268 (122)
20th percentile	$24,128 (63)

CHILDREN	★★★★ (153)
Living with two parents	65.8% (253)
Older teens in school	86.6% (144)
Speak English very well	99.1% (179)
Poverty rate for children	15.3% (68)
No health insurance	8.8% (385)

DIVERSITY/EQUALITY	★★ (354)
Racial diversity index	10.9% (481)
Geographic diversity index	52.4% (185)
Top 20% share of income	45.5% (93)
Gender gap in earnings	36.9% (360)
White-collar gender gap	38.7% (429)

EDUCATION	★★★★ (202)
Eighth grade or less	2.6% (185)
High school diplomas	90.9% (162)
Attended college	54.6% (232)
Bachelor's degrees	20.7% (200)
Advanced degrees	5.7% (292)

EMPLOYMENT	★★ (401)
Average jobless rate	6.9% (185)
Self-employed workers	8.0% (333)
Management/financial jobs	10.6% (306)
Computer/engineering jobs	3.4% (131)
Health care jobs	3.2% (525)

GROWTH POTENTIAL	★★ (427)
Children per senior	1.30 (347)
Median age	41.7 (390)
Moved from different state	3.2% (136)
Homes built since 2000	13.9% (240)
Construction jobs	4.1% (530)

HOUSING	★★★★★ (47)
Home vacancy rate	5.6% (69)
Home ownership rate	77.5% (21)
Housing diversity index	85.1% (212)
4 or more bedrooms	18.1% (197)
Affordability/income ratio	$2,657 (315)

INCOME	★★★★ (121)
Poverty rate	10.8% (54)
Median household income	$48,472 (162)
Interest/dividends	21.4% (202)
Public assistance	10.4% (76)
Median fulltime earnings	$38,564 (203)

SENIORS	★★★★★ (29)
Seniors living alone	22.2% (41)
Poverty rate for seniors	3.8% (7)
Median income for seniors	$37,025 (115)
Seniors who work	20.0% (195)
Home ownership by seniors	87.6% (52)

STABILITY	★ (463)
25-39 age group	15.6% (474)
Born in state of residence	64.0% (398)
Same house as 1 year ago	83.8% (347)
Live and work in county	64.6% (451)
Married-couple households	54.4% (93)

TRANSPORTATION	★★ (390)
Bicycle or walk to work	2.5% (322)
Carpool to work	9.1% (419)
Public transit to work	0.3% (291)
Commute <15 minutes	40.3% (324)
Commute >45 minutes	11.5% (295)

See pages 37-130 for explanations of statistics, stars, and ranks.

Arkansas City-Winfield, KS
(Cowley County, KS)

POPULATION	
2010 census	36,311 (370)
2015 estimate	35,788 (375)
2010-2015 change	-1.4% (364)
2020 projection	35,220 (381)
2030 projection	34,016 (390)

RACE	
Whites	80.9% (319)
Blacks	2.8% (232)
Hispanics	10.0% (150)
Asians	1.6% (77)
Native Americans	1.8% (77)

AGE	
0-17 years old	24.1% (180)
18-24 years old	11.0% (115)
25-39 years old	16.6% (388)
40-54 years old	19.1% (354)
55-64 years old	12.6% (385)
65+ years old	16.7% (225)

PRIVATE SECTOR	
Businesses	729 (414)
Employees	10,727 (352)
Total wages	$392,555,074 (347)
Average weekly wages	$704 (246)

HOUSEHOLD INCOME LADDER	
95th percentile	$146,600 (205)
80th percentile	$86,827 (212)
60th percentile	$53,883 (281)
40th percentile	$36,057 (229)
20th percentile	$20,256 (220)

CHILDREN	★★★★ (163)
Living with two parents	66.4% (235)
Older teens in school	85.5% (183)
Speak English very well	98.8% (251)
Poverty rate for children	23.0% (249)
No health insurance	5.2% (197)

DIVERSITY/EQUALITY	★★★★ (196)
Racial diversity index	33.3% (225)
Geographic diversity index	52.3% (187)
Top 20% share of income	47.1% (227)
Gender gap in earnings	37.3% (374)
White-collar gender gap	21.8% (234)

EDUCATION	★★★★ (154)
Eighth grade or less	2.4% (169)
High school diplomas	91.5% (145)
Attended college	63.3% (81)
Bachelor's degrees	19.4% (235)
Advanced degrees	6.3% (234)

EMPLOYMENT	★★ (382)
Average jobless rate	7.0% (196)
Self-employed workers	8.6% (285)
Management/financial jobs	10.5% (318)
Computer/engineering jobs	2.8% (246)
Health care jobs	3.9% (488)

GROWTH POTENTIAL	★★★ (297)
Children per senior	1.44 (253)
Median age	38.2 (189)
Moved from different state	4.4% (68)
Homes built since 2000	7.7% (475)
Construction jobs	5.3% (425)

HOUSING	★★★ (279)
Home vacancy rate	12.5% (476)
Home ownership rate	67.5% (368)
Housing diversity index	83.8% (369)
4 or more bedrooms	19.9% (129)
Affordability/income ratio	$1,897 (33)

INCOME	★★★ (227)
Poverty rate	17.6% (287)
Median household income	$43,860 (264)
Interest/dividends	23.0% (157)
Public assistance	13.5% (188)
Median fulltime earnings	$37,260 (264)

SENIORS	★★★ (240)
Seniors living alone	28.6% (336)
Poverty rate for seniors	8.9% (254)
Median income for seniors	$34,500 (212)
Seniors who work	21.0% (160)
Home ownership by seniors	82.0% (274)

STABILITY	★★ (439)
25-39 age group	16.6% (388)
Born in state of residence	66.7% (367)
Same house as 1 year ago	79.2% (507)
Live and work in county	80.6% (208)
Married-couple households	50.7% (264)

TRANSPORTATION	★★★★ (208)
Bicycle or walk to work	2.7% (292)
Carpool to work	12.6% (116)
Public transit to work	0.0% (511)
Commute <15 minutes	52.9% (110)
Commute >45 minutes	11.7% (300)

See pages 37-130 for explanations of statistics, stars, and ranks.

Ashland, OH
(Ashland County, OH)

POPULATION		
2010 census	53,139 (185)	
2015 estimate	53,213 (186)	
2010-2015 change	0.1% (250)	
2020 projection	53,113 (189)	
2030 projection	52,719 (196)	

RACE	
Whites	96.2% (9)
Blacks	0.8% (404)
Hispanics	1.1% (525)
Asians	0.5% (355)
Native Americans	0.1% (402)

AGE	
0-17 years old	23.1% (256)
18-24 years old	10.8% (123)
25-39 years old	16.2% (434)
40-54 years old	19.5% (301)
55-64 years old	13.5% (258)
65+ years old	16.9% (207)

PRIVATE SECTOR	
Businesses	1,008 (273)
Employees	15,960 (194)
Total wages	$580,017,201 (196)
Average weekly wages	$699 (258)

HOUSEHOLD INCOME LADDER	
95th percentile	$133,909 (377)
80th percentile	$83,381 (282)
60th percentile	$57,571 (193)
40th percentile	$38,998 (158)
20th percentile	$22,315 (122)

CHILDREN	★★ (431)
Living with two parents	75.4% (47)
Older teens in school	84.8% (207)
Speak English very well	90.5% (526)
Poverty rate for children	25.0% (298)
No health insurance	14.1% (510)

DIVERSITY/EQUALITY	★★ (353)
Racial diversity index	7.4% (537)
Geographic diversity index	28.7% (497)
Top 20% share of income	45.4% (85)
Gender gap in earnings	36.5% (354)
White-collar gender gap	11.8% (109)

EDUCATION	★★★ (238)
Eighth grade or less	3.5% (284)
High school diplomas	88.8% (240)
Attended college	48.5% (371)
Bachelor's degrees	21.5% (174)
Advanced degrees	7.2% (164)

EMPLOYMENT	★★★ (303)
Average jobless rate	7.8% (270)
Self-employed workers	6.2% (488)
Management/financial jobs	11.6% (196)
Computer/engineering jobs	3.0% (193)
Health care jobs	5.8% (209)

GROWTH POTENTIAL	★★ (421)
Children per senior	1.37 (301)
Median age	39.9 (292)
Moved from different state	1.1% (487)
Homes built since 2000	13.5% (256)
Construction jobs	5.1% (458)

HOUSING	★★★★★ (83)
Home vacancy rate	5.7% (74)
Home ownership rate	71.9% (192)
Housing diversity index	84.6% (277)
4 or more bedrooms	19.2% (150)
Affordability/income ratio	$2,517 (256)

INCOME	★★★★ (190)
Poverty rate	14.9% (189)
Median household income	$48,003 (177)
Interest/dividends	20.7% (229)
Public assistance	12.7% (155)
Median fulltime earnings	$37,106 (278)

SENIORS	★★★★★ (92)
Seniors living alone	25.4% (132)
Poverty rate for seniors	6.2% (53)
Median income for seniors	$36,667 (126)
Seniors who work	18.3% (272)
Home ownership by seniors	85.8% (115)

STABILITY	★★★ (245)
25-39 age group	16.2% (434)
Born in state of residence	84.1% (53)
Same house as 1 year ago	86.3% (232)
Live and work in county	60.6% (487)
Married-couple households	54.5% (88)

TRANSPORTATION	★★ (437)
Bicycle or walk to work	4.3% (130)
Carpool to work	7.1% (528)
Public transit to work	0.4% (219)
Commute <15 minutes	38.4% (366)
Commute >45 minutes	14.2% (395)

See pages 37-130 for explanations of statistics, stars, and ranks.

Ashtabula, OH
(Ashtabula County, OH)

POPULATION	
2010 census	101,497 (26)
2015 estimate	98,632 (31)
2010-2015 change	-2.8% (467)
2020 projection	96,377 (38)
2030 projection	91,667 (45)

RACE	
Whites	90.2% (175)
Blacks	3.4% (214)
Hispanics	3.8% (308)
Asians	0.5% (355)
Native Americans	0.1% (402)

AGE	
0-17 years old	22.8% (277)
18-24 years old	8.0% (407)
25-39 years old	16.9% (338)
40-54 years old	21.0% (107)
55-64 years old	14.5% (122)
65+ years old	16.8% (215)

PRIVATE SECTOR	
Businesses	1,864 (80)
Employees	25,799 (69)
Total wages	$898,263,816 (93)
Average weekly wages	$670 (334)

HOUSEHOLD INCOME LADDER	
95th percentile	$130,897 (420)
80th percentile	$76,833 (428)
60th percentile	$50,678 (366)
40th percentile	$31,517 (372)
20th percentile	$17,025 (365)

CHILDREN	★★ (426)
Living with two parents	61.0% (380)
Older teens in school	81.3% (357)
Speak English very well	95.7% (463)
Poverty rate for children	29.6% (392)
No health insurance	8.9% (390)

DIVERSITY/EQUALITY	★★★ (240)
Racial diversity index	18.3% (368)
Geographic diversity index	36.8% (407)
Top 20% share of income	46.0% (121)
Gender gap in earnings	31.5% (217)
White-collar gender gap	15.8% (162)

EDUCATION	★★ (413)
Eighth grade or less	3.8% (307)
High school diplomas	87.1% (301)
Attended college	43.4% (464)
Bachelor's degrees	13.7% (470)
Advanced degrees	4.2% (466)

EMPLOYMENT	★★ (392)
Average jobless rate	8.9% (351)
Self-employed workers	6.9% (435)
Management/financial jobs	10.0% (381)
Computer/engineering jobs	2.3% (354)
Health care jobs	6.1% (168)

GROWTH POTENTIAL	★★ (436)
Children per senior	1.36 (304)
Median age	41.8 (394)
Moved from different state	1.7% (355)
Homes built since 2000	9.0% (434)
Construction jobs	6.2% (295)

HOUSING	★★★ (273)
Home vacancy rate	10.4% (371)
Home ownership rate	71.2% (218)
Housing diversity index	83.6% (385)
4 or more bedrooms	17.8% (215)
Affordability/income ratio	$2,614 (297)

INCOME	★★ (386)
Poverty rate	20.1% (373)
Median household income	$40,544 (367)
Interest/dividends	16.0% (375)
Public assistance	20.5% (442)
Median fulltime earnings	$37,454 (251)

SENIORS	★★ (439)
Seniors living alone	28.7% (344)
Poverty rate for seniors	10.5% (345)
Median income for seniors	$29,899 (411)
Seniors who work	15.3% (446)
Home ownership by seniors	80.9% (339)

STABILITY	★★★ (258)
25-39 age group	16.9% (338)
Born in state of residence	78.7% (139)
Same house as 1 year ago	88.6% (101)
Live and work in county	70.2% (369)
Married-couple households	47.4% (401)

TRANSPORTATION	★ (469)
Bicycle or walk to work	2.1% (374)
Carpool to work	9.6% (378)
Public transit to work	0.8% (96)
Commute <15 minutes	35.1% (440)
Commute >45 minutes	17.4% (490)

See pages 37-130 for explanations of statistics, stars, and ranks.

Atchison, KS
(Atchison County, KS)

POPULATION

2010 census	16,924 (536)
2015 estimate	16,398 (543)
2010-2015 change	-3.1% (487)
2020 projection	15,940 (543)
2030 projection	15,019 (544)

RACE

Whites	88.2% (219)
Blacks	4.1% (185)
Hispanics	2.8% (355)
Asians	0.4% (413)
Native Americans	0.4% (203)

AGE

0-17 years old	23.7% (218)
18-24 years old	15.3% (55)
25-39 years old	15.7% (465)
40-54 years old	18.0% (450)
55-64 years old	11.8% (456)
65+ years old	15.6% (328)

PRIVATE SECTOR

Businesses	365 (538)
Employees	4,907 (531)
Total wages	$179,012,354 (521)
Average weekly wages	$702 (251)

HOUSEHOLD INCOME LADDER

95th percentile	$132,325 (396)
80th percentile	$81,600 (334)
60th percentile	$52,949 (300)
40th percentile	$35,739 (240)
20th percentile	$18,513 (288)

CHILDREN ★★★★ (119)

Living with two parents	63.5% (310)
Older teens in school	96.3% (11)
Speak English very well	99.4% (124)
Poverty rate for children	26.3% (333)
No health insurance	7.1% (324)

DIVERSITY/EQUALITY ★ (458)

Racial diversity index	21.8% (327)
Geographic diversity index	48.6% (235)
Top 20% share of income	47.5% (256)
Gender gap in earnings	47.2% (516)
White-collar gender gap	34.6% (386)

EDUCATION ★★★★ (122)

Eighth grade or less	0.8% (10)
High school diplomas	95.8% (15)

Attended college	56.6% (195)
Bachelor's degrees	21.0% (188)
Advanced degrees	7.1% (176)

EMPLOYMENT ★★★ (265)

Average jobless rate	7.3% (228)
Self-employed workers	9.5% (207)
Management/financial jobs	11.7% (185)
Computer/engineering jobs	1.5% (499)
Health care jobs	5.6% (240)

GROWTH POTENTIAL ★★★ (280)

Children per senior	1.52 (208)
Median age	35.9 (113)
Moved from different state	3.5% (109)
Homes built since 2000	9.7% (399)
Construction jobs	4.7% (487)

HOUSING ★★ (365)

Home vacancy rate	11.1% (409)
Home ownership rate	72.3% (175)
Housing diversity index	78.8% (529)
4 or more bedrooms	20.3% (121)
Affordability/income ratio	$2,022 (62)

INCOME ★★★ (240)

Poverty rate	19.2% (347)
Median household income	$43,581 (273)
Interest/dividends	22.3% (172)
Public assistance	15.0% (254)
Median fulltime earnings	$38,738 (191)

SENIORS ★★★★ (112)

Seniors living alone	31.1% (476)
Poverty rate for seniors	8.2% (196)
Median income for seniors	n.a.
Seniors who work	23.4% (98)
Home ownership by seniors	88.3% (36)

STABILITY ★ (452)

25-39 age group	15.7% (465)
Born in state of residence	68.9% (326)
Same house as 1 year ago	84.6% (319)
Live and work in county	76.1% (274)
Married-couple households	47.1% (416)

TRANSPORTATION ★★★★ (128)

Bicycle or walk to work	8.1% (29)
Carpool to work	11.7% (170)
Public transit to work	0.1% (441)
Commute <15 minutes	50.8% (137)
Commute >45 minutes	14.1% (392)

See pages 37-130 for explanations of statistics, stars, and ranks.

Athens, OH
(Athens County, OH)

POPULATION

2010 census	64,757 (121)
2015 estimate	65,886 (117)
2010-2015 change	1.7% (150)
2020 projection	66,958 (115)
2030 projection	68,889 (109)

RACE

Whites	90.1% (183)
Blacks	2.3% (267)
Hispanics	1.8% (455)
Asians	3.3% (20)
Native Americans	0.2% (300)

AGE

0-17 years old	15.4% (547)
18-24 years old	30.2% (6)
25-39 years old	17.4% (269)
40-54 years old	15.4% (530)
55-64 years old	10.6% (502)
65+ years old	11.0% (511)

PRIVATE SECTOR

Businesses	1,032 (267)
Employees	12,934 (284)
Total wages	$397,295,399 (341)
Average weekly wages	$591 (501)

HOUSEHOLD INCOME LADDER

95th percentile	$131,879 (404)
80th percentile	$76,192 (438)
60th percentile	$44,435 (484)
40th percentile	$24,651 (514)
20th percentile	$10,526 (540)

CHILDREN ★★★★ (112)

Living with two parents	62.3% (339)
Older teens in school	98.0% (4)
Speak English very well	99.4% (124)
Poverty rate for children	33.6% (467)
No health insurance	3.9% (111)

DIVERSITY/EQUALITY ★★ (435)

Racial diversity index	18.6% (366)
Geographic diversity index	45.4% (274)
Top 20% share of income	52.8% (516)
Gender gap in earnings	39.8% (431)
White-collar gender gap	6.1% (48)

EDUCATION ★★★★★ (31)

Eighth grade or less	1.2% (42)
High school diplomas	92.0% (124)
Attended college	61.8% (96)
Bachelor's degrees	30.3% (51)
Advanced degrees	14.8% (15)

EMPLOYMENT ★ (490)

Average jobless rate	10.9% (454)
Self-employed workers	6.4% (479)
Management/financial jobs	9.1% (463)
Computer/engineering jobs	3.9% (86)
Health care jobs	4.5% (419)

GROWTH POTENTIAL ★★★★ (130)

Children per senior	1.39 (286)
Median age	28.0 (13)
Moved from different state	3.7% (96)
Homes built since 2000	14.4% (222)
Construction jobs	4.7% (487)

HOUSING ★ (482)

Home vacancy rate	9.7% (334)
Home ownership rate	56.3% (531)
Housing diversity index	85.2% (190)
4 or more bedrooms	16.7% (261)
Affordability/income ratio	$3,475 (461)

INCOME ★ (489)

Poverty rate	33.0% (537)
Median household income	$33,872 (499)
Interest/dividends	16.4% (363)
Public assistance	21.0% (455)
Median fulltime earnings	$37,371 (255)

SENIORS ★★★ (278)

Seniors living alone	26.7% (217)
Poverty rate for seniors	10.7% (357)
Median income for seniors	$35,897 (157)
Seniors who work	16.7% (360)
Home ownership by seniors	82.6% (242)

STABILITY ★ (535)

25-39 age group	17.4% (269)
Born in state of residence	72.6% (267)
Same house as 1 year ago	72.0% (539)
Live and work in county	81.7% (191)
Married-couple households	40.4% (527)

TRANSPORTATION ★★★★ (124)

Bicycle or walk to work	17.6% (2)
Carpool to work	8.3% (471)
Public transit to work	0.8% (96)
Commute <15 minutes	42.5% (287)
Commute >45 minutes	10.1% (228)

See pages 37-130 for explanations of statistics, stars, and ranks.

Auburn, IN
(DeKalb County, IN)

POPULATION

2010 census	42,223 (287)
2015 estimate	42,589 (283)
2010-2015 change	0.9% (186)
2020 projection	42,851 (285)
2030 projection	43,222 (285)

RACE

Whites	95.3% (34)
Blacks	0.1% (544)
Hispanics	2.6% (378)
Asians	0.5% (355)
Native Americans	0.1% (402)

AGE

0-17 years old	25.3% (97)
18-24 years old	8.5% (330)
25-39 years old	18.1% (186)
40-54 years old	20.6% (145)
55-64 years old	13.2% (297)
65+ years old	14.3% (423)

PRIVATE SECTOR

Businesses	926 (302)
Employees	19,164 (135)
Total wages	$850,431,589 (107)
Average weekly wages	$853 (51)

HOUSEHOLD INCOME LADDER

95th percentile	$140,233 (286)
80th percentile	$86,558 (220)
60th percentile	$57,133 (203)
40th percentile	$38,641 (165)
20th percentile	$22,326 (120)

CHILDREN ★★★ (307)

Living with two parents	67.5% (207)
Older teens in school	78.1% (446)
Speak English very well	99.1% (179)
Poverty rate for children	21.4% (203)
No health insurance	9.7% (412)

DIVERSITY/EQUALITY ★★★ (296)

Racial diversity index	9.1% (514)
Geographic diversity index	42.2% (323)
Top 20% share of income	46.6% (174)
Gender gap in earnings	41.7% (467)
White-collar gender gap	2.2% (12)

EDUCATION ★★★ (264)

Eighth grade or less	3.0% (231)
High school diplomas	89.5% (215)
Attended college	51.6% (289)
Bachelor's degrees	18.0% (284)
Advanced degrees	5.2% (352)

EMPLOYMENT ★★ (375)

Average jobless rate	7.5% (242)
Self-employed workers	5.7% (515)
Management/financial jobs	9.9% (392)
Computer/engineering jobs	4.7% (40)
Health care jobs	4.5% (419)

GROWTH POTENTIAL ★★★ (275)

Children per senior	1.77 (104)
Median age	38.6 (207)
Moved from different state	1.8% (338)
Homes built since 2000	13.7% (249)
Construction jobs	5.2% (442)

HOUSING ★★★★★ (103)

Home vacancy rate	5.6% (69)
Home ownership rate	76.9% (31)
Housing diversity index	82.2% (450)
4 or more bedrooms	17.3% (232)
Affordability/income ratio	$2,278 (153)

INCOME ★★★★ (150)

Poverty rate	14.6% (178)
Median household income	$48,341 (166)
Interest/dividends	20.1% (241)
Public assistance	11.5% (112)
Median fulltime earnings	$39,930 (144)

SENIORS ★★★ (234)

Seniors living alone	28.5% (332)
Poverty rate for seniors	7.1% (101)
Median income for seniors	$34,261 (222)
Seniors who work	18.3% (272)
Home ownership by seniors	82.7% (236)

STABILITY ★★★ (222)

25-39 age group	18.1% (186)
Born in state of residence	74.5% (231)
Same house as 1 year ago	87.6% (157)
Live and work in county	61.9% (476)
Married-couple households	52.5% (171)

TRANSPORTATION ★★ (425)

Bicycle or walk to work	1.8% (409)
Carpool to work	8.1% (489)
Public transit to work	0.2% (363)
Commute <15 minutes	36.5% (410)
Commute >45 minutes	8.3% (144)

See pages 37-130 for explanations of statistics, stars, and ranks.

Austin, MN
(Mower County, MN)

POPULATION

2010 census	39,163 (323)
2015 estimate	39,116 (325)
2010-2015 change	-0.1% (266)
2020 projection	39,014 (327)
2030 projection	38,817 (328)

RACE

Whites	82.4% (297)
Blacks	3.0% (227)
Hispanics	10.9% (139)
Asians	2.1% (45)
Native Americans	0.1% (402)

AGE

0-17 years old	24.9% (131)
18-24 years old	8.9% (282)
25-39 years old	17.4% (269)
40-54 years old	18.4% (430)
55-64 years old	12.8% (356)
65+ years old	17.6% (151)

PRIVATE SECTOR

Businesses	774 (385)
Employees	13,785 (241)
Total wages	$654,659,914 (164)
Average weekly wages	$913 (33)

HOUSEHOLD INCOME LADDER

95th percentile	$152,233 (140)
80th percentile	$93,076 (115)
60th percentile	$61,942 (109)
40th percentile	$38,675 (163)
20th percentile	$19,949 (232)

CHILDREN ★★★★ (183)

Living with two parents	62.2% (344)
Older teens in school	88.0% (101)
Speak English very well	96.5% (436)
Poverty rate for children	18.8% (142)
No health insurance	5.8% (236)

DIVERSITY/EQUALITY ★★★ (266)

Racial diversity index	30.8% (248)
Geographic diversity index	50.1% (212)
Top 20% share of income	47.9% (290)
Gender gap in earnings	30.3% (175)
White-collar gender gap	36.6% (402)

EDUCATION ★★★★ (208)

Eighth grade or less	4.0% (325)
High school diplomas	89.0% (231)
Attended college	60.6% (119)
Bachelor's degrees	20.6% (204)
Advanced degrees	5.4% (334)

EMPLOYMENT ★★★★★ (95)

Average jobless rate	6.5% (157)
Self-employed workers	11.1% (115)
Management/financial jobs	11.5% (202)
Computer/engineering jobs	3.3% (145)
Health care jobs	6.4% (132)

GROWTH POTENTIAL ★★ (398)

Children per senior	1.41 (269)
Median age	39.0 (238)
Moved from different state	2.1% (269)
Homes built since 2000	9.1% (430)
Construction jobs	5.4% (413)

HOUSING ★★★★★ (97)

Home vacancy rate	7.9% (213)
Home ownership rate	71.9% (192)
Housing diversity index	83.8% (369)
4 or more bedrooms	21.8% (85)
Affordability/income ratio	$2,260 (144)

INCOME ★★★★ (115)

Poverty rate	14.0% (155)
Median household income	$49,427 (139)
Interest/dividends	25.1% (94)
Public assistance	13.1% (177)
Median fulltime earnings	$40,275 (132)

SENIORS ★★ (367)

Seniors living alone	31.7% (504)
Poverty rate for seniors	7.7% (156)
Median income for seniors	$32,866 (289)
Seniors who work	19.5% (226)
Home ownership by seniors	80.5% (356)

STABILITY ★★★ (249)

25-39 age group	17.4% (269)
Born in state of residence	68.3% (338)
Same house as 1 year ago	86.4% (225)
Live and work in county	76.6% (261)
Married-couple households	50.1% (291)

TRANSPORTATION ★★★★★ (70)

Bicycle or walk to work	4.1% (147)
Carpool to work	11.0% (229)
Public transit to work	1.8% (34)
Commute <15 minutes	60.8% (42)
Commute >45 minutes	10.1% (228)

See pages 37-130 for explanations of statistics, stars, and ranks.

Baraboo, WI
(Sauk County, WI)

POPULATION			
2010 census	61,976 (137)	Attended college	57.6% (174)
2015 estimate	63,642 (130)	Bachelor's degrees	23.5% (126)
2010-2015 change	2.7% (96)	Advanced degrees	7.0% (184)

POPULATION
2010 census 61,976 (137)
2015 estimate 63,642 (130)
2010-2015 change 2.7% (96)
2020 projection 65,658 (121)
2030 projection 69,813 (105)

RACE
Whites 91.8% (146)
Blacks 0.5% (466)
Hispanics 4.7% (260)
Asians 0.7% (241)
Native Americans 1.2% (89)

AGE
0-17 years old 23.2% (251)
18-24 years old 7.4% (489)
25-39 years old 18.5% (144)
40-54 years old 20.4% (169)
55-64 years old 13.8% (203)
65+ years old 16.6% (237)

PRIVATE SECTOR
Businesses 1,847 (82)
Employees 31,270 (34)
Total wages $1,131,349,557 (50)
Average weekly wages $696 (262)

HOUSEHOLD INCOME LADDER
95th percentile $150,192 (159)
80th percentile $90,775 (146)
60th percentile $62,286 (102)
40th percentile $41,215 (95)
20th percentile $23,397 (85)

CHILDREN ★★★★ (218)
Living with two parents 69.2% (163)
Older teens in school 80.6% (382)
Speak English very well 98.0% (341)
Poverty rate for children 18.3% (135)
No health insurance 7.6% (349)

DIVERSITY/EQUALITY ★★★★ (216)
Racial diversity index 15.5% (403)
Geographic diversity index 40.0% (351)
Top 20% share of income 45.7% (103)
Gender gap in earnings 27.2% (123)
White-collar gender gap 21.4% (225)

EDUCATION ★★★★ (139)
Eighth grade or less 2.0% (126)
High school diplomas 92.0% (124)

Attended college 57.6% (174)
Bachelor's degrees 23.5% (126)
Advanced degrees 7.0% (184)

EMPLOYMENT ★★★★ (130)
Average jobless rate 5.5% (98)
Self-employed workers 9.9% (171)
Management/financial jobs 13.6% (62)
Computer/engineering jobs 3.2% (158)
Health care jobs 4.3% (444)

GROWTH POTENTIAL ★★★ (281)
Children per senior 1.40 (279)
Median age 40.9 (350)
Moved from different state 1.4% (425)
Homes built since 2000 19.2% (103)
Construction jobs 6.0% (326)

HOUSING ★★★★ (175)
Home vacancy rate 6.1% (104)
Home ownership rate 69.2% (297)
Housing diversity index 83.7% (378)
4 or more bedrooms 20.8% (107)
Affordability/income ratio $3,265 (443)

INCOME ★★★★★ (104)
Poverty rate 12.3% (94)
Median household income $51,055 (100)
Interest/dividends 24.8% (105)
Public assistance 13.7% (197)
Median fulltime earnings $40,122 (137)

SENIORS ★★★ (222)
Seniors living alone 27.4% (263)
Poverty rate for seniors 7.9% (170)
Median income for seniors $34,454 (213)
Seniors who work 23.5% (95)
Home ownership by seniors 78.0% (454)

STABILITY ★★★★★ (58)
25-39 age group 18.5% (144)
Born in state of residence 76.0% (206)
Same house as 1 year ago 88.0% (133)
Live and work in county 77.3% (250)
Married-couple households 52.1% (190)

TRANSPORTATION ★★★ (268)
Bicycle or walk to work 5.0% (91)
Carpool to work 11.3% (201)
Public transit to work 0.2% (363)
Commute <15 minutes 43.7% (267)
Commute >45 minutes 13.8% (382)

See pages 37-130 for explanations of statistics, stars, and ranks.

Beatrice, NE
(Gage County, NE)

POPULATION

2010 census	22,311 (506)
2015 estimate	21,900 (510)
2010-2015 change	-1.8% (389)
2020 projection	21,508 (515)
2030 projection	20,696 (514)

RACE

Whites	95.3% (34)
Blacks	0.4% (499)
Hispanics	2.0% (428)
Asians	0.6% (291)
Native Americans	0.2% (300)

AGE

0-17 years old	22.0% (335)
18-24 years old	7.2% (510)
25-39 years old	14.9% (515)
40-54 years old	21.1% (97)
55-64 years old	14.6% (107)
65+ years old	20.2% (50)

PRIVATE SECTOR

Businesses	776 (384)
Employees	7,098 (473)
Total wages	$233,050,341 (480)
Average weekly wages	$631 (435)

HOUSEHOLD INCOME LADDER

95th percentile	$144,028 (242)
80th percentile	$88,787 (170)
60th percentile	$59,951 (152)
40th percentile	$38,291 (174)
20th percentile	$21,010 (187)

CHILDREN ★★★★★ (36)

Living with two parents	76.9% (31)
Older teens in school	81.8% (329)
Speak English very well	99.0% (200)
Poverty rate for children	11.7% (26)
No health insurance	1.6% (7)

DIVERSITY/EQUALITY ★★ (430)

Racial diversity index	9.1% (514)
Geographic diversity index	35.6% (429)
Top 20% share of income	45.7% (106)
Gender gap in earnings	30.4% (178)
White-collar gender gap	40.7% (452)

EDUCATION ★★★★ (168)

Eighth grade or less	3.4% (269)
High school diplomas	91.1% (156)
Attended college	61.1% (108)
Bachelor's degrees	22.3% (148)
Advanced degrees	5.7% (292)

EMPLOYMENT ★★★★★ (12)

Average jobless rate	4.3% (38)
Self-employed workers	15.6% (14)
Management/financial jobs	13.6% (62)
Computer/engineering jobs	2.9% (219)
Health care jobs	7.0% (69)

GROWTH POTENTIAL ★ (484)

Children per senior	1.09 (469)
Median age	44.6 (494)
Moved from different state	2.3% (234)
Homes built since 2000	8.5% (453)
Construction jobs	6.6% (241)

HOUSING ★★★★ (143)

Home vacancy rate	8.9% (280)
Home ownership rate	71.1% (222)
Housing diversity index	83.6% (385)
4 or more bedrooms	20.9% (103)
Affordability/income ratio	$2,166 (106)

INCOME ★★★★★ (78)

Poverty rate	9.7% (27)
Median household income	$50,010 (127)
Interest/dividends	25.9% (71)
Public assistance	9.0% (47)
Median fulltime earnings	$37,189 (271)

SENIORS ★★★ (235)

Seniors living alone	30.2% (436)
Poverty rate for seniors	9.1% (263)
Median income for seniors	$33,400 (263)
Seniors who work	25.4% (63)
Home ownership by seniors	81.1% (325)

STABILITY ★★★★ (167)

25-39 age group	14.9% (515)
Born in state of residence	79.3% (123)
Same house as 1 year ago	88.9% (86)
Live and work in county	73.7% (320)
Married-couple households	54.4% (93)

TRANSPORTATION ★★★ (249)

Bicycle or walk to work	3.0% (249)
Carpool to work	11.6% (178)
Public transit to work	0.0% (511)
Commute <15 minutes	50.1% (149)
Commute >45 minutes	11.6% (296)

See pages 37-130 for explanations of statistics, stars, and ranks.

Beaver Dam, WI
(Dodge County, WI)

POPULATION

2010 census	88,759 (50)
2015 estimate	88,502 (48)
2010-2015 change	-0.3% (279)
2020 projection	88,146 (51)
2030 projection	87,341 (58)

RACE

Whites	90.8% (166)
Blacks	2.0% (290)
Hispanics	4.4% (270)
Asians	0.6% (291)
Native Americans	0.7% (136)

AGE

0-17 years old	21.2% (397)
18-24 years old	7.6% (468)
25-39 years old	18.6% (135)
40-54 years old	22.8% (10)
55-64 years old	13.8% (203)
65+ years old	15.9% (297)

PRIVATE SECTOR

Businesses	1,618 (119)
Employees	29,348 (46)
Total wages	$1,244,703,659 (35)
Average weekly wages	$816 (69)

HOUSEHOLD INCOME LADDER

95th percentile	$142,908 (253)
80th percentile	$92,580 (120)
60th percentile	$65,148 (74)
40th percentile	$44,099 (54)
20th percentile	$25,378 (46)

CHILDREN ★★★★★ (60)

Living with two parents	70.4% (135)
Older teens in school	81.6% (341)
Speak English very well	99.0% (200)
Poverty rate for children	12.3% (33)
No health insurance	2.5% (34)

DIVERSITY/EQUALITY ★★★ (316)

Racial diversity index	17.3% (383)
Geographic diversity index	30.3% (484)
Top 20% share of income	43.3% (9)
Gender gap in earnings	34.6% (306)
White-collar gender gap	29.6% (331)

EDUCATION ★★★ (230)

Eighth grade or less	1.5% (72)
High school diplomas	91.1% (156)
Attended college	52.8% (266)
Bachelor's degrees	17.6% (301)
Advanced degrees	5.1% (364)

EMPLOYMENT ★★★ (253)

Average jobless rate	6.0% (117)
Self-employed workers	8.7% (281)
Management/financial jobs	11.3% (218)
Computer/engineering jobs	3.4% (131)
Health care jobs	4.3% (444)

GROWTH POTENTIAL ★★ (353)

Children per senior	1.33 (325)
Median age	42.0 (398)
Moved from different state	1.5% (406)
Homes built since 2000	12.5% (297)
Construction jobs	7.1% (173)

HOUSING ★★★★ (147)

Home vacancy rate	6.8% (151)
Home ownership rate	72.3% (175)
Housing diversity index	84.1% (337)
4 or more bedrooms	18.7% (171)
Affordability/income ratio	$2,847 (366)

INCOME ★★★★★ (61)

Poverty rate	9.2% (19)
Median household income	$53,783 (65)
Interest/dividends	25.0% (97)
Public assistance	11.4% (107)
Median fulltime earnings	$41,445 (80)

SENIORS ★★ (383)

Seniors living alone	28.9% (358)
Poverty rate for seniors	7.7% (156)
Median income for seniors	$32,514 (301)
Seniors who work	21.9% (132)
Home ownership by seniors	74.1% (534)

STABILITY ★★★★ (159)

25-39 age group	18.6% (135)
Born in state of residence	82.9% (68)
Same house as 1 year ago	87.6% (157)
Live and work in county	56.1% (515)
Married-couple households	53.5% (131)

TRANSPORTATION ★ (446)

Bicycle or walk to work	3.4% (199)
Carpool to work	8.1% (489)
Public transit to work	0.1% (441)
Commute <15 minutes	40.0% (329)
Commute >45 minutes	14.4% (407)

See pages 37-130 for explanations of statistics, stars, and ranks.

Bedford, IN
(Lawrence County, IN)

POPULATION	
2010 census	46,134 (246)
2015 estimate	45,495 (252)
2010-2015 change	-1.4% (364)
2020 projection	44,720 (265)
2030 projection	43,040 (286)

RACE	
Whites	96.1% (15)
Blacks	0.4% (499)
Hispanics	1.5% (480)
Asians	0.6% (291)
Native Americans	0.1% (402)

AGE	
0-17 years old	22.5% (300)
18-24 years old	7.6% (468)
25-39 years old	17.1% (308)
40-54 years old	21.0% (107)
55-64 years old	14.2% (161)
65+ years old	17.5% (158)

PRIVATE SECTOR	
Businesses	747 (403)
Employees	10,730 (351)
Total wages	$393,252,348 (345)
Average weekly wages	$705 (244)

HOUSEHOLD INCOME LADDER	
95th percentile	$132,413 (395)
80th percentile	$85,437 (241)
60th percentile	$56,754 (216)
40th percentile	$37,348 (196)
20th percentile	$21,249 (177)

CHILDREN	★★★ (308)
Living with two parents	72.1% (105)
Older teens in school	75.9% (493)
Speak English very well	98.9% (226)
Poverty rate for children	18.4% (138)
No health insurance	11.5% (459)

DIVERSITY/EQUALITY	★★★ (292)
Racial diversity index	7.6% (531)
Geographic diversity index	34.3% (446)
Top 20% share of income	44.8% (53)
Gender gap in earnings	35.8% (335)
White-collar gender gap	12.0% (113)

EDUCATION	★★★ (292)
Eighth grade or less	2.2% (152)
High school diplomas	90.6% (178)
Attended college	50.6% (311)
Bachelor's degrees	15.1% (417)
Advanced degrees	4.5% (442)

EMPLOYMENT	★★★★ (115)
Average jobless rate	6.3% (140)
Self-employed workers	8.2% (314)
Management/financial jobs	10.3% (339)
Computer/engineering jobs	4.6% (48)
Health care jobs	6.7% (104)

GROWTH POTENTIAL	★★ (357)
Children per senior	1.29 (353)
Median age	41.9 (397)
Moved from different state	0.7% (540)
Homes built since 2000	13.3% (263)
Construction jobs	7.5% (122)

HOUSING	★★★★ (114)
Home vacancy rate	8.6% (260)
Home ownership rate	77.0% (27)
Housing diversity index	86.1% (51)
4 or more bedrooms	12.6% (472)
Affordability/income ratio	$2,191 (120)

INCOME	★★★★ (193)
Poverty rate	13.0% (114)
Median household income	$45,875 (216)
Interest/dividends	18.2% (305)
Public assistance	12.5% (148)
Median fulltime earnings	$38,368 (208)

SENIORS	★★★★★ (106)
Seniors living alone	25.7% (154)
Poverty rate for seniors	8.4% (214)
Median income for seniors	$33,647 (255)
Seniors who work	22.4% (122)
Home ownership by seniors	85.3% (131)

STABILITY	★★★★ (111)
25-39 age group	17.1% (308)
Born in state of residence	80.4% (104)
Same house as 1 year ago	89.4% (64)
Live and work in county	62.4% (471)
Married-couple households	55.5% (59)

TRANSPORTATION	★ (524)
Bicycle or walk to work	1.4% (472)
Carpool to work	8.9% (439)
Public transit to work	0.3% (291)
Commute <15 minutes	34.3% (453)
Commute >45 minutes	17.2% (486)

See pages 37-130 for explanations of statistics, stars, and ranks.

Bellefontaine, OH
(Logan County, OH)

POPULATION			Attended college	41.9% (491)
2010 census	45,858 (251)		Bachelor's degrees	17.1% (322)
2015 estimate	45,386 (255)		Advanced degrees	5.9% (272)
2010-2015 change	-1.0% (326)		**EMPLOYMENT**	**★★★ (263)**
2020 projection	44,970 (262)		Average jobless rate	7.6% (250)
2030 projection	43,960 (273)		Self-employed workers	8.7% (281)
			Management/financial jobs	11.9% (165)
RACE			Computer/engineering jobs	3.2% (158)
Whites	94.1% (73)		Health care jobs	4.7% (385)
Blacks	1.9% (295)		**GROWTH POTENTIAL**	**★★ (416)**
Hispanics	1.3% (503)		Children per senior	1.51 (210)
Asians	0.7% (241)		Median age	40.7 (341)
Native Americans	0.2% (300)		Moved from different state	1.0% (504)
			Homes built since 2000	11.6% (330)
AGE			Construction jobs	5.6% (392)
0-17 years old	24.3% (164)		**HOUSING**	**★★★★ (150)**
18-24 years old	7.6% (468)		Home vacancy rate	7.7% (199)
25-39 years old	17.4% (269)		Home ownership rate	73.6% (132)
40-54 years old	20.3% (186)		Housing diversity index	84.4% (299)
55-64 years old	14.3% (148)		4 or more bedrooms	16.0% (293)
65+ years old	16.1% (286)		Affordability/income ratio	$2,398 (213)
PRIVATE SECTOR			**INCOME**	**★★★★ (154)**
Businesses	795 (376)		Poverty rate	14.5% (176)
Employees	17,165 (167)		Median household income	$49,783 (135)
Total wages	$750,405,979 (135)		Interest/dividends	20.3% (238)
Average weekly wages	$841 (57)		Public assistance	14.4% (225)
			Median fulltime earnings	$41,044 (95)
HOUSEHOLD INCOME LADDER			**SENIORS**	**★★★★ (111)**
95th percentile	$143,382 (250)		Seniors living alone	26.8% (222)
80th percentile	$88,512 (174)		Poverty rate for seniors	7.1% (101)
60th percentile	$60,881 (134)		Median income for seniors	$35,938 (155)
40th percentile	$40,731 (106)		Seniors who work	17.8% (299)
20th percentile	$21,722 (151)		Home ownership by seniors	87.5% (56)
CHILDREN	**★★★ (301)**		**STABILITY**	**★★★★ (168)**
Living with two parents	64.6% (280)		25-39 age group	17.4% (269)
Older teens in school	83.1% (271)		Born in state of residence	85.0% (45)
Speak English very well	95.8% (459)		Same house as 1 year ago	87.8% (149)
Poverty rate for children	21.7% (211)		Live and work in county	65.8% (440)
No health insurance	7.5% (344)		Married-couple households	50.8% (256)
DIVERSITY/EQUALITY	**★ (504)**		**TRANSPORTATION**	**★★ (352)**
Racial diversity index	11.4% (476)		Bicycle or walk to work	1.8% (409)
Geographic diversity index	27.2% (507)		Carpool to work	12.9% (106)
Top 20% share of income	46.8% (200)		Public transit to work	0.3% (291)
Gender gap in earnings	37.1% (366)		Commute <15 minutes	32.8% (479)
White-collar gender gap	33.9% (381)		Commute >45 minutes	11.1% (275)
EDUCATION	**★★★ (313)**			
Eighth grade or less	2.6% (185)			
High school diplomas	91.0% (160)			

See pages 37-130 for explanations of statistics, stars, and ranks.

Bemidji, MN
(Beltrami County, MN)

POPULATION

2010 census	44,442 (266)
2015 estimate	45,672 (250)
2010-2015 change	2.8% (94)
2020 projection	46,965 (237)
2030 projection	49,666 (220)

RACE

Whites	73.4% (369)
Blacks	0.8% (404)
Hispanics	1.9% (442)
Asians	1.0% (158)
Native Americans	20.0% (6)

AGE

0-17 years old	25.2% (108)
18-24 years old	14.5% (61)
25-39 years old	17.2% (290)
40-54 years old	16.7% (508)
55-64 years old	12.3% (414)
65+ years old	14.0% (438)

PRIVATE SECTOR

Businesses	1,035 (263)
Employees	14,032 (232)
Total wages	$487,414,822 (252)
Average weekly wages	$668 (338)

HOUSEHOLD INCOME LADDER

95th percentile	$142,820 (255)
80th percentile	$85,839 (233)
60th percentile	$55,976 (226)
40th percentile	$36,131 (227)
20th percentile	$19,222 (256)

CHILDREN ★★ (349)

Living with two parents	52.8% (486)
Older teens in school	87.5% (112)
Speak English very well	99.7% (57)
Poverty rate for children	23.6% (260)
No health insurance	11.7% (466)

DIVERSITY/EQUALITY ★★★ (232)

Racial diversity index	42.0% (175)
Geographic diversity index	40.0% (351)
Top 20% share of income	47.9% (285)
Gender gap in earnings	22.3% (61)
White-collar gender gap	43.1% (470)

EDUCATION ★★★★★ (71)

Eighth grade or less	1.0% (20)
High school diplomas	91.7% (135)
Attended college	66.7% (40)
Bachelor's degrees	25.4% (101)
Advanced degrees	8.5% (103)

EMPLOYMENT ★★★ (323)

Average jobless rate	10.6% (446)
Self-employed workers	8.5% (290)
Management/financial jobs	10.3% (339)
Computer/engineering jobs	3.0% (193)
Health care jobs	6.4% (132)

GROWTH POTENTIAL ★★★★★ (71)

Children per senior	1.81 (93)
Median age	33.3 (62)
Moved from different state	1.9% (310)
Homes built since 2000	20.7% (83)
Construction jobs	7.3% (151)

HOUSING ★★★★ (148)

Home vacancy rate	6.6% (136)
Home ownership rate	69.1% (298)
Housing diversity index	85.1% (212)
4 or more bedrooms	21.2% (96)
Affordability/income ratio	$3,325 (446)

INCOME ★★★ (281)

Poverty rate	18.8% (329)
Median household income	$44,757 (237)
Interest/dividends	18.7% (286)
Public assistance	15.9% (290)
Median fulltime earnings	$37,063 (282)

SENIORS ★★★★ (170)

Seniors living alone	25.5% (142)
Poverty rate for seniors	9.4% (282)
Median income for seniors	$38,993 (73)
Seniors who work	19.8% (206)
Home ownership by seniors	80.7% (350)

STABILITY ★★★ (289)

25-39 age group	17.2% (290)
Born in state of residence	76.1% (205)
Same house as 1 year ago	84.7% (314)
Live and work in county	84.2% (144)
Married-couple households	44.6% (471)

TRANSPORTATION ★★★★★ (90)

Bicycle or walk to work	4.3% (130)
Carpool to work	12.0% (141)
Public transit to work	2.1% (31)
Commute <15 minutes	46.1% (230)
Commute >45 minutes	9.5% (203)

See pages 37-130 for explanations of statistics, stars, and ranks.

Big Rapids, MI
(Mecosta County, MI)

POPULATION	
2010 census	42,798 (279)
2015 estimate	43,067 (279)
2010-2015 change	0.6% (209)
2020 projection	43,397 (280)
2030 projection	43,919 (275)

RACE	
Whites	91.7% (147)
Blacks	2.7% (241)
Hispanics	2.0% (428)
Asians	0.9% (178)
Native Americans	0.5% (174)

AGE	
0-17 years old	19.1% (498)
18-24 years old	19.7% (28)
25-39 years old	14.7% (523)
40-54 years old	17.3% (487)
55-64 years old	12.8% (356)
65+ years old	16.4% (255)

PRIVATE SECTOR	
Businesses	623 (460)
Employees	8,692 (427)
Total wages	$307,655,147 (426)
Average weekly wages	$681 (311)

HOUSEHOLD INCOME LADDER	
95th percentile	$136,011 (342)
80th percentile	$80,868 (354)
60th percentile	$51,632 (339)
40th percentile	$34,028 (288)
20th percentile	$17,199 (350)

CHILDREN	★★★ (238)
Living with two parents	69.1% (164)
Older teens in school	89.2% (77)
Speak English very well	97.6% (375)
Poverty rate for children	31.2% (427)
No health insurance	7.7% (352)

DIVERSITY/EQUALITY	★★★ (255)
Racial diversity index	15.7% (399)
Geographic diversity index	30.1% (485)
Top 20% share of income	47.2% (236)
Gender gap in earnings	30.4% (178)
White-collar gender gap	4.6% (39)

EDUCATION	★★★★ (132)
Eighth grade or less	2.1% (136)
High school diplomas	90.9% (162)
Attended college	57.3% (181)
Bachelor's degrees	23.3% (130)
Advanced degrees	8.7% (96)

EMPLOYMENT	★ (480)
Average jobless rate	12.2% (497)
Self-employed workers	9.1% (243)
Management/financial jobs	8.9% (483)
Computer/engineering jobs	3.2% (158)
Health care jobs	4.6% (401)

GROWTH POTENTIAL	★★★ (261)
Children per senior	1.17 (435)
Median age	35.7 (109)
Moved from different state	1.6% (383)
Homes built since 2000	17.5% (140)
Construction jobs	5.6% (392)

HOUSING	★★★★★ (62)
Home vacancy rate	5.9% (88)
Home ownership rate	74.5% (98)
Housing diversity index	85.4% (156)
4 or more bedrooms	19.0% (159)
Affordability/income ratio	$2,638 (305)

INCOME	★★ (341)
Poverty rate	23.1% (448)
Median household income	$41,889 (327)
Interest/dividends	21.0% (214)
Public assistance	18.0% (371)
Median fulltime earnings	$37,595 (242)

SENIORS	★★★★ (160)
Seniors living alone	27.2% (254)
Poverty rate for seniors	8.0% (177)
Median income for seniors	$36,801 (121)
Seniors who work	14.2% (496)
Home ownership by seniors	88.1% (39)

STABILITY	★ (460)
25-39 age group	14.7% (523)
Born in state of residence	83.2% (66)
Same house as 1 year ago	82.0% (439)
Live and work in county	68.9% (390)
Married-couple households	50.0% (296)

TRANSPORTATION	★★★ (252)
Bicycle or walk to work	6.2% (55)
Carpool to work	9.9% (348)
Public transit to work	0.8% (96)
Commute <15 minutes	44.6% (251)
Commute >45 minutes	15.6% (443)

See pages 37-130 for explanations of statistics, stars, and ranks.

Boone, IA
(Boone County, IA)

POPULATION

2010 census	26,306 (469)
2015 estimate	26,643 (466)
2010-2015 change	1.3% (167)
2020 projection	26,784 (461)
2030 projection	26,907 (457)

RACE

Whites	95.0% (46)
Blacks	0.9% (388)
Hispanics	2.3% (398)
Asians	0.3% (473)
Native Americans	0.2% (300)

AGE

0-17 years old	22.6% (291)
18-24 years old	8.0% (407)
25-39 years old	17.8% (227)
40-54 years old	20.2% (202)
55-64 years old	14.7% (97)
65+ years old	16.8% (215)

PRIVATE SECTOR

Businesses	653 (450)
Employees	7,225 (466)
Total wages	$258,626,154 (465)
Average weekly wages	$688 (290)

HOUSEHOLD INCOME LADDER

95th percentile	$146,670 (202)
80th percentile	$96,358 (79)
60th percentile	$64,029 (84)
40th percentile	$42,443 (72)
20th percentile	$24,002 (67)

CHILDREN ★★★★★ (22)

Living with two parents	71.0% (118)
Older teens in school	93.6% (25)
Speak English very well	99.3% (142)
Poverty rate for children	12.3% (33)
No health insurance	4.7% (166)

DIVERSITY/EQUALITY ★★ (369)

Racial diversity index	9.7% (500)
Geographic diversity index	36.1% (420)
Top 20% share of income	44.2% (32)
Gender gap in earnings	38.3% (402)
White-collar gender gap	28.0% (309)

EDUCATION ★★★★★ (83)

Eighth grade or less	1.1% (26)
High school diplomas	95.1% (27)
Attended college	64.7% (64)
Bachelor's degrees	24.7% (116)
Advanced degrees	6.4% (229)

EMPLOYMENT ★★★★★ (63)

Average jobless rate	4.7% (54)
Self-employed workers	9.6% (200)
Management/financial jobs	12.6% (111)
Computer/engineering jobs	4.7% (40)
Health care jobs	5.8% (209)

GROWTH POTENTIAL ★★★ (317)

Children per senior	1.35 (313)
Median age	41.3 (371)
Moved from different state	3.4% (118)
Homes built since 2000	10.6% (374)
Construction jobs	6.3% (284)

HOUSING ★★★★ (216)

Home vacancy rate	7.7% (199)
Home ownership rate	75.4% (69)
Housing diversity index	79.2% (523)
4 or more bedrooms	20.9% (103)
Affordability/income ratio	$2,257 (142)

INCOME ★★★★★ (60)

Poverty rate	10.1% (34)
Median household income	$52,985 (74)
Interest/dividends	25.2% (87)
Public assistance	11.1% (96)
Median fulltime earnings	$42,508 (53)

SENIORS ★★★★★ (86)

Seniors living alone	28.8% (355)
Poverty rate for seniors	5.4% (29)
Median income for seniors	$37,634 (99)
Seniors who work	23.0% (113)
Home ownership by seniors	85.1% (137)

STABILITY ★★ (404)

25-39 age group	17.8% (227)
Born in state of residence	79.0% (132)
Same house as 1 year ago	83.7% (353)
Live and work in county	53.3% (530)
Married-couple households	52.3% (180)

TRANSPORTATION ★★★ (315)

Bicycle or walk to work	2.3% (348)
Carpool to work	10.6% (271)
Public transit to work	0.5% (178)
Commute <15 minutes	41.0% (317)
Commute >45 minutes	10.1% (228)

See pages 37-130 for explanations of statistics, stars, and ranks.

Brainerd, MN
(Cass and Crow Wing Counties, MN)

POPULATION		
2010 census	91,067 (43)	
2015 estimate	92,134 (45)	
2010-2015 change	1.2% (173)	
2020 projection	93,816 (41)	
2030 projection	97,309 (32)	

RACE		
Whites	92.0% (135)	
Blacks	0.5% (466)	
Hispanics	1.4% (488)	
Asians	0.5% (355)	
Native Americans	4.0% (42)	

AGE		
0-17 years old	22.0% (335)	
18-24 years old	7.1% (515)	
25-39 years old	15.5% (484)	
40-54 years old	19.3% (323)	
55-64 years old	15.1% (74)	
65+ years old	21.0% (34)	

PRIVATE SECTOR		
Businesses	2,650 (30)	
Employees	30,027 (42)	
Total wages	$995,947,443 (70)	
Average weekly wages	$638 (417)	

HOUSEHOLD INCOME LADDER		
95th percentile	$153,748 (124)	
80th percentile	$89,279 (166)	
60th percentile	$59,408 (159)	
40th percentile	$38,770 (159)	
20th percentile	$21,788 (149)	

CHILDREN	★★★★ (133)	
Living with two parents	68.6% (177)	
Older teens in school	83.3% (263)	
Speak English very well	99.6% (77)	
Poverty rate for children	18.7% (141)	
No health insurance	5.4% (209)	

DIVERSITY/EQUALITY	★★ (424)	
Racial diversity index	15.2% (409)	
Geographic diversity index	37.1% (402)	
Top 20% share of income	48.4% (318)	
Gender gap in earnings	31.2% (210)	
White-collar gender gap	31.0% (354)	

EDUCATION	★★★★★ (97)	
Eighth grade or less	0.9% (16)	
High school diplomas	94.1% (54)	
Attended college	64.0% (72)	
Bachelor's degrees	22.3% (148)	
Advanced degrees	6.6% (211)	

EMPLOYMENT	★★★★★ (64)	
Average jobless rate	6.2% (131)	
Self-employed workers	13.5% (42)	
Management/financial jobs	13.1% (78)	
Computer/engineering jobs	2.5% (307)	
Health care jobs	6.0% (181)	

GROWTH POTENTIAL	★★★★ (209)	
Children per senior	1.05 (485)	
Median age	44.9 (496)	
Moved from different state	1.6% (383)	
Homes built since 2000	22.5% (64)	
Construction jobs	9.1% (40)	

HOUSING	★★★★★ (45)	
Home vacancy rate	3.9% (7)	
Home ownership rate	77.1% (26)	
Housing diversity index	85.4% (156)	
4 or more bedrooms	20.7% (110)	
Affordability/income ratio	$3,646 (477)	

INCOME	★★★★ (127)	
Poverty rate	12.9% (113)	
Median household income	$48,249 (167)	
Interest/dividends	22.4% (169)	
Public assistance	11.1% (96)	
Median fulltime earnings	$39,654 (152)	

SENIORS	★★★★★ (105)	
Seniors living alone	25.1% (120)	
Poverty rate for seniors	7.5% (140)	
Median income for seniors	$37,500 (102)	
Seniors who work	17.3% (324)	
Home ownership by seniors	85.7% (118)	

STABILITY	★★★★ (155)	
25-39 age group	15.5% (484)	
Born in state of residence	78.1% (153)	
Same house as 1 year ago	88.3% (115)	
Live and work in county	76.5% (263)	
Married-couple households	53.2% (143)	

TRANSPORTATION	★★★ (326)	
Bicycle or walk to work	2.6% (308)	
Carpool to work	9.6% (378)	
Public transit to work	0.6% (141)	
Commute <15 minutes	40.7% (321)	
Commute >45 minutes	9.8% (218)	

See pages 37-130 for explanations of statistics, stars, and ranks.

Branson, MO
(Stone and Taney Counties, MO)

POPULATION			Attended college	50.3% (321)
2010 census	83,877 (58)		Bachelor's degrees	17.2% (315)
2015 estimate	85,535 (56)		Advanced degrees	4.8% (405)
2010-2015 change	2.0% (128)		**EMPLOYMENT**	★★★ (299)
2020 projection	89,123 (48)		Average jobless rate	9.6% (402)
2030 projection	97,020 (33)		Self-employed workers	13.6% (38)
RACE			Management/financial jobs	11.7% (185)
Whites	92.0% (135)		Computer/engineering jobs	1.9% (441)
Blacks	0.6% (438)		Health care jobs	3.8% (494)
Hispanics	4.0% (296)		**GROWTH POTENTIAL**	★★★★ (112)
Asians	0.6% (291)		Children per senior	0.92 (523)
Native Americans	0.5% (174)		Median age	45.4 (504)
AGE			Moved from different state	5.0% (51)
0-17 years old	20.0% (458)		Homes built since 2000	28.7% (15)
18-24 years old	8.6% (317)		Construction jobs	8.3% (67)
25-39 years old	15.5% (484)		**HOUSING**	★ (513)
40-54 years old	18.9% (376)		Home vacancy rate	8.7% (268)
55-64 years old	15.1% (74)		Home ownership rate	67.1% (382)
65+ years old	21.8% (24)		Housing diversity index	79.0% (525)
PRIVATE SECTOR			4 or more bedrooms	14.9% (363)
Businesses	2,547 (33)		Affordability/income ratio	$3,422 (457)
Employees	30,438 (41)		**INCOME**	★★ (349)
Total wages	$865,074,878 (102)		Poverty rate	18.1% (300)
Average weekly wages	$547 (535)		Median household income	$39,096 (402)
HOUSEHOLD INCOME LADDER			Interest/dividends	23.3% (147)
95th percentile	$135,287 (355)		Public assistance	16.3% (305)
80th percentile	$72,967 (486)		Median fulltime earnings	$30,683 (533)
60th percentile	$47,322 (438)		**SENIORS**	★★★★★ (91)
40th percentile	$31,497 (373)		Seniors living alone	22.3% (45)
20th percentile	$18,674 (282)		Poverty rate for seniors	8.3% (202)
CHILDREN	★★ (371)		Median income for seniors	$35,441 (172)
Living with two parents	66.5% (231)		Seniors who work	20.3% (185)
Older teens in school	78.5% (438)		Home ownership by seniors	83.3% (206)
Speak English very well	99.5% (96)		**STABILITY**	★ (517)
Poverty rate for children	26.6% (341)		25-39 age group	15.5% (484)
No health insurance	12.0% (471)		Born in state of residence	45.1% (504)
DIVERSITY/EQUALITY	★★★★ (115)		Same house as 1 year ago	81.3% (470)
Racial diversity index	15.1% (413)		Live and work in county	74.9% (291)
Geographic diversity index	71.0% (39)		Married-couple households	53.2% (143)
Top 20% share of income	48.0% (292)		**TRANSPORTATION**	★★★ (230)
Gender gap in earnings	31.4% (213)		Bicycle or walk to work	3.1% (232)
White-collar gender gap	16.4% (173)		Carpool to work	16.0% (32)
EDUCATION	★★★ (305)		Public transit to work	0.7% (119)
Eighth grade or less	2.1% (136)		Commute <15 minutes	34.5% (448)
High school diplomas	87.3% (296)		Commute >45 minutes	13.9% (387)

See pages 37-130 for explanations of statistics, stars, and ranks.

Brookings, SD
(Brookings County, SD)

POPULATION

2010 census	31,965 (415)
2015 estimate	33,897 (395)
2010-2015 change	6.0% (32)
2020 projection	35,832 (372)
2030 projection	39,855 (321)

RACE

Whites	91.2% (159)
Blacks	1.3% (351)
Hispanics	2.3% (398)
Asians	2.9% (25)
Native Americans	0.6% (150)

AGE

0-17 years old	19.6% (478)
18-24 years old	28.1% (9)
25-39 years old	18.7% (127)
40-54 years old	13.9% (546)
55-64 years old	9.7% (532)
65+ years old	10.1% (528)

PRIVATE SECTOR

Businesses	996 (280)
Employees	13,599 (253)
Total wages	$539,117,449 (221)
Average weekly wages	$762 (139)

HOUSEHOLD INCOME LADDER

95th percentile	$157,696 (111)
80th percentile	$93,750 (108)
60th percentile	$59,091 (161)
40th percentile	$39,920 (131)
20th percentile	$21,278 (173)

CHILDREN ★★★★★ (8)

Living with two parents	73.3% (76)
Older teens in school	97.9% (5)
Speak English very well	98.8% (251)
Poverty rate for children	9.3% (10)
No health insurance	6.6% (293)

DIVERSITY/EQUALITY ★★ (397)

Racial diversity index	16.6% (387)
Geographic diversity index	57.7% (137)
Top 20% share of income	49.1% (363)
Gender gap in earnings	39.0% (421)
White-collar gender gap	32.8% (373)

EDUCATION ★★★★★ (12)

Eighth grade or less	1.7% (97)
High school diplomas	95.9% (14)
Attended college	72.7% (16)
Bachelor's degrees	43.1% (13)
Advanced degrees	12.4% (33)

EMPLOYMENT ★★★★★ (52)

Average jobless rate	3.1% (12)
Self-employed workers	10.6% (135)
Management/financial jobs	13.1% (78)
Computer/engineering jobs	7.0% (10)
Health care jobs	3.2% (525)

GROWTH POTENTIAL ★★★★★ (29)

Children per senior	1.94 (66)
Median age	26.4 (8)
Moved from different state	7.3% (19)
Homes built since 2000	19.8% (94)
Construction jobs	5.3% (425)

HOUSING ★★★★ (123)

Home vacancy rate	5.4% (55)
Home ownership rate	59.5% (510)
Housing diversity index	85.3% (170)
4 or more bedrooms	27.2% (27)
Affordability/income ratio	$3,115 (421)

INCOME ★★★★ (111)

Poverty rate	16.3% (234)
Median household income	$50,082 (124)
Interest/dividends	23.5% (142)
Public assistance	7.2% (24)
Median fulltime earnings	$38,636 (196)

SENIORS ★★★★★ (67)

Seniors living alone	30.0% (427)
Poverty rate for seniors	4.3% (11)
Median income for seniors	$41,786 (46)
Seniors who work	32.5% (12)
Home ownership by seniors	76.9% (493)

STABILITY ★ (508)

25-39 age group	18.7% (127)
Born in state of residence	58.5% (434)
Same house as 1 year ago	70.5% (544)
Live and work in county	88.7% (83)
Married-couple households	45.4% (456)

TRANSPORTATION ★★★★★ (12)

Bicycle or walk to work	9.6% (16)
Carpool to work	10.2% (312)
Public transit to work	0.4% (219)
Commute <15 minutes	65.9% (15)
Commute >45 minutes	5.3% (38)

See pages 37-130 for explanations of statistics, stars, and ranks.

Bucyrus, OH
(Crawford County, OH)

POPULATION

2010 census	43,784 (273)
2015 estimate	42,306 (288)
2010-2015 change	-3.4% (501)
2020 projection	40,927 (301)
2030 projection	38,168 (339)

RACE

Whites	96.0% (21)
Blacks	0.7% (423)
Hispanics	1.4% (488)
Asians	0.4% (413)
Native Americans	0.0% (523)

AGE

0-17 years old	22.3% (312)
18-24 years old	7.9% (424)
25-39 years old	16.5% (403)
40-54 years old	20.0% (233)
55-64 years old	14.3% (148)
65+ years old	19.0% (80)

PRIVATE SECTOR

Businesses	805 (370)
Employees	11,430 (329)
Total wages	$406,873,980 (329)
Average weekly wages	$685 (300)

HOUSEHOLD INCOME LADDER

95th percentile	$121,372 (505)
80th percentile	$76,959 (423)
60th percentile	$50,575 (368)
40th percentile	$32,730 (334)
20th percentile	$18,979 (266)

CHILDREN ★★★★ (172)

Living with two parents	67.8% (200)
Older teens in school	82.2% (311)
Speak English very well	99.4% (124)
Poverty rate for children	25.7% (315)
No health insurance	3.7% (98)

DIVERSITY/EQUALITY ★ (449)

Racial diversity index	7.8% (529)
Geographic diversity index	28.8% (495)
Top 20% share of income	47.7% (266)
Gender gap in earnings	33.8% (280)
White-collar gender gap	20.0% (207)

EDUCATION ★★★ (314)

Eighth grade or less	1.1% (26)
High school diplomas	90.4% (188)
Attended college	48.1% (381)
Bachelor's degrees	13.4% (482)
Advanced degrees	4.2% (466)

EMPLOYMENT ★★ (408)

Average jobless rate	8.1% (298)
Self-employed workers	6.6% (461)
Management/financial jobs	10.9% (263)
Computer/engineering jobs	1.9% (441)
Health care jobs	5.3% (286)

GROWTH POTENTIAL ★ (531)

Children per senior	1.17 (435)
Median age	42.6 (437)
Moved from different state	0.8% (524)
Homes built since 2000	7.2% (500)
Construction jobs	5.6% (392)

HOUSING ★★ (349)

Home vacancy rate	10.4% (371)
Home ownership rate	68.6% (321)
Housing diversity index	82.0% (458)
4 or more bedrooms	16.5% (267)
Affordability/income ratio	$2,125 (92)

INCOME ★★★ (268)

Poverty rate	16.4% (241)
Median household income	$40,795 (362)
Interest/dividends	22.4% (169)
Public assistance	16.3% (305)
Median fulltime earnings	$36,037 (333)

SENIORS ★★ (413)

Seniors living alone	30.5% (451)
Poverty rate for seniors	10.2% (334)
Median income for seniors	$31,805 (329)
Seniors who work	14.5% (478)
Home ownership by seniors	83.9% (183)

STABILITY ★★★ (307)

25-39 age group	16.5% (403)
Born in state of residence	83.9% (57)
Same house as 1 year ago	86.8% (206)
Live and work in county	58.8% (496)
Married-couple households	51.5% (226)

TRANSPORTATION ★★★ (282)

Bicycle or walk to work	3.1% (232)
Carpool to work	10.4% (289)
Public transit to work	0.3% (291)
Commute <15 minutes	42.5% (287)
Commute >45 minutes	9.3% (188)

See pages 37-130 for explanations of statistics, stars, and ranks.

Burlington, IA-IL
(Des Moines County, IA, and Henderson County, IL)

POPULATION

2010 census	47,656 (225)
2015 estimate	47,050 (235)
2010-2015 change	-1.3% (355)
2020 projection	46,178 (245)
2030 projection	44,257 (270)

RACE

Whites	89.6% (191)
Blacks	4.6% (173)
Hispanics	2.7% (361)
Asians	0.6% (291)
Native Americans	0.2% (300)

AGE

0-17 years old	22.4% (306)
18-24 years old	7.4% (489)
25-39 years old	16.9% (338)
40-54 years old	19.7% (273)
55-64 years old	14.5% (122)
65+ years old	19.2% (72)

PRIVATE SECTOR

Businesses	1,387 (156)
Employees	21,051 (113)
Total wages	$811,019,749 (114)
Average weekly wages	$741 (176)

HOUSEHOLD INCOME LADDER

95th percentile	$136,409 (337)
80th percentile	$84,700 (257)
60th percentile	$55,333 (238)
40th percentile	$36,294 (222)
20th percentile	$20,253 (221)

CHILDREN ★★★★ (114)

Living with two parents	59.9% (399)
Older teens in school	88.6% (90)
Speak English very well	99.5% (96)
Poverty rate for children	21.9% (218)
No health insurance	2.4% (28)

DIVERSITY/EQUALITY ★★ (400)

Racial diversity index	19.4% (355)
Geographic diversity index	46.4% (261)
Top 20% share of income	47.1% (224)
Gender gap in earnings	37.2% (372)
White-collar gender gap	38.3% (426)

EDUCATION ★★★★ (163)

Eighth grade or less	1.6% (84)
High school diplomas	92.4% (115)
Attended college	58.6% (153)
Bachelor's degrees	20.8% (194)
Advanced degrees	5.5% (318)

EMPLOYMENT ★★★★ (211)

Average jobless rate	6.4% (147)
Self-employed workers	8.5% (290)
Management/financial jobs	10.1% (365)
Computer/engineering jobs	3.3% (145)
Health care jobs	6.0% (181)

GROWTH POTENTIAL ★★ (430)

Children per senior	1.17 (435)
Median age	43.1 (453)
Moved from different state	2.3% (234)
Homes built since 2000	7.3% (496)
Construction jobs	7.4% (134)

HOUSING ★★★ (236)

Home vacancy rate	8.2% (234)
Home ownership rate	74.5% (98)
Housing diversity index	80.3% (505)
4 or more bedrooms	18.5% (178)
Affordability/income ratio	$2,162 (105)

INCOME ★★★ (223)

Poverty rate	14.4% (172)
Median household income	$44,735 (241)
Interest/dividends	22.5% (168)
Public assistance	16.7% (319)
Median fulltime earnings	$37,887 (226)

SENIORS ★★★★ (188)

Seniors living alone	30.3% (440)
Poverty rate for seniors	6.9% (84)
Median income for seniors	$35,048 (185)
Seniors who work	20.5% (180)
Home ownership by seniors	84.7% (155)

STABILITY ★★★ (324)

25-39 age group	16.9% (338)
Born in state of residence	70.5% (301)
Same house as 1 year ago	85.7% (272)
Live and work in county	77.4% (248)
Married-couple households	47.8% (390)

TRANSPORTATION ★★★★ (176)

Bicycle or walk to work	3.4% (199)
Carpool to work	9.4% (394)
Public transit to work	0.4% (219)
Commute <15 minutes	52.2% (118)
Commute >45 minutes	6.5% (71)

See pages 37-130 for explanations of statistics, stars, and ranks.

Cadillac, MI
(Missaukee and Wexford Counties, MI)

POPULATION

2010 census	47,584 (226)
2015 estimate	47,906 (228)
2010-2015 change	0.7% (202)
2020 projection	48,565 (227)
2030 projection	49,763 (218)

RACE

Whites	94.9% (51)
Blacks	0.5% (466)
Hispanics	2.0% (428)
Asians	0.6% (291)
Native Americans	0.6% (150)

AGE

0-17 years old	23.5% (232)
18-24 years old	7.4% (489)
25-39 years old	17.0% (317)
40-54 years old	20.0% (233)
55-64 years old	14.5% (122)
65+ years old	17.6% (151)

PRIVATE SECTOR

Businesses	1,013 (272)
Employees	13,769 (243)
Total wages	$482,662,869 (258)
Average weekly wages	$674 (325)

HOUSEHOLD INCOME LADDER

95th percentile	$125,292 (484)
80th percentile	$74,013 (473)
60th percentile	$50,410 (371)
40th percentile	$33,695 (300)
20th percentile	$19,126 (258)

CHILDREN ★★★ (288)

Living with two parents	67.2% (214)
Older teens in school	78.9% (430)
Speak English very well	98.8% (251)
Poverty rate for children	26.0% (327)
No health insurance	6.7% (296)

DIVERSITY/EQUALITY ★ (498)

Racial diversity index	9.9% (496)
Geographic diversity index	24.6% (531)
Top 20% share of income	46.2% (133)
Gender gap in earnings	39.8% (431)
White-collar gender gap	27.6% (304)

EDUCATION ★★★ (269)

Eighth grade or less	2.4% (169)
High school diplomas	90.3% (192)
Attended college	51.4% (295)
Bachelor's degrees	16.2% (360)
Advanced degrees	4.8% (405)

EMPLOYMENT ★★★ (305)

Average jobless rate	9.9% (417)
Self-employed workers	10.2% (155)
Management/financial jobs	11.3% (218)
Computer/engineering jobs	2.8% (246)
Health care jobs	5.1% (319)

GROWTH POTENTIAL ★ (496)

Children per senior	1.33 (325)
Median age	42.2 (412)
Moved from different state	1.0% (504)
Homes built since 2000	12.2% (306)
Construction jobs	4.8% (480)

HOUSING ★★★★★ (43)

Home vacancy rate	6.2% (109)
Home ownership rate	78.4% (15)
Housing diversity index	86.0% (71)
4 or more bedrooms	15.5% (324)
Affordability/income ratio	$2,311 (169)

INCOME ★★ (345)

Poverty rate	17.2% (270)
Median household income	$41,403 (340)
Interest/dividends	18.9% (279)
Public assistance	18.6% (389)
Median fulltime earnings	$34,813 (393)

SENIORS ★★★★★ (83)

Seniors living alone	22.9% (58)
Poverty rate for seniors	7.3% (119)
Median income for seniors	$33,893 (241)
Seniors who work	15.3% (446)
Home ownership by seniors	89.1% (23)

STABILITY ★★★★★ (105)

25-39 age group	17.0% (317)
Born in state of residence	86.6% (21)
Same house as 1 year ago	87.1% (192)
Live and work in county	66.9% (419)
Married-couple households	54.5% (88)

TRANSPORTATION ★★★ (298)

Bicycle or walk to work	3.5% (189)
Carpool to work	11.2% (211)
Public transit to work	0.2% (363)
Commute <15 minutes	41.8% (303)
Commute >45 minutes	11.7% (300)

See pages 37-130 for explanations of statistics, stars, and ranks.

Cambridge, OH
(Guernsey County, OH)

POPULATION

2010 census	40,087 (314)
2015 estimate	39,258 (320)
2010-2015 change	-2.1% (418)
2020 projection	38,404 (334)
2030 projection	36,620 (351)

RACE

Whites	95.1% (42)
Blacks	1.5% (329)
Hispanics	1.0% (530)
Asians	0.3% (473)
Native Americans	0.1% (402)

AGE

0-17 years old	23.3% (246)
18-24 years old	7.8% (447)
25-39 years old	16.3% (418)
40-54 years old	21.1% (97)
55-64 years old	14.4% (136)
65+ years old	17.1% (186)

PRIVATE SECTOR

Businesses	835 (355)
Employees	13,324 (266)
Total wages	$521,036,041 (228)
Average weekly wages	$752 (157)

HOUSEHOLD INCOME LADDER

95th percentile	$131,173 (414)
80th percentile	$79,951 (371)
60th percentile	$51,208 (354)
40th percentile	$32,344 (348)
20th percentile	$17,512 (342)

CHILDREN ★★ (380)

Living with two parents	64.4% (283)
Older teens in school	76.8% (474)
Speak English very well	97.9% (352)
Poverty rate for children	33.7% (468)
No health insurance	5.4% (209)

DIVERSITY/EQUALITY ★ (481)

Racial diversity index	9.5% (505)
Geographic diversity index	32.5% (457)
Top 20% share of income	47.1% (231)
Gender gap in earnings	40.2% (442)
White-collar gender gap	24.2% (262)

EDUCATION ★★ (382)

Eighth grade or less	2.6% (185)
High school diplomas	86.8% (314)

Attended college	45.2% (435)
Bachelor's degrees	13.5% (478)
Advanced degrees	5.0% (378)

EMPLOYMENT ★★ (419)

Average jobless rate	11.7% (481)
Self-employed workers	8.2% (314)
Management/financial jobs	8.4% (510)
Computer/engineering jobs	2.3% (354)
Health care jobs	7.2% (58)

GROWTH POTENTIAL ★★ (424)

Children per senior	1.36 (304)
Median age	42.2 (412)
Moved from different state	1.0% (504)
Homes built since 2000	10.8% (364)
Construction jobs	6.7% (219)

HOUSING ★★★ (263)

Home vacancy rate	10.7% (390)
Home ownership rate	73.0% (151)
Housing diversity index	83.6% (385)
4 or more bedrooms	16.0% (293)
Affordability/income ratio	$2,336 (183)

INCOME ★★ (370)

Poverty rate	19.9% (366)
Median household income	$40,930 (355)
Interest/dividends	16.4% (363)
Public assistance	19.9% (424)
Median fulltime earnings	$38,060 (220)

SENIORS ★★ (378)

Seniors living alone	28.6% (336)
Poverty rate for seniors	8.9% (254)
Median income for seniors	$30,432 (391)
Seniors who work	14.1% (500)
Home ownership by seniors	83.5% (197)

STABILITY ★★★★ (198)

25-39 age group	16.3% (418)
Born in state of residence	81.6% (91)
Same house as 1 year ago	88.6% (101)
Live and work in county	72.0% (341)
Married-couple households	49.7% (311)

TRANSPORTATION ★ (519)

Bicycle or walk to work	1.6% (443)
Carpool to work	7.1% (528)
Public transit to work	0.4% (219)
Commute <15 minutes	35.9% (421)
Commute >45 minutes	14.4% (407)

See pages 37-130 for explanations of statistics, stars, and ranks.

Canton, IL
(Fulton County, IL)

POPULATION

2010 census	37,069 (355)
2015 estimate	35,699 (376)
2010-2015 change	-3.7% (513)
2020 projection	34,485 (390)
2030 projection	32,066 (409)

RACE

Whites	92.2% (128)
Blacks	3.5% (209)
Hispanics	2.7% (361)
Asians	0.4% (413)
Native Americans	0.1% (402)

AGE

0-17 years old	20.3% (445)
18-24 years old	8.0% (407)
25-39 years old	19.0% (104)
40-54 years old	20.2% (202)
55-64 years old	14.0% (182)
65+ years old	18.5% (104)

PRIVATE SECTOR

Businesses	635 (455)
Employees	6,082 (506)
Total wages	$186,979,791 (516)
Average weekly wages	$591 (501)

HOUSEHOLD INCOME LADDER

95th percentile	$126,174 (479)
80th percentile	$82,531 (303)
60th percentile	$55,838 (230)
40th percentile	$36,452 (217)
20th percentile	$20,068 (225)

CHILDREN ★★★★ (136)

Living with two parents	63.1% (320)
Older teens in school	82.3% (304)
Speak English very well	99.2% (163)
Poverty rate for children	18.4% (138)
No health insurance	2.3% (20)

DIVERSITY/EQUALITY ★★ (436)

Racial diversity index	14.8% (418)
Geographic diversity index	25.4% (521)
Top 20% share of income	44.7% (50)
Gender gap in earnings	36.0% (339)
White-collar gender gap	32.9% (374)

EDUCATION ★★★ (255)

Eighth grade or less	2.6% (185)
High school diplomas	89.3% (223)
Attended college	55.9% (205)
Bachelor's degrees	17.0% (328)
Advanced degrees	4.3% (456)

EMPLOYMENT ★★★★ (193)

Average jobless rate	7.9% (286)
Self-employed workers	8.0% (333)
Management/financial jobs	10.9% (263)
Computer/engineering jobs	2.9% (219)
Health care jobs	7.0% (69)

GROWTH POTENTIAL ★ (529)

Children per senior	1.10 (464)
Median age	42.2 (412)
Moved from different state	1.1% (487)
Homes built since 2000	4.9% (540)
Construction jobs	6.1% (310)

HOUSING ★★★ (249)

Home vacancy rate	9.0% (287)
Home ownership rate	75.3% (72)
Housing diversity index	80.1% (512)
4 or more bedrooms	16.8% (258)
Affordability/income ratio	$1,769 (19)

INCOME ★★★★ (186)

Poverty rate	14.2% (160)
Median household income	$46,083 (211)
Interest/dividends	22.8% (162)
Public assistance	14.5% (234)
Median fulltime earnings	$37,886 (227)

SENIORS ★★★ (260)

Seniors living alone	28.1% (306)
Poverty rate for seniors	8.3% (202)
Median income for seniors	$33,276 (269)
Seniors who work	16.1% (400)
Home ownership by seniors	84.9% (145)

STABILITY ★★★ (228)

25-39 age group	19.0% (104)
Born in state of residence	86.1% (26)
Same house as 1 year ago	86.4% (225)
Live and work in county	54.5% (524)
Married-couple households	50.3% (284)

TRANSPORTATION ★ (505)

Bicycle or walk to work	3.1% (232)
Carpool to work	11.4% (190)
Public transit to work	0.3% (291)
Commute <15 minutes	37.9% (378)
Commute >45 minutes	24.0% (543)

See pages 37-130 for explanations of statistics, stars, and ranks.

Carroll, IA
(Carroll County, IA)

POPULATION

2010 census	20,816 (522)
2015 estimate	20,498 (521)
2010-2015 change	-1.5% (373)
2020 projection	20,165 (522)
2030 projection	19,401 (524)

RACE

Whites	95.7% (25)
Blacks	1.5% (329)
Hispanics	2.1% (416)
Asians	0.1% (529)
Native Americans	0.1% (402)

AGE

0-17 years old	24.2% (172)
18-24 years old	7.4% (489)
25-39 years old	15.9% (453)
40-54 years old	19.7% (273)
55-64 years old	13.9% (192)
65+ years old	18.9% (85)

PRIVATE SECTOR

Businesses	901 (311)
Employees	10,397 (363)
Total wages	$377,612,357 (357)
Average weekly wages	$698 (259)

HOUSEHOLD INCOME LADDER

95th percentile	$153,922 (123)
80th percentile	$92,462 (121)
60th percentile	$64,119 (83)
40th percentile	$38,066 (180)
20th percentile	$20,414 (210)

CHILDREN ★★★★★ (19)

Living with two parents	72.8% (83)
Older teens in school	86.1% (164)
Speak English very well	99.8% (38)
Poverty rate for children	11.3% (23)
No health insurance	1.0% (2)

DIVERSITY/EQUALITY ★ (464)

Racial diversity index	8.3% (526)
Geographic diversity index	28.2% (502)
Top 20% share of income	46.7% (187)
Gender gap in earnings	27.5% (126)
White-collar gender gap	37.8% (417)

EDUCATION ★★★★ (134)

Eighth grade or less	1.3% (52)
High school diplomas	96.1% (11)
Attended college	59.0% (144)
Bachelor's degrees	21.9% (165)
Advanced degrees	4.9% (396)

EMPLOYMENT ★★★★★ (28)

Average jobless rate	3.3% (16)
Self-employed workers	16.6% (10)
Management/financial jobs	13.9% (50)
Computer/engineering jobs	1.5% (499)
Health care jobs	6.2% (156)

GROWTH POTENTIAL ★ (505)

Children per senior	1.28 (357)
Median age	42.3 (427)
Moved from different state	1.3% (452)
Homes built since 2000	10.3% (384)
Construction jobs	5.0% (467)

HOUSING ★★★★★ (14)

Home vacancy rate	7.6% (193)
Home ownership rate	74.7% (89)
Housing diversity index	83.6% (385)
4 or more bedrooms	31.9% (5)
Affordability/income ratio	$2,239 (137)

INCOME ★★★★★ (65)

Poverty rate	10.1% (34)
Median household income	$50,559 (111)
Interest/dividends	28.0% (37)
Public assistance	9.7% (57)
Median fulltime earnings	$38,894 (183)

SENIORS ★ (483)

Seniors living alone	35.0% (542)
Poverty rate for seniors	9.7% (301)
Median income for seniors	$29,630 (418)
Seniors who work	21.2% (153)
Home ownership by seniors	77.9% (458)

STABILITY ★★★★★ (20)

25-39 age group	15.9% (453)
Born in state of residence	84.1% (53)
Same house as 1 year ago	90.0% (44)
Live and work in county	88.3% (86)
Married-couple households	53.0% (152)

TRANSPORTATION ★★★★★ (104)

Bicycle or walk to work	4.2% (142)
Carpool to work	7.6% (510)
Public transit to work	0.5% (178)
Commute <15 minutes	64.0% (24)
Commute >45 minutes	4.7% (26)

See pages 37-130 for explanations of statistics, stars, and ranks.

Celina, OH
(Mercer County, OH)

POPULATION

2010 census	40,814 (304)
2015 estimate	40,968 (302)
2010-2015 change	0.4% (228)
2020 projection	40,927 (301)
2030 projection	40,686 (310)

RACE

Whites	96.2% (9)
Blacks	0.4% (499)
Hispanics	1.7% (464)
Asians	0.8% (201)
Native Americans	0.1% (402)

AGE

0-17 years old	25.7% (81)
18-24 years old	8.0% (407)
25-39 years old	16.3% (418)
40-54 years old	19.8% (261)
55-64 years old	13.9% (192)
65+ years old	16.4% (255)

PRIVATE SECTOR

Businesses	969 (287)
Employees	16,785 (175)
Total wages	$633,615,702 (173)
Average weekly wages	$726 (203)

HOUSEHOLD INCOME LADDER

95th percentile	$141,737 (268)
80th percentile	$94,326 (95)
60th percentile	$64,137 (82)
40th percentile	$42,457 (71)
20th percentile	$23,795 (74)

CHILDREN ★★★★★ (13)

Living with two parents	80.9% (8)
Older teens in school	87.9% (103)
Speak English very well	99.0% (200)
Poverty rate for children	10.0% (14)
No health insurance	4.6% (159)

DIVERSITY/EQUALITY ★ (524)

Racial diversity index	7.4% (537)
Geographic diversity index	26.6% (509)
Top 20% share of income	44.0% (26)
Gender gap in earnings	44.7% (499)
White-collar gender gap	41.8% (464)

EDUCATION ★★★★ (187)

Eighth grade or less	1.1% (26)
High school diplomas	95.5% (18)

Attended college	48.6% (367)
Bachelor's degrees	18.0% (284)
Advanced degrees	6.3% (234)

EMPLOYMENT ★★★ (255)

Average jobless rate	5.5% (98)
Self-employed workers	9.0% (254)
Management/financial jobs	10.9% (263)
Computer/engineering jobs	2.7% (270)
Health care jobs	4.7% (385)

GROWTH POTENTIAL ★★★ (308)

Children per senior	1.57 (186)
Median age	40.1 (309)
Moved from different state	1.5% (406)
Homes built since 2000	12.0% (315)
Construction jobs	6.5% (253)

HOUSING ★★★★★ (11)

Home vacancy rate	4.5% (17)
Home ownership rate	76.6% (38)
Housing diversity index	86.3% (36)
4 or more bedrooms	19.6% (135)
Affordability/income ratio	$2,452 (226)

INCOME ★★★★★ (63)

Poverty rate	8.4% (13)
Median household income	$53,099 (72)
Interest/dividends	24.5% (115)
Public assistance	9.2% (49)
Median fulltime earnings	$39,439 (159)

SENIORS ★★ (397)

Seniors living alone	32.1% (514)
Poverty rate for seniors	5.8% (45)
Median income for seniors	$33,310 (268)
Seniors who work	18.0% (287)
Home ownership by seniors	78.5% (434)

STABILITY ★★★★★ (47)

25-39 age group	16.3% (418)
Born in state of residence	85.2% (44)
Same house as 1 year ago	89.0% (79)
Live and work in county	68.6% (395)
Married-couple households	57.9% (21)

TRANSPORTATION ★★★ (299)

Bicycle or walk to work	2.0% (386)
Carpool to work	7.8% (504)
Public transit to work	0.4% (219)
Commute <15 minutes	48.6% (184)
Commute >45 minutes	6.8% (80)

See pages 37-130 for explanations of statistics, stars, and ranks.

Centralia, IL
(Marion County, IL)

POPULATION

2010 census	39,437 (319)
2015 estimate	38,339 (335)
2010-2015 change	-2.8% (467)
2020 projection	37,178 (358)
2030 projection	34,872 (377)

RACE

Whites	91.9% (141)
Blacks	3.7% (202)
Hispanics	1.7% (464)
Asians	0.7% (241)
Native Americans	0.2% (300)

AGE

0-17 years old	23.0% (259)
18-24 years old	8.3% (362)
25-39 years old	16.8% (359)
40-54 years old	20.0% (233)
55-64 years old	13.9% (192)
65+ years old	18.0% (122)

PRIVATE SECTOR

Businesses	872 (330)
Employees	11,077 (341)
Total wages	$405,010,269 (331)
Average weekly wages	$703 (249)

HOUSEHOLD INCOME LADDER

95th percentile	$134,391 (369)
80th percentile	$82,220 (320)
60th percentile	$52,499 (310)
40th percentile	$33,194 (317)
20th percentile	$18,082 (314)

CHILDREN ★★★ (303)

Living with two parents	58.2% (445)
Older teens in school	82.9% (283)
Speak English very well	99.9% (19)
Poverty rate for children	31.0% (421)
No health insurance	5.0% (181)

DIVERSITY/EQUALITY ★★ (346)

Racial diversity index	15.3% (405)
Geographic diversity index	33.1% (454)
Top 20% share of income	46.8% (192)
Gender gap in earnings	33.3% (266)
White-collar gender gap	19.1% (196)

EDUCATION ★★★ (241)

Eighth grade or less	2.4% (169)
High school diplomas	90.7% (173)
Attended college	57.7% (171)
Bachelor's degrees	15.3% (412)
Advanced degrees	4.6% (431)

EMPLOYMENT ★★ (354)

Average jobless rate	9.6% (402)
Self-employed workers	7.2% (410)
Management/financial jobs	8.5% (505)
Computer/engineering jobs	2.3% (354)
Health care jobs	7.8% (28)

GROWTH POTENTIAL ★ (501)

Children per senior	1.28 (357)
Median age	41.7 (390)
Moved from different state	1.9% (310)
Homes built since 2000	10.8% (364)
Construction jobs	4.3% (514)

HOUSING ★★★★ (113)

Home vacancy rate	10.4% (371)
Home ownership rate	74.6% (91)
Housing diversity index	86.6% (12)
4 or more bedrooms	13.6% (424)
Affordability/income ratio	$1,624 (9)

INCOME ★★★ (323)

Poverty rate	18.6% (322)
Median household income	$42,238 (312)
Interest/dividends	19.9% (247)
Public assistance	19.9% (424)
Median fulltime earnings	$37,559 (243)

SENIORS ★★ (346)

Seniors living alone	29.8% (422)
Poverty rate for seniors	7.1% (101)
Median income for seniors	$31,602 (346)
Seniors who work	15.9% (418)
Home ownership by seniors	82.5% (251)

STABILITY ★★ (353)

25-39 age group	16.8% (359)
Born in state of residence	81.1% (98)
Same house as 1 year ago	84.9% (306)
Live and work in county	70.4% (363)
Married-couple households	47.3% (409)

TRANSPORTATION ★★★ (310)

Bicycle or walk to work	2.2% (358)
Carpool to work	10.2% (312)
Public transit to work	0.5% (178)
Commute <15 minutes	44.6% (251)
Commute >45 minutes	10.3% (237)

See pages 37-130 for explanations of statistics, stars, and ranks.

Charleston-Mattoon, IL
(Coles and Cumberland Counties, IL)

POPULATION	
2010 census	64,921 (120)
2015 estimate	63,419 (132)
2010-2015 change	-2.3% (436)
2020 projection	62,333 (136)
2030 projection	60,046 (152)

RACE	
Whites	92.3% (124)
Blacks	2.9% (229)
Hispanics	2.1% (416)
Asians	1.0% (158)
Native Americans	0.2% (300)

AGE	
0-17 years old	19.0% (501)
18-24 years old	18.6% (32)
25-39 years old	17.6% (248)
40-54 years old	17.2% (494)
55-64 years old	12.4% (408)
65+ years old	15.2% (354)

PRIVATE SECTOR	
Businesses	1,342 (166)
Employees	21,167 (112)
Total wages	$758,309,726 (131)
Average weekly wages	$689 (289)

HOUSEHOLD INCOME LADDER	
95th percentile	$140,629 (282)
80th percentile	$82,197 (322)
60th percentile	$51,373 (348)
40th percentile	$31,347 (378)
20th percentile	$16,658 (377)

CHILDREN	★★★★★ (93)
Living with two parents	64.3% (288)
Older teens in school	93.7% (24)
Speak English very well	98.0% (341)
Poverty rate for children	24.8% (293)
No health insurance	3.5% (82)

DIVERSITY/EQUALITY	★ (526)
Racial diversity index	14.6% (422)
Geographic diversity index	33.7% (449)
Top 20% share of income	50.6% (452)
Gender gap in earnings	38.0% (392)
White-collar gender gap	30.7% (349)

EDUCATION	★★★★★ (106)
Eighth grade or less	2.3% (161)
High school diplomas	92.5% (110)
Attended college	61.5% (105)
Bachelor's degrees	23.3% (130)
Advanced degrees	8.8% (92)

EMPLOYMENT	★★ (357)
Average jobless rate	9.3% (387)
Self-employed workers	9.8% (186)
Management/financial jobs	10.9% (263)
Computer/engineering jobs	2.6% (288)
Health care jobs	4.6% (401)

GROWTH POTENTIAL	★★★ (299)
Children per senior	1.25 (385)
Median age	35.0 (91)
Moved from different state	2.5% (203)
Homes built since 2000	9.7% (399)
Construction jobs	5.7% (373)

HOUSING	★★★ (240)
Home vacancy rate	7.2% (172)
Home ownership rate	65.2% (431)
Housing diversity index	85.7% (108)
4 or more bedrooms	13.4% (433)
Affordability/income ratio	$2,271 (148)

INCOME	★★★ (324)
Poverty rate	21.1% (403)
Median household income	$40,512 (368)
Interest/dividends	21.5% (194)
Public assistance	16.0% (295)
Median fulltime earnings	$35,833 (342)

SENIORS	★★★ (279)
Seniors living alone	29.0% (366)
Poverty rate for seniors	7.0% (93)
Median income for seniors	$36,207 (147)
Seniors who work	15.3% (446)
Home ownership by seniors	82.6% (242)

STABILITY	★ (468)
25-39 age group	17.6% (248)
Born in state of residence	80.8% (102)
Same house as 1 year ago	76.7% (525)
Live and work in county	76.7% (259)
Married-couple households	45.2% (461)

TRANSPORTATION	★★★★★ (81)
Bicycle or walk to work	6.9% (43)
Carpool to work	10.1% (322)
Public transit to work	0.8% (96)
Commute <15 minutes	50.8% (137)
Commute >45 minutes	7.2% (91)

See pages 37-130 for explanations of statistics, stars, and ranks.

Chillicothe, OH
(Ross County, OH)

POPULATION	
2010 census	78,064 (72)
2015 estimate	77,170 (78)
2010-2015 change	-1.1% (335)
2020 projection	77,251 (77)
2030 projection	77,116 (84)

RACE	
Whites	89.9% (186)
Blacks	5.2% (155)
Hispanics	1.1% (525)
Asians	0.5% (355)
Native Americans	0.0% (523)

AGE	
0-17 years old	21.9% (344)
18-24 years old	8.0% (407)
25-39 years old	19.1% (95)
40-54 years old	22.4% (17)
55-64 years old	13.7% (225)
65+ years old	14.8% (384)

PRIVATE SECTOR	
Businesses	1,238 (191)
Employees	21,341 (107)
Total wages	$868,012,087 (99)
Average weekly wages	$782 (119)

HOUSEHOLD INCOME LADDER	
95th percentile	$139,685 (294)
80th percentile	$86,536 (221)
60th percentile	$54,521 (263)
40th percentile	$35,018 (261)
20th percentile	$19,558 (241)

CHILDREN	★★★ (256)
Living with two parents	62.3% (339)
Older teens in school	82.0% (319)
Speak English very well	99.2% (163)
Poverty rate for children	28.0% (368)
No health insurance	4.4% (145)

DIVERSITY/EQUALITY	★★ (437)
Racial diversity index	18.8% (363)
Geographic diversity index	26.6% (509)
Top 20% share of income	47.3% (244)
Gender gap in earnings	32.5% (242)
White-collar gender gap	29.0% (322)

EDUCATION	★★ (357)
Eighth grade or less	2.8% (205)
High school diplomas	86.8% (314)
Attended college	45.6% (430)
Bachelor's degrees	15.5% (409)
Advanced degrees	5.6% (304)

EMPLOYMENT	★★ (433)
Average jobless rate	11.3% (466)
Self-employed workers	5.3% (537)
Management/financial jobs	9.4% (444)
Computer/engineering jobs	3.7% (103)
Health care jobs	6.5% (121)

GROWTH POTENTIAL	★★ (396)
Children per senior	1.48 (227)
Median age	40.6 (335)
Moved from different state	0.9% (515)
Homes built since 2000	12.2% (306)
Construction jobs	5.9% (345)

HOUSING	★★★★ (199)
Home vacancy rate	10.0% (347)
Home ownership rate	71.7% (199)
Housing diversity index	85.8% (97)
4 or more bedrooms	16.0% (293)
Affordability/income ratio	$2,545 (269)

INCOME	★★★ (312)
Poverty rate	19.3% (348)
Median household income	$43,345 (281)
Interest/dividends	17.8% (316)
Public assistance	20.9% (452)
Median fulltime earnings	$41,059 (94)

SENIORS	★★ (347)
Seniors living alone	26.6% (209)
Poverty rate for seniors	9.3% (276)
Median income for seniors	$32,360 (309)
Seniors who work	14.0% (503)
Home ownership by seniors	82.0% (274)

STABILITY	★★★★★ (73)
25-39 age group	19.1% (95)
Born in state of residence	85.3% (41)
Same house as 1 year ago	85.6% (277)
Live and work in county	70.8% (357)
Married-couple households	51.8% (206)

TRANSPORTATION	★ (499)
Bicycle or walk to work	1.8% (409)
Carpool to work	9.8% (358)
Public transit to work	0.7% (119)
Commute <15 minutes	30.7% (514)
Commute >45 minutes	16.5% (468)

See pages 37-130 for explanations of statistics, stars, and ranks.

Clinton, IA
(Clinton County, IA)

POPULATION

2010 census	49,116 (217)
2015 estimate	47,768 (230)
2010-2015 change	-2.7% (459)
2020 projection	46,524 (241)
2030 projection	43,880 (276)

RACE

Whites	91.7% (147)
Blacks	2.7% (241)
Hispanics	2.9% (350)
Asians	0.7% (241)
Native Americans	0.4% (203)

AGE

0-17 years old	23.0% (259)
18-24 years old	8.1% (396)
25-39 years old	16.3% (418)
40-54 years old	20.8% (122)
55-64 years old	14.0% (182)
65+ years old	17.8% (137)

PRIVATE SECTOR

Businesses	1,331 (168)
Employees	19,380 (132)
Total wages	$740,125,584 (140)
Average weekly wages	$734 (190)

HOUSEHOLD INCOME LADDER

95th percentile	$152,989 (133)
80th percentile	$97,710 (69)
60th percentile	$63,253 (94)
40th percentile	$39,331 (145)
20th percentile	$20,358 (212)

CHILDREN ★★★★★ (73)

Living with two parents	63.3% (316)
Older teens in school	88.3% (94)
Speak English very well	99.5% (96)
Poverty rate for children	20.0% (167)
No health insurance	1.8% (9)

DIVERSITY/EQUALITY ★ (454)

Racial diversity index	15.7% (399)
Geographic diversity index	42.4% (316)
Top 20% share of income	46.9% (206)
Gender gap in earnings	47.0% (514)
White-collar gender gap	25.4% (277)

EDUCATION ★★★★ (128)

Eighth grade or less	1.4% (60)
High school diplomas	93.9% (61)
Attended college	61.9% (95)
Bachelor's degrees	21.9% (165)
Advanced degrees	5.9% (272)

EMPLOYMENT ★★★★ (157)

Average jobless rate	4.8% (58)
Self-employed workers	8.4% (297)
Management/financial jobs	12.2% (139)
Computer/engineering jobs	3.2% (158)
Health care jobs	5.0% (339)

GROWTH POTENTIAL ★★ (417)

Children per senior	1.29 (353)
Median age	42.1 (408)
Moved from different state	2.9% (165)
Homes built since 2000	8.6% (449)
Construction jobs	6.1% (310)

HOUSING ★★★★★ (95)

Home vacancy rate	5.8% (79)
Home ownership rate	73.7% (129)
Housing diversity index	81.9% (461)
4 or more bedrooms	20.8% (107)
Affordability/income ratio	$2,180 (113)

INCOME ★★★★ (117)

Poverty rate	13.9% (151)
Median household income	$50,498 (114)
Interest/dividends	23.9% (130)
Public assistance	15.0% (254)
Median fulltime earnings	$42,200 (61)

SENIORS ★★★ (221)

Seniors living alone	28.7% (344)
Poverty rate for seniors	8.4% (214)
Median income for seniors	$34,818 (197)
Seniors who work	21.9% (132)
Home ownership by seniors	81.3% (316)

STABILITY ★★★ (272)

25-39 age group	16.3% (418)
Born in state of residence	74.2% (240)
Same house as 1 year ago	87.6% (157)
Live and work in county	75.1% (287)
Married-couple households	49.0% (349)

TRANSPORTATION ★★★ (261)

Bicycle or walk to work	2.8% (279)
Carpool to work	8.3% (471)
Public transit to work	1.0% (69)
Commute <15 minutes	48.6% (184)
Commute >45 minutes	9.2% (182)

See pages 37-130 for explanations of statistics, stars, and ranks.

Coffeyville, KS
(Montgomery County, KS)

POPULATION

2010 census	35,471 (380)
2015 estimate	33,314 (402)
2010-2015 change	-6.1% (546)
2020 projection	31,812 (421)
2030 projection	28,925 (433)

RACE

Whites	80.4% (322)
Blacks	5.1% (160)
Hispanics	6.0% (222)
Asians	1.1% (139)
Native Americans	2.7% (58)

AGE

0-17 years old	23.7% (218)
18-24 years old	9.6% (189)
25-39 years old	17.1% (308)
40-54 years old	18.3% (439)
55-64 years old	13.3% (282)
65+ years old	17.9% (132)

PRIVATE SECTOR

Businesses	851 (343)
Employees	13,176 (273)
Total wages	$459,184,065 (285)
Average weekly wages	$670 (334)

HOUSEHOLD INCOME LADDER

95th percentile	$120,869 (508)
80th percentile	$76,867 (426)
60th percentile	$49,164 (397)
40th percentile	$32,423 (343)
20th percentile	$16,057 (406)

CHILDREN ★★★ (272)

Living with two parents	60.7% (386)
Older teens in school	85.6% (179)
Speak English very well	98.8% (251)
Poverty rate for children	26.3% (333)
No health insurance	7.2% (330)

DIVERSITY/EQUALITY ★★★★ (201)

Racial diversity index	34.4% (219)
Geographic diversity index	57.8% (136)
Top 20% share of income	46.8% (200)
Gender gap in earnings	35.2% (318)
White-collar gender gap	34.0% (382)

EDUCATION ★★★★ (206)

Eighth grade or less	2.7% (195)
High school diplomas	89.7% (211)
Attended college	59.5% (139)
Bachelor's degrees	18.2% (277)
Advanced degrees	5.4% (334)

EMPLOYMENT ★★ (379)

Average jobless rate	8.7% (340)
Self-employed workers	8.1% (323)
Management/financial jobs	9.6% (427)
Computer/engineering jobs	2.8% (246)
Health care jobs	5.5% (250)

GROWTH POTENTIAL ★ (460)

Children per senior	1.32 (334)
Median age	39.4 (262)
Moved from different state	3.0% (157)
Homes built since 2000	5.6% (533)
Construction jobs	4.9% (473)

HOUSING ★ (510)

Home vacancy rate	16.3% (540)
Home ownership rate	69.5% (287)
Housing diversity index	80.6% (502)
4 or more bedrooms	13.7% (415)
Affordability/income ratio	$1,718 (15)

INCOME ★★★ (305)

Poverty rate	19.0% (338)
Median household income	$41,083 (352)
Interest/dividends	21.2% (209)
Public assistance	15.9% (290)
Median fulltime earnings	$35,668 (352)

SENIORS ★ (453)

Seniors living alone	31.3% (486)
Poverty rate for seniors	9.1% (263)
Median income for seniors	$32,963 (286)
Seniors who work	19.2% (234)
Home ownership by seniors	76.5% (500)

STABILITY ★★ (382)

25-39 age group	17.1% (308)
Born in state of residence	61.6% (412)
Same house as 1 year ago	83.6% (359)
Live and work in county	85.9% (119)
Married-couple households	47.4% (401)

TRANSPORTATION ★★★★ (116)

Bicycle or walk to work	5.7% (64)
Carpool to work	9.8% (358)
Public transit to work	0.1% (441)
Commute <15 minutes	54.0% (95)
Commute >45 minutes	6.6% (74)

See pages 37-130 for explanations of statistics, stars, and ranks.

Coldwater, MI
(Branch County, MI)

POPULATION

2010 census	45,248 (256)
2015 estimate	43,664 (276)
2010-2015 change	-3.5% (508)
2020 projection	42,769 (287)
2030 projection	40,903 (305)

RACE

Whites	91.3% (155)
Blacks	2.3% (267)
Hispanics	4.3% (279)
Asians	0.5% (355)
Native Americans	0.2% (300)

AGE

0-17 years old	23.8% (206)
18-24 years old	8.0% (407)
25-39 years old	17.5% (258)
40-54 years old	20.4% (169)
55-64 years old	13.9% (192)
65+ years old	16.3% (268)

PRIVATE SECTOR

Businesses	711 (422)
Employees	10,174 (370)
Total wages	$367,206,085 (366)
Average weekly wages	$694 (272)

HOUSEHOLD INCOME LADDER

95th percentile	$137,354 (320)
80th percentile	$81,474 (337)
60th percentile	$55,230 (241)
40th percentile	$35,970 (234)
20th percentile	$20,418 (209)

CHILDREN ★★ (433)

Living with two parents	69.3% (161)
Older teens in school	76.2% (486)
Speak English very well	95.2% (473)
Poverty rate for children	27.8% (363)
No health insurance	10.1% (425)

DIVERSITY/EQUALITY ★★ (344)

Racial diversity index	16.4% (391)
Geographic diversity index	42.0% (327)
Top 20% share of income	46.1% (126)
Gender gap in earnings	30.5% (183)
White-collar gender gap	37.6% (415)

EDUCATION ★★ (352)

Eighth grade or less	3.5% (284)
High school diplomas	89.5% (215)
Attended college	50.0% (334)
Bachelor's degrees	13.7% (470)
Advanced degrees	4.3% (456)

EMPLOYMENT ★★ (361)

Average jobless rate	7.0% (196)
Self-employed workers	8.3% (302)
Management/financial jobs	9.8% (408)
Computer/engineering jobs	2.5% (307)
Health care jobs	5.0% (339)

GROWTH POTENTIAL ★ (475)

Children per senior	1.45 (244)
Median age	40.6 (335)
Moved from different state	1.4% (425)
Homes built since 2000	9.3% (420)
Construction jobs	4.8% (480)

HOUSING ★★★★★ (61)

Home vacancy rate	7.9% (213)
Home ownership rate	76.4% (43)
Housing diversity index	85.5% (143)
4 or more bedrooms	18.0% (202)
Affordability/income ratio	$2,145 (98)

INCOME ★★★ (301)

Poverty rate	17.7% (290)
Median household income	$44,373 (254)
Interest/dividends	16.7% (354)
Public assistance	15.8% (286)
Median fulltime earnings	$36,581 (312)

SENIORS ★★★ (238)

Seniors living alone	24.4% (94)
Poverty rate for seniors	9.8% (308)
Median income for seniors	$31,556 (350)
Seniors who work	16.0% (410)
Home ownership by seniors	84.0% (179)

STABILITY ★★★★ (146)

25-39 age group	17.5% (258)
Born in state of residence	74.6% (228)
Same house as 1 year ago	89.0% (79)
Live and work in county	65.9% (436)
Married-couple households	53.7% (123)

TRANSPORTATION ★★ (411)

Bicycle or walk to work	2.9% (265)
Carpool to work	10.0% (337)
Public transit to work	0.4% (219)
Commute <15 minutes	34.3% (453)
Commute >45 minutes	13.0% (356)

See pages 37-130 for explanations of statistics, stars, and ranks.

Columbus, NE
(Platte County, NE)

POPULATION

2010 census	32,237 (414)
2015 estimate	32,847 (409)
2010-2015 change	1.9% (136)
2020 projection	33,384 (400)
2030 projection	34,397 (383)

RACE

Whites	81.7% (307)
Blacks	0.3% (519)
Hispanics	15.9% (99)
Asians	0.6% (291)
Native Americans	0.1% (402)

AGE

0-17 years old	26.2% (63)
18-24 years old	8.7% (299)
25-39 years old	17.1% (308)
40-54 years old	19.6% (289)
55-64 years old	13.1% (318)
65+ years old	15.4% (344)

PRIVATE SECTOR

Businesses	1,134 (224)
Employees	16,011 (192)
Total wages	$622,994,529 (177)
Average weekly wages	$748 (160)

HOUSEHOLD INCOME LADDER

95th percentile	$154,638 (119)
80th percentile	$92,451 (122)
60th percentile	$66,267 (64)
40th percentile	$45,800 (42)
20th percentile	$24,745 (51)

CHILDREN ★★★★ (120)

Living with two parents	70.4% (135)
Older teens in school	84.7% (210)
Speak English very well	96.6% (430)
Poverty rate for children	11.5% (25)
No health insurance	6.4% (276)

DIVERSITY/EQUALITY ★★★ (313)

Racial diversity index	30.7% (249)
Geographic diversity index	43.2% (308)
Top 20% share of income	43.5% (12)
Gender gap in earnings	32.3% (234)
White-collar gender gap	57.4% (536)

EDUCATION ★★★★ (185)

Eighth grade or less	5.1% (390)
High school diplomas	89.5% (215)
Attended college	61.8% (96)
Bachelor's degrees	21.8% (167)
Advanced degrees	6.6% (211)

EMPLOYMENT ★★★★ (182)

Average jobless rate	4.5% (47)
Self-employed workers	9.9% (171)
Management/financial jobs	10.7% (287)
Computer/engineering jobs	3.9% (86)
Health care jobs	4.0% (476)

GROWTH POTENTIAL ★★★★ (196)

Children per senior	1.70 (133)
Median age	38.0 (184)
Moved from different state	1.4% (425)
Homes built since 2000	9.8% (395)
Construction jobs	8.2% (78)

HOUSING ★★★★★ (4)

Home vacancy rate	4.6% (20)
Home ownership rate	72.8% (160)
Housing diversity index	85.2% (190)
4 or more bedrooms	26.2% (35)
Affordability/income ratio	$2,223 (130)

INCOME ★★★★★ (47)

Poverty rate	8.5% (14)
Median household income	$56,318 (45)
Interest/dividends	27.7% (41)
Public assistance	6.5% (16)
Median fulltime earnings	$37,528 (245)

SENIORS ★★★★ (211)

Seniors living alone	31.4% (495)
Poverty rate for seniors	8.3% (202)
Median income for seniors	$34,405 (215)
Seniors who work	31.1% (17)
Home ownership by seniors	77.2% (478)

STABILITY ★★★★★ (36)

25-39 age group	17.1% (308)
Born in state of residence	74.4% (235)
Same house as 1 year ago	87.1% (192)
Live and work in county	86.0% (116)
Married-couple households	55.2% (65)

TRANSPORTATION ★★★★★ (60)

Bicycle or walk to work	4.3% (130)
Carpool to work	11.9% (145)
Public transit to work	0.0% (511)
Commute <15 minutes	61.4% (38)
Commute >45 minutes	4.0% (13)

See pages 37-130 for explanations of statistics, stars, and ranks.

Connersville, IN
(Fayette County, IN)

POPULATION

2010 census	24,277 (486)
2015 estimate	23,434 (492)
2010-2015 change	-3.5% (508)
2020 projection	22,596 (500)
2030 projection	20,917 (512)

RACE

Whites	96.0% (21)
Blacks	2.0% (290)
Hispanics	1.0% (530)
Asians	0.3% (473)
Native Americans	0.0% (523)

AGE

0-17 years old	22.7% (284)
18-24 years old	7.7% (454)
25-39 years old	16.8% (359)
40-54 years old	20.2% (202)
55-64 years old	14.7% (97)
65+ years old	18.0% (122)

PRIVATE SECTOR

Businesses	397 (535)
Employees	5,223 (524)
Total wages	$178,999,825 (522)
Average weekly wages	$659 (368)

HOUSEHOLD INCOME LADDER

95th percentile	$119,200 (522)
80th percentile	$72,798 (487)
60th percentile	$48,163 (420)
40th percentile	$31,005 (387)
20th percentile	$16,415 (388)

CHILDREN ★★★ (309)

Living with two parents	57.1% (459)
Older teens in school	84.7% (210)
Speak English very well	99.4% (124)
Poverty rate for children	29.9% (400)
No health insurance	5.9% (244)

DIVERSITY/EQUALITY ★★★ (326)

Racial diversity index	7.8% (529)
Geographic diversity index	45.8% (269)
Top 20% share of income	48.0% (299)
Gender gap in earnings	34.9% (313)
White-collar gender gap	11.6% (105)

EDUCATION ★ (468)

Eighth grade or less	3.3% (259)
High school diplomas	84.7% (380)
Attended college	41.9% (491)
Bachelor's degrees	10.7% (535)
Advanced degrees	2.8% (540)

EMPLOYMENT ★ (474)

Average jobless rate	12.1% (493)
Self-employed workers	7.8% (355)
Management/financial jobs	7.9% (530)
Computer/engineering jobs	2.2% (381)
Health care jobs	6.8% (91)

GROWTH POTENTIAL ★ (537)

Children per senior	1.26 (378)
Median age	42.2 (412)
Moved from different state	0.8% (524)
Homes built since 2000	6.1% (525)
Construction jobs	5.3% (425)

HOUSING ★★ (345)

Home vacancy rate	12.7% (483)
Home ownership rate	68.9% (308)
Housing diversity index	84.2% (325)
4 or more bedrooms	15.4% (329)
Affordability/income ratio	$2,080 (73)

INCOME ★ (444)

Poverty rate	20.6% (392)
Median household income	$39,379 (398)
Interest/dividends	13.1% (467)
Public assistance	22.1% (478)
Median fulltime earnings	$36,308 (316)

SENIORS ★★ (352)

Seniors living alone	27.0% (239)
Poverty rate for seniors	7.9% (170)
Median income for seniors	$31,404 (354)
Seniors who work	16.4% (383)
Home ownership by seniors	79.4% (400)

STABILITY ★ (454)

25-39 age group	16.8% (359)
Born in state of residence	71.6% (286)
Same house as 1 year ago	85.9% (257)
Live and work in county	62.0% (474)
Married-couple households	48.0% (378)

TRANSPORTATION ★ (494)

Bicycle or walk to work	2.0% (386)
Carpool to work	10.8% (249)
Public transit to work	0.3% (291)
Commute <15 minutes	41.2% (314)
Commute >45 minutes	21.7% (533)

See pages 37-130 for explanations of statistics, stars, and ranks.

Coshocton, OH
(Coshocton County, OH)

POPULATION

2010 census	36,901 (360)
2015 estimate	36,569 (366)
2010-2015 change	-0.9% (323)
2020 projection	36,195 (366)
2030 projection	35,319 (370)

RACE

Whites	96.2% (9)
Blacks	1.1% (367)
Hispanics	0.9% (535)
Asians	0.4% (413)
Native Americans	0.1% (402)

AGE

0-17 years old	23.6% (228)
18-24 years old	7.7% (454)
25-39 years old	16.8% (359)
40-54 years old	20.3% (186)
55-64 years old	14.3% (148)
65+ years old	17.3% (172)

PRIVATE SECTOR

Businesses	627 (458)
Employees	9,457 (393)
Total wages	$432,847,966 (303)
Average weekly wages	$880 (44)

HOUSEHOLD INCOME LADDER

95th percentile	$127,329 (467)
80th percentile	$78,658 (388)
60th percentile	$51,086 (358)
40th percentile	$33,557 (307)
20th percentile	$19,554 (242)

CHILDREN ★ (468)

Living with two parents	74.7% (57)
Older teens in school	79.7% (407)
Speak English very well	92.4% (515)
Poverty rate for children	24.2% (278)
No health insurance	16.7% (533)

DIVERSITY/EQUALITY ★ (550)

Racial diversity index	7.4% (537)
Geographic diversity index	21.1% (548)
Top 20% share of income	44.8% (57)
Gender gap in earnings	49.5% (524)
White-collar gender gap	52.5% (520)

EDUCATION ★ (477)

Eighth grade or less	5.1% (390)
High school diplomas	86.2% (333)
Attended college	37.7% (531)
Bachelor's degrees	12.5% (507)
Advanced degrees	3.6% (505)

EMPLOYMENT ★★ (430)

Average jobless rate	7.8% (270)
Self-employed workers	10.1% (158)
Management/financial jobs	8.5% (505)
Computer/engineering jobs	2.0% (420)
Health care jobs	4.5% (419)

GROWTH POTENTIAL ★ (469)

Children per senior	1.37 (301)
Median age	41.5 (380)
Moved from different state	0.6% (546)
Homes built since 2000	10.5% (377)
Construction jobs	5.8% (360)

HOUSING ★★★★ (187)

Home vacancy rate	7.4% (180)
Home ownership rate	74.4% (103)
Housing diversity index	81.8% (466)
4 or more bedrooms	17.4% (226)
Affordability/income ratio	$2,314 (173)

INCOME ★★★ (300)

Poverty rate	16.1% (228)
Median household income	$41,701 (330)
Interest/dividends	18.6% (288)
Public assistance	18.7% (393)
Median fulltime earnings	$37,662 (239)

SENIORS ★★★ (283)

Seniors living alone	27.1% (247)
Poverty rate for seniors	6.9% (84)
Median income for seniors	$31,676 (338)
Seniors who work	16.7% (360)
Home ownership by seniors	81.5% (305)

STABILITY ★★★★★ (53)

25-39 age group	16.8% (359)
Born in state of residence	88.6% (4)
Same house as 1 year ago	88.1% (126)
Live and work in county	70.3% (366)
Married-couple households	55.0% (74)

TRANSPORTATION ★★ (392)

Bicycle or walk to work	3.7% (173)
Carpool to work	9.1% (419)
Public transit to work	0.4% (219)
Commute <15 minutes	39.2% (343)
Commute >45 minutes	13.9% (387)

See pages 37-130 for explanations of statistics, stars, and ranks.

Crawfordsville, IN
(Montgomery County, IN)

POPULATION

2010 census	38,124 (340)
2015 estimate	38,227 (337)
2010-2015 change	0.3% (237)
2020 projection	38,076 (342)
2030 projection	37,636 (343)

RACE

Whites	92.5% (116)
Blacks	0.9% (388)
Hispanics	4.5% (265)
Asians	0.5% (355)
Native Americans	0.3% (231)

AGE

0-17 years old	23.3% (246)
18-24 years old	9.9% (168)
25-39 years old	16.4% (411)
40-54 years old	20.9% (112)
55-64 years old	13.1% (318)
65+ years old	16.4% (255)

PRIVATE SECTOR

Businesses	797 (375)
Employees	13,774 (242)
Total wages	$562,476,292 (206)
Average weekly wages	$785 (110)

HOUSEHOLD INCOME LADDER

95th percentile	$134,471 (368)
80th percentile	$85,602 (238)
60th percentile	$57,805 (189)
40th percentile	$39,136 (153)
20th percentile	$22,559 (113)

CHILDREN ★★★★ (178)

Living with two parents	65.6% (256)
Older teens in school	87.3% (124)
Speak English very well	98.6% (278)
Poverty rate for children	23.8% (268)
No health insurance	6.5% (282)

DIVERSITY/EQUALITY ★★★ (298)

Racial diversity index	14.2% (432)
Geographic diversity index	39.8% (357)
Top 20% share of income	43.9% (25)
Gender gap in earnings	34.3% (296)
White-collar gender gap	31.5% (359)

EDUCATION ★★ (331)

Eighth grade or less	2.2% (152)
High school diplomas	88.7% (245)
Attended college	46.8% (400)
Bachelor's degrees	16.3% (357)
Advanced degrees	4.6% (431)

EMPLOYMENT ★ (468)

Average jobless rate	6.9% (185)
Self-employed workers	7.3% (401)
Management/financial jobs	9.4% (444)
Computer/engineering jobs	2.9% (219)
Health care jobs	3.3% (517)

GROWTH POTENTIAL ★★ (373)

Children per senior	1.42 (267)
Median age	40.2 (317)
Moved from different state	1.9% (310)
Homes built since 2000	8.9% (439)
Construction jobs	6.4% (270)

HOUSING ★★★ (231)

Home vacancy rate	9.0% (287)
Home ownership rate	71.0% (229)
Housing diversity index	83.4% (396)
4 or more bedrooms	16.9% (255)
Affordability/income ratio	$2,294 (162)

INCOME ★★★★ (200)

Poverty rate	14.2% (160)
Median household income	$48,213 (169)
Interest/dividends	19.9% (247)
Public assistance	13.5% (188)
Median fulltime earnings	$37,131 (274)

SENIORS ★★★ (292)

Seniors living alone	27.1% (247)
Poverty rate for seniors	8.0% (177)
Median income for seniors	$33,055 (279)
Seniors who work	19.8% (206)
Home ownership by seniors	78.7% (427)

STABILITY ★★★ (260)

25-39 age group	16.4% (411)
Born in state of residence	76.6% (188)
Same house as 1 year ago	83.5% (366)
Live and work in county	73.5% (323)
Married-couple households	53.8% (116)

TRANSPORTATION ★★ (341)

Bicycle or walk to work	4.5% (117)
Carpool to work	9.9% (348)
Public transit to work	0.3% (291)
Commute <15 minutes	42.7% (282)
Commute >45 minutes	15.1% (426)

See pages 37-130 for explanations of statistics, stars, and ranks.

Decatur, IN
(Adams County, IN)

POPULATION		
2010 census	34,387 (388)	
2015 estimate	34,980 (382)	
2010-2015 change	1.7% (150)	
2020 projection	35,324 (378)	
2030 projection	35,890 (365)	

RACE	
Whites	94.1% (73)
Blacks	0.7% (423)
Hispanics	4.4% (270)
Asians	0.3% (473)
Native Americans	0.1% (402)

AGE	
0-17 years old	31.3% (11)
18-24 years old	8.3% (362)
25-39 years old	16.6% (388)
40-54 years old	18.0% (450)
55-64 years old	11.5% (478)
65+ years old	14.3% (423)

PRIVATE SECTOR	
Businesses	669 (446)
Employees	11,291 (336)
Total wages	$389,489,503 (349)
Average weekly wages	$663 (352)

HOUSEHOLD INCOME LADDER	
95th percentile	$136,410 (336)
80th percentile	$82,983 (293)
60th percentile	$58,840 (165)
40th percentile	$38,097 (178)
20th percentile	$21,459 (165)

CHILDREN	★ (536)
Living with two parents	80.8% (9)
Older teens in school	68.8% (535)
Speak English very well	86.8% (538)
Poverty rate for children	27.3% (353)
No health insurance	34.9% (551)

DIVERSITY/EQUALITY	★ (517)
Racial diversity index	11.2% (477)
Geographic diversity index	24.1% (533)
Top 20% share of income	46.4% (153)
Gender gap in earnings	34.7% (308)
White-collar gender gap	41.3% (459)

EDUCATION	★ (451)
Eighth grade or less	8.9% (505)
High school diplomas	85.6% (357)
Attended college	44.5% (444)
Bachelor's degrees	16.1% (366)
Advanced degrees	5.0% (378)

EMPLOYMENT	★★★★ (198)
Average jobless rate	6.2% (131)
Self-employed workers	11.8% (81)
Management/financial jobs	10.4% (332)
Computer/engineering jobs	3.2% (158)
Health care jobs	4.3% (444)

GROWTH POTENTIAL	★★★★★ (100)
Children per senior	2.19 (41)
Median age	33.8 (70)
Moved from different state	1.5% (406)
Homes built since 2000	9.5% (408)
Construction jobs	8.3% (67)

HOUSING	★★★★★ (20)
Home vacancy rate	5.9% (88)
Home ownership rate	78.4% (15)
Housing diversity index	83.2% (405)
4 or more bedrooms	25.1% (41)
Affordability/income ratio	$2,426 (220)

INCOME	★★★★ (158)
Poverty rate	16.3% (234)
Median household income	$48,188 (171)
Interest/dividends	23.2% (151)
Public assistance	10.3% (72)
Median fulltime earnings	$36,992 (287)

SENIORS	★ (459)
Seniors living alone	32.1% (514)
Poverty rate for seniors	5.1% (22)
Median income for seniors	$31,856 (325)
Seniors who work	18.5% (268)
Home ownership by seniors	74.0% (536)

STABILITY	★★★★★ (26)
25-39 age group	16.6% (388)
Born in state of residence	86.7% (18)
Same house as 1 year ago	89.5% (61)
Live and work in county	68.5% (398)
Married-couple households	58.5% (16)

TRANSPORTATION	★★★★ (163)
Bicycle or walk to work	2.4% (331)
Carpool to work	17.5% (19)
Public transit to work	0.0% (511)
Commute <15 minutes	43.4% (273)
Commute >45 minutes	12.5% (334)

See pages 37-130 for explanations of statistics, stars, and ranks.

Defiance, OH
(Defiance County, OH)

POPULATION

2010 census	39,037 (326)
2015 estimate	38,352 (333)
2010-2015 change	-1.8% (389)
2020 projection	37,738 (346)
2030 projection	36,407 (354)

RACE

Whites	87.0% (241)
Blacks	1.7% (315)
Hispanics	9.5% (157)
Asians	0.4% (413)
Native Americans	0.3% (231)

AGE

0-17 years old	23.8% (206)
18-24 years old	9.3% (217)
25-39 years old	17.3% (280)
40-54 years old	19.3% (323)
55-64 years old	14.0% (182)
65+ years old	16.3% (268)

PRIVATE SECTOR

Businesses	780 (382)
Employees	13,730 (246)
Total wages	$578,862,473 (198)
Average weekly wages	$811 (76)

HOUSEHOLD INCOME LADDER

95th percentile	$136,513 (334)
80th percentile	$87,203 (197)
60th percentile	$60,301 (143)
40th percentile	$40,236 (124)
20th percentile	$24,173 (62)

CHILDREN ★★★★ (145)

Living with two parents	63.3% (316)
Older teens in school	87.4% (116)
Speak English very well	99.4% (124)
Poverty rate for children	20.4% (176)
No health insurance	5.8% (236)

DIVERSITY/EQUALITY ★★★★ (215)

Racial diversity index	23.4% (308)
Geographic diversity index	41.9% (329)
Top 20% share of income	43.9% (24)
Gender gap in earnings	36.8% (359)
White-collar gender gap	24.6% (265)

EDUCATION ★★★★ (215)

Eighth grade or less	1.9% (114)
High school diplomas	91.6% (141)

Attended college	50.8% (306)
Bachelor's degrees	18.4% (268)
Advanced degrees	6.3% (234)

EMPLOYMENT ★★ (417)

Average jobless rate	8.4% (323)
Self-employed workers	6.0% (502)
Management/financial jobs	10.1% (365)
Computer/engineering jobs	2.4% (336)
Health care jobs	5.7% (222)

GROWTH POTENTIAL ★ (457)

Children per senior	1.46 (237)
Median age	39.7 (279)
Moved from different state	1.4% (425)
Homes built since 2000	9.5% (408)
Construction jobs	4.9% (473)

HOUSING ★★★★★ (93)

Home vacancy rate	8.0% (223)
Home ownership rate	74.9% (83)
Housing diversity index	84.1% (337)
4 or more bedrooms	18.7% (171)
Affordability/income ratio	$2,149 (101)

INCOME ★★★★ (139)

Poverty rate	13.4% (135)
Median household income	$50,663 (108)
Interest/dividends	20.8% (224)
Public assistance	12.7% (155)
Median fulltime earnings	$39,645 (153)

SENIORS ★★★★★ (104)

Seniors living alone	23.3% (63)
Poverty rate for seniors	6.0% (49)
Median income for seniors	$37,018 (116)
Seniors who work	16.4% (383)
Home ownership by seniors	83.1% (217)

STABILITY ★★★ (311)

25-39 age group	17.3% (280)
Born in state of residence	74.8% (224)
Same house as 1 year ago	85.5% (280)
Live and work in county	63.2% (462)
Married-couple households	52.1% (190)

TRANSPORTATION ★★ (367)

Bicycle or walk to work	2.7% (292)
Carpool to work	6.9% (533)
Public transit to work	0.4% (219)
Commute <15 minutes	44.5% (254)
Commute >45 minutes	9.0% (175)

See pages 37-130 for explanations of statistics, stars, and ranks.

Dickinson, ND
(Stark County, ND)

POPULATION

2010 census	24,199 (487)
2015 estimate	32,154 (418)
2010-2015 change	32.9% (2)
2020 projection	39,561 (318)
2030 projection	52,025 (203)

RACE

Whites	90.3% (173)
Blacks	1.1% (367)
Hispanics	4.4% (270)
Asians	1.3% (112)
Native Americans	0.9% (115)

AGE

0-17 years old	23.9% (194)
18-24 years old	10.5% (136)
25-39 years old	22.0% (20)
40-54 years old	18.6% (412)
55-64 years old	11.8% (456)
65+ years old	13.3% (465)

PRIVATE SECTOR

Businesses	1,495 (135)
Employees	19,951 (126)
Total wages	$1,291,948,376 (32)
Average weekly wages	$1,245 (3)

HOUSEHOLD INCOME LADDER

95th percentile	$200,146 (18)
80th percentile	$121,575 (11)
60th percentile	$87,043 (9)
40th percentile	$57,772 (9)
20th percentile	$30,560 (14)

CHILDREN ★★★★★ (103)

Living with two parents	79.6% (14)
Older teens in school	81.5% (345)
Speak English very well	97.5% (388)
Poverty rate for children	4.9% (1)
No health insurance	11.7% (466)

DIVERSITY/EQUALITY ★ (442)

Racial diversity index	18.2% (372)
Geographic diversity index	55.2% (153)
Top 20% share of income	45.3% (80)
Gender gap in earnings	48.2% (520)
White-collar gender gap	45.3% (482)

EDUCATION ★★★★★ (79)

Eighth grade or less	1.6% (84)
High school diplomas	94.2% (53)

Attended college	65.4% (54)
Bachelor's degrees	26.4% (93)
Advanced degrees	6.8% (191)

EMPLOYMENT ★★★★★ (83)

Average jobless rate	2.8% (6)
Self-employed workers	12.5% (56)
Management/financial jobs	12.9% (92)
Computer/engineering jobs	3.3% (145)
Health care jobs	3.6% (508)

GROWTH POTENTIAL ★★★★★ (33)

Children per senior	1.79 (99)
Median age	35.0 (91)
Moved from different state	7.4% (16)
Homes built since 2000	18.7% (115)
Construction jobs	8.4% (64)

HOUSING ★★★★★ (81)

Home vacancy rate	8.2% (234)
Home ownership rate	68.7% (317)
Housing diversity index	84.2% (325)
4 or more bedrooms	28.4% (18)
Affordability/income ratio	$2,860 (371)

INCOME ★★★★★ (5)

Poverty rate	6.7% (4)
Median household income	$72,099 (7)
Interest/dividends	28.1% (35)
Public assistance	7.2% (24)
Median fulltime earnings	$49,423 (16)

SENIORS ★★★ (314)

Seniors living alone	28.3% (318)
Poverty rate for seniors	13.3% (455)
Median income for seniors	$37,203 (111)
Seniors who work	26.5% (42)
Home ownership by seniors	76.1% (510)

STABILITY ★★★★★ (22)

25-39 age group	22.0% (20)
Born in state of residence	64.1% (397)
Same house as 1 year ago	82.1% (434)
Live and work in county	92.0% (46)
Married-couple households	52.6% (167)

TRANSPORTATION ★★★★ (146)

Bicycle or walk to work	2.8% (279)
Carpool to work	10.1% (322)
Public transit to work	0.3% (291)
Commute <15 minutes	61.8% (37)
Commute >45 minutes	8.3% (144)

See pages 37-130 for explanations of statistics, stars, and ranks.

Dixon, IL
(Lee County, IL)

POPULATION	
2010 census	36,031 (375)
2015 estimate	34,584 (388)
2010-2015 change	-4.0% (521)
2020 projection	33,634 (396)
2030 projection	31,730 (412)

RACE	
Whites	87.1% (239)
Blacks	5.0% (164)
Hispanics	5.6% (233)
Asians	0.9% (178)
Native Americans	0.2% (300)

AGE	
0-17 years old	20.4% (437)
18-24 years old	8.4% (349)
25-39 years old	18.2% (167)
40-54 years old	21.6% (50)
55-64 years old	14.3% (148)
65+ years old	17.0% (197)

PRIVATE SECTOR	
Businesses	721 (420)
Employees	10,311 (366)
Total wages	$413,882,574 (322)
Average weekly wages	$772 (126)

HOUSEHOLD INCOME LADDER	
95th percentile	$158,397 (105)
80th percentile	$94,108 (98)
60th percentile	$63,245 (95)
40th percentile	$41,659 (86)
20th percentile	$23,149 (93)

CHILDREN	★★★★★ (51)
Living with two parents	69.7% (150)
Older teens in school	89.0% (80)
Speak English very well	98.9% (226)
Poverty rate for children	13.7% (52)
No health insurance	4.8% (173)

DIVERSITY/EQUALITY	★★ (418)
Racial diversity index	23.5% (307)
Geographic diversity index	32.9% (455)
Top 20% share of income	45.5% (86)
Gender gap in earnings	34.3% (296)
White-collar gender gap	44.5% (475)

EDUCATION	★★★★ (210)
Eighth grade or less	2.4% (169)
High school diplomas	89.1% (229)
Attended college	54.7% (230)
Bachelor's degrees	18.9% (254)
Advanced degrees	6.7% (205)

EMPLOYMENT	★★★★ (216)
Average jobless rate	7.5% (242)
Self-employed workers	8.3% (302)
Management/financial jobs	11.6% (196)
Computer/engineering jobs	3.1% (180)
Health care jobs	5.8% (209)

GROWTH POTENTIAL	★ (517)
Children per senior	1.20 (417)
Median age	42.2 (412)
Moved from different state	1.2% (474)
Homes built since 2000	9.5% (408)
Construction jobs	5.1% (458)

HOUSING	★★★★ (173)
Home vacancy rate	8.3% (241)
Home ownership rate	74.1% (115)
Housing diversity index	81.3% (484)
4 or more bedrooms	20.1% (122)
Affordability/income ratio	$2,169 (107)

INCOME	★★★★★ (77)
Poverty rate	11.1% (59)
Median household income	$52,379 (82)
Interest/dividends	23.2% (151)
Public assistance	11.1% (96)
Median fulltime earnings	$41,202 (88)

SENIORS	★★★★ (140)
Seniors living alone	29.4% (394)
Poverty rate for seniors	5.4% (29)
Median income for seniors	$39,460 (63)
Seniors who work	19.9% (201)
Home ownership by seniors	82.8% (232)

STABILITY	★★★★ (208)
25-39 age group	18.2% (167)
Born in state of residence	81.4% (95)
Same house as 1 year ago	86.8% (206)
Live and work in county	60.4% (491)
Married-couple households	51.9% (199)

TRANSPORTATION	★ (460)
Bicycle or walk to work	2.2% (358)
Carpool to work	8.3% (471)
Public transit to work	0.4% (219)
Commute <15 minutes	41.1% (316)
Commute >45 minutes	15.7% (445)

See pages 37-130 for explanations of statistics, stars, and ranks.

Dodge City, KS
(Ford County, KS)

POPULATION

2010 census	33,848 (396)
2015 estimate	34,536 (389)
2010-2015 change	2.0% (128)
2020 projection	35,051 (382)
2030 projection	36,008 (358)

RACE

Whites	41.8% (509)
Blacks	2.3% (267)
Hispanics	52.8% (24)
Asians	1.3% (112)
Native Americans	0.4% (203)

AGE

0-17 years old	30.7% (14)
18-24 years old	10.6% (131)
25-39 years old	20.3% (54)
40-54 years old	18.7% (399)
55-64 years old	9.6% (536)
65+ years old	10.2% (524)

PRIVATE SECTOR

Businesses	760 (392)
Employees	14,734 (217)
Total wages	$526,203,852 (226)
Average weekly wages	$687 (295)

HOUSEHOLD INCOME LADDER

95th percentile	$143,805 (244)
80th percentile	$86,476 (222)
60th percentile	$61,968 (108)
40th percentile	$40,490 (113)
20th percentile	$22,684 (110)

CHILDREN ★ (524)

Living with two parents	64.9% (274)
Older teens in school	75.6% (498)
Speak English very well	88.5% (531)
Poverty rate for children	27.8% (363)
No health insurance	11.4% (456)

DIVERSITY/EQUALITY ★★★★★ (48)

Racial diversity index	54.6% (59)
Geographic diversity index	66.4% (67)
Top 20% share of income	45.2% (69)
Gender gap in earnings	27.0% (118)
White-collar gender gap	44.6% (477)

EDUCATION ★ (530)

Eighth grade or less	19.4% (542)
High school diplomas	66.6% (543)

Attended college	45.5% (432)
Bachelor's degrees	17.8% (290)
Advanced degrees	5.0% (378)

EMPLOYMENT ★ (503)

Average jobless rate	6.4% (147)
Self-employed workers	7.2% (410)
Management/financial jobs	8.6% (498)
Computer/engineering jobs	1.3% (519)
Health care jobs	3.7% (503)

GROWTH POTENTIAL ★★★★★ (98)

Children per senior	3.01 (14)
Median age	30.9 (38)
Moved from different state	3.0% (157)
Homes built since 2000	7.6% (483)
Construction jobs	4.6% (494)

HOUSING ★★★★★ (102)

Home vacancy rate	6.0% (95)
Home ownership rate	61.2% (488)
Housing diversity index	85.2% (190)
4 or more bedrooms	22.8% (69)
Affordability/income ratio	$1,960 (44)

INCOME ★★★ (262)

Poverty rate	18.2% (304)
Median household income	$50,777 (105)
Interest/dividends	16.9% (345)
Public assistance	12.1% (137)
Median fulltime earnings	$33,573 (437)

SENIORS ★★★★★ (110)

Seniors living alone	26.8% (222)
Poverty rate for seniors	4.0% (8)
Median income for seniors	$37,434 (108)
Seniors who work	30.4% (22)
Home ownership by seniors	72.4% (544)

STABILITY ★★★★★ (27)

25-39 age group	20.3% (54)
Born in state of residence	52.4% (476)
Same house as 1 year ago	86.2% (237)
Live and work in county	92.6% (39)
Married-couple households	55.2% (65)

TRANSPORTATION ★★★★★ (41)

Bicycle or walk to work	1.8% (409)
Carpool to work	14.8% (50)
Public transit to work	0.4% (219)
Commute <15 minutes	66.3% (13)
Commute >45 minutes	5.2% (37)

See pages 37-130 for explanations of statistics, stars, and ranks.

Effingham, IL
(Effingham County, IL)

POPULATION

2010 census	34,242 (390)
2015 estimate	34,371 (391)
2010-2015 change	0.4% (228)
2020 projection	34,214 (393)
2030 projection	33,786 (397)

RACE

Whites	96.5% (5)
Blacks	0.3% (519)
Hispanics	1.9% (442)
Asians	0.6% (291)
Native Americans	0.1% (402)

AGE

0-17 years old	24.0% (184)
18-24 years old	8.6% (317)
25-39 years old	18.8% (121)
40-54 years old	19.1% (354)
55-64 years old	13.1% (318)
65+ years old	16.3% (268)

PRIVATE SECTOR

Businesses	1,174 (211)
Employees	18,450 (148)
Total wages	$662,042,738 (159)
Average weekly wages	$690 (285)

HOUSEHOLD INCOME LADDER

95th percentile	$165,634 (70)
80th percentile	$93,958 (103)
60th percentile	$63,870 (86)
40th percentile	$41,789 (80)
20th percentile	$23,481 (82)

CHILDREN ★★★★★ (50)

Living with two parents	69.9% (146)
Older teens in school	86.7% (141)
Speak English very well	99.4% (124)
Poverty rate for children	16.1% (83)
No health insurance	2.8% (50)

DIVERSITY/EQUALITY ★ (544)

Racial diversity index	6.8% (543)
Geographic diversity index	26.3% (514)
Top 20% share of income	47.6% (261)
Gender gap in earnings	35.6% (330)
White-collar gender gap	52.5% (520)

EDUCATION ★★★★★ (93)

Eighth grade or less	1.1% (26)
High school diplomas	94.7% (40)
Attended college	61.8% (96)
Bachelor's degrees	24.6% (118)
Advanced degrees	6.8% (191)

EMPLOYMENT ★★★★★ (94)

Average jobless rate	5.4% (89)
Self-employed workers	10.3% (150)
Management/financial jobs	11.2% (229)
Computer/engineering jobs	3.6% (112)
Health care jobs	6.3% (144)

GROWTH POTENTIAL ★★★ (234)

Children per senior	1.47 (234)
Median age	38.9 (228)
Moved from different state	1.1% (487)
Homes built since 2000	13.2% (271)
Construction jobs	7.8% (98)

HOUSING ★★★★★ (25)

Home vacancy rate	7.3% (176)
Home ownership rate	79.1% (8)
Housing diversity index	86.3% (36)
4 or more bedrooms	19.3% (145)
Affordability/income ratio	$2,455 (232)

INCOME ★★★★★ (69)

Poverty rate	10.6% (47)
Median household income	$52,224 (85)
Interest/dividends	30.6% (18)
Public assistance	10.5% (81)
Median fulltime earnings	$36,254 (321)

SENIORS ★★ (366)

Seniors living alone	35.3% (544)
Poverty rate for seniors	7.8% (163)
Median income for seniors	$32,813 (293)
Seniors who work	19.6% (221)
Home ownership by seniors	85.0% (142)

STABILITY ★★★★★ (3)

25-39 age group	18.8% (121)
Born in state of residence	85.4% (39)
Same house as 1 year ago	88.4% (109)
Live and work in county	85.7% (123)
Married-couple households	54.0% (108)

TRANSPORTATION ★★★ (250)

Bicycle or walk to work	1.8% (409)
Carpool to work	9.8% (358)
Public transit to work	0.4% (219)
Commute <15 minutes	48.1% (194)
Commute >45 minutes	6.8% (80)

See pages 37-130 for explanations of statistics, stars, and ranks.

Emporia, KS
(Lyon County, KS)

POPULATION	
2010 census	33,690 (398)
2015 estimate	33,339 (400)
2010-2015 change	-1.0% (326)
2020 projection	32,325 (415)
2030 projection	30,317 (423)

RACE	
Whites	72.2% (376)
Blacks	2.3% (267)
Hispanics	20.4% (76)
Asians	2.0% (51)
Native Americans	0.2% (300)

AGE	
0-17 years old	22.7% (284)
18-24 years old	18.1% (37)
25-39 years old	17.0% (317)
40-54 years old	17.1% (500)
55-64 years old	12.0% (438)
65+ years old	13.2% (470)

PRIVATE SECTOR	
Businesses	805 (370)
Employees	11,128 (339)
Total wages	$342,518,048 (389)
Average weekly wages	$592 (498)

HOUSEHOLD INCOME LADDER	
95th percentile	$137,276 (322)
80th percentile	$76,021 (440)
60th percentile	$48,619 (409)
40th percentile	$32,779 (332)
20th percentile	$17,177 (352)

CHILDREN	★★ (357)
Living with two parents	60.6% (390)
Older teens in school	81.0% (366)
Speak English very well	96.5% (436)
Poverty rate for children	25.2% (304)
No health insurance	7.0% (319)

DIVERSITY/EQUALITY	★★★★★ (106)
Racial diversity index	43.5% (164)
Geographic diversity index	52.7% (181)
Top 20% share of income	47.8% (280)
Gender gap in earnings	35.7% (331)
White-collar gender gap	12.8% (125)

EDUCATION	★★★★ (174)
Eighth grade or less	5.0% (385)
High school diplomas	88.8% (240)
Attended college	56.1% (202)
Bachelor's degrees	25.4% (101)
Advanced degrees	8.1% (120)

EMPLOYMENT	★ (446)
Average jobless rate	7.2% (218)
Self-employed workers	7.6% (376)
Management/financial jobs	9.0% (475)
Computer/engineering jobs	2.0% (420)
Health care jobs	4.8% (369)

GROWTH POTENTIAL	★★★★★ (104)
Children per senior	1.71 (127)
Median age	32.5 (52)
Moved from different state	4.6% (65)
Homes built since 2000	8.4% (455)
Construction jobs	7.2% (162)

HOUSING	★★ (432)
Home vacancy rate	11.6% (441)
Home ownership rate	59.7% (507)
Housing diversity index	83.2% (405)
4 or more bedrooms	19.2% (150)
Affordability/income ratio	$2,334 (182)

INCOME	★★ (344)
Poverty rate	21.5% (416)
Median household income	$40,021 (380)
Interest/dividends	19.9% (247)
Public assistance	14.0% (207)
Median fulltime earnings	$34,344 (408)

SENIORS	★★ (375)
Seniors living alone	29.7% (416)
Poverty rate for seniors	9.4% (282)
Median income for seniors	$36,348 (146)
Seniors who work	22.3% (124)
Home ownership by seniors	74.6% (530)

STABILITY	★ (490)
25-39 age group	17.0% (317)
Born in state of residence	67.1% (362)
Same house as 1 year ago	76.9% (523)
Live and work in county	87.8% (92)
Married-couple households	44.5% (474)

TRANSPORTATION	★★★★★ (47)
Bicycle or walk to work	4.8% (98)
Carpool to work	14.0% (66)
Public transit to work	0.4% (219)
Commute <15 minutes	63.8% (27)
Commute >45 minutes	9.3% (188)

See pages 37-130 for explanations of statistics, stars, and ranks.

Escanaba, MI
(Delta County, MI)

POPULATION	
2010 census	37,069 (355)
2015 estimate	36,377 (368)
2010-2015 change	-1.9% (399)
2020 projection	35,769 (374)
2030 projection	34,478 (381)

RACE	
Whites	93.7% (83)
Blacks	0.2% (537)
Hispanics	1.0% (530)
Asians	0.3% (473)
Native Americans	1.9% (72)

AGE	
0-17 years old	20.5% (433)
18-24 years old	7.3% (503)
25-39 years old	15.1% (507)
40-54 years old	19.9% (250)
55-64 years old	16.7% (23)
65+ years old	20.6% (42)

PRIVATE SECTOR	
Businesses	963 (288)
Employees	11,733 (318)
Total wages	$424,851,943 (309)
Average weekly wages	$696 (262)

HOUSEHOLD INCOME LADDER	
95th percentile	$126,558 (473)
80th percentile	$80,604 (360)
60th percentile	$52,050 (316)
40th percentile	$32,311 (350)
20th percentile	$17,426 (344)

CHILDREN	★★★★★ (109)
Living with two parents	70.2% (141)
Older teens in school	89.4% (76)
Speak English very well	99.9% (19)
Poverty rate for children	24.5% (286)
No health insurance	6.4% (276)

DIVERSITY/EQUALITY	★★ (420)
Racial diversity index	12.1% (462)
Geographic diversity index	32.7% (456)
Top 20% share of income	46.1% (125)
Gender gap in earnings	37.8% (385)
White-collar gender gap	25.6% (281)

EDUCATION	★★★★ (150)
Eighth grade or less	1.2% (42)
High school diplomas	94.8% (36)
Attended college	61.2% (107)
Bachelor's degrees	19.5% (233)
Advanced degrees	4.6% (431)

EMPLOYMENT	★★ (333)
Average jobless rate	9.2% (377)
Self-employed workers	8.5% (290)
Management/financial jobs	9.1% (463)
Computer/engineering jobs	2.3% (354)
Health care jobs	6.9% (79)

GROWTH POTENTIAL	★ (519)
Children per senior	0.99 (506)
Median age	46.4 (518)
Moved from different state	2.0% (288)
Homes built since 2000	9.8% (395)
Construction jobs	6.5% (253)

HOUSING	★★★★ (127)
Home vacancy rate	8.7% (268)
Home ownership rate	78.6% (10)
Housing diversity index	84.7% (260)
4 or more bedrooms	14.5% (377)
Affordability/income ratio	$2,424 (219)

INCOME	★★★ (235)
Poverty rate	17.2% (270)
Median household income	$42,031 (319)
Interest/dividends	23.3% (147)
Public assistance	17.5% (358)
Median fulltime earnings	$40,407 (125)

SENIORS	★ (447)
Seniors living alone	29.7% (416)
Poverty rate for seniors	10.7% (357)
Median income for seniors	$29,865 (414)
Seniors who work	11.6% (545)
Home ownership by seniors	85.1% (137)

STABILITY	★★★★ (140)
25-39 age group	15.1% (507)
Born in state of residence	81.0% (100)
Same house as 1 year ago	87.4% (173)
Live and work in county	86.8% (103)
Married-couple households	50.1% (291)

TRANSPORTATION	★★★★ (169)
Bicycle or walk to work	3.5% (189)
Carpool to work	10.8% (249)
Public transit to work	0.7% (119)
Commute <15 minutes	49.5% (163)
Commute >45 minutes	8.8% (165)

See pages 37-130 for explanations of statistics, stars, and ranks.

Fairfield, IA
(Jefferson County, IA)

POPULATION		Attended college	68.1% (32)
2010 census	16,843 (538)	Bachelor's degrees	32.3% (40)
2015 estimate	17,555 (536)	Advanced degrees	13.6% (23)
2010-2015 change	4.2% (55)	**EMPLOYMENT**	★★★★★ **(38)**
2020 projection	18,094 (533)	Average jobless rate	6.4% (147)
2030 projection	19,107 (525)	Self-employed workers	14.6% (22)
		Management/financial jobs	15.1% (29)
RACE		Computer/engineering jobs	5.0% (30)
Whites	82.3% (298)	Health care jobs	4.1% (462)
Blacks	1.4% (340)		
Hispanics	3.0% (343)	**GROWTH POTENTIAL**	★ **(466)**
Asians	7.9% (5)	Children per senior	1.07 (477)
Native Americans	0.1% (402)	Median age	42.5 (432)
		Moved from different state	3.6% (104)
AGE		Homes built since 2000	11.4% (338)
0-17 years old	18.5% (517)	Construction jobs	4.6% (494)
18-24 years old	11.2% (110)		
25-39 years old	18.0% (201)	**HOUSING**	★★★★ **(209)**
40-54 years old	16.6% (511)	Home vacancy rate	5.1% (39)
55-64 years old	18.3% (5)	Home ownership rate	66.5% (405)
65+ years old	17.3% (172)	Housing diversity index	82.7% (429)
		4 or more bedrooms	17.4% (226)
PRIVATE SECTOR		Affordability/income ratio	$2,354 (195)
Businesses	749 (401)		
Employees	6,363 (496)	**INCOME**	★★★★ **(142)**
Total wages	$228,200,954 (485)	Poverty rate	15.0% (190)
Average weekly wages	$690 (285)	Median household income	$42,899 (292)
		Interest/dividends	33.1% (5)
HOUSEHOLD INCOME LADDER		Public assistance	15.7% (280)
95th percentile	$147,923 (183)	Median fulltime earnings	$37,122 (276)
80th percentile	$87,596 (190)		
60th percentile	$55,126 (246)	**SENIORS**	★★★★ **(145)**
40th percentile	$33,556 (308)	Seniors living alone	28.7% (344)
20th percentile	$17,686 (332)	Poverty rate for seniors	7.9% (170)
		Median income for seniors	n.a.
CHILDREN	★★★★ **(190)**	Seniors who work	30.4% (22)
Living with two parents	69.6% (151)	Home ownership by seniors	77.2% (478)
Older teens in school	79.8% (405)		
Speak English very well	99.4% (124)	**STABILITY**	★★★ **(292)**
Poverty rate for children	20.6% (182)	25-39 age group	18.0% (201)
No health insurance	6.4% (276)	Born in state of residence	56.4% (453)
		Same house as 1 year ago	86.6% (213)
DIVERSITY/EQUALITY	★★★ **(267)**	Live and work in county	83.4% (155)
Racial diversity index	31.3% (242)	Married-couple households	48.0% (378)
Geographic diversity index	64.2% (81)		
Top 20% share of income	51.3% (480)	**TRANSPORTATION**	★★★★★ **(93)**
Gender gap in earnings	49.9% (527)	Bicycle or walk to work	7.6% (36)
White-collar gender gap	1.2% (9)	Carpool to work	6.1% (546)
		Public transit to work	0.1% (441)
EDUCATION	★★★★★ **(22)**	Commute <15 minutes	63.5% (29)
Eighth grade or less	0.6% (7)	Commute >45 minutes	5.6% (43)
High school diplomas	96.4% (9)		

See pages 37-130 for explanations of statistics, stars, and ranks.

Fairmont, MN
(Martin County, MN)

POPULATION	
2010 census	20,840 (521)
2015 estimate	20,022 (525)
2010-2015 change	-3.9% (517)
2020 projection	19,374 (526)
2030 projection	18,134 (530)

RACE	
Whites	94.0% (75)
Blacks	0.3% (519)
Hispanics	3.9% (302)
Asians	0.5% (355)
Native Americans	0.2% (300)

AGE	
0-17 years old	21.6% (366)
18-24 years old	7.0% (521)
25-39 years old	15.0% (511)
40-54 years old	19.4% (315)
55-64 years old	15.4% (66)
65+ years old	21.5% (25)

PRIVATE SECTOR	
Businesses	593 (474)
Employees	7,350 (459)
Total wages	$282,255,846 (447)
Average weekly wages	$739 (180)

HOUSEHOLD INCOME LADDER	
95th percentile	$175,173 (43)
80th percentile	$90,780 (145)
60th percentile	$62,257 (103)
40th percentile	$41,176 (97)
20th percentile	$21,552 (160)

CHILDREN	★★★★★ (82)
Living with two parents	67.9% (198)
Older teens in school	86.0% (166)
Speak English very well	99.9% (19)
Poverty rate for children	17.6% (112)
No health insurance	5.0% (181)

DIVERSITY/EQUALITY	★ (491)
Racial diversity index	11.5% (473)
Geographic diversity index	41.1% (338)
Top 20% share of income	47.0% (211)
Gender gap in earnings	39.3% (425)
White-collar gender gap	40.1% (448)

EDUCATION	★★★★ (172)
Eighth grade or less	0.8% (10)
High school diplomas	93.5% (75)
Attended college	57.6% (174)
Bachelor's degrees	20.8% (194)
Advanced degrees	3.7% (498)

EMPLOYMENT	★★★★★ (15)
Average jobless rate	3.5% (20)
Self-employed workers	16.8% (9)
Management/financial jobs	15.6% (22)
Computer/engineering jobs	3.0% (193)
Health care jobs	4.8% (369)

GROWTH POTENTIAL	★ (528)
Children per senior	1.00 (503)
Median age	45.4 (504)
Moved from different state	2.3% (234)
Homes built since 2000	6.2% (522)
Construction jobs	6.3% (284)

HOUSING	★★★★★ (84)
Home vacancy rate	8.5% (253)
Home ownership rate	73.8% (126)
Housing diversity index	82.5% (441)
4 or more bedrooms	24.1% (48)
Affordability/income ratio	$2,051 (68)

INCOME	★★★★★ (74)
Poverty rate	11.4% (66)
Median household income	$51,391 (92)
Interest/dividends	25.0% (97)
Public assistance	8.9% (44)
Median fulltime earnings	$39,186 (172)

SENIORS	★★ (340)
Seniors living alone	31.9% (509)
Poverty rate for seniors	8.2% (196)
Median income for seniors	$36,623 (130)
Seniors who work	25.1% (70)
Home ownership by seniors	75.4% (520)

STABILITY	★★★★ (205)
25-39 age group	15.0% (511)
Born in state of residence	75.0% (221)
Same house as 1 year ago	88.7% (95)
Live and work in county	82.1% (179)
Married-couple households	50.5% (271)

TRANSPORTATION	★★★★ (152)
Bicycle or walk to work	3.3% (211)
Carpool to work	9.7% (369)
Public transit to work	1.0% (69)
Commute <15 minutes	52.1% (123)
Commute >45 minutes	7.4% (99)

See pages 37-130 for explanations of statistics, stars, and ranks.

Faribault-Northfield, MN
(Rice County, MN)

POPULATION	
2010 census	64,142 (126)
2015 estimate	65,400 (121)
2010-2015 change	2.0% (128)
2020 projection	67,233 (113)
2030 projection	71,063 (101)

RACE	
Whites	84.4% (273)
Blacks	3.8% (198)
Hispanics	7.8% (186)
Asians	2.4% (33)
Native Americans	0.5% (174)

AGE	
0-17 years old	22.4% (306)
18-24 years old	14.8% (60)
25-39 years old	16.9% (338)
40-54 years old	20.5% (151)
55-64 years old	11.8% (456)
65+ years old	13.6% (454)

PRIVATE SECTOR	
Businesses	1,376 (159)
Employees	20,264 (124)
Total wages	$858,332,835 (105)
Average weekly wages	$815 (71)

HOUSEHOLD INCOME LADDER	
95th percentile	$175,025 (44)
80th percentile	$105,057 (38)
60th percentile	$72,379 (28)
40th percentile	$46,817 (32)
20th percentile	$25,995 (36)

CHILDREN	★★★★★ (66)
Living with two parents	73.6% (72)
Older teens in school	94.1% (19)
Speak English very well	98.7% (265)
Poverty rate for children	16.0% (81)
No health insurance	10.3% (428)

DIVERSITY/EQUALITY	★★★ (231)
Racial diversity index	27.9% (270)
Geographic diversity index	50.9% (198)
Top 20% share of income	46.7% (183)
Gender gap in earnings	38.0% (392)
White-collar gender gap	23.1% (251)

EDUCATION	★★★★★ (78)
Eighth grade or less	2.9% (217)
High school diplomas	91.5% (145)
Attended college	61.6% (102)
Bachelor's degrees	28.1% (74)
Advanced degrees	9.9% (64)

EMPLOYMENT	★★★★★ (73)
Average jobless rate	5.6% (106)
Self-employed workers	10.8% (125)
Management/financial jobs	13.0% (86)
Computer/engineering jobs	4.8% (37)
Health care jobs	5.0% (339)

GROWTH POTENTIAL	★★★★★ (110)
Children per senior	1.65 (148)
Median age	36.4 (128)
Moved from different state	3.2% (136)
Homes built since 2000	21.1% (78)
Construction jobs	6.2% (295)

HOUSING	★★★★★ (16)
Home vacancy rate	5.2% (46)
Home ownership rate	73.9% (122)
Housing diversity index	84.5% (287)
4 or more bedrooms	29.0% (13)
Affordability/income ratio	$3,107 (419)

INCOME	★★★★★ (33)
Poverty rate	11.4% (66)
Median household income	$59,598 (26)
Interest/dividends	24.3% (122)
Public assistance	8.8% (42)
Median fulltime earnings	$46,282 (25)

SENIORS	★★★ (273)
Seniors living alone	29.3% (389)
Poverty rate for seniors	8.5% (223)
Median income for seniors	$37,599 (100)
Seniors who work	25.3% (67)
Home ownership by seniors	75.1% (524)

STABILITY	★★ (360)
25-39 age group	16.9% (338)
Born in state of residence	68.3% (338)
Same house as 1 year ago	83.7% (353)
Live and work in county	66.9% (419)
Married-couple households	54.6% (84)

TRANSPORTATION	★★ (351)
Bicycle or walk to work	5.5% (73)
Carpool to work	8.6% (457)
Public transit to work	0.8% (96)
Commute <15 minutes	42.2% (294)
Commute >45 minutes	17.1% (483)

See pages 37-130 for explanations of statistics, stars, and ranks.

Farmington, MO
(St. Francois County, MO)

POPULATION

2010 census	65,359 (119)
2015 estimate	66,520 (114)
2010-2015 change	1.8% (142)
2020 projection	68,365 (109)
2030 projection	72,027 (98)

RACE

Whites	92.3% (124)
Blacks	4.8% (170)
Hispanics	1.4% (488)
Asians	0.4% (413)
Native Americans	0.3% (231)

AGE

0-17 years old	21.2% (397)
18-24 years old	9.2% (234)
25-39 years old	21.1% (39)
40-54 years old	21.4% (67)
55-64 years old	12.3% (414)
65+ years old	14.8% (384)

PRIVATE SECTOR

Businesses	1,684 (105)
Employees	16,973 (170)
Total wages	$491,454,286 (250)
Average weekly wages	$557 (529)

HOUSEHOLD INCOME LADDER

95th percentile	$123,860 (492)
80th percentile	$75,643 (446)
60th percentile	$48,155 (421)
40th percentile	$31,806 (368)
20th percentile	$16,796 (369)

CHILDREN ★★★ (279)

Living with two parents	67.3% (209)
Older teens in school	75.7% (497)
Speak English very well	99.9% (19)
Poverty rate for children	25.9% (321)
No health insurance	5.5% (218)

DIVERSITY/EQUALITY ★★★ (223)

Racial diversity index	14.5% (425)
Geographic diversity index	34.6% (443)
Top 20% share of income	46.8% (203)
Gender gap in earnings	25.6% (97)
White-collar gender gap	11.6% (105)

EDUCATION ★★ (387)

Eighth grade or less	3.5% (284)
High school diplomas	83.4% (411)
Attended college	49.5% (345)
Bachelor's degrees	14.0% (462)
Advanced degrees	5.1% (364)

EMPLOYMENT ★★ (376)

Average jobless rate	8.3% (314)
Self-employed workers	6.2% (488)
Management/financial jobs	7.9% (530)
Computer/engineering jobs	2.1% (399)
Health care jobs	7.9% (26)

GROWTH POTENTIAL ★★★★ (171)

Children per senior	1.43 (261)
Median age	38.9 (228)
Moved from different state	1.9% (310)
Homes built since 2000	18.5% (119)
Construction jobs	7.3% (151)

HOUSING ★★★ (277)

Home vacancy rate	7.7% (199)
Home ownership rate	66.3% (410)
Housing diversity index	85.1% (212)
4 or more bedrooms	14.1% (398)
Affordability/income ratio	$2,604 (290)

INCOME ★ (455)

Poverty rate	19.3% (348)
Median household income	$39,741 (388)
Interest/dividends	13.2% (463)
Public assistance	21.0% (455)
Median fulltime earnings	$32,592 (467)

SENIORS ★ (479)

Seniors living alone	30.4% (447)
Poverty rate for seniors	9.9% (315)
Median income for seniors	$30,656 (385)
Seniors who work	14.4% (485)
Home ownership by seniors	78.1% (450)

STABILITY ★★★★ (137)

25-39 age group	21.1% (39)
Born in state of residence	80.1% (111)
Same house as 1 year ago	80.2% (495)
Live and work in county	74.7% (299)
Married-couple households	49.4% (330)

TRANSPORTATION ★★ (403)

Bicycle or walk to work	0.9% (521)
Carpool to work	13.5% (83)
Public transit to work	0.0% (511)
Commute <15 minutes	41.5% (308)
Commute >45 minutes	16.7% (477)

See pages 37-130 for explanations of statistics, stars, and ranks.

Fergus Falls, MN
(Otter Tail County, MN)

POPULATION	
2010 census	57,303 (163)
2015 estimate	57,716 (159)
2010-2015 change	0.7% (202)
2020 projection	57,736 (161)
2030 projection	57,779 (161)

RACE	
Whites	93.7% (83)
Blacks	1.2% (361)
Hispanics	3.0% (343)
Asians	0.6% (291)
Native Americans	0.3% (231)

AGE	
0-17 years old	21.4% (379)
18-24 years old	7.0% (521)
25-39 years old	14.0% (541)
40-54 years old	19.8% (261)
55-64 years old	15.7% (52)
65+ years old	22.0% (23)

PRIVATE SECTOR	
Businesses	1,569 (124)
Employees	18,640 (145)
Total wages	$661,798,703 (160)
Average weekly wages	$683 (305)

HOUSEHOLD INCOME LADDER	
95th percentile	$160,257 (94)
80th percentile	$93,776 (105)
60th percentile	$63,572 (91)
40th percentile	$41,694 (84)
20th percentile	$22,131 (132)

CHILDREN	★★★★★ (52)
Living with two parents	77.0% (29)
Older teens in school	84.6% (214)
Speak English very well	97.6% (375)
Poverty rate for children	12.3% (33)
No health insurance	4.5% (150)

DIVERSITY/EQUALITY	★ (482)
Racial diversity index	12.1% (462)
Geographic diversity index	44.4% (291)
Top 20% share of income	46.8% (203)
Gender gap in earnings	36.2% (346)
White-collar gender gap	47.5% (495)

EDUCATION	★★★★★ (82)
Eighth grade or less	1.6% (84)
High school diplomas	93.6% (68)
Attended college	66.2% (45)
Bachelor's degrees	25.5% (100)
Advanced degrees	6.8% (191)

EMPLOYMENT	★★★★★ (25)
Average jobless rate	4.4% (42)
Self-employed workers	14.6% (22)
Management/financial jobs	14.3% (42)
Computer/engineering jobs	2.7% (270)
Health care jobs	6.4% (132)

GROWTH POTENTIAL	★★ (367)
Children per senior	0.97 (513)
Median age	46.7 (523)
Moved from different state	1.7% (355)
Homes built since 2000	17.4% (145)
Construction jobs	8.2% (78)

HOUSING	★★★★★ (8)
Home vacancy rate	5.0% (33)
Home ownership rate	78.5% (13)
Housing diversity index	86.2% (43)
4 or more bedrooms	23.5% (56)
Affordability/income ratio	$3,149 (427)

INCOME	★★★★★ (55)
Poverty rate	10.0% (31)
Median household income	$52,365 (83)
Interest/dividends	27.9% (39)
Public assistance	9.3% (50)
Median fulltime earnings	$40,608 (114)

SENIORS	★★★ (255)
Seniors living alone	26.5% (201)
Poverty rate for seniors	9.2% (270)
Median income for seniors	$36,021 (153)
Seniors who work	21.6% (142)
Home ownership by seniors	77.7% (464)

STABILITY	★★★★ (147)
25-39 age group	14.0% (541)
Born in state of residence	72.5% (270)
Same house as 1 year ago	89.5% (61)
Live and work in county	78.4% (237)
Married-couple households	57.0% (31)

TRANSPORTATION	★★★★ (154)
Bicycle or walk to work	4.9% (96)
Carpool to work	11.5% (184)
Public transit to work	0.9% (83)
Commute <15 minutes	47.5% (202)
Commute >45 minutes	11.2% (278)

See pages 37-130 for explanations of statistics, stars, and ranks.

Findlay, OH
(Hancock County, OH)

POPULATION

2010 census	74,782 (83)
2015 estimate	75,573 (85)
2010-2015 change	1.1% (181)
2020 projection	76,106 (84)
2030 projection	76,915 (86)

RACE

Whites	90.2% (175)
Blacks	1.3% (351)
Hispanics	4.9% (254)
Asians	1.7% (69)
Native Americans	0.1% (402)

AGE

0-17 years old	22.8% (277)
18-24 years old	9.7% (183)
25-39 years old	18.5% (144)
40-54 years old	20.2% (202)
55-64 years old	13.3% (282)
65+ years old	15.5% (333)

PRIVATE SECTOR

Businesses	1,678 (106)
Employees	41,294 (11)
Total wages	$1,927,507,671 (10)
Average weekly wages	$898 (35)

HOUSEHOLD INCOME LADDER

95th percentile	$168,550 (60)
80th percentile	$95,400 (86)
60th percentile	$61,911 (111)
40th percentile	$40,566 (111)
20th percentile	$22,756 (105)

CHILDREN ★★★★★ (62)

Living with two parents	68.0% (195)
Older teens in school	90.4% (60)
Speak English very well	99.5% (96)
Poverty rate for children	20.3% (173)
No health insurance	4.1% (126)

DIVERSITY/EQUALITY ★★ (371)

Racial diversity index	18.3% (368)
Geographic diversity index	36.8% (407)
Top 20% share of income	47.0% (216)
Gender gap in earnings	40.4% (445)
White-collar gender gap	17.9% (187)

EDUCATION ★★★★★ (64)

| Eighth grade or less | 1.2% (42) |
| High school diplomas | 93.2% (88) |

Attended college	59.8% (129)
Bachelor's degrees	27.9% (76)
Advanced degrees	10.1% (56)

EMPLOYMENT ★★★★ (138)

Average jobless rate	6.9% (185)
Self-employed workers	6.2% (488)
Management/financial jobs	15.6% (22)
Computer/engineering jobs	4.5% (58)
Health care jobs	4.3% (444)

GROWTH POTENTIAL ★★ (387)

Children per senior	1.47 (234)
Median age	39.2 (248)
Moved from different state	2.7% (179)
Homes built since 2000	11.8% (321)
Construction jobs	4.3% (514)

HOUSING ★★★★★ (99)

Home vacancy rate	5.8% (79)
Home ownership rate	70.6% (249)
Housing diversity index	84.2% (325)
4 or more bedrooms	19.7% (132)
Affordability/income ratio	$2,497 (248)

INCOME ★★★★★ (87)

Poverty rate	13.9% (151)
Median household income	$50,895 (103)
Interest/dividends	24.4% (119)
Public assistance	10.8% (89)
Median fulltime earnings	$41,990 (64)

SENIORS ★★★★ (183)

Seniors living alone	30.5% (451)
Poverty rate for seniors	4.7% (13)
Median income for seniors	$35,587 (166)
Seniors who work	23.1% (107)
Home ownership by seniors	80.6% (353)

STABILITY ★★★★★ (102)

25-39 age group	18.5% (144)
Born in state of residence	78.9% (136)
Same house as 1 year ago	84.3% (333)
Live and work in county	81.8% (186)
Married-couple households	50.5% (271)

TRANSPORTATION ★★★★ (197)

Bicycle or walk to work	2.8% (279)
Carpool to work	9.5% (388)
Public transit to work	0.3% (291)
Commute <15 minutes	50.6% (143)
Commute >45 minutes	6.0% (53)

See pages 37-130 for explanations of statistics, stars, and ranks.

Fort Dodge, IA
(Webster County, IA)

POPULATION

2010 census	38,013 (342)
2015 estimate	37,071 (355)
2010-2015 change	-2.5% (451)
2020 projection	36,080 (368)
2030 projection	33,980 (392)

RACE

Whites	88.9% (207)
Blacks	4.0% (189)
Hispanics	4.2% (287)
Asians	1.1% (139)
Native Americans	0.3% (231)

AGE

0-17 years old	21.7% (359)
18-24 years old	10.9% (119)
25-39 years old	17.7% (236)
40-54 years old	18.8% (386)
55-64 years old	13.9% (192)
65+ years old	17.0% (197)

PRIVATE SECTOR

Businesses	1,155 (215)
Employees	16,041 (190)
Total wages	$676,951,481 (156)
Average weekly wages	$812 (75)

HOUSEHOLD INCOME LADDER

95th percentile	$145,913 (215)
80th percentile	$84,017 (272)
60th percentile	$53,361 (289)
40th percentile	$33,740 (298)
20th percentile	$18,406 (295)

CHILDREN ★★★★ (137)

Living with two parents	62.0% (353)
Older teens in school	87.5% (112)
Speak English very well	98.2% (320)
Poverty rate for children	21.4% (203)
No health insurance	2.7% (43)

DIVERSITY/EQUALITY ★ (483)

Racial diversity index	20.6% (340)
Geographic diversity index	36.9% (405)
Top 20% share of income	48.2% (306)
Gender gap in earnings	36.7% (358)
White-collar gender gap	39.0% (433)

EDUCATION ★★★★ (162)

Eighth grade or less	1.9% (114)
High school diplomas	92.0% (124)
Attended college	63.1% (82)
Bachelor's degrees	19.6% (229)
Advanced degrees	5.0% (378)

EMPLOYMENT ★★★★★ (101)

Average jobless rate	8.4% (323)
Self-employed workers	11.6% (90)
Management/financial jobs	14.2% (44)
Computer/engineering jobs	2.4% (336)
Health care jobs	5.9% (193)

GROWTH POTENTIAL ★★★ (329)

Children per senior	1.28 (357)
Median age	39.7 (279)
Moved from different state	3.6% (104)
Homes built since 2000	6.1% (525)
Construction jobs	6.8% (204)

HOUSING ★★★ (323)

Home vacancy rate	9.1% (296)
Home ownership rate	67.7% (356)
Housing diversity index	80.8% (497)
4 or more bedrooms	18.8% (168)
Affordability/income ratio	$2,026 (65)

INCOME ★★★★ (207)

Poverty rate	15.2% (199)
Median household income	$42,408 (304)
Interest/dividends	22.7% (163)
Public assistance	16.4% (309)
Median fulltime earnings	$40,493 (120)

SENIORS ★★ (411)

Seniors living alone	31.3% (486)
Poverty rate for seniors	7.6% (145)
Median income for seniors	$28,325 (452)
Seniors who work	20.8% (166)
Home ownership by seniors	79.1% (414)

STABILITY ★★★ (280)

25-39 age group	17.7% (236)
Born in state of residence	78.6% (145)
Same house as 1 year ago	82.4% (422)
Live and work in county	87.3% (97)
Married-couple households	44.1% (479)

TRANSPORTATION ★★★★ (205)

Bicycle or walk to work	2.7% (292)
Carpool to work	7.4% (518)
Public transit to work	0.4% (219)
Commute <15 minutes	56.3% (78)
Commute >45 minutes	5.6% (43)

See pages 37-130 for explanations of statistics, stars, and ranks.

Fort Leonard Wood, MO
(Pulaski County, MO)

POPULATION	
2010 census	52,274 (192)
2015 estimate	53,221 (185)
2010-2015 change	1.8% (142)
2020 projection	55,653 (172)
2030 projection	60,689 (149)

RACE	
Whites	70.2% (392)
Blacks	11.2% (110)
Hispanics	10.3% (147)
Asians	3.4% (17)
Native Americans	0.8% (125)

AGE	
0-17 years old	23.2% (251)
18-24 years old	23.4% (18)
25-39 years old	24.0% (8)
40-54 years old	14.8% (537)
55-64 years old	7.4% (549)
65+ years old	7.2% (550)

PRIVATE SECTOR	
Businesses	738 (411)
Employees	7,416 (457)
Total wages	$190,649,438 (511)
Average weekly wages	$494 (547)

HOUSEHOLD INCOME LADDER	
95th percentile	$129,219 (440)
80th percentile	$83,819 (276)
60th percentile	$58,020 (181)
40th percentile	$40,144 (127)
20th percentile	$22,490 (117)

CHILDREN	★★★ (281)
Living with two parents	76.7% (34)
Older teens in school	53.2% (551)
Speak English very well	98.4% (300)
Poverty rate for children	18.1% (127)
No health insurance	5.6% (225)

DIVERSITY/EQUALITY	★★★★★ (3)
Racial diversity index	48.1% (128)
Geographic diversity index	80.7% (4)
Top 20% share of income	42.2% (3)
Gender gap in earnings	32.3% (234)
White-collar gender gap	12.0% (113)

EDUCATION	★★★★★ (91)
Eighth grade or less	2.1% (136)
High school diplomas	91.2% (153)
Attended college	62.4% (92)
Bachelor's degrees	25.7% (97)
Advanced degrees	9.1% (83)

EMPLOYMENT	★ (494)
Average jobless rate	12.7% (512)
Self-employed workers	5.7% (515)
Management/financial jobs	10.7% (287)
Computer/engineering jobs	2.3% (354)
Health care jobs	5.8% (209)

GROWTH POTENTIAL	★★★★★ (4)
Children per senior	3.21 (9)
Median age	26.8 (10)
Moved from different state	30.9% (1)
Homes built since 2000	39.4% (4)
Construction jobs	5.4% (413)

HOUSING	★ (549)
Home vacancy rate	14.7% (531)
Home ownership rate	48.6% (548)
Housing diversity index	77.7% (536)
4 or more bedrooms	22.1% (80)
Affordability/income ratio	$2,708 (331)

INCOME	★★★ (259)
Poverty rate	13.2% (123)
Median household income	$47,931 (178)
Interest/dividends	14.7% (418)
Public assistance	13.0% (169)
Median fulltime earnings	$33,991 (422)

SENIORS	★★★★★ (59)
Seniors living alone	23.4% (65)
Poverty rate for seniors	6.6% (68)
Median income for seniors	$38,444 (85)
Seniors who work	15.2% (452)
Home ownership by seniors	89.2% (22)

STABILITY	★★ (388)
25-39 age group	24.0% (8)
Born in state of residence	30.5% (543)
Same house as 1 year ago	56.9% (551)
Live and work in county	93.6% (24)
Married-couple households	51.9% (199)

TRANSPORTATION	★★★★ (184)
Bicycle or walk to work	1.6% (443)
Carpool to work	14.0% (66)
Public transit to work	0.4% (219)
Commute <15 minutes	35.4% (433)
Commute >45 minutes	3.7% (12)

See pages 37-130 for explanations of statistics, stars, and ranks.

Fort Madison-Keokuk, IA-IL-MO
(Lee County, IA, Hancock County, IL, and Clark County, MO)

POPULATION	
2010 census	62,105 (136)
2015 estimate	60,433 (147)
2010-2015 change	-2.7% (459)
2020 projection	58,655 (153)
2030 projection	55,016 (185)

RACE	
Whites	93.5% (91)
Blacks	1.9% (295)
Hispanics	2.4% (389)
Asians	0.4% (413)
Native Americans	0.1% (402)

AGE	
0-17 years old	21.6% (366)
18-24 years old	7.7% (454)
25-39 years old	16.2% (434)
40-54 years old	20.2% (202)
55-64 years old	14.8% (91)
65+ years old	19.5% (64)

PRIVATE SECTOR	
Businesses	1,556 (126)
Employees	19,038 (140)
Total wages	$805,080,860 (116)
Average weekly wages	$813 (74)

HOUSEHOLD INCOME LADDER	
95th percentile	$128,030 (455)
80th percentile	$81,604 (333)
60th percentile	$54,505 (264)
40th percentile	$36,194 (226)
20th percentile	$21,063 (184)

CHILDREN	★★★★ (208)
Living with two parents	65.9% (247)
Older teens in school	80.0% (397)
Speak English very well	99.3% (142)
Poverty rate for children	22.1% (224)
No health insurance	5.0% (181)

DIVERSITY/EQUALITY	★★ (402)
Racial diversity index	12.5% (456)
Geographic diversity index	52.8% (178)
Top 20% share of income	44.5% (42)
Gender gap in earnings	41.6% (465)
White-collar gender gap	46.2% (490)

EDUCATION	★★★★ (186)
Eighth grade or less	1.4% (60)
High school diplomas	93.6% (68)
Attended college	56.9% (188)
Bachelor's degrees	18.4% (268)
Advanced degrees	4.5% (442)

EMPLOYMENT	★★★ (285)
Average jobless rate	7.7% (260)
Self-employed workers	10.4% (145)
Management/financial jobs	10.5% (318)
Computer/engineering jobs	2.0% (420)
Health care jobs	5.4% (273)

GROWTH POTENTIAL	★ (497)
Children per senior	1.11 (457)
Median age	44.0 (477)
Moved from different state	2.2% (248)
Homes built since 2000	7.6% (483)
Construction jobs	6.4% (270)

HOUSING	★★★ (243)
Home vacancy rate	9.7% (334)
Home ownership rate	76.2% (49)
Housing diversity index	80.3% (505)
4 or more bedrooms	17.7% (220)
Affordability/income ratio	$1,891 (30)

INCOME	★★★★ (208)
Poverty rate	14.8% (187)
Median household income	$44,745 (238)
Interest/dividends	21.6% (193)
Public assistance	14.1% (212)
Median fulltime earnings	$37,795 (230)

SENIORS	★★★★ (148)
Seniors living alone	25.6% (149)
Poverty rate for seniors	9.5% (291)
Median income for seniors	$34,417 (214)
Seniors who work	20.9% (165)
Home ownership by seniors	84.3% (173)

STABILITY	★★ (371)
25-39 age group	16.2% (434)
Born in state of residence	63.1% (403)
Same house as 1 year ago	89.6% (57)
Live and work in county	66.2% (432)
Married-couple households	51.4% (231)

TRANSPORTATION	★★ (363)
Bicycle or walk to work	2.9% (265)
Carpool to work	7.8% (504)
Public transit to work	0.2% (363)
Commute <15 minutes	43.9% (262)
Commute >45 minutes	9.6% (210)

See pages 37-130 for explanations of statistics, stars, and ranks.

Frankfort, IN
(Clinton County, IN)

POPULATION

2010 census	33,224 (401)
2015 estimate	32,609 (412)
2010-2015 change	-1.9% (399)
2020 projection	31,924 (419)
2030 projection	30,486 (421)

RACE

Whites	83.8% (282)
Blacks	0.7% (423)
Hispanics	14.5% (107)
Asians	0.4% (413)
Native Americans	0.2% (300)

AGE

0-17 years old	26.1% (66)
18-24 years old	8.5% (330)
25-39 years old	17.1% (308)
40-54 years old	20.1% (221)
55-64 years old	12.9% (343)
65+ years old	15.3% (348)

PRIVATE SECTOR

Businesses	539 (500)
Employees	9,291 (403)
Total wages	$354,623,820 (379)
Average weekly wages	$734 (190)

HOUSEHOLD INCOME LADDER

95th percentile	$137,993 (311)
80th percentile	$88,500 (175)
60th percentile	$60,938 (132)
40th percentile	$40,107 (129)
20th percentile	$23,123 (96)

CHILDREN ★★ (374)

Living with two parents	68.3% (185)
Older teens in school	76.6% (479)
Speak English very well	93.0% (508)
Poverty rate for children	21.3% (200)
No health insurance	6.9% (307)

DIVERSITY/EQUALITY ★★★★ (160)

Racial diversity index	27.7% (274)
Geographic diversity index	39.9% (354)
Top 20% share of income	44.4% (38)
Gender gap in earnings	38.3% (402)
White-collar gender gap	11.5% (103)

EDUCATION ★ (443)

Eighth grade or less	6.7% (459)
High school diplomas	86.8% (314)
Attended college	43.1% (470)
Bachelor's degrees	15.7% (399)
Advanced degrees	4.1% (472)

EMPLOYMENT ★ (453)

Average jobless rate	7.3% (228)
Self-employed workers	7.0% (428)
Management/financial jobs	9.0% (475)
Computer/engineering jobs	2.9% (219)
Health care jobs	4.2% (454)

GROWTH POTENTIAL ★★ (331)

Children per senior	1.71 (127)
Median age	38.4 (202)
Moved from different state	0.8% (524)
Homes built since 2000	6.7% (509)
Construction jobs	6.9% (198)

HOUSING ★★★★ (202)

Home vacancy rate	10.8% (397)
Home ownership rate	72.4% (170)
Housing diversity index	82.1% (454)
4 or more bedrooms	21.8% (85)
Affordability/income ratio	$2,024 (63)

INCOME ★★★★ (199)

Poverty rate	14.1% (157)
Median household income	$48,478 (161)
Interest/dividends	18.4% (296)
Public assistance	11.8% (122)
Median fulltime earnings	$36,770 (305)

SENIORS ★★★★★ (103)

Seniors living alone	24.9% (113)
Poverty rate for seniors	7.2% (114)
Median income for seniors	$34,893 (193)
Seniors who work	20.0% (195)
Home ownership by seniors	84.5% (165)

STABILITY ★★★ (269)

25-39 age group	17.1% (308)
Born in state of residence	76.8% (180)
Same house as 1 year ago	87.5% (165)
Live and work in county	57.8% (504)
Married-couple households	53.9% (113)

TRANSPORTATION ★★★ (319)

Bicycle or walk to work	1.2% (492)
Carpool to work	15.6% (39)
Public transit to work	0.0% (511)
Commute <15 minutes	37.4% (390)
Commute >45 minutes	13.2% (363)

See pages 37-130 for explanations of statistics, stars, and ranks.

Freeport, IL
(Stephenson County, IL)

POPULATION

2010 census	47,711 (223)
2015 estimate	45,749 (249)
2010-2015 change	-4.1% (522)
2020 projection	44,124 (273)
2030 projection	40,910 (303)

RACE

Whites	84.1% (277)
Blacks	9.1% (118)
Hispanics	3.3% (324)
Asians	0.8% (201)
Native Americans	0.1% (402)

AGE

0-17 years old	21.8% (351)
18-24 years old	7.9% (424)
25-39 years old	15.1% (507)
40-54 years old	20.4% (169)
55-64 years old	14.6% (107)
65+ years old	20.2% (50)

PRIVATE SECTOR

Businesses	1,077 (251)
Employees	14,087 (231)
Total wages	$587,318,048 (194)
Average weekly wages	$802 (86)

HOUSEHOLD INCOME LADDER

95th percentile	$138,081 (310)
80th percentile	$85,197 (250)
60th percentile	$54,451 (268)
40th percentile	$35,408 (252)
20th percentile	$20,230 (223)

CHILDREN ★★★★ (148)

Living with two parents	52.5% (490)
Older teens in school	88.3% (94)
Speak English very well	99.8% (38)
Poverty rate for children	22.1% (224)
No health insurance	1.4% (5)

DIVERSITY/EQUALITY ★★★★ (173)

Racial diversity index	28.3% (268)
Geographic diversity index	42.4% (316)
Top 20% share of income	46.6% (170)
Gender gap in earnings	30.4% (178)
White-collar gender gap	16.6% (176)

EDUCATION ★★★★ (160)

Eighth grade or less	1.1% (26)
High school diplomas	92.9% (98)
Attended college	60.5% (120)
Bachelor's degrees	18.2% (277)
Advanced degrees	5.4% (334)

EMPLOYMENT ★★★★ (192)

Average jobless rate	9.9% (417)
Self-employed workers	11.2% (108)
Management/financial jobs	13.0% (86)
Computer/engineering jobs	2.6% (288)
Health care jobs	5.3% (286)

GROWTH POTENTIAL ★ (546)

Children per senior	1.08 (471)
Median age	44.3 (487)
Moved from different state	1.3% (452)
Homes built since 2000	4.6% (543)
Construction jobs	5.7% (373)

HOUSING ★★ (338)

Home vacancy rate	9.3% (305)
Home ownership rate	70.7% (244)
Housing diversity index	80.1% (512)
4 or more bedrooms	18.0% (202)
Affordability/income ratio	$2,182 (116)

INCOME ★★★★ (206)

Poverty rate	15.0% (190)
Median household income	$45,331 (227)
Interest/dividends	25.2% (87)
Public assistance	17.0% (334)
Median fulltime earnings	$37,220 (268)

SENIORS ★★★★★ (101)

Seniors living alone	28.2% (311)
Poverty rate for seniors	7.0% (93)
Median income for seniors	$39,117 (70)
Seniors who work	22.7% (114)
Home ownership by seniors	83.8% (186)

STABILITY ★★ (421)

25-39 age group	15.1% (507)
Born in state of residence	73.9% (247)
Same house as 1 year ago	85.8% (264)
Live and work in county	74.8% (294)
Married-couple households	48.0% (378)

TRANSPORTATION ★★★★ (219)

Bicycle or walk to work	3.4% (199)
Carpool to work	10.9% (239)
Public transit to work	0.8% (96)
Commute <15 minutes	45.3% (243)
Commute >45 minutes	10.3% (237)

See pages 37-130 for explanations of statistics, stars, and ranks.

Fremont, NE
(Dodge County, NE)

POPULATION

2010 census	36,691 (364)
2015 estimate	36,706 (363)
2010-2015 change	0.0% (255)
2020 projection	36,668 (361)
2030 projection	36,506 (353)

RACE

Whites	86.1% (254)
Blacks	0.4% (499)
Hispanics	10.9% (139)
Asians	0.8% (201)
Native Americans	0.1% (402)

AGE

0-17 years old	23.5% (232)
18-24 years old	8.6% (317)
25-39 years old	18.4% (151)
40-54 years old	18.4% (430)
55-64 years old	12.5% (396)
65+ years old	18.6% (101)

PRIVATE SECTOR

Businesses	1,111 (238)
Employees	13,955 (234)
Total wages	$471,980,376 (273)
Average weekly wages	$650 (389)

HOUSEHOLD INCOME LADDER

95th percentile	$143,964 (243)
80th percentile	$85,037 (253)
60th percentile	$56,960 (207)
40th percentile	$39,629 (138)
20th percentile	$23,149 (93)

CHILDREN ★★★★ **(144)**

Living with two parents	68.1% (192)
Older teens in school	85.8% (172)
Speak English very well	96.4% (440)
Poverty rate for children	13.4% (50)
No health insurance	6.7% (296)

DIVERSITY/EQUALITY ★★★ **(239)**

Racial diversity index	24.6% (298)
Geographic diversity index	45.0% (280)
Top 20% share of income	46.4% (148)
Gender gap in earnings	37.1% (366)
White-collar gender gap	18.5% (193)

EDUCATION ★★★ **(249)**

Eighth grade or less	4.6% (361)
High school diplomas	88.5% (253)
Attended college	55.4% (215)
Bachelor's degrees	20.2% (216)
Advanced degrees	5.7% (292)

EMPLOYMENT ★★ **(350)**

Average jobless rate	5.1% (69)
Self-employed workers	7.4% (393)
Management/financial jobs	11.8% (173)
Computer/engineering jobs	1.8% (457)
Health care jobs	4.1% (462)

GROWTH POTENTIAL ★★ **(395)**

Children per senior	1.27 (370)
Median age	39.4 (262)
Moved from different state	1.6% (383)
Homes built since 2000	8.7% (445)
Construction jobs	6.6% (241)

HOUSING ★★★★★ **(89)**

Home vacancy rate	5.0% (33)
Home ownership rate	66.6% (404)
Housing diversity index	84.2% (325)
4 or more bedrooms	21.7% (90)
Affordability/income ratio	$2,323 (177)

INCOME ★★★★★ **(95)**

Poverty rate	11.4% (66)
Median household income	$49,068 (147)
Interest/dividends	24.3% (122)
Public assistance	10.0% (63)
Median fulltime earnings	$39,108 (175)

SENIORS ★★★★ **(215)**

Seniors living alone	26.6% (209)
Poverty rate for seniors	8.8% (250)
Median income for seniors	$34,068 (233)
Seniors who work	27.3% (35)
Home ownership by seniors	75.2% (522)

STABILITY ★★★★ **(171)**

25-39 age group	18.4% (151)
Born in state of residence	72.8% (263)
Same house as 1 year ago	85.8% (264)
Live and work in county	72.1% (337)
Married-couple households	52.3% (180)

TRANSPORTATION ★★★★ **(211)**

Bicycle or walk to work	3.5% (189)
Carpool to work	9.7% (369)
Public transit to work	0.2% (363)
Commute <15 minutes	54.0% (95)
Commute >45 minutes	9.6% (210)

See pages 37-130 for explanations of statistics, stars, and ranks.

Fremont, OH
(Sandusky County, OH)

POPULATION			
2010 census	60,944 (144)	Attended college	52.5% (272)
2015 estimate	59,679 (150)	Bachelor's degrees	15.8% (391)
2010-2015 change	-2.1% (418)	Advanced degrees	5.2% (352)
2020 projection	58,499 (154)	**EMPLOYMENT**	**★★ (431)**
2030 projection	55,981 (174)	Average jobless rate	7.6% (250)
		Self-employed workers	6.4% (479)
RACE		Management/financial jobs	8.5% (505)
Whites	85.3% (263)	Computer/engineering jobs	3.3% (145)
Blacks	3.1% (222)	Health care jobs	5.2% (307)
Hispanics	9.4% (159)	**GROWTH POTENTIAL**	**★ (453)**
Asians	0.4% (413)	Children per senior	1.41 (269)
Native Americans	0.2% (300)	Median age	41.3 (371)
		Moved from different state	1.1% (487)
AGE		Homes built since 2000	9.2% (427)
0-17 years old	23.4% (240)	Construction jobs	6.0% (326)
18-24 years old	8.0% (407)	**HOUSING**	**★★★★ (184)**
25-39 years old	16.9% (338)	Home vacancy rate	8.2% (234)
40-54 years old	20.7% (132)	Home ownership rate	74.2% (110)
55-64 years old	14.4% (136)	Housing diversity index	82.8% (426)
65+ years old	16.6% (237)	4 or more bedrooms	17.0% (247)
		Affordability/income ratio	$2,332 (181)
PRIVATE SECTOR		**INCOME**	**★★★★ (157)**
Businesses	1,301 (176)	Poverty rate	14.3% (168)
Employees	22,857 (90)	Median household income	$47,209 (188)
Total wages	$873,725,927 (98)	Interest/dividends	20.3% (238)
Average weekly wages	$735 (187)	Public assistance	13.0% (169)
		Median fulltime earnings	$40,658 (111)
HOUSEHOLD INCOME LADDER		**SENIORS**	**★★★ (265)**
95th percentile	$137,360 (319)	Seniors living alone	30.0% (427)
80th percentile	$88,229 (183)	Poverty rate for seniors	7.7% (156)
60th percentile	$57,031 (205)	Median income for seniors	$33,975 (235)
40th percentile	$38,327 (173)	Seniors who work	17.4% (318)
20th percentile	$20,579 (203)	Home ownership by seniors	84.7% (155)
CHILDREN	**★★★ (253)**	**STABILITY**	**★★★★ (179)**
Living with two parents	58.8% (433)	25-39 age group	16.9% (338)
Older teens in school	80.5% (384)	Born in state of residence	84.2% (51)
Speak English very well	99.3% (142)	Same house as 1 year ago	89.0% (79)
Poverty rate for children	21.9% (218)	Live and work in county	67.7% (410)
No health insurance	4.5% (150)	Married-couple households	49.5% (323)
DIVERSITY/EQUALITY	**★★ (336)**	**TRANSPORTATION**	**★★ (334)**
Racial diversity index	26.2% (285)	Bicycle or walk to work	2.6% (308)
Geographic diversity index	28.5% (499)	Carpool to work	7.6% (510)
Top 20% share of income	45.1% (64)	Public transit to work	0.6% (141)
Gender gap in earnings	40.9% (454)	Commute <15 minutes	44.6% (251)
White-collar gender gap	17.8% (185)	Commute >45 minutes	8.7% (158)
EDUCATION	**★★★ (236)**		
Eighth grade or less	2.2% (152)		
High school diplomas	92.9% (98)		

See pages 37-130 for explanations of statistics, stars, and ranks.

Galesburg, IL
(Knox County, IL)

POPULATION

2010 census	52,919 (188)
2015 estimate	51,441 (202)
2010-2015 change	-2.8% (467)
2020 projection	49,949 (212)
2030 projection	46,961 (247)

RACE

Whites	83.9% (280)
Blacks	8.3% (126)
Hispanics	5.3% (244)
Asians	0.8% (201)
Native Americans	0.1% (402)

AGE

0-17 years old	20.0% (458)
18-24 years old	10.2% (151)
25-39 years old	17.2% (290)
40-54 years old	18.9% (376)
55-64 years old	14.2% (161)
65+ years old	19.3% (68)

PRIVATE SECTOR

Businesses	1,033 (265)
Employees	16,014 (191)
Total wages	$510,036,037 (238)
Average weekly wages	$612 (464)

HOUSEHOLD INCOME LADDER

95th percentile	$131,012 (416)
80th percentile	$81,145 (348)
60th percentile	$50,125 (381)
40th percentile	$31,457 (374)
20th percentile	$17,417 (345)

CHILDREN ★★★ (274)

Living with two parents	57.6% (455)
Older teens in school	85.8% (172)
Speak English very well	97.8% (361)
Poverty rate for children	30.5% (413)
No health insurance	3.0% (59)

DIVERSITY/EQUALITY ★★★ (321)

Racial diversity index	28.6% (264)
Geographic diversity index	36.5% (416)
Top 20% share of income	47.4% (250)
Gender gap in earnings	36.3% (350)
White-collar gender gap	20.9% (219)

EDUCATION ★★★★ (199)

Eighth grade or less	2.2% (152)
High school diplomas	89.3% (223)

Attended college	55.7% (209)
Bachelor's degrees	19.2% (241)
Advanced degrees	6.6% (211)

EMPLOYMENT ★★★ (233)

Average jobless rate	7.4% (237)
Self-employed workers	8.8% (273)
Management/financial jobs	9.9% (392)
Computer/engineering jobs	2.4% (336)
Health care jobs	6.8% (91)

GROWTH POTENTIAL ★ (549)

Children per senior	1.04 (487)
Median age	42.1 (408)
Moved from different state	1.1% (487)
Homes built since 2000	5.5% (534)
Construction jobs	4.4% (509)

HOUSING ★★ (396)

Home vacancy rate	8.6% (260)
Home ownership rate	66.7% (399)
Housing diversity index	80.4% (504)
4 or more bedrooms	15.6% (320)
Affordability/income ratio	$2,011 (59)

INCOME ★★★ (310)

Poverty rate	18.8% (329)
Median household income	$39,976 (383)
Interest/dividends	21.0% (214)
Public assistance	17.2% (344)
Median fulltime earnings	$36,855 (297)

SENIORS ★ (485)

Seniors living alone	33.7% (536)
Poverty rate for seniors	7.9% (170)
Median income for seniors	$31,717 (335)
Seniors who work	16.6% (367)
Home ownership by seniors	77.1% (486)

STABILITY ★★★ (243)

25-39 age group	17.2% (290)
Born in state of residence	79.0% (132)
Same house as 1 year ago	88.7% (95)
Live and work in county	80.0% (219)
Married-couple households	42.7% (499)

TRANSPORTATION ★★★★ (206)

Bicycle or walk to work	5.2% (85)
Carpool to work	8.2% (480)
Public transit to work	0.5% (178)
Commute <15 minutes	52.2% (118)
Commute >45 minutes	10.4% (248)

See pages 37-130 for explanations of statistics, stars, and ranks.

Garden City, KS
(Finney and Kearny Counties, KS)

POPULATION

2010 census	40,753 (305)
2015 estimate	41,074 (300)
2010-2015 change	0.8% (194)
2020 projection	40,658 (308)
2030 projection	39,731 (322)

RACE

Whites	46.4% (498)
Blacks	2.0% (290)
Hispanics	46.2% (29)
Asians	3.7% (15)
Native Americans	0.3% (231)

AGE

0-17 years old	31.2% (12)
18-24 years old	10.2% (151)
25-39 years old	20.4% (52)
40-54 years old	18.2% (441)
55-64 years old	10.3% (510)
65+ years old	9.6% (538)

PRIVATE SECTOR

Businesses	1,146 (217)
Employees	16,043 (189)
Total wages	$586,900,947 (195)
Average weekly wages	$704 (246)

HOUSEHOLD INCOME LADDER

95th percentile	$159,131 (102)
80th percentile	$91,645 (132)
60th percentile	$60,945 (131)
40th percentile	$40,961 (100)
20th percentile	$25,440 (44)

CHILDREN ★★ **(411)**

Living with two parents	66.1% (245)
Older teens in school	81.0% (366)
Speak English very well	90.7% (524)
Poverty rate for children	23.8% (268)
No health insurance	7.2% (330)

DIVERSITY/EQUALITY ★★★★★ **(93)**

Racial diversity index	56.9% (31)
Geographic diversity index	64.1% (82)
Top 20% share of income	46.7% (176)
Gender gap in earnings	33.7% (276)
White-collar gender gap	43.3% (471)

EDUCATION ★ **(513)**

Eighth grade or less	15.0% (533)
High school diplomas	72.5% (533)

Attended college	49.5% (345)
Bachelor's degrees	19.0% (248)
Advanced degrees	6.4% (229)

EMPLOYMENT ★★ **(407)**

Average jobless rate	4.4% (42)
Self-employed workers	9.5% (207)
Management/financial jobs	11.0% (252)
Computer/engineering jobs	0.8% (543)
Health care jobs	3.0% (535)

GROWTH POTENTIAL ★★★★★ **(67)**

Children per senior	3.24 (8)
Median age	30.6 (32)
Moved from different state	2.5% (203)
Homes built since 2000	7.5% (487)
Construction jobs	6.1% (310)

HOUSING ★★★★★ **(28)**

Home vacancy rate	5.1% (39)
Home ownership rate	63.4% (470)
Housing diversity index	85.3% (170)
4 or more bedrooms	29.3% (9)
Affordability/income ratio	$2,322 (175)

INCOME ★★★ **(256)**

Poverty rate	16.4% (241)
Median household income	$49,388 (140)
Interest/dividends	15.8% (385)
Public assistance	12.9% (164)
Median fulltime earnings	$35,172 (377)

SENIORS ★★★★ **(157)**

Seniors living alone	27.6% (269)
Poverty rate for seniors	12.5% (436)
Median income for seniors	$39,274 (68)
Seniors who work	31.7% (15)
Home ownership by seniors	76.6% (498)

STABILITY ★★★★★ **(43)**

25-39 age group	20.4% (52)
Born in state of residence	56.6% (448)
Same house as 1 year ago	85.5% (280)
Live and work in county	90.0% (63)
Married-couple households	53.3% (140)

TRANSPORTATION ★★★★★ **(30)**

Bicycle or walk to work	3.2% (225)
Carpool to work	15.8% (35)
Public transit to work	0.6% (141)
Commute <15 minutes	58.3% (58)
Commute >45 minutes	5.3% (38)

See pages 37-130 for explanations of statistics, stars, and ranks.

Grand Rapids, MN
(Itasca County, MN)

POPULATION

2010 census	45,058 (259)
2015 estimate	45,435 (254)
2010-2015 change	0.8% (194)
2020 projection	45,702 (250)
2030 projection	46,235 (255)

RACE

Whites	92.3% (124)
Blacks	0.5% (466)
Hispanics	1.2% (513)
Asians	0.5% (355)
Native Americans	3.2% (47)

AGE

0-17 years old	21.3% (383)
18-24 years old	7.0% (521)
25-39 years old	14.9% (515)
40-54 years old	19.6% (289)
55-64 years old	16.7% (23)
65+ years old	20.4% (45)

PRIVATE SECTOR

Businesses	1,018 (270)
Employees	13,022 (278)
Total wages	$517,114,389 (232)
Average weekly wages	$764 (133)

HOUSEHOLD INCOME LADDER

95th percentile	$138,919 (302)
80th percentile	$85,498 (240)
60th percentile	$57,692 (191)
40th percentile	$39,658 (137)
20th percentile	$21,464 (164)

CHILDREN ★★★★ (141)

Living with two parents	71.4% (113)
Older teens in school	87.2% (130)
Speak English very well	99.7% (57)
Poverty rate for children	20.8% (187)
No health insurance	9.3% (401)

DIVERSITY/EQUALITY ★★★ (273)

Racial diversity index	14.6% (422)
Geographic diversity index	34.0% (448)
Top 20% share of income	45.6% (100)
Gender gap in earnings	36.9% (360)
White-collar gender gap	8.4% (68)

EDUCATION ★★★★★ (90)

Eighth grade or less	0.5% (2)
High school diplomas	95.0% (31)
Attended college	65.6% (49)
Bachelor's degrees	22.2% (153)
Advanced degrees	6.2% (243)

EMPLOYMENT ★★★★ (116)

Average jobless rate	7.1% (208)
Self-employed workers	10.3% (150)
Management/financial jobs	10.3% (339)
Computer/engineering jobs	3.5% (122)
Health care jobs	6.9% (79)

GROWTH POTENTIAL ★★ (378)

Children per senior	1.04 (487)
Median age	45.9 (511)
Moved from different state	2.0% (288)
Homes built since 2000	16.6% (164)
Construction jobs	7.5% (122)

HOUSING ★★★★★ (29)

Home vacancy rate	4.2% (9)
Home ownership rate	79.5% (4)
Housing diversity index	86.4% (26)
4 or more bedrooms	17.0% (247)
Affordability/income ratio	$3,256 (442)

INCOME ★★★★ (133)

Poverty rate	13.6% (142)
Median household income	$47,761 (181)
Interest/dividends	22.7% (163)
Public assistance	12.2% (138)
Median fulltime earnings	$40,388 (126)

SENIORS ★★★ (250)

Seniors living alone	26.4% (193)
Poverty rate for seniors	7.2% (114)
Median income for seniors	$37,060 (113)
Seniors who work	14.5% (478)
Home ownership by seniors	81.2% (322)

STABILITY ★★★★★ (80)

25-39 age group	14.9% (515)
Born in state of residence	80.3% (107)
Same house as 1 year ago	87.3% (181)
Live and work in county	84.0% (145)
Married-couple households	55.7% (53)

TRANSPORTATION ★★★ (291)

Bicycle or walk to work	3.7% (173)
Carpool to work	10.3% (299)
Public transit to work	1.0% (69)
Commute <15 minutes	38.2% (373)
Commute >45 minutes	11.7% (300)

See pages 37-130 for explanations of statistics, stars, and ranks.

Great Bend, KS
(Barton County, KS)

POPULATION

2010 census	27,674 (460)
2015 estimate	27,103 (464)
2010-2015 change	-2.1% (418)
2020 projection	26,539 (462)
2030 projection	25,387 (469)

RACE

Whites	82.6% (295)
Blacks	1.3% (351)
Hispanics	14.0% (111)
Asians	0.2% (509)
Native Americans	0.1% (402)

AGE

0-17 years old	24.5% (149)
18-24 years old	9.0% (265)
25-39 years old	16.8% (359)
40-54 years old	18.6% (412)
55-64 years old	13.7% (225)
65+ years old	17.3% (172)

PRIVATE SECTOR

Businesses	921 (305)
Employees	10,301 (367)
Total wages	$376,407,898 (358)
Average weekly wages	$703 (249)

HOUSEHOLD INCOME LADDER

95th percentile	$135,776 (347)
80th percentile	$82,335 (315)
60th percentile	$56,457 (220)
40th percentile	$36,389 (219)
20th percentile	$19,614 (239)

CHILDREN ★★★★ (177)

Living with two parents	65.4% (260)
Older teens in school	87.4% (116)
Speak English very well	98.2% (320)
Poverty rate for children	22.6% (238)
No health insurance	6.5% (282)

DIVERSITY/EQUALITY ★★ (428)

Racial diversity index	29.8% (254)
Geographic diversity index	46.7% (259)
Top 20% share of income	47.4% (246)
Gender gap in earnings	40.0% (438)
White-collar gender gap	45.9% (487)

EDUCATION ★★★ (315)

Eighth grade or less	4.5% (354)
High school diplomas	87.0% (309)
Attended college	55.9% (205)
Bachelor's degrees	17.6% (301)
Advanced degrees	4.3% (456)

EMPLOYMENT ★★★★ (126)

Average jobless rate	6.8% (179)
Self-employed workers	10.3% (150)
Management/financial jobs	12.1% (149)
Computer/engineering jobs	2.2% (381)
Health care jobs	6.5% (121)

GROWTH POTENTIAL ★★★ (316)

Children per senior	1.41 (269)
Median age	39.3 (256)
Moved from different state	3.2% (136)
Homes built since 2000	3.6% (547)
Construction jobs	7.4% (134)

HOUSING ★★★★ (130)

Home vacancy rate	8.1% (227)
Home ownership rate	67.4% (371)
Housing diversity index	84.3% (314)
4 or more bedrooms	20.4% (118)
Affordability/income ratio	$1,845 (20)

INCOME ★★★★ (181)

Poverty rate	15.9% (219)
Median household income	$44,013 (260)
Interest/dividends	23.4% (146)
Public assistance	12.0% (132)
Median fulltime earnings	$38,201 (212)

SENIORS ★★ (342)

Seniors living alone	30.8% (462)
Poverty rate for seniors	9.9% (315)
Median income for seniors	$32,031 (318)
Seniors who work	21.5% (144)
Home ownership by seniors	81.7% (294)

STABILITY ★★★★ (193)

25-39 age group	16.8% (359)
Born in state of residence	71.8% (278)
Same house as 1 year ago	84.3% (333)
Live and work in county	88.2% (90)
Married-couple households	50.1% (291)

TRANSPORTATION ★★★★ (129)

Bicycle or walk to work	3.5% (189)
Carpool to work	11.3% (201)
Public transit to work	0.1% (441)
Commute <15 minutes	58.2% (60)
Commute >45 minutes	7.9% (126)

See pages 37-130 for explanations of statistics, stars, and ranks.

Greensburg, IN
(Decatur County, IN)

POPULATION		Attended college	48.2% (379)
2010 census	25,740 (477)	Bachelor's degrees	17.6% (301)
2015 estimate	26,521 (468)	Advanced degrees	5.5% (318)
2010-2015 change	3.0% (86)		
2020 projection	27,021 (460)	**EMPLOYMENT**	**★★★ (237)**
2030 projection	27,955 (445)	Average jobless rate	6.3% (140)
		Self-employed workers	8.1% (323)
RACE		Management/financial jobs	12.5% (119)
Whites	95.3% (34)	Computer/engineering jobs	3.8% (96)
Blacks	0.6% (438)	Health care jobs	3.9% (488)
Hispanics	1.8% (455)		
Asians	1.3% (112)	**GROWTH POTENTIAL**	**★★★ (302)**
Native Americans	0.1% (402)	Children per senior	1.64 (153)
		Median age	39.5 (270)
AGE		Moved from different state	2.1% (269)
0-17 years old	24.9% (131)	Homes built since 2000	12.2% (306)
18-24 years old	7.9% (424)	Construction jobs	5.6% (392)
25-39 years old	17.7% (236)		
40-54 years old	21.3% (73)	**HOUSING**	**★★★ (241)**
55-64 years old	13.0% (334)	Home vacancy rate	8.1% (227)
65+ years old	15.2% (354)	Home ownership rate	70.2% (264)
		Housing diversity index	84.4% (299)
PRIVATE SECTOR		4 or more bedrooms	13.7% (415)
Businesses	592 (476)	Affordability/income ratio	$2,311 (169)
Employees	11,989 (310)		
Total wages	$490,484,248 (251)	**INCOME**	**★★★★ (159)**
Average weekly wages	$787 (108)	Poverty rate	14.2% (160)
		Median household income	$49,799 (132)
HOUSEHOLD INCOME LADDER		Interest/dividends	19.7% (259)
95th percentile	$140,192 (288)	Public assistance	11.0% (94)
80th percentile	$85,388 (243)	Median fulltime earnings	$37,827 (229)
60th percentile	$58,124 (179)		
40th percentile	$40,540 (112)	**SENIORS**	**★★★★★ (74)**
20th percentile	$23,427 (83)	Seniors living alone	24.6% (100)
		Poverty rate for seniors	7.1% (101)
CHILDREN	**★★★ (318)**	Median income for seniors	$38,271 (88)
Living with two parents	61.1% (378)	Seniors who work	19.7% (214)
Older teens in school	81.0% (366)	Home ownership by seniors	85.2% (132)
Speak English very well	100.0% (1)		
Poverty rate for children	22.7% (242)	**STABILITY**	**★★★★ (206)**
No health insurance	9.7% (412)	25-39 age group	17.7% (236)
		Born in state of residence	79.1% (130)
DIVERSITY/EQUALITY	**★★★ (325)**	Same house as 1 year ago	84.5% (325)
Racial diversity index	9.1% (514)	Live and work in county	70.4% (363)
Geographic diversity index	36.2% (419)	Married-couple households	52.3% (180)
Top 20% share of income	43.8% (19)		
Gender gap in earnings	32.4% (239)	**TRANSPORTATION**	**★★ (388)**
White-collar gender gap	30.3% (342)	Bicycle or walk to work	2.0% (386)
		Carpool to work	7.9% (498)
EDUCATION	**★★★ (256)**	Public transit to work	0.6% (141)
Eighth grade or less	1.8% (102)	Commute <15 minutes	47.0% (216)
High school diplomas	90.3% (192)	Commute >45 minutes	12.7% (343)

See pages 37-130 for explanations of statistics, stars, and ranks.

Greenville, OH
(Darke County, OH)

POPULATION

2010 census	52,959 (187)
2015 estimate	52,076 (198)
2010-2015 change	-1.7% (384)
2020 projection	51,396 (204)
2030 projection	49,870 (216)

RACE

Whites	96.5% (5)
Blacks	0.6% (438)
Hispanics	1.4% (488)
Asians	0.3% (473)
Native Americans	0.2% (300)

AGE

0-17 years old	24.4% (155)
18-24 years old	7.6% (468)
25-39 years old	15.9% (453)
40-54 years old	20.4% (169)
55-64 years old	13.6% (247)
65+ years old	18.0% (122)

PRIVATE SECTOR

Businesses	1,094 (246)
Employees	16,100 (188)
Total wages	$593,912,011 (189)
Average weekly wages	$709 (234)

HOUSEHOLD INCOME LADDER

95th percentile	$133,825 (379)
80th percentile	$82,460 (308)
60th percentile	$54,115 (277)
40th percentile	$35,548 (250)
20th percentile	$21,034 (186)

CHILDREN ★★★★★ (83)

Living with two parents	72.6% (92)
Older teens in school	84.1% (237)
Speak English very well	99.7% (57)
Poverty rate for children	19.7% (160)
No health insurance	4.7% (166)

DIVERSITY/EQUALITY ★ (496)

Racial diversity index	6.8% (543)
Geographic diversity index	34.4% (444)
Top 20% share of income	46.1% (128)
Gender gap in earnings	37.5% (375)
White-collar gender gap	39.3% (438)

EDUCATION ★★ (346)

Eighth grade or less	1.4% (60)
High school diplomas	91.2% (153)
Attended college	42.4% (483)
Bachelor's degrees	13.4% (482)
Advanced degrees	4.7% (419)

EMPLOYMENT ★★★ (249)

Average jobless rate	7.6% (250)
Self-employed workers	10.5% (139)
Management/financial jobs	11.3% (218)
Computer/engineering jobs	2.5% (307)
Health care jobs	4.9% (355)

GROWTH POTENTIAL ★★ (374)

Children per senior	1.36 (304)
Median age	41.8 (394)
Moved from different state	1.8% (338)
Homes built since 2000	6.7% (509)
Construction jobs	7.8% (98)

HOUSING ★★★ (283)

Home vacancy rate	6.8% (151)
Home ownership rate	72.1% (181)
Housing diversity index	80.6% (502)
4 or more bedrooms	16.4% (272)
Affordability/income ratio	$2,462 (238)

INCOME ★★★★ (175)

Poverty rate	13.3% (130)
Median household income	$44,632 (245)
Interest/dividends	21.5% (194)
Public assistance	11.8% (122)
Median fulltime earnings	$37,555 (244)

SENIORS ★★★★ (205)

Seniors living alone	28.9% (358)
Poverty rate for seniors	5.2% (25)
Median income for seniors	$33,406 (261)
Seniors who work	19.3% (232)
Home ownership by seniors	82.2% (264)

STABILITY ★★★ (257)

25-39 age group	15.9% (453)
Born in state of residence	80.1% (111)
Same house as 1 year ago	87.3% (181)
Live and work in county	61.7% (478)
Married-couple households	54.6% (84)

TRANSPORTATION ★★ (410)

Bicycle or walk to work	2.5% (322)
Carpool to work	8.2% (480)
Public transit to work	1.0% (69)
Commute <15 minutes	37.2% (396)
Commute >45 minutes	12.8% (346)

See pages 37-130 for explanations of statistics, stars, and ranks.

Hannibal, MO
(Marion and Ralls Counties, MO)

POPULATION

2010 census	38,948 (330)
2015 estimate	39,076 (326)
2010-2015 change	0.3% (237)
2020 projection	38,981 (328)
2030 projection	38,687 (330)

RACE

Whites	91.9% (141)
Blacks	4.1% (185)
Hispanics	1.4% (488)
Asians	0.6% (291)
Native Americans	0.6% (150)

AGE

0-17 years old	23.2% (251)
18-24 years old	8.7% (299)
25-39 years old	17.0% (317)
40-54 years old	20.0% (233)
55-64 years old	13.9% (192)
65+ years old	17.1% (186)

PRIVATE SECTOR

Businesses	1,078 (250)
Employees	14,688 (219)
Total wages	$517,891,188 (230)
Average weekly wages	$678 (318)

HOUSEHOLD INCOME LADDER

95th percentile	$132,558 (393)
80th percentile	$78,716 (387)
60th percentile	$53,295 (293)
40th percentile	$35,491 (251)
20th percentile	$19,443 (249)

CHILDREN   ★★★ (294)

Living with two parents	59.1% (425)
Older teens in school	79.7% (407)
Speak English very well	99.5% (96)
Poverty rate for children	23.8% (268)
No health insurance	5.7% (233)

DIVERSITY/EQUALITY   ★★★ (234)

Racial diversity index	15.3% (405)
Geographic diversity index	49.1% (227)
Top 20% share of income	46.3% (146)
Gender gap in earnings	35.8% (335)
White-collar gender gap	16.1% (167)

EDUCATION   ★★★ (257)

Eighth grade or less	2.7% (195)
High school diplomas	88.0% (267)
Attended college	48.3% (374)
Bachelor's degrees	19.7% (227)
Advanced degrees	6.5% (220)

EMPLOYMENT   ★★★★ (165)

Average jobless rate	6.9% (185)
Self-employed workers	9.1% (243)
Management/financial jobs	11.2% (229)
Computer/engineering jobs	2.3% (354)
Health care jobs	6.8% (91)

GROWTH POTENTIAL   ★★★ (322)

Children per senior	1.36 (304)
Median age	40.9 (350)
Moved from different state	2.2% (248)
Homes built since 2000	11.8% (321)
Construction jobs	6.7% (219)

HOUSING   ★★★★ (177)

Home vacancy rate	6.5% (130)
Home ownership rate	69.0% (303)
Housing diversity index	84.7% (260)
4 or more bedrooms	15.7% (315)
Affordability/income ratio	$2,501 (249)

INCOME   ★★★ (254)

Poverty rate	16.7% (255)
Median household income	$42,464 (301)
Interest/dividends	21.1% (210)
Public assistance	12.4% (143)
Median fulltime earnings	$34,557 (401)

SENIORS   ★★★ (244)

Seniors living alone	25.9% (164)
Poverty rate for seniors	10.8% (365)
Median income for seniors	$33,961 (237)
Seniors who work	22.0% (130)
Home ownership by seniors	80.0% (375)

STABILITY   ★★ (334)

25-39 age group	17.0% (317)
Born in state of residence	67.8% (350)
Same house as 1 year ago	88.3% (115)
Live and work in county	65.9% (436)
Married-couple households	50.4% (278)

TRANSPORTATION   ★★★ (240)

Bicycle or walk to work	3.3% (211)
Carpool to work	8.7% (453)
Public transit to work	0.4% (219)
Commute <15 minutes	50.3% (145)
Commute >45 minutes	8.3% (144)

See pages 37-130 for explanations of statistics, stars, and ranks.

Hastings, NE
(Adams County, NE)

POPULATION

2010 census	31,364 (427)
2015 estimate	31,587 (422)
2010-2015 change	0.7% (202)
2020 projection	31,740 (422)
2030 projection	31,972 (410)

RACE

Whites	87.7% (229)
Blacks	0.8% (404)
Hispanics	8.6% (172)
Asians	1.3% (112)
Native Americans	0.1% (402)

AGE

0-17 years old	23.5% (232)
18-24 years old	11.8% (90)
25-39 years old	17.2% (290)
40-54 years old	18.2% (441)
55-64 years old	12.9% (343)
65+ years old	16.3% (268)

PRIVATE SECTOR

Businesses	1,136 (222)
Employees	13,016 (280)
Total wages	$455,891,067 (288)
Average weekly wages	$674 (325)

HOUSEHOLD INCOME LADDER

95th percentile	$159,750 (100)
80th percentile	$91,132 (139)
60th percentile	$63,222 (96)
40th percentile	$39,809 (133)
20th percentile	$22,728 (107)

CHILDREN ★★★★★ (38)

Living with two parents	75.5% (44)
Older teens in school	92.9% (32)
Speak English very well	98.9% (226)
Poverty rate for children	15.9% (75)
No health insurance	6.7% (296)

DIVERSITY/EQUALITY ★ (501)

Racial diversity index	22.3% (319)
Geographic diversity index	44.5% (290)
Top 20% share of income	49.6% (406)
Gender gap in earnings	32.8% (249)
White-collar gender gap	52.1% (517)

EDUCATION ★★★★★ (101)

Eighth grade or less	4.3% (343)
High school diplomas	93.3% (85)
Attended college	64.3% (69)
Bachelor's degrees	25.0% (108)
Advanced degrees	8.5% (103)

EMPLOYMENT ★★★★★ (68)

Average jobless rate	5.5% (98)
Self-employed workers	12.2% (67)
Management/financial jobs	14.1% (46)
Computer/engineering jobs	2.3% (354)
Health care jobs	5.7% (222)

GROWTH POTENTIAL ★★★★ (219)

Children per senior	1.44 (253)
Median age	37.8 (174)
Moved from different state	2.6% (187)
Homes built since 2000	8.3% (459)
Construction jobs	8.0% (89)

HOUSING ★★★★★ (65)

Home vacancy rate	6.0% (95)
Home ownership rate	69.5% (287)
Housing diversity index	84.4% (299)
4 or more bedrooms	21.9% (82)
Affordability/income ratio	$2,060 (70)

INCOME ★★★★★ (97)

Poverty rate	11.8% (82)
Median household income	$50,635 (109)
Interest/dividends	25.6% (80)
Public assistance	9.9% (59)
Median fulltime earnings	$37,232 (267)

SENIORS ★★ (425)

Seniors living alone	36.3% (546)
Poverty rate for seniors	8.2% (196)
Median income for seniors	$32,509 (302)
Seniors who work	26.8% (39)
Home ownership by seniors	77.0% (490)

STABILITY ★★★ (234)

25-39 age group	17.2% (290)
Born in state of residence	73.3% (254)
Same house as 1 year ago	83.5% (366)
Live and work in county	82.9% (166)
Married-couple households	49.9% (302)

TRANSPORTATION ★★★★ (118)

Bicycle or walk to work	2.9% (265)
Carpool to work	9.0% (435)
Public transit to work	0.4% (219)
Commute <15 minutes	61.4% (38)
Commute >45 minutes	4.6% (24)

See pages 37-130 for explanations of statistics, stars, and ranks.

Hays, KS
(Ellis County, KS)

POPULATION

2010 census	28,452 (451)
2015 estimate	29,029 (442)
2010-2015 change	2.0% (128)
2020 projection	29,289 (437)
2030 projection	29,738 (426)

RACE

Whites	90.5% (171)
Blacks	1.1% (367)
Hispanics	5.5% (237)
Asians	1.5% (85)
Native Americans	0.2% (300)

AGE

0-17 years old	21.3% (383)
18-24 years old	18.2% (35)
25-39 years old	19.1% (95)
40-54 years old	15.8% (524)
55-64 years old	11.7% (463)
65+ years old	13.9% (444)

PRIVATE SECTOR

Businesses	1,089 (248)
Employees	12,576 (295)
Total wages	$451,044,204 (292)
Average weekly wages	$690 (285)

HOUSEHOLD INCOME LADDER

95th percentile	$156,913 (114)
80th percentile	$87,725 (188)
60th percentile	$57,980 (182)
40th percentile	$35,061 (259)
20th percentile	$19,710 (238)

CHILDREN ★★★★★ (48)

Living with two parents	69.4% (156)
Older teens in school	90.2% (63)
Speak English very well	98.8% (251)
Poverty rate for children	12.7% (47)
No health insurance	5.1% (188)

DIVERSITY/EQUALITY ★ (500)

Racial diversity index	17.7% (378)
Geographic diversity index	38.5% (379)
Top 20% share of income	49.9% (419)
Gender gap in earnings	33.0% (261)
White-collar gender gap	39.9% (446)

EDUCATION ★★★★★ (27)

Eighth grade or less	2.0% (126)
High school diplomas	95.2% (23)

Attended college	71.4% (24)
Bachelor's degrees	35.5% (26)
Advanced degrees	10.1% (56)

EMPLOYMENT ★★★★★ (75)

Average jobless rate	4.5% (47)
Self-employed workers	10.6% (135)
Management/financial jobs	12.3% (133)
Computer/engineering jobs	2.7% (270)
Health care jobs	6.6% (114)

GROWTH POTENTIAL ★★★★ (211)

Children per senior	1.54 (197)
Median age	32.2 (49)
Moved from different state	3.2% (136)
Homes built since 2000	9.3% (420)
Construction jobs	5.2% (442)

HOUSING ★★★★★ (60)

Home vacancy rate	5.6% (69)
Home ownership rate	63.6% (466)
Housing diversity index	86.0% (71)
4 or more bedrooms	29.4% (8)
Affordability/income ratio	$3,295 (445)

INCOME ★★★★ (135)

Poverty rate	15.6% (214)
Median household income	$45,579 (221)
Interest/dividends	25.9% (71)
Public assistance	7.1% (23)
Median fulltime earnings	$35,768 (344)

SENIORS ★★★ (295)

Seniors living alone	31.4% (495)
Poverty rate for seniors	8.1% (187)
Median income for seniors	$33,943 (239)
Seniors who work	25.5% (61)
Home ownership by seniors	78.1% (450)

STABILITY ★★ (347)

25-39 age group	19.1% (95)
Born in state of residence	77.7% (163)
Same house as 1 year ago	75.9% (531)
Live and work in county	93.2% (33)
Married-couple households	43.3% (489)

TRANSPORTATION ★★★★★ (73)

Bicycle or walk to work	3.5% (189)
Carpool to work	7.9% (498)
Public transit to work	0.4% (219)
Commute <15 minutes	74.4% (2)
Commute >45 minutes	3.1% (8)

See pages 37-130 for explanations of statistics, stars, and ranks.

Hillsdale, MI
(Hillsdale County, MI)

POPULATION		Attended college	49.4% (348)
2010 census	46,688 (238)	Bachelor's degrees	16.0% (372)
2015 estimate	45,941 (245)	Advanced degrees	5.4% (334)
2010-2015 change	-1.6% (381)	**EMPLOYMENT**	★★★ **(316)**
2020 projection	45,518 (254)	Average jobless rate	9.0% (358)
2030 projection	44,511 (268)	Self-employed workers	10.6% (135)
		Management/financial jobs	9.9% (392)
RACE		Computer/engineering jobs	2.3% (354)
Whites	95.4% (31)	Health care jobs	5.5% (250)
Blacks	0.6% (438)		
Hispanics	2.0% (428)	**GROWTH POTENTIAL**	★ **(477)**
Asians	0.3% (473)	Children per senior	1.33 (325)
Native Americans	0.5% (174)	Median age	42.0 (398)
		Moved from different state	2.4% (218)
AGE		Homes built since 2000	11.2% (351)
0-17 years old	22.7% (284)	Construction jobs	4.3% (514)
18-24 years old	9.8% (176)		
25-39 years old	15.0% (511)	**HOUSING**	★★★★★ **(35)**
40-54 years old	20.8% (122)	Home vacancy rate	6.3% (122)
55-64 years old	14.7% (97)	Home ownership rate	77.3% (23)
65+ years old	17.0% (197)	Housing diversity index	84.1% (337)
		4 or more bedrooms	21.4% (94)
PRIVATE SECTOR		Affordability/income ratio	$2,352 (193)
Businesses	708 (424)		
Employees	10,415 (362)	**INCOME**	★★★ **(317)**
Total wages	$423,995,955 (311)	Poverty rate	20.1% (373)
Average weekly wages	$783 (116)	Median household income	$41,961 (324)
		Interest/dividends	19.8% (254)
HOUSEHOLD INCOME LADDER		Public assistance	16.7% (319)
95th percentile	$135,020 (360)	Median fulltime earnings	$36,800 (304)
80th percentile	$77,837 (404)		
60th percentile	$51,616 (340)	**SENIORS**	★★★★ **(121)**
40th percentile	$33,588 (305)	Seniors living alone	24.8% (111)
20th percentile	$19,503 (244)	Poverty rate for seniors	8.7% (241)
		Median income for seniors	$33,682 (253)
CHILDREN	★★ **(360)**	Seniors who work	17.2% (330)
Living with two parents	71.3% (114)	Home ownership by seniors	88.0% (41)
Older teens in school	84.9% (201)		
Speak English very well	97.3% (399)	**STABILITY**	★★★ **(283)**
Poverty rate for children	32.3% (450)	25-39 age group	15.0% (511)
No health insurance	12.4% (482)	Born in state of residence	77.4% (172)
		Same house as 1 year ago	87.6% (157)
DIVERSITY/EQUALITY	★ **(469)**	Live and work in county	65.7% (443)
Racial diversity index	8.9% (518)	Married-couple households	54.7% (80)
Geographic diversity index	38.0% (391)		
Top 20% share of income	46.7% (186)	**TRANSPORTATION**	★★ **(369)**
Gender gap in earnings	35.2% (318)	Bicycle or walk to work	4.6% (110)
White-collar gender gap	37.4% (412)	Carpool to work	9.9% (348)
		Public transit to work	0.2% (363)
EDUCATION	★★★ **(324)**	Commute <15 minutes	35.8% (426)
Eighth grade or less	3.5% (284)	Commute >45 minutes	13.2% (363)
High school diplomas	88.4% (257)		

See pages 37-130 for explanations of statistics, stars, and ranks.

Holland, MI
(Allegan County, MI)

POPULATION

2010 census	111,408 (17)
2015 estimate	114,625 (16)
2010-2015 change	2.9% (92)
2020 projection	117,972 (15)
2030 projection	124,532 (14)

RACE

Whites	89.1% (202)
Blacks	1.4% (340)
Hispanics	7.0% (201)
Asians	0.7% (241)
Native Americans	0.5% (174)

AGE

0-17 years old	25.1% (116)
18-24 years old	7.9% (424)
25-39 years old	17.0% (317)
40-54 years old	21.5% (57)
55-64 years old	13.8% (203)
65+ years old	14.6% (400)

PRIVATE SECTOR

Businesses	2,051 (57)
Employees	33,008 (27)
Total wages	$1,479,708,183 (19)
Average weekly wages	$862 (48)

HOUSEHOLD INCOME LADDER

95th percentile	$152,913 (134)
80th percentile	$95,642 (83)
60th percentile	$64,942 (75)
40th percentile	$44,050 (56)
20th percentile	$24,400 (58)

CHILDREN ★★★★★ (57)

Living with two parents	76.7% (34)
Older teens in school	81.7% (337)
Speak English very well	98.9% (226)
Poverty rate for children	17.1% (99)
No health insurance	2.5% (34)

DIVERSITY/EQUALITY ★ (460)

Racial diversity index	20.1% (347)
Geographic diversity index	33.5% (450)
Top 20% share of income	45.7% (103)
Gender gap in earnings	42.8% (481)
White-collar gender gap	34.9% (389)

EDUCATION ★★★★ (178)

Eighth grade or less	2.0% (126)
High school diplomas	91.9% (128)
Attended college	54.0% (243)
Bachelor's degrees	21.5% (174)
Advanced degrees	6.2% (243)

EMPLOYMENT ★★★★ (147)

Average jobless rate	6.1% (121)
Self-employed workers	8.9% (266)
Management/financial jobs	12.4% (126)
Computer/engineering jobs	3.9% (86)
Health care jobs	4.8% (369)

GROWTH POTENTIAL ★★★★ (214)

Children per senior	1.72 (122)
Median age	40.0 (303)
Moved from different state	1.1% (487)
Homes built since 2000	17.7% (137)
Construction jobs	6.7% (219)

HOUSING ★★★★★ (2)

Home vacancy rate	5.0% (33)
Home ownership rate	80.9% (2)
Housing diversity index	85.7% (108)
4 or more bedrooms	22.9% (67)
Affordability/income ratio	$2,587 (286)

INCOME ★★★★★ (92)

Poverty rate	12.7% (105)
Median household income	$54,264 (61)
Interest/dividends	21.0% (214)
Public assistance	12.6% (150)
Median fulltime earnings	$42,558 (52)

SENIORS ★★★★★ (66)

Seniors living alone	23.6% (73)
Poverty rate for seniors	7.6% (145)
Median income for seniors	$36,653 (127)
Seniors who work	17.0% (341)
Home ownership by seniors	88.7% (28)

STABILITY ★★★★ (197)

25-39 age group	17.0% (317)
Born in state of residence	81.0% (100)
Same house as 1 year ago	88.4% (109)
Live and work in county	45.2% (547)
Married-couple households	60.3% (9)

TRANSPORTATION ★ (510)

Bicycle or walk to work	1.7% (428)
Carpool to work	8.0% (493)
Public transit to work	0.2% (363)
Commute <15 minutes	28.5% (533)
Commute >45 minutes	10.9% (268)

See pages 37-130 for explanations of statistics, stars, and ranks.

Houghton, MI
(Houghton and Keweenaw Counties, MI)

POPULATION

2010 census	38,784 (332)
2015 estimate	38,548 (330)
2010-2015 change	-0.6% (298)
2020 projection	38,637 (333)
2030 projection	38,698 (329)

RACE

Whites	92.9% (110)
Blacks	0.7% (423)
Hispanics	1.4% (488)
Asians	2.7% (29)
Native Americans	0.4% (203)

AGE

0-17 years old	20.2% (452)
18-24 years old	20.0% (26)
25-39 years old	15.0% (511)
40-54 years old	15.8% (524)
55-64 years old	12.5% (396)
65+ years old	16.5% (247)

PRIVATE SECTOR

Businesses	875 (328)
Employees	8,592 (432)
Total wages	$272,990,655 (452)
Average weekly wages	$611 (467)

HOUSEHOLD INCOME LADDER

95th percentile	$127,331 (466)
80th percentile	$77,272 (419)
60th percentile	$48,127 (422)
40th percentile	$30,064 (420)
20th percentile	$16,335 (394)

CHILDREN ★★★★★ (55)

Living with two parents	75.4% (47)
Older teens in school	86.5% (149)
Speak English very well	99.0% (200)
Poverty rate for children	18.4% (138)
No health insurance	4.2% (134)

DIVERSITY/EQUALITY ★★★★ (141)

Racial diversity index	13.6% (437)
Geographic diversity index	40.0% (351)
Top 20% share of income	48.6% (328)
Gender gap in earnings	2.6% (5)
White-collar gender gap	19.3% (199)

EDUCATION ★★★★★ (29)

Eighth grade or less	1.1% (26)
High school diplomas	94.9% (34)

Attended college	64.6% (66)
Bachelor's degrees	33.1% (34)
Advanced degrees	11.9% (39)

EMPLOYMENT ★★★★★ (93)

Average jobless rate	7.2% (218)
Self-employed workers	8.0% (333)
Management/financial jobs	11.7% (185)
Computer/engineering jobs	7.2% (9)
Health care jobs	5.1% (319)

GROWTH POTENTIAL ★★★ (222)

Children per senior	1.23 (393)
Median age	34.1 (78)
Moved from different state	3.9% (82)
Homes built since 2000	9.9% (389)
Construction jobs	5.9% (345)

HOUSING ★★ (428)

Home vacancy rate	8.5% (253)
Home ownership rate	69.5% (287)
Housing diversity index	75.9% (543)
4 or more bedrooms	18.4% (183)
Affordability/income ratio	$2,501 (249)

INCOME ★★★ (288)

Poverty rate	21.1% (403)
Median household income	$37,779 (432)
Interest/dividends	23.8% (135)
Public assistance	14.6% (240)
Median fulltime earnings	$37,035 (284)

SENIORS ★ (473)

Seniors living alone	31.3% (486)
Poverty rate for seniors	9.4% (282)
Median income for seniors	$31,600 (347)
Seniors who work	12.9% (526)
Home ownership by seniors	80.1% (369)

STABILITY ★★ (358)

25-39 age group	15.0% (511)
Born in state of residence	76.4% (195)
Same house as 1 year ago	83.6% (359)
Live and work in county	88.7% (83)
Married-couple households	46.8% (425)

TRANSPORTATION ★★★★★ (8)

Bicycle or walk to work	11.1% (10)
Carpool to work	12.1% (135)
Public transit to work	0.9% (83)
Commute <15 minutes	56.9% (72)
Commute >45 minutes	4.5% (21)

See pages 37-130 for explanations of statistics, stars, and ranks.

Huntington, IN
(Huntington County, IN)

POPULATION

2010 census	37,124 (353)
2015 estimate	36,630 (365)
2010-2015 change	-1.3% (355)
2020 projection	35,843 (371)
2030 projection	34,201 (388)

RACE

Whites	95.6% (26)
Blacks	0.7% (423)
Hispanics	2.0% (428)
Asians	0.8% (201)
Native Americans	0.4% (203)

AGE

0-17 years old	22.6% (291)
18-24 years old	10.1% (157)
25-39 years old	17.5% (258)
40-54 years old	20.7% (132)
55-64 years old	13.5% (258)
65+ years old	15.5% (333)

PRIVATE SECTOR

Businesses	821 (363)
Employees	12,800 (285)
Total wages	$448,123,753 (294)
Average weekly wages	$673 (327)

HOUSEHOLD INCOME LADDER

95th percentile	$127,438 (463)
80th percentile	$83,262 (286)
60th percentile	$56,828 (212)
40th percentile	$38,174 (176)
20th percentile	$22,554 (114)

CHILDREN ★★★★ (117)

Living with two parents	72.5% (97)
Older teens in school	85.0% (197)
Speak English very well	99.7% (57)
Poverty rate for children	16.4% (86)
No health insurance	8.5% (379)

DIVERSITY/EQUALITY ★★ (394)

Racial diversity index	8.6% (523)
Geographic diversity index	37.4% (398)
Top 20% share of income	43.3% (8)
Gender gap in earnings	42.4% (477)
White-collar gender gap	30.9% (353)

EDUCATION ★★★★ (204)

Eighth grade or less	1.4% (60)
High school diplomas	91.5% (145)

Attended college	50.2% (325)
Bachelor's degrees	19.1% (245)
Advanced degrees	6.3% (234)

EMPLOYMENT ★★★ (311)

Average jobless rate	7.4% (237)
Self-employed workers	7.5% (385)
Management/financial jobs	11.3% (218)
Computer/engineering jobs	2.9% (219)
Health care jobs	5.1% (319)

GROWTH POTENTIAL ★★ (388)

Children per senior	1.45 (244)
Median age	39.8 (285)
Moved from different state	2.2% (248)
Homes built since 2000	11.2% (351)
Construction jobs	5.1% (458)

HOUSING ★★★★ (174)

Home vacancy rate	6.4% (127)
Home ownership rate	75.8% (60)
Housing diversity index	79.5% (522)
4 or more bedrooms	19.2% (150)
Affordability/income ratio	$2,128 (93)

INCOME ★★★★ (162)

Poverty rate	12.0% (85)
Median household income	$46,945 (194)
Interest/dividends	20.2% (240)
Public assistance	11.1% (96)
Median fulltime earnings	$36,830 (300)

SENIORS ★★★★ (175)

Seniors living alone	27.5% (264)
Poverty rate for seniors	7.3% (119)
Median income for seniors	$32,381 (307)
Seniors who work	18.7% (259)
Home ownership by seniors	86.0% (102)

STABILITY ★★★★ (218)

25-39 age group	17.5% (258)
Born in state of residence	78.2% (150)
Same house as 1 year ago	84.6% (319)
Live and work in county	63.9% (455)
Married-couple households	55.3% (62)

TRANSPORTATION ★★★ (314)

Bicycle or walk to work	3.7% (173)
Carpool to work	8.9% (439)
Public transit to work	0.2% (363)
Commute <15 minutes	42.7% (282)
Commute >45 minutes	9.4% (197)

See pages 37-130 for explanations of statistics, stars, and ranks.

Huron, SD
(Beadle County, SD)

POPULATION	
2010 census	17,398 (535)
2015 estimate	18,372 (531)
2010-2015 change	5.6% (37)
2020 projection	19,126 (528)
2030 projection	20,633 (515)

RACE	
Whites	81.2% (315)
Blacks	0.2% (537)
Hispanics	8.9% (168)
Asians	7.8% (6)
Native Americans	1.2% (89)

AGE	
0-17 years old	25.3% (97)
18-24 years old	7.7% (454)
25-39 years old	17.9% (214)
40-54 years old	19.6% (289)
55-64 years old	13.3% (282)
65+ years old	16.2% (279)

PRIVATE SECTOR	
Businesses	602 (469)
Employees	7,244 (464)
Total wages	$264,221,855 (461)
Average weekly wages	$701 (254)

HOUSEHOLD INCOME LADDER	
95th percentile	$141,668 (270)
80th percentile	$89,366 (164)
60th percentile	$57,737 (190)
40th percentile	$35,638 (247)
20th percentile	$20,298 (219)

CHILDREN	★★ (386)
Living with two parents	72.5% (97)
Older teens in school	83.8% (245)
Speak English very well	86.3% (541)
Poverty rate for children	34.1% (470)
No health insurance	2.3% (20)

DIVERSITY/EQUALITY	★★★ (261)
Racial diversity index	32.6% (229)
Geographic diversity index	53.4% (166)
Top 20% share of income	46.0% (122)
Gender gap in earnings	42.1% (474)
White-collar gender gap	32.7% (371)

EDUCATION	★★ (420)
Eighth grade or less	10.5% (515)
High school diplomas	84.0% (400)
Attended college	54.5% (233)
Bachelor's degrees	20.7% (200)
Advanced degrees	4.2% (466)

EMPLOYMENT	★★★★★ (91)
Average jobless rate	2.9% (8)
Self-employed workers	13.2% (48)
Management/financial jobs	12.8% (100)
Computer/engineering jobs	3.0% (193)
Health care jobs	3.3% (517)

GROWTH POTENTIAL	★★ (358)
Children per senior	1.56 (189)
Median age	39.0 (238)
Moved from different state	3.4% (118)
Homes built since 2000	9.0% (434)
Construction jobs	4.6% (494)

HOUSING	★★★★ (134)
Home vacancy rate	5.5% (60)
Home ownership rate	65.2% (431)
Housing diversity index	84.0% (344)
4 or more bedrooms	19.6% (135)
Affordability/income ratio	$2,086 (77)

INCOME	★★★ (273)
Poverty rate	20.8% (397)
Median household income	$46,267 (208)
Interest/dividends	21.5% (194)
Public assistance	17.1% (338)
Median fulltime earnings	$37,615 (241)

SENIORS	★★ (417)
Seniors living alone	32.9% (527)
Poverty rate for seniors	10.9% (370)
Median income for seniors	$32,877 (288)
Seniors who work	29.7% (27)
Home ownership by seniors	73.3% (540)

STABILITY	★★★★ (169)
25-39 age group	17.9% (214)
Born in state of residence	66.2% (372)
Same house as 1 year ago	84.1% (344)
Live and work in county	89.7% (68)
Married-couple households	50.3% (284)

TRANSPORTATION	★★★★★ (15)
Bicycle or walk to work	3.3% (211)
Carpool to work	12.5% (121)
Public transit to work	1.7% (36)
Commute <15 minutes	66.1% (14)
Commute >45 minutes	3.5% (11)

See pages 37-130 for explanations of statistics, stars, and ranks.

Hutchinson, KS
(Reno County, KS)

POPULATION	
2010 census	64,511 (125)
2015 estimate	63,718 (129)
2010-2015 change	-1.2% (345)
2020 projection	62,886 (133)
2030 projection	61,097 (146)

RACE	
Whites	85.2% (266)
Blacks	2.9% (229)
Hispanics	8.8% (170)
Asians	0.6% (291)
Native Americans	0.4% (203)

AGE	
0-17 years old	23.2% (251)
18-24 years old	9.1% (251)
25-39 years old	18.2% (167)
40-54 years old	18.2% (441)
55-64 years old	13.7% (225)
65+ years old	17.6% (151)

PRIVATE SECTOR	
Businesses	1,595 (120)
Employees	21,907 (99)
Total wages	$773,315,558 (125)
Average weekly wages	$679 (315)

HOUSEHOLD INCOME LADDER	
95th percentile	$139,150 (301)
80th percentile	$82,984 (292)
60th percentile	$56,156 (224)
40th percentile	$37,617 (192)
20th percentile	$21,314 (171)

CHILDREN	★★★★★ (64)
Living with two parents	74.9% (52)
Older teens in school	87.4% (116)
Speak English very well	99.4% (124)
Poverty rate for children	15.8% (73)
No health insurance	7.3% (333)

DIVERSITY/EQUALITY	★★★ (269)
Racial diversity index	26.5% (281)
Geographic diversity index	43.6% (301)
Top 20% share of income	46.5% (161)
Gender gap in earnings	37.9% (389)
White-collar gender gap	22.2% (239)

EDUCATION	★★★★ (176)
Eighth grade or less	3.1% (238)
High school diplomas	89.0% (231)
Attended college	62.8% (85)
Bachelor's degrees	20.6% (204)
Advanced degrees	6.0% (264)

EMPLOYMENT	★★★★ (195)
Average jobless rate	5.7% (109)
Self-employed workers	8.8% (273)
Management/financial jobs	12.0% (156)
Computer/engineering jobs	3.0% (193)
Health care jobs	4.8% (369)

GROWTH POTENTIAL	★★ (365)
Children per senior	1.32 (334)
Median age	39.5 (270)
Moved from different state	2.8% (171)
Homes built since 2000	6.2% (522)
Construction jobs	6.6% (241)

HOUSING	★★★ (270)
Home vacancy rate	10.2% (358)
Home ownership rate	67.2% (379)
Housing diversity index	84.2% (325)
4 or more bedrooms	16.9% (255)
Affordability/income ratio	$2,078 (72)

INCOME	★★★★ (183)
Poverty rate	12.2% (91)
Median household income	$45,288 (229)
Interest/dividends	22.6% (166)
Public assistance	13.0% (169)
Median fulltime earnings	$35,851 (341)

SENIORS	★★★★ (201)
Seniors living alone	26.8% (222)
Poverty rate for seniors	7.8% (163)
Median income for seniors	$35,251 (181)
Seniors who work	23.3% (103)
Home ownership by seniors	77.8% (461)

STABILITY	★★★★ (156)
25-39 age group	18.2% (167)
Born in state of residence	74.0% (245)
Same house as 1 year ago	80.7% (489)
Live and work in county	86.7% (104)
Married-couple households	52.3% (180)

TRANSPORTATION	★★★★ (200)
Bicycle or walk to work	2.1% (374)
Carpool to work	9.9% (348)
Public transit to work	0.6% (141)
Commute <15 minutes	52.8% (114)
Commute >45 minutes	7.7% (115)

See pages 37-130 for explanations of statistics, stars, and ranks.

Hutchinson, MN
(McLeod County, MN)

POPULATION

2010 census	36,651 (365)
2015 estimate	35,932 (373)
2010-2015 change	-2.0% (412)
2020 projection	35,644 (376)
2030 projection	35,078 (374)

RACE

Whites	92.4% (121)
Blacks	0.4% (499)
Hispanics	5.3% (244)
Asians	0.6% (291)
Native Americans	0.2% (300)

AGE

0-17 years old	24.1% (180)
18-24 years old	7.6% (468)
25-39 years old	18.6% (135)
40-54 years old	20.0% (233)
55-64 years old	12.7% (375)
65+ years old	17.1% (186)

PRIVATE SECTOR

Businesses	877 (326)
Employees	15,362 (203)
Total wages	$647,851,308 (166)
Average weekly wages	$811 (76)

HOUSEHOLD INCOME LADDER

95th percentile	$153,117 (131)
80th percentile	$97,013 (75)
60th percentile	$66,843 (55)
40th percentile	$46,744 (33)
20th percentile	$26,005 (35)

CHILDREN ★★★★★ (77)

Living with two parents	72.3% (101)
Older teens in school	82.9% (283)
Speak English very well	97.9% (352)
Poverty rate for children	11.8% (28)
No health insurance	4.7% (166)

DIVERSITY/EQUALITY ★★★ (279)

Racial diversity index	14.3% (427)
Geographic diversity index	32.3% (460)
Top 20% share of income	43.8% (17)
Gender gap in earnings	30.9% (198)
White-collar gender gap	28.3% (315)

EDUCATION ★★★★ (142)

Eighth grade or less	1.8% (102)
High school diplomas	94.3% (47)
Attended college	61.1% (108)
Bachelor's degrees	20.4% (213)
Advanced degrees	5.5% (318)

EMPLOYMENT ★★★★★ (72)

Average jobless rate	4.5% (47)
Self-employed workers	9.3% (224)
Management/financial jobs	12.2% (139)
Computer/engineering jobs	4.6% (48)
Health care jobs	5.9% (193)

GROWTH POTENTIAL ★★ (371)

Children per senior	1.41 (269)
Median age	39.9 (292)
Moved from different state	0.7% (540)
Homes built since 2000	14.2% (231)
Construction jobs	5.9% (345)

HOUSING ★★★★★ (1)

Home vacancy rate	4.5% (17)
Home ownership rate	76.2% (49)
Housing diversity index	86.1% (51)
4 or more bedrooms	26.7% (32)
Affordability/income ratio	$2,642 (307)

INCOME ★★★★★ (32)

Poverty rate	8.1% (11)
Median household income	$56,128 (46)
Interest/dividends	27.5% (44)
Public assistance	7.2% (24)
Median fulltime earnings	$41,746 (67)

SENIORS ★★★★ (214)

Seniors living alone	29.1% (371)
Poverty rate for seniors	5.5% (36)
Median income for seniors	$36,422 (140)
Seniors who work	23.1% (107)
Home ownership by seniors	77.1% (486)

STABILITY ★★★★★ (84)

25-39 age group	18.6% (135)
Born in state of residence	81.6% (91)
Same house as 1 year ago	87.3% (181)
Live and work in county	66.6% (425)
Married-couple households	53.4% (134)

TRANSPORTATION ★★ (399)

Bicycle or walk to work	3.8% (161)
Carpool to work	9.3% (401)
Public transit to work	0.3% (291)
Commute <15 minutes	45.2% (244)
Commute >45 minutes	17.5% (493)

See pages 37-130 for explanations of statistics, stars, and ranks.

Ionia, MI
(Ionia County, MI)

POPULATION

2010 census	63,905 (128)
2015 estimate	64,223 (126)
2010-2015 change	0.5% (219)
2020 projection	64,687 (126)
2030 projection	65,418 (125)

RACE

Whites	88.4% (216)
Blacks	3.1% (222)
Hispanics	4.7% (260)
Asians	0.3% (473)
Native Americans	0.7% (136)

AGE

0-17 years old	23.6% (228)
18-24 years old	9.3% (217)
25-39 years old	19.8% (64)
40-54 years old	22.1% (25)
55-64 years old	12.6% (385)
65+ years old	12.6% (482)

PRIVATE SECTOR

Businesses	851 (343)
Employees	16,294 (185)
Total wages	$445,863,235 (296)
Average weekly wages	$526 (539)

HOUSEHOLD INCOME LADDER

95th percentile	$134,684 (365)
80th percentile	$86,686 (218)
60th percentile	$59,832 (155)
40th percentile	$39,523 (140)
20th percentile	$21,660 (154)

CHILDREN ★★★★★ (74)

Living with two parents	72.6% (92)
Older teens in school	83.3% (263)
Speak English very well	99.3% (142)
Poverty rate for children	19.5% (152)
No health insurance	2.7% (43)

DIVERSITY/EQUALITY ★★★★ (220)

Racial diversity index	21.4% (333)
Geographic diversity index	22.2% (543)
Top 20% share of income	43.6% (13)
Gender gap in earnings	30.5% (183)
White-collar gender gap	14.7% (148)

EDUCATION ★★★ (303)

Eighth grade or less	2.8% (205)
High school diplomas	89.0% (231)
Attended college	53.0% (262)
Bachelor's degrees	15.7% (399)
Advanced degrees	4.3% (456)

EMPLOYMENT ★ (451)

Average jobless rate	10.4% (437)
Self-employed workers	6.6% (461)
Management/financial jobs	10.7% (287)
Computer/engineering jobs	3.2% (158)
Health care jobs	4.6% (401)

GROWTH POTENTIAL ★★★★ (204)

Children per senior	1.87 (77)
Median age	37.9 (179)
Moved from different state	1.6% (383)
Homes built since 2000	13.7% (249)
Construction jobs	6.3% (284)

HOUSING ★★★★★ (41)

Home vacancy rate	7.5% (186)
Home ownership rate	78.5% (13)
Housing diversity index	84.3% (314)
4 or more bedrooms	21.1% (98)
Affordability/income ratio	$2,239 (137)

INCOME ★★★★ (194)

Poverty rate	15.1% (196)
Median household income	$49,124 (146)
Interest/dividends	20.8% (224)
Public assistance	18.4% (381)
Median fulltime earnings	$41,202 (88)

SENIORS ★★★★ (168)

Seniors living alone	27.0% (239)
Poverty rate for seniors	7.6% (145)
Median income for seniors	$34,792 (199)
Seniors who work	15.0% (459)
Home ownership by seniors	87.5% (56)

STABILITY ★★★★ (194)

25-39 age group	19.8% (64)
Born in state of residence	88.0% (7)
Same house as 1 year ago	84.9% (306)
Live and work in county	46.4% (544)
Married-couple households	54.4% (93)

TRANSPORTATION ★ (471)

Bicycle or walk to work	2.8% (279)
Carpool to work	12.2% (132)
Public transit to work	0.5% (178)
Commute <15 minutes	28.3% (534)
Commute >45 minutes	19.1% (510)

See pages 37-130 for explanations of statistics, stars, and ranks.

Iron Mountain, MI-WI
(Dickinson County, MI, and Florence County, WI)

POPULATION

2010 census	30,591 (431)
2015 estimate	30,252 (433)
2010-2015 change	-1.1% (335)
2020 projection	29,629 (433)
2030 projection	28,339 (437)

RACE

Whites	96.1% (15)
Blacks	0.4% (499)
Hispanics	1.2% (513)
Asians	0.5% (355)
Native Americans	0.5% (174)

AGE

0-17 years old	19.9% (465)
18-24 years old	7.0% (521)
25-39 years old	14.6% (527)
40-54 years old	21.6% (50)
55-64 years old	16.5% (27)
65+ years old	20.5% (44)

PRIVATE SECTOR

Businesses	940 (297)
Employees	11,756 (315)
Total wages	$462,409,230 (280)
Average weekly wages	$756 (152)

HOUSEHOLD INCOME LADDER

95th percentile	$141,475 (273)
80th percentile	$82,320 (318)
60th percentile	$52,301 (312)
40th percentile	$34,830 (268)
20th percentile	$19,007 (265)

CHILDREN ★★★★★ (34)

Living with two parents	68.0% (195)
Older teens in school	90.8% (57)
Speak English very well	99.5% (96)
Poverty rate for children	14.3% (58)
No health insurance	2.5% (34)

DIVERSITY/EQUALITY ★ (441)

Racial diversity index	7.6% (531)
Geographic diversity index	45.0% (280)
Top 20% share of income	48.7% (336)
Gender gap in earnings	36.4% (352)
White-collar gender gap	25.1% (272)

EDUCATION ★★★★ (125)

Eighth grade or less	1.1% (26)
High school diplomas	94.5% (42)
Attended college	57.1% (185)
Bachelor's degrees	22.2% (153)
Advanced degrees	7.1% (176)

EMPLOYMENT ★★★★ (121)

Average jobless rate	7.1% (208)
Self-employed workers	8.2% (314)
Management/financial jobs	10.3% (339)
Computer/engineering jobs	3.1% (180)
Health care jobs	8.2% (15)

GROWTH POTENTIAL ★ (461)

Children per senior	0.97 (513)
Median age	47.3 (529)
Moved from different state	3.1% (147)
Homes built since 2000	11.4% (338)
Construction jobs	7.2% (162)

HOUSING ★★★★★ (9)

Home vacancy rate	5.5% (60)
Home ownership rate	82.0% (1)
Housing diversity index	85.9% (83)
4 or more bedrooms	15.9% (303)
Affordability/income ratio	$2,025 (64)

INCOME ★★★★ (148)

Poverty rate	13.1% (119)
Median household income	$44,742 (239)
Interest/dividends	26.3% (66)
Public assistance	14.8% (249)
Median fulltime earnings	$38,805 (185)

SENIORS ★★★★ (197)

Seniors living alone	27.9% (290)
Poverty rate for seniors	8.6% (234)
Median income for seniors	$32,005 (320)
Seniors who work	14.8% (465)
Home ownership by seniors	89.5% (19)

STABILITY ★★★★ (220)

25-39 age group	14.6% (527)
Born in state of residence	71.1% (289)
Same house as 1 year ago	90.2% (41)
Live and work in county	79.4% (224)
Married-couple households	51.7% (212)

TRANSPORTATION ★★★ (247)

Bicycle or walk to work	2.7% (292)
Carpool to work	7.3% (523)
Public transit to work	0.3% (291)
Commute <15 minutes	54.3% (92)
Commute >45 minutes	6.5% (71)

See pages 37-130 for explanations of statistics, stars, and ranks.

Jackson, OH
(Jackson County, OH)

POPULATION

2010 census	33,225 (400)
2015 estimate	32,596 (413)
2010-2015 change	-1.9% (399)
2020 projection	32,235 (416)
2030 projection	31,419 (415)

RACE

Whites	96.2% (9)
Blacks	0.6% (438)
Hispanics	0.9% (535)
Asians	0.1% (529)
Native Americans	0.0% (523)

AGE

0-17 years old	24.2% (172)
18-24 years old	8.2% (379)
25-39 years old	18.1% (186)
40-54 years old	20.5% (151)
55-64 years old	13.8% (203)
65+ years old	15.3% (348)

PRIVATE SECTOR

Businesses	624 (459)
Employees	8,803 (420)
Total wages	$294,713,534 (440)
Average weekly wages	$644 (405)

HOUSEHOLD INCOME LADDER

95th percentile	$130,695 (422)
80th percentile	$76,567 (432)
60th percentile	$48,415 (412)
40th percentile	$30,592 (399)
20th percentile	$14,866 (456)

CHILDREN ★★★ (280)

Living with two parents	64.9% (274)
Older teens in school	84.4% (226)
Speak English very well	98.2% (320)
Poverty rate for children	33.3% (466)
No health insurance	4.8% (173)

DIVERSITY/EQUALITY ★★★ (317)

Racial diversity index	7.4% (537)
Geographic diversity index	31.3% (473)
Top 20% share of income	48.0% (295)
Gender gap in earnings	29.2% (156)
White-collar gender gap	4.4% (30)

EDUCATION ★★★ (327)

Eighth grade or less	3.4% (269)
High school diplomas	86.2% (333)
Attended college	45.6% (430)
Bachelor's degrees	18.6% (265)
Advanced degrees	6.6% (211)

EMPLOYMENT ★ (441)

Average jobless rate	11.5% (474)
Self-employed workers	4.4% (549)
Management/financial jobs	8.4% (510)
Computer/engineering jobs	2.9% (219)
Health care jobs	8.1% (16)

GROWTH POTENTIAL ★★★ (246)

Children per senior	1.59 (175)
Median age	39.5 (270)
Moved from different state	1.4% (425)
Homes built since 2000	14.9% (206)
Construction jobs	6.7% (219)

HOUSING ★★★★ (195)

Home vacancy rate	9.0% (287)
Home ownership rate	67.7% (356)
Housing diversity index	85.7% (108)
4 or more bedrooms	16.8% (258)
Affordability/income ratio	$2,311 (169)

INCOME ★★ (426)

Poverty rate	23.5% (457)
Median household income	$39,460 (395)
Interest/dividends	15.9% (380)
Public assistance	21.5% (467)
Median fulltime earnings	$37,731 (233)

SENIORS ★ (465)

Seniors living alone	30.8% (462)
Poverty rate for seniors	12.0% (413)
Median income for seniors	$31,651 (342)
Seniors who work	18.1% (284)
Home ownership by seniors	79.2% (406)

STABILITY ★★★ (242)

25-39 age group	18.1% (186)
Born in state of residence	82.1% (81)
Same house as 1 year ago	85.9% (257)
Live and work in county	69.0% (388)
Married-couple households	47.4% (401)

TRANSPORTATION ★ (457)

Bicycle or walk to work	2.4% (331)
Carpool to work	12.0% (141)
Public transit to work	0.3% (291)
Commute <15 minutes	37.2% (396)
Commute >45 minutes	20.1% (518)

See pages 37-130 for explanations of statistics, stars, and ranks.

Jacksonville, IL
(Morgan and Scott Counties, IL)

POPULATION
2010 census	40,902 (301)
2015 estimate	39,920 (314)
2010-2015 change	-2.4% (443)
2020 projection	38,853 (331)
2030 projection	36,682 (350)

RACE
Whites	90.2% (175)
Blacks	5.2% (155)
Hispanics	2.2% (406)
Asians	0.5% (355)
Native Americans	0.1% (402)

AGE
0-17 years old	20.7% (420)
18-24 years old	10.5% (136)
25-39 years old	17.0% (317)
40-54 years old	20.2% (202)
55-64 years old	13.5% (258)
65+ years old	18.0% (122)

PRIVATE SECTOR
Businesses	852 (342)
Employees	12,714 (290)
Total wages	$459,683,560 (284)
Average weekly wages	$695 (268)

HOUSEHOLD INCOME LADDER
95th percentile	$150,941 (153)
80th percentile	$90,903 (143)
60th percentile	$58,804 (166)
40th percentile	$36,733 (211)
20th percentile	$20,752 (195)

CHILDREN ★★★★★ (79)
Living with two parents	62.0% (353)
Older teens in school	87.3% (124)
Speak English very well	99.6% (77)
Poverty rate for children	18.9% (145)
No health insurance	1.9% (11)

DIVERSITY/EQUALITY ★★ (438)
Racial diversity index	18.3% (368)
Geographic diversity index	29.5% (491)
Top 20% share of income	46.8% (194)
Gender gap in earnings	34.1% (291)
White-collar gender gap	32.1% (366)

EDUCATION ★★★★ (156)
Eighth grade or less	1.8% (102)
High school diplomas	92.9% (98)

Attended college	52.5% (272)
Bachelor's degrees	22.8% (135)
Advanced degrees	7.3% (157)

EMPLOYMENT ★★★★ (207)
Average jobless rate	8.4% (323)
Self-employed workers	9.3% (224)
Management/financial jobs	13.3% (70)
Computer/engineering jobs	1.7% (470)
Health care jobs	5.9% (193)

GROWTH POTENTIAL ★ (483)
Children per senior	1.15 (442)
Median age	41.3 (371)
Moved from different state	1.8% (338)
Homes built since 2000	8.3% (459)
Construction jobs	5.7% (373)

HOUSING ★★★★ (178)
Home vacancy rate	9.0% (287)
Home ownership rate	70.1% (267)
Housing diversity index	84.6% (277)
4 or more bedrooms	17.0% (247)
Affordability/income ratio	$2,100 (82)

INCOME ★★★★ (172)
Poverty rate	14.3% (168)
Median household income	$46,087 (210)
Interest/dividends	21.5% (194)
Public assistance	14.7% (243)
Median fulltime earnings	$40,156 (136)

SENIORS ★★★ (303)
Seniors living alone	27.9% (290)
Poverty rate for seniors	9.7% (301)
Median income for seniors	$35,461 (171)
Seniors who work	20.2% (187)
Home ownership by seniors	78.8% (425)

STABILITY ★★ (345)
25-39 age group	17.0% (317)
Born in state of residence	83.6% (61)
Same house as 1 year ago	82.3% (426)
Live and work in county	69.6% (377)
Married-couple households	49.4% (330)

TRANSPORTATION ★★★ (231)
Bicycle or walk to work	4.6% (110)
Carpool to work	10.0% (337)
Public transit to work	0.3% (291)
Commute <15 minutes	49.9% (154)
Commute >45 minutes	11.9% (308)

See pages 37-130 for explanations of statistics, stars, and ranks.

Jamestown, ND
(Stutsman County, ND)

POPULATION	
2010 census	21,100 (519)
2015 estimate	21,103 (518)
2010-2015 change	0.0% (255)
2020 projection	21,227 (516)
2030 projection	18,657 (527)

RACE	
Whites	93.6% (87)
Blacks	0.5% (466)
Hispanics	2.0% (428)
Asians	0.6% (291)
Native Americans	1.5% (80)

AGE	
0-17 years old	20.6% (423)
18-24 years old	10.5% (136)
25-39 years old	18.0% (201)
40-54 years old	18.8% (386)
55-64 years old	14.9% (90)
65+ years old	17.2% (182)

PRIVATE SECTOR	
Businesses	813 (365)
Employees	9,438 (394)
Total wages	$384,078,546 (351)
Average weekly wages	$783 (116)

HOUSEHOLD INCOME LADDER	
95th percentile	$156,474 (115)
80th percentile	$97,510 (71)
60th percentile	$63,778 (88)
40th percentile	$41,746 (81)
20th percentile	$23,135 (95)

CHILDREN	★★★★★ (84)
Living with two parents	63.6% (306)
Older teens in school	94.6% (16)
Speak English very well	99.7% (57)
Poverty rate for children	16.2% (85)
No health insurance	9.2% (399)

DIVERSITY/EQUALITY	★ (540)
Racial diversity index	12.3% (459)
Geographic diversity index	39.4% (367)
Top 20% share of income	47.4% (248)
Gender gap in earnings	39.8% (431)
White-collar gender gap	58.8% (541)

EDUCATION	★★★★ (133)
Eighth grade or less	1.4% (60)
High school diplomas	93.6% (68)
Attended college	58.6% (153)
Bachelor's degrees	27.0% (87)
Advanced degrees	4.4% (451)

EMPLOYMENT	★★★★★ (56)
Average jobless rate	2.5% (3)
Self-employed workers	12.2% (67)
Management/financial jobs	12.2% (139)
Computer/engineering jobs	4.0% (76)
Health care jobs	4.7% (385)

GROWTH POTENTIAL	★★ (356)
Children per senior	1.20 (417)
Median age	40.6 (335)
Moved from different state	3.9% (82)
Homes built since 2000	8.2% (462)
Construction jobs	6.2% (295)

HOUSING	★★★★★ (67)
Home vacancy rate	6.1% (104)
Home ownership rate	66.7% (399)
Housing diversity index	85.5% (143)
4 or more bedrooms	21.8% (85)
Affordability/income ratio	$2,124 (91)

INCOME	★★★★★ (73)
Poverty rate	10.9% (56)
Median household income	$52,359 (84)
Interest/dividends	24.1% (127)
Public assistance	11.5% (112)
Median fulltime earnings	$41,652 (73)

SENIORS	★ (511)
Seniors living alone	36.8% (548)
Poverty rate for seniors	12.3% (427)
Median income for seniors	$34,844 (196)
Seniors who work	25.5% (61)
Home ownership by seniors	68.5% (550)

STABILITY	★★★★★ (87)
25-39 age group	18.0% (201)
Born in state of residence	76.5% (191)
Same house as 1 year ago	86.4% (225)
Live and work in county	94.6% (15)
Married-couple households	45.3% (459)

TRANSPORTATION	★★★★★ (62)
Bicycle or walk to work	3.8% (161)
Carpool to work	8.2% (480)
Public transit to work	1.1% (58)
Commute <15 minutes	67.4% (9)
Commute >45 minutes	4.2% (17)

See pages 37-130 for explanations of statistics, stars, and ranks.

Jasper, IN
(Dubois and Pike Counties, IN)

POPULATION		Attended college	49.8% (339)
2010 census	54,734 (175)	Bachelor's degrees	18.7% (262)
2015 estimate	55,055 (173)	Advanced degrees	5.1% (364)
2010-2015 change	0.6% (209)	**EMPLOYMENT**	**★★★★ (170)**
2020 projection	55,100 (176)	Average jobless rate	3.7% (25)
2030 projection	55,020 (184)	Self-employed workers	6.4% (479)

RACE		Management/financial jobs	12.1% (149)
Whites	93.6% (87)	Computer/engineering jobs	3.9% (86)
Blacks	0.3% (519)	Health care jobs	4.8% (369)
Hispanics	5.1% (249)	**GROWTH POTENTIAL**	**★★ (435)**
Asians	0.5% (355)	Children per senior	1.49 (220)
Native Americans	0.0% (523)	Median age	41.7 (390)

AGE		Moved from different state	1.3% (452)
0-17 years old	24.2% (172)	Homes built since 2000	12.1% (310)
18-24 years old	7.6% (468)	Construction jobs	5.3% (425)
25-39 years old	16.0% (449)	**HOUSING**	**★★★★★ (57)**
40-54 years old	22.1% (25)	Home vacancy rate	7.1% (165)
55-64 years old	13.8% (203)	Home ownership rate	77.2% (24)
65+ years old	16.3% (268)	Housing diversity index	86.4% (26)

PRIVATE SECTOR		4 or more bedrooms	15.8% (307)
Businesses	1,410 (152)	Affordability/income ratio	$2,433 (222)
Employees	28,364 (53)	**INCOME**	**★★★★★ (66)**
Total wages	$1,182,282,346 (42)	Poverty rate	9.9% (28)
Average weekly wages	$802 (86)	Median household income	$51,822 (88)

HOUSEHOLD INCOME LADDER		Interest/dividends	23.5% (142)
95th percentile	$145,880 (216)	Public assistance	6.5% (16)
80th percentile	$91,339 (136)	Median fulltime earnings	$38,599 (198)
60th percentile	$64,709 (76)	**SENIORS**	**★★★★ (169)**
40th percentile	$41,335 (94)	Seniors living alone	25.7% (154)
20th percentile	$24,411 (56)	Poverty rate for seniors	7.9% (170)

CHILDREN	**★★★★ (115)**	Median income for seniors	$32,632 (297)
Living with two parents	74.8% (54)	Seniors who work	18.5% (268)
Older teens in school	82.8% (286)	Home ownership by seniors	84.5% (165)
Speak English very well	96.5% (436)	**STABILITY**	**★★★★★ (12)**
Poverty rate for children	14.3% (58)	25-39 age group	16.0% (449)
No health insurance	5.4% (209)	Born in state of residence	83.5% (62)

DIVERSITY/EQUALITY	**★ (484)**	Same house as 1 year ago	90.5% (34)
Racial diversity index	12.1% (462)	Live and work in county	76.7% (259)
Geographic diversity index	29.7% (488)	Married-couple households	59.0% (13)
Top 20% share of income	44.5% (43)	**TRANSPORTATION**	**★★ (377)**
Gender gap in earnings	38.8% (415)	Bicycle or walk to work	1.8% (409)
White-collar gender gap	41.0% (456)	Carpool to work	9.2% (408)

EDUCATION	**★★★ (286)**	Public transit to work	0.3% (291)
Eighth grade or less	3.8% (307)	Commute <15 minutes	42.0% (298)
High school diplomas	90.0% (202)	Commute >45 minutes	10.3% (237)

See pages 37-130 for explanations of statistics, stars, and ranks.

Junction City, KS
(Geary County, KS)

POPULATION

2010 census	34,362 (389)
2015 estimate	37,030 (357)
2010-2015 change	7.8% (15)
2020 projection	40,392 (311)
2030 projection	47,938 (232)

RACE

Whites	58.9% (451)
Blacks	16.2% (88)
Hispanics	14.4% (108)
Asians	3.8% (14)
Native Americans	0.7% (136)

AGE

0-17 years old	30.8% (13)
18-24 years old	15.6% (54)
25-39 years old	27.5% (2)
40-54 years old	12.4% (550)
55-64 years old	6.2% (551)
65+ years old	7.5% (548)

PRIVATE SECTOR

Businesses	680 (438)
Employees	7,591 (453)
Total wages	$232,589,503 (481)
Average weekly wages	$589 (506)

HOUSEHOLD INCOME LADDER

95th percentile	$135,962 (343)
80th percentile	$82,415 (314)
60th percentile	$50,831 (363)
40th percentile	$38,725 (162)
20th percentile	$25,932 (37)

CHILDREN ★★★ (264)

Living with two parents	72.6% (92)
Older teens in school	63.0% (546)
Speak English very well	98.5% (287)
Poverty rate for children	17.7% (116)
No health insurance	3.1% (64)

DIVERSITY/EQUALITY ★★★★★ (8)

Racial diversity index	60.1% (15)
Geographic diversity index	80.0% (7)
Top 20% share of income	46.3% (143)
Gender gap in earnings	35.7% (331)
White-collar gender gap	5.3% (44)

EDUCATION ★★★★ (129)

Eighth grade or less	2.1% (136)
High school diplomas	93.7% (65)

Attended college	65.6% (49)
Bachelor's degrees	20.7% (200)
Advanced degrees	5.8% (283)

EMPLOYMENT ★★ (390)

Average jobless rate	9.2% (377)
Self-employed workers	7.2% (410)
Management/financial jobs	9.7% (416)
Computer/engineering jobs	2.5% (307)
Health care jobs	6.2% (156)

GROWTH POTENTIAL ★★★★★ (3)

Children per senior	4.13 (2)
Median age	26.2 (5)
Moved from different state	14.5% (2)
Homes built since 2000	34.3% (8)
Construction jobs	5.4% (413)

HOUSING ★ (538)

Home vacancy rate	12.3% (469)
Home ownership rate	42.8% (551)
Housing diversity index	81.7% (470)
4 or more bedrooms	18.8% (168)
Affordability/income ratio	$3,091 (416)

INCOME ★★★ (257)

Poverty rate	12.4% (97)
Median household income	$43,992 (262)
Interest/dividends	14.2% (435)
Public assistance	10.2% (68)
Median fulltime earnings	$33,806 (429)

SENIORS ★★★★ (173)

Seniors living alone	37.0% (549)
Poverty rate for seniors	7.5% (140)
Median income for seniors	$37,042 (114)
Seniors who work	33.3% (10)
Home ownership by seniors	82.7% (236)

STABILITY ★★ (402)

25-39 age group	27.5% (2)
Born in state of residence	32.5% (539)
Same house as 1 year ago	73.0% (536)
Live and work in county	82.0% (181)
Married-couple households	56.0% (49)

TRANSPORTATION ★★★★ (165)

Bicycle or walk to work	2.1% (374)
Carpool to work	13.5% (83)
Public transit to work	0.2% (363)
Commute <15 minutes	38.0% (375)
Commute >45 minutes	3.2% (9)

See pages 37-130 for explanations of statistics, stars, and ranks.

Kearney, NE
(Buffalo and Kearney Counties, NE)

POPULATION	
2010 census	52,591 (190)
2015 estimate	55,448 (171)
2010-2015 change	5.4% (39)
2020 projection	57,599 (162)
2030 projection	62,045 (141)

RACE	
Whites	88.5% (215)
Blacks	1.0% (381)
Hispanics	7.9% (185)
Asians	1.1% (139)
Native Americans	0.2% (300)

AGE	
0-17 years old	23.5% (232)
18-24 years old	15.0% (56)
25-39 years old	19.7% (68)
40-54 years old	16.9% (504)
55-64 years old	11.7% (463)
65+ years old	13.3% (465)

PRIVATE SECTOR	
Businesses	2,038 (58)
Employees	24,614 (80)
Total wages	$898,692,313 (91)
Average weekly wages	$702 (251)

HOUSEHOLD INCOME LADDER	
95th percentile	$163,296 (78)
80th percentile	$98,519 (67)
60th percentile	$65,968 (67)
40th percentile	$42,397 (74)
20th percentile	$23,591 (78)

CHILDREN	★★★★★ (9)
Living with two parents	74.5% (61)
Older teens in school	94.1% (19)
Speak English very well	99.1% (179)
Poverty rate for children	12.4% (39)
No health insurance	4.2% (134)

DIVERSITY/EQUALITY	★ (475)
Racial diversity index	21.0% (335)
Geographic diversity index	41.3% (335)
Top 20% share of income	46.9% (209)
Gender gap in earnings	35.9% (337)
White-collar gender gap	50.6% (512)

EDUCATION	★★★★★ (32)
Eighth grade or less	1.8% (102)
High school diplomas	94.4% (44)
Attended college	70.9% (26)
Bachelor's degrees	33.4% (33)
Advanced degrees	9.3% (76)

EMPLOYMENT	★★★★★ (69)
Average jobless rate	3.5% (20)
Self-employed workers	11.2% (108)
Management/financial jobs	12.5% (119)
Computer/engineering jobs	3.2% (158)
Health care jobs	5.5% (250)

GROWTH POTENTIAL	★★★★ (121)
Children per senior	1.77 (104)
Median age	33.5 (64)
Moved from different state	3.0% (157)
Homes built since 2000	15.5% (191)
Construction jobs	6.0% (326)

HOUSING	★★★★★ (44)
Home vacancy rate	4.5% (17)
Home ownership rate	63.9% (456)
Housing diversity index	85.3% (170)
4 or more bedrooms	28.0% (21)
Affordability/income ratio	$2,727 (337)

INCOME	★★★★★ (75)
Poverty rate	12.3% (94)
Median household income	$53,460 (67)
Interest/dividends	24.5% (115)
Public assistance	7.6% (32)
Median fulltime earnings	$37,998 (222)

SENIORS	★★★★★ (61)
Seniors living alone	27.9% (290)
Poverty rate for seniors	5.5% (36)
Median income for seniors	$41,200 (49)
Seniors who work	30.9% (19)
Home ownership by seniors	78.0% (454)

STABILITY	★★★★ (139)
25-39 age group	19.7% (68)
Born in state of residence	75.7% (211)
Same house as 1 year ago	78.2% (515)
Live and work in county	86.0% (116)
Married-couple households	51.7% (212)

TRANSPORTATION	★★★★★ (50)
Bicycle or walk to work	4.8% (98)
Carpool to work	11.6% (178)
Public transit to work	0.2% (363)
Commute <15 minutes	64.2% (23)
Commute >45 minutes	4.9% (31)

See pages 37-130 for explanations of statistics, stars, and ranks.

Kendallville, IN
(Noble County, IN)

POPULATION
2010 census	47,536 (228)
2015 estimate	47,733 (231)
2010-2015 change	0.4% (228)
2020 projection	47,681 (232)
2030 projection	47,400 (240)

RACE
Whites	87.9% (222)
Blacks	0.5% (466)
Hispanics	10.0% (150)
Asians	0.6% (291)
Native Americans	0.1% (402)

AGE
0-17 years old	25.7% (81)
18-24 years old	8.5% (330)
25-39 years old	18.6% (135)
40-54 years old	19.9% (250)
55-64 years old	13.3% (282)
65+ years old	13.9% (444)

PRIVATE SECTOR
Businesses	799 (372)
Employees	16,781 (176)
Total wages	$619,302,868 (179)
Average weekly wages	$710 (232)

HOUSEHOLD INCOME LADDER
95th percentile	$143,675 (247)
80th percentile	$87,536 (191)
60th percentile	$60,326 (142)
40th percentile	$40,795 (104)
20th percentile	$22,380 (118)

CHILDREN ★★★ (299)
Living with two parents	67.8% (200)
Older teens in school	82.0% (319)
Speak English very well	95.6% (466)
Poverty rate for children	18.3% (135)
No health insurance	9.4% (406)

DIVERSITY/EQUALITY ★★ (381)
Racial diversity index	21.7% (328)
Geographic diversity index	40.4% (344)
Top 20% share of income	45.3% (76)
Gender gap in earnings	41.8% (468)
White-collar gender gap	32.7% (371)

EDUCATION ★ (441)
Eighth grade or less	6.6% (452)
High school diplomas	84.7% (380)
Attended college	46.4% (409)
Bachelor's degrees	15.6% (407)
Advanced degrees	4.0% (478)

EMPLOYMENT ★★ (421)
Average jobless rate	8.8% (344)
Self-employed workers	6.6% (461)
Management/financial jobs	10.6% (306)
Computer/engineering jobs	2.8% (246)
Health care jobs	4.9% (355)

GROWTH POTENTIAL ★★★ (243)
Children per senior	1.85 (84)
Median age	37.9 (179)
Moved from different state	1.4% (425)
Homes built since 2000	12.3% (303)
Construction jobs	6.0% (326)

HOUSING ★★★★★ (72)
Home vacancy rate	4.7% (22)
Home ownership rate	75.1% (80)
Housing diversity index	84.4% (299)
4 or more bedrooms	15.8% (307)
Affordability/income ratio	$2,291 (161)

INCOME ★★★★ (141)
Poverty rate	12.2% (91)
Median household income	$49,331 (143)
Interest/dividends	19.6% (263)
Public assistance	11.2% (104)
Median fulltime earnings	$38,951 (180)

SENIORS ★★★ (241)
Seniors living alone	28.2% (311)
Poverty rate for seniors	6.1% (51)
Median income for seniors	$32,711 (296)
Seniors who work	18.9% (247)
Home ownership by seniors	81.5% (305)

STABILITY ★★★ (232)
25-39 age group	18.6% (135)
Born in state of residence	76.2% (201)
Same house as 1 year ago	84.3% (333)
Live and work in county	57.5% (509)
Married-couple households	55.7% (53)

TRANSPORTATION ★★ (389)
Bicycle or walk to work	2.4% (331)
Carpool to work	11.1% (221)
Public transit to work	0.0% (511)
Commute <15 minutes	36.4% (411)
Commute >45 minutes	11.8% (306)

See pages 37-130 for explanations of statistics, stars, and ranks.

Kennett, MO
(Dunklin County, MO)

POPULATION

2010 census	31,953 (416)
2015 estimate	30,895 (428)
2010-2015 change	-3.3% (495)
2020 projection	29,681 (432)
2030 projection	27,318 (453)

RACE

Whites	81.7% (307)
Blacks	9.8% (116)
Hispanics	6.1% (218)
Asians	0.4% (413)
Native Americans	0.3% (231)

AGE

0-17 years old	25.9% (72)
18-24 years old	8.5% (330)
25-39 years old	15.9% (453)
40-54 years old	20.0% (233)
55-64 years old	12.7% (375)
65+ years old	17.1% (186)

PRIVATE SECTOR

Businesses	1,542 (127)
Employees	8,306 (439)
Total wages	$200,791,701 (508)
Average weekly wages	$465 (549)

HOUSEHOLD INCOME LADDER

95th percentile	$115,229 (536)
80th percentile	$65,598 (530)
60th percentile	$38,345 (537)
40th percentile	$23,388 (529)
20th percentile	$12,737 (506)

CHILDREN ★ (448)

Living with two parents	60.7% (386)
Older teens in school	76.6% (479)
Speak English very well	99.3% (142)
Poverty rate for children	39.3% (511)
No health insurance	7.5% (344)

DIVERSITY/EQUALITY ★★ (360)

Racial diversity index	31.9% (238)
Geographic diversity index	49.5% (217)
Top 20% share of income	51.2% (477)
Gender gap in earnings	28.9% (151)
White-collar gender gap	36.5% (400)

EDUCATION ★ (502)

Eighth grade or less	6.1% (429)
High school diplomas	77.9% (508)
Attended college	38.6% (528)
Bachelor's degrees	12.6% (504)
Advanced degrees	5.3% (347)

EMPLOYMENT ★ (472)

Average jobless rate	8.1% (298)
Self-employed workers	7.6% (376)
Management/financial jobs	10.2% (357)
Computer/engineering jobs	1.1% (532)
Health care jobs	4.6% (401)

GROWTH POTENTIAL ★★ (432)

Children per senior	1.51 (210)
Median age	39.8 (285)
Moved from different state	2.8% (171)
Homes built since 2000	6.6% (513)
Construction jobs	4.9% (473)

HOUSING ★★ (435)

Home vacancy rate	11.1% (409)
Home ownership rate	63.1% (471)
Housing diversity index	85.7% (108)
4 or more bedrooms	9.5% (541)
Affordability/income ratio	$2,172 (108)

INCOME ★ (529)

Poverty rate	27.7% (510)
Median household income	$31,077 (530)
Interest/dividends	12.4% (483)
Public assistance	27.4% (528)
Median fulltime earnings	$31,585 (515)

SENIORS ★ (543)

Seniors living alone	32.7% (523)
Poverty rate for seniors	19.0% (532)
Median income for seniors	$23,805 (515)
Seniors who work	16.2% (398)
Home ownership by seniors	77.2% (478)

STABILITY ★ (519)

25-39 age group	15.9% (453)
Born in state of residence	67.8% (350)
Same house as 1 year ago	83.6% (359)
Live and work in county	70.0% (372)
Married-couple households	43.2% (491)

TRANSPORTATION ★★ (333)

Bicycle or walk to work	1.6% (443)
Carpool to work	10.6% (271)
Public transit to work	0.2% (363)
Commute <15 minutes	49.2% (170)
Commute >45 minutes	12.6% (336)

See pages 37-130 for explanations of statistics, stars, and ranks.

Kirksville, MO
(Adair and Schuyler Counties, MO)

POPULATION	
2010 census	30,038 (434)
2015 estimate	29,814 (435)
2010-2015 change	-0.7% (303)
2020 projection	29,589 (434)
2030 projection	29,071 (432)

RACE	
Whites	92.4% (121)
Blacks	1.8% (309)
Hispanics	2.2% (406)
Asians	2.3% (36)
Native Americans	0.3% (231)

AGE	
0-17 years old	19.4% (489)
18-24 years old	25.5% (17)
25-39 years old	14.4% (534)
40-54 years old	15.3% (531)
55-64 years old	10.9% (496)
65+ years old	14.5% (412)

PRIVATE SECTOR	
Businesses	696 (431)
Employees	7,939 (448)
Total wages	$232,231,234 (482)
Average weekly wages	$563 (526)

HOUSEHOLD INCOME LADDER	
95th percentile	$142,006 (264)
80th percentile	$76,316 (436)
60th percentile	$47,183 (440)
40th percentile	$26,307 (493)
20th percentile	$13,040 (502)

CHILDREN	★★★★ (186)
Living with two parents	70.1% (142)
Older teens in school	91.5% (47)
Speak English very well	97.0% (413)
Poverty rate for children	22.6% (238)
No health insurance	10.5% (437)

DIVERSITY/EQUALITY	★★ (409)
Racial diversity index	14.5% (425)
Geographic diversity index	55.4% (151)
Top 20% share of income	51.1% (472)
Gender gap in earnings	32.8% (249)
White-collar gender gap	30.2% (341)

EDUCATION	★★★★★ (59)
Eighth grade or less	2.4% (169)
High school diplomas	90.6% (178)
Attended college	56.5% (196)
Bachelor's degrees	29.7% (55)
Advanced degrees	13.9% (21)

EMPLOYMENT	★★★★ (201)
Average jobless rate	7.8% (270)
Self-employed workers	9.5% (207)
Management/financial jobs	11.4% (210)
Computer/engineering jobs	3.2% (158)
Health care jobs	5.5% (250)

GROWTH POTENTIAL	★★★★ (141)
Children per senior	1.34 (321)
Median age	29.9 (27)
Moved from different state	4.8% (61)
Homes built since 2000	12.6% (294)
Construction jobs	4.7% (487)

HOUSING	★★ (383)
Home vacancy rate	10.5% (381)
Home ownership rate	60.8% (494)
Housing diversity index	85.6% (127)
4 or more bedrooms	17.1% (239)
Affordability/income ratio	$2,780 (353)

INCOME	★★ (382)
Poverty rate	26.0% (486)
Median household income	$37,514 (438)
Interest/dividends	23.2% (151)
Public assistance	13.8% (202)
Median fulltime earnings	$32,605 (466)

SENIORS	★★★ (307)
Seniors living alone	30.9% (469)
Poverty rate for seniors	8.8% (250)
Median income for seniors	$29,890 (412)
Seniors who work	24.0% (89)
Home ownership by seniors	81.5% (305)

STABILITY	★ (546)
25-39 age group	14.4% (534)
Born in state of residence	63.0% (404)
Same house as 1 year ago	70.6% (543)
Live and work in county	81.7% (191)
Married-couple households	45.0% (465)

TRANSPORTATION	★★★★★ (79)
Bicycle or walk to work	7.8% (32)
Carpool to work	10.4% (289)
Public transit to work	0.2% (363)
Commute <15 minutes	57.2% (68)
Commute >45 minutes	9.3% (188)

See pages 37-130 for explanations of statistics, stars, and ranks.

Lebanon, MO
(Laclede County, MO)

POPULATION

2010 census	35,571 (379)
2015 estimate	35,473 (378)
2010-2015 change	-0.3% (279)
2020 projection	35,642 (377)
2030 projection	35,893 (364)

RACE

Whites	94.0% (75)
Blacks	0.5% (466)
Hispanics	2.2% (406)
Asians	0.7% (241)
Native Americans	0.5% (174)

AGE

0-17 years old	24.2% (172)
18-24 years old	8.1% (396)
25-39 years old	17.9% (214)
40-54 years old	20.6% (145)
55-64 years old	12.9% (343)
65+ years old	16.3% (268)

PRIVATE SECTOR

Businesses	758 (394)
Employees	11,271 (338)
Total wages	$357,513,671 (373)
Average weekly wages	$610 (471)

HOUSEHOLD INCOME LADDER

95th percentile	$127,902 (456)
80th percentile	$73,606 (478)
60th percentile	$48,019 (426)
40th percentile	$30,335 (406)
20th percentile	$17,166 (354)

CHILDREN ★★★ (260)

Living with two parents	65.9% (247)
Older teens in school	83.9% (243)
Speak English very well	99.9% (19)
Poverty rate for children	28.1% (370)
No health insurance	8.2% (366)

DIVERSITY/EQUALITY ★★★ (253)

Racial diversity index	11.5% (473)
Geographic diversity index	53.2% (172)
Top 20% share of income	46.3% (145)
Gender gap in earnings	40.5% (449)
White-collar gender gap	13.4% (133)

EDUCATION ★★ (403)

Eighth grade or less	2.9% (217)
High school diplomas	83.4% (411)
Attended college	45.7% (429)
Bachelor's degrees	15.1% (417)
Advanced degrees	4.5% (442)

EMPLOYMENT ★★★ (326)

Average jobless rate	8.8% (344)
Self-employed workers	10.9% (120)
Management/financial jobs	11.2% (229)
Computer/engineering jobs	3.6% (112)
Health care jobs	3.3% (517)

GROWTH POTENTIAL ★★★ (324)

Children per senior	1.48 (227)
Median age	39.8 (285)
Moved from different state	2.6% (187)
Homes built since 2000	17.5% (140)
Construction jobs	4.1% (530)

HOUSING ★★★ (275)

Home vacancy rate	10.8% (397)
Home ownership rate	70.1% (267)
Housing diversity index	85.2% (190)
4 or more bedrooms	15.8% (307)
Affordability/income ratio	$2,604 (290)

INCOME ★★ (419)

Poverty rate	19.5% (358)
Median household income	$39,712 (389)
Interest/dividends	16.7% (354)
Public assistance	19.0% (399)
Median fulltime earnings	$32,126 (490)

SENIORS ★★ (422)

Seniors living alone	26.8% (222)
Poverty rate for seniors	11.7% (397)
Median income for seniors	$28,114 (454)
Seniors who work	17.5% (310)
Home ownership by seniors	79.9% (377)

STABILITY ★★★★ (149)

25-39 age group	17.9% (214)
Born in state of residence	66.0% (375)
Same house as 1 year ago	84.9% (306)
Live and work in county	81.2% (200)
Married-couple households	53.8% (116)

TRANSPORTATION ★★★ (327)

Bicycle or walk to work	2.4% (331)
Carpool to work	13.2% (94)
Public transit to work	0.1% (441)
Commute <15 minutes	38.6% (360)
Commute >45 minutes	12.8% (346)

See pages 37-130 for explanations of statistics, stars, and ranks.

Lexington, NE
(Dawson and Gosper Counties, NE)

POPULATION

2010 census	26,370 (468)
2015 estimate	25,859 (474)
2010-2015 change	-1.9% (399)
2020 projection	25,475 (474)
2030 projection	24,661 (475)

RACE

Whites	64.5% (419)
Blacks	4.0% (189)
Hispanics	30.4% (50)
Asians	0.1% (529)
Native Americans	0.5% (174)

AGE

0-17 years old	27.6% (37)
18-24 years old	8.3% (362)
25-39 years old	17.4% (269)
40-54 years old	19.4% (315)
55-64 years old	12.2% (424)
65+ years old	15.1% (363)

PRIVATE SECTOR

Businesses	900 (312)
Employees	9,436 (395)
Total wages	$311,012,430 (421)
Average weekly wages	$634 (425)

HOUSEHOLD INCOME LADDER

95th percentile	$140,203 (287)
80th percentile	$83,986 (274)
60th percentile	$58,155 (176)
40th percentile	$39,269 (148)
20th percentile	$23,646 (76)

CHILDREN ★★★ (292)

Living with two parents	73.6% (72)
Older teens in school	85.6% (179)
Speak English very well	90.3% (527)
Poverty rate for children	21.6% (210)
No health insurance	6.6% (293)

DIVERSITY/EQUALITY ★★★★ (176)

Racial diversity index	49.0% (122)
Geographic diversity index	55.9% (146)
Top 20% share of income	44.4% (37)
Gender gap in earnings	34.6% (306)
White-collar gender gap	55.5% (529)

EDUCATION ★ (522)

Eighth grade or less	15.0% (533)
High school diplomas	76.5% (518)
Attended college	45.8% (426)
Bachelor's degrees	15.9% (382)
Advanced degrees	5.2% (352)

EMPLOYMENT ★★★ (270)

Average jobless rate	4.8% (58)
Self-employed workers	13.0% (52)
Management/financial jobs	10.5% (318)
Computer/engineering jobs	1.0% (536)
Health care jobs	3.8% (494)

GROWTH POTENTIAL ★★★ (230)

Children per senior	1.83 (88)
Median age	37.0 (143)
Moved from different state	2.0% (288)
Homes built since 2000	8.1% (465)
Construction jobs	6.7% (219)

HOUSING ★★★★★ (82)

Home vacancy rate	8.2% (234)
Home ownership rate	68.0% (343)
Housing diversity index	84.8% (248)
4 or more bedrooms	22.7% (72)
Affordability/income ratio	$1,851 (24)

INCOME ★★★ (228)

Poverty rate	14.6% (178)
Median household income	$48,739 (153)
Interest/dividends	19.2% (272)
Public assistance	11.4% (107)
Median fulltime earnings	$33,422 (442)

SENIORS ★★★ (223)

Seniors living alone	28.2% (311)
Poverty rate for seniors	10.0% (321)
Median income for seniors	$33,526 (257)
Seniors who work	30.3% (24)
Home ownership by seniors	75.8% (514)

STABILITY ★★★★ (144)

25-39 age group	17.4% (269)
Born in state of residence	64.4% (394)
Same house as 1 year ago	84.7% (314)
Live and work in county	83.6% (151)
Married-couple households	54.9% (75)

TRANSPORTATION ★★★★★ (29)

Bicycle or walk to work	3.9% (158)
Carpool to work	17.5% (19)
Public transit to work	0.1% (441)
Commute <15 minutes	62.4% (35)
Commute >45 minutes	9.4% (197)

See pages 37-130 for explanations of statistics, stars, and ranks.

Liberal, KS
(Seward County, KS)

POPULATION	
2010 census	22,952 (495)
2015 estimate	23,152 (497)
2010-2015 change	0.9% (186)
2020 projection	23,156 (495)
2030 projection	23,102 (492)

RACE	
Whites	33.7% (525)
Blacks	3.5% (209)
Hispanics	58.3% (16)
Asians	2.9% (25)
Native Americans	0.7% (136)

AGE	
0-17 years old	31.6% (10)
18-24 years old	11.4% (104)
25-39 years old	21.6% (28)
40-54 years old	17.6% (470)
55-64 years old	9.3% (539)
65+ years old	8.6% (546)

PRIVATE SECTOR	
Businesses	577 (484)
Employees	9,137 (410)
Total wages	$320,533,112 (407)
Average weekly wages	$675 (320)

HOUSEHOLD INCOME LADDER	
95th percentile	$140,259 (285)
80th percentile	$86,985 (204)
60th percentile	$57,831 (187)
40th percentile	$39,732 (134)
20th percentile	$23,568 (81)

CHILDREN	★ (487)
Living with two parents	58.6% (437)
Older teens in school	85.3% (193)
Speak English very well	86.2% (543)
Poverty rate for children	28.2% (373)
No health insurance	8.2% (366)

DIVERSITY/EQUALITY	★★★★★ (2)
Racial diversity index	54.4% (63)
Geographic diversity index	72.7% (24)
Top 20% share of income	45.2% (70)
Gender gap in earnings	23.6% (73)
White-collar gender gap	4.5% (36)

EDUCATION	★ (542)
Eighth grade or less	22.1% (546)
High school diplomas	62.8% (549)
Attended college	39.0% (525)
Bachelor's degrees	11.4% (526)
Advanced degrees	3.1% (524)

EMPLOYMENT	★ (518)
Average jobless rate	9.0% (358)
Self-employed workers	7.1% (421)
Management/financial jobs	7.1% (545)
Computer/engineering jobs	2.0% (420)
Health care jobs	4.7% (385)

GROWTH POTENTIAL	★★★★★ (39)
Children per senior	3.70 (3)
Median age	29.4 (22)
Moved from different state	4.2% (70)
Homes built since 2000	6.7% (509)
Construction jobs	7.3% (151)

HOUSING	★★★★ (115)
Home vacancy rate	6.9% (158)
Home ownership rate	67.6% (362)
Housing diversity index	84.8% (248)
4 or more bedrooms	18.3% (192)
Affordability/income ratio	$1,848 (22)

INCOME	★★ (350)
Poverty rate	19.1% (341)
Median household income	$47,134 (189)
Interest/dividends	13.4% (458)
Public assistance	13.8% (202)
Median fulltime earnings	$32,771 (461)

SENIORS	★★★★ (153)
Seniors living alone	31.9% (509)
Poverty rate for seniors	8.3% (202)
Median income for seniors	$36,967 (117)
Seniors who work	35.3% (5)
Home ownership by seniors	79.2% (406)

STABILITY	★★★ (273)
25-39 age group	21.6% (28)
Born in state of residence	43.9% (508)
Same house as 1 year ago	83.3% (382)
Live and work in county	87.4% (95)
Married-couple households	46.6% (431)

TRANSPORTATION	★★★★★ (11)
Bicycle or walk to work	3.4% (199)
Carpool to work	24.2% (1)
Public transit to work	0.2% (363)
Commute <15 minutes	69.8% (7)
Commute >45 minutes	7.6% (111)

See pages 37-130 for explanations of statistics, stars, and ranks.

Lincoln, IL
(Logan County, IL)

POPULATION		Attended college	57.8% (169)
2010 census	30,305 (432)	Bachelor's degrees	17.4% (308)
2015 estimate	29,494 (439)	Advanced degrees	4.3% (456)
2010-2015 change	-2.7% (459)		
2020 projection	28,544 (442)	**EMPLOYMENT**	★★★★ (175)
2030 projection	26,687 (460)	Average jobless rate	7.8% (270)
		Self-employed workers	9.1% (243)
RACE		Management/financial jobs	14.5% (38)
Whites	77.2% (345)	Computer/engineering jobs	2.5% (307)
Blacks	11.6% (107)	Health care jobs	4.9% (355)
Hispanics	4.1% (292)		
Asians	0.9% (178)	**GROWTH POTENTIAL**	★ (534)
Native Americans	0.2% (300)	Children per senior	1.16 (439)
		Median age	39.7 (279)
AGE		Moved from different state	1.7% (355)
0-17 years old	19.3% (492)	Homes built since 2000	3.9% (546)
18-24 years old	11.1% (113)	Construction jobs	4.7% (487)
25-39 years old	20.0% (58)		
40-54 years old	20.1% (221)	**HOUSING**	★★★ (322)
55-64 years old	12.8% (356)	Home vacancy rate	7.8% (205)
65+ years old	16.7% (225)	Home ownership rate	67.8% (349)
		Housing diversity index	82.1% (454)
PRIVATE SECTOR		4 or more bedrooms	13.6% (424)
Businesses	563 (494)	Affordability/income ratio	$1,957 (40)
Employees	7,231 (465)		
Total wages	$269,085,895 (455)	**INCOME**	★★★★ (120)
Average weekly wages	$716 (223)	Poverty rate	14.2% (160)
		Median household income	$50,539 (113)
HOUSEHOLD INCOME LADDER		Interest/dividends	23.3% (147)
95th percentile	$146,824 (200)	Public assistance	14.6% (240)
80th percentile	$90,493 (151)	Median fulltime earnings	$42,358 (57)
60th percentile	$61,666 (118)		
40th percentile	$38,415 (169)	**SENIORS**	★★★★★ (71)
20th percentile	$19,013 (264)	Seniors living alone	28.0% (296)
		Poverty rate for seniors	5.4% (29)
CHILDREN	★★★ (269)	Median income for seniors	$40,746 (55)
Living with two parents	68.2% (189)	Seniors who work	20.6% (173)
Older teens in school	58.6% (549)	Home ownership by seniors	85.6% (120)
Speak English very well	99.1% (179)		
Poverty rate for children	17.7% (116)	**STABILITY**	★★ (355)
No health insurance	2.2% (15)	25-39 age group	20.0% (58)
		Born in state of residence	82.0% (85)
DIVERSITY/EQUALITY	★★ (348)	Same house as 1 year ago	76.1% (529)
Racial diversity index	38.5% (192)	Live and work in county	67.3% (414)
Geographic diversity index	31.8% (465)	Married-couple households	50.5% (271)
Top 20% share of income	46.8% (192)		
Gender gap in earnings	33.7% (276)	**TRANSPORTATION**	★★★★ (182)
White-collar gender gap	37.7% (416)	Bicycle or walk to work	4.5% (117)
		Carpool to work	12.3% (130)
EDUCATION	★★★ (261)	Public transit to work	0.8% (96)
Eighth grade or less	2.2% (152)	Commute <15 minutes	49.4% (165)
High school diplomas	86.5% (327)	Commute >45 minutes	14.4% (407)

See pages 37-130 for explanations of statistics, stars, and ranks.

Logansport, IN
(Cass County, IN)

POPULATION		Attended college	44.7% (441)
2010 census	38,966 (328)	Bachelor's degrees	14.7% (431)
2015 estimate	37,979 (341)	Advanced degrees	4.1% (472)
2010-2015 change	-2.5% (451)		
2020 projection	36,801 (360)	**EMPLOYMENT**	**★★ (439)**
2030 projection	34,425 (382)	Average jobless rate	8.7% (340)
		Self-employed workers	6.8% (446)
RACE		Management/financial jobs	9.8% (408)
Whites	81.8% (304)	Computer/engineering jobs	1.7% (470)
Blacks	1.4% (340)	Health care jobs	5.8% (209)
Hispanics	13.6% (114)		
Asians	1.4% (99)	**GROWTH POTENTIAL**	**★ (478)**
Native Americans	0.3% (231)	Children per senior	1.54 (197)
		Median age	40.1 (309)
AGE		Moved from different state	0.9% (515)
0-17 years old	24.4% (155)	Homes built since 2000	6.1% (525)
18-24 years old	8.5% (330)	Construction jobs	5.4% (413)
25-39 years old	17.1% (308)		
40-54 years old	21.1% (97)	**HOUSING**	**★★★ (297)**
55-64 years old	13.2% (297)	Home vacancy rate	8.4% (245)
65+ years old	15.8% (305)	Home ownership rate	75.4% (69)
		Housing diversity index	77.7% (536)
PRIVATE SECTOR		4 or more bedrooms	18.6% (174)
Businesses	680 (438)	Affordability/income ratio	$1,948 (39)
Employees	11,353 (333)		
Total wages	$380,798,069 (353)	**INCOME**	**★★★ (298)**
Average weekly wages	$645 (402)	Poverty rate	15.6% (214)
		Median household income	$42,290 (309)
HOUSEHOLD INCOME LADDER		Interest/dividends	15.9% (380)
95th percentile	$131,324 (411)	Public assistance	12.7% (155)
80th percentile	$76,718 (429)	Median fulltime earnings	$34,026 (421)
60th percentile	$52,507 (309)		
40th percentile	$35,010 (262)	**SENIORS**	**★★★ (248)**
20th percentile	$21,678 (153)	Seniors living alone	31.7% (504)
		Poverty rate for seniors	6.3% (54)
CHILDREN	**★★★ (298)**	Median income for seniors	$32,441 (304)
Living with two parents	68.8% (172)	Seniors who work	18.9% (247)
Older teens in school	86.2% (158)	Home ownership by seniors	85.9% (105)
Speak English very well	94.7% (482)		
Poverty rate for children	23.7% (266)	**STABILITY**	**★★★ (237)**
No health insurance	9.0% (393)	25-39 age group	17.1% (308)
		Born in state of residence	75.7% (211)
DIVERSITY/EQUALITY	**★★★★ (195)**	Same house as 1 year ago	85.6% (277)
Racial diversity index	31.2% (246)	Live and work in county	69.9% (373)
Geographic diversity index	41.5% (334)	Married-couple households	52.5% (171)
Top 20% share of income	47.1% (231)		
Gender gap in earnings	34.2% (293)	**TRANSPORTATION**	**★★★ (325)**
White-collar gender gap	13.1% (127)	Bicycle or walk to work	1.5% (457)
		Carpool to work	10.8% (249)
EDUCATION	**★ (458)**	Public transit to work	0.8% (96)
Eighth grade or less	6.4% (446)	Commute <15 minutes	41.5% (308)
High school diplomas	83.5% (410)	Commute >45 minutes	10.9% (268)

See pages 37-130 for explanations of statistics, stars, and ranks.

Ludington, MI
(Mason County, MI)

POPULATION
2010 census	28,705 (447)
2015 estimate	28,783 (446)
2010-2015 change	0.3% (237)
2020 projection	28,958 (440)
2030 projection	29,206 (430)

RACE
Whites	91.9% (141)
Blacks	0.9% (388)
Hispanics	4.3% (279)
Asians	0.6% (291)
Native Americans	0.7% (136)

AGE
0-17 years old	20.8% (417)
18-24 years old	7.7% (454)
25-39 years old	14.9% (515)
40-54 years old	19.5% (301)
55-64 years old	16.5% (27)
65+ years old	20.7% (40)

PRIVATE SECTOR
Businesses	679 (441)
Employees	8,795 (421)
Total wages	$315,506,417 (414)
Average weekly wages	$690 (285)

HOUSEHOLD INCOME LADDER
95th percentile	$131,753 (405)
80th percentile	$79,988 (369)
60th percentile	$51,778 (333)
40th percentile	$32,741 (333)
20th percentile	$19,059 (262)

CHILDREN ★★ (332)
Living with two parents	59.4% (419)
Older teens in school	81.5% (345)
Speak English very well	99.1% (179)
Poverty rate for children	31.4% (433)
No health insurance	5.2% (197)

DIVERSITY/EQUALITY ★★ (410)
Racial diversity index	15.3% (405)
Geographic diversity index	31.7% (468)
Top 20% share of income	49.0% (356)
Gender gap in earnings	28.4% (144)
White-collar gender gap	24.6% (265)

EDUCATION ★★★★ (111)
Eighth grade or less	1.5% (72)
High school diplomas	93.8% (63)

Attended college	61.1% (108)
Bachelor's degrees	21.0% (188)
Advanced degrees	7.8% (129)

EMPLOYMENT ★★★ (264)
Average jobless rate	10.7% (450)
Self-employed workers	11.2% (108)
Management/financial jobs	12.0% (156)
Computer/engineering jobs	2.7% (270)
Health care jobs	5.2% (307)

GROWTH POTENTIAL ★ (472)
Children per senior	1.01 (500)
Median age	45.7 (510)
Moved from different state	1.9% (310)
Homes built since 2000	14.6% (213)
Construction jobs	6.3% (284)

HOUSING ★★★★★ (70)
Home vacancy rate	6.7% (141)
Home ownership rate	75.0% (81)
Housing diversity index	85.6% (127)
4 or more bedrooms	19.4% (142)
Affordability/income ratio	$2,853 (370)

INCOME ★★★ (270)
Poverty rate	17.2% (270)
Median household income	$42,024 (320)
Interest/dividends	24.9% (100)
Public assistance	19.1% (406)
Median fulltime earnings	$36,262 (320)

SENIORS ★★★★ (200)
Seniors living alone	26.6% (209)
Poverty rate for seniors	6.4% (57)
Median income for seniors	$34,333 (219)
Seniors who work	15.5% (436)
Home ownership by seniors	83.5% (197)

STABILITY ★★★ (259)
25-39 age group	14.9% (515)
Born in state of residence	82.1% (81)
Same house as 1 year ago	84.3% (333)
Live and work in county	81.9% (184)
Married-couple households	50.8% (256)

TRANSPORTATION ★★★★ (216)
Bicycle or walk to work	2.7% (292)
Carpool to work	8.8% (448)
Public transit to work	0.8% (96)
Commute <15 minutes	47.6% (199)
Commute >45 minutes	6.2% (64)

See pages 37-130 for explanations of statistics, stars, and ranks.

Macomb, IL
(McDonough County, IL)

POPULATION	
2010 census	32,612 (408)
2015 estimate	31,333 (426)
2010-2015 change	-3.9% (517)
2020 projection	30,180 (430)
2030 projection	27,916 (446)

RACE	
Whites	88.4% (216)
Blacks	4.7% (171)
Hispanics	2.7% (361)
Asians	2.0% (51)
Native Americans	0.2% (300)

AGE	
0-17 years old	16.4% (545)
18-24 years old	26.3% (12)
25-39 years old	15.8% (460)
40-54 years old	15.1% (532)
55-64 years old	11.7% (463)
65+ years old	14.8% (384)

PRIVATE SECTOR	
Businesses	614 (465)
Employees	7,390 (458)
Total wages	$229,871,357 (483)
Average weekly wages	$598 (491)

HOUSEHOLD INCOME LADDER	
95th percentile	$148,793 (175)
80th percentile	$84,977 (254)
60th percentile	$52,716 (306)
40th percentile	$29,853 (428)
20th percentile	$13,919 (479)

CHILDREN	★★★★★ (20)
Living with two parents	68.2% (189)
Older teens in school	97.5% (8)
Speak English very well	99.8% (38)
Poverty rate for children	19.9% (163)
No health insurance	2.7% (43)

DIVERSITY/EQUALITY	★★ (364)
Racial diversity index	21.5% (331)
Geographic diversity index	37.9% (392)
Top 20% share of income	49.8% (417)
Gender gap in earnings	28.3% (140)
White-collar gender gap	24.7% (268)

EDUCATION	★★★★★ (19)
Eighth grade or less	0.9% (16)
High school diplomas	93.1% (91)
Attended college	67.7% (35)
Bachelor's degrees	36.1% (23)
Advanced degrees	16.2% (11)

EMPLOYMENT	★★ (426)
Average jobless rate	9.4% (394)
Self-employed workers	7.7% (362)
Management/financial jobs	10.7% (287)
Computer/engineering jobs	3.4% (131)
Health care jobs	4.0% (476)

GROWTH POTENTIAL	★★ (352)
Children per senior	1.10 (464)
Median age	30.7 (33)
Moved from different state	2.5% (203)
Homes built since 2000	9.6% (404)
Construction jobs	3.9% (538)

HOUSING	★ (460)
Home vacancy rate	13.6% (507)
Home ownership rate	63.7% (462)
Housing diversity index	82.6% (433)
4 or more bedrooms	18.4% (183)
Affordability/income ratio	$2,230 (134)

INCOME	★★★ (276)
Poverty rate	23.0% (444)
Median household income	$40,314 (374)
Interest/dividends	24.6% (113)
Public assistance	14.8% (249)
Median fulltime earnings	$37,722 (235)

SENIORS	★★★★ (164)
Seniors living alone	29.4% (394)
Poverty rate for seniors	5.4% (29)
Median income for seniors	$38,720 (77)
Seniors who work	19.8% (206)
Home ownership by seniors	81.8% (286)

STABILITY	★ (493)
25-39 age group	15.8% (460)
Born in state of residence	77.8% (159)
Same house as 1 year ago	76.6% (526)
Live and work in county	87.1% (99)
Married-couple households	43.8% (484)

TRANSPORTATION	★★★★★ (25)
Bicycle or walk to work	8.8% (23)
Carpool to work	8.1% (489)
Public transit to work	1.1% (58)
Commute <15 minutes	62.9% (31)
Commute >45 minutes	5.7% (48)

See pages 37-130 for explanations of statistics, stars, and ranks.

Madison, IN
(Jefferson County, IN)

POPULATION

2010 census	32,428 (411)
2015 estimate	32,416 (415)
2010-2015 change	0.0% (255)
2020 projection	32,235 (416)
2030 projection	31,747 (411)

RACE

Whites	93.4% (94)
Blacks	1.9% (295)
Hispanics	2.4% (389)
Asians	0.8% (201)
Native Americans	0.2% (300)

AGE

0-17 years old	21.6% (366)
18-24 years old	10.7% (124)
25-39 years old	16.9% (338)
40-54 years old	21.5% (57)
55-64 years old	13.7% (225)
65+ years old	15.7% (318)

PRIVATE SECTOR

Businesses	617 (462)
Employees	10,270 (368)
Total wages	$397,255,534 (342)
Average weekly wages	$744 (168)

HOUSEHOLD INCOME LADDER

95th percentile	$137,282 (321)
80th percentile	$83,367 (283)
60th percentile	$55,022 (248)
40th percentile	$37,286 (199)
20th percentile	$21,505 (163)

CHILDREN ★★★★ (204)

Living with two parents	59.7% (408)
Older teens in school	83.2% (268)
Speak English very well	99.8% (38)
Poverty rate for children	20.3% (173)
No health insurance	5.5% (218)

DIVERSITY/EQUALITY ★★★★★ (102)

Racial diversity index	12.6% (453)
Geographic diversity index	48.1% (241)
Top 20% share of income	43.8% (21)
Gender gap in earnings	32.8% (249)
White-collar gender gap	6.2% (50)

EDUCATION ★★★ (304)

Eighth grade or less	3.4% (269)
High school diplomas	88.9% (236)
Attended college	49.0% (355)
Bachelor's degrees	17.1% (322)
Advanced degrees	5.6% (304)

EMPLOYMENT ★★ (438)

Average jobless rate	9.2% (377)
Self-employed workers	6.0% (502)
Management/financial jobs	7.9% (530)
Computer/engineering jobs	3.3% (145)
Health care jobs	6.3% (144)

GROWTH POTENTIAL ★★ (411)

Children per senior	1.38 (291)
Median age	40.7 (341)
Moved from different state	2.7% (179)
Homes built since 2000	10.7% (370)
Construction jobs	5.0% (467)

HOUSING ★★★★ (215)

Home vacancy rate	7.8% (205)
Home ownership rate	71.8% (196)
Housing diversity index	84.9% (235)
4 or more bedrooms	13.1% (448)
Affordability/income ratio	$2,452 (226)

INCOME ★★★ (222)

Poverty rate	14.5% (176)
Median household income	$45,718 (218)
Interest/dividends	18.6% (288)
Public assistance	13.5% (188)
Median fulltime earnings	$38,077 (219)

SENIORS ★★★ (288)

Seniors living alone	28.8% (355)
Poverty rate for seniors	9.3% (276)
Median income for seniors	$39,400 (65)
Seniors who work	18.3% (272)
Home ownership by seniors	79.6% (388)

STABILITY ★★ (399)

25-39 age group	16.9% (338)
Born in state of residence	69.8% (312)
Same house as 1 year ago	83.5% (366)
Live and work in county	73.9% (313)
Married-couple households	49.3% (333)

TRANSPORTATION ★ (452)

Bicycle or walk to work	2.7% (292)
Carpool to work	9.3% (401)
Public transit to work	0.3% (291)
Commute <15 minutes	38.9% (353)
Commute >45 minutes	16.0% (453)

See pages 37-130 for explanations of statistics, stars, and ranks.

Manitowoc, WI
(Manitowoc County, WI)

POPULATION	
2010 census	81,442 (64)
2015 estimate	79,806 (69)
2010-2015 change	-2.0% (412)
2020 projection	78,110 (76)
2030 projection	74,746 (91)

RACE	
Whites	91.7% (147)
Blacks	0.4% (499)
Hispanics	3.5% (318)
Asians	2.7% (29)
Native Americans	0.5% (174)

AGE	
0-17 years old	21.4% (379)
18-24 years old	7.6% (468)
25-39 years old	16.0% (449)
40-54 years old	21.7% (42)
55-64 years old	15.1% (74)
65+ years old	18.2% (111)

PRIVATE SECTOR	
Businesses	1,742 (95)
Employees	29,702 (43)
Total wages	$1,229,025,959 (36)
Average weekly wages	$796 (97)

HOUSEHOLD INCOME LADDER	
95th percentile	$141,581 (272)
80th percentile	$90,075 (154)
60th percentile	$60,183 (147)
40th percentile	$39,008 (157)
20th percentile	$23,079 (98)

CHILDREN	★★★★★ (59)
Living with two parents	74.2% (65)
Older teens in school	81.8% (329)
Speak English very well	98.7% (265)
Poverty rate for children	15.0% (63)
No health insurance	2.5% (34)

DIVERSITY/EQUALITY	★★ (355)
Racial diversity index	15.7% (399)
Geographic diversity index	27.4% (506)
Top 20% share of income	45.0% (61)
Gender gap in earnings	35.1% (316)
White-collar gender gap	22.9% (249)

EDUCATION	★★★★ (180)
Eighth grade or less	1.9% (114)
High school diplomas	92.1% (122)
Attended college	55.9% (205)
Bachelor's degrees	21.0% (188)
Advanced degrees	5.5% (318)

EMPLOYMENT	★★★★ (194)
Average jobless rate	5.7% (109)
Self-employed workers	8.2% (314)
Management/financial jobs	10.8% (280)
Computer/engineering jobs	3.7% (103)
Health care jobs	5.3% (286)

GROWTH POTENTIAL	★ (538)
Children per senior	1.18 (427)
Median age	44.2 (484)
Moved from different state	0.9% (515)
Homes built since 2000	9.0% (434)
Construction jobs	5.3% (425)

HOUSING	★★★★★ (91)
Home vacancy rate	6.4% (127)
Home ownership rate	75.2% (76)
Housing diversity index	83.5% (391)
4 or more bedrooms	19.6% (135)
Affordability/income ratio	$2,618 (298)

INCOME	★★★★★ (67)
Poverty rate	10.0% (31)
Median household income	$48,398 (165)
Interest/dividends	26.8% (56)
Public assistance	10.5% (81)
Median fulltime earnings	$41,111 (90)

SENIORS	★★ (431)
Seniors living alone	30.4% (447)
Poverty rate for seniors	8.4% (214)
Median income for seniors	$30,724 (382)
Seniors who work	16.0% (410)
Home ownership by seniors	80.1% (369)

STABILITY	★★★★★ (23)
25-39 age group	16.0% (449)
Born in state of residence	84.8% (46)
Same house as 1 year ago	93.1% (6)
Live and work in county	77.3% (250)
Married-couple households	53.4% (134)

TRANSPORTATION	★★★ (290)
Bicycle or walk to work	3.3% (211)
Carpool to work	7.8% (504)
Public transit to work	0.4% (219)
Commute <15 minutes	46.0% (233)
Commute >45 minutes	7.7% (115)

See pages 37-130 for explanations of statistics, stars, and ranks.

Marietta, OH
(Washington County, OH)

POPULATION		
2010 census	61,778	(138)
2015 estimate	61,112	(140)
2010-2015 change	-1.1%	(335)
2020 projection	60,263	(146)
2030 projection	58,381	(159)

RACE		
Whites	95.4%	(31)
Blacks	1.1%	(367)
Hispanics	1.0%	(530)
Asians	0.7%	(241)
Native Americans	0.2%	(300)

AGE		
0-17 years old	20.2%	(452)
18-24 years old	9.2%	(234)
25-39 years old	16.4%	(411)
40-54 years old	20.5%	(151)
55-64 years old	15.0%	(87)
65+ years old	18.7%	(97)

PRIVATE SECTOR		
Businesses	1,465	(144)
Employees	22,144	(95)
Total wages	$972,119,018	(76)
Average weekly wages	$844	(55)

HOUSEHOLD INCOME LADDER		
95th percentile	$144,421	(238)
80th percentile	$85,894	(232)
60th percentile	$54,382	(270)
40th percentile	$34,199	(281)
20th percentile	$18,371	(298)

CHILDREN	★★★★★ (90)	
Living with two parents	69.9%	(146)
Older teens in school	84.9%	(201)
Speak English very well	99.8%	(38)
Poverty rate for children	21.5%	(206)
No health insurance	3.7%	(98)

DIVERSITY/EQUALITY	★★ (422)	
Racial diversity index	8.9%	(518)
Geographic diversity index	53.3%	(169)
Top 20% share of income	47.7%	(273)
Gender gap in earnings	40.5%	(449)
White-collar gender gap	30.8%	(350)

EDUCATION	★★★★ (183)	
Eighth grade or less	1.5%	(72)
High school diplomas	92.2%	(120)
Attended college	54.0%	(243)
Bachelor's degrees	19.2%	(241)
Advanced degrees	6.3%	(234)

EMPLOYMENT	★★★★ (196)	
Average jobless rate	6.8%	(179)
Self-employed workers	6.9%	(435)
Management/financial jobs	10.5%	(318)
Computer/engineering jobs	4.3%	(63)
Health care jobs	6.1%	(168)

GROWTH POTENTIAL	★ (445)	
Children per senior	1.08	(471)
Median age	43.6	(468)
Moved from different state	3.1%	(147)
Homes built since 2000	9.1%	(430)
Construction jobs	6.5%	(253)

HOUSING	★★★★★ (100)	
Home vacancy rate	8.6%	(260)
Home ownership rate	75.2%	(76)
Housing diversity index	85.4%	(156)
4 or more bedrooms	18.1%	(197)
Affordability/income ratio	$2,544	(268)

INCOME	★★★ (231)	
Poverty rate	16.4%	(241)
Median household income	$43,509	(277)
Interest/dividends	20.6%	(231)
Public assistance	15.4%	(274)
Median fulltime earnings	$39,849	(145)

SENIORS	★★★ (321)	
Seniors living alone	26.6%	(209)
Poverty rate for seniors	10.0%	(321)
Median income for seniors	$33,764	(247)
Seniors who work	15.4%	(441)
Home ownership by seniors	82.1%	(268)

STABILITY	★★★ (328)	
25-39 age group	16.4%	(411)
Born in state of residence	62.0%	(411)
Same house as 1 year ago	88.7%	(95)
Live and work in county	70.3%	(366)
Married-couple households	51.8%	(206)

TRANSPORTATION	★★ (423)	
Bicycle or walk to work	3.0%	(249)
Carpool to work	8.2%	(480)
Public transit to work	0.2%	(363)
Commute <15 minutes	33.9%	(463)
Commute >45 minutes	9.5%	(203)

See pages 37-130 for explanations of statistics, stars, and ranks.

Marinette, WI-MI
(Marinette County, WI, and Menominee County, MI)

POPULATION	
2010 census	65,778 (116)
2015 estimate	64,432 (124)
2010-2015 change	-2.0% (412)
2020 projection	62,962 (131)
2030 projection	60,011 (153)

RACE	
Whites	95.0% (46)
Blacks	0.3% (519)
Hispanics	1.5% (480)
Asians	0.4% (413)
Native Americans	1.0% (103)

AGE	
0-17 years old	19.7% (473)
18-24 years old	7.4% (489)
25-39 years old	14.6% (527)
40-54 years old	20.8% (122)
55-64 years old	16.4% (30)
65+ years old	21.1% (29)

PRIVATE SECTOR	
Businesses	1,563 (125)
Employees	22,134 (96)
Total wages	$855,669,647 (106)
Average weekly wages	$743 (169)

HOUSEHOLD INCOME LADDER	
95th percentile	$122,002 (501)
80th percentile	$77,347 (415)
60th percentile	$51,853 (323)
40th percentile	$33,349 (313)
20th percentile	$18,372 (297)

CHILDREN	★★★★ (123)
Living with two parents	62.0% (353)
Older teens in school	88.9% (82)
Speak English very well	99.0% (200)
Poverty rate for children	22.4% (232)
No health insurance	3.1% (64)

DIVERSITY/EQUALITY	★★ (405)
Racial diversity index	9.7% (500)
Geographic diversity index	51.4% (194)
Top 20% share of income	45.9% (120)
Gender gap in earnings	46.4% (512)
White-collar gender gap	27.2% (299)

EDUCATION	★★★ (222)
Eighth grade or less	1.1% (26)
High school diplomas	93.6% (68)
Attended college	54.3% (238)
Bachelor's degrees	15.9% (382)
Advanced degrees	4.1% (472)

EMPLOYMENT	★★★ (266)
Average jobless rate	7.8% (270)
Self-employed workers	9.3% (224)
Management/financial jobs	9.8% (408)
Computer/engineering jobs	3.7% (103)
Health care jobs	5.3% (286)

GROWTH POTENTIAL	★ (488)
Children per senior	0.93 (519)
Median age	47.3 (529)
Moved from different state	2.5% (203)
Homes built since 2000	14.6% (213)
Construction jobs	6.2% (295)

HOUSING	★★★★★ (77)
Home vacancy rate	6.3% (122)
Home ownership rate	76.7% (36)
Housing diversity index	86.2% (43)
4 or more bedrooms	13.3% (437)
Affordability/income ratio	$2,461 (237)

INCOME	★★★★ (185)
Poverty rate	14.1% (157)
Median household income	$42,056 (318)
Interest/dividends	21.8% (188)
Public assistance	14.7% (243)
Median fulltime earnings	$41,009 (96)

SENIORS	★ (441)
Seniors living alone	31.5% (498)
Poverty rate for seniors	9.2% (270)
Median income for seniors	$28,339 (451)
Seniors who work	15.2% (452)
Home ownership by seniors	83.9% (183)

STABILITY	★ (474)
25-39 age group	14.6% (527)
Born in state of residence	63.3% (402)
Same house as 1 year ago	88.9% (86)
Live and work in county	67.0% (417)
Married-couple households	48.7% (356)

TRANSPORTATION	★★★ (257)
Bicycle or walk to work	3.3% (211)
Carpool to work	10.5% (280)
Public transit to work	0.3% (291)
Commute <15 minutes	47.6% (199)
Commute >45 minutes	10.5% (254)

See pages 37-130 for explanations of statistics, stars, and ranks.

Marion, IN
(Grant County, IN)

POPULATION	
2010 census	70,061 (100)
2015 estimate	67,979 (110)
2010-2015 change	-3.0% (481)
2020 projection	65,778 (118)
2030 projection	61,364 (144)
RACE	
Whites	85.8% (257)
Blacks	6.6% (139)
Hispanics	4.0% (296)
Asians	0.7% (241)
Native Americans	0.2% (300)
AGE	
0-17 years old	21.0% (411)
18-24 years old	13.5% (66)
25-39 years old	15.4% (490)
40-54 years old	19.2% (336)
55-64 years old	13.5% (258)
65+ years old	17.3% (172)
PRIVATE SECTOR	
Businesses	1,165 (213)
Employees	23,755 (84)
Total wages	$875,245,184 (97)
Average weekly wages	$709 (234)
HOUSEHOLD INCOME LADDER	
95th percentile	$121,403 (504)
80th percentile	$75,497 (451)
60th percentile	$49,049 (402)
40th percentile	$32,324 (349)
20th percentile	$18,472 (290)
CHILDREN	★★★ (251)
Living with two parents	57.2% (457)
Older teens in school	87.3% (124)
Speak English very well	99.6% (77)
Poverty rate for children	28.6% (381)
No health insurance	5.4% (209)
DIVERSITY/EQUALITY	★★★★ (136)
Racial diversity index	25.7% (288)
Geographic diversity index	44.9% (283)
Top 20% share of income	46.1% (129)
Gender gap in earnings	34.0% (289)
White-collar gender gap	7.9% (63)
EDUCATION	★★★ (242)
Eighth grade or less	2.1% (136)
High school diplomas	89.5% (215)

Attended college	48.9% (357)
Bachelor's degrees	18.4% (268)
Advanced degrees	6.5% (220)
EMPLOYMENT	★ (452)
Average jobless rate	8.8% (344)
Self-employed workers	5.4% (535)
Management/financial jobs	9.7% (416)
Computer/engineering jobs	2.0% (420)
Health care jobs	6.0% (181)
GROWTH POTENTIAL	★ (518)
Children per senior	1.22 (401)
Median age	40.0 (303)
Moved from different state	2.9% (165)
Homes built since 2000	8.0% (469)
Construction jobs	3.3% (546)
HOUSING	★★★★ (169)
Home vacancy rate	8.0% (223)
Home ownership rate	69.7% (281)
Housing diversity index	84.7% (260)
4 or more bedrooms	15.8% (307)
Affordability/income ratio	$2,055 (69)
INCOME	★★ (359)
Poverty rate	18.7% (326)
Median household income	$40,294 (375)
Interest/dividends	16.8% (349)
Public assistance	17.0% (334)
Median fulltime earnings	$35,206 (375)
SENIORS	★★ (405)
Seniors living alone	31.0% (475)
Poverty rate for seniors	8.7% (241)
Median income for seniors	$31,911 (323)
Seniors who work	15.8% (423)
Home ownership by seniors	82.4% (257)
STABILITY	★★ (385)
25-39 age group	15.4% (490)
Born in state of residence	72.6% (267)
Same house as 1 year ago	85.0% (299)
Live and work in county	82.3% (178)
Married-couple households	47.4% (401)
TRANSPORTATION	★★★ (255)
Bicycle or walk to work	4.6% (110)
Carpool to work	8.0% (493)
Public transit to work	0.5% (178)
Commute <15 minutes	48.8% (178)
Commute >45 minutes	9.9% (225)

See pages 37-130 for explanations of statistics, stars, and ranks.

Marion, OH
(Marion County, OH)

POPULATION	
2010 census	66,501 (113)
2015 estimate	65,355 (122)
2010-2015 change	-1.7% (384)
2020 projection	64,469 (127)
2030 projection	62,471 (135)

RACE	
Whites	89.1% (202)
Blacks	5.7% (148)
Hispanics	2.4% (389)
Asians	0.5% (355)
Native Americans	0.1% (402)

AGE	
0-17 years old	21.3% (383)
18-24 years old	8.7% (299)
25-39 years old	19.4% (78)
40-54 years old	21.3% (73)
55-64 years old	13.8% (203)
65+ years old	15.5% (333)

PRIVATE SECTOR	
Businesses	1,128 (228)
Employees	20,218 (125)
Total wages	$765,229,979 (129)
Average weekly wages	$728 (198)

HOUSEHOLD INCOME LADDER	
95th percentile	$136,084 (341)
80th percentile	$84,272 (271)
60th percentile	$53,331 (290)
40th percentile	$34,043 (287)
20th percentile	$19,445 (248)

CHILDREN	★★★ (254)
Living with two parents	59.7% (408)
Older teens in school	83.8% (245)
Speak English very well	99.5% (96)
Poverty rate for children	28.6% (381)
No health insurance	4.2% (134)

DIVERSITY/EQUALITY	★★★ (257)
Racial diversity index	20.2% (345)
Geographic diversity index	30.4% (481)
Top 20% share of income	46.7% (176)
Gender gap in earnings	25.4% (94)
White-collar gender gap	20.2% (211)

EDUCATION	★★ (355)
Eighth grade or less	1.9% (114)
High school diplomas	87.7% (280)
Attended college	47.0% (397)
Bachelor's degrees	13.0% (493)
Advanced degrees	5.0% (378)

EMPLOYMENT	★★ (359)
Average jobless rate	9.6% (402)
Self-employed workers	5.8% (508)
Management/financial jobs	10.5% (318)
Computer/engineering jobs	2.9% (219)
Health care jobs	6.7% (104)

GROWTH POTENTIAL	★ (533)
Children per senior	1.38 (291)
Median age	40.4 (325)
Moved from different state	1.5% (406)
Homes built since 2000	7.4% (491)
Construction jobs	3.5% (544)

HOUSING	★★ (357)
Home vacancy rate	11.3% (426)
Home ownership rate	67.9% (347)
Housing diversity index	82.4% (444)
4 or more bedrooms	17.9% (209)
Affordability/income ratio	$2,244 (139)

INCOME	★★★ (316)
Poverty rate	18.8% (329)
Median household income	$42,966 (291)
Interest/dividends	18.9% (279)
Public assistance	20.3% (437)
Median fulltime earnings	$39,236 (169)

SENIORS	★★ (357)
Seniors living alone	29.4% (394)
Poverty rate for seniors	7.5% (140)
Median income for seniors	$33,716 (251)
Seniors who work	19.2% (234)
Home ownership by seniors	77.8% (461)

STABILITY	★★★★ (188)
25-39 age group	19.4% (78)
Born in state of residence	82.9% (68)
Same house as 1 year ago	80.8% (486)
Live and work in county	73.4% (326)
Married-couple households	50.4% (278)

TRANSPORTATION	★★ (438)
Bicycle or walk to work	1.5% (457)
Carpool to work	9.8% (358)
Public transit to work	0.7% (119)
Commute <15 minutes	38.5% (364)
Commute >45 minutes	14.9% (420)

See pages 37-130 for explanations of statistics, stars, and ranks.

Marquette, MI
(Marquette County, MI)

POPULATION

2010 census	67,077 (111)
2015 estimate	67,215 (111)
2010-2015 change	0.2% (241)
2020 projection	67,794 (110)
2030 projection	68,706 (111)

RACE

Whites	92.5% (116)
Blacks	1.6% (320)
Hispanics	1.4% (488)
Asians	0.8% (201)
Native Americans	1.3% (86)

AGE

0-17 years old	18.2% (523)
18-24 years old	15.8% (53)
25-39 years old	16.9% (338)
40-54 years old	18.4% (430)
55-64 years old	14.7% (97)
65+ years old	16.0% (291)

PRIVATE SECTOR

Businesses	1,478 (139)
Employees	21,612 (100)
Total wages	$830,210,769 (112)
Average weekly wages	$739 (180)

HOUSEHOLD INCOME LADDER

95th percentile	$147,884 (184)
80th percentile	$87,851 (187)
60th percentile	$55,221 (242)
40th percentile	$36,069 (228)
20th percentile	$17,775 (328)

CHILDREN ★★★★★ (24)

Living with two parents	72.6% (92)
Older teens in school	94.0% (22)
Speak English very well	99.5% (96)
Poverty rate for children	17.7% (116)
No health insurance	4.0% (118)

DIVERSITY/EQUALITY ★★ (334)

Racial diversity index	14.3% (427)
Geographic diversity index	36.6% (414)
Top 20% share of income	48.4% (317)
Gender gap in earnings	37.1% (366)
White-collar gender gap	3.3% (20)

EDUCATION ★★★★★ (40)

Eighth grade or less	0.9% (16)
High school diplomas	96.0% (12)
Attended college	65.1% (60)
Bachelor's degrees	30.1% (52)
Advanced degrees	8.8% (92)

EMPLOYMENT ★★★★ (137)

Average jobless rate	8.1% (298)
Self-employed workers	8.3% (302)
Management/financial jobs	10.0% (381)
Computer/engineering jobs	3.4% (131)
Health care jobs	8.1% (16)

GROWTH POTENTIAL ★★ (376)

Children per senior	1.14 (446)
Median age	39.1 (244)
Moved from different state	2.8% (171)
Homes built since 2000	8.9% (439)
Construction jobs	6.2% (295)

HOUSING ★★★ (230)

Home vacancy rate	6.7% (141)
Home ownership rate	68.6% (321)
Housing diversity index	85.1% (212)
4 or more bedrooms	14.6% (373)
Affordability/income ratio	$2,894 (376)

INCOME ★★★★ (191)

Poverty rate	17.0% (262)
Median household income	$45,409 (225)
Interest/dividends	21.7% (190)
Public assistance	14.5% (234)
Median fulltime earnings	$40,930 (101)

SENIORS ★★ (435)

Seniors living alone	29.7% (416)
Poverty rate for seniors	7.5% (140)
Median income for seniors	$36,964 (118)
Seniors who work	11.9% (541)
Home ownership by seniors	77.7% (464)

STABILITY ★★★★ (126)

25-39 age group	16.9% (338)
Born in state of residence	78.8% (138)
Same house as 1 year ago	83.3% (382)
Live and work in county	95.9% (10)
Married-couple households	47.9% (387)

TRANSPORTATION ★★★★★ (96)

Bicycle or walk to work	7.0% (41)
Carpool to work	9.1% (419)
Public transit to work	0.6% (141)
Commute <15 minutes	50.9% (135)
Commute >45 minutes	6.1% (59)

See pages 37-130 for explanations of statistics, stars, and ranks.

Marshall, MN
(Lyon County, MN)

POPULATION	
2010 census	25,857 (475)
2015 estimate	25,673 (477)
2010-2015 change	-0.7% (303)
2020 projection	25,637 (473)
2030 projection	25,564 (467)

RACE	
Whites	86.6% (245)
Blacks	2.8% (232)
Hispanics	6.3% (212)
Asians	3.3% (20)
Native Americans	0.5% (174)

AGE	
0-17 years old	24.6% (144)
18-24 years old	11.7% (94)
25-39 years old	19.3% (85)
40-54 years old	18.2% (441)
55-64 years old	12.2% (424)
65+ years old	14.0% (438)

PRIVATE SECTOR	
Businesses	741 (409)
Employees	11,921 (311)
Total wages	$472,483,631 (271)
Average weekly wages	$762 (139)

HOUSEHOLD INCOME LADDER	
95th percentile	$177,758 (41)
80th percentile	$97,439 (72)
60th percentile	$64,494 (79)
40th percentile	$41,809 (79)
20th percentile	$21,688 (152)

CHILDREN	★★★★ (116)
Living with two parents	69.9% (146)
Older teens in school	87.4% (116)
Speak English very well	97.0% (413)
Poverty rate for children	20.2% (171)
No health insurance	4.1% (126)

DIVERSITY/EQUALITY	★★ (377)
Racial diversity index	24.4% (300)
Geographic diversity index	42.3% (321)
Top 20% share of income	48.9% (354)
Gender gap in earnings	33.9% (284)
White-collar gender gap	29.3% (324)

EDUCATION	★★★★★ (89)
Eighth grade or less	2.7% (195)
High school diplomas	94.0% (57)
Attended college	62.5% (89)
Bachelor's degrees	28.2% (72)
Advanced degrees	7.1% (176)

EMPLOYMENT	★★★★★ (34)
Average jobless rate	5.3% (82)
Self-employed workers	13.4% (46)
Management/financial jobs	16.0% (15)
Computer/engineering jobs	3.9% (86)
Health care jobs	4.8% (369)

GROWTH POTENTIAL	★★★★ (188)
Children per senior	1.76 (111)
Median age	35.1 (94)
Moved from different state	1.9% (310)
Homes built since 2000	11.5% (333)
Construction jobs	6.4% (270)

HOUSING	★★★★★ (50)
Home vacancy rate	9.2% (302)
Home ownership rate	67.7% (356)
Housing diversity index	86.0% (71)
4 or more bedrooms	29.2% (11)
Affordability/income ratio	$2,591 (287)

INCOME	★★★★★ (91)
Poverty rate	14.1% (157)
Median household income	$51,600 (90)
Interest/dividends	25.5% (82)
Public assistance	10.9% (91)
Median fulltime earnings	$40,000 (140)

SENIORS	★★★ (301)
Seniors living alone	31.2% (479)
Poverty rate for seniors	8.4% (214)
Median income for seniors	$36,105 (151)
Seniors who work	25.8% (55)
Home ownership by seniors	76.3% (505)

STABILITY	★★★★★ (32)
25-39 age group	19.3% (85)
Born in state of residence	74.6% (228)
Same house as 1 year ago	85.0% (299)
Live and work in county	91.5% (50)
Married-couple households	50.3% (284)

TRANSPORTATION	★★★★★ (18)
Bicycle or walk to work	4.7% (106)
Carpool to work	13.2% (94)
Public transit to work	0.9% (83)
Commute <15 minutes	62.6% (33)
Commute >45 minutes	4.3% (19)

See pages 37-130 for explanations of statistics, stars, and ranks.

Marshall, MO
(Saline County, MO)

POPULATION	
2010 census	23,370 (492)
2015 estimate	23,258 (494)
2010-2015 change	-0.5% (292)
2020 projection	23,004 (496)
2030 projection	22,446 (499)

RACE	
Whites	81.4% (311)
Blacks	4.9% (168)
Hispanics	9.2% (163)
Asians	1.5% (85)
Native Americans	0.2% (300)

AGE	
0-17 years old	23.0% (259)
18-24 years old	11.8% (90)
25-39 years old	16.9% (338)
40-54 years old	19.2% (336)
55-64 years old	12.7% (375)
65+ years old	16.4% (255)

PRIVATE SECTOR	
Businesses	521 (510)
Employees	6,969 (476)
Total wages	$229,203,970 (484)
Average weekly wages	$632 (432)

HOUSEHOLD INCOME LADDER	
95th percentile	$128,890 (444)
80th percentile	$73,224 (483)
60th percentile	$49,095 (400)
40th percentile	$32,373 (345)
20th percentile	$18,647 (283)

CHILDREN	★★★★ (125)
Living with two parents	63.6% (306)
Older teens in school	92.4% (36)
Speak English very well	98.3% (312)
Poverty rate for children	25.7% (315)
No health insurance	3.9% (111)

DIVERSITY/EQUALITY	★★★ (228)
Racial diversity index	32.6% (229)
Geographic diversity index	45.1% (279)
Top 20% share of income	46.8% (196)
Gender gap in earnings	26.3% (108)
White-collar gender gap	39.0% (433)

EDUCATION	★★★ (248)
Eighth grade or less	4.4% (346)
High school diplomas	88.4% (257)
Attended college	50.3% (321)
Bachelor's degrees	20.4% (213)
Advanced degrees	7.4% (149)

EMPLOYMENT	★★★★ (185)
Average jobless rate	5.5% (98)
Self-employed workers	9.4% (216)
Management/financial jobs	11.8% (173)
Computer/engineering jobs	1.4% (510)
Health care jobs	6.0% (181)

GROWTH POTENTIAL	★★ (377)
Children per senior	1.40 (279)
Median age	38.2 (189)
Moved from different state	1.9% (310)
Homes built since 2000	8.6% (449)
Construction jobs	5.8% (360)

HOUSING	★★★★ (217)
Home vacancy rate	10.2% (358)
Home ownership rate	67.8% (349)
Housing diversity index	85.3% (170)
4 or more bedrooms	18.1% (197)
Affordability/income ratio	$2,237 (136)

INCOME	★★ (361)
Poverty rate	17.3% (280)
Median household income	$40,101 (379)
Interest/dividends	17.5% (329)
Public assistance	15.3% (272)
Median fulltime earnings	$32,064 (493)

SENIORS	★★ (432)
Seniors living alone	29.4% (394)
Poverty rate for seniors	11.6% (392)
Median income for seniors	$29,974 (409)
Seniors who work	21.1% (156)
Home ownership by seniors	78.2% (445)

STABILITY	★★ (363)
25-39 age group	16.9% (338)
Born in state of residence	73.0% (259)
Same house as 1 year ago	82.0% (439)
Live and work in county	83.7% (148)
Married-couple households	47.3% (409)

TRANSPORTATION	★★★★★ (76)
Bicycle or walk to work	3.5% (189)
Carpool to work	11.8% (152)
Public transit to work	1.1% (58)
Commute <15 minutes	59.0% (51)
Commute >45 minutes	7.7% (115)

See pages 37-130 for explanations of statistics, stars, and ranks.

Marshalltown, IA
(Marshall County, IA)

POPULATION	
2010 census	40,648 (306)
2015 estimate	40,746 (307)
2010-2015 change	0.2% (241)
2020 projection	40,851 (304)
2030 projection	40,819 (306)

RACE	
Whites	74.6% (359)
Blacks	1.6% (320)
Hispanics	19.3% (80)
Asians	2.9% (25)
Native Americans	0.3% (231)

AGE	
0-17 years old	25.0% (126)
18-24 years old	8.4% (349)
25-39 years old	17.4% (269)
40-54 years old	18.7% (399)
55-64 years old	13.5% (258)
65+ years old	16.9% (207)

PRIVATE SECTOR	
Businesses	929 (301)
Employees	14,517 (221)
Total wages	$615,460,870 (181)
Average weekly wages	$815 (71)

HOUSEHOLD INCOME LADDER	
95th percentile	$146,211 (210)
80th percentile	$90,792 (144)
60th percentile	$63,397 (93)
40th percentile	$44,103 (53)
20th percentile	$25,135 (48)

CHILDREN	★★★ (265)
Living with two parents	65.0% (270)
Older teens in school	82.3% (304)
Speak English very well	91.4% (518)
Poverty rate for children	16.9% (94)
No health insurance	2.6% (40)

DIVERSITY/EQUALITY	★★★★★ (75)
Racial diversity index	40.5% (186)
Geographic diversity index	48.0% (245)
Top 20% share of income	43.8% (18)
Gender gap in earnings	31.4% (213)
White-collar gender gap	25.7% (284)

EDUCATION	★★ (419)
Eighth grade or less	10.8% (521)
High school diplomas	82.0% (445)
Attended college	53.8% (249)
Bachelor's degrees	20.8% (194)
Advanced degrees	5.7% (292)

EMPLOYMENT	★★★ (300)
Average jobless rate	6.3% (140)
Self-employed workers	7.1% (421)
Management/financial jobs	11.0% (252)
Computer/engineering jobs	3.2% (158)
Health care jobs	4.9% (355)

GROWTH POTENTIAL	★★★ (286)
Children per senior	1.48 (227)
Median age	38.9 (228)
Moved from different state	2.1% (269)
Homes built since 2000	8.4% (455)
Construction jobs	7.2% (162)

HOUSING	★★★★ (165)
Home vacancy rate	7.5% (186)
Home ownership rate	72.5% (167)
Housing diversity index	80.8% (497)
4 or more bedrooms	21.0% (100)
Affordability/income ratio	$1,959 (42)

INCOME	★★★★ (130)
Poverty rate	11.1% (59)
Median household income	$53,351 (70)
Interest/dividends	21.5% (194)
Public assistance	15.1% (262)
Median fulltime earnings	$39,002 (177)

SENIORS	★★★★ (138)
Seniors living alone	24.9% (113)
Poverty rate for seniors	5.4% (29)
Median income for seniors	$36,415 (141)
Seniors who work	18.6% (265)
Home ownership by seniors	80.5% (356)

STABILITY	★★★★★ (108)
25-39 age group	17.4% (269)
Born in state of residence	70.8% (295)
Same house as 1 year ago	85.0% (299)
Live and work in county	81.7% (191)
Married-couple households	55.1% (69)

TRANSPORTATION	★★★★★ (65)
Bicycle or walk to work	3.8% (161)
Carpool to work	16.4% (28)
Public transit to work	0.3% (291)
Commute <15 minutes	55.1% (90)
Commute >45 minutes	10.0% (227)

See pages 37-130 for explanations of statistics, stars, and ranks.

Maryville, MO
(Nodaway County, MO)

POPULATION

2010 census	23,370 (492)
2015 estimate	22,810 (500)
2010-2015 change	-2.4% (443)
2020 projection	22,455 (504)
2030 projection	21,710 (508)

RACE

Whites	93.0% (108)
Blacks	2.7% (241)
Hispanics	1.5% (480)
Asians	1.7% (69)
Native Americans	0.3% (231)

AGE

0-17 years old	17.0% (537)
18-24 years old	29.1% (8)
25-39 years old	15.3% (493)
40-54 years old	14.8% (537)
55-64 years old	10.1% (519)
65+ years old	13.8% (448)

PRIVATE SECTOR

Businesses	471 (520)
Employees	5,529 (520)
Total wages	$174,061,079 (524)
Average weekly wages	$605 (479)

HOUSEHOLD INCOME LADDER

95th percentile	$119,504 (519)
80th percentile	$74,093 (471)
60th percentile	$45,926 (462)
40th percentile	$27,203 (479)
20th percentile	$14,475 (466)

CHILDREN ★★★★ (131)

Living with two parents	65.9% (247)
Older teens in school	95.8% (12)
Speak English very well	99.0% (200)
Poverty rate for children	28.9% (385)
No health insurance	6.9% (307)

DIVERSITY/EQUALITY ★ (511)

Racial diversity index	13.4% (440)
Geographic diversity index	51.6% (192)
Top 20% share of income	48.0% (297)
Gender gap in earnings	42.2% (476)
White-collar gender gap	47.7% (497)

EDUCATION ★★★★★ (105)

Eighth grade or less	1.6% (84)
High school diplomas	93.5% (75)
Attended college	53.4% (257)
Bachelor's degrees	25.7% (97)
Advanced degrees	9.5% (73)

EMPLOYMENT ★★★ (261)

Average jobless rate	7.2% (218)
Self-employed workers	11.8% (81)
Management/financial jobs	10.4% (332)
Computer/engineering jobs	2.7% (270)
Health care jobs	4.3% (444)

GROWTH POTENTIAL ★★★★★ (66)

Children per senior	1.24 (390)
Median age	28.3 (16)
Moved from different state	5.4% (41)
Homes built since 2000	15.0% (204)
Construction jobs	6.4% (270)

HOUSING ★★ (420)

Home vacancy rate	8.2% (234)
Home ownership rate	53.9% (538)
Housing diversity index	85.2% (190)
4 or more bedrooms	19.4% (142)
Affordability/income ratio	$3,194 (431)

INCOME ★★ (440)

Poverty rate	28.6% (515)
Median household income	$35,854 (472)
Interest/dividends	19.5% (264)
Public assistance	13.5% (188)
Median fulltime earnings	$32,195 (486)

SENIORS ★★★ (276)

Seniors living alone	25.6% (149)
Poverty rate for seniors	14.5% (481)
Median income for seniors	$35,057 (184)
Seniors who work	19.9% (201)
Home ownership by seniors	83.0% (221)

STABILITY ★ (539)

25-39 age group	15.3% (493)
Born in state of residence	65.8% (379)
Same house as 1 year ago	69.8% (546)
Live and work in county	86.1% (113)
Married-couple households	45.2% (461)

TRANSPORTATION ★★★★★ (37)

Bicycle or walk to work	8.4% (25)
Carpool to work	11.0% (229)
Public transit to work	0.2% (363)
Commute <15 minutes	60.8% (42)
Commute >45 minutes	7.4% (99)

See pages 37-130 for explanations of statistics, stars, and ranks.

Mason City, IA
(Cerro Gordo and Worth Counties, IA)

POPULATION	
2010 census	51,749 (197)
2015 estimate	50,586 (210)
2010-2015 change	-2.2% (427)
2020 projection	49,320 (219)
2030 projection	46,613 (248)

RACE	
Whites	92.5% (116)
Blacks	1.2% (361)
Hispanics	4.0% (296)
Asians	1.0% (158)
Native Americans	0.1% (402)

AGE	
0-17 years old	21.0% (411)
18-24 years old	8.0% (407)
25-39 years old	15.7% (465)
40-54 years old	20.7% (132)
55-64 years old	15.3% (68)
65+ years old	19.2% (72)

PRIVATE SECTOR	
Businesses	1,746 (93)
Employees	23,018 (88)
Total wages	$914,550,426 (90)
Average weekly wages	$764 (133)

HOUSEHOLD INCOME LADDER	
95th percentile	$153,428 (126)
80th percentile	$88,473 (176)
60th percentile	$57,268 (199)
40th percentile	$37,327 (197)
20th percentile	$20,353 (213)

CHILDREN	★★★★★ (56)
Living with two parents	66.5% (231)
Older teens in school	87.2% (130)
Speak English very well	99.4% (124)
Poverty rate for children	16.7% (89)
No health insurance	2.0% (13)

DIVERSITY/EQUALITY	★ (472)
Racial diversity index	14.2% (432)
Geographic diversity index	38.8% (373)
Top 20% share of income	48.7% (332)
Gender gap in earnings	30.9% (198)
White-collar gender gap	39.6% (442)

EDUCATION	★★★★★ (96)
Eighth grade or less	1.1% (26)
High school diplomas	95.2% (23)
Attended college	65.5% (52)
Bachelor's degrees	22.3% (148)
Advanced degrees	5.7% (292)

EMPLOYMENT	★★★★★ (60)
Average jobless rate	4.5% (47)
Self-employed workers	10.7% (129)
Management/financial jobs	12.0% (156)
Computer/engineering jobs	2.9% (219)
Health care jobs	7.1% (63)

GROWTH POTENTIAL	★ (536)
Children per senior	1.10 (464)
Median age	44.3 (487)
Moved from different state	1.4% (425)
Homes built since 2000	7.7% (475)
Construction jobs	5.7% (373)

HOUSING	★★★★ (139)
Home vacancy rate	5.3% (50)
Home ownership rate	72.1% (181)
Housing diversity index	82.0% (458)
4 or more bedrooms	19.3% (145)
Affordability/income ratio	$2,430 (221)

INCOME	★★★★ (143)
Poverty rate	13.2% (123)
Median household income	$46,334 (206)
Interest/dividends	25.9% (71)
Public assistance	14.4% (225)
Median fulltime earnings	$38,581 (201)

SENIORS	★★★ (266)
Seniors living alone	30.9% (469)
Poverty rate for seniors	8.7% (241)
Median income for seniors	$34,712 (202)
Seniors who work	22.5% (120)
Home ownership by seniors	81.9% (280)

STABILITY	★★★ (224)
25-39 age group	15.7% (465)
Born in state of residence	76.8% (180)
Same house as 1 year ago	88.8% (93)
Live and work in county	81.4% (199)
Married-couple households	47.4% (401)

TRANSPORTATION	★★★★ (127)
Bicycle or walk to work	4.5% (117)
Carpool to work	9.1% (419)
Public transit to work	1.0% (69)
Commute <15 minutes	51.0% (131)
Commute >45 minutes	6.1% (59)

See pages 37-130 for explanations of statistics, stars, and ranks.

McPherson, KS
(McPherson County, KS)

POPULATION

2010 census	29,180 (441)
2015 estimate	28,941 (443)
2010-2015 change	-0.8% (314)
2020 projection	28,452 (445)
2030 projection	27,429 (451)

RACE

Whites	92.2% (128)
Blacks	1.0% (381)
Hispanics	3.9% (302)
Asians	0.7% (241)
Native Americans	0.5% (174)

AGE

0-17 years old	23.0% (259)
18-24 years old	8.9% (282)
25-39 years old	15.7% (465)
40-54 years old	19.7% (273)
55-64 years old	13.8% (203)
65+ years old	18.8% (94)

PRIVATE SECTOR

Businesses	853 (341)
Employees	13,190 (272)
Total wages	$612,409,965 (182)
Average weekly wages	$893 (37)

HOUSEHOLD INCOME LADDER

95th percentile	$159,262 (101)
80th percentile	$100,513 (56)
60th percentile	$67,334 (53)
40th percentile	$45,836 (40)
20th percentile	$29,487 (16)

CHILDREN ★★★★★ (37)

Living with two parents	76.9% (31)
Older teens in school	80.7% (379)
Speak English very well	100.0% (1)
Poverty rate for children	9.4% (11)
No health insurance	3.4% (79)

DIVERSITY/EQUALITY ★ (456)

Racial diversity index	14.8% (418)
Geographic diversity index	43.6% (301)
Top 20% share of income	44.6% (44)
Gender gap in earnings	49.6% (525)
White-collar gender gap	34.9% (389)

EDUCATION ★★★★★ (76)

Eighth grade or less	2.9% (217)
High school diplomas	92.5% (110)
Attended college	65.1% (60)
Bachelor's degrees	29.5% (59)
Advanced degrees	7.7% (133)

EMPLOYMENT ★★★★★ (33)

Average jobless rate	3.1% (12)
Self-employed workers	12.5% (56)
Management/financial jobs	18.1% (9)
Computer/engineering jobs	2.6% (288)
Health care jobs	4.7% (385)

GROWTH POTENTIAL ★ (455)

Children per senior	1.22 (401)
Median age	42.0 (398)
Moved from different state	2.0% (288)
Homes built since 2000	10.4% (381)
Construction jobs	5.8% (360)

HOUSING ★★★★★ (5)

Home vacancy rate	6.7% (141)
Home ownership rate	76.0% (57)
Housing diversity index	84.5% (287)
4 or more bedrooms	28.8% (15)
Affordability/income ratio	$2,368 (198)

INCOME ★★★★★ (24)

Poverty rate	7.2% (6)
Median household income	$56,128 (46)
Interest/dividends	28.6% (29)
Public assistance	6.7% (20)
Median fulltime earnings	$43,150 (46)

SENIORS ★★★★★ (50)

Seniors living alone	26.0% (172)
Poverty rate for seniors	6.8% (77)
Median income for seniors	$39,854 (62)
Seniors who work	26.4% (43)
Home ownership by seniors	83.0% (221)

STABILITY ★★★★★ (106)

25-39 age group	15.7% (465)
Born in state of residence	73.9% (247)
Same house as 1 year ago	86.2% (237)
Live and work in county	82.6% (170)
Married-couple households	56.5% (38)

TRANSPORTATION ★★★★★ (89)

Bicycle or walk to work	4.7% (106)
Carpool to work	9.5% (388)
Public transit to work	0.1% (441)
Commute <15 minutes	60.6% (44)
Commute >45 minutes	4.5% (21)

See pages 37-130 for explanations of statistics, stars, and ranks.

Menomonie, WI
(Dunn County, WI)

POPULATION

2010 census	43,857 (270)
2015 estimate	44,497 (269)
2010-2015 change	1.5% (160)
2020 projection	45,380 (256)
2030 projection	47,159 (244)

RACE

Whites	93.3% (98)
Blacks	0.6% (438)
Hispanics	1.7% (464)
Asians	2.0% (51)
Native Americans	0.3% (231)

AGE

0-17 years old	20.0% (458)
18-24 years old	19.2% (30)
25-39 years old	16.9% (338)
40-54 years old	17.9% (454)
55-64 years old	12.0% (438)
65+ years old	14.0% (438)

PRIVATE SECTOR

Businesses	846 (347)
Employees	13,648 (249)
Total wages	$511,468,042 (236)
Average weekly wages	$721 (215)

HOUSEHOLD INCOME LADDER

95th percentile	$146,302 (207)
80th percentile	$90,928 (142)
60th percentile	$61,155 (126)
40th percentile	$40,211 (125)
20th percentile	$21,989 (140)

CHILDREN ★★★★★ (30)

Living with two parents	73.2% (78)
Older teens in school	95.0% (14)
Speak English very well	97.6% (375)
Poverty rate for children	14.6% (61)
No health insurance	4.8% (173)

DIVERSITY/EQUALITY ★★ (367)

Racial diversity index	12.8% (447)
Geographic diversity index	49.3% (223)
Top 20% share of income	46.2% (131)
Gender gap in earnings	39.7% (429)
White-collar gender gap	31.2% (356)

EDUCATION ★★★★★ (58)

Eighth grade or less	1.3% (52)
High school diplomas	95.1% (27)

Attended college	63.7% (76)
Bachelor's degrees	27.1% (86)
Advanced degrees	9.3% (76)

EMPLOYMENT ★★★★★ (92)

Average jobless rate	6.1% (121)
Self-employed workers	11.2% (108)
Management/financial jobs	12.1% (149)
Computer/engineering jobs	4.3% (63)
Health care jobs	5.1% (319)

GROWTH POTENTIAL ★★★★ (125)

Children per senior	1.43 (261)
Median age	34.1 (78)
Moved from different state	3.8% (89)
Homes built since 2000	18.3% (126)
Construction jobs	5.8% (360)

HOUSING ★★★★★ (101)

Home vacancy rate	5.2% (46)
Home ownership rate	67.6% (362)
Housing diversity index	84.7% (260)
4 or more bedrooms	23.0% (65)
Affordability/income ratio	$3,087 (415)

INCOME ★★★★ (123)

Poverty rate	15.1% (196)
Median household income	$49,788 (134)
Interest/dividends	27.0% (51)
Public assistance	14.1% (212)
Median fulltime earnings	$39,761 (149)

SENIORS ★★★ (261)

Seniors living alone	26.8% (222)
Poverty rate for seniors	8.1% (187)
Median income for seniors	$33,692 (252)
Seniors who work	21.1% (156)
Home ownership by seniors	78.4% (435)

STABILITY ★ (511)

25-39 age group	16.9% (338)
Born in state of residence	67.4% (354)
Same house as 1 year ago	77.2% (521)
Live and work in county	65.3% (446)
Married-couple households	51.4% (231)

TRANSPORTATION ★★★ (225)

Bicycle or walk to work	8.3% (27)
Carpool to work	9.4% (394)
Public transit to work	0.1% (441)
Commute <15 minutes	37.4% (390)
Commute >45 minutes	11.1% (275)

See pages 37-130 for explanations of statistics, stars, and ranks.

Merrill, WI
(Lincoln County, WI)

POPULATION

2010 census	28,743 (446)
2015 estimate	27,980 (451)
2010-2015 change	-2.7% (459)
2020 projection	27,126 (458)
2030 projection	25,466 (468)

RACE

Whites	96.1% (15)
Blacks	0.5% (466)
Hispanics	1.3% (503)
Asians	0.4% (413)
Native Americans	0.2% (300)

AGE

0-17 years old	20.2% (452)
18-24 years old	6.8% (527)
25-39 years old	14.8% (520)
40-54 years old	23.1% (5)
55-64 years old	15.5% (59)
65+ years old	19.4% (65)

PRIVATE SECTOR

Businesses	666 (447)
Employees	9,021 (412)
Total wages	$348,343,387 (383)
Average weekly wages	$743 (169)

HOUSEHOLD INCOME LADDER

95th percentile	$139,605 (295)
80th percentile	$89,729 (158)
60th percentile	$60,235 (146)
40th percentile	$39,276 (147)
20th percentile	$22,493 (116)

CHILDREN ★★★★★ (71)

Living with two parents	70.4% (135)
Older teens in school	82.6% (293)
Speak English very well	99.4% (124)
Poverty rate for children	12.4% (39)
No health insurance	4.6% (159)

DIVERSITY/EQUALITY ★★★ (281)

Racial diversity index	7.6% (531)
Geographic diversity index	31.6% (469)
Top 20% share of income	44.0% (28)
Gender gap in earnings	32.3% (234)
White-collar gender gap	18.1% (189)

EDUCATION ★★★★ (201)

Eighth grade or less	1.2% (42)
High school diplomas	93.3% (85)
Attended college	55.2% (216)
Bachelor's degrees	16.7% (344)
Advanced degrees	4.8% (405)

EMPLOYMENT ★★★★ (158)

Average jobless rate	6.1% (121)
Self-employed workers	9.8% (186)
Management/financial jobs	10.6% (306)
Computer/engineering jobs	2.9% (219)
Health care jobs	6.1% (168)

GROWTH POTENTIAL ★ (539)

Children per senior	1.04 (487)
Median age	46.1 (514)
Moved from different state	0.8% (524)
Homes built since 2000	12.9% (280)
Construction jobs	5.4% (413)

HOUSING ★★★★★ (54)

Home vacancy rate	5.0% (33)
Home ownership rate	75.5% (67)
Housing diversity index	86.4% (26)
4 or more bedrooms	15.3% (333)
Affordability/income ratio	$2,667 (319)

INCOME ★★★★★ (96)

Poverty rate	10.2% (39)
Median household income	$49,721 (136)
Interest/dividends	24.6% (113)
Public assistance	12.3% (140)
Median fulltime earnings	$39,421 (161)

SENIORS ★★ (399)

Seniors living alone	27.2% (254)
Poverty rate for seniors	7.9% (170)
Median income for seniors	$30,698 (384)
Seniors who work	15.2% (452)
Home ownership by seniors	78.4% (435)

STABILITY ★★★ (285)

25-39 age group	14.8% (520)
Born in state of residence	81.8% (88)
Same house as 1 year ago	88.6% (101)
Live and work in county	63.1% (464)
Married-couple households	53.4% (134)

TRANSPORTATION ★★ (343)

Bicycle or walk to work	2.2% (358)
Carpool to work	10.1% (322)
Public transit to work	0.5% (178)
Commute <15 minutes	38.4% (366)
Commute >45 minutes	9.8% (218)

See pages 37-130 for explanations of statistics, stars, and ranks.

Mexico, MO
(Audrain County, MO)

POPULATION

2010 census	25,529 (478)
2015 estimate	26,096 (471)
2010-2015 change	2.2% (118)
2020 projection	26,170 (468)
2030 projection	26,238 (464)

RACE

Whites	87.4% (234)
Blacks	6.6% (139)
Hispanics	2.8% (355)
Asians	0.1% (529)
Native Americans	0.1% (402)

AGE

0-17 years old	23.8% (206)
18-24 years old	8.2% (379)
25-39 years old	18.9% (111)
40-54 years old	19.9% (250)
55-64 years old	12.8% (356)
65+ years old	16.5% (247)

PRIVATE SECTOR

Businesses	572 (488)
Employees	7,116 (472)
Total wages	$236,050,443 (478)
Average weekly wages	$638 (417)

HOUSEHOLD INCOME LADDER

95th percentile	$113,835 (540)
80th percentile	$75,007 (457)
60th percentile	$50,349 (374)
40th percentile	$32,301 (351)
20th percentile	$19,294 (253)

CHILDREN ★★ (435)

Living with two parents	64.4% (283)
Older teens in school	76.7% (476)
Speak English very well	98.6% (278)
Poverty rate for children	28.5% (377)
No health insurance	11.8% (469)

DIVERSITY/EQUALITY ★★★ (318)

Racial diversity index	23.0% (314)
Geographic diversity index	37.6% (397)
Top 20% share of income	44.9% (60)
Gender gap in earnings	31.9% (223)
White-collar gender gap	37.8% (417)

EDUCATION ★★ (436)

Eighth grade or less	4.0% (325)
High school diplomas	85.8% (352)
Attended college	40.9% (503)
Bachelor's degrees	12.9% (497)
Advanced degrees	4.7% (419)

EMPLOYMENT ★★ (345)

Average jobless rate	8.8% (344)
Self-employed workers	9.7% (196)
Management/financial jobs	11.4% (210)
Computer/engineering jobs	1.4% (510)
Health care jobs	5.3% (286)

GROWTH POTENTIAL ★★ (372)

Children per senior	1.44 (253)
Median age	39.2 (248)
Moved from different state	3.1% (147)
Homes built since 2000	9.9% (389)
Construction jobs	4.8% (480)

HOUSING ★★★★ (161)

Home vacancy rate	9.4% (309)
Home ownership rate	70.3% (256)
Housing diversity index	86.6% (12)
4 or more bedrooms	15.3% (333)
Affordability/income ratio	$2,225 (131)

INCOME ★★ (342)

Poverty rate	18.5% (317)
Median household income	$41,310 (343)
Interest/dividends	19.1% (273)
Public assistance	13.7% (197)
Median fulltime earnings	$31,928 (501)

SENIORS ★★ (343)

Seniors living alone	29.1% (371)
Poverty rate for seniors	11.5% (388)
Median income for seniors	$29,808 (415)
Seniors who work	19.0% (243)
Home ownership by seniors	84.8% (150)

STABILITY ★★★★ (183)

25-39 age group	18.9% (111)
Born in state of residence	78.2% (150)
Same house as 1 year ago	83.2% (388)
Live and work in county	74.6% (301)
Married-couple households	50.3% (284)

TRANSPORTATION ★★★★ (198)

Bicycle or walk to work	3.6% (180)
Carpool to work	10.5% (280)
Public transit to work	0.7% (119)
Commute <15 minutes	51.0% (131)
Commute >45 minutes	11.2% (278)

See pages 37-130 for explanations of statistics, stars, and ranks.

Minot, ND
(McHenry, Renville, and Ward Counties, ND)

POPULATION	
2010 census	69,540 (102)
2015 estimate	79,814 (68)
2010-2015 change	14.8% (6)
2020 projection	88,958 (49)
2030 projection	96,151 (37)

RACE	
Whites	87.0% (241)
Blacks	2.7% (241)
Hispanics	4.4% (270)
Asians	1.3% (112)
Native Americans	1.2% (89)

AGE	
0-17 years old	23.3% (246)
18-24 years old	14.9% (57)
25-39 years old	21.6% (28)
40-54 years old	17.2% (494)
55-64 years old	10.5% (505)
65+ years old	12.5% (484)

PRIVATE SECTOR	
Businesses	2,721 (27)
Employees	31,229 (35)
Total wages	$1,519,042,797 (18)
Average weekly wages	$935 (26)

HOUSEHOLD INCOME LADDER	
95th percentile	$185,880 (34)
80th percentile	$108,359 (27)
60th percentile	$74,649 (24)
40th percentile	$48,776 (25)
20th percentile	$28,915 (17)

CHILDREN	★★★★★ (100)
Living with two parents	75.8% (40)
Older teens in school	72.2% (519)
Speak English very well	99.5% (96)
Poverty rate for children	10.3% (16)
No health insurance	3.5% (82)

DIVERSITY/EQUALITY	★★★ (305)
Racial diversity index	23.9% (305)
Geographic diversity index	61.3% (114)
Top 20% share of income	46.6% (173)
Gender gap in earnings	37.0% (364)
White-collar gender gap	44.5% (475)

EDUCATION	★★★★★ (66)
Eighth grade or less	1.1% (26)
High school diplomas	95.2% (23)
Attended college	66.7% (40)
Bachelor's degrees	27.0% (87)
Advanced degrees	6.8% (191)

EMPLOYMENT	★★★★★ (61)
Average jobless rate	2.6% (4)
Self-employed workers	10.1% (158)
Management/financial jobs	14.1% (46)
Computer/engineering jobs	3.1% (180)
Health care jobs	5.1% (319)

GROWTH POTENTIAL	★★★★★ (20)
Children per senior	1.86 (82)
Median age	32.1 (48)
Moved from different state	8.5% (10)
Homes built since 2000	22.0% (69)
Construction jobs	7.7% (109)

HOUSING	★★★★ (210)
Home vacancy rate	10.0% (347)
Home ownership rate	63.7% (462)
Housing diversity index	85.2% (190)
4 or more bedrooms	24.9% (44)
Affordability/income ratio	$2,905 (380)

INCOME	★★★★★ (30)
Poverty rate	7.9% (10)
Median household income	$61,213 (23)
Interest/dividends	22.9% (159)
Public assistance	5.7% (12)
Median fulltime earnings	$42,056 (62)

SENIORS	★★★ (252)
Seniors living alone	32.0% (512)
Poverty rate for seniors	7.3% (119)
Median income for seniors	$36,507 (137)
Seniors who work	26.3% (45)
Home ownership by seniors	78.2% (445)

STABILITY	★★★★ (211)
25-39 age group	21.6% (28)
Born in state of residence	58.9% (427)
Same house as 1 year ago	77.3% (519)
Live and work in county	89.7% (68)
Married-couple households	49.8% (307)

TRANSPORTATION	★★★ (233)
Bicycle or walk to work	3.1% (232)
Carpool to work	10.4% (289)
Public transit to work	0.2% (363)
Commute <15 minutes	50.7% (141)
Commute >45 minutes	9.8% (218)

See pages 37-130 for explanations of statistics, stars, and ranks.

Mitchell, SD
(Davison and Hanson Counties, SD)

POPULATION

2010 census	22,835 (498)
2015 estimate	23,243 (495)
2010-2015 change	1.8% (142)
2020 projection	23,482 (490)
2030 projection	23,860 (481)

RACE

Whites	92.5% (116)
Blacks	0.9% (388)
Hispanics	2.0% (428)
Asians	0.2% (509)
Native Americans	3.0% (52)

AGE

0-17 years old	24.3% (164)
18-24 years old	10.5% (136)
25-39 years old	17.2% (290)
40-54 years old	18.4% (430)
55-64 years old	13.1% (318)
65+ years old	16.5% (247)

PRIVATE SECTOR

Businesses	865 (335)
Employees	11,574 (324)
Total wages	$430,530,107 (305)
Average weekly wages	$715 (225)

HOUSEHOLD INCOME LADDER

95th percentile	$142,200 (263)
80th percentile	$92,355 (124)
60th percentile	$61,457 (122)
40th percentile	$40,308 (120)
20th percentile	$22,231 (128)

CHILDREN ★★★★★ (88)

Living with two parents	73.6% (72)
Older teens in school	80.9% (370)
Speak English very well	98.5% (287)
Poverty rate for children	16.6% (88)
No health insurance	3.5% (82)

DIVERSITY/EQUALITY ★★★ (282)

Racial diversity index	14.3% (427)
Geographic diversity index	42.3% (321)
Top 20% share of income	44.8% (56)
Gender gap in earnings	27.4% (125)
White-collar gender gap	38.8% (431)

EDUCATION ★★★★★ (38)

Eighth grade or less	2.4% (169)
High school diplomas	94.5% (42)
Attended college	72.4% (17)
Bachelor's degrees	30.9% (47)
Advanced degrees	8.2% (114)

EMPLOYMENT ★★★★★ (32)

Average jobless rate	3.0% (11)
Self-employed workers	12.3% (62)
Management/financial jobs	13.9% (50)
Computer/engineering jobs	5.1% (28)
Health care jobs	4.7% (385)

GROWTH POTENTIAL ★★★★★ (92)

Children per senior	1.47 (234)
Median age	37.8 (174)
Moved from different state	4.0% (79)
Homes built since 2000	14.0% (238)
Construction jobs	9.5% (31)

HOUSING ★★★★★ (26)

Home vacancy rate	3.6% (4)
Home ownership rate	65.2% (431)
Housing diversity index	83.9% (360)
4 or more bedrooms	29.8% (7)
Affordability/income ratio	$2,552 (271)

INCOME ★★★★★ (108)

Poverty rate	12.5% (101)
Median household income	$51,245 (96)
Interest/dividends	26.9% (53)
Public assistance	12.7% (155)
Median fulltime earnings	$36,988 (290)

SENIORS ★ (512)

Seniors living alone	32.3% (519)
Poverty rate for seniors	12.2% (422)
Median income for seniors	$33,253 (270)
Seniors who work	20.7% (170)
Home ownership by seniors	66.7% (551)

STABILITY ★★★ (276)

25-39 age group	17.2% (290)
Born in state of residence	74.4% (235)
Same house as 1 year ago	81.2% (474)
Live and work in county	82.5% (172)
Married-couple households	50.5% (271)

TRANSPORTATION ★★★★★ (72)

Bicycle or walk to work	5.3% (79)
Carpool to work	9.1% (419)
Public transit to work	0.3% (291)
Commute <15 minutes	66.8% (10)
Commute >45 minutes	6.4% (67)

See pages 37-130 for explanations of statistics, stars, and ranks.

Moberly, MO
(Randolph County, MO)

POPULATION

2010 census	25,414 (479)
2015 estimate	25,104 (483)
2010-2015 change	-1.2% (345)
2020 projection	24,751 (484)
2030 projection	24,009 (479)

RACE

Whites	89.5% (195)
Blacks	4.9% (168)
Hispanics	1.8% (455)
Asians	0.6% (291)
Native Americans	0.5% (174)

AGE

0-17 years old	22.6% (291)
18-24 years old	9.4% (203)
25-39 years old	20.0% (58)
40-54 years old	20.3% (186)
55-64 years old	12.5% (396)
65+ years old	15.1% (363)

PRIVATE SECTOR

Businesses	575 (485)
Employees	7,301 (463)
Total wages	$258,143,624 (466)
Average weekly wages	$680 (313)

HOUSEHOLD INCOME LADDER

95th percentile	$128,060 (454)
80th percentile	$77,273 (418)
60th percentile	$48,956 (404)
40th percentile	$30,597 (398)
20th percentile	$16,207 (401)

CHILDREN ★★★★ **(143)**

Living with two parents	60.8% (382)
Older teens in school	88.4% (93)
Speak English very well	99.7% (57)
Poverty rate for children	24.7% (290)
No health insurance	3.6% (93)

DIVERSITY/EQUALITY ★★ **(350)**

Racial diversity index	19.5% (353)
Geographic diversity index	42.4% (316)
Top 20% share of income	47.3% (242)
Gender gap in earnings	37.2% (372)
White-collar gender gap	24.4% (264)

EDUCATION ★★ **(373)**

Eighth grade or less	3.7% (303)
High school diplomas	87.1% (301)
Attended college	50.2% (325)
Bachelor's degrees	13.6% (474)
Advanced degrees	4.3% (456)

EMPLOYMENT ★★ **(435)**

Average jobless rate	8.9% (351)
Self-employed workers	7.5% (385)
Management/financial jobs	11.4% (210)
Computer/engineering jobs	2.1% (399)
Health care jobs	4.3% (444)

GROWTH POTENTIAL ★★★ **(296)**

Children per senior	1.49 (220)
Median age	38.4 (202)
Moved from different state	2.5% (203)
Homes built since 2000	12.7% (290)
Construction jobs	5.4% (413)

HOUSING ★★ **(379)**

Home vacancy rate	16.2% (539)
Home ownership rate	72.5% (167)
Housing diversity index	85.2% (190)
4 or more bedrooms	15.1% (347)
Affordability/income ratio	$2,260 (144)

INCOME ★★ **(392)**

Poverty rate	19.1% (341)
Median household income	$37,832 (430)
Interest/dividends	16.8% (349)
Public assistance	18.5% (385)
Median fulltime earnings	$34,808 (394)

SENIORS ★★ **(419)**

Seniors living alone	26.9% (230)
Poverty rate for seniors	12.2% (422)
Median income for seniors	$29,044 (432)
Seniors who work	14.7% (467)
Home ownership by seniors	82.6% (242)

STABILITY ★★★★ **(121)**

25-39 age group	20.0% (58)
Born in state of residence	74.5% (231)
Same house as 1 year ago	83.8% (347)
Live and work in county	73.4% (326)
Married-couple households	51.5% (226)

TRANSPORTATION ★★ **(347)**

Bicycle or walk to work	2.0% (386)
Carpool to work	9.9% (348)
Public transit to work	0.2% (363)
Commute <15 minutes	49.1% (173)
Commute >45 minutes	13.1% (359)

See pages 37-130 for explanations of statistics, stars, and ranks.

Mount Pleasant, MI
(Isabella County, MI)

POPULATION		Attended college	63.4% (78)
2010 census	70,311 (98)	Bachelor's degrees	28.7% (66)
2015 estimate	70,698 (100)	Advanced degrees	11.7% (40)
2010-2015 change	0.6% (209)		
2020 projection	72,215 (94)	**EMPLOYMENT**	★ **(479)**
2030 projection	75,080 (89)	Average jobless rate	11.3% (466)
		Self-employed workers	7.7% (362)
RACE		Management/financial jobs	11.3% (218)
Whites	86.4% (250)	Computer/engineering jobs	2.5% (307)
Blacks	2.6% (247)	Health care jobs	4.0% (476)
Hispanics	3.7% (311)		
Asians	1.7% (69)	**GROWTH POTENTIAL**	★★★★★ **(109)**
Native Americans	2.7% (58)	Children per senior	1.64 (153)
		Median age	26.3 (6)
AGE		Moved from different state	2.4% (218)
0-17 years old	17.4% (533)	Homes built since 2000	18.2% (128)
18-24 years old	30.5% (5)	Construction jobs	4.3% (514)
25-39 years old	16.6% (388)		
40-54 years old	14.9% (536)	**HOUSING**	★★★★ **(218)**
55-64 years old	10.0% (521)	Home vacancy rate	5.5% (60)
65+ years old	10.6% (519)	Home ownership rate	60.2% (501)
		Housing diversity index	85.2% (190)
PRIVATE SECTOR		4 or more bedrooms	21.3% (95)
Businesses	1,260 (188)	Affordability/income ratio	$3,111 (420)
Employees	19,904 (127)		
Total wages	$654,047,798 (165)	**INCOME**	★★ **(404)**
Average weekly wages	$632 (432)	Poverty rate	30.2% (524)
		Median household income	$39,377 (399)
HOUSEHOLD INCOME LADDER		Interest/dividends	22.2% (174)
95th percentile	$142,607 (257)	Public assistance	18.6% (389)
80th percentile	$82,669 (300)	Median fulltime earnings	$37,337 (258)
60th percentile	$50,865 (361)		
40th percentile	$30,375 (405)	**SENIORS**	★★★★ **(204)**
20th percentile	$15,134 (449)	Seniors living alone	28.4% (325)
		Poverty rate for seniors	7.8% (163)
CHILDREN	★★★★ **(149)**	Median income for seniors	$37,222 (110)
Living with two parents	62.5% (334)	Seniors who work	17.5% (310)
Older teens in school	93.4% (28)	Home ownership by seniors	83.5% (197)
Speak English very well	98.9% (226)		
Poverty rate for children	24.8% (293)	**STABILITY**	★ **(529)**
No health insurance	6.9% (307)	25-39 age group	16.6% (388)
		Born in state of residence	83.5% (62)
DIVERSITY/EQUALITY	★★ **(431)**	Same house as 1 year ago	70.4% (545)
Racial diversity index	24.9% (294)	Live and work in county	80.5% (212)
Geographic diversity index	29.7% (488)	Married-couple households	40.7% (519)
Top 20% share of income	51.2% (476)		
Gender gap in earnings	32.7% (245)	**TRANSPORTATION**	★★★★★ **(56)**
White-collar gender gap	14.3% (144)	Bicycle or walk to work	8.9% (21)
		Carpool to work	8.4% (466)
EDUCATION	★★★★★ **(47)**	Public transit to work	1.3% (51)
Eighth grade or less	1.4% (60)	Commute <15 minutes	52.9% (110)
High school diplomas	92.5% (110)	Commute >45 minutes	7.7% (115)

See pages 37-130 for explanations of statistics, stars, and ranks.

Mount Vernon, IL
(Jefferson County, IL)

POPULATION	
2010 census	38,827 (331)
2015 estimate	38,353 (332)
2010-2015 change	-1.2% (345)
2020 projection	37,577 (348)
2030 projection	35,984 (360)

RACE	
Whites	86.2% (253)
Blacks	7.9% (128)
Hispanics	2.3% (398)
Asians	1.1% (139)
Native Americans	0.1% (402)

AGE	
0-17 years old	21.8% (351)
18-24 years old	8.8% (292)
25-39 years old	18.5% (144)
40-54 years old	20.1% (221)
55-64 years old	13.5% (258)
65+ years old	17.3% (172)

PRIVATE SECTOR	
Businesses	903 (310)
Employees	16,739 (178)
Total wages	$692,483,472 (152)
Average weekly wages	$796 (97)

HOUSEHOLD INCOME LADDER	
95th percentile	$145,060 (228)
80th percentile	$87,146 (200)
60th percentile	$54,306 (273)
40th percentile	$34,115 (284)
20th percentile	$17,901 (323)

CHILDREN	★★★ (266)
Living with two parents	65.9% (247)
Older teens in school	81.4% (350)
Speak English very well	98.4% (300)
Poverty rate for children	26.2% (328)
No health insurance	6.0% (248)

DIVERSITY/EQUALITY	★★ (426)
Racial diversity index	24.9% (294)
Geographic diversity index	34.8% (438)
Top 20% share of income	48.3% (312)
Gender gap in earnings	40.9% (454)
White-collar gender gap	22.2% (239)

EDUCATION	★★★ (221)
Eighth grade or less	3.0% (231)
High school diplomas	88.7% (245)
Attended college	58.3% (163)
Bachelor's degrees	17.6% (301)
Advanced degrees	6.1% (250)

EMPLOYMENT	★★ (332)
Average jobless rate	9.2% (377)
Self-employed workers	9.1% (243)
Management/financial jobs	9.4% (444)
Computer/engineering jobs	2.6% (288)
Health care jobs	6.2% (156)

GROWTH POTENTIAL	★★ (428)
Children per senior	1.26 (378)
Median age	40.7 (341)
Moved from different state	1.7% (355)
Homes built since 2000	12.5% (297)
Construction jobs	5.4% (413)

HOUSING	★★★★★ (74)
Home vacancy rate	7.1% (165)
Home ownership rate	73.0% (151)
Housing diversity index	86.7% (6)
4 or more bedrooms	14.6% (373)
Affordability/income ratio	$2,019 (61)

INCOME	★★★ (265)
Poverty rate	17.0% (262)
Median household income	$43,247 (284)
Interest/dividends	21.4% (202)
Public assistance	18.8% (394)
Median fulltime earnings	$38,607 (197)

SENIORS	★★ (410)
Seniors living alone	29.1% (371)
Poverty rate for seniors	10.6% (350)
Median income for seniors	$31,303 (360)
Seniors who work	16.7% (360)
Home ownership by seniors	81.3% (316)

STABILITY	★★★★★ (101)
25-39 age group	18.5% (144)
Born in state of residence	80.0% (115)
Same house as 1 year ago	84.4% (331)
Live and work in county	83.6% (151)
Married-couple households	49.2% (340)

TRANSPORTATION	★★★ (318)
Bicycle or walk to work	2.4% (331)
Carpool to work	9.2% (408)
Public transit to work	0.4% (219)
Commute <15 minutes	42.1% (296)
Commute >45 minutes	8.0% (131)

See pages 37-130 for explanations of statistics, stars, and ranks.

Mount Vernon, OH
(Knox County, OH)

POPULATION	
2010 census	60,921 (145)
2015 estimate	61,061 (141)
2010-2015 change	0.2% (241)
2020 projection	62,063 (137)
2030 projection	63,854 (133)

RACE	
Whites	95.6% (26)
Blacks	0.9% (388)
Hispanics	1.4% (488)
Asians	0.4% (413)
Native Americans	0.1% (402)

AGE	
0-17 years old	23.4% (240)
18-24 years old	11.9% (88)
25-39 years old	15.9% (453)
40-54 years old	19.5% (301)
55-64 years old	13.5% (258)
65+ years old	15.8% (305)

PRIVATE SECTOR	
Businesses	1,034 (264)
Employees	17,724 (157)
Total wages	$723,266,966 (144)
Average weekly wages	$785 (110)

HOUSEHOLD INCOME LADDER	
95th percentile	$146,271 (209)
80th percentile	$86,992 (203)
60th percentile	$58,445 (174)
40th percentile	$40,136 (128)
20th percentile	$20,929 (190)

CHILDREN	★★ (345)
Living with two parents	71.5% (111)
Older teens in school	83.0% (276)
Speak English very well	96.8% (421)
Poverty rate for children	23.3% (252)
No health insurance	13.8% (506)

DIVERSITY/EQUALITY	★★ (393)
Racial diversity index	8.5% (525)
Geographic diversity index	38.6% (378)
Top 20% share of income	46.6% (167)
Gender gap in earnings	38.1% (396)
White-collar gender gap	20.1% (209)

EDUCATION	★★★ (223)
Eighth grade or less	4.0% (325)
High school diplomas	90.7% (173)
Attended college	50.2% (325)
Bachelor's degrees	22.3% (148)
Advanced degrees	6.7% (205)

EMPLOYMENT	★★★★ (139)
Average jobless rate	6.6% (161)
Self-employed workers	10.5% (139)
Management/financial jobs	12.8% (100)
Computer/engineering jobs	2.9% (219)
Health care jobs	5.0% (339)

GROWTH POTENTIAL	★★★★ (198)
Children per senior	1.48 (227)
Median age	38.7 (211)
Moved from different state	2.0% (288)
Homes built since 2000	16.9% (155)
Construction jobs	6.8% (204)

HOUSING	★★★★ (120)
Home vacancy rate	7.5% (186)
Home ownership rate	70.8% (239)
Housing diversity index	84.6% (277)
4 or more bedrooms	21.1% (98)
Affordability/income ratio	$2,730 (338)

INCOME	★★★★ (168)
Poverty rate	15.3% (204)
Median household income	$48,533 (159)
Interest/dividends	24.8% (105)
Public assistance	14.4% (225)
Median fulltime earnings	$37,141 (273)

SENIORS	★★★ (281)
Seniors living alone	28.0% (296)
Poverty rate for seniors	9.0% (260)
Median income for seniors	$37,121 (112)
Seniors who work	17.2% (330)
Home ownership by seniors	81.1% (325)

STABILITY	★★★ (305)
25-39 age group	15.9% (453)
Born in state of residence	77.6% (167)
Same house as 1 year ago	84.5% (325)
Live and work in county	68.5% (398)
Married-couple households	53.8% (116)

TRANSPORTATION	★ (441)
Bicycle or walk to work	5.3% (79)
Carpool to work	10.8% (249)
Public transit to work	0.3% (291)
Commute <15 minutes	35.3% (436)
Commute >45 minutes	21.2% (525)

See pages 37-130 for explanations of statistics, stars, and ranks.

Muscatine, IA
(Muscatine County, IA)

POPULATION

2010 census	42,745 (281)
2015 estimate	43,011 (280)
2010-2015 change	0.6% (209)
2020 projection	43,175 (281)
2030 projection	43,254 (284)

RACE

Whites	78.9% (333)
Blacks	1.5% (329)
Hispanics	16.9% (90)
Asians	1.3% (112)
Native Americans	0.2% (300)

AGE

0-17 years old	25.5% (90)
18-24 years old	8.4% (349)
25-39 years old	18.3% (159)
40-54 years old	19.8% (261)
55-64 years old	13.1% (318)
65+ years old	14.9% (374)

PRIVATE SECTOR

Businesses	1,113 (237)
Employees	20,483 (119)
Total wages	$973,422,815 (75)
Average weekly wages	$914 (32)

HOUSEHOLD INCOME LADDER

95th percentile	$148,802 (173)
80th percentile	$94,747 (92)
60th percentile	$65,853 (68)
40th percentile	$42,700 (70)
20th percentile	$23,982 (68)

CHILDREN ★★★★★ (106)

Living with two parents	67.3% (209)
Older teens in school	86.3% (155)
Speak English very well	97.6% (375)
Poverty rate for children	19.0% (147)
No health insurance	3.0% (59)

DIVERSITY/EQUALITY ★★★★ (218)

Racial diversity index	34.8% (215)
Geographic diversity index	48.0% (245)
Top 20% share of income	44.9% (58)
Gender gap in earnings	36.3% (350)
White-collar gender gap	36.9% (406)

EDUCATION ★★★ (287)

Eighth grade or less	5.3% (402)
High school diplomas	88.1% (263)
Attended college	55.0% (224)
Bachelor's degrees	19.7% (227)
Advanced degrees	5.1% (364)

EMPLOYMENT ★★★ (258)

Average jobless rate	4.6% (52)
Self-employed workers	6.9% (435)
Management/financial jobs	12.4% (126)
Computer/engineering jobs	4.8% (37)
Health care jobs	2.7% (542)

GROWTH POTENTIAL ★★★ (291)

Children per senior	1.71 (127)
Median age	38.2 (189)
Moved from different state	1.4% (425)
Homes built since 2000	11.7% (324)
Construction jobs	5.8% (360)

HOUSING ★★★★ (151)

Home vacancy rate	7.5% (186)
Home ownership rate	73.9% (122)
Housing diversity index	81.7% (470)
4 or more bedrooms	20.9% (103)
Affordability/income ratio	$2,364 (196)

INCOME ★★★★★ (80)

Poverty rate	12.4% (97)
Median household income	$53,676 (66)
Interest/dividends	25.1% (94)
Public assistance	11.9% (127)
Median fulltime earnings	$40,451 (122)

SENIORS ★★★★★ (38)

Seniors living alone	24.6% (100)
Poverty rate for seniors	5.3% (26)
Median income for seniors	$41,107 (51)
Seniors who work	21.5% (144)
Home ownership by seniors	85.1% (137)

STABILITY ★★★★★ (33)

25-39 age group	18.3% (159)
Born in state of residence	70.7% (299)
Same house as 1 year ago	89.9% (50)
Live and work in county	76.5% (263)
Married-couple households	55.2% (65)

TRANSPORTATION ★★★★ (202)

Bicycle or walk to work	2.5% (322)
Carpool to work	10.3% (299)
Public transit to work	0.3% (291)
Commute <15 minutes	49.2% (170)
Commute >45 minutes	6.4% (67)

See pages 37-130 for explanations of statistics, stars, and ranks.

New Castle, IN
(Henry County, IN)

POPULATION	
2010 census	49,462 (214)
2015 estimate	48,985 (218)
2010-2015 change	-1.0% (326)
2020 projection	48,639 (225)
2030 projection	47,779 (235)

RACE	
Whites	94.0% (75)
Blacks	1.7% (315)
Hispanics	1.6% (472)
Asians	0.4% (413)
Native Americans	0.3% (231)

AGE	
0-17 years old	21.2% (397)
18-24 years old	8.2% (379)
25-39 years old	17.1% (308)
40-54 years old	22.3% (19)
55-64 years old	13.6% (247)
65+ years old	17.6% (151)

PRIVATE SECTOR	
Businesses	742 (408)
Employees	10,078 (373)
Total wages	$312,968,139 (419)
Average weekly wages	$597 (493)

HOUSEHOLD INCOME LADDER	
95th percentile	$127,357 (465)
80th percentile	$80,558 (362)
60th percentile	$51,293 (350)
40th percentile	$33,559 (306)
20th percentile	$18,445 (292)

CHILDREN	★★★ (275)
Living with two parents	62.8% (323)
Older teens in school	83.0% (276)
Speak English very well	99.6% (77)
Poverty rate for children	23.5% (255)
No health insurance	8.8% (385)

DIVERSITY/EQUALITY	★★★ (322)
Racial diversity index	11.5% (473)
Geographic diversity index	35.8% (425)
Top 20% share of income	48.7% (332)
Gender gap in earnings	27.6% (130)
White-collar gender gap	12.1% (118)

EDUCATION	★★ (339)
Eighth grade or less	2.9% (217)
High school diplomas	88.7% (245)
Attended college	46.8% (400)
Bachelor's degrees	16.5% (350)
Advanced degrees	4.7% (419)

EMPLOYMENT	★★★ (291)
Average jobless rate	10.6% (446)
Self-employed workers	9.2% (231)
Management/financial jobs	11.4% (210)
Computer/engineering jobs	2.4% (336)
Health care jobs	6.3% (144)

GROWTH POTENTIAL	★ (527)
Children per senior	1.21 (411)
Median age	42.2 (412)
Moved from different state	0.8% (524)
Homes built since 2000	7.7% (475)
Construction jobs	5.3% (425)

HOUSING	★★★ (321)
Home vacancy rate	13.6% (507)
Home ownership rate	73.5% (137)
Housing diversity index	84.1% (337)
4 or more bedrooms	15.2% (344)
Affordability/income ratio	$2,189 (119)

INCOME	★★★ (278)
Poverty rate	16.3% (234)
Median household income	$41,855 (328)
Interest/dividends	16.3% (366)
Public assistance	13.6% (195)
Median fulltime earnings	$36,831 (299)

SENIORS	★★ (401)
Seniors living alone	27.3% (260)
Poverty rate for seniors	9.4% (282)
Median income for seniors	$31,780 (331)
Seniors who work	14.6% (472)
Home ownership by seniors	79.9% (377)

STABILITY	★★ (435)
25-39 age group	17.1% (308)
Born in state of residence	79.2% (125)
Same house as 1 year ago	84.9% (306)
Live and work in county	52.8% (533)
Married-couple households	50.6% (267)

TRANSPORTATION	★ (535)
Bicycle or walk to work	1.8% (409)
Carpool to work	8.4% (466)
Public transit to work	0.3% (291)
Commute <15 minutes	34.8% (442)
Commute >45 minutes	19.9% (516)

See pages 37-130 for explanations of statistics, stars, and ranks.

New Philadelphia-Dover, OH
(Tuscarawas County, OH)

POPULATION

2010 census	92,582 (40)
2015 estimate	92,916 (44)
2010-2015 change	0.4% (228)
2020 projection	93,141 (44)
2030 projection	93,216 (41)

RACE

Whites	95.2% (38)
Blacks	0.8% (404)
Hispanics	2.3% (398)
Asians	0.4% (413)
Native Americans	0.3% (231)

AGE

0-17 years old	23.1% (256)
18-24 years old	7.8% (447)
25-39 years old	17.9% (214)
40-54 years old	19.5% (301)
55-64 years old	14.4% (136)
65+ years old	17.4% (165)

PRIVATE SECTOR

Businesses	2,113 (54)
Employees	31,632 (33)
Total wages	$1,160,974,523 (49)
Average weekly wages	$706 (240)

HOUSEHOLD INCOME LADDER

95th percentile	$137,559 (315)
80th percentile	$84,386 (265)
60th percentile	$55,331 (239)
40th percentile	$36,898 (205)
20th percentile	$19,835 (235)

CHILDREN ★★★ (232)

Living with two parents	71.9% (107)
Older teens in school	82.7% (289)
Speak English very well	96.3% (442)
Poverty rate for children	20.8% (187)
No health insurance	7.7% (352)

DIVERSITY/EQUALITY ★ (547)

Racial diversity index	9.3% (509)
Geographic diversity index	25.4% (521)
Top 20% share of income	46.7% (179)
Gender gap in earnings	41.4% (464)
White-collar gender gap	53.1% (523)

EDUCATION ★★ (389)

Eighth grade or less	4.4% (346)
High school diplomas	87.8% (274)
Attended college	43.6% (459)
Bachelor's degrees	16.0% (372)
Advanced degrees	4.8% (405)

EMPLOYMENT ★★★ (315)

Average jobless rate	7.0% (196)
Self-employed workers	6.5% (474)
Management/financial jobs	9.0% (475)
Computer/engineering jobs	2.9% (219)
Health care jobs	6.7% (104)

GROWTH POTENTIAL ★ (456)

Children per senior	1.33 (325)
Median age	41.0 (357)
Moved from different state	1.1% (487)
Homes built since 2000	11.5% (333)
Construction jobs	5.5% (404)

HOUSING ★★★★ (162)

Home vacancy rate	5.5% (60)
Home ownership rate	70.3% (256)
Housing diversity index	83.9% (360)
4 or more bedrooms	15.8% (307)
Affordability/income ratio	$2,452 (226)

INCOME ★★★★ (202)

Poverty rate	14.0% (155)
Median household income	$45,310 (228)
Interest/dividends	21.1% (210)
Public assistance	14.0% (207)
Median fulltime earnings	$37,512 (246)

SENIORS ★★★ (289)

Seniors living alone	27.8% (283)
Poverty rate for seniors	7.7% (156)
Median income for seniors	$32,860 (290)
Seniors who work	17.7% (302)
Home ownership by seniors	81.3% (316)

STABILITY ★★★★★ (37)

25-39 age group	17.9% (214)
Born in state of residence	86.1% (26)
Same house as 1 year ago	88.3% (115)
Live and work in county	71.0% (355)
Married-couple households	54.0% (108)

TRANSPORTATION ★★ (368)

Bicycle or walk to work	2.7% (292)
Carpool to work	9.5% (388)
Public transit to work	0.3% (291)
Commute <15 minutes	39.1% (348)
Commute >45 minutes	10.7% (262)

See pages 37-130 for explanations of statistics, stars, and ranks.

Newton, IA
(Jasper County, IA)

POPULATION

2010 census	36,842 (361)
2015 estimate	36,827 (360)
2010-2015 change	0.0% (255)
2020 projection	36,585 (363)
2030 projection	35,896 (363)

RACE

Whites	94.9% (51)
Blacks	1.5% (329)
Hispanics	1.7% (464)
Asians	0.6% (291)
Native Americans	0.2% (300)

AGE

0-17 years old	22.2% (320)
18-24 years old	7.6% (468)
25-39 years old	17.4% (269)
40-54 years old	21.4% (67)
55-64 years old	13.7% (225)
65+ years old	17.7% (142)

PRIVATE SECTOR

Businesses	833 (356)
Employees	8,875 (416)
Total wages	$302,993,336 (431)
Average weekly wages	$657 (373)

HOUSEHOLD INCOME LADDER

95th percentile	$142,227 (262)
80th percentile	$94,046 (100)
60th percentile	$66,711 (58)
40th percentile	$43,516 (66)
20th percentile	$25,107 (49)

CHILDREN ★★★★★ (23)

Living with two parents	72.3% (101)
Older teens in school	87.1% (133)
Speak English very well	99.9% (19)
Poverty rate for children	11.1% (22)
No health insurance	2.4% (28)

DIVERSITY/EQUALITY ★★★★ (209)

Racial diversity index	9.9% (496)
Geographic diversity index	31.6% (469)
Top 20% share of income	44.3% (34)
Gender gap in earnings	34.3% (296)
White-collar gender gap	3.3% (20)

EDUCATION ★★★★ (169)

Eighth grade or less	0.8% (10)
High school diplomas	95.5% (18)
Attended college	58.4% (161)
Bachelor's degrees	20.0% (222)
Advanced degrees	3.1% (524)

EMPLOYMENT ★★★★ (111)

Average jobless rate	5.4% (89)
Self-employed workers	10.1% (158)
Management/financial jobs	13.4% (67)
Computer/engineering jobs	4.6% (48)
Health care jobs	3.7% (503)

GROWTH POTENTIAL ★ (451)

Children per senior	1.26 (378)
Median age	42.2 (412)
Moved from different state	1.4% (425)
Homes built since 2000	10.7% (370)
Construction jobs	6.2% (295)

HOUSING ★★★★ (145)

Home vacancy rate	9.4% (309)
Home ownership rate	73.0% (151)
Housing diversity index	84.0% (344)
4 or more bedrooms	19.0% (159)
Affordability/income ratio	$2,139 (97)

INCOME ★★★★★ (72)

Poverty rate	9.6% (23)
Median household income	$55,033 (53)
Interest/dividends	25.5% (82)
Public assistance	14.4% (225)
Median fulltime earnings	$41,004 (97)

SENIORS ★★★★★ (88)

Seniors living alone	25.9% (164)
Poverty rate for seniors	7.1% (101)
Median income for seniors	$38,987 (74)
Seniors who work	23.1% (107)
Home ownership by seniors	82.3% (261)

STABILITY ★★★ (304)

25-39 age group	17.4% (269)
Born in state of residence	82.1% (81)
Same house as 1 year ago	84.2% (341)
Live and work in county	56.1% (515)
Married-couple households	54.3% (99)

TRANSPORTATION ★★ (364)

Bicycle or walk to work	2.3% (348)
Carpool to work	11.4% (190)
Public transit to work	0.6% (141)
Commute <15 minutes	38.9% (353)
Commute >45 minutes	14.2% (395)

See pages 37-130 for explanations of statistics, stars, and ranks.

New Ulm, MN
(Brown County, MN)

POPULATION

2010 census	25,893 (474)
2015 estimate	25,313 (482)
2010-2015 change	-2.2% (427)
2020 projection	24,765 (483)
2030 projection	23,716 (484)

RACE

Whites	94.5% (61)
Blacks	0.4% (499)
Hispanics	3.7% (311)
Asians	0.5% (355)
Native Americans	0.1% (402)

AGE

0-17 years old	21.6% (366)
18-24 years old	9.7% (183)
25-39 years old	15.4% (490)
40-54 years old	19.4% (315)
55-64 years old	14.3% (148)
65+ years old	19.7% (59)

PRIVATE SECTOR

Businesses	749 (401)
Employees	12,136 (306)
Total wages	$467,176,093 (278)
Average weekly wages	$740 (178)

HOUSEHOLD INCOME LADDER

95th percentile	$165,380 (72)
80th percentile	$91,759 (130)
60th percentile	$64,423 (80)
40th percentile	$41,625 (87)
20th percentile	$23,179 (91)

CHILDREN   ★★★★★ **(21)**

Living with two parents	72.8% (83)
Older teens in school	90.5% (59)
Speak English very well	98.5% (287)
Poverty rate for children	8.1% (5)
No health insurance	4.3% (140)

DIVERSITY/EQUALITY   ★ **(523)**

Racial diversity index	10.6% (485)
Geographic diversity index	32.3% (460)
Top 20% share of income	46.2% (132)
Gender gap in earnings	39.8% (431)
White-collar gender gap	45.7% (484)

EDUCATION   ★★★★★ **(85)**

Eighth grade or less	1.1% (26)
High school diplomas	95.5% (18)

Attended college	62.0% (93)
Bachelor's degrees	25.0% (108)
Advanced degrees	6.7% (205)

EMPLOYMENT   ★★★★★ **(43)**

Average jobless rate	3.2% (14)
Self-employed workers	14.6% (22)
Management/financial jobs	13.2% (73)
Computer/engineering jobs	2.7% (270)
Health care jobs	5.0% (339)

GROWTH POTENTIAL   ★ **(476)**

Children per senior	1.10 (464)
Median age	43.5 (464)
Moved from different state	2.2% (248)
Homes built since 2000	7.7% (475)
Construction jobs	6.7% (219)

HOUSING   ★★★★★ **(18)**

Home vacancy rate	6.5% (130)
Home ownership rate	77.7% (19)
Housing diversity index	82.5% (441)
4 or more bedrooms	28.0% (21)
Affordability/income ratio	$2,386 (207)

INCOME   ★★★★★ **(39)**

Poverty rate	7.8% (8)
Median household income	$52,598 (78)
Interest/dividends	30.0% (25)
Public assistance	8.1% (34)
Median fulltime earnings	$39,671 (151)

SENIORS   ★★★ **(320)**

Seniors living alone	30.1% (433)
Poverty rate for seniors	8.6% (234)
Median income for seniors	$34,713 (201)
Seniors who work	21.0% (160)
Home ownership by seniors	79.5% (394)

STABILITY   ★★★★★ **(55)**

25-39 age group	15.4% (490)
Born in state of residence	81.5% (93)
Same house as 1 year ago	89.6% (57)
Live and work in county	85.6% (125)
Married-couple households	52.5% (171)

TRANSPORTATION   ★★★★★ **(55)**

Bicycle or walk to work	6.4% (52)
Carpool to work	8.2% (480)
Public transit to work	0.6% (141)
Commute <15 minutes	63.9% (26)
Commute >45 minutes	4.7% (26)

See pages 37-130 for explanations of statistics, stars, and ranks.

Norfolk, NE
(Madison, Pierce, and Stanton Counties, NE)

POPULATION

2010 census	48,271 (220)
2015 estimate	48,184 (225)
2010-2015 change	-0.2% (273)
2020 projection	47,595 (233)
2030 projection	46,338 (254)

RACE

Whites	85.4% (262)
Blacks	0.8% (404)
Hispanics	11.0% (138)
Asians	0.6% (291)
Native Americans	0.9% (115)

AGE

0-17 years old	25.0% (126)
18-24 years old	9.2% (234)
25-39 years old	17.4% (269)
40-54 years old	19.6% (289)
55-64 years old	12.9% (343)
65+ years old	15.8% (305)

PRIVATE SECTOR

Businesses	1,772 (90)
Employees	20,607 (118)
Total wages	$775,128,012 (124)
Average weekly wages	$723 (211)

HOUSEHOLD INCOME LADDER

95th percentile	$150,197 (158)
80th percentile	$92,677 (119)
60th percentile	$61,896 (113)
40th percentile	$41,389 (93)
20th percentile	$22,650 (112)

CHILDREN ★★★★ (129)

Living with two parents	69.4% (156)
Older teens in school	86.8% (139)
Speak English very well	97.9% (352)
Poverty rate for children	18.2% (128)
No health insurance	6.2% (262)

DIVERSITY/EQUALITY ★★ (427)

Racial diversity index	25.8% (286)
Geographic diversity index	43.6% (301)
Top 20% share of income	46.7% (176)
Gender gap in earnings	37.5% (375)
White-collar gender gap	47.0% (493)

EDUCATION ★★★★ (135)

Eighth grade or less	3.4% (269)
High school diplomas	92.1% (122)

Attended college	64.0% (72)
Bachelor's degrees	22.6% (142)
Advanced degrees	6.6% (211)

EMPLOYMENT ★★★★★ (46)

Average jobless rate	3.3% (16)
Self-employed workers	12.7% (54)
Management/financial jobs	11.9% (165)
Computer/engineering jobs	2.4% (336)
Health care jobs	6.9% (79)

GROWTH POTENTIAL ★★★ (257)

Children per senior	1.59 (175)
Median age	38.3 (197)
Moved from different state	2.2% (248)
Homes built since 2000	9.9% (389)
Construction jobs	6.7% (219)

HOUSING ★★★★★ (38)

Home vacancy rate	5.9% (88)
Home ownership rate	69.1% (298)
Housing diversity index	84.6% (277)
4 or more bedrooms	25.5% (38)
Affordability/income ratio	$2,196 (123)

INCOME ★★★★★ (110)

Poverty rate	13.2% (123)
Median household income	$51,361 (94)
Interest/dividends	24.1% (127)
Public assistance	9.9% (59)
Median fulltime earnings	$37,274 (262)

SENIORS ★★★★ (143)

Seniors living alone	26.0% (172)
Poverty rate for seniors	9.1% (263)
Median income for seniors	$35,827 (160)
Seniors who work	25.6% (57)
Home ownership by seniors	79.6% (388)

STABILITY ★★★★ (150)

25-39 age group	17.4% (269)
Born in state of residence	73.9% (247)
Same house as 1 year ago	85.9% (257)
Live and work in county	74.0% (310)
Married-couple households	54.1% (105)

TRANSPORTATION ★★★★ (120)

Bicycle or walk to work	2.8% (279)
Carpool to work	10.9% (239)
Public transit to work	0.2% (363)
Commute <15 minutes	58.1% (62)
Commute >45 minutes	5.7% (48)

See pages 37-130 for explanations of statistics, stars, and ranks.

North Platte, NE
(Lincoln, Logan, and McPherson Counties, NE)

POPULATION

2010 census	37,590 (346)
2015 estimate	36,908 (358)
2010-2015 change	-1.8% (389)
2020 projection	36,613 (362)
2030 projection	35,948 (361)

RACE

Whites	89.2% (199)
Blacks	0.8% (404)
Hispanics	7.8% (186)
Asians	0.5% (355)
Native Americans	0.2% (300)

AGE

0-17 years old	24.5% (149)
18-24 years old	7.4% (489)
25-39 years old	17.7% (236)
40-54 years old	19.2% (336)
55-64 years old	14.3% (148)
65+ years old	16.9% (207)

PRIVATE SECTOR

Businesses	1,286 (180)
Employees	11,993 (309)
Total wages	$411,982,402 (324)
Average weekly wages	$661 (360)

HOUSEHOLD INCOME LADDER

95th percentile	$145,475 (222)
80th percentile	$93,129 (114)
60th percentile	$60,112 (148)
40th percentile	$40,835 (103)
20th percentile	$21,396 (169)

CHILDREN ★★★★★ (46)

Living with two parents	72.8% (83)
Older teens in school	89.6% (72)
Speak English very well	100.0% (1)
Poverty rate for children	18.2% (128)
No health insurance	5.0% (181)

DIVERSITY/EQUALITY ★ (525)

Racial diversity index	19.8% (350)
Geographic diversity index	47.7% (249)
Top 20% share of income	47.0% (213)
Gender gap in earnings	52.7% (535)
White-collar gender gap	46.0% (489)

EDUCATION ★★★★ (141)

Eighth grade or less	3.0% (231)
High school diplomas	92.6% (107)

Attended college	64.6% (66)
Bachelor's degrees	21.5% (174)
Advanced degrees	5.8% (283)

EMPLOYMENT ★★★★ (178)

Average jobless rate	4.1% (35)
Self-employed workers	9.9% (171)
Management/financial jobs	11.0% (252)
Computer/engineering jobs	1.7% (470)
Health care jobs	5.5% (250)

GROWTH POTENTIAL ★★ (433)

Children per senior	1.45 (244)
Median age	40.2 (317)
Moved from different state	2.6% (187)
Homes built since 2000	8.7% (445)
Construction jobs	4.8% (480)

HOUSING ★★★★ (170)

Home vacancy rate	7.2% (172)
Home ownership rate	66.5% (405)
Housing diversity index	84.2% (325)
4 or more bedrooms	19.2% (150)
Affordability/income ratio	$2,277 (152)

INCOME ★★★★ (116)

Poverty rate	12.8% (109)
Median household income	$50,196 (121)
Interest/dividends	19.7% (259)
Public assistance	12.0% (132)
Median fulltime earnings	$42,395 (56)

SENIORS ★★ (426)

Seniors living alone	33.5% (535)
Poverty rate for seniors	8.7% (241)
Median income for seniors	$31,174 (365)
Seniors who work	23.8% (92)
Home ownership by seniors	77.5% (471)

STABILITY ★★★★★ (48)

25-39 age group	17.7% (236)
Born in state of residence	70.5% (301)
Same house as 1 year ago	87.3% (181)
Live and work in county	94.4% (17)
Married-couple households	50.5% (271)

TRANSPORTATION ★★★★ (114)

Bicycle or walk to work	3.1% (232)
Carpool to work	9.3% (401)
Public transit to work	0.3% (291)
Commute <15 minutes	60.3% (45)
Commute >45 minutes	4.2% (17)

See pages 37-130 for explanations of statistics, stars, and ranks.

North Vernon, IN
(Jennings County, IN)

POPULATION

2010 census	28,525 (450)
2015 estimate	27,897 (455)
2010-2015 change	-2.2% (427)
2020 projection	27,446 (455)
2030 projection	26,483 (461)

RACE

Whites	95.5% (29)
Blacks	1.4% (340)
Hispanics	2.3% (398)
Asians	0.2% (509)
Native Americans	0.1% (402)

AGE

0-17 years old	24.8% (135)
18-24 years old	8.7% (299)
25-39 years old	17.3% (280)
40-54 years old	21.9% (38)
55-64 years old	12.8% (356)
65+ years old	14.4% (419)

PRIVATE SECTOR

Businesses	353 (540)
Employees	6,006 (508)
Total wages	$216,206,532 (499)
Average weekly wages	$692 (277)

HOUSEHOLD INCOME LADDER

95th percentile	$122,339 (498)
80th percentile	$80,589 (361)
60th percentile	$54,543 (262)
40th percentile	$37,411 (194)
20th percentile	$19,250 (255)

CHILDREN ★★★ (250)

Living with two parents	63.9% (301)
Older teens in school	80.4% (386)
Speak English very well	99.7% (57)
Poverty rate for children	22.5% (235)
No health insurance	6.8% (302)

DIVERSITY/EQUALITY ★★★★ (172)

Racial diversity index	8.7% (521)
Geographic diversity index	35.8% (425)
Top 20% share of income	44.8% (53)
Gender gap in earnings	30.4% (178)
White-collar gender gap	2.5% (17)

EDUCATION ★ (455)

Eighth grade or less	3.6% (292)
High school diplomas	86.6% (322)
Attended college	39.8% (519)
Bachelor's degrees	11.3% (529)
Advanced degrees	3.4% (514)

EMPLOYMENT ★ (509)

Average jobless rate	9.7% (409)
Self-employed workers	5.4% (535)
Management/financial jobs	11.0% (252)
Computer/engineering jobs	1.6% (486)
Health care jobs	4.2% (454)

GROWTH POTENTIAL ★★★★ (213)

Children per senior	1.72 (122)
Median age	39.4 (262)
Moved from different state	1.8% (338)
Homes built since 2000	12.1% (310)
Construction jobs	7.4% (134)

HOUSING ★★★★ (116)

Home vacancy rate	8.5% (253)
Home ownership rate	75.8% (60)
Housing diversity index	84.9% (235)
4 or more bedrooms	15.4% (329)
Affordability/income ratio	$2,133 (95)

INCOME ★★★ (289)

Poverty rate	15.9% (219)
Median household income	$44,736 (240)
Interest/dividends	15.6% (390)
Public assistance	15.7% (280)
Median fulltime earnings	$36,710 (307)

SENIORS ★★★ (251)

Seniors living alone	29.2% (381)
Poverty rate for seniors	8.9% (254)
Median income for seniors	$33,901 (240)
Seniors who work	15.8% (423)
Home ownership by seniors	87.2% (63)

STABILITY ★★ (426)

25-39 age group	17.3% (280)
Born in state of residence	79.2% (125)
Same house as 1 year ago	86.2% (237)
Live and work in county	47.8% (541)
Married-couple households	51.4% (231)

TRANSPORTATION ★ (511)

Bicycle or walk to work	1.4% (472)
Carpool to work	9.7% (369)
Public transit to work	0.6% (141)
Commute <15 minutes	28.3% (534)
Commute >45 minutes	14.9% (420)

See pages 37-130 for explanations of statistics, stars, and ranks.

Norwalk, OH
(Huron County, OH)

POPULATION	
2010 census	59,626 (154)
2015 estimate	58,469 (156)
2010-2015 change	-1.9% (399)
2020 projection	57,494 (163)
2030 projection	55,355 (180)

RACE	
Whites	90.9% (164)
Blacks	1.1% (367)
Hispanics	6.0% (222)
Asians	0.3% (473)
Native Americans	0.1% (402)

AGE	
0-17 years old	25.1% (116)
18-24 years old	8.1% (396)
25-39 years old	18.2% (167)
40-54 years old	20.1% (221)
55-64 years old	13.6% (247)
65+ years old	14.9% (374)

PRIVATE SECTOR	
Businesses	1,127 (230)
Employees	17,836 (155)
Total wages	$698,732,542 (150)
Average weekly wages	$753 (155)

HOUSEHOLD INCOME LADDER	
95th percentile	$136,904 (329)
80th percentile	$86,708 (217)
60th percentile	$59,996 (151)
40th percentile	$39,507 (141)
20th percentile	$22,060 (137)

CHILDREN	★★★★ (165)
Living with two parents	67.0% (217)
Older teens in school	86.3% (155)
Speak English very well	97.5% (388)
Poverty rate for children	19.8% (162)
No health insurance	6.2% (262)

DIVERSITY/EQUALITY	★★ (358)
Racial diversity index	17.0% (385)
Geographic diversity index	31.2% (474)
Top 20% share of income	44.6% (47)
Gender gap in earnings	39.9% (435)
White-collar gender gap	22.6% (242)

EDUCATION	★★ (372)
Eighth grade or less	3.9% (316)
High school diplomas	90.6% (178)
Attended college	43.6% (459)
Bachelor's degrees	14.2% (454)
Advanced degrees	4.8% (405)

EMPLOYMENT	★★ (411)
Average jobless rate	7.2% (218)
Self-employed workers	7.4% (393)
Management/financial jobs	9.1% (463)
Computer/engineering jobs	2.2% (381)
Health care jobs	5.3% (286)

GROWTH POTENTIAL	★★★ (225)
Children per senior	1.69 (137)
Median age	38.8 (217)
Moved from different state	1.1% (487)
Homes built since 2000	9.3% (420)
Construction jobs	8.3% (67)

HOUSING	★★★★ (176)
Home vacancy rate	9.1% (296)
Home ownership rate	70.7% (244)
Housing diversity index	83.4% (396)
4 or more bedrooms	20.6% (114)
Affordability/income ratio	$2,382 (204)

INCOME	★★★★ (203)
Poverty rate	13.5% (137)
Median household income	$48,745 (152)
Interest/dividends	19.5% (264)
Public assistance	17.1% (338)
Median fulltime earnings	$39,169 (173)

SENIORS	★★★ (326)
Seniors living alone	27.1% (247)
Poverty rate for seniors	8.0% (177)
Median income for seniors	$34,119 (229)
Seniors who work	14.2% (496)
Home ownership by seniors	81.2% (322)

STABILITY	★★★★ (207)
25-39 age group	18.2% (167)
Born in state of residence	82.5% (75)
Same house as 1 year ago	86.4% (225)
Live and work in county	58.3% (501)
Married-couple households	52.9% (157)

TRANSPORTATION	★★★ (317)
Bicycle or walk to work	3.7% (173)
Carpool to work	9.7% (369)
Public transit to work	0.8% (96)
Commute <15 minutes	40.3% (324)
Commute >45 minutes	12.2% (321)

See pages 37-130 for explanations of statistics, stars, and ranks.

Oskaloosa, IA
(Mahaska County, IA)

POPULATION			
2010 census	22,381 (503)	Attended college	59.7% (134)
2015 estimate	22,324 (505)	Bachelor's degrees	24.9% (111)
2010-2015 change	-0.3% (279)	Advanced degrees	6.1% (250)
2020 projection	22,198 (507)	**EMPLOYMENT**	★★★★ (161)
2030 projection	21,819 (506)	Average jobless rate	8.0% (291)
		Self-employed workers	9.9% (171)
RACE		Management/financial jobs	13.4% (67)
Whites	94.4% (66)	Computer/engineering jobs	3.7% (103)
Blacks	1.3% (351)	Health care jobs	4.5% (419)
Hispanics	1.9% (442)		
Asians	1.2% (125)	**GROWTH POTENTIAL**	★★★ (294)
Native Americans	0.1% (402)	Children per senior	1.41 (269)
		Median age	39.8 (285)
AGE		Moved from different state	2.8% (171)
0-17 years old	23.9% (194)	Homes built since 2000	9.0% (434)
18-24 years old	9.3% (217)	Construction jobs	6.9% (198)
25-39 years old	17.0% (317)		
40-54 years old	19.5% (301)	**HOUSING**	★★★★ (137)
55-64 years old	13.4% (274)	Home vacancy rate	6.8% (151)
65+ years old	16.9% (207)	Home ownership rate	70.3% (256)
		Housing diversity index	82.5% (441)
PRIVATE SECTOR		4 or more bedrooms	21.0% (100)
Businesses	588 (480)	Affordability/income ratio	$2,180 (113)
Employees	6,518 (492)		
Total wages	$225,178,340 (488)	**INCOME**	★★★★ (137)
Average weekly wages	$664 (344)	Poverty rate	14.7% (182)
		Median household income	$48,726 (154)
HOUSEHOLD INCOME LADDER		Interest/dividends	24.8% (105)
95th percentile	$143,731 (245)	Public assistance	16.2% (301)
80th percentile	$87,133 (202)	Median fulltime earnings	$41,874 (66)
60th percentile	$57,498 (196)		
40th percentile	$38,390 (172)	**SENIORS**	★★ (384)
20th percentile	$19,865 (233)	Seniors living alone	29.6% (413)
		Poverty rate for seniors	11.8% (401)
CHILDREN	★★★★★ (40)	Median income for seniors	$33,386 (264)
Living with two parents	70.4% (135)	Seniors who work	26.2% (46)
Older teens in school	87.4% (116)	Home ownership by seniors	74.9% (526)
Speak English very well	99.1% (179)		
Poverty rate for children	17.4% (109)	**STABILITY**	★★★ (322)
No health insurance	0.8% (1)	25-39 age group	17.0% (317)
		Born in state of residence	80.0% (115)
DIVERSITY/EQUALITY	★ (548)	Same house as 1 year ago	84.9% (306)
Racial diversity index	10.8% (482)	Live and work in county	62.7% (467)
Geographic diversity index	34.8% (438)	Married-couple households	51.5% (226)
Top 20% share of income	47.9% (284)		
Gender gap in earnings	44.6% (496)	**TRANSPORTATION**	★★★★ (113)
White-collar gender gap	55.8% (531)	Bicycle or walk to work	5.3% (79)
		Carpool to work	11.4% (190)
EDUCATION	★★★★ (114)	Public transit to work	0.8% (96)
Eighth grade or less	1.3% (52)	Commute <15 minutes	47.3% (204)
High school diplomas	94.0% (57)	Commute >45 minutes	8.0% (131)

See pages 37-130 for explanations of statistics, stars, and ranks.

Ottawa, KS
(Franklin County, KS)

POPULATION

2010 census	25,992 (473)
2015 estimate	25,609 (478)
2010-2015 change	-1.5% (373)
2020 projection	25,350 (476)
2030 projection	24,777 (474)

RACE

Whites	91.2% (159)
Blacks	1.2% (361)
Hispanics	3.9% (302)
Asians	0.2% (509)
Native Americans	0.4% (203)

AGE

0-17 years old	25.0% (126)
18-24 years old	9.1% (251)
25-39 years old	17.0% (317)
40-54 years old	20.5% (151)
55-64 years old	13.2% (297)
65+ years old	15.3% (348)

PRIVATE SECTOR

Businesses	587 (481)
Employees	7,329 (460)
Total wages	$264,130,661 (462)
Average weekly wages	$693 (274)

HOUSEHOLD INCOME LADDER

95th percentile	$151,773 (143)
80th percentile	$89,271 (167)
60th percentile	$62,484 (100)
40th percentile	$41,969 (77)
20th percentile	$24,280 (60)

CHILDREN ★★★★★ (69)

Living with two parents	73.1% (79)
Older teens in school	87.1% (133)
Speak English very well	99.3% (142)
Poverty rate for children	19.6% (155)
No health insurance	5.1% (188)

DIVERSITY/EQUALITY ★★ (388)

Racial diversity index	16.6% (387)
Geographic diversity index	48.6% (235)
Top 20% share of income	45.3% (73)
Gender gap in earnings	37.1% (366)
White-collar gender gap	45.5% (483)

EDUCATION ★★★★ (115)

Eighth grade or less	1.0% (20)
High school diplomas	94.0% (57)
Attended college	61.5% (105)
Bachelor's degrees	21.7% (169)
Advanced degrees	6.5% (220)

EMPLOYMENT ★★★ (324)

Average jobless rate	6.9% (185)
Self-employed workers	7.0% (428)
Management/financial jobs	10.1% (365)
Computer/engineering jobs	3.6% (112)
Health care jobs	5.1% (319)

GROWTH POTENTIAL ★★★★ (146)

Children per senior	1.63 (158)
Median age	39.0 (238)
Moved from different state	3.0% (157)
Homes built since 2000	13.2% (271)
Construction jobs	8.0% (89)

HOUSING ★★★★ (203)

Home vacancy rate	10.1% (352)
Home ownership rate	71.8% (196)
Housing diversity index	84.9% (235)
4 or more bedrooms	17.1% (239)
Affordability/income ratio	$2,406 (216)

INCOME ★★★★ (165)

Poverty rate	13.1% (119)
Median household income	$51,081 (98)
Interest/dividends	17.6% (325)
Public assistance	13.7% (197)
Median fulltime earnings	$39,779 (148)

SENIORS ★★★★ (128)

Seniors living alone	25.4% (132)
Poverty rate for seniors	7.1% (101)
Median income for seniors	$34,240 (223)
Seniors who work	27.0% (37)
Home ownership by seniors	77.6% (466)

STABILITY ★★★ (231)

25-39 age group	17.0% (317)
Born in state of residence	69.6% (317)
Same house as 1 year ago	86.2% (237)
Live and work in county	60.9% (484)
Married-couple households	58.5% (16)

TRANSPORTATION ★★ (418)

Bicycle or walk to work	3.5% (189)
Carpool to work	10.5% (280)
Public transit to work	0.6% (141)
Commute <15 minutes	40.0% (329)
Commute >45 minutes	18.9% (509)

See pages 37-130 for explanations of statistics, stars, and ranks.

Ottawa-Peru, IL
(Bureau, LaSalle, and Putnam Counties, IL)

POPULATION		ATTENDED COLLEGE	
Attended college		55.1% (221)	

POPULATION	
2010 census	154,908 (4)
2015 estimate	150,564 (4)
2010-2015 change	-2.8% (467)
2020 projection	147,385 (6)
2030 projection	140,870 (9)

RACE	
Whites	87.6% (230)
Blacks	1.9% (295)
Hispanics	8.5% (173)
Asians	0.7% (241)
Native Americans	0.1% (402)

AGE	
0-17 years old	22.2% (320)
18-24 years old	8.2% (379)
25-39 years old	17.0% (317)
40-54 years old	20.7% (132)
55-64 years old	14.1% (174)
65+ years old	17.7% (142)

PRIVATE SECTOR	
Businesses	3,574 (12)
Employees	47,391 (7)
Total wages	$1,986,809,202 (8)
Average weekly wages	$806 (83)

HOUSEHOLD INCOME LADDER	
95th percentile	$153,375 (127)
80th percentile	$96,126 (82)
60th percentile	$62,457 (101)
40th percentile	$40,107 (129)
20th percentile	$21,509 (162)

CHILDREN	★★★★ (162)
Living with two parents	66.9% (220)
Older teens in school	83.2% (268)
Speak English very well	98.0% (341)
Poverty rate for children	20.4% (176)
No health insurance	4.1% (126)

DIVERSITY/EQUALITY	★ (507)
Racial diversity index	22.5% (317)
Geographic diversity index	30.0% (487)
Top 20% share of income	46.4% (148)
Gender gap in earnings	43.8% (490)
White-collar gender gap	39.4% (440)

EDUCATION	★★★ (231)
Eighth grade or less	2.5% (180)
High school diplomas	90.5% (186)
Attended college	55.1% (221)
Bachelor's degrees	17.5% (307)
Advanced degrees	5.5% (318)

EMPLOYMENT	★★ (371)
Average jobless rate	9.3% (387)
Self-employed workers	7.5% (385)
Management/financial jobs	10.3% (339)
Computer/engineering jobs	2.5% (307)
Health care jobs	6.0% (181)

GROWTH POTENTIAL	★ (479)
Children per senior	1.25 (385)
Median age	42.2 (412)
Moved from different state	1.2% (474)
Homes built since 2000	9.3% (420)
Construction jobs	6.0% (326)

HOUSING	★★★★ (190)
Home vacancy rate	9.7% (334)
Home ownership rate	73.9% (122)
Housing diversity index	83.2% (405)
4 or more bedrooms	18.4% (183)
Affordability/income ratio	$2,329 (180)

INCOME	★★★★★ (102)
Poverty rate	13.0% (114)
Median household income	$50,717 (106)
Interest/dividends	24.3% (122)
Public assistance	13.0% (169)
Median fulltime earnings	$41,423 (81)

SENIORS	★★★★ (178)
Seniors living alone	28.1% (306)
Poverty rate for seniors	6.8% (77)
Median income for seniors	$35,937 (156)
Seniors who work	19.8% (206)
Home ownership by seniors	82.8% (232)

STABILITY	★★★★ (153)
25-39 age group	17.0% (317)
Born in state of residence	83.3% (65)
Same house as 1 year ago	89.2% (72)
Live and work in county	66.9% (419)
Married-couple households	50.8% (256)

TRANSPORTATION	★★ (378)
Bicycle or walk to work	2.8% (279)
Carpool to work	9.6% (378)
Public transit to work	0.4% (219)
Commute <15 minutes	42.9% (280)
Commute >45 minutes	13.8% (382)

See pages 37-130 for explanations of statistics, stars, and ranks.

Ottumwa, IA
(Davis and Wapello Counties, IA)

POPULATION	
2010 census	44,378 (268)
2015 estimate	43,942 (274)
2010-2015 change	-1.0% (326)
2020 projection	43,539 (279)
2030 projection	42,501 (292)

RACE	
Whites	87.9% (222)
Blacks	1.7% (315)
Hispanics	8.2% (177)
Asians	0.8% (201)
Native Americans	0.1% (402)

AGE	
0-17 years old	23.8% (206)
18-24 years old	9.0% (265)
25-39 years old	17.8% (227)
40-54 years old	18.9% (376)
55-64 years old	13.8% (203)
65+ years old	16.7% (225)

PRIVATE SECTOR	
Businesses	1,041 (261)
Employees	14,922 (212)
Total wages	$558,993,753 (208)
Average weekly wages	$720 (217)

HOUSEHOLD INCOME LADDER	
95th percentile	$137,412 (316)
80th percentile	$82,601 (301)
60th percentile	$54,882 (252)
40th percentile	$33,773 (296)
20th percentile	$18,380 (296)

CHILDREN	★ (510)
Living with two parents	67.4% (208)
Older teens in school	68.6% (537)
Speak English very well	93.7% (499)
Poverty rate for children	26.7% (344)
No health insurance	12.1% (473)

DIVERSITY/EQUALITY	★★ (339)
Racial diversity index	22.0% (324)
Geographic diversity index	43.0% (310)
Top 20% share of income	47.8% (278)
Gender gap in earnings	32.0% (227)
White-collar gender gap	30.6% (347)

EDUCATION	★★ (332)
Eighth grade or less	6.3% (439)
High school diplomas	87.5% (286)
Attended college	53.9% (247)
Bachelor's degrees	17.7% (295)
Advanced degrees	5.6% (304)

EMPLOYMENT	★★ (344)
Average jobless rate	7.3% (228)
Self-employed workers	8.8% (273)
Management/financial jobs	11.1% (240)
Computer/engineering jobs	1.6% (486)
Health care jobs	5.1% (319)

GROWTH POTENTIAL	★★★ (303)
Children per senior	1.43 (261)
Median age	39.5 (270)
Moved from different state	2.2% (248)
Homes built since 2000	6.8% (508)
Construction jobs	7.6% (110)

HOUSING	★★★ (229)
Home vacancy rate	7.9% (213)
Home ownership rate	74.3% (105)
Housing diversity index	81.3% (484)
4 or more bedrooms	15.1% (347)
Affordability/income ratio	$1,926 (35)

INCOME	★★★ (313)
Poverty rate	18.8% (329)
Median household income	$43,138 (287)
Interest/dividends	19.9% (247)
Public assistance	19.0% (399)
Median fulltime earnings	$37,359 (257)

SENIORS	★★ (423)
Seniors living alone	31.7% (504)
Poverty rate for seniors	10.6% (350)
Median income for seniors	$29,590 (419)
Seniors who work	19.8% (206)
Home ownership by seniors	81.8% (286)

STABILITY	★★★★ (131)
25-39 age group	17.8% (227)
Born in state of residence	74.4% (235)
Same house as 1 year ago	85.8% (264)
Live and work in county	79.4% (224)
Married-couple households	51.4% (231)

TRANSPORTATION	★★★★ (143)
Bicycle or walk to work	3.1% (232)
Carpool to work	12.5% (121)
Public transit to work	0.5% (178)
Commute <15 minutes	49.3% (166)
Commute >45 minutes	7.9% (126)

See pages 37-130 for explanations of statistics, stars, and ranks.

Owatonna, MN
(Steele County, MN)

POPULATION	
2010 census	36,576 (367)
2015 estimate	36,755 (362)
2010-2015 change	0.5% (219)
2020 projection	37,235 (356)
2030 projection	38,219 (337)

RACE	
Whites	87.9% (222)
Blacks	2.5% (253)
Hispanics	7.1% (197)
Asians	0.9% (178)
Native Americans	0.1% (402)

AGE	
0-17 years old	25.6% (85)
18-24 years old	8.0% (407)
25-39 years old	16.6% (388)
40-54 years old	21.3% (73)
55-64 years old	12.8% (356)
65+ years old	15.5% (333)

PRIVATE SECTOR	
Businesses	871 (331)
Employees	19,423 (131)
Total wages	$767,027,442 (128)
Average weekly wages	$759 (147)

HOUSEHOLD INCOME LADDER	
95th percentile	$164,646 (73)
80th percentile	$100,131 (59)
60th percentile	$70,809 (37)
40th percentile	$46,510 (35)
20th percentile	$25,057 (50)

CHILDREN	★★★★★ (33)
Living with two parents	71.0% (118)
Older teens in school	91.3% (49)
Speak English very well	99.2% (163)
Poverty rate for children	15.9% (75)
No health insurance	3.0% (59)

DIVERSITY/EQUALITY	★★★★ (219)
Racial diversity index	22.1% (323)
Geographic diversity index	40.8% (339)
Top 20% share of income	45.5% (90)
Gender gap in earnings	35.1% (316)
White-collar gender gap	16.8% (178)

EDUCATION	★★★★★ (80)
Eighth grade or less	1.7% (97)
High school diplomas	94.3% (47)
Attended college	61.6% (102)
Bachelor's degrees	27.9% (76)
Advanced degrees	7.2% (164)

EMPLOYMENT	★★★★★ (89)
Average jobless rate	4.9% (63)
Self-employed workers	7.9% (345)
Management/financial jobs	14.3% (42)
Computer/engineering jobs	5.0% (30)
Health care jobs	4.5% (419)

GROWTH POTENTIAL	★★★ (269)
Children per senior	1.65 (148)
Median age	39.8 (285)
Moved from different state	1.6% (383)
Homes built since 2000	16.4% (172)
Construction jobs	5.6% (392)

HOUSING	★★★★★ (3)
Home vacancy rate	5.3% (50)
Home ownership rate	76.4% (43)
Housing diversity index	85.6% (127)
4 or more bedrooms	27.2% (27)
Affordability/income ratio	$2,601 (289)

INCOME	★★★★★ (41)
Poverty rate	10.4% (43)
Median household income	$57,858 (33)
Interest/dividends	25.0% (97)
Public assistance	8.9% (44)
Median fulltime earnings	$43,214 (45)

SENIORS	★ (456)
Seniors living alone	32.7% (523)
Poverty rate for seniors	9.4% (282)
Median income for seniors	$34,547 (210)
Seniors who work	18.9% (247)
Home ownership by seniors	77.4% (476)

STABILITY	★★★★ (118)
25-39 age group	16.6% (388)
Born in state of residence	75.7% (211)
Same house as 1 year ago	87.0% (198)
Live and work in county	77.9% (246)
Married-couple households	53.9% (113)

TRANSPORTATION	★★★ (276)
Bicycle or walk to work	1.9% (401)
Carpool to work	7.4% (518)
Public transit to work	0.6% (141)
Commute <15 minutes	56.2% (83)
Commute >45 minutes	8.9% (171)

See pages 37-130 for explanations of statistics, stars, and ranks.

Owosso, MI
(Shiawassee County, MI)

POPULATION	
2010 census	70,648 (97)
2015 estimate	68,619 (106)
2010-2015 change	-2.9% (477)
2020 projection	67,316 (112)
2030 projection	64,556 (131)

RACE	
Whites	94.5% (61)
Blacks	0.5% (466)
Hispanics	2.7% (361)
Asians	0.4% (413)
Native Americans	0.4% (203)

AGE	
0-17 years old	22.7% (284)
18-24 years old	8.8% (292)
25-39 years old	16.9% (338)
40-54 years old	21.6% (50)
55-64 years old	14.2% (161)
65+ years old	15.9% (297)

PRIVATE SECTOR	
Businesses	1,025 (269)
Employees	13,405 (259)
Total wages	$460,582,140 (282)
Average weekly wages	$661 (360)

HOUSEHOLD INCOME LADDER	
95th percentile	$136,473 (335)
80th percentile	$88,079 (186)
60th percentile	$57,882 (185)
40th percentile	$38,461 (168)
20th percentile	$21,443 (167)

CHILDREN	★★★★ (130)
Living with two parents	70.7% (127)
Older teens in school	84.0% (239)
Speak English very well	99.4% (124)
Poverty rate for children	21.4% (203)
No health insurance	5.2% (197)

DIVERSITY/EQUALITY	★ (476)
Racial diversity index	10.6% (485)
Geographic diversity index	23.1% (541)
Top 20% share of income	45.1% (68)
Gender gap in earnings	35.3% (321)
White-collar gender gap	33.2% (376)

EDUCATION	★★★★ (181)
Eighth grade or less	1.3% (52)
High school diplomas	92.9% (98)
Attended college	59.3% (142)
Bachelor's degrees	16.7% (344)
Advanced degrees	5.2% (352)

EMPLOYMENT	★★★ (247)
Average jobless rate	10.3% (432)
Self-employed workers	8.9% (266)
Management/financial jobs	11.8% (173)
Computer/engineering jobs	3.7% (103)
Health care jobs	5.7% (222)

GROWTH POTENTIAL	★★ (333)
Children per senior	1.42 (267)
Median age	41.5 (380)
Moved from different state	1.5% (406)
Homes built since 2000	9.7% (399)
Construction jobs	7.6% (110)

HOUSING	★★★★★ (51)
Home vacancy rate	7.1% (165)
Home ownership rate	76.1% (55)
Housing diversity index	85.1% (212)
4 or more bedrooms	18.9% (164)
Affordability/income ratio	$2,179 (112)

INCOME	★★★★ (196)
Poverty rate	14.4% (172)
Median household income	$48,233 (168)
Interest/dividends	18.6% (288)
Public assistance	15.9% (290)
Median fulltime earnings	$40,595 (115)

SENIORS	★★★★★ (81)
Seniors living alone	22.2% (41)
Poverty rate for seniors	5.7% (42)
Median income for seniors	$37,469 (105)
Seniors who work	14.0% (503)
Home ownership by seniors	85.6% (120)

STABILITY	★★★ (268)
25-39 age group	16.9% (338)
Born in state of residence	87.5% (10)
Same house as 1 year ago	87.6% (157)
Live and work in county	47.4% (542)
Married-couple households	54.9% (75)

TRANSPORTATION	★ (520)
Bicycle or walk to work	3.1% (232)
Carpool to work	10.1% (322)
Public transit to work	0.4% (219)
Commute <15 minutes	30.6% (515)
Commute >45 minutes	20.3% (519)

See pages 37-130 for explanations of statistics, stars, and ranks.

Parsons, KS
(Labette County, KS)

POPULATION

2010 census	21,607 (513)
2015 estimate	20,803 (520)
2010-2015 change	-3.7% (513)
2020 projection	20,018 (524)
2030 projection	18,492 (529)

RACE

Whites	85.3% (263)
Blacks	3.4% (214)
Hispanics	4.3% (279)
Asians	0.3% (473)
Native Americans	1.0% (103)

AGE

0-17 years old	23.7% (218)
18-24 years old	8.8% (292)
25-39 years old	16.7% (375)
40-54 years old	19.7% (273)
55-64 years old	13.7% (225)
65+ years old	17.4% (165)

PRIVATE SECTOR

Businesses	453 (526)
Employees	6,515 (493)
Total wages	$219,404,953 (494)
Average weekly wages	$648 (397)

HOUSEHOLD INCOME LADDER

95th percentile	$122,725 (497)
80th percentile	$78,314 (397)
60th percentile	$52,026 (318)
40th percentile	$32,638 (335)
20th percentile	$17,919 (322)

CHILDREN ★★★ (283)

Living with two parents	62.9% (322)
Older teens in school	86.8% (139)
Speak English very well	98.1% (331)
Poverty rate for children	23.6% (260)
No health insurance	9.9% (420)

DIVERSITY/EQUALITY ★★★★ (163)

Racial diversity index	26.6% (280)
Geographic diversity index	49.4% (222)
Top 20% share of income	45.3% (74)
Gender gap in earnings	30.5% (183)
White-collar gender gap	28.7% (319)

EDUCATION ★★★★ (161)

Eighth grade or less	3.2% (250)
High school diplomas	90.8% (167)
Attended college	59.7% (134)
Bachelor's degrees	21.3% (182)
Advanced degrees	7.2% (164)

EMPLOYMENT ★★★★ (183)

Average jobless rate	5.3% (82)
Self-employed workers	7.6% (376)
Management/financial jobs	11.3% (218)
Computer/engineering jobs	1.7% (470)
Health care jobs	6.9% (79)

GROWTH POTENTIAL ★ (511)

Children per senior	1.36 (304)
Median age	40.6 (335)
Moved from different state	2.1% (269)
Homes built since 2000	6.9% (506)
Construction jobs	4.2% (524)

HOUSING ★★ (403)

Home vacancy rate	15.0% (534)
Home ownership rate	69.3% (294)
Housing diversity index	83.5% (391)
4 or more bedrooms	14.9% (363)
Affordability/income ratio	$1,694 (13)

INCOME ★★★ (277)

Poverty rate	17.8% (292)
Median household income	$41,439 (338)
Interest/dividends	20.1% (241)
Public assistance	11.6% (116)
Median fulltime earnings	$33,453 (440)

SENIORS ★★ (380)

Seniors living alone	28.5% (332)
Poverty rate for seniors	8.5% (223)
Median income for seniors	$31,000 (373)
Seniors who work	17.2% (330)
Home ownership by seniors	79.7% (385)

STABILITY ★★★ (225)

25-39 age group	16.7% (375)
Born in state of residence	69.2% (324)
Same house as 1 year ago	85.5% (280)
Live and work in county	83.6% (151)
Married-couple households	50.6% (267)

TRANSPORTATION ★★★★ (179)

Bicycle or walk to work	3.6% (180)
Carpool to work	8.3% (471)
Public transit to work	0.2% (363)
Commute <15 minutes	59.0% (51)
Commute >45 minutes	7.5% (105)

See pages 37-130 for explanations of statistics, stars, and ranks.

Pella, IA
(Marion County, IA)

POPULATION

2010 census	33,309 (399)
2015 estimate	33,294 (403)
2010-2015 change	0.0% (255)
2020 projection	33,233 (404)
2030 projection	32,922 (402)

RACE

Whites	95.1% (42)
Blacks	0.5% (466)
Hispanics	1.8% (455)
Asians	1.0% (158)
Native Americans	0.2% (300)

AGE

0-17 years old	24.3% (164)
18-24 years old	10.7% (124)
25-39 years old	15.8% (460)
40-54 years old	20.3% (186)
55-64 years old	12.6% (385)
65+ years old	16.2% (279)

PRIVATE SECTOR

Businesses	922 (304)
Employees	15,008 (209)
Total wages	$670,522,044 (157)
Average weekly wages	$859 (50)

HOUSEHOLD INCOME LADDER

95th percentile	$144,866 (230)
80th percentile	$95,078 (87)
60th percentile	$67,018 (54)
40th percentile	$45,815 (41)
20th percentile	$25,379 (45)

CHILDREN ★★★★★ (1)

Living with two parents	78.8% (16)
Older teens in school	93.2% (31)
Speak English very well	99.2% (163)
Poverty rate for children	12.1% (31)
No health insurance	1.9% (11)

DIVERSITY/EQUALITY ★ (499)

Racial diversity index	9.5% (505)
Geographic diversity index	38.1% (390)
Top 20% share of income	43.7% (14)
Gender gap in earnings	44.6% (496)
White-collar gender gap	48.0% (501)

EDUCATION ★★★★★ (74)

Eighth grade or less	2.1% (136)
High school diplomas	94.3% (47)

Attended college	63.8% (75)
Bachelor's degrees	28.1% (74)
Advanced degrees	7.5% (142)

EMPLOYMENT ★★★★★ (51)

Average jobless rate	4.0% (32)
Self-employed workers	9.7% (196)
Management/financial jobs	14.6% (34)
Computer/engineering jobs	4.2% (66)
Health care jobs	5.5% (250)

GROWTH POTENTIAL ★★ (392)

Children per senior	1.50 (216)
Median age	39.2 (248)
Moved from different state	2.0% (288)
Homes built since 2000	13.6% (251)
Construction jobs	4.2% (524)

HOUSING ★★★★★ (23)

Home vacancy rate	5.5% (60)
Home ownership rate	74.0% (120)
Housing diversity index	85.4% (156)
4 or more bedrooms	23.1% (63)
Affordability/income ratio	$2,510 (252)

INCOME ★★★★★ (59)

Poverty rate	9.9% (28)
Median household income	$54,693 (57)
Interest/dividends	24.8% (105)
Public assistance	11.3% (106)
Median fulltime earnings	$42,789 (49)

SENIORS ★★★★ (203)

Seniors living alone	28.4% (325)
Poverty rate for seniors	5.9% (47)
Median income for seniors	$35,784 (161)
Seniors who work	25.0% (71)
Home ownership by seniors	75.9% (513)

STABILITY ★★★★ (136)

25-39 age group	15.8% (460)
Born in state of residence	77.7% (163)
Same house as 1 year ago	84.5% (325)
Live and work in county	75.9% (276)
Married-couple households	57.9% (21)

TRANSPORTATION ★★★ (289)

Bicycle or walk to work	5.4% (75)
Carpool to work	9.0% (435)
Public transit to work	0.4% (219)
Commute <15 minutes	50.1% (149)
Commute >45 minutes	15.8% (446)

See pages 37-130 for explanations of statistics, stars, and ranks.

Peru, IN
(Miami County, IN)

POPULATION

2010 census	36,903 (359)
2015 estimate	35,862 (374)
2010-2015 change	-2.8% (467)
2020 projection	34,852 (384)
2030 projection	32,799 (403)

RACE

Whites	89.8% (188)
Blacks	5.0% (164)
Hispanics	2.7% (361)
Asians	0.4% (413)
Native Americans	1.0% (103)

AGE

0-17 years old	22.0% (335)
18-24 years old	9.2% (234)
25-39 years old	18.7% (127)
40-54 years old	21.6% (50)
55-64 years old	13.3% (282)
65+ years old	15.3% (348)

PRIVATE SECTOR

Businesses	528 (506)
Employees	6,745 (482)
Total wages	$226,100,802 (486)
Average weekly wages	$645 (402)

HOUSEHOLD INCOME LADDER

95th percentile	$126,162 (480)
80th percentile	$83,168 (290)
60th percentile	$56,164 (223)
40th percentile	$35,714 (242)
20th percentile	$21,264 (175)

CHILDREN ★★★★ (169)

Living with two parents	66.8% (224)
Older teens in school	82.1% (313)
Speak English very well	99.3% (142)
Poverty rate for children	22.2% (228)
No health insurance	4.5% (150)

DIVERSITY/EQUALITY ★ (474)

Racial diversity index	19.0% (361)
Geographic diversity index	37.4% (398)
Top 20% share of income	45.9% (115)
Gender gap in earnings	36.6% (356)
White-collar gender gap	49.4% (508)

EDUCATION ★★ (431)

Eighth grade or less	3.3% (259)
High school diplomas	85.6% (357)
Attended college	44.2% (451)
Bachelor's degrees	12.2% (512)
Advanced degrees	3.7% (498)

EMPLOYMENT ★★ (420)

Average jobless rate	9.4% (394)
Self-employed workers	7.0% (428)
Management/financial jobs	8.8% (488)
Computer/engineering jobs	1.9% (441)
Health care jobs	6.8% (91)

GROWTH POTENTIAL ★★ (401)

Children per senior	1.44 (253)
Median age	40.1 (309)
Moved from different state	1.2% (474)
Homes built since 2000	7.4% (491)
Construction jobs	6.8% (204)

HOUSING ★★★ (257)

Home vacancy rate	11.2% (423)
Home ownership rate	73.0% (151)
Housing diversity index	81.3% (484)
4 or more bedrooms	19.9% (129)
Affordability/income ratio	$1,892 (31)

INCOME ★★★ (249)

Poverty rate	15.2% (199)
Median household income	$45,184 (232)
Interest/dividends	18.2% (305)
Public assistance	16.9% (327)
Median fulltime earnings	$38,917 (182)

SENIORS ★★★★ (152)

Seniors living alone	25.8% (160)
Poverty rate for seniors	8.4% (214)
Median income for seniors	$34,557 (209)
Seniors who work	18.3% (272)
Home ownership by seniors	85.2% (132)

STABILITY ★★ (335)

25-39 age group	18.7% (127)
Born in state of residence	78.2% (150)
Same house as 1 year ago	84.5% (325)
Live and work in county	50.1% (539)
Married-couple households	53.6% (129)

TRANSPORTATION ★ (445)

Bicycle or walk to work	2.2% (358)
Carpool to work	9.2% (408)
Public transit to work	0.3% (291)
Commute <15 minutes	32.3% (489)
Commute >45 minutes	11.2% (278)

See pages 37-130 for explanations of statistics, stars, and ranks.

Pierre, SD
(Hughes, Stanley, and Sully Counties, SD)

POPULATION	
2010 census	21,361 (517)
2015 estimate	21,935 (508)
2010-2015 change	2.7% (96)
2020 projection	22,301 (505)
2030 projection	22,949 (493)

RACE	
Whites	84.3% (275)
Blacks	0.6% (438)
Hispanics	2.4% (389)
Asians	0.4% (413)
Native Americans	9.2% (21)

AGE	
0-17 years old	23.8% (206)
18-24 years old	7.2% (510)
25-39 years old	19.2% (88)
40-54 years old	20.4% (169)
55-64 years old	14.2% (161)
65+ years old	15.2% (354)

PRIVATE SECTOR	
Businesses	945 (295)
Employees	8,368 (438)
Total wages	$304,571,787 (429)
Average weekly wages	$700 (256)

HOUSEHOLD INCOME LADDER	
95th percentile	$167,625 (64)
80th percentile	$103,623 (44)
60th percentile	$71,680 (33)
40th percentile	$47,208 (30)
20th percentile	$25,880 (39)

CHILDREN	★★★★★ (11)
Living with two parents	78.0% (20)
Older teens in school	90.4% (60)
Speak English very well	100.0% (1)
Poverty rate for children	13.9% (55)
No health insurance	4.0% (118)

DIVERSITY/EQUALITY	★★★★ (127)
Racial diversity index	27.9% (270)
Geographic diversity index	44.9% (283)
Top 20% share of income	45.9% (118)
Gender gap in earnings	23.3% (68)
White-collar gender gap	27.0% (297)

EDUCATION	★★★★★ (46)
Eighth grade or less	2.3% (161)
High school diplomas	92.3% (117)
Attended college	65.3% (55)
Bachelor's degrees	33.6% (32)
Advanced degrees	10.0% (61)

EMPLOYMENT	★★★★★ (22)
Average jobless rate	2.8% (6)
Self-employed workers	8.8% (273)
Management/financial jobs	21.3% (4)
Computer/engineering jobs	5.9% (14)
Health care jobs	4.5% (419)

GROWTH POTENTIAL	★★★★ (215)
Children per senior	1.56 (189)
Median age	39.8 (285)
Moved from different state	2.8% (171)
Homes built since 2000	14.6% (213)
Construction jobs	6.6% (241)

HOUSING	★★★★★ (64)
Home vacancy rate	7.7% (199)
Home ownership rate	68.3% (332)
Housing diversity index	85.5% (143)
4 or more bedrooms	26.8% (30)
Affordability/income ratio	$2,742 (342)

INCOME	★★★★★ (53)
Poverty rate	9.5% (22)
Median household income	$58,827 (28)
Interest/dividends	21.5% (194)
Public assistance	8.3% (37)
Median fulltime earnings	$41,551 (77)

SENIORS	★★★★ (113)
Seniors living alone	29.4% (394)
Poverty rate for seniors	7.4% (128)
Median income for seniors	$42,321 (44)
Seniors who work	31.1% (17)
Home ownership by seniors	75.3% (521)

STABILITY	★★★★★ (90)
25-39 age group	19.2% (88)
Born in state of residence	72.1% (273)
Same house as 1 year ago	84.6% (319)
Live and work in county	81.6% (195)
Married-couple households	51.6% (218)

TRANSPORTATION	★★★★★ (21)
Bicycle or walk to work	3.5% (189)
Carpool to work	11.6% (178)
Public transit to work	0.5% (178)
Commute <15 minutes	71.7% (4)
Commute >45 minutes	2.2% (2)

See pages 37-130 for explanations of statistics, stars, and ranks.

Pittsburg, KS
(Crawford County, KS)

POPULATION			Attended college	66.9% (39)
2010 census	39,134 (325)		Bachelor's degrees	31.1% (46)
2015 estimate	39,217 (322)		Advanced degrees	10.6% (47)

POPULATION		Attended college	66.9% (39)
2010 census	39,134 (325)	Bachelor's degrees	31.1% (46)
2015 estimate	39,217 (322)	Advanced degrees	10.6% (47)
2010-2015 change	0.2% (241)	**EMPLOYMENT**	**★★★★ (168)**
2020 projection	39,057 (326)	Average jobless rate	5.6% (106)
2030 projection	38,641 (331)	Self-employed workers	8.8% (273)
RACE		Management/financial jobs	11.8% (173)
Whites	87.9% (222)	Computer/engineering jobs	2.5% (307)
Blacks	2.1% (283)	Health care jobs	5.8% (209)
Hispanics	5.0% (252)	**GROWTH POTENTIAL**	**★★★★ (117)**
Asians	1.5% (85)	Children per senior	1.49 (220)
Native Americans	0.5% (174)	Median age	32.6 (54)
AGE		Moved from different state	5.0% (51)
0-17 years old	21.7% (359)	Homes built since 2000	13.8% (246)
18-24 years old	18.3% (33)	Construction jobs	5.7% (373)
25-39 years old	18.1% (186)	**HOUSING**	**★ (481)**
40-54 years old	16.4% (518)	Home vacancy rate	12.7% (483)
55-64 years old	11.0% (495)	Home ownership rate	61.1% (489)
65+ years old	14.6% (400)	Housing diversity index	85.0% (226)
PRIVATE SECTOR		4 or more bedrooms	12.6% (472)
Businesses	909 (307)	Affordability/income ratio	$2,351 (191)
Employees	12,572 (296)	**INCOME**	**★★ (355)**
Total wages	$399,584,579 (337)	Poverty rate	22.0% (427)
Average weekly wages	$611 (467)	Median household income	$36,534 (457)
HOUSEHOLD INCOME LADDER		Interest/dividends	18.3% (299)
95th percentile	$135,676 (349)	Public assistance	12.9% (164)
80th percentile	$76,344 (434)	Median fulltime earnings	$35,374 (366)
60th percentile	$47,017 (444)	**SENIORS**	**★ (460)**
40th percentile	$28,461 (451)	Seniors living alone	31.9% (509)
20th percentile	$15,588 (428)	Poverty rate for seniors	9.6% (295)
CHILDREN	**★★★★★ (70)**	Median income for seniors	$29,567 (420)
Living with two parents	71.8% (108)	Seniors who work	20.5% (180)
Older teens in school	91.2% (51)	Home ownership by seniors	77.9% (458)
Speak English very well	98.9% (226)	**STABILITY**	**★★ (431)**
Poverty rate for children	20.0% (167)	25-39 age group	18.1% (186)
No health insurance	6.7% (296)	Born in state of residence	64.6% (391)
DIVERSITY/EQUALITY	**★★★ (227)**	Same house as 1 year ago	80.2% (495)
Racial diversity index	22.3% (319)	Live and work in county	84.3% (143)
Geographic diversity index	54.4% (158)	Married-couple households	45.4% (456)
Top 20% share of income	49.1% (369)	**TRANSPORTATION**	**★★★★ (183)**
Gender gap in earnings	35.5% (327)	Bicycle or walk to work	3.1% (232)
White-collar gender gap	11.9% (112)	Carpool to work	8.3% (471)
EDUCATION	**★★★★★ (54)**	Public transit to work	0.3% (291)
Eighth grade or less	3.1% (238)	Commute <15 minutes	56.9% (72)
High school diplomas	91.7% (135)	Commute >45 minutes	6.1% (59)

See pages 37-130 for explanations of statistics, stars, and ranks.

Platteville, WI
(Grant County, WI)

POPULATION

2010 census	51,208 (201)
2015 estimate	52,250 (196)
2010-2015 change	2.0% (128)
2020 projection	53,218 (187)
2030 projection	55,163 (182)

RACE

Whites	95.6% (26)
Blacks	1.3% (351)
Hispanics	1.4% (488)
Asians	0.8% (201)
Native Americans	0.1% (402)

AGE

0-17 years old	20.6% (423)
18-24 years old	17.6% (39)
25-39 years old	15.3% (493)
40-54 years old	17.6% (470)
55-64 years old	12.7% (375)
65+ years old	16.1% (286)

PRIVATE SECTOR

Businesses	1,212 (204)
Employees	13,569 (255)
Total wages	$457,600,772 (287)
Average weekly wages	$649 (393)

HOUSEHOLD INCOME LADDER

95th percentile	$137,147 (325)
80th percentile	$86,388 (225)
60th percentile	$58,909 (163)
40th percentile	$39,152 (152)
20th percentile	$22,283 (123)

CHILDREN ★★★★★ (101)

Living with two parents	77.1% (27)
Older teens in school	89.8% (68)
Speak English very well	96.0% (453)
Poverty rate for children	17.3% (107)
No health insurance	8.4% (371)

DIVERSITY/EQUALITY ★★★ (244)

Racial diversity index	8.6% (523)
Geographic diversity index	47.2% (255)
Top 20% share of income	44.3% (33)
Gender gap in earnings	26.8% (114)
White-collar gender gap	36.2% (398)

EDUCATION ★★★★ (140)

Eighth grade or less	2.6% (185)
High school diplomas	93.5% (75)
Attended college	57.8% (169)
Bachelor's degrees	22.0% (159)
Advanced degrees	7.3% (157)

EMPLOYMENT ★★★★★ (78)

Average jobless rate	4.6% (52)
Self-employed workers	13.8% (35)
Management/financial jobs	12.5% (119)
Computer/engineering jobs	3.1% (180)
Health care jobs	4.4% (433)

GROWTH POTENTIAL ★★★ (274)

Children per senior	1.28 (357)
Median age	36.1 (118)
Moved from different state	2.4% (218)
Homes built since 2000	13.3% (263)
Construction jobs	5.6% (392)

HOUSING ★★★★★ (75)

Home vacancy rate	6.0% (95)
Home ownership rate	70.8% (239)
Housing diversity index	84.4% (299)
4 or more bedrooms	22.9% (67)
Affordability/income ratio	$2,715 (334)

INCOME ★★★★ (126)

Poverty rate	15.4% (211)
Median household income	$49,067 (148)
Interest/dividends	27.6% (43)
Public assistance	10.2% (68)
Median fulltime earnings	$36,300 (317)

SENIORS ★★★ (233)

Seniors living alone	28.0% (296)
Poverty rate for seniors	9.8% (308)
Median income for seniors	$34,175 (225)
Seniors who work	21.0% (160)
Home ownership by seniors	82.6% (242)

STABILITY ★ (484)

25-39 age group	15.3% (493)
Born in state of residence	68.6% (334)
Same house as 1 year ago	82.0% (439)
Live and work in county	68.0% (406)
Married-couple households	51.7% (212)

TRANSPORTATION ★★★★ (164)

Bicycle or walk to work	7.8% (32)
Carpool to work	9.1% (419)
Public transit to work	0.3% (291)
Commute <15 minutes	44.9% (247)
Commute >45 minutes	10.1% (228)

See pages 37-130 for explanations of statistics, stars, and ranks.

Plymouth, IN
(Marshall County, IN)

POPULATION

2010 census	47,051 (232)
2015 estimate	46,857 (237)
2010-2015 change	-0.4% (286)
2020 projection	46,602 (240)
2030 projection	45,928 (256)

RACE

Whites	88.6% (213)
Blacks	0.6% (438)
Hispanics	9.1% (164)
Asians	0.7% (241)
Native Americans	0.1% (402)

AGE

0-17 years old	25.8% (75)
18-24 years old	8.5% (330)
25-39 years old	16.2% (434)
40-54 years old	20.6% (145)
55-64 years old	13.2% (297)
65+ years old	15.7% (318)

PRIVATE SECTOR

Businesses	963 (288)
Employees	17,274 (164)
Total wages	$621,661,306 (178)
Average weekly wages	$692 (277)

HOUSEHOLD INCOME LADDER

95th percentile	$139,924 (291)
80th percentile	$88,246 (182)
60th percentile	$59,929 (153)
40th percentile	$38,394 (171)
20th percentile	$22,264 (124)

CHILDREN ★★ (364)

Living with two parents	75.4% (47)
Older teens in school	77.1% (471)
Speak English very well	94.8% (480)
Poverty rate for children	15.9% (75)
No health insurance	14.2% (513)

DIVERSITY/EQUALITY ★★★ (249)

Racial diversity index	20.7% (338)
Geographic diversity index	40.5% (342)
Top 20% share of income	45.6% (99)
Gender gap in earnings	34.8% (310)
White-collar gender gap	20.5% (214)

EDUCATION ★★ (386)

Eighth grade or less	6.9% (467)
High school diplomas	85.4% (363)
Attended college	47.3% (392)
Bachelor's degrees	18.4% (268)
Advanced degrees	5.9% (272)

EMPLOYMENT ★★ (378)

Average jobless rate	8.3% (314)
Self-employed workers	7.5% (385)
Management/financial jobs	11.8% (173)
Computer/engineering jobs	1.7% (470)
Health care jobs	5.2% (307)

GROWTH POTENTIAL ★★ (332)

Children per senior	1.64 (153)
Median age	39.5 (270)
Moved from different state	1.2% (474)
Homes built since 2000	11.3% (344)
Construction jobs	6.0% (326)

HOUSING ★★★★★ (34)

Home vacancy rate	6.2% (109)
Home ownership rate	76.9% (31)
Housing diversity index	84.4% (299)
4 or more bedrooms	21.9% (82)
Affordability/income ratio	$2,539 (263)

INCOME ★★★★ (113)

Poverty rate	12.1% (88)
Median household income	$48,485 (160)
Interest/dividends	22.4% (169)
Public assistance	10.5% (81)
Median fulltime earnings	$39,698 (150)

SENIORS ★★★★ (187)

Seniors living alone	28.7% (344)
Poverty rate for seniors	9.2% (270)
Median income for seniors	$33,223 (271)
Seniors who work	19.8% (206)
Home ownership by seniors	86.9% (71)

STABILITY ★★★★ (182)

25-39 age group	16.2% (434)
Born in state of residence	76.3% (198)
Same house as 1 year ago	89.6% (57)
Live and work in county	64.5% (453)
Married-couple households	54.8% (78)

TRANSPORTATION ★★★ (259)

Bicycle or walk to work	4.8% (98)
Carpool to work	11.8% (152)
Public transit to work	0.2% (363)
Commute <15 minutes	41.5% (308)
Commute >45 minutes	12.6% (336)

See pages 37-130 for explanations of statistics, stars, and ranks.

Pontiac, IL
(Livingston County, IL)

POPULATION

2010 census	38,950 (329)
2015 estimate	36,671 (364)
2010-2015 change	-5.9% (540)
2020 projection	34,897 (383)
2030 projection	31,497 (414)

RACE

Whites	89.2% (199)
Blacks	5.4% (153)
Hispanics	4.3% (279)
Asians	0.3% (473)
Native Americans	0.0% (523)

AGE

0-17 years old	21.2% (397)
18-24 years old	8.4% (349)
25-39 years old	18.7% (127)
40-54 years old	21.3% (73)
55-64 years old	13.8% (203)
65+ years old	16.7% (225)

PRIVATE SECTOR

Businesses	842 (351)
Employees	11,313 (334)
Total wages	$482,862,393 (257)
Average weekly wages	$821 (64)

HOUSEHOLD INCOME LADDER

95th percentile	$149,346 (169)
80th percentile	$96,521 (78)
60th percentile	$65,283 (73)
40th percentile	$43,529 (65)
20th percentile	$22,690 (108)

CHILDREN ★★★★ (111)

Living with two parents	66.6% (228)
Older teens in school	82.9% (283)
Speak English very well	99.5% (96)
Poverty rate for children	17.6% (112)
No health insurance	3.5% (82)

DIVERSITY/EQUALITY ★ (541)

Racial diversity index	20.0% (349)
Geographic diversity index	28.3% (501)
Top 20% share of income	45.9% (115)
Gender gap in earnings	46.8% (513)
White-collar gender gap	52.1% (517)

EDUCATION ★★★ (276)

Eighth grade or less	2.9% (217)
High school diplomas	88.8% (240)
Attended college	51.6% (289)
Bachelor's degrees	16.1% (366)
Advanced degrees	5.8% (283)

EMPLOYMENT ★★★ (244)

Average jobless rate	6.3% (140)
Self-employed workers	9.8% (186)
Management/financial jobs	11.7% (185)
Computer/engineering jobs	2.5% (307)
Health care jobs	4.5% (419)

GROWTH POTENTIAL ★ (463)

Children per senior	1.27 (370)
Median age	41.3 (371)
Moved from different state	0.8% (524)
Homes built since 2000	6.4% (516)
Construction jobs	7.1% (173)

HOUSING ★★★★ (149)

Home vacancy rate	7.4% (180)
Home ownership rate	73.1% (148)
Housing diversity index	81.7% (470)
4 or more bedrooms	19.6% (135)
Affordability/income ratio	$1,976 (50)

INCOME ★★★★★ (68)

Poverty rate	11.6% (74)
Median household income	$54,254 (62)
Interest/dividends	24.9% (100)
Public assistance	13.4% (185)
Median fulltime earnings	$43,301 (42)

SENIORS ★★★★★ (93)

Seniors living alone	29.3% (389)
Poverty rate for seniors	5.0% (17)
Median income for seniors	$38,969 (75)
Seniors who work	21.7% (138)
Home ownership by seniors	84.9% (145)

STABILITY ★★★★ (138)

25-39 age group	18.7% (127)
Born in state of residence	84.3% (50)
Same house as 1 year ago	84.6% (319)
Live and work in county	70.5% (362)
Married-couple households	50.5% (271)

TRANSPORTATION ★★★ (258)

Bicycle or walk to work	4.1% (147)
Carpool to work	10.4% (289)
Public transit to work	0.1% (441)
Commute <15 minutes	51.8% (126)
Commute >45 minutes	13.1% (359)

See pages 37-130 for explanations of statistics, stars, and ranks.

Poplar Bluff, MO
(Butler County, MO)

POPULATION			
2010 census	42,794 (280)	Attended college	48.3% (374)
2015 estimate	42,951 (281)	Bachelor's degrees	16.4% (354)
2010-2015 change	0.4% (228)	Advanced degrees	5.9% (272)

POPULATION
2010 census 42,794 (280)
2015 estimate 42,951 (281)
2010-2015 change 0.4% (228)
2020 projection 42,954 (283)
2030 projection 42,848 (287)

RACE
Whites 89.5% (195)
Blacks 5.6% (150)
Hispanics 1.7% (464)
Asians 0.6% (291)
Native Americans 0.5% (174)

AGE
0-17 years old 23.3% (246)
18-24 years old 8.4% (349)
25-39 years old 18.4% (151)
40-54 years old 18.9% (376)
55-64 years old 13.9% (192)
65+ years old 17.1% (186)

PRIVATE SECTOR
Businesses 1,471 (142)
Employees 15,428 (201)
Total wages $472,175,579 (272)
Average weekly wages $589 (506)

HOUSEHOLD INCOME LADDER
95th percentile $121,076 (507)
80th percentile $71,530 (496)
60th percentile $44,136 (490)
40th percentile $28,571 (446)
20th percentile $15,236 (445)

CHILDREN ★★★★ (209)
Living with two parents 62.2% (344)
Older teens in school 85.2% (195)
Speak English very well 99.8% (38)
Poverty rate for children 31.1% (423)
No health insurance 3.2% (69)

DIVERSITY/EQUALITY ★★★ (327)
Racial diversity index 19.5% (353)
Geographic diversity index 42.5% (315)
Top 20% share of income 48.8% (347)
Gender gap in earnings 30.2% (172)
White-collar gender gap 21.7% (232)

EDUCATION ★★ (359)
Eighth grade or less 3.3% (259)
High school diplomas 84.3% (393)

Attended college 48.3% (374)
Bachelor's degrees 16.4% (354)
Advanced degrees 5.9% (272)

EMPLOYMENT ★★★★ (186)
Average jobless rate 9.4% (394)
Self-employed workers 10.5% (139)
Management/financial jobs 10.1% (365)
Computer/engineering jobs 1.7% (470)
Health care jobs 8.0% (19)

GROWTH POTENTIAL ★★ (383)
Children per senior 1.36 (304)
Median age 40.0 (303)
Moved from different state 2.2% (248)
Homes built since 2000 14.0% (238)
Construction jobs 4.8% (480)

HOUSING ★★ (405)
Home vacancy rate 13.1% (494)
Home ownership rate 65.1% (434)
Housing diversity index 85.6% (127)
4 or more bedrooms 15.3% (333)
Affordability/income ratio $2,611 (296)

INCOME ★ (478)
Poverty rate 21.3% (411)
Median household income $35,738 (474)
Interest/dividends 15.0% (410)
Public assistance 22.9% (494)
Median fulltime earnings $31,599 (513)

SENIORS ★ (480)
Seniors living alone 29.2% (381)
Poverty rate for seniors 14.8% (485)
Median income for seniors $29,295 (427)
Seniors who work 18.8% (253)
Home ownership by seniors 78.7% (427)

STABILITY ★★★★★ (99)
25-39 age group 18.4% (151)
Born in state of residence 74.3% (239)
Same house as 1 year ago 83.1% (394)
Live and work in county 90.9% (54)
Married-couple households 49.9% (302)

TRANSPORTATION ★★★★ (199)
Bicycle or walk to work 1.9% (401)
Carpool to work 10.2% (312)
Public transit to work 0.7% (119)
Commute <15 minutes 48.1% (194)
Commute >45 minutes 6.0% (53)

See pages 37-130 for explanations of statistics, stars, and ranks.

Port Clinton, OH
(Ottawa County, OH)

POPULATION

2010 census	41,428 (297)
2015 estimate	40,877 (304)
2010-2015 change	-1.3% (355)
2020 projection	40,390 (312)
2030 projection	39,291 (325)

RACE

Whites	92.6% (114)
Blacks	0.9% (388)
Hispanics	4.8% (256)
Asians	0.4% (413)
Native Americans	0.0% (523)

AGE

0-17 years old	19.8% (468)
18-24 years old	6.6% (535)
25-39 years old	14.6% (527)
40-54 years old	20.8% (122)
55-64 years old	17.0% (16)
65+ years old	21.2% (27)

PRIVATE SECTOR

Businesses	1,002 (279)
Employees	11,272 (337)
Total wages	$446,957,709 (295)
Average weekly wages	$763 (135)

HOUSEHOLD INCOME LADDER

95th percentile	$170,641 (55)
80th percentile	$103,785 (43)
60th percentile	$65,846 (69)
40th percentile	$43,903 (60)
20th percentile	$26,215 (34)

CHILDREN ★★★★ (155)

Living with two parents	66.9% (220)
Older teens in school	77.8% (457)
Speak English very well	99.3% (142)
Poverty rate for children	17.8% (120)
No health insurance	2.8% (50)

DIVERSITY/EQUALITY ★ (447)

Racial diversity index	14.0% (435)
Geographic diversity index	28.9% (493)
Top 20% share of income	45.6% (101)
Gender gap in earnings	43.6% (489)
White-collar gender gap	20.7% (216)

EDUCATION ★★★★★ (100)

Eighth grade or less	1.1% (26)
High school diplomas	94.8% (36)
Attended college	58.5% (157)
Bachelor's degrees	22.8% (135)
Advanced degrees	8.0% (123)

EMPLOYMENT ★★★★★ (107)

Average jobless rate	5.5% (98)
Self-employed workers	7.2% (410)
Management/financial jobs	12.6% (111)
Computer/engineering jobs	3.5% (122)
Health care jobs	6.6% (114)

GROWTH POTENTIAL ★ (510)

Children per senior	0.93 (519)
Median age	47.3 (529)
Moved from different state	1.0% (504)
Homes built since 2000	13.6% (251)
Construction jobs	7.1% (173)

HOUSING ★★★★★ (17)

Home vacancy rate	4.8% (27)
Home ownership rate	79.5% (4)
Housing diversity index	86.1% (51)
4 or more bedrooms	17.8% (215)
Affordability/income ratio	$2,574 (282)

INCOME ★★★★★ (48)

Poverty rate	10.7% (52)
Median household income	$53,914 (64)
Interest/dividends	25.8% (77)
Public assistance	10.4% (76)
Median fulltime earnings	$45,164 (31)

SENIORS ★★★★★ (40)

Seniors living alone	25.5% (142)
Poverty rate for seniors	4.9% (16)
Median income for seniors	n.a.
Seniors who work	21.8% (135)
Home ownership by seniors	86.2% (90)

STABILITY ★★★ (318)

25-39 age group	14.6% (527)
Born in state of residence	83.9% (57)
Same house as 1 year ago	90.0% (44)
Live and work in county	51.5% (536)
Married-couple households	55.1% (69)

TRANSPORTATION ★ (508)

Bicycle or walk to work	1.2% (492)
Carpool to work	5.8% (551)
Public transit to work	1.1% (58)
Commute <15 minutes	34.2% (456)
Commute >45 minutes	12.3% (325)

See pages 37-130 for explanations of statistics, stars, and ranks.

Portsmouth, OH
(Scioto County, OH)

POPULATION

2010 census	79,499 (69)
2015 estimate	76,825 (79)
2010-2015 change	-3.4% (501)
2020 projection	75,206 (88)
2030 projection	71,821 (99)

RACE

Whites	93.6% (87)
Blacks	2.6% (247)
Hispanics	1.2% (513)
Asians	0.4% (413)
Native Americans	0.4% (203)

AGE

0-17 years old	22.1% (330)
18-24 years old	9.6% (189)
25-39 years old	19.0% (104)
40-54 years old	19.6% (289)
55-64 years old	13.4% (274)
65+ years old	16.2% (279)

PRIVATE SECTOR

Businesses	1,296 (177)
Employees	18,529 (147)
Total wages	$631,675,224 (174)
Average weekly wages	$656 (378)

HOUSEHOLD INCOME LADDER

95th percentile	$136,993 (327)
80th percentile	$78,410 (395)
60th percentile	$46,785 (447)
40th percentile	$26,183 (494)
20th percentile	$13,619 (488)

CHILDREN ★★★★ (217)

Living with two parents	58.0% (448)
Older teens in school	90.1% (65)
Speak English very well	99.8% (38)
Poverty rate for children	33.0% (464)
No health insurance	4.0% (118)

DIVERSITY/EQUALITY ★ (445)

Racial diversity index	12.3% (459)
Geographic diversity index	31.0% (477)
Top 20% share of income	49.9% (423)
Gender gap in earnings	38.7% (411)
White-collar gender gap	4.5% (36)

EDUCATION ★★ (362)

Eighth grade or less	3.1% (238)
High school diplomas	86.2% (333)
Attended college	46.2% (414)
Bachelor's degrees	15.4% (410)
Advanced degrees	5.9% (272)

EMPLOYMENT ★★★ (282)

Average jobless rate	9.6% (402)
Self-employed workers	4.6% (545)
Management/financial jobs	9.7% (416)
Computer/engineering jobs	2.8% (246)
Health care jobs	10.5% (1)

GROWTH POTENTIAL ★ (444)

Children per senior	1.36 (304)
Median age	39.5 (270)
Moved from different state	1.4% (425)
Homes built since 2000	8.4% (455)
Construction jobs	5.7% (373)

HOUSING ★★ (343)

Home vacancy rate	11.4% (432)
Home ownership rate	68.5% (328)
Housing diversity index	85.0% (226)
4 or more bedrooms	14.2% (392)
Affordability/income ratio	$2,512 (253)

INCOME ★ (476)

Poverty rate	25.3% (479)
Median household income	$35,903 (471)
Interest/dividends	13.1% (467)
Public assistance	27.4% (528)
Median fulltime earnings	$40,354 (129)

SENIORS ★ (531)

Seniors living alone	30.8% (462)
Poverty rate for seniors	13.1% (450)
Median income for seniors	$27,046 (476)
Seniors who work	12.2% (539)
Home ownership by seniors	77.5% (471)

STABILITY ★★★★ (112)

25-39 age group	19.0% (104)
Born in state of residence	82.2% (79)
Same house as 1 year ago	87.7% (154)
Live and work in county	75.0% (289)
Married-couple households	46.5% (432)

TRANSPORTATION ★ (522)

Bicycle or walk to work	3.3% (211)
Carpool to work	6.0% (547)
Public transit to work	0.3% (291)
Commute <15 minutes	31.7% (505)
Commute >45 minutes	14.2% (395)

See pages 37-130 for explanations of statistics, stars, and ranks.

Quincy, IL-MO
(Adams County, IL, and Lewis County, MO)

POPULATION

2010 census	77,314 (76)
2015 estimate	77,220 (77)
2010-2015 change	-0.1% (266)
2020 projection	76,558 (82)
2030 projection	75,011 (90)

RACE

Whites	92.5% (116)
Blacks	3.7% (202)
Hispanics	1.4% (488)
Asians	0.8% (201)
Native Americans	0.1% (402)

AGE

0-17 years old	22.8% (277)
18-24 years old	9.0% (265)
25-39 years old	17.8% (227)
40-54 years old	19.1% (354)
55-64 years old	13.3% (282)
65+ years old	18.1% (117)

PRIVATE SECTOR

Businesses	1,977 (62)
Employees	30,704 (38)
Total wages	$1,209,500,051 (37)
Average weekly wages	$758 (148)

HOUSEHOLD INCOME LADDER

95th percentile	$138,774 (303)
80th percentile	$84,008 (273)
60th percentile	$56,052 (225)
40th percentile	$36,472 (215)
20th percentile	$20,046 (228)

CHILDREN ★★★★★ (87)

Living with two parents	70.5% (131)
Older teens in school	86.4% (152)
Speak English very well	98.3% (312)
Poverty rate for children	19.7% (160)
No health insurance	4.0% (118)

DIVERSITY/EQUALITY ★★★ (294)

Racial diversity index	14.3% (427)
Geographic diversity index	43.6% (301)
Top 20% share of income	46.2% (133)
Gender gap in earnings	34.5% (301)
White-collar gender gap	22.0% (238)

EDUCATION ★★★★ (126)

Eighth grade or less	1.5% (72)
High school diplomas	93.5% (75)
Attended college	58.7% (151)
Bachelor's degrees	22.5% (143)
Advanced degrees	7.2% (164)

EMPLOYMENT ★★★★ (173)

Average jobless rate	6.7% (169)
Self-employed workers	9.4% (216)
Management/financial jobs	11.5% (202)
Computer/engineering jobs	2.1% (399)
Health care jobs	6.4% (132)

GROWTH POTENTIAL ★★ (437)

Children per senior	1.26 (378)
Median age	40.4 (325)
Moved from different state	2.0% (288)
Homes built since 2000	11.3% (344)
Construction jobs	5.2% (442)

HOUSING ★★★★ (117)

Home vacancy rate	7.8% (205)
Home ownership rate	71.1% (222)
Housing diversity index	85.3% (170)
4 or more bedrooms	18.0% (202)
Affordability/income ratio	$2,336 (183)

INCOME ★★★★ (198)

Poverty rate	14.2% (160)
Median household income	$45,726 (217)
Interest/dividends	22.7% (163)
Public assistance	14.2% (215)
Median fulltime earnings	$36,883 (296)

SENIORS ★★★ (254)

Seniors living alone	27.6% (269)
Poverty rate for seniors	7.8% (163)
Median income for seniors	$33,731 (250)
Seniors who work	22.6% (116)
Home ownership by seniors	78.2% (445)

STABILITY ★★★★★ (38)

25-39 age group	17.8% (227)
Born in state of residence	72.6% (267)
Same house as 1 year ago	89.2% (72)
Live and work in county	86.5% (108)
Married-couple households	51.4% (231)

TRANSPORTATION ★★★★ (159)

Bicycle or walk to work	3.4% (199)
Carpool to work	9.8% (358)
Public transit to work	0.6% (141)
Commute <15 minutes	48.3% (189)
Commute >45 minutes	5.0% (33)

See pages 37-130 for explanations of statistics, stars, and ranks.

Red Wing, MN
(Goodhue County, MN)

POPULATION		
2010 census	46,183 (243)	
2015 estimate	46,435 (241)	
2010-2015 change	0.5% (219)	
2020 projection	46,693 (239)	
2030 projection	47,208 (243)	

RACE		
Whites	92.7% (113)	
Blacks	1.1% (367)	
Hispanics	3.1% (333)	
Asians	0.6% (291)	
Native Americans	1.1% (96)	

AGE		
0-17 years old	22.9% (270)	
18-24 years old	7.3% (503)	
25-39 years old	16.8% (359)	
40-54 years old	20.6% (145)	
55-64 years old	14.5% (122)	
65+ years old	17.9% (132)	

PRIVATE SECTOR		
Businesses	1,220 (202)	
Employees	17,536 (161)	
Total wages	$806,545,939 (115)	
Average weekly wages	$884 (40)	

HOUSEHOLD INCOME LADDER		
95th percentile	$173,282 (49)	
80th percentile	$106,542 (32)	
60th percentile	$71,164 (35)	
40th percentile	$44,800 (47)	
20th percentile	$24,402 (57)	

CHILDREN	★★★★★ (98)	
Living with two parents	68.1% (192)	
Older teens in school	86.3% (155)	
Speak English very well	99.0% (200)	
Poverty rate for children	17.1% (99)	
No health insurance	5.3% (206)	

DIVERSITY/EQUALITY	★ (477)	
Racial diversity index	13.9% (436)	
Geographic diversity index	39.6% (361)	
Top 20% share of income	46.5% (164)	
Gender gap in earnings	37.5% (375)	
White-collar gender gap	42.4% (466)	

EDUCATION	★★★★★ (88)	
Eighth grade or less	1.1% (26)	
High school diplomas	95.0% (31)	
Attended college	64.7% (64)	
Bachelor's degrees	24.0% (123)	
Advanced degrees	6.3% (234)	

EMPLOYMENT	★★★★★ (29)	
Average jobless rate	5.3% (82)	
Self-employed workers	12.1% (71)	
Management/financial jobs	15.2% (27)	
Computer/engineering jobs	4.0% (76)	
Health care jobs	6.3% (144)	

GROWTH POTENTIAL	★★ (385)	
Children per senior	1.28 (357)	
Median age	43.0 (450)	
Moved from different state	1.7% (355)	
Homes built since 2000	15.9% (179)	
Construction jobs	6.0% (326)	

HOUSING	★★★★★ (13)	
Home vacancy rate	5.1% (39)	
Home ownership rate	75.8% (60)	
Housing diversity index	84.7% (260)	
4 or more bedrooms	27.5% (25)	
Affordability/income ratio	$3,140 (426)	

INCOME	★★★★★ (27)	
Poverty rate	11.2% (61)	
Median household income	$57,062 (38)	
Interest/dividends	27.8% (40)	
Public assistance	7.0% (21)	
Median fulltime earnings	$45,222 (30)	

SENIORS	★★★★ (180)	
Seniors living alone	29.1% (371)	
Poverty rate for seniors	6.0% (49)	
Median income for seniors	$38,674 (78)	
Seniors who work	24.7% (77)	
Home ownership by seniors	77.1% (486)	

STABILITY	★★★★ (201)	
25-39 age group	16.8% (359)	
Born in state of residence	76.3% (198)	
Same house as 1 year ago	88.4% (109)	
Live and work in county	63.6% (458)	
Married-couple households	54.2% (102)	

TRANSPORTATION	★★ (374)	
Bicycle or walk to work	4.4% (123)	
Carpool to work	8.7% (453)	
Public transit to work	1.1% (58)	
Commute <15 minutes	39.9% (333)	
Commute >45 minutes	16.5% (468)	

See pages 37-130 for explanations of statistics, stars, and ranks.

Richmond, IN
(Wayne County, IN)

POPULATION	
2010 census	68,917 (105)
2015 estimate	67,001 (112)
2010-2015 change	-2.8% (467)
2020 projection	64,942 (124)
2030 projection	60,796 (148)

RACE	
Whites	88.8% (208)
Blacks	4.7% (171)
Hispanics	2.7% (361)
Asians	0.8% (201)
Native Americans	0.1% (402)

AGE	
0-17 years old	22.4% (306)
18-24 years old	9.3% (217)
25-39 years old	16.9% (338)
40-54 years old	20.4% (169)
55-64 years old	13.5% (258)
65+ years old	17.5% (158)

PRIVATE SECTOR	
Businesses	1,401 (154)
Employees	25,409 (72)
Total wages	$922,739,652 (88)
Average weekly wages	$698 (259)

HOUSEHOLD INCOME LADDER	
95th percentile	$130,245 (430)
80th percentile	$77,457 (408)
60th percentile	$47,960 (427)
40th percentile	$30,185 (413)
20th percentile	$16,498 (386)

CHILDREN	★ (497)
Living with two parents	56.9% (461)
Older teens in school	78.5% (438)
Speak English very well	96.9% (419)
Poverty rate for children	33.0% (464)
No health insurance	12.7% (489)

DIVERSITY/EQUALITY	★★ (340)
Racial diversity index	20.8% (337)
Geographic diversity index	48.1% (241)
Top 20% share of income	50.7% (456)
Gender gap in earnings	33.6% (271)
White-collar gender gap	16.2% (171)

EDUCATION	★★★ (283)
Eighth grade or less	3.2% (250)
High school diplomas	86.4% (331)
Attended college	49.6% (342)
Bachelor's degrees	18.2% (277)
Advanced degrees	6.8% (191)

EMPLOYMENT	★★★ (314)
Average jobless rate	9.0% (358)
Self-employed workers	6.3% (484)
Management/financial jobs	9.7% (416)
Computer/engineering jobs	2.8% (246)
Health care jobs	7.4% (49)

GROWTH POTENTIAL	★ (465)
Children per senior	1.28 (357)
Median age	40.9 (350)
Moved from different state	3.6% (104)
Homes built since 2000	6.7% (509)
Construction jobs	4.6% (494)

HOUSING	★★ (346)
Home vacancy rate	11.6% (441)
Home ownership rate	68.4% (329)
Housing diversity index	84.0% (344)
4 or more bedrooms	16.0% (293)
Affordability/income ratio	$2,395 (212)

INCOME	★★ (356)
Poverty rate	21.1% (403)
Median household income	$38,494 (418)
Interest/dividends	19.1% (273)
Public assistance	17.1% (338)
Median fulltime earnings	$36,537 (314)

SENIORS	★★ (421)
Seniors living alone	29.3% (389)
Poverty rate for seniors	9.4% (282)
Median income for seniors	$31,019 (371)
Seniors who work	16.0% (410)
Home ownership by seniors	80.1% (369)

STABILITY	★★ (376)
25-39 age group	16.9% (338)
Born in state of residence	70.3% (305)
Same house as 1 year ago	83.2% (388)
Live and work in county	82.4% (174)
Married-couple households	46.9% (419)

TRANSPORTATION	★★ (338)
Bicycle or walk to work	3.0% (249)
Carpool to work	7.6% (510)
Public transit to work	0.5% (178)
Commute <15 minutes	44.8% (249)
Commute >45 minutes	9.5% (203)

See pages 37-130 for explanations of statistics, stars, and ranks.

Rochelle, IL
(Ogle County, IL)

POPULATION
2010 census	53,497 (182)
2015 estimate	51,659 (200)
2010-2015 change	-3.4% (501)
2020 projection	50,477 (210)
2030 projection	48,073 (230)

RACE
Whites	88.0% (221)
Blacks	1.0% (381)
Hispanics	9.4% (159)
Asians	0.3% (473)
Native Americans	0.0% (523)

AGE
0-17 years old	23.4% (240)
18-24 years old	8.0% (407)
25-39 years old	16.5% (403)
40-54 years old	21.9% (38)
55-64 years old	13.3% (282)
65+ years old	16.8% (215)

PRIVATE SECTOR
Businesses	1,074 (253)
Employees	13,345 (264)
Total wages	$601,712,607 (185)
Average weekly wages	$867 (47)

HOUSEHOLD INCOME LADDER
95th percentile	$161,733 (89)
80th percentile	$105,216 (35)
60th percentile	$68,148 (45)
40th percentile	$43,939 (59)
20th percentile	$24,017 (66)

CHILDREN ★★★★★ (29)
Living with two parents	74.2% (65)
Older teens in school	89.8% (68)
Speak English very well	97.7% (370)
Poverty rate for children	13.7% (52)
No health insurance	2.4% (28)

DIVERSITY/EQUALITY ★★ (349)
Racial diversity index	21.6% (330)
Geographic diversity index	39.9% (354)
Top 20% share of income	45.0% (63)
Gender gap in earnings	40.8% (453)
White-collar gender gap	29.8% (337)

EDUCATION ★★★★ (149)
Eighth grade or less	3.1% (238)
High school diplomas	91.1% (156)
Attended college	60.1% (126)
Bachelor's degrees	22.2% (153)
Advanced degrees	7.4% (149)

EMPLOYMENT ★★★★ (214)
Average jobless rate	8.0% (291)
Self-employed workers	7.4% (393)
Management/financial jobs	12.6% (111)
Computer/engineering jobs	2.7% (270)
Health care jobs	6.2% (156)

GROWTH POTENTIAL ★★ (408)
Children per senior	1.39 (286)
Median age	41.5 (380)
Moved from different state	1.7% (355)
Homes built since 2000	13.0% (276)
Construction jobs	5.5% (404)

HOUSING ★★★★★ (33)
Home vacancy rate	6.6% (136)
Home ownership rate	75.9% (58)
Housing diversity index	84.6% (277)
4 or more bedrooms	23.0% (65)
Affordability/income ratio	$2,552 (271)

INCOME ★★★★★ (49)
Poverty rate	10.6% (47)
Median household income	$54,849 (55)
Interest/dividends	25.5% (82)
Public assistance	11.2% (104)
Median fulltime earnings	$45,229 (29)

SENIORS ★★★★ (177)
Seniors living alone	31.3% (486)
Poverty rate for seniors	6.3% (54)
Median income for seniors	$34,793 (198)
Seniors who work	20.1% (192)
Home ownership by seniors	86.8% (72)

STABILITY ★★ (377)
25-39 age group	16.5% (403)
Born in state of residence	76.7% (185)
Same house as 1 year ago	88.1% (126)
Live and work in county	50.1% (539)
Married-couple households	54.0% (108)

TRANSPORTATION ★ (459)
Bicycle or walk to work	2.0% (386)
Carpool to work	10.1% (322)
Public transit to work	0.4% (219)
Commute <15 minutes	32.4% (487)
Commute >45 minutes	14.3% (402)

See pages 37-130 for explanations of statistics, stars, and ranks.

Rolla, MO
(Phelps County, MO)

POPULATION

2010 census	45,156 (258)
2015 estimate	44,794 (264)
2010-2015 change	-0.8% (314)
2020 projection	44,960 (263)
2030 projection	45,166 (261)

RACE

Whites	89.1% (202)
Blacks	2.3% (267)
Hispanics	2.4% (389)
Asians	3.4% (17)
Native Americans	0.6% (150)

AGE

0-17 years old	21.3% (383)
18-24 years old	17.0% (45)
25-39 years old	17.2% (290)
40-54 years old	17.7% (464)
55-64 years old	12.2% (424)
65+ years old	14.6% (400)

PRIVATE SECTOR

Businesses	1,139 (220)
Employees	12,144 (304)
Total wages	$398,536,883 (338)
Average weekly wages	$631 (435)

HOUSEHOLD INCOME LADDER

95th percentile	$145,076 (227)
80th percentile	$82,420 (313)
60th percentile	$51,374 (347)
40th percentile	$32,906 (329)
20th percentile	$16,639 (378)

CHILDREN ★★★★ (157)

Living with two parents	65.1% (268)
Older teens in school	91.6% (45)
Speak English very well	97.8% (361)
Poverty rate for children	22.7% (242)
No health insurance	7.1% (324)

DIVERSITY/EQUALITY ★★★★★ (57)

Racial diversity index	20.3% (343)
Geographic diversity index	53.9% (165)
Top 20% share of income	49.1% (374)
Gender gap in earnings	15.2% (16)
White-collar gender gap	1.1% (7)

EDUCATION ★★★★★ (72)

Eighth grade or less	3.6% (292)
High school diplomas	89.7% (211)
Attended college	57.3% (181)
Bachelor's degrees	29.7% (55)
Advanced degrees	13.0% (27)

EMPLOYMENT ★★★★ (120)

Average jobless rate	7.0% (196)
Self-employed workers	5.7% (515)
Management/financial jobs	12.3% (133)
Computer/engineering jobs	6.1% (13)
Health care jobs	5.8% (209)

GROWTH POTENTIAL ★★★★★ (101)

Children per senior	1.46 (237)
Median age	34.4 (83)
Moved from different state	5.3% (44)
Homes built since 2000	20.8% (81)
Construction jobs	5.0% (467)

HOUSING ★★ (381)

Home vacancy rate	11.2% (423)
Home ownership rate	61.1% (489)
Housing diversity index	85.4% (156)
4 or more bedrooms	18.4% (183)
Affordability/income ratio	$2,751 (346)

INCOME ★★★ (282)

Poverty rate	19.4% (353)
Median household income	$41,618 (332)
Interest/dividends	21.0% (214)
Public assistance	13.3% (182)
Median fulltime earnings	$35,044 (382)

SENIORS ★★★★ (210)

Seniors living alone	26.1% (179)
Poverty rate for seniors	9.7% (301)
Median income for seniors	$35,857 (158)
Seniors who work	18.7% (259)
Home ownership by seniors	82.1% (268)

STABILITY ★ (483)

25-39 age group	17.2% (290)
Born in state of residence	65.9% (376)
Same house as 1 year ago	75.9% (531)
Live and work in county	82.7% (167)
Married-couple households	48.6% (358)

TRANSPORTATION ★★★★ (142)

Bicycle or walk to work	4.0% (155)
Carpool to work	11.8% (152)
Public transit to work	0.4% (219)
Commute <15 minutes	50.2% (146)
Commute >45 minutes	8.4% (148)

See pages 37-130 for explanations of statistics, stars, and ranks.

Salem, OH
(Columbiana County, OH)

POPULATION	
2010 census	107,841 (18)
2015 estimate	104,806 (22)
2010-2015 change	-2.8% (467)
2020 projection	102,032 (28)
2030 projection	96,313 (35)

RACE	
Whites	94.4% (66)
Blacks	2.2% (276)
Hispanics	1.4% (488)
Asians	0.3% (473)
Native Americans	0.1% (402)

AGE	
0-17 years old	21.1% (407)
18-24 years old	7.6% (468)
25-39 years old	17.3% (280)
40-54 years old	21.2% (85)
55-64 years old	15.1% (74)
65+ years old	17.8% (137)

PRIVATE SECTOR	
Businesses	1,988 (61)
Employees	25,826 (68)
Total wages	$882,495,817 (96)
Average weekly wages	$657 (373)

HOUSEHOLD INCOME LADDER	
95th percentile	$138,481 (305)
80th percentile	$82,314 (319)
60th percentile	$55,394 (236)
40th percentile	$36,024 (231)
20th percentile	$19,861 (234)

CHILDREN	★★★ (231)
Living with two parents	62.3% (339)
Older teens in school	84.6% (214)
Speak English very well	98.9% (226)
Poverty rate for children	23.8% (268)
No health insurance	6.2% (262)

DIVERSITY/EQUALITY	★ (513)
Racial diversity index	10.8% (482)
Geographic diversity index	38.3% (385)
Top 20% share of income	47.5% (254)
Gender gap in earnings	39.9% (435)
White-collar gender gap	38.8% (431)

EDUCATION	★★ (342)
Eighth grade or less	1.8% (102)
High school diplomas	89.8% (207)
Attended college	44.4% (447)
Bachelor's degrees	14.6% (435)
Advanced degrees	4.7% (419)

EMPLOYMENT	★★ (416)
Average jobless rate	9.0% (358)
Self-employed workers	6.9% (435)
Management/financial jobs	10.8% (280)
Computer/engineering jobs	2.3% (354)
Health care jobs	5.2% (307)

GROWTH POTENTIAL	★ (508)
Children per senior	1.19 (423)
Median age	43.2 (456)
Moved from different state	2.4% (218)
Homes built since 2000	8.6% (449)
Construction jobs	5.1% (458)

HOUSING	★★★★ (220)
Home vacancy rate	8.0% (223)
Home ownership rate	71.1% (222)
Housing diversity index	84.5% (287)
4 or more bedrooms	13.7% (415)
Affordability/income ratio	$2,272 (149)

INCOME	★★★ (253)
Poverty rate	15.4% (211)
Median household income	$44,497 (250)
Interest/dividends	18.7% (286)
Public assistance	17.9% (368)
Median fulltime earnings	$39,237 (168)

SENIORS	★★★★ (185)
Seniors living alone	26.4% (193)
Poverty rate for seniors	7.7% (156)
Median income for seniors	$32,976 (284)
Seniors who work	19.7% (214)
Home ownership by seniors	83.0% (221)

STABILITY	★★ (417)
25-39 age group	17.3% (280)
Born in state of residence	77.5% (168)
Same house as 1 year ago	86.0% (250)
Live and work in county	53.1% (532)
Married-couple households	50.8% (256)

TRANSPORTATION	★ (493)
Bicycle or walk to work	2.1% (374)
Carpool to work	8.9% (439)
Public transit to work	0.5% (178)
Commute <15 minutes	33.7% (465)
Commute >45 minutes	15.8% (446)

See pages 37-130 for explanations of statistics, stars, and ranks.

Salina, KS
(Ottawa and Saline Counties, KS)

POPULATION

2010 census	61,697 (139)
2015 estimate	61,666 (136)
2010-2015 change	-0.1% (266)
2020 projection	61,551 (139)
2030 projection	61,179 (145)

RACE

Whites	82.2% (299)
Blacks	2.9% (229)
Hispanics	9.8% (155)
Asians	2.3% (36)
Native Americans	0.4% (203)

AGE

0-17 years old	24.5% (149)
18-24 years old	9.5% (197)
25-39 years old	18.1% (186)
40-54 years old	19.3% (323)
55-64 years old	13.0% (334)
65+ years old	15.7% (318)

PRIVATE SECTOR

Businesses	1,648 (113)
Employees	26,940 (62)
Total wages	$975,520,309 (73)
Average weekly wages	$696 (262)

HOUSEHOLD INCOME LADDER

95th percentile	$151,716 (144)
80th percentile	$86,944 (207)
60th percentile	$57,816 (188)
40th percentile	$37,922 (184)
20th percentile	$21,899 (141)

CHILDREN ★★★★ (173)

Living with two parents	62.8% (323)
Older teens in school	88.9% (82)
Speak English very well	98.8% (251)
Poverty rate for children	24.3% (280)
No health insurance	5.9% (244)

DIVERSITY/EQUALITY ★★★ (248)

Racial diversity index	31.3% (242)
Geographic diversity index	48.9% (230)
Top 20% share of income	47.9% (286)
Gender gap in earnings	25.1% (89)
White-collar gender gap	41.6% (463)

EDUCATION ★★★★ (144)

Eighth grade or less	2.9% (217)
High school diplomas	90.4% (188)
Attended college	59.7% (134)
Bachelor's degrees	23.4% (127)
Advanced degrees	7.5% (142)

EMPLOYMENT ★★★★★ (71)

Average jobless rate	5.0% (66)
Self-employed workers	10.1% (158)
Management/financial jobs	13.6% (62)
Computer/engineering jobs	2.1% (399)
Health care jobs	6.9% (79)

GROWTH POTENTIAL ★★★ (263)

Children per senior	1.56 (189)
Median age	38.0 (184)
Moved from different state	2.4% (218)
Homes built since 2000	7.7% (475)
Construction jobs	7.0% (185)

HOUSING ★★★★★ (73)

Home vacancy rate	6.2% (109)
Home ownership rate	67.4% (371)
Housing diversity index	86.1% (51)
4 or more bedrooms	21.2% (96)
Affordability/income ratio	$2,469 (241)

INCOME ★★★★ (180)

Poverty rate	15.3% (204)
Median household income	$48,123 (173)
Interest/dividends	21.4% (202)
Public assistance	10.4% (76)
Median fulltime earnings	$35,930 (337)

SENIORS ★★★★ (123)

Seniors living alone	28.3% (318)
Poverty rate for seniors	5.7% (42)
Median income for seniors	$35,399 (176)
Seniors who work	25.0% (71)
Home ownership by seniors	81.1% (325)

STABILITY ★★★★ (199)

25-39 age group	18.1% (186)
Born in state of residence	70.2% (307)
Same house as 1 year ago	84.6% (319)
Live and work in county	86.5% (108)
Married-couple households	47.6% (395)

TRANSPORTATION ★★★★ (133)

Bicycle or walk to work	2.5% (322)
Carpool to work	9.1% (419)
Public transit to work	0.5% (178)
Commute <15 minutes	59.0% (51)
Commute >45 minutes	4.3% (19)

See pages 37-130 for explanations of statistics, stars, and ranks.

Sandusky, OH
(Erie County, OH)

POPULATION	
2010 census	77,079 (78)
2015 estimate	75,550 (86)
2010-2015 change	-2.0% (412)
2020 projection	74,026 (90)
2030 projection	70,828 (103)

RACE	
Whites	84.1% (277)
Blacks	8.3% (126)
Hispanics	3.9% (302)
Asians	0.6% (291)
Native Americans	0.2% (300)

AGE	
0-17 years old	21.3% (383)
18-24 years old	7.9% (424)
25-39 years old	16.3% (418)
40-54 years old	20.3% (186)
55-64 years old	15.3% (68)
65+ years old	18.9% (85)

PRIVATE SECTOR	
Businesses	1,832 (84)
Employees	31,726 (31)
Total wages	$1,097,868,948 (55)
Average weekly wages	$665 (343)

HOUSEHOLD INCOME LADDER	
95th percentile	$152,333 (139)
80th percentile	$90,969 (141)
60th percentile	$60,005 (150)
40th percentile	$39,464 (142)
20th percentile	$22,258 (125)

CHILDREN	★★★★ (158)
Living with two parents	61.9% (359)
Older teens in school	83.7% (251)
Speak English very well	99.9% (19)
Poverty rate for children	19.0% (147)
No health insurance	4.7% (166)

DIVERSITY/EQUALITY	★★★ (256)
Racial diversity index	28.3% (268)
Geographic diversity index	34.8% (438)
Top 20% share of income	47.7% (271)
Gender gap in earnings	38.3% (402)
White-collar gender gap	4.9% (41)

EDUCATION	★★★★ (127)
Eighth grade or less	1.2% (42)
High school diplomas	92.6% (107)
Attended college	55.5% (213)
Bachelor's degrees	22.5% (143)
Advanced degrees	8.4% (106)

EMPLOYMENT	★★★ (226)
Average jobless rate	7.7% (260)
Self-employed workers	7.7% (362)
Management/financial jobs	11.0% (252)
Computer/engineering jobs	2.3% (354)
Health care jobs	7.0% (69)

GROWTH POTENTIAL	★ (547)
Children per senior	1.12 (455)
Median age	44.0 (477)
Moved from different state	1.7% (355)
Homes built since 2000	7.4% (491)
Construction jobs	4.1% (530)

HOUSING	★★★★ (138)
Home vacancy rate	7.1% (165)
Home ownership rate	68.6% (321)
Housing diversity index	85.4% (156)
4 or more bedrooms	19.4% (142)
Affordability/income ratio	$2,737 (341)

INCOME	★★★★ (136)
Poverty rate	12.4% (97)
Median household income	$48,011 (176)
Interest/dividends	23.0% (157)
Public assistance	15.5% (277)
Median fulltime earnings	$41,314 (86)

SENIORS	★★★ (280)
Seniors living alone	29.0% (366)
Poverty rate for seniors	6.3% (54)
Median income for seniors	$36,397 (144)
Seniors who work	16.6% (367)
Home ownership by seniors	80.6% (353)

STABILITY	★★ (387)
25-39 age group	16.3% (418)
Born in state of residence	80.1% (111)
Same house as 1 year ago	86.0% (250)
Live and work in county	69.1% (386)
Married-couple households	47.0% (417)

TRANSPORTATION	★★★ (303)
Bicycle or walk to work	3.2% (225)
Carpool to work	10.0% (337)
Public transit to work	0.7% (119)
Commute <15 minutes	42.3% (292)
Commute >45 minutes	11.4% (292)

See pages 37-130 for explanations of statistics, stars, and ranks.

Sault Ste. Marie, MI
(Chippewa County, MI)

POPULATION

2010 census	38,520 (334)
2015 estimate	38,033 (339)
2010-2015 change	-1.3% (355)
2020 projection	37,442 (349)
2030 projection	36,152 (357)

RACE

Whites	70.7% (384)
Blacks	6.5% (142)
Hispanics	1.6% (472)
Asians	0.9% (178)
Native Americans	14.8% (10)

AGE

0-17 years old	20.2% (452)
18-24 years old	11.7% (94)
25-39 years old	19.2% (88)
40-54 years old	20.0% (233)
55-64 years old	13.1% (318)
65+ years old	15.8% (305)

PRIVATE SECTOR

Businesses	728 (415)
Employees	6,464 (494)
Total wages	$179,145,508 (520)
Average weekly wages	$533 (538)

HOUSEHOLD INCOME LADDER

95th percentile	$123,944 (490)
80th percentile	$78,756 (386)
60th percentile	$51,429 (346)
40th percentile	$32,551 (336)
20th percentile	$17,116 (357)

CHILDREN ★★★ (297)

Living with two parents	60.1% (395)
Older teens in school	83.5% (255)
Speak English very well	99.5% (96)
Poverty rate for children	28.6% (381)
No health insurance	6.5% (282)

DIVERSITY/EQUALITY ★★★★★ (94)

Racial diversity index	47.1% (135)
Geographic diversity index	35.3% (433)
Top 20% share of income	47.0% (213)
Gender gap in earnings	25.5% (96)
White-collar gender gap	16.2% (171)

EDUCATION ★★★★ (193)

Eighth grade or less	1.8% (102)
High school diplomas	90.6% (178)
Attended college	54.3% (238)
Bachelor's degrees	19.1% (245)
Advanced degrees	6.5% (220)

EMPLOYMENT ★★ (364)

Average jobless rate	11.7% (481)
Self-employed workers	9.4% (216)
Management/financial jobs	10.0% (381)
Computer/engineering jobs	1.9% (441)
Health care jobs	6.9% (79)

GROWTH POTENTIAL ★★★ (309)

Children per senior	1.28 (357)
Median age	39.0 (238)
Moved from different state	2.4% (218)
Homes built since 2000	14.5% (220)
Construction jobs	5.7% (373)

HOUSING ★★★★ (121)

Home vacancy rate	6.5% (130)
Home ownership rate	70.3% (256)
Housing diversity index	86.6% (12)
4 or more bedrooms	14.7% (370)
Affordability/income ratio	$2,531 (260)

INCOME ★★★ (292)

Poverty rate	18.9% (334)
Median household income	$41,993 (321)
Interest/dividends	22.2% (174)
Public assistance	17.4% (352)
Median fulltime earnings	$36,088 (330)

SENIORS ★★★ (328)

Seniors living alone	27.8% (283)
Poverty rate for seniors	8.1% (187)
Median income for seniors	$31,856 (325)
Seniors who work	16.3% (391)
Home ownership by seniors	81.6% (299)

STABILITY ★★★★★ (49)

25-39 age group	19.2% (88)
Born in state of residence	79.9% (117)
Same house as 1 year ago	82.7% (411)
Live and work in county	93.2% (33)
Married-couple households	49.0% (349)

TRANSPORTATION ★★★★★ (44)

Bicycle or walk to work	5.6% (69)
Carpool to work	12.9% (106)
Public transit to work	0.8% (96)
Commute <15 minutes	55.1% (90)
Commute >45 minutes	6.3% (65)

See pages 37-130 for explanations of statistics, stars, and ranks.

Scottsbluff, NE
(Banner, Scotts Bluff, and Sioux Counties, NE)

POPULATION	
2010 census	38,971 (327)
2015 estimate	38,309 (336)
2010-2015 change	-1.7% (384)
2020 projection	37,757 (345)
2030 projection	36,596 (352)

RACE	
Whites	74.9% (358)
Blacks	0.7% (423)
Hispanics	21.4% (72)
Asians	0.7% (241)
Native Americans	0.9% (115)

AGE	
0-17 years old	24.3% (164)
18-24 years old	8.5% (330)
25-39 years old	18.1% (186)
40-54 years old	17.7% (464)
55-64 years old	13.7% (225)
65+ years old	17.6% (151)

PRIVATE SECTOR	
Businesses	1,466 (143)
Employees	13,841 (238)
Total wages	$495,252,965 (248)
Average weekly wages	$688 (290)

HOUSEHOLD INCOME LADDER	
95th percentile	$148,975 (172)
80th percentile	$86,610 (219)
60th percentile	$54,683 (258)
40th percentile	$36,054 (230)
20th percentile	$20,990 (188)

CHILDREN	★★★ (221)
Living with two parents	62.7% (328)
Older teens in school	87.7% (107)
Speak English very well	98.0% (341)
Poverty rate for children	22.2% (228)
No health insurance	7.7% (352)

DIVERSITY/EQUALITY	★★★ (323)
Racial diversity index	39.3% (188)
Geographic diversity index	55.0% (154)
Top 20% share of income	49.0% (360)
Gender gap in earnings	32.1% (230)
White-collar gender gap	47.8% (498)

EDUCATION	★★★★ (179)
Eighth grade or less	4.4% (346)
High school diplomas	88.1% (263)
Attended college	61.1% (108)
Bachelor's degrees	22.4% (145)
Advanced degrees	7.3% (157)

EMPLOYMENT	★★★★★ (104)
Average jobless rate	5.3% (82)
Self-employed workers	11.6% (90)
Management/financial jobs	12.7% (103)
Computer/engineering jobs	1.5% (499)
Health care jobs	6.0% (181)

GROWTH POTENTIAL	★★★ (251)
Children per senior	1.38 (291)
Median age	39.3 (256)
Moved from different state	3.8% (89)
Homes built since 2000	7.2% (500)
Construction jobs	7.3% (151)

HOUSING	★★★★ (112)
Home vacancy rate	8.6% (260)
Home ownership rate	68.7% (317)
Housing diversity index	84.9% (235)
4 or more bedrooms	22.8% (69)
Affordability/income ratio	$2,338 (185)

INCOME	★★★★ (211)
Poverty rate	13.6% (142)
Median household income	$45,933 (215)
Interest/dividends	20.5% (236)
Public assistance	12.0% (132)
Median fulltime earnings	$35,058 (381)

SENIORS	★★★★ (139)
Seniors living alone	30.3% (440)
Poverty rate for seniors	7.6% (145)
Median income for seniors	$34,386 (217)
Seniors who work	30.9% (19)
Home ownership by seniors	79.8% (382)

STABILITY	★★★★ (127)
25-39 age group	18.1% (186)
Born in state of residence	64.5% (392)
Same house as 1 year ago	85.9% (257)
Live and work in county	91.8% (47)
Married-couple households	49.1% (345)

TRANSPORTATION	★★★★★ (105)
Bicycle or walk to work	3.3% (211)
Carpool to work	10.9% (239)
Public transit to work	0.3% (291)
Commute <15 minutes	58.1% (62)
Commute >45 minutes	5.3% (38)

See pages 37-130 for explanations of statistics, stars, and ranks.

Sedalia, MO
(Pettis County, MO)

POPULATION

2010 census	42,201 (288)
2015 estimate	42,255 (289)
2010-2015 change	0.1% (250)
2020 projection	42,473 (288)
2030 projection	42,803 (288)

RACE

Whites	85.8% (257)
Blacks	2.8% (232)
Hispanics	8.1% (180)
Asians	0.6% (291)
Native Americans	0.2% (300)

AGE

0-17 years old	25.2% (108)
18-24 years old	8.9% (282)
25-39 years old	18.3% (159)
40-54 years old	20.0% (233)
55-64 years old	12.5% (396)
65+ years old	15.0% (371)

PRIVATE SECTOR

Businesses	1,124 (231)
Employees	16,108 (187)
Total wages	$510,168,188 (237)
Average weekly wages	$609 (473)

HOUSEHOLD INCOME LADDER

95th percentile	$131,385 (410)
80th percentile	$74,445 (466)
60th percentile	$49,495 (392)
40th percentile	$31,989 (363)
20th percentile	$18,765 (278)

CHILDREN ★★★ (234)

Living with two parents	70.9% (122)
Older teens in school	84.9% (201)
Speak English very well	96.0% (453)
Poverty rate for children	24.2% (278)
No health insurance	6.9% (307)

DIVERSITY/EQUALITY ★★ (343)

Racial diversity index	25.6% (290)
Geographic diversity index	50.2% (210)
Top 20% share of income	47.8% (280)
Gender gap in earnings	33.6% (271)
White-collar gender gap	39.7% (444)

EDUCATION ★★ (350)

Eighth grade or less	6.8% (463)
High school diplomas	83.9% (403)
Attended college	55.0% (224)
Bachelor's degrees	18.9% (254)
Advanced degrees	6.1% (250)

EMPLOYMENT ★★★ (296)

Average jobless rate	6.4% (147)
Self-employed workers	8.8% (273)
Management/financial jobs	10.3% (339)
Computer/engineering jobs	2.3% (354)
Health care jobs	5.3% (286)

GROWTH POTENTIAL ★★★ (244)

Children per senior	1.68 (141)
Median age	37.5 (162)
Moved from different state	2.4% (218)
Homes built since 2000	13.6% (251)
Construction jobs	5.3% (425)

HOUSING ★★★★ (198)

Home vacancy rate	9.8% (341)
Home ownership rate	68.0% (343)
Housing diversity index	86.4% (26)
4 or more bedrooms	17.4% (226)
Affordability/income ratio	$2,540 (266)

INCOME ★★ (371)

Poverty rate	18.1% (300)
Median household income	$39,928 (384)
Interest/dividends	18.8% (284)
Public assistance	16.4% (309)
Median fulltime earnings	$31,949 (497)

SENIORS ★★★ (284)

Seniors living alone	26.1% (179)
Poverty rate for seniors	11.9% (408)
Median income for seniors	$32,255 (312)
Seniors who work	20.1% (192)
Home ownership by seniors	82.1% (268)

STABILITY ★★★★ (189)

25-39 age group	18.3% (159)
Born in state of residence	69.1% (325)
Same house as 1 year ago	81.5% (460)
Live and work in county	84.8% (137)
Married-couple households	52.4% (177)

TRANSPORTATION ★★★★ (203)

Bicycle or walk to work	2.0% (386)
Carpool to work	11.2% (211)
Public transit to work	0.6% (141)
Commute <15 minutes	46.1% (230)
Commute >45 minutes	6.9% (82)

See pages 37-130 for explanations of statistics, stars, and ranks.

Seymour, IN
(Jackson County, IN)

POPULATION	
2010 census	42,376 (284)
2015 estimate	44,069 (271)
2010-2015 change	4.0% (61)
2020 projection	45,158 (259)
2030 projection	47,246 (242)

RACE	
Whites	90.2% (175)
Blacks	0.8% (404)
Hispanics	6.1% (218)
Asians	1.4% (99)
Native Americans	0.2% (300)

AGE	
0-17 years old	24.3% (164)
18-24 years old	8.2% (379)
25-39 years old	20.0% (58)
40-54 years old	20.0% (233)
55-64 years old	12.6% (385)
65+ years old	15.0% (371)

PRIVATE SECTOR	
Businesses	905 (309)
Employees	17,505 (162)
Total wages	$726,065,372 (143)
Average weekly wages	$798 (93)

HOUSEHOLD INCOME LADDER	
95th percentile	$128,082 (452)
80th percentile	$84,427 (264)
60th percentile	$56,990 (206)
40th percentile	$37,158 (202)
20th percentile	$21,540 (161)

CHILDREN	★★★ (229)
Living with two parents	68.8% (172)
Older teens in school	81.5% (345)
Speak English very well	99.1% (179)
Poverty rate for children	21.0% (193)
No health insurance	8.5% (379)

DIVERSITY/EQUALITY	★★★ (306)
Racial diversity index	18.2% (372)
Geographic diversity index	38.7% (375)
Top 20% share of income	44.0% (28)
Gender gap in earnings	31.8% (221)
White-collar gender gap	39.2% (436)

EDUCATION	★★ (363)
Eighth grade or less	3.0% (231)
High school diplomas	90.2% (196)

Attended college	42.7% (479)
Bachelor's degrees	15.9% (382)
Advanced degrees	4.7% (419)

EMPLOYMENT	★★★ (281)
Average jobless rate	7.3% (228)
Self-employed workers	6.8% (446)
Management/financial jobs	11.7% (185)
Computer/engineering jobs	3.9% (86)
Health care jobs	4.8% (369)

GROWTH POTENTIAL	★★★ (301)
Children per senior	1.62 (164)
Median age	38.3 (197)
Moved from different state	1.4% (425)
Homes built since 2000	15.3% (195)
Construction jobs	5.0% (467)

HOUSING	★★★★ (140)
Home vacancy rate	8.9% (280)
Home ownership rate	74.2% (110)
Housing diversity index	86.5% (19)
4 or more bedrooms	13.6% (424)
Affordability/income ratio	$2,387 (208)

INCOME	★★★ (234)
Poverty rate	14.8% (187)
Median household income	$47,000 (192)
Interest/dividends	17.5% (329)
Public assistance	12.7% (155)
Median fulltime earnings	$36,667 (308)

SENIORS	★★★★ (115)
Seniors living alone	26.1% (179)
Poverty rate for seniors	7.1% (101)
Median income for seniors	$33,564 (256)
Seniors who work	20.0% (195)
Home ownership by seniors	85.9% (105)

STABILITY	★★★★★ (29)
25-39 age group	20.0% (58)
Born in state of residence	77.5% (168)
Same house as 1 year ago	86.4% (225)
Live and work in county	73.8% (317)
Married-couple households	54.5% (88)

TRANSPORTATION	★★★ (330)
Bicycle or walk to work	1.8% (409)
Carpool to work	10.2% (312)
Public transit to work	0.4% (219)
Commute <15 minutes	43.1% (277)
Commute >45 minutes	9.8% (218)

See pages 37-130 for explanations of statistics, stars, and ranks.

Shawano, WI
(Menominee and Shawano Counties, WI)

POPULATION	
2010 census	46,181 (244)
2015 estimate	45,877 (246)
2010-2015 change	-0.7% (303)
2020 projection	45,602 (253)
2030 projection	45,050 (263)

RACE	
Whites	80.0% (326)
Blacks	0.3% (519)
Hispanics	2.9% (350)
Asians	0.7% (241)
Native Americans	14.4% (11)

AGE	
0-17 years old	22.9% (270)
18-24 years old	7.6% (468)
25-39 years old	15.3% (493)
40-54 years old	21.4% (67)
55-64 years old	13.7% (225)
65+ years old	19.0% (80)

PRIVATE SECTOR	
Businesses	1,015 (271)
Employees	9,908 (378)
Total wages	$305,188,138 (428)
Average weekly wages	$592 (498)

HOUSEHOLD INCOME LADDER	
95th percentile	$137,883 (313)
80th percentile	$83,651 (281)
60th percentile	$56,780 (215)
40th percentile	$37,641 (190)
20th percentile	$21,828 (146)

CHILDREN	★★★ (277)
Living with two parents	65.9% (247)
Older teens in school	78.8% (433)
Speak English very well	99.1% (179)
Poverty rate for children	20.7% (185)
No health insurance	8.3% (370)

DIVERSITY/EQUALITY	★★★★ (166)
Racial diversity index	33.8% (221)
Geographic diversity index	24.7% (530)
Top 20% share of income	45.9% (118)
Gender gap in earnings	25.8% (102)
White-collar gender gap	13.7% (138)

EDUCATION	★★★★ (220)
Eighth grade or less	1.4% (60)
High school diplomas	93.5% (75)
Attended college	50.4% (319)
Bachelor's degrees	16.9% (334)
Advanced degrees	5.4% (334)

EMPLOYMENT	★★★★ (143)
Average jobless rate	6.0% (117)
Self-employed workers	11.9% (78)
Management/financial jobs	12.7% (103)
Computer/engineering jobs	2.3% (354)
Health care jobs	4.5% (419)

GROWTH POTENTIAL	★ (454)
Children per senior	1.21 (411)
Median age	43.3 (460)
Moved from different state	0.9% (515)
Homes built since 2000	15.2% (199)
Construction jobs	5.9% (345)

HOUSING	★★★★★ (39)
Home vacancy rate	5.4% (55)
Home ownership rate	75.7% (64)
Housing diversity index	85.3% (170)
4 or more bedrooms	20.6% (114)
Affordability/income ratio	$2,749 (345)

INCOME	★★★★ (140)
Poverty rate	13.3% (130)
Median household income	$46,677 (199)
Interest/dividends	27.2% (47)
Public assistance	13.3% (182)
Median fulltime earnings	$36,899 (294)

SENIORS	★★★ (227)
Seniors living alone	25.7% (154)
Poverty rate for seniors	9.5% (291)
Median income for seniors	$31,018 (372)
Seniors who work	18.7% (259)
Home ownership by seniors	83.8% (186)

STABILITY	★★★ (254)
25-39 age group	15.3% (493)
Born in state of residence	86.4% (22)
Same house as 1 year ago	88.9% (86)
Live and work in county	59.7% (493)
Married-couple households	52.9% (157)

TRANSPORTATION	★★ (356)
Bicycle or walk to work	3.8% (161)
Carpool to work	10.7% (260)
Public transit to work	0.3% (291)
Commute <15 minutes	39.2% (343)
Commute >45 minutes	14.3% (402)

See pages 37-130 for explanations of statistics, stars, and ranks.

Sidney, OH
(Shelby County, OH)

POPULATION

2010 census	49,423 (215)
2015 estimate	48,901 (219)
2010-2015 change	-1.1% (335)
2020 projection	48,627 (226)
2030 projection	47,896 (233)

RACE

Whites	93.4% (94)
Blacks	2.5% (253)
Hispanics	1.5% (480)
Asians	0.7% (241)
Native Americans	0.3% (231)

AGE

0-17 years old	26.3% (57)
18-24 years old	7.9% (424)
25-39 years old	16.8% (359)
40-54 years old	21.6% (50)
55-64 years old	13.2% (297)
65+ years old	14.1% (431)

PRIVATE SECTOR

Businesses	938 (298)
Employees	24,713 (78)
Total wages	$1,191,392,391 (38)
Average weekly wages	$927 (27)

HOUSEHOLD INCOME LADDER

95th percentile	$157,814 (109)
80th percentile	$96,146 (81)
60th percentile	$66,740 (57)
40th percentile	$44,609 (49)
20th percentile	$26,597 (30)

CHILDREN ★★★★★ (25)

Living with two parents	71.6% (110)
Older teens in school	89.5% (75)
Speak English very well	99.7% (57)
Poverty rate for children	14.2% (57)
No health insurance	2.6% (40)

DIVERSITY/EQUALITY ★ (493)

Racial diversity index	12.7% (452)
Geographic diversity index	28.4% (500)
Top 20% share of income	46.4% (150)
Gender gap in earnings	41.8% (468)
White-collar gender gap	28.1% (310)

EDUCATION ★★★★ (209)

Eighth grade or less	1.5% (72)
High school diplomas	92.0% (124)

Attended college	49.4% (348)
Bachelor's degrees	17.7% (295)
Advanced degrees	6.9% (186)

EMPLOYMENT ★★★★ (219)

Average jobless rate	6.7% (169)
Self-employed workers	6.8% (446)
Management/financial jobs	12.6% (111)
Computer/engineering jobs	4.0% (76)
Health care jobs	4.8% (369)

GROWTH POTENTIAL ★★★ (292)

Children per senior	1.87 (77)
Median age	38.9 (228)
Moved from different state	1.1% (487)
Homes built since 2000	11.1% (356)
Construction jobs	5.9% (345)

HOUSING ★★★★★ (80)

Home vacancy rate	6.3% (122)
Home ownership rate	70.9% (232)
Housing diversity index	86.3% (36)
4 or more bedrooms	16.9% (255)
Affordability/income ratio	$2,383 (205)

INCOME ★★★★★ (71)

Poverty rate	10.3% (41)
Median household income	$54,550 (58)
Interest/dividends	21.4% (202)
Public assistance	9.9% (59)
Median fulltime earnings	$41,481 (79)

SENIORS ★★★★★ (108)

Seniors living alone	25.6% (149)
Poverty rate for seniors	7.1% (101)
Median income for seniors	$36,628 (129)
Seniors who work	19.1% (238)
Home ownership by seniors	84.8% (150)

STABILITY ★★★★★ (40)

25-39 age group	16.8% (359)
Born in state of residence	84.2% (51)
Same house as 1 year ago	88.3% (115)
Live and work in county	71.2% (354)
Married-couple households	57.1% (29)

TRANSPORTATION ★★ (332)

Bicycle or walk to work	1.8% (409)
Carpool to work	8.2% (480)
Public transit to work	0.2% (363)
Commute <15 minutes	46.2% (229)
Commute >45 minutes	7.2% (91)

See pages 37-130 for explanations of statistics, stars, and ranks.

Sikeston, MO
(Scott County, MO)

POPULATION

2010 census	39,191 (322)
2015 estimate	39,008 (327)
2010-2015 change	-0.5% (292)
2020 projection	38,357 (336)
2030 projection	36,985 (346)

RACE

Whites	84.1% (277)
Blacks	11.3% (109)
Hispanics	2.1% (416)
Asians	0.4% (413)
Native Americans	0.3% (231)

AGE

0-17 years old	24.0% (184)
18-24 years old	8.4% (349)
25-39 years old	17.9% (214)
40-54 years old	20.0% (233)
55-64 years old	13.2% (297)
65+ years old	16.4% (255)

PRIVATE SECTOR

Businesses	1,313 (172)
Employees	13,136 (274)
Total wages	$443,830,752 (297)
Average weekly wages	$650 (389)

HOUSEHOLD INCOME LADDER

95th percentile	$130,588 (423)
80th percentile	$77,429 (409)
60th percentile	$47,066 (443)
40th percentile	$31,213 (384)
20th percentile	$16,137 (404)

CHILDREN ★★★ (313)

Living with two parents	59.4% (419)
Older teens in school	77.9% (452)
Speak English very well	99.9% (19)
Poverty rate for children	27.6% (357)
No health insurance	4.2% (134)

DIVERSITY/EQUALITY ★★ (414)

Racial diversity index	27.9% (270)
Geographic diversity index	41.3% (335)
Top 20% share of income	47.8% (277)
Gender gap in earnings	38.2% (399)
White-collar gender gap	37.5% (414)

EDUCATION ★★ (396)

Eighth grade or less	2.8% (205)
High school diplomas	85.9% (345)
Attended college	43.7% (456)
Bachelor's degrees	14.0% (462)
Advanced degrees	4.6% (431)

EMPLOYMENT ★★★ (236)

Average jobless rate	6.8% (179)
Self-employed workers	7.3% (401)
Management/financial jobs	9.5% (440)
Computer/engineering jobs	2.0% (420)
Health care jobs	7.8% (28)

GROWTH POTENTIAL ★★ (338)

Children per senior	1.46 (237)
Median age	39.7 (279)
Moved from different state	1.7% (355)
Homes built since 2000	10.0% (388)
Construction jobs	6.5% (253)

HOUSING ★★★★ (196)

Home vacancy rate	7.8% (205)
Home ownership rate	68.1% (339)
Housing diversity index	85.6% (127)
4 or more bedrooms	15.2% (344)
Affordability/income ratio	$2,408 (217)

INCOME ★ (461)

Poverty rate	19.6% (360)
Median household income	$39,162 (401)
Interest/dividends	15.2% (401)
Public assistance	23.1% (498)
Median fulltime earnings	$32,113 (491)

SENIORS ★ (498)

Seniors living alone	31.3% (486)
Poverty rate for seniors	13.6% (463)
Median income for seniors	$28,056 (458)
Seniors who work	19.2% (234)
Home ownership by seniors	78.4% (435)

STABILITY ★★ (331)

25-39 age group	17.9% (214)
Born in state of residence	75.2% (219)
Same house as 1 year ago	85.9% (257)
Live and work in county	62.0% (474)
Married-couple households	50.0% (296)

TRANSPORTATION ★★★★ (215)

Bicycle or walk to work	0.8% (531)
Carpool to work	14.1% (61)
Public transit to work	0.2% (363)
Commute <15 minutes	43.0% (278)
Commute >45 minutes	7.1% (88)

See pages 37-130 for explanations of statistics, stars, and ranks.

Spearfish, SD
(Lawrence County, SD)

POPULATION		Attended college	64.4% (68)
2010 census	24,097 (488)	Bachelor's degrees	31.2% (45)
2015 estimate	24,827 (485)	Advanced degrees	9.1% (83)
2010-2015 change	3.0% (86)		
2020 projection	25,696 (472)	**EMPLOYMENT**	★★★★★ **(59)**
2030 projection	27,400 (452)	Average jobless rate	3.8% (28)
		Self-employed workers	13.1% (49)
RACE		Management/financial jobs	12.5% (119)
Whites	91.3% (155)	Computer/engineering jobs	2.9% (219)
Blacks	0.4% (499)	Health care jobs	5.4% (273)
Hispanics	3.1% (333)		
Asians	0.8% (201)	**GROWTH POTENTIAL**	★★★★★ **(63)**
Native Americans	3.1% (49)	Children per senior	1.07 (477)
		Median age	41.5 (380)
AGE		Moved from different state	5.6% (36)
0-17 years old	18.6% (509)	Homes built since 2000	22.1% (68)
18-24 years old	13.0% (71)	Construction jobs	9.9% (21)
25-39 years old	16.3% (418)		
40-54 years old	18.5% (425)	**HOUSING**	★★★ **(233)**
55-64 years old	16.1% (42)	Home vacancy rate	5.5% (60)
65+ years old	17.5% (158)	Home ownership rate	66.9% (392)
		Housing diversity index	83.8% (369)
PRIVATE SECTOR		4 or more bedrooms	22.0% (81)
Businesses	1,120 (233)	Affordability/income ratio	$3,954 (494)
Employees	9,862 (381)		
Total wages	$319,439,044 (410)	**INCOME**	★★★★ **(179)**
Average weekly wages	$623 (447)	Poverty rate	13.1% (119)
		Median household income	$45,548 (222)
HOUSEHOLD INCOME LADDER		Interest/dividends	22.2% (174)
95th percentile	$153,941 (122)	Public assistance	11.4% (107)
80th percentile	$90,696 (147)	Median fulltime earnings	$35,732 (347)
60th percentile	$58,148 (178)		
40th percentile	$37,627 (191)	**SENIORS**	★★★ **(304)**
20th percentile	$20,630 (201)	Seniors living alone	29.2% (381)
		Poverty rate for seniors	7.4% (128)
CHILDREN	★★★★ **(127)**	Median income for seniors	$32,207 (314)
Living with two parents	70.6% (128)	Seniors who work	21.7% (138)
Older teens in school	84.7% (210)	Home ownership by seniors	78.7% (427)
Speak English very well	99.0% (200)		
Poverty rate for children	13.4% (50)	**STABILITY**	★ **(479)**
No health insurance	8.6% (384)	25-39 age group	16.3% (418)
		Born in state of residence	56.5% (451)
DIVERSITY/EQUALITY	★★★ **(259)**	Same house as 1 year ago	81.4% (465)
Racial diversity index	16.4% (391)	Live and work in county	79.8% (221)
Geographic diversity index	61.5% (109)	Married-couple households	49.7% (311)
Top 20% share of income	48.0% (292)		
Gender gap in earnings	33.6% (271)	**TRANSPORTATION**	★★★★★ **(10)**
White-collar gender gap	29.3% (324)	Bicycle or walk to work	9.1% (19)
		Carpool to work	14.6% (52)
EDUCATION	★★★★★ **(36)**	Public transit to work	0.5% (178)
Eighth grade or less	0.7% (9)	Commute <15 minutes	58.2% (60)
High school diplomas	96.7% (7)	Commute >45 minutes	8.4% (148)

See pages 37-130 for explanations of statistics, stars, and ranks.

Spencer, IA
(Clay County, IA)

POPULATION	
2010 census	16,667 (539)
2015 estimate	16,507 (542)
2010-2015 change	-1.0% (326)
2020 projection	16,247 (542)
2030 projection	15,647 (543)

RACE	
Whites	94.6% (59)
Blacks	0.6% (438)
Hispanics	3.0% (343)
Asians	0.6% (291)
Native Americans	0.1% (402)

AGE	
0-17 years old	22.8% (277)
18-24 years old	7.4% (489)
25-39 years old	17.2% (290)
40-54 years old	18.8% (386)
55-64 years old	14.7% (97)
65+ years old	19.1% (76)

PRIVATE SECTOR	
Businesses	680 (438)
Employees	7,138 (471)
Total wages	$272,140,815 (454)
Average weekly wages	$733 (192)

HOUSEHOLD INCOME LADDER	
95th percentile	$139,604 (296)
80th percentile	$93,777 (104)
60th percentile	$61,265 (125)
40th percentile	$40,693 (107)
20th percentile	$21,877 (143)

CHILDREN	★★★★★ (41)
Living with two parents	69.8% (149)
Older teens in school	92.0% (38)
Speak English very well	99.9% (19)
Poverty rate for children	20.1% (170)
No health insurance	3.2% (69)

DIVERSITY/EQUALITY	★★ (352)
Racial diversity index	10.4% (490)
Geographic diversity index	42.2% (323)
Top 20% share of income	45.1% (67)
Gender gap in earnings	34.5% (301)
White-collar gender gap	33.4% (377)

EDUCATION	★★★★ (175)
Eighth grade or less	2.1% (136)
High school diplomas	93.8% (63)
Attended college	60.9% (114)
Bachelor's degrees	20.5% (207)
Advanced degrees	3.4% (514)

EMPLOYMENT	★★★★★ (67)
Average jobless rate	3.8% (28)
Self-employed workers	13.7% (37)
Management/financial jobs	12.4% (126)
Computer/engineering jobs	2.2% (381)
Health care jobs	5.3% (286)

GROWTH POTENTIAL	★ (486)
Children per senior	1.19 (423)
Median age	42.2 (412)
Moved from different state	2.3% (234)
Homes built since 2000	8.7% (445)
Construction jobs	5.3% (425)

HOUSING	★★★★★ (96)
Home vacancy rate	9.9% (345)
Home ownership rate	74.5% (98)
Housing diversity index	84.6% (277)
4 or more bedrooms	21.0% (100)
Affordability/income ratio	$2,193 (122)

INCOME	★★★★★ (83)
Poverty rate	11.5% (71)
Median household income	$50,389 (116)
Interest/dividends	26.5% (62)
Public assistance	10.2% (68)
Median fulltime earnings	$38,592 (200)

SENIORS	★★★ (264)
Seniors living alone	32.7% (523)
Poverty rate for seniors	8.3% (202)
Median income for seniors	$37,590 (101)
Seniors who work	22.4% (122)
Home ownership by seniors	82.1% (268)

STABILITY	★★★★ (190)
25-39 age group	17.2% (290)
Born in state of residence	74.2% (240)
Same house as 1 year ago	84.2% (341)
Live and work in county	82.4% (174)
Married-couple households	51.0% (248)

TRANSPORTATION	★★★★★ (78)
Bicycle or walk to work	5.0% (91)
Carpool to work	11.9% (145)
Public transit to work	0.3% (291)
Commute <15 minutes	58.5% (56)
Commute >45 minutes	7.5% (105)

See pages 37-130 for explanations of statistics, stars, and ranks.

Spirit Lake, IA
(Dickinson County, IA)

POPULATION

2010 census	16,667 (539)
2015 estimate	17,111 (539)
2010-2015 change	2.7% (96)
2020 projection	17,308 (536)
2030 projection	17,613 (533)

RACE

Whites	96.7% (3)
Blacks	0.3% (519)
Hispanics	1.6% (472)
Asians	0.4% (413)
Native Americans	0.1% (402)

AGE

0-17 years old	19.3% (492)
18-24 years old	6.2% (543)
25-39 years old	15.7% (465)
40-54 years old	18.4% (430)
55-64 years old	16.8% (21)
65+ years old	23.6% (13)

PRIVATE SECTOR

Businesses	811 (367)
Employees	8,578 (433)
Total wages	$312,897,617 (420)
Average weekly wages	$701 (254)

HOUSEHOLD INCOME LADDER

95th percentile	$197,892 (20)
80th percentile	$105,500 (34)
60th percentile	$67,743 (49)
40th percentile	$46,394 (36)
20th percentile	$24,317 (59)

CHILDREN ★★★★★ (44)

Living with two parents	75.5% (44)
Older teens in school	78.9% (430)
Speak English very well	100.0% (1)
Poverty rate for children	6.1% (2)
No health insurance	4.5% (150)

DIVERSITY/EQUALITY ★ (528)

Racial diversity index	6.5% (548)
Geographic diversity index	46.0% (267)
Top 20% share of income	48.6% (327)
Gender gap in earnings	38.0% (392)
White-collar gender gap	48.9% (506)

EDUCATION ★★★★★ (30)

Eighth grade or less	0.5% (2)
High school diplomas	97.2% (4)
Attended college	71.7% (21)
Bachelor's degrees	29.0% (62)
Advanced degrees	8.7% (96)

EMPLOYMENT ★★★★★ (6)

Average jobless rate	3.8% (28)
Self-employed workers	17.0% (7)
Management/financial jobs	16.7% (11)
Computer/engineering jobs	3.1% (180)
Health care jobs	5.9% (193)

GROWTH POTENTIAL ★★ (344)

Children per senior	0.82 (534)
Median age	48.7 (539)
Moved from different state	2.1% (269)
Homes built since 2000	18.8% (112)
Construction jobs	9.1% (40)

HOUSING ★★★★★ (42)

Home vacancy rate	7.3% (176)
Home ownership rate	75.5% (67)
Housing diversity index	85.7% (108)
4 or more bedrooms	23.6% (53)
Affordability/income ratio	$2,930 (387)

INCOME ★★★★★ (25)

Poverty rate	6.6% (2)
Median household income	$57,265 (37)
Interest/dividends	31.4% (10)
Public assistance	8.4% (39)
Median fulltime earnings	$40,954 (100)

SENIORS ★★★★★ (20)

Seniors living alone	24.7% (105)
Poverty rate for seniors	5.0% (17)
Median income for seniors	$43,893 (37)
Seniors who work	25.9% (51)
Home ownership by seniors	84.7% (155)

STABILITY ★★★★ (174)

25-39 age group	15.7% (465)
Born in state of residence	70.1% (308)
Same house as 1 year ago	86.4% (225)
Live and work in county	78.6% (236)
Married-couple households	56.3% (43)

TRANSPORTATION ★★★★ (144)

Bicycle or walk to work	3.4% (199)
Carpool to work	9.2% (408)
Public transit to work	0.6% (141)
Commute <15 minutes	53.6% (100)
Commute >45 minutes	5.1% (36)

See pages 37-130 for explanations of statistics, stars, and ranks.

Sterling, IL
(Whiteside County, IL)

POPULATION

2010 census	58,498 (157)
2015 estimate	57,079 (165)
2010-2015 change	-2.4% (443)
2020 projection	55,632 (173)
2030 projection	52,689 (197)

RACE

Whites	85.0% (267)
Blacks	1.6% (320)
Hispanics	11.6% (130)
Asians	0.5% (355)
Native Americans	0.2% (300)

AGE

0-17 years old	22.9% (270)
18-24 years old	7.9% (424)
25-39 years old	15.8% (460)
40-54 years old	20.5% (151)
55-64 years old	14.3% (148)
65+ years old	18.6% (101)

PRIVATE SECTOR

Businesses	1,229 (194)
Employees	16,212 (186)
Total wages	$547,501,924 (214)
Average weekly wages	$649 (393)

HOUSEHOLD INCOME LADDER

95th percentile	$145,744 (218)
80th percentile	$86,936 (208)
60th percentile	$58,803 (167)
40th percentile	$38,176 (175)
20th percentile	$22,238 (126)

CHILDREN ★★★★ (134)

Living with two parents	65.0% (270)
Older teens in school	83.7% (251)
Speak English very well	98.6% (278)
Poverty rate for children	18.0% (125)
No health insurance	3.3% (72)

DIVERSITY/EQUALITY ★★★ (283)

Racial diversity index	26.4% (283)
Geographic diversity index	44.1% (293)
Top 20% share of income	46.3% (146)
Gender gap in earnings	40.0% (438)
White-collar gender gap	22.7% (245)

EDUCATION ★★★★ (192)

Eighth grade or less	2.7% (195)
High school diplomas	91.2% (153)

Attended college	58.2% (166)
Bachelor's degrees	18.0% (284)
Advanced degrees	6.1% (250)

EMPLOYMENT ★★ (360)

Average jobless rate	8.1% (298)
Self-employed workers	6.8% (446)
Management/financial jobs	9.9% (392)
Computer/engineering jobs	3.0% (193)
Health care jobs	5.8% (209)

GROWTH POTENTIAL ★ (535)

Children per senior	1.23 (393)
Median age	42.7 (442)
Moved from different state	1.0% (504)
Homes built since 2000	7.6% (483)
Construction jobs	5.1% (458)

HOUSING ★★★★★ (63)

Home vacancy rate	7.2% (172)
Home ownership rate	75.3% (72)
Housing diversity index	85.1% (212)
4 or more bedrooms	18.2% (194)
Affordability/income ratio	$2,093 (80)

INCOME ★★★★ (128)

Poverty rate	12.0% (85)
Median household income	$47,401 (183)
Interest/dividends	23.5% (142)
Public assistance	13.5% (188)
Median fulltime earnings	$40,060 (139)

SENIORS ★★★★ (179)

Seniors living alone	30.2% (436)
Poverty rate for seniors	5.1% (22)
Median income for seniors	$36,547 (135)
Seniors who work	19.2% (234)
Home ownership by seniors	83.7% (190)

STABILITY ★★★ (277)

25-39 age group	15.8% (460)
Born in state of residence	72.8% (263)
Same house as 1 year ago	90.4% (36)
Live and work in county	68.4% (400)
Married-couple households	50.2% (290)

TRANSPORTATION ★★★ (284)

Bicycle or walk to work	2.4% (331)
Carpool to work	9.8% (358)
Public transit to work	0.3% (291)
Commute <15 minutes	46.5% (225)
Commute >45 minutes	9.0% (175)

See pages 37-130 for explanations of statistics, stars, and ranks.

Stevens Point, WI
(Portage County, WI)

POPULATION	
2010 census	70,019 (101)
2015 estimate	70,408 (102)
2010-2015 change	0.6% (209)
2020 projection	70,717 (99)
2030 projection	71,267 (100)

RACE	
Whites	92.0% (135)
Blacks	0.6% (438)
Hispanics	2.9% (350)
Asians	2.7% (29)
Native Americans	0.4% (203)

AGE	
0-17 years old	19.9% (465)
18-24 years old	16.9% (46)
25-39 years old	16.7% (375)
40-54 years old	19.4% (315)
55-64 years old	12.9% (343)
65+ years old	14.1% (431)

PRIVATE SECTOR	
Businesses	1,583 (121)
Employees	29,213 (47)
Total wages	$1,176,553,123 (44)
Average weekly wages	$775 (122)

HOUSEHOLD INCOME LADDER	
95th percentile	$151,500 (145)
80th percentile	$94,376 (94)
60th percentile	$63,654 (90)
40th percentile	$41,421 (91)
20th percentile	$22,087 (136)

CHILDREN	★★★★★ (17)
Living with two parents	76.9% (31)
Older teens in school	91.2% (51)
Speak English very well	97.5% (388)
Poverty rate for children	13.2% (49)
No health insurance	2.4% (28)

DIVERSITY/EQUALITY	★★★ (268)
Racial diversity index	15.2% (409)
Geographic diversity index	37.9% (392)
Top 20% share of income	46.2% (139)
Gender gap in earnings	36.0% (339)
White-collar gender gap	10.3% (91)

EDUCATION	★★★★★ (43)
Eighth grade or less	1.3% (52)
High school diplomas	94.7% (40)
Attended college	63.7% (76)
Bachelor's degrees	31.7% (42)
Advanced degrees	9.5% (73)

EMPLOYMENT	★★★★ (171)
Average jobless rate	7.2% (218)
Self-employed workers	8.3% (302)
Management/financial jobs	12.9% (92)
Computer/engineering jobs	4.7% (40)
Health care jobs	4.3% (444)

GROWTH POTENTIAL	★★★ (270)
Children per senior	1.41 (269)
Median age	36.2 (122)
Moved from different state	1.7% (355)
Homes built since 2000	16.6% (164)
Construction jobs	5.0% (467)

HOUSING	★★★★★ (108)
Home vacancy rate	5.4% (55)
Home ownership rate	68.6% (321)
Housing diversity index	85.5% (143)
4 or more bedrooms	19.7% (132)
Affordability/income ratio	$2,939 (390)

INCOME	★★★★★ (98)
Poverty rate	15.1% (196)
Median household income	$51,613 (89)
Interest/dividends	24.9% (100)
Public assistance	12.2% (138)
Median fulltime earnings	$41,959 (65)

SENIORS	★★★ (298)
Seniors living alone	28.0% (296)
Poverty rate for seniors	8.2% (196)
Median income for seniors	$36,674 (125)
Seniors who work	17.3% (324)
Home ownership by seniors	79.3% (403)

STABILITY	★★★ (265)
25-39 age group	16.7% (375)
Born in state of residence	77.8% (159)
Same house as 1 year ago	82.0% (439)
Live and work in county	80.1% (216)
Married-couple households	51.1% (245)

TRANSPORTATION	★★★★ (141)
Bicycle or walk to work	7.8% (32)
Carpool to work	8.3% (471)
Public transit to work	0.5% (178)
Commute <15 minutes	45.6% (240)
Commute >45 minutes	7.8% (122)

See pages 37-130 for explanations of statistics, stars, and ranks.

Storm Lake, IA
(Buena Vista County, IA)

POPULATION

2010 census	20,260 (526)
2015 estimate	20,493 (522)
2010-2015 change	1.2% (173)
2020 projection	20,562 (521)
2030 projection	20,580 (516)

RACE

Whites	63.9% (424)
Blacks	2.7% (241)
Hispanics	24.3% (62)
Asians	8.5% (3)
Native Americans	0.0% (523)

AGE

0-17 years old	25.3% (97)
18-24 years old	11.6% (98)
25-39 years old	16.7% (375)
40-54 years old	19.2% (336)
55-64 years old	12.6% (385)
65+ years old	14.6% (400)

PRIVATE SECTOR

Businesses	594 (473)
Employees	9,242 (404)
Total wages	$329,697,630 (399)
Average weekly wages	$686 (297)

HOUSEHOLD INCOME LADDER

95th percentile	$147,344 (193)
80th percentile	$88,652 (172)
60th percentile	$57,447 (198)
40th percentile	$40,241 (123)
20th percentile	$23,156 (92)

CHILDREN ★★★ (302)

Living with two parents	67.6% (204)
Older teens in school	87.1% (133)
Speak English very well	87.7% (534)
Poverty rate for children	17.3% (107)
No health insurance	4.5% (150)

DIVERSITY/EQUALITY ★★ (351)

Racial diversity index	52.5% (90)
Geographic diversity index	61.9% (104)
Top 20% share of income	48.5% (322)
Gender gap in earnings	38.4% (406)
White-collar gender gap	65.9% (550)

EDUCATION ★ (484)

Eighth grade or less	12.9% (529)
High school diplomas	77.3% (513)
Attended college	50.2% (325)
Bachelor's degrees	19.5% (233)
Advanced degrees	6.8% (191)

EMPLOYMENT ★★★ (221)

Average jobless rate	3.7% (25)
Self-employed workers	11.6% (90)
Management/financial jobs	10.6% (306)
Computer/engineering jobs	1.9% (441)
Health care jobs	3.9% (488)

GROWTH POTENTIAL ★★★ (265)

Children per senior	1.73 (120)
Median age	35.9 (113)
Moved from different state	4.2% (70)
Homes built since 2000	6.5% (515)
Construction jobs	4.6% (494)

HOUSING ★★★★★ (79)

Home vacancy rate	5.4% (55)
Home ownership rate	68.9% (308)
Housing diversity index	83.3% (402)
4 or more bedrooms	22.4% (76)
Affordability/income ratio	$2,156 (103)

INCOME ★★★★ (184)

Poverty rate	12.6% (103)
Median household income	$48,195 (170)
Interest/dividends	22.9% (159)
Public assistance	13.0% (169)
Median fulltime earnings	$34,160 (417)

SENIORS ★★★★ (163)

Seniors living alone	29.5% (405)
Poverty rate for seniors	9.6% (295)
Median income for seniors	$38,929 (76)
Seniors who work	28.3% (30)
Home ownership by seniors	78.8% (425)

STABILITY ★★ (357)

25-39 age group	16.7% (375)
Born in state of residence	59.0% (426)
Same house as 1 year ago	81.0% (478)
Live and work in county	89.5% (74)
Married-couple households	51.8% (206)

TRANSPORTATION ★★★★★ (5)

Bicycle or walk to work	6.2% (55)
Carpool to work	18.3% (14)
Public transit to work	0.1% (441)
Commute <15 minutes	66.4% (12)
Commute >45 minutes	4.0% (13)

See pages 37-130 for explanations of statistics, stars, and ranks.

Sturgis, MI
(St. Joseph County, MI)

POPULATION			
2010 census	61,295 (142)		
2015 estimate	61,018 (143)		
2010-2015 change	-0.5% (292)		
2020 projection	60,813 (142)		
2030 projection	60,206 (151)		

RACE
Whites	87.2% (236)
Blacks	2.8% (232)
Hispanics	7.2% (194)
Asians	0.6% (291)
Native Americans	0.3% (231)

AGE
0-17 years old	25.3% (97)
18-24 years old	8.2% (379)
25-39 years old	17.4% (269)
40-54 years old	19.7% (273)
55-64 years old	13.5% (258)
65+ years old	16.0% (291)

PRIVATE SECTOR
Businesses	3,062 (19)
Employees	20,476 (120)
Total wages	$791,527,523 (120)
Average weekly wages	$743 (169)

HOUSEHOLD INCOME LADDER
95th percentile	$128,909 (443)
80th percentile	$78,995 (382)
60th percentile	$53,188 (295)
40th percentile	$36,447 (218)
20th percentile	$20,770 (194)

CHILDREN ★★★ (320)
Living with two parents	64.8% (276)
Older teens in school	82.8% (286)
Speak English very well	97.1% (408)
Poverty rate for children	26.7% (344)
No health insurance	7.5% (344)

DIVERSITY/EQUALITY ★★★★ (132)
Racial diversity index	23.3% (309)
Geographic diversity index	48.8% (233)
Top 20% share of income	45.6% (94)
Gender gap in earnings	34.2% (293)
White-collar gender gap	12.0% (113)

EDUCATION ★★ (378)
Eighth grade or less	4.5% (354)
High school diplomas	87.0% (309)
Attended college	49.1% (354)
Bachelor's degrees	14.6% (435)
Advanced degrees	4.8% (405)

EMPLOYMENT ★ (444)
Average jobless rate	8.6% (335)
Self-employed workers	7.7% (362)
Management/financial jobs	9.9% (392)
Computer/engineering jobs	3.0% (193)
Health care jobs	4.1% (462)

GROWTH POTENTIAL ★ (450)
Children per senior	1.58 (182)
Median age	39.2 (248)
Moved from different state	1.9% (310)
Homes built since 2000	9.6% (404)
Construction jobs	4.0% (536)

HOUSING ★★★★★ (36)
Home vacancy rate	7.5% (186)
Home ownership rate	75.0% (81)
Housing diversity index	86.3% (36)
4 or more bedrooms	20.7% (110)
Affordability/income ratio	$2,383 (205)

INCOME ★★★ (283)
Poverty rate	17.2% (270)
Median household income	$44,449 (251)
Interest/dividends	18.8% (284)
Public assistance	15.9% (290)
Median fulltime earnings	$35,758 (346)

SENIORS ★★★★ (154)
Seniors living alone	25.2% (124)
Poverty rate for seniors	8.4% (214)
Median income for seniors	$33,164 (273)
Seniors who work	17.4% (318)
Home ownership by seniors	86.0% (102)

STABILITY ★★★ (233)
25-39 age group	17.4% (269)
Born in state of residence	68.9% (326)
Same house as 1 year ago	87.1% (192)
Live and work in county	69.2% (382)
Married-couple households	53.0% (152)

TRANSPORTATION ★★★ (237)
Bicycle or walk to work	3.8% (161)
Carpool to work	13.3% (88)
Public transit to work	0.2% (363)
Commute <15 minutes	37.4% (390)
Commute >45 minutes	10.3% (237)

See pages 37-130 for explanations of statistics, stars, and ranks.

Taylorville, IL
(Christian County, IL)

POPULATION	
2010 census	34,800 (387)
2015 estimate	33,642 (398)
2010-2015 change	-3.3% (495)
2020 projection	32,590 (414)
2030 projection	30,489 (420)

RACE	
Whites	95.2% (38)
Blacks	1.7% (315)
Hispanics	1.5% (480)
Asians	0.5% (355)
Native Americans	0.1% (402)

AGE	
0-17 years old	21.5% (373)
18-24 years old	8.2% (379)
25-39 years old	17.8% (227)
40-54 years old	20.5% (151)
55-64 years old	13.7% (225)
65+ years old	18.2% (111)

PRIVATE SECTOR	
Businesses	726 (416)
Employees	8,625 (431)
Total wages	$308,570,649 (425)
Average weekly wages	$688 (290)

HOUSEHOLD INCOME LADDER	
95th percentile	$141,089 (277)
80th percentile	$87,220 (196)
60th percentile	$54,919 (251)
40th percentile	$36,235 (224)
20th percentile	$20,352 (214)

CHILDREN	★★★ (225)
Living with two parents	61.2% (377)
Older teens in school	79.2% (421)
Speak English very well	99.4% (124)
Poverty rate for children	21.9% (218)
No health insurance	3.4% (79)

DIVERSITY/EQUALITY	★ (470)
Racial diversity index	9.3% (509)
Geographic diversity index	25.4% (521)
Top 20% share of income	45.6% (97)
Gender gap in earnings	37.8% (385)
White-collar gender gap	26.8% (295)

EDUCATION	★★★ (318)
Eighth grade or less	1.9% (114)
High school diplomas	90.0% (202)
Attended college	47.9% (385)
Bachelor's degrees	15.1% (417)
Advanced degrees	4.3% (456)

EMPLOYMENT	★★★★ (181)
Average jobless rate	5.4% (89)
Self-employed workers	8.9% (266)
Management/financial jobs	12.2% (139)
Computer/engineering jobs	1.8% (457)
Health care jobs	5.7% (222)

GROWTH POTENTIAL	★★ (403)
Children per senior	1.18 (427)
Median age	42.0 (398)
Moved from different state	1.8% (338)
Homes built since 2000	8.3% (459)
Construction jobs	7.6% (110)

HOUSING	★★★★ (213)
Home vacancy rate	7.8% (205)
Home ownership rate	74.6% (91)
Housing diversity index	81.9% (461)
4 or more bedrooms	14.2% (392)
Affordability/income ratio	$1,849 (23)

INCOME	★★★ (230)
Poverty rate	14.6% (178)
Median household income	$45,334 (226)
Interest/dividends	18.6% (288)
Public assistance	15.0% (254)
Median fulltime earnings	$38,768 (188)

SENIORS	★★★ (317)
Seniors living alone	31.2% (479)
Poverty rate for seniors	7.8% (163)
Median income for seniors	$33,849 (244)
Seniors who work	18.0% (287)
Home ownership by seniors	83.3% (206)

STABILITY	★★★ (264)
25-39 age group	17.8% (227)
Born in state of residence	86.1% (26)
Same house as 1 year ago	87.9% (140)
Live and work in county	59.1% (494)
Married-couple households	47.9% (387)

TRANSPORTATION	★★ (416)
Bicycle or walk to work	1.6% (443)
Carpool to work	11.6% (178)
Public transit to work	0.9% (83)
Commute <15 minutes	39.3% (341)
Commute >45 minutes	18.0% (499)

See pages 37-130 for explanations of statistics, stars, and ranks.

Tiffin, OH
(Seneca County, OH)

POPULATION		
2010 census	56,745 (164)	
2015 estimate	55,610 (170)	
2010-2015 change	-2.0% (412)	
2020 projection	54,515 (183)	
2030 projection	52,222 (201)	

RACE		
Whites	90.6% (169)	
Blacks	2.4% (263)	
Hispanics	4.8% (256)	
Asians	0.6% (291)	
Native Americans	0.1% (402)	

AGE		
0-17 years old	22.8% (277)	
18-24 years old	10.9% (119)	
25-39 years old	17.2% (290)	
40-54 years old	19.2% (336)	
55-64 years old	14.1% (174)	
65+ years old	15.8% (305)	

PRIVATE SECTOR		
Businesses	1,055 (257)	
Employees	16,451 (183)	
Total wages	$558,771,582 (209)	
Average weekly wages	$653 (385)	

HOUSEHOLD INCOME LADDER		
95th percentile	$132,975 (386)	
80th percentile	$83,846 (275)	
60th percentile	$55,926 (229)	
40th percentile	$36,463 (216)	
20th percentile	$20,412 (211)	

CHILDREN	★★★★ (124)	
Living with two parents	62.7% (328)	
Older teens in school	90.0% (67)	
Speak English very well	99.7% (57)	
Poverty rate for children	27.2% (352)	
No health insurance	2.7% (43)	

DIVERSITY/EQUALITY	★★★ (310)	
Racial diversity index	17.6% (380)	
Geographic diversity index	23.9% (535)	
Top 20% share of income	46.8% (200)	
Gender gap in earnings	33.9% (284)	
White-collar gender gap	4.2% (28)	

EDUCATION	★★★ (232)	
Eighth grade or less	1.0% (20)	
High school diplomas	93.1% (91)	
Attended college	49.6% (342)	
Bachelor's degrees	15.9% (382)	
Advanced degrees	5.5% (318)	

EMPLOYMENT	★★ (395)	
Average jobless rate	8.1% (298)	
Self-employed workers	6.7% (457)	
Management/financial jobs	9.8% (408)	
Computer/engineering jobs	3.0% (193)	
Health care jobs	5.3% (286)	

GROWTH POTENTIAL	★ (452)	
Children per senior	1.44 (253)	
Median age	39.0 (238)	
Moved from different state	1.5% (406)	
Homes built since 2000	6.1% (525)	
Construction jobs	5.6% (392)	

HOUSING	★★★ (296)	
Home vacancy rate	8.8% (273)	
Home ownership rate	71.3% (215)	
Housing diversity index	80.0% (514)	
4 or more bedrooms	19.2% (150)	
Affordability/income ratio	$2,132 (94)	

INCOME	★★★ (244)	
Poverty rate	16.9% (259)	
Median household income	$45,444 (224)	
Interest/dividends	20.4% (237)	
Public assistance	16.1% (300)	
Median fulltime earnings	$38,107 (217)	

SENIORS	★★★ (319)	
Seniors living alone	29.7% (416)	
Poverty rate for seniors	6.6% (68)	
Median income for seniors	$32,614 (298)	
Seniors who work	16.7% (360)	
Home ownership by seniors	82.0% (274)	

STABILITY	★★★ (287)	
25-39 age group	17.2% (290)	
Born in state of residence	87.0% (16)	
Same house as 1 year ago	86.0% (250)	
Live and work in county	57.9% (503)	
Married-couple households	50.8% (256)	

TRANSPORTATION	★★ (357)	
Bicycle or walk to work	4.4% (123)	
Carpool to work	7.2% (527)	
Public transit to work	0.3% (291)	
Commute <15 minutes	40.0% (329)	
Commute >45 minutes	9.8% (218)	

See pages 37-130 for explanations of statistics, stars, and ranks.

Traverse City, MI
(Benzie, Grand Traverse, Kalkaska, and Leelanau Counties, MI)

POPULATION
2010 census	143,372 (7)
2015 estimate	148,334 (5)
2010-2015 change	3.5% (70)
2020 projection	153,682 (4)
2030 projection	164,583 (5)

RACE
Whites	92.9% (110)
Blacks	1.0% (381)
Hispanics	2.6% (378)
Asians	0.7% (241)
Native Americans	1.4% (84)

AGE
0-17 years old	20.5% (433)
18-24 years old	7.4% (489)
25-39 years old	17.0% (317)
40-54 years old	20.3% (186)
55-64 years old	15.9% (50)
65+ years old	19.0% (80)

PRIVATE SECTOR
Businesses	4,450 (5)
Employees	53,595 (5)
Total wages	$2,123,864,614 (6)
Average weekly wages	$762 (139)

HOUSEHOLD INCOME LADDER
95th percentile	$161,164 (90)
80th percentile	$93,560 (109)
60th percentile	$62,148 (105)
40th percentile	$41,846 (78)
20th percentile	$23,610 (77)

CHILDREN ★★★★★ (99)
Living with two parents	70.9% (122)
Older teens in school	83.1% (271)
Speak English very well	98.3% (312)
Poverty rate for children	15.0% (63)
No health insurance	4.8% (173)

DIVERSITY/EQUALITY ★★ (386)
Racial diversity index	13.6% (437)
Geographic diversity index	34.7% (441)
Top 20% share of income	48.9% (352)
Gender gap in earnings	29.7% (166)
White-collar gender gap	19.5% (201)

EDUCATION ★★★★★ (45)
Eighth grade or less	1.5% (72)
High school diplomas	93.7% (65)
Attended college	65.3% (55)
Bachelor's degrees	28.6% (68)
Advanced degrees	10.8% (44)

EMPLOYMENT ★★★★★ (48)
Average jobless rate	7.3% (228)
Self-employed workers	12.3% (62)
Management/financial jobs	13.5% (66)
Computer/engineering jobs	3.3% (145)
Health care jobs	7.2% (58)

GROWTH POTENTIAL ★★ (359)
Children per senior	1.08 (471)
Median age	44.5 (493)
Moved from different state	2.1% (269)
Homes built since 2000	18.0% (134)
Construction jobs	6.7% (219)

HOUSING ★★★★★ (69)
Home vacancy rate	5.9% (88)
Home ownership rate	79.3% (7)
Housing diversity index	84.7% (260)
4 or more bedrooms	18.5% (178)
Affordability/income ratio	$3,247 (440)

INCOME ★★★★★ (93)
Poverty rate	11.7% (77)
Median household income	$51,125 (97)
Interest/dividends	26.4% (65)
Public assistance	12.8% (162)
Median fulltime earnings	$39,105 (176)

SENIORS ★★★★★ (46)
Seniors living alone	25.7% (154)
Poverty rate for seniors	5.5% (36)
Median income for seniors	$41,117 (50)
Seniors who work	19.6% (221)
Home ownership by seniors	87.1% (69)

STABILITY ★★★★★ (103)
25-39 age group	17.0% (317)
Born in state of residence	80.2% (109)
Same house as 1 year ago	87.0% (198)
Live and work in county	76.4% (265)
Married-couple households	52.9% (157)

TRANSPORTATION ★★★ (287)
Bicycle or walk to work	3.3% (211)
Carpool to work	10.8% (249)
Public transit to work	0.9% (83)
Commute <15 minutes	34.0% (460)
Commute >45 minutes	9.3% (188)

See pages 37-130 for explanations of statistics, stars, and ranks.

Urbana, OH
(Champaign County, OH)

POPULATION	
2010 census	40,097 (313)
2015 estimate	38,987 (328)
2010-2015 change	-2.8% (467)
2020 projection	38,345 (337)
2030 projection	36,927 (347)

RACE	
Whites	93.7% (83)
Blacks	1.9% (295)
Hispanics	1.4% (488)
Asians	0.4% (413)
Native Americans	0.1% (402)

AGE	
0-17 years old	23.6% (228)
18-24 years old	8.6% (317)
25-39 years old	16.3% (418)
40-54 years old	22.0% (31)
55-64 years old	13.4% (274)
65+ years old	16.0% (291)

PRIVATE SECTOR	
Businesses	599 (470)
Employees	8,765 (425)
Total wages	$347,786,615 (384)
Average weekly wages	$763 (135)

HOUSEHOLD INCOME LADDER	
95th percentile	$140,648 (281)
80th percentile	$88,227 (184)
60th percentile	$61,607 (121)
40th percentile	$41,585 (88)
20th percentile	$22,895 (101)

CHILDREN	★★★★ (216)
Living with two parents	67.9% (198)
Older teens in school	77.4% (463)
Speak English very well	99.2% (163)
Poverty rate for children	20.6% (182)
No health insurance	5.2% (197)

DIVERSITY/EQUALITY	★★★ (230)
Racial diversity index	12.1% (462)
Geographic diversity index	28.7% (497)
Top 20% share of income	42.8% (5)
Gender gap in earnings	34.3% (296)
White-collar gender gap	13.1% (127)

EDUCATION	★★★ (281)
Eighth grade or less	1.8% (102)
High school diplomas	91.1% (156)
Attended college	46.8% (400)
Bachelor's degrees	17.1% (322)
Advanced degrees	4.7% (419)

EMPLOYMENT	★★ (424)
Average jobless rate	9.1% (370)
Self-employed workers	6.8% (446)
Management/financial jobs	11.1% (240)
Computer/engineering jobs	2.9% (219)
Health care jobs	4.5% (419)

GROWTH POTENTIAL	★ (489)
Children per senior	1.48 (227)
Median age	41.2 (368)
Moved from different state	1.7% (355)
Homes built since 2000	9.4% (414)
Construction jobs	4.2% (524)

HOUSING	★★★★ (163)
Home vacancy rate	7.9% (213)
Home ownership rate	73.5% (137)
Housing diversity index	83.2% (405)
4 or more bedrooms	18.1% (197)
Affordability/income ratio	$2,417 (218)

INCOME	★★★★ (147)
Poverty rate	12.4% (97)
Median household income	$50,974 (102)
Interest/dividends	18.9% (279)
Public assistance	15.1% (262)
Median fulltime earnings	$41,316 (85)

SENIORS	★★★★★ (48)
Seniors living alone	25.9% (164)
Poverty rate for seniors	3.6% (5)
Median income for seniors	$36,761 (123)
Seniors who work	21.6% (142)
Home ownership by seniors	85.8% (115)

STABILITY	★★ (424)
25-39 age group	16.3% (418)
Born in state of residence	84.0% (55)
Same house as 1 year ago	84.7% (314)
Live and work in county	45.4% (546)
Married-couple households	55.1% (69)

TRANSPORTATION	★ (530)
Bicycle or walk to work	2.4% (331)
Carpool to work	7.7% (509)
Public transit to work	0.3% (291)
Commute <15 minutes	29.9% (525)
Commute >45 minutes	16.3% (464)

See pages 37-130 for explanations of statistics, stars, and ranks.

Van Wert, OH
(Van Wert County, OH)

POPULATION

2010 census	28,744 (445)
2015 estimate	28,562 (449)
2010-2015 change	-0.6% (298)
2020 projection	28,169 (447)
2030 projection	27,293 (454)

RACE

Whites	94.7% (55)
Blacks	0.9% (388)
Hispanics	2.8% (355)
Asians	0.3% (473)
Native Americans	0.2% (300)

AGE

0-17 years old	23.7% (218)
18-24 years old	7.9% (424)
25-39 years old	16.8% (359)
40-54 years old	20.1% (221)
55-64 years old	13.8% (203)
65+ years old	17.7% (142)

PRIVATE SECTOR

Businesses	534 (503)
Employees	9,370 (398)
Total wages	$327,769,755 (401)
Average weekly wages	$673 (327)

HOUSEHOLD INCOME LADDER

95th percentile	$128,683 (446)
80th percentile	$83,236 (287)
60th percentile	$58,581 (171)
40th percentile	$39,284 (146)
20th percentile	$23,112 (97)

CHILDREN ★★★★★ (61)

Living with two parents	68.3% (185)
Older teens in school	91.6% (45)
Speak English very well	99.7% (57)
Poverty rate for children	18.2% (128)
No health insurance	6.2% (262)

DIVERSITY/EQUALITY ★ (509)

Racial diversity index	10.2% (493)
Geographic diversity index	36.8% (407)
Top 20% share of income	46.2% (133)
Gender gap in earnings	38.8% (415)
White-collar gender gap	44.8% (478)

EDUCATION ★★★★ (188)

Eighth grade or less	0.8% (10)
High school diplomas	93.9% (61)

Attended college	48.8% (362)
Bachelor's degrees	17.7% (295)
Advanced degrees	6.9% (186)

EMPLOYMENT ★★★ (318)

Average jobless rate	7.5% (242)
Self-employed workers	8.3% (302)
Management/financial jobs	8.9% (483)
Computer/engineering jobs	3.1% (180)
Health care jobs	5.9% (193)

GROWTH POTENTIAL ★ (498)

Children per senior	1.34 (321)
Median age	41.5 (380)
Moved from different state	2.2% (248)
Homes built since 2000	6.3% (518)
Construction jobs	5.1% (458)

HOUSING ★★★★★ (68)

Home vacancy rate	7.6% (193)
Home ownership rate	75.7% (64)
Housing diversity index	82.8% (426)
4 or more bedrooms	21.9% (82)
Affordability/income ratio	$1,993 (54)

INCOME ★★★★ (169)

Poverty rate	12.8% (109)
Median household income	$48,060 (174)
Interest/dividends	19.9% (247)
Public assistance	13.1% (177)
Median fulltime earnings	$37,915 (225)

SENIORS ★★★★ (159)

Seniors living alone	27.1% (247)
Poverty rate for seniors	5.9% (47)
Median income for seniors	$33,890 (242)
Seniors who work	16.3% (391)
Home ownership by seniors	85.9% (105)

STABILITY ★★★ (235)

25-39 age group	16.8% (359)
Born in state of residence	78.1% (153)
Same house as 1 year ago	86.6% (213)
Live and work in county	61.2% (482)
Married-couple households	55.1% (69)

TRANSPORTATION ★★★ (304)

Bicycle or walk to work	2.7% (292)
Carpool to work	9.6% (378)
Public transit to work	0.1% (441)
Commute <15 minutes	46.8% (219)
Commute >45 minutes	9.4% (197)

See pages 37-130 for explanations of statistics, stars, and ranks.

Vermillion, SD
(Clay County, SD)

POPULATION

2010 census	13,864 (546)
2015 estimate	13,964 (547)
2010-2015 change	0.7% (202)
2020 projection	13,979 (547)
2030 projection	13,945 (546)

RACE

Whites	88.8% (208)
Blacks	1.5% (329)
Hispanics	2.5% (384)
Asians	2.1% (45)
Native Americans	2.9% (55)

AGE

0-17 years old	16.9% (538)
18-24 years old	32.8% (2)
25-39 years old	16.8% (359)
40-54 years old	13.7% (548)
55-64 years old	9.2% (542)
65+ years old	10.5% (521)

PRIVATE SECTOR

Businesses	340 (542)
Employees	3,297 (546)
Total wages	$89,300,811 (549)
Average weekly wages	$521 (541)

HOUSEHOLD INCOME LADDER

95th percentile	$153,313 (129)
80th percentile	$84,375 (267)
60th percentile	$44,803 (480)
40th percentile	$28,295 (455)
20th percentile	$13,869 (480)

CHILDREN ★★★★★ (7)

Living with two parents	78.2% (19)
Older teens in school	96.4% (10)
Speak English very well	99.3% (142)
Poverty rate for children	21.0% (193)
No health insurance	2.7% (43)

DIVERSITY/EQUALITY ★★ (432)

Racial diversity index	20.9% (336)
Geographic diversity index	64.7% (77)
Top 20% share of income	52.0% (501)
Gender gap in earnings	34.7% (308)
White-collar gender gap	40.6% (451)

EDUCATION ★★★★★ (6)

Eighth grade or less	1.1% (26)
High school diplomas	97.5% (2)

Attended college	72.8% (14)
Bachelor's degrees	48.6% (8)
Advanced degrees	22.4% (3)

EMPLOYMENT ★★★★ (215)

Average jobless rate	6.8% (179)
Self-employed workers	12.2% (67)
Management/financial jobs	9.8% (408)
Computer/engineering jobs	2.9% (219)
Health care jobs	4.8% (369)

GROWTH POTENTIAL ★★★★★ (38)

Children per senior	1.60 (169)
Median age	25.2 (4)
Moved from different state	9.6% (6)
Homes built since 2000	15.9% (179)
Construction jobs	4.9% (473)

HOUSING ★★★ (312)

Home vacancy rate	5.5% (60)
Home ownership rate	51.5% (544)
Housing diversity index	84.3% (314)
4 or more bedrooms	26.0% (36)
Affordability/income ratio	$3,688 (479)

INCOME ★★ (381)

Poverty rate	27.6% (509)
Median household income	$36,608 (454)
Interest/dividends	23.8% (135)
Public assistance	15.2% (266)
Median fulltime earnings	$35,228 (373)

SENIORS ★★★★★ (14)

Seniors living alone	24.6% (100)
Poverty rate for seniors	2.7% (2)
Median income for seniors	$50,903 (10)
Seniors who work	32.2% (13)
Home ownership by seniors	76.6% (498)

STABILITY ★ (551)

25-39 age group	16.8% (359)
Born in state of residence	50.2% (485)
Same house as 1 year ago	64.7% (549)
Live and work in county	75.9% (276)
Married-couple households	39.6% (531)

TRANSPORTATION ★★★★★ (17)

Bicycle or walk to work	17.4% (3)
Carpool to work	9.1% (419)
Public transit to work	0.4% (219)
Commute <15 minutes	71.0% (5)
Commute >45 minutes	8.6% (154)

See pages 37-130 for explanations of statistics, stars, and ranks.

Vincennes, IN
(Knox County, IN)

POPULATION	
2010 census	38,440 (335)
2015 estimate	37,927 (344)
2010-2015 change	-1.3% (355)
2020 projection	37,314 (353)
2030 projection	35,988 (359)

RACE	
Whites	93.2% (103)
Blacks	3.0% (227)
Hispanics	1.8% (455)
Asians	0.7% (241)
Native Americans	0.1% (402)

AGE	
0-17 years old	21.4% (379)
18-24 years old	13.2% (69)
25-39 years old	16.4% (411)
40-54 years old	19.4% (315)
55-64 years old	13.2% (297)
65+ years old	16.5% (247)

PRIVATE SECTOR	
Businesses	886 (322)
Employees	13,208 (271)
Total wages	$474,480,788 (268)
Average weekly wages	$691 (282)

HOUSEHOLD INCOME LADDER	
95th percentile	$136,854 (330)
80th percentile	$79,431 (379)
60th percentile	$53,510 (288)
40th percentile	$33,875 (293)
20th percentile	$18,254 (303)

CHILDREN	★★★★★ (89)
Living with two parents	66.3% (241)
Older teens in school	95.8% (12)
Speak English very well	99.6% (77)
Poverty rate for children	23.5% (255)
No health insurance	8.0% (362)

DIVERSITY/EQUALITY	★ (455)
Racial diversity index	13.0% (443)
Geographic diversity index	36.0% (421)
Top 20% share of income	46.8% (188)
Gender gap in earnings	33.8% (280)
White-collar gender gap	38.2% (424)

EDUCATION	★★★ (250)
Eighth grade or less	1.8% (102)
High school diplomas	89.4% (220)
Attended college	54.5% (233)
Bachelor's degrees	15.7% (399)
Advanced degrees	5.1% (364)

EMPLOYMENT	★★★★ (218)
Average jobless rate	6.1% (121)
Self-employed workers	7.2% (410)
Management/financial jobs	10.8% (280)
Computer/engineering jobs	2.3% (354)
Health care jobs	6.8% (91)

GROWTH POTENTIAL	★ (487)
Children per senior	1.30 (347)
Median age	39.2 (248)
Moved from different state	2.0% (288)
Homes built since 2000	7.9% (470)
Construction jobs	4.3% (514)

HOUSING	★ (470)
Home vacancy rate	11.5% (436)
Home ownership rate	66.0% (415)
Housing diversity index	82.1% (454)
4 or more bedrooms	12.1% (492)
Affordability/income ratio	$1,982 (52)

INCOME	★★★ (302)
Poverty rate	15.9% (219)
Median household income	$42,725 (295)
Interest/dividends	16.0% (375)
Public assistance	14.3% (220)
Median fulltime earnings	$35,230 (372)

SENIORS	★★★ (305)
Seniors living alone	30.6% (454)
Poverty rate for seniors	8.1% (187)
Median income for seniors	$31,831 (327)
Seniors who work	22.6% (116)
Home ownership by seniors	80.5% (356)

STABILITY	★★★ (306)
25-39 age group	16.4% (411)
Born in state of residence	79.0% (132)
Same house as 1 year ago	83.8% (347)
Live and work in county	78.1% (243)
Married-couple households	48.6% (358)

TRANSPORTATION	★★ (336)
Bicycle or walk to work	2.5% (322)
Carpool to work	8.3% (471)
Public transit to work	0.2% (363)
Commute <15 minutes	45.7% (237)
Commute >45 minutes	8.8% (165)

See pages 37-130 for explanations of statistics, stars, and ranks.

Wabash, IN
(Wabash County, IN)

POPULATION	
2010 census	32,888 (406)
2015 estimate	32,138 (420)
2010-2015 change	-2.3% (436)
2020 projection	31,149 (427)
2030 projection	29,140 (431)

RACE	
Whites	94.7% (55)
Blacks	0.8% (404)
Hispanics	2.3% (398)
Asians	0.3% (473)
Native Americans	0.7% (136)

AGE	
0-17 years old	21.8% (351)
18-24 years old	10.0% (163)
25-39 years old	15.5% (484)
40-54 years old	19.8% (261)
55-64 years old	13.7% (225)
65+ years old	19.1% (76)

PRIVATE SECTOR	
Businesses	698 (428)
Employees	10,799 (349)
Total wages	$370,448,961 (363)
Average weekly wages	$660 (364)

HOUSEHOLD INCOME LADDER	
95th percentile	$128,625 (447)
80th percentile	$80,626 (359)
60th percentile	$54,186 (276)
40th percentile	$37,752 (186)
20th percentile	$21,203 (182)

CHILDREN	★★★★ (121)
Living with two parents	69.6% (151)
Older teens in school	87.8% (105)
Speak English very well	99.8% (38)
Poverty rate for children	25.7% (315)
No health insurance	5.1% (188)

DIVERSITY/EQUALITY	★ (534)
Racial diversity index	10.2% (493)
Geographic diversity index	37.0% (403)
Top 20% share of income	45.0% (62)
Gender gap in earnings	42.1% (474)
White-collar gender gap	59.0% (542)

EDUCATION	★★★★ (219)
Eighth grade or less	2.4% (169)
High school diplomas	90.8% (167)
Attended college	49.9% (335)
Bachelor's degrees	19.3% (239)
Advanced degrees	6.8% (191)

EMPLOYMENT	★★★ (279)
Average jobless rate	7.0% (196)
Self-employed workers	7.7% (362)
Management/financial jobs	10.9% (263)
Computer/engineering jobs	2.3% (354)
Health care jobs	6.0% (181)

GROWTH POTENTIAL	★ (545)
Children per senior	1.14 (446)
Median age	42.4 (429)
Moved from different state	2.1% (269)
Homes built since 2000	6.1% (525)
Construction jobs	4.1% (530)

HOUSING	★★★ (224)
Home vacancy rate	5.9% (88)
Home ownership rate	74.1% (115)
Housing diversity index	79.0% (525)
4 or more bedrooms	18.2% (194)
Affordability/income ratio	$2,083 (75)

INCOME	★★★★ (192)
Poverty rate	14.4% (172)
Median household income	$45,649 (219)
Interest/dividends	21.9% (187)
Public assistance	11.7% (120)
Median fulltime earnings	$36,011 (335)

SENIORS	★★★★ (130)
Seniors living alone	26.8% (222)
Poverty rate for seniors	6.4% (57)
Median income for seniors	n.a.
Seniors who work	17.6% (306)
Home ownership by seniors	85.2% (132)

STABILITY	★★★ (261)
25-39 age group	15.5% (484)
Born in state of residence	78.5% (146)
Same house as 1 year ago	84.3% (333)
Live and work in county	74.1% (308)
Married-couple households	54.1% (105)

TRANSPORTATION	★★★ (292)
Bicycle or walk to work	3.9% (158)
Carpool to work	6.2% (543)
Public transit to work	0.5% (178)
Commute <15 minutes	50.1% (149)
Commute >45 minutes	8.4% (148)

See pages 37-130 for explanations of statistics, stars, and ranks.

Wahpeton, ND-MN
(Richland County, ND, and Wilkin County, MN)

POPULATION

2010 census	22,897 (497)
2015 estimate	22,798 (501)
2010-2015 change	-0.4% (286)
2020 projection	22,512 (503)
2030 projection	19,828 (521)

RACE

Whites	93.2% (103)
Blacks	0.4% (499)
Hispanics	2.4% (389)
Asians	0.3% (473)
Native Americans	2.3% (67)

AGE

0-17 years old	22.1% (330)
18-24 years old	12.3% (80)
25-39 years old	15.2% (498)
40-54 years old	19.8% (261)
55-64 years old	14.5% (122)
65+ years old	16.2% (279)

PRIVATE SECTOR

Businesses	747 (403)
Employees	7,445 (456)
Total wages	$299,734,185 (436)
Average weekly wages	$774 (123)

HOUSEHOLD INCOME LADDER

95th percentile	$158,269 (107)
80th percentile	$97,679 (70)
60th percentile	$66,503 (59)
40th percentile	$44,136 (52)
20th percentile	$24,068 (64)

CHILDREN ★★★★★ (16)

Living with two parents	78.4% (17)
Older teens in school	87.8% (105)
Speak English very well	100.0% (1)
Poverty rate for children	12.7% (47)
No health insurance	3.7% (98)

DIVERSITY/EQUALITY ★★ (395)

Racial diversity index	13.0% (443)
Geographic diversity index	57.4% (139)
Top 20% share of income	44.9% (58)
Gender gap in earnings	38.9% (418)
White-collar gender gap	52.3% (519)

EDUCATION ★★★★ (112)

Eighth grade or less	1.6% (84)
High school diplomas	94.4% (44)

Attended college	68.0% (33)
Bachelor's degrees	22.1% (158)
Advanced degrees	4.6% (431)

EMPLOYMENT ★★★★★ (9)

Average jobless rate	2.7% (5)
Self-employed workers	16.4% (13)
Management/financial jobs	16.1% (14)
Computer/engineering jobs	2.6% (288)
Health care jobs	5.3% (286)

GROWTH POTENTIAL ★★★★ (206)

Children per senior	1.36 (304)
Median age	40.9 (350)
Moved from different state	5.3% (44)
Homes built since 2000	9.6% (404)
Construction jobs	7.2% (162)

HOUSING ★★★★★ (12)

Home vacancy rate	8.6% (260)
Home ownership rate	72.6% (165)
Housing diversity index	85.0% (226)
4 or more bedrooms	29.3% (9)
Affordability/income ratio	$1,979 (51)

INCOME ★★★★★ (46)

Poverty rate	10.5% (44)
Median household income	$54,020 (63)
Interest/dividends	27.3% (46)
Public assistance	8.2% (36)
Median fulltime earnings	$42,299 (59)

SENIORS ★★ (396)

Seniors living alone	30.9% (469)
Poverty rate for seniors	9.6% (295)
Median income for seniors	$35,142 (183)
Seniors who work	23.4% (98)
Home ownership by seniors	75.2% (522)

STABILITY ★ (501)

25-39 age group	15.2% (498)
Born in state of residence	51.4% (481)
Same house as 1 year ago	86.9% (202)
Live and work in county	62.5% (470)
Married-couple households	53.2% (143)

TRANSPORTATION ★★★★ (140)

Bicycle or walk to work	5.6% (69)
Carpool to work	10.2% (312)
Public transit to work	0.1% (441)
Commute <15 minutes	56.5% (77)
Commute >45 minutes	10.3% (237)

See pages 37-130 for explanations of statistics, stars, and ranks.

Wapakoneta, OH
(Auglaize County, OH)

POPULATION		
2010 census	45,949 (249)	
2015 estimate	45,876 (247)	
2010-2015 change	-0.2% (273)	
2020 projection	45,694 (251)	
2030 projection	45,154 (262)	

RACE		
Whites	96.5% (5)	
Blacks	0.5% (466)	
Hispanics	1.4% (488)	
Asians	0.5% (355)	
Native Americans	0.2% (300)	

AGE		
0-17 years old	24.5% (149)	
18-24 years old	8.0% (407)	
25-39 years old	16.4% (411)	
40-54 years old	20.6% (145)	
55-64 years old	14.0% (182)	
65+ years old	16.5% (247)	

PRIVATE SECTOR		
Businesses	949 (293)	
Employees	18,610 (146)	
Total wages	$771,603,750 (126)	
Average weekly wages	$797 (95)	

HOUSEHOLD INCOME LADDER		
95th percentile	$147,844 (185)	
80th percentile	$96,744 (76)	
60th percentile	$66,291 (63)	
40th percentile	$42,300 (75)	
20th percentile	$25,706 (41)	

CHILDREN	★★★★★ (6)	
Living with two parents	77.6% (23)	
Older teens in school	89.6% (72)	
Speak English very well	99.5% (96)	
Poverty rate for children	11.7% (26)	
No health insurance	2.4% (28)	

DIVERSITY/EQUALITY	★ (485)	
Racial diversity index	6.8% (543)	
Geographic diversity index	23.4% (539)	
Top 20% share of income	43.3% (9)	
Gender gap in earnings	42.7% (479)	
White-collar gender gap	30.5% (344)	

EDUCATION	★★★★ (146)	
Eighth grade or less	1.0% (20)	
High school diplomas	95.7% (16)	
Attended college	55.2% (216)	
Bachelor's degrees	19.4% (235)	
Advanced degrees	6.4% (229)	

EMPLOYMENT	★★★★ (156)	
Average jobless rate	5.0% (66)	
Self-employed workers	7.1% (421)	
Management/financial jobs	11.5% (202)	
Computer/engineering jobs	3.6% (112)	
Health care jobs	5.9% (193)	

GROWTH POTENTIAL	★★ (425)	
Children per senior	1.48 (227)	
Median age	41.0 (357)	
Moved from different state	1.0% (504)	
Homes built since 2000	10.9% (361)	
Construction jobs	5.8% (360)	

HOUSING	★★★★★ (48)	
Home vacancy rate	5.4% (55)	
Home ownership rate	74.2% (110)	
Housing diversity index	85.1% (212)	
4 or more bedrooms	19.3% (145)	
Affordability/income ratio	$2,456 (234)	

INCOME	★★★★★ (57)	
Poverty rate	8.9% (17)	
Median household income	$54,274 (60)	
Interest/dividends	24.5% (115)	
Public assistance	10.1% (66)	
Median fulltime earnings	$41,743 (68)	

SENIORS	★★ (370)	
Seniors living alone	31.3% (486)	
Poverty rate for seniors	6.7% (73)	
Median income for seniors	$32,825 (291)	
Seniors who work	18.8% (253)	
Home ownership by seniors	79.5% (394)	

STABILITY	★★★★ (119)	
25-39 age group	16.4% (411)	
Born in state of residence	87.3% (12)	
Same house as 1 year ago	89.4% (64)	
Live and work in county	56.6% (513)	
Married-couple households	56.7% (34)	

TRANSPORTATION	★★ (381)	
Bicycle or walk to work	2.6% (308)	
Carpool to work	6.4% (541)	
Public transit to work	0.2% (363)	
Commute <15 minutes	42.3% (292)	
Commute >45 minutes	6.9% (82)	

See pages 37-130 for explanations of statistics, stars, and ranks.

Warrensburg, MO
(Johnson County, MO)

POPULATION
2010 census	52,595 (189)
2015 estimate	53,951 (179)
2010-2015 change	2.6% (103)
2020 projection	54,561 (182)
2030 projection	55,659 (176)

RACE
Whites	86.5% (248)
Blacks	4.4% (179)
Hispanics	3.8% (308)
Asians	1.7% (69)
Native Americans	0.6% (150)

AGE
0-17 years old	22.0% (335)
18-24 years old	20.8% (25)
25-39 years old	19.1% (95)
40-54 years old	16.6% (511)
55-64 years old	10.0% (521)
65+ years old	11.4% (501)

PRIVATE SECTOR
Businesses	991 (282)
Employees	9,194 (406)
Total wages	$265,389,742 (460)
Average weekly wages	$555 (530)

HOUSEHOLD INCOME LADDER
95th percentile	$141,441 (274)
80th percentile	$90,328 (153)
60th percentile	$60,240 (145)
40th percentile	$39,704 (135)
20th percentile	$20,882 (191)

CHILDREN ★★★★★ (49)
Living with two parents	77.3% (26)
Older teens in school	85.5% (183)
Speak English very well	98.7% (265)
Poverty rate for children	16.9% (94)
No health insurance	3.7% (98)

DIVERSITY/EQUALITY ★★★★★ (58)
Racial diversity index	24.7% (297)
Geographic diversity index	64.5% (79)
Top 20% share of income	44.8% (53)
Gender gap in earnings	35.3% (321)
White-collar gender gap	9.9% (89)

EDUCATION ★★★★★ (63)
Eighth grade or less	1.7% (97)
High school diplomas	92.6% (107)
Attended college	64.1% (71)
Bachelor's degrees	27.5% (83)
Advanced degrees	9.9% (64)

EMPLOYMENT ★★ (366)
Average jobless rate	8.0% (291)
Self-employed workers	8.0% (333)
Management/financial jobs	10.3% (339)
Computer/engineering jobs	4.0% (76)
Health care jobs	4.0% (476)

GROWTH POTENTIAL ★★★★★ (27)
Children per senior	1.93 (68)
Median age	29.7 (25)
Moved from different state	5.9% (31)
Homes built since 2000	23.2% (48)
Construction jobs	6.7% (219)

HOUSING ★★★ (307)
Home vacancy rate	5.8% (79)
Home ownership rate	60.4% (499)
Housing diversity index	83.7% (378)
4 or more bedrooms	18.4% (183)
Affordability/income ratio	$2,840 (364)

INCOME ★★★ (236)
Poverty rate	17.0% (262)
Median household income	$49,792 (133)
Interest/dividends	18.5% (294)
Public assistance	13.4% (185)
Median fulltime earnings	$36,109 (328)

SENIORS ★★★★★ (28)
Seniors living alone	21.4% (27)
Poverty rate for seniors	6.5% (67)
Median income for seniors	$43,519 (38)
Seniors who work	21.3% (152)
Home ownership by seniors	84.8% (150)

STABILITY ★ (507)
25-39 age group	19.1% (95)
Born in state of residence	55.2% (461)
Same house as 1 year ago	73.2% (534)
Live and work in county	71.8% (346)
Married-couple households	53.1% (148)

TRANSPORTATION ★★★ (308)
Bicycle or walk to work	5.4% (75)
Carpool to work	9.2% (408)
Public transit to work	0.2% (363)
Commute <15 minutes	46.9% (217)
Commute >45 minutes	14.6% (414)

See pages 37-130 for explanations of statistics, stars, and ranks.

Warsaw, IN
(Kosciusko County, IN)

POPULATION			
2010 census	77,358 (74)	Attended college	50.5% (314)
2015 estimate	78,620 (72)	Bachelor's degrees	21.7% (169)
2010-2015 change	1.6% (157)	Advanced degrees	6.7% (205)

POPULATION
2010 census — 77,358 (74)
2015 estimate — 78,620 (72)
2010-2015 change — 1.6% (157)
2020 projection — 79,450 (73)
2030 projection — 80,844 (73)

RACE
Whites — 89.0% (205)
Blacks — 0.7% (423)
Hispanics — 7.8% (186)
Asians — 1.0% (158)
Native Americans — 0.3% (231)

AGE
0-17 years old — 24.8% (135)
18-24 years old — 9.4% (203)
25-39 years old — 18.1% (186)
40-54 years old — 20.0% (233)
55-64 years old — 13.2% (297)
65+ years old — 14.6% (400)

PRIVATE SECTOR
Businesses — 1,823 (86)
Employees — 33,989 (23)
Total wages — $1,944,324,105 (9)
Average weekly wages — $1,100 (9)

HOUSEHOLD INCOME LADDER
95th percentile — $171,015 (54)
80th percentile — $95,040 (90)
60th percentile — $63,211 (97)
40th percentile — $44,472 (50)
20th percentile — $25,850 (40)

CHILDREN ★★★ (252)
Living with two parents — 74.8% (54)
Older teens in school — 82.1% (313)
Speak English very well — 96.1% (446)
Poverty rate for children — 15.9% (75)
No health insurance — 11.8% (469)

DIVERSITY/EQUALITY ★ (471)
Racial diversity index — 20.2% (345)
Geographic diversity index — 47.3% (254)
Top 20% share of income — 47.0% (220)
Gender gap in earnings — 42.0% (471)
White-collar gender gap — 44.9% (479)

EDUCATION ★★★ (260)
Eighth grade or less — 4.3% (343)
High school diplomas — 86.7% (319)

Attended college — 50.5% (314)
Bachelor's degrees — 21.7% (169)
Advanced degrees — 6.7% (205)

EMPLOYMENT ★★ (355)
Average jobless rate — 6.5% (157)
Self-employed workers — 6.9% (435)
Management/financial jobs — 10.6% (306)
Computer/engineering jobs — 4.0% (76)
Health care jobs — 3.9% (488)

GROWTH POTENTIAL ★★★ (284)
Children per senior — 1.70 (133)
Median age — 37.9 (179)
Moved from different state — 2.1% (269)
Homes built since 2000 — 14.4% (222)
Construction jobs — 4.6% (494)

HOUSING ★★★★★ (31)
Home vacancy rate — 6.3% (122)
Home ownership rate — 76.5% (41)
Housing diversity index — 86.0% (71)
4 or more bedrooms — 19.2% (150)
Affordability/income ratio — $2,516 (255)

INCOME ★★★★★ (82)
Poverty rate — 11.4% (66)
Median household income — $52,821 (75)
Interest/dividends — 21.5% (194)
Public assistance — 9.1% (48)
Median fulltime earnings — $40,573 (116)

SENIORS ★★★★★ (65)
Seniors living alone — 25.4% (132)
Poverty rate for seniors — 6.8% (77)
Median income for seniors — $36,403 (143)
Seniors who work — 21.1% (156)
Home ownership by seniors — 87.2% (63)

STABILITY ★★★★★ (44)
25-39 age group — 18.1% (186)
Born in state of residence — 71.0% (293)
Same house as 1 year ago — 86.6% (213)
Live and work in county — 76.2% (269)
Married-couple households — 58.3% (18)

TRANSPORTATION ★★★ (271)
Bicycle or walk to work — 3.3% (211)
Carpool to work — 11.8% (152)
Public transit to work — 0.2% (363)
Commute <15 minutes — 39.1% (348)
Commute >45 minutes — 9.3% (188)

See pages 37-130 for explanations of statistics, stars, and ranks.

Washington, IN
(Daviess County, IN)

POPULATION

2010 census	31,648 (421)
2015 estimate	32,906 (407)
2010-2015 change	4.0% (61)
2020 projection	33,921 (394)
2030 projection	35,911 (362)

RACE

Whites	93.0% (108)
Blacks	1.4% (340)
Hispanics	4.5% (265)
Asians	0.3% (473)
Native Americans	0.0% (523)

AGE

0-17 years old	29.1% (24)
18-24 years old	8.9% (282)
25-39 years old	17.2% (290)
40-54 years old	18.5% (425)
55-64 years old	12.0% (438)
65+ years old	14.3% (423)

PRIVATE SECTOR

Businesses	826 (358)
Employees	9,497 (392)
Total wages	$310,434,728 (422)
Average weekly wages	$629 (439)

HOUSEHOLD INCOME LADDER

95th percentile	$147,534 (192)
80th percentile	$84,879 (255)
60th percentile	$56,945 (209)
40th percentile	$39,101 (154)
20th percentile	$22,038 (138)

CHILDREN   ★ **(471)**

Living with two parents	81.1% (7)
Older teens in school	57.7% (550)
Speak English very well	95.7% (463)
Poverty rate for children	17.5% (111)
No health insurance	21.8% (550)

DIVERSITY/EQUALITY   ★ **(488)**

Racial diversity index	13.3% (441)
Geographic diversity index	25.7% (518)
Top 20% share of income	45.1% (65)
Gender gap in earnings	42.6% (478)
White-collar gender gap	30.1% (339)

EDUCATION   ★ **(531)**

Eighth grade or less	14.9% (532)
High school diplomas	74.3% (528)
Attended college	40.8% (504)
Bachelor's degrees	14.7% (431)
Advanced degrees	5.4% (334)

EMPLOYMENT   ★★★ **(240)**

Average jobless rate	5.4% (89)
Self-employed workers	10.5% (139)
Management/financial jobs	10.3% (339)
Computer/engineering jobs	2.3% (354)
Health care jobs	4.8% (369)

GROWTH POTENTIAL   ★★★★★ **(52)**

Children per senior	2.04 (55)
Median age	35.0 (91)
Moved from different state	0.9% (515)
Homes built since 2000	15.1% (202)
Construction jobs	11.2% (9)

HOUSING   ★★★★★ **(55)**

Home vacancy rate	6.2% (109)
Home ownership rate	72.4% (170)
Housing diversity index	85.4% (156)
4 or more bedrooms	20.0% (127)
Affordability/income ratio	$2,328 (179)

INCOME   ★★★★ **(171)**

Poverty rate	13.2% (123)
Median household income	$47,342 (184)
Interest/dividends	18.3% (299)
Public assistance	10.6% (84)
Median fulltime earnings	$37,714 (236)

SENIORS   ★★ **(424)**

Seniors living alone	28.9% (358)
Poverty rate for seniors	10.0% (321)
Median income for seniors	$31,348 (357)
Seniors who work	21.0% (160)
Home ownership by seniors	75.6% (518)

STABILITY   ★★★★★ **(24)**

25-39 age group	17.2% (290)
Born in state of residence	85.9% (32)
Same house as 1 year ago	87.9% (140)
Live and work in county	68.6% (395)
Married-couple households	59.8% (11)

TRANSPORTATION   ★★★★ **(191)**

Bicycle or walk to work	3.4% (199)
Carpool to work	16.9% (24)
Public transit to work	0.4% (219)
Commute <15 minutes	43.4% (273)
Commute >45 minutes	16.5% (468)

See pages 37-130 for explanations of statistics, stars, and ranks.

Washington Court House, OH
(Fayette County, OH)

POPULATION

2010 census	29,030 (443)
2015 estimate	28,679 (447)
2010-2015 change	-1.2% (345)
2020 projection	28,519 (443)
2030 projection	28,109 (442)

RACE

Whites	93.3% (98)
Blacks	1.9% (295)
Hispanics	1.8% (455)
Asians	0.6% (291)
Native Americans	0.1% (402)

AGE

0-17 years old	24.0% (184)
18-24 years old	7.6% (468)
25-39 years old	17.0% (317)
40-54 years old	21.5% (57)
55-64 years old	13.7% (225)
65+ years old	16.2% (279)

PRIVATE SECTOR

Businesses	590 (477)
Employees	9,614 (385)
Total wages	$301,277,177 (434)
Average weekly wages	$603 (485)

HOUSEHOLD INCOME LADDER

95th percentile	$128,534 (449)
80th percentile	$77,846 (403)
60th percentile	$50,371 (373)
40th percentile	$33,437 (312)
20th percentile	$18,423 (294)

CHILDREN ★★★ (323)

Living with two parents	57.7% (453)
Older teens in school	81.1% (364)
Speak English very well	98.0% (341)
Poverty rate for children	28.0% (368)
No health insurance	4.0% (118)

DIVERSITY/EQUALITY ★ (531)

Racial diversity index	12.8% (447)
Geographic diversity index	25.4% (521)
Top 20% share of income	47.1% (230)
Gender gap in earnings	33.9% (284)
White-collar gender gap	48.5% (504)

EDUCATION ★★ (381)

Eighth grade or less	2.3% (161)
High school diplomas	88.2% (260)
Attended college	43.7% (456)
Bachelor's degrees	15.1% (417)
Advanced degrees	3.9% (489)

EMPLOYMENT ★★ (373)

Average jobless rate	8.6% (335)
Self-employed workers	8.9% (266)
Management/financial jobs	11.1% (240)
Computer/engineering jobs	2.2% (381)
Health care jobs	4.7% (385)

GROWTH POTENTIAL ★★ (347)

Children per senior	1.49 (220)
Median age	41.1 (362)
Moved from different state	1.7% (355)
Homes built since 2000	14.3% (227)
Construction jobs	5.7% (373)

HOUSING ★★★ (328)

Home vacancy rate	6.5% (130)
Home ownership rate	60.1% (502)
Housing diversity index	86.1% (51)
4 or more bedrooms	12.3% (482)
Affordability/income ratio	$2,652 (314)

INCOME ★★ (364)

Poverty rate	18.4% (315)
Median household income	$40,503 (369)
Interest/dividends	16.0% (375)
Public assistance	19.6% (416)
Median fulltime earnings	$37,671 (238)

SENIORS ★★ (428)

Seniors living alone	29.1% (371)
Poverty rate for seniors	8.7% (241)
Median income for seniors	$30,032 (407)
Seniors who work	17.8% (299)
Home ownership by seniors	77.9% (458)

STABILITY ★★ (369)

25-39 age group	17.0% (317)
Born in state of residence	86.1% (26)
Same house as 1 year ago	83.6% (359)
Live and work in county	64.1% (454)
Married-couple households	48.8% (354)

TRANSPORTATION ★ (468)

Bicycle or walk to work	2.2% (358)
Carpool to work	9.1% (419)
Public transit to work	0.5% (178)
Commute <15 minutes	41.8% (303)
Commute >45 minutes	18.6% (505)

See pages 37-130 for explanations of statistics, stars, and ranks.

Watertown, SD
(Codington County, SD)

POPULATION

2010 census	27,227 (462)
2015 estimate	27,939 (454)
2010-2015 change	2.6% (103)
2020 projection	28,498 (444)
2030 projection	29,513 (428)

RACE

Whites	93.5% (91)
Blacks	0.4% (499)
Hispanics	1.9% (442)
Asians	0.2% (509)
Native Americans	2.5% (60)

AGE

0-17 years old	24.4% (155)
18-24 years old	9.0% (265)
25-39 years old	19.8% (64)
40-54 years old	18.7% (399)
55-64 years old	13.0% (334)
65+ years old	15.2% (354)

PRIVATE SECTOR

Businesses	1,161 (214)
Employees	13,807 (239)
Total wages	$509,443,997 (239)
Average weekly wages	$710 (232)

HOUSEHOLD INCOME LADDER

95th percentile	$144,206 (240)
80th percentile	$85,602 (238)
60th percentile	$61,770 (114)
40th percentile	$40,795 (104)
20th percentile	$22,663 (111)

CHILDREN ★★★★★ (26)

Living with two parents	66.4% (235)
Older teens in school	92.0% (38)
Speak English very well	99.0% (200)
Poverty rate for children	9.1% (9)
No health insurance	3.5% (82)

DIVERSITY/EQUALITY ★★ (415)

Racial diversity index	12.5% (456)
Geographic diversity index	42.8% (311)
Top 20% share of income	46.8% (198)
Gender gap in earnings	34.8% (310)
White-collar gender gap	36.5% (400)

EDUCATION ★★★★ (198)

Eighth grade or less	1.8% (102)
High school diplomas	93.6% (68)

Attended college	54.4% (236)
Bachelor's degrees	20.5% (207)
Advanced degrees	4.0% (478)

EMPLOYMENT ★★★★ (166)

Average jobless rate	2.9% (8)
Self-employed workers	11.2% (108)
Management/financial jobs	11.7% (185)
Computer/engineering jobs	2.7% (270)
Health care jobs	3.3% (517)

GROWTH POTENTIAL ★★★ (283)

Children per senior	1.60 (169)
Median age	38.0 (184)
Moved from different state	1.6% (383)
Homes built since 2000	13.9% (240)
Construction jobs	5.5% (404)

HOUSING ★★★★★ (15)

Home vacancy rate	3.3% (2)
Home ownership rate	67.7% (356)
Housing diversity index	85.5% (143)
4 or more bedrooms	28.3% (19)
Affordability/income ratio	$2,975 (398)

INCOME ★★★★ (149)

Poverty rate	10.3% (41)
Median household income	$48,912 (151)
Interest/dividends	23.2% (151)
Public assistance	12.8% (162)
Median fulltime earnings	$34,876 (390)

SENIORS ★ (448)

Seniors living alone	32.4% (521)
Poverty rate for seniors	9.9% (315)
Median income for seniors	$36,149 (148)
Seniors who work	26.0% (47)
Home ownership by seniors	70.8% (547)

STABILITY ★★★★★ (95)

25-39 age group	19.8% (64)
Born in state of residence	73.4% (252)
Same house as 1 year ago	82.8% (406)
Live and work in county	92.1% (44)
Married-couple households	46.9% (419)

TRANSPORTATION ★★★★★ (98)

Bicycle or walk to work	2.3% (348)
Carpool to work	10.0% (337)
Public transit to work	0.2% (363)
Commute <15 minutes	65.4% (17)
Commute >45 minutes	4.1% (16)

See pages 37-130 for explanations of statistics, stars, and ranks.

Watertown-Fort Atkinson, WI
(Jefferson County, WI)

POPULATION	
2010 census	83,686 (59)
2015 estimate	84,559 (60)
2010-2015 change	1.0% (185)
2020 projection	85,842 (57)
2030 projection	88,375 (55)

RACE	
Whites	90.2% (175)
Blacks	0.8% (404)
Hispanics	6.9% (202)
Asians	0.7% (241)
Native Americans	0.1% (402)

AGE	
0-17 years old	22.7% (284)
18-24 years old	10.2% (151)
25-39 years old	18.1% (186)
40-54 years old	21.2% (85)
55-64 years old	13.5% (258)
65+ years old	14.3% (423)

PRIVATE SECTOR	
Businesses	1,872 (79)
Employees	28,958 (49)
Total wages	$1,111,261,933 (53)
Average weekly wages	$738 (185)

HOUSEHOLD INCOME LADDER	
95th percentile	$157,794 (110)
80th percentile	$99,974 (60)
60th percentile	$69,584 (40)
40th percentile	$46,943 (31)
20th percentile	$27,653 (22)

CHILDREN	★★★★★ (35)
Living with two parents	73.7% (70)
Older teens in school	89.0% (80)
Speak English very well	99.0% (200)
Poverty rate for children	14.7% (62)
No health insurance	3.3% (72)

DIVERSITY/EQUALITY	★★★ (233)
Racial diversity index	18.1% (375)
Geographic diversity index	37.8% (396)
Top 20% share of income	43.4% (11)
Gender gap in earnings	31.6% (218)
White-collar gender gap	29.7% (333)

EDUCATION	★★★★ (137)
Eighth grade or less	2.7% (195)
High school diplomas	92.9% (98)
Attended college	58.9% (145)
Bachelor's degrees	23.8% (124)
Advanced degrees	6.8% (191)

EMPLOYMENT	★★★★ (112)
Average jobless rate	5.5% (98)
Self-employed workers	7.7% (362)
Management/financial jobs	13.1% (78)
Computer/engineering jobs	3.8% (96)
Health care jobs	5.7% (222)

GROWTH POTENTIAL	★★★ (252)
Children per senior	1.58 (182)
Median age	39.1 (244)
Moved from different state	1.6% (383)
Homes built since 2000	14.8% (208)
Construction jobs	6.3% (284)

HOUSING	★★★★★ (104)
Home vacancy rate	4.2% (9)
Home ownership rate	71.4% (209)
Housing diversity index	83.9% (360)
4 or more bedrooms	19.6% (135)
Affordability/income ratio	$3,042 (407)

INCOME	★★★★★ (56)
Poverty rate	10.6% (47)
Median household income	$56,877 (40)
Interest/dividends	26.6% (60)
Public assistance	11.5% (112)
Median fulltime earnings	$41,610 (75)

SENIORS	★★★ (267)
Seniors living alone	29.2% (381)
Poverty rate for seniors	8.3% (202)
Median income for seniors	$38,293 (87)
Seniors who work	22.3% (124)
Home ownership by seniors	77.2% (478)

STABILITY	★★★ (244)
25-39 age group	18.1% (186)
Born in state of residence	77.9% (158)
Same house as 1 year ago	86.9% (202)
Live and work in county	53.4% (529)
Married-couple households	54.7% (80)

TRANSPORTATION	★★ (371)
Bicycle or walk to work	4.2% (142)
Carpool to work	10.0% (337)
Public transit to work	0.4% (219)
Commute <15 minutes	37.9% (378)
Commute >45 minutes	14.5% (411)

See pages 37-130 for explanations of statistics, stars, and ranks.

West Plains, MO
(Howell County, MO)

POPULATION

2010 census	40,400 (308)
2015 estimate	40,117 (313)
2010-2015 change	-0.7% (303)
2020 projection	40,140 (314)
2030 projection	40,085 (317)

RACE

Whites	94.9% (51)
Blacks	0.3% (519)
Hispanics	1.9% (442)
Asians	0.6% (291)
Native Americans	0.5% (174)

AGE

0-17 years old	24.5% (149)
18-24 years old	8.1% (396)
25-39 years old	16.8% (359)
40-54 years old	19.6% (289)
55-64 years old	12.8% (356)
65+ years old	18.2% (111)

PRIVATE SECTOR

Businesses	1,124 (231)
Employees	12,714 (290)
Total wages	$409,239,642 (327)
Average weekly wages	$619 (450)

HOUSEHOLD INCOME LADDER

95th percentile	$122,237 (499)
80th percentile	$66,938 (526)
60th percentile	$41,761 (511)
40th percentile	$25,694 (503)
20th percentile	$13,774 (483)

CHILDREN ★★★ (306)

Living with two parents	64.2% (291)
Older teens in school	80.0% (397)
Speak English very well	99.8% (38)
Poverty rate for children	31.4% (433)
No health insurance	5.6% (225)

DIVERSITY/EQUALITY ★★★ (284)

Racial diversity index	9.9% (496)
Geographic diversity index	59.9% (123)
Top 20% share of income	50.2% (437)
Gender gap in earnings	30.8% (190)
White-collar gender gap	18.1% (189)

EDUCATION ★★★ (239)

Eighth grade or less	1.9% (114)
High school diplomas	88.0% (267)
Attended college	50.2% (325)
Bachelor's degrees	16.5% (350)
Advanced degrees	7.7% (133)

EMPLOYMENT ★★★★ (203)

Average jobless rate	8.3% (314)
Self-employed workers	10.7% (129)
Management/financial jobs	8.6% (498)
Computer/engineering jobs	2.1% (399)
Health care jobs	7.7% (35)

GROWTH POTENTIAL ★★★ (327)

Children per senior	1.35 (313)
Median age	40.6 (335)
Moved from different state	1.6% (383)
Homes built since 2000	18.7% (115)
Construction jobs	5.2% (442)

HOUSING ★★★ (239)

Home vacancy rate	7.4% (180)
Home ownership rate	67.0% (386)
Housing diversity index	85.3% (170)
4 or more bedrooms	17.4% (226)
Affordability/income ratio	$3,136 (425)

INCOME ★ (481)

Poverty rate	23.2% (452)
Median household income	$32,784 (509)
Interest/dividends	18.2% (305)
Public assistance	23.0% (496)
Median fulltime earnings	$31,097 (526)

SENIORS ★ (522)

Seniors living alone	26.6% (209)
Poverty rate for seniors	16.1% (504)
Median income for seniors	$26,560 (484)
Seniors who work	12.9% (526)
Home ownership by seniors	76.8% (495)

STABILITY ★★★ (226)

25-39 age group	16.8% (359)
Born in state of residence	60.0% (419)
Same house as 1 year ago	84.4% (331)
Live and work in county	89.4% (78)
Married-couple households	52.5% (171)

TRANSPORTATION ★★★ (300)

Bicycle or walk to work	1.6% (443)
Carpool to work	9.2% (408)
Public transit to work	0.1% (441)
Commute <15 minutes	48.8% (178)
Commute >45 minutes	7.4% (99)

See pages 37-130 for explanations of statistics, stars, and ranks.

Whitewater-Elkhorn, WI
(Walworth County, WI)

POPULATION

2010 census	102,228 (25)
2015 estimate	102,804 (27)
2010-2015 change	0.6% (209)
2020 projection	103,686 (24)
2030 projection	105,356 (29)

RACE

Whites	85.7% (260)
Blacks	0.9% (388)
Hispanics	10.9% (139)
Asians	1.0% (158)
Native Americans	0.1% (402)

AGE

0-17 years old	22.3% (312)
18-24 years old	12.5% (77)
25-39 years old	16.8% (359)
40-54 years old	20.2% (202)
55-64 years old	13.5% (258)
65+ years old	14.7% (389)

PRIVATE SECTOR

Businesses	2,514 (34)
Employees	33,711 (25)
Total wages	$1,182,927,904 (41)
Average weekly wages	$675 (320)

HOUSEHOLD INCOME LADDER

95th percentile	$165,807 (69)
80th percentile	$101,358 (51)
60th percentile	$66,800 (56)
40th percentile	$42,819 (69)
20th percentile	$23,423 (84)

CHILDREN ★★★★★ (78)

Living with two parents	69.5% (154)
Older teens in school	87.6% (110)
Speak English very well	97.2% (403)
Poverty rate for children	16.7% (89)
No health insurance	3.7% (98)

DIVERSITY/EQUALITY ★★★★ (143)

Racial diversity index	25.3% (292)
Geographic diversity index	58.0% (132)
Top 20% share of income	47.2% (238)
Gender gap in earnings	33.8% (280)
White-collar gender gap	16.9% (180)

EDUCATION ★★★★★ (104)

Eighth grade or less	3.1% (238)
High school diplomas	90.8% (167)
Attended college	60.2% (125)
Bachelor's degrees	27.3% (85)
Advanced degrees	9.1% (83)

EMPLOYMENT ★★★★ (150)

Average jobless rate	7.2% (218)
Self-employed workers	9.9% (171)
Management/financial jobs	12.9% (92)
Computer/engineering jobs	3.5% (122)
Health care jobs	4.8% (369)

GROWTH POTENTIAL ★★★★ (142)

Children per senior	1.51 (210)
Median age	38.9 (228)
Moved from different state	3.4% (118)
Homes built since 2000	16.9% (155)
Construction jobs	7.2% (162)

HOUSING ★★★★★ (98)

Home vacancy rate	5.1% (39)
Home ownership rate	68.1% (339)
Housing diversity index	85.8% (97)
4 or more bedrooms	22.6% (74)
Affordability/income ratio	$3,548 (465)

INCOME ★★★★★ (76)

Poverty rate	13.5% (137)
Median household income	$53,445 (68)
Interest/dividends	25.6% (80)
Public assistance	11.9% (127)
Median fulltime earnings	$41,349 (84)

SENIORS ★★★★ (172)

Seniors living alone	29.2% (381)
Poverty rate for seniors	6.9% (84)
Median income for seniors	$39,026 (72)
Seniors who work	23.7% (93)
Home ownership by seniors	79.2% (406)

STABILITY ★ (495)

25-39 age group	16.8% (359)
Born in state of residence	58.4% (435)
Same house as 1 year ago	83.0% (397)
Live and work in county	62.7% (467)
Married-couple households	51.8% (206)

TRANSPORTATION ★★ (426)

Bicycle or walk to work	4.4% (123)
Carpool to work	9.1% (419)
Public transit to work	0.8% (96)
Commute <15 minutes	36.6% (407)
Commute >45 minutes	17.7% (497)

See pages 37-130 for explanations of statistics, stars, and ranks.

Williston, ND
(Williams County, ND)

POPULATION

2010 census	22,398 (502)
2015 estimate	35,294 (380)
2010-2015 change	57.6% (1)
2020 projection	49,045 (222)
2030 projection	82,273 (67)

RACE

Whites	86.8% (244)
Blacks	1.8% (309)
Hispanics	4.5% (265)
Asians	0.4% (413)
Native Americans	4.1% (41)

AGE

0-17 years old	25.1% (116)
18-24 years old	9.9% (168)
25-39 years old	24.2% (7)
40-54 years old	18.6% (412)
55-64 years old	11.9% (447)
65+ years old	10.3% (522)

PRIVATE SECTOR

Businesses	2,324 (43)
Employees	33,793 (24)
Total wages	$2,695,544,781 (3)
Average weekly wages	$1,534 (2)

HOUSEHOLD INCOME LADDER

95th percentile	>$250,000 (1)
80th percentile	$153,948 (3)
60th percentile	$106,784 (3)
40th percentile	$71,278 (4)
20th percentile	$36,450 (6)

CHILDREN ★★★★ (118)

Living with two parents	75.7% (41)
Older teens in school	83.1% (271)
Speak English very well	99.9% (19)
Poverty rate for children	12.6% (44)
No health insurance	10.7% (441)

DIVERSITY/EQUALITY ★ (490)

Racial diversity index	24.2% (303)
Geographic diversity index	61.5% (109)
Top 20% share of income	48.8% (345)
Gender gap in earnings	54.8% (542)
White-collar gender gap	37.2% (409)

EDUCATION ★★★★★ (110)

Eighth grade or less	1.6% (84)
High school diplomas	92.9% (98)

Attended college	66.6% (43)
Bachelor's degrees	22.4% (145)
Advanced degrees	6.0% (264)

EMPLOYMENT ★★★★★ (21)

Average jobless rate	1.7% (1)
Self-employed workers	16.6% (10)
Management/financial jobs	14.6% (34)
Computer/engineering jobs	3.2% (158)
Health care jobs	4.0% (476)

GROWTH POTENTIAL ★★★★★ (2)

Children per senior	2.44 (30)
Median age	32.6 (54)
Moved from different state	9.5% (7)
Homes built since 2000	28.2% (17)
Construction jobs	9.8% (24)

HOUSING ★★★★ (207)

Home vacancy rate	8.9% (280)
Home ownership rate	64.0% (454)
Housing diversity index	83.2% (405)
4 or more bedrooms	24.1% (48)
Affordability/income ratio	$2,288 (159)

INCOME ★★★★★ (7)

Poverty rate	10.1% (34)
Median household income	$88,013 (3)
Interest/dividends	28.4% (30)
Public assistance	7.7% (33)
Median fulltime earnings	$56,718 (2)

SENIORS ★★★★★ (24)

Seniors living alone	25.3% (127)
Poverty rate for seniors	5.4% (29)
Median income for seniors	$50,898 (11)
Seniors who work	28.0% (33)
Home ownership by seniors	78.9% (422)

STABILITY ★★★★★ (92)

25-39 age group	24.2% (7)
Born in state of residence	57.4% (441)
Same house as 1 year ago	76.5% (528)
Live and work in county	95.6% (12)
Married-couple households	50.3% (284)

TRANSPORTATION ★★★★ (151)

Bicycle or walk to work	5.2% (85)
Carpool to work	9.9% (348)
Public transit to work	0.0% (511)
Commute <15 minutes	57.2% (68)
Commute >45 minutes	9.7% (214)

See pages 37-130 for explanations of statistics, stars, and ranks.

Willmar, MN
(Kandiyohi County, MN)

POPULATION			
2010 census	42,239 (286)		
2015 estimate	42,542 (285)		
2010-2015 change	0.7% (202)		
2020 projection	42,785 (286)		
2030 projection	43,281 (283)		

RACE
Whites	83.7% (284)
Blacks	2.8% (232)
Hispanics	11.6% (130)
Asians	0.6% (291)
Native Americans	0.3% (231)

AGE
0-17 years old	23.8% (206)
18-24 years old	8.9% (282)
25-39 years old	17.6% (248)
40-54 years old	18.6% (412)
55-64 years old	14.2% (161)
65+ years old	16.9% (207)

PRIVATE SECTOR
Businesses	1,226 (196)
Employees	19,063 (138)
Total wages	$665,893,561 (158)
Average weekly wages	$672 (330)

HOUSEHOLD INCOME LADDER
95th percentile	$157,345 (113)
80th percentile	$95,432 (84)
60th percentile	$63,684 (89)
40th percentile	$42,177 (76)
20th percentile	$23,277 (88)

CHILDREN ★★★★★ (85)
Living with two parents	71.1% (117)
Older teens in school	87.3% (124)
Speak English very well	98.2% (320)
Poverty rate for children	17.6% (112)
No health insurance	5.5% (218)

DIVERSITY/EQUALITY ★★ (356)
Racial diversity index	28.5% (265)
Geographic diversity index	39.9% (354)
Top 20% share of income	47.5% (256)
Gender gap in earnings	32.3% (234)
White-collar gender gap	37.8% (417)

EDUCATION ★★★★ (138)
Eighth grade or less	3.4% (269)
High school diplomas	90.0% (202)
Attended college	65.6% (49)
Bachelor's degrees	22.7% (139)
Advanced degrees	6.9% (186)

EMPLOYMENT ★★★★★ (53)
Average jobless rate	4.8% (58)
Self-employed workers	11.8% (81)
Management/financial jobs	12.4% (126)
Computer/engineering jobs	3.2% (158)
Health care jobs	6.7% (104)

GROWTH POTENTIAL ★★★★ (200)
Children per senior	1.41 (269)
Median age	39.9 (292)
Moved from different state	1.9% (310)
Homes built since 2000	13.9% (240)
Construction jobs	8.3% (67)

HOUSING ★★★★★ (7)
Home vacancy rate	4.9% (31)
Home ownership rate	72.6% (165)
Housing diversity index	86.2% (43)
4 or more bedrooms	27.7% (24)
Affordability/income ratio	$3,055 (410)

INCOME ★★★★★ (105)
Poverty rate	11.7% (77)
Median household income	$52,632 (77)
Interest/dividends	22.9% (159)
Public assistance	11.9% (127)
Median fulltime earnings	$38,753 (190)

SENIORS ★★★★★ (89)
Seniors living alone	24.4% (94)
Poverty rate for seniors	6.4% (57)
Median income for seniors	$39,190 (69)
Seniors who work	23.3% (103)
Home ownership by seniors	79.1% (414)

STABILITY ★★★★★ (16)
25-39 age group	17.6% (248)
Born in state of residence	76.7% (185)
Same house as 1 year ago	87.8% (149)
Live and work in county	86.1% (113)
Married-couple households	55.8% (52)

TRANSPORTATION ★★★★ (190)
Bicycle or walk to work	2.8% (279)
Carpool to work	8.2% (480)
Public transit to work	1.0% (69)
Commute <15 minutes	53.9% (98)
Commute >45 minutes	7.2% (91)

See pages 37-130 for explanations of statistics, stars, and ranks.

Wilmington, OH
(Clinton County, OH)

POPULATION	
2010 census	42,040 (290)
2015 estimate	41,917 (290)
2010-2015 change	-0.3% (279)
2020 projection	41,827 (294)
2030 projection	41,490 (300)

RACE	
Whites	93.5% (91)
Blacks	2.5% (253)
Hispanics	1.6% (472)
Asians	0.3% (473)
Native Americans	0.1% (402)

AGE	
0-17 years old	24.2% (172)
18-24 years old	9.6% (189)
25-39 years old	16.9% (338)
40-54 years old	20.9% (112)
55-64 years old	13.6% (247)
65+ years old	14.7% (389)

PRIVATE SECTOR	
Businesses	725 (417)
Employees	13,716 (247)
Total wages	$576,282,362 (201)
Average weekly wages	$808 (78)

HOUSEHOLD INCOME LADDER	
95th percentile	$144,756 (233)
80th percentile	$86,932 (209)
60th percentile	$57,499 (195)
40th percentile	$37,663 (189)
20th percentile	$20,423 (208)

CHILDREN	★★★★ (142)
Living with two parents	63.5% (310)
Older teens in school	88.2% (97)
Speak English very well	99.3% (142)
Poverty rate for children	21.7% (211)
No health insurance	5.6% (225)

DIVERSITY/EQUALITY	★★★ (315)
Racial diversity index	12.4% (458)
Geographic diversity index	31.8% (465)
Top 20% share of income	46.8% (188)
Gender gap in earnings	37.6% (379)
White-collar gender gap	2.6% (18)

EDUCATION	★★★ (246)
Eighth grade or less	1.6% (84)
High school diplomas	90.7% (173)
Attended college	50.8% (306)
Bachelor's degrees	16.7% (344)
Advanced degrees	5.3% (347)

EMPLOYMENT	★★★ (273)
Average jobless rate	9.2% (377)
Self-employed workers	7.6% (376)
Management/financial jobs	11.3% (218)
Computer/engineering jobs	4.8% (37)
Health care jobs	4.9% (355)

GROWTH POTENTIAL	★★★ (255)
Children per senior	1.64 (153)
Median age	39.3 (256)
Moved from different state	1.7% (355)
Homes built since 2000	14.6% (213)
Construction jobs	6.1% (310)

HOUSING	★★★ (290)
Home vacancy rate	9.4% (309)
Home ownership rate	64.4% (450)
Housing diversity index	85.8% (97)
4 or more bedrooms	16.0% (293)
Affordability/income ratio	$2,565 (280)

INCOME	★★★ (251)
Poverty rate	15.9% (219)
Median household income	$46,787 (197)
Interest/dividends	17.2% (339)
Public assistance	17.2% (344)
Median fulltime earnings	$39,222 (170)

SENIORS	★★ (332)
Seniors living alone	28.9% (358)
Poverty rate for seniors	7.6% (145)
Median income for seniors	$34,589 (208)
Seniors who work	17.9% (292)
Home ownership by seniors	79.2% (406)

STABILITY	★★★ (263)
25-39 age group	16.9% (338)
Born in state of residence	82.0% (85)
Same house as 1 year ago	86.0% (250)
Live and work in county	63.4% (461)
Married-couple households	52.0% (194)

TRANSPORTATION	★ (538)
Bicycle or walk to work	3.1% (232)
Carpool to work	7.3% (523)
Public transit to work	0.3% (291)
Commute <15 minutes	36.2% (414)
Commute >45 minutes	21.9% (535)

See pages 37-130 for explanations of statistics, stars, and ranks.

Winona, MN
(Winona County, MN)

POPULATION	
2010 census	51,461 (199)
2015 estimate	50,885 (207)
2010-2015 change	-1.1% (335)
2020 projection	50,538 (209)
2030 projection	49,860 (217)

RACE	
Whites	92.0% (135)
Blacks	1.4% (340)
Hispanics	2.7% (361)
Asians	2.6% (32)
Native Americans	0.4% (203)

AGE	
0-17 years old	18.5% (517)
18-24 years old	21.0% (24)
25-39 years old	16.3% (418)
40-54 years old	17.1% (500)
55-64 years old	12.5% (396)
65+ years old	14.6% (400)

PRIVATE SECTOR	
Businesses	1,075 (252)
Employees	21,607 (101)
Total wages	$817,177,608 (113)
Average weekly wages	$727 (200)

HOUSEHOLD INCOME LADDER	
95th percentile	$159,851 (98)
80th percentile	$93,508 (110)
60th percentile	$61,752 (116)
40th percentile	$39,414 (144)
20th percentile	$20,785 (193)

CHILDREN	★★★★★ (31)
Living with two parents	80.8% (9)
Older teens in school	92.3% (37)
Speak English very well	96.8% (421)
Poverty rate for children	11.9% (29)
No health insurance	6.8% (302)

DIVERSITY/EQUALITY	★★★★ (178)
Racial diversity index	15.2% (409)
Geographic diversity index	53.3% (169)
Top 20% share of income	46.4% (152)
Gender gap in earnings	25.0% (87)
White-collar gender gap	27.2% (299)

EDUCATION	★★★★★ (48)
Eighth grade or less	1.9% (114)
High school diplomas	94.3% (47)
Attended college	67.2% (36)
Bachelor's degrees	30.0% (53)
Advanced degrees	9.3% (76)

EMPLOYMENT	★★★★★ (79)
Average jobless rate	6.2% (131)
Self-employed workers	10.4% (145)
Management/financial jobs	13.1% (78)
Computer/engineering jobs	4.7% (40)
Health care jobs	5.1% (319)

GROWTH POTENTIAL	★★★ (313)
Children per senior	1.27 (370)
Median age	33.9 (76)
Moved from different state	3.8% (89)
Homes built since 2000	10.3% (384)
Construction jobs	3.9% (538)

HOUSING	★★★★ (124)
Home vacancy rate	5.8% (79)
Home ownership rate	69.9% (275)
Housing diversity index	82.6% (433)
4 or more bedrooms	24.7% (45)
Affordability/income ratio	$3,045 (408)

INCOME	★★★★★ (94)
Poverty rate	14.7% (182)
Median household income	$50,547 (112)
Interest/dividends	25.2% (87)
Public assistance	7.4% (28)
Median fulltime earnings	$38,120 (216)

SENIORS	★★★★ (198)
Seniors living alone	29.1% (371)
Poverty rate for seniors	8.5% (223)
Median income for seniors	$37,840 (95)
Seniors who work	23.4% (98)
Home ownership by seniors	79.7% (385)

STABILITY	★ (448)
25-39 age group	16.3% (418)
Born in state of residence	62.3% (410)
Same house as 1 year ago	82.3% (426)
Live and work in county	79.3% (229)
Married-couple households	49.5% (323)

TRANSPORTATION	★★★★★ (51)
Bicycle or walk to work	8.0% (31)
Carpool to work	8.7% (453)
Public transit to work	1.9% (33)
Commute <15 minutes	52.9% (110)
Commute >45 minutes	7.7% (115)

See pages 37-130 for explanations of statistics, stars, and ranks.

Wisconsin Rapids-Marshfield, WI
(Wood County, WI)

POPULATION

2010 census	74,749 (84)
2015 estimate	73,435 (89)
2010-2015 change	-1.8% (389)
2020 projection	72,097 (95)
2030 projection	69,422 (107)

RACE

Whites	93.2% (103)
Blacks	0.5% (466)
Hispanics	2.6% (378)
Asians	2.0% (51)
Native Americans	0.7% (136)

AGE

0-17 years old	22.1% (330)
18-24 years old	7.5% (483)
25-39 years old	16.5% (403)
40-54 years old	21.3% (73)
55-64 years old	14.5% (122)
65+ years old	18.1% (117)

PRIVATE SECTOR

Businesses	1,782 (89)
Employees	32,230 (28)
Total wages	$1,344,554,550 (28)
Average weekly wages	$802 (86)

HOUSEHOLD INCOME LADDER

95th percentile	$144,605 (234)
80th percentile	$87,160 (199)
60th percentile	$60,256 (144)
40th percentile	$38,736 (161)
20th percentile	$22,144 (131)

CHILDREN ★★★★★ (75)

Living with two parents	70.8% (125)
Older teens in school	84.8% (207)
Speak English very well	97.6% (375)
Poverty rate for children	15.8% (73)
No health insurance	2.8% (50)

DIVERSITY/EQUALITY ★★★ (278)

Racial diversity index	13.0% (443)
Geographic diversity index	32.5% (457)
Top 20% share of income	45.8% (112)
Gender gap in earnings	33.4% (268)
White-collar gender gap	11.7% (108)

EDUCATION ★★★★ (116)

Eighth grade or less	1.3% (52)
High school diplomas	94.8% (36)

Attended college	59.8% (129)
Bachelor's degrees	21.5% (174)
Advanced degrees	7.0% (184)

EMPLOYMENT ★★★★★ (86)

Average jobless rate	6.6% (161)
Self-employed workers	8.1% (323)
Management/financial jobs	11.1% (240)
Computer/engineering jobs	4.1% (70)
Health care jobs	7.9% (26)

GROWTH POTENTIAL ★ (495)

Children per senior	1.22 (401)
Median age	43.4 (462)
Moved from different state	1.2% (474)
Homes built since 2000	10.8% (364)
Construction jobs	5.8% (360)

HOUSING ★★★★★ (27)

Home vacancy rate	5.0% (33)
Home ownership rate	74.5% (98)
Housing diversity index	86.6% (12)
4 or more bedrooms	18.2% (194)
Affordability/income ratio	$2,453 (230)

INCOME ★★★★★ (99)

Poverty rate	11.0% (58)
Median household income	$48,961 (150)
Interest/dividends	25.2% (87)
Public assistance	14.0% (207)
Median fulltime earnings	$41,078 (91)

SENIORS ★★ (377)

Seniors living alone	29.5% (405)
Poverty rate for seniors	7.4% (128)
Median income for seniors	$33,152 (274)
Seniors who work	17.3% (324)
Home ownership by seniors	78.6% (432)

STABILITY ★★★★★ (82)

25-39 age group	16.5% (403)
Born in state of residence	81.4% (95)
Same house as 1 year ago	89.2% (72)
Live and work in county	79.4% (224)
Married-couple households	51.0% (248)

TRANSPORTATION ★★★★ (196)

Bicycle or walk to work	5.2% (85)
Carpool to work	8.5% (462)
Public transit to work	0.2% (363)
Commute <15 minutes	50.2% (146)
Commute >45 minutes	8.2% (138)

See pages 37-130 for explanations of statistics, stars, and ranks.

Wooster, OH
(Wayne County, OH)

POPULATION			Attended college	47.2% (394)
2010 census	114,520 (15)		Bachelor's degrees	22.8% (135)
2015 estimate	116,063 (15)		Advanced degrees	8.2% (114)
2010-2015 change	1.3% (167)		**EMPLOYMENT**	★★★★★ (90)
2020 projection	117,092 (16)		Average jobless rate	4.8% (58)
2030 projection	118,724 (17)		Self-employed workers	11.4% (103)
			Management/financial jobs	10.9% (263)
RACE			Computer/engineering jobs	4.6% (48)
Whites	94.2% (70)		Health care jobs	5.0% (339)
Blacks	1.6% (320)			
Hispanics	1.7% (464)		**GROWTH POTENTIAL**	★★★ (318)
Asians	0.8% (201)		Children per senior	1.58 (182)
Native Americans	0.2% (300)		Median age	38.8 (217)
			Moved from different state	1.3% (452)
AGE			Homes built since 2000	12.5% (297)
0-17 years old	24.8% (135)		Construction jobs	5.8% (360)
18-24 years old	10.1% (157)			
25-39 years old	16.3% (418)		**HOUSING**	★★★★★ (37)
40-54 years old	19.9% (250)		Home vacancy rate	5.1% (39)
55-64 years old	13.3% (282)		Home ownership rate	73.1% (148)
65+ years old	15.7% (318)		Housing diversity index	85.9% (83)
			4 or more bedrooms	20.8% (107)
PRIVATE SECTOR			Affordability/income ratio	$2,693 (326)
Businesses	2,482 (35)			
Employees	39,408 (15)		**INCOME**	★★★★★ (106)
Total wages	$1,637,332,777 (14)		Poverty rate	13.2% (123)
Average weekly wages	$799 (90)		Median household income	$50,383 (117)
			Interest/dividends	24.4% (119)
HOUSEHOLD INCOME LADDER			Public assistance	12.4% (143)
95th percentile	$148,797 (174)		Median fulltime earnings	$40,349 (130)
80th percentile	$90,631 (149)			
60th percentile	$60,974 (128)		**SENIORS**	★★★★★ (102)
40th percentile	$40,960 (101)		Seniors living alone	25.9% (164)
20th percentile	$23,589 (79)		Poverty rate for seniors	5.3% (26)
			Median income for seniors	$36,649 (128)
CHILDREN	★ (491)		Seniors who work	20.8% (166)
Living with two parents	77.7% (21)		Home ownership by seniors	82.4% (257)
Older teens in school	78.3% (441)			
Speak English very well	88.1% (532)		**STABILITY**	★★★★★ (97)
Poverty rate for children	20.4% (176)		25-39 age group	16.3% (418)
No health insurance	16.8% (534)		Born in state of residence	81.7% (89)
			Same house as 1 year ago	86.5% (219)
DIVERSITY/EQUALITY	★ (536)		Live and work in county	70.6% (361)
Racial diversity index	11.2% (477)		Married-couple households	57.6% (24)
Geographic diversity index	32.4% (459)			
Top 20% share of income	45.6% (94)		**TRANSPORTATION**	★★★ (283)
Gender gap in earnings	45.6% (507)		Bicycle or walk to work	5.7% (64)
White-collar gender gap	47.1% (494)		Carpool to work	9.1% (419)
			Public transit to work	0.2% (363)
EDUCATION	★★★ (302)		Commute <15 minutes	39.6% (336)
Eighth grade or less	7.0% (472)		Commute >45 minutes	10.4% (248)
High school diplomas	86.6% (322)			

See pages 37-130 for explanations of statistics, stars, and ranks.

Worthington, MN
(Nobles County, MN)

POPULATION
2010 census	21,378 (516)
2015 estimate	21,770 (512)
2010-2015 change	1.8% (142)
2020 projection	22,075 (511)
2030 projection	22,695 (497)

RACE
Whites	62.5% (432)
Blacks	3.9% (195)
Hispanics	25.3% (58)
Asians	5.8% (11)
Native Americans	0.2% (300)

AGE
0-17 years old	26.3% (57)
18-24 years old	9.4% (203)
25-39 years old	18.7% (127)
40-54 years old	17.7% (464)
55-64 years old	12.8% (356)
65+ years old	15.2% (354)

PRIVATE SECTOR
Businesses	559 (496)
Employees	8,822 (419)
Total wages	$347,351,060 (385)
Average weekly wages	$757 (150)

HOUSEHOLD INCOME LADDER
95th percentile	$162,106 (86)
80th percentile	$89,415 (163)
60th percentile	$61,918 (110)
40th percentile	$40,442 (115)
20th percentile	$21,660 (154)

CHILDREN ★★ **(406)**
Living with two parents	61.5% (367)
Older teens in school	77.4% (463)
Speak English very well	94.7% (482)
Poverty rate for children	22.4% (232)
No health insurance	7.7% (352)

DIVERSITY/EQUALITY ★★★★★ **(105)**
Racial diversity index	54.0% (68)
Geographic diversity index	64.8% (75)
Top 20% share of income	46.5% (164)
Gender gap in earnings	26.1% (106)
White-collar gender gap	57.0% (534)

EDUCATION ★ **(511)**
Eighth grade or less	12.0% (527)
High school diplomas	79.5% (490)
Attended college	47.7% (388)
Bachelor's degrees	14.5% (443)
Advanced degrees	3.5% (511)

EMPLOYMENT ★★★★ **(127)**
Average jobless rate	6.9% (185)
Self-employed workers	14.6% (22)
Management/financial jobs	12.2% (139)
Computer/engineering jobs	1.8% (457)
Health care jobs	4.6% (401)

GROWTH POTENTIAL ★★★★ **(158)**
Children per senior	1.74 (113)
Median age	36.6 (134)
Moved from different state	3.7% (96)
Homes built since 2000	7.9% (470)
Construction jobs	7.2% (162)

HOUSING ★★★★★ **(24)**
Home vacancy rate	6.6% (136)
Home ownership rate	72.1% (181)
Housing diversity index	84.5% (287)
4 or more bedrooms	26.0% (36)
Affordability/income ratio	$2,112 (85)

INCOME ★★★★ **(155)**
Poverty rate	15.6% (214)
Median household income	$50,625 (110)
Interest/dividends	25.7% (79)
Public assistance	12.7% (155)
Median fulltime earnings	$35,300 (368)

SENIORS ★★★★★ **(90)**
Seniors living alone	27.7% (278)
Poverty rate for seniors	8.4% (214)
Median income for seniors	$33,788 (245)
Seniors who work	26.0% (47)
Home ownership by seniors	86.1% (93)

STABILITY ★★★★ **(186)**
25-39 age group	18.7% (127)
Born in state of residence	54.3% (466)
Same house as 1 year ago	85.4% (285)
Live and work in county	82.0% (181)
Married-couple households	53.9% (113)

TRANSPORTATION ★★★★★ **(33)**
Bicycle or walk to work	4.3% (130)
Carpool to work	17.7% (18)
Public transit to work	0.3% (291)
Commute <15 minutes	56.1% (84)
Commute >45 minutes	8.8% (165)

See pages 37-130 for explanations of statistics, stars, and ranks.

Yankton, SD
(Yankton County, SD)

POPULATION

2010 census	22,438 (501)
2015 estimate	22,702 (502)
2010-2015 change	1.2% (173)
2020 projection	22,946 (497)
2030 projection	23,332 (488)

RACE

Whites	90.2% (175)
Blacks	2.0% (290)
Hispanics	3.3% (324)
Asians	0.8% (201)
Native Americans	2.2% (70)

AGE

0-17 years old	21.4% (379)
18-24 years old	8.7% (299)
25-39 years old	18.9% (111)
40-54 years old	20.4% (169)
55-64 years old	13.8% (203)
65+ years old	16.7% (225)

PRIVATE SECTOR

Businesses	769 (388)
Employees	10,732 (350)
Total wages	$418,210,450 (316)
Average weekly wages	$749 (159)

HOUSEHOLD INCOME LADDER

95th percentile	$164,233 (74)
80th percentile	$91,478 (135)
60th percentile	$60,487 (140)
40th percentile	$36,809 (206)
20th percentile	$19,508 (243)

CHILDREN ★★★★★ (72)

Living with two parents	71.0% (118)
Older teens in school	81.6% (341)
Speak English very well	99.5% (96)
Poverty rate for children	18.0% (125)
No health insurance	1.8% (9)

DIVERSITY/EQUALITY ★★ (392)

Racial diversity index	18.4% (367)
Geographic diversity index	53.1% (173)
Top 20% share of income	50.6% (450)
Gender gap in earnings	20.7% (51)
White-collar gender gap	49.9% (510)

EDUCATION ★★★★★ (103)

Eighth grade or less	2.0% (126)
High school diplomas	93.3% (85)
Attended college	59.8% (129)
Bachelor's degrees	27.9% (76)
Advanced degrees	6.8% (191)

EMPLOYMENT ★★★★★ (4)

Average jobless rate	3.6% (24)
Self-employed workers	15.1% (17)
Management/financial jobs	13.8% (54)
Computer/engineering jobs	3.4% (131)
Health care jobs	8.0% (19)

GROWTH POTENTIAL ★★★★ (194)

Children per senior	1.28 (357)
Median age	40.8 (347)
Moved from different state	3.5% (109)
Homes built since 2000	12.8% (286)
Construction jobs	8.2% (78)

HOUSING ★★★★★ (30)

Home vacancy rate	5.1% (39)
Home ownership rate	67.4% (371)
Housing diversity index	86.2% (43)
4 or more bedrooms	25.2% (40)
Affordability/income ratio	$2,671 (320)

INCOME ★★★★ (144)

Poverty rate	14.2% (160)
Median household income	$48,176 (172)
Interest/dividends	26.8% (56)
Public assistance	15.4% (274)
Median fulltime earnings	$38,295 (209)

SENIORS ★★★★ (119)

Seniors living alone	24.3% (93)
Poverty rate for seniors	9.7% (301)
Median income for seniors	$35,412 (175)
Seniors who work	25.9% (51)
Home ownership by seniors	79.9% (377)

STABILITY ★★★★ (132)

25-39 age group	18.9% (111)
Born in state of residence	63.8% (400)
Same house as 1 year ago	83.6% (359)
Live and work in county	89.1% (80)
Married-couple households	50.9% (253)

TRANSPORTATION ★★★★★ (48)

Bicycle or walk to work	5.4% (75)
Carpool to work	9.0% (435)
Public transit to work	0.9% (83)
Commute <15 minutes	68.2% (8)
Commute >45 minutes	5.7% (48)

See pages 37-130 for explanations of statistics, stars, and ranks.

Zanesville, OH
(Muskingum County, OH)

POPULATION	
2010 census	86,074 (55)
2015 estimate	86,290 (55)
2010-2015 change	0.3% (237)
2020 projection	86,504 (54)
2030 projection	86,596 (60)

RACE	
Whites	92.0% (135)
Blacks	3.3% (217)
Hispanics	0.9% (535)
Asians	0.4% (413)
Native Americans	0.2% (300)

AGE	
0-17 years old	23.4% (240)
18-24 years old	9.2% (234)
25-39 years old	17.0% (317)
40-54 years old	20.5% (151)
55-64 years old	13.7% (225)
65+ years old	16.3% (268)

PRIVATE SECTOR	
Businesses	1,687 (104)
Employees	27,032 (61)
Total wages	$1,019,364,579 (67)
Average weekly wages	$725 (207)

HOUSEHOLD INCOME LADDER	
95th percentile	$132,186 (399)
80th percentile	$79,580 (378)
60th percentile	$51,497 (345)
40th percentile	$31,743 (369)
20th percentile	$17,383 (348)

CHILDREN	★★★ (239)
Living with two parents	58.9% (431)
Older teens in school	84.4% (226)
Speak English very well	99.7% (57)
Poverty rate for children	28.1% (370)
No health insurance	3.9% (111)

DIVERSITY/EQUALITY	★★ (403)
Racial diversity index	15.1% (413)
Geographic diversity index	25.3% (526)
Top 20% share of income	46.6% (174)
Gender gap in earnings	38.1% (396)
White-collar gender gap	13.5% (135)

EDUCATION	★★★ (300)
Eighth grade or less	1.9% (114)
High school diplomas	88.7% (245)
Attended college	48.1% (381)
Bachelor's degrees	16.0% (372)
Advanced degrees	5.4% (334)

EMPLOYMENT	★★ (383)
Average jobless rate	8.3% (314)
Self-employed workers	6.5% (474)
Management/financial jobs	8.6% (498)
Computer/engineering jobs	1.9% (441)
Health care jobs	7.4% (49)

GROWTH POTENTIAL	★★ (412)
Children per senior	1.44 (253)
Median age	40.3 (319)
Moved from different state	0.8% (524)
Homes built since 2000	12.0% (315)
Construction jobs	5.8% (360)

HOUSING	★★★ (250)
Home vacancy rate	7.6% (193)
Home ownership rate	66.8% (396)
Housing diversity index	85.1% (212)
4 or more bedrooms	15.1% (347)
Affordability/income ratio	$2,640 (306)

INCOME	★★ (395)
Poverty rate	18.6% (322)
Median household income	$41,130 (349)
Interest/dividends	15.4% (396)
Public assistance	22.7% (492)
Median fulltime earnings	$37,063 (282)

SENIORS	★ (445)
Seniors living alone	28.1% (306)
Poverty rate for seniors	8.3% (202)
Median income for seniors	$29,546 (421)
Seniors who work	14.6% (472)
Home ownership by seniors	78.4% (435)

STABILITY	★★★★ (195)
25-39 age group	17.0% (317)
Born in state of residence	86.1% (26)
Same house as 1 year ago	85.2% (294)
Live and work in county	77.3% (250)
Married-couple households	48.0% (378)

TRANSPORTATION	★ (506)
Bicycle or walk to work	2.4% (331)
Carpool to work	8.5% (462)
Public transit to work	0.3% (291)
Commute <15 minutes	32.6% (484)
Commute >45 minutes	15.1% (426)

See pages 37-130 for explanations of statistics, stars, and ranks.

7

WEST

★★★★★

MICROPOLITAN
AMERICA

Aberdeen, WA
(Grays Harbor County, WA)

POPULATION	
2010 census	72,797 (90)
2015 estimate	71,122 (99)
2010-2015 change	-2.3% (436)
2020 projection	70,626 (101)
2030 projection	69,874 (104)

RACE	
Whites	80.1% (325)
Blacks	1.1% (367)
Hispanics	9.6% (156)
Asians	1.8% (60)
Native Americans	4.0% (42)

AGE	
0-17 years old	21.2% (397)
18-24 years old	7.9% (424)
25-39 years old	18.1% (186)
40-54 years old	19.0% (364)
55-64 years old	15.6% (56)
65+ years old	18.2% (111)

PRIVATE SECTOR	
Businesses	2,371 (40)
Employees	15,641 (199)
Total wages	$543,459,392 (217)
Average weekly wages	$668 (338)

HOUSEHOLD INCOME LADDER	
95th percentile	$132,693 (390)
80th percentile	$85,370 (245)
60th percentile	$53,738 (285)
40th percentile	$34,766 (269)
20th percentile	$18,902 (272)

CHILDREN	★★ (375)
Living with two parents	58.5% (440)
Older teens in school	78.8% (433)
Speak English very well	97.2% (403)
Poverty rate for children	24.8% (293)
No health insurance	7.1% (324)

DIVERSITY/EQUALITY	★★★★★ (65)
Racial diversity index	34.6% (218)
Geographic diversity index	55.6% (149)
Top 20% share of income	46.9% (208)
Gender gap in earnings	27.8% (133)
White-collar gender gap	13.8% (139)

EDUCATION	★★★ (294)
Eighth grade or less	4.1% (332)
High school diplomas	88.5% (253)
Attended college	57.5% (178)
Bachelor's degrees	14.7% (431)
Advanced degrees	4.9% (396)

EMPLOYMENT	★ (520)
Average jobless rate	14.3% (531)
Self-employed workers	8.8% (273)
Management/financial jobs	9.1% (463)
Computer/engineering jobs	2.7% (270)
Health care jobs	4.4% (433)

GROWTH POTENTIAL	★★ (380)
Children per senior	1.16 (439)
Median age	42.7 (442)
Moved from different state	1.7% (355)
Homes built since 2000	14.7% (210)
Construction jobs	6.7% (219)

HOUSING	★★ (374)
Home vacancy rate	9.6% (327)
Home ownership rate	67.8% (349)
Housing diversity index	85.2% (190)
4 or more bedrooms	15.6% (320)
Affordability/income ratio	$3,636 (475)

INCOME	★★ (339)
Poverty rate	18.1% (300)
Median household income	$43,538 (275)
Interest/dividends	16.3% (366)
Public assistance	22.7% (492)
Median fulltime earnings	$40,858 (103)

SENIORS	★★ (350)
Seniors living alone	28.0% (296)
Poverty rate for seniors	8.5% (223)
Median income for seniors	$34,785 (200)
Seniors who work	14.0% (503)
Home ownership by seniors	81.3% (316)

STABILITY	★★ (374)
25-39 age group	18.1% (186)
Born in state of residence	64.0% (398)
Same house as 1 year ago	83.3% (382)
Live and work in county	83.1% (161)
Married-couple households	46.0% (443)

TRANSPORTATION	★★★ (223)
Bicycle or walk to work	2.9% (265)
Carpool to work	13.9% (72)
Public transit to work	1.6% (38)
Commute <15 minutes	41.4% (312)
Commute >45 minutes	16.4% (466)

See pages 37-130 for explanations of statistics, stars, and ranks.

Alamogordo, NM
(Otero County, NM)

POPULATION

2010 census	63,797 (129)
2015 estimate	64,362 (125)
2010-2015 change	0.9% (186)
2020 projection	63,552 (130)
2030 projection	61,721 (142)

RACE

Whites	51.1% (482)
Blacks	3.5% (209)
Hispanics	36.1% (43)
Asians	1.1% (139)
Native Americans	6.2% (29)

AGE

0-17 years old	24.2% (172)
18-24 years old	11.3% (106)
25-39 years old	19.0% (104)
40-54 years old	17.8% (462)
55-64 years old	11.9% (447)
65+ years old	15.7% (318)

PRIVATE SECTOR

Businesses	1,005 (277)
Employees	11,445 (328)
Total wages	$360,162,999 (371)
Average weekly wages	$605 (479)

HOUSEHOLD INCOME LADDER

95th percentile	$130,235 (431)
80th percentile	$77,229 (420)
60th percentile	$49,645 (390)
40th percentile	$30,924 (388)
20th percentile	$16,296 (398)

CHILDREN ★ **(482)**

Living with two parents	56.0% (473)
Older teens in school	79.9% (401)
Speak English very well	95.1% (476)
Poverty rate for children	34.1% (470)
No health insurance	8.5% (379)

DIVERSITY/EQUALITY ★★★★★ **(10)**

Racial diversity index	60.3% (14)
Geographic diversity index	77.5% (12)
Top 20% share of income	47.1% (226)
Gender gap in earnings	31.0% (204)
White-collar gender gap	11.5% (103)

EDUCATION ★★ **(365)**

Eighth grade or less	6.3% (439)
High school diplomas	83.8% (405)
Attended college	53.9% (247)
Bachelor's degrees	15.9% (382)
Advanced degrees	6.6% (211)

EMPLOYMENT ★ **(526)**

Average jobless rate	12.7% (512)
Self-employed workers	6.3% (484)
Management/financial jobs	8.9% (483)
Computer/engineering jobs	3.4% (131)
Health care jobs	4.1% (462)

GROWTH POTENTIAL ★★★★★ **(37)**

Children per senior	1.54 (197)
Median age	35.6 (105)
Moved from different state	7.6% (14)
Homes built since 2000	15.7% (186)
Construction jobs	9.0% (47)

HOUSING ★★ **(380)**

Home vacancy rate	9.6% (327)
Home ownership rate	64.3% (451)
Housing diversity index	84.6% (277)
4 or more bedrooms	14.0% (401)
Affordability/income ratio	$2,559 (278)

INCOME ★★ **(424)**

Poverty rate	23.1% (448)
Median household income	$39,775 (386)
Interest/dividends	18.6% (288)
Public assistance	18.3% (380)
Median fulltime earnings	$32,359 (475)

SENIORS ★★ **(339)**

Seniors living alone	28.2% (311)
Poverty rate for seniors	11.8% (401)
Median income for seniors	$34,521 (211)
Seniors who work	14.0% (503)
Home ownership by seniors	85.6% (120)

STABILITY ★ **(443)**

25-39 age group	19.0% (104)
Born in state of residence	38.3% (525)
Same house as 1 year ago	81.3% (470)
Live and work in county	89.8% (66)
Married-couple households	48.6% (358)

TRANSPORTATION ★★★★★ **(80)**

Bicycle or walk to work	3.1% (232)
Carpool to work	17.3% (21)
Public transit to work	0.6% (141)
Commute <15 minutes	43.9% (262)
Commute >45 minutes	8.2% (138)

See pages 37-130 for explanations of statistics, stars, and ranks.

Astoria, OR
(Clatsop County, OR)

POPULATION

2010 census	37,039 (358)
2015 estimate	37,831 (347)
2010-2015 change	2.1% (125)
2020 projection	38,344 (338)
2030 projection	39,454 (324)

RACE

Whites	86.4% (250)
Blacks	0.7% (423)
Hispanics	8.1% (180)
Asians	1.1% (139)
Native Americans	0.3% (231)

AGE

0-17 years old	19.8% (468)
18-24 years old	8.3% (362)
25-39 years old	17.8% (227)
40-54 years old	18.7% (399)
55-64 years old	16.9% (18)
65+ years old	18.5% (104)

PRIVATE SECTOR

Businesses	1,525 (129)
Employees	14,878 (214)
Total wages	$508,470,769 (240)
Average weekly wages	$657 (373)

HOUSEHOLD INCOME LADDER

95th percentile	$151,368 (147)
80th percentile	$92,281 (127)
60th percentile	$57,896 (184)
40th percentile	$36,734 (210)
20th percentile	$21,563 (159)

CHILDREN ★★★ (223)

Living with two parents	66.8% (224)
Older teens in school	82.2% (311)
Speak English very well	97.3% (399)
Poverty rate for children	22.3% (230)
No health insurance	5.2% (197)

DIVERSITY/EQUALITY ★★★★ (116)

Racial diversity index	24.6% (298)
Geographic diversity index	68.8% (52)
Top 20% share of income	46.7% (182)
Gender gap in earnings	31.0% (204)
White-collar gender gap	30.4% (343)

EDUCATION ★★★★★ (86)

Eighth grade or less	2.2% (152)
High school diplomas	91.7% (135)
Attended college	66.6% (43)
Bachelor's degrees	23.4% (127)
Advanced degrees	8.6% (99)

EMPLOYMENT ★★★★ (163)

Average jobless rate	7.6% (250)
Self-employed workers	11.6% (90)
Management/financial jobs	11.8% (173)
Computer/engineering jobs	2.5% (307)
Health care jobs	5.4% (273)

GROWTH POTENTIAL ★★★★ (208)

Children per senior	1.07 (477)
Median age	43.9 (475)
Moved from different state	6.8% (28)
Homes built since 2000	14.2% (231)
Construction jobs	6.8% (204)

HOUSING ★ (516)

Home vacancy rate	9.6% (327)
Home ownership rate	60.7% (495)
Housing diversity index	85.6% (127)
4 or more bedrooms	16.6% (264)
Affordability/income ratio	$5,312 (531)

INCOME ★★★★ (220)

Poverty rate	15.8% (217)
Median household income	$46,408 (203)
Interest/dividends	24.7% (109)
Public assistance	19.0% (399)
Median fulltime earnings	$38,573 (202)

SENIORS ★★ (354)

Seniors living alone	29.8% (422)
Poverty rate for seniors	7.0% (93)
Median income for seniors	$36,579 (131)
Seniors who work	18.9% (247)
Home ownership by seniors	76.4% (502)

STABILITY ★ (465)

25-39 age group	17.8% (227)
Born in state of residence	46.3% (500)
Same house as 1 year ago	79.5% (504)
Live and work in county	93.7% (22)
Married-couple households	47.4% (401)

TRANSPORTATION ★★★★★ (31)

Bicycle or walk to work	8.9% (21)
Carpool to work	11.8% (152)
Public transit to work	1.1% (58)
Commute <15 minutes	48.8% (178)
Commute >45 minutes	7.1% (88)

See pages 37-130 for explanations of statistics, stars, and ranks.

Blackfoot, ID
(Bingham County, ID)

POPULATION		Attended college	58.5% (157)
2010 census	45,607 (253)	Bachelor's degrees	17.8% (290)
2015 estimate	44,990 (260)	Advanced degrees	4.7% (419)
2010-2015 change	-1.4% (364)	**EMPLOYMENT**	★★★★ (135)
2020 projection	44,434 (268)	Average jobless rate	7.1% (208)
2030 projection	43,301 (282)	Self-employed workers	9.6% (200)
RACE		Management/financial jobs	12.6% (111)
Whites	74.5% (361)	Computer/engineering jobs	3.6% (112)
Blacks	0.3% (519)	Health care jobs	5.3% (286)
Hispanics	17.7% (89)	**GROWTH POTENTIAL**	★★★★★ (48)
Asians	0.7% (241)	Children per senior	2.56 (28)
Native Americans	5.0% (32)	Median age	32.9 (58)
AGE		Moved from different state	2.2% (248)
0-17 years old	32.0% (7)	Homes built since 2000	16.7% (162)
18-24 years old	8.4% (349)	Construction jobs	7.6% (110)
25-39 years old	18.4% (151)	**HOUSING**	★★★★★ (6)
40-54 years old	17.3% (487)	Home vacancy rate	6.7% (141)
55-64 years old	11.3% (486)	Home ownership rate	74.1% (115)
65+ years old	12.5% (484)	Housing diversity index	85.7% (108)
PRIVATE SECTOR		4 or more bedrooms	34.9% (4)
Businesses	990 (283)	Affordability/income ratio	$2,819 (361)
Employees	10,383 (364)	**INCOME**	★★★★ (195)
Total wages	$356,566,705 (375)	Poverty rate	13.5% (137)
Average weekly wages	$660 (364)	Median household income	$50,155 (122)
HOUSEHOLD INCOME LADDER		Interest/dividends	21.1% (210)
95th percentile	$144,310 (239)	Public assistance	14.5% (234)
80th percentile	$91,649 (131)	Median fulltime earnings	$35,600 (356)
60th percentile	$61,406 (123)	**SENIORS**	★★★★★ (32)
40th percentile	$41,664 (85)	Seniors living alone	22.0% (35)
20th percentile	$22,800 (104)	Poverty rate for seniors	6.9% (84)
CHILDREN	★★★★ (201)	Median income for seniors	$35,566 (170)
Living with two parents	75.6% (43)	Seniors who work	20.6% (173)
Older teens in school	79.5% (414)	Home ownership by seniors	88.8% (27)
Speak English very well	97.2% (403)	**STABILITY**	★★★★★ (34)
Poverty rate for children	18.8% (142)	25-39 age group	18.4% (151)
No health insurance	7.7% (352)	Born in state of residence	67.5% (353)
DIVERSITY/EQUALITY	★★ (390)	Same house as 1 year ago	87.9% (140)
Racial diversity index	41.1% (182)	Live and work in county	66.5% (427)
Geographic diversity index	50.8% (200)	Married-couple households	62.6% (6)
Top 20% share of income	43.8% (20)	**TRANSPORTATION**	★★★★ (168)
Gender gap in earnings	47.0% (514)	Bicycle or walk to work	2.4% (331)
White-collar gender gap	62.5% (544)	Carpool to work	9.6% (378)
EDUCATION	★★ (335)	Public transit to work	3.0% (13)
Eighth grade or less	6.3% (439)	Commute <15 minutes	46.6% (224)
High school diplomas	85.9% (345)	Commute >45 minutes	12.4% (331)

See pages 37-130 for explanations of statistics, stars, and ranks.

Bozeman, MT
(Gallatin County, MT)

POPULATION	
2010 census	89,513 (46)
2015 estimate	100,739 (29)
2010-2015 change	12.5% (7)
2020 projection	112,664 (17)
2030 projection	140,788 (10)

RACE	
Whites	92.6% (114)
Blacks	0.4% (499)
Hispanics	3.1% (333)
Asians	1.3% (112)
Native Americans	0.9% (115)

AGE	
0-17 years old	20.6% (423)
18-24 years old	16.3% (49)
25-39 years old	23.2% (14)
40-54 years old	17.4% (485)
55-64 years old	11.7% (463)
65+ years old	10.7% (517)

PRIVATE SECTOR	
Businesses	5,872 (2)
Employees	44,127 (8)
Total wages	$1,704,252,996 (12)
Average weekly wages	$743 (169)

HOUSEHOLD INCOME LADDER	
95th percentile	$184,341 (35)
80th percentile	$103,501 (45)
60th percentile	$67,621 (50)
40th percentile	$43,981 (58)
20th percentile	$24,714 (53)

CHILDREN	★★★★★ (14)
Living with two parents	79.8% (12)
Older teens in school	93.8% (23)
Speak English very well	99.1% (179)
Poverty rate for children	10.7% (20)
No health insurance	7.8% (357)

DIVERSITY/EQUALITY	★★★★ (217)
Racial diversity index	14.1% (434)
Geographic diversity index	72.6% (27)
Top 20% share of income	49.5% (397)
Gender gap in earnings	30.8% (190)
White-collar gender gap	27.6% (304)

EDUCATION	★★★★★ (2)
Eighth grade or less	0.6% (7)
High school diplomas	97.5% (2)
Attended college	78.7% (5)
Bachelor's degrees	48.8% (7)
Advanced degrees	15.3% (14)

EMPLOYMENT	★★★★★ (7)
Average jobless rate	6.3% (140)
Self-employed workers	15.3% (15)
Management/financial jobs	14.6% (34)
Computer/engineering jobs	7.6% (5)
Health care jobs	5.2% (307)

GROWTH POTENTIAL	★★★★★ (11)
Children per senior	1.92 (69)
Median age	33.2 (61)
Moved from different state	6.1% (29)
Homes built since 2000	33.7% (9)
Construction jobs	9.5% (31)

HOUSING	★ (483)
Home vacancy rate	5.3% (50)
Home ownership rate	61.5% (485)
Housing diversity index	80.0% (514)
4 or more bedrooms	23.4% (59)
Affordability/income ratio	$4,887 (522)

INCOME	★★★★★ (37)
Poverty rate	13.2% (123)
Median household income	$55,553 (49)
Interest/dividends	30.4% (21)
Public assistance	5.7% (12)
Median fulltime earnings	$40,797 (107)

SENIORS	★★★★★ (36)
Seniors living alone	25.5% (142)
Poverty rate for seniors	4.0% (8)
Median income for seniors	$45,618 (24)
Seniors who work	24.5% (79)
Home ownership by seniors	79.5% (394)

STABILITY	★★★ (240)
25-39 age group	23.2% (14)
Born in state of residence	42.8% (514)
Same house as 1 year ago	76.6% (526)
Live and work in county	94.1% (18)
Married-couple households	49.3% (333)

TRANSPORTATION	★★★★★ (49)
Bicycle or walk to work	10.5% (13)
Carpool to work	9.8% (358)
Public transit to work	0.7% (119)
Commute <15 minutes	47.3% (204)
Commute >45 minutes	5.3% (38)

See pages 37-130 for explanations of statistics, stars, and ranks.

Breckenridge, CO
(Summit County, CO)

POPULATION

2010 census	27,994 (455)
2015 estimate	30,257 (432)
2010-2015 change	8.1% (14)
2020 projection	32,703 (410)
2030 projection	38,305 (335)

RACE

Whites	81.0% (317)
Blacks	1.2% (361)
Hispanics	14.7% (106)
Asians	1.3% (112)
Native Americans	0.2% (300)

AGE

0-17 years old	16.9% (538)
18-24 years old	9.0% (265)
25-39 years old	27.3% (3)
40-54 years old	22.1% (25)
55-64 years old	15.1% (74)
65+ years old	9.7% (535)

PRIVATE SECTOR

Businesses	2,165 (50)
Employees	17,940 (154)
Total wages	$645,872,903 (168)
Average weekly wages	$692 (277)

HOUSEHOLD INCOME LADDER

95th percentile	$213,654 (12)
80th percentile	$126,093 (8)
60th percentile	$83,492 (12)
40th percentile	$52,663 (15)
20th percentile	$31,896 (8)

CHILDREN ★ **(445)**

Living with two parents	72.2% (104)
Older teens in school	75.3% (499)
Speak English very well	97.0% (413)
Poverty rate for children	19.6% (155)
No health insurance	19.3% (545)

DIVERSITY/EQUALITY ★★★★★ **(12)**

Racial diversity index	32.2% (234)
Geographic diversity index	81.6% (3)
Top 20% share of income	47.9% (283)
Gender gap in earnings	17.4% (28)
White-collar gender gap	11.8% (109)

EDUCATION ★★★★★ **(17)**

Eighth grade or less	4.0% (325)
High school diplomas	94.1% (54)

Attended college	75.7% (8)
Bachelor's degrees	46.1% (10)
Advanced degrees	13.1% (26)

EMPLOYMENT ★★★★★ **(50)**

Average jobless rate	4.7% (54)
Self-employed workers	13.9% (34)
Management/financial jobs	13.8% (54)
Computer/engineering jobs	4.1% (70)
Health care jobs	4.3% (444)

GROWTH POTENTIAL ★★★★★ **(30)**

Children per senior	1.74 (113)
Median age	37.1 (149)
Moved from different state	5.6% (36)
Homes built since 2000	18.9% (110)
Construction jobs	11.9% (5)

HOUSING ★ **(539)**

Home vacancy rate	7.6% (193)
Home ownership rate	66.3% (410)
Housing diversity index	77.6% (539)
4 or more bedrooms	20.1% (122)
Affordability/income ratio	$7,043 (548)

INCOME ★★★★★ **(14)**

Poverty rate	13.7% (145)
Median household income	$67,983 (13)
Interest/dividends	31.0% (14)
Public assistance	3.2% (4)
Median fulltime earnings	$41,205 (87)

SENIORS ★★★★★ **(4)**

Seniors living alone	16.5% (1)
Poverty rate for seniors	6.4% (57)
Median income for seniors	$68,015 (4)
Seniors who work	39.3% (2)
Home ownership by seniors	79.8% (382)

STABILITY ★★★ **(282)**

25-39 age group	27.3% (3)
Born in state of residence	26.8% (547)
Same house as 1 year ago	78.6% (514)
Live and work in county	93.1% (35)
Married-couple households	49.6% (317)

TRANSPORTATION ★★★★★ **(6)**

Bicycle or walk to work	10.5% (13)
Carpool to work	10.0% (337)
Public transit to work	6.0% (8)
Commute <15 minutes	48.6% (184)
Commute >45 minutes	6.4% (67)

See pages 37-130 for explanations of statistics, stars, and ranks.

Brookings, OR
(Curry County, OR)

POPULATION	
2010 census	22,364 (504)
2015 estimate	22,483 (504)
2010-2015 change	0.5% (219)
2020 projection	22,547 (502)
2030 projection	22,711 (496)

RACE	
Whites	87.5% (232)
Blacks	0.3% (519)
Hispanics	6.3% (212)
Asians	0.6% (291)
Native Americans	1.9% (72)

AGE	
0-17 years old	15.5% (546)
18-24 years old	5.5% (551)
25-39 years old	12.4% (549)
40-54 years old	17.3% (487)
55-64 years old	18.9% (2)
65+ years old	30.5% (1)

PRIVATE SECTOR	
Businesses	753 (397)
Employees	5,042 (526)
Total wages	$160,692,148 (529)
Average weekly wages	$613 (462)

HOUSEHOLD INCOME LADDER	
95th percentile	$130,349 (427)
80th percentile	$77,996 (401)
60th percentile	$49,844 (388)
40th percentile	$30,864 (389)
20th percentile	$17,717 (330)

CHILDREN	★★ (336)
Living with two parents	56.2% (471)
Older teens in school	76.6% (479)
Speak English very well	99.0% (200)
Poverty rate for children	17.8% (120)
No health insurance	7.0% (319)

DIVERSITY/EQUALITY	★★★★ (142)
Racial diversity index	22.9% (316)
Geographic diversity index	69.7% (46)
Top 20% share of income	46.6% (166)
Gender gap in earnings	37.9% (389)
White-collar gender gap	24.0% (258)

EDUCATION	★★★★ (130)
Eighth grade or less	2.1% (136)
High school diplomas	91.4% (151)

Attended college	62.9% (84)
Bachelor's degrees	22.0% (159)
Advanced degrees	7.3% (157)

EMPLOYMENT	★★★★★ (87)
Average jobless rate	11.3% (466)
Self-employed workers	14.0% (33)
Management/financial jobs	10.7% (287)
Computer/engineering jobs	2.4% (336)
Health care jobs	8.7% (6)

GROWTH POTENTIAL	★ (485)
Children per senior	0.51 (551)
Median age	54.6 (551)
Moved from different state	7.4% (16)
Homes built since 2000	14.7% (210)
Construction jobs	5.3% (425)

HOUSING	★ (545)
Home vacancy rate	8.9% (280)
Home ownership rate	65.4% (425)
Housing diversity index	84.4% (299)
4 or more bedrooms	6.8% (551)
Affordability/income ratio	$5,337 (532)

INCOME	★★★★ (213)
Poverty rate	16.6% (252)
Median household income	$40,884 (358)
Interest/dividends	28.4% (30)
Public assistance	19.7% (418)
Median fulltime earnings	$40,212 (134)

SENIORS	★ (495)
Seniors living alone	29.7% (416)
Poverty rate for seniors	11.1% (378)
Median income for seniors	n.a.
Seniors who work	11.8% (542)
Home ownership by seniors	80.1% (369)

STABILITY	★ (548)
25-39 age group	12.4% (549)
Born in state of residence	29.3% (545)
Same house as 1 year ago	83.0% (397)
Live and work in county	89.8% (66)
Married-couple households	46.3% (437)

TRANSPORTATION	★★★★★ (26)
Bicycle or walk to work	8.3% (27)
Carpool to work	9.2% (408)
Public transit to work	0.0% (511)
Commute <15 minutes	64.5% (21)
Commute >45 minutes	3.3% (10)

See pages 37-130 for explanations of statistics, stars, and ranks.

Burley, ID
(Cassia and Minidoka Counties, ID)

POPULATION	
2010 census	43,021 (277)
2015 estimate	43,967 (273)
2010-2015 change	2.2% (118)
2020 projection	44,337 (270)
2030 projection	45,045 (264)

RACE	
Whites	68.0% (400)
Blacks	0.1% (544)
Hispanics	29.6% (52)
Asians	0.4% (413)
Native Americans	0.6% (150)

AGE	
0-17 years old	30.6% (15)
18-24 years old	9.0% (265)
25-39 years old	17.8% (227)
40-54 years old	16.9% (504)
55-64 years old	11.6% (471)
65+ years old	14.0% (438)

PRIVATE SECTOR	
Businesses	1,283 (182)
Employees	15,254 (205)
Total wages	$533,235,131 (224)
Average weekly wages	$672 (330)

HOUSEHOLD INCOME LADDER	
95th percentile	$128,066 (453)
80th percentile	$79,811 (374)
60th percentile	$54,579 (259)
40th percentile	$36,388 (220)
20th percentile	$20,667 (200)

CHILDREN	★★ (436)
Living with two parents	72.8% (83)
Older teens in school	78.2% (442)
Speak English very well	93.2% (505)
Poverty rate for children	24.0% (274)
No health insurance	12.7% (489)

DIVERSITY/EQUALITY	★★ (421)
Racial diversity index	45.0% (149)
Geographic diversity index	59.9% (123)
Top 20% share of income	45.7% (102)
Gender gap in earnings	50.4% (528)
White-collar gender gap	67.3% (551)

EDUCATION	★ (488)
Eighth grade or less	11.3% (524)
High school diplomas	78.9% (499)
Attended college	52.6% (270)
Bachelor's degrees	16.5% (350)
Advanced degrees	4.6% (431)

EMPLOYMENT	★★★ (306)
Average jobless rate	5.2% (76)
Self-employed workers	11.1% (115)
Management/financial jobs	11.0% (252)
Computer/engineering jobs	2.4% (336)
Health care jobs	3.0% (535)

GROWTH POTENTIAL	★★★★ (147)
Children per senior	2.19 (41)
Median age	33.7 (68)
Moved from different state	3.1% (147)
Homes built since 2000	11.3% (344)
Construction jobs	4.7% (487)

HOUSING	★★★★★ (22)
Home vacancy rate	6.1% (104)
Home ownership rate	72.3% (175)
Housing diversity index	85.8% (97)
4 or more bedrooms	25.5% (38)
Affordability/income ratio	$2,632 (302)

INCOME	★★★ (287)
Poverty rate	16.6% (252)
Median household income	$45,287 (230)
Interest/dividends	17.6% (325)
Public assistance	12.3% (140)
Median fulltime earnings	$32,449 (470)

SENIORS	★★★★ (167)
Seniors living alone	26.7% (217)
Poverty rate for seniors	10.2% (334)
Median income for seniors	$30,535 (390)
Seniors who work	22.2% (126)
Home ownership by seniors	86.4% (82)

STABILITY	★★★★ (135)
25-39 age group	17.8% (227)
Born in state of residence	59.2% (425)
Same house as 1 year ago	85.7% (272)
Live and work in county	69.3% (381)
Married-couple households	61.5% (7)

TRANSPORTATION	★★★★ (117)
Bicycle or walk to work	3.1% (232)
Carpool to work	12.9% (106)
Public transit to work	0.1% (441)
Commute <15 minutes	50.5% (144)
Commute >45 minutes	5.4% (42)

See pages 37-130 for explanations of statistics, stars, and ranks.

Butte-Silver Bow, MT
(Silver Bow County, MT)

POPULATION

2010 census	34,200 (392)
2015 estimate	34,622 (387)
2010-2015 change	1.2% (173)
2020 projection	34,737 (386)
2030 projection	34,936 (375)

RACE

Whites	91.4% (154)
Blacks	0.5% (466)
Hispanics	4.0% (296)
Asians	0.7% (241)
Native Americans	1.5% (80)

AGE

0-17 years old	20.4% (437)
18-24 years old	12.1% (85)
25-39 years old	16.9% (338)
40-54 years old	19.3% (323)
55-64 years old	14.7% (97)
65+ years old	16.7% (225)

PRIVATE SECTOR

Businesses	1,225 (197)
Employees	13,508 (257)
Total wages	$518,309,870 (229)
Average weekly wages	$738 (185)

HOUSEHOLD INCOME LADDER

95th percentile	$144,592 (235)
80th percentile	$83,131 (291)
60th percentile	$48,192 (418)
40th percentile	$30,083 (417)
20th percentile	$15,139 (447)

CHILDREN ★★ (376)

Living with two parents	61.3% (373)
Older teens in school	70.9% (527)
Speak English very well	99.5% (96)
Poverty rate for children	26.2% (328)
No health insurance	5.2% (197)

DIVERSITY/EQUALITY ★★★ (312)

Racial diversity index	16.2% (395)
Geographic diversity index	50.5% (206)
Top 20% share of income	51.0% (469)
Gender gap in earnings	24.7% (85)
White-collar gender gap	22.9% (249)

EDUCATION ★★★★★ (109)

Eighth grade or less	2.0% (126)
High school diplomas	93.1% (91)
Attended college	59.7% (134)
Bachelor's degrees	25.7% (97)
Advanced degrees	7.3% (157)

EMPLOYMENT ★★★★★ (41)

Average jobless rate	7.0% (196)
Self-employed workers	10.1% (158)
Management/financial jobs	12.8% (100)
Computer/engineering jobs	4.6% (48)
Health care jobs	8.0% (19)

GROWTH POTENTIAL ★★ (390)

Children per senior	1.22 (401)
Median age	40.6 (335)
Moved from different state	4.2% (70)
Homes built since 2000	9.0% (434)
Construction jobs	5.1% (458)

HOUSING ★ (491)

Home vacancy rate	8.4% (245)
Home ownership rate	64.6% (447)
Housing diversity index	79.2% (523)
4 or more bedrooms	19.2% (150)
Affordability/income ratio	$3,393 (452)

INCOME ★★★ (320)

Poverty rate	20.1% (373)
Median household income	$37,749 (433)
Interest/dividends	21.5% (194)
Public assistance	17.7% (361)
Median fulltime earnings	$38,248 (211)

SENIORS ★ (504)

Seniors living alone	35.4% (545)
Poverty rate for seniors	8.2% (196)
Median income for seniors	$31,804 (330)
Seniors who work	18.8% (253)
Home ownership by seniors	74.7% (529)

STABILITY ★ (480)

25-39 age group	16.9% (338)
Born in state of residence	68.0% (347)
Same house as 1 year ago	80.8% (486)
Live and work in county	91.0% (52)
Married-couple households	39.6% (531)

TRANSPORTATION ★★★★ (111)

Bicycle or walk to work	3.5% (189)
Carpool to work	10.2% (312)
Public transit to work	0.4% (219)
Commute <15 minutes	58.0% (65)
Commute >45 minutes	5.6% (43)

See pages 37-130 for explanations of statistics, stars, and ranks.

Cañon City, CO
(Fremont County, CO)

POPULATION	
2010 census	46,824 (236)
2015 estimate	46,692 (238)
2010-2015 change	-0.3% (279)
2020 projection	46,167 (246)
2030 projection	45,242 (260)

RACE	
Whites	78.0% (339)
Blacks	5.1% (160)
Hispanics	13.0% (119)
Asians	0.7% (241)
Native Americans	1.3% (86)

AGE	
0-17 years old	16.7% (542)
18-24 years old	6.7% (531)
25-39 years old	21.8% (24)
40-54 years old	20.7% (132)
55-64 years old	14.6% (107)
65+ years old	19.4% (65)

PRIVATE SECTOR	
Businesses	849 (346)
Employees	8,107 (445)
Total wages	$246,370,203 (473)
Average weekly wages	$584 (510)

HOUSEHOLD INCOME LADDER	
95th percentile	$126,398 (475)
80th percentile	$75,636 (447)
60th percentile	$49,062 (401)
40th percentile	$32,834 (331)
20th percentile	$18,081 (315)

CHILDREN	★★★ (261)
Living with two parents	57.9% (450)
Older teens in school	88.2% (97)
Speak English very well	98.8% (251)
Poverty rate for children	29.4% (390)
No health insurance	5.6% (225)

DIVERSITY/EQUALITY	★★★★★ (11)
Racial diversity index	37.2% (202)
Geographic diversity index	72.8% (22)
Top 20% share of income	47.4% (247)
Gender gap in earnings	16.4% (19)
White-collar gender gap	8.6% (71)

EDUCATION	★★ (404)
Eighth grade or less	4.7% (366)
High school diplomas	86.2% (333)
Attended college	46.3% (412)
Bachelor's degrees	13.5% (478)
Advanced degrees	5.0% (378)

EMPLOYMENT	★★ (396)
Average jobless rate	9.2% (377)
Self-employed workers	8.1% (323)
Management/financial jobs	10.2% (357)
Computer/engineering jobs	1.7% (470)
Health care jobs	5.9% (193)

GROWTH POTENTIAL	★★ (350)
Children per senior	0.86 (530)
Median age	43.5 (464)
Moved from different state	3.5% (109)
Homes built since 2000	16.5% (167)
Construction jobs	6.6% (241)

HOUSING	★★★ (327)
Home vacancy rate	8.8% (273)
Home ownership rate	70.9% (232)
Housing diversity index	85.1% (212)
4 or more bedrooms	15.7% (315)
Affordability/income ratio	$3,921 (491)

INCOME	★★★ (279)
Poverty rate	17.4% (283)
Median household income	$40,423 (370)
Interest/dividends	19.4% (269)
Public assistance	15.5% (277)
Median fulltime earnings	$37,483 (247)

SENIORS	★★★ (253)
Seniors living alone	28.0% (296)
Poverty rate for seniors	7.0% (93)
Median income for seniors	$32,600 (299)
Seniors who work	17.3% (324)
Home ownership by seniors	83.2% (210)

STABILITY	★★★ (246)
25-39 age group	21.8% (24)
Born in state of residence	44.4% (506)
Same house as 1 year ago	82.1% (434)
Live and work in county	80.1% (216)
Married-couple households	51.8% (206)

TRANSPORTATION	★★★ (312)
Bicycle or walk to work	4.5% (117)
Carpool to work	11.8% (152)
Public transit to work	0.4% (219)
Commute <15 minutes	43.7% (267)
Commute >45 minutes	17.2% (486)

See pages 37-130 for explanations of statistics, stars, and ranks.

Carlsbad-Artesia, NM
(Eddy County, NM)

POPULATION

2010 census	53,829 (179)
2015 estimate	57,578 (162)
2010-2015 change	7.0% (21)
2020 projection	60,020 (149)
2030 projection	64,955 (129)

RACE

Whites	50.1% (485)
Blacks	1.3% (351)
Hispanics	45.9% (30)
Asians	0.6% (291)
Native Americans	1.2% (89)

AGE

0-17 years old	26.1% (66)
18-24 years old	9.0% (265)
25-39 years old	19.4% (78)
40-54 years old	18.8% (386)
55-64 years old	12.8% (356)
65+ years old	13.9% (444)

PRIVATE SECTOR

Businesses	1,517 (130)
Employees	24,620 (79)
Total wages	$1,360,922,877 (23)
Average weekly wages	$1,063 (13)

HOUSEHOLD INCOME LADDER

95th percentile	$168,705 (59)
80th percentile	$104,384 (41)
60th percentile	$70,435 (38)
40th percentile	$44,209 (51)
20th percentile	$23,575 (80)

CHILDREN ★★★ (244)

Living with two parents	61.4% (370)
Older teens in school	79.3% (419)
Speak English very well	98.2% (320)
Poverty rate for children	12.5% (42)
No health insurance	7.4% (341)

DIVERSITY/EQUALITY ★★ (335)

Racial diversity index	53.8% (70)
Geographic diversity index	59.6% (127)
Top 20% share of income	48.6% (328)
Gender gap in earnings	52.2% (533)
White-collar gender gap	36.8% (404)

EDUCATION ★★★ (297)

Eighth grade or less	3.9% (316)
High school diplomas	85.2% (368)
Attended college	51.5% (291)
Bachelor's degrees	17.7% (295)
Advanced degrees	7.1% (176)

EMPLOYMENT ★★ (338)

Average jobless rate	5.8% (113)
Self-employed workers	7.6% (376)
Management/financial jobs	11.7% (185)
Computer/engineering jobs	2.8% (246)
Health care jobs	3.8% (494)

GROWTH POTENTIAL ★★★★ (116)

Children per senior	1.87 (77)
Median age	36.5 (131)
Moved from different state	3.5% (109)
Homes built since 2000	11.9% (318)
Construction jobs	7.5% (122)

HOUSING ★★★★ (141)

Home vacancy rate	9.0% (287)
Home ownership rate	73.0% (151)
Housing diversity index	86.3% (36)
4 or more bedrooms	14.2% (392)
Affordability/income ratio	$2,204 (125)

INCOME ★★★★★ (81)

Poverty rate	11.3% (65)
Median household income	$56,618 (42)
Interest/dividends	16.0% (375)
Public assistance	13.0% (169)
Median fulltime earnings	$46,380 (24)

SENIORS ★★★★ (122)

Seniors living alone	26.8% (222)
Poverty rate for seniors	9.8% (308)
Median income for seniors	$35,675 (162)
Seniors who work	20.2% (187)
Home ownership by seniors	87.7% (48)

STABILITY ★★★★★ (57)

25-39 age group	19.4% (78)
Born in state of residence	59.9% (420)
Same house as 1 year ago	86.2% (237)
Live and work in county	96.2% (8)
Married-couple households	49.8% (307)

TRANSPORTATION ★★★★ (192)

Bicycle or walk to work	2.0% (386)
Carpool to work	10.8% (249)
Public transit to work	0.4% (219)
Commute <15 minutes	53.6% (100)
Commute >45 minutes	7.8% (122)

See pages 37-130 for explanations of statistics, stars, and ranks.

Cedar City, UT
(Iron County, UT)

POPULATION	
2010 census	46,163 (245)
2015 estimate	48,368 (223)
2010-2015 change	4.8% (42)
2020 projection	51,652 (203)
2030 projection	59,101 (155)

RACE	
Whites	86.6% (245)
Blacks	0.6% (438)
Hispanics	8.1% (180)
Asians	1.1% (139)
Native Americans	2.3% (67)

AGE	
0-17 years old	29.4% (21)
18-24 years old	16.3% (49)
25-39 years old	19.2% (88)
40-54 years old	14.3% (542)
55-64 years old	9.7% (532)
65+ years old	11.1% (509)

PRIVATE SECTOR	
Businesses	1,323 (171)
Employees	12,091 (308)
Total wages	$355,075,759 (377)
Average weekly wages	$565 (524)

HOUSEHOLD INCOME LADDER	
95th percentile	$146,740 (201)
80th percentile	$80,637 (358)
60th percentile	$53,324 (291)
40th percentile	$34,084 (285)
20th percentile	$18,169 (310)

CHILDREN	★★★ (241)
Living with two parents	84.1% (3)
Older teens in school	80.2% (392)
Speak English very well	99.4% (124)
Poverty rate for children	22.9% (246)
No health insurance	14.5% (520)

DIVERSITY/EQUALITY	★ (478)
Racial diversity index	24.3% (301)
Geographic diversity index	59.0% (129)
Top 20% share of income	47.7% (271)
Gender gap in earnings	48.4% (522)
White-collar gender gap	48.0% (501)

EDUCATION	★★★★★ (57)
Eighth grade or less	1.5% (72)
High school diplomas	91.9% (128)
Attended college	67.9% (34)
Bachelor's degrees	28.6% (68)
Advanced degrees	9.3% (76)

EMPLOYMENT	★★★ (287)
Average jobless rate	10.5% (441)
Self-employed workers	9.9% (171)
Management/financial jobs	13.3% (70)
Computer/engineering jobs	2.7% (270)
Health care jobs	4.6% (401)

GROWTH POTENTIAL	★★★★★ (8)
Children per senior	2.66 (26)
Median age	28.1 (15)
Moved from different state	4.9% (57)
Homes built since 2000	28.3% (16)
Construction jobs	7.6% (110)

HOUSING	★★ (333)
Home vacancy rate	8.9% (280)
Home ownership rate	63.6% (466)
Housing diversity index	81.1% (492)
4 or more bedrooms	29.1% (12)
Affordability/income ratio	$3,783 (489)

INCOME	★★★ (264)
Poverty rate	21.0% (400)
Median household income	$43,855 (265)
Interest/dividends	17.2% (339)
Public assistance	12.9% (164)
Median fulltime earnings	$39,939 (143)

SENIORS	★★★★★ (21)
Seniors living alone	21.2% (23)
Poverty rate for seniors	6.4% (57)
Median income for seniors	$44,701 (30)
Seniors who work	21.2% (153)
Home ownership by seniors	85.4% (129)

STABILITY	★★★★★ (51)
25-39 age group	19.2% (88)
Born in state of residence	57.8% (437)
Same house as 1 year ago	83.0% (397)
Live and work in county	88.3% (86)
Married-couple households	58.7% (14)

TRANSPORTATION	★★★★★ (24)
Bicycle or walk to work	6.7% (48)
Carpool to work	14.2% (58)
Public transit to work	0.5% (178)
Commute <15 minutes	63.8% (27)
Commute >45 minutes	10.4% (248)

See pages 37-130 for explanations of statistics, stars, and ranks.

Centralia, WA
(Lewis County, WA)

POPULATION			
2010 census	75,455 (81)	Attended college	57.6% (174)
2015 estimate	75,882 (82)	Bachelor's degrees	14.6% (435)
2010-2015 change	0.6% (209)	Advanced degrees	5.5% (318)
2020 projection	76,812 (81)	**EMPLOYMENT**	★ (454)
2030 projection	78,977 (82)	Average jobless rate	12.1% (493)

POPULATION
2010 census — 75,455 (81)
2015 estimate — 75,882 (82)
2010-2015 change — 0.6% (209)
2020 projection — 76,812 (81)
2030 projection — 78,977 (82)

RACE
Whites — 84.7% (269)
Blacks — 0.7% (423)
Hispanics — 9.5% (157)
Asians — 1.2% (125)
Native Americans — 0.6% (150)

AGE
0-17 years old — 22.2% (320)
18-24 years old — 8.3% (362)
25-39 years old — 16.6% (388)
40-54 years old — 19.4% (315)
55-64 years old — 14.6% (107)
65+ years old — 18.9% (85)

PRIVATE SECTOR
Businesses — 2,328 (42)
Employees — 19,055 (139)
Total wages — $712,518,549 (147)
Average weekly wages — $719 (218)

HOUSEHOLD INCOME LADDER
95th percentile — $138,263 (308)
80th percentile — $85,069 (251)
60th percentile — $54,847 (253)
40th percentile — $35,760 (238)
20th percentile — $19,823 (236)

CHILDREN — ★★★ (328)
Living with two parents — 66.2% (244)
Older teens in school — 75.3% (499)
Speak English very well — 95.7% (463)
Poverty rate for children — 21.0% (193)
No health insurance — 5.1% (188)

DIVERSITY/EQUALITY — ★★★★★ (84)
Racial diversity index — 27.2% (279)
Geographic diversity index — 58.3% (131)
Top 20% share of income — 45.8% (108)
Gender gap in earnings — 39.5% (428)
White-collar gender gap — 3.5% (23)

EDUCATION — ★★★ (289)
Eighth grade or less — 4.3% (343)
High school diplomas — 88.0% (267)

Attended college — 57.6% (174)
Bachelor's degrees — 14.6% (435)
Advanced degrees — 5.5% (318)

EMPLOYMENT — ★ (454)
Average jobless rate — 12.1% (493)
Self-employed workers — 9.0% (254)
Management/financial jobs — 10.3% (339)
Computer/engineering jobs — 2.5% (307)
Health care jobs — 4.9% (355)

GROWTH POTENTIAL — ★★★ (323)
Children per senior — 1.18 (427)
Median age — 42.8 (447)
Moved from different state — 2.5% (203)
Homes built since 2000 — 16.4% (172)
Construction jobs — 6.5% (253)

HOUSING — ★★★ (315)
Home vacancy rate — 6.8% (151)
Home ownership rate — 67.4% (371)
Housing diversity index — 85.5% (143)
4 or more bedrooms — 15.3% (333)
Affordability/income ratio — $3,946 (493)

INCOME — ★★★ (243)
Poverty rate — 16.3% (234)
Median household income — $44,100 (257)
Interest/dividends — 23.1% (155)
Public assistance — 22.9% (494)
Median fulltime earnings — $41,995 (63)

SENIORS — ★★★★ (186)
Seniors living alone — 26.2% (186)
Poverty rate for seniors — 6.9% (84)
Median income for seniors — $37,793 (96)
Seniors who work — 15.0% (459)
Home ownership by seniors — 82.9% (225)

STABILITY — ★★ (437)
25-39 age group — 16.6% (388)
Born in state of residence — 61.0% (416)
Same house as 1 year ago — 82.8% (406)
Live and work in county — 75.5% (282)
Married-couple households — 51.0% (248)

TRANSPORTATION — ★★ (346)
Bicycle or walk to work — 2.7% (292)
Carpool to work — 13.3% (88)
Public transit to work — 1.1% (58)
Commute <15 minutes — 32.9% (477)
Commute >45 minutes — 16.5% (468)

See pages 37-130 for explanations of statistics, stars, and ranks.

Clearlake, CA
(Lake County, CA)

POPULATION

2010 census	64,665 (123)
2015 estimate	64,591 (123)
2010-2015 change	-0.1% (266)
2020 projection	65,337 (122)
2030 projection	66,963 (119)

RACE

Whites	72.6% (374)
Blacks	2.1% (283)
Hispanics	18.5% (85)
Asians	1.5% (85)
Native Americans	3.0% (52)

AGE

0-17 years old	20.4% (437)
18-24 years old	7.7% (454)
25-39 years old	15.7% (465)
40-54 years old	19.3% (323)
55-64 years old	17.1% (15)
65+ years old	19.8% (58)

PRIVATE SECTOR

Businesses	2,789 (26)
Employees	11,539 (325)
Total wages	$381,097,130 (352)
Average weekly wages	$635 (422)

HOUSEHOLD INCOME LADDER

95th percentile	$134,377 (370)
80th percentile	$78,903 (384)
60th percentile	$47,136 (442)
40th percentile	$27,572 (467)
20th percentile	$15,430 (438)

CHILDREN ★ **(520)**

Living with two parents	52.8% (486)
Older teens in school	81.4% (350)
Speak English very well	92.3% (516)
Poverty rate for children	32.8% (461)
No health insurance	11.4% (456)

DIVERSITY/EQUALITY ★★★★★ **(23)**

Racial diversity index	43.7% (161)
Geographic diversity index	54.4% (158)
Top 20% share of income	49.4% (393)
Gender gap in earnings	10.5% (10)
White-collar gender gap	8.6% (71)

EDUCATION ★★ **(391)**

Eighth grade or less	5.3% (402)
High school diplomas	84.4% (389)
Attended college	55.7% (209)
Bachelor's degrees	13.7% (470)
Advanced degrees	4.0% (478)

EMPLOYMENT ★★ **(397)**

Average jobless rate	14.6% (532)
Self-employed workers	12.2% (67)
Management/financial jobs	11.3% (218)
Computer/engineering jobs	3.0% (193)
Health care jobs	4.6% (401)

GROWTH POTENTIAL ★★ **(413)**

Children per senior	1.03 (492)
Median age	45.5 (508)
Moved from different state	1.7% (355)
Homes built since 2000	15.2% (199)
Construction jobs	7.4% (134)

HOUSING ★ **(536)**

Home vacancy rate	9.1% (296)
Home ownership rate	63.0% (475)
Housing diversity index	85.2% (190)
4 or more bedrooms	7.0% (550)
Affordability/income ratio	$4,618 (518)

INCOME ★★ **(338)**

Poverty rate	24.7% (475)
Median household income	$35,578 (476)
Interest/dividends	19.5% (264)
Public assistance	14.5% (234)
Median fulltime earnings	$40,844 (104)

SENIORS ★★★ **(285)**

Seniors living alone	29.2% (381)
Poverty rate for seniors	9.8% (308)
Median income for seniors	$34,932 (192)
Seniors who work	20.6% (173)
Home ownership by seniors	81.5% (305)

STABILITY ★ **(536)**

25-39 age group	15.7% (465)
Born in state of residence	66.1% (373)
Same house as 1 year ago	80.4% (492)
Live and work in county	77.1% (256)
Married-couple households	40.4% (527)

TRANSPORTATION ★★ **(440)**

Bicycle or walk to work	3.8% (161)
Carpool to work	11.8% (152)
Public transit to work	0.8% (96)
Commute <15 minutes	33.7% (465)
Commute >45 minutes	21.3% (528)

See pages 37-130 for explanations of statistics, stars, and ranks.

Clovis, NM
(Curry County, NM)

POPULATION
2010 census	48,376 (219)
2015 estimate	50,398 (211)
2010-2015 change	4.2% (55)
2020 projection	51,194 (206)
2030 projection	52,616 (198)

RACE
Whites	50.1% (485)
Blacks	5.7% (148)
Hispanics	39.9% (36)
Asians	1.6% (77)
Native Americans	0.6% (150)

AGE
0-17 years old	27.2% (41)
18-24 years old	12.6% (76)
25-39 years old	21.4% (33)
40-54 years old	17.6% (470)
55-64 years old	9.9% (524)
65+ years old	11.3% (504)

PRIVATE SECTOR
Businesses	1,111 (238)
Employees	13,929 (235)
Total wages	$476,698,123 (263)
Average weekly wages	$658 (370)

HOUSEHOLD INCOME LADDER
95th percentile	$146,280 (208)
80th percentile	$84,876 (256)
60th percentile	$51,590 (341)
40th percentile	$32,044 (360)
20th percentile	$16,879 (368)

CHILDREN ★★ (402)
Living with two parents	62.8% (323)
Older teens in school	79.1% (424)
Speak English very well	96.1% (446)
Poverty rate for children	32.6% (457)
No health insurance	5.8% (236)

DIVERSITY/EQUALITY ★★★★★ (68)
Racial diversity index	58.6% (18)
Geographic diversity index	71.3% (36)
Top 20% share of income	49.7% (409)
Gender gap in earnings	40.2% (442)
White-collar gender gap	17.0% (181)

EDUCATION ★★★ (237)
Eighth grade or less	6.4% (446)
High school diplomas	83.7% (406)
Attended college	59.5% (139)
Bachelor's degrees	21.7% (169)
Advanced degrees	8.4% (106)

EMPLOYMENT ★ (465)
Average jobless rate	9.1% (370)
Self-employed workers	6.3% (484)
Management/financial jobs	10.7% (287)
Computer/engineering jobs	2.5% (307)
Health care jobs	4.4% (433)

GROWTH POTENTIAL ★★★★★ (26)
Children per senior	2.41 (33)
Median age	30.7 (33)
Moved from different state	7.8% (12)
Homes built since 2000	13.8% (246)
Construction jobs	7.0% (185)

HOUSING ★★ (395)
Home vacancy rate	9.7% (334)
Home ownership rate	58.4% (518)
Housing diversity index	86.1% (51)
4 or more bedrooms	17.3% (232)
Affordability/income ratio	$3,057 (411)

INCOME ★★ (407)
Poverty rate	21.0% (400)
Median household income	$41,084 (351)
Interest/dividends	15.6% (390)
Public assistance	16.7% (319)
Median fulltime earnings	$32,281 (482)

SENIORS ★★ (388)
Seniors living alone	28.4% (325)
Poverty rate for seniors	10.6% (350)
Median income for seniors	$29,038 (433)
Seniors who work	17.9% (292)
Home ownership by seniors	82.0% (274)

STABILITY ★★ (346)
25-39 age group	21.4% (33)
Born in state of residence	47.1% (495)
Same house as 1 year ago	76.8% (524)
Live and work in county	91.6% (48)
Married-couple households	48.8% (354)

TRANSPORTATION ★★★★ (121)
Bicycle or walk to work	2.6% (308)
Carpool to work	10.1% (322)
Public transit to work	0.3% (291)
Commute <15 minutes	54.2% (93)
Commute >45 minutes	2.5% (3)

See pages 37-130 for explanations of statistics, stars, and ranks.

Coos Bay, OR
(Coos County, OR)

POPULATION

2010 census	63,043 (133)
2015 estimate	63,121 (135)
2010-2015 change	0.1% (250)
2020 projection	62,772 (134)
2030 projection	62,188 (138)

RACE

Whites	85.8% (257)
Blacks	0.6% (438)
Hispanics	5.9% (227)
Asians	1.4% (99)
Native Americans	2.5% (60)

AGE

0-17 years old	18.6% (509)
18-24 years old	7.5% (483)
25-39 years old	15.2% (498)
40-54 years old	18.5% (425)
55-64 years old	16.9% (18)
65+ years old	23.3% (18)

PRIVATE SECTOR

Businesses	1,727 (96)
Employees	16,408 (184)
Total wages	$540,644,502 (219)
Average weekly wages	$634 (425)

HOUSEHOLD INCOME LADDER

95th percentile	$132,901 (388)
80th percentile	$73,285 (482)
60th percentile	$47,219 (439)
40th percentile	$30,860 (391)
20th percentile	$16,576 (380)

CHILDREN ★★★ (321)

Living with two parents	63.3% (316)
Older teens in school	76.3% (484)
Speak English very well	98.6% (278)
Poverty rate for children	25.2% (304)
No health insurance	5.1% (188)

DIVERSITY/EQUALITY ★★★★ (170)

Racial diversity index	25.8% (286)
Geographic diversity index	67.0% (61)
Top 20% share of income	50.3% (446)
Gender gap in earnings	25.7% (100)
White-collar gender gap	26.9% (296)

EDUCATION ★★★★ (212)

Eighth grade or less	2.3% (161)
High school diplomas	89.3% (223)

Attended college	56.7% (193)
Bachelor's degrees	17.8% (290)
Advanced degrees	6.2% (243)

EMPLOYMENT ★★ (339)

Average jobless rate	11.7% (481)
Self-employed workers	12.1% (71)
Management/financial jobs	10.1% (365)
Computer/engineering jobs	2.9% (219)
Health care jobs	5.1% (319)

GROWTH POTENTIAL ★ (520)

Children per senior	0.80 (536)
Median age	48.1 (534)
Moved from different state	3.1% (147)
Homes built since 2000	11.1% (356)
Construction jobs	6.4% (270)

HOUSING ★ (442)

Home vacancy rate	8.7% (268)
Home ownership rate	65.0% (436)
Housing diversity index	86.5% (19)
4 or more bedrooms	13.3% (437)
Affordability/income ratio	$4,417 (511)

INCOME ★★ (376)

Poverty rate	18.3% (309)
Median household income	$38,605 (414)
Interest/dividends	23.9% (130)
Public assistance	25.8% (517)
Median fulltime earnings	$36,136 (325)

SENIORS ★★ (387)

Seniors living alone	27.6% (269)
Poverty rate for seniors	10.9% (370)
Median income for seniors	$33,521 (258)
Seniors who work	16.0% (410)
Home ownership by seniors	80.2% (368)

STABILITY ★ (472)

25-39 age group	15.2% (498)
Born in state of residence	47.7% (492)
Same house as 1 year ago	83.5% (366)
Live and work in county	95.2% (14)
Married-couple households	46.9% (419)

TRANSPORTATION ★★★★★ (84)

Bicycle or walk to work	5.3% (79)
Carpool to work	12.7% (115)
Public transit to work	1.0% (69)
Commute <15 minutes	48.3% (189)
Commute >45 minutes	8.6% (154)

See pages 37-130 for explanations of statistics, stars, and ranks.

Craig, CO
(Moffat County, CO)

POPULATION

2010 census	13,795 (548)
2015 estimate	12,937 (551)
2010-2015 change	-6.2% (548)
2020 projection	12,589 (550)
2030 projection	11,955 (550)

RACE

Whites	82.2% (299)
Blacks	0.5% (466)
Hispanics	14.3% (109)
Asians	1.5% (85)
Native Americans	1.0% (103)

AGE

0-17 years old	26.1% (66)
18-24 years old	8.2% (379)
25-39 years old	19.3% (85)
40-54 years old	19.7% (273)
55-64 years old	14.5% (122)
65+ years old	12.1% (494)

PRIVATE SECTOR

Businesses	417 (534)
Employees	3,667 (544)
Total wages	$170,502,624 (526)
Average weekly wages	$894 (36)

HOUSEHOLD INCOME LADDER

95th percentile	$146,402 (206)
80th percentile	$94,012 (101)
60th percentile	$65,551 (71)
40th percentile	$40,397 (117)
20th percentile	$20,051 (227)

CHILDREN ★★ (344)

Living with two parents	76.5% (37)
Older teens in school	68.4% (539)
Speak English very well	98.1% (331)
Poverty rate for children	13.8% (54)
No health insurance	12.3% (479)

DIVERSITY/EQUALITY ★★★ (329)

Racial diversity index	30.3% (252)
Geographic diversity index	63.9% (85)
Top 20% share of income	44.4% (39)
Gender gap in earnings	46.2% (511)
White-collar gender gap	53.1% (523)

EDUCATION ★★★ (329)

Eighth grade or less	2.6% (185)
High school diplomas	90.6% (178)
Attended college	50.5% (314)
Bachelor's degrees	14.5% (443)
Advanced degrees	3.6% (505)

EMPLOYMENT ★★ (331)

Average jobless rate	5.9% (115)
Self-employed workers	10.7% (129)
Management/financial jobs	10.4% (332)
Computer/engineering jobs	1.6% (486)
Health care jobs	4.1% (462)

GROWTH POTENTIAL ★★★★★ (95)

Children per senior	2.15 (44)
Median age	37.1 (149)
Moved from different state	2.6% (187)
Homes built since 2000	9.4% (414)
Construction jobs	9.0% (47)

HOUSING ★ (443)

Home vacancy rate	13.9% (514)
Home ownership rate	69.9% (275)
Housing diversity index	81.7% (470)
4 or more bedrooms	22.7% (72)
Affordability/income ratio	$3,421 (456)

INCOME ★★★★ (118)

Poverty rate	11.4% (66)
Median household income	$51,387 (93)
Interest/dividends	15.5% (393)
Public assistance	14.2% (215)
Median fulltime earnings	$45,813 (26)

SENIORS ★★★★★ (97)

Seniors living alone	33.7% (536)
Poverty rate for seniors	6.4% (57)
Median income for seniors	$29,491 (423)
Seniors who work	30.1% (25)
Home ownership by seniors	89.9% (17)

STABILITY ★★ (379)

25-39 age group	19.3% (85)
Born in state of residence	55.9% (456)
Same house as 1 year ago	80.6% (491)
Live and work in county	77.4% (248)
Married-couple households	51.4% (231)

TRANSPORTATION ★★★★★ (39)

Bicycle or walk to work	7.2% (40)
Carpool to work	18.0% (16)
Public transit to work	0.7% (119)
Commute <15 minutes	56.3% (78)
Commute >45 minutes	17.5% (493)

See pages 37-130 for explanations of statistics, stars, and ranks.

Crescent City, CA
(Del Norte County, CA)

POPULATION	
2010 census	28,610 (449)
2015 estimate	27,254 (461)
2010-2015 change	-4.7% (529)
2020 projection	26,487 (463)
2030 projection	25,122 (470)

RACE	
Whites	63.3% (428)
Blacks	2.8% (232)
Hispanics	19.1% (82)
Asians	2.4% (33)
Native Americans	4.8% (35)

AGE	
0-17 years old	21.2% (397)
18-24 years old	8.3% (362)
25-39 years old	21.7% (26)
40-54 years old	20.3% (186)
55-64 years old	13.7% (225)
65+ years old	14.8% (384)

PRIVATE SECTOR	
Businesses	690 (433)
Employees	4,207 (542)
Total wages	$127,133,792 (544)
Average weekly wages	$581 (514)

HOUSEHOLD INCOME LADDER	
95th percentile	$145,633 (219)
80th percentile	$82,431 (311)
60th percentile	$51,823 (327)
40th percentile	$30,071 (419)
20th percentile	$15,006 (452)

CHILDREN	★★ (338)
Living with two parents	51.8% (493)
Older teens in school	82.3% (304)
Speak English very well	98.4% (300)
Poverty rate for children	29.0% (386)
No health insurance	2.9% (56)

DIVERSITY/EQUALITY	★★★★★ (64)
Racial diversity index	55.3% (49)
Geographic diversity index	52.9% (175)
Top 20% share of income	50.1% (434)
Gender gap in earnings	17.3% (25)
White-collar gender gap	27.7% (307)

EDUCATION	★ (460)
Eighth grade or less	6.6% (452)
High school diplomas	79.7% (484)

Attended college	50.8% (306)
Bachelor's degrees	13.4% (482)
Advanced degrees	4.6% (431)

EMPLOYMENT	★★★ (328)
Average jobless rate	11.5% (474)
Self-employed workers	9.9% (171)
Management/financial jobs	12.5% (119)
Computer/engineering jobs	3.0% (193)
Health care jobs	4.7% (385)

GROWTH POTENTIAL	★★ (334)
Children per senior	1.43 (261)
Median age	38.8 (217)
Moved from different state	2.6% (187)
Homes built since 2000	16.5% (167)
Construction jobs	4.0% (536)

HOUSING	★ (526)
Home vacancy rate	9.3% (305)
Home ownership rate	60.6% (496)
Housing diversity index	86.0% (71)
4 or more bedrooms	9.4% (542)
Affordability/income ratio	$4,497 (512)

INCOME	★★★ (271)
Poverty rate	21.8% (424)
Median household income	$40,847 (359)
Interest/dividends	18.5% (294)
Public assistance	16.9% (327)
Median fulltime earnings	$43,810 (39)

SENIORS	★ (490)
Seniors living alone	33.4% (533)
Poverty rate for seniors	12.1% (416)
Median income for seniors	n.a.
Seniors who work	18.8% (253)
Home ownership by seniors	79.9% (377)

STABILITY	★★★ (236)
25-39 age group	21.7% (26)
Born in state of residence	67.0% (363)
Same house as 1 year ago	78.7% (512)
Live and work in county	93.4% (27)
Married-couple households	42.0% (506)

TRANSPORTATION	★★★★★ (16)
Bicycle or walk to work	5.0% (91)
Carpool to work	13.7% (77)
Public transit to work	0.6% (141)
Commute <15 minutes	61.1% (40)
Commute >45 minutes	2.9% (7)

See pages 37-130 for explanations of statistics, stars, and ranks.

Deming, NM
(Luna County, NM)

POPULATION	
2010 census	25,095 (481)
2015 estimate	24,518 (487)
2010-2015 change	-2.3% (436)
2020 projection	23,670 (489)
2030 projection	21,970 (502)

RACE	
Whites	33.0% (528)
Blacks	1.0% (381)
Hispanics	64.1% (14)
Asians	0.5% (355)
Native Americans	0.9% (115)

AGE	
0-17 years old	26.6% (55)
18-24 years old	9.0% (265)
25-39 years old	15.4% (490)
40-54 years old	16.7% (508)
55-64 years old	11.9% (447)
65+ years old	20.3% (49)

PRIVATE SECTOR	
Businesses	464 (524)
Employees	5,730 (516)
Total wages	$148,906,064 (534)
Average weekly wages	$500 (544)

HOUSEHOLD INCOME LADDER	
95th percentile	$105,054 (550)
80th percentile	$56,444 (550)
60th percentile	$35,632 (548)
40th percentile	$21,814 (540)
20th percentile	$11,612 (532)

CHILDREN	★ (535)
Living with two parents	59.6% (414)
Older teens in school	71.1% (526)
Speak English very well	87.7% (534)
Poverty rate for children	39.0% (508)
No health insurance	4.3% (140)

DIVERSITY/EQUALITY	★★★★ (123)
Racial diversity index	48.0% (129)
Geographic diversity index	72.1% (30)
Top 20% share of income	49.3% (386)
Gender gap in earnings	45.5% (506)
White-collar gender gap	17.5% (183)

EDUCATION	★ (540)
Eighth grade or less	17.3% (538)
High school diplomas	69.1% (538)
Attended college	36.8% (536)
Bachelor's degrees	11.4% (526)
Advanced degrees	5.0% (378)

EMPLOYMENT	★ (547)
Average jobless rate	13.8% (525)
Self-employed workers	7.7% (362)
Management/financial jobs	8.7% (493)
Computer/engineering jobs	1.0% (536)
Health care jobs	3.3% (517)

GROWTH POTENTIAL	★★★ (233)
Children per senior	1.31 (344)
Median age	39.0 (238)
Moved from different state	3.3% (129)
Homes built since 2000	14.2% (231)
Construction jobs	6.4% (270)

HOUSING	★ (503)
Home vacancy rate	13.9% (514)
Home ownership rate	67.4% (371)
Housing diversity index	85.3% (170)
4 or more bedrooms	9.0% (545)
Affordability/income ratio	$2,981 (400)

INCOME	★ (539)
Poverty rate	29.6% (522)
Median household income	$27,476 (544)
Interest/dividends	13.2% (463)
Public assistance	30.0% (537)
Median fulltime earnings	$26,761 (550)

SENIORS	★ (540)
Seniors living alone	31.5% (498)
Poverty rate for seniors	19.3% (536)
Median income for seniors	$24,401 (509)
Seniors who work	15.6% (432)
Home ownership by seniors	80.1% (369)

STABILITY	★ (526)
25-39 age group	15.4% (490)
Born in state of residence	47.7% (492)
Same house as 1 year ago	82.1% (434)
Live and work in county	88.5% (85)
Married-couple households	44.7% (468)

TRANSPORTATION	★★★★★ (94)
Bicycle or walk to work	1.5% (457)
Carpool to work	15.6% (39)
Public transit to work	1.4% (46)
Commute <15 minutes	56.7% (75)
Commute >45 minutes	12.7% (343)

See pages 37-130 for explanations of statistics, stars, and ranks.

Durango, CO
(La Plata County, CO)

POPULATION	
2010 census	51,334 (200)
2015 estimate	54,688 (174)
2010-2015 change	6.5% (27)
2020 projection	58,069 (158)
2030 projection	65,642 (123)

RACE	
Whites	79.6% (330)
Blacks	0.4% (499)
Hispanics	12.5% (123)
Asians	0.8% (201)
Native Americans	5.0% (32)

AGE	
0-17 years old	19.6% (478)
18-24 years old	10.5% (136)
25-39 years old	21.2% (37)
40-54 years old	19.5% (301)
55-64 years old	15.6% (56)
65+ years old	13.5% (459)

PRIVATE SECTOR	
Businesses	2,421 (38)
Employees	20,268 (123)
Total wages	$867,713,329 (100)
Average weekly wages	$823 (61)

HOUSEHOLD INCOME LADDER	
95th percentile	$186,075 (33)
80th percentile	$110,423 (23)
60th percentile	$72,549 (27)
40th percentile	$49,345 (22)
20th percentile	$26,826 (26)

CHILDREN	★★★★★ (97)
Living with two parents	73.4% (75)
Older teens in school	82.4% (301)
Speak English very well	99.0% (200)
Poverty rate for children	10.2% (15)
No health insurance	8.2% (366)

DIVERSITY/EQUALITY	★★★★★ (28)
Racial diversity index	34.8% (215)
Geographic diversity index	76.9% (15)
Top 20% share of income	46.6% (168)
Gender gap in earnings	29.2% (156)
White-collar gender gap	15.7% (159)

EDUCATION	★★★★★ (8)
Eighth grade or less	1.9% (114)
High school diplomas	94.8% (36)
Attended college	75.2% (10)
Bachelor's degrees	42.6% (14)
Advanced degrees	14.1% (18)

EMPLOYMENT	★★★★★ (8)
Average jobless rate	5.2% (76)
Self-employed workers	12.5% (56)
Management/financial jobs	15.7% (19)
Computer/engineering jobs	5.5% (22)
Health care jobs	6.4% (132)

GROWTH POTENTIAL	★★★★★ (43)
Children per senior	1.45 (244)
Median age	38.8 (217)
Moved from different state	7.1% (22)
Homes built since 2000	22.3% (66)
Construction jobs	8.2% (78)

HOUSING	★ (486)
Home vacancy rate	6.6% (136)
Home ownership rate	67.0% (386)
Housing diversity index	83.2% (405)
4 or more bedrooms	16.6% (264)
Affordability/income ratio	$5,519 (536)

INCOME	★★★★★ (22)
Poverty rate	10.6% (47)
Median household income	$60,278 (24)
Interest/dividends	30.1% (23)
Public assistance	6.3% (15)
Median fulltime earnings	$42,413 (55)

SENIORS	★★★★★ (7)
Seniors living alone	22.2% (41)
Poverty rate for seniors	4.8% (15)
Median income for seniors	$52,276 (7)
Seniors who work	25.9% (51)
Home ownership by seniors	86.1% (93)

STABILITY	★★ (386)
25-39 age group	21.2% (37)
Born in state of residence	34.9% (534)
Same house as 1 year ago	78.9% (511)
Live and work in county	92.6% (39)
Married-couple households	49.7% (311)

TRANSPORTATION	★★★★★ (54)
Bicycle or walk to work	9.1% (19)
Carpool to work	11.3% (201)
Public transit to work	2.2% (30)
Commute <15 minutes	36.8% (402)
Commute >45 minutes	8.8% (165)

See pages 37-130 for explanations of statistics, stars, and ranks.

Edwards, CO
(Eagle County, CO)

POPULATION

2010 census	52,197 (195)
2015 estimate	53,605 (182)
2010-2015 change	2.7% (96)
2020 projection	56,254 (170)
2030 projection	62,105 (140)

RACE

Whites	67.0% (404)
Blacks	0.6% (438)
Hispanics	30.0% (51)
Asians	1.1% (139)
Native Americans	0.3% (231)

AGE

0-17 years old	23.4% (240)
18-24 years old	7.9% (424)
25-39 years old	26.5% (5)
40-54 years old	22.7% (13)
55-64 years old	12.1% (430)
65+ years old	7.4% (549)

PRIVATE SECTOR

Businesses	3,317 (15)
Employees	27,909 (54)
Total wages	$1,188,318,427 (39)
Average weekly wages	$819 (66)

HOUSEHOLD INCOME LADDER

95th percentile	>$250,000 (1)
80th percentile	$138,742 (5)
60th percentile	$89,460 (6)
40th percentile	$59,202 (6)
20th percentile	$38,057 (4)

CHILDREN ★★★ (255)

Living with two parents	80.4% (11)
Older teens in school	85.8% (172)
Speak English very well	91.3% (519)
Poverty rate for children	11.9% (29)
No health insurance	13.2% (500)

DIVERSITY/EQUALITY ★★★★★ (19)

Racial diversity index	46.1% (142)
Geographic diversity index	80.7% (4)
Top 20% share of income	50.0% (432)
Gender gap in earnings	18.5% (35)
White-collar gender gap	14.3% (144)

EDUCATION ★★★★★ (39)

Eighth grade or less	6.0% (424)
High school diplomas	88.9% (236)
Attended college	71.1% (25)
Bachelor's degrees	45.9% (11)
Advanced degrees	10.5% (48)

EMPLOYMENT ★★★★★ (35)

Average jobless rate	4.4% (42)
Self-employed workers	13.4% (46)
Management/financial jobs	18.3% (8)
Computer/engineering jobs	3.0% (193)
Health care jobs	4.5% (419)

GROWTH POTENTIAL ★★★★★ (12)

Children per senior	3.14 (11)
Median age	35.6 (105)
Moved from different state	4.2% (70)
Homes built since 2000	22.7% (55)
Construction jobs	11.2% (9)

HOUSING ★★ (440)

Home vacancy rate	4.7% (22)
Home ownership rate	67.1% (382)
Housing diversity index	78.2% (533)
4 or more bedrooms	27.5% (25)
Affordability/income ratio	$5,808 (540)

INCOME ★★★★★ (11)

Poverty rate	9.2% (19)
Median household income	$72,214 (6)
Interest/dividends	27.2% (47)
Public assistance	3.8% (8)
Median fulltime earnings	$44,175 (36)

SENIORS ★★★★★ (3)

Seniors living alone	18.6% (7)
Poverty rate for seniors	7.7% (156)
Median income for seniors	$64,500 (6)
Seniors who work	40.5% (1)
Home ownership by seniors	86.7% (76)

STABILITY ★★★★★ (45)

25-39 age group	26.5% (5)
Born in state of residence	32.6% (538)
Same house as 1 year ago	88.7% (95)
Live and work in county	83.7% (148)
Married-couple households	54.3% (99)

TRANSPORTATION ★★★★★ (101)

Bicycle or walk to work	3.2% (225)
Carpool to work	11.0% (229)
Public transit to work	7.6% (4)
Commute <15 minutes	37.8% (381)
Commute >45 minutes	9.2% (182)

See pages 37-130 for explanations of statistics, stars, and ranks.

Elko, NV
(Elko and Eureka Counties, NV)

POPULATION

2010 census	50,805 (206)
2015 estimate	53,951 (179)
2010-2015 change	6.2% (30)
2020 projection	55,385 (175)
2030 projection	58,578 (158)

RACE

Whites	68.4% (399)
Blacks	1.1% (367)
Hispanics	23.3% (66)
Asians	1.1% (139)
Native Americans	5.0% (32)

AGE

0-17 years old	28.0% (32)
18-24 years old	9.4% (203)
25-39 years old	20.8% (47)
40-54 years old	20.7% (132)
55-64 years old	12.0% (438)
65+ years old	9.2% (541)

PRIVATE SECTOR

Businesses	1,385 (157)
Employees	22,145 (94)
Total wages	$1,251,481,998 (34)
Average weekly wages	$1,087 (10)

HOUSEHOLD INCOME LADDER

95th percentile	$197,587 (22)
80th percentile	$119,436 (15)
60th percentile	$83,927 (10)
40th percentile	$58,121 (7)
20th percentile	$33,102 (7)

CHILDREN ★★★★ (206)

Living with two parents	77.0% (29)
Older teens in school	81.6% (341)
Speak English very well	97.8% (361)
Poverty rate for children	15.2% (67)
No health insurance	12.3% (479)

DIVERSITY/EQUALITY ★★★★ (169)

Racial diversity index	47.5% (132)
Geographic diversity index	69.5% (48)
Top 20% share of income	43.2% (7)
Gender gap in earnings	59.5% (550)
White-collar gender gap	37.2% (409)

EDUCATION ★★★ (319)

Eighth grade or less	5.8% (413)
High school diplomas	84.3% (393)
Attended college	57.7% (171)
Bachelor's degrees	18.5% (267)
Advanced degrees	5.6% (304)

EMPLOYMENT ★★ (389)

Average jobless rate	5.5% (98)
Self-employed workers	5.7% (515)
Management/financial jobs	11.2% (229)
Computer/engineering jobs	5.2% (26)
Health care jobs	2.2% (549)

GROWTH POTENTIAL ★★★★★ (36)

Children per senior	3.05 (12)
Median age	33.8 (70)
Moved from different state	4.9% (57)
Homes built since 2000	14.2% (231)
Construction jobs	7.0% (185)

HOUSING ★★★★ (125)

Home vacancy rate	4.7% (22)
Home ownership rate	70.3% (256)
Housing diversity index	81.3% (484)
4 or more bedrooms	22.8% (69)
Affordability/income ratio	$2,533 (261)

INCOME ★★★★★ (19)

Poverty rate	10.9% (56)
Median household income	$71,462 (9)
Interest/dividends	17.7% (321)
Public assistance	6.6% (18)
Median fulltime earnings	$52,344 (9)

SENIORS ★★★★★ (6)

Seniors living alone	22.3% (45)
Poverty rate for seniors	6.4% (57)
Median income for seniors	$49,667 (14)
Seniors who work	29.6% (28)
Home ownership by seniors	85.9% (105)

STABILITY ★★★★ (187)

25-39 age group	20.8% (47)
Born in state of residence	32.7% (537)
Same house as 1 year ago	84.3% (333)
Live and work in county	82.7% (167)
Married-couple households	57.7% (23)

TRANSPORTATION ★★★★★ (64)

Bicycle or walk to work	8.1% (29)
Carpool to work	14.6% (52)
Public transit to work	12.2% (2)
Commute <15 minutes	44.8% (249)
Commute >45 minutes	24.3% (544)

See pages 37-130 for explanations of statistics, stars, and ranks.

Ellensburg, WA
(Kittitas County, WA)

POPULATION		Attended college	65.7% (47)
2010 census	40,915 (300)	Bachelor's degrees	34.5% (30)
2015 estimate	43,269 (277)	Advanced degrees	10.3% (51)
2010-2015 change	5.8% (34)		

EMPLOYMENT	★★★★ (119)
Average jobless rate	7.8% (270)
Self-employed workers	14.6% (22)
Management/financial jobs	11.4% (210)
Computer/engineering jobs	4.1% (70)
Health care jobs	3.9% (488)

POPULATION
2020 projection 46,043 (247)
2030 projection 52,339 (199)

RACE
Whites 84.6% (270)
Blacks 0.9% (388)
Hispanics 8.5% (173)
Asians 2.3% (36)
Native Americans 0.8% (125)

GROWTH POTENTIAL ★★★★★ (68)
Children per senior 1.27 (370)
Median age 33.0 (59)
Moved from different state 3.4% (118)
Homes built since 2000 24.8% (36)
Construction jobs 6.8% (204)

AGE
0-17 years old 18.0% (527)
18-24 years old 22.6% (19)
25-39 years old 16.5% (403)
40-54 years old 16.6% (511)
55-64 years old 12.2% (424)
65+ years old 14.1% (431)

HOUSING ★ (529)
Home vacancy rate 6.0% (95)
Home ownership rate 57.6% (528)
Housing diversity index 84.3% (314)
4 or more bedrooms 13.5% (431)
Affordability/income ratio $5,228 (530)

PRIVATE SECTOR
Businesses 1,356 (164)
Employees 10,218 (369)
Total wages $313,553,143 (418)
Average weekly wages $590 (504)

INCOME ★★★★ (197)
Poverty rate 22.2% (430)
Median household income $46,458 (202)
Interest/dividends 24.1% (127)
Public assistance 14.7% (243)
Median fulltime earnings $42,321 (58)

HOUSEHOLD INCOME LADDER
95th percentile $147,141 (197)
80th percentile $89,483 (162)
60th percentile $59,037 (162)
40th percentile $34,965 (263)
20th percentile $16,686 (374)

SENIORS ★★★★★ (78)
Seniors living alone 28.6% (336)
Poverty rate for seniors 6.4% (57)
Median income for seniors $44,405 (34)
Seniors who work 24.4% (82)
Home ownership by seniors 81.0% (335)

CHILDREN ★★★★★ (43)
Living with two parents 74.7% (57)
Older teens in school 91.5% (47)
Speak English very well 98.4% (300)
Poverty rate for children 17.1% (99)
No health insurance 5.2% (197)

STABILITY ★ (534)
25-39 age group 16.5% (403)
Born in state of residence 62.8% (406)
Same house as 1 year ago 70.8% (542)
Live and work in county 84.7% (139)
Married-couple households 45.4% (456)

DIVERSITY/EQUALITY ★★★ (301)
Racial diversity index 27.6% (275)
Geographic diversity index 57.0% (140)
Top 20% share of income 47.2% (235)
Gender gap in earnings 54.1% (539)
White-collar gender gap 12.0% (113)

TRANSPORTATION ★★★★★ (91)
Bicycle or walk to work 12.3% (6)
Carpool to work 9.1% (419)
Public transit to work 0.8% (96)
Commute <15 minutes 54.2% (93)
Commute >45 minutes 13.7% (379)

EDUCATION ★★★★★ (53)
Eighth grade or less 3.2% (250)
High school diplomas 90.8% (167)

See pages 37-130 for explanations of statistics, stars, and ranks.

Española, NM
(Rio Arriba County, NM)

POPULATION

2010 census	40,246 (310)
2015 estimate	39,465 (318)
2010-2015 change	-1.9% (399)
2020 projection	38,096 (341)
2030 projection	35,358 (369)

RACE

Whites	13.1% (546)
Blacks	0.4% (499)
Hispanics	71.5% (10)
Asians	0.4% (413)
Native Americans	14.0% (13)

AGE

0-17 years old	24.3% (164)
18-24 years old	8.6% (317)
25-39 years old	17.0% (317)
40-54 years old	19.9% (250)
55-64 years old	14.3% (148)
65+ years old	15.9% (297)

PRIVATE SECTOR

Businesses	598 (471)
Employees	5,211 (525)
Total wages	$158,610,031 (530)
Average weekly wages	$585 (509)

HOUSEHOLD INCOME LADDER

95th percentile	$152,768 (136)
80th percentile	$76,927 (424)
60th percentile	$45,144 (475)
40th percentile	$27,647 (466)
20th percentile	$12,524 (508)

CHILDREN ★ **(488)**

Living with two parents	49.9% (507)
Older teens in school	76.2% (486)
Speak English very well	98.9% (226)
Poverty rate for children	30.6% (416)
No health insurance	9.8% (417)

DIVERSITY/EQUALITY ★★★★ **(144)**

Racial diversity index	45.2% (147)
Geographic diversity index	38.5% (379)
Top 20% share of income	52.4% (512)
Gender gap in earnings	1.8% (2)
White-collar gender gap	24.8% (270)

EDUCATION ★★ **(385)**

Eighth grade or less	5.8% (413)
High school diplomas	83.0% (420)
Attended college	51.8% (285)
Bachelor's degrees	16.3% (357)
Advanced degrees	5.6% (304)

EMPLOYMENT ★★★ **(277)**

Average jobless rate	11.4% (473)
Self-employed workers	6.6% (461)
Management/financial jobs	15.8% (17)
Computer/engineering jobs	4.6% (48)
Health care jobs	3.8% (494)

GROWTH POTENTIAL ★★★ **(231)**

Children per senior	1.53 (206)
Median age	40.1 (309)
Moved from different state	0.8% (524)
Homes built since 2000	12.9% (280)
Construction jobs	8.4% (64)

HOUSING ★ **(506)**

Home vacancy rate	16.7% (542)
Home ownership rate	77.6% (20)
Housing diversity index	84.4% (299)
4 or more bedrooms	13.4% (433)
Affordability/income ratio	$4,319 (507)

INCOME ★ **(467)**

Poverty rate	23.7% (462)
Median household income	$36,098 (465)
Interest/dividends	8.9% (537)
Public assistance	16.8% (324)
Median fulltime earnings	$35,630 (355)

SENIORS ★★★★ **(212)**

Seniors living alone	22.6% (52)
Poverty rate for seniors	13.9% (469)
Median income for seniors	$29,867 (413)
Seniors who work	14.6% (472)
Home ownership by seniors	89.4% (20)

STABILITY ★★ **(395)**

25-39 age group	17.0% (317)
Born in state of residence	77.7% (163)
Same house as 1 year ago	93.9% (3)
Live and work in county	58.7% (497)
Married-couple households	41.3% (511)

TRANSPORTATION ★ **(501)**

Bicycle or walk to work	1.0% (512)
Carpool to work	11.4% (190)
Public transit to work	1.6% (38)
Commute <15 minutes	31.9% (502)
Commute >45 minutes	22.2% (536)

See pages 37-130 for explanations of statistics, stars, and ranks.

Eureka-Arcata-Fortuna, CA
(Humboldt County, CA)

POPULATION
2010 census	134,623 (10)
2015 estimate	135,727 (9)
2010-2015 change	0.8% (194)
2020 projection	137,593 (10)
2030 projection	141,790 (8)

RACE
Whites	75.7% (356)
Blacks	1.1% (367)
Hispanics	10.6% (145)
Asians	2.9% (25)
Native Americans	4.6% (36)

AGE
0-17 years old	19.6% (478)
18-24 years old	13.3% (68)
25-39 years old	20.2% (56)
40-54 years old	17.6% (470)
55-64 years old	14.6% (107)
65+ years old	14.7% (389)

PRIVATE SECTOR
Businesses	4,340 (6)
Employees	34,291 (22)
Total wages	$1,187,177,637 (40)
Average weekly wages	$666 (342)

HOUSEHOLD INCOME LADDER
95th percentile	$146,970 (199)
80th percentile	$83,776 (278)
60th percentile	$52,158 (313)
40th percentile	$32,918 (326)
20th percentile	$17,440 (343)

CHILDREN ★★ (384)
Living with two parents	57.9% (450)
Older teens in school	83.6% (254)
Speak English very well	97.1% (408)
Poverty rate for children	23.7% (266)
No health insurance	10.8% (445)

DIVERSITY/EQUALITY ★★★★★ (107)
Racial diversity index	41.0% (183)
Geographic diversity index	51.5% (193)
Top 20% share of income	49.3% (386)
Gender gap in earnings	29.3% (160)
White-collar gender gap	11.4% (102)

EDUCATION ★★★★★ (92)
Eighth grade or less	2.8% (205)
High school diplomas	90.0% (202)
Attended college	65.7% (47)
Bachelor's degrees	27.5% (83)
Advanced degrees	8.3% (112)

EMPLOYMENT ★★★★ (123)
Average jobless rate	10.5% (441)
Self-employed workers	12.9% (53)
Management/financial jobs	12.4% (126)
Computer/engineering jobs	4.4% (60)
Health care jobs	5.0% (339)

GROWTH POTENTIAL ★★★ (259)
Children per senior	1.33 (325)
Median age	37.4 (160)
Moved from different state	2.3% (234)
Homes built since 2000	8.8% (443)
Construction jobs	7.4% (134)

HOUSING ★ (537)
Home vacancy rate	8.2% (234)
Home ownership rate	54.9% (536)
Housing diversity index	86.8% (3)
4 or more bedrooms	11.8% (503)
Affordability/income ratio	$6,619 (546)

INCOME ★★★ (224)
Poverty rate	21.4% (412)
Median household income	$42,197 (313)
Interest/dividends	25.2% (87)
Public assistance	11.9% (127)
Median fulltime earnings	$38,599 (198)

SENIORS ★★★★ (149)
Seniors living alone	27.5% (264)
Poverty rate for seniors	7.0% (93)
Median income for seniors	$40,136 (57)
Seniors who work	21.8% (135)
Home ownership by seniors	79.6% (388)

STABILITY ★★★ (281)
25-39 age group	20.2% (56)
Born in state of residence	68.3% (338)
Same house as 1 year ago	79.3% (506)
Live and work in county	98.0% (5)
Married-couple households	40.6% (521)

TRANSPORTATION ★★★★★ (22)
Bicycle or walk to work	9.2% (17)
Carpool to work	10.1% (322)
Public transit to work	1.8% (34)
Commute <15 minutes	49.3% (166)
Commute >45 minutes	6.1% (59)

See pages 37-130 for explanations of statistics, stars, and ranks.

Evanston, WY
(Uinta County, WY)

POPULATION

2010 census	21,118 (518)
2015 estimate	20,822 (519)
2010-2015 change	-1.4% (364)
2020 projection	20,727 (520)
2030 projection	20,551 (517)

RACE

Whites	87.8% (228)
Blacks	0.2% (537)
Hispanics	8.9% (168)
Asians	0.1% (529)
Native Americans	0.4% (203)

AGE

0-17 years old	29.6% (20)
18-24 years old	8.1% (396)
25-39 years old	19.8% (64)
40-54 years old	18.6% (412)
55-64 years old	13.6% (247)
65+ years old	10.2% (524)

PRIVATE SECTOR

Businesses	732 (413)
Employees	6,529 (491)
Total wages	$276,192,608 (451)
Average weekly wages	$814 (73)

HOUSEHOLD INCOME LADDER

95th percentile	$161,855 (88)
80th percentile	$105,570 (33)
60th percentile	$67,769 (48)
40th percentile	$45,451 (43)
20th percentile	$23,002 (100)

CHILDREN ★★★★ (171)

Living with two parents	77.5% (24)
Older teens in school	80.1% (396)
Speak English very well	98.4% (300)
Poverty rate for children	18.3% (135)
No health insurance	8.8% (385)

DIVERSITY/EQUALITY ★ (462)

Racial diversity index	22.0% (324)
Geographic diversity index	65.8% (70)
Top 20% share of income	46.2% (136)
Gender gap in earnings	56.3% (546)
White-collar gender gap	45.8% (486)

EDUCATION ★★★★ (197)

Eighth grade or less	2.8% (205)
High school diplomas	91.6% (141)
Attended college	55.9% (205)
Bachelor's degrees	20.1% (220)
Advanced degrees	5.6% (304)

EMPLOYMENT ★★★★ (197)

Average jobless rate	4.4% (42)
Self-employed workers	9.1% (243)
Management/financial jobs	13.1% (78)
Computer/engineering jobs	2.1% (399)
Health care jobs	4.1% (462)

GROWTH POTENTIAL ★★★★★ (35)

Children per senior	2.90 (20)
Median age	34.6 (84)
Moved from different state	5.4% (41)
Homes built since 2000	13.8% (246)
Construction jobs	7.1% (173)

HOUSING ★★★★ (194)

Home vacancy rate	8.3% (241)
Home ownership rate	73.0% (151)
Housing diversity index	80.3% (505)
4 or more bedrooms	26.8% (30)
Affordability/income ratio	$3,124 (423)

INCOME ★★★★★ (64)

Poverty rate	13.7% (145)
Median household income	$56,569 (43)
Interest/dividends	20.1% (241)
Public assistance	7.4% (28)
Median fulltime earnings	$43,846 (38)

SENIORS ★★★★★ (64)

Seniors living alone	24.4% (94)
Poverty rate for seniors	10.0% (321)
Median income for seniors	$36,494 (138)
Seniors who work	25.4% (63)
Home ownership by seniors	85.6% (120)

STABILITY ★★★ (308)

25-39 age group	19.8% (64)
Born in state of residence	34.9% (534)
Same house as 1 year ago	81.0% (478)
Live and work in county	83.2% (159)
Married-couple households	57.5% (26)

TRANSPORTATION ★★★★★ (43)

Bicycle or walk to work	3.4% (199)
Carpool to work	13.1% (98)
Public transit to work	2.8% (16)
Commute <15 minutes	62.7% (32)
Commute >45 minutes	13.8% (382)

See pages 37-130 for explanations of statistics, stars, and ranks.

Fallon, NV
(Churchill County, NV)

POPULATION	
2010 census	24,877 (482)
2015 estimate	24,200 (488)
2010-2015 change	-2.7% (459)
2020 projection	23,305 (494)
2030 projection	21,687 (509)

RACE	
Whites	74.6% (359)
Blacks	2.1% (283)
Hispanics	13.1% (118)
Asians	3.0% (23)
Native Americans	4.4% (38)

AGE	
0-17 years old	23.6% (228)
18-24 years old	9.3% (217)
25-39 years old	18.8% (121)
40-54 years old	18.1% (446)
55-64 years old	13.1% (318)
65+ years old	17.0% (197)

PRIVATE SECTOR	
Businesses	617 (462)
Employees	5,999 (509)
Total wages	$251,822,093 (470)
Average weekly wages	$807 (81)

HOUSEHOLD INCOME LADDER	
95th percentile	$145,259 (225)
80th percentile	$96,310 (80)
60th percentile	$57,451 (197)
40th percentile	$37,887 (185)
20th percentile	$21,225 (179)

CHILDREN	★★ (398)
Living with two parents	65.2% (266)
Older teens in school	77.0% (473)
Speak English very well	97.6% (375)
Poverty rate for children	20.8% (187)
No health insurance	12.5% (485)

DIVERSITY/EQUALITY	★★★★★ (27)
Racial diversity index	42.2% (172)
Geographic diversity index	72.8% (22)
Top 20% share of income	45.3% (76)
Gender gap in earnings	39.7% (429)
White-collar gender gap	6.9% (54)

EDUCATION	★★★ (254)
Eighth grade or less	3.3% (259)
High school diplomas	90.4% (188)

Attended college	55.7% (209)
Bachelor's degrees	15.7% (399)
Advanced degrees	5.1% (364)

EMPLOYMENT	★ (447)
Average jobless rate	11.9% (488)
Self-employed workers	8.3% (302)
Management/financial jobs	11.2% (229)
Computer/engineering jobs	1.7% (470)
Health care jobs	5.5% (250)

GROWTH POTENTIAL	★★★★★ (91)
Children per senior	1.39 (286)
Median age	38.9 (228)
Moved from different state	7.0% (23)
Homes built since 2000	20.2% (89)
Construction jobs	6.2% (295)

HOUSING	★ (508)
Home vacancy rate	11.3% (426)
Home ownership rate	61.4% (487)
Housing diversity index	82.7% (429)
4 or more bedrooms	15.7% (315)
Affordability/income ratio	$3,185 (428)

INCOME	★★★ (233)
Poverty rate	15.9% (219)
Median household income	$47,415 (182)
Interest/dividends	18.2% (305)
Public assistance	15.5% (277)
Median fulltime earnings	$39,238 (167)

SENIORS	★★★★ (184)
Seniors living alone	26.2% (186)
Poverty rate for seniors	6.8% (77)
Median income for seniors	$39,324 (66)
Seniors who work	15.7% (427)
Home ownership by seniors	81.5% (305)

STABILITY	★ (515)
25-39 age group	18.8% (121)
Born in state of residence	32.5% (539)
Same house as 1 year ago	77.3% (519)
Live and work in county	86.3% (111)
Married-couple households	49.7% (311)

TRANSPORTATION	★★★ (279)
Bicycle or walk to work	3.0% (249)
Carpool to work	11.4% (190)
Public transit to work	0.1% (441)
Commute <15 minutes	48.9% (176)
Commute >45 minutes	12.8% (346)

See pages 37-130 for explanations of statistics, stars, and ranks.

Fernley, NV
(Lyon County, NV)

POPULATION	
2010 census	51,980 (196)
2015 estimate	52,585 (193)
2010-2015 change	1.2% (173)
2020 projection	54,779 (178)
2030 projection	59,649 (154)

RACE	
Whites	76.7% (347)
Blacks	0.8% (404)
Hispanics	15.6% (102)
Asians	1.4% (99)
Native Americans	2.3% (67)

AGE	
0-17 years old	23.0% (259)
18-24 years old	7.1% (515)
25-39 years old	16.6% (388)
40-54 years old	19.6% (289)
55-64 years old	14.8% (91)
65+ years old	18.8% (94)

PRIVATE SECTOR	
Businesses	958 (291)
Employees	9,340 (399)
Total wages	$370,736,343 (361)
Average weekly wages	$763 (135)

HOUSEHOLD INCOME LADDER	
95th percentile	$134,638 (366)
80th percentile	$88,273 (181)
60th percentile	$57,523 (194)
40th percentile	$40,680 (108)
20th percentile	$23,044 (99)

CHILDREN	★★ (370)
Living with two parents	65.3% (263)
Older teens in school	81.8% (329)
Speak English very well	97.8% (361)
Poverty rate for children	22.0% (221)
No health insurance	13.8% (506)

DIVERSITY/EQUALITY	★★★★★ (51)
Racial diversity index	38.6% (191)
Geographic diversity index	72.0% (31)
Top 20% share of income	44.1% (30)
Gender gap in earnings	37.7% (382)
White-collar gender gap	25.9% (287)

EDUCATION	★★ (358)
Eighth grade or less	5.9% (420)
High school diplomas	85.2% (368)
Attended college	54.3% (238)
Bachelor's degrees	16.2% (360)
Advanced degrees	5.7% (292)

EMPLOYMENT	★ (527)
Average jobless rate	13.6% (524)
Self-employed workers	6.9% (435)
Management/financial jobs	8.5% (505)
Computer/engineering jobs	4.7% (40)
Health care jobs	3.3% (517)

GROWTH POTENTIAL	★★★★★ (49)
Children per senior	1.22 (401)
Median age	43.2 (456)
Moved from different state	5.5% (39)
Homes built since 2000	39.9% (3)
Construction jobs	9.3% (38)

HOUSING	★ (514)
Home vacancy rate	11.3% (426)
Home ownership rate	70.2% (264)
Housing diversity index	74.7% (548)
4 or more bedrooms	15.3% (333)
Affordability/income ratio	$2,787 (356)

INCOME	★★★★ (201)
Poverty rate	16.5% (246)
Median household income	$47,255 (186)
Interest/dividends	17.5% (329)
Public assistance	14.2% (215)
Median fulltime earnings	$41,701 (70)

SENIORS	★★★★★ (37)
Seniors living alone	19.6% (11)
Poverty rate for seniors	7.4% (128)
Median income for seniors	$40,801 (54)
Seniors who work	16.1% (400)
Home ownership by seniors	86.1% (93)

STABILITY	★ (550)
25-39 age group	16.6% (388)
Born in state of residence	26.5% (548)
Same house as 1 year ago	81.5% (460)
Live and work in county	46.4% (544)
Married-couple households	52.0% (194)

TRANSPORTATION	★ (533)
Bicycle or walk to work	1.1% (501)
Carpool to work	13.9% (72)
Public transit to work	0.2% (363)
Commute <15 minutes	27.7% (537)
Commute >45 minutes	28.3% (548)

See pages 37-130 for explanations of statistics, stars, and ranks.

Fort Morgan, CO
(Morgan County, CO)

POPULATION	
2010 census	28,159 (453)
2015 estimate	28,360 (450)
2010-2015 change	0.7% (202)
2020 projection	28,380 (446)
2030 projection	28,496 (435)

RACE	
Whites	60.5% (442)
Blacks	2.5% (253)
Hispanics	35.0% (45)
Asians	0.4% (413)
Native Americans	0.5% (174)

AGE	
0-17 years old	26.8% (51)
18-24 years old	8.9% (282)
25-39 years old	18.3% (159)
40-54 years old	19.1% (354)
55-64 years old	11.7% (463)
65+ years old	15.1% (363)

PRIVATE SECTOR	
Businesses	682 (437)
Employees	9,897 (379)
Total wages	$406,757,926 (330)
Average weekly wages	$790 (106)

HOUSEHOLD INCOME LADDER	
95th percentile	$142,561 (258)
80th percentile	$86,962 (206)
60th percentile	$59,480 (158)
40th percentile	$39,163 (151)
20th percentile	$23,301 (86)

CHILDREN	★★★ (267)
Living with two parents	63.6% (306)
Older teens in school	87.6% (110)
Speak English very well	92.3% (516)
Poverty rate for children	16.0% (81)
No health insurance	6.9% (307)

DIVERSITY/EQUALITY	★★★★★ (31)
Racial diversity index	51.1% (104)
Geographic diversity index	63.3% (90)
Top 20% share of income	44.3% (36)
Gender gap in earnings	29.5% (165)
White-collar gender gap	29.4% (328)

EDUCATION	★ (481)
Eighth grade or less	10.5% (515)
High school diplomas	80.0% (479)
Attended college	50.8% (306)
Bachelor's degrees	14.6% (435)
Advanced degrees	5.6% (304)

EMPLOYMENT	★★★ (321)
Average jobless rate	6.2% (131)
Self-employed workers	10.9% (120)
Management/financial jobs	9.6% (427)
Computer/engineering jobs	2.8% (246)
Health care jobs	3.8% (494)

GROWTH POTENTIAL	★★★★ (166)
Children per senior	1.77 (104)
Median age	36.4 (128)
Moved from different state	2.6% (187)
Homes built since 2000	14.4% (222)
Construction jobs	6.0% (326)

HOUSING	★★★★ (111)
Home vacancy rate	6.2% (109)
Home ownership rate	64.7% (443)
Housing diversity index	85.9% (83)
4 or more bedrooms	23.5% (56)
Affordability/income ratio	$3,003 (406)

INCOME	★★★★ (212)
Poverty rate	11.6% (74)
Median household income	$48,450 (164)
Interest/dividends	16.9% (345)
Public assistance	14.3% (220)
Median fulltime earnings	$36,989 (288)

SENIORS	★★★ (313)
Seniors living alone	25.4% (132)
Poverty rate for seniors	9.4% (282)
Median income for seniors	$31,309 (359)
Seniors who work	23.4% (98)
Home ownership by seniors	74.9% (526)

STABILITY	★★★★ (216)
25-39 age group	18.3% (159)
Born in state of residence	57.5% (440)
Same house as 1 year ago	81.3% (470)
Live and work in county	89.6% (72)
Married-couple households	53.6% (129)

TRANSPORTATION	★★★★★ (42)
Bicycle or walk to work	4.8% (98)
Carpool to work	17.3% (21)
Public transit to work	0.1% (441)
Commute <15 minutes	57.5% (67)
Commute >45 minutes	10.3% (237)

See pages 37-130 for explanations of statistics, stars, and ranks.

Gallup, NM
(McKinley County, NM)

POPULATION

2010 census	71,492 (91)
2015 estimate	76,708 (80)
2010-2015 change	7.3% (19)
2020 projection	79,002 (74)
2030 projection	83,460 (65)

RACE

Whites	9.9% (548)
Blacks	0.8% (404)
Hispanics	13.9% (113)
Asians	0.9% (178)
Native Americans	72.3% (1)

AGE

0-17 years old	30.5% (16)
18-24 years old	11.3% (106)
25-39 years old	19.7% (68)
40-54 years old	17.9% (454)
55-64 years old	10.4% (506)
65+ years old	10.2% (524)

PRIVATE SECTOR

Businesses	1,106 (242)
Employees	13,313 (267)
Total wages	$342,475,829 (390)
Average weekly wages	$495 (546)

HOUSEHOLD INCOME LADDER

95th percentile	$124,714 (488)
80th percentile	$67,315 (521)
60th percentile	$39,094 (533)
40th percentile	$21,172 (543)
20th percentile	$9,154 (550)

CHILDREN   ★ (545)

Living with two parents	47.2% (520)
Older teens in school	80.2% (392)
Speak English very well	96.8% (421)
Poverty rate for children	44.2% (531)
No health insurance	16.6% (531)

DIVERSITY/EQUALITY   ★★★★★ (99)

Racial diversity index	44.8% (153)
Geographic diversity index	37.4% (398)
Top 20% share of income	52.3% (510)
Gender gap in earnings	10.1% (9)
White-collar gender gap	12.7% (123)

EDUCATION   ★ (498)

Eighth grade or less	5.1% (390)
High school diplomas	78.2% (506)
Attended college	42.9% (473)
Bachelor's degrees	11.2% (531)
Advanced degrees	4.0% (478)

EMPLOYMENT   ★ (545)

Average jobless rate	15.5% (539)
Self-employed workers	6.0% (502)
Management/financial jobs	7.2% (544)
Computer/engineering jobs	2.1% (399)
Health care jobs	5.5% (250)

GROWTH POTENTIAL   ★★★★★ (62)

Children per senior	2.99 (16)
Median age	30.8 (36)
Moved from different state	2.0% (288)
Homes built since 2000	12.4% (301)
Construction jobs	5.9% (345)

HOUSING   ★ (478)

Home vacancy rate	20.0% (549)
Home ownership rate	73.1% (148)
Housing diversity index	83.0% (417)
4 or more bedrooms	14.4% (381)
Affordability/income ratio	$2,374 (201)

INCOME   ★ (540)

Poverty rate	37.5% (549)
Median household income	$28,772 (541)
Interest/dividends	7.4% (546)
Public assistance	26.4% (521)
Median fulltime earnings	$31,153 (523)

SENIORS   ★ (464)

Seniors living alone	24.6% (100)
Poverty rate for seniors	30.9% (548)
Median income for seniors	$23,070 (519)
Seniors who work	16.8% (356)
Home ownership by seniors	87.2% (63)

STABILITY   ★★★★★ (54)

25-39 age group	19.7% (68)
Born in state of residence	77.8% (159)
Same house as 1 year ago	91.6% (19)
Live and work in county	90.0% (63)
Married-couple households	39.1% (535)

TRANSPORTATION   ★★★ (262)

Bicycle or walk to work	4.3% (130)
Carpool to work	12.5% (121)
Public transit to work	0.4% (219)
Commute <15 minutes	44.4% (256)
Commute >45 minutes	15.2% (430)

See pages 37-130 for explanations of statistics, stars, and ranks.

Gardnerville Ranchos, NV
(Douglas County, NV)

POPULATION	
2010 census	46,997 (233)
2015 estimate	47,710 (232)
2010-2015 change	1.5% (160)
2020 projection	47,560 (234)
2030 projection	47,427 (237)

RACE	
Whites	81.7% (307)
Blacks	0.5% (466)
Hispanics	11.9% (127)
Asians	1.4% (99)
Native Americans	1.9% (72)

AGE	
0-17 years old	18.6% (509)
18-24 years old	6.4% (542)
25-39 years old	14.1% (538)
40-54 years old	19.9% (250)
55-64 years old	17.5% (7)
65+ years old	23.5% (15)

PRIVATE SECTOR	
Businesses	1,829 (85)
Employees	16,481 (182)
Total wages	$680,640,057 (155)
Average weekly wages	$794 (101)

HOUSEHOLD INCOME LADDER	
95th percentile	$192,688 (29)
80th percentile	$108,193 (28)
60th percentile	$71,203 (34)
40th percentile	$47,994 (26)
20th percentile	$26,817 (27)

CHILDREN	★★★ (257)
Living with two parents	68.3% (185)
Older teens in school	87.4% (116)
Speak English very well	98.1% (331)
Poverty rate for children	16.4% (86)
No health insurance	14.7% (522)

DIVERSITY/EQUALITY	★★★★★ (46)
Racial diversity index	31.7% (240)
Geographic diversity index	69.3% (49)
Top 20% share of income	48.5% (320)
Gender gap in earnings	27.0% (118)
White-collar gender gap	8.0% (64)

EDUCATION	★★★★★ (61)
Eighth grade or less	2.0% (126)
High school diplomas	93.6% (68)
Attended college	69.8% (28)
Bachelor's degrees	25.2% (106)
Advanced degrees	9.0% (87)

EMPLOYMENT	★★★★ (144)
Average jobless rate	8.5% (332)
Self-employed workers	10.1% (158)
Management/financial jobs	14.6% (34)
Computer/engineering jobs	4.4% (60)
Health care jobs	3.7% (503)

GROWTH POTENTIAL	★★★ (238)
Children per senior	0.79 (538)
Median age	49.4 (542)
Moved from different state	5.0% (51)
Homes built since 2000	22.7% (55)
Construction jobs	8.1% (86)

HOUSING	★ (462)
Home vacancy rate	5.7% (74)
Home ownership rate	69.4% (293)
Housing diversity index	79.8% (520)
4 or more bedrooms	18.7% (171)
Affordability/income ratio	$4,647 (519)

INCOME	★★★★★ (21)
Poverty rate	10.6% (47)
Median household income	$58,535 (31)
Interest/dividends	31.2% (13)
Public assistance	8.9% (44)
Median fulltime earnings	$45,390 (28)

SENIORS	★★★★★ (13)
Seniors living alone	18.9% (9)
Poverty rate for seniors	5.0% (17)
Median income for seniors	$51,872 (9)
Seniors who work	17.4% (318)
Home ownership by seniors	86.4% (82)

STABILITY	★ (541)
25-39 age group	14.1% (538)
Born in state of residence	17.6% (551)
Same house as 1 year ago	85.4% (285)
Live and work in county	59.8% (492)
Married-couple households	56.1% (46)

TRANSPORTATION	★★ (405)
Bicycle or walk to work	2.6% (308)
Carpool to work	11.3% (201)
Public transit to work	0.3% (291)
Commute <15 minutes	36.7% (405)
Commute >45 minutes	15.2% (430)

See pages 37-130 for explanations of statistics, stars, and ranks.

Gillette, WY
(Campbell County, WY)

POPULATION	
2010 census	46,133 (247)
2015 estimate	49,220 (216)
2010-2015 change	6.7% (25)
2020 projection	53,344 (186)
2030 projection	62,698 (134)

RACE	
Whites	87.9% (222)
Blacks	0.8% (404)
Hispanics	8.2% (177)
Asians	0.6% (291)
Native Americans	1.0% (103)

AGE	
0-17 years old	28.0% (32)
18-24 years old	9.1% (251)
25-39 years old	23.4% (13)
40-54 years old	20.5% (151)
55-64 years old	12.3% (414)
65+ years old	6.6% (551)

PRIVATE SECTOR	
Businesses	1,707 (99)
Employees	22,887 (89)
Total wages	$1,359,051,684 (25)
Average weekly wages	$1,142 (8)

HOUSEHOLD INCOME LADDER	
95th percentile	$181,552 (38)
80th percentile	$127,547 (7)
60th percentile	$93,072 (5)
40th percentile	$66,565 (5)
20th percentile	$37,581 (5)

CHILDREN	★★★★★ (92)
Living with two parents	72.0% (106)
Older teens in school	84.6% (214)
Speak English very well	98.5% (287)
Poverty rate for children	8.4% (6)
No health insurance	9.1% (397)

DIVERSITY/EQUALITY	★★★★★ (92)
Racial diversity index	22.0% (324)
Geographic diversity index	71.6% (35)
Top 20% share of income	41.6% (1)
Gender gap in earnings	54.9% (543)
White-collar gender gap	13.9% (140)

EDUCATION	★★★★ (203)
Eighth grade or less	2.2% (152)
High school diplomas	91.8% (132)
Attended college	57.7% (171)
Bachelor's degrees	19.0% (248)
Advanced degrees	4.4% (451)

EMPLOYMENT	★★ (400)
Average jobless rate	4.0% (32)
Self-employed workers	6.5% (474)
Management/financial jobs	10.1% (365)
Computer/engineering jobs	3.2% (158)
Health care jobs	3.1% (531)

GROWTH POTENTIAL	★★★★★ (5)
Children per senior	4.24 (1)
Median age	32.7 (56)
Moved from different state	7.0% (23)
Homes built since 2000	35.8% (7)
Construction jobs	7.2% (162)

HOUSING	★★★★ (192)
Home vacancy rate	7.0% (162)
Home ownership rate	72.3% (175)
Housing diversity index	76.6% (541)
4 or more bedrooms	27.9% (23)
Affordability/income ratio	$2,651 (313)

INCOME	★★★★★ (10)
Poverty rate	7.2% (6)
Median household income	$80,060 (5)
Interest/dividends	17.3% (336)
Public assistance	3.0% (2)
Median fulltime earnings	$54,198 (5)

SENIORS	★★★★★ (23)
Seniors living alone	25.5% (142)
Poverty rate for seniors	5.0% (17)
Median income for seniors	$46,849 (20)
Seniors who work	31.2% (16)
Home ownership by seniors	78.7% (427)

STABILITY	★★★★★ (41)
25-39 age group	23.4% (13)
Born in state of residence	40.1% (520)
Same house as 1 year ago	79.7% (501)
Live and work in county	97.2% (6)
Married-couple households	56.2% (45)

TRANSPORTATION	★★★★ (161)
Bicycle or walk to work	1.5% (457)
Carpool to work	10.6% (271)
Public transit to work	2.5% (22)
Commute <15 minutes	47.1% (213)
Commute >45 minutes	10.1% (228)

See pages 37-130 for explanations of statistics, stars, and ranks.

Glenwood Springs, CO
(Garfield and Pitkin Counties, CO)

POPULATION			
2010 census	73,537 (88)	Attended college	65.2% (57)
2015 estimate	75,882 (82)	Bachelor's degrees	35.8% (24)
2010-2015 change	3.2% (74)	Advanced degrees	10.2% (53)

POPULATION
2010 census — 73,537 (88)
2015 estimate — 75,882 (82)
2010-2015 change — 3.2% (74)
2020 projection — 79,857 (71)
2030 projection — 88,648 (54)

RACE
Whites — 72.8% (373)
Blacks — 0.6% (438)
Hispanics — 23.8% (63)
Asians — 0.9% (178)
Native Americans — 0.6% (150)

AGE
0-17 years old — 24.0% (184)
18-24 years old — 7.9% (424)
25-39 years old — 21.7% (26)
40-54 years old — 21.5% (57)
55-64 years old — 13.7% (225)
65+ years old — 11.3% (504)

PRIVATE SECTOR
Businesses — 4,249 (9)
Employees — 34,340 (20)
Total wages — $1,643,781,457 (13)
Average weekly wages — $921 (28)

HOUSEHOLD INCOME LADDER
95th percentile — $204,673 (14)
80th percentile — $114,374 (21)
60th percentile — $76,425 (21)
40th percentile — $49,585 (21)
20th percentile — $28,383 (20)

CHILDREN ★★★ (226)
Living with two parents — 77.1% (27)
Older teens in school — 90.2% (63)
Speak English very well — 96.7% (428)
Poverty rate for children — 14.3% (58)
No health insurance — 19.4% (546)

DIVERSITY/EQUALITY ★★★★ (153)
Racial diversity index — 41.3% (181)
Geographic diversity index — 78.1% (10)
Top 20% share of income — 51.4% (484)
Gender gap in earnings — 30.6% (187)
White-collar gender gap — 35.3% (395)

EDUCATION ★★★★★ (69)
Eighth grade or less — 4.7% (366)
High school diplomas — 87.7% (280)
Attended college — 65.2% (57)
Bachelor's degrees — 35.8% (24)
Advanced degrees — 10.2% (53)

EMPLOYMENT ★★★★★ (70)
Average jobless rate — 7.1% (208)
Self-employed workers — 14.4% (29)
Management/financial jobs — 15.7% (19)
Computer/engineering jobs — 2.8% (246)
Health care jobs — 3.9% (488)

GROWTH POTENTIAL ★★★★★ (18)
Children per senior — 2.13 (46)
Median age — 37.1 (149)
Moved from different state — 4.6% (65)
Homes built since 2000 — 26.4% (31)
Construction jobs — 13.9% (2)

HOUSING ★ (495)
Home vacancy rate — 8.1% (227)
Home ownership rate — 64.8% (438)
Housing diversity index — 82.0% (458)
4 or more bedrooms — 22.3% (78)
Affordability/income ratio — $5,375 (533)

INCOME ★★★★★ (34)
Poverty rate — 11.6% (74)
Median household income — $59,875 (25)
Interest/dividends — 23.1% (155)
Public assistance — 6.6% (18)
Median fulltime earnings — $44,986 (32)

SENIORS ★★★★★ (22)
Seniors living alone — 25.3% (127)
Poverty rate for seniors — 10.0% (321)
Median income for seniors — $49,370 (16)
Seniors who work — 34.6% (6)
Home ownership by seniors — 81.9% (280)

STABILITY ★★★ (288)
25-39 age group — 21.7% (26)
Born in state of residence — 38.6% (524)
Same house as 1 year ago — 82.3% (426)
Live and work in county — 79.4% (224)
Married-couple households — 52.5% (171)

TRANSPORTATION ★★★★★ (86)
Bicycle or walk to work — 8.4% (25)
Carpool to work — 12.5% (121)
Public transit to work — 6.8% (5)
Commute <15 minutes — 35.9% (421)
Commute >45 minutes — 19.6% (513)

See pages 37-130 for explanations of statistics, stars, and ranks.

Grants, NM
(Cibola County, NM)

POPULATION	
2010 census	27,213 (463)
2015 estimate	27,329 (460)
2010-2015 change	0.4% (228)
2020 projection	27,029 (459)
2030 projection	26,329 (462)

RACE	
Whites	20.9% (540)
Blacks	0.9% (388)
Hispanics	37.5% (42)
Asians	0.7% (241)
Native Americans	38.5% (3)

AGE	
0-17 years old	24.2% (172)
18-24 years old	9.5% (197)
25-39 years old	20.5% (50)
40-54 years old	18.8% (386)
55-64 years old	12.8% (356)
65+ years old	14.2% (429)

PRIVATE SECTOR	
Businesses	329 (545)
Employees	4,830 (532)
Total wages	$169,639,502 (527)
Average weekly wages	$675 (320)

HOUSEHOLD INCOME LADDER	
95th percentile	$114,826 (537)
80th percentile	$69,871 (505)
60th percentile	$44,149 (489)
40th percentile	$26,035 (499)
20th percentile	$15,167 (446)

CHILDREN	★ (499)
Living with two parents	38.2% (541)
Older teens in school	88.6% (90)
Speak English very well	97.1% (408)
Poverty rate for children	45.5% (536)
No health insurance	6.2% (262)

DIVERSITY/EQUALITY	★★★★★ (9)
Racial diversity index	66.7% (4)
Geographic diversity index	49.2% (224)
Top 20% share of income	48.0% (291)
Gender gap in earnings	16.4% (19)
White-collar gender gap	4.4% (30)

EDUCATION	★ (467)
Eighth grade or less	4.6% (361)
High school diplomas	83.1% (417)
Attended college	46.7% (403)
Bachelor's degrees	11.2% (531)
Advanced degrees	2.9% (534)

EMPLOYMENT	★ (514)
Average jobless rate	15.3% (537)
Self-employed workers	10.3% (150)
Management/financial jobs	9.7% (416)
Computer/engineering jobs	1.4% (510)
Health care jobs	5.1% (319)

GROWTH POTENTIAL	★★★ (242)
Children per senior	1.70 (133)
Median age	36.2 (122)
Moved from different state	2.0% (288)
Homes built since 2000	12.9% (280)
Construction jobs	5.3% (425)

HOUSING	★★★ (318)
Home vacancy rate	13.1% (494)
Home ownership rate	74.2% (110)
Housing diversity index	84.2% (325)
4 or more bedrooms	15.5% (324)
Affordability/income ratio	$2,552 (271)

INCOME	★ (528)
Poverty rate	29.3% (520)
Median household income	$34,565 (492)
Interest/dividends	10.8% (517)
Public assistance	24.7% (512)
Median fulltime earnings	$30,134 (540)

SENIORS	★★★★ (161)
Seniors living alone	25.6% (149)
Poverty rate for seniors	12.8% (442)
Median income for seniors	$28,347 (448)
Seniors who work	20.6% (173)
Home ownership by seniors	90.8% (8)

STABILITY	★★★★ (196)
25-39 age group	20.5% (50)
Born in state of residence	69.8% (312)
Same house as 1 year ago	87.5% (165)
Live and work in county	84.6% (141)
Married-couple households	39.6% (531)

TRANSPORTATION	★★★★ (139)
Bicycle or walk to work	2.1% (374)
Carpool to work	18.6% (11)
Public transit to work	0.4% (219)
Commute <15 minutes	49.9% (154)
Commute >45 minutes	15.4% (436)

See pages 37-130 for explanations of statistics, stars, and ranks.

Hailey, ID
(Blaine, Camas, and Lincoln Counties, ID)

POPULATION

2010 census	27,701 (459)
2015 estimate	27,955 (453)
2010-2015 change	0.9% (186)
2020 projection	28,109 (449)
2030 projection	28,406 (436)

RACE

Whites	75.8% (355)
Blacks	0.1% (544)
Hispanics	21.9% (70)
Asians	1.0% (158)
Native Americans	0.3% (231)

AGE

0-17 years old	25.1% (116)
18-24 years old	6.6% (535)
25-39 years old	16.9% (338)
40-54 years old	22.1% (25)
55-64 years old	14.8% (91)
65+ years old	14.6% (400)

PRIVATE SECTOR

Businesses	1,691 (103)
Employees	12,212 (301)
Total wages	$473,424,189 (269)
Average weekly wages	$746 (163)

HOUSEHOLD INCOME LADDER

95th percentile	$203,983 (15)
80th percentile	$99,180 (63)
60th percentile	$67,776 (47)
40th percentile	$42,427 (73)
20th percentile	$24,560 (54)

CHILDREN ★ (454)

Living with two parents	71.3% (114)
Older teens in school	74.4% (505)
Speak English very well	93.4% (501)
Poverty rate for children	20.4% (176)
No health insurance	13.4% (503)

DIVERSITY/EQUALITY ★★★★ (137)

Racial diversity index	37.7% (197)
Geographic diversity index	74.8% (17)
Top 20% share of income	50.3% (445)
Gender gap in earnings	31.0% (204)
White-collar gender gap	31.4% (357)

EDUCATION ★★★★ (131)

Eighth grade or less	7.7% (484)
High school diplomas	87.1% (301)
Attended college	64.3% (69)
Bachelor's degrees	34.2% (31)
Advanced degrees	8.3% (112)

EMPLOYMENT ★★★★★ (45)

Average jobless rate	4.4% (42)
Self-employed workers	17.2% (6)
Management/financial jobs	13.2% (73)
Computer/engineering jobs	4.6% (48)
Health care jobs	3.1% (531)

GROWTH POTENTIAL ★★★★★ (54)

Children per senior	1.72 (122)
Median age	41.4 (376)
Moved from different state	3.9% (82)
Homes built since 2000	19.7% (97)
Construction jobs	10.6% (12)

HOUSING ★★ (426)

Home vacancy rate	5.9% (88)
Home ownership rate	66.8% (396)
Housing diversity index	81.5% (478)
4 or more bedrooms	23.4% (59)
Affordability/income ratio	$5,727 (537)

INCOME ★★★★★ (107)

Poverty rate	11.5% (71)
Median household income	$53,013 (73)
Interest/dividends	19.1% (273)
Public assistance	7.3% (27)
Median fulltime earnings	$37,219 (269)

SENIORS ★★★★★ (30)

Seniors living alone	28.4% (325)
Poverty rate for seniors	7.6% (145)
Median income for seniors	$44,407 (33)
Seniors who work	32.6% (11)
Home ownership by seniors	84.0% (179)

STABILITY ★★ (367)

25-39 age group	16.9% (338)
Born in state of residence	37.6% (528)
Same house as 1 year ago	86.5% (219)
Live and work in county	87.4% (95)
Married-couple households	53.7% (123)

TRANSPORTATION ★★★★ (112)

Bicycle or walk to work	5.9% (60)
Carpool to work	10.2% (312)
Public transit to work	2.3% (26)
Commute <15 minutes	47.3% (204)
Commute >45 minutes	13.0% (356)

See pages 37-130 for explanations of statistics, stars, and ranks.

Heber, UT
(Wasatch County, UT)

POPULATION

2010 census	23,530 (489)
2015 estimate	29,161 (440)
2010-2015 change	23.9% (3)
2020 projection	35,258 (380)
2030 projection	51,718 (206)

RACE

Whites	84.2% (276)
Blacks	0.1% (544)
Hispanics	13.2% (117)
Asians	1.4% (99)
Native Americans	0.1% (402)

AGE

0-17 years old	33.1% (5)
18-24 years old	7.9% (424)
25-39 years old	22.0% (20)
40-54 years old	17.7% (464)
55-64 years old	10.2% (516)
65+ years old	9.1% (543)

PRIVATE SECTOR

Businesses	893 (317)
Employees	6,267 (497)
Total wages	$221,743,568 (492)
Average weekly wages	$680 (313)

HOUSEHOLD INCOME LADDER

95th percentile	$195,163 (27)
80th percentile	$117,639 (16)
60th percentile	$82,263 (14)
40th percentile	$55,306 (12)
20th percentile	$31,863 (9)

CHILDREN ★★★★ (182)

Living with two parents	82.2% (5)
Older teens in school	78.2% (442)
Speak English very well	96.6% (430)
Poverty rate for children	12.3% (33)
No health insurance	11.4% (456)

DIVERSITY/EQUALITY ★★ (383)

Racial diversity index	27.3% (278)
Geographic diversity index	58.5% (130)
Top 20% share of income	44.7% (49)
Gender gap in earnings	52.1% (532)
White-collar gender gap	43.8% (473)

EDUCATION ★★★★★ (35)

Eighth grade or less	2.3% (161)
High school diplomas	91.5% (145)

Attended college	72.2% (19)
Bachelor's degrees	32.9% (36)
Advanced degrees	10.2% (53)

EMPLOYMENT ★★★★★ (11)

Average jobless rate	4.7% (54)
Self-employed workers	15.3% (15)
Management/financial jobs	14.1% (46)
Computer/engineering jobs	5.2% (26)
Health care jobs	5.3% (286)

GROWTH POTENTIAL ★★★★★ (9)

Children per senior	3.63 (5)
Median age	33.0 (59)
Moved from different state	3.9% (82)
Homes built since 2000	41.7% (1)
Construction jobs	8.6% (61)

HOUSING ★★★ (298)

Home vacancy rate	5.5% (60)
Home ownership rate	73.0% (151)
Housing diversity index	74.8% (547)
4 or more bedrooms	44.2% (1)
Affordability/income ratio	$4,765 (520)

INCOME ★★★★★ (15)

Poverty rate	10.0% (31)
Median household income	$66,486 (15)
Interest/dividends	20.6% (231)
Public assistance	5.8% (14)
Median fulltime earnings	$49,436 (15)

SENIORS ★★★★★ (1)

Seniors living alone	18.8% (8)
Poverty rate for seniors	4.7% (13)
Median income for seniors	n.a.
Seniors who work	28.2% (31)
Home ownership by seniors	92.0% (5)

STABILITY ★★★★★ (83)

25-39 age group	22.0% (20)
Born in state of residence	61.5% (413)
Same house as 1 year ago	83.7% (353)
Live and work in county	51.1% (537)
Married-couple households	64.7% (2)

TRANSPORTATION ★ (482)

Bicycle or walk to work	1.8% (409)
Carpool to work	9.7% (369)
Public transit to work	0.5% (178)
Commute <15 minutes	37.5% (387)
Commute >45 minutes	18.0% (499)

See pages 37-130 for explanations of statistics, stars, and ranks.

Helena, MT
(Jefferson and Lewis and Clark Counties, MT)

POPULATION

2010 census	74,801 (82)
2015 estimate	78,063 (74)
2010-2015 change	4.4% (54)
2020 projection	81,586 (67)
2030 projection	89,043 (53)

RACE

Whites	92.0% (135)
Blacks	0.4% (499)
Hispanics	2.8% (355)
Asians	0.6% (291)
Native Americans	2.1% (71)

AGE

0-17 years old	21.9% (344)
18-24 years old	8.2% (379)
25-39 years old	17.4% (269)
40-54 years old	20.3% (186)
55-64 years old	16.4% (30)
65+ years old	15.7% (318)

PRIVATE SECTOR

Businesses	2,882 (22)
Employees	26,525 (64)
Total wages	$1,024,055,796 (66)
Average weekly wages	$742 (173)

HOUSEHOLD INCOME LADDER

95th percentile	$163,702 (77)
80th percentile	$100,646 (55)
60th percentile	$68,841 (43)
40th percentile	$45,946 (37)
20th percentile	$26,688 (29)

CHILDREN ★★★★★ (96)

Living with two parents	70.3% (140)
Older teens in school	82.5% (296)
Speak English very well	99.9% (19)
Poverty rate for children	15.1% (65)
No health insurance	5.6% (225)

DIVERSITY/EQUALITY ★★★★★ (26)

Racial diversity index	15.2% (409)
Geographic diversity index	62.3% (100)
Top 20% share of income	44.4% (40)
Gender gap in earnings	23.4% (70)
White-collar gender gap	0.3% (2)

EDUCATION ★★★★★ (14)

Eighth grade or less	1.2% (42)
High school diplomas	95.2% (23)

Attended college	72.4% (17)
Bachelor's degrees	38.1% (19)
Advanced degrees	12.6% (29)

EMPLOYMENT ★★★★★ (3)

Average jobless rate	5.1% (69)
Self-employed workers	10.9% (120)
Management/financial jobs	19.5% (6)
Computer/engineering jobs	7.9% (3)
Health care jobs	5.9% (193)

GROWTH POTENTIAL ★★★★ (172)

Children per senior	1.40 (279)
Median age	42.0 (398)
Moved from different state	3.8% (89)
Homes built since 2000	19.1% (105)
Construction jobs	6.8% (204)

HOUSING ★★★★★ (71)

Home vacancy rate	4.1% (8)
Home ownership rate	71.5% (204)
Housing diversity index	85.1% (212)
4 or more bedrooms	23.4% (59)
Affordability/income ratio	$3,725 (481)

INCOME ★★★★★ (44)

Poverty rate	11.8% (82)
Median household income	$56,935 (39)
Interest/dividends	27.7% (41)
Public assistance	9.6% (56)
Median fulltime earnings	$42,847 (47)

SENIORS ★★★★★ (68)

Seniors living alone	24.7% (105)
Poverty rate for seniors	6.6% (68)
Median income for seniors	$46,104 (21)
Seniors who work	21.7% (138)
Home ownership by seniors	78.7% (427)

STABILITY ★★ (338)

25-39 age group	17.4% (269)
Born in state of residence	56.9% (444)
Same house as 1 year ago	82.4% (422)
Live and work in county	87.0% (100)
Married-couple households	50.8% (256)

TRANSPORTATION ★★★★★ (92)

Bicycle or walk to work	5.6% (69)
Carpool to work	11.8% (152)
Public transit to work	0.5% (178)
Commute <15 minutes	45.4% (242)
Commute >45 minutes	4.9% (31)

See pages 37-130 for explanations of statistics, stars, and ranks.

Hermiston-Pendleton, OR
(Morrow and Umatilla Counties, OR)

POPULATION		
2010 census	87,062 (53)	
2015 estimate	87,721 (51)	
2010-2015 change	0.8% (194)	
2020 projection	88,178 (50)	
2030 projection	89,262 (51)	

RACE		
Whites	67.0% (404)	
Blacks	0.7% (423)	
Hispanics	26.4% (54)	
Asians	0.9% (178)	
Native Americans	1.9% (72)	

AGE		
0-17 years old	26.3% (57)	
18-24 years old	9.4% (203)	
25-39 years old	18.6% (135)	
40-54 years old	19.5% (301)	
55-64 years old	12.6% (385)	
65+ years old	13.6% (454)	

PRIVATE SECTOR		
Businesses	2,291 (45)	
Employees	27,291 (57)	
Total wages	$1,019,111,061 (68)	
Average weekly wages	$718 (219)	

HOUSEHOLD INCOME LADDER		
95th percentile	$137,393 (318)	
80th percentile	$86,776 (214)	
60th percentile	$57,872 (186)	
40th percentile	$37,706 (188)	
20th percentile	$20,592 (202)	

CHILDREN	★★ (415)	
Living with two parents	60.7% (386)	
Older teens in school	83.7% (251)	
Speak English very well	91.3% (519)	
Poverty rate for children	26.5% (340)	
No health insurance	6.2% (262)	

DIVERSITY/EQUALITY	★★★★★ (59)	
Racial diversity index	48.0% (129)	
Geographic diversity index	68.7% (54)	
Top 20% share of income	45.5% (86)	
Gender gap in earnings	35.9% (337)	
White-collar gender gap	32.4% (369)	

EDUCATION	★★ (430)	
Eighth grade or less	8.4% (497)	
High school diplomas	82.3% (437)	
Attended college	53.5% (255)	
Bachelor's degrees	14.9% (424)	
Advanced degrees	5.5% (318)	

EMPLOYMENT	★★ (410)	
Average jobless rate	9.3% (387)	
Self-employed workers	8.6% (285)	
Management/financial jobs	11.0% (252)	
Computer/engineering jobs	3.1% (180)	
Health care jobs	3.8% (494)	

GROWTH POTENTIAL	★★★★ (199)	
Children per senior	1.94 (66)	
Median age	36.2 (122)	
Moved from different state	3.4% (118)	
Homes built since 2000	11.2% (351)	
Construction jobs	4.8% (480)	

HOUSING	★★★★ (208)	
Home vacancy rate	6.2% (109)	
Home ownership rate	63.6% (466)	
Housing diversity index	86.1% (51)	
4 or more bedrooms	17.1% (239)	
Affordability/income ratio	$2,907 (382)	

INCOME	★★★ (321)	
Poverty rate	17.4% (283)	
Median household income	$48,614 (156)	
Interest/dividends	18.9% (279)	
Public assistance	23.1% (498)	
Median fulltime earnings	$36,770 (305)	

SENIORS	★★★ (263)	
Seniors living alone	25.7% (154)	
Poverty rate for seniors	8.6% (234)	
Median income for seniors	$34,852 (195)	
Seniors who work	21.5% (144)	
Home ownership by seniors	76.4% (502)	

STABILITY	★★ (432)	
25-39 age group	18.6% (135)	
Born in state of residence	44.7% (505)	
Same house as 1 year ago	81.9% (450)	
Live and work in county	81.5% (197)	
Married-couple households	50.9% (253)	

TRANSPORTATION	★★★★ (136)	
Bicycle or walk to work	4.8% (98)	
Carpool to work	11.2% (211)	
Public transit to work	0.5% (178)	
Commute <15 minutes	47.1% (213)	
Commute >45 minutes	7.3% (95)	

See pages 37-130 for explanations of statistics, stars, and ranks.

Hilo, HI
(Hawaii County, HI)

POPULATION

2010 census	185,079 (3)
2015 estimate	196,428 (2)
2010-2015 change	6.1% (31)
2020 projection	210,431 (2)
2030 projection	242,308 (1)

RACE

Whites	30.8% (530)
Blacks	0.6% (438)
Hispanics	12.2% (125)
Asians	32.5% (2)
Native Americans	0.3% (231)

AGE

0-17 years old	22.3% (312)
18-24 years old	8.2% (379)
25-39 years old	18.1% (186)
40-54 years old	18.6% (412)
55-64 years old	16.0% (46)
65+ years old	16.8% (215)

PRIVATE SECTOR

Businesses	4,768 (4)
Employees	54,545 (4)
Total wages	$2,034,834,831 (7)
Average weekly wages	$717 (221)

HOUSEHOLD INCOME LADDER

95th percentile	$172,924 (50)
80th percentile	$100,744 (53)
60th percentile	$64,294 (81)
40th percentile	$39,663 (136)
20th percentile	$18,722 (281)

CHILDREN ★★ (385)

Living with two parents	61.5% (367)
Older teens in school	74.4% (505)
Speak English very well	97.0% (413)
Poverty rate for children	29.6% (392)
No health insurance	3.6% (93)

DIVERSITY/EQUALITY ★★★★★ (16)

Racial diversity index	72.9% (1)
Geographic diversity index	63.3% (90)
Top 20% share of income	48.9% (349)
Gender gap in earnings	21.3% (52)
White-collar gender gap	19.2% (197)

EDUCATION ★★★★★ (77)

Eighth grade or less	1.5% (72)
High school diplomas	93.0% (96)
Attended college	60.7% (117)
Bachelor's degrees	27.0% (87)
Advanced degrees	8.8% (92)

EMPLOYMENT ★★★★ (148)

Average jobless rate	8.1% (298)
Self-employed workers	11.9% (78)
Management/financial jobs	12.5% (119)
Computer/engineering jobs	3.1% (180)
Health care jobs	4.8% (369)

GROWTH POTENTIAL ★★★★ (115)

Children per senior	1.32 (334)
Median age	41.1 (362)
Moved from different state	3.7% (96)
Homes built since 2000	24.5% (39)
Construction jobs	7.5% (122)

HOUSING ★ (530)

Home vacancy rate	8.6% (260)
Home ownership rate	66.4% (409)
Housing diversity index	81.9% (461)
4 or more bedrooms	16.0% (293)
Affordability/income ratio	$5,790 (539)

INCOME ★★★ (239)

Poverty rate	19.5% (358)
Median household income	$52,108 (86)
Interest/dividends	22.1% (181)
Public assistance	19.9% (424)
Median fulltime earnings	$39,120 (174)

SENIORS ★★★★★ (45)

Seniors living alone	20.0% (14)
Poverty rate for seniors	9.2% (270)
Median income for seniors	$44,528 (32)
Seniors who work	20.7% (170)
Home ownership by seniors	81.1% (325)

STABILITY ★★★★ (117)

25-39 age group	18.1% (186)
Born in state of residence	57.4% (441)
Same house as 1 year ago	87.1% (192)
Live and work in county	98.2% (4)
Married-couple households	48.0% (378)

TRANSPORTATION ★★ (331)

Bicycle or walk to work	2.9% (265)
Carpool to work	13.3% (88)
Public transit to work	1.4% (46)
Commute <15 minutes	31.8% (503)
Commute >45 minutes	16.5% (468)

See pages 37-130 for explanations of statistics, stars, and ranks.

Hobbs, NM
(Lea County, NM)

POPULATION
2010 census	64,727 (122)
2015 estimate	71,180 (97)
2010-2015 change	10.0% (10)
2020 projection	76,821 (80)
2030 projection	89,113 (52)

RACE
Whites	39.4% (515)
Blacks	3.2% (220)
Hispanics	54.5% (21)
Asians	0.2% (509)
Native Americans	0.7% (136)

AGE
0-17 years old	29.8% (19)
18-24 years old	10.1% (157)
25-39 years old	21.1% (39)
40-54 years old	17.9% (454)
55-64 years old	10.3% (510)
65+ years old	10.7% (517)

PRIVATE SECTOR
Businesses	1,844 (83)
Employees	27,747 (56)
Total wages	$1,456,669,357 (20)
Average weekly wages	$1,010 (18)

HOUSEHOLD INCOME LADDER
95th percentile	$173,847 (47)
80th percentile	$105,131 (36)
60th percentile	$72,173 (30)
40th percentile	$44,682 (48)
20th percentile	$23,210 (89)

CHILDREN ★ (490)
Living with two parents	62.1% (349)
Older teens in school	71.7% (523)
Speak English very well	94.6% (485)
Poverty rate for children	21.8% (216)
No health insurance	12.0% (471)

DIVERSITY/EQUALITY ★★★ (242)
Racial diversity index	54.6% (59)
Geographic diversity index	71.0% (39)
Top 20% share of income	46.4% (158)
Gender gap in earnings	53.0% (537)
White-collar gender gap	46.9% (492)

EDUCATION ★ (523)
Eighth grade or less	9.9% (511)
High school diplomas	74.3% (528)
Attended college	41.9% (491)
Bachelor's degrees	13.1% (491)
Advanced degrees	4.9% (396)

EMPLOYMENT ★★ (414)
Average jobless rate	5.9% (115)
Self-employed workers	7.8% (355)
Management/financial jobs	10.6% (306)
Computer/engineering jobs	2.4% (336)
Health care jobs	3.4% (513)

GROWTH POTENTIAL ★★★★★ (42)
Children per senior	2.79 (23)
Median age	31.8 (46)
Moved from different state	3.3% (129)
Homes built since 2000	9.3% (420)
Construction jobs	7.8% (98)

HOUSING ★★ (336)
Home vacancy rate	12.3% (469)
Home ownership rate	69.5% (287)
Housing diversity index	84.6% (277)
4 or more bedrooms	12.9% (458)
Affordability/income ratio	$1,888 (29)

INCOME ★★★★ (145)
Poverty rate	15.0% (190)
Median household income	$57,533 (35)
Interest/dividends	11.1% (509)
Public assistance	13.0% (169)
Median fulltime earnings	$44,704 (33)

SENIORS ★★★★ (171)
Seniors living alone	23.5% (69)
Poverty rate for seniors	10.6% (350)
Median income for seniors	$31,765 (334)
Seniors who work	21.4% (148)
Home ownership by seniors	82.6% (242)

STABILITY ★★★★★ (18)
25-39 age group	21.1% (39)
Born in state of residence	43.2% (512)
Same house as 1 year ago	88.1% (126)
Live and work in county	93.7% (22)
Married-couple households	55.6% (56)

TRANSPORTATION ★★★★ (186)
Bicycle or walk to work	2.2% (358)
Carpool to work	11.4% (190)
Public transit to work	0.6% (141)
Commute <15 minutes	49.8% (159)
Commute >45 minutes	7.9% (126)

See pages 37-130 for explanations of statistics, stars, and ranks.

Hood River, OR
(Hood River County, OR)

POPULATION

2010 census	22,346 (505)
2015 estimate	23,137 (498)
2010-2015 change	3.5% (70)
2020 projection	23,985 (487)
2030 projection	25,827 (465)

RACE

Whites	64.8% (417)
Blacks	0.5% (466)
Hispanics	30.5% (48)
Asians	1.8% (60)
Native Americans	0.7% (136)

AGE

0-17 years old	24.8% (135)
18-24 years old	8.2% (379)
25-39 years old	18.2% (167)
40-54 years old	21.7% (42)
55-64 years old	13.2% (297)
65+ years old	14.0% (438)

PRIVATE SECTOR

Businesses	1,221 (201)
Employees	11,737 (317)
Total wages	$396,966,101 (343)
Average weekly wages	$650 (389)

HOUSEHOLD INCOME LADDER

95th percentile	$195,482 (26)
80th percentile	$98,262 (68)
60th percentile	$67,489 (52)
40th percentile	$47,332 (29)
20th percentile	$25,266 (47)

CHILDREN ★★ (369)

Living with two parents	72.6% (92)
Older teens in school	84.9% (201)
Speak English very well	86.7% (539)
Poverty rate for children	23.5% (255)
No health insurance	7.1% (324)

DIVERSITY/EQUALITY ★★★★★ (103)

Racial diversity index	48.6% (126)
Geographic diversity index	72.7% (24)
Top 20% share of income	48.7% (339)
Gender gap in earnings	29.3% (160)
White-collar gender gap	42.4% (466)

EDUCATION ★★★ (270)

Eighth grade or less	11.9% (526)
High school diplomas	80.0% (479)
Attended college	55.5% (213)
Bachelor's degrees	31.8% (41)
Advanced degrees	10.0% (61)

EMPLOYMENT ★★★★★ (23)

Average jobless rate	5.1% (69)
Self-employed workers	11.7% (86)
Management/financial jobs	12.7% (103)
Computer/engineering jobs	5.7% (19)
Health care jobs	6.8% (91)

GROWTH POTENTIAL ★★★★ (153)

Children per senior	1.78 (102)
Median age	39.4 (262)
Moved from different state	2.7% (179)
Homes built since 2000	19.7% (97)
Construction jobs	5.9% (345)

HOUSING ★★ (411)

Home vacancy rate	6.1% (104)
Home ownership rate	64.9% (437)
Housing diversity index	85.5% (143)
4 or more bedrooms	17.7% (220)
Affordability/income ratio	$5,755 (538)

INCOME ★★★★ (131)

Poverty rate	14.3% (168)
Median household income	$55,827 (48)
Interest/dividends	26.9% (53)
Public assistance	14.7% (243)
Median fulltime earnings	$35,437 (364)

SENIORS ★★★★ (155)

Seniors living alone	29.4% (394)
Poverty rate for seniors	4.6% (12)
Median income for seniors	$45,403 (25)
Seniors who work	23.1% (107)
Home ownership by seniors	74.5% (531)

STABILITY ★★★★ (160)

25-39 age group	18.2% (167)
Born in state of residence	44.1% (507)
Same house as 1 year ago	92.2% (13)
Live and work in county	83.9% (146)
Married-couple households	51.4% (231)

TRANSPORTATION ★★★★★ (35)

Bicycle or walk to work	8.8% (23)
Carpool to work	11.2% (211)
Public transit to work	0.1% (441)
Commute <15 minutes	57.2% (68)
Commute >45 minutes	6.1% (59)

See pages 37-130 for explanations of statistics, stars, and ranks.

Jackson, WY-ID
(Teton County, WY, and Teton County, ID)

POPULATION	
2010 census	31,464 (426)
2015 estimate	33,689 (397)
2010-2015 change	7.1% (20)
2020 projection	36,403 (364)
2030 projection	42,540 (291)

RACE	
Whites	81.1% (316)
Blacks	0.2% (537)
Hispanics	15.9% (99)
Asians	1.3% (112)
Native Americans	0.3% (231)

AGE	
0-17 years old	22.0% (335)
18-24 years old	6.0% (546)
25-39 years old	27.2% (4)
40-54 years old	21.9% (38)
55-64 years old	12.7% (375)
65+ years old	10.3% (522)

PRIVATE SECTOR	
Businesses	2,680 (28)
Employees	19,662 (130)
Total wages	$778,797,411 (122)
Average weekly wages	$762 (139)

HOUSEHOLD INCOME LADDER	
95th percentile	>$250,000 (1)
80th percentile	$125,194 (9)
60th percentile	$82,746 (13)
40th percentile	$56,143 (10)
20th percentile	$31,703 (11)

CHILDREN	★★★★ (147)
Living with two parents	76.2% (39)
Older teens in school	82.5% (296)
Speak English very well	96.2% (443)
Poverty rate for children	10.6% (19)
No health insurance	9.4% (406)

DIVERSITY/EQUALITY	★★★★★ (89)
Racial diversity index	31.7% (240)
Geographic diversity index	81.8% (2)
Top 20% share of income	51.4% (483)
Gender gap in earnings	23.7% (75)
White-collar gender gap	28.6% (317)

EDUCATION	★★★★★ (16)
Eighth grade or less	2.6% (185)
High school diplomas	94.4% (44)
Attended college	75.3% (9)
Bachelor's degrees	50.0% (5)
Advanced degrees	12.2% (35)

EMPLOYMENT	★★★★★ (49)
Average jobless rate	4.3% (38)
Self-employed workers	12.5% (56)
Management/financial jobs	19.5% (6)
Computer/engineering jobs	2.6% (288)
Health care jobs	4.1% (462)

GROWTH POTENTIAL	★★★★★ (10)
Children per senior	2.14 (45)
Median age	36.8 (138)
Moved from different state	7.2% (20)
Homes built since 2000	28.2% (17)
Construction jobs	10.0% (17)

HOUSING	★ (531)
Home vacancy rate	9.8% (341)
Home ownership rate	64.0% (454)
Housing diversity index	79.8% (520)
4 or more bedrooms	24.0% (51)
Affordability/income ratio	$6,031 (542)

INCOME	★★★★★ (6)
Poverty rate	8.5% (14)
Median household income	$68,318 (12)
Interest/dividends	30.8% (15)
Public assistance	3.7% (6)
Median fulltime earnings	$44,153 (37)

SENIORS	★★★★★ (5)
Seniors living alone	25.5% (142)
Poverty rate for seniors	3.3% (3)
Median income for seniors	$65,134 (5)
Seniors who work	34.1% (8)
Home ownership by seniors	83.7% (190)

STABILITY	★★★★ (154)
25-39 age group	27.2% (4)
Born in state of residence	26.2% (549)
Same house as 1 year ago	84.7% (314)
Live and work in county	85.1% (134)
Married-couple households	51.7% (212)

TRANSPORTATION	★★★★★ (7)
Bicycle or walk to work	11.2% (9)
Carpool to work	10.7% (260)
Public transit to work	6.3% (6)
Commute <15 minutes	52.3% (117)
Commute >45 minutes	9.6% (210)

See pages 37-130 for explanations of statistics, stars, and ranks.

Juneau, AK
(Juneau City and Borough, AK)

POPULATION	
2010 census	31,275 (428)
2015 estimate	32,756 (410)
2010-2015 change	4.7% (45)
2020 projection	33,325 (403)
2030 projection	34,368 (385)

RACE	
Whites	66.0% (409)
Blacks	1.2% (361)
Hispanics	6.1% (218)
Asians	7.3% (9)
Native Americans	11.8% (18)

AGE	
0-17 years old	22.6% (291)
18-24 years old	9.0% (265)
25-39 years old	22.2% (19)
40-54 years old	22.0% (31)
55-64 years old	14.6% (107)
65+ years old	9.7% (535)

PRIVATE SECTOR	
Businesses	1,056 (256)
Employees	10,966 (343)
Total wages	$483,468,525 (256)
Average weekly wages	$848 (52)

HOUSEHOLD INCOME LADDER	
95th percentile	$225,829 (9)
80th percentile	$140,078 (4)
60th percentile	$99,873 (4)
40th percentile	$72,702 (3)
20th percentile	$43,058 (2)

CHILDREN	★★★★ (168)
Living with two parents	64.7% (278)
Older teens in school	87.2% (130)
Speak English very well	98.5% (287)
Poverty rate for children	11.0% (21)
No health insurance	11.1% (450)

DIVERSITY/EQUALITY	★★★★★ (5)
Racial diversity index	53.6% (73)
Geographic diversity index	74.7% (18)
Top 20% share of income	43.7% (15)
Gender gap in earnings	25.2% (90)
White-collar gender gap	15.8% (162)

EDUCATION	★★★★★ (13)
Eighth grade or less	1.3% (52)
High school diplomas	95.1% (27)
Attended college	73.9% (12)
Bachelor's degrees	37.4% (21)
Advanced degrees	12.6% (29)

EMPLOYMENT	★★★★★ (18)
Average jobless rate	5.2% (76)
Self-employed workers	9.2% (231)
Management/financial jobs	20.4% (5)
Computer/engineering jobs	7.6% (5)
Health care jobs	4.6% (401)

GROWTH POTENTIAL	★★★★★ (94)
Children per senior	2.32 (34)
Median age	37.0 (143)
Moved from different state	4.8% (61)
Homes built since 2000	9.6% (404)
Construction jobs	6.7% (219)

HOUSING	★★ (402)
Home vacancy rate	4.7% (22)
Home ownership rate	63.7% (462)
Housing diversity index	81.4% (479)
4 or more bedrooms	17.8% (215)
Affordability/income ratio	$3,773 (488)

INCOME	★★★★★ (2)
Poverty rate	6.6% (2)
Median household income	$85,746 (4)
Interest/dividends	50.6% (1)
Public assistance	10.4% (76)
Median fulltime earnings	$54,253 (4)

SENIORS	★★★★★ (9)
Seniors living alone	22.3% (45)
Poverty rate for seniors	2.2% (1)
Median income for seniors	$69,148 (2)
Seniors who work	34.4% (7)
Home ownership by seniors	76.3% (505)

STABILITY	★★★★ (141)
25-39 age group	22.2% (19)
Born in state of residence	39.8% (523)
Same house as 1 year ago	81.5% (460)
Live and work in county	99.1% (1)
Married-couple households	49.4% (330)

TRANSPORTATION	★★★★★ (3)
Bicycle or walk to work	7.3% (39)
Carpool to work	16.3% (30)
Public transit to work	4.5% (10)
Commute <15 minutes	51.6% (127)
Commute >45 minutes	2.5% (3)

See pages 37-130 for explanations of statistics, stars, and ranks.

Kalispell, MT
(Flathead County, MT)

POPULATION

2010 census	90,928 (44)
2015 estimate	96,165 (36)
2010-2015 change	5.8% (34)
2020 projection	102,413 (27)
2030 projection	116,045 (20)

RACE

Whites	93.3% (98)
Blacks	0.3% (519)
Hispanics	2.6% (378)
Asians	0.5% (355)
Native Americans	1.5% (80)

AGE

0-17 years old	22.6% (291)
18-24 years old	7.6% (468)
25-39 years old	17.3% (280)
40-54 years old	19.9% (250)
55-64 years old	16.1% (42)
65+ years old	16.4% (255)

PRIVATE SECTOR

Businesses	4,239 (10)
Employees	35,806 (18)
Total wages	$1,346,483,002 (27)
Average weekly wages	$723 (211)

HOUSEHOLD INCOME LADDER

95th percentile	$160,181 (96)
80th percentile	$87,333 (194)
60th percentile	$58,262 (175)
40th percentile	$38,611 (166)
20th percentile	$21,443 (167)

CHILDREN ★★★★ (167)

Living with two parents	74.5% (61)
Older teens in school	77.1% (471)
Speak English very well	99.7% (57)
Poverty rate for children	18.2% (128)
No health insurance	6.9% (307)

DIVERSITY/EQUALITY ★★★★ (135)

Racial diversity index	12.8% (447)
Geographic diversity index	69.3% (49)
Top 20% share of income	49.5% (397)
Gender gap in earnings	30.7% (189)
White-collar gender gap	8.7% (76)

EDUCATION ★★★★★ (60)

Eighth grade or less	0.5% (2)
High school diplomas	95.3% (21)
Attended college	65.5% (52)
Bachelor's degrees	28.3% (70)
Advanced degrees	7.3% (157)

EMPLOYMENT ★★★★★ (31)

Average jobless rate	7.0% (196)
Self-employed workers	14.4% (29)
Management/financial jobs	13.8% (54)
Computer/engineering jobs	3.6% (112)
Health care jobs	6.8% (91)

GROWTH POTENTIAL ★★★★★ (61)

Children per senior	1.38 (291)
Median age	42.1 (408)
Moved from different state	4.7% (64)
Homes built since 2000	24.3% (40)
Construction jobs	9.5% (31)

HOUSING ★★★ (330)

Home vacancy rate	6.0% (95)
Home ownership rate	70.9% (232)
Housing diversity index	83.7% (378)
4 or more bedrooms	18.6% (174)
Affordability/income ratio	$4,838 (521)

INCOME ★★★★★ (79)

Poverty rate	13.3% (130)
Median household income	$47,851 (180)
Interest/dividends	30.5% (19)
Public assistance	9.4% (51)
Median fulltime earnings	$37,726 (234)

SENIORS ★★★★ (129)

Seniors living alone	25.0% (118)
Poverty rate for seniors	7.6% (145)
Median income for seniors	$38,297 (86)
Seniors who work	20.1% (192)
Home ownership by seniors	81.1% (325)

STABILITY ★★★★ (123)

25-39 age group	17.3% (280)
Born in state of residence	47.0% (496)
Same house as 1 year ago	87.3% (181)
Live and work in county	95.5% (13)
Married-couple households	54.6% (84)

TRANSPORTATION ★★★ (246)

Bicycle or walk to work	4.2% (142)
Carpool to work	8.0% (493)
Public transit to work	0.7% (119)
Commute <15 minutes	42.2% (294)
Commute >45 minutes	6.6% (74)

See pages 37-130 for explanations of statistics, stars, and ranks.

Kapaa, HI
(Kauai County, HI)

POPULATION

2010 census	67,091 (110)
2015 estimate	71,735 (96)
2010-2015 change	6.9% (22)
2020 projection	76,397 (83)
2030 projection	86,938 (59)

RACE

Whites	30.1% (531)
Blacks	0.6% (438)
Hispanics	10.5% (146)
Asians	42.7% (1)
Native Americans	0.2% (300)

AGE

0-17 years old	22.3% (312)
18-24 years old	7.4% (489)
25-39 years old	18.0% (201)
40-54 years old	20.4% (169)
55-64 years old	15.1% (74)
65+ years old	16.7% (225)

PRIVATE SECTOR

Businesses	2,269 (47)
Employees	26,065 (65)
Total wages	$1,029,894,973 (65)
Average weekly wages	$760 (145)

HOUSEHOLD INCOME LADDER

95th percentile	$196,588 (24)
80th percentile	$115,478 (19)
60th percentile	$79,396 (18)
40th percentile	$52,065 (17)
20th percentile	$28,322 (21)

CHILDREN ★★★★ (194)

Living with two parents	68.9% (168)
Older teens in school	73.9% (511)
Speak English very well	97.4% (395)
Poverty rate for children	12.5% (42)
No health insurance	3.9% (111)

DIVERSITY/EQUALITY ★★★★★ (1)

Racial diversity index	69.1% (3)
Geographic diversity index	66.2% (68)
Top 20% share of income	45.6% (98)
Gender gap in earnings	11.3% (11)
White-collar gender gap	7.7% (60)

EDUCATION ★★★★★ (73)

Eighth grade or less	2.4% (169)
High school diplomas	94.3% (47)
Attended college	63.4% (78)
Bachelor's degrees	27.6% (79)
Advanced degrees	8.2% (114)

EMPLOYMENT ★★★★ (146)

Average jobless rate	5.4% (89)
Self-employed workers	10.8% (125)
Management/financial jobs	11.7% (185)
Computer/engineering jobs	3.2% (158)
Health care jobs	4.6% (401)

GROWTH POTENTIAL ★★★★ (210)

Children per senior	1.33 (325)
Median age	41.6 (387)
Moved from different state	3.4% (118)
Homes built since 2000	15.6% (189)
Construction jobs	7.4% (134)

HOUSING ★ (547)

Home vacancy rate	11.6% (441)
Home ownership rate	61.6% (484)
Housing diversity index	82.4% (444)
4 or more bedrooms	16.5% (267)
Affordability/income ratio	$7,382 (550)

INCOME ★★★★★ (31)

Poverty rate	10.7% (52)
Median household income	$65,101 (18)
Interest/dividends	31.4% (10)
Public assistance	11.6% (116)
Median fulltime earnings	$40,094 (138)

SENIORS ★★★★★ (18)

Seniors living alone	17.2% (2)
Poverty rate for seniors	6.9% (84)
Median income for seniors	$50,357 (12)
Seniors who work	22.1% (129)
Home ownership by seniors	79.0% (417)

STABILITY ★★★★★ (31)

25-39 age group	18.0% (201)
Born in state of residence	54.6% (465)
Same house as 1 year ago	88.0% (133)
Live and work in county	99.1% (1)
Married-couple households	54.7% (80)

TRANSPORTATION ★★★ (313)

Bicycle or walk to work	4.1% (147)
Carpool to work	10.9% (239)
Public transit to work	1.1% (58)
Commute <15 minutes	33.2% (473)
Commute >45 minutes	12.8% (346)

See pages 37-130 for explanations of statistics, stars, and ranks.

Ketchikan, AK
(Ketchikan Gateway Borough, AK)

POPULATION	
2010 census	13,477 (551)
2015 estimate	13,709 (548)
2010-2015 change	1.7% (150)
2020 projection	13,657 (548)
2030 projection	13,503 (548)

RACE	
Whites	65.0% (416)
Blacks	0.4% (499)
Hispanics	4.8% (256)
Asians	7.4% (8)
Native Americans	13.6% (15)

AGE	
0-17 years old	23.0% (259)
18-24 years old	8.9% (282)
25-39 years old	19.6% (71)
40-54 years old	21.4% (67)
55-64 years old	15.5% (59)
65+ years old	11.5% (499)

PRIVATE SECTOR	
Businesses	572 (488)
Employees	5,328 (522)
Total wages	$221,099,104 (493)
Average weekly wages	$798 (93)

HOUSEHOLD INCOME LADDER	
95th percentile	$201,938 (16)
80th percentile	$117,281 (17)
60th percentile	$80,804 (17)
40th percentile	$51,075 (19)
20th percentile	$29,797 (15)

CHILDREN	★★ (362)
Living with two parents	68.4% (181)
Older teens in school	68.1% (540)
Speak English very well	99.6% (77)
Poverty rate for children	15.6% (71)
No health insurance	10.7% (441)

DIVERSITY/EQUALITY	★★★★★ (4)
Racial diversity index	54.3% (66)
Geographic diversity index	72.7% (24)
Top 20% share of income	45.3% (76)
Gender gap in earnings	24.5% (81)
White-collar gender gap	6.1% (48)

EDUCATION	★★★★ (120)
Eighth grade or less	1.5% (72)
High school diplomas	93.0% (96)
Attended college	59.4% (141)
Bachelor's degrees	22.8% (135)
Advanced degrees	7.5% (142)

EMPLOYMENT	★★★ (224)
Average jobless rate	7.9% (286)
Self-employed workers	9.3% (224)
Management/financial jobs	12.0% (156)
Computer/engineering jobs	3.2% (158)
Health care jobs	5.0% (339)

GROWTH POTENTIAL	★★★★★ (74)
Children per senior	2.00 (61)
Median age	38.7 (211)
Moved from different state	5.3% (44)
Homes built since 2000	8.1% (465)
Construction jobs	9.1% (40)

HOUSING	★ (472)
Home vacancy rate	8.8% (273)
Home ownership rate	58.8% (514)
Housing diversity index	85.4% (156)
4 or more bedrooms	16.1% (286)
Affordability/income ratio	$3,932 (492)

INCOME	★★★★★ (16)
Poverty rate	12.1% (88)
Median household income	$64,222 (20)
Interest/dividends	47.8% (2)
Public assistance	15.2% (266)
Median fulltime earnings	$48,190 (19)

SENIORS	★★★★★ (63)
Seniors living alone	29.2% (381)
Poverty rate for seniors	3.5% (4)
Median income for seniors	$44,750 (28)
Seniors who work	31.8% (14)
Home ownership by seniors	74.1% (534)

STABILITY	★★ (403)
25-39 age group	19.6% (71)
Born in state of residence	41.4% (518)
Same house as 1 year ago	79.5% (504)
Live and work in county	98.8% (3)
Married-couple households	46.7% (427)

TRANSPORTATION	★★★★★ (1)
Bicycle or walk to work	11.1% (10)
Carpool to work	18.4% (13)
Public transit to work	3.0% (13)
Commute <15 minutes	60.3% (45)
Commute >45 minutes	1.2% (1)

See pages 37-130 for explanations of statistics, stars, and ranks.

Klamath Falls, OR
(Klamath County, OR)

POPULATION

2010 census	66,380 (115)
2015 estimate	66,016 (116)
2010-2015 change	-0.5% (292)
2020 projection	65,673 (119)
2030 projection	65,105 (128)

RACE

Whites	79.7% (328)
Blacks	0.8% (404)
Hispanics	11.6% (130)
Asians	1.2% (125)
Native Americans	3.1% (49)

AGE

0-17 years old	21.7% (359)
18-24 years old	9.0% (265)
25-39 years old	16.5% (403)
40-54 years old	18.9% (376)
55-64 years old	15.1% (74)
65+ years old	18.7% (97)

PRIVATE SECTOR

Businesses	1,752 (91)
Employees	17,296 (163)
Total wages	$592,761,864 (192)
Average weekly wages	$659 (368)

HOUSEHOLD INCOME LADDER

95th percentile	$135,780 (346)
80th percentile	$79,658 (377)
60th percentile	$49,889 (387)
40th percentile	$32,363 (347)
20th percentile	$17,645 (335)

CHILDREN ★★★★ (210)

Living with two parents	64.0% (297)
Older teens in school	84.5% (220)
Speak English very well	97.8% (361)
Poverty rate for children	24.4% (284)
No health insurance	4.4% (145)

DIVERSITY/EQUALITY ★★★★★ (81)

Racial diversity index	34.9% (213)
Geographic diversity index	67.0% (61)
Top 20% share of income	47.7% (273)
Gender gap in earnings	26.9% (116)
White-collar gender gap	28.2% (314)

EDUCATION ★★★★ (170)

Eighth grade or less	3.1% (238)
High school diplomas	88.8% (240)

Attended college	60.7% (117)
Bachelor's degrees	20.5% (207)
Advanced degrees	7.2% (164)

EMPLOYMENT ★★ (372)

Average jobless rate	12.4% (506)
Self-employed workers	9.0% (254)
Management/financial jobs	11.2% (229)
Computer/engineering jobs	4.1% (70)
Health care jobs	4.8% (369)

GROWTH POTENTIAL ★★ (440)

Children per senior	1.16 (439)
Median age	42.5 (432)
Moved from different state	3.5% (109)
Homes built since 2000	14.2% (231)
Construction jobs	4.3% (514)

HOUSING ★★ (419)

Home vacancy rate	9.6% (327)
Home ownership rate	64.8% (438)
Housing diversity index	86.1% (51)
4 or more bedrooms	13.7% (415)
Affordability/income ratio	$3,756 (484)

INCOME ★★ (412)

Poverty rate	19.3% (348)
Median household income	$40,336 (372)
Interest/dividends	21.1% (210)
Public assistance	27.3% (527)
Median fulltime earnings	$35,663 (353)

SENIORS ★★★★ (216)

Seniors living alone	25.4% (132)
Poverty rate for seniors	8.0% (177)
Median income for seniors	$35,585 (167)
Seniors who work	14.4% (485)
Home ownership by seniors	83.1% (217)

STABILITY ★ (458)

25-39 age group	16.5% (403)
Born in state of residence	47.3% (494)
Same house as 1 year ago	82.0% (439)
Live and work in county	93.5% (26)
Married-couple households	48.2% (373)

TRANSPORTATION ★★★★ (119)

Bicycle or walk to work	5.2% (85)
Carpool to work	10.9% (239)
Public transit to work	0.3% (291)
Commute <15 minutes	51.0% (131)
Commute >45 minutes	7.3% (95)

See pages 37-130 for explanations of statistics, stars, and ranks.

La Grande, OR
(Union County, OR)

POPULATION

2010 census	25,748 (476)
2015 estimate	25,790 (475)
2010-2015 change	0.2% (241)
2020 projection	25,929 (471)
2030 projection	26,258 (463)

RACE

Whites	89.7% (189)
Blacks	0.6% (438)
Hispanics	4.4% (270)
Asians	2.2% (40)
Native Americans	0.8% (125)

AGE

0-17 years old	22.2% (320)
18-24 years old	11.5% (100)
25-39 years old	16.4% (411)
40-54 years old	17.3% (487)
55-64 years old	14.6% (107)
65+ years old	18.0% (122)

PRIVATE SECTOR

Businesses	873 (329)
Employees	7,662 (452)
Total wages	$266,705,985 (458)
Average weekly wages	$669 (336)

HOUSEHOLD INCOME LADDER

95th percentile	$150,417 (157)
80th percentile	$84,386 (265)
60th percentile	$54,081 (278)
40th percentile	$33,860 (294)
20th percentile	$17,900 (324)

CHILDREN ★★★★ (205)

Living with two parents	74.6% (59)
Older teens in school	83.3% (263)
Speak English very well	98.9% (226)
Poverty rate for children	22.9% (246)
No health insurance	10.0% (424)

DIVERSITY/EQUALITY ★ (505)

Racial diversity index	19.2% (358)
Geographic diversity index	61.2% (117)
Top 20% share of income	50.0% (427)
Gender gap in earnings	44.6% (496)
White-collar gender gap	46.8% (491)

EDUCATION ★★★★★ (102)

Eighth grade or less	2.0% (126)
High school diplomas	93.4% (82)
Attended college	62.0% (93)
Bachelor's degrees	23.8% (124)
Advanced degrees	7.8% (129)

EMPLOYMENT ★★★★ (152)

Average jobless rate	7.1% (208)
Self-employed workers	11.9% (78)
Management/financial jobs	10.5% (318)
Computer/engineering jobs	4.0% (76)
Health care jobs	4.8% (369)

GROWTH POTENTIAL ★★ (354)

Children per senior	1.23 (393)
Median age	40.0 (303)
Moved from different state	3.4% (118)
Homes built since 2000	11.4% (338)
Construction jobs	5.5% (404)

HOUSING ★★ (438)

Home vacancy rate	8.4% (245)
Home ownership rate	63.8% (460)
Housing diversity index	84.1% (337)
4 or more bedrooms	15.5% (324)
Affordability/income ratio	$3,724 (480)

INCOME ★★★ (290)

Poverty rate	18.6% (322)
Median household income	$43,822 (267)
Interest/dividends	24.4% (119)
Public assistance	22.3% (482)
Median fulltime earnings	$37,760 (231)

SENIORS ★★★ (306)

Seniors living alone	25.4% (132)
Poverty rate for seniors	9.3% (276)
Median income for seniors	$33,508 (259)
Seniors who work	16.7% (360)
Home ownership by seniors	79.4% (400)

STABILITY ★★ (365)

25-39 age group	16.4% (411)
Born in state of residence	55.1% (463)
Same house as 1 year ago	81.6% (456)
Live and work in county	93.4% (27)
Married-couple households	51.4% (231)

TRANSPORTATION ★★★★★ (14)

Bicycle or walk to work	10.9% (12)
Carpool to work	10.3% (299)
Public transit to work	1.0% (69)
Commute <15 minutes	59.9% (48)
Commute >45 minutes	6.6% (74)

See pages 37-130 for explanations of statistics, stars, and ranks.

Laramie, WY
(Albany County, WY)

POPULATION			Attended college	82.5% (2)
2010 census	36,299 (371)		Bachelor's degrees	50.9% (4)
2015 estimate	37,956 (342)		Advanced degrees	21.5% (4)
2010-2015 change	4.6% (47)		**EMPLOYMENT**	★★★★★ **(58)**
2020 projection	39,294 (323)		Average jobless rate	4.7% (54)
2030 projection	42,142 (293)		Self-employed workers	11.2% (108)
			Management/financial jobs	11.0% (252)
RACE			Computer/engineering jobs	6.3% (11)
Whites	83.4% (286)		Health care jobs	5.0% (339)
Blacks	1.3% (351)			
Hispanics	9.1% (164)		**GROWTH POTENTIAL**	★★★★★ **(23)**
Asians	3.1% (22)		Children per senior	1.82 (90)
Native Americans	0.7% (136)		Median age	26.6 (9)
			Moved from different state	10.2% (5)
AGE			Homes built since 2000	22.6% (59)
0-17 years old	16.6% (543)		Construction jobs	5.4% (413)
18-24 years old	29.5% (7)			
25-39 years old	20.9% (44)		**HOUSING**	★ **(448)**
40-54 years old	13.8% (547)		Home vacancy rate	6.8% (151)
55-64 years old	10.1% (519)		Home ownership rate	48.5% (549)
65+ years old	9.1% (543)		Housing diversity index	85.3% (170)
			4 or more bedrooms	25.0% (43)
PRIVATE SECTOR			Affordability/income ratio	$5,045 (526)
Businesses	1,209 (205)			
Employees	9,690 (384)		**INCOME**	★★★★ **(174)**
Total wages	$310,063,285 (423)		Poverty rate	26.9% (504)
Average weekly wages	$615 (456)		Median household income	$42,834 (294)
			Interest/dividends	27.1% (50)
HOUSEHOLD INCOME LADDER			Public assistance	4.6% (10)
95th percentile	$166,528 (66)		Median fulltime earnings	$38,801 (186)
80th percentile	$89,667 (159)			
60th percentile	$53,022 (296)		**SENIORS**	★★★★★ **(52)**
40th percentile	$30,504 (401)		Seniors living alone	29.0% (366)
20th percentile	$14,808 (458)		Poverty rate for seniors	8.0% (177)
			Median income for seniors	$47,112 (19)
CHILDREN	★★★★★ **(10)**		Seniors who work	28.2% (31)
Living with two parents	78.3% (18)		Home ownership by seniors	81.7% (294)
Older teens in school	97.3% (9)			
Speak English very well	98.3% (312)		**STABILITY**	★ **(537)**
Poverty rate for children	21.5% (206)		25-39 age group	20.9% (44)
No health insurance	3.1% (64)		Born in state of residence	38.2% (526)
			Same house as 1 year ago	68.4% (547)
DIVERSITY/EQUALITY	★★★★ **(161)**		Live and work in county	93.6% (24)
Racial diversity index	29.4% (259)		Married-couple households	39.2% (534)
Geographic diversity index	74.3% (20)			
Top 20% share of income	52.3% (508)		**TRANSPORTATION**	★★★★★ **(4)**
Gender gap in earnings	36.1% (343)		Bicycle or walk to work	15.5% (5)
White-collar gender gap	8.8% (77)		Carpool to work	11.3% (201)
			Public transit to work	2.8% (16)
EDUCATION	★★★★★ **(1)**		Commute <15 minutes	72.4% (3)
Eighth grade or less	0.5% (2)		Commute >45 minutes	4.8% (29)
High school diplomas	97.6% (1)			

See pages 37-130 for explanations of statistics, stars, and ranks.

Las Vegas, NM
(San Miguel County, NM)

POPULATION

2010 census	29,393 (440)
2015 estimate	27,967 (452)
2010-2015 change	-4.9% (531)
2020 projection	26,485 (464)
2030 projection	23,658 (485)

RACE

Whites	19.0% (542)
Blacks	1.3% (351)
Hispanics	76.9% (8)
Asians	1.0% (158)
Native Americans	0.9% (115)

AGE

0-17 years old	20.6% (423)
18-24 years old	11.3% (106)
25-39 years old	14.3% (535)
40-54 years old	21.7% (42)
55-64 years old	14.8% (91)
65+ years old	17.4% (165)

PRIVATE SECTOR

Businesses	551 (498)
Employees	5,014 (528)
Total wages	$118,715,195 (546)
Average weekly wages	$455 (550)

HOUSEHOLD INCOME LADDER

95th percentile	$110,605 (547)
80th percentile	$63,960 (535)
60th percentile	$37,034 (541)
40th percentile	$21,614 (541)
20th percentile	$10,010 (544)

CHILDREN ★ (539)

Living with two parents	43.9% (530)
Older teens in school	86.6% (144)
Speak English very well	85.5% (544)
Poverty rate for children	38.7% (505)
No health insurance	9.7% (412)

DIVERSITY/EQUALITY ★ (487)

Racial diversity index	37.2% (202)
Geographic diversity index	45.4% (274)
Top 20% share of income	53.0% (520)
Gender gap in earnings	25.7% (100)
White-collar gender gap	55.1% (528)

EDUCATION ★★★★ (216)

Eighth grade or less	2.9% (217)
High school diplomas	87.2% (299)
Attended college	56.9% (188)
Bachelor's degrees	18.4% (268)
Advanced degrees	7.2% (164)

EMPLOYMENT ★★ (335)

Average jobless rate	6.4% (147)
Self-employed workers	5.8% (508)
Management/financial jobs	12.9% (92)
Computer/engineering jobs	3.0% (193)
Health care jobs	4.1% (462)

GROWTH POTENTIAL ★★ (429)

Children per senior	1.18 (427)
Median age	42.5 (432)
Moved from different state	2.5% (203)
Homes built since 2000	10.4% (381)
Construction jobs	6.2% (295)

HOUSING ★ (533)

Home vacancy rate	17.9% (546)
Home ownership rate	72.1% (181)
Housing diversity index	85.3% (170)
4 or more bedrooms	10.2% (529)
Affordability/income ratio	$4,145 (503)

INCOME ★ (526)

Poverty rate	29.7% (523)
Median household income	$29,237 (537)
Interest/dividends	9.6% (533)
Public assistance	24.2% (510)
Median fulltime earnings	$34,170 (416)

SENIORS ★ (526)

Seniors living alone	31.5% (498)
Poverty rate for seniors	19.1% (533)
Median income for seniors	$23,356 (518)
Seniors who work	14.4% (485)
Home ownership by seniors	86.1% (93)

STABILITY ★ (502)

25-39 age group	14.3% (535)
Born in state of residence	72.7% (265)
Same house as 1 year ago	91.8% (17)
Live and work in county	74.5% (303)
Married-couple households	31.9% (548)

TRANSPORTATION ★★★ (241)

Bicycle or walk to work	4.9% (96)
Carpool to work	10.4% (289)
Public transit to work	0.4% (219)
Commute <15 minutes	53.6% (100)
Commute >45 minutes	16.0% (453)

See pages 37-130 for explanations of statistics, stars, and ranks.

Los Alamos, NM
(Los Alamos County, NM)

POPULATION

2010 census	17,950 (532)
2015 estimate	17,785 (534)
2010-2015 change	-0.9% (323)
2020 projection	17,174 (538)
2030 projection	15,946 (540)

RACE

Whites	73.9% (365)
Blacks	0.5% (466)
Hispanics	16.2% (94)
Asians	6.8% (10)
Native Americans	1.0% (103)

AGE

0-17 years old	23.5% (232)
18-24 years old	5.7% (550)
25-39 years old	16.3% (418)
40-54 years old	22.8% (10)
55-64 years old	15.1% (74)
65+ years old	16.6% (237)

PRIVATE SECTOR

Businesses	387 (536)
Employees	13,574 (254)
Total wages	$1,111,845,915 (52)
Average weekly wages	$1,575 (1)

HOUSEHOLD INCOME LADDER

95th percentile	>$250,000 (1)
80th percentile	$176,866 (2)
60th percentile	$121,215 (1)
40th percentile	$84,845 (1)
20th percentile	$41,682 (3)

CHILDREN ★★★★★ (3)

Living with two parents	84.3% (2)
Older teens in school	94.7% (15)
Speak English very well	95.4% (470)
Poverty rate for children	7.7% (4)
No health insurance	3.6% (93)

DIVERSITY/EQUALITY ★★★★★ (76)

Racial diversity index	42.3% (171)
Geographic diversity index	80.6% (6)
Top 20% share of income	43.0% (6)
Gender gap in earnings	56.3% (546)
White-collar gender gap	26.3% (290)

EDUCATION ★★★★★ (4)

Eighth grade or less	1.5% (72)
High school diplomas	97.1% (5)
Attended college	87.5% (1)
Bachelor's degrees	65.0% (1)
Advanced degrees	39.8% (1)

EMPLOYMENT ★★★★★ (27)

Average jobless rate	3.5% (20)
Self-employed workers	4.5% (547)
Management/financial jobs	23.3% (1)
Computer/engineering jobs	30.9% (1)
Health care jobs	5.6% (240)

GROWTH POTENTIAL ★ (481)

Children per senior	1.41 (269)
Median age	43.5 (464)
Moved from different state	5.1% (50)
Homes built since 2000	11.7% (324)
Construction jobs	1.1% (551)

HOUSING ★★★★★ (21)

Home vacancy rate	4.4% (14)
Home ownership rate	74.2% (110)
Housing diversity index	83.7% (378)
4 or more bedrooms	26.3% (34)
Affordability/income ratio	$2,690 (323)

INCOME ★★★★★ (1)

Poverty rate	6.1% (1)
Median household income	$101,934 (1)
Interest/dividends	46.4% (3)
Public assistance	2.4% (1)
Median fulltime earnings	$87,975 (1)

SENIORS ★★★★★ (12)

Seniors living alone	22.4% (49)
Poverty rate for seniors	3.6% (5)
Median income for seniors	$89,293 (1)
Seniors who work	21.0% (160)
Home ownership by seniors	86.2% (90)

STABILITY ★★★★ (177)

25-39 age group	16.3% (418)
Born in state of residence	32.5% (539)
Same house as 1 year ago	88.7% (95)
Live and work in county	93.4% (27)
Married-couple households	59.6% (12)

TRANSPORTATION ★★★★★ (36)

Bicycle or walk to work	5.3% (79)
Carpool to work	8.4% (466)
Public transit to work	4.2% (12)
Commute <15 minutes	47.5% (202)
Commute >45 minutes	4.7% (26)

See pages 37-130 for explanations of statistics, stars, and ranks.

Montrose, CO
(Montrose County, CO)

POPULATION

2010 census	41,276 (299)
2015 estimate	40,946 (303)
2010-2015 change	-0.8% (314)
2020 projection	41,938 (293)
2030 projection	44,104 (272)

RACE

Whites	76.4% (350)
Blacks	0.5% (466)
Hispanics	20.2% (77)
Asians	0.7% (241)
Native Americans	0.3% (231)

AGE

0-17 years old	22.8% (277)
18-24 years old	6.8% (527)
25-39 years old	16.1% (442)
40-54 years old	18.9% (376)
55-64 years old	15.1% (74)
65+ years old	20.4% (45)

PRIVATE SECTOR

Businesses	1,255 (189)
Employees	11,023 (342)
Total wages	$379,778,514 (354)
Average weekly wages	$663 (352)

HOUSEHOLD INCOME LADDER

95th percentile	$130,569 (425)
80th percentile	$85,788 (235)
60th percentile	$54,454 (267)
40th percentile	$34,214 (280)
20th percentile	$19,578 (240)

CHILDREN   ★ (457)

Living with two parents	72.8% (83)
Older teens in school	80.5% (384)
Speak English very well	95.0% (477)
Poverty rate for children	29.9% (400)
No health insurance	15.8% (528)

DIVERSITY/EQUALITY   ★★★★★ (55)

Racial diversity index	37.5% (199)
Geographic diversity index	72.6% (27)
Top 20% share of income	45.8% (108)
Gender gap in earnings	32.4% (239)
White-collar gender gap	25.8% (286)

EDUCATION   ★★★ (244)

Eighth grade or less	6.1% (429)
High school diplomas	87.5% (286)
Attended college	55.0% (224)
Bachelor's degrees	22.0% (159)
Advanced degrees	7.2% (164)

EMPLOYMENT   ★★★★ (145)

Average jobless rate	10.2% (427)
Self-employed workers	14.7% (21)
Management/financial jobs	12.4% (126)
Computer/engineering jobs	2.3% (354)
Health care jobs	5.2% (307)

GROWTH POTENTIAL   ★★★★★ (57)

Children per senior	1.11 (457)
Median age	44.2 (484)
Moved from different state	4.5% (67)
Homes built since 2000	26.9% (29)
Construction jobs	11.3% (8)

HOUSING   ★★ (361)

Home vacancy rate	6.2% (109)
Home ownership rate	70.1% (267)
Housing diversity index	82.3% (448)
4 or more bedrooms	18.5% (178)
Affordability/income ratio	$4,339 (508)

INCOME   ★★★ (221)

Poverty rate	19.0% (338)
Median household income	$43,999 (261)
Interest/dividends	28.2% (34)
Public assistance	16.0% (295)
Median fulltime earnings	$36,936 (293)

SENIORS   ★★★ (258)

Seniors living alone	26.7% (217)
Poverty rate for seniors	8.6% (234)
Median income for seniors	$34,669 (204)
Seniors who work	20.2% (187)
Home ownership by seniors	79.1% (414)

STABILITY   ★ (457)

25-39 age group	16.1% (442)
Born in state of residence	45.8% (503)
Same house as 1 year ago	82.0% (439)
Live and work in county	83.0% (165)
Married-couple households	54.4% (93)

TRANSPORTATION   ★★★★ (125)

Bicycle or walk to work	3.3% (211)
Carpool to work	14.0% (66)
Public transit to work	0.2% (363)
Commute <15 minutes	53.7% (99)
Commute >45 minutes	10.3% (237)

See pages 37-130 for explanations of statistics, stars, and ranks.

Moscow, ID
(Latah County, ID)

POPULATION

2010 census	37,244 (349)
2015 estimate	38,778 (329)
2010-2015 change	4.1% (57)
2020 projection	39,299 (322)
2030 projection	40,324 (313)

RACE

Whites	89.9% (186)
Blacks	0.6% (438)
Hispanics	4.0% (296)
Asians	2.2% (40)
Native Americans	0.6% (150)

AGE

0-17 years old	18.6% (509)
18-24 years old	25.7% (15)
25-39 years old	19.2% (88)
40-54 years old	14.5% (540)
55-64 years old	10.7% (500)
65+ years old	11.3% (504)

PRIVATE SECTOR

Businesses	948 (294)
Employees	8,512 (436)
Total wages	$242,850,736 (474)
Average weekly wages	$549 (532)

HOUSEHOLD INCOME LADDER

95th percentile	$146,071 (211)
80th percentile	$86,884 (210)
60th percentile	$54,804 (255)
40th percentile	$32,469 (340)
20th percentile	$16,052 (407)

CHILDREN ★★★★★ (12)

Living with two parents	82.4% (4)
Older teens in school	93.5% (27)
Speak English very well	98.4% (300)
Poverty rate for children	17.1% (99)
No health insurance	4.7% (166)

DIVERSITY/EQUALITY ★★★★★ (95)

Racial diversity index	18.9% (362)
Geographic diversity index	68.4% (55)
Top 20% share of income	49.4% (392)
Gender gap in earnings	25.3% (93)
White-collar gender gap	13.1% (127)

EDUCATION ★★★★★ (3)

Eighth grade or less	0.9% (16)
High school diplomas	96.6% (8)
Attended college	79.4% (4)
Bachelor's degrees	47.9% (9)
Advanced degrees	17.6% (7)

EMPLOYMENT ★★★★★ (81)

Average jobless rate	7.6% (250)
Self-employed workers	10.0% (168)
Management/financial jobs	12.6% (111)
Computer/engineering jobs	7.6% (5)
Health care jobs	4.1% (462)

GROWTH POTENTIAL ★★★★★ (44)

Children per senior	1.64 (153)
Median age	28.5 (17)
Moved from different state	8.8% (9)
Homes built since 2000	17.0% (154)
Construction jobs	4.4% (509)

HOUSING ★ (473)

Home vacancy rate	5.3% (50)
Home ownership rate	54.0% (537)
Housing diversity index	84.8% (248)
4 or more bedrooms	18.5% (178)
Affordability/income ratio	$4,503 (514)

INCOME ★★★★ (188)

Poverty rate	21.6% (419)
Median household income	$42,439 (303)
Interest/dividends	24.7% (109)
Public assistance	10.3% (72)
Median fulltime earnings	$40,502 (119)

SENIORS ★★★★ (125)

Seniors living alone	27.2% (254)
Poverty rate for seniors	7.3% (119)
Median income for seniors	$41,569 (48)
Seniors who work	24.3% (83)
Home ownership by seniors	78.1% (450)

STABILITY ★ (543)

25-39 age group	19.2% (88)
Born in state of residence	40.0% (522)
Same house as 1 year ago	71.0% (541)
Live and work in county	73.5% (323)
Married-couple households	46.3% (437)

TRANSPORTATION ★★★★★ (27)

Bicycle or walk to work	15.9% (4)
Carpool to work	12.9% (106)
Public transit to work	0.7% (119)
Commute <15 minutes	49.0% (174)
Commute >45 minutes	8.6% (154)

See pages 37-130 for explanations of statistics, stars, and ranks.

Moses Lake, WA
(Grant County, WA)

POPULATION

2010 census	89,120 (47)
2015 estimate	93,259 (42)
2010-2015 change	4.6% (47)
2020 projection	98,515 (34)
2030 projection	110,341 (23)

RACE

Whites	56.0% (469)
Blacks	0.6% (438)
Hispanics	39.7% (38)
Asians	1.1% (139)
Native Americans	0.9% (115)

AGE

0-17 years old	30.3% (18)
18-24 years old	9.9% (168)
25-39 years old	19.0% (104)
40-54 years old	17.6% (470)
55-64 years old	10.8% (497)
65+ years old	12.4% (487)

PRIVATE SECTOR

Businesses	3,126 (18)
Employees	30,968 (36)
Total wages	$1,044,909,904 (62)
Average weekly wages	$649 (393)

HOUSEHOLD INCOME LADDER

95th percentile	$151,139 (150)
80th percentile	$86,399 (224)
60th percentile	$58,476 (172)
40th percentile	$37,711 (187)
20th percentile	$21,883 (142)

CHILDREN ★★ **(389)**

Living with two parents	70.6% (128)
Older teens in school	80.9% (370)
Speak English very well	88.8% (530)
Poverty rate for children	22.8% (244)
No health insurance	6.1% (258)

DIVERSITY/EQUALITY ★★★★ **(130)**

Racial diversity index	52.8% (85)
Geographic diversity index	65.4% (71)
Top 20% share of income	45.3% (74)
Gender gap in earnings	41.0% (456)
White-collar gender gap	45.9% (487)

EDUCATION ★ **(517)**

Eighth grade or less	15.9% (537)
High school diplomas	75.5% (521)
Attended college	49.7% (340)
Bachelor's degrees	16.6% (348)
Advanced degrees	5.5% (318)

EMPLOYMENT ★ **(464)**

Average jobless rate	10.1% (423)
Self-employed workers	7.7% (362)
Management/financial jobs	12.3% (133)
Computer/engineering jobs	2.9% (219)
Health care jobs	2.9% (537)

GROWTH POTENTIAL ★★★★★ **(78)**

Children per senior	2.44 (30)
Median age	32.2 (49)
Moved from different state	3.1% (147)
Homes built since 2000	19.2% (103)
Construction jobs	4.1% (530)

HOUSING ★★★ **(300)**

Home vacancy rate	6.3% (122)
Home ownership rate	60.5% (497)
Housing diversity index	84.9% (235)
4 or more bedrooms	18.9% (164)
Affordability/income ratio	$3,233 (437)

INCOME ★★ **(336)**

Poverty rate	17.9% (297)
Median household income	$48,714 (155)
Interest/dividends	16.1% (372)
Public assistance	21.6% (470)
Median fulltime earnings	$37,296 (261)

SENIORS ★★ **(344)**

Seniors living alone	25.5% (142)
Poverty rate for seniors	10.8% (365)
Median income for seniors	$33,889 (243)
Seniors who work	17.5% (310)
Home ownership by seniors	78.4% (435)

STABILITY ★★★★★ **(107)**

25-39 age group	19.0% (104)
Born in state of residence	54.0% (468)
Same house as 1 year ago	83.1% (394)
Live and work in county	93.1% (35)
Married-couple households	54.7% (80)

TRANSPORTATION ★★★★★ **(68)**

Bicycle or walk to work	3.2% (225)
Carpool to work	13.2% (94)
Public transit to work	2.6% (20)
Commute <15 minutes	44.9% (247)
Commute >45 minutes	7.9% (126)

See pages 37-130 for explanations of statistics, stars, and ranks.

Mountain Home, ID
(Elmore County, ID)

POPULATION

2010 census	27,038 (465)
2015 estimate	25,876 (473)
2010-2015 change	-4.3% (526)
2020 projection	24,847 (482)
2030 projection	22,888 (494)

RACE

Whites	74.1% (364)
Blacks	2.4% (263)
Hispanics	16.1% (97)
Asians	3.4% (17)
Native Americans	1.2% (89)

AGE

0-17 years old	26.7% (52)
18-24 years old	13.5% (66)
25-39 years old	21.6% (28)
40-54 years old	16.6% (511)
55-64 years old	9.9% (524)
65+ years old	11.6% (498)

PRIVATE SECTOR

Businesses	526 (508)
Employees	4,673 (533)
Total wages	$137,847,412 (539)
Average weekly wages	$567 (522)

HOUSEHOLD INCOME LADDER

95th percentile	$130,911 (419)
80th percentile	$82,446 (309)
60th percentile	$53,589 (286)
40th percentile	$35,685 (244)
20th percentile	$21,305 (172)

CHILDREN ★★ (373)

Living with two parents	76.7% (34)
Older teens in school	59.8% (548)
Speak English very well	95.9% (457)
Poverty rate for children	22.5% (235)
No health insurance	6.6% (293)

DIVERSITY/EQUALITY ★★★★★ (22)

Racial diversity index	42.2% (172)
Geographic diversity index	79.1% (8)
Top 20% share of income	45.9% (117)
Gender gap in earnings	33.1% (262)
White-collar gender gap	14.4% (147)

EDUCATION ★★★ (265)

Eighth grade or less	5.6% (410)
High school diplomas	87.7% (280)
Attended college	60.8% (116)
Bachelor's degrees	16.7% (344)
Advanced degrees	5.5% (318)

EMPLOYMENT ★★ (370)

Average jobless rate	8.4% (323)
Self-employed workers	9.2% (231)
Management/financial jobs	11.9% (165)
Computer/engineering jobs	2.1% (399)
Health care jobs	4.1% (462)

GROWTH POTENTIAL ★★★★★ (19)

Children per senior	2.30 (36)
Median age	30.8 (36)
Moved from different state	9.1% (8)
Homes built since 2000	27.0% (27)
Construction jobs	5.1% (458)

HOUSING ★ (507)

Home vacancy rate	11.7% (451)
Home ownership rate	58.8% (514)
Housing diversity index	82.6% (433)
4 or more bedrooms	18.3% (192)
Affordability/income ratio	$3,086 (414)

INCOME ★★★ (330)

Poverty rate	16.1% (228)
Median household income	$43,848 (266)
Interest/dividends	14.7% (418)
Public assistance	13.3% (182)
Median fulltime earnings	$32,899 (457)

SENIORS ★ (452)

Seniors living alone	31.2% (479)
Poverty rate for seniors	10.6% (350)
Median income for seniors	$29,656 (417)
Seniors who work	14.4% (485)
Home ownership by seniors	84.2% (175)

STABILITY ★★★ (252)

25-39 age group	21.6% (28)
Born in state of residence	31.5% (542)
Same house as 1 year ago	78.1% (516)
Live and work in county	85.7% (123)
Married-couple households	58.6% (15)

TRANSPORTATION ★★★★ (158)

Bicycle or walk to work	3.2% (225)
Carpool to work	11.9% (145)
Public transit to work	0.4% (219)
Commute <15 minutes	51.2% (130)
Commute >45 minutes	8.7% (158)

See pages 37-130 for explanations of statistics, stars, and ranks.

Newport, OR
(Lincoln County, OR)

POPULATION

2010 census	46,034 (248)
2015 estimate	47,038 (236)
2010-2015 change	2.2% (118)
2020 projection	47,739 (231)
2030 projection	49,252 (223)

RACE

Whites	83.3% (288)
Blacks	0.3% (519)
Hispanics	8.4% (175)
Asians	1.4% (99)
Native Americans	3.0% (52)

AGE

0-17 years old	17.2% (535)
18-24 years old	6.6% (535)
25-39 years old	14.5% (531)
40-54 years old	18.4% (430)
55-64 years old	19.3% (1)
65+ years old	24.0% (12)

PRIVATE SECTOR

Businesses	1,697 (102)
Employees	13,801 (240)
Total wages	$439,480,692 (300)
Average weekly wages	$612 (464)

HOUSEHOLD INCOME LADDER

95th percentile	$142,810 (256)
80th percentile	$81,345 (341)
60th percentile	$51,235 (353)
40th percentile	$33,678 (301)
20th percentile	$18,851 (275)

CHILDREN ★ (441)

Living with two parents	61.7% (366)
Older teens in school	76.0% (490)
Speak English very well	97.9% (352)
Poverty rate for children	24.3% (280)
No health insurance	12.4% (482)

DIVERSITY/EQUALITY ★★★★★ (72)

Racial diversity index	29.7% (256)
Geographic diversity index	70.3% (42)
Top 20% share of income	48.1% (302)
Gender gap in earnings	32.8% (249)
White-collar gender gap	12.4% (121)

EDUCATION ★★★★ (182)

Eighth grade or less	3.5% (284)
High school diplomas	87.8% (274)
Attended college	58.3% (163)
Bachelor's degrees	20.7% (200)
Advanced degrees	8.2% (114)

EMPLOYMENT ★★★★ (122)

Average jobless rate	7.9% (286)
Self-employed workers	13.5% (42)
Management/financial jobs	12.2% (139)
Computer/engineering jobs	2.9% (219)
Health care jobs	4.9% (355)

GROWTH POTENTIAL ★ (526)

Children per senior	0.72 (544)
Median age	50.4 (546)
Moved from different state	3.9% (82)
Homes built since 2000	14.6% (213)
Construction jobs	5.7% (373)

HOUSING ★ (500)

Home vacancy rate	6.1% (104)
Home ownership rate	63.8% (460)
Housing diversity index	85.2% (190)
4 or more bedrooms	12.0% (496)
Affordability/income ratio	$5,204 (529)

INCOME ★★★ (291)

Poverty rate	16.9% (259)
Median household income	$42,101 (317)
Interest/dividends	26.5% (62)
Public assistance	22.3% (482)
Median fulltime earnings	$35,334 (367)

SENIORS ★★★ (225)

Seniors living alone	28.7% (344)
Poverty rate for seniors	7.8% (163)
Median income for seniors	$37,876 (93)
Seniors who work	19.7% (214)
Home ownership by seniors	80.6% (353)

STABILITY ★ (505)

25-39 age group	14.5% (531)
Born in state of residence	43.6% (510)
Same house as 1 year ago	83.5% (366)
Live and work in county	93.9% (20)
Married-couple households	47.2% (413)

TRANSPORTATION ★★★★★ (28)

Bicycle or walk to work	5.6% (69)
Carpool to work	14.0% (66)
Public transit to work	2.3% (26)
Commute <15 minutes	49.9% (154)
Commute >45 minutes	9.2% (182)

See pages 37-130 for explanations of statistics, stars, and ranks.

Nogales, AZ
(Santa Cruz County, AZ)

POPULATION

2010 census	47,420 (229)
2015 estimate	46,461 (240)
2010-2015 change	-2.0% (412)
2020 projection	46,497 (242)
2030 projection	46,579 (249)

RACE

Whites	15.6% (545)
Blacks	0.2% (537)
Hispanics	82.8% (5)
Asians	1.0% (158)
Native Americans	0.1% (402)

AGE

0-17 years old	28.8% (25)
18-24 years old	9.5% (197)
25-39 years old	15.2% (498)
40-54 years old	19.0% (364)
55-64 years old	12.3% (414)
65+ years old	15.3% (348)

PRIVATE SECTOR

Businesses	1,102 (243)
Employees	9,917 (377)
Total wages	$340,572,929 (391)
Average weekly wages	$660 (364)

HOUSEHOLD INCOME LADDER

95th percentile	$143,449 (249)
80th percentile	$78,491 (392)
60th percentile	$50,839 (362)
40th percentile	$30,228 (410)
20th percentile	$15,766 (417)

CHILDREN ★ **(502)**

Living with two parents	59.5% (415)
Older teens in school	90.1% (65)
Speak English very well	81.2% (546)
Poverty rate for children	29.8% (398)
No health insurance	13.0% (496)

DIVERSITY/EQUALITY ★★★★ **(133)**

Racial diversity index	29.0% (262)
Geographic diversity index	71.9% (33)
Top 20% share of income	49.3% (384)
Gender gap in earnings	34.8% (310)
White-collar gender gap	19.8% (203)

EDUCATION ★★ **(437)**

Eighth grade or less	9.4% (508)
High school diplomas	77.9% (508)
Attended college	49.9% (335)
Bachelor's degrees	22.0% (159)
Advanced degrees	6.2% (243)

EMPLOYMENT ★★ **(367)**

Average jobless rate	11.3% (466)
Self-employed workers	13.1% (49)
Management/financial jobs	11.5% (202)
Computer/engineering jobs	2.3% (354)
Health care jobs	3.6% (508)

GROWTH POTENTIAL ★★★★★ **(103)**

Children per senior	1.89 (72)
Median age	36.5 (131)
Moved from different state	2.7% (179)
Homes built since 2000	25.1% (35)
Construction jobs	5.2% (442)

HOUSING ★ **(485)**

Home vacancy rate	9.1% (296)
Home ownership rate	66.0% (415)
Housing diversity index	83.0% (417)
4 or more bedrooms	12.1% (492)
Affordability/income ratio	$3,413 (454)

INCOME ★ **(486)**

Poverty rate	23.5% (457)
Median household income	$40,140 (377)
Interest/dividends	12.1% (489)
Public assistance	24.9% (514)
Median fulltime earnings	$33,598 (436)

SENIORS ★ **(513)**

Seniors living alone	21.1% (21)
Poverty rate for seniors	20.1% (541)
Median income for seniors	$28,059 (457)
Seniors who work	16.4% (383)
Home ownership by seniors	72.5% (543)

STABILITY ★★ **(373)**

25-39 age group	15.2% (498)
Born in state of residence	46.3% (500)
Same house as 1 year ago	87.5% (165)
Live and work in county	86.0% (116)
Married-couple households	53.7% (123)

TRANSPORTATION ★★ **(400)**

Bicycle or walk to work	2.4% (331)
Carpool to work	9.8% (358)
Public transit to work	0.2% (363)
Commute <15 minutes	35.9% (421)
Commute >45 minutes	10.9% (268)

See pages 37-130 for explanations of statistics, stars, and ranks.

Oak Harbor, WA
(Island County, WA)

POPULATION

2010 census	78,506 (71)
2015 estimate	80,593 (67)
2010-2015 change	2.7% (96)
2020 projection	82,192 (65)
2030 projection	85,771 (61)

RACE

Whites	80.9% (319)
Blacks	2.8% (232)
Hispanics	6.6% (207)
Asians	5.1% (12)
Native Americans	1.0% (103)

AGE

0-17 years old	19.4% (489)
18-24 years old	9.2% (234)
25-39 years old	17.2% (290)
40-54 years old	17.6% (470)
55-64 years old	15.5% (59)
65+ years old	21.2% (27)

PRIVATE SECTOR

Businesses	1,900 (74)
Employees	10,800 (348)
Total wages	$336,727,880 (395)
Average weekly wages	$600 (487)

HOUSEHOLD INCOME LADDER

95th percentile	$171,715 (51)
80th percentile	$107,770 (29)
60th percentile	$72,630 (26)
40th percentile	$47,475 (27)
20th percentile	$26,776 (28)

CHILDREN ★★★★ (174)

Living with two parents	75.0% (51)
Older teens in school	72.4% (518)
Speak English very well	99.1% (179)
Poverty rate for children	13.9% (55)
No health insurance	5.8% (236)

DIVERSITY/EQUALITY ★★★★★ (29)

Racial diversity index	33.6% (222)
Geographic diversity index	77.5% (12)
Top 20% share of income	46.2% (137)
Gender gap in earnings	36.9% (360)
White-collar gender gap	5.4% (45)

EDUCATION ★★★★★ (37)

Eighth grade or less	1.6% (84)
High school diplomas	94.9% (34)

Attended college	71.5% (23)
Bachelor's degrees	28.7% (66)
Advanced degrees	8.9% (90)

EMPLOYMENT ★★★★★ (76)

Average jobless rate	9.0% (358)
Self-employed workers	10.0% (168)
Management/financial jobs	12.9% (92)
Computer/engineering jobs	5.0% (30)
Health care jobs	6.7% (104)

GROWTH POTENTIAL ★★★★ (134)

Children per senior	0.91 (526)
Median age	44.0 (477)
Moved from different state	6.9% (25)
Homes built since 2000	21.0% (79)
Construction jobs	7.5% (122)

HOUSING ★ (476)

Home vacancy rate	6.2% (109)
Home ownership rate	67.8% (349)
Housing diversity index	83.3% (402)
4 or more bedrooms	13.8% (409)
Affordability/income ratio	$4,946 (523)

INCOME ★★★★★ (17)

Poverty rate	9.6% (23)
Median household income	$58,815 (29)
Interest/dividends	30.5% (19)
Public assistance	10.9% (91)
Median fulltime earnings	$49,109 (17)

SENIORS ★★★★★ (17)

Seniors living alone	24.2% (89)
Poverty rate for seniors	4.0% (8)
Median income for seniors	$49,984 (13)
Seniors who work	19.7% (214)
Home ownership by seniors	85.9% (105)

STABILITY ★ (500)

25-39 age group	17.2% (290)
Born in state of residence	36.9% (531)
Same house as 1 year ago	82.7% (411)
Live and work in county	67.6% (412)
Married-couple households	56.3% (43)

TRANSPORTATION ★★ (355)

Bicycle or walk to work	4.1% (147)
Carpool to work	9.7% (369)
Public transit to work	3.0% (13)
Commute <15 minutes	37.0% (399)
Commute >45 minutes	23.0% (539)

See pages 37-130 for explanations of statistics, stars, and ranks.

Ontario, OR-ID
(Malheur County, OR, and Payette County, ID)

POPULATION

2010 census	53,936 (178)
2015 estimate	53,276 (184)
2010-2015 change	-1.2% (345)
2020 projection	52,621 (193)
2030 projection	51,389 (208)

RACE

Whites	69.6% (395)
Blacks	0.7% (423)
Hispanics	25.7% (56)
Asians	1.1% (139)
Native Americans	0.6% (150)

AGE

0-17 years old	25.8% (75)
18-24 years old	9.1% (251)
25-39 years old	18.5% (144)
40-54 years old	18.7% (399)
55-64 years old	11.8% (456)
65+ years old	16.2% (279)

PRIVATE SECTOR

Businesses	1,437 (151)
Employees	14,300 (227)
Total wages	$455,754,433 (289)
Average weekly wages	$613 (462)

HOUSEHOLD INCOME LADDER

95th percentile	$126,617 (472)
80th percentile	$76,667 (430)
60th percentile	$50,040 (383)
40th percentile	$31,195 (386)
20th percentile	$15,801 (413)

CHILDREN ★★ (440)

Living with two parents	69.0% (166)
Older teens in school	80.3% (388)
Speak English very well	95.2% (473)
Poverty rate for children	30.8% (420)
No health insurance	12.2% (478)

DIVERSITY/EQUALITY ★★★★ (200)

Racial diversity index	44.9% (150)
Geographic diversity index	68.0% (57)
Top 20% share of income	47.7% (273)
Gender gap in earnings	29.8% (167)
White-collar gender gap	57.4% (536)

EDUCATION ★★ (409)

Eighth grade or less	6.9% (467)
High school diplomas	84.2% (396)

Attended college	54.0% (243)
Bachelor's degrees	14.5% (443)
Advanced degrees	4.5% (442)

EMPLOYMENT ★★★ (256)

Average jobless rate	10.7% (450)
Self-employed workers	14.3% (31)
Management/financial jobs	13.0% (86)
Computer/engineering jobs	1.4% (510)
Health care jobs	4.2% (454)

GROWTH POTENTIAL ★★★★ (161)

Children per senior	1.60 (169)
Median age	36.8 (138)
Moved from different state	5.7% (33)
Homes built since 2000	12.9% (280)
Construction jobs	4.8% (480)

HOUSING ★★★ (223)

Home vacancy rate	7.7% (199)
Home ownership rate	66.9% (392)
Housing diversity index	86.2% (43)
4 or more bedrooms	17.7% (220)
Affordability/income ratio	$3,238 (438)

INCOME ★ (457)

Poverty rate	22.4% (435)
Median household income	$39,652 (390)
Interest/dividends	17.8% (316)
Public assistance	23.6% (505)
Median fulltime earnings	$33,268 (445)

SENIORS ★★ (392)

Seniors living alone	26.8% (222)
Poverty rate for seniors	12.8% (442)
Median income for seniors	$33,758 (248)
Seniors who work	19.9% (201)
Home ownership by seniors	77.5% (471)

STABILITY ★ (509)

25-39 age group	18.5% (144)
Born in state of residence	37.1% (530)
Same house as 1 year ago	82.3% (426)
Live and work in county	66.8% (423)
Married-couple households	52.9% (157)

TRANSPORTATION ★★★★★ (109)

Bicycle or walk to work	5.5% (73)
Carpool to work	12.4% (128)
Public transit to work	0.2% (363)
Commute <15 minutes	48.3% (189)
Commute >45 minutes	7.7% (115)

See pages 37-130 for explanations of statistics, stars, and ranks.

Othello, WA
(Adams County, WA)

POPULATION

2010 census	18,728 (531)
2015 estimate	19,254 (528)
2010-2015 change	2.8% (94)
2020 projection	20,077 (523)
2030 projection	21,919 (504)

RACE

Whites	36.2% (518)
Blacks	0.2% (537)
Hispanics	61.5% (15)
Asians	0.8% (201)
Native Americans	0.1% (402)

AGE

0-17 years old	35.2% (1)
18-24 years old	9.9% (168)
25-39 years old	18.0% (201)
40-54 years old	17.0% (502)
55-64 years old	9.8% (530)
65+ years old	10.1% (528)

PRIVATE SECTOR

Businesses	793 (377)
Employees	6,251 (500)
Total wages	$224,624,098 (489)
Average weekly wages	$691 (282)

HOUSEHOLD INCOME LADDER

95th percentile	$145,940 (214)
80th percentile	$81,256 (344)
60th percentile	$56,933 (210)
40th percentile	$36,524 (214)
20th percentile	$21,765 (150)

CHILDREN ★ (532)

Living with two parents	67.0% (217)
Older teens in school	68.0% (542)
Speak English very well	79.0% (548)
Poverty rate for children	27.6% (357)
No health insurance	9.3% (401)

DIVERSITY/EQUALITY ★★★★ (193)

Racial diversity index	49.0% (122)
Geographic diversity index	63.4% (88)
Top 20% share of income	44.6% (48)
Gender gap in earnings	40.4% (445)
White-collar gender gap	55.6% (530)

EDUCATION ★ (538)

Eighth grade or less	25.8% (549)
High school diplomas	65.9% (545)
Attended college	41.8% (494)
Bachelor's degrees	13.9% (466)
Advanced degrees	4.8% (405)

EMPLOYMENT ★ (510)

Average jobless rate	9.6% (402)
Self-employed workers	8.0% (333)
Management/financial jobs	9.9% (392)
Computer/engineering jobs	2.0% (420)
Health care jobs	3.2% (525)

GROWTH POTENTIAL ★★★★ (114)

Children per senior	3.49 (6)
Median age	28.9 (19)
Moved from different state	1.3% (452)
Homes built since 2000	12.7% (290)
Construction jobs	3.3% (546)

HOUSING ★★★★★ (94)

Home vacancy rate	6.0% (95)
Home ownership rate	65.3% (429)
Housing diversity index	86.1% (51)
4 or more bedrooms	23.1% (63)
Affordability/income ratio	$2,972 (397)

INCOME ★★ (427)

Poverty rate	21.4% (412)
Median household income	$46,564 (201)
Interest/dividends	13.4% (458)
Public assistance	21.2% (461)
Median fulltime earnings	$33,631 (434)

SENIORS ★★★ (308)

Seniors living alone	26.3% (190)
Poverty rate for seniors	13.5% (461)
Median income for seniors	$35,637 (164)
Seniors who work	25.9% (51)
Home ownership by seniors	75.5% (519)

STABILITY ★★★★★ (68)

25-39 age group	18.0% (201)
Born in state of residence	55.7% (459)
Same house as 1 year ago	89.9% (50)
Live and work in county	77.3% (250)
Married-couple households	58.1% (19)

TRANSPORTATION ★★★★★ (87)

Bicycle or walk to work	2.9% (265)
Carpool to work	15.3% (42)
Public transit to work	0.5% (178)
Commute <15 minutes	49.7% (161)
Commute >45 minutes	7.4% (99)

See pages 37-130 for explanations of statistics, stars, and ranks.

Pahrump, NV
(Nye County, NV)

POPULATION	
2010 census	43,946 (269)
2015 estimate	42,477 (286)
2010-2015 change	-3.3% (495)
2020 projection	42,192 (292)
2030 projection	41,776 (296)

RACE	
Whites	77.8% (341)
Blacks	2.5% (253)
Hispanics	14.2% (110)
Asians	1.7% (69)
Native Americans	1.8% (77)

AGE	
0-17 years old	18.8% (504)
18-24 years old	6.1% (545)
25-39 years old	12.2% (550)
40-54 years old	19.0% (364)
55-64 years old	17.2% (13)
65+ years old	26.6% (6)

PRIVATE SECTOR	
Businesses	824 (361)
Employees	9,332 (401)
Total wages	$467,898,198 (277)
Average weekly wages	$964 (21)

HOUSEHOLD INCOME LADDER	
95th percentile	$139,265 (300)
80th percentile	$78,901 (385)
60th percentile	$51,262 (352)
40th percentile	$34,949 (264)
20th percentile	$19,482 (245)

CHILDREN	★ (503)
Living with two parents	60.1% (395)
Older teens in school	72.9% (516)
Speak English very well	99.1% (179)
Poverty rate for children	34.7% (472)
No health insurance	12.7% (489)

DIVERSITY/EQUALITY	★★★★★ (24)
Racial diversity index	37.3% (201)
Geographic diversity index	78.0% (11)
Top 20% share of income	46.4% (156)
Gender gap in earnings	37.1% (366)
White-collar gender gap	1.4% (10)

EDUCATION	★★ (399)
Eighth grade or less	2.9% (217)
High school diplomas	85.2% (368)
Attended college	48.9% (357)
Bachelor's degrees	12.5% (507)
Advanced degrees	3.7% (498)

EMPLOYMENT	★ (525)
Average jobless rate	13.4% (522)
Self-employed workers	7.5% (385)
Management/financial jobs	9.7% (416)
Computer/engineering jobs	3.5% (122)
Health care jobs	3.3% (517)

GROWTH POTENTIAL	★★★★ (144)
Children per senior	0.71 (545)
Median age	50.8 (549)
Moved from different state	5.2% (47)
Homes built since 2000	36.0% (6)
Construction jobs	8.9% (51)

HOUSING	★ (502)
Home vacancy rate	11.4% (432)
Home ownership rate	70.5% (250)
Housing diversity index	75.1% (546)
4 or more bedrooms	16.0% (293)
Affordability/income ratio	$2,539 (263)

INCOME	★★★ (269)
Poverty rate	18.2% (304)
Median household income	$41,712 (329)
Interest/dividends	19.5% (264)
Public assistance	15.7% (280)
Median fulltime earnings	$38,832 (184)

SENIORS	★★★★ (136)
Seniors living alone	21.5% (31)
Poverty rate for seniors	9.0% (260)
Median income for seniors	$37,885 (92)
Seniors who work	13.4% (520)
Home ownership by seniors	83.8% (186)

STABILITY	★ (549)
25-39 age group	12.2% (550)
Born in state of residence	19.6% (550)
Same house as 1 year ago	82.1% (434)
Live and work in county	77.2% (255)
Married-couple households	52.2% (188)

TRANSPORTATION	★★★★ (220)
Bicycle or walk to work	3.3% (211)
Carpool to work	14.5% (55)
Public transit to work	1.1% (58)
Commute <15 minutes	49.8% (159)
Commute >45 minutes	19.9% (516)

See pages 37-130 for explanations of statistics, stars, and ranks.

Payson, AZ
(Gila County, AZ)

POPULATION

2010 census	53,597 (180)
2015 estimate	53,159 (187)
2010-2015 change	-0.8% (314)
2020 projection	52,462 (195)
2030 projection	51,120 (209)

RACE

Whites	63.7% (427)
Blacks	0.6% (438)
Hispanics	18.6% (84)
Asians	0.6% (291)
Native Americans	15.1% (9)

AGE

0-17 years old	20.5% (433)
18-24 years old	7.2% (510)
25-39 years old	12.8% (548)
40-54 years old	17.6% (470)
55-64 years old	16.2% (38)
65+ years old	25.6% (10)

PRIVATE SECTOR

Businesses	871 (331)
Employees	9,565 (388)
Total wages	$396,177,964 (344)
Average weekly wages	$797 (95)

HOUSEHOLD INCOME LADDER

95th percentile	$122,797 (495)
80th percentile	$77,394 (412)
60th percentile	$47,777 (429)
40th percentile	$31,450 (375)
20th percentile	$17,561 (338)

CHILDREN ★ (513)

Living with two parents	49.3% (512)
Older teens in school	81.9% (325)
Speak English very well	99.5% (96)
Poverty rate for children	38.5% (504)
No health insurance	14.3% (516)

DIVERSITY/EQUALITY ★★★★★ (18)

Racial diversity index	53.7% (71)
Geographic diversity index	66.2% (68)
Top 20% share of income	46.5% (159)
Gender gap in earnings	32.7% (245)
White-collar gender gap	2.3% (15)

EDUCATION ★★ (340)

Eighth grade or less	3.8% (307)
High school diplomas	84.1% (398)
Attended college	53.3% (259)
Bachelor's degrees	15.2% (415)
Advanced degrees	6.1% (250)

EMPLOYMENT ★ (484)

Average jobless rate	12.8% (514)
Self-employed workers	7.5% (385)
Management/financial jobs	9.1% (463)
Computer/engineering jobs	2.1% (399)
Health care jobs	6.4% (132)

GROWTH POTENTIAL ★★ (431)

Children per senior	0.80 (536)
Median age	48.6 (537)
Moved from different state	1.9% (310)
Homes built since 2000	15.5% (191)
Construction jobs	8.7% (58)

HOUSING ★★ (388)

Home vacancy rate	8.8% (273)
Home ownership rate	72.7% (162)
Housing diversity index	83.7% (378)
4 or more bedrooms	11.1% (519)
Affordability/income ratio	$3,376 (451)

INCOME ★★ (378)

Poverty rate	22.7% (441)
Median household income	$39,751 (387)
Interest/dividends	19.0% (278)
Public assistance	20.0% (430)
Median fulltime earnings	$38,006 (221)

SENIORS ★★★★ (126)

Seniors living alone	23.5% (69)
Poverty rate for seniors	8.9% (254)
Median income for seniors	$36,543 (136)
Seniors who work	15.4% (441)
Home ownership by seniors	86.1% (93)

STABILITY ★ (498)

25-39 age group	12.8% (548)
Born in state of residence	53.4% (471)
Same house as 1 year ago	87.4% (173)
Live and work in county	85.1% (134)
Married-couple households	48.2% (373)

TRANSPORTATION ★★★★ (181)

Bicycle or walk to work	3.4% (199)
Carpool to work	12.1% (135)
Public transit to work	0.4% (219)
Commute <15 minutes	53.2% (107)
Commute >45 minutes	12.0% (311)

See pages 37-130 for explanations of statistics, stars, and ranks.

Portales, NM
(Roosevelt County, NM)

POPULATION

2010 census	19,846 (528)
2015 estimate	19,120 (529)
2010-2015 change	-3.7% (513)
2020 projection	18,461 (531)
2030 projection	17,137 (536)

RACE

Whites	54.2% (474)
Blacks	2.2% (276)
Hispanics	40.1% (35)
Asians	0.6% (291)
Native Americans	1.1% (96)

AGE

0-17 years old	25.7% (81)
18-24 years old	18.2% (35)
25-39 years old	18.9% (111)
40-54 years old	15.0% (534)
55-64 years old	10.0% (521)
65+ years old	12.2% (492)

PRIVATE SECTOR

Businesses	370 (537)
Employees	4,274 (541)
Total wages	$121,407,680 (545)
Average weekly wages	$546 (536)

HOUSEHOLD INCOME LADDER

95th percentile	$126,256 (478)
80th percentile	$75,736 (444)
60th percentile	$44,683 (482)
40th percentile	$26,897 (489)
20th percentile	$14,908 (455)

CHILDREN ★★ (354)

Living with two parents	65.9% (247)
Older teens in school	84.0% (239)
Speak English very well	97.7% (370)
Poverty rate for children	37.0% (495)
No health insurance	6.9% (307)

DIVERSITY/EQUALITY ★★★★ (206)

Racial diversity index	54.4% (63)
Geographic diversity index	68.8% (52)
Top 20% share of income	49.1% (372)
Gender gap in earnings	43.2% (483)
White-collar gender gap	39.5% (441)

EDUCATION ★★★ (271)

Eighth grade or less	8.4% (497)
High school diplomas	82.3% (437)
Attended college	57.4% (179)
Bachelor's degrees	22.9% (134)
Advanced degrees	9.0% (87)

EMPLOYMENT ★ (508)

Average jobless rate	9.7% (409)
Self-employed workers	7.9% (345)
Management/financial jobs	9.2% (459)
Computer/engineering jobs	2.8% (246)
Health care jobs	3.1% (531)

GROWTH POTENTIAL ★★★★★ (55)

Children per senior	2.11 (47)
Median age	29.4 (22)
Moved from different state	5.0% (51)
Homes built since 2000	13.2% (271)
Construction jobs	5.8% (360)

HOUSING ★ (504)

Home vacancy rate	11.5% (436)
Home ownership rate	58.4% (518)
Housing diversity index	86.3% (36)
4 or more bedrooms	12.1% (492)
Affordability/income ratio	$3,334 (447)

INCOME ★ (484)

Poverty rate	26.3% (490)
Median household income	$35,546 (478)
Interest/dividends	14.1% (439)
Public assistance	18.0% (371)
Median fulltime earnings	$30,821 (531)

SENIORS ★ (519)

Seniors living alone	33.3% (531)
Poverty rate for seniors	14.1% (472)
Median income for seniors	$28,005 (459)
Seniors who work	15.1% (455)
Home ownership by seniors	80.5% (356)

STABILITY ★ (518)

25-39 age group	18.9% (111)
Born in state of residence	49.8% (488)
Same house as 1 year ago	79.9% (499)
Live and work in county	73.0% (329)
Married-couple households	45.5% (453)

TRANSPORTATION ★★★★★ (46)

Bicycle or walk to work	5.9% (60)
Carpool to work	12.6% (116)
Public transit to work	0.1% (441)
Commute <15 minutes	57.0% (71)
Commute >45 minutes	4.5% (21)

See pages 37-130 for explanations of statistics, stars, and ranks.

Port Angeles, WA
(Clallam County, WA)

POPULATION

2010 census	71,404 (92)
2015 estimate	73,486 (88)
2010-2015 change	2.9% (92)
2020 projection	75,687 (86)
2030 projection	80,564 (74)

RACE

Whites	83.8% (282)
Blacks	0.8% (404)
Hispanics	5.7% (231)
Asians	1.5% (85)
Native Americans	4.4% (38)

AGE

0-17 years old	17.8% (530)
18-24 years old	7.3% (503)
25-39 years old	14.5% (531)
40-54 years old	17.3% (487)
55-64 years old	16.9% (18)
65+ years old	26.2% (7)

PRIVATE SECTOR

Businesses	2,299 (44)
Employees	14,943 (210)
Total wages	$459,960,880 (283)
Average weekly wages	$592 (498)

HOUSEHOLD INCOME LADDER

95th percentile	$148,341 (179)
80th percentile	$86,709 (216)
60th percentile	$57,060 (204)
40th percentile	$37,137 (203)
20th percentile	$20,699 (197)

CHILDREN ★★★ (258)

Living with two parents	62.2% (344)
Older teens in school	84.0% (239)
Speak English very well	97.9% (352)
Poverty rate for children	22.4% (232)
No health insurance	6.9% (307)

DIVERSITY/EQUALITY ★★★★★ (69)

Racial diversity index	29.1% (261)
Geographic diversity index	69.7% (46)
Top 20% share of income	47.1% (228)
Gender gap in earnings	30.0% (170)
White-collar gender gap	20.3% (212)

EDUCATION ★★★★ (119)

Eighth grade or less	2.0% (126)
High school diplomas	92.3% (117)
Attended college	64.0% (72)
Bachelor's degrees	21.2% (185)
Advanced degrees	7.4% (149)

EMPLOYMENT ★★★★ (217)

Average jobless rate	9.9% (417)
Self-employed workers	11.8% (81)
Management/financial jobs	10.3% (339)
Computer/engineering jobs	3.4% (131)
Health care jobs	5.7% (222)

GROWTH POTENTIAL ★ (493)

Children per senior	0.68 (547)
Median age	50.1 (544)
Moved from different state	3.3% (129)
Homes built since 2000	16.9% (155)
Construction jobs	6.7% (219)

HOUSING ★★ (439)

Home vacancy rate	6.9% (158)
Home ownership rate	69.8% (279)
Housing diversity index	84.6% (277)
4 or more bedrooms	11.5% (514)
Affordability/income ratio	$4,594 (517)

INCOME ★★★★ (124)

Poverty rate	15.0% (190)
Median household income	$47,253 (187)
Interest/dividends	30.1% (23)
Public assistance	16.5% (313)
Median fulltime earnings	$40,513 (117)

SENIORS ★★★★ (166)

Seniors living alone	27.6% (269)
Poverty rate for seniors	7.4% (128)
Median income for seniors	$42,268 (45)
Seniors who work	15.8% (423)
Home ownership by seniors	82.9% (225)

STABILITY ★ (469)

25-39 age group	14.5% (531)
Born in state of residence	47.8% (491)
Same house as 1 year ago	85.8% (264)
Live and work in county	93.4% (27)
Married-couple households	47.2% (413)

TRANSPORTATION ★★★★★ (66)

Bicycle or walk to work	5.7% (64)
Carpool to work	10.3% (299)
Public transit to work	2.5% (22)
Commute <15 minutes	49.9% (154)
Commute >45 minutes	9.4% (197)

See pages 37-130 for explanations of statistics, stars, and ranks.

Price, UT
(Carbon County, UT)

POPULATION	
2010 census	21,403 (514)
2015 estimate	20,479 (523)
2010-2015 change	-4.3% (526)
2020 projection	19,822 (525)
2030 projection	18,629 (528)

RACE	
Whites	83.4% (286)
Blacks	0.7% (423)
Hispanics	13.0% (119)
Asians	0.7% (241)
Native Americans	0.5% (174)

AGE	
0-17 years old	26.9% (47)
18-24 years old	10.3% (146)
25-39 years old	19.1% (95)
40-54 years old	15.7% (527)
55-64 years old	13.3% (282)
65+ years old	14.6% (400)

PRIVATE SECTOR	
Businesses	538 (501)
Employees	6,565 (490)
Total wages	$280,117,496 (448)
Average weekly wages	$821 (64)

HOUSEHOLD INCOME LADDER	
95th percentile	$133,760 (380)
80th percentile	$88,405 (178)
60th percentile	$59,391 (160)
40th percentile	$35,871 (236)
20th percentile	$18,587 (286)

CHILDREN	★★★★★ (53)
Living with two parents	76.4% (38)
Older teens in school	88.9% (82)
Speak English very well	99.8% (38)
Poverty rate for children	18.2% (128)
No health insurance	7.0% (319)

DIVERSITY/EQUALITY	★★ (359)
Racial diversity index	28.7% (263)
Geographic diversity index	42.2% (323)
Top 20% share of income	43.8% (21)
Gender gap in earnings	57.0% (548)
White-collar gender gap	21.5% (226)

EDUCATION	★★★★ (189)
Eighth grade or less	1.4% (60)
High school diplomas	90.4% (188)
Attended college	63.4% (78)
Bachelor's degrees	16.0% (372)
Advanced degrees	4.6% (431)

EMPLOYMENT	★ (449)
Average jobless rate	7.4% (237)
Self-employed workers	6.1% (495)
Management/financial jobs	8.7% (493)
Computer/engineering jobs	3.3% (145)
Health care jobs	4.7% (385)

GROWTH POTENTIAL	★★★★ (220)
Children per senior	1.84 (86)
Median age	35.1 (94)
Moved from different state	2.2% (248)
Homes built since 2000	8.8% (443)
Construction jobs	5.9% (345)

HOUSING	★★★★★ (90)
Home vacancy rate	9.9% (345)
Home ownership rate	71.1% (222)
Housing diversity index	84.4% (299)
4 or more bedrooms	26.9% (29)
Affordability/income ratio	$2,642 (307)

INCOME	★★★★ (173)
Poverty rate	15.3% (204)
Median household income	$46,900 (196)
Interest/dividends	19.8% (254)
Public assistance	14.1% (212)
Median fulltime earnings	$41,384 (83)

SENIORS	★★★ (224)
Seniors living alone	30.8% (462)
Poverty rate for seniors	6.6% (68)
Median income for seniors	$31,647 (343)
Seniors who work	17.0% (341)
Home ownership by seniors	88.2% (37)

STABILITY	★★★★★ (56)
25-39 age group	19.1% (95)
Born in state of residence	74.5% (231)
Same house as 1 year ago	82.2% (432)
Live and work in county	89.5% (74)
Married-couple households	52.7% (166)

TRANSPORTATION	★★★★★ (52)
Bicycle or walk to work	3.0% (249)
Carpool to work	13.3% (88)
Public transit to work	0.6% (141)
Commute <15 minutes	64.9% (18)
Commute >45 minutes	6.7% (77)

See pages 37-130 for explanations of statistics, stars, and ranks.

Prineville, OR
(Crook County, OR)

POPULATION	
2010 census	20,978 (520)
2015 estimate	21,630 (514)
2010-2015 change	3.1% (78)
2020 projection	22,159 (508)
2030 projection	23,290 (490)

RACE	
Whites	88.8% (208)
Blacks	0.3% (519)
Hispanics	7.4% (190)
Asians	0.4% (413)
Native Americans	0.9% (115)

AGE	
0-17 years old	19.9% (465)
18-24 years old	5.8% (548)
25-39 years old	15.2% (498)
40-54 years old	19.0% (364)
55-64 years old	16.6% (25)
65+ years old	23.4% (17)

PRIVATE SECTOR	
Businesses	569 (490)
Employees	4,630 (534)
Total wages	$192,814,824 (510)
Average weekly wages	$801 (89)

HOUSEHOLD INCOME LADDER	
95th percentile	$126,531 (474)
80th percentile	$75,853 (443)
60th percentile	$48,398 (413)
40th percentile	$31,270 (382)
20th percentile	$18,111 (312)

CHILDREN	★★ (372)
Living with two parents	74.6% (59)
Older teens in school	68.0% (542)
Speak English very well	98.0% (341)
Poverty rate for children	28.2% (373)
No health insurance	6.5% (282)

DIVERSITY/EQUALITY	★★★★ (122)
Racial diversity index	20.5% (342)
Geographic diversity index	62.4% (98)
Top 20% share of income	46.4% (153)
Gender gap in earnings	33.6% (271)
White-collar gender gap	18.2% (192)

EDUCATION	★★ (364)
Eighth grade or less	3.2% (250)
High school diplomas	89.1% (229)
Attended college	51.8% (285)
Bachelor's degrees	14.1% (457)
Advanced degrees	2.8% (540)

EMPLOYMENT	★★ (434)
Average jobless rate	13.5% (523)
Self-employed workers	12.4% (61)
Management/financial jobs	11.1% (240)
Computer/engineering jobs	1.8% (457)
Health care jobs	4.4% (433)

GROWTH POTENTIAL	★★ (370)
Children per senior	0.85 (532)
Median age	48.1 (534)
Moved from different state	2.5% (203)
Homes built since 2000	26.0% (32)
Construction jobs	6.2% (295)

HOUSING	★ (468)
Home vacancy rate	5.2% (46)
Home ownership rate	68.7% (317)
Housing diversity index	81.9% (461)
4 or more bedrooms	13.1% (448)
Affordability/income ratio	$4,498 (513)

INCOME	★★ (435)
Poverty rate	19.4% (353)
Median household income	$37,106 (441)
Interest/dividends	21.3% (206)
Public assistance	25.8% (517)
Median fulltime earnings	$33,453 (440)

SENIORS	★★ (337)
Seniors living alone	24.8% (111)
Poverty rate for seniors	10.5% (345)
Median income for seniors	$34,629 (206)
Seniors who work	14.7% (467)
Home ownership by seniors	79.5% (394)

STABILITY	★ (496)
25-39 age group	15.2% (498)
Born in state of residence	54.1% (467)
Same house as 1 year ago	81.0% (478)
Live and work in county	73.2% (328)
Married-couple households	54.8% (78)

TRANSPORTATION	★★ (350)
Bicycle or walk to work	4.2% (142)
Carpool to work	9.6% (378)
Public transit to work	0.0% (511)
Commute <15 minutes	46.7% (223)
Commute >45 minutes	15.1% (426)

See pages 37-130 for explanations of statistics, stars, and ranks.

Pullman, WA
(Whitman County, WA)

POPULATION

2010 census	44,776 (264)
2015 estimate	48,177 (226)
2010-2015 change	7.6% (16)
2020 projection	50,793 (208)
2030 projection	56,646 (170)

RACE

Whites	80.3% (323)
Blacks	2.1% (283)
Hispanics	5.4% (240)
Asians	7.8% (6)
Native Americans	0.4% (203)

AGE

0-17 years old	15.0% (550)
18-24 years old	37.0% (1)
25-39 years old	17.0% (317)
40-54 years old	12.9% (549)
55-64 years old	8.5% (547)
65+ years old	9.7% (535)

PRIVATE SECTOR

Businesses	1,223 (200)
Employees	10,167 (371)
Total wages	$373,113,355 (360)
Average weekly wages	$706 (240)

HOUSEHOLD INCOME LADDER

95th percentile	$167,508 (65)
80th percentile	$89,734 (157)
60th percentile	$48,874 (405)
40th percentile	$26,325 (492)
20th percentile	$12,472 (509)

CHILDREN ★★★★★ (18)

Living with two parents	75.1% (50)
Older teens in school	98.6% (3)
Speak English very well	96.8% (421)
Poverty rate for children	19.3% (150)
No health insurance	2.9% (56)

DIVERSITY/EQUALITY ★★ (429)

Racial diversity index	34.4% (219)
Geographic diversity index	68.1% (56)
Top 20% share of income	53.2% (522)
Gender gap in earnings	43.3% (487)
White-collar gender gap	34.7% (387)

EDUCATION ★★★★★ (5)

Eighth grade or less	1.0% (20)
High school diplomas	96.0% (12)

Attended college	81.4% (3)
Bachelor's degrees	52.7% (2)
Advanced degrees	24.9% (2)

EMPLOYMENT ★★★★★ (85)

Average jobless rate	8.8% (344)
Self-employed workers	9.6% (200)
Management/financial jobs	13.7% (59)
Computer/engineering jobs	9.4% (2)
Health care jobs	4.0% (476)

GROWTH POTENTIAL ★★★★★ (73)

Children per senior	1.54 (197)
Median age	24.2 (2)
Moved from different state	7.7% (13)
Homes built since 2000	16.9% (155)
Construction jobs	2.3% (549)

HOUSING ★ (461)

Home vacancy rate	7.1% (165)
Home ownership rate	44.5% (550)
Housing diversity index	85.6% (127)
4 or more bedrooms	23.3% (62)
Affordability/income ratio	$4,963 (524)

INCOME ★★★ (307)

Poverty rate	31.2% (528)
Median household income	$36,631 (451)
Interest/dividends	26.3% (66)
Public assistance	12.9% (164)
Median fulltime earnings	$41,067 (92)

SENIORS ★★★ (226)

Seniors living alone	30.4% (447)
Poverty rate for seniors	7.1% (101)
Median income for seniors	$44,144 (35)
Seniors who work	24.1% (86)
Home ownership by seniors	74.2% (533)

STABILITY ★ (544)

25-39 age group	17.0% (317)
Born in state of residence	50.0% (487)
Same house as 1 year ago	60.4% (550)
Live and work in county	89.5% (74)
Married-couple households	40.6% (521)

TRANSPORTATION ★★★★★ (2)

Bicycle or walk to work	19.6% (1)
Carpool to work	13.5% (83)
Public transit to work	5.4% (9)
Commute <15 minutes	58.3% (58)
Commute >45 minutes	5.0% (33)

See pages 37-130 for explanations of statistics, stars, and ranks.

Red Bluff, CA
(Tehama County, CA)

POPULATION

2010 census	63,463 (130)
2015 estimate	63,308 (134)
2010-2015 change	-0.2% (273)
2020 projection	64,355 (128)
2030 projection	66,693 (122)

RACE

Whites	70.1% (393)
Blacks	0.5% (466)
Hispanics	23.5% (65)
Asians	1.5% (85)
Native Americans	1.8% (77)

AGE

0-17 years old	24.2% (172)
18-24 years old	8.1% (396)
25-39 years old	17.1% (308)
40-54 years old	19.7% (273)
55-64 years old	13.6% (247)
65+ years old	17.3% (172)

PRIVATE SECTOR

Businesses	1,652 (110)
Employees	13,313 (267)
Total wages	$513,337,195 (234)
Average weekly wages	$742 (173)

HOUSEHOLD INCOME LADDER

95th percentile	$145,286 (224)
80th percentile	$83,783 (277)
60th percentile	$52,044 (317)
40th percentile	$32,916 (327)
20th percentile	$18,973 (267)

CHILDREN ★★ (347)

Living with two parents	65.6% (256)
Older teens in school	85.9% (169)
Speak English very well	94.3% (492)
Poverty rate for children	27.6% (357)
No health insurance	8.4% (371)

DIVERSITY/EQUALITY ★★★★ (159)

Racial diversity index	45.2% (147)
Geographic diversity index	46.4% (261)
Top 20% share of income	47.8% (279)
Gender gap in earnings	32.7% (245)
White-collar gender gap	23.8% (257)

EDUCATION ★★ (432)

Eighth grade or less	6.9% (467)
High school diplomas	82.3% (437)
Attended college	53.0% (262)
Bachelor's degrees	14.4% (448)
Advanced degrees	4.4% (451)

EMPLOYMENT ★ (467)

Average jobless rate	13.2% (520)
Self-employed workers	11.7% (86)
Management/financial jobs	11.7% (185)
Computer/engineering jobs	1.9% (441)
Health care jobs	3.4% (513)

GROWTH POTENTIAL ★★★★ (190)

Children per senior	1.40 (279)
Median age	40.5 (329)
Moved from different state	1.7% (355)
Homes built since 2000	18.2% (128)
Construction jobs	7.8% (98)

HOUSING ★ (447)

Home vacancy rate	8.5% (253)
Home ownership rate	67.5% (368)
Housing diversity index	85.5% (143)
4 or more bedrooms	11.7% (505)
Affordability/income ratio	$4,183 (504)

INCOME ★★★ (325)

Poverty rate	19.8% (364)
Median household income	$41,001 (353)
Interest/dividends	16.8% (349)
Public assistance	14.8% (249)
Median fulltime earnings	$37,365 (256)

SENIORS ★★★★ (174)

Seniors living alone	23.6% (73)
Poverty rate for seniors	10.2% (334)
Median income for seniors	$35,370 (178)
Seniors who work	17.4% (318)
Home ownership by seniors	83.5% (197)

STABILITY ★★ (398)

25-39 age group	17.1% (308)
Born in state of residence	72.3% (271)
Same house as 1 year ago	83.1% (394)
Live and work in county	68.8% (392)
Married-couple households	50.8% (256)

TRANSPORTATION ★★★ (256)

Bicycle or walk to work	4.4% (123)
Carpool to work	13.0% (101)
Public transit to work	0.4% (219)
Commute <15 minutes	35.2% (437)
Commute >45 minutes	11.6% (296)

See pages 37-130 for explanations of statistics, stars, and ranks.

Rexburg, ID
(Fremont and Madison Counties, ID)

POPULATION

2010 census	50,778 (207)
2015 estimate	51,092 (205)
2010-2015 change	0.6% (209)
2020 projection	52,388 (196)
2030 projection	55,140 (183)

RACE

Whites	88.7% (212)
Blacks	0.6% (438)
Hispanics	8.1% (180)
Asians	1.0% (158)
Native Americans	0.1% (402)

AGE

0-17 years old	27.4% (39)
18-24 years old	25.7% (15)
25-39 years old	18.9% (111)
40-54 years old	12.0% (551)
55-64 years old	7.3% (550)
65+ years old	8.6% (546)

PRIVATE SECTOR

Businesses	1,237 (192)
Employees	13,627 (252)
Total wages	$402,631,453 (332)
Average weekly wages	$568 (521)

HOUSEHOLD INCOME LADDER

95th percentile	$134,310 (372)
80th percentile	$81,102 (349)
60th percentile	$48,189 (419)
40th percentile	$29,672 (431)
20th percentile	$15,768 (416)

CHILDREN ★★★★★ (28)

Living with two parents	89.1% (1)
Older teens in school	92.7% (34)
Speak English very well	98.0% (341)
Poverty rate for children	22.3% (230)
No health insurance	6.9% (307)

DIVERSITY/EQUALITY ★ (542)

Racial diversity index	20.6% (340)
Geographic diversity index	63.2% (92)
Top 20% share of income	49.7% (411)
Gender gap in earnings	51.6% (531)
White-collar gender gap	64.4% (547)

EDUCATION ★★★★★ (49)

Eighth grade or less	3.0% (231)
High school diplomas	93.7% (65)
Attended college	73.1% (13)
Bachelor's degrees	29.3% (61)
Advanced degrees	8.7% (96)

EMPLOYMENT ★★★★★ (109)

Average jobless rate	9.2% (377)
Self-employed workers	14.3% (31)
Management/financial jobs	12.9% (92)
Computer/engineering jobs	4.2% (66)
Health care jobs	4.0% (476)

GROWTH POTENTIAL ★★★★★ (1)

Children per senior	3.19 (10)
Median age	24.1 (1)
Moved from different state	13.3% (3)
Homes built since 2000	32.1% (12)
Construction jobs	6.2% (295)

HOUSING ★ (464)

Home vacancy rate	7.8% (205)
Home ownership rate	58.1% (520)
Housing diversity index	80.8% (497)
4 or more bedrooms	28.3% (19)
Affordability/income ratio	$4,505 (515)

INCOME ★★ (406)

Poverty rate	29.4% (521)
Median household income	$37,272 (440)
Interest/dividends	19.8% (254)
Public assistance	10.6% (84)
Median fulltime earnings	$32,732 (463)

SENIORS ★★★★★ (26)

Seniors living alone	23.9% (80)
Poverty rate for seniors	5.3% (26)
Median income for seniors	$38,528 (81)
Seniors who work	25.3% (67)
Home ownership by seniors	86.8% (72)

STABILITY ★★ (420)

25-39 age group	18.9% (111)
Born in state of residence	50.7% (484)
Same house as 1 year ago	68.4% (547)
Live and work in county	71.4% (351)
Married-couple households	71.0% (1)

TRANSPORTATION ★★★★★ (13)

Bicycle or walk to work	11.4% (8)
Carpool to work	13.2% (94)
Public transit to work	0.6% (141)
Commute <15 minutes	55.4% (87)
Commute >45 minutes	7.0% (86)

See pages 37-130 for explanations of statistics, stars, and ranks.

Riverton, WY
(Fremont County, WY)

POPULATION	
2010 census	40,123 (311)
2015 estimate	40,315 (311)
2010-2015 change	0.5% (219)
2020 projection	40,556 (309)
2030 projection	41,070 (302)

RACE	
Whites	70.5% (387)
Blacks	0.5% (466)
Hispanics	6.6% (207)
Asians	0.7% (241)
Native Americans	18.9% (7)

AGE	
0-17 years old	25.2% (108)
18-24 years old	8.5% (330)
25-39 years old	18.2% (167)
40-54 years old	18.0% (450)
55-64 years old	14.3% (148)
65+ years old	15.8% (305)

PRIVATE SECTOR	
Businesses	1,537 (128)
Employees	10,604 (356)
Total wages	$413,485,923 (323)
Average weekly wages	$750 (158)

HOUSEHOLD INCOME LADDER	
95th percentile	$158,294 (106)
80th percentile	$98,770 (64)
60th percentile	$64,679 (77)
40th percentile	$41,440 (89)
20th percentile	$22,119 (133)

CHILDREN	★★ (394)
Living with two parents	59.7% (408)
Older teens in school	79.9% (401)
Speak English very well	99.8% (38)
Poverty rate for children	20.9% (191)
No health insurance	14.2% (513)

DIVERSITY/EQUALITY	★★★★★ (44)
Racial diversity index	46.2% (141)
Geographic diversity index	67.0% (61)
Top 20% share of income	45.3% (80)
Gender gap in earnings	35.5% (327)
White-collar gender gap	21.0% (220)

EDUCATION	★★★★ (113)
Eighth grade or less	1.0% (20)
High school diplomas	92.9% (98)
Attended college	63.0% (83)
Bachelor's degrees	21.3% (182)
Advanced degrees	6.9% (186)

EMPLOYMENT	★★★★★ (96)
Average jobless rate	7.8% (270)
Self-employed workers	13.6% (38)
Management/financial jobs	13.1% (78)
Computer/engineering jobs	2.5% (307)
Health care jobs	5.4% (273)

GROWTH POTENTIAL	★★★★ (124)
Children per senior	1.59 (175)
Median age	38.2 (189)
Moved from different state	3.4% (118)
Homes built since 2000	13.6% (251)
Construction jobs	8.3% (67)

HOUSING	★★★★ (159)
Home vacancy rate	6.2% (109)
Home ownership rate	70.9% (232)
Housing diversity index	84.9% (235)
4 or more bedrooms	20.0% (127)
Affordability/income ratio	$3,534 (464)

INCOME	★★★★★ (54)
Poverty rate	14.2% (160)
Median household income	$52,773 (76)
Interest/dividends	33.0% (6)
Public assistance	10.2% (68)
Median fulltime earnings	$40,630 (112)

SENIORS	★★★★★ (98)
Seniors living alone	28.4% (325)
Poverty rate for seniors	5.5% (36)
Median income for seniors	$34,967 (191)
Seniors who work	26.0% (47)
Home ownership by seniors	82.5% (251)

STABILITY	★★★ (291)
25-39 age group	18.2% (167)
Born in state of residence	50.1% (486)
Same house as 1 year ago	83.0% (397)
Live and work in county	93.8% (21)
Married-couple households	49.5% (323)

TRANSPORTATION	★★★★★ (69)
Bicycle or walk to work	4.6% (110)
Carpool to work	12.5% (121)
Public transit to work	1.1% (58)
Commute <15 minutes	56.6% (76)
Commute >45 minutes	8.9% (171)

See pages 37-130 for explanations of statistics, stars, and ranks.

Rock Springs, WY
(Sweetwater County, WY)

POPULATION

2010 census	43,806 (272)
2015 estimate	44,626 (265)
2010-2015 change	1.9% (136)
2020 projection	45,607 (252)
2030 projection	47,667 (236)

RACE

Whites	79.9% (327)
Blacks	0.8% (404)
Hispanics	15.8% (101)
Asians	1.4% (99)
Native Americans	0.2% (300)

AGE

0-17 years old	26.9% (47)
18-24 years old	9.4% (203)
25-39 years old	22.8% (16)
40-54 years old	18.9% (376)
55-64 years old	12.8% (356)
65+ years old	9.2% (541)

PRIVATE SECTOR

Businesses	1,581 (122)
Employees	19,110 (137)
Total wages	$1,168,140,398 (46)
Average weekly wages	$1,176 (7)

HOUSEHOLD INCOME LADDER

95th percentile	$169,871 (57)
80th percentile	$117,033 (18)
60th percentile	$83,854 (11)
40th percentile	$55,887 (11)
20th percentile	$30,837 (12)

CHILDREN ★★★★★ (91)

Living with two parents	73.3% (76)
Older teens in school	85.5% (183)
Speak English very well	98.1% (331)
Poverty rate for children	17.0% (97)
No health insurance	5.8% (236)

DIVERSITY/EQUALITY ★★★★ (149)

Racial diversity index	33.6% (222)
Geographic diversity index	71.3% (36)
Top 20% share of income	42.2% (4)
Gender gap in earnings	55.8% (545)
White-collar gender gap	31.4% (357)

EDUCATION ★★★★ (207)

Eighth grade or less	3.1% (238)
High school diplomas	90.7% (173)
Attended college	56.2% (200)
Bachelor's degrees	20.2% (216)
Advanced degrees	5.5% (318)

EMPLOYMENT ★ (471)

Average jobless rate	5.4% (89)
Self-employed workers	5.6% (523)
Management/financial jobs	9.4% (444)
Computer/engineering jobs	3.3% (145)
Health care jobs	3.1% (531)

GROWTH POTENTIAL ★★★★★ (17)

Children per senior	2.94 (18)
Median age	33.6 (66)
Moved from different state	7.2% (20)
Homes built since 2000	17.7% (137)
Construction jobs	7.8% (98)

HOUSING ★★★★ (168)

Home vacancy rate	9.5% (317)
Home ownership rate	71.0% (229)
Housing diversity index	83.2% (405)
4 or more bedrooms	24.0% (51)
Affordability/income ratio	$2,766 (351)

INCOME ★★★★★ (13)

Poverty rate	11.5% (71)
Median household income	$69,022 (11)
Interest/dividends	18.9% (279)
Public assistance	4.4% (9)
Median fulltime earnings	$53,503 (7)

SENIORS ★★★★★ (73)

Seniors living alone	30.0% (427)
Poverty rate for seniors	6.9% (84)
Median income for seniors	$40,086 (58)
Seniors who work	24.8% (74)
Home ownership by seniors	86.1% (93)

STABILITY ★★★★★ (67)

25-39 age group	22.8% (16)
Born in state of residence	41.6% (517)
Same house as 1 year ago	80.2% (495)
Live and work in county	96.3% (7)
Married-couple households	54.4% (93)

TRANSPORTATION ★★★★★ (67)

Bicycle or walk to work	2.6% (308)
Carpool to work	15.7% (36)
Public transit to work	2.4% (25)
Commute <15 minutes	49.5% (163)
Commute >45 minutes	12.4% (331)

See pages 37-130 for explanations of statistics, stars, and ranks.

Roseburg, OR
(Douglas County, OR)

POPULATION

2010 census	107,667 (19)
2015 estimate	107,685 (20)
2010-2015 change	0.0% (255)
2020 projection	108,166 (23)
2030 projection	109,321 (25)

RACE

Whites	88.8% (208)
Blacks	0.3% (519)
Hispanics	5.2% (247)
Asians	0.9% (178)
Native Americans	1.3% (86)

AGE

0-17 years old	19.7% (473)
18-24 years old	7.2% (510)
25-39 years old	15.3% (493)
40-54 years old	18.7% (399)
55-64 years old	16.2% (38)
65+ years old	22.9% (20)

PRIVATE SECTOR

Businesses	2,854 (24)
Employees	28,589 (52)
Total wages	$1,040,548,005 (63)
Average weekly wages	$700 (256)

HOUSEHOLD INCOME LADDER

95th percentile	$132,187 (398)
80th percentile	$79,197 (380)
60th percentile	$51,122 (356)
40th percentile	$32,983 (324)
20th percentile	$18,357 (300)

CHILDREN ★★ (340)

Living with two parents	62.1% (349)
Older teens in school	81.8% (329)
Speak English very well	99.6% (77)
Poverty rate for children	30.0% (404)
No health insurance	8.4% (371)

DIVERSITY/EQUALITY ★★★★ (113)

Racial diversity index	20.7% (338)
Geographic diversity index	67.2% (60)
Top 20% share of income	47.0% (216)
Gender gap in earnings	38.3% (402)
White-collar gender gap	10.4% (93)

EDUCATION ★★★★ (191)

Eighth grade or less	1.7% (97)
High school diplomas	90.8% (167)
Attended college	59.9% (127)
Bachelor's degrees	16.1% (366)
Advanced degrees	5.7% (292)

EMPLOYMENT ★★ (348)

Average jobless rate	12.2% (497)
Self-employed workers	10.4% (145)
Management/financial jobs	11.4% (210)
Computer/engineering jobs	3.6% (112)
Health care jobs	4.7% (385)

GROWTH POTENTIAL ★ (503)

Children per senior	0.86 (530)
Median age	46.9 (526)
Moved from different state	2.9% (165)
Homes built since 2000	14.6% (213)
Construction jobs	5.7% (373)

HOUSING ★★ (398)

Home vacancy rate	7.4% (180)
Home ownership rate	67.4% (371)
Housing diversity index	85.5% (143)
4 or more bedrooms	12.7% (466)
Affordability/income ratio	$4,108 (501)

INCOME ★★ (374)

Poverty rate	19.3% (348)
Median household income	$41,312 (342)
Interest/dividends	19.1% (273)
Public assistance	23.9% (508)
Median fulltime earnings	$38,135 (215)

SENIORS ★★★★ (208)

Seniors living alone	23.0% (61)
Poverty rate for seniors	7.7% (156)
Median income for seniors	$36,562 (134)
Seniors who work	12.8% (530)
Home ownership by seniors	81.1% (325)

STABILITY ★ (453)

25-39 age group	15.3% (493)
Born in state of residence	46.8% (499)
Same house as 1 year ago	83.6% (359)
Live and work in county	92.7% (38)
Married-couple households	50.1% (291)

TRANSPORTATION ★★★★ (217)

Bicycle or walk to work	3.8% (161)
Carpool to work	11.9% (145)
Public transit to work	0.2% (363)
Commute <15 minutes	42.6% (284)
Commute >45 minutes	9.1% (180)

See pages 37-130 for explanations of statistics, stars, and ranks.

Roswell, NM
(Chaves County, NM)

POPULATION	
2010 census	65,645 (117)
2015 estimate	65,764 (118)
2010-2015 change	0.2% (241)
2020 projection	65,661 (120)
2030 projection	65,193 (127)

RACE	
Whites	41.6% (510)
Blacks	1.6% (320)
Hispanics	54.2% (22)
Asians	0.7% (241)
Native Americans	0.7% (136)

AGE	
0-17 years old	27.1% (43)
18-24 years old	10.5% (136)
25-39 years old	17.9% (214)
40-54 years old	18.1% (446)
55-64 years old	12.0% (438)
65+ years old	14.4% (419)

PRIVATE SECTOR	
Businesses	1,640 (115)
Employees	17,618 (159)
Total wages	$558,677,912 (210)
Average weekly wages	$610 (471)

HOUSEHOLD INCOME LADDER	
95th percentile	$137,889 (312)
80th percentile	$85,050 (252)
60th percentile	$51,795 (330)
40th percentile	$31,883 (366)
20th percentile	$17,543 (339)

CHILDREN	★★ (417)
Living with two parents	60.0% (398)
Older teens in school	82.4% (301)
Speak English very well	94.8% (480)
Poverty rate for children	32.7% (459)
No health insurance	6.4% (276)

DIVERSITY/EQUALITY	★★★★★ (83)
Racial diversity index	53.3% (75)
Geographic diversity index	64.3% (80)
Top 20% share of income	48.8% (340)
Gender gap in earnings	36.1% (343)
White-collar gender gap	21.6% (229)

EDUCATION	★ (445)
Eighth grade or less	9.2% (507)
High school diplomas	79.6% (486)
Attended college	52.4% (276)
Bachelor's degrees	17.7% (295)
Advanced degrees	5.4% (334)

EMPLOYMENT	★★ (346)
Average jobless rate	7.6% (250)
Self-employed workers	9.2% (231)
Management/financial jobs	11.3% (218)
Computer/engineering jobs	2.6% (288)
Health care jobs	4.1% (462)

GROWTH POTENTIAL	★★★★ (178)
Children per senior	1.88 (76)
Median age	34.8 (88)
Moved from different state	3.5% (109)
Homes built since 2000	7.7% (475)
Construction jobs	5.8% (360)

HOUSING	★★★ (305)
Home vacancy rate	10.7% (390)
Home ownership rate	66.7% (399)
Housing diversity index	86.1% (51)
4 or more bedrooms	14.2% (392)
Affordability/income ratio	$2,454 (231)

INCOME	★★ (400)
Poverty rate	21.9% (426)
Median household income	$40,630 (366)
Interest/dividends	15.4% (396)
Public assistance	19.9% (424)
Median fulltime earnings	$37,244 (266)

SENIORS	★★ (333)
Seniors living alone	27.7% (278)
Poverty rate for seniors	13.4% (457)
Median income for seniors	$32,731 (294)
Seniors who work	20.6% (173)
Home ownership by seniors	82.5% (251)

STABILITY	★★ (362)
25-39 age group	17.9% (214)
Born in state of residence	56.6% (448)
Same house as 1 year ago	83.2% (388)
Live and work in county	87.2% (98)
Married-couple households	48.1% (376)

TRANSPORTATION	★★★★ (218)
Bicycle or walk to work	2.6% (308)
Carpool to work	11.3% (201)
Public transit to work	0.4% (219)
Commute <15 minutes	48.9% (176)
Commute >45 minutes	9.5% (203)

See pages 37-130 for explanations of statistics, stars, and ranks.

Ruidoso, NM
(Lincoln County, NM)

POPULATION

2010 census	20,497 (525)
2015 estimate	19,420 (527)
2010-2015 change	-5.3% (536)
2020 projection	18,474 (530)
2030 projection	16,648 (537)

RACE

Whites	64.0% (422)
Blacks	0.6% (438)
Hispanics	31.2% (47)
Asians	0.2% (509)
Native Americans	2.5% (60)

AGE

0-17 years old	18.7% (507)
18-24 years old	6.0% (546)
25-39 years old	14.3% (535)
40-54 years old	18.0% (450)
55-64 years old	17.9% (6)
65+ years old	25.3% (11)

PRIVATE SECTOR

Businesses	698 (428)
Employees	5,265 (523)
Total wages	$142,368,153 (537)
Average weekly wages	$520 (542)

HOUSEHOLD INCOME LADDER

95th percentile	$160,018 (97)
80th percentile	$85,246 (248)
60th percentile	$48,331 (415)
40th percentile	$30,006 (423)
20th percentile	$16,407 (389)

CHILDREN ★★★ (278)

Living with two parents	67.7% (202)
Older teens in school	83.1% (271)
Speak English very well	92.9% (509)
Poverty rate for children	20.2% (171)
No health insurance	5.2% (197)

DIVERSITY/EQUALITY ★★★★ (211)

Racial diversity index	49.2% (119)
Geographic diversity index	73.0% (21)
Top 20% share of income	53.4% (528)
Gender gap in earnings	37.7% (382)
White-collar gender gap	25.6% (281)

EDUCATION ★★★★ (167)

Eighth grade or less	4.0% (325)
High school diplomas	89.0% (231)
Attended college	60.9% (114)
Bachelor's degrees	24.3% (122)
Advanced degrees	6.5% (220)

EMPLOYMENT ★★★★★ (77)

Average jobless rate	7.3% (228)
Self-employed workers	13.1% (49)
Management/financial jobs	15.9% (16)
Computer/engineering jobs	2.4% (336)
Health care jobs	4.6% (401)

GROWTH POTENTIAL ★★★ (271)

Children per senior	0.74 (541)
Median age	50.4 (546)
Moved from different state	4.2% (70)
Homes built since 2000	17.4% (145)
Construction jobs	10.0% (17)

HOUSING ★★ (366)

Home vacancy rate	11.1% (409)
Home ownership rate	79.0% (9)
Housing diversity index	84.0% (344)
4 or more bedrooms	13.6% (424)
Affordability/income ratio	$3,977 (495)

INCOME ★★★ (241)

Poverty rate	16.5% (246)
Median household income	$40,708 (365)
Interest/dividends	26.8% (56)
Public assistance	15.2% (266)
Median fulltime earnings	$34,500 (404)

SENIORS ★★★★★ (55)

Seniors living alone	25.9% (164)
Poverty rate for seniors	10.1% (332)
Median income for seniors	n.a.
Seniors who work	20.2% (187)
Home ownership by seniors	91.7% (6)

STABILITY ★ (512)

25-39 age group	14.3% (535)
Born in state of residence	43.2% (512)
Same house as 1 year ago	86.1% (245)
Live and work in county	85.1% (134)
Married-couple households	47.6% (395)

TRANSPORTATION ★★★★★ (103)

Bicycle or walk to work	4.3% (130)
Carpool to work	16.0% (32)
Public transit to work	0.0% (511)
Commute <15 minutes	51.9% (125)
Commute >45 minutes	12.0% (311)

See pages 37-130 for explanations of statistics, stars, and ranks.

Safford, AZ
(Graham County, AZ)

POPULATION

2010 census	37,220 (350)
2015 estimate	37,666 (349)
2010-2015 change	1.2% (173)
2020 projection	38,379 (335)
2030 projection	39,879 (320)

RACE

Whites	51.7% (480)
Blacks	1.9% (295)
Hispanics	31.8% (46)
Asians	0.8% (201)
Native Americans	12.9% (17)

AGE

0-17 years old	27.8% (36)
18-24 years old	11.3% (106)
25-39 years old	21.3% (36)
40-54 years old	17.2% (494)
55-64 years old	10.3% (510)
65+ years old	12.0% (495)

PRIVATE SECTOR

Businesses	451 (529)
Employees	5,800 (514)
Total wages	$218,940,570 (497)
Average weekly wages	$726 (203)

HOUSEHOLD INCOME LADDER

95th percentile	$137,231 (323)
80th percentile	$83,691 (279)
60th percentile	$56,385 (221)
40th percentile	$36,744 (208)
20th percentile	$18,123 (311)

CHILDREN ★★ (377)

Living with two parents	62.0% (353)
Older teens in school	85.0% (197)
Speak English very well	99.2% (163)
Poverty rate for children	29.1% (387)
No health insurance	13.1% (498)

DIVERSITY/EQUALITY ★★★★★ (54)

Racial diversity index	61.4% (11)
Geographic diversity index	52.5% (183)
Top 20% share of income	45.4% (83)
Gender gap in earnings	41.2% (459)
White-collar gender gap	13.6% (136)

EDUCATION ★★ (367)

Eighth grade or less	3.9% (316)
High school diplomas	86.4% (331)
Attended college	53.0% (262)
Bachelor's degrees	12.6% (504)
Advanced degrees	4.7% (419)

EMPLOYMENT ★ (535)

Average jobless rate	14.1% (528)
Self-employed workers	4.6% (545)
Management/financial jobs	9.6% (427)
Computer/engineering jobs	3.6% (112)
Health care jobs	4.4% (433)

GROWTH POTENTIAL ★★★★★ (40)

Children per senior	2.31 (35)
Median age	32.0 (47)
Moved from different state	3.7% (96)
Homes built since 2000	22.6% (59)
Construction jobs	6.0% (326)

HOUSING ★★★★ (126)

Home vacancy rate	5.9% (88)
Home ownership rate	70.7% (244)
Housing diversity index	84.2% (325)
4 or more bedrooms	19.0% (159)
Affordability/income ratio	$2,683 (322)

INCOME ★★ (372)

Poverty rate	22.6% (438)
Median household income	$45,964 (214)
Interest/dividends	12.8% (474)
Public assistance	22.4% (489)
Median fulltime earnings	$42,478 (54)

SENIORS ★★★ (268)

Seniors living alone	29.0% (366)
Poverty rate for seniors	10.7% (357)
Median income for seniors	$32,031 (318)
Seniors who work	16.1% (400)
Home ownership by seniors	88.7% (28)

STABILITY ★★★★★ (71)

25-39 age group	21.3% (36)
Born in state of residence	66.9% (364)
Same house as 1 year ago	82.3% (426)
Live and work in county	81.8% (186)
Married-couple households	52.4% (177)

TRANSPORTATION ★★★★ (175)

Bicycle or walk to work	3.3% (211)
Carpool to work	14.0% (66)
Public transit to work	1.2% (54)
Commute <15 minutes	46.9% (217)
Commute >45 minutes	15.2% (430)

See pages 37-130 for explanations of statistics, stars, and ranks.

Sandpoint, ID
(Bonner County, ID)

POPULATION

2010 census	40,877 (302)
2015 estimate	41,859 (291)
2010-2015 change	2.4% (111)
2020 projection	42,466 (289)
2030 projection	43,665 (279)

RACE

Whites	93.8% (80)
Blacks	0.1% (544)
Hispanics	2.7% (361)
Asians	0.6% (291)
Native Americans	0.5% (174)

AGE

0-17 years old	20.6% (423)
18-24 years old	6.2% (543)
25-39 years old	14.7% (523)
40-54 years old	19.8% (261)
55-64 years old	18.4% (4)
65+ years old	20.2% (50)

PRIVATE SECTOR

Businesses	1,454 (146)
Employees	10,714 (353)
Total wages	$342,677,176 (388)
Average weekly wages	$615 (456)

HOUSEHOLD INCOME LADDER

95th percentile	$147,773 (188)
80th percentile	$82,162 (324)
60th percentile	$51,926 (321)
40th percentile	$33,141 (319)
20th percentile	$17,050 (363)

CHILDREN ★★★★ (219)

Living with two parents	70.5% (131)
Older teens in school	81.4% (350)
Speak English very well	100.0% (1)
Poverty rate for children	19.3% (150)
No health insurance	10.5% (437)

DIVERSITY/EQUALITY ★★★★ (167)

Racial diversity index	11.9% (468)
Geographic diversity index	69.0% (51)
Top 20% share of income	49.1% (364)
Gender gap in earnings	38.0% (392)
White-collar gender gap	3.5% (23)

EDUCATION ★★★★ (164)

Eighth grade or less	2.0% (126)
High school diplomas	91.5% (145)
Attended college	59.9% (127)
Bachelor's degrees	20.8% (194)
Advanced degrees	5.6% (304)

EMPLOYMENT ★★★★★ (108)

Average jobless rate	6.2% (131)
Self-employed workers	15.0% (20)
Management/financial jobs	13.2% (73)
Computer/engineering jobs	2.6% (288)
Health care jobs	3.4% (513)

GROWTH POTENTIAL ★★★★ (159)

Children per senior	1.02 (497)
Median age	47.2 (528)
Moved from different state	4.0% (79)
Homes built since 2000	24.1% (42)
Construction jobs	8.8% (55)

HOUSING ★★ (372)

Home vacancy rate	6.8% (151)
Home ownership rate	72.7% (162)
Housing diversity index	82.9% (422)
4 or more bedrooms	18.9% (164)
Affordability/income ratio	$5,011 (525)

INCOME ★★★ (229)

Poverty rate	15.3% (204)
Median household income	$42,171 (315)
Interest/dividends	21.3% (206)
Public assistance	12.9% (164)
Median fulltime earnings	$37,066 (281)

SENIORS ★★★★ (162)

Seniors living alone	22.9% (58)
Poverty rate for seniors	9.4% (282)
Median income for seniors	$34,371 (218)
Seniors who work	16.9% (348)
Home ownership by seniors	83.4% (202)

STABILITY ★ (506)

25-39 age group	14.7% (523)
Born in state of residence	30.3% (544)
Same house as 1 year ago	85.7% (272)
Live and work in county	81.2% (200)
Married-couple households	54.0% (108)

TRANSPORTATION ★★ (386)

Bicycle or walk to work	4.0% (155)
Carpool to work	11.0% (229)
Public transit to work	0.4% (219)
Commute <15 minutes	38.1% (374)
Commute >45 minutes	17.1% (483)

See pages 37-130 for explanations of statistics, stars, and ranks.

Shelton, WA
(Mason County, WA)

POPULATION	
2010 census	60,699 (146)
2015 estimate	61,023 (142)
2010-2015 change	0.5% (219)
2020 projection	62,913 (132)
2030 projection	67,103 (118)

RACE	
Whites	81.9% (302)
Blacks	1.0% (381)
Hispanics	8.7% (171)
Asians	1.7% (69)
Native Americans	2.5% (60)

AGE	
0-17 years old	19.6% (478)
18-24 years old	7.6% (468)
25-39 years old	16.8% (359)
40-54 years old	19.2% (336)
55-64 years old	16.4% (30)
65+ years old	20.4% (45)

PRIVATE SECTOR	
Businesses	1,225 (197)
Employees	8,246 (441)
Total wages	$266,585,538 (459)
Average weekly wages	$622 (448)

HOUSEHOLD INCOME LADDER	
95th percentile	$149,816 (165)
80th percentile	$91,183 (138)
60th percentile	$60,783 (137)
40th percentile	$40,305 (121)
20th percentile	$20,324 (215)

CHILDREN	★★ (346)
Living with two parents	62.5% (334)
Older teens in school	83.4% (258)
Speak English very well	97.6% (375)
Poverty rate for children	26.3% (333)
No health insurance	9.6% (411)

DIVERSITY/EQUALITY	★★★★★ (17)
Racial diversity index	31.9% (238)
Geographic diversity index	63.4% (88)
Top 20% share of income	46.6% (170)
Gender gap in earnings	17.9% (32)
White-collar gender gap	3.0% (19)

EDUCATION	★★★ (307)
Eighth grade or less	4.0% (325)
High school diplomas	86.9% (313)
Attended college	56.2% (200)
Bachelor's degrees	15.9% (382)
Advanced degrees	5.1% (364)

EMPLOYMENT	★★ (415)
Average jobless rate	12.9% (516)
Self-employed workers	10.5% (139)
Management/financial jobs	12.3% (133)
Computer/engineering jobs	2.9% (219)
Health care jobs	3.8% (494)

GROWTH POTENTIAL	★★ (375)
Children per senior	0.96 (515)
Median age	45.4 (504)
Moved from different state	2.5% (203)
Homes built since 2000	19.4% (100)
Construction jobs	6.5% (253)

HOUSING	★★ (335)
Home vacancy rate	6.4% (127)
Home ownership rate	77.0% (27)
Housing diversity index	83.5% (391)
4 or more bedrooms	10.5% (525)
Affordability/income ratio	$4,053 (499)

INCOME	★★★★ (153)
Poverty rate	17.2% (270)
Median household income	$50,406 (115)
Interest/dividends	24.7% (109)
Public assistance	18.5% (385)
Median fulltime earnings	$42,817 (48)

SENIORS	★★★★★ (43)
Seniors living alone	21.4% (27)
Poverty rate for seniors	5.6% (40)
Median income for seniors	$42,486 (43)
Seniors who work	12.8% (530)
Home ownership by seniors	87.7% (48)

STABILITY	★ (520)
25-39 age group	16.8% (359)
Born in state of residence	55.9% (456)
Same house as 1 year ago	83.3% (382)
Live and work in county	57.7% (507)
Married-couple households	51.2% (242)

TRANSPORTATION	★ (453)
Bicycle or walk to work	1.6% (443)
Carpool to work	15.7% (36)
Public transit to work	1.5% (42)
Commute <15 minutes	26.0% (545)
Commute >45 minutes	25.4% (546)

See pages 37-130 for explanations of statistics, stars, and ranks.

Sheridan, WY
(Sheridan County, WY)

POPULATION

2010 census	29,116 (442)
2015 estimate	30,009 (434)
2010-2015 change	3.1% (78)
2020 projection	30,677 (429)
2030 projection	32,080 (408)

RACE

Whites	91.7% (147)
Blacks	0.8% (404)
Hispanics	4.2% (287)
Asians	0.7% (241)
Native Americans	1.1% (96)

AGE

0-17 years old	21.9% (344)
18-24 years old	7.9% (424)
25-39 years old	17.2% (290)
40-54 years old	19.2% (336)
55-64 years old	16.3% (35)
65+ years old	17.5% (158)

PRIVATE SECTOR

Businesses	1,330 (169)
Employees	9,989 (376)
Total wages	$353,613,531 (380)
Average weekly wages	$681 (311)

HOUSEHOLD INCOME LADDER

95th percentile	$174,010 (45)
80th percentile	$100,270 (58)
60th percentile	$68,321 (44)
40th percentile	$43,013 (67)
20th percentile	$23,866 (73)

CHILDREN ★★★★★ (2)

Living with two parents	74.9% (52)
Older teens in school	93.6% (25)
Speak English very well	99.9% (19)
Poverty rate for children	10.5% (18)
No health insurance	2.4% (28)

DIVERSITY/EQUALITY ★★★★ (134)

Racial diversity index	15.7% (399)
Geographic diversity index	71.7% (34)
Top 20% share of income	45.5% (86)
Gender gap in earnings	36.0% (339)
White-collar gender gap	27.4% (301)

EDUCATION ★★★★★ (33)

Eighth grade or less	0.8% (10)
High school diplomas	95.6% (17)

Attended college	69.7% (29)
Bachelor's degrees	29.5% (59)
Advanced degrees	9.7% (68)

EMPLOYMENT ★★★★★ (2)

Average jobless rate	3.4% (19)
Self-employed workers	13.6% (38)
Management/financial jobs	15.0% (31)
Computer/engineering jobs	5.7% (19)
Health care jobs	7.1% (63)

GROWTH POTENTIAL ★★★★★ (77)

Children per senior	1.25 (385)
Median age	42.2 (412)
Moved from different state	4.9% (57)
Homes built since 2000	18.5% (119)
Construction jobs	10.3% (13)

HOUSING ★★★★ (142)

Home vacancy rate	5.2% (46)
Home ownership rate	68.3% (332)
Housing diversity index	85.2% (190)
4 or more bedrooms	23.6% (53)
Affordability/income ratio	$4,111 (502)

INCOME ★★★★★ (26)

Poverty rate	8.3% (12)
Median household income	$55,455 (50)
Interest/dividends	25.1% (94)
Public assistance	5.0% (11)
Median fulltime earnings	$45,436 (27)

SENIORS ★★★ (286)

Seniors living alone	32.5% (522)
Poverty rate for seniors	7.0% (93)
Median income for seniors	$35,340 (179)
Seniors who work	25.4% (63)
Home ownership by seniors	78.2% (445)

STABILITY ★★ (393)

25-39 age group	17.2% (290)
Born in state of residence	40.4% (519)
Same house as 1 year ago	82.3% (426)
Live and work in county	92.4% (41)
Married-couple households	53.3% (140)

TRANSPORTATION ★★★★★ (88)

Bicycle or walk to work	4.8% (98)
Carpool to work	10.9% (239)
Public transit to work	0.3% (291)
Commute <15 minutes	58.8% (55)
Commute >45 minutes	6.9% (82)

See pages 37-130 for explanations of statistics, stars, and ranks.

Show Low, AZ
(Navajo County, AZ)

POPULATION

2010 census	107,449 (20)
2015 estimate	108,277 (18)
2010-2015 change	0.8% (194)
2020 projection	108,367 (22)
2030 projection	108,554 (27)

RACE

Whites	42.6% (508)
Blacks	0.5% (466)
Hispanics	11.1% (137)
Asians	0.7% (241)
Native Americans	43.1% (2)

AGE

0-17 years old	28.3% (28)
18-24 years old	9.3% (217)
25-39 years old	17.0% (317)
40-54 years old	17.6% (470)
55-64 years old	12.6% (385)
65+ years old	15.2% (354)

PRIVATE SECTOR

Businesses	1,492 (136)
Employees	17,271 (165)
Total wages	$623,749,418 (175)
Average weekly wages	$695 (268)

HOUSEHOLD INCOME LADDER

95th percentile	$132,485 (394)
80th percentile	$73,053 (485)
60th percentile	$46,780 (448)
40th percentile	$26,915 (486)
20th percentile	$13,197 (498)

CHILDREN ★ (541)

Living with two parents	50.7% (503)
Older teens in school	75.2% (501)
Speak English very well	94.7% (482)
Poverty rate for children	40.4% (518)
No health insurance	12.9% (494)

DIVERSITY/EQUALITY ★★★★ (146)

Racial diversity index	62.0% (8)
Geographic diversity index	50.5% (206)
Top 20% share of income	50.0% (426)
Gender gap in earnings	32.0% (227)
White-collar gender gap	29.3% (324)

EDUCATION ★★ (390)

Eighth grade or less	4.2% (337)
High school diplomas	84.1% (398)
Attended college	52.5% (272)
Bachelor's degrees	13.2% (489)
Advanced degrees	4.6% (431)

EMPLOYMENT ★ (483)

Average jobless rate	19.8% (548)
Self-employed workers	10.6% (135)
Management/financial jobs	10.4% (332)
Computer/engineering jobs	2.0% (420)
Health care jobs	5.6% (240)

GROWTH POTENTIAL ★★★★★ (51)

Children per senior	1.87 (77)
Median age	35.7 (109)
Moved from different state	2.3% (234)
Homes built since 2000	24.7% (37)
Construction jobs	8.2% (78)

HOUSING ★★ (431)

Home vacancy rate	10.3% (366)
Home ownership rate	70.0% (272)
Housing diversity index	81.8% (466)
4 or more bedrooms	14.7% (370)
Affordability/income ratio	$2,906 (381)

INCOME ★ (507)

Poverty rate	30.6% (526)
Median household income	$35,921 (470)
Interest/dividends	12.6% (480)
Public assistance	27.4% (528)
Median fulltime earnings	$36,222 (323)

SENIORS ★★★★ (182)

Seniors living alone	20.0% (14)
Poverty rate for seniors	15.4% (495)
Median income for seniors	$32,071 (316)
Seniors who work	14.7% (467)
Home ownership by seniors	88.4% (31)

STABILITY ★★★★ (212)

25-39 age group	17.0% (317)
Born in state of residence	68.3% (338)
Same house as 1 year ago	86.1% (245)
Live and work in county	91.0% (52)
Married-couple households	46.9% (419)

TRANSPORTATION ★★★★★ (110)

Bicycle or walk to work	4.4% (123)
Carpool to work	14.2% (58)
Public transit to work	1.6% (38)
Commute <15 minutes	48.3% (189)
Commute >45 minutes	14.5% (411)

See pages 37-130 for explanations of statistics, stars, and ranks.

Silver City, NM
(Grant County, NM)

POPULATION

2010 census	29,514 (437)
2015 estimate	28,609 (448)
2010-2015 change	-3.1% (487)
2020 projection	27,326 (456)
2030 projection	24,831 (473)

RACE

Whites	47.6% (494)
Blacks	0.5% (466)
Hispanics	49.2% (27)
Asians	0.1% (529)
Native Americans	0.7% (136)

AGE

0-17 years old	21.7% (359)
18-24 years old	7.9% (424)
25-39 years old	15.3% (493)
40-54 years old	15.6% (528)
55-64 years old	16.0% (46)
65+ years old	23.5% (15)

PRIVATE SECTOR

Businesses	651 (451)
Employees	6,262 (499)
Total wages	$246,456,138 (472)
Average weekly wages	$757 (150)

HOUSEHOLD INCOME LADDER

95th percentile	$141,435 (275)
80th percentile	$78,449 (394)
60th percentile	$46,959 (445)
40th percentile	$29,962 (426)
20th percentile	$16,528 (385)

CHILDREN ★★ (403)

Living with two parents	51.8% (493)
Older teens in school	76.8% (474)
Speak English very well	98.9% (226)
Poverty rate for children	31.1% (423)
No health insurance	3.3% (72)

DIVERSITY/EQUALITY ★★★★★ (37)

Racial diversity index	53.1% (80)
Geographic diversity index	64.1% (82)
Top 20% share of income	50.7% (461)
Gender gap in earnings	26.4% (109)
White-collar gender gap	4.5% (36)

EDUCATION ★★★★★ (99)

Eighth grade or less	3.8% (307)
High school diplomas	88.2% (260)
Attended college	60.3% (123)
Bachelor's degrees	24.4% (120)
Advanced degrees	12.4% (33)

EMPLOYMENT ★★★★★ (84)

Average jobless rate	9.7% (409)
Self-employed workers	11.7% (86)
Management/financial jobs	12.0% (156)
Computer/engineering jobs	3.5% (122)
Health care jobs	7.5% (44)

GROWTH POTENTIAL ★★ (389)

Children per senior	0.92 (523)
Median age	46.5 (521)
Moved from different state	2.6% (187)
Homes built since 2000	13.3% (263)
Construction jobs	8.3% (67)

HOUSING ★★★ (317)

Home vacancy rate	11.1% (409)
Home ownership rate	74.8% (88)
Housing diversity index	86.4% (26)
4 or more bedrooms	11.8% (503)
Affordability/income ratio	$3,466 (460)

INCOME ★★ (351)

Poverty rate	20.8% (397)
Median household income	$38,311 (421)
Interest/dividends	20.7% (229)
Public assistance	20.3% (437)
Median fulltime earnings	$38,385 (207)

SENIORS ★★★★ (142)

Seniors living alone	25.9% (164)
Poverty rate for seniors	8.1% (187)
Median income for seniors	$35,015 (188)
Seniors who work	14.6% (472)
Home ownership by seniors	88.6% (30)

STABILITY ★★ (414)

25-39 age group	15.3% (493)
Born in state of residence	55.9% (456)
Same house as 1 year ago	87.7% (154)
Live and work in county	95.7% (11)
Married-couple households	43.3% (489)

TRANSPORTATION ★★★★ (177)

Bicycle or walk to work	3.6% (180)
Carpool to work	10.6% (271)
Public transit to work	0.4% (219)
Commute <15 minutes	47.6% (199)
Commute >45 minutes	6.9% (82)

See pages 37-130 for explanations of statistics, stars, and ranks.

Sonora, CA
(Tuolumne County, CA)

POPULATION	
2010 census	55,365 (169)
2015 estimate	53,709 (181)
2010-2015 change	-3.0% (481)
2020 projection	52,524 (194)
2030 projection	50,334 (214)

RACE	
Whites	81.4% (311)
Blacks	1.8% (309)
Hispanics	11.4% (136)
Asians	1.5% (85)
Native Americans	1.5% (80)

AGE	
0-17 years old	16.8% (540)
18-24 years old	7.6% (468)
25-39 years old	16.6% (388)
40-54 years old	18.8% (386)
55-64 years old	17.5% (7)
65+ years old	22.7% (21)

PRIVATE SECTOR	
Businesses	1,445 (148)
Employees	11,683 (319)
Total wages	$434,591,890 (302)
Average weekly wages	$715 (225)

HOUSEHOLD INCOME LADDER	
95th percentile	$164,177 (75)
80th percentile	$93,753 (107)
60th percentile	$59,905 (154)
40th percentile	$39,024 (156)
20th percentile	$22,098 (135)

CHILDREN	★★★★ (146)
Living with two parents	69.4% (156)
Older teens in school	81.1% (364)
Speak English very well	99.2% (163)
Poverty rate for children	15.9% (75)
No health insurance	6.3% (271)

DIVERSITY/EQUALITY	★★★★ (191)
Racial diversity index	32.3% (233)
Geographic diversity index	47.8% (247)
Top 20% share of income	48.2% (306)
Gender gap in earnings	29.3% (160)
White-collar gender gap	21.8% (234)

EDUCATION	★★★★ (171)
Eighth grade or less	1.8% (102)
High school diplomas	90.6% (178)
Attended college	60.4% (122)
Bachelor's degrees	18.9% (254)
Advanced degrees	5.9% (272)

EMPLOYMENT	★★★★ (140)
Average jobless rate	12.9% (516)
Self-employed workers	11.6% (90)
Management/financial jobs	13.4% (67)
Computer/engineering jobs	4.2% (66)
Health care jobs	5.9% (193)

GROWTH POTENTIAL	★ (515)
Children per senior	0.74 (541)
Median age	48.6 (537)
Moved from different state	1.2% (474)
Homes built since 2000	11.5% (333)
Construction jobs	8.4% (64)

HOUSING	★ (471)
Home vacancy rate	5.6% (69)
Home ownership rate	68.4% (329)
Housing diversity index	84.3% (314)
4 or more bedrooms	11.7% (505)
Affordability/income ratio	$5,154 (528)

INCOME	★★★★★ (43)
Poverty rate	13.9% (151)
Median household income	$50,306 (118)
Interest/dividends	30.3% (22)
Public assistance	10.3% (72)
Median fulltime earnings	$46,782 (23)

SENIORS	★★★★★ (99)
Seniors living alone	24.1% (86)
Poverty rate for seniors	7.2% (114)
Median income for seniors	$40,392 (56)
Seniors who work	15.9% (418)
Home ownership by seniors	84.3% (173)

STABILITY	★★★ (239)
25-39 age group	16.6% (388)
Born in state of residence	71.2% (288)
Same house as 1 year ago	83.8% (347)
Live and work in county	85.4% (131)
Married-couple households	50.6% (267)

TRANSPORTATION	★★ (397)
Bicycle or walk to work	2.6% (308)
Carpool to work	10.8% (249)
Public transit to work	0.3% (291)
Commute <15 minutes	38.7% (359)
Commute >45 minutes	14.5% (411)

See pages 37-130 for explanations of statistics, stars, and ranks.

Steamboat Springs, CO
(Routt County, CO)

POPULATION	
2010 census	23,509 (490)
2015 estimate	24,130 (489)
2010-2015 change	2.6% (103)
2020 projection	25,219 (477)
2030 projection	27,618 (448)

RACE	
Whites	90.2% (175)
Blacks	0.4% (499)
Hispanics	6.8% (203)
Asians	1.0% (158)
Native Americans	0.2% (300)

AGE	
0-17 years old	19.8% (468)
18-24 years old	8.3% (362)
25-39 years old	21.6% (28)
40-54 years old	22.8% (10)
55-64 years old	16.4% (30)
65+ years old	11.0% (511)

PRIVATE SECTOR	
Businesses	1,658 (108)
Employees	12,319 (300)
Total wages	$539,195,707 (220)
Average weekly wages	$842 (56)

HOUSEHOLD INCOME LADDER	
95th percentile	$226,863 (8)
80th percentile	$114,838 (20)
60th percentile	$77,384 (20)
40th percentile	$49,297 (23)
20th percentile	$26,929 (24)

CHILDREN	★★★★★ (5)
Living with two parents	79.0% (15)
Older teens in school	89.1% (78)
Speak English very well	98.7% (265)
Poverty rate for children	9.0% (8)
No health insurance	2.2% (15)

DIVERSITY/EQUALITY	★★★★ (112)
Racial diversity index	18.1% (375)
Geographic diversity index	78.2% (9)
Top 20% share of income	50.2% (436)
Gender gap in earnings	20.3% (46)
White-collar gender gap	30.8% (350)

EDUCATION	★★★★★ (7)
Eighth grade or less	1.1% (26)
High school diplomas	96.8% (6)
Attended college	76.4% (7)
Bachelor's degrees	49.7% (6)
Advanced degrees	14.2% (17)

EMPLOYMENT	★★★★★ (42)
Average jobless rate	4.0% (32)
Self-employed workers	12.3% (62)
Management/financial jobs	14.5% (38)
Computer/engineering jobs	2.8% (246)
Health care jobs	5.7% (222)

GROWTH POTENTIAL	★★★★★ (34)
Children per senior	1.80 (96)
Median age	40.1 (309)
Moved from different state	4.4% (68)
Homes built since 2000	27.2% (26)
Construction jobs	9.9% (21)

HOUSING	★ (515)
Home vacancy rate	10.9% (400)
Home ownership rate	69.1% (298)
Housing diversity index	80.7% (501)
4 or more bedrooms	22.6% (74)
Affordability/income ratio	$6,074 (543)

INCOME	★★★★★ (20)
Poverty rate	10.2% (39)
Median household income	$64,963 (19)
Interest/dividends	24.9% (100)
Public assistance	3.7% (6)
Median fulltime earnings	$42,578 (51)

SENIORS	★★★★★ (49)
Seniors living alone	28.7% (344)
Poverty rate for seniors	10.7% (357)
Median income for seniors	$48,184 (17)
Seniors who work	29.8% (26)
Home ownership by seniors	82.2% (264)

STABILITY	★★★ (164)
25-39 age group	21.6% (28)
Born in state of residence	36.6% (532)
Same house as 1 year ago	83.0% (397)
Live and work in county	96.2% (8)
Married-couple households	50.8% (256)

TRANSPORTATION	★★★★★ (9)
Bicycle or walk to work	9.2% (17)
Carpool to work	11.1% (221)
Public transit to work	2.7% (18)
Commute <15 minutes	49.3% (166)
Commute >45 minutes	6.0% (53)

See pages 37-130 for explanations of statistics, stars, and ranks.

Sterling, CO
(Logan County, CO)

POPULATION

2010 census	22,709 (499)
2015 estimate	22,036 (507)
2010-2015 change	-3.0% (481)
2020 projection	21,976 (513)
2030 projection	21,929 (503)

RACE

Whites	78.5% (334)
Blacks	1.4% (340)
Hispanics	15.4% (103)
Asians	2.2% (40)
Native Americans	1.2% (89)

AGE

0-17 years old	19.5% (486)
18-24 years old	13.6% (64)
25-39 years old	18.8% (121)
40-54 years old	19.0% (364)
55-64 years old	13.3% (282)
65+ years old	15.8% (305)

PRIVATE SECTOR

Businesses	611 (466)
Employees	6,039 (507)
Total wages	$207,784,586 (503)
Average weekly wages	$662 (358)

HOUSEHOLD INCOME LADDER

95th percentile	$149,662 (167)
80th percentile	$86,457 (223)
60th percentile	$55,377 (237)
40th percentile	$34,544 (273)
20th percentile	$18,076 (316)

CHILDREN ★★★★ (213)

Living with two parents	69.5% (154)
Older teens in school	85.8% (172)
Speak English very well	100.0% (1)
Poverty rate for children	26.2% (328)
No health insurance	9.4% (406)

DIVERSITY/EQUALITY ★★★ (275)

Racial diversity index	35.9% (210)
Geographic diversity index	61.2% (117)
Top 20% share of income	49.0% (360)
Gender gap in earnings	41.2% (459)
White-collar gender gap	30.5% (344)

EDUCATION ★★★ (277)

Eighth grade or less	4.8% (374)
High school diplomas	88.3% (259)

Attended college	57.6% (174)
Bachelor's degrees	15.1% (417)
Advanced degrees	6.0% (264)

EMPLOYMENT ★★★★ (209)

Average jobless rate	9.0% (358)
Self-employed workers	12.3% (62)
Management/financial jobs	11.8% (173)
Computer/engineering jobs	1.3% (519)
Health care jobs	5.9% (193)

GROWTH POTENTIAL ★ (473)

Children per senior	1.23 (393)
Median age	37.6 (168)
Moved from different state	2.1% (269)
Homes built since 2000	7.6% (483)
Construction jobs	4.4% (509)

HOUSING ★★★ (299)

Home vacancy rate	8.7% (268)
Home ownership rate	66.2% (413)
Housing diversity index	84.8% (248)
4 or more bedrooms	17.0% (247)
Affordability/income ratio	$2,947 (394)

INCOME ★★★★ (189)

Poverty rate	16.9% (259)
Median household income	$42,319 (307)
Interest/dividends	23.3% (147)
Public assistance	11.8% (122)
Median fulltime earnings	$38,987 (178)

SENIORS ★★★★★ (60)

Seniors living alone	22.4% (49)
Poverty rate for seniors	8.1% (187)
Median income for seniors	$32,287 (311)
Seniors who work	24.0% (89)
Home ownership by seniors	85.6% (120)

STABILITY ★★ (368)

25-39 age group	18.8% (121)
Born in state of residence	58.6% (431)
Same house as 1 year ago	79.7% (501)
Live and work in county	86.7% (104)
Married-couple households	49.2% (340)

TRANSPORTATION ★★★★★ (38)

Bicycle or walk to work	4.3% (130)
Carpool to work	14.6% (52)
Public transit to work	0.3% (291)
Commute <15 minutes	64.8% (19)
Commute >45 minutes	8.1% (135)

See pages 37-130 for explanations of statistics, stars, and ranks.

Summit Park, UT
(Summit County, UT)

POPULATION

2010 census	36,324 (369)
2015 estimate	39,633 (316)
2010-2015 change	9.1% (11)
2020 projection	42,287 (291)
2030 projection	48,298 (229)

RACE

Whites	84.9% (268)
Blacks	0.5% (466)
Hispanics	11.6% (130)
Asians	2.0% (51)
Native Americans	0.2% (300)

AGE

0-17 years old	26.7% (52)
18-24 years old	7.7% (454)
25-39 years old	18.2% (167)
40-54 years old	24.3% (2)
55-64 years old	14.0% (182)
65+ years old	9.3% (540)

PRIVATE SECTOR

Businesses	2,578 (31)
Employees	22,720 (91)
Total wages	$937,225,426 (82)
Average weekly wages	$793 (103)

HOUSEHOLD INCOME LADDER

95th percentile	>$250,000 (1)
80th percentile	$178,719 (1)
60th percentile	$112,935 (2)
40th percentile	$74,304 (2)
20th percentile	$43,919 (1)

CHILDREN ★★★★★ (94)

Living with two parents	81.9% (6)
Older teens in school	79.7% (407)
Speak English very well	97.2% (403)
Poverty rate for children	9.6% (13)
No health insurance	8.4% (371)

DIVERSITY/EQUALITY ★ (465)

Racial diversity index	26.5% (281)
Geographic diversity index	75.3% (16)
Top 20% share of income	52.1% (505)
Gender gap in earnings	43.2% (483)
White-collar gender gap	48.2% (503)

EDUCATION ★★★★★ (9)

Eighth grade or less	4.4% (346)
High school diplomas	93.4% (82)

Attended college	78.7% (5)
Bachelor's degrees	51.3% (3)
Advanced degrees	19.0% (6)

EMPLOYMENT ★★★★★ (1)

Average jobless rate	3.2% (14)
Self-employed workers	16.6% (10)
Management/financial jobs	22.4% (2)
Computer/engineering jobs	5.9% (14)
Health care jobs	5.4% (273)

GROWTH POTENTIAL ★★★★★ (31)

Children per senior	2.88 (21)
Median age	38.2 (189)
Moved from different state	3.9% (82)
Homes built since 2000	27.8% (20)
Construction jobs	6.7% (219)

HOUSING ★★★ (287)

Home vacancy rate	4.8% (27)
Home ownership rate	74.6% (91)
Housing diversity index	78.5% (532)
4 or more bedrooms	36.0% (3)
Affordability/income ratio	$5,419 (534)

INCOME ★★★★★ (3)

Poverty rate	7.8% (8)
Median household income	$91,773 (2)
Interest/dividends	28.1% (35)
Public assistance	3.6% (5)
Median fulltime earnings	$56,116 (3)

SENIORS ★★★★★ (2)

Seniors living alone	17.9% (4)
Poverty rate for seniors	7.4% (128)
Median income for seniors	$68,495 (3)
Seniors who work	35.7% (3)
Home ownership by seniors	87.8% (46)

STABILITY ★★★★ (125)

25-39 age group	18.2% (167)
Born in state of residence	42.8% (514)
Same house as 1 year ago	87.9% (140)
Live and work in county	71.9% (344)
Married-couple households	63.8% (3)

TRANSPORTATION ★★ (387)

Bicycle or walk to work	2.8% (279)
Carpool to work	7.5% (515)
Public transit to work	2.3% (26)
Commute <15 minutes	33.7% (465)
Commute >45 minutes	14.2% (395)

See pages 37-130 for explanations of statistics, stars, and ranks.

Susanville, CA
(Lassen County, CA)

POPULATION

2010 census	34,895 (384)
2015 estimate	31,345 (425)
2010-2015 change	-10.2% (550)
2020 projection	29,271 (438)
2030 projection	25,617 (466)

RACE

Whites	65.9% (411)
Blacks	8.4% (124)
Hispanics	18.3% (87)
Asians	2.1% (45)
Native Americans	2.8% (56)

AGE

0-17 years old	15.1% (549)
18-24 years old	11.9% (88)
25-39 years old	27.9% (1)
40-54 years old	21.3% (73)
55-64 years old	12.4% (408)
65+ years old	11.4% (501)

PRIVATE SECTOR

Businesses	567 (492)
Employees	4,292 (540)
Total wages	$142,043,242 (538)
Average weekly wages	$636 (421)

HOUSEHOLD INCOME LADDER

95th percentile	$160,264 (93)
80th percentile	$95,061 (89)
60th percentile	$64,004 (85)
40th percentile	$41,432 (90)
20th percentile	$21,584 (157)

CHILDREN ★★★ (285)

Living with two parents	66.9% (220)
Older teens in school	76.0% (490)
Speak English very well	98.7% (265)
Poverty rate for children	23.6% (260)
No health insurance	5.6% (225)

DIVERSITY/EQUALITY ★★★★★ (7)

Racial diversity index	52.3% (93)
Geographic diversity index	50.0% (214)
Top 20% share of income	45.8% (114)
Gender gap in earnings	7.8% (6)
White-collar gender gap	8.2% (66)

EDUCATION ★ (486)

Eighth grade or less	4.9% (380)
High school diplomas	78.7% (500)
Attended college	49.2% (352)
Bachelor's degrees	10.5% (537)
Advanced degrees	3.2% (521)

EMPLOYMENT ★ (500)

Average jobless rate	10.9% (454)
Self-employed workers	5.7% (515)
Management/financial jobs	10.0% (381)
Computer/engineering jobs	1.8% (457)
Health care jobs	5.4% (273)

GROWTH POTENTIAL ★★★ (320)

Children per senior	1.32 (334)
Median age	37.0 (143)
Moved from different state	2.0% (288)
Homes built since 2000	13.1% (274)
Construction jobs	5.3% (425)

HOUSING ★ (487)

Home vacancy rate	13.6% (507)
Home ownership rate	65.1% (434)
Housing diversity index	85.9% (83)
4 or more bedrooms	13.3% (437)
Affordability/income ratio	$3,354 (449)

INCOME ★★★★★ (90)

Poverty rate	16.4% (241)
Median household income	$51,555 (91)
Interest/dividends	16.1% (372)
Public assistance	11.4% (107)
Median fulltime earnings	$50,150 (12)

SENIORS ★★★ (296)

Seniors living alone	28.4% (325)
Poverty rate for seniors	8.1% (187)
Median income for seniors	$37,854 (94)
Seniors who work	17.4% (318)
Home ownership by seniors	79.0% (417)

STABILITY ★★★★★ (89)

25-39 age group	27.9% (1)
Born in state of residence	69.3% (323)
Same house as 1 year ago	72.2% (537)
Live and work in county	92.2% (43)
Married-couple households	51.5% (226)

TRANSPORTATION ★★★★ (187)

Bicycle or walk to work	5.0% (91)
Carpool to work	11.4% (190)
Public transit to work	1.3% (51)
Commute <15 minutes	41.0% (317)
Commute >45 minutes	12.2% (321)

See pages 37-130 for explanations of statistics, stars, and ranks.

Taos, NM
(Taos County, NM)

POPULATION

2010 census	32,937 (403)
2015 estimate	32,907 (406)
2010-2015 change	-0.1% (266)
2020 projection	32,740 (409)
2030 projection	32,275 (405)

RACE

Whites	35.9% (519)
Blacks	0.4% (499)
Hispanics	56.2% (19)
Asians	0.8% (201)
Native Americans	5.1% (31)

AGE

0-17 years old	19.3% (492)
18-24 years old	6.8% (527)
25-39 years old	14.7% (523)
40-54 years old	20.8% (122)
55-64 years old	17.4% (10)
65+ years old	21.0% (34)

PRIVATE SECTOR

Businesses	1,130 (226)
Employees	8,379 (437)
Total wages	$239,658,219 (475)
Average weekly wages	$550 (531)

HOUSEHOLD INCOME LADDER

95th percentile	$148,202 (181)
80th percentile	$75,526 (450)
60th percentile	$45,404 (472)
40th percentile	$26,966 (485)
20th percentile	$13,813 (481)

CHILDREN ★ (465)

Living with two parents	53.5% (484)
Older teens in school	72.0% (521)
Speak English very well	98.9% (226)
Poverty rate for children	38.8% (506)
No health insurance	2.6% (40)

DIVERSITY/EQUALITY ★★★★★ (40)

Racial diversity index	55.2% (50)
Geographic diversity index	63.8% (86)
Top 20% share of income	51.5% (488)
Gender gap in earnings	25.9% (103)
White-collar gender gap	3.8% (26)

EDUCATION ★★★★★ (108)

Eighth grade or less	3.7% (303)
High school diplomas	88.9% (236)
Attended college	62.8% (85)
Bachelor's degrees	25.9% (96)
Advanced degrees	9.8% (66)

EMPLOYMENT ★★★★ (154)

Average jobless rate	10.7% (450)
Self-employed workers	13.5% (42)
Management/financial jobs	10.5% (318)
Computer/engineering jobs	3.9% (86)
Health care jobs	5.7% (222)

GROWTH POTENTIAL ★★★ (307)

Children per senior	0.92 (523)
Median age	46.8 (524)
Moved from different state	3.1% (147)
Homes built since 2000	16.8% (159)
Construction jobs	8.5% (63)

HOUSING ★ (527)

Home vacancy rate	11.4% (432)
Home ownership rate	72.1% (181)
Housing diversity index	84.7% (260)
4 or more bedrooms	10.4% (526)
Affordability/income ratio	$5,910 (541)

INCOME ★★ (433)

Poverty rate	24.2% (469)
Median household income	$36,582 (456)
Interest/dividends	17.8% (316)
Public assistance	19.0% (399)
Median fulltime earnings	$34,774 (398)

SENIORS ★★★★ (191)

Seniors living alone	26.4% (193)
Poverty rate for seniors	15.1% (492)
Median income for seniors	$31,653 (341)
Seniors who work	24.2% (85)
Home ownership by seniors	87.2% (63)

STABILITY ★ (471)

25-39 age group	14.7% (523)
Born in state of residence	56.8% (446)
Same house as 1 year ago	87.3% (181)
Live and work in county	93.3% (31)
Married-couple households	41.5% (510)

TRANSPORTATION ★★★★ (150)

Bicycle or walk to work	5.4% (75)
Carpool to work	12.0% (141)
Public transit to work	0.8% (96)
Commute <15 minutes	41.9% (300)
Commute >45 minutes	9.7% (214)

See pages 37-130 for explanations of statistics, stars, and ranks.

The Dalles, OR
(Wasco County, OR)

POPULATION

2010 census	25,213 (480)
2015 estimate	25,775 (476)
2010-2015 change	2.2% (118)
2020 projection	26,309 (465)
2030 projection	27,459 (450)

RACE

Whites	76.1% (352)
Blacks	0.4% (499)
Hispanics	16.5% (93)
Asians	1.5% (85)
Native Americans	3.6% (45)

AGE

0-17 years old	22.5% (300)
18-24 years old	8.4% (349)
25-39 years old	17.7% (236)
40-54 years old	17.2% (494)
55-64 years old	14.8% (91)
65+ years old	19.3% (68)

PRIVATE SECTOR

Businesses	914 (306)
Employees	9,194 (406)
Total wages	$317,269,591 (413)
Average weekly wages	$664 (344)

HOUSEHOLD INCOME LADDER

95th percentile	$139,772 (293)
80th percentile	$81,940 (326)
60th percentile	$52,922 (301)
40th percentile	$36,016 (232)
20th percentile	$21,586 (156)

CHILDREN ★★★★ (170)

Living with two parents	70.0% (143)
Older teens in school	84.2% (232)
Speak English very well	96.2% (443)
Poverty rate for children	20.7% (185)
No health insurance	4.5% (150)

DIVERSITY/EQUALITY ★★★★ (140)

Racial diversity index	39.2% (189)
Geographic diversity index	65.0% (74)
Top 20% share of income	47.0% (211)
Gender gap in earnings	31.6% (218)
White-collar gender gap	41.3% (459)

EDUCATION ★★ (334)

Eighth grade or less	8.2% (496)
High school diplomas	84.5% (388)
Attended college	58.2% (166)
Bachelor's degrees	19.1% (245)
Advanced degrees	6.6% (211)

EMPLOYMENT ★★★ (225)

Average jobless rate	9.0% (358)
Self-employed workers	11.5% (99)
Management/financial jobs	11.2% (229)
Computer/engineering jobs	2.3% (354)
Health care jobs	5.6% (240)

GROWTH POTENTIAL ★★★ (330)

Children per senior	1.17 (435)
Median age	41.0 (357)
Moved from different state	3.5% (109)
Homes built since 2000	13.0% (276)
Construction jobs	5.9% (345)

HOUSING ★★★ (310)

Home vacancy rate	7.9% (213)
Home ownership rate	64.5% (449)
Housing diversity index	86.4% (26)
4 or more bedrooms	18.5% (178)
Affordability/income ratio	$4,026 (498)

INCOME ★★★ (272)

Poverty rate	16.1% (228)
Median household income	$43,422 (278)
Interest/dividends	22.2% (174)
Public assistance	20.0% (430)
Median fulltime earnings	$37,332 (260)

SENIORS ★★ (359)

Seniors living alone	24.4% (94)
Poverty rate for seniors	8.7% (241)
Median income for seniors	$35,603 (165)
Seniors who work	16.9% (348)
Home ownership by seniors	73.7% (538)

STABILITY ★★★★ (209)

25-39 age group	17.7% (236)
Born in state of residence	53.4% (471)
Same house as 1 year ago	87.9% (140)
Live and work in county	83.1% (161)
Married-couple households	52.3% (180)

TRANSPORTATION ★★★★★ (34)

Bicycle or walk to work	5.3% (79)
Carpool to work	11.8% (152)
Public transit to work	1.6% (38)
Commute <15 minutes	59.3% (49)
Commute >45 minutes	7.3% (95)

See pages 37-130 for explanations of statistics, stars, and ranks.

Truckee-Grass Valley, CA
(Nevada County, CA)

POPULATION

2010 census	98,764 (32)
2015 estimate	98,877 (30)
2010-2015 change	0.1% (250)
2020 projection	99,766 (32)
2030 projection	101,792 (30)

RACE

Whites	85.7% (260)
Blacks	0.5% (466)
Hispanics	9.0% (166)
Asians	1.5% (85)
Native Americans	0.9% (115)

AGE

0-17 years old	18.1% (526)
18-24 years old	6.9% (526)
25-39 years old	14.9% (515)
40-54 years old	19.2% (336)
55-64 years old	18.6% (3)
65+ years old	22.3% (22)

PRIVATE SECTOR

Businesses	3,330 (14)
Employees	23,971 (82)
Total wages	$957,234,540 (78)
Average weekly wages	$768 (130)

HOUSEHOLD INCOME LADDER

95th percentile	$190,137 (31)
80th percentile	$110,191 (24)
60th percentile	$71,123 (36)
40th percentile	$45,102 (44)
20th percentile	$25,602 (43)

CHILDREN ★★★★ (132)

Living with two parents	73.9% (68)
Older teens in school	84.3% (229)
Speak English very well	98.5% (287)
Poverty rate for children	17.1% (99)
No health insurance	7.9% (359)

DIVERSITY/EQUALITY ★★★★ (186)

Racial diversity index	25.7% (288)
Geographic diversity index	55.8% (147)
Top 20% share of income	48.4% (319)
Gender gap in earnings	31.4% (213)
White-collar gender gap	18.7% (195)

EDUCATION ★★★★★ (28)

Eighth grade or less	2.2% (152)
High school diplomas	93.6% (68)
Attended college	74.2% (11)
Bachelor's degrees	33.0% (35)
Advanced degrees	10.9% (42)

EMPLOYMENT ★★★★★ (5)

Average jobless rate	9.8% (415)
Self-employed workers	17.4% (4)
Management/financial jobs	15.5% (24)
Computer/engineering jobs	6.3% (11)
Health care jobs	6.8% (91)

GROWTH POTENTIAL ★★ (434)

Children per senior	0.81 (535)
Median age	49.0 (540)
Moved from different state	1.9% (310)
Homes built since 2000	14.5% (220)
Construction jobs	9.0% (47)

HOUSING ★★ (385)

Home vacancy rate	4.2% (9)
Home ownership rate	72.4% (170)
Housing diversity index	83.0% (417)
4 or more bedrooms	15.7% (315)
Affordability/income ratio	$6,139 (544)

INCOME ★★★★★ (18)

Poverty rate	12.7% (105)
Median household income	$56,521 (44)
Interest/dividends	30.8% (15)
Public assistance	7.5% (31)
Median fulltime earnings	$49,043 (18)

SENIORS ★★★★★ (41)

Seniors living alone	23.8% (78)
Poverty rate for seniors	7.3% (119)
Median income for seniors	$46,011 (22)
Seniors who work	19.1% (238)
Home ownership by seniors	84.9% (145)

STABILITY ★★ (392)

25-39 age group	14.9% (515)
Born in state of residence	64.8% (388)
Same house as 1 year ago	87.8% (149)
Live and work in county	73.5% (323)
Married-couple households	51.9% (199)

TRANSPORTATION ★★ (365)

Bicycle or walk to work	3.6% (180)
Carpool to work	9.2% (408)
Public transit to work	1.3% (51)
Commute <15 minutes	37.5% (387)
Commute >45 minutes	15.1% (426)

See pages 37-130 for explanations of statistics, stars, and ranks.

Twin Falls, ID
(Jerome and Twin Falls Counties, ID)

POPULATION

2010 census	99,604 (30)
2015 estimate	105,189 (21)
2010-2015 change	5.6% (37)
2020 projection	110,624 (19)
2030 projection	122,259 (15)

RACE

Whites	77.4% (343)
Blacks	0.4% (499)
Hispanics	19.0% (83)
Asians	1.2% (125)
Native Americans	0.6% (150)

AGE

0-17 years old	28.5% (26)
18-24 years old	9.2% (234)
25-39 years old	19.6% (71)
40-54 years old	17.5% (483)
55-64 years old	11.3% (486)
65+ years old	14.0% (438)

PRIVATE SECTOR

Businesses	3,260 (16)
Employees	40,843 (14)
Total wages	$1,348,184,561 (26)
Average weekly wages	$635 (422)

HOUSEHOLD INCOME LADDER

95th percentile	$134,192 (373)
80th percentile	$79,874 (373)
60th percentile	$52,967 (298)
40th percentile	$35,323 (256)
20th percentile	$21,059 (185)

CHILDREN ★★★ (305)

Living with two parents	73.7% (70)
Older teens in school	82.5% (296)
Speak English very well	94.5% (486)
Poverty rate for children	20.6% (182)
No health insurance	10.4% (434)

DIVERSITY/EQUALITY ★★★ (277)

Racial diversity index	36.4% (208)
Geographic diversity index	64.7% (77)
Top 20% share of income	47.2% (236)
Gender gap in earnings	43.2% (483)
White-collar gender gap	42.7% (469)

EDUCATION ★★ (398)

Eighth grade or less	7.7% (484)
High school diplomas	82.5% (431)
Attended college	54.8% (229)
Bachelor's degrees	17.1% (322)
Advanced degrees	5.2% (352)

EMPLOYMENT ★★★★ (124)

Average jobless rate	6.0% (117)
Self-employed workers	12.0% (75)
Management/financial jobs	11.9% (165)
Computer/engineering jobs	2.4% (336)
Health care jobs	5.3% (286)

GROWTH POTENTIAL ★★★★★ (86)

Children per senior	2.03 (57)
Median age	33.8 (70)
Moved from different state	3.1% (147)
Homes built since 2000	21.9% (70)
Construction jobs	5.1% (458)

HOUSING ★★★★ (135)

Home vacancy rate	6.2% (109)
Home ownership rate	65.7% (419)
Housing diversity index	85.0% (226)
4 or more bedrooms	24.4% (46)
Affordability/income ratio	$3,343 (448)

INCOME ★★★ (311)

Poverty rate	15.9% (219)
Median household income	$43,523 (276)
Interest/dividends	17.4% (334)
Public assistance	14.7% (243)
Median fulltime earnings	$33,153 (449)

SENIORS ★★★★ (206)

Seniors living alone	25.0% (118)
Poverty rate for seniors	11.6% (392)
Median income for seniors	$31,639 (344)
Seniors who work	22.2% (126)
Home ownership by seniors	82.6% (242)

STABILITY ★★★★ (185)

25-39 age group	19.6% (71)
Born in state of residence	53.4% (471)
Same house as 1 year ago	82.0% (439)
Live and work in county	81.6% (195)
Married-couple households	56.1% (46)

TRANSPORTATION ★★★★ (138)

Bicycle or walk to work	3.8% (161)
Carpool to work	10.8% (249)
Public transit to work	0.4% (219)
Commute <15 minutes	50.1% (149)
Commute >45 minutes	5.9% (51)

See pages 37-130 for explanations of statistics, stars, and ranks.

Ukiah, CA
(Mendocino County, CA)

POPULATION		Attended college	58.9% (145)
2010 census	87,841 (52)	Bachelor's degrees	20.5% (207)
2015 estimate	87,649 (52)	Advanced degrees	6.2% (243)
2010-2015 change	-0.2% (273)		
2020 projection	87,526 (52)	**EMPLOYMENT**	★★★★ (177)
2030 projection	87,546 (57)	Average jobless rate	12.2% (497)
		Self-employed workers	15.1% (17)
RACE		Management/financial jobs	13.0% (86)
Whites	66.7% (406)	Computer/engineering jobs	3.2% (158)
Blacks	0.6% (438)	Health care jobs	4.2% (454)
Hispanics	23.6% (64)		
Asians	2.1% (45)	**GROWTH POTENTIAL**	★★★ (325)
Native Americans	3.4% (46)	Children per senior	1.20 (417)
		Median age	42.2 (412)
AGE		Moved from different state	2.2% (248)
0-17 years old	21.8% (351)	Homes built since 2000	9.3% (420)
18-24 years old	8.2% (379)	Construction jobs	8.3% (67)
25-39 years old	17.2% (290)		
40-54 years old	18.7% (399)	**HOUSING**	★ (544)
55-64 years old	16.0% (46)	Home vacancy rate	6.9% (158)
65+ years old	18.1% (117)	Home ownership rate	57.9% (524)
		Housing diversity index	85.2% (190)
PRIVATE SECTOR		4 or more bedrooms	8.4% (547)
Businesses	3,917 (11)	Affordability/income ratio	$7,175 (549)
Employees	24,910 (76)		
Total wages	$849,150,499 (108)	**INCOME**	★★★★ (214)
Average weekly wages	$656 (378)	Poverty rate	20.4% (388)
		Median household income	$42,980 (290)
HOUSEHOLD INCOME LADDER		Interest/dividends	24.9% (100)
95th percentile	$149,762 (166)	Public assistance	12.6% (150)
80th percentile	$86,188 (228)	Median fulltime earnings	$38,791 (187)
60th percentile	$54,483 (266)		
40th percentile	$32,112 (356)	**SENIORS**	★★★ (324)
20th percentile	$17,627 (336)	Seniors living alone	29.1% (371)
		Poverty rate for seniors	9.1% (263)
CHILDREN	★ (442)	Median income for seniors	$37,780 (97)
Living with two parents	58.8% (433)	Seniors who work	24.1% (86)
Older teens in school	81.7% (337)	Home ownership by seniors	74.0% (536)
Speak English very well	92.7% (511)		
Poverty rate for children	28.1% (370)	**STABILITY**	★★ (356)
No health insurance	7.3% (333)	25-39 age group	17.2% (290)
		Born in state of residence	66.9% (364)
DIVERSITY/EQUALITY	★★★★★ (90)	Same house as 1 year ago	83.5% (366)
Racial diversity index	49.7% (115)	Live and work in county	93.0% (37)
Geographic diversity index	53.4% (166)	Married-couple households	43.2% (491)
Top 20% share of income	50.9% (466)		
Gender gap in earnings	25.0% (87)	**TRANSPORTATION**	★★★★★ (63)
White-collar gender gap	15.4% (155)	Bicycle or walk to work	7.5% (37)
		Carpool to work	11.8% (152)
EDUCATION	★★★ (263)	Public transit to work	0.6% (141)
Eighth grade or less	6.6% (452)	Commute <15 minutes	53.5% (103)
High school diplomas	86.5% (327)	Commute >45 minutes	9.3% (188)

See pages 37-130 for explanations of statistics, stars, and ranks.

Vernal, UT
(Uintah County, UT)

POPULATION

2010 census	32,588 (409)
2015 estimate	37,928 (343)
2010-2015 change	16.4% (5)
2020 projection	42,864 (284)
2030 projection	54,931 (186)

RACE

Whites	82.2% (299)
Blacks	0.5% (466)
Hispanics	8.0% (184)
Asians	0.6% (291)
Native Americans	7.0% (28)

AGE

0-17 years old	33.8% (2)
18-24 years old	9.2% (234)
25-39 years old	23.6% (12)
40-54 years old	15.1% (532)
55-64 years old	9.2% (542)
65+ years old	9.1% (543)

PRIVATE SECTOR

Businesses	1,229 (194)
Employees	10,845 (346)
Total wages	$516,121,936 (233)
Average weekly wages	$915 (30)

HOUSEHOLD INCOME LADDER

95th percentile	$183,988 (37)
80th percentile	$106,989 (31)
60th percentile	$77,473 (19)
40th percentile	$54,106 (13)
20th percentile	$30,603 (13)

CHILDREN ★★★★★ (95)

Living with two parents	79.7% (13)
Older teens in school	81.5% (345)
Speak English very well	98.7% (265)
Poverty rate for children	9.4% (11)
No health insurance	10.4% (434)

DIVERSITY/EQUALITY ★★ (373)

Racial diversity index	31.3% (242)
Geographic diversity index	49.2% (224)
Top 20% share of income	44.7% (50)
Gender gap in earnings	63.3% (551)
White-collar gender gap	27.7% (307)

EDUCATION ★★★ (295)

Eighth grade or less	2.1% (136)
High school diplomas	88.0% (267)
Attended college	53.7% (251)
Bachelor's degrees	16.2% (360)
Advanced degrees	4.1% (472)

EMPLOYMENT ★★★ (245)

Average jobless rate	5.1% (69)
Self-employed workers	8.5% (290)
Management/financial jobs	10.7% (287)
Computer/engineering jobs	4.0% (76)
Health care jobs	4.0% (476)

GROWTH POTENTIAL ★★★★★ (15)

Children per senior	3.70 (3)
Median age	29.7 (25)
Moved from different state	3.9% (82)
Homes built since 2000	33.1% (10)
Construction jobs	5.6% (392)

HOUSING ★★★★ (197)

Home vacancy rate	11.7% (451)
Home ownership rate	76.2% (49)
Housing diversity index	79.9% (517)
4 or more bedrooms	28.9% (14)
Affordability/income ratio	$2,835 (362)

INCOME ★★★★★ (9)

Poverty rate	9.3% (21)
Median household income	$66,815 (14)
Interest/dividends	26.9% (53)
Public assistance	8.5% (41)
Median fulltime earnings	$50,087 (13)

SENIORS ★★★★★ (25)

Seniors living alone	23.9% (80)
Poverty rate for seniors	8.0% (177)
Median income for seniors	$38,510 (83)
Seniors who work	21.5% (144)
Home ownership by seniors	93.4% (1)

STABILITY ★★★★★ (1)

25-39 age group	23.6% (12)
Born in state of residence	68.9% (326)
Same house as 1 year ago	85.5% (280)
Live and work in county	89.5% (74)
Married-couple households	60.5% (8)

TRANSPORTATION ★★★★ (166)

Bicycle or walk to work	2.9% (265)
Carpool to work	11.6% (178)
Public transit to work	0.9% (83)
Commute <15 minutes	53.5% (103)
Commute >45 minutes	11.6% (296)

See pages 37-130 for explanations of statistics, stars, and ranks.

Winnemucca, NV
(Humboldt County, NV)

POPULATION

2010 census	16,528 (542)
2015 estimate	17,019 (541)
2010-2015 change	3.0% (86)
2020 projection	17,104 (539)
2030 projection	17,337 (535)

RACE

Whites	66.4% (407)
Blacks	0.5% (466)
Hispanics	25.5% (57)
Asians	0.4% (413)
Native Americans	4.5% (37)

AGE

0-17 years old	27.9% (34)
18-24 years old	9.0% (265)
25-39 years old	19.3% (85)
40-54 years old	20.2% (202)
55-64 years old	13.7% (225)
65+ years old	9.9% (532)

PRIVATE SECTOR

Businesses	496 (516)
Employees	6,374 (495)
Total wages	$360,381,666 (370)
Average weekly wages	$1,087 (10)

HOUSEHOLD INCOME LADDER

95th percentile	$160,185 (95)
80th percentile	$107,300 (30)
60th percentile	$75,125 (22)
40th percentile	$52,045 (18)
20th percentile	$26,472 (31)

CHILDREN ★★ (335)

Living with two parents	68.4% (181)
Older teens in school	83.3% (263)
Speak English very well	96.6% (430)
Poverty rate for children	12.1% (31)
No health insurance	16.6% (531)

DIVERSITY/EQUALITY ★★★★★ (73)

Racial diversity index	49.1% (121)
Geographic diversity index	70.3% (42)
Top 20% share of income	41.8% (2)
Gender gap in earnings	54.2% (540)
White-collar gender gap	30.8% (350)

EDUCATION ★★ (428)

Eighth grade or less	6.6% (452)
High school diplomas	84.8% (377)
Attended college	47.9% (385)
Bachelor's degrees	14.0% (462)
Advanced degrees	5.1% (364)

EMPLOYMENT ★ (507)

Average jobless rate	7.8% (270)
Self-employed workers	6.4% (479)
Management/financial jobs	6.9% (547)
Computer/engineering jobs	5.9% (14)
Health care jobs	2.0% (550)

GROWTH POTENTIAL ★★★★★ (102)

Children per senior	2.83 (22)
Median age	35.3 (100)
Moved from different state	5.4% (41)
Homes built since 2000	12.8% (286)
Construction jobs	2.8% (548)

HOUSING ★★★ (268)

Home vacancy rate	10.3% (366)
Home ownership rate	73.4% (142)
Housing diversity index	83.6% (385)
4 or more bedrooms	15.3% (333)
Affordability/income ratio	$2,452 (226)

INCOME ★★★★★ (38)

Poverty rate	10.5% (44)
Median household income	$65,212 (17)
Interest/dividends	13.3% (462)
Public assistance	10.0% (63)
Median fulltime earnings	$53,244 (8)

SENIORS ★★★★★ (11)

Seniors living alone	19.9% (12)
Poverty rate for seniors	8.1% (187)
Median income for seniors	n.a.
Seniors who work	30.5% (21)
Home ownership by seniors	84.6% (159)

STABILITY ★★ (336)

25-39 age group	19.3% (85)
Born in state of residence	37.7% (527)
Same house as 1 year ago	83.3% (382)
Live and work in county	89.1% (80)
Married-couple households	51.4% (231)

TRANSPORTATION ★★★★ (123)

Bicycle or walk to work	3.7% (173)
Carpool to work	15.4% (41)
Public transit to work	14.5% (1)
Commute <15 minutes	46.0% (233)
Commute >45 minutes	31.1% (550)

See pages 37-130 for explanations of statistics, stars, and ranks.